LETTERS
OF A DEAD MAN

LETTERS
OF A DEAD MAN

Prince Hermann von Pückler-Muskau, *author*

Linda B. Parshall, *editor and translator*

Published in association with the Stiftung Fürst-Pückler-Park Bad Muskau
and the Foundation for Landscape Studies, New York

DUMBARTON OAKS RESEARCH LIBRARY AND COLLECTION
WASHINGTON, D.C.

Printed in China by Everbest Printing Company.

LIBRARY OF CONGRESS CATALOGING-IN-PUBLICATION DATA

Pückler-Muskau, Hermann, Fürst von, 1785–1871.

Letters of a dead man / Prince Hermann von Pückler-Muskau, author; Linda B. Parshall, editor and translator.

    pages cm. — (ex horto: Dumbarton Oaks texts in garden and landscape studies)

    Includes bibliographical references and index.

        ISBN 978-0-88402-411-8 (hardcover : alk. paper)

1. Pückler-Muskau, Hermann, Fürst von, 1785–1871—Correspondence.

2. Authors, German—19th century—Correspondence.

3. Authors, German—19th century—Biography.

I. Parshall, Linda B., editor, translator.

II. Title.

PT2449.P7Z48 2016

838´.709—dc23

[B]

        2015021791

FRONT COVER: *Charvolants* (carriages drawn by kites), 1827 (FIG. 66).

BACK COVER: (top) *Waterloo Bridge*, 1825 (FIG. 4); (bottom) *Cross Section of the Thames Tunnel*, 1828 (FIG. 43).

FRONTISPIECE: *The Prince of Pückler-Muskau.* © Goethe University, Frankfurt.

Book and cover design and type composition: Melissa Tandysh

www.doaks.org/publications

EX HORTO DUMBARTON OAKS TEXTS IN GARDEN AND LANDSCAPE STUDIES

Contents

List of Illustrations

All photographs from the Memory Albums are © Stiftung Fürst-Pückler-Museum Park und Schloss Branitz (photographer Thomas Kläber); the photographs from Memory Albums II and III are published courtesy of Hermann Sylvius Graf von Pückler.

Preface

THE NAME OF PRINCE HERMANN VON PÜCKLER-MUSKAU IS LITERALLY ON THE tongues of most Germans at some point in their lives. A frozen dessert, similar to Neapolitan ice cream in the United States, was named Fürst Pückler in his honor in a book by a royal Prussian *chef de cuisine*, Louis Ferdinand Jungius, in 1839. The prince is also widely—if a bit less popularly—known in Germany as one of the great landscape designers of the nineteenth century, as a literary phenomenon, and as a lively and candid, if sometimes caustic, observer of people and the places they inhabit. In the English-speaking world, he still commands some attention as a landscape designer, although not to the degree he once did. His literary reputation, meanwhile, based chiefly on his *Letters of a Dead Man,* is in eclipse. Dumbarton Oaks is pleased to publish this first full translation of his letters, in the hopes of bringing renewed international attention to Pückler as a writer, landscape critic, social observer, and designer, restoring him in some measure to the stature he held among his contemporaries and in the late nineteenth century.

There are many reasons to publish a new and full translation of *Letters of a Dead Man.* To begin with, there is the curious tale of their origin. As detailed in Linda Parshall's illuminating and engaging introduction to this book, they tell the story of Pückler's extended tour of England, Wales, and Ireland in the middle years of the 1820s. He was nearly bankrupt from the expense of creating a vast landscape park at his estate in Muskau, so he divorced his wife and set off for England to find a wealthy new bride. At the risk of giving away the ending, Pückler failed at his quest. But the letters he sent home to his ex-wife—with whom he remained close for the rest of his life—became a literary sensation. Full of trenchant and often witty observations on the people, customs, and landscapes of the British Isles, they were edited and published to great acclaim in Germany in 1830 as *Briefe eines Verstorbenen (Letters of a Dead Man).* Moving from the fashionable circles of London and the extensive grounds of English country houses to the rugged fastnesses of Wales and Ireland, the book was part travel journal, part memoir, and part epistolary novel. It captivated readers and reviewers, including notable German literati Johann Wolfgang von Goethe and Heinrich Heine, and Pückler's fortunes began to rise. Two years later, an abridged and expurgated version appeared in English as *Tour in England, Ireland, and France, in the Years 1828 and 1829* edited and translated by Sarah Austin. This too was a great success, as it was issued in England and the United States, reprinted many times, and helped to bring Pückler to the attention of landscape designers and reformers, including Frederick Law Olmsted, Charles Eliot, and Margaret Fuller. So while Pückler did not find a bride, his travels provided financial salvation—for a time.

Despite the great success of *Briefe eines Verstorbenen* and, later, *Tour in England, Ireland, and France,* Pückler's letters remain surprisingly unknown outside of Germany today. They deserve a wider audience. Social historians, for instance, should be fascinated by his discussions of class, education, and industrialization as well as of contemporaneous political topics—especially Irish emancipation. Literary scholars will have much to discover in his sharp wit, turns of phrase, and erudition. Art historians may wish to consult the meticulous inventories of collections at the many country houses he visited. They might also be intrigued by the illustrations in this volume, which are nearly all contemporaneous with Pückler's travels, many from prints and books he collected himself, and others modern photographs of the works of art he saw and particularly admired. What makes these letters especially compelling, however, is the way in which this rich detail is situated in the landscape. Rather than serving as mere backdrops to a series of entertaining and wide-ranging insights, the physical surroundings are brought forward in Pückler's prose as actors and characters in their own right.

Thus, we hope and expect that these letters will be especially valuable to students of the physical environment, particularly landscape historians. Following on the heels of a newly published translation by John Hargraves of Pückler's design treatise, *Hints on Landscape Gardening*, this translation will greatly expand access to Pückler's extensive comments on English cities, parks, and gardens. The letters reveal their author as a keen observer of designed landscapes, helping us to understand better how the general principles of design found in *Hints* compare with detailed descriptions of the English sources he used as models. Possibly the most compelling aspect of this translation, however, is the vividness with which the letters convey the social mores that animated these spaces during his time. Much of today's scholarship in garden and landscape studies is directed toward themes of use and reception, and Parshall's translation will be a welcome new source for comparative research on social histories of nineteenth-century landscapes.

Letters of a Dead Man is the fourth volume in a new series of translations issued by Dumbarton Oaks. Titled *ex horto*, the series presents classic and rare texts on garden history and on the philosophy, art, and techniques of landscape architecture, making available in English both works in manuscript that have never been published and books that have long been out of print. These volumes will eventually constitute a library of historical sources that have defined the core of the field, providing unprecedented access to the foundational literature of garden and landscape studies.

Letters of a Dead Man is a monumental work, far larger in scope than previous titles in *ex horto*. We are pleased to present the text in its entirety, however. Given the range of the content and the quality of Linda Parshall's translation, there will certainly be readers who tackle the whole volume. But it will be equally valuable for the many others who will read just a few letters at a time or consult specific passages in relation to other research projects. The contents are so extensive that they constitute a trove to be mined for many purposes, and for projects from a wide range of disciplines. We are grateful to Elizabeth Barlow Rogers and the Foundation for Landscape Studies for instigating the project and providing crucial early support for the translation and editing. We are equally grateful to Cord Panning and the Stiftung Fürst-Pückler-Park Bad Muskau for their financial contribution to the publication. Jan Ziolkowski, director of Dumbarton Oaks, was quick to see the value of the project and was unstinting in his support. Kathy Sparkes, director of publications, and Sara Taylor, art and archaeology editor, saw this complex project through to a spectacular conclusion. Linda Parshall did a remarkable job rendering Pückler's sometimes difficult sentences into modern English; the result is often poetic, and it captures the flavor of the original both in rhythm and tone. We hope that this book will go some distance toward restoring Pückler's literary standing in the English-speaking world and will create a renewed appreciation of the rich interplay between his writings and his achievements as a landscape designer.

John Beardsley
Dumbarton Oaks

Forewords

PRINCE HERMANN VON PÜCKLER-MUSKAU'S EXTRAORDINARY LANDSCAPE PARK and pleasure ground stretches over three square miles in Upper Lusatia, a historical region now comprised in part of the German state of Saxony and in a portion of Lower Silesia lying east of the Polish border at the River Neisse. A prime example of Romanticism in landscape design, it incorporates aspects of Humphry Repton's Picturesque style into a personal idiom deeply rooted in nature. In addition, it includes artfully orchestrated views of the scenery beyond its borders. Comprised of forests, pastureland, farms, the village of Bad Muskau, and in the distance the prince's alum works, this was Pückler's ancestral estate, the ownership of which involved sound overall management and, with regard to his park and pleasure ground, daily maintenance and upkeep.

How does this extraordinary place fit into the history of landscape design? Further, an American might wonder what similarities a latter-day aristocratic landowner's plan of his personal domain could possibly have with a democratic public park. And yet, the broad sweeping meadows, trees planted in groves, artfully engineered water bodies, and arrangement of scenic prospects that Frederick Law Olmsted and Calvert Vaux created in the heart of New York City cannot help but be compared with the same features found in Muskau Park in Germany.

This begs the question of direct influence: might Muskau have served as a kind of Romantic park prototype when Central Park was created some two decades later? The answer, however, is no. Although the German park had reached a splendid maturity when the financially straitened Pückler sold it to the prince of the Netherlands in 1845, it is impossible to conclude if, when they conceived their Greensward plan for Central Park, Olmsted and Vaux had seen Muskau Park, since neither had traveled on the Continent or visited the great parks and gardens of Europe. Like Pückler, however, their sensibilities had been nourished by their connections with England.

An Englishman by birth, Vaux was a Victorian architect in the Picturesque style, as can be seen in the Belvedere and other structures he designed in Central Park and elsewhere. In Olmsted's first book, *Walks and Talks of an American Farmer in England*, published in 1852 before he had any inkling of what his future lifetime profession would be, we find—along with observations on agricultural practices and land management—appreciative descriptions of landscape scenery and an occasional rapturous response to the sublime in nature. Thus, in aesthetic predisposition these two Americans had much in common with their still unknown German counterpart.

It was only after taking up residence in Brookline, Massachusetts, and founding an architectural practice there, that Olmsted discerned an actual correspondence in his style of landscape design and that of Pückler, as evinced by his recommendation to his protégé in the firm, Charles Eliot, that he include Muskau as part of his itinerary of European parks. The American connection with Muskau was further reinforced by Vaux's apprentice and later partner, the landscape architect Samuel Parsons. After visiting Muskau in 1917, Parsons commissioned an English edition of *Andeutungen über Landschaftsgärtnerei* (*Hints on Landscape Gardening*), Pückler's 1834 book that described his ongoing plans for Muskau Park. A new translation of this important work, accompanied by reproductions of the handsome colored lithographic plates from the German original, has recently been published by the Foundation for Landscape Studies in association with Birkhäuser. It was logical, therefore, that this scholarly organization should wish to further Pückler's reputation among Anglophone readers by supporting the publication of a new translation of the first and most famous of his numerous books, his *Briefe eines Verstorbenen* (*Letters of a Dead Man*) of 1830.

The effort to realize this intention began ten years ago. In 2006, while attending a conference titled "Pückler and America" held in Muskau Park, the project crystalized when I recognized Linda Parshall, a fellow speaker and a landscape historian noted for her publication in 2001 of the first English translation of C. C. L. Hirschfeld's *Theory of Garden Art*. As we gazed across one of Pückler's long meadows at the restored castle, we began to discuss the desirability of a new version of *Letters of a Dead Man* that would better capture the full range of Pückler's adventures in England than the expurgated 1832 translation by Sarah Austin.

At my suggestion, the awards committee of the Foundation for Landscape Studies subsequently approved a grant for what Parshall and I assumed at the time would be an abridged version of *Letters of a Dead Man*. As it turned out, she discovered such a rich and vivid account of Regency society and mores interlarded with numerous landscape observations that she felt compelled to undertake the monumental task of translating Pückler's entire opus. The present eminently readable and thoroughly annotated translation with its excellent apparatus will, therefore, prove instructive with regard to period and place both for the general reader as well as for the specialist in landscape or cultural history.

Now, thanks to substantial funding from the Stiftung Fürst-Pückler-Park Bad Muskau and to the Foundation for Landscape Studies' partnership with Dumbarton Oaks of Harvard University in publishing this important work, we can collectively celebrate the much-deserved advancement of Pückler's reputation in America and the rest of the English-speaking world. It is our hope that current and future readers will derive from this new translation both literary delight as well as insight into the character and genius of one of history's greatest landscape designers.

Elizabeth Barlow Rogers
Foundation for Landscape Studies

IN THE LAST FEW YEARS, THE THREE LARGE PARKS CLOSELY LINKED TO PRINCE Pückler-Muskau have enjoyed increasing renown owing to their extensive and spectacular restorations. The political changes that began in 1989 made it possible for the Berlin Wall to be removed from Babelsberg Park, thereby magnificently uniting not only Berlin but also the cultural landscape of Potsdam. Around the same time, Branitz Park shed the constraints of a former GDR museum, with its typical focus on pre- and early history, and has now developed into an authentic Pückler site, providing vivid insight into the life of the celebrated prince and his obsession with parks, while also making significant archival material available for research. At Muskau Park, the epic landscape that had been torn asunder by a national border as a consequence of World War II has been wonderfully rejoined, as visionary Polish and German conservators reopened views and rebuilt bridges to create an aesthetic whole.

In recent years, the Pückler phenomenon has come ever more clearly into public view through numerous media reports, exhibitions, and publications as well as by the listing of Babelsberg Park and Muskau Park as UNESCO World Heritage Sites. Pückler's fame seems to be more widespread than ever before. Yet a closer examination reveals that the audience has grown mostly in German-speaking countries and primarily in relation to Pückler's activities in landscape and garden art. In other countries, the eccentric prince parades in the spotlight of only a handful of specialists and initiated few. He is scarcely visible as a literary figure, and when so, it is primarily with reference to his garden book, *Hints on Landscape Gardening*, in which he presents, with eloquent language and inviting lithographs, his definitive vision for Muskau Park. In contrast, the *Letters of a Dead Man*, despite being one of the most significant examples of German travel literature of the nineteenth century and surpassing *Hints* in its literary value, remains largely unknown outside Germany.

Introducing the "green prince," or "Muskau Pasha," to a larger international audience is the aim of the administrations of the three Pückler parks in Potsdam-Babelsberg, Cottbus-Branitz, and Bad Muskau-Łęknica (Poland). In addition to the ongoing research and restoration of the parks, the administrators place great importance on the concise translation of Pückler's most significant publications into major languages. English, as the lingua franca of our age, is at the forefront of this effort. So we feel especially grateful to Elizabeth Barlow Rogers and the Foundation for Landscape Studies for having published in 2014, together with Birkhäuser Publishers, the lavishly illustrated and newly translated *Hints on Landscape Gardening*. And it was Elizabeth Barlow Rogers, who, in her enthusiasm for Muskau Park, encouraged Linda Parshall to put her meticulous translating skills to work in *Letters of a Dead Man*. We are also deeply appreciative that Dumbarton Oaks entered into this project, directing the challenging task of publishing the letters in such an exemplary manner. That the Stiftung Fürst-Pückler-Park Bad Muskau was invited to cooperate with this group is an exceptional honor, and it makes us feel very confident regarding the international reception of Prince Pückler-Muskau in the years to come.

Cord Panning
Stiftung Fürst-Pückler-Park Bad Muskau

Acknowledgments

IN JUNE 2006, AN INTERNATIONAL CONFERENCE ON "PÜCKLER AND AMERICA" was held at Muskau Park, where I was first urged to undertake a translation of Pückler's letters. Little did I expect that this project would extend over several years and yield an illustrated volume of such magnitude. Among the many friends and colleagues who encouraged me during this undertaking, first mention goes to Elizabeth Barlow Rogers of the Foundation for Landscape Studies, who initially proposed this translation and has never ceased to champion it. I must also single out Cord Panning of the Stiftung Fürst-Pückler-Park Bad Muskau, who became a good friend during the course of the project; his unwavering support and expertise have been helpful at every turn. I am grateful not only for the personal commitment of these two people but also for the generous subventions provided by their respective foundations.

My research on European landscape history is indebted to the long-term support of Dumbarton Oaks, which makes it a special privilege and honor to be publishing this volume in the *ex horto* series. I thank those at Dumbarton Oaks who have been vital in seeing the publication through to completion, above all John Beardsley, Sara Taylor, and Kathy Sparkes. I wish to acknowledge the generosity of the Stiftung Fürst-Pückler-Museum Park und Schloss Branitz, and of Hermann Sylvius Graf von Pückler, for providing photos from the Memory Albums. The staff at Branitz were generous with their time and expertise both during and after my research visits. Special mention goes to Christian Friedrich and Anne Schäfer, as well as to Beate Schneider for her assistance with the photography. I am happy to acknowledge the munificence of the many other museums, libraries, and cultural institutions that provided high-resolution images of objects in their collections at little or no cost. This now widespread practice—pioneered by the British Museum—has been a vital benefit to researchers the world over. The internet was also crucial to my research, providing access to primary material in early books and journals, as well as serendipitous finds such as playbills and menus.

It was during my first fellowship at Dumbarton Oaks in the late 1980s that John Dixon Hunt encouraged me to pursue German landscape history. He has remained a good friend and colleague. My interests moved from the eighteenth century to Pückler's writings during a second Dumbarton Oaks fellowship, in 1999–2000, and for that edifying year I would like to acknowledge Michel Conan, then director of Garden and Landscape Studies, and my exceptional cofellows Shirine Hamadeh and Betsey Robinson. Others who have made contributions—both scholarly and personal—include Sarah Blake, Mary Crettier, Samuel Danon, Sonja Duempelmann, Christof Mauch, Therese O'Malley, and Nicholas Penny. Special recognition goes to Peter James Bowman, an authority on Pückler's English adventures, whose open generosity in sharing his notes and other primary research materials has been invaluable. And for their faithful endurance in helping to decode many a knotty passage in Pückler's German prose, I am grateful to Regina Hanemann and Peter Schmidt. Finally, I am indebted to my husband, Peter, whose infinite patience, meticulous editing, and steadfast confidence in the project made this book possible.

Linda B. Parshall

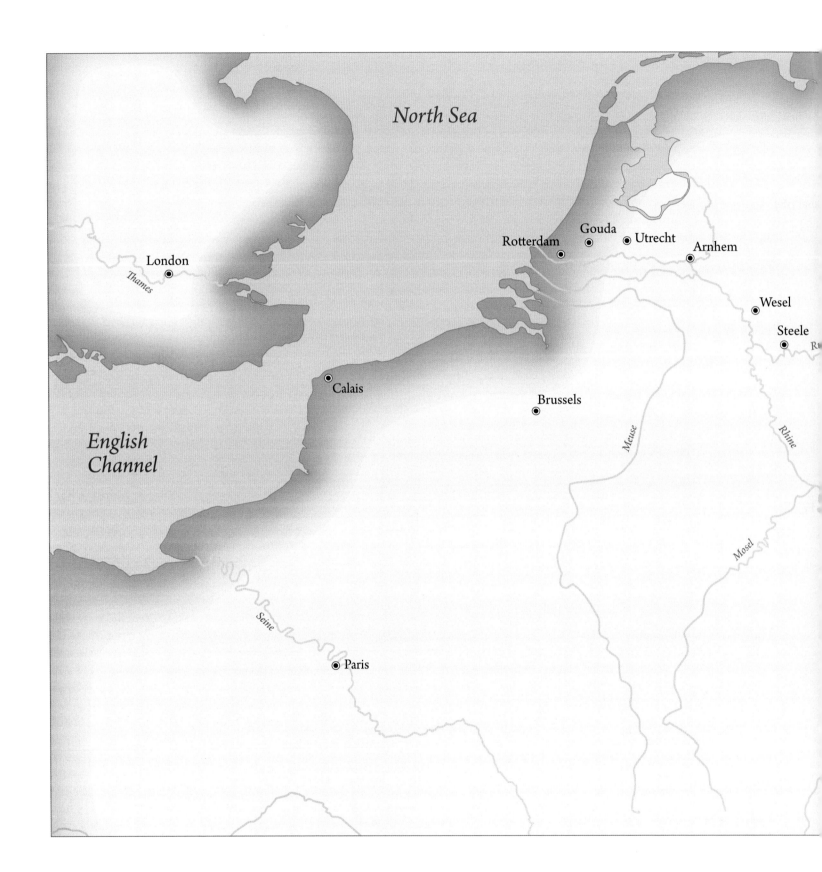

North Sea

London
Thames

English
Channel

Calais

Rotterdam
Gouda
Utrecht
Arnhem

Wesel

Steele

Brussels

Meuse

Rhine

Mosel

Seine

Paris

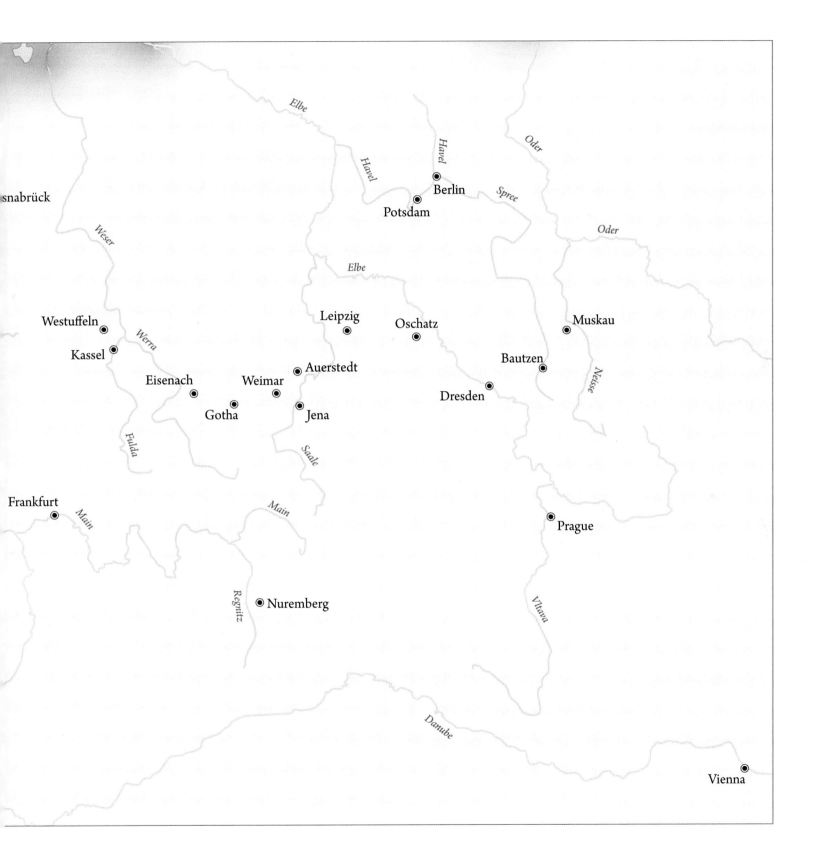

snabrück

Elbe

Havel

Havel

Oder

Berlin

Spree

Potsdam

Oder

Weser

Elbe

Westuffeln

Werra

Leipzig

Oschatz

Muskau

Kassel

Bautzen

Eisenach

Weimar

Auerstedt

Dresden

Neisse

Gotha

Jena

Saale

Frankfurt

Main

Main

Fulda

Vltava

Prague

Regnitz

Nuremberg

Danube

Vienna

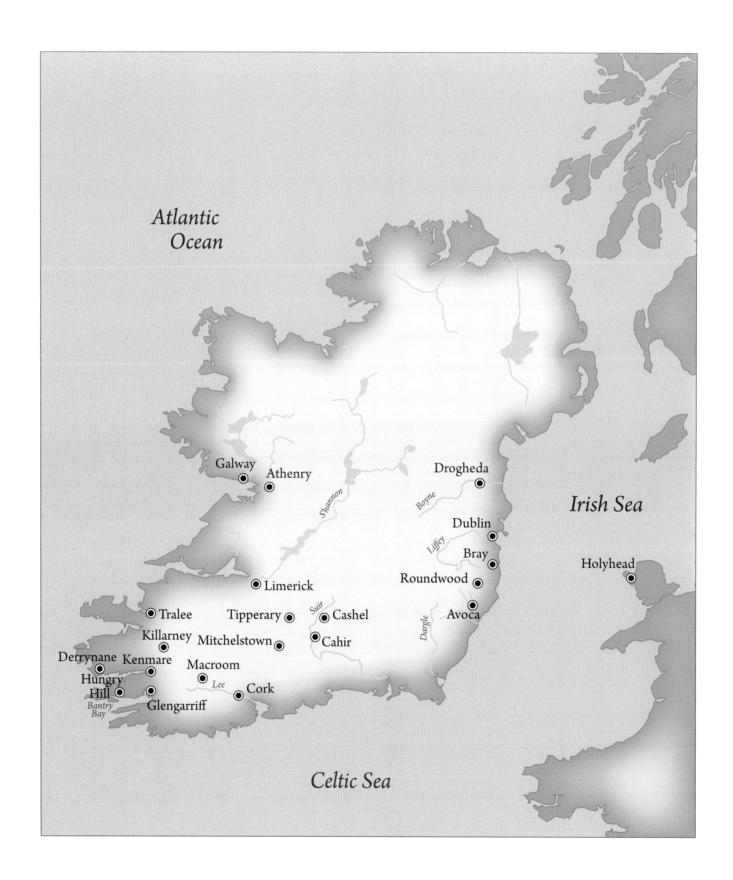

Atlantic
Ocean

Galway
Athenry
Drogheda

Irish Sea

Shannon

Boyne

Dublin

Liffey

Bray

Holyhead

Roundwood

Limerick

Tralee
Tipperary
Suir
Cashel
Avoca

Killarney
Mitchelstown
Cahir

Dargle

Derrynane
Kenmare
Macroom

Hungry
Hill
Lee
Cork

Glengarriff

*Bantry
Bay*

Celtic Sea

Tweed

Tyne

Tees

Irish Sea

North Sea

Dublin

Holyhead

⊙ Guisborough
⊙ Whitby
Castle
Howard
Ripon ⊙
Ouse
⊙ Scarborough
⊙ Flamborough
York ⊙
Derwent
Leeds

Chester ⊙
Sheffield ⊙
⊙ Doncaster

Llangollen ⊙
Dee
Newport ⊙
Trent
Nottingham ⊙

WALES

Shrewsbury

Severn

Wye

Birmingham ⊙
Avon

Hereford ⊙
Warwick ⊙
⊙ Newmarket

Monmouth ⊙
Stratford-
upon-Avon
Stowe ⊙
Woburn ⊙
⊙ Audley End

Chepstow ⊙
Oxford ⊙
⊙ Hatfield

Bristol ⊙
London
Bath
Windsor ⊙
Thames
⊙ Salisbury
Cobham ⊙
Medway
⊙ Dover

Brighton ⊙

Calais ⊙

English Channel

INTRODUCTION

Gentle Reader, I presume thou wilt be very inquisitive to know what antic or personate actor this is, that so insolently intrudes upon this common theatre to the world's view, arrogating another man's name; whence he is, why he doth it, and what he hath to say.

—ROBERT BURTON, *The Anatomy of Melancholy*, 1621[1]

When Prince Hermann von Pückler-Muskau set off for a lengthy tour of England in September 1826, his main purpose was not to chronicle his adventures but to find a wealthy wife. That he was recently divorced did not seem an insurmountable problem. He and Lucie, his wife of almost nine years,[2] had made a mutual decision to dissolve their marriage expressly in the hope of his making an auspicious second match—for how else could they save their beloved Muskau Park (Figure 1)? The elaborate plans for transforming two thousand acres near the southwestern corner of Pückler's vast realm into an ideal landscape garden were well underway but far from fully realized, and the couple's financial situation was precarious. Lucie would remain at Muskau and oversee the landscaping project, and the two would stay in touch through the regular exchange of letters—Pückler keeping her apprised of his adventures and the progress of the bride quest, Lucie keeping him up-to-date about happenings at home.

Pückler was by no means alone in regarding Britain as the premier location for securing a fortune: it boasted an inordinate number of millionaires, the majority in the vicinity of London. Low taxes allowed the wealthy, especially the landed aristocracy, to grow wealthier, and the nouveaux riches were happy to see their daughters acquire a noble title. The prince was already deeply interested in British politics, industry, and finance (to say nothing of the world of the London fashionables), and he was eager to visit the landscape parks that were his preferred models for Muskau. He would have a great deal to write home about.

The prince did not see Muskau again for nearly two and a half years. During this time, he wrote Lucie faithfully and extensively, describing his journey from its beginnings in Germany and Holland, through England, Wales, and Ireland, to its conclusion in France. The bulk of the letters tell of his lengthy stay in Britain: the near successes and repeated disappointments he was dealt as a suitor; the innumerable balls he attended; the evenings of theater and music he enjoyed; the factories and mines he toured; the towns, churches, houses, and gardens he visited; the art

1

*View from the
Belvedere on
Lucknitz Hill,
Muskau.*

collections he studied; the meals he consumed; the politicians he met; the weather he braved; and the landscapes he passed through, often enrapturing and sometimes forbidding.[3]

The bride search, however, was ultimately a failure. Why—given his charm, good looks, entertaining wit, and impressive title—was Pückler unsuccessful? More than one factor worked against him. Though admirably fit and vital, he was over forty—not as young as the vaguely thirty years that he made himself out to be (dyed hair notwithstanding)—and he was a bit too dandified to suit some tastes. His marital status represented a greater obstacle. Although divorce was not uncommon in Prussia, it required an act of Parliament in Britain and hence was rare; many among the nobility, including royalty, simply avoided it, having a second or third unofficial union instead.[4] Pückler's matrimonial hopes were further undermined when word got out that he was not only divorced but still close to his ex-wife, who was waiting at home to receive him along with a young heiress. A friend warned him that most English girls would see themselves as no more than a mistress were they to be taken on as a second wife. He recognized the danger and tried to discount rumors about his intentions, complaining bitterly about the way scandal-mongering newspapers snooped into private lives, spread inflammatory tales, and tarnished reputations.[5]

At the close of Pückler's lengthy sojourn in Britain, he returned alone to Muskau and Lucie. The couple's financial situation was more untenable than ever, not least because of the cost of his journey. Yet a new means of rescue emerged: his voluminous letters might be published. That this idea took hold was partly due to Karl August Varnhagen von Ense and his wife Rahel, who carried significant cultural weight in Berlin and who were acquaintances of Lucie and Pückler.[6] Rahel, of Jewish heritage, had become a highly influential presence in the intellectual circles of Berlin and maintained one of the city's most important salons, which Pückler attended along with many of the most renowned thinkers of the time.[7] Her husband, a writer especially recognized for his biographies, was to become Pückler's lifelong friend. The Varnhagens were familiar with the plans for Muskau, and in July 1828, when the prince was still in Ireland, they went to visit Lucie. Passing through the Muskau landscape, they were deeply impressed by the transformations already achieved. And, as Lucie read aloud to them from her husband's epistles, Varnhagen felt increasing admiration and affection for the man whose presence he sensed not only in his park but also in his writing—in the appealing candor and naturalness of the reporting, the serendipitous choices of subject, the mercurial shifts in mood, and the fluid, unselfconscious ease and poetry of the style. He also approved of Pückler's fresh, liberal-minded stance on contemporary social and political issues.[8]

Clearly the letters could, and should, be published, yet serious editing was required. Once Pückler returned home and settled on the idea, he undertook the task with the assistance of Lucie and, later, Varnhagen. The objective was not only to refine the prose but to protect the author's identity. An unnamed "Editor"—Pückler himself—was invented, and a preface was composed with a web of deceptive assertions: that the editor had been a close friend of the recently deceased author, that this gentleman's personal correspondence was being presented unabridged, and that there had been no improvements or embellishments to the content. In truth, the letters were shortened to half their original length, significantly polished, in places rewritten, and occasionally augmented.[9] Many a tedious detail was removed, proper names of most people and locations (including Muskau) were replaced with initials, and the bride hunt was expunged from the record. The result was at once an adventure story, a travel book, and an exposé of the lives of the rich and famous.

Presented to the public in 1830 under the beguiling title *Briefe eines Verstorbenen* (*Letters of a Dead Man*), the first two volumes were not just an enormous success, they were a sensation. In an affront to chronology, however, they contained the second half of the letters.[10] These encompass the more venturous segment of Pückler's travels—his wild journey through Wales and Ireland—replete with rugged landscapes, boisterous rustics, near-death encounters, romantic escapades, political rivalries, and even ghostly apparitions. The two volumes created the initial stir, a reception surpassing Pückler's most extravagant dreams. The earlier letters, which cover his more lengthy stay among the fashionable society of Brighton and London, necessarily required more careful expurgation to eliminate traces of the bride hunt and to protect the many prominent individuals involved. The shift of focus to the lifestyle of the upper classes proved no obstacle to the popularity of *Letters of a Dead Man,* however; indeed, it probably had the opposite effect, for sales continued to rise when the final two volumes appeared in the following year.[11]

Varnhagen's enthusiastic support was a factor in this success, as he not only wrote a glowing review but also exercised his considerable influence in eliciting responses from two of the most famous German writers of the era, Johann Wolfgang von Goethe and Heinrich Heine. Both men were happy to comply. Goethe, already in his eighties, was very taken with the unknown author and his ability to sweep the reader off into romantically charged landscapes, the motley population of a crowded inn, or learned exchanges in a great man's dining room. Heine, solely on the basis of Varnhagen's high regard, inserted an endorsement into the preface to his own travel book, which was just then going to press, and even selected a passage from *Letters of a Dead Man* as an epigraph. Later, when he actually got around to reading Pückler's volumes for himself, he was delighted to conclude that his praise had been fully justified.[12]

These and many other favorable reactions helped further sales, but the popularity of *Letters of a Dead Man* is best explained by the scope of their content and the candid, yet oftentimes coy, narration. Pückler's ease of movement among the British upper classes, his frequently volatile and sometimes vulnerable personality, his quirkiness and underlying arrogance, and the seductive grace and naturalness of his writing bring many a dinner party, horserace, or theater performance to life. Yet these letters appealed not just as fine examples of the form. From a literary point of view, they represent a remarkable amalgam of genres much in vogue at the time. First, they satisfied what since the late eighteenth century had become a near cultic taste for travel literature.[13] They also gratified another literary enthusiasm, the so-called *Briefwut* or letter-frenzy, an infatuation with reading and writing letters that was markedly bolstered by increasing literacy rates and a more efficient postal network.[14] Likewise, they constituted a kind of memoir or diary; Pückler asserts that his letters take the place of a journal, and he presents them as factual, if sometimes embroidered, accounts of his experiences abroad. The influence of two other genres—the short story and the novel, particularly the epistolary novel—can also be sensed in the extraordinary synthesis of reportage and quasifiction that gives his communications their particular flare. Many passages are narrative tours de force, tales—some repeated secondhand, or so Pückler claims—that can stand alone with their self-contained plots and extended story lines. Finally, the numerous vignettes of upper-class life constitute a kind of "silver fork novel," a popular subgenre exposing the formalities and foibles of the rich and famous, likewise often romans à clef. In its multifacetedness, *Letters of a Dead Man* conveys the diversity of Pückler's narrative persona.

All four volumes were in demand, and the coffers at Muskau began to fill again. There were numerous reprintings and translations.[15] The English version, *Tour in England, Ireland, and France,* was met with immediate success and countless reviews; within a year, it was reissued in the United States, and it was reprinted eight times in a matter of months.[16] Pückler was inordinately fortunate to have a writer of great skill to provide his entrée to the English-speaking world, for the *Tour* was a superb rendering by Sarah Austin, a woman who had already achieved considerable renown as an editor, writer, and translator. Educated in Germany, she was widely read and a fine stylist who knew her audience and revised the text accordingly—cutting where she saw fit, censoring the content, and softening the tone to better appeal to British sensibilities; she frequently excised much of the narrator's acerbity and ironic commentary (even regarding the weather!)[17] Although Pückler was initially scandalized by her editorial interventions, he abandoned his criticism when he saw the sales figures. Austin had a further and quite personal incentive to refine the chronicler's voice, however: she quickly discovered the identity of the far-from-deceased author and initiated a lengthy correspondence with him that developed into an epistolary love affair of its own.[18]

In *Letters of a Dead Man*, Pückler presents himself as a gentleman and man of the world, a droll wit gifted with an analytical intelligence, great charm, and social aplomb. The portrait that emerges is of a connoisseur of the arts, a gourmand, an accomplished horseman, an energetic and intrepid walker, and a bit of a rake. He is a devoted reader as well, and we regularly see him engrossed in a book, sometimes while bouncing along through the night in his carriage. We witness his compassionate side, his concern for the mistreatment of prostitutes and the abuse of animals; we endure his cranky self-centeredness as he bemoans his chronic physical and psychic ailments. But, above all, he is the consummate traveler, affectionately characterized by Heine as "his Serene Highness . . . the romantic Anacharsis—he, most fashionable of eccentric men— Diogenes on horseback."[19]

From Count to Prince: The Way to Britain

Hermann Ludwig Heinrich von Pückler (1785–1871) was born on the family estate of Muskau, about one hundred miles southeast of Berlin. He was the first child and the only surviving son of Imperial Count Ludwig Carl Hans Erdmann von Pückler (1754–1811) and his considerably younger wife, Clementine von Callenberg (1770–1850).[20] The pretty and vivacious Clementine was fourteen when she married the stodgy thirty-year-old count and fifteen when Hermann was born. The precocious, headstrong boy was often censured, rarely indulged, and generally ignored by his parents, who were busy dealing with the growing tensions in their own relationship. Pückler, thus, had little experience with family life.[21] At the age of five, he was entrusted to a tutor, and at seven, he was dispatched to a series of boarding schools, first to the Moravian academy in nearby Uhyst, where he stayed for five years, an experience that he suggests scarred him for life.[22] Once his mother obtained a divorce and left Muskau in 1799 (having given birth to four more children), his relationship with his father grew more difficult, prompting him to set off on his own peripatetic adventures. First, at the age of sixteen, he enrolled at Leipzig University, purportedly to study law but abandoning that course after a year of carousing to spend two years in Dresden as an officer in the Saxon cavalry. When his inherent prodigality soon caused him to move again, his father thought seriously about disinheriting him. Returning to Muskau was unthinkable, so the young Pückler spent the years from 1804 to 1810 in straitened circumstances, living very modestly in a series of European capitals and finally undertaking a walking trip— a necessarily low-budget version of a Grand Tour—through Germany, France, Switzerland, and Italy. Throughout these years, his indulgences and intemperate conduct involved him in duels, flirtations, and gambling—all of this adding to his reputation for profligacy. He was twenty-six years old when his father died in 1811.

Hermann was now Count von Pückler-Muskau, the lord of two domains: by far the largest one, his childhood home of Muskau, came to him from his mother's side; from his father's side, he inherited Branitz, an estate located just over twenty miles to the west, near Cottbus.[23] It did not take long for Pückler to discover that his father's legacy included enormous debts, the result of years of financial mismanagement. Branitz was not particularly productive and was, in any case, leased, but Muskau, an ancient imperial estate of the Holy Roman Empire, should have turned a profit. Encompassing nearly two hundred square miles of sandy, pine-covered hills dotted with lakes and traversed by the Neisse River, Muskau included a town (today Bad Muskau) and over forty villages. Although its status as an independent territory (*Grafschaft*) had been relinquished as a result of the mediatization of the German states in the early nineteenth century, its population of over eight thousand made it larger than many German principalities.[24] And it boasted a number of enterprises: several mills, brickworks, beekeeping and candle-making operations, productive timberland, fisheries with over one hundred fifty ponds and sixteen lakes, and mines yielding alum, granite, porphyry, and other metals. There was ample game, thousands of sheep, and a brewery that made a highly prized Weizenbier. These and other undertakings brought in various kinds of income (there was a fish tax, for instance), yet not enough to make up for the deep losses incurred under his father's stewardship, which were only augmented by Pückler's own inclination to spend beyond his means.[25]

Pückler's persistent ambition was to create a magnificent park at Muskau, an idea fostered throughout his earlier *Wanderjahre,* when he visited important gardens and country estates.

Before he could make headway on this project, however, the ongoing Napoleonic Wars intervened. This conflict had already brought about the dissolution of the Holy Roman Empire in 1806, which placed the once independent Muskau under Saxon rule. Since Saxony had allied itself with Napoleon's Confederation of the Rhine, Pückler now found himself obliged to provide billeting for soldiers of the French army at Muskau; he was even put under house arrest for a time due to suspected Prussian sympathies.[26] Only when the confederation was dissolved in 1813 could he serve once more as a soldier in the armies against Napoleon, which he did with some distinction, and at the end of hostilities in 1814, he traveled to England in the retinue of the victorious Russian tsar and Prussian king.

This was his first sojourn in England; it lasted for nine months, during which time he observed and admired the social whirl, emulated the manners and dress of the many important people he met, attended the theater, admired the burgeoning industry, and even purchased several English horses to take home with him. Most important for his landscaping project were his visits to the many large parks in the vicinity of London, the natural-looking "landscape gardens" that had brought England considerable fame and that Pückler saw as paradigms for Muskau. He spent weeks exploring dozens of estates, both on his own and in the company of his friend Leopold Schefer, whom he had appointed as park superintendent at Muskau and whom he sent for so that the two could tour properties together.[27] Aware that his landscaping plans would only add to his financial woes, he set his sights on a lucrative marriage, and it seemed success was near when he entered into a contract with the older and very wealthy widow Lady Lansdowne. Although the arrangement was ultimately scuttled by her family, she remained a loyal friend and helpful adviser during his second trip to England more than a decade later.[28]

When Pückler returned to Muskau in the spring of 1815, he was full of ideas for his park, yet it was clear that his lavish plans far outstripped his means. Redirecting streams, sculpting hills and dales, and planting and transplanting innumerable trees were expensive propositions. He also intended to renovate several existing structures and to build new ones (many designs were prepared by his friend Friedrich Schinkel, one of Germany's greatest architects). Meanwhile, he lost more of his seignorial rights and privileges when the Congress of Vienna awarded certain Saxon territories, including Muskau, to Prussia as a way of punishing Saxony for having sided with Napoleon.

In the following year, however, Pückler's personal and financial future began to look rosier, for he was then courting Lucie von Pappenheim, the daughter of Karl August von Hardenberg, the chancellor of Prussia. A well-educated, sophisticated, and charismatic woman who was nine years older than Pückler, Lucie had money in her own right and was expected to inherit a substantial fortune from her father.[29] Having left her previous husband after six years of marriage, she had been living independently for over a decade, and since 1815 she was residing in Berlin with Adelheid, her daughter, and Helmina, her ward. She undertook formal divorce proceedings soon after meeting Pückler, and the two were married in late 1817. Although their relationship may not have been sexual, it was deeply devoted, as indicated by their nicknames for each other: he was "Lou," perhaps from Ludwig but more likely from "loup" (wolf) or "filou" (rascal); Lucie, addressed in *Letters of a Dead Man* as Julie, possibly an allusion to the heroine of Rousseau's *La nouvelle Héloïse*, was "Schnucke" (a type of small German sheep).[30] Pückler had found not only a soul mate who shared his enthusiasm for creating a park but an intelligent, cultured, and generous companion for the rest of his years.

Regrettably, her significant fortune offered only a temporary reprieve to his financial difficulties, for they quickly depleted the funds she had brought to the match. The future still held the promise of Lucie's expected inheritance from her father, but when he died in 1822 they discovered that Hardenberg had disinherited his daughter in favor of a mistress. Meanwhile, Count Pückler got a boost in rank, for Prussia granted him the title of prince as a gesture to mollify him for the sovereign rights he had lost seven years before. Although this was the highest noble rank he could attain, it neither made him royal nor improved his fortunes. Yet it did lift his standing, especially in England, where anyone carrying the title of prince claimed great respect. Thus, in the following year, Lucie suggested that they seek a divorce, freeing him to seek a wealthy English bride; by the time it was granted in early 1826, the two were grudging but ready to carry out their plan. Having sold many of their worldly goods to stay afloat, they now parted with even more possessions in order to pay for what would be an expensive journey. With great reluctance and a vow to remain together in the future, whatever their official status, they set off on September 7, 1826. Lucie went as far as Bautzen, about thirty-five miles southwest of Muskau, and then turned back, while Pückler and his manservant Berndt continued on to Dresden. That evening, comfortably settled in an inn, he took up his pen to write his first letter home, beginning a faithful correspondence that would carry Lucie with him on his month-long journey across Germany and the Netherlands, his twenty-seven months in England, Wales, and Ireland, and his homeward passage via Paris (see pages xviii–xix).

Letters of a Dead Man

Of the several perspectives we gain through Pückler's chronicle of his journey to the British Isles, one of the most interesting is that of a Continental educated in the climate of the Enlightenment who encounters the society and culture of the preeminent nation of Europe. As Pückler's own biography vividly illustrates, he came to maturity in a fragmented, politically decentralized, and unstable area disrupted by the Napoleonic Wars, a realm slowly contemplating the possibilities of nationhood. Pückler considered himself a liberal thinker, up-to-date in his views on responsible leadership, social justice, and stewardship of the land, and much engaged by the potentialities of industry. Yet in numerous ways he remained a figure of the eighteenth century and what he saw as its romantic ideals. Raised a Protestant, he declares himself repeatedly as a man of belief and often displays an intense pantheistic reverence for nature, although he had a deeply skeptical view of organized religion. Pückler was an aristocrat from a political culture that had not yet engaged in true democracy, and like most of his class he looked upon the consequences of the French Revolution with a mix of unease and admiration. In England, he encountered a constitutional monarchy that had been in place for centuries, a country with vast international reach led by an aristocracy in possession of unimaginable wealth and extravagant land holdings, and a military that had proven instrumental in the defeat of Napoleon. Pückler could only see such a country as in many respects a model (both pro and con) for the future of Germany. All of this is reflected directly and indirectly in the published letters. But throughout his journey, and despite his close and, indeed, intimate experience of the British and the Irish, Pückler retained his objectivity along with his antipathies and affections. The result is a penetrating, astute, and very often witty panorama of a society bound by impossible wealth and the constraints of a rigid aristocratic tradition yet also seeming to hold the keys to the future.

Pückler's chronicle of his nearly two years in and around London describes a frenzied social life led at a hectic pace, packed with a myriad of personalities and events, and punctuated by idle moments of leisure. He arrives in London early in the fall, well ahead of the social season, which leaves him time to explore, to accustom himself to local habits and modish expectations, and to improve his English. He settles initially at the Clarendon Hotel on New Bond Street, close to Hyde Park and its bridleways, an ideal place to be seen.[31] His daily routine is quickly established: he gets up late, reads three or four newspapers over breakfast, checks his visiting book to see what he has scheduled, and then spends several hours riding around town, returning to his hotel to change in preparation for dinner, the theater, or a small exclusive party. He is soon admitted to the Travellers Club, where he spends time dining, gambling, adjusting to the idiosyncrasies of the house rules, and admiring the peculiarities of English customs, including the refined art of sitting: "It is a pleasure simply to *watch* an Englishman seated, or better reclined, in front of the fire in one of their bed-like chairs. Attached to the armrest is a device resembling a music stand equipped with a candlestick . . . In addition, an unusual contraption . . . receives one or both of his feet. The hat on his head consummates this enviable image of bliss" (63).[32] Elsewhere, we are treated to a description of a formal dinner in a great house that concludes, after the ladies adjourn to the library, with the entire company of men standing to relieve themselves in their individual chamber pots (165). The abundant detail and personal tenor of Pückler's descriptions bring people and places to life with singular immediacy. We are with him as he attends the theater, rides in his carriage, walks through the streets of London, visits a prison, or follows Parliamentary debates.

Pückler's main, albeit unmentioned, task awaited him in the scintillating arena of the Season, those months of feverish activity when the upper classes moved from their country houses to "town" in order to congregate at balls, dinners, and soirées as well as to entertain and court one another. There the display of wealth and position—along with those who hoped to acquire it—could be seen in its full regalia. Pückler leaps boldly into the fray, passing out and receiving as many visiting cards as possible and attending as many social events as he could manage, both private parties and the exclusive Almack's (balls for which invitations had to be gained through "Lady Patronesses"). Back in London after the preseason in Brighton, he records his first full day's activities: twenty-two social calls, dinner at a club, then a ball, and finally a soirée. He would likely have returned to his lodgings in time for breakfast, though he might first have taken a ride in a park at sunrise. Pückler describes intimate dinners with political and social notables, a breakfast for two thousand people at Kew Gardens, and balls so crowded that it is impossible to move, much less dance (an entertainment that Pückler habitually declines). He finds staircases chockfull of guests who will never catch a glimpse of their host, and outside streets so jammed with a gridlock of carriages that mayhem ensues. Over time, his schedule begins to wear heavily on him, which is hardly surprising considering its intensity, and he regularly seeks relief in long, early excursions into the countryside on horseback to watch the dawn: "My morning ride thus took me a good twenty miles from the city . . . that vast Babylon stretching out interminably before me with its thousand towers and hundred thousand sins, its fog and smoke, its treasures and miseries . . . its eternal sameness of dinners and parties!" (196–97).

Pückler had other ways of distracting himself from the restrictions of proper society, and his accounts are an important source for understanding early nineteenth-century popular culture. First, there is the theater, which he at times seems to attend almost nightly. It is a passion for him. London offered wildly popular and flourishing spectacles that were attended by all, from the more adventurous among the aristocracy to the plebeians, including pickpockets and prostitutes. Pückler is drawn to performances on every level, from popular musicals and vaudeville to animal acts and acrobats. He finds a grotesque street performance of *Punch and Judy* as engaging as a Shakespearean tragedy or an opera at Covent Garden. The rowdy, ill-mannered audiences, unimaginable on the Continent, come as a surprise, however. Pückler had regularly visited the theater in Berlin and Paris; he read the reviews of theatrical performances and was fully informed about various actors, actresses, singers, and playwrights. He digresses at length on a production of *Othello*, and at one point delivers a virtual dissertation on the dramatic subtleties of *Macbeth* with a startling defense of the Lady herself.[33] He was also an avid reader, and he had more than enough material to occupy him, for in 1826 alone London boasted 11 public reading rooms, 179 different newspapers and magazines, and well over 1,000 published books.

Throughout his London sojourn, Pückler makes periodic trips to other towns and to the countryside, where he visits estates, attends the races, tours factories and mines, and explores ruined castles, always taking note of the natural scene. He does not travel light, an extensive wardrobe being de rigueur: informal breakfast attire, riding duds, dinner clothes, and special dancing pumps, not to mention fox hunting paraphernalia, all of which might be needed. Luckily, Pückler is a virtuoso in the art of travel, and all his provisions are readily accessible—simply watching him unpack his efficiently composed baggage is a treat in itself. He convinces us that a traveler's life in nineteenth-century England had its hardships but also its luxuries—who could resist a triple layer of mattresses, a bathtub of Chinese porcelain, or an English breakfast?

A large tea urn stood in the middle of the table decoratively surrounded by a silver teapot, a *Spühlnapf,* and a milk jug. Three small Wedgewood plates with the same number of knives and forks and two large cups of lovely porcelain . . . an inviting platter with boiled eggs and another with toasted *oreilles de cochon à la Sainte-Ménéhould.* There were muffins on a dish kept warm by hot water; a second dish held cold ham; there was fluffy white bread, both dry and buttered toast, the best fresh butter in an elegant crystal container, handy salt and pepper casters, English mustard as well as *moutarde de maille,* and finally, a silver tea caddy with very good green and black tea (104).

Landscape gardens, of course, are of particular importance for him, so in mid-December he sets off on an organized tour of famous properties. Convinced that "a brief stay here can help a good gardener advance further in his discipline than ten years of study at home" (98), he brings his head gardener from Muskau to accompany him,[34] meanwhile gently teasing Lucie: "Given your aversion to moving on foot . . . it would therefore require at least 170 years for you to visit all the parks in England, of which there must be a hundred thousand, since no matter where one goes, the place is teeming with them" (104). Pückler never tires of the parks, and the descriptions of his country visits are replete with ribald anecdotes, including being turned away by cantankerous landlords, climbing over fences, bribing gatekeepers, dodging behind copses of trees to avoid detection, and even playing the occasional practical joke. More commonly, he is granted a generous welcome and shown around the great estates by the chatelaines or the owners themselves. He is much intrigued by these massive piles and their individual histories, and he makes a point of complimenting the arrays of ancient weaponry and ancestral portraits in vast entry halls.

As someone who claims a pedigree dating back to a character from the *Nibelungenlied,* he does not hide his admiration for the venerable lineage enjoyed by English families and the estates and artifacts that testify to it.[35]

The visits to country houses also offer Pückler the chance to indulge his love of the fine arts, a passion that in some respects rivals his devotion to gardens, nature, and the theater. Important collections of paintings always draw his full attention, and when possible he takes the time to dwell on particular works. He knew a lot about the Old Masters, had an excellent memory for them, and was capable of delivering informed opinions about the genuineness of a Titian or a Raphael. Visits to collections also offered him occasions to present Lucie with a no doubt unneeded history lesson or a random discourse on virtue. Pückler takes self-conscious delight in unveiling the secrets he finds concealed in the visages of kings and princes or in discovering in portraits of Machiavelli or Oliver Cromwell a complete outline of each man's character (and, by extension, an entire corpus of thought and the impact of a career). Indeed, sometimes in the course of his telling, the line between art and life seems to blur altogether. Among the more astonishing moments in *Letters of a Dead Man* is a voluptuous passage in which he describes a painting that seems in nearly every detail to be a reincarnation of Titian's *Venus of Urbino* (193–94). In fact, this is a barely disguised account of his visit to a prostitute, which the original letter makes explicit, earning him a sharp reprimand from Lucie.[36]

As would be expected of an alert and interested traveler during the rise of mechanized industry, Pückler took an interest in the factories of England. His principality at home included a number of villages with small industries and mines as well as peasant farmers, and as he tours the country he inquires about local conditions, labor relations, and land holdings. He visits a number of manufacturing operations in places like Birmingham and Sheffield, establishments that greatly impressed him with their complex machinery driven by steam power, their well-coordinated routines, and their astounding variety of products. He takes special pride in forging a button for Lucie on one such machine. Despite some deplorable conditions he encounters in the plants, Pückler comes to belittle the plight of the English workmen, concluding that they are pampered and overfed: "What *we* call affluence is here considered to be the bare essentials and is manifest across all classes" (384).[37] Needless to say, this unsympathetic impression of the consequences of the Industrial Revolution is markedly different from what his countryman Friedrich Engels would report from his time in Manchester less than two decades later. Yet Pückler manages to find romance in a nighttime view of Leeds, its belching smokestacks evoking not misery and oppression but a vision of splendor:

> A hundred red fires flashed up through the haze, and as many chimneys were lined up among them, exhaling black smoke. In such a setting the colossal five-story factories looked stunning. From every window two lights shone for the workers who toiled until deep in the night. To add a touch of the romantic to all this tumult of activity and industrial illumination, two ancient Gothic churches rose high above the houses, and in the blue dome of the heavens, the golden light of the moon poured down a majestic calm onto their spires, as if to temper the feverish labor below (296).[38]

How things were governed was a constant matter of importance to Pückler, and as it happened he was in London during a crucial moment of succession within the Tory leadership involving such figures as George Canning, the Duke of Wellington, and Robert Peel. He attended a number of the debates in Parliament, fascinated by a form of government he had not had the opportunity to study elsewhere, certainly not in Germany, and his accounts of these, like his assessment of the rhetorical skills of various speakers, are pointed. Although he mocks the bizarre behavior and indecorousness he witnesses in the lower chamber, he nonetheless greatly respects a system of governance that succeeds in recruiting talent and encouraging argument rather than relying on established authority and bureaucracy.[39]

Despite its many highpoints, Pückler's lengthy sojourn in London and its environs comes to be tainted with melancholy—a not uncommon disposition for someone whose emotions tended to swing from vibrant enthusiasm to gloomy introspection. His moods are something he addresses often, and at times, either the landscape or the city becomes a metaphor for his state of mind, occasionally with a solipsism that comes close to poetry. By July 1828, Pückler is through with the metropolis and determined to leave it, first arranging for his carriage, horses, and some birds to be sent to Lucie. As he prepares to depart for Wales, his tone darkens and he concludes his last communication from London with remarkable bitterness. We know in hindsight that his departure was in various respects a capitulation, an acknowledgment that his search for a wife had been a failure—but this is a side of the story he cannot tell in the published letters. And he was by this time also anxious about money, for keeping up with London high society had seriously strained his finances. This too he omits from *Letters of a Dead Man*, although he occasionally complains of rumors circling around him and, in one case, he becomes quite specific, confessing that he is threatened with public scandal at being wrongly implicated in the near drowning of a close female acquaintance (379–81).[40]

Yet however much we may know about the spoken and unspoken reasons for his cynicism, Pückler's final denunciation of the English upper classes still comes as a shock, for he unleashes a tirade against them for "true vulgarity, a crass immorality, an undisguised arrogance, and an uncouth disregard of good-heartedness—all of it striving for the luster of an empty refinement" (374). It is a heavy indictment given Pückler's customary aloofness—often witty or sarcastic but rarely intemperate. We cannot but sense a measure of self-condemnation, for he too had done his best to excel at the game he now condemns. He longs to be away and on his own: "Somewhere Lord Byron says about himself that only in solitude is his soul released to its full sphere of activity. I now see that this truth applies to lesser mortals as well, for it is the same with me. In the aggravations of society, I feel only half of my soul and am appalled at the thought of having to be amiable!" (381).

Pückler sets off for Wales, and as the distance from London increases, so does his mood improve and the pace of his life decelerate; he is at last free to follow his own inclinations. Large estates pass by unvisited as he concentrates his attention on landscape, picturesque ruins, and ancient churches, sometimes forsaking his carriage altogether and continuing for miles on foot, happy to be alone. The letters from these three or four weeks are often contemplative and inward looking as well as rich in anecdote and personal encounters. There are breathtaking descriptions, perhaps the most beautiful in all of his letters. Pückler confronts formidable mountain barriers, undertakes ascents along treacherous precipices, and becomes engulfed in horrific bouts of violent weather. On the one hand, Wales resembles a friendlier and more hospitable England, the people gracious and seemingly content with their lot. On the other hand, it is a wild and spirit-inhabited land quite unlike anything he has ever seen. Pückler's visit to Wales and then Ireland lasted only about six months, but it constitutes fully half of the published text. Accordingly, these letters can seem almost leisurely in their sense of time and place. They are also more occupied with political and religious issues than with the world of high society.

The industrial advances he witnesses in England and Wales exemplify modernity and the promise of increased well-being for all. Ireland, however, presents a very different picture—an agrarian economy consumed by poverty with little prospect of bettering its plight. The wealthy landowners are mostly English, Protestant, and typically absentee among a population that is overwhelmingly Irish and Catholic. The best part of the land had long been appropriated by the British, who rented out small parcels at rates considerably greater than what they were able to exact in England. Moreover, the Irish counties were heavily taxed to support an Anglican clergy, who were also mainly absentee and, as Pückler understands it, inclined to use their sinecures to underwrite lavish lifestyles at home.[41] Although he initially admired the English system of land tenure, the injustice being imposed on the Irish peasantry provokes him to reexamine his views: "That is Ireland! Neglected or oppressed by the government, degraded by the stupid intolerance of the English priesthood, abandoned by the rich landowners, and stigmatized by poverty and the poison of whisky. It is the home of naked, miserable wretches" (484).[42]

The harshness of this statement obscures Pückler's eventual identification with the Irish lot, which comes quickly and with great passion. He is determined to seek out Daniel O'Connell, the herculean leader of the Catholic emancipation movement, a man of imposing stature and eloquence (Figure 97). The pilgrimage to O'Connell's "solitary stronghold" at Derrynane is nothing short of thrilling (Figure 96). Battling through a furious downpour, Pückler is abandoned by his guide, nearly blown off his horse and drowned, rescued by a ghostly figure in black, and forced to proceed on foot carrying his saddle. Finally arriving in the dark of night, he is warmly welcomed by O'Connell into the house, where he enjoys an excellent dinner and well-aged wine (518–21).

O'Connell is presented as a model of enlightened leadership. Pückler is deeply impressed by the man and his rhetoric, both on his visit to Derrynane and in a later meeting, when the prince listens as he addresses the Catholic Association. Pückler also spends considerable time with a number of prominent Catholic clergymen, who greet him as a distinguished and sympathetic emissary. Among them he finds not only generosity, good humor, and a lack of pretension but also an unexpected liberality. These are qualities that he comes to admire in the Irish; he particularly appreciates their warmth, vivacity, and self-effacing wit, although he finds the peasantry prone to excessive drink and perpetual shillelagh battles. In Ireland, he seems to discover the alter ego of the English, and it pleases him greatly. When Pückler leaves O'Connell's company, the two of them ride together as far as a stream in spate and a half-destroyed bridge. There they bid farewell: "I could not help telling this champion of the rights of his fellow countrymen how much I hoped that, when next I saw him, he and his supporters would have succeeded in destroying the fortress of English intolerance, just as the torrent, in forcing its own path, had broken down the decayed walls of the bridge. And so we parted" (526).

Surrounded by symptoms of sectarian conflict in a culture ridden with superstition, Pückler's own reflections on the subject of piety and religious belief come across with unusual force. Although deeply averse to the "cultic" aspects of religion, he discovers much to like in the venerable traditions and the artistry of Catholic ritual. Anglican services seem apathetic and hypocritical by comparison. At one point, he meets—or more likely conjures up—the proverbially loquacious and irreverent Catholic priest, a "Dublin cleric" who brazenly declares that:

"For the most part, religious systems remain the most monstrous and strange amalgams of the sublime and the ridiculous, of eternal truth and blind ignorance, of genuine philosophy and patent idolatry . . . The question is whether Newton's discovery of the secrets of the heavens, or the inventors of the compass and the printing press, have not been a greater benefit to mankind than were the many founders of religions who demanded allegiance to their banner alone" (599). Whether this unnamed priest existed or not, Pückler is undoubtedly retailing his own opinions on the subject of religion, although, as if to underscore the point and simultaneously bring it into question, he follows this monologue with a personal observation: "That Jesuitical dogmas will no longer rule the world, and that freedom of the press will perform unimagined miracles— of that I am perfectly convinced. But people will still be people, and as a result I fear that force and deception will always prevail over reason." In either case, and against expectation, it is the long-suffering and yet spirited Irish who ultimately sustain Pückler's confidence in mankind.

The Irish adventures are so various and so frequently extraordinary, indeed so often hilarious, that they contain much of the best of Pückler's writing, which is further enriched by the spectacular and varied landscapes. Considered as a corpus, *Letters of a Dead Man* conveys an articulate, if often contradictory portrait of their author as much as of Britain and its people. Thus, from an intensely personal perspective, we are granted a wide-angle view of a society on the threshold of the Victorian era and in command of a vast empire. In Pückler's last letter, written from Paris, he acknowledges this larger dimension of his undertaking with a wonderfully apt metaphor. First, he comments on the current fashion for panoramas of various sorts, or what he amusingly refers to as the "amas"; he has just toured several of these venues, not only the more familiar cycloramas and dioramas, but also a georama (in the center of the globe) (Figure 126), a neorama (from the interior of Saint Peter's, the center of Christendom), a cosmorama (in the center of the cosmos), and a uranorama (in the center of the solar system), and he concludes, "So I started the day in the middle of the earth, next admired the various splendors of its surface, and ended up, after a brief visit to all the planets, in the sun" (688). Thus, in a single inspired stroke, and with a sly nod to Dante, Pückler gathers the universe around him to position his own story within the great human comedy itself.

Beyond *Letters of a Dead Man*: The Rest of the Biography

The trip to Britain saved Muskau Park—without the help of a young heiress—and the extraordinary reception of *Letters of a Dead Man* restored Pückler's spirits in other respects as well. He reveled in the heady gossip over his anonymity, which of course actually made him quite famous. Two additional publications appeared in 1834, the first a motley collection of short pieces that titillated Germany as much as *Letters of a Dead Man* had done, and that soon appeared in French and English translations.[43] The second was his important treatise *Andeutungen über Landschaftsgärtnerei* (*Hints on Landscape Gardening*), an elegantly produced and lavishly illustrated handbook on how to build and maintain a landscape park.[44] Centered on Pückler's creation at Muskau, it is both a technical guide and a personal reminiscence, and it brought him and his garden more renown while bolstering his standing as a landscapist and writer.

The success of *Letters of a Dead Man*, along with Pückler's inherent restlessness, provided the impetus for further travels, this time to more exotic locales; his costume of nankeen trousers and a Turkish fez with a blue tassel set the tone. Although he had long wished to visit America, those plans were interrupted by a challenge to a duel. Once that was settled in his favor, he set off in 1834 for what turned out to be six years of travel. After a few months in France, he headed to North Africa, spending time in Algiers and Tunis, before proceeding to Malta and Greece. In the course of these adventures he became ill and was twice delayed by outbreaks of cholera and the plague. On the move again, he spent nearly six months in Egypt, where he was befriended by the powerful Muhammad Ali Pasha. He also toured Sudan, Palestine, Lebanon, Syria, and Turkey.[45] Throughout these many—and very costly—adventures, Pückler never stopped writing, keeping copious journals and rarely neglecting daily letters to Lucie. The result was several sets of volumes that brought in enough additional income to sustain life at Muskau for a few years longer, although nothing among his extensive literary endeavors could equal the personal investment and wealth of observation that gave *Letters of a Dead Man* its well-deserved reputation.[46]

Thus, his financial situation continued to deteriorate, finally leaving him with only two options: bankruptcy or selling the entire principality. With some hesitation, he and Lucie chose the latter, and a buyer was found in 1845. Once their obligations were paid off, the couple moved to Branitz, the estate that his father had essentially abandoned upon marrying Pückler's mother. Much smaller than Muskau, and without its dramatic topography, Branitz presented a different challenge, one that the prince undertook at first with reluctance and then with the full force of his creativity and enthusiasm.

Pückler's preoccupation with nature, landscape, and gardening was lifelong. He describes himself more than once in *Letters of a Dead Man* as a "parkomaniac," an epithet he bore with pride. Pückler conceived the parks at Muskau and Branitz as enduring monuments, and it is thus fitting that both remain to testify to his success.[47] His accomplishments as a designer eventually captured the attention of the most influential landscapists in the United States, including Charles Eliot (1859–1897) and Frederick Law Olmsted (1822–1903). *Hints on Landscape Gardening* was eventually translated into English as well, and Muskau Park became yet more widely known abroad.[48] Somewhat reduced in scale, the park is now a UNESCO World Heritage Site that stretches over nearly fifteen hundred acres of modern-day Germany and Poland. Having survived the political and military ravaging of the twentieth century, which for a time transformed the Neisse River into an armed border, the park is again a unified whole. Restored and tended, its buildings renovated and its once sundered expanses joined by rebuilt bridges and unbroken pathways, it is a reasonable approximation of Pückler's original dreamscape. Branitz, too, has been beautifully preserved and restored, and there, curiously arising from the center of a small lake, stands the final tribute to his eccentricity, a grassy pyramid that he contrived for his burial place, the "tumulus" as he called it, where he and Lucie still rest today.

NOTES TO THE INTRODUCTION

1 Robert Burton, "Democritus Junior to the Reader," in *The Anatomy of Melancholy* (London: J. M. Dent, and New York: E. P. Dutton, 1932), 1:15.

2 Pückler's wife was Countess Lucie von Pappenheim, née Hardenberg (1776–1854), see pages xxviii–xxix and xxxviii, note 29.

3 Pückler's original letters are held in the Varnhagen Collection of the Biblioteka Jagiellońska (Jagiellonian Library), Kraków, Poland; microfilm copies are in the Pückler Archive, Branitz. Some of the correspondence not included in *Briefe eines Verstorbenen* (see pages xxv and xxxvii, note 10) was published after Pückler's death by Varnhagen von Ense's niece Ludmilla Assing (1821–1880) in *Briefwechsel und Tagebücher des Fürsten Hermann von Pückler-Muskau*, 9 vols. (1873; repr., Bern: Herbert Lang, 1971). Assing also published a two-volume biography of the prince. Lucie's letters from before 1834 were burned.

4 The divorce laws in Britain were not reformed until the middle of the nineteenth century, beginning with the first Matrimonial Causes Act of 1857. Until then, proceedings were rare, costly, and nearly always initiated by husbands; from 1700 to 1857, there were only 314 such acts of Parliament, of which at most eight were petitions by wives. Proven adultery was the only admissible basis, and for a woman to submit a claim, life-threatening cruelty had to be verified as well.

5 See pages 71–72.

6 The support of Varnhagen and his wife Rahel, née Levin (1771–1833) was very important to the success of *Letters of a Dead Man*.

7 Hannah Arendt's biography—*Rahel Varnhagen: The Life of a Jewess*, trans. Richard and Clara Winston (London: East and West Library, 1957)—was published first in English, with the German original appearing in 1959. A revised edition was issued by Johns Hopkins University Press in 2000.

8 Pückler was pleased to hear of Varnhagen's reaction to Muskau, see page 467.

9 Indeed, the ghost of the supposedly deceased author admits to such interventions and more in the convoluted Second Preface by the Editor, where he is conjured up by the Editor.

10 *Briefe eines Verstorbenen: Ein fragmentarisches Tagebuch aus England, Wales, Irland und Frankreich, geschrieben in den Jahren 1828 und 1829*, 2 vols. (Munich: Franckh, 1830). In the present translation, the forty-eight letters are in their original chronological order.

11 *Briefe eines Verstorbenen: Ein fragmentarisches Tagebuch aus Deutschland, Holland und England, geschrieben in den Jahren 1826, 1827, und 1828*, 2 vols. (Stuttgart: Hallberger, 1831). Modern editions include: *Briefe eines Verstorbenen*, ed. Therese Erler (Berlin: Rütten and Loening, 1987); *Briefe eines Verstorbenen*, ed. Günter J. Vaupel (Frankfurt: Insel, 1991); and *Briefe eines Verstorbenen*, ed. Heinz Ohff (Berlin: Propyläen, 1986 and 2006). For an up-to-date bibliography, see Peter James Bowman, *The Fortune Hunter: A German Prince in Regency England* (Oxford: Signal Books, 2010).

12 Varnhagen's lengthy review appeared in the *Jahrbücher für wissenschaftliche Kritik* (1830), nos. 56–59, cols. 446–468, and (1831), cols. 913–924. Goethe's review ("Briefe eines Verstorbenen," *Jahrbücher für wissenschaftliche Kritik* [1830], nos. 56–59, cols. 468–472) inspires the self-proclaimed editor of *Letters of a Dead Man* to summon Pückler's ghost in the Second Preface so that he can pass on the happy news. Heinrich Heine's response appeared in *Reisebilder II, 1828–1831: Kommentar,* ed. Christa Stöcker (Berlin: Akademie-Verlag, 2003), 506. The English translation is in part four of *Heinrich Heine's Pictures of Travel*, 9th ed. (Philadelphia: Schaefer and Koradi, 1882), 411.

13 Some German universities had even begun offering courses on the art of traveling.

14 Literacy rates were soaring; by the end of the eighteenth century, Prussia boasted about eighty percent literacy, England and Wales seventy percent—numbers that included more and more women. The postal service was equally impressive: in London, there were as many as a dozen mail deliveries a day (an early augury of email), and outside the capital post coaches crisscrossed the countryside on high-quality roads, carrying letters, packages, and travelers in relative comfort and at considerable speed. The system was so effective that Pückler sent his own carriage home part way through his trip and took to riding in mail coaches, often sitting outside where he had a splendid view.

15 The abridged French translation is *Mémoires et voyages du prince Puckler-Muskau: Lettres postumes sur l'Angleterre, l'Irlande, la France, la Hollande, et l'Allemagne*, 5 vols. (Paris: H. Fournier Je, 1832–1833). It also appeared almost immediately in Swedish and Dutch.

16 As with the original German publication, the first two volumes contained the later letters and had a different title in the first editions: *Tour in England, Ireland, and France, in the Years 1828 and 1829: With Remarks on the Manners and Customs of the Inhabitants, and Anecdotes of Distinguished Public Characters; In a Series of Letters; By a German Prince*, trans. Sarah Austin (London: E. Wilson, 1832). The second two volumes appeared in the same year and bore the title *Tour in Germany, Holland, and England in the Years 1826, 1827, and 1828, With Remarks on the Manners and Customs of the Inhabitants, and Anecdotes of Distinguished Public Characters; In a Series of Letters; By a German Prince*, trans. Sarah Austin (London: E. Wilson, 1832). All four volumes were republished in Philadelphia in 1833, and many excerpts were published in various periodicals. For additional editions, see page xlv, note 2.

17 For an overview of Austin's editing, see pages xli–xlii.

18 Austin writes in her introduction that rumors have named Prince Pückler-Muskau as the anonymous author, but she does not admit sure knowledge of this fact. She does, however, add "by a German Prince" to her title, and the multitude of reviews in British periodicals did not fail to name him openly. On the reception of the *Tour* and Austin's relationship with Pückler, see Bowman, *The Fortune Hunter*, 164–69, 210–11; and E. M. Butler, *A Regency Visitor: The English Tour of Prince Pückler-Muskau Described in his Letters, 1826–1828* (New York: Dutton, 1958), 15–26. For a fascinating account of Austin's lengthy correspondence with Pückler, see Lotte Hamburger and Joseph Hamburger, *Contemplating Adultery: The Secret Life of a Victorian Woman* (London: Macmillan, 1992).

19 Heinrich Heine, *Lutetia*, 1854; the original German text was translated in *French Affairs: Letters from Paris*, trans. Charles Godfrey Leland (New York: United States Book Company, 1893), 2:28. These passages appear in the lengthy "Letter of Dedication to His Serene Highness The Prince Pückler Muskau," 17–32.

20 The story of Prince Pückler's life has been told numerous times, in English most fully in the engaging biography by Eliza M. Butler, *The Tempestuous Prince, Hermann Pückler-Muskau* (London and New York: Longmans Green, 1929), which shocked and captivated in equal measure when it appeared; and recently in Bowman, *The Fortune Hunter*, which, though focusing on Pückler's bride search in England, also offers a comprehensive and entertaining account of his years before and after that adventure.

21 His maternal grandfather, Hermann von Callenberg, who died in 1795, was the exception, often serving as Pückler's advocate.

22 The German name for Moravians is Herrnhuter, and Pückler later called this academy the "Herrnhuter Hypocrite Institution."

23 His titles included Standesherr von Muskau (mediatized lord of Muskau) and Erbherr auf Branitz (hereditary lord of Branitz).

24 Pückler's father had been the *Reichsgraf* (imperial count) of Muskau, a sovereign position that meant he was answerable only and directly to the Holy Roman Emperor and not subject to any other secular authority. When the Holy Roman Empire was dissolved by Napoleon, however, all such positions were mediatized—that is, no longer direct—and the ruler of Muskau owed allegiance to Saxony. The inhabitants of the region spoke German or Sorbian (Wendish), a West Slavic language that is now protected as a minority language in Germany.

25 A description written by a soldier billeted at Muskau in 1812 tells of extreme poverty among the Wendish population.

26 As many as forty thousand soldiers were billeted at Muskau; these included Russian and Prussian troops as well as those fighting for Napoleon. See the afterword to *Briefe eines Verstorbenen*, ed. Günter J. Vaupel (Frankfurt: Insel, 1991), 2:701.

27 Leopold Schefer (1784–1862) was a German poet and novelist who resided in Muskau and served for a time as manager of Muskau and Branitz.

28 Pückler's near marriage to Lady Lansdowne is told in detail in Bowman, *The Fortune Hunter*, ch. 2.

29 Married at the age of twenty to Count Carl Theodor von Pappenheim, Lucie separated from him six years later and resided at his estate at Dennenlohe until she moved to Berlin, where she met Pückler in 1816. She divorced Pappenheim the following year.

30 The name Julie may be an allusion to Jean-Jacques Rousseau's epistolary novel *Julie, ou La nouvelle Héloise* (Amsterdam, 1761), in which a central element is the heroine's picturesque garden.

31 Before long he would move to less expensive rooms, rented from a milliner, on Albemarle Street.

32 Unlike coffee houses on the Continent, English gentlemen's clubs were exclusive, admitting only upper-crust men and rarely foreigners. In London, Pückler was also admitted to the United Service Club, but he far preferred the Travellers Club, which he describes at length in entertaining detail.

33 On Macbeth, see pages 310–13; on *Othello*, see pages 348–49.

34 Just as he earlier brought Schefer to England, he now sent for Jacob Heinrich Rehder, who was instrumental in the transformation of Muskau Park; see page xxxix, note 48.

35 Pückler proposes that his family is descended from Rüdiger, a hero in the *Nibelungenlied,* the famous Middle High German epic of ca. 1200; see *Hints on Landscape Gardening: Together with a Description of Their Practical Application in Muskau,* trans. John Hargraves (Basel: Birkhäuser, in association with the Foundation for Landscape Studies, 2014), 88n.

36 See pages 193–94. Typically for the era, Pückler's moral code did not preclude sexual encounters. He comments more than once—sometimes with sympathy, sometimes with dismay—on the spectacle of widespread prostitution in London. This was a widely known phenomenon, and it gave rise to helpful guidebooks such as *Harris's List of Covent Garden Ladies,* an annotated directory published annually from 1757 to 1795.

37 This comment is made in connection with Birmingham, which he describes positively here but negatively earlier (127–28), although generally with begrudging admiration (134).

38 He is similarly romantic about the smokestacks of Birmingham (127).

39 He writes: "This double senate of the English people, whatever its human failings, is something extraordinarily magnificent; and when you look at its workings from up close, you begin to understand why the English *nation* is still the first on the planet" (209). For an excellent summary of Pückler's view on the British and Prussian systems of government, see Bowman, *The Fortune Hunter,* 105–7.

40 She was, in fact, a niece of Napoleon.

41 See pages 552–54. Pückler includes a chart of these inequities in the diocese of Cashel, where Catholics make up 97 percent of the population but where Protestant clerics, supported by enforced tithing, outnumber Catholic priests by four to one (see page 560).

42 His initial admiration is clear: "When a great man calls a village his own, this does not mean, as with us, that he merely has dominion over it . . . [in England] they are kings in the bosom of domesticity and live placidly in the quiet assurance that their property is inviolable . . . When you consider this, I say, you must admit that England is a blessed land, if not a perfect one" (pages 59 and 444–45).

43 *Tutti Frutti,* 5 vols., trans. Edmund Spencer (1834; repr., New York: Harper, 1834).

44 *Andeutungen über Landschaftsgärtnerei, verbunden mit der Beschreibung ihrer praktischen Anwendung in Muskau* (Stuttgart: Hallberger'sche Verlagshandlung, 1834). For the recent English translation, see note 35.

45 In Lebanon, he stayed for over a week with Lady Hester Stanhope, whose ability to "go native" (see Pückler's account on pages 192–93), provided a model for his own penchant for native garb. For a detailed and entertaining overview of these travels, see Butler, *The Tempestuous Prince,* ch. 3.

46 His published works make up twenty-nine volumes.

47 That work continued on his plans for Muskau after his departure was due to the loyalty of his head gardener Rehder and Rehder's apprentice and successor Eduard Petzold (1815–1891), as both men were kept on by the new owners. Furthermore, Petzold himself became a recognized landscape designer, and his writings were significant in establishing Pückler's legacy. See Linda B. Parshall, introduction to *Hints on Landscape Gardening,* 16–17. Pückler went on to produce designs for other parks, including Babelsberg and Ettersburg. Rehder's influence also endured through his grandson Alfred Rehder (1863–1949), who, after being trained in Germany, worked at Harvard's Arnold Arboretum for fifty-one years. See Gerhard Rehder, "The Making of a Botanist," *Arnoldia* 32 (1972): 141–56.

48 There had been a French translation in 1847, but English speakers, many of whom visited the park, had to wait seventy years for *Hints on Landscape Gardening,* trans. Bernhard Sickert (Boston and New York: Houghton Mifflin, 1917), now superseded by John Hargrave's translation of 2014 (see note 35, above).

TRANSLATOR'S PREFACE

This is the first unabridged English translation of Prince Hermann von Pückler-Muskau's *Briefe eines Verstorbenen*. It is based on the original four-volume German publication, except that here the chronological order has been restored, thus allowing the reader to follow the author's adventures in their proper sequence. Although there are no omissions from the German version of *Letters of a Dead Man*, there are a few additions and other adjustments: where I am able to do so, I give full names for the individuals and places that Pückler identifies only with initials; I have relocated a few footnotes, placed the First Preface by the Editor at the beginning of the book, and relegated the Second Preface by the Editor to the end as a kind of postscript. Otherwise, this translation follows the text that Pückler himself shepherded into print.[1]

It must be stressed that *Letters of a Dead Man*, although taken from the actual letters that Pückler wrote to his wife Lucie, was nonetheless scrupulously recast for publication and properly honed for an early nineteenth-century reading public. In spite of the claims made in the prefaces and footnotes, the letters were not published "exactly as they were originally written." This is not to say that they are fabrications, but simply that Pückler reworked them, sometimes extensively, before sending them into the world. The originals, although at points racier and more candid, are twice as long, loosely composed, and full of details that would hold little interest for a general reader; furthermore, they contain some passages that are excessively intimate and confessional, as well as others that might make the author appear more mean-spirited and at times more salacious than he would wish. The edited letters, on the other hand, are very much a polished construction, not only revised but also augmented and harmonized.

Nearly two centuries have passed since *Briefe eines Verstorbenen* was translated into English by Pückler's contemporary, Sarah Austin. Her edition—*Tour in England, Ireland, and France* (published in 1832)—is justifiably celebrated and has until now been the sole means for readers of English to enjoy Pückler's letters in anything approaching their entirety. Although Austin's prose can often be difficult for a modern reader to parse, her language has a flair, facility, and period flavor that do ample justice to Pückler's style.[2]

Austin was very good at gauging her readership: the *Tour* was the *succès de scandal* of the time, and part of its success was due to her meticulous management of the text. Pückler had amended his original letters to remove much that was invasive, insulting, or overly revelatory, but Austin went even further. Despite her claim to have retained every opinion "without the least attempt at change or coloring," save the rare intervention to "obscure" a passage that might be seen as "objectionably personal," her emendations were, in fact, legion.[3] These extend from changing or eliding a few words to eliminating entire pages. (For example, she omits the Second Preface by the Editor altogether.) Not only did Austin seek to provide a text that did not offend her readers, she was intent on polishing the character of the author, with whom she had fallen in love.[4] Perhaps as a consequence of that alone she was particularly averse to sexual innuendos and the praise of female beauty. She even went so far as to cut a suggestive line from Shakespeare's *Othello* and to omit a discussion of the sex life of frogs. Austin shielded the identity of certain individuals even more carefully than Pückler did by further removing or altering initials, indications of rank, and place names, and she often tempered his opinions about religion and politics. Anecdotes were relocated from one letter to another, and the embittered diatribe that Pückler delivered on his departure from London was reduced nearly by half. Austin cut a nine-page discussion of the Paris theater, eliminated a reference to O'Connell's blond wig, and omitted a description of a certain gentleman's "calf enhancers." We miss hearing about the reuse of soiled tablecloths in country houses and the mistreatment of foreigners at the Travellers Club. The list of her interventions is long and by itself constitutes a lesson in a pre-Victorian sense of propriety.

This translation restores all of Austin's omissions and palliations. My goal has been to provide a complete text that captures the appeal of *Letters of a Dead Man*, not just in their content but in their language, and to render Pückler's words in an idiom that is modern without sacrificing the period charm of the original. The challenge for any translator is preserving the various aspects of a writing style—in this case, doing justice to Pückler's eloquence, wit, and lightly-worn erudition, maintaining the lushness of his descriptions and the freshness of his dialogues, and expressing this in fluid and accessible English. In a discussion of Shakespeare, Pückler himself muses on the proper goal of translation, concluding that it should aim for authenticity and spontaneity. This has also been my ambition: a translation that remains as close as possible to the prototype without being constrained by it, that portrays its spirit and sense in natural-sounding prose. Of course, any translation is necessarily an interpretation, and certain compromises are unavoidable: puns are nearly impossible to convey, allusions often need explanation, unintentionally obscure passages ask for clarification. Meanwhile, I have somewhat tempered Pückler's prolixity, varied his vocabulary in accordance with English preference, and removed many word repetitions and superfluous adjectives and adverbs. I have shortened his typically lengthy German sentences (which can reach twenty lines or more) and introduced additional paragraph breaks. I have employed traditional English punctuation and avoided the constant use of dashes in the original. I have corrected Pückler's facts only rarely, and if so, mention this in an endnote.

Letters of a Dead Man contains many lively interpolations by the so-called Editor, both in his additions (he contributed two prefaces and many footnotes) and his excisions (he cut various passages "to protect the reader," indicating them by lines of dots). This supposed friend of the dead man is, of course, an invention of Pückler himself, a lively Doppelgänger who weaves in and out of the letters adding commentary, updates, and analyses. The reader should consider his contributions both antic and instructive, which is certainly how Pückler meant them.

————

The countless English words and short phrases set off by quotation marks or italics in the original German publication are simply included here unmarked. Longer English passages are much less frequent and often awkwardly phrased, revealing Pückler's imperfect control of the language. These I have occasionally improved.

Pückler was much more comfortable in French, something that is clear from the ease and regularity with which he inserted phrases and even short dialogues in that language throughout *Briefe eines Verstorbenen*. For the reader's convenience, I have translated many of these without noting it. In some instances, however, I have kept the French, not only to retain the effect but also to show the particular ways in which the language served Pückler's purposes—for example, as a signal of intimacy (particularly with Lucie), as a gesture of coyness, or as an attempt at masking indiscretion. These, as well as words or phrases in other foreign languages, are generally translated in the endnotes unless they are included in Webster's Encyclopedic Unabridged Dictionary of the English Language or are otherwise easily understood.

Pückler often includes a translation or summary of something that he has heard or read in English. A number of these are careful translations of identifiable texts, while others are abridged or variously altered. Meanwhile, it is clear from the content and consistency of style that many of the passages he claims to have taken from elsewhere are, in fact, conflations or fabrications by Pückler himself. As he confesses to Lucie at one point, "Whenever I send you excerpts, you can never be sure who wrote them" (240). I have tried to find the English source of each translation. Whenever I was successful and discovered that Pückler's rendering was a close approximation of it, I simply quoted the original; when he provided only a very loose paraphrase, I retranslated his German version of the text back into English. In both cases, a reference to the source is provided in an endnote.

To save repeating information in the endnotes, I have compiled annotated indexes of proper names and places (including names of characters in plays, the subjects of portraits, the places referred to in literary works, and the like). The footnotes added by the Editor appear at the bottom of the pages, as in the original publication. My own commentary is in the endnotes, marked in the text by Arabic numerals. I have updated the spelling of proper names and places; converted Pückler's measures into miles, yards, and acres; and given temperatures in Fahrenheit. All quotations from the Bible are from the King James Version.

The original edition of *Briefe eines Verstorbenen* was reprinted many times in the 1830s. There were numerous errors in the earliest volumes; indeed, in his Postscript, the Editor complains bitterly about the number of misprints introduced into the first published half of the letters. Since many of these were quickly corrected, modern German editions are generally based on the second and third printings. Of these, I relied on Günter J. Vaupel's 1991 edition and Heinz Ohff's 1986 edition.[5] The former publication has useful notes and interesting illustrations, and it is augmented by selections from additional letters by Pückler.[6] Although the latter publication has extensive notes, it must be consulted with care, for the text and notes contain errors that have not been rectified in the "new and revised" edition.

Note on the Illustrations

Some of the early editions of *Briefe eines Verstorbenen* included a small number of tipped-in plates, but apart from these Pückler's published letters were not illustrated. The language of the letters, however, is often intensely visual, full of evocative descriptions of people, landscapes, buildings, and works of art. Furthermore, Pückler assiduously documented his journey by collecting prints, drawings, booklets, and even the occasional pressed flower. After his return to Muskau, he pasted these souvenirs into four large leather-bound volumes (22 × 15 inches [56 × 38 cm]), his so-called Memory Albums. There he disposed nearly one thousand items in the order of his travels, annotating the pages, sometimes at length, in his delicate script.[7] The value of these mementos as pictorial supplements to the letters led to the idea of including a selection of illustrations to amplify Pückler's written account. About forty percent of the images in this translation are taken from the Memory Albums; the remainder were selected from sources roughly contemporary with Pückler's time in the British Isles, although I have taken occasional liberties with strict chronology in order to provide examples best suited to specific passages.

NOTES TO THE TRANSLATOR'S PREFACE

1 Although the second half of the letters were published first, I have put them in chronological order. This has meant that a few of the footnotes inserted by the Editor at the first instance of a word or phrase have been moved to accommodate the reordering. Pückler's sense of propriety led him to disguise many people and places by using only initials, a convention of nineteenth-century literature that lent an air of credibility while piquing the reader's interest. The majority of the names newly identified in this publication are due to the work of Peter James Bowman.

2 On Austin's translation, see page xxvi. Parts of her translation have been reprinted elsewhere. A few passages appeared in periodicals such as *The Athenaeum; Journal of English and Foreign Literature, Science, and the Fine Arts;* and *The Literary Gazette: A Weekly Journal of Literature, Science, and the Fine Arts.* An abridged version of the London letters (renumbered) can be found in Butler, *A Regency Visitor.* Flora Brennan, trans., *Puckler's Progress: The Adventures of Prince Pückler-Muskau in England, Wales, and Ireland as Told in Letters to His Former Wife, 1826–1829* (London: Collins, 1987), is another much abridged version, primarily containing the London letters and also renumbered differently; it includes Brennan's own translations as well as excerpts from Austin's *Tour.*

3 Austin makes these assertions in her prefaces.

4 See page xxvi.

5 See page xxxvii, note 11.

6 These are taken from Assing's posthumous edition, *Briefwechsel und Tagebücher des Fürsten Hermann von Pückler-Muskau.*

7 See, for instance, Figures 15 and 35. The albums now reside at Branitz Park and Castle, Pückler's estate near Cottbus, Germany. A selection of pages from all four volumes, along with a group of scholarly essays, were published in *Englandsouvenirs: Fürst Pücklers Reise 1826–1829* (Zittau: Graphische Werkstätten, 2005). Some images from the albums also appear in Bowman, *The Fortune Hunter;* and in *Reisebriefe aus England und Irland: Eine Auswahl aus den Briefen eines Verstorbenen* (Berlin: Aufbau-Verlag, 1992).

Letters of a Dead Man

FIRST PREFACE BY THE EDITOR

The letters we present here are exceptional, because they appear exactly as originally written, with only a very few, unimportant differences.[1]

It is easy to see that they were not intended for publication. However, the author's death has alleviated many concerns. And since his letters not only contain much interesting commentary, but also express a genuine individuality and are written with unvarnished frankness and complete impartiality—not common elements in our literature—we felt that their publication would not prove superfluous.

I must admit that, during his lifetime, the now-deceased gentleman had the misfortune of going about things differently from other people, which is perhaps why he was so often unsuccessful in his endeavors. Many of his acquaintances considered him a singular character, but alas *artificial*, and in this they did him a disservice. There was no one more genuine in his eccentricities, whether or not he appeared so; no one was more artless, where others thought they saw deliberation.

A similarly awkward fate is now haunting the publication of his letters, since certain circumstances, which cannot be explained here, made it necessary, against all custom, to print the last two parts first, so that they become the beginning.* [2] If these are well received, then we hope to follow them quickly with the rest, which will also prove capable of standing on their own. For the reader's convenience, we have preceded each letter with a short list of contents; we have also included a few notes throughout *ad modum Minelli*,[3] for which we ask your forgiveness and indulgence.

B——, October 30th, 1829

---

* In doing this, we are offering a special opportunity to all potential reviewers to let their wit shine forth. They could say, for example, that this work must certainly be called original, because it is *provisional,* having leapt with its two legs into the world, while leaving the head behind for the next performance.

LIST OF LETTERS AND TOPICS

Germany. Epistolary topics. Liston the actor. Madame Vestris and her lovely legs. The man whose way home was lit. *Manger et digérer* [Eating and digesting]. Sentimental outpouring. Unpleasant newspapers. Drury Lane. Braham, the Wandering Jew. Miss Paton. The raucous lower orders in the theater. Hetaerae and hierodules in that same place; their vulgarity and originality.

LETTER 6.
Hurdy-gurdies. Punch. Collapsing houses. The King in Parliament. Contrasts. The opera. Figaro without singers. English melodies. Charles Kemble. Old Zieten's costume. A diplomatic *bon mot*. Practical philosophy. Falstaff, as he is and ought to be. About the king in Hamlet. The brilliant performer from Newfoundland. Small circles in the big world. How the day passes here. Language learning. The author of Anastasius. His antique furniture. Oberon. The rocky chorus. Introduction to the king. Further incidents at the levee. Dinner at Mr. Rothschild's. True piety. His elegant friends. The King of Burma's state carriage. Mathews "at home."

LETTER 7.
The auctioneer. The lady Napoleonist. French theater. A rout. Lady Charlotte Bury. She is a Brownonian. Politics and conversation. The English fog-sun. The pickled hand and the corpse at the window. Modern knights of St John. Small park tour. A chain of scythes. English liberality. Richmond. Adelphi. A splendid drunkard. Musings. The diorama.

LETTER 8.
Professional travel. Gothic and Italian villas. The Priory. Cassiobury Park. Tasteful splendor. Drawings by Denon. Flower garden. Ashridge. Modern Gothic. Woburn Abbey.

LETTER 9.
Warwick Castle. Feudal grandeur. The baronial hall. Paintings. Leamington spa. Guy's Cliffe. His cave. Monument to Gaveston. Tombs of Beauchamp and Leicester. The ruins of Kenilworth. Elizabeth's balcony. The past. Birmingham. Mr. Thomasson's factory. Aston Hall. Cromwell. Chester. The county jail. Festivities of the rogues and villains.

LETTER 10.
Hawkstone Park. Unusually lovely natural landscape. Copper cliffs. The Red Castle and the New Zealander's hut. Yet more factories. Dangerous work. The room where Shakespeare was born. His grave. Various parks. Judith by Cigoli. Blenheim. Vandalism. Pictures. Oxford. Its Gothic appearance. The sovereigns as doctors and Blücher as apothecary. The museum. Tredescant and his dodo bird. The blue dung beetle as nobleman. Elizabeth's riding spats and the locks of her admirers. The library. Manuscripts. Stowe. Excess. Louis XVIII's lindens.

LETTER 11.
The conversational flair of the French. Escapade at the Duke of York's. English mourning. Journal excerpts. A cosmorama with kitchen fire. The boot-polish purveyor's sporting match. Visit to Cobham Hall. Paintings. The most beautiful woman. Life in an English country house. The park.

LETTER 12.

Brighton. Sunset. Oriental baths. On gourmands and heroes. A ride along the sea. Almack's ball. The wife of the governor of Mauritius. The romantic Scotsman. Sermons and preachers. The windmill. The society at Count Flahaut's. The highland brothers and the bloody hand. Private balls. The Garden Odysseus. Innocent politics.

LETTER 13.

The persuasiveness of beggars. Tea-kettle pantomime and jugglers. Dream visions. The fancy ball. Miss Fremantle. Social observations. Ball delights. Cloud pictures. The French doctor. Amateur concerts. The black people. Chinese feet. Opera, and park time.

LETTER 14.

Technical aspects of local society. Good food. Captain Parry and his ship. The Horse Guards' mess. Gambling. Females of middle age. Monkeys and ponies. The great dentist. Lady Stanhope in Syria. Adam is still alive. Tipu Sahib's shawl. A Titian Venus. Reality and art. Flight homeward. The lord mayor's dinner. Sea, fire, life. The estimable artistic couple. The houses of Lord Hertford and the banker Hope. Difficulties of English behavior. The Persian chargé d'affaires. Politeness of English princes. A ride in the countryside.

LETTER 15.

Correspondence. The lord mayor's dinner. The flying privy. The perils of fog. Freedom of the press. Unusual customs. Liston. The Areopagus. Almack's. Speedy travel. An afternoon at Parliament. Melodrama. Lady politicians. A *white* head. Brilliant parties. A new chariot of Venus. Coachmen's exploits. A dinner at the Duke of Clarence's. The homemade horse. Gold and silver. A lady's bazaar. Archbishops' aprons. Music of old. Industry in the City. The true aristocrats of religion. Dream fantasies.

LETTER 16.

Mr. Hope's art collection. A dandy's fashion necessities. Ladies' conference. Style of invitation. The Ascot races. The charming fairy and her country abode. The immortal Rousseau. Purse theft. A life-saving oven. English cavalry. The tailors' Hussars. Balls. Disenchantment. Two thousand breakfast guests. Colossal pineapples. Tyrolean singers. Duke of Northumberland's palace. Persian politics and fertility. Flower table. Children's balls. Art and nature. Greenwich. Execution. Court pleasures. King's Bench and Newgate. The uncommon philosopher. Vauxhall. Battle of Waterloo. The phrenologist. Characteristics. Mr. Nash's library. St Giles. Art exhibition. Pounds and thalers. Excerpts. Gossip. The tunnel. Good parody of *Der Freischütz*. Haymarket Theater. Courtesans. Bedlam. The last Stuart. Ominous funeral processions. Barclay's Brewery. West India docks. Delightful scam. Moonlit ride. A Harpagon from Isfahan. The self-beheading peasant. New organ. Miss Linwood. Canning's death. *Vivian Grey*. Respect for the public. Newspaper article. A walk with young ladies.

LETTER 17.

Short tour in a diving bell. Private conflagration. Counterfeit mermaid. Clever orangutan. Outlandish wounds. Living skeleton. Herr von S—— and his adventures. Salt Hill. Stoke Park.

Dropmore. Windsor Castle. Eton. St Leonard's Hill. The giraffe. Surreptitious drive through Virginia Water. Lord Harcourt's fear of the King. Lord Byron. An old lady's curious bed companion. The chapel. The English military. Anecdote about Canning. The races at Egham. Dwarf trees. Adventure by moonlight.

LETTER 18.
How a park should be. The comforts of friendship. Hatfield and Burghley House. Doncaster races. Finery in the countryside. Madame de Maintenon. Pointless talent. York Minster. A city walk. Skeleton of a Roman woman. Clifford's Tower. County jail. Thieves' wardrobe. Climbing a tower. Town hall and coats-of-arms of many lord mayors. Archbishop's seat. His kitchen garden. An odd case of distraction. Castle Howard. Painted memoirs. Bad climate. Two old women. Scarborough sand. Rock bridge. Lighthouse at Flamborough Head.

LETTER 19.
Whitby. What is remarkable about a duke. Ruins. Museum. Alum works. Lord Mulgrave's mansion and park. Fountains Abbey. Seven aged virgins, though not in uniform. Catacombs at Ripon. Harrogate spa. World's End. The old general. Harewood Park. Hunting dogs. Wooden draperies. Leeds. Turk grinding coffee. Cloth mills. Temple Newsam. Disppointment. Wentworth House. Sheffield, city of knives and shears. Wild animals. Lord Middleton's country house. St Albans Abbey. The Duke of Bedford's leg bone as shillelagh. Return to London.

LETTER 20.
Excursion to Brighton. Arundel Castle. Petworth House. A few portraits. Hotspur's sword. The elderly Whalebone. The lucky Duchess. Those born in October. Don Juan's further adventures in hell. A novel set in 2200. Rules of proper behavior. Political tinkerers. The license of English actors. Young as Percy. Sensible ensemble acting. Contemporary miracles. A domestic ball. About *Macbeth*. Macready in this role. Nervous invalids. Enchantments of the streets. Pleasant nighttime excursions. More about Hatfield. Persian treasures. About Turkey. Panshanger Park.

LETTER 21.
Billy the rat exterminator. Animal tragedy. The newest Roscius. Original sin. Austrian philosophy. Colors of the days. The dangers of Friday. Unpleasant Christmas present. Don Miguel. Portuguese etiquette. Comical occurrence at the theater. Festivities to honor the Infante. The charming adjutant. Anecdote by Sir Walter Scott. Disadvantages of sandy lands. India House. Tipu Sahib. Pastimes. Shawls. Journey in a steam-powered carriage and in one pulled by a kite. Romantic foxhunt. Famous foxhunting cleric. Illness. Recommendation concerning blotting paper. Advantages of being filled with air. Instruction. Reconvalescence.

LETTER 22.
The rich Thellusson. The dandy in America. English justice. "A Chancery Suit." The magicians are becoming dramatic, too. Mr. Carr's painting collection. General Lejeune's genre pictures. Collapse of the Brunswick Theater. The courtier. Mina, Arguelles, and Valdes. On performing and translating Shakespeare. Kean, Young, and Kemble in *Othello.*

Llyweln's loyal companion and his tragic end. Devil's Bridge. Tan-y-Bwlch. Its lovely park. Drained sea. Giant dam. Tremadog. Recollections of sand, dirt and home. Evening fancy. Philosophical nuggets. The owner of Penrhyn Castle. Road at Penmaenmawr. Conwy Castle with thirty-two towers. Contentment villa. The queen's closet. A fish called plaice. Hookes with forty-one sons. Gothic mania. Respectable Englishmen.

LETTER 28.
Vie de château. The cathedral in St Asaph. Tabernacle. Earnest belief. Denbigh Castle. Casino amid the ruins. Harpists competition and chorus. Romantic valley. Delightful Fanny. Her dairy and aviary. Bird paradise. Horseback excursion and fantastic region. Short sojourn in Craig-y-Don. Newspaper article. Fish dinner. Fortunate circumstances of the middle class. Preconceived notions about England. Isle of Anglesey. Parys Mines. On producing copper. New inventions. Holyhead. Lighthouse. Appalling cliffs, and seagulls in training. Hanging footbridge. Stormy crossing to Ireland. First impressions. Exhibition of fruit and flowers. The former are consumed. City walk and tour of various sights. Viceroy's castle and neo-Gothic chapel. University. My cicerone. Organ from the Armada. Archimedes' burning glass. Portraits of Swift and Burke. Battle of Navarino. Phoenix Park. Characteristics of the populace. Lady B—. The meaning of "character" in England. The Liffey. W—Park. Charming entrance. The Three Rocks. Beautiful view. The half-naked peasant girl. Wooden Capuchins. The dandy. The comfortable arrangements of the English aristocracy. Visit to the countryside. First meeting with Lady Morgan. Mishap on an evening ride. More about the Irish muse.

LETTER 29.
Ride to County Wicklow. Bray. Student accessories. English piety. Killruddery. Glen of the Downs. Pavilion and tiger. Valley of Dunran. The Giant. The Devil's Glen. Spooky chasm. Kühleborn. Rural meal in Rosanna. Tourists. Avondale, an Eden by moonlight. Avoca Inn. Meeting of the Waters. Castle Howard. Beautiful portrait of Mary Stuart. Park of Ballyarthur. The ha-ha. My horse plays blind man's bluff. Shelton Abbey. The negro porter. Loss of my pocketbook. What a gentleman is. The valley of Glenmalure. Entering a lead mine. The military road. Sun behind black masses of clouds. Seven Churches. Ivy-covered gate. Mysterious towers with no entryway. The black lake of St Kevin. The giant Fionn mac Cumhaill and the king's love-struck daughter. Her tragic end and the saint's excessive abstinence. Irish habits of dress. A recitation of Walter Scott and Moore. Bog and will-o'-the-wisps. A night on straw. Foggy heath. First rays of the sun over the lake and valley of Luggala. Romantic solitude. Portrait in stone. Powerscourt Park. Intolerance, sanctimony, and Sunday. Sugar Loaf. Rich land. Rest by a brook. Lord Byron.

LETTER 30.
Domestic affairs. The Donnybrook fair. Amorous couple. Powerscourt. The Dargle and Lover's Leap. Waterfall. Gallop with my guide behind me. Moonlit ride back. Life in the Bray inn, with an account of some English customs. Grand Duke of Weimar. Advantages of traveling discreetly. Industrious beggars. Kingston. Harbor construction. Machinery. Ghost ship. Tasteless monument to the king. Excellent road to Dublin. English riders and splendid clowns. The dance of the sea anemones.

LETTER 31.

The young clergyman. Trip west with him. Peculiar landscape. Sojourn at Captain Berming-
ham's. Life of true Irishmen. They are not excessively studied/meticulous. Church service in
Tuam. Galway racecourse. Similarities between the common folk and savages. City of Galway.
Lack of reading material there. The races. One rider's accident. The spectators' indifference.
The beautiful African. Athenry spa town, like a Polish village. Palace of King John. The abbey.
Escorted by the folk. Whiskey. Prague and Karlsbad as Bohemian villages. Asses a curiosity.
Castle Hackett. The fairy queen. She fetches herself a lover. Magnificent sunset. The meaning of
"good temper." Cong. Irish wit. The Pigeon Hole. Subterranean river. Meg Merrilies. Illuminated
rock vaulting. Enchanted trout beneath the earth. Lake Corrib with 365 islands. Ruins of a monastery. How the Irish bury their dead. The captain's good-heartedness.

LETTER 32.

Hors d'oeuvre. Adventure with the gypsy. How to recover one's soul. More about the beautiful
African. Shooting a pistol. Blue and black eyes. The devil's Sunday dress. Mr. L——. The stupid
fury of the Orangemen. Beautifully designed bodies of water. Picture gallery at Mount Bellew.
Peter with a scarlet wig by Rubens. Winter landscape by Ruisdael. Superb portrait of a Jew by
Rembrandt. Irish hunters. Departure by means of a letter-post cart. The engaging Irishman.
Certain revelation. Crossbones. Their history. The Punch Bowl. Lord Gort's park. My post-horses
want to stay there. The Irish postal service in general.

LETTER 33.

Limerick. Old-fashioned character of the city. Catholics and Protestants. Deputation and offer
of the Order of the Liberator. O'Connell's cousin. Cathedral. People believe I am Napoleon's
son. I switch my manservant and retreat. Conversation in the diligence. The Shannon resembles
an American river. Industrious beggars in Listowel. Twelve rainbows on a single day. Killarney.
Lake voyage in a storm. The dandy and the manufacturer. Danger of drowning. Innisfallen
Island. O'Donoghue's white horse. His ghostly story. The old boatman and his adventure.
Fashion magazine from hell. Muckross Abbey. The large yew. Decree of the priests. O'Sullivan's
Cascade. The young Sunday's-child. The wager. Addressing Ross Castle. Two Englishmen too
many. The Knight of the Gap. Madman's rock. Fanferluche. Park at Brandon Castle. A bugler.
The Eagle's Nest and Coleman's Leap. Dinner. Fresh salmon roasted over arbutus sticks. Home-
ward journey. Melancholy thoughts. Moonlit baptismal ceremony with whiskey. Julie Island.
Trip to Kenmare. Shillelagh battle. Nighttime ride to Glengariff. Bizarre road. Colonel White's
park, a model. The owner's family. Lord Bantry's shooting lodge. Storm. Sinister mood. Rock
basin, tempest, invocation, apparition of . . .

LETTER 34.

Who the Black Huntsman really was. Return to Kenmare. An Irish messenger. Invitation to
O'Connell's. Ride to his enchanted castle. Adventurous travel. Blackwater Bridge. Last tree to
be seen. Chaos from now on. Fearsome coast. Road ending in the sea. Expensive good advice.
Rescued by a smuggler. Crossing the mountain pass in blackest night. Udolpho's mysteries.
Derrynane Abbey. Light. A man in a dressing gown. O'Connell the Great Agitator. Various

about him. Father L'Estrange, his confessor. O'Connell as chieftain, dispensing justice to his subjects. His religious tolerance. Departure from Derrynane. O'Connell accompanies me. New Jupiter in the form of a bull. Danish forts. Farewell. Irish modes of transport. Courtesy of the Irish lower classes. Rectified incident. The innkeeper's daughter at Kenmare. Hungry Hill and its majestic waterfall. O'Rourke's eagle. Modern Ganymede. Seals below my window. Their love of music. Domestic worship service. Pious discussion of the Flood, the Last Judgment, and the Apocalypse. Praise of the splendid region, a place to build cottages.

Letter 35.
Honeycombs in the open air. Egyptian lotus. Visit to a pair of eagles. Their romantic dwelling and their unusual instinct. Local wild huntsmen. The caverns of Sugarloaf. Tracks of the fairy queen's carriage. Dangers of hunting in these mountains. Fog, bogs, and wild bulls. The taming of one. A folktale.

Letter 36.
Idolization of Sunday in England. Miraculous conversion of a Protestant to Catholicism. Trip in a mountain cart. The Whiteboys. Macroom. The naive mother and the unruly child in a jingle. The strong Danish king. Cork. Crossing the sea to Cobh. Magnificent approach from the seaward side. Folko's castle by the sea. Monkstown. Extraordinary illumination with two complete rainbows. Cobh's amphitheater. Unfulfilled expectation of fish. Illuminated nighttime vista. The stars. Departure with the mail coach. Mitchelstown and its castle. Novella material. Exceptional weather for Ireland. The soldier from O'Connell's militia. The Galtee Mountains. Cahir. Another of King John's castles. Lord Glengall's beautiful park. The equipage of a prince in Cashel. Power of habit—the secret of all education. A club dinner.

Letter 37.
Rock of Cashel, one of the most remarkable ruins in Ireland. The Devil's Bite. Old Saxon architecture. Bell of the Inquisition. Statue of Saint Patrick and the throne of Scone. Hore Abbey and Athassel Priory. The plight of Catholics in Tipperary. Ludicrous newspaper article concerning me. My rejoinder.

Letter 38.
Natural history of the swan. Holy Cross and its monuments. Dinner with eighteen clerics and our conversation. The Wends and the Irish. List of Catholic and Protestant parishes in the diocese of Cashel. Curious details and commentary. Well-intentioned exorcism. A break-neck hunt. The wandering bog. Horse feats. Life of a country squire. Strange address to Parliament. Castle in the air. Poteen enthusiasm. Distinguished Irishmen. A good rule.

Letter 39.
Two brothers. Material life. "Devils." The pretty hostess. The piper. The robbers. The duped lawyer. Oyster secrets. Johnny's adventure at Holy Cross. The murder of Baker. Cousin R——. Sergeant Scully. The motionless rooster. Fitzpatrick and his bagpipe.

The Letters

Dresden, September 8th, 1826

M<small>Y PRECIOUS FRIEND!</small>
The love you expressed as we parted in Bautzen made me so happy and so miserable that I have not yet recovered. I still see your sorrowful image standing before me; I still read the deep pain in your glances and your tears; and my own heart tells me only too clearly what you must have felt. May God soon grant us a reunion as joyful as our parting was sad! For the moment I can only remind you of what I have said so often: if I did not know that you, my dearest friend, were with me in this world, I could take no unclouded pleasure in its joys. Therefore if you love me, you will tend to your health, keep yourself amused as much as you can, and not neglect to follow doctor's orders either.

Hoping to vanquish the melancholy that is spreading gloom over every aspect of my journey, I turned to your Sévigné for assistance. Her relationship with her daughter has much in common with yours and mine except that I am more deeply connected to you than Madame de Grignan is to her own mother. You resemble the charming Sévigné as if she were one of your ancestors. Whatever advantages she has over you arise from her era and education; you have others. And what in her appears not so much classical as finished and restrained is in your case richer and steeped in the infinite—it has become romantic. I opened the book at random and, aptly enough, landed on this passage:

> N'aimons jamais, ou n'aimons guères,
> Il est dangereux d'aimer tant.[1]

To which she adds, with emotion: "For myself, I prefer the disease to the cure, and I find it sweeter to part from those I love than to love them halfheartedly."[2]

To have written you just a few lines is already a consolation. Now that I am conversing with you again, I feel closer to you also. I have no travel adventures to relate as yet; my own emotions have been so engrossing that I am hardly aware of the places I have passed through.

Dresden seemed less cheerful to me than usual, and I thanked God when I was comfortably settled in my room at the inn. The storm that blew directly in my face all day long has left me overheated and exhausted and, as you know, I am not well anyway, so I need the rest.

May heaven send you a peaceful night in M—— and an affectionate dream of your friend![3]

VOUS AVEZ SANS *doute cuit toutes sortes de bouillons amers, ainsi que moi.*[4] Nevertheless, I got up in better spirits and better health than yesterday, and immediately proceeded to organize my things and make all the little arrangements required in preparation for a long journey. In the evening I felt quite exhausted again, and dreading a recurrence of my nervous hypochondriac indisposition, which you have christened my *maladie imaginaire*, I sent for *Hofrat* W——, the favorite physician of strangers passing through here. Aside from his skill, he is amusing and merry company. You know my way of using doctors. Nobody can be of a more homoeopathic nature, for as a rule I am half-cured merely by talking to them about my malady and its remedies; if I then swallow anything they prescribe, it is only in infinitesimal amounts. This was the case today, and after a few hours that W—— seasoned with many a piquant anecdote as he sat at my bedside, I supped with an improved appetite and slept quite well until late morning. When I opened my eyes they fell on a short letter from you! Faithful Berndt had placed it on my blanket, knowing there could be no happier way for me to begin the day. Next to the pleasure of hearing from you, only one other remains: writing to you.

Please continue to express your feelings so openly and do not spare mine. I am well aware that your letters will resemble a somber landscape for a long time still, but I will be comforted if, just occasionally, I glimpse a sweet ray of sunlight penetrating the gloom.

Leipzig, September 11th, 1826

IN A VERY pretty room, with a well-waxed parquet floor, elegant furniture, silk drapes, and everything still in its first *fraicheur*, the waiter is right now laying the table for my dinner while I write you these few words.

I left Dresden at ten o'clock this morning in a fairly good mood, painting colorful fantasies of the future. But my longing for you, good Julie,* tugs painfully at my heart, and I am compelled to measure my dull and joyless solitude against the intense delight I would have felt in making this trip with you and under more fortunate circumstances.

There is little to say of the road thus far. Nothing about it is at all romantic—even the vineyards stretching all the way to Meissen exhibit more sand than green. Although too open, the landscape is sometimes pleasing in its freshness and fertility, such as near Oschatz, where Collmberg, beautifully covered with brush, looks down on the countryside like a youthful head of curls! The roadway is good and it seems that in Saxony, too, the mail service is improving now that the excellent Nagler has introduced a new postal era in Prussia. Still, I find nothing more amusing than the cheerful enthusiasm of Berndt. He goads both the willing and the phlegmatic indefatigably, behaving as if he has already toured the whole world with me and, it goes without saying, has found things everywhere to be better than at home.

Given the delicate state of my health, the comfort of an English carriage is a real blessing. In general I pride myself on my command of the art of traveling, particularly my ability to combine the utmost comfort with the least possible inconvenience and loss of time. This includes

---

* This name is fictitious, because we are not authorized to print the real one. Hence we have also had to mask a few other names and allusions to social relationships.—*The Editor.*

bringing along the greatest imaginable number of things and, for lengthy trips, often precious and familiar mementos. I have managed the task perfectly this time. Before I packed in Dresden, people thought my room a warehouse. Now everything has disappeared into the sundry receptacles in the carriage, without giving it that heavy, overloaded appearance that so easily frightens our mail coach drivers and announces you to the innkeeper as someone embarking on a Grand Tour. Every item is discretely placed and easily accessible, so that once I have arrived at my night's lodging, it takes only a few minutes for all my household affairs to be reestablished in the new location. And on the road the enormous, bright-crystal windows are unobstructed by any luggage or racks, thus providing a view as accessible as from an open *calèche* while still allowing me to be Lord of the Temperature.

As for those people on the high seats at the rear of the carriage, they overlook all the luggage and the horses but are unable to cast intrusive glances inside or overhear a conversation taking place there (one never knows if state secrets might be debated once we arrive in the land of the Brobdingnagians or the Lilliputians).[5] I could deliver a course of lectures on this subject, one not at all inconsequential for travelers. I am being so long-winded now only in order to give you a full picture of me, navigating the world in my nomadic dwelling as each day the ever-changing post horses carry me farther away from you.

The proprietor of the Hôtel de Saxe, certainly one of the best inns in Germany, is an old acquaintance of mine. He even earned a right to my gratitude when I was a student in Leipzig, for I enjoyed many a merry and sometimes boisterous meal at his house. So today I invited him to share my more solitary repast and relate a few stories about the old days and the wild ways of the young. Unfortunately, the situation has become more serious *everywhere*. At one time pleasure was all but an occupation in itself; it was the focus of one's thoughts, the subject of one's studies. Whoever persisted in dancing could easily find the music. Nowadays pleasure is found only in business; to feel happy otherwise, if achievable at all, requires serious stimulation.

Weimar, September 13th, 1826, evening

I WILL NOT burden you with a tirade about the battlefields of Leipzig and Lützen, a description of the puny-looking monument to Gustavus Adolphus, or an account of the meager beauties of the region around Schulpforta. I had hoped to purchase a book in Weißenfels where the great Müllner once lived, but was amazed to find not a single bookshop. People must be afraid that he will slap them with a lawsuit!

I stepped onto the plains of Jena and Auerstedt with exactly the same emotions a Frenchman in the Grande Armée must have felt as he strode over the fields of Rossbach between 1806 and 1812—because the last victory, like the last laugh, is always the best. Then, after so many reminiscences of former battles, I was welcomed by smiling Weimar, the seat of the Muses, and I blessed that noble prince who has made this town a monument to *peace* and helped light a literary beacon that, with its varicolored flame, has for so long illuminated our way in Germany.[6]

On the following day I presented myself to this great prince, my former commander, and all the other high-ranking ladies and gentlemen of his entourage. I found them little changed, although the court had been augmented by two engaging princesses who, even if they had been born into the lowest level of commoners, would have distinguished themselves through their charm and refined manners. People here still display a courteousness to strangers that has gone completely out of style elsewhere. I had scarcely been announced when a footman appeared to inform me that he and his equipage were at my disposal for the duration of my stay, and he also extended a standing invitation to dinner.

The next day the grand duke was kind enough to show me his private library, which is elegantly arranged and houses a particularly fine collection of English engravings. He laughed heartily when I told him about a report I had read recently in a Parisian newspaper claiming that he had ordered Schiller's remains exhumed so that the skeleton could be placed *in natura* in his library. In fact I saw only a bust of Schiller there, one of several such statues decorating the rooms—although, if I heard correctly, his skull is encased in the pedestal, certainly an odd way of showing respect!

I visited the park again with renewed enthusiasm.[7] The region is not especially picturesque, but the grounds are so intelligently laid out, the separate sections so aptly and handsomely realized, that they impart a feeling of contentment rarely found, even where nature has proven more generous. A new addition was a small botanical garden laid out in a wide circle with a magnificent ancient tree at its center. Organized according to the Linnean system, it contains individual specimens of every tree, shrub, and plant that can survive outdoors in this climate. There can be no more pleasant place for botanical study than the seat beneath this old tree. Like a venerable patriarch it gazes down upon the younger botanical generations of every shape, foliage, blossom, and color. In the course of my excursions I also visited a model farm belonging to the grand duke where the Swiss cows are colossal in size but give little milk, transplantations of things foreign being generally unsuccessful. Farther along was a charming pheasant run abounding with gold and silver pheasants and white deer. A bizarre sight is provided by a large "turkey tree." The keeper has trained seventy to eighty of these ponderous birds to move their way up onto the branches of an old linden. Festooned with such strange fruits, the tree takes on a wonderfully exotic appearance.

Because meals are served very early at this court, I hardly had time to get myself *en costume* and, arriving a bit late, found a large party already gathered. I noticed several Englishmen who are quite sensibly studying German here, where they are welcomed with unstinting hospitality, instead of investing great effort in the ungainly dialect of Dresden. The table conversation quickly became animated. You are familiar with the grand duke's joviality, and in this regard he is exactly like his friend, the unforgettable king of Bavaria. We repeated many amusing anecdotes from the days when I still had the honor of being his adjutant, and afterward I just had to ride my grand hobbyhorse—my outing in a hot-air balloon.[8] More interesting were Duke Bernhard's tales of his journey through North and South America, which I understand we will soon see in print along with remarks by Goethe.[9] Bernhard occupies an elevated station by dint of his birth, but he stands still higher as a man. No one could offer the free Americans a more favorable image of a German prince than he, with the matchless dignity of his manners, his genuine liberality, and his unassuming affability.

In the evening there was a large gathering, by its nature not likely to be very enjoyable. Yet at the card table I found myself seated across from the grand duchess and was at once filled with delight. Who has not heard of this noble and excellent German woman?[10] She impressed even Napoleon with her quiet serenity and is loved by everyone lucky enough to experience her gentle and endearing presence! We were sitting, as I said, at the gaming table, but we paid little attention to the rules of whist and spent most of our time in merry conversation.

At a court visited by so many foreigners, peculiar and eccentric characters are bound to turn up and provide material for piquant anecdotes, tempting even for those of us least inclined to scandalmongering. I heard several extremely funny yarns when the card game was over and I was back mixing with the other guests. One concerned an odd visiting card I was shown, which probably owes its existence to a story once circulated by an Englishman, a tale that then inspired Baron J——, notorious for his droll humor, to replicate the incident. As sacrificial lamb he chose one of his table companions, a former captain, who was unaccustomed to the world and its ways, and told the man, who led a solitary life in D——, that courtesy now required him to make a round of social calls in the city. The innocent captain dutifully replied that he knew nothing about such matters but would gladly follow the baron's guidance.

"Very good," came the response, "I will take care of everything, including the visiting cards, which must be in French and must mention under whom you used to serve. I'll pick you up in my carriage three days from now and you should be wearing your uniform."

The visiting cards were duly sent out in advance of their arrival, and everything happened as planned. You can imagine the amusement on the faces of those they visited, since the cards read as follows: "Le Baron de J—— pour présenter *feu* Monsieur le Capitaine de M—— jadis au service de plusieurs membres de la confédération du Rhin."[11]

September 14th, 1826

THIS EVENING I paid my visit to Goethe. He received me in a dimly lit room, its *clair-obscur* arranged with a certain artistic style. The handsome old man with his Jovian countenance looked truly impressive. Age has only changed but scarcely weakened him. He is perhaps not as lively as he once was, but all the more steady and serene; his conversation is now imbued more with a sense of lofty tranquility than with the sparkling fire that sometimes came over him in his moments of grandeur. I was profoundly happy at his good health and jokingly mentioned how pleased I was to find him, our spiritual king, just as majestic and fit as ever.

"Oh, you are too gracious in granting me such a title," he replied in his still-perceptible south German manner, accompanied by a satirical, north German smile.

"No," I insisted, from the bottom of my heart, "not just a king, but even a despot, given that you have compelled all of Europe to be swept along with you."

He bowed politely, questioned me about a few topics related to my earlier sojourn in Weimar, and then said many kind things about Muskau and my efforts there, remarking delicately how commendable it was to awaken, by whatever means, the sense of beauty, since aspects of the good and everything noble will always emerge from the beautiful of their own accord. Finally, at my request, he even offered some encouragement that he might one day visit us. You can imagine, dearest, the eagerness with which I took this up, even if it was just a *façon de parler.*

Next our conversation turned to Sir Walter Scott. Goethe was not very enthusiastic about the Great Unknown.[12] He said he was in no doubt whatsoever that Scott wrote his novels the way the old painters produced their paintings in collaboration with their pupils; that is, *he* provided the plan and major ideas, the skeleton of the scenes, but then had his pupils execute them, merely retouching a bit at the end. It was almost as if Goethe thought it was not worthwhile for a man of such eminence to spend time on so many fastidious details.*

———————————

* Sir Walter's official explanation, a claim not yet issued at the time of this conversation, was that all his writings were by him alone.—*The Editor.*

"If I had been interested only in making a profit," he added, "I would have sent things out anonymously with Lenz and others. Indeed, I might still be doing so, and people would be racking their brains about who the author might be. But the results would be nothing more than factory products."

I later remarked that it was refreshing for Germans to observe how our literature was now conquering foreign nations, "and here," I added, "*our* Napoleon will meet no Waterloo."

"Of course," he responded, ignoring my fairly insipid compliment, "quite apart from what we ourselves produce, we have already attained a very high level of culture through assimilating literature from abroad. Soon other nations will be studying German, for it must be dawning on them that this will spare them the trouble of learning all but a few other languages. Do we not already have superb German translations of the most distinguished works? The ancient classics, the masterpieces of modern Europe, the literatures of India and the Orient—have they not all been more brilliantly rendered by the richness and versatility of the German language, by devoted German diligence, by our genius that has succeeded in penetrating these works more deeply than could be true of other languages? France's former dominance in the world of letters," he continued, "was considerably indebted to the fact that it was the first to produce passable translations from the Greek and Latin. But how thoroughly has it now been surpassed by Germany!"

In the political realm Goethe seemed to set little store in popular constitutional theories. Meanwhile I defended my own views with some warmth. Here he turned to his favorite idea, which he repeated several times, namely, that each of us should be concerned only with the continued influence we exert and carry forward, with true constancy and love, in our own special sphere, be it large or small. Such an attitude would benefit everyone, no matter what form of government prevailed. For his part, he said he acted no differently. And, he added good-naturedly, this was just what I had done in Muskau, undistracted by other demands. I replied, in a very modest way, that however true and noble this principle might be, I nonetheless believed that a constitutional form of government was needed to bring it into being, because such a government alone could offer every citizen the assurance of greater security for himself and his property; could motivate the necessary energy and enthusiasm, as well as a dependable patriotism. These circumstances would in turn provide a more solid and universal foundation for quiet activity within each individual's circle. Finally, though perhaps rather ineptly, I invoked England as proof of my claim. Goethe responded at once, saying that my example was not the best choice, because there was no country in which selfishness was more dominant and perhaps no other population intrinsically less humane in its political and private relationships.* He insisted that salvation did not come from the outside, no matter what the form of government, but from the inside, through the wisdom and restrained pursuits of each individual, acting within his own circle. This, he said, would always remain the essential element in human happiness and was the easiest and simplest to achieve.

After this he spoke of Lord Byron with great affection—almost like a father speaking about his son—which buoyed my already immense enthusiasm for that great English poet. One thing he disputed was the foolish claim that *Manfred* is a parroting of *Faust*.[13] Yet it did strike him as interesting that Byron unconsciously made use of the same mask of Mephistopheles as he had, although admittedly Byron played it out completely differently. He regretted very much that the

---

* Here I almost suspect that my departed friend has simply put his own opinions into Goethe's mouth.
—*The Editor.*

two had never met, and he severely condemned the English nation—with full justification—for having judged their great countryman so ungenerously and understood him so little. But on this topic Goethe has already pronounced so thoroughly and so beautifully that I needn't add anything further. At the end I mentioned the production of *Faust* at a private theater in Berlin with music by Prince Radziwill and praised the gripping effect of some parts of the performance. "Well," said Goethe soberly, "it is a peculiar undertaking, but all viewpoints and experiments should be praised."

I am annoyed by the weakness of my memory, for I cannot recall any more of our lively conversation. I took leave of the great man—third in the league after Homer and Shakespeare—with enormous love and respect. His name will shine through all eternity, as long as the German tongue survives, and if I had a little bit of Mephistopheles in me, I would have called out from the staircase:

> It is very kind of a great lord
> To speak so humanely with a poor devil.* [14]

September 15th, 1826, evening

TODAY I WAS invited to dine at the hereditary grand duke's in the Belvedere, [15] so I set off at two o'clock on a well-maintained road. The weather has been wonderful since I arrived—days of crystal, as your Sévigné says, where one feels neither heat nor cold, days that only spring or autumn can offer.

The hereditary grand duke and his wife live in the Belvedere like private citizens, receiving their guests without high-flown etiquette but with the most attentive courtesy. The grand duchess seemed still very dispirited by the emperor's death, [16] but later, when the conversation became more animated, she gave the company a gripping description of the floods in Saint Petersburg, which she had witnessed with her own eyes. I have always admired the excellent education and broad knowledge that distinguish the princesses of Russia; in the case of the grand duchess's sister, the late queen of Württemberg, [17] it could even have been called erudition. I once had a letter to deliver to her in Frankfurt, and as she took it from me, she requested that I remain in the circle until the others around her were dismissed. The first turn fell to a professor from the Pestalozzi school, and he seemed to know less about his own system than the queen did (at that time she was still the Grand Duchess Catherine). She repeatedly corrected his circuitous answers with the utmost clarity! A diplomat was next, and he in his sphere likewise received, as much as the general conversation allowed, the finest and most eloquent responses. After this she began an exhaustive discussion with a famous economist from A——. The remarkable audience culminated with her profound and brilliant reflections in a lively exchange with a well-known philosopher.

Following dinner the hereditary grand duke toured us through his greenhouses, which are, after Schönbrunn, the most comprehensive in Germany. You know, dear Julie, that I place

---

* I do not think that the venerable man will take offense at the publication of this exchange. Every word, even an insignificant one, that falls from his lips is a precious gift for so many of us, and if my late friend misunderstood him at some point, or transmitted his words without perfect accuracy, at least these comments contain nothing that, in my opinion, could be called an indiscretion.—*The Editor.*

little value on mere rarity, taking delight only in things of *beauty*, in the plant world as elsewhere. Hence many of the treasures were lost on me. I could not share in the rapture that overtook several connoisseurs caught up in the sight of a stick six inches tall, which, although bearing no more than five leaves and no blossoms, had cost sixty guineas and was not to be found in any other German conservatory. On the other hand I was truly delighted by a red cactus grandiflora that was in full, marvelous bloom, and a host of other showy, gorgeous plants. I gazed in awe at the magnificent specimen of a huge breadfruit tree and amused myself by coloring my fingers carmine red from touching the cochineals inhabiting another cactus.[18] Altogether this collection of plants includes more than sixty thousand different varieties. The orangery is magnificent as well, and shelters a veteran with a trunk one and one-half yards in circumference that has already endured for five hundred and fifty northern summers.

I spent the evening at Herr August von Goethe's, a witty man and an old friend of Madame Schopenhauer, who is also a benevolent supporter of mine. Frau von Goethe came in later and augmented our company most pleasantly. She is a cheerful, original, and intelligent woman, and the praise her father-in-law has rightfully lavished on her has not been completely without effect. She seemed delighted that the English author of *Granby*,[19] who had studied German in Weimar, had just sent her a first copy of his novel. I found the offering fairly insignificant and told her I hoped the author was more interesting than his work. I may have said this with a touch of pique, because the English are flattered too much here—as, indeed, they are all over the Continent— and God knows how inappropriately!

September 16th, 1826

AFTER TAKING LEAVE of all the ladies and gentlemen of the house this morning, I devoted the rest of the day to my friend Sp——, who with his family exemplifies how well modest domesticity and kindheartedness can persist at court and in the fashionable world. A young Englishman, who serves as secretary to Mr. Canning and speaks German like his mother tongue, entertained us with humorous anecdotes about English society, bitterly rebuking its ponderousness and ill nature, while at the same time finding the means to say pleasing things about the Germans, particularly those who were present! *Only when they are abroad, however, do the English make these kinds of judgments.* Once they have returned home they quickly assume their customary coldness and haughty indifference, consider foreigners lesser beings, and laugh derisively at the German bonhomie they praised so heartily when they were its beneficiaries. Meanwhile they accept the absurd reverence we grant to the very notion of an Englishman as nothing more than a well-deserved tribute.

This is my last letter from here, dear Julie. Tomorrow *very early*—not with the cockcrow but according to *my* calendar, namely at noon—I plan to depart and will scarcely stop until I reach London. Please, I beg you, take care of your health and keep your spirits as cheerful as you can, relying on that wonderful strength that the creator has granted you: *to be master of one's own self.* But do not therefore love me the less—for your love is the source of *my* strength.

Your faithful Lou

Wesel, September 20th, 1826

$\mathcal{B}$ELOVED FRIEND!

After saying goodbye to Goethe and his family and paying a final visit to a genteel and charming painter in her studio, I was filled with pleasant memories as I departed the German Athens.

In Gotha I tarried just long enough to visit an old friend and comrade-in-arms, the Baron von L——, a minister and astronomer (a rare conflation of heaven and earth). I found him still suffering from the aftermath of his unhappy duel in Paris, though he was bearing the misfortune with a calm sagacity, a quality he maintains in every aspect of his life.

It was already dark when I reached Eisenach, where I was to deliver something from the grand duke to another of my former comrades. I found his house brightly lit, heard dance music, and entered to find a large gathering of people, who looked on my traveling clothes and hunting cap with astonishment. They were celebrating the wedding of the daughter of the house, and once he recognized me, her father welcomed me heartily. I excused myself to the bride for my *lack of a wedding garment*,[1] drank a glass of iced punch to her welfare, another to her father's, danced a *polonaise*, and disappeared *à la française*.[2]

Immediately thereafter I performed my bedtime ablutions and settled down for a comfortable rest in my carriage. When I awoke I was just one station away from Kassel, at the same spot where ten years ago we made an awkward entrée with a broken shaft sticking straight up from our carriage and our driver seemingly mounted upon it. I breakfasted there, reminiscing about that trip, and continued on, passing through the melancholy beauty of the capital and then through a splendid beech wood gleaming like green gold in the bright sunshine. I indulged in some romantic musings near Westuffeln while pondering a conical mountain appointed with ancient, moss-covered ruins, and then hurried across a long, monotonous landscape to arrive for my dinner in the ancient bishopric of Osnabrück.

In a carriage one always sleeps better the second night, because the movement has the same effect—at least on me—as a cradle on a child. I felt very well and cheerful the following morning and noticed that the entire landscape was gradually assuming a Dutch character. Old-fashioned houses with multiple gables and sash windows; a more phlegmatic people speaking an incomprehensible Plattdeutsch in no way inferior to Dutch in its melodiousness; better furnished rooms (but still without Dutch cleanliness); tea instead of coffee; everywhere excellent fresh butter and cream; and last but not least, more cheating by the innkeepers! Everything seemed to add fresh nuances to this colorful world.

The regions we moved through were graceful and gentle, especially near Steele an der Ruhr, a perfect place to retreat into cheerful solitude from the bustle of the world. I feasted my eyes on the succulent vegetation and on the luxurious oak and beech woods that crowned the hills on left and right, sometimes moving down to arch over the road before retreating again into the distance. The fields they bordered were amazingly fertile, shaded with brown and red where the earth had been freshly plowed, shimmering in light or dark green where covered by the young winter crops and fresh clover. Every village is surrounded by a grove of trees in lovely full leaf, and nothing can surpass the luxuriance of the meadows where the Ruhr winds its extraordinarily serpentine course. I thought with a smile that if a man were told he was destined to die on the Ruhr, he should ensconce himself here and make the most of such a prophecy. Toward evening, as I was still reflecting on how this smiling landscape compared to our own gloomy pine forests, a tongue of familiar land suddenly appeared as if by magic incantation, a reminder of home with sand, pines, and withered birches paralleling the road as far as the eye could see. Ten minutes later we were once again greeted by verdant meadows and proud beeches. So what revolution thrust that stretch of sand into the midst of all this lushness?

A few miles from Wesel, however, the entire countryside becomes *tout de bon* like ours at home, and since the good road ends here, you find yourself wading in the gritty sand of Berlin. Unfortunately I arrived one day too late to catch the steamboat, otherwise I would have reached London just four and one-half days after leaving Weimar. Now I have to travel overland to Rotterdam, where I will await the departure of the next ship.

Rotterdam, September 25th, 1826

MY JOURNEY FROM Wesel to Arnhem was rather boring.[3] The horses plodded along in the endless sand of an uncompelling landscape. Except for the large brickworks—which I looked at carefully, since they are so much preferable to ours—there was nothing interesting along the way. Thus the truly magical effect of the extensive garden stretching between Arnhem and Rotterdam is all the more rewarding. On a road built of clinkers (very hard-baked bricks) covered with fine sand—an unsurpassed road that shows not a hint of tracks—the carriage rolled on with that steady, gentle murmur of the wheels so inviting to the play of the imagination.

This endless park is devoid of cliffs and mountains, yet as the road climbs the occasional high embankment; as numerous groupings of substantial country estates, buildings, and towers come into view; as colossal stands of trees rise from meadows and plains or loom above clear lakes, the landscape displays variations in height and depth that rival scenes of the most picturesque type. In fact, its distinguishing quality is exactly this unbelievable movement and diversity of elements that never fail to rivet one's attention. Cities and villages, palaces with their plush environs, villas of every architectural style with the loveliest flower gardens, vast expanses of grassland with thousands of grazing cattle, lakes twenty miles in circumference that have gradually emerged from the cutting of peat, countless islands where the towering reeds—meticulously cultivated for thatching roofs—provide dwelling places for a myriad of waterfowl—everything joins hands in *one* joyous dance and you are there, swept along by winged horses, as in a dream. Meanwhile new palaces and still other cities loom on the horizon, their high Gothic towers melting into the clouds in the crepuscular distance. Yet close by, an often-grotesque and constantly shifting cast of characters undermines all continuity. At one moment there may be strange carriages without any shafts, richly ornamented with carvings and gold, driven by coachmen seated on narrow platforms and dressed in blue waistcoats, short black pants, black stockings, and shoes with enormous silver buckles; or perhaps women may ramble along on foot, all wearing six-inch-long earrings in gold and silver and, on their heads, Chinese summer hats like rooftops. Then come yews pruned into dragons and fabulous monsters, or linden trunks coated with white and colored oil paint; chimneys decorated in an Asian style with many little towers; houses intentionally built on a slant; gardens where life-size marble statues in the costumes of the old French court lurk in the shrubbery. And there are the many two- to three-foot-high brass vessels, polished like mirrors and gleaming like pure gold, which stand in the green meadows along the road and serve the modest purpose of receiving milk from the cows being diligently tended by young girls and boys. In short, a multitude of strange and fantastic images unfurl in a constant succession of scenes before your eyes, imbuing the whole thing with a completely foreign character. Now imagine this picture framed in the golden light of the most brilliant sunshine, set about with the lushest of vegetation—from gigantic oaks, maples, ashes, and beeches down to displays of the most precious flowers of the conservatory—and you will be able to conjure up a vivid idea of this wonderful part of Holland and the intense enjoyment of yesterday's journey.

Regarding the variety of the landscape and its vegetation, there was but one feature that seemed exceptional, although no less interesting or pleasant. Namely, stretching out more than eighteen miles between Arnhem and Utrecht you find the same sand as on the Lüneburg Heath, as bad as on the worst plains of the Mark Brandenburg. In spite of this, and proving what can be achieved by sensible cultivation, the scrawny heather and pines (all that this ground can yield on its own) are accompanied by the most diverse plantings of oaks, white and copper beeches, birches, poplars, etc., all growing happily. Where the soil is too poor they serve only as shrubs and are cut down every five or six years; on occasion, where the soil is somewhat better, they are left to continue growing. The entirety of this magnificent road is bordered by dense, well-maintained rows of trees, and I found it extraordinary that the oaks and beeches seemed to thrive even more than birches and poplars in spite of the dry sand. A great number of meticulously tidy Dutch houses and villas stood in the middle of this desolate heath; several were still under construction, as were the grounds surrounding them. I could not understand why so many people had chosen such inhospitable terrain for luxurious establishments, but I learned that the government has wisely ceded the entire tract, until now judged useless and left untouched, to the adjoining property holders and other wealthy individuals. The land was granted for fifty years, free of any charges or taxes, the only condition being that it had to be immediately planted or cultivated. Eventually the descendants of the present holders will pay a very low, proportionate rent. After what I have seen here, I am convinced that in a hundred years most of our hungry pinewoods could be transformed into productive land in the same way, thus regenerating the whole, moribund region.

Utrecht is gracefully built, and like all Dutch towns, a model of cleanliness. The diversity and colorful appearance of the houses and the narrow, crooked streets with their old-fashioned layout strike me as much more gemütlich than all those "beautiful cities" where everything crosses at right angles like a mathematical diagram and one takes in the whole dreary length of every street at one glance. Since Utrecht is the farthest above sea level of any town in Holland, the air is very healthy. The environs are charming, and I was told that because the wealthiest country gentry sojourn here, it boasts a lively society in the winter and spring. Commerce, on the other hand, is inconsequential; the allure of the place and its inhabitants is more an aristocratic one.

From here I went to Gouda, which has a cathedral renowned for its exquisite stained glass.[4] Not long ago an Englishman offered, to no avail, eighty thousand guilders for one of the windows, which is the equal of a miniature painting in its execution and gleams with an indescribable blaze of color; indeed, the jewels and pearls on the priests' garments rival real ones. Another of the windows was donated by Philip II, and shortly thereafter half of it was shattered by a lightning strike, something that must have been viewed as portentous at the time. Philip himself is portrayed in it wearing a mantle of true purple—not the normal red, but a shimmering color between violet and crimson, more beautiful than anything I have ever seen in old glass. A third window bears a portrait of the duke of Alba. The windows are unusually large and in most cases immaculately preserved; all date from the fifteenth or sixteenth century except for one, which was painted in the seventeenth century and, being far inferior to the others not only in the glow of its colors but also in its draftsmanship and originality, very much betrays the decline of this art form.

Anyone who has seen Gouda can save himself the trouble of a visit to the leaning tower of Pisa because here half the city seems to have been constructed according to a similar principle. Although it might be easy to credit the Dutch (who in many respects could be considered the Chinese of Europe) with having purposefully chosen such a bizarre design for their houses, in fact the startling tilt of the buildings is probably due to the unstable, boggy ground.* Almost all the houses stand with their gables toward the street, and every one of them is differently decorated. In the narrowest lanes they almost touch one another at the top, forming a triangle over your head, something that instills a certain apprehension as you walk along beneath them.

Since it was a Sunday, I found the town full of people, although their joviality was quiet and understated. Most stood around idly, gawked a bit, but politely removed their hats as my carriage passed by.

Before reaching Rotterdam you drive along a lengthy row of country houses, all fronted by successive parterres of flowers and separated from the road on both sides by a narrow canal. Each house is approached over a substantial drawbridge, contrasting oddly with the insignificance of the watercourse (in an emergency, a hearty leap would get you from one bank to the other). The towering windmills outside the town are also baroque. They are frequently gilded and adorned with the most outlandish carvings, and some of them have walls so finely overlain with reeds that from a distance they look fur-covered. Others resemble the scaly body of a crocodile; yet others a Chinese bell tower. But all together they create a very striking effect. In between you can glimpse ships' masts jutting up from the harbor and see the enormous glass-covered sheds where the warships are built, heralding a maritime and commercial city.

I soon found myself in a long, very busy street. A tall tower displaying a clock face of black with numbers and hands in fire red served as a *point de vue*. It took me a good quarter hour to reach the Hôtel des Bains on the quay, where I am now comfortably installed. From my window I overlook a broad expanse of water and four steamers, one of which will take me to England the day after tomorrow. Boats are rowing busily back and forth, and the crowds hurry restlessly along

---

* I remember reading about a Greek monastery in Wallachia with four towers that looked as if they were about to collapse at any moment. But this was an optical illusion produced by the oblique orientation of the windows and the friezes encircling the towers.

LETTERS OF A DEAD MAN

the quay, which is decoratively bordered by towering elms that must have been planted already in Erasmus's time. After a little walk beneath these trees, I ate a good meal and then continued writing this interminable letter, which is unfortunately going to cost more in postage than it is worth! My health is still not all I might wish, but getting better day by day. I may be cured by the sea and by a few glasses of seawater, which I will drink as soon as I find myself rocking on the waves.

September 26th, 1826

THE LIFESTYLE HERE has a lot in common with the English. People get up late, dine at the communal table at four o'clock, and drink tea in the evening. Otherwise there are not many diversions for foreign visitors in this big city, since there is not even a permanent theater. From time to time a company from The Hague puts on a few performances in an inferior establishment. In Rotterdam everything appears to center on commerce and accordingly the population seeks recreation in domestic pleasures inaccessible to the mere passing traveler.

I went into the countinghouse of a Jewish banker to change some English currency. In spite of the insignificance of the sum, he behaved with extreme deference and after carefully counting out the money, accompanied me to the door. I was therefore more than a little surprised when I learned from my hired servant that this man's fortune has been estimated at two million guilders. It seems the bankers here have not acquired the arrogance of those in other countries.

Next I visited the arsenal, insignificant compared to English establishments of its kind. Many of the sheds are covered with pasteboard, which looks good and is supposed to be very durable. It is made by taking squares of normal, strong pasteboard and dipping them repeatedly into a vat of simmering wood tar until they are permeated and covered on both sides, after which the panels are hung in the sun to dry. These are then laid out on a very flat roof, overlapped like copper plates, and nailed to the boards underneath, which they protect from moisture for many years. According to the marine officials, such a roof is supposed to last far longer than shingles or the very best tarred sailcloth.

In one of the rooms I found something interesting: the detailed model of a warship that could be completely dismantled; it had been built for the naval school in Delft, where it helped make the lessons extremely clear. The king's golden barge, perhaps not the equal of Cleopatra's in magnificence, is nonetheless displayed with great self-satisfaction by the good Dutch folk, although it is rotting away here in this dry setting, being only rarely used.

The environs of Rotterdam are famous for pretty country girls and succulent fruit, which (I mean the latter, of course!) represent a not insignificant export to England. Nowhere else can you find such enormous grapes, for instance; at the market I saw a lot of them for sale that were like plums in size and appearance. Continuing my leisurely stroll I came upon a placard advertising a panorama of Etna; I entered in the wake of a group of ladies, and ah!—I lost my heart. The most captivating girl I have ever seen smiled at me from the foot of the fire-spitting mountain; her eyes must have gotten their fervor from the mountain's eternal flames, while her mischievous lips bloomed like the red flowers of the resplendent oleander beside her. She had the sweetest foot, the most sensuous and perfectly proportioned figure—if not divine, she was certainly the most seductive of mortals. Was this a Dutch woman? Oh no, a true Sicilian, but alas!—only painted! Her triumphant glances mocked me from her leafy bower as I departed that paradise. Since we no longer live in the time of Pygmalion, such creatures can never be brought to life, never seduced.

2

Still, fate may yet allow me to meet her original somewhere. In any case, such a hopeful vision is not an unpleasant traveling companion. What a shame, however, that I must now carry it along with me to the land of mist and fog, instead of entering the beautiful realm of fire that is aflame from *two* sides, burned by a warmer sun above and by the magical embers below. Already tomorrow the cold sea will be surging around me as I leave dear Holland, but I will not subscribe to the cry of that naughty Voltaire: "Adieu canards, canaux, canailles!"[5]

I will not write again until London, where I must decide whether or not to make an extended stay. In the meanwhile I am enclosing a lithograph of my steamship (Figure 2).[6] The spot where I am standing is marked with a †, the way knights of old used to sign their names. With a little help from your imagination, you will see me waving my handkerchief and sending you a thousand adoring and heartfelt thoughts from afar.

Your faithful Lou

London, October 5th, 1826

$\mathscr{I}$ HAD A MISERABLE crossing. A squall, wretched seasickness, forty hours instead of twenty and, not least, running aground on a sandbank in the Thames where we were trapped for six hours before being lifted by the tide. These were the unpleasant *événements* of the trip.

I do not know whether I looked at everything with rose-colored glasses ten years ago when I last visited England, or whether in the interim my imagination has painted that distant image with more appealing colors. In any event, this time I found the views on both sides of the river neither as fresh nor as picturesque. There were, however, occasional glimpses of appealing country estates and splendid groups of trees, although these often had their foliage lopped off as in northern Germany, which disfigures the landscape. But the view is not as dreary as it might be (in otherwise so-beautiful Silesia, for instance) because there are so *many* trees in the abundant hedgerows that surround every field and because care is taken to leave at least the topmost crowns intact.

Among the passengers was an Englishman recently returned from Herrnhut who had also visited the spa at Muskau. Remaining anonymous, I was entertained by his opinion of our park and its environs. You can judge how greatly taste can vary and how little this should disturb us by hearing of this man's profound admiration for those drab regions simply because of the immensity of the evergreen woods, by which he meant the monotonous stretches of pine forest that we find so intolerable. In England—where pines are painstakingly planted in the parks, even though they tend not to thrive—they are a precious rarity.

An American passenger was very indignant over having gotten seasick on this miserable crossing, something he had never experienced sailing from America to Rotterdam. And a plantation owner from Demerara, who was always freezing, whined even more loudly about the abolition of the slave trade, a loss that, in *his* opinion, would soon bring about the total ruin of the colonies. "A slave or native never works if he doesn't have to," he said, "and he doesn't need to work in order to live, for the superb land and climate supply him with food and shelter. Europeans, however, *cannot* work in the heat, so all that is left is the simple choice: colonies *with* slaves or *no* colonies. Everyone knows this perfectly well, but people have entirely other intentions that they try to tuck away behind the window dressing of their philanthropy."

These were his words. He went on to assert that, because it was to the advantage of their masters, slaves were treated far better than, for example, the peasants of Ireland; and he claimed to have often seen servants treated much worse in Europe. "There may be the occasional exception," he admitted, "but nothing that warrants general consideration."

I tried to steer the discussion away from this topic, one so painful for any person of good-will, and asked him to tell me about life in Guyana and the splendor of its primeval forests, a much more interesting conversation that filled me with a kind of nostalgia for those wonders of nature in a place where all things are more magnificent and only human beings ignoble.

The ludicrous figure on our journey was an English lady who attempted, with unusual volubility and at every opportunity, to enter into conversation *en français*. No longer in the bloom of youth, she managed to remedy this defect, even on board ship, by taking extreme care with her appearance; one of the passengers claimed she had "a crack" in her neck, a newly invented kind of screw with which wrinkles can be winched up. Late in the morning, when the rest of us—all more or less miserable—finally appeared on deck, we found her already ensconced there and in an elegant *négligé*. My moans elicited a cheerful response, delivered in her broad dialect:

"Comment, comment, vous n'avez pas pu dormir? Moi parfaitement, très comfortable. J'étais très chaudement couchée entre deux matelots, et je m'en porte à merveille."
"Madame," I said, "on comprend que vous ne craignez pas la mer."[1]

In the middle of the second night we anchored near London Bridge. This is the worst thing that can happen, because the customs officials strictly prohibit anything being taken off the ship until they have finished the inspections, yet their offices are not open until ten o'clock in the morning. Not wanting to leave my German servants alone with the carriage and my effects, and having also neglected to arrange accommodations for myself or to contact the ambassador to release me from the inspection, I was compelled to find a bed for the night in a squalid sailors' tavern on the waterfront with nothing but the clothes on my back. The next morning, however, when I was present for the inspection of my things, I found that the trusty key of gold proved effective once again, saving me from a long wait and additional impediments. Even a few dozen French gloves lying in all innocence on top of my clothes went unnoticed—my guinea seemed to make them invisible.

I hurried as fast as I could to get out of the filthy City and its anthill-like hubbub, but I had to travel another half stage with the post horses before reaching the west end of town and the Clarendon Hotel, where I had previously stayed.[2] My former host at that establishment, a Swiss, had in the meantime departed England for another country, I do not yet know which. His son had taken over and received me with all the deference that distinguishes English innkeepers and, in fact, everyone else here who depends on the money of others. He would also shortly render me a real service because after resting for scarcely an hour, I realized that in the confusion of the night, I had left a purse with eighty sovereigns in a drawer in my quayside sleeping quarters. Monsieur Jaquier, who knew the lay of the land in England, shrugged his shoulders but nonetheless sent a trustworthy man down to the harbor to try and recover what I had lost. The disorderliness that reigned in that seedy inn on the outskirts of town came in very handy. Our messenger found my room not yet straightened up and, no doubt to the employees' disappointment, the purse was still lying untouched in the very drawer I had described.

London is presently so devoid of elegance and people of fashion, that you hardly see a carriage drive past and rarely an ambassador among the *beau monde*. Meanwhile this monstrous city is filled with dirt and fog, and the macadamized streets are like rutted country roads because the old pavement was ripped out and replaced by fragments of granite filled in with gravel.

Admittedly this affords a gentler ride and muffles the noise, but in the winter it turns the place into a half bog. Without the excellent sidewalks people would have to go around on stilts, as they do in the *département* of Landes near Bordeaux. The lower-class Englishwomen wear something similar on their big feet, but made of iron.

Yet London is significantly improved with the new Regent Street, Portland Place, and Regent's Park. Now for the first time it looks like a royal capital instead of just a vast metropolis of shopkeepers, to use Napoleon's expression. Poor Mr. Nash—an influential architect to the king and the man responsible for most of these ameliorations—is badly treated by many cognoscenti but is, in my opinion, greatly deserving of the nation's gratitude for having conceived and executed such colossal plans for the beautification of its major city, although it cannot be denied that his buildings are a jumble of every possible style, and that the mishmash often appears more baroque than ingenious. Much is still in the planning stages, of course, but given the general building frenzy and the great wealth of the English, it will soon be fully realized. The details should not be examined too closely, it's true. The steeple serving as a focal point in Regent's Street, for instance, ends in a needle-like spire, and the building's torso and roof seem to be in perpetual conflict about where one ends and the other begins.[3] It is a strange architectural miscarriage and prompted a delectable caricature in which a good likeness of the diminutive, wizened-looking Mr. Nash, dressed in riding boots and spurs, is shown skewered on the spire. The inscription below reads "NASHIONAL TASTE!!!" (Figure 3).

Many similar perversities could be listed. For instance: the four flattened figures squashed against the wall of a balcony adorning the largest mansion on Regent's Park. Their significance remains a mystery. They seem to be wearing something like bathrobes, so at least you can infer that they are intended to represent human figures. Perhaps they are emblems of a hospital because, as in Potsdam, these ostensible palaces are granted unity and eminence only through their facades, while in actuality they are made up of a lot of small buildings serving all kinds of commercial purposes as well as housing hundreds of different proprietors.

On the other hand, the pastoral layout of the park is flawless, and this also originated with Mr. Nash, especially the tracts of water. Here art is perfectly concealed by the appearance of untouched nature. You believe that you are looking at a broad river flowing for miles between

3

Nashional Taste.

4

Waterloo Bridge.

S.ᵗ Martin's   Adelphi

luxuriously leafy banks until, in the distance, it separates into several branches. What you actually have before you is a laboriously excavated channel of water, still and enclosed, although clear. A landscape as appealing as this, with hills rising in the distance and surrounded by a mile-long circle of magnificent buildings, is no doubt a design worthy of a major capital, and once the young trees have become ancient giants, it will not find its match anywhere. In order to create all this, many old streets were torn up, and during the last ten years more than sixty thousand new houses were constructed in this part of town. A particular beauty of these new streets is that they are broad, to be sure, but—like the paths in a park—they do not always run in straight lines. Instead they make occasional curves that break the uniformity. By the time London has docks, and if the buildings around St Paul's Church are cleared (something the talented Colonel Trench has planned), then no other city will be able to match it in *magnificence,* just as it already now surpasses every other in *size.*

     Of all the new bridges, Waterloo is paramount, although the entrepreneurs supposedly lost three hundred thousand pounds in its construction (Figure 4). Twelve hundred feet in length with solid balustrades of granite, it is little trafficked and, fog permitting, makes an enjoyable

St. Pauls
Covent Garden   Savoy   Covent Garden
Theatre   Lancaster Place   Drury Lane
Theatre

WATERLOO   BRIDGE

walk, offering the most beautiful views of the splendid mixture of palaces, bridges, ships, and towers along the river. The contraption used here for collecting the bridge tolls was new to me. You must pass through an iron turnstile in the form of a cross, as is normal, but this one is set up so that it moves only a quarter turn each time, just enough to allow one person through. And at the moment it completes this quarter turn, a mechanism beneath the bridge lets a token fall into a sealed container. Next to this turnstile is a similar device for carriages and wagons, so the proprietors need only count the coins in the evening to know exactly how many pedestrians and horses have passed over the bridge each day. The cost is one penny for a pedestrian and three for a horse. They had planned on taking in three hundred pounds a day, but rarely collect more than fifty.

October 7th, 1826

WHAT WOULD REALLY appeal to you is the spotlessness of the houses, the extreme comfort of the furniture, and the manners and courtesy of the servant classes. True, you must pay six times as much for every luxury (the basic necessities are not *that* much more expensive than at home), but you gain six times the comfort. The inns, too, are far more opulent and well appointed than on the Continent. The beds, for example, consist of three mattresses lying on top of each other and are big enough to accommodate two or three people. Each bed has curtains that hang from a rectangular canopy resting on four strong, mahogany columns, and when you pull them closed you find yourself in something like a small closet that in France would be considered a quite commodious dwelling for a single person. In German and French hotels, and even in many private houses, you find just one pathetic water bottle on your washstand, with a single faience or silver pitcher and basin next to an elongated face towel. Here there are small tubs of genuine Chinese porcelain in which you can easily immerse half your body, faucets that immediately deliver all the water you want, a half dozen generous towels, a good number of large and small crystal bottles, a tall cheval glass, foot basins, and so on, all of elegant design. This is not to list the other unmentionable amenities necessary for one's daily ablutions.

Everything is so agreeably presented that the minute you wake up you are seized by the desire for a bath. If you need anything at all, the mere ring of your bell will summon a neatly dressed girl who will curtsy deeply, or a respectful waiter with the decorum and attire of a practiced *valet de chambre*. What a contrast to an unkempt fellow in a cropped jacket and green apron who asks you with the most insolent pretense of being helpful, "Was schaffen's, Ihr Gnoden," or "Haben *Sie* hier jeklingelt?"[4] and then runs off before finding out what you wanted! Good carpets cover the floors of every room, and in the brightly polished steel grate there is a jolly fire burning, unlike the filthy planks or the smoking, evil-smelling stoves in so many of our own country's inns.

When you go out, you never find a grimy staircase or one so poorly lit that the only thing visible is the gloom. Moreover, the greatest tranquility and discretion reign throughout the building both day and night. In many hotels a spacious set of rooms will even have its own staircase, so you needn't encounter anyone. At meals a guest is granted a profusion of white table linen and brilliantly polished silverware, along with a well-equipped *plat de ménage* and an elegance in the presentation of the food that leaves nothing to be desired. The serving staff are never intrusive yet always there if you need them. The innkeeper himself usually appears at the beginning of the meal to ask whether everything is satisfactory. In short, there is nothing lacking in the good inns here that a prosperous, well-traveled gentleman expects in his own house, and the service can be even more attentive. Admittedly the bill reflects it, and even the waiters must be paid almost as much as one's own servants. In the top hotels a waiter is not satisfied with a tip of less than two pounds per week for himself alone. More than in any other country, gratuities are the order of the day, and they are demanded with surprising impudence, even in church!

Today I visited a few bazaars; these have become ever more prevalent in the past few years and are extremely convenient for buyers. The so-called horse bazaar is built on an enormous scale and daily attracts a very motley crowd. It occupies several rambling buildings, and in the first of the endless galleries and rooms you find displays of many hundreds of carriages and harnesses of every kind, new as well as old ones at all prices, and polished up to look pristine. In other galleries you see porcelain wares, finery, crystal, mirrors, hardware, toys, even tropical birds and butterfly collections—everything is for sale. Finally, in the center of the complex are the rooms of a coffeehouse where a glazed arcade runs all the way around an open area. Here, while enjoying a leisurely breakfast (albeit in very mixed company), you can watch while various horses are led out and out up for auction. Anyone wanting to sell his horses can, for a predetermined fee, have them sent here, where they are kept in the many adjacent stalls and are very well tended. If a horse has been warranted sound by the auctioneer, you can feel quite secure about your purchase, since the owners of the establishment have to stand by it. As a rule, you do not find the best here but certainly the cheapest, and for many this alone is a good thing; even better is the enormous convenience of being able to acquire everything you need quickly and in the same place. There are already many such bazaars, as I have said, and they are definitely worth a short promenade. Owing to the excellent, conveniently laid-out sidewalks; the colorful, ever-changing street scenes; and the many luxurious shops, strolling through London is very pleasant for a foreign visitor, especially in the evenings. In addition to the radiance of the gaslights,[5] large glass balls of deep red, blue, and green hang in front of the many apothecary shops, beacons that can be seen for miles. They serve as guiding stars, although they can be misleading if you accidentally confuse one with the other.

Among all the shops, the most visually seductive are those selling beautiful English crystal. Real diamonds could hardly be more dazzling than the lustrous collections of some of these manufacturers. I also saw a number of pieces worked in rose red and other colored glass, although I was surprised that the designs had not evolved. The chandeliers, for instance, are just as monotonous as ever, and yet I would have thought this kind of thing could perhaps be made in the shape of a sun with radiating beams or a flower bouquet, instead of the same old crown form; or that wall sconces of glowing colors fashioned like jewelry set with brilliant gems could generate unexpected effects in rooms decorated, for example, in an Oriental style.

In other shops you see fascinating displays of all the instruments of modern agriculture and mechanics, from gigantic sowing machines and devices for uprooting old trees down to tiny pruning shears. Throughout these spacious premises you find everything arrayed with the same degree of care, even among the butchers, fishmongers, and potato sellers. The shops of the ironmongers and lamp sellers are also worth a visit since they are well stocked with all that is new and useful, things not easily found in such quantity or with such convenience anywhere on the Continent. As for the traveler who wishes to limit his company to the salons and his own kind of people, hoping to see only genteel attractions, he had better stay at home!

I finished the day with a ride to the soldiers' hospital in Chelsea where I felt profoundly happy to see the old warriors well cared for and living in a palace set amid meticulously tended gardens, with the most beautiful, closely mowed bowling greens and tall allées of chestnut trees that would make a minor sovereign proud. Then at eight o'clock I had dinner at the Austrian ambassador's, a meal distinguished not just by the amiability of the host but also by the authentic Metternich-Johannisberger,[6] a nectar for which even the most inveterate liberal must give the great minister his due. I found your friend Berndt there; the forty-year-old lad passed on many warm greetings to you. He is just the same as ever and regaled me at length with his sartorial woes. It seems that out of boredom here, he has become dreadfully thin. Indeed his tailor found him significantly stouter in one spot only, namely where he had been wearing calf enhancers!

It is too soon to tell you much about local society. Once I have been here for a while and experienced the season, I will be able to report in more detail. As long as London remains a Palmyra in its isolation from the fashionable world, I will content myself with descriptions of those places I come across accidentally or choose to seek out.

A FEW DAYS ago I took advantage of the somewhat brighter weather to visit Chiswick, a villa belonging to the duke of Devonshire. It is considered the most elegant estate of its type in all of England, and I had only seen it briefly several years ago at a party given by the duke. I was not able to look at the paintings this time either because a guest was living in the house. I found many changes in the garden, however, though hardly for the better, because it is now ruled by a mixture of regularity and irregularity that yields an unpleasant effect. There is everywhere evidence of the ugly fashion now widespread in England of planting nothing but single, isolated trees more or less in rows all over the pleasure ground,* which makes the lawns look like nurseries. In the shrubberies the bushes are trimmed on every side so they cannot touch their neighbors; the ground around them is carefully cleaned every day; and the strips of grass are edged into stiff lines so that you see more black earth than green foliage. Consequently the unconstrained beauty of nature's forms is utterly suppressed.

Mr. Nash is the only one who works on an entirely different principle in the laying out of grounds, and the new gardens at Buckingham House are true models for all planters.

What most favors English gardeners is the mild climate. Cherry and Portuguese laurels, azaleas, and rhododendrons never freeze and provide—both winter and summer—magnificent undergrowth, as well as luxuriant blossoms and berries.

Magnolias seldom need to be covered, and even camellias overwinter in sheltered spots beneath a simple raffia mat. The lawns, too, maintain their beautiful green throughout the winter. Indeed they tend to be far lovelier and thicker than during the dry summers when, as I recall, I have often seen them looking even worse than in the Mark Brandenburg. But now in the autumn all the vegetation is at the peak of exuberant splendor.

In front of the house at Chiswick there is a tall, isolated tree, and its effect is lovely: the trunk has been smoothly pruned up to the crown so you can stand beneath the limbs and overlook the entire garden and part of the park—a good hint for landscape gardeners and one I suggest you make use of in Muskau. The allée of cedars (a tree that unfortunately cannot survive outdoors at home) is famous and matches the height of ancient firs. Colossal yew hedges also testify to the length of time this estate has been carefully tended, while the new greenhouses and conservatories demonstrate the good taste of the current owner better than the pleasure ground does. It is odd that in England orange trees cannot be grown to any significant size. This part of the nursery is a bit stark, whereas the flower gardens are still blooming in profusion. The beds are sparsely set out so that each individual plant can spread freely, except for those in which just *a single* kind of flower is grown. Here the goal is to keep the whole area as densely planted as possible, and consequently these beds are by far the loveliest. In the greenhouses I saw my first example of the great Providence pineapple, which has produced fruits weighing up to twelve pounds.

There is a small zoo attached to Chiswick where a tame elephant performs all sorts of tricks and calmly allows itself to be ridden around on an open stretch of lawn. Its neighbor is a llama, an animal of a much less benign nature. Its weapon is an extremely foul-smelling saliva that it can

---

* A "pleasure ground" is an area that is fenced, carefully tended, and adorned with flowers, which serves as a transition between the park and the actual gardens.—*The Editor.*

spit over a distance of several yards at any heckler. Its aim is so precise and its charges so sudden and quick that most adversaries have difficulty escaping the projectile.

Unfortunately Chiswick boasts only stagnant, slimy water, which is sometimes so depleted that if the elephant were excessively thirsty, it could guzzle up the last drops in a jiffy.

After an hour of rapid travel past a succession of delightful villas and country houses of every kind, passing through a swarm of riders, country wagons, traveling carriages, and coal carts hauled by gigantic horses, interspersed with occasional beautiful views of the Thames, I arrived back at Hyde Park Corner and plunged again into the labyrinth of the vast metropolis.

The following day I visited the City with my hired servant, a Swiss man who has not only traveled in Egypt, Syria, Siberia, and America, but has also published a Russian post book,[7] delivered the first report to London about Tettenborn's capture of Hamburg, and imported a live specimen of a Cossack. In addition, having recently purchased Napoleon's coronation robes in Paris, he displayed them here for an entrance fee of five shillings. Meanwhile he is fluent in most European languages and a real bargain at a half guinea a day. He can serve as a physician as well, for he has collected so many secret formulas and arcana on his travels that he possesses wonderful household remedies for every possible malady, not to mention, so he claims, a thousand recipes for making punch. Guided by this universal genius, I went first to the Royal Exchange.

Elsewhere the stock exchanges are simply mercantile, whereas here they have a thoroughly historic character. The imposing statues of English rulers are posted all around, those of Henry VIII and Elizabeth being especially prominent. Along with the ancient and dignified architecture, these awaken poetic sentiments that take on a deeper significance at the thought of the immeasurable global commerce centered in London. Yet the traders who populate this scene and bring it to life return you to the realm of the ordinary soon enough, for here self-interest flashes vividly from every eye. In this respect the Exchange, like the entire City, has an almost sinister aspect, not so different from the restless and desolate scramblings of the ghosts of the damned (Figure 5).

The great courtyard of the Exchange is surrounded by covered arcades with inscriptions directing the merchants of all nations toward their appropriate meeting places. In the center is a statue of Charles II, who built this palace.[8] In posture and gesture it captures the man exactly as history describes him: not handsome but not without grace, and with an endemic levity in his features that makes him look half-grave, as if in mockery. This levity could not be amended because it was rooted in mediocrity, and thus made this king as engaging and careless as a *roué* as he was bad as a ruler. In the niches that encircle the second story of the building are the busts of other English monarchs. I have already mentioned Henry VIII and Queen Elizabeth—both would be striking even without the associations attached to them: Henry fat and comfy while looking cruel in a gemütlich way; Elizabeth manly in her magnificence, yet with a female malice. The busts were certainly made after the best Holbeinian originals. On this same floor is the famous Lloyd's Coffee House, the filthiest venue of its kind in London, which looks nothing like a place where, every day, deals amounting to millions of pounds are concluded. Admittedly you do see more pens and paper than refreshments.

Nearby is the beautiful and gargantuan Bank of England, containing a host of large and small rooms that are mostly lit from above and meant to house its various offices. Here hundreds of clerks are at work alongside one another, routinely conducting their colossal transactions. A poor, awestruck German can find it difficult to follow the maxim *nil admirari*,[9] especially while

5

*The Royal Exchange
and* Nero.

THE ROYAL EXCHANGE.

NERO.

gaping at the piles of gold and barrels of silver in the Bullion Office where the ingots are stored, imagining that he is faced with the treasures of *One Thousand and One Nights.*

From here I went to the town hall where the Lord Mayor, presently a bookseller, was dispensing justice. He looks impressive in his blue mantle and gold chain and knows how to assume a thoroughly regal demeanor. In my opinion he performed his duty as well as any regular judicial officer, for ever since the time of Sancho Panza, it has been evident that a healthy measure of common sense can often recognize what is *right* more successfully than studied expertise can, which becomes myopic from too many excessively ground eyeglasses. In like manner, parenthetically, I myself usually prefer the *artistic* judgment of a cultured, unstudied mind to that of an art expert who is seduced by a name, or that of a self-made artist who is excessively impressed by challenges he has overcome.

The venue was an undistinguished room half filled with the lowliest riffraff, and at issue the most common subject in England: thievery. The transgressor, who appeared serene in his boredom, confessed after only a slight hesitation, and the drama came quickly to an end.

So we wandered on through the tumultuous City, a place where you can disappear like an atom if you fail to look both right and left so as not to be skewered by the shaft of a cabriolet passing too near the sidewalk or crushed to death by the overturning cab of a diligence. We came once again to an extremely dark and shabby coffeehouse, this one called Garroway's, a miserable spot where properties and palaces, often valued in the hundred thousands, are auctioned off daily. Seating ourselves with all seriousness, as if eager to make comparable acquisitions, we admired the auctioneer's exceptional charm and his astonishing skill at arousing the desire to buy. He was dressed in refined black, wore a wig, and stood on a raised lectern like a professor. He presented every piece of property with a delightful introduction seasoned by droll remarks, and he praised each item so compellingly that the naïve buyer would swear it was being sold for the most recklessly trifling sum.

My hired lackey told me that this famous auctioneer had recently been involved in an awkward case. It seems he had heaped tremendous praise on a country estate for the romantic hanging wood located nearby, a type of woodland very popular in England and generally understood to include weeping willows, weeping birches, weeping ashes, spruces, and the like. Once the unwary purchaser had been seduced into buying the estate (it is peculiarly English that nearly all purchases are transacted without any actual inspection of the offered property), he visited his newly acquired plot of land only to find it almost completely denuded of trees and with no hanging wood in the vicinity save a gallows! So there you have English humor, and so much for legality!

How could I leave the City without having visited its master, a true "lion" (the English expression for anything extraordinary), in a word, Rothschild? (Figure 6).

In this part of town, too, he occupies an unassuming place (his mansion is located in the West End), and my access to this chief ally of the Holy Alliance was considerably impeded by the freight wagon loaded with silver ingots that blocked the small courtyard of his office. There I also found the Russian consul in the process of making a courtesy call. A fine and clever man, he knew how to play his role perfectly and to combine it with all due respect *cum dignitate.* This was made all the more difficult because the brilliant autocrat of the City is himself quite informal. After I had handed him my letter of credit he commented ironically that we were wealthy and fortunate people to be traveling around amusing ourselves, while the burdens of the world lay on him, poor man. He went on to complain bitterly that no miserable wretch ever came to England

without wanting something from him. Just yesterday, he said, another Russian had again come begging, a remark that brought a bittersweet expression to the consul's face. "And," he added, "the Germans never give me any peace at all!"

Now it was my turn to remain unruffled. As the conversation turned to politics, we were both happy to admit that without him Europe would not be able to carry on. He modestly brushed this off and said with a smile: "Oh, no, now you're only joking. I am nothing more than a servant with whom people are content because he does his job well, and to whom they acknowledge their gratitude by allowing him to accrue a morsel or two."

This was delivered in a totally idiosyncratic mixture of half English, half German—the English with a heavy German accent—but with an impressive self-assurance that seemed to find it not worth trifling over. Such a truly original language struck me as perfectly characteristic of a man whose genius and, in a way, greatness of character cannot be disputed.

Having begun, appropriately in England, at the Royal Exchange, where the merchants are on view, I closed my tour at Exeter Change,[10] where the display is of exotic animals, rather like representatives of the Colonies (Figure 7). Here I met another lion, but this time a real one named Nero who, besides his docility, has the merit of already having provided the nation with six generations of young English lions, a rarity in our latitudes. He is of gargantuan size and dignified appearance, but now rests on his laurels and sleeps like a king most of the day. If he wakes up in a bad mood, his roar causes the slats of his ancient cage to shudder and the lowlier animals in his vicinity to shake as well. These are creatures of all sorts: elephants, tigers, leopards, hyenas, zebras, apes, ostriches, condors, parrots, and birds from every zone (Figures 5 and 8). Strangely they live not on the ground level but on the second and third floors, which means you can ride around up there on a tame elephant—one is always saddled and ready—and enjoy a lovely view into the distance. The shops on the ground floor are known for having a large selection and relatively cheap prices, and as I recall the ambassador of the late king of Württemberg was busier here than in St James's and Downing Street.[11] Indeed at one time he was in great danger of losing his position because of the wretched death of a large, rare tortoise.

On the way back to my hotel we went by a palace that inspired my widely traveled cicerone, Mr. Tournier, to tell me the following story. If he embroidered it, I beg you to blame him, not me.

6

Nathan Rothschild in Profile (A View from the Royal Exchange).

This palace is, namely, the house of the Montagu family (relocated by Shakespeare to Verona). The young heir had been abducted when he was just one year old, and nothing had been heard of him since. After eight years of futile inquiries by the despairing mother, the neighborhood chimney sweep sent a small boy to clean the flue in Lady Montagu's bedroom, and through a lucky accident—by dint of a mark near his eye and an ensuing investigation—the prodigal son was recognized. (This anecdote later inspired a well-known French musical comedy.) Out of gratitude for her unexpected happiness, Lady Montagu instituted an annual festival on the anniversary of this joyful event. I believe something similar still takes place today. She used to invite every member of the London chimney sweeps' guild to a celebration in the large garden adjoining her palace, where she and all of her staff catered to these people.

As the years passed the boy turned into a distinguished but wild and eccentric youth, who took enormous pleasure in unusual acts of bravado. He found the best opportunity for these in perpetual travels to unfamiliar foreign lands, where he was always accompanied by a dear friend, a certain Mr. Barnett. Thus he had already seen the most remote spots in the world when Tournier, according to his own account, accompanied him as his manservant to Switzerland in 1790. Having arrived in Schaffhausen, the lord fastened on the unhappy idea of riding

7

Exeter Change.

8

*Exeter Change Interior
Showing Nero.*

down the Rhine Falls in a boat. The leading clergyman of the town, along with other acquaintances, begged the young hothead not to undertake such an insane venture, but in vain. The Schaffhausen city militia was even called in, but either he eluded their vigilance, or they were no better at frightening him than the Leipzig militia had been at controlling the local students.[12] In any case, after he had done a kind of trial run by sending out an empty boat as an augury—which luckily came through with its wooden life intact—Montagu followed in the company of his friend. Mr. Barnett had also done his best to dissuade the headstrong lord from his plan. But Montagu challenged him: "What's this, Barnett? You've trekked all over the whole globe with me, faithfully endured every peril by my side, and now you want to abandon me over this childish nonsense?" Thus compelled to give in, Barnett shrugged his shoulders and climbed into the ill-fated boat.

The daredevils floated off gently, at first moving slowly toward the precipice but then with ever more wrenching speed, while hundreds of apprehensive spectators looked on. What everyone had predicted happened. As the boat touched the edge of the rocks it swung around, and the two men appeared just once more between the boulders. The thunder of the raging water muffled their cries for help, which could be heard only indistinctly and intermittently. Soon they disappeared entirely, and though months were spent searching for their bodies along the whole length of the Rhine, all the way to the mouth in Holland, and though vast sums were offered for their retrieval, they were never recovered. Now they slumber unrecognized in the crystal deep.

It is strange that on the same day that witnessed their deaths, the ancestral residence of the Montagu's in Sussex burned to the ground. The unhappy mother survived the death of her twice-lost son by just a year.[13]

If Grillparzer can be believed, at least *one* unforgiving ancestress was implicated, perhaps even from the time of Romeo.[14]

October 13th, 1826

EXHAUSTED FROM THE tour the day before yesterday, I spent the next morning within my own four walls, but in the evening went to the English opera, which is located in the Strand not far from the menagerie, whose inhabitants are thus conveniently available. The theater is neither elegant nor large, but the actors are not at all bad. No opera was being performed; instead there were hideous melodramas: first *Frankenstein*, where a man is created by black magic and without female agency, which accordingly turns out very badly; then the *Vampyre* after the well-known story falsely ascribed to Lord Byron.[15] The leading role in both is played by Mr. Cook who is distinguished by his handsome appearance, very talented acting, and extremely genteel and noble demeanor. The whole ensemble gave exemplary performances, but the pieces were so silly and absurd that you could not possibly hold out to the end. Not only were the heat, the vapors, and the audience far from enjoyable, but the show lasted from seven o'clock until half past twelve, too long even if it had been superb.

The next day I drove to Hampton Court to visit the castle, the stud farm, and my old friend Lady Lansdowne. Of these three I found the first the least changed and the famous grapevine in the garden even more weighed down with fruit.[16] All told, it bore far more than a thousand clusters and completely filled the greenhouse (seventy-five feet long by twenty-five feet wide) that is dedicated solely to that vine. Its brown trunk stood in one corner like the somber progenitor of a proud race, quite lost and inconspicuous, as if it no longer had any relationship to the magnificent vaults of leaves and fruit that owed it their entire existence.

Most of the rooms in the palace are still furnished exactly as they were when William III left them 120 years ago. The frayed chairs and carpets are intentionally kept this way. Many interesting paintings adorn the walls, above all the famous cartoons by Raphael, which, however, are soon going to be moved from here to the king's new palace.[17] You have heard all this described so often that I will refrain from repetition, but let me mention just two beautiful portraits, one of Wolsey, the proud builder of this palace, and one of Henry VIII, his treacherous master. Both are excellent and very characteristic. Remember that fat lawyer we had so much trouble getting rid of, the one with the bestial expression, sensual, as bloodthirsty as can be? Adroit, pedantic, full of intellect and cunning joined to unbridled arrogance, he nonetheless bore an overriding tendency to the common and was still, in a truly naïve way, free of any conscience. Put a green frockcoat with mother-of-pearl buttons on the portrait of Henry and there he is, perfectly portrayed.

Nature always reveals itself in varying nuances that evolve in different stages. So it is, too, with the fate of mankind and the world.

During the night I almost succumbed to death by suffocation, since the idiotic servant I had brought along from home, no doubt too well hosted by an English comrade earlier in the evening, decided to take some coals out of the fireplace while I was already asleep and left them on a lacquered tray next to the hearth. Luckily I was awakened by frightful fumes and an infernal stench, just as I was dreaming that I was one of Henry VIII's courtiers, and on the Field of the Cloth of Gold,[18] where I had just made a conquest of a French beauty—otherwise I would have kissed my imaginary bride only in heaven.

The place where you abide, my dear one, seems very like that heaven to me—just as far away and just as sweet; and so I send you a kiss of peace across the sea and close this, my first epistle from England, with wishes for your health and blessing.

Your most affectionate, devoted Lou

London, October 15th, 1826

𝒯HE CLIMATE HERE seems not to agree with me at all, because I have been feeling unwell ever since I disembarked. However, as long as I do not have to stay in my room, I can manage. To cure myself I go out riding in the delightfully cultivated environs of London, and I make excursions within the city as well.

It was recently the British Museum's turn, and there I found a peculiar mishmash of art objects and *naturalia*, curiosities, books, and models housed in a deplorable building.[1] At the entrance, above the staircase, two enormous giraffes stand like stuffed sentries, or better, emblems of English taste! Granted, there is much of interest in the various rooms, but I must reluctantly confess that, unless in the best of moods, excessive exposure to such remarkable things gives me indigestion. Among these antediluvian remains was a monstrous but well-preserved set of stag's antlers some six times larger than any in the stag gallery of our friend C——'s castle. In the antiquities gallery (which looks like a barn) I was delighted to find the splendid Elgin Marbles, as they are known here. If only it were possible to see this lost world of ancient art in all its splendor with the monuments intact! That would be worth the effort. But, parenthetically, the isolated torsos provide only the kind of pleasure we might feel at seeing a gorgeous woman who has lost a leg, both arms, and her eyes.

A bust of Hippocrates particularly appealed to me as a perfect representation of the professional physician. At the mere sight of such a visage here in England, people involuntarily reach into their pockets.* I also gazed at the famous Portland Vase with all due enthusiasm. I am sending you two special publications about the vase and the Elgin Marbles, quite well illustrated, but I must now take my leave and have my things packed, because I intend to head to Newmarket tomorrow to spend a few days there during the horse races (Figure 9).

Newmarket, October 19th, 1826

The beauty of the countryside and the exceptional charm of the places I passed through today once again filled me with pleasure. These fertile and orderly landscapes adorned with thousands of delightful country houses, and the incessant throng of elegant carriages, riders, and well-dressed pedestrians are all quite particular to England. This image of perfection, however,

---

* English physicians are accustomed to receiving a guinea at every visit. One of them assured me that whenever he was sick and wrote himself a prescription, he never failed to take a guinea from his own left pocket and move it to his right.—*The Editor.*

harbors one flaw: everything is too well cultivated, too perfect, and therefore always and everywhere the same and, consequently, tiring. More than that, it can even be revolting, just as the aroma from a plate of delicacies can be nauseating on a full stomach. This may also help explain the English love of travel. For it is generally true that a life of unmixed bliss eventually becomes intolerable—perhaps the very reason why the dear Lord chased our ancestor Adam out of paradise: to save him from dying of boredom!

But today cast a certain admixture of shadows over my progress. The intense competition to get to the races left me with nothing but exhausted horses at every station and sometimes no horses at all. Thus, by English standards, I had a miserable trip and only arrived in Newmarket late at night. There was no accommodation to be had at any inn, and so I counted myself lucky

to find a small room in a private house for just five guineas a week. Fortunately I ran into an old acquaintance there, the son of a minor Hungarian magnate.[2] His *joie de vivre* and unassuming nature make him reliably cheery and universally liked. I admire such natures because they possess all that I lack.

On the following morning we rode out together to orient ourselves somewhat. Each day here resembles the next just like one egg resembles another. At eight thirty you see a few hundred racehorses, each covered with a blanket, taking their morning promenade on a treeless hill. They are strewn across the grassy slope like a herd of cattle. Some move at a walk, others at a slow or intermediate gallop, but never at a full run. An overseer riding a small pony usually accompanies all those belonging to the same owner or boarding with the same training groom. The racehorses themselves are ridden by small, scantily clothed boys who sit atop the blankets. Occasionally, much to the amusement of the spectators, one of them will get thrown. After this review—certainly a matter of great interest to a horse enthusiast—everyone has breakfast and then spends another half hour or so at the horse auction conducted by the renowned Mr. Tattersall. This takes place nearly every day on the open street; afterward all proceed by horseback or carriage to the races.

These begin fairly promptly at noon. An immeasurable grassy plain covered with fine, thick turf provides the battlefield where various distances are run, from a minimum of half a mile to a maximum of five miles, always in a straight line. Toward its end the course is bounded on both sides by ropes, beyond which are three or four rows of carriages, mainly unharnessed, each packed with spectators from top to bottom, inside and out. At the finish line is a little wooden hut quite like what shepherds use in many parts of Germany. This is mounted on wheels so it can easily be moved if the end post needs to be placed nearer or farther away. The judge sits inside where he has a view of the exact finish line, marked by a post planted opposite him. It is crucial that he be certain which horse's nose crosses the line first, for as little as one inch is often decisive.

The jockeys here are especially skillful in disclosing as little as possible about the true swiftness of their mounts, urging them on just enough to win. If they see they have no chance, they prefer to hang well back, whereas those still battling for victory keep in a tight race to the finish line. Only in Germany and France do you see the grotesque spectacle of a jockey left a thousand paces behind, who nonetheless works away at his horse like a steam engine with his spurs and crop. In the case of a tie, the two horses must run again, something that happens often. In these cases the judge is under oath, and there is no appealing his verdict.

English jockeys are not small boys, as foreigners occasionally assume, but often diminutive old men of sixty. They have their own club and are the best practical riders I know. Always as small and slight as possible, they labor constantly at reducing their weight by induced sweating, purging, and the like. You will remember that I myself once owned racehorses, and for a while kept a Newmarket jockey in my service, who, among other accomplishments, won a significant bet for me in Vienna. I was always much amused when he put himself in training and, after being fortified with several laxatives, would drape himself in three or four heavy furs and ride off for some distance at a trot in the most extreme heat until the sweat was streaming off him and he nearly sank to the ground from exhaustion. It made him happy, and the more miserable he felt, the more contented he was.

But this, too, depends upon local regulations that stipulate how much weight a horse is supposed to carry. As on any occasion where a lot of money is at stake, it is inadvisable for a jockey to take off too many pounds, for then he must add lead weights to the girth, something that is unpleasant for both horse and rider.*

---

* Let me take this opportunity to advise those of my Berlin friends who would like their horses to compete in local races, that they have them trained only by well-recommended English grooms. As has been repeatedly demonstrated to me, our grooms, without exception, have no understanding at all of the matter. They believe they have trained a horse once it has become a skeleton, when bloodletting, purging, and daily racing around have robbed it of the strengths that genuine training could have increased by tenfold. Both well and poorly trained horses look equally lean, I admit, but with the latter it is the leanness of misery and debilitation, with the former just the absence of unnecessary flesh and fat, along with the highest development and power in the muscles and lungs.—*The Editor.*

At a certain distance from the finish line toward the entry point, another white post stands about a hundred paces off to the side; this is the betting post. Here the bettors assemble after watching the horses being saddled in the stable, having satisfied themselves about all the prevailing conditions, and perhaps also giving a wave to the jockeys. Many would find the activity at the betting post to be the most disconcerting of all. With the cacophony and shouting, it has much in common with a Jewish synagogue, except that the passion is more visible. Among the participants are the leading peers of England and their liveried servants, as well as the most disreputable sharpers and blacklegs. In short, all those who have the money to gamble claim equal rights here, and there is no essential difference in their appearance, nor in the way they treat one another. Most carry notebooks, and each man yells out his offers. Then when an offer is accepted, both men note this immediately in their books. Dukes, lords, stable lads, rogues are all frantically bellowing and betting against each other with a volubility and technical vocabulary impenetrable to the neophyte foreigner. Suddenly a cry rings out: "The horses have started!"

The crowd scatters quickly, but the devoted bettors meet up again at the ropes encircling the track. Amid the carriages and riders you can see a multitude of telescopes, opera glasses, and lorgnettes focused on the jockeys approaching in the distance. They bear down on you with the speed of the wind, and for a few moments an anxious silence envelops the colorful throng, while a mounted overseer keeps the track clear, nonchalantly brandishing his whip to drive back any interlopers. But the quiet is brief, and soon the wildest tumult erupts once more, a mixture of loud cheers and laments, curses and shouts of approval, resounding from every side, back and forth, bellowed by men and women alike. You hear the bettors screaming furiously: "Ten to four on the Admiral, a hundred to one on Putana," "Smallbeer against the field," "Karo-Bube wins," and so forth; and you've hardly noticed the word "done" pronounced here and there when the noble beasts have suddenly arrived,[3] passed by in a heartbeat, and at the next moment are at the finish, where either destiny or skill or fraud will have prevailed. The big losers stare rigidly ahead for a moment, the winners exult at full volume, many put a good face on it, but all of them now run quickly after the jockeys to watch while they are weighed and the horses unsaddled, many with the hope that an irregularity might still give them a win. In a quarter hour the same game begins anew with other horses, in a sequence to be repeated six or seven times. *Voilà les courses de Newmarket.*

The first day I was so clairvoyant that I guessed the winner correctly three times merely from what I intuited and appraised during the saddling, and I won a considerable amount. But after that things went as they usually do at games, and on the following days I lost all my winnings and as much again. Anyone who wins here regularly is sure of what he is doing *beforehand,* and it is well-known that many of the English nobility have very loose principles on this point.

Among the onlookers I found several acquaintances from earlier days, and they allowed me to see their racehorses in the stable, considered a great privilege. They also offered to procure my entrée to the local club, but this holds out no real benefit since the place is nothing but a gambling establishment, something one has to particularly beware of in England.

It is regarded as a national trait and a reflection of the generally mercantile spirit here that anything is allowed before a race, yet serious altercations can arise about the legitimacy of the betting—which is often carried out at enormous speed and amid the greatest confusion. On the other hand it often happens that someone who has lost more than he can pay simply vanishes quietly before the settlement date; that is, he declares bankruptcy and hides himself away on the

Continent either forever, or until he is capable of paying up. When this kind of thing occurs, the habitués call it a bad meet.

On the very first day of my stay in Newmarket, my Hungarian friend introduced me to the family of a rich merchant from the vicinity. All of them came to the races every day and brought along their house guests, including several very pretty girls, returning afterward to their nearby estate.[4] We were invited to dine there the next day and to stay the following day as well, which we accepted with pleasure.

We set off on horseback at around five o'clock. The beginning of our host's property was marked by a broad double allée of young, newly planted beech trees, and this led us after approximately a half hour to the park entrance, a kind of triumphal arch bordered laterally by two pavilions joined to the wooden railings enclosing the park. For some distance beyond the gate, however, the railings had been planted on both sides so that the entrance pavilions appeared to be standing isolated in the woods, which made for a very good effect. The way then led us for a while through thick brush until we reached a meadow dotted with groups of trees, the chief ingredient of any English park. Soon we caught sight of the illuminated house in the distance, with the tall trees and shrubberies of the pleasure ground spreading out behind it. We nearly had to leap over a few cows lying in front of the doorstep, a peculiarity already condemned by Repton. Such things come about because the park—that is, the ornamented pasture—is customarily allowed to extend on at least one, and most often two, sides, all the way up to the residence. Having the pleasure ground and garden encircle the house would be far more suitable, since it seems to me that the greatest enjoyment comes from *distant* views of cattle, not from their immediate proximity with all its unpleasant side effects.

We found a rather numerous party made up of the master and mistress of the household, both middle-aged; their eldest married daughter and her husband; and two younger, not-very-appealing daughters. Also in attendance was a baronet from the neighborhood with his pretty wife and her equally charming sister, who was, however, very melancholic, having recently returned from India without success.* And there was a much acclaimed Miss Brummell (who often moves in higher circles than this),[5] three other negligible gentlemen, the son of the house, and finally a London fop of the second rank, who could well serve as a study for an aspiring dandy of the City.

The baronet had served in Germany and, as he told us, was there awarded the Cross of Maria Theresia, although he declined to wear it because he now considered it a juvenile bauble unsuited to his agrarian occupations. He was a modest and friendly man, who, being most familiar with the Continent, seemed to have been specially assigned to do us the honors of the house. We, however, chose to be instructed in *English* customs by his wife and sister-in-law.

According to local custom, a visit from two noblemen (even *foreigners,* although they rank 15 percent lower than the native-born variety) is an honor for a house of lower standing such as this one, and we were therefore tremendously celebrated; even the dandy, as far as the rules of his métier allowed, was charming and attentive. It is a nearly universal weakness of the non-noble

---

* It is customary to ship an annual transport of impoverished young English ladies to India, where such merchandise is rarer, and thus, if possible, to be rid of them—a speculation that is usually successful. To be a returnee, however, is a sad state of affairs!

English to boast about their distinguished acquaintances. Meanwhile the nobility* does the same with the fashionables or exclusives—a caste of its own, a state within a state. The exclusives themselves exercise a still more despotic power in society and pay no attention even to rank, still less to wealth, but simply find it possible to situate their existence in the above-mentioned national weakness.

It is therefore a joy for the English of the middle rank to travel on the Continent, where they can easily make genteel acquaintances and, once they have returned home, talk about them as intimate friends. Our hostess soon gave us a small specimen of this:

"Do you know the queen of Bavaria?" she asked. To my response that I had once had the honor of being presented to her, she continued, "She is a great friend of mine," exactly as if speaking about the wife of one of her husband's business associates. She immediately produced, from among the many baubles that she had draped over herself, a portrait of said queen who, she declared, had presented it to her. This may well have been true, because her daughter showed us a letter from one of the princesses (the daughters of Her Majesty) containing very intimate communications about her marriage and domestic arrangements, a document that has probably served as a showpiece for some time already to indulge the vanity of its possessor. Is it not extraordinary that our grand Germans, many of whom treat their own countrymen with disdainful arrogance, never fail to treat all English natives, however lacking in intellectual distinction, as if they were equals? And this just because of their Englishness, without questioning in the least whether their standing at home justifies such special favor! Nothing makes us appear more inferior in the eyes of the English than our abject obsession with foreigners; and it is all the more humiliating because it really comes down to the profound respect we all have, from the highest ranks to the very lowest, for English money.

Here in England it takes a significant fortune to have a house in the country since custom demands a great deal of luxury; and in keeping with this expectation, the same appointments must appear at the shopkeeper's domicile as at the duke's: an attractively decorated house with elegant furnishings, an opulent table service, servants in the latest and finest uniforms, a profusion of dishes and foreign wines at every meal, select and costly desserts, and in everything the appearance of affluence and "plenty," as the English call it. As long as guests are present this sort of life carries on, and then afterward, when left to themselves, many families will compensate by resorting to the most meager food. This is why no one can simply arrive at a country house without being invited. Furthermore, invitations are usually specific as to the day and hour since one's acquaintances tend to be numerous, making it essential that time and space be carefully allotted so that the departure of one person will make room for the next. You can hardly call this true hospitality; it is rather a way for the owner to put his resources on display for as many visitors as possible. Once a family has kept a house open for a month or longer, they themselves go out visiting for the rest of the time; but that single, hospitable month has already cost them the annual revenue of one of our rich landowners at home.

Since you have never been in England, let me write a few words describing the progress of an English dinner, which is, as I have said, more or less the same everywhere. You love the intricacies of everyday life and have often told me you miss them in most travel descriptions, even

---

* You know that in England only the families of peers are counted as nobility. From the baronet on, all the rest are just part of the "gentry," a word we might best translate as *Honoratioren* (notables).

though nothing gives a more vivid picture of a foreign land. So I hope you will not think I am going into too much petty detail.

As in France, a gentleman conducts a lady to the table on his arm, not by the hand, and is liberated from those antiquated bows and curtsies still exchanged in much of the most elegant German society each time a lady has been accompanied in. On the other hand, there is much anxiety about rank, although the English show little understanding of how to assess it with regard to foreigners. I cursed my own station today because it got me seated next to the hostess, whereas my friend very wisely inserted himself between the two beautiful sisters. When you enter the dining room you find the entire first course, except for the *relevés,* already set out on the table, just as in France; and as soon as the covers have been removed after the soup, you serve yourself from the dish in front of you and offer some to your neighbor.* If you want anything else, you must ask for it across the table or send a servant to fetch it. Because this is such a tiresome practice, some of the most elegant and widely traveled people here have adopted the more convenient German custom of having the dishes taken around by the servants.

When wine is served at dinner, it is common practice for two people to empty their glasses simultaneously. Both of you raise your glasses, look fixedly at one another, give a nod, and only then gravely drink up. Many outlandish customs of South Sea Islanders are surely less ludicrous! It is a courtesy to engage someone in this ritual, and often a messenger must be dispatched from the other end of the table to announce to B that A would like to raise a glass with him, after which awkward attempts are made to catch the other's eye until finally, like Chinese pagoda dolls,[6] the two perform the obligatory ceremony of nodding with great formality. If you are inclined to enjoy more wine, but the company is small and you have already shared a drink with every acquaintance, you must wait for dessert or be courageous enough to defy convention.

After the second course and an interim dessert of cheese, salad, raw celery, and similar treats (these sometimes accompanied by ale which is twenty to thirty years old and so strong that, if poured on the fire, ignites like brandy), the tablecloth is removed and the dessert set out; in the best houses this is often placed on a second even finer cloth lying under the first; in other establishments it may be set directly on the polished tabletop. This course consists of every possible hothouse fruit of extraordinary quality, Indian and local compotes, digestive ginger, frozen treats, etc. Fresh glasses are placed in front of each guest, and small fringed napkins are laid down along with the dessert plates and silverware. Three bottles of wine are set before the host, usually claret (Bordeaux), port, and Madeira. He pushes these along to his neighbor on the left, either on coasters or in a little silver wagon on wheels. Every man pours for himself, and if a lady sitting next to him would like some, he pours for her as well, and so on, until the circuit has been made—at which point it all starts over again. Luckily some crystal pitchers of ice water allow foreigners to mix a little antidote into their brandy, a very prevalent drink here. The servants all leave the room once dessert has been served; if more wine is needed, the butler is rung for, and he brings it in alone. The ladies remain seated for another quarter hour and are occasionally offered special servings of sweet wine, after which they leave the table. The gentlemen rise with them, one opens the door, and as soon as the ladies have been shown out, the men form a cozier group, the host takes the place of the hostess, and the discussion turns to daily concerns; any foreigner

———————————

* A good English education therefore includes the art of carving, something much neglected in Germany.

LETTERS OF A DEAD MAN

is now pretty much forgotten and must be satisfied with just listening. Anyone, however, is free to follow the ladies whenever he likes, an opportunity that Count Batthyány and I made the quickest possible use of, all the more so considering that this is now stylish, whereas excessive drinking is becoming unfashionable. For the same reason the dandy had preceded us to the salon, where we found the ladies grouped around a large table, awaiting us with coffee and tea.*

When the entire company was reunited, everyone broke up into whatever groups they liked, with no inhibitions. Some made music (whereby the melancholic beauty played an organ that was probably installed there for religious purposes); others enjoyed a game of whist; here and there a sweet couple whispered in a window recess; several talked politics. Only the dandy remained alone. Sunk deep in a large armchair, he had placed his elegantly shod right foot on his left knee and was apparently so engrossed in Mme de Staël's book *De l'Allemagne* that he no longer took the slightest notice of the society surrounding him.

On the whole I have to admit that the comely young man achieved a fairly good imitation of the best of his type. Perhaps I was seduced into this favorable opinion because he spoke so much at dinner about the great Goethe and praised his *Fost* [*sic*],⁷ both having been made fashionable in England by Lord Byron. The dandy, Mr. Moseley, seemed especially fond of *Fost* because of what he judged to be its aesthetic inclination, for he spent, as he told us, half his life in Paris and declared himself to be a freethinker.

The next day, after a communal breakfast, we and the ladies went for a ride in the park, which has nothing worthwhile to see except perhaps the river-like canal filled with slimy, stagnant water. It cost five thousand pounds to excavate and would have been better left undone. Accordingly we were all the more gratified by the hothouses and fruit gardens. The hothouses, a hobby of the owner, are heated by steam using a highly ingenious mechanism that he himself invented, whereby the simple turn of a handle can immediately increase or decrease the temperature as desired.

These spacious, elegant structures were filled with twenty-three different kinds of pineapple, and above them, hanging down from the glass ceiling, were hundreds of enormous clusters of dark blue grapes. Along a wall in the fruit gardens we admired the pears, which are extremely flavorful and grow to seven inches in length and sixteen in circumference.

Many of the gentlemen now went off on a hunt, but we opted for the domestic company. The amusing Batthyány had become the darling of the ladies and left them all downcast on our departure after dinner at one o'clock in the morning, this time in a post chaise. It was inevitable that on such a long journey we were compelled to laugh as we reviewed the many ridiculous

---

* When leaving the king's presence, ladies must go out backward (as one of them assured me) so as not to turn the wrong side to His Majesty, something that is against the strictly observed laws of etiquette in England. This has evolved into a kind of military maneuver, which can be quite embarrassing to a young woman new to the practice. The ladies close ranks with their backs to the exit, toward which they retreat in a diagonal line. As soon as the wing commandress reaches the door, she turns around to the right and passes through, followed in sequence by the others. Lady C is in command. As they arrive in the ladies' part of the house, they find a number of elegant porcelain vases, also all ordered in rank and file. *Après cela* they sip at a glass of liqueur, sit down for tea or coffee, and the female conversation begins. You know what this usually consists of: clothes, scandal, and love. "Such is the custom of Branksome Hall." [The elegant porcelain vases are a euphemistic way to describe chamber pots. The quotation, a popular refrain of the time, is from Sir Walter Scott's "The Lay of the Last Minstrel."—*Translator.*]

things we'd seen, although as a genuine Berliner, I did feel quite ashamed to be making fun of our hosts and their company instead of feeling profound gratitude for the hospitality. But today's world is corrupt, and besides, hospitality born of ostentation can only expect such a response. Our reputations were surely faring no better in the house we had just left.

At the races the next morning we saw the young ladies again and bet gloves with them until we lost, then delighted them with others we had smuggled in from Paris.[8] But we turned down a second invitation to go to the country since we were already scheduled to attend a gentlemen's dinner and Count Batthyány intended to ride off in the evening to a fox hunt in Melton. I, too, am going to be leaving Newmarket and will continue my letter in London.

Epping Place, October 20th, 1826

I DID NOT get as far as I had hoped and was compelled to spend the night here because the two parks I visited consumed half the day. But the effort was richly rewarded since the first of them was Audley End, Lord Braybrooke's estate, which can claim a place among the most impressive in the whole country (Figure 10). Its approach road has deep ha-has on either side that protect the park and yet allow a full view of it. You first look over an expansive green landscape with a splendidly shaped body of water at its center; this is wide and river-like, although unfortunately covered with duckweed because there is too little influx. Near the opposite bank is the magnificent Gothic palace that was originally built by the Earl of Suffolk. It was supposedly three times as large then, but it is still imposing and picturesque, with a multitude of towers, projections, and diverse lofty windows. Even though Lady Braybrooke was at home, I was granted the very rare permission to tour it.

I stepped into a wide but extremely plain entrance hall, the primary decoration being a few sets of antlers from giant stags of a primeval era that had been unearthed here. The furnishing consisted of massive benches and chairs on which the family arms were painted in bright colors. Other objects on view were some very old paintings, a Gothic lamp, and a large table made out of two pieces of shell marble polished only on the top surface; the rest was left roughly chiseled. There were a dozen leather fire buckets also painted with colorful crests. The ceiling was of wood with deep coffers and old, faded paint. It was evident at first glance that you had not stepped into a house built yesterday.

A tall, heavy door of carved oak led from here into the barons' hall, a large room with colossal windows extending from floor to ceiling and on one side giving an unobstructed view of the landscape (Figure 11). Many full-length ancestral portraits, some painted by Van Dyck, hung on the opposite wall, and between them arose a colossal marble fireplace bearing the Suffolk arms in richly colored stucco. The third wall, where we had entered, was covered in elaborate carvings in high relief with the figures half life-size as you see them in the choirs of Gothic churches. Across from this was another tall double door that led into the dining room and on either side an open staircase ascending to the second floor.

The dining room contains portraits of Suffolk and Queen Elizabeth. Her red hair, pale complexion, and artificial gaze, as well as her extravagant finery, do not give a very flattering impression of the gallant and vain maiden queen.

Upstairs is a long, narrow gallery full of antiquities, as well as pretty little odds and ends including, in the center, a large wind chart connected to the weather vane so it can tell the

hunters every morning which way the wind is blowing.* This gallery serves as a parlor. Most English country houses and palaces have adopted the good practice of identifying just *one* main room as a gathering place, a much more successful way to keep people together.

The chapel is modern but richly and tastefully decorated. If the chaplain is away, the master of the house, in keeping with ancient custom, delivers a sermon and conducts the worship service here at nine thirty every morning, with all the family and servants in obligatory attendance.

The park is large but crisscrossed by a disturbing complex of fences in order to allocate a particular terrain to each kind of animal—sheep, cows, horses, and deer. There are four to five hundred head of deer, and they almost always graze in close proximity, more like a tame herd than our idea of wild game. The flavor of the meat is also unlike that of their relatives living free in the woods of our homeland, quite the way that feral cattle are said to have a different taste. The areas with good cover for partridges and hares are also fenced, since the low brush would otherwise be eaten by the cattle. This is why the majority of English parks consist only of meadows with discrete groups of trees so tall that the animals cannot reach their branches.

10

Audley End.

---

* Not a bad thing to introduce at court.—*The Editor.*

Audley End,
The Great Hall.

The extensive vistas are impressive at first, but soon become tiring because of their uniformity. Nor do I find that the many enclosures and fences are flattering to the landscape, for every young tree planted on the plain must be surrounded by a high fence to protect it from the foraging animals.

Two separate temples and an obelisk, both of which can be reached only by walking across the grass, looked very out of place in the midst of this pasture. The distant Gothic tower of the Walden church, rising picturesquely above the crowns of the oaks, was distinctly more appropriate.[9] On the other hand I found the flower garden and the pheasant run extremely beautiful. The garden forms a large oval, densely surrounded by a natural evergreen wall of yews, cherry laurels, rhododendrons, cedars, cypresses, large boxwoods, hollies, etc., with very tall forest trees behind. A brook with a grotto and waterfall flows across the fine, velvety lawn, on which rare and splendid plants and flower beds of all shapes and colors have been set out in lovely groupings.

The pheasant run, a good half-hour away, is a little wood, shady and dense, filled with varied and rather sizeable trees, and surrounded by a wall. You can only get there by going across the sodden grass because the gravel path does not begin until the small entrance gate. This is an economic measure since roads are extremely expensive to build and maintain here, which is why most parks usually boast only *one* drive to the house, and why the footpaths end at the iron fence of the pleasure ground. English ladies are less afraid than ours of exposing their dainty feet to the wet.

The path I just mentioned brought me under a graceful, vaulted bower and, after various meanders, quite unexpectedly to the ivy-clad portal of a small building adjoined by the game-keeper's dwelling, even more hidden among the trees. This man opened the entry portal from the inside, and an astonishing sight now unfolded before us. We stepped into a small, open room where we found freestanding columns completely draped in thick Old Blush roses; between the columns on the right we could see a large aviary filled with parrots, and on the left an equally capacious nesting place with canaries, goldfinches, and other tiny birds. In front of us was a sweeping lawn sprinkled with evergreen shrubs and, as backdrop, a tall wood into which a few very narrow observation points had been artfully cut to provide views toward a distant village and a solitary church tower.

On this open plot of grass the gamekeeper now called together clouds of golden, silver, and multicolored pheasants, along with some exotic fowl, tame ravens, unusual doves, and other birds. They are all regularly fed here, and they bustled around in a bright, colorful throng, their varied movements and gestures heightened by the zeal of their appetites. They formed a very peculiar spectacle. A golden pheasant cock behaved in an especially comical way because, like an outdated dandy, he seemed to be paying court to all the hens. The utterly preposterous contortions and airs he adopted in the process compelled my old Berndt to such laughter that the English servants, accustomed to maintaining an attitude of slavish reverence before their masters, were amazed by his impropriety, although it amused *me* at least as much as the dandified pheasant's Pantalone-like antics among the hens.[10] There are more than five hundred gold and silver pheasants in this wood. Immediately after they hatch, just *one* of their wings is cut to hinder them from flying; hence they live here both summer and winter. Yet this climate is so mild that not even a shed is needed to protect them from the cold.

So as not to tire you, I will skip the description of the second park, Short Grove, which had little to recommend it and looked very neglected. The house offered one nice idea: the exterior of the main door was covered with mirrors, and the reflections afforded a lovely painting of the area as you approached the entrance. The fully furnished castle with park, greenhouses, etc., had just been rented (for the moderate price of four hundred pounds a year)—a very common practice here when the owners are off traveling. We would not want to adopt this system, but on the other hand parts of our city dwellings are almost always rented out, while the master and mistress occupy only the *bel étage*. The English, in turn, find this very strange, and it must be said that it is highly inconvenient; several families living in *one* house seldom encourages either cleanliness or tidiness.

The great wealth of the English landowners always astounds people from the Continent, where these days it is chiefly the landowners who constitute the poorest class and are those least protected by laws and institutions. Here, however, everything accrues to their benefit. It is extremely difficult for a man living on his income to acquire a freehold, since nearly all the land belongs to the crown or the higher nobility, who as a rule only give it out on a kind of hereditary leasehold. Thus, for example, when a great man calls a village his own, this does not mean, as with us, that he merely has dominion over it. Every house is actually his property and has been granted to the occupant only for a certain period of time, as I will explain. It is easy to envision what immense and ever-increasing revenues this must generate in a country that is already so industrialized, and you cannot help admiring the way the aristocracy has collaborated for centuries in order to shape English institutions to their advantage.

The free purchase of a piece of land involves a number of difficult conditions and in any case can only involve such high prices that smaller capitalists cannot participate. Since that is simply how it is, they find the hereditary leasehold more advantageous to them personally and consistently prefer it. But the leaseholds here are very different from what we are accustomed to at home. Namely, the requisite land is conveyed to the tenant for a period of ninety-nine years with the agreement that he pay the landowner a certain annual rent: in the case of houses so and so much per foot of frontage, from a few shillings up to five and ten guilders; in the case of larger pieces of property, so and so much per acre.

Meanwhile the tenant does what he wants with it, builds whatever he likes, lays out gardens, parks, etc. At the end of the ninety-nine years, however, everything there, just as it is, including anything nailed down, reverts to the family of the landowner. Furthermore the tenant is required to maintain his house in excellent condition, even repaint it every seven years, an expectation encouraged by visitations from the police. He can, by the way, sell the property to someone else during the period allotted to him, but only up to the fixed date when the actual owner will repossess it. In this way all the rural towns, villas, and the like that you see belong house by house to the great landowners. Although the tenants can usually reacquire the property after the term has expired, they will pay two or three times the rent for it, depending on how much the value of the property has risen in the interim and how much they themselves have improved it. These conditions even obtain throughout most of London, which also belongs to particular noblemen; Lord Grosvenor alone is said to take in more than one hundred thousand pounds sterling in yearly ground rents. Therefore, apart from the aristocracy, almost no one living in a house in London is its actual owner. Even Rothschild the banker does not own his own house. And when someone "buys" one, according to common practice, he is asked for how long. The price varies depending on whether it is being purchased firsthand, in such cases usually for a rent, or second- or thirdhand, then for a sum of money. This practice means that most of the profits of industry fall invariably to the aristocracy and thereby increase the immeasurable influence that they already exert on the government of the country.[11]

London, October 21st, 1826

THIS AFTERNOON I arrived back here safely through an incessant downpour, restored myself with a good dinner at the club, and in the evening won six times my travel costs at whist—"may good fortune stay with me this time!" I am well, in love with life, and find that I miss nothing—except you.

With circumstances so favorably joined, let me end my letter, which has once again swollen into a packet.

Eternally, your faithfully devoted Lou

London, November 20th, 1826

BELOVED FRIEND,

I would like to advise travelers to foreign countries never to take along servants from home, particularly if they imagine that it will help save money, nowadays always an important objective. In fact, *one* servant costs more than *four* extravagances, and in addition you place an often debilitating burden on yourself.

This conclusion arose from the trials of my old manservant, who is on the verge of falling into a fit of English spleen from the daily challenges he faces here, in particular that of obtaining soup at his midday meal; the very memory of this beloved dish brings tears to his eyes. He reminds me of the Prussian soldiers who, drowning in rivers of champagne, bludgeoned the French peasants for not serving them Stettin beer.

It is true that the middle-class English, being accustomed to a nutritious diet of meat, are unfamiliar with the broths and water-based soups of the North. What goes by this name here is a relatively expensive concoction, something like a witch's brew, made of all sorts of peppers and spices from both the East and West Indies. The image of my stalwart valet putting the first spoonful in his mouth called to mind Peregrine Pickle's infamous encounter with an ancient Roman soup,[1] and it transformed my annoyance with him into hearty laughter. But I can see that in due course his loyalty to me will be dashed against this rock. We Germans are peculiar in our insistence on keeping to the familiar, whether it be in regard to faith, love, or for that matter soup.

In the absence of society, the various clubs are a great convenience. Although it did not used to be the case, foreigners can now gain access to them, and the ambassador saw to it that

---

* Some letters have been excluded here because they contain only personal remarks. I mention this simply to explain a twenty-day silence to the lovely ladies among my readers, who have certainly shared my delight at the punctuality observed by the late writer in corresponding with his absent friend. These hiatuses will occur intermittently whenever I feel obliged to omit portions of the letters. To avoid tedium I have only rarely inserted rows of dots to indicate these excisions—for example, the *less interesting* banalities of daily life or the *overly interesting* chronicles of certain scandals. A short satirical account of one such scandal in another letter played very poorly, so I dare not risk it again. The sweetest ladies in Sandomir excommunicated the poor author. I am told by my correspondent there that "everyone is asking: have you read the letters of a dead man? These women are unstoppable." Nobody understands a joke any more in this world gone sad! Every pleasantry is received in a dour mood and stamped as an intentional insult. Nowadays Aristophanes would be slapped with twenty lawsuits and thrown out of the country.—*The Editor.* [Pückler's letters were originally published starting with Letter 25, hence the first sentence above appeared in a footnote to Letter 27. The remainder of this note probably refers to the "Observations" (pages 402–7) and the response (pages 416–19).—*Translator.*]

I was admitted to two: the United Service Club where, except for foreign ambassadors, only military officers are allowed; and the Travellers Club, to which every educated foreigner who comes well recommended is admitted. However every three months one must, in a rather humiliating way, apply to the Travellers Club to have the permission renewed, a stipulation enforced with near ill-mannered severity.

In Germany people have little notion of the elegance and comfort of English club society or the strictness of the club rules. Everything required for luxury and convenience, without resort to pomp, can be found here just as in the best-kept private house. Stairs and rooms are always adorned with fresh carpets, and rugs (dressed sheepskins with brightly colored wool) are laid down in front of the doors to prevent drafts; marble mantelpieces, lovely mirrors (always of one piece, considered part of solid English luxury), and a general abundance of furnishing make every living area extremely accommodating. Even scales are not lacking, so that you can daily ascertain your own weight, a favorite hobby of the English. You never see the numerous staff without shoes, and they are always neatly dressed in civilian costume or livery. A porter is unfailingly at his post ready to deal with greatcoats and umbrellas. Umbrellas deserve close attention in England since they are, alas, essential in these parts and are stolen everywhere in the most shameless fashion if you do not pay strict attention to their safekeeping. This has become so notorious that a recent newspaper published a report about a certain League of Virtue distributing prizes for the most noble deed:

"The choice became very difficult the last time, for just as they were about to crown someone for paying his tailor's bills promptly for a number of years in a row, it was established that another man had *twice* returned umbrellas people had left at his house. The members of the League were stunned to silence by this unprecedented act, amazed that so much noblemindedness was still to be found in Israel, but then burst into loud and enthusiastic applause, leaving no doubt about who would wear the victor's crown."

In the elegant and well-furnished library there is always someone at hand to find whatever books you request. The periodicals are all carefully arranged in the reading room, and in the nearby *Carten*-room* is a selection of the newest and best of them. The rolled-up maps are hung on top of each other in descending lengths against the walls, so that one can easily be drawn down over the others by a cord at the center. A simple mechanism allows a tug on the cord at the side to roll it back up again with great speed. The name of each country is written in such large letters on its mahogany rod that even the uppermost inscription is easy to read. Thus a great many maps can be hung in an extremely small room, and any one of them can be displayed whenever you need it without disrupting the others.

The table, by which I mean the food (the primary concern for most people, not least for me) is usually prepared by French cooks and is as good and as reasonably priced as one can expect in London. Since the club acquires its own wines and sells them at cost, they are very drinkable and inexpensive. However a gourmand almost never finds the best wines in London, even in superior establishments. This is due to the strange English habit (and these people cling to their habits

---

* Here I will mention that ever since Prussia was promised a constitution (*Charte*), my deceased friend adopted the following orthography for the homonyms to distinguish the three terms: *Carte* for geographical charts and *Karte* for playing cards. He still hopes that this proviso will not prove futile.—*The Editor.* [In 1810, Frederick William III had promised to give Prussia a constitution, but he did not follow through.—*Translator.*]

like an oyster to its shell) of ordering wine only through London suppliers; they themselves never import it directly from the countries where it is made, as we tend to do. Furthermore the dealers do not hesitate to adulterate it. One such man was recently accused of having so-and-so many thousand bottles of claret and port in his cellars on which he had never paid duty, and he escaped punishment by testifying that he had fabricated all of those wines himself in London. So you can imagine what concoctions are served here under the appealing name of Champagne or Lafitte. In any case, the dealers almost never purchase the best vintages available abroad, since they would make too little profit or none at all; and when they do purchase good wine, it is only in order to make the poor ones tolerable.

Please excuse this digression that you, who drink only water, cannot find very interesting. But you know that I am writing for us both, and I confess that to me the subject is not insignificant. I enjoy the taste of wine.

But back to the clubs. To begin with, you can observe the diversity of English customs much better here than in the fashionable world beyond, which always seems more or less predictable; whereas the same people, many of whom are part of that world, behave with fewer inhibitions in a club. A foreigner is bound to admire the refinement evidenced in the English art of sitting, and it must also be admitted that anyone unfamiliar with the ingenuity of English chairs is truly missing out on a good part of earthly delight, for they come in all shapes and are designed for every degree of fatigue, malady, or peculiarity of constitution. It is a pleasure simply to *watch* an Englishman seated, or better reclined, in front of the fire in one of their bed-like chairs. Attached to the armrest is a device resembling a music stand equipped with a candlestick, and this is set up before him in such a way that with the slightest touch he can move it closer or farther away, or push it to the left or right just as he likes. In addition, an unusual contraption, of which several are always waiting by the large fireplace, receives one or both of his feet. The hat on his head consummates this enviable image of bliss.

The latter behatted condition is the most difficult to assume for anyone brought up in the old school. I cannot suppress a provincial shudder when, stepping into the brilliantly illuminated salon of the club in the evening and finding elegantly dressed dukes, ambassadors, and lords seated at the card tables, I must—if I wish to imitate the fashionables—keep my hat on. I step up to a whist party, nod at this one or that, and then (perhaps after selecting a newspaper) collapse onto a sofa. After some time has passed, I can nonchalantly toss the hat down (which I have no doubt found outrageously annoying). Or, if I plan to stay for only a few minutes, there is no reason for removing it at all.

Various mannerisms—the custom of half reclining instead of sitting, of occasionally stretching out full length on the carpet at the feet of the ladies, of crossing one leg over the other so that you hold one foot in your hand, of putting your hands in the armholes of your vest, and so forth—all these postures have already migrated into the best and most exclusive circles. It is therefore quite possible that keeping your hat on will also bring you this honor. All the more so because Paris, once the model of proper conduct for all of Europe, has adopted the opposite stance and now mimics the English. And often in a rather grotesque way that frequently outstrips the original.

At the Travellers Club I was particularly amused to observe one distinguished foreigner from the South who was playing cards and, like the Chinese, was repeatedly and audibly releasing certain sounds through his open mouth that would once have been unacceptable in a tavern. It is likely he intended this as a satire on the loose customs and the noble crassness of outward appearances here, yet such habits, however unappetizing, are symptomatic of the Travellers Club.

On the other hand, great offense is taken in the dining room (which is basically nothing but an elegant restaurant and, accordingly, requires paying one's bill when the meal is over) if a foreigner reprimands a waiter for giving him bad service, making him wait a long time, or bringing one thing instead of another. It is much the same if one places an order in a loud and imperious fashion, even though the English themselves very often indulge in such behavior, and do so far more regularly when abroad. Furthermore it is viewed not just as unseemly but downright embarrassing for someone to read during dinner. It is simply not the fashion in England. Since I myself am supremely guilty of this and other rude habits, I have already noticed several signs of disapproval from one or another righteous and unimpeachable islander passing by and shaking his head. In general you must take care to avoid doing anything differently from the English, and yet you must not imitate them in everything, because no race is more intolerant. Most do not suffer foreigners gladly, and thus they consider it an extraordinary favor to give us entrée into their exclusive societies. Nevertheless that we are allowed to visit their clubs is at the least greatly convenient, not to say economical, given the costliness of English inns and the paucity of restaurants and coffeehouses like those one finds on the Continent.

Among the egregious transgressions against English conventions, those most likely to result in permanent banishment are the following: to put a knife in your mouth as if it were a fork; to pick up sugar or asparagus with your hands; and, worst of all, to spit anywhere in a room. These rules are certainly praiseworthy, and cultured people the world over avoid similar practices, though customs can vary a lot. For instance, Marshal Richelieu detected an adventurer passing himself off as a man of distinction merely by seeing him pick up olives with a fork and *not with his fingers*! The ridiculous thing is the extraordinary importance given to these infractions here, particularly the third crime mentioned above, which is so pedantically frowned upon that you could search throughout London in vain to find a shop with anything like a spittoon. An indignant Dutch visitor, much discomfited by this, maintained that the Englishman's only spittoon was his stomach.

These are, I repeat, more than just trivial matters, whereas in foreign countries the finest rules of decorum almost always have to do with trivialities. If I were to give a few general guidelines to a young traveler, I would advise him to treat people brutally in Naples, be natural in Rome, not talk politics in Austria, give himself no airs in France, give himself a lot of them in Germany, and by no means ever spit in England! Thus admonished, a young man would go a long way in the world.

What is justly admirable in England is the expedience and economy of daily life and public institutions, along with an unstinting resolve to follow the rules. In Germany all good institutions soon wither away, and only *new* brooms sweep clean. Here things are completely different. On the other hand, no one person is responsible for everything, but strictly for what his office entails and no more. The treatment of servants is just as admirable as the manner in which they themselves carry out their duties. Each one has his or her stipulated sphere of activity where the most attentive performance is required, and in the case of neglect, it is always known who is answerable. At the same time the servants are granted reasonable freedom and a certain amount of time to themselves, something their masters scrupulously respect.

In general the serving classes are treated far more decently and with far more consideration than at home. On the other hand, they are so thoroughly excluded from all manner of familiarity, and required to pay so much reverence to their masters, that they are regarded more as machines than human beings. This and their good pay are doubtless responsible for the fact that, *relatively* speaking, it is the serving class in England that, in its way, represents the most visible standard of decorum.

It would be forgivable if a foreigner occasionally mistook a *valet de chambre* for a master, presuming the visitor considered *courtesy* and a suave bearing to be the distinguishing traits of gentility. Indeed, whatever their other admirable and essential qualities, these assets are not to be found among most of the upper-class citizenry. Of course there is the odd brilliant exception. The cockiness of the males, though it often borders on crassness, is not so unbecoming, nor is their high opinion of themselves. But these traits are deleterious in females, as are Englishwomen's vain attempts to affect Continental grace and lightheartedness.

Earlier I praised the expedience of the establishments here, and as evidence I will describe the organization of the card room in the Travellers Club. This is not an actual gambling club but, as the name implies, one intended for travelers. Therefore its *full* members can only be those who have traveled a certain number of miles on the Continent or, better yet, have gone on even longer expeditions. Their travels have not made them any less English, however, not that I mean this as a criticism. In any event, although it is not a gambling club, at the Travellers whist and écarté, but not hazard, are played for very high stakes.

In our casinos, private parties, etc., anybody intent on playing must always conscientiously seek out a game first, and if the tables are occupied, wait patiently, perhaps for hours, until a place is open. Here it is the law that every man who arrives at any table may join that game as soon as a rubber is concluded, and then whoever has already played two rubbers in succession must quit. This offers the advantage that if you have lost at a table that you then deem unlucky, you can go look for something better at another.

In the center of the room a clerk is stationed at a desk, and he rings a bell as soon as you need a waiter. He also delivers the bill. And if a dispute arises, he goes to fetch the classic treatises on whist, for not the slightest transgression of the rules is allowed without the designated punishment. Admittedly this is painful for anyone playing solely for amusement, but it is actually sensible and builds good players. The same clerk passes out the markers to each participant. The club itself is the common payer, which avoids the unpleasantness of having to face a nasty defaulter—someone who loses a lot but never pays up—and there are just as many of these in England as elsewhere. Cash never makes an appearance (very agreeable if for no other reason than mere cleanliness); instead, as soon as each player sits down at the table, he is given a little basket containing tokens of various shapes with the value of each marked on it in numerals, and these are noted by the clerk in his book. If the player loses his tokens he requests more, and so forth. Before departing you consult with the accountant, either to verify your losses or, if you have won, to deliver the tokens acquired. In either case you are handed a record of the results on a card, a duplicate of the calculations in the clerk's account book. If you owe more than one hundred pounds you must make your payment to the clerk the following morning, whereas if you have winnings to claim, you can turn in your tokens at any time.

To be perfectly honest, although the native English are attended to by the clerk, this last rule is very poorly observed in the Travellers Club when it comes to foreigners, very likely with the tacit acquiescence of the management. There have already been several occasions when I myself and several of my friends were unable to receive any payment, I for weeks and they for months, yet our losses were always demanded with great punctuality. In response to our objections, the clerk insisted that this or that Englishman owed six hundred pounds, another owed one thousand pounds and more, or had gone away on a journey without paying, and therefore these sums could not be collected just now, their arrears making it impossible for the pay desk to fulfill its obligations at the moment, etc. Everyone says this is a glaring exception and never occurs in the other clubs—exactly the reason it deserves public rebuke.

It would be highly desirable for us to imitate the organization of the English clubs in our German cities. Although ours would be less luxurious because we are poorer, the proposition is very feasible. It would also repay the English in like manner, to the extent that we would not be eternally on our knees in such childlike admiration of their money and their name. Rather, with true humanity and still more civility than is shown us in England, we should let them see that we *Germans* are our own masters *in Germany*, and that consequently we can demand more respect than those who only come here to save money or civilize themselves a little by forming distinguished liaisons (barred to them in the middle ranks at home) or convince themselves that, as far as the *physical* enjoyment of life goes, we remain semibarbarians.

As I have already said, it is astonishing that for us the term "Englishman" serves in lieu of the highest title, an indisputable sign that treating us badly is enough to gain our veneration. This is why a man who would barely be admitted into the most inferior circles in England, where the whole of society from top to bottom is so brusquely aristocratic, is immediately feted and indulged in German lands by the courts and the highest-ranking nobility. His every wish is granted, and all of his offenses and awkwardnesses are viewed as charmingly quaint tokens of English eccentricity, until by chance a truly eminent Englishman shows up, and people are astonished to learn that they have been conferring all that honor on a mere ensign on half pay, or even a rich tailor or shoemaker. Still, such lowly Englishmen are at least polite, whereas the impertinence of many aristocrats is truly beyond belief.

I know of an amiable prince of royal blood from one of the largest towns in Germany who still suffers from excessive Anglomania because he has not seen the English in their own country and therefore judges them in accord with his own good-natured chivalry. He quite reasonably also loves their horses and carriages. Once he sent an Englishman an invitation to a hunt, a viscount who had just arrived and had not yet been presented to him. The viscount responded that he could not possibly accept, since the prince was totally unknown to him. No such courteous invitation would ever be extended to a foreigner in England, where a great man considers his summons to a single *midday meal* as the finest compliment he can bestow, even on high-ranking foreigners, but never without a long previous acquaintance or a substantial letter of introduction. (The English are more generous with invitations to soirées, routs,[2] and the like, where they need to fill up space). If by some miracle such a courteous offer were to be made in England, not a single well-bred man on the entire Continent could respond in the manner of this boorish lord.*

---

* Let me note here, once and for all, that whoever judges England only on the basis of his sojourn there in 1813 has to be entirely wrong, because that was an era of enthusiasm and boundless joy across the entire nation at having been delivered, by us, from their most dangerous enemy, which made them, for the first and perhaps last time, universally amiable. [Pückler first went to England in 1814.—*Translator.*]

IN ORDER TO carry out your commission, I paid a visit to Lottum yesterday morning, but did not find him at home. Instead, to my great delight, there was a letter from you, which I was so impatient to read that I stayed right there in his room and attentively read through it two or three times. I am so grateful for your love, and how you try to spare me any unpleasantness and entertain me only with cheering news. But please do not spare me so much that it might jeopardize our plans for Muskau. You give a far better account of the contents of my letters than they themselves possibly can, and it is an endearing failing on your part to overvalue me so sweetly. Love paints the most trivial things with magical colors and makes them glorious; but I should also concede that our closeness has given you an acquaintance with certain qualities in me that may have some genuine value, qualities that do not disclose themselves to most people but rather retreat quickly, like the mimosa, from the world's coarse touch. This comforts me. What hurts me, however, is your remark that you find everything *you* write so vacuous, that you believe the pain of being separated from me has made you feebleminded. Do I ask for platitudes? What I value is the familiar chitchat that runs blithely along expressing itself naturally in such a profound and warmhearted manner. I am especially happy with your responses to what I send you, for they mirror my own sentiments just as I expect them to.

Go along to the capital with your lady friend. It will distract you and at the same time permit you to take care of some matters for us there. *Les absents ont tort,*[3] do not forget that. I must disapprove of B——'s frivolity. Anyone who pays no attention to his own reputation in the world, even if inside he is an angel of goodness and virtue; anyone who does not care what people say about him or indeed finds it only amusing, will in no time lose his good reputation, human malice being what it is. He will soon be in more or less the same position as Peter Schlemihl once he had given away his shadow: at first he considered it unimportant to relinquish something so inconsequential, but later he could hardly bear its loss. Only in the deepest solitude, far from all the world, striding restlessly from the North to the South Pole in his seven-league boots, and living exclusively for science, could he find a bit of serenity.

At the end of your letter, as I clearly see, melancholy regains the upper hand, and I know how to talk about this too, *mais il faut du courage.*[4] In every life there are times of trial that must be endured, when the oft-bitter cup must be emptied to the last drop. If the sun transfigures the evening, then we cannot complain about the noonday heat.

But enough of these somber topics. Let me take you to the Haymarket Theater, which I recently visited while the famous Liston was enchanting the public for the 102nd time in the role of Paul Pry, a kind of meddlesome busybody. This actor, who is said to have earned a fortune of six thousand louis d'or in annual income, is one of those I would call a *natural* comic. He is of the same breed as Unzelmann and Wurm, who used to be in Berlin, or Bösenberg and Döring in Dresden. These are actors without any depth of study in their art who, through their droll manner and the inexhaustible whimsy that flows from them so naturally, evoke laughter just by appearing on stage! Of course they are often hypochondriacs in real life, which is also said of Liston (Figure 12).

The notorious Madame Vestris, who formerly caused such a furor, was also engaged there, and although she has faded somewhat, she still looks very appealing on the stage. An excellent singer and even better actress, in every respect she is even more beloved by the English public than Liston is. Her beautiful legs are especially famous and are a "standing" topic in the theatrical

12

John Liston.

Mr LISTON.

LETTERS OF A DEAD MAN

reviews in the newspapers; she often puts them on display while dressed in male attire. They are of such elegant proportions, so sweetly muscular, that the sight of them is ravishing for an art lover. Her poise and the unfailing wit of her acting are thereby truly enchanting, although she is often a bit too lusty and flirtatious with the audience. It can be said that in many ways Madame Vestris belongs to all of Europe. Her father, Bartolozzi, was Italian, a quite well-known engraver in the so-called stipple manner; her mother was German and a great virtuoso on the piano; her husband was the splendid French dancer Vestris. She herself is English. Whatever else may seem to be lacking in her international relations has no doubt been adequately compensated for by hundreds of prominent lovers. Madame Vestris also speaks a number of foreign languages with perfect fluency. One of the songs she sings in the German "Broom Girl" is "Ach du lieber Augustin," with a correct and clear accent and the most delightful sauciness (Figure 13).[5]

The following anecdote, recently conveyed to me as reliably authentic, illustrates just how elegant she once was in her métier, and how much the English Croesus corrupted her. A stranger who heard that Madame Vestris was not always unkind sent her a fifty-pound banknote on the occasion of her benefit performance,[6] with the written request that he be allowed to pick up his ticket that evening. His wish was granted and the young man appeared at the appointed hour with the confidence and demeanor of a conqueror. The outcome, however, was not what he had expected. Madame Vestris received him with a very grave, measured expression and directed him in silence to a chair, where the surprised man seated himself all the more perplexed, since he saw his open banknote in her beautiful hand.

"Sir," she said, "this morning you sent me this note for an entry ticket to my benefit concert, and it is *too much* for such a ticket. If, however, you have associated other hopes with it, then I must in all honesty assure you that it is by far *too little*. Therefore allow me to light your way home with it."

With these words she set the note aflame on a nearby candle, opened the door, and lit the way down the steps for the unhappy tempter who painfully stuttered his excuses.

A dinner today at our ambassador's—which was, incidentally, an especially coveted invitation—prevented me from going to the theater. I have neglected it much too much until now and have therefore promised myself to pursue it more insistently so that, bit by bit, I can give you more detailed reports.

MADAME VESTRIS.

AS

A BROOM GIRL.

13

Madame Vestris, as a Broom Girl.

We were just among ourselves, and the company was unusually merry. One of those present was a certain great gourmand, and much teased, *sans en perdre un coup de dent*.[7] Finally Prince Esterházy assured him that if he ever landed in purgatory his punishment would doubtless be to watch the blessed eat without cease in his presence, while he himself would have to do the digesting on their behalf.

Shortly after this, people started talking about old Lord P——, who felt so unlucky at being childless, especially since he had married a young woman in order not to be. "Oh, n'importe," the Prince said, "son frère a des enfants tous les ans, et cela revient au même pour la famille."

"Pour la famille, oui," I responded, "mais pas pour lui. Son frère mange et lui digère."[8]

This joke caused a ripple and, along with the bubbling champagne, a hundred better ones were contrived by the other guests. But my letter would become a vade mecum if I were to relate them all.

Lord Clanwilliam was there as well, and although he treats me in a very friendly way, I know on good authority that he tries to do me harm in society . . . .
. . . . *

A man with a warmer heart would have spoken to me face-to-face about this alleged injustice. But diplomats are much too glad to incorporate elements of fish blood into their organization, and so the noble lord has preferred secret intrigues. Luckily I can laugh about such underhanded maneuvers. It is hard to do much serious damage to a man like me—someone who is not looking for anything and fears little; who is interested in the fashionable world only to the extent that from time to time he delves into it to experiment with some self-assessment as well as a bit of surveillance on others; who is independent as far as necessities go; and who has only a few, albeit very reliable friends.

In addition, experience has cooled me down; my blood no longer seethes with unbearable heat; yet I have not lost my lightness of spirit nor my capacity to love deeply. Given this, I enjoy life more now than in the bloom of my youth and would not want to return to that intoxicated state. Indeed my current disposition means that I feel absolutely no dread of old age, and I am convinced that I will also discover many wonderful things in *that* epoch, when it arrives, facets I have not foreseen, which go unrecognized by those who want to stay forever young. Recently I read a few pretty English verses that touched on something similar, and I have translated them with a thought to you, my more than motherly friend, who so often regrets the departure of youth. These are the words so deeply felt:

> Ist gleich die trübe Wange bleich,
> Das Auge nicht mehr hell,
> Und nahet schon das ernste Reich,
> Wo Jugend fliehet schnell!
> Doch lächelt Dir die Wange noch,
> Das Auge kennt die Träne noch,
> Das Herz schlägt noch so warm und frei

---

* These and similar passages have been omitted, since they refer to nothing more than family affairs and can be of no interest to the reader.—*The Editor*.

Als in des Lebens grünstem Mai.
So denk' denn nicht, daß nur die Jugend
Und Schönheit Segen leiht—
Zeit lehrt die Seele schön're Tugend,
In Jahren treuer Zärtlichkeit.
Und selbst wenn einst die Nacht von oben
Verdunkelnd Deine Brust umfängt,
Wird noch durch Liebeshand gehoben
Dein Haupt zur ew'gen Ruh' gesenkt.
O, so auch blinkt der Abendstern,
Ist gleich dahin der Sonne Licht,
Noch sanft und warm aus hoher Fern',
Und Tagesglanz entbehrst Du nicht.[9]

Yes, my beloved Julie, thus has time taught us through years of faithful tenderness—that nothing can have more value than this, and we have become, each for the other, an evening star, its mild glow richly rivaling the radiance of the midday sun, which scorches as often as it warms.

Lottum and I drove home, sat by a cozy fire, and had a long talk about the affairs of our country, which are in some ways so oppressive. Lottum is very kind to me, and I am doubly attached to him, first because of his own amiability and sincerity, and second out of gratitude to his excellent father, to whom we owe more thanks than we do to yours, although he had no other motive than an impartial love of justice.

November 23rd, 1826

IT IS AN odd tradition in England that newspapers persistently interfere in people's private lives. Anyone of significance finds himself identified by name in connection with the most insipid trivialities—attendance at a dinner or a soirée, for example—which foreigners read about with great satisfaction. And should he do anything of the slightest importance, he will find himself utterly exposed and judged impulsively. The system is easily manipulated by those seeking to gain friends or further personal hostilities. Indeed many people find newspapers a good place to publish articles to their own advantage, articles *they themselves* plant; and foreign delegations vigorously exploit this opportunity.

You see what a dangerous weapon the press can be, but luckily the poison comes with its own antidote: the equanimity and general indifference with which this kind of thing is received by the English public. A newspaper article that would drive a Continental into hiding for three months will only provoke a glimmer of schadenfreude here and within twenty-four hours be forgotten.

For example, almost every day over the last four weeks the papers have been mocking a local lord for some duel that he seems to have performed without heroism. The most hurtful inferences have been published about the caliber of his courage, and yet he remains utterly unself-conscious and sociable. The English would like to deliver me such a low blow, since they obstinately believe, as they do of any marriageable man who arrives here, that I have come for the sole purpose of looking for a rich Englishwoman to be my wife. A satirical article alluding to this matter was extracted from some rumor mill at home and placed in several English newspapers. Luckily I was already briefed on this tactic a long time ago by an old practitioner and therefore was the first to laugh and laughed the loudest, while publically retailing innocuous jokes against myself and others. This is the only way to face ridicule, for if you act hurt or embarrassed, the poison is proven effective; otherwise it evaporates like water on a red-hot stone. This the English understand perfectly.

As intended, I spent the evening at Drury Lane where, to my astonishment, I saw the elderly Braham as lead singer and lover in the exact role I had seen him play in a benefit performance twelve years ago, on the day before I departed England. He was already an old man then, and now the applause was just as fervent, and I found little difference in his singing, except that he screamed a bit louder and indulged in more coloratura to cover any deficiency in his voice. He is a Jew and, I think, a wandering one, since he never seems to age.[10] He is a true representative of the English manner of singing and, in his renditions of popular songs, enthusiastically revered by the public. His great vocal power and facility and his thorough knowledge of music are undeniable, but his technique is utterly tasteless.

The prima donna was Miss Paton, a quite pleasant but unexceptional singer, not unattractive, with a good figure, and very popular. What *we* might find strange is that, although married to Lord William Lennox, whose name she has taken in her private life, she remains Miss Paton on stage and is paid accordingly—probably necessary, given her husband's poverty.*

Most striking to foreigners attending the theater here is the incredible crudeness and ill-mannered behavior of the audiences. Hence the best society tends to frequent the Italian opera, visiting the national theater only rarely and never in large groups, a circumstance that may be either good or bad for theatrical productions in general. English liberty can degenerate into the most vulgar license, and one often hears a stentorian voice delivering an obscenity at the most poignant moment in a tragedy or during the most captivating cadenza of a soprano or tenor. Depending on the mood of those standing around in the gallery and the upper loges, this will be followed by laughter and whoops of approval or by the offender being thrashed and expelled. Regardless of which, you can no longer hear a thing from the stage, where, out of long experience, the actors and singers simply refuse to be interrupted but proceed calmly declaiming or warbling on *comme si de rien n'était*.[11] And this does not happen just *once* but twenty times during a performance, amusing many in the audience more than the show itself. While some hang their coats and vests over the third-rank loges and sit around in their shirtsleeves, you will often see others casually toss the remnants of their snacks (sometimes more than just orange peels) onto the heads of those below in the parterre or launch them dexterously into one of the boxes. All this can be found in Great Britain's national theater, in short, the same antics that the journeymen at the famous Wisotzky's in Berlin are said to employ as a way to enliven a phlegmatic harmonic society.

A second reason for respectable families to avoid the theater is the assemblage of several hundred ladies of easy virtue who appear in every gradation, beginning with the amusing woman whose expenses run to six thousand pounds a year and who has her own box, down to those who bivouac on the streets in the open air and, during the intermissions, crowd into the lavishly decorated foyers, where they parade all their effrontery without a smidgen of restraint.

---

* Admittedly our delightful Sontag, the queen of song, recently did likewise by entering into a left-handed marriage with Count Carlo Rossi. [A left-handed or morganatic marriage, in which the groom holds his bride's right hand with his left, is a union between people of different social stature, often performed sub rosa in order to protect the husband's rank and privilege. In this case, Sontag, a commoner and, worse, an actress, married a nobleman.—*Translator*.]

It is strange that one does not see such brazen conduct so publically flaunted anywhere but in pious and proper England. In the theater it is often scarcely possible to fend off these repugnant priestesses of Venus, especially when they are drunk, which is quite regularly the case. They also beg shamelessly. You often find a very pretty, well-dressed young woman suddenly accepting a shilling or a sixpence like the lowliest panhandler so she can enjoy a half glass of rum or ginger beer at the buffet. And so it goes, I repeat, in the national theater of England, where their greatest dramatic talents are developed, where immortal artists such as Garrick, Mrs. Siddons, and Miss O'Neill once enchanted us with their majesty, and where heroes like Kean, Kemble, and Young are still performing! Such indignities offer additional proof that Napoleon was right to call the English a nation of prosaic shopkeepers. Given all I have seen, one might dispute the claim to an authentic love of art here, although this crudeness is almost never involved with the performance itself; at most it might indicate a cabal of some sort related to a particular actor, but the motives are unrelated to what happens on the stage.

A certain ambassador accompanied me to the theater, and while we were walking around in the foyer and inspecting those present, he related a number of not uninteresting particulars concerning various of the beauties filing past. What I found most remarkable about these lovely creatures was their unbelievable lightheartedness as well as their amazing reversals of fortune.

"That one with the soulful eyes," he said, "has just come from the King's Bench prison, where she was locked up for a year as a result of debts of eight thousand pounds; yet she managed to continue her trade there and, God knows how, finally found the means to have herself freed. She is sentimental, an odd defect for her position,* and when in such a mood she gives a lover ten times more than she gets from her *entreteneur*. I know very distinguished people," he added, "who have taken irresponsible advantage of this kind of weakness, and I have no doubt that at the first such instance she will move back into her quarters in the sanctuary of the King's Bench."

"Then there is the somewhat faded lovely over here," he continued. "I saw her ten years ago living with a degree of luxury that few of my colleagues could match. But far from putting aside some of her riches, she was constantly tossing it all out the window with genuine passion. Now she'll be very obliged if you deign to help her out with a shilling."

Afterward he showed me the opposite case: a captivating woman of the utmost propriety seated in one of the first boxes. She was married to a man with twenty thousand pounds a year, yet until recently would have given her all for a guinea. Such marriages are altogether more common here than elsewhere and, strangely enough, they tend to turn out very well. Like the fourth example my companion called to my attention, a noted ballerina who had also married extremely well and was living happily with her husband, although he had recently gone bankrupt, thus casting her into poverty once again. Indeed he had landed her in a position possibly even more precarious than she had been in before. That was a good test for her head and her heart, which— at least in the case of *this* dancer—must have needed as much training as her legs had.

The licentiousness I have described invades the stage itself, where vulgar double entendres abound in words and actions. It confirms all one reads in old memoirs about what the Virgin Queen had to endure.

Adieu.
Eternally, your Lou

---

* I nearly believe the baron wanted me to understand that he knew this from experience.

London, November 25th, 1826

*M*OST BELOVED!

From time to time I feel a real need to spend a day alone at home in a kind of wistful brooding, reliving memories old and new in their full panoply of sentiments. Through the interplay of so many colors, *a single* misty hue gradually suffuses it all, and finally the dissonances of life blend into a mild, unfocused emotion. Such a mood is surprisingly encouraged by something I usually find utterly insufferable: the hurdy-gurdies that play day and night in every street, grinding out hundreds of melodies in a wild, intermingling whirl, until all the music gets lost in a dreamy ringing in the ears.

More amusing is a very different kind of local street performance, a genuine national comedy that deserves our close attention, and today it sent me a merry diversion from just below my windows. This is the English Punch (entirely different from the Italian Pulcinella), whose faithful portrait I include here in the margin, at the very moment he is beating his wife to death (Figure 14).[1]

The most godless comedic figure I have ever come across, he is a character with no more conscience than the piece of wood he is made of, and perhaps not altogether different from the class of people he represents in this nation.

Punch, like his namesake, is an admixture of arrack, lemon, and sugar; he is strong, sour, and sweet; and at the same time has a character largely indifferent to the intoxication he induces. He is, moreover, the most consummate egoist on earth, *et ne doute jamais de rien.*[2] With his indomitable merriness and irrepressible humor, he conquers all, laughs at the law, at those around him, and even at the devil himself. Punch unveils to us what an Englishman *is* and what he *aspires* to be—on the native side: self-interestedness, stamina, mettle, and, if needed, reckless determination; on the foreign: unflappable levity and a ready wit. But allow me to portray him further in his own words, and to disclose a few additional bits of information from his biography.

First of all, as a descendant of Pulcinella from Acerra he is undoubtedly a nobleman of the old school—Harlequin, Clown, the German Kasperle, and others can be counted among his cousins. Because of his great daring, however, Punch is best suited to be head of this family. Devout he is not, but as a good Englishman he goes to church on Sundays, though he may follow this by murdering a priest whom he finds tedious because of his unrelenting attempts to convert him. No doubt about it: Punch is a wild character, not very moral, and not for nothing made of wood. He is the best of all boxers because he does not feel any blows, and those he delivers are impossible to withstand. At the same time he is a true Turk in his low estimation of human life; he suffers no dissent and has no fear, not even of the devil. On the other hand, you must esteem his great qualities! His heart's admirable callousness and his inveterate high spirits, his valiant

zu Briefe eines Verstorbenen III Thl.

14

Punch and Judy.

selfishness, his unruffled self-satisfaction, his unfailing wit, and the consummate slyness that allows him to escape from every *mauvais pas* and emerge triumphant over all comers—these qualities cast a radiant luster over the many liberties he takes with human life. People have seen him as a conflation of Richard III and Falstaff, not altogether unjustly. In appearance, too, he combines the bent legs and the hunchback of Richard with the corpulence of Falstaff, complemented by a long Italian nose and black eyes that spit fire.

His accommodation is a box on four poles with the requisite interior decorations, a theater that can be set up in a few seconds any place you like. A drapery hanging down over the poles hides his "soul," who controls the puppet and lends him his requisite lines. Hence a drama that is performed daily on the street will vary according to the talent of the puppeteer interpreting it for the public, but the order of events is essentially the same and goes roughly like this:

As the curtain rises you hear Punch behind the scenes warbling away at the little French song "Marlbrough s'en va-t-en guerre."[3] He then appears on the stage, dancing and in high spirits, and proceeds in droll verses to inform the spectators about what kind of crea-ture he is. He proclaims himself a cheerful, amusing fellow who likes a good joke but cannot make much sense of other people, and if he is ever inclined to be gentle, it is only concerning the fair sex. Punch squanders his money and seeks only to laugh his way through life and get as fat as possible. He admits to being a tempter and seducer of young girls and fond of sumptuous eating and drinking as long as it is available, but if he has nothing, he is also prepared to subsist on tree bark. And if death were to come for him, well, that would mean nothing more than an end to the comedy of Punch (an outlook that bears the unquestionable taint of atheism).

After this monologue he calls backstage for Judy, his young wife, but she does not listen and finally sends her dog out instead. Punch fawns on him, but the nasty cur bites him firmly on the nose and will not let go for ages until, after a preposterous tussle and a slew of aggressive, not to say indiscreet jokes, he finally fends off the dog and gives him a good drubbing.

While all this racket is going on, Scaramouche, a family friend, enters carrying a large stick and immediately interrogates Punch about why he is beating Judy's favorite dog, an animal that has *never* bitten anyone.

"I, too, have *never* beaten a dog," Punch responds, "but" he continues, "what's that you're holding in your hand, dear Scaramouche?"

"Oh, it's nothing but a fiddle. Perhaps you would like to test its tone? Just come over here and examine this marvelous instrument."

"Thank you, thank you so much, dear Scaramouche," Punch responds modestly, "I can already distinguish the tones quite well from a distance."

But Scaramouche will not be put off, and while he is dancing around swinging his stick, accompanying himself with his own singing, he passes close to Punch and, as if by chance, gives him a huge bang on the head. Punch acts as if he has noticed nothing, but he also starts to dance and, seizing his advantage, suddenly rips the stick out of Scaramouche's hand and delivers him such a blow that poor Scaramouche's head rolls off at his feet. Where Punch delivers a blow, no grass can grow!

"Ha, ha!" he calls out laughing, "did you hear the fiddle, my good Scaramouche, and what a lovely tone it has! As long as you live, my boy, you'll never hear one more beautiful. But where is my Judy, then. My sweet Judy, why haven't you come?"

Meanwhile Punch hides Scaramouche's corpse behind a curtain, and Judy, the female pendant of her husband, just as hunchbacked and with an even more monstrous nose, comes on stage. A tenderly comic scene follows, after which Punch asks to see his child. Judy goes to fetch it, and during her absence Punch waxes ecstatic in a second monologue about his happiness as a husband and father. When the little monster arrives, the parents can hardly contain themselves for joy, lavishing it with the most affectionate names and caresses. Then Judy exits again to tend to domestic affairs, leaving the suckling babe in its father's arms. Punch plays with it in a clumsy attempt to imitate a nanny, but the child is very naughty and issues a pitiful scream. At first Punch tries to soothe it but then grows impatient and strikes it; this elicits louder screams, and when the child deposits something in Punch's hands, he becomes furious and with a slew of curses throws the child out the window onto the street, where it lands with a broken neck amid the spectators. Punch bends far out over the edge of the stage to look at it, grimaces, shakes his head, starts laughing, and then begins to sing and dance:

> *Eia popeia,* it's over with the babe
> You filthy little thing, get out and away.
> Soon I'll make another—not hard for me to do.
> It's easy enough to find others just like you.[4]

Now Judy returns and asks in consternation for her darling. "It has gone to sleep," Punch answers impassively, but after continued interrogation he must finally admit that the child fell out the window while he was playing with it. Judy goes wild, tears at her hair, and deluges the evil tyrant with the most appalling accusations. In vain he promises her *la pace di Marcolfa,** but she will not listen and instead runs off uttering violent threats.

Punch holds his belly for laughter, dances around and, in his exuberance, hits his own head against the wall in time with the song he sings:

---

* "The peace of Marcolfa" is well-known in Italy. The good wife of the honorable Bertoldo (in the old novel of this name) said to the queen: if you and your husband have been arguing during the day, make *peace* again in the evening, and she found this peace so pleasant that she often started arguments during the day for that reason alone.

What a mad ruckus for *nothing* at all,
For the sake of a miniature, miserable squirt!
Just you wait, Judy, for I will convert you,
And teach you a different set of mores soon.

Meanwhile, Judy has arrived from behind armed him with a broomstick and immediately starts working him over with all her might. At first he offers friendly words, promises never again to throw a child out a window, begs her not to take the "joke" too far—but since none of this is any use, he again loses his patience and ends it, as he did with Scaramouche, by beating poor Judy to death.

"Now, dear Judy," he says in a very pleasant tone, "our argument is over. If you are satisfied, then I am too. So get up again, dear Judy. Oh, quit shamming! This is just another of your tricks! What? You don't want to get up? Well then, I'll put you down!" And with this Punch flings her after her child down onto the street and, not even bothering to look at her, bursts out in his usual guffaws. He cries: "To lose a wife is a *bonne fortune,*" and then sings:

Who'd want to be plagued with a wife,
When he could set himself free,
Slay her with a stick or a knife,
And toss her into the sea.

In the second act we find Punch in the midst of a rendezvous with his mistress, Polly, whom he is courting in a not particularly decorous manner, insisting that only *she* can banish his cares and if he had as many wives as Solomon, he would murder them all for her sake.[5] After this a courtier and friend of Polly's pays him a visit; Punch does not kill his guest this time but merely toys with him a bit, then gets bored and declares that he'll take advantage of the beautiful weather and go for a ride. A wild stallion is brought on stage, and for a while Punch prances around on him in a ridiculous way until at last he is thrown off by the untamable beast's horrendous bucking. He cries out for help and his friend the doctor, who fortunately happens to be passing by, quickly runs over. Punch lies there as if he were dead and moans appallingly. The doctor tries to calm him, feels for his pulse, and asks:

"Where were you actually hurt? Here?"
"No, lower."
"In the chest?"
"No, lower."
"Is your leg broken?"
"No, higher."
"Well then, where?"

But at that instant Punch gives the poor doctor a crashing blow to a certain part of the body, leaps up laughing, and sings as he dances:

Here's the spot where the wound did fall,
And now through sympathy is healed in all.

I only fell onto nice green grass.
You think I'm made of glass, you ass?

The furious doctor runs off without another word and shortly thereafter returns carrying a big stick with a golden knob and cries out, "Here, dear Punch, I'm bringing some wholesome medicine for you alone!" Then he lets loose even more forcefully than Judy did, beating the stick like a threshing flail on Punch's shoulders.

"Oh, woe," Punch cries, "a thousand thanks, but I'm already healthy, I can't tolerate any medicine at all, it immediately gives me a headache and a pain in my hip."

"Ah, that's only because you've always taken doses that were too small," the doctor says, interrupting him, "take just a little bit more, and you'll soon be better."

Punch. Sure, that's how you doctors always talk, but try it once yourself.

Doctor. We doctors never take our own medicine. But *you* need at least a few more doses.

Punch looks defeated, falls down exhausted, and begs for mercy. But just when the gullible doctor bends down over him, Punch dives at his arms with lightning speed, wrestles with him, and finally snatches the stick and proceeds to imperil the doctor's life. "Now," he cries, "you'll really have to try a bit of your own lovely medicine, most worthy doctor, just a tiny bit, most honorable friend. Like this . . . and this . . ."

"Oh God, he's killing me . . ." screams the doctor.

"Not worth mentioning, it's just so conventional. Doctors always die when they take their own medicine. It's just jolly, here, *one* more, and then the *last* pill." He pushes the point of the stick into his opponent's stomach: "Do you feel the effects of these beneficial pills in your insides?"

The doctor falls down dead.

Punch, laughing: "Now, my good friend, cure yourself, if you can!"

(*Exits singing and dancing.*)

After several more adventures, all with similar tragic endings, Justice finally awakens and sends a constable to arrest Punch. This man finds him, as always, in the best of spirits and just about to make music, as he terms it, with the help of a large cowbell (actually a very naïve admission of the nation's musical capacity). The dialog is short and concise:

Constable. Mr. Punch, set the music and singing aside for a bit, for I've come to have you sing your last tune.

Punch. Who the devil are you?

Constable. Don't you know me?

Punch. Not at all, and furthermore I don't feel the need to get to know you.

Constable. Oh, but you must. I'm the constable.

Punch. And who, pray tell, sent for you?

Constable. *I* have been sent to fetch *you*.

Punch. *Allons*, I don't need you, not at all; I can take care of my own affairs. Thank you very much. I don't need a constable.

Constable. Yes, but it so happens that the constable needs you.

Punch. The devil he does! And for what, might I ask?

Constable. Oh, just to have you hanged. You beat Scaramouche to death, your wife and child, the doctor . . .

PUNCH. Who the devil cares about that? If you stay here much longer, I'll handle you the same way.

CONSTABLE. Don't go joking around. You've committed murder, and here's the warrant for your arrest.

PUNCH. And I've a warrant for you, too, which I'm informing you of right now.

Punch grabs the bell he's been holding behind his back and brings it down on the constable's occiput so hard that, like his fated predecessors, he sinks lifeless to the ground. At this Punch bounds off with a capriole and can be heard yodeling backstage:

> The jug goes to water
> Until the time it's smashed
> For a jolly squanderer
> There's no cause to be abashed.

The next officer of the court sent to arrest Punch after the death of the constable suffers the same fate. Finally the hangman himself lies in wait for Punch who, in his merry obliviousness, runs straight into him. At this encounter he seems taken aback for the first time, swallows his pride, and flatters Mr. Ketsch with all his might, calling him his old friend and also inquiring warmly how his dear wife, Mistress Ketsch, is getting along.

The hangman quickly leads him to understand that all friendship must now come to an end and charges him with being a wicked man for having killed so many people, even his own wife and child.

"As far as the latter two go, they were my property," Punch says in his own defense, "and it must be left up to each individual to make the best use of his property as he sees fit."

"And why did you kill the poor doctor who came to help you?"

"Only out of self-defense, most worthy Mr. Ketsch, because he also wanted to kill me."

"How?"

"He offered me some of his medicine."

But none of these excuses helps him at all. Three or four men jump out, tie Punch up, and Mr. Ketch leads him off to prison.

In the next scene we see him at the back of the stage with his head sticking out of an iron grate, rubbing his long nose on the bars. Most indignant and sullen, he sings a little song in his customary manner in order to pass the time. Mr. Ketch appears and with his assistants erects a gallows in front of the prison. Punch descends into misery. This is not remorse but a flush of great love and longing for his Polly. Soon again he plucks up his courage and even manages a few *bons mots* about the pretty gallows, musing that it looks like a tree transplanted there to improve his view. "How beautiful it will be," he exclaims, "when it finally has leaves and fruit!"

Now a few men bring in a coffin and place it at the foot of the gallows. "Well, what's that supposed to mean?" Punch asks. "Ah ha, that must be the basket to hold the fruit."

Meanwhile Ketch returns and after greeting Punch and unlocking the door, politely announces that everything is ready; Punch can come out whenever he likes. You can imagine that he is not very eager to accept the invitation. After some to-ing and fro-ing, Ketch finally calls out with impatience: "Nothing more can be done now, you must come out and be hanged."

Punch. Oh, will you really be so cruel?

Ketch. Why were you so cruel as to murder your wife and child?

Punch. But is that a reason for you to be cruel, too, and why do you have to murder me, as well?*

Ketch offers no other reason than that he is the stronger of the two, and drags Punch out by the hair as he begs for mercy and promises to reform. "Now, dear Punch," Ketch says cold-bloodedly, "please be so good as to place your head in this noose, and everything will come quickly to an end." Punch acts as if he is inept and repeatedly fails to put his head properly in the noose.

"My God, how clumsy you are," Ketch shouts, "*this* is the way you poke your head in." (*He shows him how.*)

"*This way,* and pull it tight," cries Punch, who gets a firm hold on the careless hangman, ties him up with all his force, and speedily hangs him on the gallows, after which he hides behind the wall.

Two people arrive to take down the dead body and, believing it is the criminal, place him in the coffin and carry him off, while Punch laughs up his sleeve and dances away in glee.

Yet the most difficult battle still awaits, because now the devil himself arrives to fetch him. Although in vain, Punch makes a most perceptive comment: "It's a very stupid devil who would want to take away his best friend on earth."

The devil, seeing no sense in this, reaches out for him with his ghoulish talons and is on the verge of carrying him off, as he once did Faust. But Punch is not so easily bamboozled! Once again he grasps his murderous stick and defends himself vigorously, even against the devil. A frightful battle begins and—who would have thought it possible!—Punch, repeatedly skirting death, emerges the jubilant victor! He skewers the black devil with his stick, lifts him high in the air and spins him around, whooping with joy, singing, and laughing more heartily than ever:

Long live Punch, misery is no more,
Hooray, the devil's dead!

I leave to you all the philosophical inferences that can be gleaned from Punch's life story. It might be particularly interesting to investigate what sort of influence the daily repetitions of this popular folk play have on the morality of the English lower classes.**

In closing, for the sake of tragic justice, I am sketching a second portrait of Punch on the margin, sitting in prison as the gallows is carried on stage.

You must wait until my next letter for the details you've requested about B——, that pious soul whom I totally forgot in my preoccupation with the more interesting sinner, Punch. Adieu for now.

---

* What an excellent argument against capital punishment.

** This reminds me of the old anecdote involving a similar performance on the Piazza San Marco in Venice. Pulcinella was behaving very badly when a little priest showed up to deliver an extemporaneous evening sermon. But he attracted only a very small crowd because everyone's attention was riveted on the buffoon. "*Ah birbanti!*" the indignant preacher finally cried out in his stentorian voice, holding his tiny crucifix aloft: "*Lasciate quel c . . . , venite qua, ecco il vero Pulcinella!*" [Ah, scoundrels, leave that fool! Come over here! This is the true Pulcinella!—*Translator.*]

YOU WILL RECALL what I wrote you a while ago about the way land is sold, or better leased. Since property owners can count on ninety-nine years of possession at best, they build as cheaply as possible, with the consequence that one's life is often in danger in a London house. Just last night, for instance, a relatively new building, quite nearby in St James Street, suddenly collapsed like a house of cards and took half of the house next door along with it. It is said that a number of people were seriously injured, but most had time to escape, ominous signs having alerted them. Given the speed of construction here, there is no doubt the edifice will be back up in four weeks, although just as unstable as before.

A few days ago I was present during an interesting opening of Parliament at which King George IV performed in person, a ceremony that has not taken place for several years. The peers were assembled in the center of the chamber of the House of Lords, their red mantles thrown carelessly over their normal morning attire. The king's throne stood against the far wall; many bejeweled ladies sat on tiered seats to the left; to the right were the diplomatic corps and foreigners; opposite the throne was a barrier, and behind it were the members of the House of Commons dressed in the bourgeois fashion of our day. The exterior of the house chamber and the staircases swarmed with servants and heralds in fourteenth-century costume.

At two o'clock a salvo of cannons announced the approach of the king in full regalia. Many magnificent carriages and horses made up the procession. I have already included an illustration in my Memory Album,* and under it for contrast I have placed a triumphal entry of Caesar (Figure 15). Looking at these pictures you cannot help but wonder whether humankind has made any progress at all. It scarcely seems the case in the realm of artistic taste, especially if you consider the two figures who occupy the loftiest positions in their respective ceremonies. I mean the royal coachman and Caesar himself!

The king appeared around two thirty and was the only person in full ceremonial dress. Covered from head to toe in the regal vestments of old, with a crown on his head and a scepter in his hand, he looked pale and bloated and had to sit on his throne for a long time before he could catch his breath enough to read his speech. During this period he cast friendly glances and affable salutations toward some of the most favored ladies. Lord Liverpool stood on one side of him holding the sword of state and the speech; the duke of Wellington stood on his other side. All three looked so miserable, ash gray, and decrepit that I felt I had never seen human greatness displayed to less effect. Indeed I was profoundly struck by the tragic side of the many comedies we act out here below. On the other hand it was pure comedy to see the most powerful monarch on earth as the leading actor before an audience he believes so inferior to him! In fact, the whole tableau of entering and exiting, like the royal costume itself, is strikingly reminiscent of the way historical dramas are usually performed here. The only thing missing from this otherwise perfect

---

* It was my deceased friend's inspiration to provide an extra something that has afforded his bereaved family a wistful pleasure. He filled many large folio albums with drawings, engravings, autographs, and occasionally small brochures. Moreover, instead of the usual disorganized muddle one finds in such compendia, he included only those things he had experienced himself, and in the same order that he saw them. He also accompanied every picture with a note, so that the totality gives a short, logically consistent summary of his activities, a true "life atlas," as he sometimes used to call it.—*The Editor.*

illusion was that obligatory flourish of trumpets that always accompanies the comings and goings of a Shakespearean king.

By the way, in spite of his deficiencies, King George read the banal speech with great propriety and a fine voice, but also with a regal nonchalance, although we shall overlook whether His Majesty misspoke his lines or was slow to decipher a word. Meanwhile you could clearly tell that the monarch was delighted when the chore had ended, as his exit proceeded in a sprightlier manner than his entrance!

Since my last letter I have been to the theater twice, something you cannot manage if you have an invitation somewhere because the dinner hours are so late. I saw Mozart's *Figaro* advertised at Drury Lane, and although glad to hear the sweet tones of my homeland again, I was not a little surprised by the egregious treatment that his immortal masterpiece had to endure. You will scarcely believe me, but neither the count nor the countess sang, nor did Figaro. Instead, these parts were given to mere actors, and their main arias—with certain of the words altered—were performed by the other singers. Furthermore some English folk songs had been inserted and were crooned by the gardener in renderings about as flattering to Mozart's music as a pitch plaster on the face of Venus.[6] In addition, the entire opera was "arranged" by a Mr. Bishop, something I saw noted on the placard and initially did not understand. It means that it was made more fitting for English ears by the most tasteless and vulgar modifications.

The national music of England, whose ungraceful melodies no one could fail to recognize, is, to my mind, exceptionally repugnant, an expression of brutal emotion in pain and passion that smacks of roast beef, plum pudding, and porter. So you can imagine what a pleasant effect it engendered by being amalgamated with the sweet compositions of the master. *Je n'y pouvais tenir*[7]—to me poor Mozart was martyred on the cross, and I suffered along with him.

This dreadful state of affairs is all the more deplorable since there is no lack of commendable singers here, both male and female, and if things were handled more judiciously, very good performances could be mounted. Though frankly, even if the theater were put in order, it would require a new Orpheus to finally tame the English audiences.

The performance was far better at Covent Garden where Charles Kemble, one of the top English actors, gave a superb interpretation of Charles II. Kemble is a man of the best education who has always lived in very good society and was therefore in a position to represent the monarch in a *kingly* manner. In this case that simply means with all the *aisance*[8] typical among people of high standing. He knows how to add an engaging dimension to Charles II's levity without ever, even in moments of greatest abandon, losing that inborn sovereign dignity that is so hard to imitate. His costume appeared as if it had been cut out of the frame of an old painting, even down to the smallest detail; all the other players were dressed with the same care, which is why Kemble is also much to be praised as a stage manager.

I must say, however, that in the next piece, where Frederick the Great was the main character, the same exactness and knowledge no longer prevailed as far as *foreign* costumes went; indeed both the king and his entourage seemed to have borrowed their wardrobe from a harlequin pantomime. Zieten, for one, showed up in a tall grenadier's cap, and Seydlitz appeared with long locks *à la Murat* and just as many medals as that kingly trouper used to wear, which in those days were not at all fashionable in such profusion, nor were they yet simply an article of one's attire, as is nowadays the case.[9]

15

Procession of George IV to the House of Peers and *Triumphal Entry of Caesar.*

I OFTEN DINE at Prince E——'s, the very model of a diplomat, whose dignified bearing is complemented by a pleasant and easy manner. He shows us how a man can be liked by everyone if he understands how to make himself approachable, yet without allowing his own worth to be undervalued—*un vrai Seigneur,*[10] something increasingly rare in this world. Likely no other foreigner has ever been quite so successful at accommodating English presumption without losing face. It requires infinite tact, the lighter touch of a southern German, and an extraordinarily shrewd mind hidden behind a modest bonhomie, all of this reinforced by a great name and enormous wealth.

The other members of the diplomatic corps, with few exceptions, retreat into the background in comparison, and most of the plenipotentiaries here disappear entirely into the crowd.

Among the ambassadors, however, there is a woman who does play an important role . . . . But more details about this another time. I was only talking about the diplomats because at today's gathering I heard some-one relate a pretty *bon mot*; indeed it was uttered by a man whom you know. Count H—— was previously an ambassador to a German court well-known for its frugality, not to say stinginess. On some solemn occasion, he was given a gift of a box bearing a portrait of the sovereign sur-rounded by extremely small diamonds. A short time later one of his colleagues asked to see the present he had received. "Vous ne trouverez pas le portrait ressemblant," the Count said, as he handed over the box, "mais les diamants."[11]

I am also delighted to see old Elliot from time to time, who, along with Lord St Herbert (just as dry as he is interesting and so often mentioned in Ségur's memoirs),[12] is one of the doyens of English diplomacy and still recalls his sojourn in Dresden with great fondness. He has several engaging daughters and finds it difficult to maintain his family in a manner appropriate to their rank because he is not compensated with English liberality for such long service.* Another interesting figure is the Chevalier L—— M——, who was much esteemed by the king (then Prince of Wales) and who deserves mention first because he wines and dines his friends as well as a much-liked Amphitryon, and second because he is among the most original of men and one of the few *truly practical* philosophers I have ever come across.

All the prejudices of the masses seem not to exist for him, and no one can be more difficult to impress, neither the great lords of heaven nor those of this world. Although already sixty and for the majority of his later years a martyr to the unspeakable pain of gout and stones,[13] no one has ever heard him complain; nor has it dampened his jolly disposition even for a moment. One must admit there are natural personalities and temperaments that are worth one hundred thousand thalers a year.

I first got to know him some time ago, shortly after he had undergone a major operation to remove his stones, something the surgeon had not wanted to undertake; he considered it life-threatening given the weakness of the patient, who basically forced him to proceed, however. He was not yet able to leave his bed and looked like a dead man. As I entered I involuntarily put on a grieving face, intending to express my sympathy, but he interrupted me with a laugh and said I should cheer up. What could not be changed, he later explained, simply had to be endured, and better in good spirits than not. As for what had happened to him, he had every reason to laugh, at least about his physicians. They had decisively given him up for dead at least ten times, yet almost all of them had gone to the devil before him. "Moreover," he added with resignation, "I've enjoyed my life as few others have and must also get to know its darker side."

Amid all these joys and sorrows, the fun-loving man has remained very well preserved, and now that he is back on his feet again, he looks hardly older than forty with his artful wig and his spirited, vibrant face that must once have been handsome.

December 3rd, 1826

KEMBLE GAVE ME great pleasure again today, this time as Falstaff (Figure 16). There is no doubt that even the finest dramatic poet needs an actor to consummate his work. I have never understood the true nature of this notorious knight so well, nor has his outward demeanor ever been so vivid. Now I have seen him reborn, as it were, through Kemble. His costume and makeup were certainly striking, but by no means as caricatured as we see on our German stages; even less did he look like a man without rank or breeding, a *farceur*, the way Devrient, for instance, portrays him in Berlin. Falstaff, though possessing a vulgar soul, is still by habit and inclination a very-practiced courtier, and the coarseness that he often affects in the prince's company is at least as much an amusing ruse as it is a reflection of his own disposition. Princes, after all, given the

---

* There is a telling anecdote concerning the affable character of this old man. When he departed Dresden twenty years ago, a large number of boxes containing his effects were left behind. He was finally induced to entrust someone with the examination of their contents, and this person, who was familiar with the limitations of the owner's assets, was not a little amazed to find, still carefully wrapped, all the gifts he had been given when he was the English ambassador, set with jewels of considerable value.

16

*Charles Kemble
as Falstaff in Henry IV.*

loftiness and sobriety of their position, often love vulgarity merely for the sake of contrast. Kemble lends the character especially subtle nuances, for in these situations he retains the natural, invincible jolliness; the witty presence of mind; and the delightful drollness that make Falstaff so likeable as a companion; indeed near indispensable. Yet at court in the presence of the king and serious, dignified men, or when clowning around with the prince and his companions, or finally when they are alone, he is entirely different. In the first case you see a comical figure—somewhat resembling the Maréchal de Bassompierre—ludicrously fat but distinguished and decorous, always a joker, but with *bon ton,* never lacking the respect owed to the place and people he is with. In the second phase he lets himself go much further, taking every uncouth liberty, but always with a noticeable deference that flatters and elevates the prince, simply assuming only the privileges of a court fool allowed to say whatever pops into his head. Only in the final phase do we see Falstaff in full dishabille, with all pretense stripped away. Like a pig in a puddle he wallows quite contentedly in the mire; yet *even so* remains witty and arouses more laughter than repugnance. This is the great art of the poet who, even when faced with the most horrible monstrosities of sin and disgrace, knows how to grant them a kind of divinity that stirs our interest and, almost to our amazement, attracts us. This is the dramatic truth, the creative power of his portrayals, about which Walter Scott says so elegantly, "It allows me to compare Shakespeare only with that man in the *Arabian Nights* who could transpose himself into any body he chose and imitate its feelings and actions."

It occurs to me that there is only *one* character in this immortal poet's works whom I have always found to be somewhat distorted and generally of less interest than the others. This is the king in *Hamlet.* Just to mention one trait: it seems entirely false, psychologically, when the author has the king kneel down and exclaim "I cannot pray." The king is never presented to us as an irreligious man or a brooding skeptic, but merely as a coarse, carnal *criminal,* and (as we ourselves experience every day) such a person, even if he is one of the worst, can pray very well and very fervently, can even ask that his crimes be successful. It reminds me of the woman who, after a gang of thieves had been captured, was found alone in their cave, kneeling in ardent prayer, and asking God's blessing for the expedition she thought the thieves were just then involved in, asking that it turn out well and result in much booty.

In fact, the aim of officially prescribed prayer is often not much better—just think of the historical examples! No, the criminal king can pray. But in this tragedy, the figure who *cannot* pray is Hamlet. It is only the unbeliever, the one who wants to get to the bottom of everything, the spiritual chemist who watches the collapse of one apparently solid structure after the other, only he—unless he succeeds through divine power in erecting something indestructible inside himself * (and Hamlet has evidently not gotten this far)—only he, I say, can no longer *pray,* for

---

* How does this happen? Surely only when it is finally acknowledged that religion is related to nothing but the heart and emotions, and that the head is only suited to serve as a watchman in front of the sanctuary, armed with the sword of reason to protect it from its hereditary enemies: superstition and intolerance. If we are not satisfied with this and want to comprehend what, according to our nature, is incomprehensible to us, then we will go astray every time, whether we seek refuge in a so-called positive religion or in a system of speculative philosophy. Both are unsatisfying as soon as a person tries to make them into something more than an intriguing game of *fancy* or *reason.* Yet the innate *feeling* of God, of love, and of goodness in every *healthy* state of mind becomes clear to people of the lowest *and* highest mental capacities with equal and unalterable certitude. It engages them not only as a matter of faith, but as the true essence of their beings, as their actual selves, independent of reason or understanding, although both of these, on reflection, must finally enter in and confirm it.

he cannot see the point of it. He cannot deny that when he prays, he is doing no more than putting on an act for himself. This is a difficult transition, which is blamed on the poor creature by those very ones whose false teachings forced the child into his procrustean bed, often making it impossible for his shortened limbs ever to achieve their natural length.

But back to the play. It closed with a melodrama in which a large Newfoundland dog performed admirably, defending the flag for a long time, pursuing the enemy, and afterward, wounded, bleeding, and lame, reappearing on the stage and dying there, masterfully, with one last, inspired twitch of his tail. You could have sworn that the animal understood *at least* as well as any of his human comrades, how he was supposed to act.

I left the theater in such a good mood that afterward at the club I won eight rubbers at whist; it seems that cheerfulness and confidence can also conjure up luck at the table! But good night for today.

December 4th, 1826

WITH THE OPENING of Parliament, the upper levels of society are beginning to liven up a bit, even though London is still largely empty. Right now the most elegant ladies of the premium circles are giving special, small parties, far more difficult of access for many Englishmen than for high-ranking foreigners, because, as I have already mentioned, the despotism of fashion rules with an iron scepter in this free country, and it extends through all classes to a degree we Continentals cannot conceive of.

But before I allow myself to indulge in generalities, let me give you a brief description of my way of life here in London. I get up late, read—as a halfway-nationalized Englishman—three or four newspapers over breakfast. Afterward I glance at my visiting book to see what appointments are scheduled, and then I either drive to them in my cabriolet or ride. Even in the city, picturesque moments occur along the way, in particular the blood-red sun, which is battling against the wintry fogs, often engendering curiously striking and sometimes bizarre effects of light. Once my visits are over, I ride around for several hours in the splendid environs of London, returning at dusk to work a bit; dress for dinner, which happens at seven or eight. I spend the rest of the evening either at the theater or a small, exclusive party. The ludicrous routs (where one can hardly find a spot on the stairs, must shove or be shoved the entire time, and unfailingly suffer in a hothouse atmosphere) have not yet begun. In England, however, with the exception of a few diplomatic houses, you cannot appear anywhere in the evening unless you have been specially invited.

Things move along rather informally at these small parties, yet general conversation does not take place here. Customarily each gentleman selects a lady who particularly interests him and scarcely leaves her side the entire evening. This may leave some beautiful women sitting alone and condemned to silence, but they do not reveal their discomfort even by the slightest expression, for they are passive by nature. Everyone of course speaks French here, too—*tant bien que mal.* But at length the ladies become bored with the unending *gêne,*[14] and therefore a man who can speak English even tolerably well has no small advantage. I have not found that these women laugh at a foreign accent or at words and phrases used incorrectly, a failing attributed to the men in England. On the contrary, to have a conversation with Englishwomen is the most pleasant and reliable way to learn their language. I am firmly convinced that you benefit fully from teachers and grammar only after private practice has already acquainted you with a new tongue. For anyone with the requisite patience, however, it may be useful to start by memorizing the dictionary, as Prince Czartoryski recommends.

You can see that this life is rather *dolce far niente*,[15] though for me not so *dolce*, because I am fond of society only in intimate circles and become attached to new acquaintances with difficulty—these days hardly at all. Yet the ennui that assails me is so clearly registered on my undiplomatic face that it is readily conveyed to others, as infectious as a yawn. Here and there I find an exception, such as today when I met Mr. Morier, the witty and engaging author of *Hajji Baba*, as well as Mr. Hope, alleged author of the still more ingenious *Anastasius*. This latter book is worthy of Byron. Many people claim that Mr. Hope, who displays more reserve than brilliance in his outward demeanor, could not possibly have written it. This doubt is based especially on the fact that Mr. Hope published an earlier work on furniture, a book that contrasts profoundly in style and content with the heady *Anastasius*, which overflows with thought and feeling. For this reason an acquaintance of mine said: "One or the other. Either *Anastasius* is by him or the furniture book is—not both." But really, such disparate material requires disparate handling, and what I observed in Mr. Hope, perhaps with a kind of involuntary predilection, was a not-at-all ordinary man. He is very rich, and his house overflows with art treasures and luxury, a topic I may return to later. I do not admire the application of his theory of furniture, however, which is modeled on antiquity, given that his chairs are ungovernable. Other trophy-like arrays look silly, and the sofas are like miniature buildings with such sharp edges protruding all over the place that if you were to sit down carelessly, you might be impaled.

When I got home, late, I found your letter, which pleased me more than anything else, as does every message from you. But do not tell me that the pain of our separation weighs you down so profoundly, at least do not let it be weightier than something a joyful reunion can alleviate. This is probably no longer far off. It demonstrates little Christian confidence, my dear, that you start referring to immortality when things do not go exactly as we would wish. No, I confess it: even given all my momentary bouts of melancholy, I am on the whole quite disposed to earthly things, and "this span of life," as you call it, is still extremely dear to my heart. Of course, if you, my devoted tutelary goddess, were at the same time also Fortuna, then I would likely fare better than anyone on earth, "et toutes les étoiles pâliraient devant la mienne"[16]—but just the fact that you love me means you *are* my Fortuna, and I could not ask for a better one.

So do not let yourself be thrown off balance by your own fits of melancholy or mine. As for me, you already know: a mere trifle can raise the barometer of my soul, and a trifle can just as well cause it to fall. It is true, I was granted an all too delicate moral constitution, one not designed for simple contentment, something that requires tougher nerves.

December 5th, 1826

OBERON, WEBER'S SWAN song, filled the evening for me today. The performance left much to be desired as far as the music and singing were concerned, but the opera was extremely well done for London. The decorations were the best of their type, especially in the scene where the spirits are summoned. These did not appear in the usual costume of fire-red trousers and jackets, their heads topped with flames and the snaky hair of the Furies. Instead the broad rocky cave that took up the whole stage suddenly metamorphosed, each piece of rock turning into some fantastic and frightful shape or visage, glowing in bright flames and sallow flashes, from which here and there an entire figure would bend forward, grinning, while the unearthly voices of the rocky chorus reverberated all around. The opera itself I consider one of Weber's weaker accomplishments. Yet certain parts of it are lovely, particularly the introduction, which has something truly elfin about it. I am not so fond of the overture, though it is highly praised by connoisseurs.

I should have begun by telling you that I was presented to the king this morning at a big levee.[17] Here I must also relate an oddity stemming from the very strange and voluntary seclusion of the current monarch, namely that our own secretary of legation was presented along with me, and for the *first* time, even though he has already been serving here in this capacity for two years. His Majesty possesses a very good memory and immediately recalled my earlier sojourn in England, although he had the date wrong by several years. I took the opportunity to deliver my compliments about the substantial improvements in London since that time, thanks almost solely to the king himself. Then, following his gracious reply, I moved on and took up a comfortable position from which I could overlook the entire spectacle at my ease. It was all rather bizarre.

Each person in turn approached the king (who remained seated because of his sickliness), made a bow, was spoken to or not, and then either joined the row on the other side of the room or promptly departed. All those who had been appointed to something or other knelt down before the king and kissed his hand, which provoked the American envoy next me to make a satyr-like face. The clerics and lawyers in their black gowns and white-powdered wigs, both short and long, looked very eccentric. One of them involuntarily became the object of persistent and near universal guffaws. He fell to his knees because he was supposed to be "knighted," as the English put it. In this posture, and with the long fleece on his head, he looked remarkably like a ram led to the slaughtering block. His Majesty signaled the field marshall general to hand him his sword but the hearty warrior could not extract it from its sheath—this had probably never happened before. He tugged and yanked, all for naught. The king waiting with outstretched arm, the duke struggling with all his might, the unhappy martyr bending over in mute submission as if his end were now approaching, and all around the brilliant court in anxious expectation—it was a tableau worthy of Gilray's brush. At last the weapon of state leapt from the scabbard like a bolt of lightning, and His Majesty seized it impatiently. Alas, since His Highness's arm had seemingly fallen asleep during the long delay, the first strike connected not with the new knight but with his old wig, which for a moment shrouded both king and subject in a column of powder!

December 6th, 1826

MR. ROTHSCHILD INVITED me some time ago to visit him at his country estate, and today I was free to drive out there for dinner with my friend Lottum. The *royal* banker, who has not yet bought himself a *ducal* seat, lives in a charming villa. A few directors of the East India Company were there too, as well as several members of the Rothschild family along with others of their religion whom I liked very much. I have high esteem for this family in general because they have remained Jews. Only a fool can respect Jews less than those of other beliefs because of their religion, but apostates encounter a prejudice that is hard to overcome.

There are three circumstances, however, that would definitely incline me to allow Jews to change their religion. First, if they were truly convinced that they could be saved only in the name of Christianity; second, if their daughters wanted to marry a Christian and could not do so by any other means; third, if a Jew were elected a king over Christians. This is not altogether an impossibility, since in recent times men far more lowly than Jewish barons, and, notoriously, some with no religion at all,* have ascended to the throne.

Mr. Rothschild himself was in a very good mood, amusing and voluble. It was fun to listen as he explicated the paintings in his dining room for us—all portraits of European sovereigns and their prime ministers, which he had received as gifts. He spoke about each of these men as though they were his best friends and, to a certain degree, his equals. "Yes," he exclaimed, "that one there once pressed me for a loan, and the same week that his handwritten letter arrived, his father wrote me from Rome, also in his own hand, insisting that I should for heaven's sake not get involved. There could be no man more treacherous than his son to get mixed up with. *C'était sans doute très catholique*,[18] but the letter was probably written by old K——, who hated her son so much that, as everyone knows, she tended to say of him unjustly: Il a le cœur d'un t . . . , avec la figure d'un â . . .[19]

Now the others had their turn . . . . In the end, however, he humbly claimed to be no more than an obedient, well-paid functionary; a mere servant of those plenipotentiaries, all of whom he admired equally, whatever their politics. After all, he added with a laugh, "I never like to quarrel with my bread and butter."

It is quite prudent of Rothschild that he has accepted neither a title nor a medal, thus maintaining a far more honorable independence. He is certainly indebted to the good advice of his engaging and perceptive wife, also of his faith, who may well surpass him in tact and worldliness, if not in shrewdness and business acumen.

Before heading into the countryside this evening, we were enticed to alight from our coach to see the captured state carriage of another monarch of Asiatic origin: the king of Burma (Figure 17).[20] Thickly encrusted with gold and jewels valued at six thousand pounds, it glowed radiantly in the candlelight and, with its baldachin-like, pyramidal form, looked even more tasteful than our official carriages. There were some odd attendants seated on it: two small boys and two peacocks carved in wood and beautifully painted and varnished. Two white elephants were pulling the coach when it was captured, and fifteen thousand precious stones—both large and small, but uncut—still adorn the gilded wood and gold plate from which it is made. Many valuable Burmese weapons were arrayed as trophies all around the spacious room, lending the whole display exceptional interest. Since you always get your money's worth at such occasions here, there was a Poecilorama set up in the adjoining room showing Burmese and other Indian views that, with the help of artificial illumination, underwent several transformations and produced strikingly vivid landscape effects.[21]

I do not know why such things are not used more often to embellish a room. At a party, for instance, a room decorated in this way would certainly offer worthier variety than the banal embellishments of colorful curtains, citrus trees, and flowers that one normally sees.

------

* From the perspective of the pious, it is unclear whether it is worse to have no religion at all or be from some other sect. At any rate, Louis XIV, himself a religious hero, chose the second option. When the duke of Orléans recommended someone to him as ambassador to Spain, the king agreed to the appointment but then revoked it the next day because he had heard that the individual in question was a Jansenist. "Not at all, Your Majesty," the duke assured him, "as far as I know, he doesn't even believe in God." "Can I count on that?" the king asked with supreme gravity. "Of course," the duke responded with a smile. "Well then, he may retain the post in God's name."

THE RATH, OR BURMESE IMPERIAL STATE CARRIAGE.

December 8th, 1826

RETURNING RATHER LATE from dinner at Mr. de Polignac's, a truly charming but also highly orthodox representative of the ancien régime, I managed to arrive at the theater in time to find the renowned Mathews "at home" after the main performance.[22] The curtain had been lowered, and Mr. Mathews was sitting in front of it, above the orchestra, at a large table draped with rugs. He began rather discursively by telling the audience that he had just come back from a trip to Paris, where he had met many a quaint character and lived through many a humorous adventure. He now moved imperceptibly from narration into an utterly dramatic performance in which, with a prodigious display of talent and memory, he let what he had experienced actually happen to him before the spectators' eyes. He totally altered his face, his language, indeed his entire appearance with such lightning speed that you would not have thought it possible. The props consisted of no more than a cap, a cloak, a false nose, a wig, and so forth, which he pulled out from under the rugs and, with these simple things, instantly created the most flawless impersonations.

The applause was boisterous, and the laughter did not stop. The main characters, who appeared in multiple intrigues, were: an old Englishman who condemns everything from abroad and finds it all better at home; a lady from the provinces who, in order to learn French, never appears on the street without a dictionary in her hand, harasses the passersby with incessant questions, and never misses an opportunity to assist other English people with her knowledge. In the process, however, as you can well imagine, she always comes up with the most distorted, burlesque, and often ambiguous utterances. There was also a dandy from the City intent on affecting *le grand air*; and his opposite, a fat farmer from Yorkshire, who plays something like the role of Pächter Feldkümmel.[23] For me the most amusing vignette was an English lecture on craniology delivered by Spurzheim. The striking similarity to the man himself (well-known in England), including all his mannerisms and his German accent, was so perfect that the theater quaked with guffaws.

Other impersonations were not as satisfying, including that of Talma, whose standing is beyond the reach of a mere mimic, however talented. Besides, the great tragedian's death is all too recent, and thus the pain felt by all lovers of art over his irreparable loss is still too profound for them to be entertained by a parody.

The curtain now rose for the conclusion, a small farce that Mathews again performed alone, commanding seven to eight different roles, not counting a dog and a child, which were acted by puppets, although he barked and prattled their lines just as masterfully as he spoke the others. Playing a French tutor traveling with a ten-year-old lord, he begins by locking the lad in a guitar case so he can save his fare for the diligence, a fee he will nonetheless pass on to the distinguished papa. Each time he arrives at a station he allows the youngster out, first to let him get a breath of fresh air and second to go over his lessons. Here he proves himself a perfect ventriloquist and conducts the conversation with consummate hilarity. It becomes especially funny when the lad balks at having to crawl back into the guitar case, his mutterings and laments, like the waltz in *Der Freischütz*, fading gradually away, until the container is latched and the final pleas trickle out like a faint echo.

Many adventures befall the speeding diligence and its passengers, until at last an old maid appears (Mathews again) and, against the rules, tries to smuggle her favorite dog into the carriage. She, too, decides that the guitar case is the place to hide her darling, but she sets about her task with such alacrity that she fails to notice it is already occupied. Scarcely has she set the case down than the dog starts to growl and bark, the boy begins to howl, and she screams for help. This trio drove the gallery mad with delight!

The whole performance is, as you can see, not of the highest aesthetic standard, and in fact more geared to the English stomach. Indeed, it is almost painful to see such extraordinary skill devoted to such silly antics, yet his talent is superb, and you have to marvel at the physical energy required to carry it off: several hours of constant speaking interspersed with exhausting costume changes, and all without a hitch.

Wishing to avoid a similar strain on your patience, I will now close and hope most sincerely that my modest peep show of this city, as I unroll it before you, is not boring. You have requested pictures of daily life; you are not expecting a statistical handbook nor a topography, a regular accounting of all the so-called highlights of London nor a systematic disquisition on England. Nor am I in a position to deliver such things. So please continue to be gracious about the plain cooking I send you, which is occasionally, at least, spiced up with a small peppercorn.

Your faithful Lou

LETTER 7

London, December 12th, 1826

*D*EAREST FRIEND!

The local auctions are interesting, primarily because of the many unusual and costly objects that appear daily and can often be acquired very cheaply due to the dynamic volatility of life here and the perpetual decline and collapse of fortunes. A second factor, as I have mentioned, is the brilliance of the auctioneers, who embellish their monologues free of charge with far more wit than ours would, even for serious money.

This morning I watched the sale of an East Indian cabinet containing some admirable works of art. It had belonged to a bankrupt nabob. "The owner of these treasures," said the auctioneer, "expended a lot of effort for nothing: in the end, gentlemen, nothing for *him*, that is, but a lot for you. Doubtless he once had more money than sense; now he certainly has more sense than money." He later remarked that "modesty" and "merit" have nothing in common except that both start with an *m*. He bantered on at length in this manner, making similar plays on words, and at the close he asked, "What helps the poor to live? What gives them health, nourishment, and comfort? Not generosity, which does little. It is vanity alone—and not the vanity of the destitute, those poor devils, but of the rich. So, gentlemen, show some of this laudable vanity and buy something to indulge it! Then, involuntarily, you will earn God's blessing."

Jawohl, I thought, you are correct there, you old joker. Because our dear Lord really did organize the world such that good constantly arises out of evil. Indeed, evil only emerges so that good can be revealed in the act of vanquishing it. One must moralize at every opportunity!

I dined at the house of a distinguished lady, who talked to me throughout the meal about nothing but Napoleon, and was so smitten with him, to an English extreme, that she even found the means to commend the execution of the duc d'Enghien and the emperor's acts of perfidy in Spain.[1]

Although I no longer go that far, I am also, as you know, an admirer of the colossal greatness of this man. And I delighted my table companion with an eyewitness account of Napoleon's erstwhile magnificence, during those days of splendor in France when Caesar himself marveled at his grandeur;

> When ambassadors from so many different kings came
> To pay him homage in the name of the universe.[2]

In fact, I would not want to overlook any of his later mishaps *for the sake of his own fame* nor any of his transgressions for the *tragic interest* they inspired. He knew how to endure the *coups d'épée* as well as the *coups d'épingles* with equal dignity,[3] and in keeping with his exalted life, he set down an exalted epitaph for himself: "Je lègue l'opprobre de ma mort à l'Angleterre."[4]

This much is certain: he is still too close to judge impartially, and experience has taught us that mortal combat was declared less against his despotic principles than his personal self-aggrandizement. Nowadays, thank God, such principles lack every bit of the energy *he* invested in them, which is a great gain for humanity.*

There is now a French theater here that is visited only by the best society, although it is little more than a small and poorly lit private stage. The actors Perlet and Laporte are its mainstays and are excellent performers. Laporte also plays roles on the English stage with French self-assurance and believes that if the audience laughs at his accent and French mannerisms, they are merely acknowledging his comic power.

I went to the theater along with Mrs. Wilmot-Horton, wife of the well-known minister and parliamentary orator, and afterward followed her to the first true rout that I have experienced during this sojourn. It was in a house totally unknown to me, because it is customary here to bring friends along to such parties and introduce them to the hostess, who never imagines they might fill her small premises to the point of suffocation. The more the merrier. And for her vanity to be fully satisfied, a brawl must erupt among the carriages in front of her house, leaving some of them dashed to pieces and a few of the men and horses injured, so the next day's *Morning Post* can trumpet the ultrafashionable soirée held by Lady Vain or Lady Foolish.

Nonetheless, on the stairs (I never got any further that evening), I made a more interesting acquaintance than I expected in Lady Charlotte Bury, who has attained some renown as a writer. Once a famous beauty, she is the sister of a duke and has now married the private tutor of her children.[5] I visited her the following day and found that everything in her house was entirely in nuances of brown: furniture, curtains, rugs, her own and her children's clothes—not a single deviation of hue. The room boasted no mirrors or pictures but was decorated solely with plaster casts of classical busts and bas-reliefs. This is a new kind of Brownomania.[6] As a writer, Lady Bury is not an adherent of the old school, and if I wanted to group her with a true, spiritual Brownonian such as Lady Morgan, then I would compare the latter to a glass of well-aged Madeira that has crossed the equator more than once, whereas I would compare Lady Bury to a spring of crystal-clear water in a charming landscape; or I would compare the one with an incandescent double carnation and the other with a delicate violet.

Shortly thereafter the famous bookseller C—— entered the brown room. He has gotten rich through the works of Sir Walter Scott, although he initially rejected the manuscript of *Waverley*, the author's first and best book, finally giving Scott no more than forty pounds for it.[7] I assume that Lady Bury has reason to get more satisfaction from him, and so I discreetly departed, leaving her alone with the businessman.

---

* Unfortunately the recent memoirs of Mr. de Bourrienne are less revealing than we had expected about Napoleon's true essence. Bourrienne portrays Napoleon as though he were Bourrienne. If a dwarf runs around a giant's feet for a hundred years, still he will not be tall enough to look him in the eye. But Bourrienne is correct about one thing, a subject not beyond his short reach, namely, that the principal foe that actually struck Napoleon down was the *commercial class*, driven to extremes so apolitically. Today the commercial class is more powerful than the church or military and will yield to nothing except public opinion, should the latter ever declare itself to be in opposition.—*The Editor*. [The Editor is not alone in considering Bourrienne's memoirs (10 vols., 1829–31) unreliable.—*Translator*.]

EVERY SOCIAL CIRCLE is hugely agitated at the moment over the affairs of Portugal,[8] and today, in a box at the French theater, the Marquis of Palmela read us the English declaration that has just been published. Politics is a main ingredient of society here, as it is starting to be in Paris and someday will be in our somnolent Germany as well, because the whole world is heading in that direction. But more frivolous pleasures are suffering in the process, and the art of conversation, as it once prevailed in France, may soon be completely lost. Here, I believe, it probably never existed anyway, unless, perhaps, during the time of Charles II. In addition these people are too slavishly subject to established practices, too deliberate in their enjoyments, too steeped in prejudice, and, finally, insufficiently vibrant to achieve that unaffected freedom of mind, which is the necessary basis of engaging sociability. I must confess that I know of no more monotonous and smug society than that which prevails at the highest ranks here; the few exceptions are found mostly among foreigners, or people who have lived a long time on the Continent. A petrified, stone-cold spirit of caste and fashion governs everything; it makes the upper classes dull and the lower ranks comical. Genuine, heartfelt civility and cheerful bonhomie are *entirely* missing; and little has been adopted from foreign nations: neither French levity nor Italian *sprezzatura*, but at most just German stiffness and unease, masked by arrogance and hauteur.

In spite of all this, the halo of a firmly anchored aristocracy and extravagant wealth (accompanied, it cannot be denied, by excellent taste in spending it) has branded this the grand world of Europe par excellence, to which all nations extend some degree of priority. The fact that foreigners are personally uncomfortable in England is evident from the fact that they are so scarce, and rarely stay for long when they come. Every one of them thanks God from the bottom of his heart when he escapes English society, even though his vanity will later cause him to praise this uninvigorating, foggy sun whose rays lent him barely any comfort at all.

The English seem much more loveable as well as loving in their domestic and most intimate relations, although here too there is a preponderance of the baroque—for example, the widespread custom among the upper classes that the sons, once they have fledged, must leave the parental nest and live on their own, and are not allowed to return to their parents' home without a formal invitation, even if just for a meal. I recently found a touching example of conjugal love described in a newspaper account: shortly before the Marquess of Hastings died in Malta, he decreed that immediately after his death, his right hand should be chopped off, brined, and sent to his wife as a memento. In a similar vein, a gentlemen of my acquaintance cut off his dead mother's head (out of genuine tenderness and after receiving her prior permission) so that he could kiss her skull for the rest of his life. Other Englishmen, I believe, would rather go to hell than allow anyone to get too near their corpse with a scalpel—after all, the resurrection men have to live too![9] There are laws requiring the most scrupulous adherence to every provision of the deceased, however mad; as long as it conforms to the laws, it must be carried out. There is a mansion in England where a well-dressed corpse has been standing at a window for the last half century, gazing out over his former property undisturbed. How very much that man must have loved domesticity!

Just as I was about to describe a few more English eccentrics, my long-awaited head gardener entered the room and brought me letters from you.[10] What a shame that you were unable to include yourself in that large packet (with all your *fraîcheur*, of course, and not like Lord Hasting's hand), or dwell in a dainty little box, like Goethe's delightful *Erdgeist*.[11] Then I could call for you whenever I needed you and share every pleasure without these lengthy intervals that compel you to suffer the gloom besetting my letter of fourteen days before or evoke your merry response to something happy just when I am once again laboring under the most horrible attack of spleen. As you very rightly say, an old letter is often comparable to an old corpse that, long forgotten, is fished up out of the sea.

What makes me laugh and at the same time feel annoyed is that once again, as is your wont, you write with almost no details about my beloved Muskau; instead you send me long excerpts from an *African* travel description, which I already read here in the original ages ago. Next time I will certainly pay you back tit for tat. Anyway I am just now studying a very interesting work: the Prussian drill manual of 1805, from which I can send you the most ingenious selections as soon as I run out of other material. Oh, you good lamb, you will often be shorn with these African tidings, all the more so since the last shearing happened some time ago.[12] You must be sitting as deep in wool as the Knights of St John in B——, who, while making a show of their double crosses, sat on their sacks of wool and waited for the highest bidder. The seat of the English lord chancellor is also a wool sack,[13] but of a somewhat more genteel nature, resembling the Golden Fleece more than the potato sacks people sit on while consuming the dish we call "poor knights."[14]

I now go on almost daily excursions to parks with Rehder in order to make his presence in England as useful as possible; a brief stay here can help a good gardener advance further in his discipline than ten years of study at home. There are many interesting properties within a short distance from London, all reachable by the most charming and busy roads. Most special is Lord Mansfield's villa,[15] its decoration due to the good taste of his wife. Syon House, which belongs to the Duke of Northumberland, was laid out by Capability Brown and is well worth seeing for its magnificent greenhouses and multitude of gigantic, nonnative trees living in the open air, none of which could tolerate our climate. Here you also see whole groves of rhododendrons, camellias, and jimson weed, which are only partially covered in winter, and all kinds of lovely evergreens growing exuberantly and profusely in every season. The greenhouses and hothouses, which throw up a facade three hundred feet long, are built of nothing but stone, iron, and glass—a type of construction that here, to top it all off, is cheaper than wood!

I was intrigued by a kind of chain made by using scythes as links. This is employed each year in early July to remove aquatic plants from broad expanses of standing water (a flaw in most English parks); all that is required is simply to drag it along the bottom like a trawl. Every day from five to nine o'clock, twelve men are engaged in mowing the vast pleasure ground, the result being that you never see any tall grass and there is no need for the unpleasantness of customary mowing, which makes a mess of the garden for several days in a row. Admittedly only one section can be taken care of each day, but designated areas are completed all at one go, and the mowers return soon enough that the difference is not conspicuous. Economically these short grass clippings are a total loss, it is true, but beauty and utility cannot always be united, and in a *pleasure* garden the latter must naturally come second, or really you shouldn't have one at all.

Kew, which lies on the opposite side of the river, contains what is arguably the most complete collection of exotic plants in Europe. The park also benefits greatly from a lovely site on the Thames, although it is otherwise somewhat neglected. Here you find yews as big as our firs and very fine specimens of holly and evergreen oaks; otherwise the old queen's grounds are not very tasteful.

Wimbledon Park, meanwhile, spreads out over several hills and is thick with striking groups of trees. It offers gorgeous views, although unfortunately suffers from a certain degree of monotony.

Very close by, almost in the London suburbs, is Chiswick House, and its architecture is not without interest. Several years ago I had the kind of unpleasant adventure there that is too characteristic of England not to relate to you, although in itself it is less than piquant:

The trepidation, indeed I might say jealousy, with which the wealthy English often close off their property, even from nothing more than the profaning *gaze* of a stranger, is sometimes truly amusing. It can also become depressing, as I experienced fourteen years ago and was vividly reminded of today when I saw the old building again. I had gone for a ride one day in the vicinity of London and, attracted by the sight of this estate, asked the porter, who was standing by the park lodge, whether he could allow me to look at the gardens. He made a big fuss but finally remembered that his lord was ill and keeping to his room, hence would not encounter me, so he decided to accept the offered tip and opened the forbidden gate, meanwhile keeping an eye on my horse. I had been strolling around for a quarter of an hour and had just examined the well-tended pleasure ground when a somewhat portly figure in a shirt came into view at a window of the residence across from me. He seemed to be running around apprehensively, but finally threw the window open with some vehemence and, as a large bell began to ring loudly, yelled at me with barely suppressed fury: "*Qui êtes-vous, Monsieur? Que cherchez-vous ici?*"[16] I considered it ridiculous to return his shout over such a distance, but I also soon found it unnecessary since, alarmed by the clanging of the bell, servants were already scrambling toward me from all sides. One of them now repeated the question to me ex officio, and through him I let the owner know, in brief, that I was a foreigner who had been lured in by my passion for gardens; that I had not, in fact, climbed over the wall, as he seemed to believe, but had simply entered through the gate, where my horse was still standing; that I also felt profound regret at having caused him such anxiety in his sickly state, and only hoped that this would have no significant consequences for him; that I would now offer my best respects and immediately depart from the forbidden garden. I got back to my horse right away and rode off laughing, for this was the amusing side of the affair. But about two weeks later my path happened to take me past the same estate. I approached the lodge again and rang the bell. A stranger appeared, and out of a sense of mischief I enquired after the health of the lord and whether it was possible to visit the garden. "God forbid!" came the answer, "not at any price!" And now to my true distress I learned from this new servant that his predecessor, poor devil, had just been sent off with his wife and children, although he had served here for many years, simply because he had allowed a stranger in without permission. And yet this unforgiving gentleman is another of the genuine patent liberals in England.[17] What would an illiberal man have done, I wonder?

I will not say anything about the enchanting valley of Richmond. Every travel writer goes into ecstasy about it, and justifiably so, but the descriptions do not always awaken the same feeling in the reader. So I will abstain and simply remark that the excellent aristocratic inn, the Star and Garter, from which you overlook this paradise while your physical needs are being perfectly attended to, makes its own contribution to the enjoyment. Solitude and tranquility, combined with every comfort in an indescribably beautiful spot, are a powerful invitation to the enjoyment of life, and it is said that many a young man from London celebrates his private *Honigmonate* here in secret without the blessings of a priest.[18] We innocents, however, celebrated nothing more than magnificent nature, and your loyal gardeners called out in unison: "If only . . ." You know how the rest of the sentence goes.

In the evening I took Rehder to the Adelphi Theater, which is small and charming, distinguished by first-rate machinery, and at the moment boasts several excellent actors as well. One of them, in a not bad play, performed the role of a drunkard more naturally than I have ever seen it done. It is true, of course, that he has more opportunity to study this state of mind here, for much the same reason that the ancients were better at representing nudes than our artists are. They saw them more often. One feature very well taken from life was the drunkard's tender passion for a poor young girl in his rooming house. When sober he always found other pursuits, but whenever he was drunk, he attended to her with tears of affection for his first love. And happily, in that same mood, he brought himself to marry her.

December 23rd, 1826

THANK YOU FOR the news from Berlin. I am especially pleased by Alexander von Humboldt's appointment.[19] It must be a joy for every patriot to see a man like him finally established in his native country, which is so very rightly proud of his fame throughout the world. It must also be a happy occasion for many circles there, who will at last be given a sprinkling of salt, the lack of which has left them unpalatable for much too long.

Since you are aware of my views on such matters, you can imagine how sad I felt about the good and noble king's accident,[20] which I had already heard about from Lottum. But I hope to God that his strong constitution and the help of skillful men will avert any remaining trouble. It is certainly splendid that this occasion led an entire people to exclaim wholeheartedly "May heaven preserve our dear monarch!"

As for my own frame of mind—likely a result of the perpetual fogs, often so severe that all the streetlamps have to be lit at midday, and even then one cannot see a thing—I remain more or less in the same state of gloom. *Le pire est, que je suis tantôt trop, et tantôt trop peu sensible à l'opinion et aux procédés des autres.*[21] Unfortunately moods control me with a despotic power, making me not only sad and happy but, alas, clever and foolish as well. In my more sensitive moments I sometimes feel as though I have climbed up a rope ladder until my hands have gone numb and now, after dangling on high for a long time and vainly struggling to move farther, am about to be forced to let go and gently sink back to the lowest rung again. And perhaps, once again descended to the level of the common and insignificant, I will feel more serene than when I was up above in the stormy winds and, with fewer *hopes*, may perhaps be surrounded by a happier if also simpler *reality*. But away with such musings! They do no good at all. And even fears of a *real* impending misfortune should be expelled from one's mind. For why torment oneself with worry over what *might* happen, something that, even if only a dream phantom, can nonetheless steal so much enjoyment from the present.

In all such frames of mind *your* image is my greatest comfort, and in the end it is to you, my only and eternal friend, to whom I always turn with brimming eyes and heartfelt gratitude for your all-encompassing love, goodness, and forbearance. On your faithful breast, I lay my misery as well as my joy and aspirations, which without you would be meaningless, even were they to be brilliantly realized.

But I must leave you now, since it is my duty to attend a large party where I am destined, as in life, to become lost in the crowd. This is my last foray into the social world for the time being, because I am preparing to set off on a park and garden tour with Rehder, which will probably take us a month. This time of year is absolutely the best for anyone who wants to study these places, since the leafless trees allow for open views on every side; and thus in just a single circuit of a designed landscape you can see everything; understand the effects that have been achieved; evaluate the entirety like a plan on paper; and in addition recognize all the plantings in their intended order.

Meanwhile we visited the parks in the city yesterday, Kensington among others, and, with particular care, Regent's Park, where we also saw the diorama that has been set up there. This went far beyond my expectation and surpassed all such displays I have seen before; the senses could not possibly be more effectively deceived. Indeed even though you are well aware of the illusion, it is a struggle to convince yourself that this is all it is. The painting depicts the interior of a large abbey church, seemingly in its true dimensions. A side door stands open. Ivy creeps through the windows and the sun occasionally shines through the door, its bright glance illuminating the remnants of colorful glass panes that twinkle behind some cobwebs. Through the last window on the opposite side you see the overgrown cloister garden and watch as clouds in the sky above it gust by and obscure the sunlight, throwing deep shadows into the deathly still church. There the crumbled but magnificent monument of an ancient knight still stands in somber majesty, and the stones of the surrounding floor are broken up as if someone had dug for treasure there.

Since our departure is set for tomorrow, I am sending this letter off, even though it has not yet accrued its customary corpulence. How slender yours are by comparison! Someday, if our descendants should turn up the musty correspondence of their ancestors in a corner of the old library, they will be overcome by astonishment at my extravagance and your parsimony. Apropos, do not distract yourself too much in Berlin, and do not forget, even for a moment,

the most faithful of your friends.

Watford, December 25th, 1826

*D*EARLY DEVOTED ONE,

We finally set off this morning in terrible rainy weather. But just ten miles from London we got down to business, visiting two villas and a fairly large park in the pleasant hamlet of Stanmore. The first was constructed entirely in the *rural* Gothic style, with peaked, ornate, tiled roofs, a genre English architects are very happy with and, I might say, find *comfortable*. The interior was also charmingly done in the same style, yet extremely livable and inviting. Even the doors in the walls enclosing the kitchen garden were topped by old windows of colored glass that emerged unexpectedly amid the flourishing vegetation. The little flower garden, surrounded by pebble paths, was likewise outfitted with beds of a Gothic shape and had a playfulness that did not look bad at all.

The second villa, in Italian taste, presented quite a different picture, with large vases in front filled not with flowers but with pyramids of small pumpkins and hulls of yellow and green Seville oranges. The gardens were embellished, or rather disfigured, by a few too many carved wooden statues painted white, among them a lion lunging out abruptly in a vain attempt to instill horror and, just as ineffectually, a Cupid hanging from the branches, threatening to shoot arrows at the passersby.

The Priory,[1] a former monastery but now the castle and park of Lord Aberdeen, offers much worth seeing. The multitude of magnificent spruces and other conifers is more reminiscent of foreign climes than is usual here. The simple palace is almost totally screened on all sides by trees, both tall and short, so that you only catch an occasional glimpse of its loveliness glimmering through the lower branches or towering above the tallest. This is always very advantageous to buildings, especially old ones. In general you seldom find those long, narrow, uninterrupted vistas across level stretches of lawn that are the triumph of our garden designers, but only serve to make what's distant seem closer than it really is. We walked around the grounds for quite a long time while some young ladies and the sons of the family, pretty lads, swarmed around us on small Scottish ponies. Finally one of the boys joined us as a guide and showed us the interior of the house as well; its dark exterior walls were luxuriously covered all the way to the roof with ivy, espaliered pomegranate trees, and Old Blush roses.

We only left the park at dusk and within a half hour reached the little town of Watford, where I am now resting in a fine inn. Rehder takes this opportunity to send you his humble greetings and is writing in his journal with an industriousness that makes me chuckle.

I forgot to mention that while in the Priory (I am stealing this from Rehder's journal) we saw a single rhododendron standing in the open that measured fifteen feet in height and, with its thick branches, more than twenty-five feet in circumference. Such vegetation is a greater invitation to "parkomania" than anything on offer at home!

WE HAVE DONE the calculations, dear Julie, and concluded that if you were with us (a desire ever harbored by your loyal servants), given your aversion to moving on foot, you could see at most a quarter of a park each day. It would therefore require at least 170 years for you to visit all the parks in England, of which there must be a hundred thousand, since no matter where one goes, the place is teeming with them. Naturally we are only paying attention to the largest ones or to small villas if something happens to strike us or catch our eye *en passant*. Yet today we saw so much that was magnificent and so many lofty residences that we remain utterly entranced, for as you know, I have never managed to abide by the *nil admirari* rule, which deprives us of every sincere delight.[2]

Before I begin my description I must also do justice to the excellent inns found everywhere in the countryside here, even in the smallest villages. All of them are run with meticulous attention to detail and are consistently clean, extravagantly comfortable, and, indeed, elegant. Furthermore, no stranger is ever expected to live, eat, and sleep in the same room, as is required in German inns, which really consist of nothing but ballrooms and bedrooms.

As a rule, the table service is of silver and porcelain, the furniture practical, the bed always excellent, and a friendly, flickering fire never far away. A detailed description of this morning's breakfast will give you the best notion of what a comfortable life is accorded to local travelers. *Nota bene*. I had ordered only tea, yet when I descended from my bedroom, here is what I found, prepared for me in this little parish hardly the size of a village: A large tea urn stood in the middle of the table decoratively surrounded by a silver teapot, a *Spühlnapf*,[3] and a milk jug. Three small Wedgewood plates with the same number of knives and forks and two large cups of lovely porcelain were all waiting to be filled. Next to them was an inviting platter with boiled eggs and another with toasted *oreilles de cochon à la Sainte-Ménéhould*.[4] There were muffins on a dish kept warm by hot water; a second dish held cold ham; there was fluffy white bread, both dry and buttered toast, the best fresh butter in an elegant crystal container, handy salt and pepper casters, English mustard as well as *moutarde de maille*, and finally a silver tea caddy with very good green and black tea. This thoroughly luxurious meal (which I hope you will feel I described as picturesquely as I would a landscape) was also relatively cheap, because its price on my bill was only two shillings (sixteen Groschen). In general, however, traveling is very expensive here, especially the post horses—which cost four times what they do at home—not to mention the tips that have to be handed out in every direction all day long.

At ten o'clock we reached Cassiobury Park, the seat of the Earl of Essex (Figure 18). I arranged to be announced, and the earl sent his son-in-law Mr. Ford (whom I had already encountered in Dresden and was pleased to meet again here) to tour me around.

The house is *modern* Gothic and magnificently furnished. You first enter a hall with colorful windows opening onto a view of an interior courtyard laid out as a flower garden. From there you go to the side through a long gallery hung with armor, and then into a stairwell of richly carved wood (with steps leading to the upper floor). From the stairwell you enter the library, which in England almost always serves as the main drawing room (Figure 19). All this is on the ground floor. The library has two small rooms looking onto the garden, both filled with rare objects. I especially admired two humorous drawings by Denon, one depicting the levee of Cardinal Bernis in Rome and the other a dinner at Voltaire's with the Abbé Maury, Diderot, Helvétius, d'Alembert, and a few other philosophers—all of them portraits.

18

Cassiobury Park,
Swiss Cottage, and
Seat of the Earl of Essex.

Great Library.
CASSIOBURY.

The Great Library
at Cassiobury.

Also interesting was a small set of Queen Antoinette's furniture on which portraits of her husband and Henri IV were mounted at several points. From the library you go into a second drawing room, just as lavishly decorated, and from there into the dining room. A greenhouse in the form of a chapel flanks both of these, and everywhere the windows extend to the floor, offering a view into the most splendid park with the river flowing through it. On a distant rise you look into a very broad allée of lindens, at the end of which the sun sets for a certain period every summer. This must provide the most magnificent natural decoration along the entire length of the greenhouse, even more so when the sun's rays are reflected back in a large mirrored door on the opposite side. The walls of these rooms are all covered in oak *boiserie* with costly cornices and carving; the furniture is of rosewood, silk, and velvet; and valuable paintings in antique gilded frames adorn the walls. The rooms are very large, even baronial, and steam heat keeps them all at a temperature of sixty-four degrees Fahrenheit.[5] The stables and household buildings are set well apart on the left, but they are connected to the main house via a crenelated wall so that the whole structure extends a good thousand feet without any break.

The flower gardens are granted a substantial space of their own (Figure 20). One section is laid out in the normal fashion, that is, with a long greenhouse at the back, and in front of it are numerous *berceaux* and shady paths around a large lawn packed with beds of every shape, as well as unusual trees and shrubs. But then came something new: a deep, isolated valley in the form of an oval, with dense stands of evergreens, laurels, and rhododendrons on all sides, and with rock-garden plants growing in an impenetrable carpet on artificial stones; behind, the crowns of tall firs and oaks swayed in the wind; and at the end of the lawn was a magnificent, freestanding linden with a bench around it. From here the gravel bed of the whole little valley was covered by an embroidered flower parterre in lovely, if completely regular, patterns. The path out of this area led through a grotto overgrown with ivy and inlaid with flint stones and shells, then into a square rose garden surrounded by a laurel hedge with a temple at its center; opposite stood a hothouse for aquatic plants. The rose beds formed a variety of intertwining figures. A thick, leafy walkway of beeches, all carefully sheared, wound its serpentine way from here into the Chinese garden, likewise surrounded by tall trees and walls. It contained a host of vases, benches, fountains, and a third greenhouse, all in the purest imitation of the Chinese style. Its beds were bordered by rings of white, blue, and red sand; baroque dwarf plants and several dozen Chinese vases stood atop pedestals sheathed in climbing periwinkle and exotic species. The windows of the greenhouse are painted to look like Chinese wallpaper, and we appeared in the bull's eye mirrors mounted in the interior as if in a camera obscura. I will not even mention all the propagation going on, or the vegetable gardens with their endless walls and rows of greenhouses to protect the flowers, etc., etc. You can judge for yourself when I repeat Mr. Ford's assurance that the maintenance of the whole park and residence comes to ten thousand pounds a year! The earl has his own people who do everything required: handymen, craftsmen, masons, carpenters, cabinetmakers, and so on, each with his own specific area of expertise. One, for instance, has the sole task of keeping the fences in shape, another the rooms, a third the furniture; an exemplary arrangement for someone living in the country.

I made my visit to the elderly earl, who is kept to his room by gout, and the friendly old man gave me the best information and, most essential of all, admittance cards for the rest of my journey.

Our tour, which took us for a long ride around the park, led first to one of its major sites, called the Swiss Cottage, charmingly tucked away beside a river in the middle of a small wood (see Figure 18). We drove to it across the lawn because, as I have mentioned, many of the parks here are treated like unbridled nature and, to save expense, often have only *a single* road leading to the residence on one side and back out again on the other. Returning to the main road, we quickly covered twenty miles through a lovely, fertile landscape rich with vegetation. By three o'clock we had reached Ashridge Park, the seat of the Earl of Bridgewater (Figure 21).

Here, dear Julie, you can accompany me more closely if you open Repton's garden book, where you will find several views and the ground plan for these captivating gardens, which old Repton laid out himself. Just remember the rosary, and you will know exactly where to look.[6]

The park (one of the largest in England) measures more than fourteen miles in circumference; and the palace, modern Gothic like Cassiobury, seems to go on endlessly with its innumerable walls, turrets, and courtyards. In all frankness I must admit that this *neo*-Gothic genre (castellated style), which in drawings has such a fairy-tale quality to it, is often in reality not only tasteless but even a bit ridiculous because of its excessive ornament and general impracticality. Amid the most serene and cultivated stretches of meadowland, strewn with a myriad of flowers,

20

Garden Scenes from
Cassiobury Park.

you become aware of a kind of fortress with a hundred towers, embrasures, and parapets, not a single one of them having the slightest function, and at their base almost nothing but walls of glass (the greenhouses and conservatories, which communicate with the rooms). This is no less ludicrous than if the owner of these sweet flower gardens happened to stroll by in a helmet and armor like Don Quixote of yesteryear! The antique, old Italian, or plainly romantic styles that have been adapted to our own era harmonize infinitely better with such surroundings, appear more welcoming, and—even though they are on a far smaller scale—more grand.[7]

On the other hand, the interior of the house was overwhelming and, indeed, truly princely. The owners have quite reasonably limited the public areas to just a few very spacious rooms. Here again you step first into a hall adorned with armor and antique furniture and then enter the stairwell, the most magnificent of its type you can imagine. Rising through three high floors and encircled by the same number of galleries, it achieves the loftiness and grandeur of a chapel. The walls are of polished stone, the banisters of gleaming brass, the beautifully carved coffers in the wooden ceiling are decorated with paintings, and on every side, through all three stories, are niches containing stone statues of the kings of England. Exiting the stairwell you enter a large room adorned with gilded furniture upholstered in red velvet. Light streams in through immense windows that take up nearly the entire front wall and afford a view onto the pleasure ground and park. On the left side is an equally large room with a billiard table and, next to it, the library. On the other side, in the same succession of rooms, you find the dining room, and behind that the splendid greenhouse and orangery through which you arrive at the chapel, resplendent with precious wood reliefs and ten authentically old stained-glass windows of great beauty. All the pews are of walnut and covered in crimson velvet.

Some lovely and interesting paintings, although mostly by modern masters, hang in the rooms. The pleasure ground and gardens are even larger than those at Cassiobury, and you will find parts of them in Repton's book, namely the American garden, the monk's garden, and the rosary, to which should be added: 1) the very elegant French garden with a covered gallery on one side, a porcelain-like decorative object with flower pots in the center, and a large parterre in which each bed contains a particular kind of flower; 2) the rock garden, where all kinds of rock plants and creepers have been brought together. One needs long exposure to great luxury even to conceive of such a diverse and perfectly maintained whole; I have to admit that our sovereigns typically possess but a fraction of what is assembled here. A few thousand head of deer and countless groups of gigantic trees decorate the park, which, except for the road that leads through it, has been left entirely to nature and the many grazing herds.

Please always accept it as a small sacrifice, dear Julie, that I provide you with faithful descriptions of such details, which may well be useful to us in our own plans and buildings and are certainly more tedious to *write* than to *read*.* To improve these accounts I am making drawings on my writing tablet of everything interesting, and these should come in useful for us someday as a stimulus to new ideas. Tomorrow we will visit Woburn Abbey, the nearby palace of the Duke of Bedford, one of the richest noblemen in England. In size and splendor it supposedly surpasses Ashridge as much as Ashridge surpasses Cassiobury. A very pleasant progression.

The inn from which I am writing is once again excellent, and I intend, after all my exertions, to do as much credit to my main meal as to breakfast; although the former is good, it is much simpler here and consists of the same dishes day after day. The eternal mutton chops and a roast chicken with bread sauce always play the main role, along with boiled vegetables and the English national sauce: melted butter and flour.

Leamington, December 27th, 1826

I NOW FIND myself in a large spa town. I have not seen much of it yet since I only just arrived at eleven at night. A large part of the day was spent in an interesting visit to Woburn Abbey. That beautiful palace has been constructed simply and nobly in the Italian style—infinitely more satisfying than the colossal, Gothic nonsense. With its stables, riding course, dance hall, sculpture and paintings gallery, conservatories and gardens, it forms a small town. For the past three hundred years, this property has been passed down through the same family, something rare *even in England*, so it is not surprising, given annual revenues of what would amount to a million in our money, that an assemblage of such magnificence has materialized here, something that far surpasses the means of any individual in our country to create. All the more so since, even where such wealth is present, we have not had the benefit of a culture that for centuries has provided the resources for such a perfect ensemble of refinement and luxury.

The palace itself is a regular quadrangle, and the *piano nobile*—in the countryside always on the ground level—forms an unbroken suite of rooms wrapping around the entire building. These apartments are adorned with valuable paintings and richly furnished with opulent materials; the ceiling and door embrasures are of white stucco with gold or exotic carved woods, everything just as simple as it is dignified. In one room there was a notable collection of miniature portraits of the family, from the first Russell (the family name of the dukes of Bedford) to the current

---

* I do not know whether the reader will also be able to accept this apology.—*The Editor.*

duke, all displayed in a row. Under such circumstances it is justifiable to feel a little proud of one's family and its nobility! The miniatures were placed very tastefully side by side, medallion-like, on a piece of crimson velvet inside a long, narrow, gilded frame. The stoves are mostly of gilt metal with high marble mantelpieces, and the bronze chandeliers are likewise richly gilded. Everything is suitably magnificent and without excess. At the end is the very inviting library divided into two large rooms, with wide French doors leading directly to the flower gardens.

To me the gardens seemed particularly captivating, yet an exact description is difficult because they are so effectively interwoven with the buildings and also so diverse. But to give you a general idea, let me just mention that all along the garden side of the different buildings—which sometimes jut forward, sometimes recede, sometimes form straight, sometimes curved lines—there is an unbroken arcade covered with roses and climbing vines and bordered by a succession of lovely plantings. Above this walkway are partly rooms and partly the most charming greenhouses, one containing nothing but heathers (*Erica*), of which hundreds were in bloom and multiplied into infinity by the mirrored walls, thus affording the most delightful sight imaginable. Directly below the heather house is the heather garden, a grassy plot with beds of different shapes, all filled with the larger varieties that can survive outdoors. At one spot the arcaded walk itself is interrupted by a towering, mirrored palm house, with the most beautiful embroidered parterres unfurling on beds of gravel that extend in front of it. This palm house is adjacent to the sculpture gallery, its walls clad in different kinds of marble and some very beautiful columns from Italy. The space contains a good many antique statues and is closed on either end by a temple: one is dedicated to freedom, with busts of Fox, Canning, and others; the second is dedicated to the graces, with a magnificent group of these goddesses by Canova.

From here the arcade leads along an immense planting of azaleas and rhododendrons bordering a hill, whereupon you reach the Chinese garden, in which the dairy is especially notable (Figure 22). This is a kind of Chinese temple with a superabundance of white marble and colored glass; at the center is a fountain; and displayed all around the walls are hundreds of large Chinese and Japanese bowls of every kind, all filled with fresh milk and cream. The consoles on which these stand are extraordinarily pretty versions of Chinese furniture. The windows are of frosted glass with Chinese paintings and seemed to glow mysteriously in the dim light.

Between here and the aviary is another pleasure ground with the most beautiful trees and a number of surprising diversions, including a sweet little children's garden and an area containing all kinds of reeds and grasses growing in small beds laid out like a chessboard. The aviary itself is dedicated to the kingdom of the birds and consists of a very large fenced area with tall plantings, a cottage, and a small pond in the middle. The fourth or fifth attendant awaited us here. (Since every one of them expects a tip, you cannot visit such an establishment for less than several pounds sterling.) He showed us a number of richly feathered parrots and other exotic fowl, each granted its own small dwelling and little garden. These bird apartments were made of interlaced oak twigs and wire; the roofs were also of wire; and the bushes as well as almost all the other plants in this precinct were evergreen. When we stepped into the space at the center, our Papageno whistled, and immediately the air above us literally went dark with a myriad of doves, chickens, and heaven knows what kinds of birds. Bolting out of every shrub were gold, silver, multicolored, and ordinary pheasants. Then a black swan galloped awkwardly toward us out of the pond, expressing its great desire to be fed in piteous, childlike tones. This lovely bird, raven black with rosy red feet and bill, was completely tame and ate its feed in transit right out of the

TO HIS GRACE the DUKE of BEDFORD, This View of the DAIRY at WOBURN ABBEY.

22

Dairy at Woburn Abbey.

keeper's pocket, never leaving us alone for a minute the whole time we were wandering around the bird paradise, except when sometimes *en passant* warding off an interloping duck or some other common rabble with a kick, or shoving his beak into the side of a more noble golden pheasant. A second interesting but imprisoned inhabitant of this place was Hero, an African crane, a creature that looks as if it were made of porcelain and often reminded me in its movements of our blessed, dancing Ballerino.[8] The keeper did not know what in its history had supplied the name.

The park, almost nineteen miles in circumference, consists not only of grassland and trees but also has a beautifully forested area and a specially fenced-in section called the "thornery," a wild wood overgrown with prickly bushes and brambles and traversed by a number of paths, with a small cottage and the loveliest little flower garden at its center. This concludes the splendors of Woburn Abbey.

But no, wait! There are still two things I must add. In the house, the trappings of which I have described to you, I also found a very functional amenity, namely, a wide, interior gallery that runs past all the rooms of the large quadrangle. A number of doors open onto this passageway, and here various collections are exhibited—partly freestanding, partly in glass cases, every so often interrupted by flower étagères. In the winter and during bad weather this affords a walk both informative and pleasant, made all the more comfortable because the entire house is kept warm by heating pipes. The second memorable thing is a fine, full-length portrait of the Earl of Essex. His figure is very attractive and slim, although his face is less distinguished: small features without much expression, small eyes, dark hair along with a big red beard, which perhaps made him particularly attractive to the queen, given her own head of red locks.

But now I have written a quarter inch off my fingers and must close. Tomorrow I visit Warwick Castle, said to be the pride of England. I am eager to see if we have yet another level to attain, since so far we have moved steadily from the beautiful to the still more beautiful. The mail is about to depart so I am enclosing this letter in one for Lottum, through whose goodness you will receive it more quickly than you did the last one.

I hope that in your peaceful solitude, you will give a thought to this wandering soul and know that even if fate were to drive him to the antipodes, his heart would always be with you.

Your Lou

℘RECIOUS JULIE!

By heaven! Now, for the first time, I am filled with tremendous enthusiasm. What I described earlier was a bright, smiling nature augmented by all that art and money can provide. Although I have seen such places before, indeed possess one myself, I left it filled with appreciation and even amazement. But what I saw today was more than this. It was a *Zauberwort* cloaked in the most captivating mantle of poetry and surrounded by all the majesty of history.[1] The vision of it still fills me with joy and astonishment.

You, knowledgeable historian and reader of memoirs, know better than I that the earls of Warwick were once the most powerful vassals in England, and that one among them, the great Beauchamp, boasted of having deposed three kings and replaced each in turn. His castle, dating from the ninth century, has been in the family since Elizabeth's reign. One tower, allegedly built by Beauchamp himself, still stands without any alterations, as colossal and mighty as a materialized apparition of ancient times.[2] Already from a distance you can see the dark mass of stone, looming over the age-old cedars of Lebanon, chestnuts, oaks, and lindens, and rising vertically from the rocks along the banks of the Avon to a height of more than two hundred feet above the water's surface (Figure 23). Two towers of differing shapes ascend almost as high again above the castle itself. In the middle of the river stands the broken pier of a bridge, overhung with trees. Farther downstream where the buildings start, the water becomes a frothing cascade that drives the wheels of the mill, itself resembling a low, projecting abutment.

Driving on, you lose sight of the castle for a while and soon find yourself in front of a high, crenellated wall of wide ashlar blocks that have become covered in moss and creepers over time. The doors of a tall iron gate open slowly onto a deeply sunken road blasted through the solid rock, again with the most luxuriant vegetation climbing the walls on either side. The carriage rolls with a muffled sound over the flat rock, shaded beneath towering vaults of ancient oaks. Suddenly, at a bend in the road, the fortress emerges from the woods, resting on a gently sloping lawn in the open light of the sky, and you find yourself at the foot of the two gargantuan towers; between them, the wide arch of the entry gate looks like nothing more than an insignificant doorway. A still greater surprise is in store as you pass through the second gate of iron grillwork and enter the castle courtyard. It is hardly possible to imagine anything more picturesque and at the same time more imposing!

Let your fantasy conjure up an area approximately twice again as large as the interior of the Colosseum in Rome, and imagine yourself there overlooking a vast courtyard, surrounded on every side by a lush, romantic forest of moss-covered trees and majestic buildings

23

View of Warwick Castle.

that, although varying in style, form *one* sublime and cohesive *whole* etched against the sky—sometimes rising, sometimes falling, like the constant undulation of the green expanses on the ground—never betraying symmetry, but rather a *loftier harmony* inherent in the works of nature alone. Your glance falls first on the large, simple carpet of lawn at your feet, around which a gently curving gravel walk leads to every entrance and exit of this gigantic structure. If you turn around, you look up at the two black towers; the oldest, called Guy's Tower, stands majestic and daunting as if cast in iron, isolated and free of any shrubs or trees. The second, built by Beauchamp, is partly obscured by a magnificent chestnut and a centuries-old pine; tendrils of broad-leafed ivy and wild vines reach out across its walls, some twining around the tower, others climbing to its highest point. On your left extend the inhabited part of the castle and the chapel, all adorned with many tall windows of different sizes and shapes; the opposite side of the enormous quadrangle, almost windowless, presents only mighty, crenellated masses of stone, picturesquely interrupted by a few larches of colossal height and some tree-like arbutuses that have grown miraculously tall in this long-sheltered site.

But now the most sublime spectacle of all is waiting just below you, if you lift your gaze. Because on this fourth side is a low, brush-covered basin forming a courtyard, into which the buildings descend for some distance until the castle's serrated walls climb back up a steep slope reminiscent of an Ionian mountain. This hill, the "Keep," is thickly overgrown with shrubs all the way to the top, although they only cover the foot of the towers and walls. Behind, looming high above all the masses of stone, are enormous primeval trees, their smooth branches looking as if they are floating in the air. At the highest point, framed on both sides by the trees, a daring bridge suddenly emerges like a sublime gateway to heaven, allowing the broadest, most radiant mass of light to break through; and you can see the clouds passing in the distance beneath the tall arch of the sky and the trees' dark, leafy crowns.

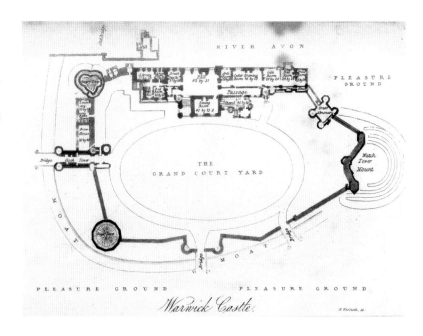

Now imagine: to survey this magical scenery *all at once,* do not forget the vestiges left by nine centuries of haughty power, of bold victories and devastating defeats, of bloody deeds and fierce grandeur, and perhaps also of gentle love and noble generosity; for these have left their *visible* traces, or at least some romantic if elusive reminder. You can then judge with what emotion I put myself in the place of the man whose memories of his forebears are rekindled daily by this spectacle, and who still resides in the same castle as the first owner of Fortress Warwick, that near-legendary Guy who lived a thousand years ago and whose weathered armor, along with hundreds of weapons of renowned ancestors, is still preserved in the ancient hall. Can there be so unpoetic a soul as not to see what a luster such reflections must confer, even on those least representative of *such* nobility?

24

*Warwick Castle,
Ground Plan.*

I am enclosing a ground plan to make my description somewhat clearer and assist your imagination (Figure 24). You must think of the river as flowing deep below the castle courtyard and invisible from the places I have listed so far. The first glimpse of it is from the windows looking out of the inhabited part of the castle (as shown in the engraving). From here you also see the magnificent park closed by woods on every side of the horizon, allowing great latitude for the play of the imagination and, quite on its own, creating a new, romantic vista.

It is only a few steps up from the court into the interior parlors, first through a passageway and then into the hall, where a row of drawing rooms stretches out on either side to a total length of 340 feet. Although these rooms are on nearly the same level as the courtyard, they are more than fifty feet above the Avon on the opposing side. The walls are from eight to fourteen feet thick and create a small, formal recess in each of the windows—themselves ten to twelve feet wide—with the most varied and lovely views of the river as it seethes wildly below and, farther along, flows off through the park in gentle curves toward the dusky horizon.

I had been moving from surprise to surprise since my very first glimpse of this castle, but all this was now surpassed, albeit in a different way, by the interior rooms. I felt myself completely transported into long-forgotten centuries when I entered the gigantic baronial hall, exactly as described by Sir Walter Scott, the walls paneled with carved cedar, hung with every kind of knightly armor, and spacious enough to feed a host of vassals. Then I saw a marble fireplace so tall that I could enter with my hat on and stand quite comfortably next to the flames blazing like a funeral pyre atop a three-hundred-year-old iron grate designed, quite curiously, in the form of a basket. To the side, in keeping with ancient custom, a cord of unsplit cedar had been stacked on a base, also of cedar, in the middle of the stone pavement, which was partly covered by faded *haute-lisse* tapestries. From time to time a servant—whose brown costume with golden knee bands, aiguillettes, and trim looked sufficiently antiquated—would feed the mighty fire with a three-foot log. The difference between the authentic feudal grandeur of bygone days and what is merely imitated in modern dalliances was evident everywhere here, and was just as striking as the difference between the moss-covered remains of a weather-beaten fortress on its rocky point and those ruins built yesterday in the pleasure garden of a newly rich commercial magnate. Almost everything in these rooms was old, magnificent, original, always tasteful, and maintained with the greatest affection. This included the most exceptional, opulent fabrics in mixtures of silk, velvet, gold, and silver all woven together; no one would be able to make such things today. The furniture consisted almost entirely of old, extremely lavish gilding; carved brown walnut and oak; or those old French cabinets and dressers inlaid with brass, the name of which escapes me at the moment.[3] There were also many fine examples of mosaics and inlaid precious woods. A fire screen with a heavy gold frame was made of a single piece of glass so clear that it seemed to disappear. A screen like this has the advantage that when you are sitting next to the flames, you can watch them without scorching your face. In one of the rooms was a state bed presented by Queen Anne to a countess of Warwick; still in good condition, it was covered in red velvet with green and blue silk embroidery.

The art treasures are beyond counting. As for the paintings, there is not a single mediocre one to be found; in fact, they are nearly all by the greatest masters and of particular interest to the family, since a number of them are portraits of their ancestors by Titian, Van Dyck, and Rubens. The greatest treasure, and truly priceless, is one of Raphael's most enchanting pictures, the beautiful Joanna of Aragon (a person difficult to locate historically) (Figure 25). This portrait exists quite unusually in four versions, each outstanding and proclaimed to be the original. Clearly three of them must be copies, yet each is nearly the equal of the others. One is in Paris, the second in Rome, the third in Vienna, the fourth here. I am familiar with all four and must unconditionally give preference to this one as the prototype.[4] There is an inexpressible, magical quality about this magnificent woman! Eyes that delve into the depths of the soul, regal majesty joined with the most feminine receptivity to love, a voluptuous fiery gaze tinged with sweet melancholy. The fullness of the most beautiful bosom; a transparent delicacy of skin; and a truth, radiance, and grace in her garments and the rest of her adornment offer a perfection that only the divine inspiration of such a genius could ever create.

Among the other remarkable portraits of particular interest due to the historical importance of the sitters were the following:

First, Machiavelli by Titian. Just as I have always imagined him—a fine, intelligent face with an element of suffering, as if mourning the contemptible side of the human race that he perceived so deeply: the servile nature that loves only when trodden upon, follows only when afraid, is loyal only when it sees an advantage. A suggestion of compassionate derision hovers over the thin lips, while the dark eye gazes meditatively inward.

It is initially striking that this great classical writer has been so long and absurdly misunderstood. We see him represented either as a moral beast (how ridiculous is Voltaire's refutation in this respect) or we hear the fantastic hypothesis that his book is a satire! On closer consideration one must conclude that only in the modern era—when we have finally begun to understand politics from an elevated, truly humane point of view—can we hope to judge Machiavelli's *Prince* correctly.

25

*Doña Isabel de
Requesens y Enríques de
Cardona-Anglesola.*

This profound and acute mind is explicating something to the "arbitrary" princes. (This is what I call all those who believe themselves princes solely *par la grâce de Dieu* and for their own sake, and those conquerors and lucky devils throughout history who, simply through blind chance, acquired whole nations that they then proceeded to regard as their own property.) Machiavelli is showing these princes the only real way for them to prosper, the exhaustive rules they must follow to maintain a power that from the very beginning thrived in the soil of sin and error. His book is and will remain for all eternity the consummate gospel for such men. And we Prussians in particular should consider ourselves fortunate that in more recent times Napoleon absorbed his Machiavelli so poorly. Had he not, we would likely still be groaning under his yoke!

Yet over this abyss, the relative truth of which is undeniable, we watch the magnificent dawn of the modern era's distinguished prince of the people![5] This new light undermines Machiavelli's entire construct of darkness, however masterfully developed; it collapses into nothingness before this sun's rays. Governance no longer depends on deceit and falsehood, on despotic might, on fear. Humanity and justice—a hundred times more powerful and beneficial for a prince and his subjects—are supplanting that tarnished brilliance, and perpetual war will be followed by eternal peace! Machiavelli sought and hoped for such change, as many passages in his book clearly indicate. Such as when he writes: "Whoever has conquered a *free* city has no *secure* means of holding onto it other than by destroying it or replacing its inhabitants; because no good deed of a sovereign will cause them *to forget their lost freedom.*"[6]

By irrefutably proving that one can acquire such a level of arbitrary power only by disregarding all morality (and what else has politics been until now?), and by offering the princes this lesson in all seriousness, he was also demonstrating all too clearly that the whole of society was founded on perdition, that it bore this principle within itself, and that no true happiness, no true civilization was possible until this was acknowledged and done away with. The revolutions of more recent times and their aftermaths have finally opened people's eyes; they will not be closed again!

The Duke of Alba, by Titian. Extremely expressive and I believe true to life, because this man was not at all just a cruel and sinister caricature. Serious, fanatical, proud, but hard as iron; effectively setting out the idea of a steadfast, loyal servant who, once he has accepted a commission, never deviates to the right or left, always unquestioning in his readiness to execute the will of his master and his God, never asking whether thousands may perish as martyrs in the process. In a word, a vigorous, not ignoble but limited, spirit, who lets others think for him and acts on behalf of a higher authority.

Henry VIII with Anne Boleyn, by Holbein.* The king, in a magnificent costume, is a fat gentleman looking rather like a butcher, whose terribly contented, even jovial, physiognomy is dominated by sensuality, cunning cruelty, and strength! You can see in all this how such a man can make people tremble and yet bind them to him. Anne Boleyn is a true English beauty with a friendly but undistinguished, almost stupid look and a figure that one still sees here often, though in different dress!

---

* Portraits of Henry VIII and Elizabeth are so abundant in England that you must forgive my repeated descriptions of outstanding examples. There is always one or another distinguishing nuance.

Cromwell, by Van Dyck. A splendid head. Something of the bronze gladiator appearance of Napoleon, but with much rougher features; behind these, however, as if behind a mask, glows a great soul. There is perhaps too little expression of enthusiasm, but in contrast his eyes contain a guile that looks almost honest and is therefore more deceptive. Yet nowhere is there a trace of cruelty, something the Protector cannot be accused of, because even the execution of the king—a brutal act, to be sure—seemed in Cromwell's mind an unavoidable and necessary political operation; it was not based on any joy in bloodshed. Cromwell's own helmet hangs beneath his portrait.

Prince Rupert, by Van Dyck. Entirely the bold soldier, every inch a cavalier! You know that in those days the king's retinue all called themselves cavaliers. But what I mean to imply here is someone distinguished and chivalric. A handsome face, dangerous to both women and enemies, and a picturesque warrior's costume and stance.

Elizabeth, by Holbein (Figure 26).[7] The best and perhaps the most faithful portrait I have ever seen of her. She is represented in her prime, rather disagreeably white with very pale reddish hair. She has almost no eyebrows, and her eyes are a bit albinotic; the excess of white gives them a false expression in spite of their artificial pleasantness. You feel that intense desires and insistent passions are hidden beneath this pallid shell like a volcano beneath the snow, and you recognize a vain wish to please in the ornately embellished costume. Portraits of her at an advanced age show a different person: severe, hard, and dangerous to approach, yet still equally overdressed.

Mary of Scotland, painted probably while she was in prison and shortly before her death, for she has the look of a forty-year-old matron. Still a genuine beauty but no longer the reckless Mary who so exuberantly enjoyed life and its charms; instead, visibly reformed by unhappiness, she is *Schiller's* Mary,[8] a noble nature who has at last found *herself* again! This is one of the more unusual pictures of this much-lamented queen, whom we are otherwise accustomed to seeing portrayed as young and radiant.

Ignatius Loyola, by Rubens. A very large, beautifully rendered picture; however you notice at once that it is only a *fiction* and not a portrait. Spiritual in a thoroughly commonplace way, the saintly expression is *vacuous*. The finest thing about the painting is the coloring.

But if I were to continue through the entire gallery, I would never finish. So allow me to lead you into the last small room where there is a lovely collection of majolica and enamels, most after drawings by Raphael. There is also a marble bust of the Black Prince,[9] a hardy soldier in head and fist, from an era when violence alone was often enough to achieve renown.

In addition to the paintings and antiquities, many valuable Etruscan vases and other works of art decorate the various rooms, and it is very commendable that they are displayed in this way and not lifelessly heaped together in a single gallery! It was pointed out to me as noteworthy evidence of the castle's careful and solid construction that, in spite of its age, when all the doors of the enfilade are closed, you can look down the entire length of 340 feet from the very last room—*through the keyholes*—and see the bust standing exactly in the middle of the room at the opposite end! Certainly a remarkable precision that our own craftsmen would find not just unfeasible, but inconceivable. Although the walls of the hall are covered with innumerable pieces of armor, the castle also boasts a separate, extraordinarily well-appointed armory. Among other things preserved there is a leather doublet stained with the blackened blood of Lord Brooke, the current earl's noteworthy ancestor, who was wearing it when he was killed in the battle of Lichfield. In one corner of the room is a quite different, indeed peculiar work of art: a long-tailed

26

Queen Elizabeth I.

monkey cast in iron, but with a perfection and abandon in its pose and limbs that is the equal of nature herself. I was extremely sorry that the lady castellan could not tell me who had made the model for this cast. He must have been a significant artist to so convincingly capture a pose that luxuriates in the most comfortable lassitude while expressing every bit of the creature's grace and suppleness.

Before leaving splendid Warwick, I climbed the highest of the two towers and, in quite fair weather, enjoyed a beautiful expansive vista in every direction. But far more captivating than this panorama was my lengthy walk in the gardens that surround the castle on two sides and in their tranquil grandeur accord perfectly with its character. The height and beauty of the trees, as well as the lushness of the vegetation and lawns, cannot be surpassed, while a host of gigantic cedars of Lebanon and the constantly altering views of the majestic castle—where the cruciform openings in its lofty battlements allow for the ever-changing play of shafts of light—wove such a sense of magic into the whole that I barely managed to tear myself away. We continued to wander the darkening pathways until the moon rose, its light making everything seem even more gigantic. It was therefore only by lamplight that we were able to see the renowned Warwick Vase (Figure 27).[10] It is covered with the most beautiful ornamentation and is colossal in size— large enough to hold several hundred gallons of water. We also saw the ancient relics kept in the porter's lodge. These consist mainly of antediluvian bulls' horns and boars' tusks, said to come from beasts that Guy, legendary Saxon ancestor of the first earls of Warwick, is supposed to have slain. The dimensions of his weaponry, also displayed here, show him to have been a giant of greater strength than nature can fashion these days.

Here, at last, I bade a reluctant farewell to Warwick Castle and tucked the memory into my heart like a dream of an exalted past. I felt in the soft moonlight like a child who sees above the treetops a fantastic Goliath from some distant era nodding his head in a friendly fashion. Such fantasies, good Julia, will accompany me as I fall asleep and be with me again tomorrow, which *also* has something romantic in store: the ruins of Kenilworth!

27

The Warwick Vase.

I WILL GO on with my narrative. The spa town of Leamington (for it is important that I say something about it, too) was just a small village thirty years ago and is now a rich and luxuriant town with ten to twelve palatial inns, four large bathhouses with colonnades and gardens, and several libraries that are connected to card and billiard rooms as well as to concert and dance halls (one of these accommodating six hundred people). In addition, a myriad of private houses solely for the use of the spa guests continually spring from the ground like mushrooms. Everything here is on a massive scale, although the waters are actually very undistinguished, a bit sulfurous and salty. The same water is used for bathing and drinking, and yet the place is teeming with visitors. The baths, as spacious as English beds, are set into the ground, girded at the top with iron plates, and lined throughout with porcelain tiles. There are also special seats on the sides.

We would do well to imitate the practical and elegant shower, which includes a machine that effortlessly moves the chairs bearing the sick and helpless into position. Rehder has made a drawing of it. The waters are taken in a large room the size of a drill hall so people have enough space to move about; and as far as I could determine, the valve handles as well as the pipes emitting the water are made of heavy silver. Like all sulfurous water, this tasted stale and dreadful.

Not far from Leamington, about an hour from Warwick, is an absolutely charming spot called Guy's Cliffe, where there is a small palace, some parts of which are as old as Warwick Castle (Figure 28).[11] Below, on the rocky shore of the picturesque Avon, is a deep cave where that same legendary Guy of Warwick, having achieved so many great exploits at home and abroad, hid himself away in order to conclude his life in pious contemplation. His inconsolable wife never stopped searching for him and finally, after two years, when she was out hunting alone, she found him lying dead in this cave and, in despair, threw herself over the rocks into the Avon. In memory of this tragic event a spacious chapel was later hewn into the rock at the same spot, and it still contains a statue of Guy that was dedicated by Henry III. Alas, the sculpture was so mutilated by Cromwell's troops that it now resembles a shapeless block. Across from the chapel are twelve monk's cells, also carved into the rock and now serving as stables. The interior of the chapel is connected to the owner's residence and has been totally restored. Part of it is several hundred years old and in the Gothic style; a later portion was built in the old Italian manner; and a third, entirely new, was designed in the Gothic style to be homogenous with the earliest part.

The exterior of the whole ensemble is extremely picturesque, and the interior is just as tasteful and attractive. I found the larger drawing room, with its two deep bay windows, particularly inviting. One of the windows stands atop the cliff that plunges thirty feet straight down to the river, which flows around a prettily shaped island near the house. Behind this a broad vista unfolds over lush meadows, beautiful trees, and, far off, a village half hidden in a wood. To the side, at a distance of about one thousand feet, you can see an ancient mill, said to be from the time of the Norman invasion. A bit farther away, but still within the park's boundaries, the picture closes with a bush-covered hill surmounted by a tall cross marking the spot where Gaveston, the infamous favorite of Edward II, was mercilessly executed after being captured by the rebellious magnates Warwick and Arundel. All these reminders, in the company of so many natural beauties, make a profound impression on the visitor. The second window, however, provided the most extreme contrast to the first. Looking out over level ground I saw nothing but a very pretty French flower garden, enclosed by tall trees; vibrant porcelain ornaments and colored sand alternated

with the blossoms. Opposite was a magnificent allée entwined with ivy pruned into pointed arches. In the room itself a cozy fire was burning; fine paintings adorned the walls; and many sofas of varying shapes, tables covered with curiosities, and sundry other pieces of furniture were scattered around in pleasant disorder, making it all look extraordinarily livable and charming.

I returned once more to the city of Warwick to visit the cathedral as well as the chapel with the grave monument to Beauchamp, the great kingmaker.[12] He erected the monument himself already during his lifetime, and he rests there to this day. The statue is of bronze and lies on top of the sarcophagus with an eagle and bear at its feet. The face is very expressive and natural. The hands are not folded, as was usual with old statues of knights, but raised a bit toward heaven, not as if the figure is about to pray but simply as if he wants to greet the dear Lord with appropriate courtesy. It is true that his head is slightly bowed, but by no means does he look submissive! Around the sides of the stone sarcophagus are the brightly painted coats-of-arms of Beauchamp's territories, and a monstrous sword still lies threateningly at his side. The splendid colored windows and myriad well-preserved and richly gilded ornaments give the whole an unusually solemn yet festive appearance. Unfortunately, about one hundred and fifty years ago, a local family was allowed to erect a monument in honor of some country squire or other from their family. This takes up the entire wall opposite the entrance, just below the largest window, and with its repugnant modern flourishes is a real blight on an otherwise lovely and harmonious ensemble.

KENILWORTH CASTLE,
CESAR'S TOWER FROM CLINTON GREEN.

Another interloper stands, or rather lies, on the side wall. But this is a man of more sterling qualities, for he is no less than the powerful Earl of Leicester, portrayed as he was in midlife. He appears to have been handsome, distinguished, and proud looking, but without the geniality in his features that the bronze image of the great Warwick so eloquently expresses.

A few posting houses beyond Leamington, in an area that is more and more desolate and poor, stands Kenilworth Castle (Figure 29).

With Walter Scott's alluring book in my hand, I stepped into these ruins, which evoke such a rush of emotions. They occupy an area more than a quarter of an hour in circumference and, although quickly deteriorating, still bear many traces of their former glory. The oldest part, built in 1120, is still standing, whereas the buildings added more recently by the Earl of Leicester are nearly level with the ground. The great lake that used to surround the castle was drained under Cromwell in the hope of finding sunken treasures there. Beyond this there was once a park thirty miles in circumference, although it, too, has long since vanished, having been turned into fields on which you see a few scattered huts. A separate and secluded part of the castle buildings, almost concealed by vines, has been transformed into a kind of outwork, and the whole stretch has a more impoverished, abandoned, and melancholy appearance than any other part of the countryside we have driven through. Yet this bleakness is not inappropriate to the scene and perhaps deepens the solemn impression of a grandeur fallen so low.

A balcony called Elizabeth's Bower still survives and, according to local legend, a figure in white is often seen there on moonlit nights, gazing down mutely and placidly into the depths. The ruins of the banquet hall with its gigantic fireplace, extensive kitchen, and wine cellars below are clearly recognizable. Indeed a few small lonesome rooms in the towers may still be in good condition, but they have been inaccessible since long ago. The mind takes delight in imagining the past through these remains, and as I clambered over the rubble I often dreamed that I had found the very spot where the nefarious Vernon treacherously pushed the most faithful and unhappy of wives into the eternal night![13] Yet now both the crimes and great deeds that occurred within these walls are equally forgotten, for time has long since covered them beneath its veil. Lost, too, is the eternal cycle of sorrows and joys, the faded splendor, the vain struggle.

The day was dreary. Black clouds rolled across the sky, and behind them a pale yellow glow occasionally broke through. The wind whispered in the ivy and whistled hollowly through the empty windows, here and there detaching a loose stone from the crumbling edifice and hurling it with a clatter down the castle wall. There was no human being to be seen; everything was desolate, eerie—a somber but exalted memorial to desolation.

Yet such moments are actually comforting! For they make you more aware of how fruitless it is to grieve over earthly things. Sorrow—like happiness—lasts only a short time. This evening I myself was again caught up in the eternal fluctuation of human life when, in garish contrast to the lifeless ruins, I was thrust into the prosaic tumult of a crowd concerned only with profit: the steaming, smoking, swarming factory town of Birmingham. The last romantic sight for me was of the fires spewing from the tall chimneys of the ironworks and lighting up the town in every direction as twilight descended. I then renounced the dalliances of my imagination until a more opportune moment.

December 30th, 1826

BIRMINGHAM IS ONE of the most impressive and also ugliest towns in England. It has 120,000 inhabitants, two-thirds of whom are certainly factory workers, and it gives the impression of being nothing but a vast atelier.

Right after breakfast I went to the factory of Mr. Thomason, our consul here. It ranks only second in size and circumference. (Unfortunately the most impressive one of all—where a thousand workers toil daily making an unimaginable array of objects ranging from steam engines with eighty horsepower to livery buttons and pins—has been hermetically sealed off to all foreigners, without exception, ever since the visit of the Austrian princes, whose retinue apparently overheard some important secrets.)

I remained absorbed for several hours in spite of the nastiness, filth, and stench of the holes that serve as the various workshops. I even made a button, which Rehder is going to bring you as a sample of my industriousness. The lower floor is far nicer, and here all the factory's products are displayed: objects made of gold, silver, or bronze; plated and lacquered wares (replicas that surpass even the Chinese originals); steel items of every shape; etc. All are arranged in stunning quantity and with remarkable elegance. There was a copy of the enormous Warwick Vase I described yesterday, in the same scale, cast in bronze and priced at four thousand pounds sterling. Also a splendid table service in silver and plate, worked in such a way that from whatever angle you see it, you can no longer distinguish the plate from the silver. Hence even the top echelons of manufacturing often mix plate with silver the way Parisian ladies mix faux stones and pearls with genuine ones.

I was introduced to a lot of new and pleasant luxuries, both large and small, and my efforts to resist the impulse to buy, an urge so well nourished here, were not totally successful! But I limited myself to trifles, and these will reach you shortly in a well-packed box.

The ironworks with its gigantic steam engines, the needle factory, the steelworks where you find an accumulation of everything from the smallest scissors to the largest fireplace mantle, entire staircases polished to the brightness of mirrors, and every nuance in between—taking all this in fills out a day very nicely. But release me from further description, it is not my métier.

December 31st, 1826

SINCE IT IS Sunday and the factories have the day off, I made an excursion to Aston Hall, the country residence of Mr. Watt. There is admittedly little to be gleaned from a gardening point of view, but the old house contains many curious portraits. Unfortunately an ignorant porter could only inform me about a few of them.

A full-length portrait of Gustavus Adolphus was extraordinarily fine. The affability, dignity, and cleverness; the clear, honest eyes that still manage to express more than that; and the placid but no less firm assurance in his whole demeanor were extremely compelling. Next to him was an excellent bust of Cromwell, which I think to be a better likeness than the painting at Warwick because it accords more with the historical character: coarse and, if you will, common features, but a craggy aspect evident in his whole countenance; here distinctly twinned with that sinister zealousness and demonic cunning that so perfectly characterize the man.

Two cannonballs that Cromwell's troops fired into the house (it was fortified at the time) smashed the banister in two places and have been left just where they fell. The banister remains unrepaired and, ludicrously enough, the whole thing, including the destroyed sections, has a new coat of white paint.

So as not to squander tomorrow as well—there is really nothing to see here besides the factories—I am thinking of heading on to Chester this evening and driving through the night. There we will visit Eaton, Lord Grosvenor's renowned park. Batthyány has described it so magnificently, and according to what I have heard, it certainly boasts everything that *money* can buy. On the following day I will return here, see the remaining factories, and then come back by way of Oxford so I can visit, along with several others, two of the greatest parks in England—Blenheim and Stowe.

Chester, January 1st, 1827

ANOTHER YEAR HAS passed! By no means the worst for me, except for being separated from you. I lit the reading lamp in the carriage and contentedly ran through Lady Morgan's latest novel while we rolled along the level road at a gallop. As soon as the hand of his watch reached midnight, Rehder conferred his New Year's wishes on you and me. Twelve hours later we arrived in Chester, a very old Baroque city.

Although we covered the eighty-nine miles from Birmingham in thirteen hours, I none-theless find that in England, like France, as you move farther away from the capital, the amenities slowly decline: the inns are no longer so good, the post horses increasingly inferior, the drivers dirtier, the dress of the people altogether shabbier, and the busy throng of life more subdued. At the same time the prices increase in inverse proportion, and you are subjected to various swin-dles that almost never occur closer to London because of the strong competition.

The weather in the new year was even more unfavorable to us than in the last: it rained the whole day. As soon as I tidied myself up a bit, we hurried off to see the marvels of Eaton Hall. I was not harboring very great expectations, but even my modest hopes were scarcely fulfilled, for the park and the gardens, albeit of enormous extent, were for my taste the least significant of their type of any I have so far described. And the house awakened the same feelings in me as Ashridge except that it was even more overloaded and far less beautiful in its interior, if a great deal more expensively furnished. I discovered all the pomp and ostentation one might imagine from a man who makes a million of our money every year, but seems not to possess an equivalent degree of taste. In this chaos of neo-Gothic flourishes, I noticed badly painted, modern glass windows and deformed tables and chairs in imitation of highly inappropriate architectural decorations; and there was not *a single* thing that I found worth sketching. It is completely incomprehensible to me how Mr. Lenné, (who must be granted full credit for the beautification of his fatherland) can have written (in the annals of the Berlin *Gartenverein*)[14] that he preferred this park to all others he had seen, a view that English critics have made some fun of. Mr. Lenné's flower garden in front of the new Palais in Potsdam is an imitation of the one here, and I must admit I would have chosen a different model, although admittedly this style is much more appropriate to the Palais than a Gothic castle.

I came upon no art treasures at all, just a few mediocre paintings by Benjamin West. Every bit of magnificence resided in the materials and money expended, such as in the colossal state-rooms and library, which could serve as a riding hippodrome. The large double portrait of the owner and his wife in the dining room is also of little interest except to their acquaintances. Lots of ghastly, miniature Gothic temples disfigure the pleasure ground, which, like the park, has no handsome trees, for the soil is poor and the whole layout does not seem to be all that old. Meanwhile the setting is tolerable, but scarcely picturesque and too flat.

Since we still had some time remaining, we visited the royal palace in Chester, which has been transformed into a superb county jail. Every aspect of its arrangement seemed to me both humane and exemplary. There is an astonishing view from the level of the *corps de logis* (where the courtrooms are) down onto the prisoners in their yards far below. Imagine a high rocky terrace crowned by a castle with two wings. The main part of the building is, as I said, reserved for the courts, which are very spacious, and the wings accommodate the prisoners incarcerated because of debts. The courtyard is laid out as a small garden where the debtors can take walks, and in the depression below the courtyard there is a kind of compound in the form of a star, divided into many compartments by high walls. Behind this lies a half-moon–shaped building where disturbers of the peace, thieves, and murderers are housed. The women are locked up at the far end on the right. Each of the individual rays of the compound includes a flower gar-den crossed with walkways and intended for the use of the prisoners, who, before sentencing, are dressed in gray, but after their conviction in half green, half red. On the lower level in each section of the rear building is a common room where a fire is lit and work done on weekdays. The cells are generous and airy, and the food varies according to the gravity of the crime: for the lowest class only bread, potatoes, and salt. Today, however, since it was New Year's, everyone had been given roast beef, plum pudding, and ale, and they were mostly, especially the women, very animated and made a horrible ruckus with cheers and toasts to the city magistrate who provided the festivities.

The view from the upper terrace is magnificent. It looks over the garden compound, jails, and lovely countryside, where you can see the river coursing along far below, just behind the prisoners' cells; to the side are the roofs and spires of the city in a picturesque jumble and in the distance, the mountains of Wales. Really, all things considered, the officials of our regional high courts at home seldom live as well as the rogues and villains do here.

I thank heaven that we are going to begin our return trip tomorrow since I have had more than my fill of worthy sights and parks. I am very much afraid that you will feel just the same about my monotonous letters. But whoever has said A must also say B, so brace yourself for another dozen parks before we get back to foggy London.

Meanwhile I am sending the present epistle to the capital today, to grant you at least a charitable interval, and I ask God to keep you under his faithful and beneficent protection.

Your eternally devoted Lou

*B*ELOVED FRIEND!

Yesterday I felt very park blaséd and believed I could no longer dredge up any serious interest in that sort of thing, but today I find myself converted. Beyond everything else I have seen I must give *first* preference to Hawkstone, not because of what it has acquired through art or magnificence or aristocratic luster, but because of what it has been granted by nature alone. For nature has accomplished something extraordinary here, indeed to such a degree that had I the power to contribute to its beauty, I cannot imagine (apart from buildings) how I would do so. Absolutely all the requisite elements for an ideal location have been united in this place, as you will gather from a simple description.

Just cast your mind's eye on a piece of land so vast that from its highest point you can sweep your gaze over fifteen different counties. Three sides of this broad panorama rise and fall like the waves of a choppy sea in a regular alteration of hills and low mountain crests. At the horizon these are framed by the extraordinary contours of the jagged rocks and towering mountains of Wales sloping down gently at either end and opening a vista on the fourth side into a verdant plain shaded by thousands of tall trees. There, in the dusky distance, the expanse blends into the clouded heavens above a white strip of fog—the sea.

The Welsh mountains are partly covered with snow, and all the arable land between here and there is so densely interwoven with hedges and trees that at a distance it gives the impression of a light wood occasionally intersected by water and innumerable meadows and fields, some bigger, some smaller. You are now standing right in the middle of this scene on a group of hills looking out over the nearby crowns of ancient beech and oak forests that alternate with the most luxuriant grassy slopes. You see cliffs criss-crossed by veins of gleaming, bright green copper that rise to five or six hundred feet and frequently form deep canyons and welcoming glens. At one of the more somber spots in this wilderness stand the age-old ruins of the Red Castle, a magnificent relic from the time of William the Conqueror.

Now just imagine that this thoroughly romantic mountainscape, looming up from the flat plain completely on its own, is embraced by the silvery bright waves of the Hawk River in a nearly perfect circle. The naturally enclosed space is in fact the park of Hawkstone, a site recognized in this area as so charming that newlyweds from the nearby cities of Liverpool and Shrewsbury have long been in the habit of spending the first weeks of their sweet happiness here, if their wedding takes place during a season of clement weather. This is perhaps why the park is dedicated, contrary to English custom, more to the public than to its owner; in fact, he does not live here at all, and his house, dilapidated and unsightly, is hidden in a corner of the park like an hors d'oeuvre. There is a fine inn, however, which supplies choice beds and reliable sustenance—in the form of food and drink—for young couples, other lovers of whatever type, and all friends of nature. Here we too set up camp and after a substantial breakfast, headed off to cover the long distance on foot since the difficult terrain is impossible to navigate in a carriage. Our clambering promenade, somewhat perilous in the winter, lasted four hours.

We walked toward the copper cliffs on very wet ground (it had, unfortunately, rained and snowed the whole night before), crossing a broad, flat meadow dotted with oaks and grazing herds. The cliffs rise up above a high hillside of old beeches like an overhanging wall, and on the top they are crowned by black conifers, which makes for a lovely sight. In this natural wall is the Grotto, the first major section of the park, approached via a dark, covered path more than a hundred feet long that has been cut into the rocks. Before reaching it you climb uphill through the woods for some time on arduous switchbacks. The Grotto consists of several caves encrusted with all kinds of stones, metallic ores, and minerals. Some openings have been made and set with small, colorful panes of glass that are polished like diamonds and in the darkness resemble Aladdin's precious jewels. An old woman, who must have been at least fifty, was our guide, and repeatedly caused us to wonder at her stamina and nimbleness as she climbed up and down the rocks in her slippers. The irregular, precipitous, and glassy steps in the rock were at times really difficult to negotiate, so that good Rehder, who into the bargain had iron heels on his boots, often managed to reach firm ground again only with the greatest effort and among bitter laments about the extraordinary difficulty of scrambling down the rocks on slippery metal.

We came to a pavilion built of boughs and branches, thatched with heather and adorned with wall hangings of moss, and here we were offered a picturesque view of a baroque-looking hill called the Temple of Patience. The path then turned toward the interior of the forest and led us to the so-called Swiss Bridge, which boldly connects two cliffs. Since the handrail has partly fallen off and the passage is quite vertiginous, this would have signaled the end of all further exploration for my good Julie (had she actually managed to reach this spot). How fine it therefore is at such moments to have so tireless a guide in the realm of imagination as you have in me, one who sweeps you across this Devil's Bridge in a flash and with little effort, and now shows you a tower-like rock looming up darkly above the shining beeches.[1] Thickly overgrown by brambles and with ivy hanging down in hundreds of garlands, it provided a fox with shelter from pursuing hounds. For many years he made it his Castle Maleperduys. This is an authenticated fact and has given the rock the name: Reynard's House. Our guide even claimed that a new occupant had taken up residence, but we saw no trace of him. We continued on uphill and down until, already quite tired, we finally reached the terrace, an open spot with beautiful prospects cut individually through the woods.

Not far away, behind some very tall trees, stands a 120-foot column dedicated to the patriarch of the owner's family, a merchant and lord mayor of London from the time of Henry III.[2] His statue crowns the column. A convenient spiral staircase in the interior takes you to the top and the marvel of a panoramic overlook of the fifteen counties I described above. From here you pass through profoundly isolated and ever wilder ravines until you reach a pretty cottage at the end of an inviting meadow valley. Various exotic animals and birds were once kept here, although now they are stuffed and mounted residents of a single room. We were amused when the young female attendant showing us around said of them, "All the animals you see here used to live before."

I will skip the greenhouse (built of chunks of rock and branches of trees) as well as the Gothic tower (a kind of summer house) and escort you again a long, long way through the woods, next over meadow-covered hills and through a narrow ravine, then laboriously back up a mountain again to the magnificent ruin, the thrillingly situated Red Castle. Its weathered walls and ramparts hewn into the cliffs extend a long way. The interior is accessible only via a narrow winding path, two feet wide and blasted into the rock. It was so dark that I found myself forced to hold onto my guide's skirts like the thread of Ariadne because I literally could not see my hand in front of my face. You exit this gorge into a picturesque, rocky passageway with high, smooth walls overarched by mountain ashes and other fruit-bearing trees. To the side is a cavern with a wide opening still closed by rusted grating. Ascending a difficult stone staircase you finally reach the topmost part of the ruin, a soaring, roofless tower with walls fifteen feet thick in which many hundred-year-old trees have taken root. Here a bottomless well seems to plunge to the very bowels of the earth, and as you look down over the solid and well-preserved barrier surrounding it, the contrast between the height of the tower above you, where the sky looks in, and the bottomless depths below you, where eternal night reigns, makes a powerful impression. You imagine that you are seeing despair and hope allegorically bound together into a *single* image. The tower and the cliff on which it stands plunge in the same perpendicular line into the vertiginous depths, toward the valley where enormous trees look like mere saplings.

Fifteen minutes and a fairly strong leap of the imagination got us from there to the hut of a New Zealander. The dwelling was built many years ago (for these sites are very old) and was modeled on a drawing of Captain Cook's. It stands on a small lake and is stocked with arrows, tomahawks, the skulls of devoured enemies, and other endearing trifles that made up the innocent indulgences of those children of nature.

Here we ended our promenade, neglecting to visit several things we deemed unworthy of this magnificent spot: a cave where a hermit automaton recites poetry; a silly rendition of Neptune carved in sandstone; a Chinese temple made of wood; and a modern citadel, also of wood, where several cannons can be fired during celebrations or by special request. These sites of pseudo-art as well as the paths leading to them have unfortunately all fallen into disrepair since the owner no longer lives here. But like the above-mentioned follies, they are but minor deficiencies in an exalted whole that radiates wondrously in all the variousness of its natural beauty.

Newport, January 3rd, 1827

IT HAS BECOME fully and earnestly winter, the earth is covered in ice and six inches of snow, and in rooms only rarely warmed by inadequate fires, the cold is almost unbearable. Having spent nearly all of today in the carriage, there is nothing further to report.

Birmingham, January 4th, 1827

WE DID NOT see anything notable along the way today either, except for driving through one park that looked as if most of it was newly laid out. A small but pretty garden offered very nice models for flower stands and trellises as well as attractive baskets, all made delicately of iron wire and covered with creeping plants. Rehder had to make drawings of them despite his icy fingers.

The inn where we ate our luncheon is more than two hundred years old, for it bore the date 1603. It was in the old style with various half-timbered designs, and the prettiest specimen of such a cottage that I have come across on our tour. Toward evening, with the cold growing more and more bitter, we reached Birmingham, where I will now have a comfortable rest.

ONCE AGAIN, as during my early sojourn here, the entire day was devoted to factories and looking at displays of their wares. But the poor workers sometimes have a bad time of it! The wages are adequate, true, yet often the tiniest oversight, the smallest error can be horrifically dangerous. For instance, today I saw someone whose job it is to hold the die during the stamping of the livery buttons, and he has already had his thumb shattered twice in the process so that it is now nothing more than a small, misshapen lump of flesh. And woe to those who let their garments come too close to the steam engines and other machines! Several have been seized by this merciless force and crushed just like an atrocious boa constrictor squeezes its helpless prey. At the same time many of the jobs are as unhealthy as those in the lead works of Siberia, and in some cases the stench is so overpowering that an unaccustomed visitor cannot tolerate it for more than a minute.

Everything has its drawbacks, including these highly developed industries, but this is not a reason to condemn them. Virtue itself, after all, is not altogether untarnished when it oversteps the bounds of moderation; and even vice has its lighter moments.

It is notable that regardless of the progress in all their inventions, the English—according to Mr. Thomason's own testimony—still cannot equal the fine iron casting of Berliners. The examples I saw were deeply inferior. Despite the fact that the English are so far ahead of us, it often seems to me as if the moment might already have arrived when *they* begin to lapse and *we* to emerge. Since they must sink from such heights and we must rise from such depths, however, it will be a long time before we achieve the same level. Still we seem to be heading toward each other, so good luck, Germany! If your people can only obtain *freedom,* then all their aspirations may be achieved.

TODAY'S JOURNEY WAS not lengthy, but it was very significant, because the place named in the dateline of my letter is Shakespeare's birthplace! How deeply moving to see these insignificant objects that centuries ago were in direct, domestic contact with such a great and beloved man, and then to visit the place where his bones have decayed for so long, thus being transported from his cradle to his grave in just moments.

Both the house he was born in and the very room where that great event took place remain almost unchanged. The modest chamber hardly differs from the middle-class rooms found in our own small towns nowadays and is aptly suited to a time when an English village bore the same level of culture as that attained by the common man in Germany today. Countless names, of kings and beggars alike, are inscribed on the walls of this small space; and though I am not particularly fond of clinging to foreign greatness in this way—rather like insects affixed to the walls of a marble palace—I could not resist the urge to add my own name to the others in a spirit of profound gratitude and reverence.

Next to the Avon, the same river that sweeps past the noble walls of Warwick Castle, stands the church where Shakespeare lies buried. A lovely remnant of antiquity, it is adorned with many notable monuments, naturally the most preeminent being of the immortal poet himself. His memorial used to be painted in bright colors and gilded, as was his bust, but due to the stupidity of a certain Malone, it was whitewashed almost one hundred years ago, which destroyed much of its special character. The bust, by the way, lacks all expression and is of no particular artistic value; it is probably a bad likeness as well. Only with a lot of effort and money was I able to acquire a small picture of it in the original colors, the last that the verger's wife had available. I am enclosing it with this letter.

I managed to find a bookshop where I bought several views of the place and objects I have mentioned. There is a large picture of Shakespeare in the city hall, painted fairly recently, and a still better one of Garrick, who looks a bit like Iffland in his features and general appearance.

Oxford, January 7th, 1827

AFTER GIVING OUR parkomania a two-day rest, we made up for lost time by visiting no fewer than four large parks today, the last of them the famous Blenheim. So let's start—but in order.

We first passed through Eatrop Park, which is remarkable for being from that transitional era when people were just starting to abandon the French manner and lost their way. Thus, instead of allées of *individual trees* they planted allées of differently shaped *clumps*, yet always in regular alternation; or they laid out groves in serpentine lines and built perpendicular mountainsides out of irregular terraces. The whole place looked totally derelict.

Ditchley Park is a more beautiful estate. Unfortunately the English climate played a nasty trick on us today. The sun had beamed down in the morning (only the second time since we left London, I think), and we were feeling triumphant, when suddenly such a fog enveloped us that for the whole rest of the day we could see no farther than a hundred steps, sometimes scarcely ten. Inside the residence we found a number of paintings, especially some beautiful portraits, although no one could tell us whom they represented. We learned nothing new regarding *our* art, but we did see something novel on the exterior of the hunting lodge, namely, in place of actual predators, six dozen rats had been nailed up, their tails and legs spread out quite elegantly.

The third in the series was Blandford Park, which belongs to Lord Churchill and is thoroughly insignificant, although we did find some splendid works of art in the house. I was especially envious of the owner for two paintings. The first represents a captivating female nude in a reclining pose who smiles mischievously through her fingers. It is ascribed, certainly incorrectly, to Michelangelo. The draftsmanship is bold, but there is also an honesty and elasticity in the flesh, a Titianesque coloration and a sweetness of expression that do not suggest Michelangelo, even though it may be unfounded to think, as many do, that no oil paintings exist by this master.

The second picture appealed to me even more: a Judith, allegedly by Cigoli, a painter whose works I do not recall having seen. I usually find this subject more repulsive than pleasant—the triumphant virgin bearing the severed, distorted head in her hand. Yet what a poetically construed expression I saw in Judith's exalted and appealing countenance! A whole world of emotions is contained in these meaningful features. The face is no longer that of a virgin but already of a youthful *woman*. Clear traces of the past are legible in her brimming eyes, and a gentle trembling around her voluptuously swollen, almost rapturous lips reveals to us that she has become acquainted with passion, if only against her will! But the love of God and fatherland was stronger in her mind, and she therefore held firm to her mission. The victim had to be sacrificed, but no *triumph* swells in her breast. Meditatively she strides forward, brooding over thoughts that may not be entirely clear to her. Her delicate hand clutches the locks of hair on this dreadful though virile and handsome head. She carries it off as if she were scarcely conscious of her actions.

I am taking careful note of all these lovely paintings so I can someday have them copied, if ever I have the leisure to do so. I much prefer good copies of *magnificent pictures* to mediocre or unappealing originals, even those by the most famous masters. Only the *poetic,* not the *technical* aspects of a work of art can truly excite me. So as not to be too prolix, I will skip over a valuable collection of drawings by Raphael, Claude Lorrain, and Rubens, as well as several interesting portraits.

The loathsome fog grew more and more dense, and so we saw Blenheim only as if at twilight. In its splendor and grandeur it must be called extraordinary, and I very much liked what I could see, or better intuit, for everything was enveloped in a magical veil through which the sun, without rays, glowed like a moon. The palace is extremely large and regular, built in the old French style unfortunately, and like a royal palace in its magnificence. The park is twenty-three miles in circumference, and the artificially excavated lake, the most splendid of its type, covers 250 acres (Figure 30).[3] The pleasure ground is equally vast, and forty people are at work every day keeping it mowed. Across from the palace is an artificial cascade where the water plunges down over immense chunks of blasted rock that were carried here from far away. The imitation of nature is so deceptive that, unless you were told, you would hardly suppose that art had any role in it.

As you wander through these grounds, you have to admire Brown's great genius. He is the Garden Shakespeare of England. And his plantings have grown tremendously large; we found, for instance, a massive, dense Portuguese laurel that was two hundred feet in circumference!

The current owner has annual revenues of seventy thousand pounds, yet he is so badly in debt that his assets are managed on behalf of his creditors, leaving him just five thousand a year for the rest of his life. What a shame that he expends this paltry amount on dismantling Brown's imposing gardens and modernizing them in accord with a newer, wretched taste, using innumerable plants, beds, and clumplettes to transform the rich vestments that Brown had lavished on nature into nothing but harlequins' jackets. A large portion of the old pleasure ground has already been destroyed in this manner, as the aged gardener showed us, almost with tears in his eyes. Several of the colossal trees had been felled and were still lying there, and a black spot on the grass marked where a laurel, almost as large as the one I just described, had been standing until very recently in all the richness of its glory. I thought with sorrow how futile it is to try to found something lasting, and in my thoughts I already envisioned that successor of mine who will one day likewise destroy my own park, which you and I together have constructed and tended with so much love!

Blenheim was mostly laid out on the same spot as the ancient royal park of Woodstock (which you will recall from Walter Scott's most recent novel), and a large section of the oak wood, probably dating from the time of the unhappy Rosamond, is still verdant, its inevitable demise happening only slowly in a century-long agony.[4] You find oaks and cedars here that are true monsters in their shape and size. Many are so densely wrapped with ivy that it has killed the trees while conveying to them new and more beautiful evergreen foliage, enveloping the weathered trunks in a magnificent natural shroud until they finally crumble into dust.

Fifteen hundred deer, a host of pheasants, and numerous herds of sheep and cattle inhabit the park. Expanses of meadowland seem to stretch out in the amorphous mist like a boundless

VIEW OF BLENHEIM, OXFORDSHIRE. THE SEAT OF HIS GRACE THE DUKE OF MARLBOROUGH.

sea, in some places as barren as a steppe, in others thickly studded with woods and groupings of trees and shrubs.

30

Blenheim Castle and Park.

Due to the owner's economic straits, the interior of the palace looks somewhat dilapidated, but it contains a lot of very valuable art treasures. One must admit that no nation has ever given one of her great men a more worthy reward in money and property than Blenheim was for the Duke of Marlborough. It can be called princely down to the smallest detail. As you enter the palace you pass first through a gate shaped like a triumphal arch, on top of which is a cistern that supplies all the buildings with water. Then you step into a spacious courtyard where the kitchens and other domestic offices are found, and from there you finally reach the great court, which affords an open view toward the park and is closed only by an iron grille. On the other side, a third courtyard forms the pendant to the first and contains the stables.

Many cupolas make the palace even more imposing. The hall, 150 feet high, is topped by one of these, making it taller than most towers. Its domed ceiling is occupied by a beautiful fresco. When we entered, a burly stove was emitting such dense smoke that we thought we'd encountered a second fog *inside* the house. A few extremely dirty, almost ragged servants—something unheard of in such establishments here—ran past us and fetched the chatelaine, who, wrapped in a Scotch plaid, with a little wand in her hand and the demeanor of a sorceress, bore down on us so majestically that one could easily mistake her for the duchess herself. The magic wand was for pointing more conveniently to the various highlights. She began by requesting that we inscribe our names in a large book, because on certain days most of Blenheim is open to the public. Unfortunately the inkwell was out of ink, so this step had to be left undone. Afterward we went through many unheated and very faded chambers decorated with numerous beautiful paintings intermixed with many a mediocre one, all generously endowed with the names Raphael, Guido, etc.[5] The gallery seemed rich in lovely and authentic Rubenses, the most appealing being his own self-portrait, a subject he repeated often; but this one was exceptionally well done. I was also intrigued by a full-length portrait of the infamous Duke of Buckingham by Van Dyck. It depicts a *roué* of a totally different kind from the modern variety, as much in his fine features as his chivalrous decorum and tasteful costume. There was a lovely Madonna by Carlo Dolci, less smooth and banal than others by this artist. A truly excellent and highly characteristic portrait of Catherine of Medici shows her as very pale, with exquisite hands, and a strange expression of cold passion, if I may put it that way, but without eliciting the unfavorable reaction one might expect. Rubens's wife, hanging next to her, represents the opposite pole: a charming Flemish housewife, somewhat common in appearance but magnificently painted and brilliantly conceived. A Philip II by Titian seemed insignificant to me, whereas two beggar boys by Murillo were outstanding. Lot and His Daughters by Rubens. The girls are somewhat less coarse and awkward than most of this artist's beauties, who have all too much affinity to the products of his homeland. But the old Lot is the incomparable model of an aged, drunken sensualist. The theme, by the way, was treated with more indecency than art should allow for sacred subjects.

Hanging in the bedroom was, strangely enough, a repulsively gruesome picture of Seneca's death in the bath, showing him already a greenish corpse. The Lot would have been more suitable here. There was a very appealing portrait of the duke's mother playing with her son by Joshua Reynolds, certainly the best of all English painters. The beauty, gentle sweetness, and childlike air of the duchess were almost worthy of a Madonna, and the little boy was a true god of love, full of mischief and grace. A large portrait of Charles I on horseback by Van Dyck is quite famous and cost ten thousand pounds, although its subject is really too hackneyed. There is also a large panel here from Raphael's earliest period, in the manner of Perugino or perhaps even by him. It represents the Virgin and Child with Saints Nicholas and John. I did not like the expression of the figures and mention the painting only out of respect for the artist's name.[6]

The library is a splendid room filled with seventeen thousand volumes. On one side is a marble statue of Queen Anne; on the other, an odd pendant, is a colossal, antique bust of Alexander, an ideal of youthful beauty that to my mind surpasses the face of the Apollo Belvedere. It is more human and yet shows a godlike man among men, albeit in a pagan, not a moral Christian sense.

It is only fair to mention the portrait that adorns the library, namely that of the great Duke of Marlborough, the person responsible for creating this amazing place. His story is notable in more than one respect, and I recommend, especially *to anyone wanting to make his fortune*, that it be carefully studied, for a lot can be learned from a character so well-suited to making progress in the world. The following little-known anecdote has always seemed remarkable to me, however insignificant the event was *an sich.*

One day when he was out riding with his retinue, the duke was surprised by a sudden rain shower. He quickly asked his groom for his overcoat, and when it was not brought immediately, he repeated the order with a certain urgency. This irritated the servant, who replied with an impertinent look, "I hope you will at least wait long enough for me to unbuckle it." The Duke, without displaying the slightest irritability, turned with a laugh to his neighbor and said, "I wouldn't want to have this man's temperament for anything in the world."

A disposition with a very similar power of self-control is revealed in the better-known story of the Countess of Castlemaine, whose petulance Churchill (the name of the duke at that time) knew how to make such good use of. It provided, in the strangest way, the foundation for the great hero's career.[7]

In the darkness of a foggy night we reached Oxford, where I alit at the Star and bolstered myself with an excellent dinner, thanks to a French cook from London who ended up here. Although I do not bestow *religious* veneration on cooks, as the ancients did, I cannot deny a small reverence for their art. *Il est beau au feu* can be said just as well about such a virtuoso in the kitchen as it can about a daring warrior.[8] As for diplomacy and politics, there is probably no minister so ungrateful as not to recognize how much he owes to his cook.

My excursion is now nearing its end, and in three days I hope to send Rehder back to you like a bee full of honey, with all the materials we have collected.

January 8th, 1827

OXFORD IS AN uncommon town. Surely such an array of magnificent Gothic buildings from three hundred to a thousand years old cannot be found clustered together in the same spot anywhere else. There are places here that transport you back to the fifteenth century because gathered around are nothing but monuments from that time, without a single modern interruption. Many, indeed most, of these old colleges and churches are also very beautiful in their details, and all are highly picturesque in effect. I have often wondered why some aspects of this architectural style have not been adopted for our modern dwellings; for example, the luminous windows sometimes alternating with large bays. Not only beautiful but practical, these are divided into two or three sections and distributed asymmetrically. Habit alone can make us tolerate the monotonous rows of rectangular holes we call windows.

I went first to the three-hundred-year old theater,[9] as they call it, built by a bishop and intended only for clerical actors. The herm-like pillars of the iron grille surrounding it are topped with the heads of Roman emperors, a strange idea, but the effect is not bad. In keeping with its origins, this theater looks more like a church, and here the emperor of Russia, the king of Prussia, and the prince regent were appointed doctors and thus compelled to appear in red doctoral robes. Their portraits have been displayed here ever since: in the center in a magnificent frame is the king of England wearing his coronation regalia, an outstanding painting by Thomas Lawrence, a rendering worthy of former times; the Russian emperor and Prussian king, also by Lawrence, hang on either side, framed much more modestly and in less fancy dress. It is not a good likeness of the king of Prussia, but I have never seen a better picture of Emperor

Alexander. Blücher likewise received the robe of doctor here, and on the occasion remarked that since the gentlemen were making sovereigns into doctors, *he* could expect no more than to become an apothecary.

At the University Stereotype Press, where it takes only five seconds to print a double-sided sheet, I again showed my spontaneity and had the honor of printing a page from the Bible, which I am sending along to you as a companion to the Birmingham button. It contains some interesting episodes about the Maccabees.

A lot of printing is done here for Bible societies, and if this continues at the same rate, we will soon reach the time prophesied by the journal *Der Katholik* in 1824: "If there ever comes a time when everyone reads the Bible, then the world will be nothing but an abode for wild animals."[10] If this means that everyone will then understand and abide by the Bible, it may be correct, because the whole of mankind might then be ripe for a loftier existence on another planet. I nonetheless agree with *Der Katholik* that the indiscriminate distribution of Bibles, even to the most ignorant savages, is throwing out the baby with the bathwater.

From here I strolled over to the museum, which houses a wide diversity of objects. Just as you enter, you see in the stairway a picture of the Battle of Pavia in which the most important figures are painted from life and named in inscriptions next to them.[11] The style is that of old miniatures, and the historical accuracy of the costumes and armor is particularly noteworthy. At the bottom is an inscription: *Comen les gens de Lempereur deffirent les francoys en lan 1525.*[12]

In the same stairway hang portraits of Cardinal Wolsey, Cardinal Richelieu, and many other historical figures. One of them is Tradescant, a famous gardener to Charles I.[13] I could hardly drag Rehder away from it; he kept contemplating the picture with what seemed a protective attitude and was especially pleased by a garland of carrots and cucumbers twined picturesquely around this forefather of gardeners. For me the most interesting thing was a creature that looked like something straight out of the *Arabian Nights*: a strange, large bird called a dodo. When alive it belonged to this gardener, and nothing like it has ever been seen again. As proof that this story was not a fable, we were shown the dodo's outlandish head and beak in the museum.[14]

In the natural history collection was an exhibit of a host of parrots, some very rare. There was also another peculiar bird with spines on its wings, which it uses like lances to impale little fish; this diminutive soldier, only six inches tall, looks uncommonly impudent, like an ostrich in miniature, only much more clever and belligerent. Also worth seeing was the platypus, a kind of colossal water rat with webbed feet and a duck's bill. It comes from Australia, that strange part of the world that produces things so alien to the rest of the natural realm that you almost suppose it belongs to a different era of creation or was once shed by a passing star and fell down to our earth.

There was a picture made of hummingbird feathers in which the colors looked supernatural. Just as surprising was the bas-relief of a magnificent knight in gilded green armor made out of the wings of rose chafers. It would be a good satire on today's country gentry if such a knight were depicted in the blue armor of the dung beetle.

There are too many different things in the curiosity cabinet to describe as a proper antiquarian would, so I must limit myself to what I found most appealing, even if not always of the greatest significance. First, then, a glove of Henry VIII's set with precious gems and an extremely well-preserved, almost Chinese-shaped easy chair of his. Further, a letter to Lord Burghley by the hand of Queen Elizabeth, very elegantly written, along with some pretty little riding spats and shoes of the Maiden Queen, which at the least reveal a most delightful foot. Finally her watch with a tasteful chain consisting of five medallions, one below the other, each containing hair of a different color, probably from her various minions. Still more remarkable is a medallion with a crude portrait in mosaic and an inscription asserting that it belonged to King Alfred. This rare remnant of ancient days was found by someone just ten years ago while plowing a field on the Isle of Athelney, where Alfred once hid away from the Danes.[15]

I will simply mention quickly: the copy of a Chinese ship (a junk) the size of a rowboat, so that one could easily take it for an excursion on the water; a model of the so-called Druidic Temple from Stonehenge; a very complete collection of fossilized bones; and so forth. Now let me lead you into the picture gallery, built by Elizabeth, and preserved entirely in statu quo. The ceiling is adorned with wooden coffers, each with a coat-of-arms, all looking very ancient and magnificent. In the foyer are very well-executed plaster models of the most famous temples of antiquity. Some of the paintings are superb. The loveliest is a portrait of Mary Queen of Scots—authentically by the hand of Zuccaro—painted immediately after her arrival from France while she was still glowing with all the freshness and indescribable charm of her youth. It is easy to understand how this woman could have only zealous admirers or rabid enemies. One almost never sees a face that is more *attractive* in the true sense of the word, or more enticing. But despite all its French gracefulness, it nonetheless reveals how headstrong her beauty was, how reckless her passions. Yet there is no trace of wickedness or vulgarity—neither the wickedness seen in Elizabeth and Catherine of Medici, nor the vulgarity in Queen Anne. She is in fact truly womanly and thus *entirely* seductive, endowed to an elevated degree with all the *virtues* and *weaknesses* of her sex. To possess such a portrait would be the greatest bliss. To possess the original might prove too much to handle!

The same artist also painted Elizabeth, a portrait that is identical to the one I described at Warwick. The Earl of Leicester, portrayed shortly before his death, is likewise of great interest. His face is both distinguished and handsome, and although it does not disclose great genius, its expression is nonetheless that of an intelligent man, dignified and powerful in his propriety. Nothing is left of the radiance of youth, although there is that certain proud ease of a confident, steadfast benevolence. In a copy of *The School of Athens* by Giulio Romano, I again admired the marvelous face of the young Duke of Urbino, an ideal of gentle, youthful beauty that the loveliest of girls might long for.[16] Most important in this collection, however, is a self-portrait by Raphael himself.[17] Garrick's portrait by Raphael Mengs did not correspond to my notion of him as much as the portrait in Stratford, but I was much pleased by Schröder's full-length picture of Charles XII (every inch a grand Don Quixote) and by a very characteristic portrait of Charles II by Peter Lely.[18] I find that the king's features, like his conception of the world, appear thoroughly French and are strikingly similar to those of Bussy Rabutin. Charles's father hangs next to him in an unusually attractive likeness. He has a handsome face, of course, with expressive eyes, but his soft, long-suffering, philosophical expression is enough to reveal that the bearer of such features would have been unequal to a man like Cromwell, not to say a match for the age in which he lived. For a man of high standing, the greatest misfortune is to be born into an unjust time yet not have the greatness to put his own stamp on it. The great philosopher Locke, painted by Gibson, looks like a gaunt bookworm. Next to him is a handsome, plump Luther by Holbein; the stately Handel, by Hudson;[19] and a portrait of Hugo Grotius with a face that is fine, sly, and yet chivalric and honorable, looking like a vigorous man of the world rather than a scholar. These are most of the objects that especially appealed to me.

TODAY I FINALLY took a stroll around Oxford, and I can barely express the kind of inner enjoyment I felt wandering from cloister to cloister in this Gothic town, recalling times long past. There is a magnificent allée of elms here that dates back to 1520, as do the buildings visible from the same promenade. Not a single tree is missing from this queen of all allées, and as it passes through the middle of a meadow bordering the water, you see a delightful landscape on one side and, on the other, part of the town with five or six exquisite Gothic towers. This is already a magnificent vista *an sich*, but today it was almost like an enchanted fairy tale, with an overcast sky across which the wind chased black, fantastic clouds like the Wild Hunt,[20] until finally a splendid rainbow arched over the whole city, as if springing up from one tower and plunging down into another.

I will take the most agreeable memories with me of all the colleges in this ancient abode of the muses: each different from the others and of a different era; each enclosing a large courtyard and decorated with magnificent towers; each with a more or less ornate church; each with a library and a picture gallery; and all, in their way, of unflagging interest. If you can bear drinking again and again from the same well, let me lead you around a bit more.

My first walk this morning was to the Radcliffe Library, a round building located more or less in the center of town and of recent date; that is, built in the previous century at Dr. Radcliffe's expense.[21] Its interior is nothing but a rotunda rising three stories up, topped by a cupola, with two rows of open galleries one above the other; the books (on medicine and natural science) are stored in the side rooms radiating out from the central circle. Casts of the best classical statues are standing against the pillars below. A small, beautifully constructed spiral staircase leads up a little side tower giving access to the last gallery, which is on the roof encircling the dome; from here you have a beautiful view of the Gothic palaces with their thousands of spires reaching toward the skies. The surrounding landscape is also pleasant, fertile, and densely treed. In this small town of only sixteen thousand inhabitants, there are twenty-four colleges (a kind of cloister for education) and thirteen churches.

From here we visited the library built by Henry VIII, which has been kept mostly in its primitive condition, both externally and internally, and houses no fewer than three hundred thousand volumes. The place is unique of its type, and the interior, too, completely transports you into bygone centuries: its cruciform shape; the strange cabinets and iron grilles—half blue, half gilded—in a form no longer seen today; the monstrous windows, as broad as three church windows together and filled with the loveliest stained glass; the colorful, gilded ceiling with innumerable coffers, each one containing the image of an open Bible with four crowns; even the old costumes still worn by the faculty who sit at the tables dressed in the garb of Luther. The imagination is extraordinarily moved by such sights! A gallery goes around midway up the tall shelves so that the higher books can be reached, and underneath it is another ceiling with painted coffers. On the railing hang the portraits of the various librarians, from the first to the last; those unlucky enough to be in modern dress look like apes among their dignified ancestors. In the central section of the room, the shelves have been set up on both sides so that they form a long passageway of enclosed spaces where anyone who wants to use the library can work undisturbed, a venerable and exemplary arrangement.

Apart from this central space, the remaining books are kept in rooms occupying the entire first floor of the square building. Very notable manuscripts and early printed books are preserved here, and one cannot but regret what German *poverty* has sacrificed to English *wealth*: for example, a splendid copy of the oldest Fust Bible of 1440,[22] which I think used to belong to our Doctor Barth and is covered with annotations in his hand. It was truly a joy for me to find a manuscript so very like the one section of Froissart in our own library (the one with miniatures on every page), adorned with the same arabesques of fruits and flowers on a gold ground and so similar in style and in the coloring of the images that it is almost certainly by the same artist. Unfortunately it bears neither a name nor date. The text is Curtius's history of Alexander, although all the figures appear in costumes from the period in which this copy was written, as is also the case with the French and English knights in the Froissart, so that Alexander, covered from head to toe in iron, takes up his lance against Darius and knocks him roughly out of his saddle.

A remarkable French manuscript containing an heroic poem is inscribed with the name of the writer and the date 1340 (an extreme rarity) and below this the name of the artist and the date 1346, suggesting that it took the latter six years to complete the miniatures, nearly all of which are painted on a very unusual, diapered background of gold, blue, and red squared off in different directions and resembling a carpet. This document is especially interesting because on every page that bears a picture, the illuminator has surrounded the text not with a border or arabesque but instead with representations of the trades, games, and diversions of his own era. A quick glance was enough to see that in addition to a host of games and activities that we no longer recognize, there were also a great many that are amazingly similar to those we enjoy now. For instance: a masked ball; *Kämmerchen vermieten*;[23] the hand game called *gioco di villano*;[24] a comparable foot game (an exercise we lads once played in order to keep warm in winter); *Hahnenschlag* and cockfights;[25] tightrope walkers and magicians; trick riders and trained horses executing much more difficult feats than anyone manages today; target practice where (*mille pardons*) you aim at a man offering his bare backside to the company (a similar target is still to be found in Brody, Lusatia); a blacksmith's shop where a horse is being shod in a shoeing frame; a freight wagon with three large cart horses harnessed one in front of the other and with side racks, harnesses, etc., all looking the same as they do today (even including the driver's costume, a blue shirt); and many other things that there is no time to list now—all this proved that many things change, but infinitely more stay the same, and perhaps on the whole our former activities look much more similar to the present than we tend to imagine.

One of the library's most elegant showpieces is a Boccaccio with extremely beautiful miniatures and superb writing. Also among its greatest rarities is a seventh-century *Acts of the Apostles* written in Latin and Greek, with each line containing just *one* word in the two languages. It is very well preserved considering its great age.

From a spot in the beautiful quadrangle of All Souls College (which is covered with the finest lawn), you have an especially splendid view of the continuous spires and facades of the ancient buildings rising over one another without the slightest intrusion of modernity. Here is yet another library of seventy thousand volumes set out in a room 120 feet long and 60 feet high. In the middle is an orrery that represents our entire solar system in an extraordinarily simple way, keeping pace with the sun and planets throughout the year.[26]

Christ Church College is a beautiful structure of more recent date, only one part of it being really ancient. The church is in the Old Saxon style, and its classical columns alternate with round and pointed arches in a way that is peculiar but not at all offensive to the eye. The famous shrine of St Frideswide is here, an exceedingly magnificent and tasteful Gothic tomb from the beginning of the eighth century, thus well-preserved for twelve hundred years.[27] It was once adorned with silver apostles and other embellishments, but these were plundered under Cromwell, just as that unhappy religious war irreparably damaged ancient monuments all over England, objects that until then had been flawlessly conserved.

There is also a charming walk at this college that I have already described to you. It led us to the Magdalene Cloister, which has been partly restored and has the highest tower of all the colleges. The restorations are being done fully in accordance with the original style and will safeguard these parts of the building for another five hundred years. Meanwhile, although only a very small fraction is complete, forty thousand pounds have already been expended. Just imagine what immense, no-longer-amassable sums would be required today to undertake such a project from the ground up! The working classes and to an extent the artists have clearly gained the advantage over consumers in our own day, and their work has become so expensive that a truly great artistic monument of this standard is now scarcely affordable. After all, even given the devaluation of money, the amount that once bought a divine work by Raphael is not enough today to buy a portrait by Thomas Lawrence.

Our walk closed with the Botanical Garden, where there was nothing worth recording. So I'll release you for now, my good Julie. *Mais c'est à y revenir demain.*[28]

Buckingham, January 10th, 1827

IT IS SINFUL how long I have been neglecting my private journal! The more bloated my travel letters to you, the more my unhappy journal shrinks. If you burn these letters, I will have no idea at all what has been happening, and just imagine how uncomfortable it is to disappear from one's own memory! Truly my imagination is such a montage of the ruins and echoes of past eras that I am already dreaming of a future in which even the ruins will come to an end and a man will have lost not just his shadow but his entire being, so he can begin a different life on new stars. Really, no matter what people say, when you lose your memory you lose everything that you are, just like an old man has lost what he was as a child. But we, dear friend of my heart, can find each other *again,* and then the bond that connects us here will of necessity be reforged there. And this will be enough for us.

Mais revenons à nos moutons—c'est à dire, parlons de nouveau de parcs.[29]

An abominable storm, rain, and darkness kept me in Oxford until three in the afternoon, when it finally cleared up enough to depart. The mail coach driver was not exactly sure about the road, which is not a main thoroughfare, and he took us on a long detour, so we did not arrive until very late. While the fire was being lit in my chamber, I went into the innkeeper's room, where I found his niece, a very pretty girl, as well as two doctors from the vicinity, with whom I spent a very enjoyable evening.

Aylesbury, January 11th, 1827

STOWE, LIKE BLENHEIM, is another specimen of English grandeur and magnificence (Figure 31). The park covers a large area of beautiful, undulating landscape with superb stands of trees. The palace is a marvelous building in Italian taste done after drawings by Chambers, and the perfectly maintained pleasure ground that surrounds it extends for twelve hundred acres. These

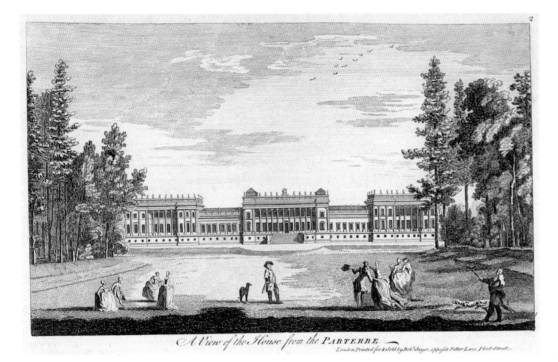

gardens were laid out long ago and, although very lovely in many respects and distinguished by a wealth of lofty trees, they are overburdened by temples and structures of every kind. It would be the greatest improvement if ten or twelve of them were torn down. Deserving of special praise is a charming flower garden thickly surrounded by tall leafy trees, firs, cedars, and shrubbery, both evergreen and deciduous. It spreads out in a regular pattern like a carpet in front of a crescent-shaped house with columns where rare birds reside. A pretty fountain splashes up in the middle of this carpet, and on both sides are two decorative aviaries made of wire mesh.

Irregular groups of flowers on the lawn form another garden, adorned with statues and with a greenhouse at its center. The surroundings are an open grove of extremely tall trees offering no further vista.

In the park is the Bourbon Tower, so named because it is surrounded by a crown of lindens planted by Louis XVIII during his lengthy sojourn at nearby Hartwell. Although of recent vintage, it has half collapsed already. I hope that this will not prove an evil premonition for the Bourbons in France, where even his own people dubbed the wise charter giver *Louis l'inévitable* and *deux fois neuf*.[30]

Also worth mentioning is a monument dedicated to the great men and women of England, with very appropriate inscriptions and busts nicely modeled after the best paintings.

The palace facade is 450 feet long, as is the uninterrupted suite of rooms in the *piano nobile* that you reach by mounting a lovely staircase on the garden side. You pass through a wide, bronze door and step into an oval hall of marble where a beautiful cupola provides the only illumination. Twenty faux-marble columns of reddish scagliola ring the hall, forming niches that house ten classical statues. The floor is paved with genuine marble and in its center is a gold grate emitting a continual supply of warm air.

It would take too long to describe each individual room. I will simply mention that they are very richly furnished in the taste that reigned nearly a century ago. The wall coverings are either heavy silk or *haute-lisse* tapestries, and all the rooms are more or less fully adorned with paintings, curiosities, and art treasures. A myriad of Chinese porcelains and other objects from that country are piled up everywhere, especially in the state bedroom, which is used only as an exhibition space and contains a splendid old bed of embroidered velvet with gold fringe. In the adjoining boudoir were many other precious objects that we could only see from a distance through a security grille. The theft of a ruby necklace that had belonged to Marie Antoinette of France explains why one is no longer allowed to enter without the duke being present.

The library, in the form of a long gallery, serves as the main entertaining room and is furnished in a modern style, full of sofas, tables, pianofortes, etc. The walls are covered with cabinets running all the way to the ceiling, and a light and elegant gallery in the middle is reached via a small spiral staircase. A large neighboring room, set up in the same way, contains nothing but portfolios of engravings, perhaps one of the richest collections in the world. This seems to be the present duke's favorite hobby.

The music room houses, in addition to every necessary musical device, a large organ. Another room on the opposite side of the palace and facing the park (actually the entrance hall where the carriages arrive) offers a view I found quite odd in its effect. Namely, you look out at a great, open expanse of lawn embraced on both sides by oak woods, and in the middle distance and beyond are a few meadows and woods alternating with each other. In the center of the lawn, totally isolated about sixty to seventy paces from the house, you see a colossal, snow white equestrian statue, admirably executed and atop a high pedestal, so that the rider seems to rest right on the treetops behind him. No building or other object is visible apart from trees, grass, and sky, and the scene is so completely deserted that the white ghost of the rider inevitably draws one's entire attention. No more perfect stage set for *Don Juan* can be imagined. It also happened that exactly today, by some lucky accident, the sky was threatening a snowstorm on this side of the palace and had become completely overcast and black. Against it the dazzling white statue stood out almost chillingly. At that moment it seemed alive, with every muscle thrown into sharp relief by the piercing light.

Among the paintings is a treasure that seems utterly unknown to our German travelers, at least I have never read anything about it: a genuine portrait of Shakespeare, painted during his lifetime by Burbage (Figure 32).[31] Of course the hypercritics in England are unwilling to recognize any *genuine* portrait of Shakespeare. Yet I find it almost impossible that someone could invent a physiognomy that so triumphantly bears the character of truth *an sich*; that so entirely expresses the greatness and originality of the man it portrays, imbuing him with all the spiritual dignity, all the brilliance, wit, subtlety, and that inexhaustible wealth of humor bestowed on no other mortal. The face is by no means what is generally called handsome, but the noble beauty of the mind behind it is apparent at a glance. That audacious intellect plays across the high forehead in flashing lights; the large, dark brown eyes are penetrating, fiery, and yet mild. Only around the lips do we see hovering a gentle mockery and benevolent slyness, but these are paired with such a sweet smile that the otherwise solemn dignity of the whole is imbued with great, engagingly human charm. Moreover the structure of the skull and brow is perfection, with no noticeable protuberances and showing all the organs so vaulted and well formed that one cannot but be astonished at the harmony of such an ideally organized head.[32] It is a joy to find the perfect unity between the *picture* of the man and his *works*.

William Shakespeare,
the "Chandos Portrait."

I was particularly attracted by the essentially German character of two excellent pictures by Albrecht Dürer, female saints in a visionary landscape.[33] They are nothing less than two authentic, Nuremberg housewives, wearing their native bonnets and portrayed after nature, good humoredly bustling about their saintly duties. Luther in a portrait by Holbein displays more spirit and less corpulence than usual.

Another notable picture by Van Dyck is the Marquis de la Vieuville, the French ambassador to Charles I, who accompanied the king into battle with chivalric spirit and was killed at Newbury.[34] His costume is peculiar yet picturesque. A white fitted doublet à la Henri IV, with a black cloak over it; short, full, black trousers falling over the knee with silvery metal points; light violet stockings with gold gussets; and white shoes with gold roses. Embroidered on the cloak is the star of the Order of the Holy Spirit, four times larger than is now common, and the blue ribbon is over the shoulder but worn lower and with the cross to the side, as is the current fashion. Narrower and smaller than nowadays, this hangs almost under his arm on the broad ribbon.

I had imagined the duc de Guise differently than this pale face with a reddish beard and hair, looking more scheming than splendid.[35] A portrait by Velásquez corresponds better to the character of the sitter, namely Count Gondomar, who as Spanish ambassador to the court of James I flattered the learned ruler with his garbled Latin, a burlesque mode in which he permitted himself to say anything he wanted. Afterward, through his Jesuitical influence, he had Sir Walter Raleigh, the favorite of Queen Elizabeth, brought to the scaffold.

A picture of Oliver Cromwell, by his court painter Richardson,[36] has a double interest for the family since it was painted for one of the duke's ancestors, who himself appears in it as a page, obligingly helping to tie a bow in the Protector's sash. This portrait does not entirely resemble others I have seen of Cromwell, but renders him as younger and of a more refined nature; hence it was probably meant to flatter, something doubly to be suspected from a *court* painter.

I will only mention two beautiful, large paintings by Teniers, one depicting three highly typical Dutch peasants who have met up in a village and are gossiping with their pipes in their mouths. Also an excellent Ruisdael; six famous Rembrandts; and Titian's mistress, painted by the artist himself, with arms and a bosom that swell out to meet an embrace. I also very much admired more recent works of art: two Sèvres cups with miniatures after Petitot by the splendid porcelain painter Madame Jaquotot. One of them portrays Ninon de Lenclos. None of the other portraits I have seen has ever matched my vision of her, whereas this one completely expresses her well-known character: she appears seductively lovely, genuinely French, as lively as quicksilver, and with a boldness that borders on impudence but is yet too noble and essentially natural to make any but an engaging impression. The second—a mellow, cheerful, and voluptuous beauty—was inscribed Françoise d'Orléans de Valois. As someone fully conversant with French genealogy and memoirs, *you* will know who she is. *Je l'ignore.* Each of these cups cost one thousand francs.

In the evening, under lovely moonlight, we drove on to Aylesbury, from where I am now writing you.

Uxbridge, January 12th, 1827

STILL HOPING TO be back in London again this evening, I am writing you a few brief words while fresh horses are being harnessed. This morning we visited Lord Carrington's park,[37] the last one—at least for the time being—a fact that should be some consolation to you. The garden has nothing special to offer. The house is once again in the popular neo-Gothic style, but since it is simpler in construction and less pretentious, it also looks less affected. It is built of rough, undressed stone. Inside there was some excellent, old stained glass, although only in the upper part of the windows; the rest were left clear to let more light into the rooms.

A good portrait of Pitt hangs in the library. The great man's features are anything but genial, and who knows whether posterity will not someday come to a similar conclusion about his *works*. I noticed something charming in the garden: a thick wreath of ivy on the grass, looking like it had been carelessly dropped and left behind by a passerby.

Our journey was supposed to close with a visit to Bulstrode, which Repton describes so extensively as the model for garden and park designs. But this cup will be taken from you, dear Julie, because the Duke of Portland sold it, and the current owner has felled the proud, giant trees over which Repton enthused so much; turned the meadows into cultivated fields; and even torn down the house in order to transform the stones into money. It was a gloomy scene of devastation, made more alarming by the strange dress of the women working there, who were wrapped from head to toe in blood red cloaks, looking like a sinister gathering of executioners.

London, January 13, 1827

UNDER BRIGHT GASLIGHT, which always looks like festive illumination here, we drove into the city, and in search of an immediate contrast to my long immersion in park-and-garden life, I got off at Covent Garden to see my first Christmas pantomime.[38] This is a very popular kind of play in England, perfect for children, and so naturally I was very happy there! Playwrights and set designers expend a lot of effort outdoing the previous year with ever-greater wonders. Before bidding you goodnight, I want to relive the play for you in a rhapsodic sketch.

As the curtain rises, the scene is filled with a dense fog that gradually dissipates, an illusion very beguilingly achieved by the use of fine gauze. In the twilight you can discern a rustic cottage, the home of an enchantress, and in the background a lake ringed by mountains and overshadowed by a few snowy peaks. Everything is still dusky and indistinct, but then as the sun comes up, it conquers the heavy morning mists, and the cottage appears in total clarity along with a far-off village. Now you spy a large rooster standing on the roof, flapping his wings, preening himself, and greeting the sun with a volley of very convincing cock-a-doodle-doos. Next to him a magpie adds its voice, strides around, and begins teasing a gigantic tomcat lying in a niche in the wall below, who responds by sleepily stretching his legs, cleaning his face, and purring contentedly. This tomcat is performed with great virtuosity by an actor who later transforms himself into Harlequin. The way he plays with a melon, the ease with which he climbs up and down the chimney, his leaps and bearing are all so natural that they can only have been derived from long study of the animals themselves. Luckily the art of acting has advanced to the point that we are no longer outdone by poodles and monkeys, but rather are capable of impersonating these celebrated animals ourselves.

Meanwhile the door opens and Mother Shipton, a terrible witch, steps out with her all-too-similar son. The domestic animals, including a large owl, immediately pay her their respects as best they can. But the witch is feeling testy, utters a curse and, with a touch of ingenious stagecraft, transforms them on the spot into figures from the commedia dell'arte. Like a metaphor of the world, they now proceed to persecute one another tirelessly until the cleverest of them finally prevails. Thus the fairy tale spins through a thousand transformations and madcap tricks, with no particular coherence other than the occasional sly allusion to current events. Best of all were the magnificent decorations and then the jokes by the machinist. One of the finest of these scenes was the witch's kitchen. A rock splits open and reveals a large cave. In its center a cord of wood is blazing away, and rotating above it on a rapidly turning spit, one sees a whole stag (complete with antlers), a whole ox, and a pig. Baking on a hearth to the right is a pie the size of a freight wagon, and steaming on the left is a plum pudding of the same dimensions. Now the *chef de cuisine* appears with a couple dozen assistants in grotesque white uniforms, each equipped with a long tail and armed with a gigantic knife and fork. The commander first has them perform a ridiculous exercise, present arms, etc., whereby they prove themselves just as proficient as the seven girls in uniform.[39] He then arranges them platoon-like so they can baste the roasts with butter, using cooking spoons on the same gargantuan scale as the other utensils, all the while diligently fanning the flames with their long tails.

The scene now shows us a lofty castle toward which the colossal dishes are conveyed like so much artillery. As they ascend in the distance, the twists and turns of the rocky road make them look smaller and smaller, until finally the pie disappears over the horizon like a setting moon.

Next we are transported to a large city with all manner of comical inscriptions on the buildings, mostly satires on the glut of new inventions and companies for every possible undertaking: for example, "Washing Company of the Three United Kingdoms," "Steamboat to America in six days," "Guaranteed way to win the lottery," "Mining shares for ten pounds each," "Become a millionaire in ten years," etc., etc. Conspicuous in the foreground is a tailor's workshop where several apprentices are diligently sewing, and affixed as an emblem over the door is a pair of scissors six yards long, pointing up. Harlequin arrives, chased by Pantaloon and Co., and leaps into the tailor's house by doing a somersault in the air and through a second-story window, which shatters with a loud noise. The pursuers, recoiling from the deadly jump, hurl themselves on top of one another and pound away with an artistic dexterity and agility that you expect only from puppets. Ladders are set up and the company climbs up into the house after Harlequin, but he has already escaped out the chimney and runs away across the rooftops. Meanwhile, hoping to see in which direction Harlequin has gone, Pantaloon peeps out of the middle window, his long chin and beard framed by the blades of the scissors. Suddenly they snap shut, and his head falls onto the street. The headless Pantaloon now dashes down the stairs and out the door in pursuit of his rolling head, which is snapped up that very moment by a poodle, who speeds off with it. Pantaloon follows behind and meets Harlequin again, who has now disguised himself as a doctor and holds a hurried consultation with three other doctors about how to help the woebegone Pantaloon. They finally agree to smear essence of Macassar oil on the bare spot where the head once was, and thanks to this operation, it slowly grows back right before the eyes of the spectators.

In the last act we are transported to the Tivoli Gardens in Paris. A hot-air balloon ascends with a lovely child on board, and as it floats from the stage and over the audience, the terrestrial set gradually sinks away. When the balloon reaches the ceiling it takes a turn around the chandelier as the stage fills with billowing clouds and a thousand twinkling stars—an ingenious illusion! As the balloon descends, the city and garden gradually reemerge. After this scene a rope is stretched out, and amid a brilliant display of fireworks, a shapely lady pushes a wheelbarrow across it to the top of a Gothic tower, while other *équilibristes* perform their riskiest stunts below.

Thunder and lightning open the finale, as the stage changes into a magnificent Chinese hall festooned with a thousand colorful paper lanterns. All magic dissolves, a benevolent sorcerer king exiles the witch to the bowels of the earth, and Harlequin, recognized to be a genuine prince, marries his Columbine.

On our way home, we witnessed another strange drama, this one gratis. A tall, glowing column of smoke rose from a chimney, turning from green to red to blue. And the closer we got, the more dense and variegated the smoke became as it swirled upward, like the Chinese fireworks we had just seen, but in color. "Probably a chemical laboratory," I said to Rehder. "I hope no serious fire arises from it." Hardly had I uttered this when my fear came true. Screams rang out on all sides, wild flames darted toward the sky, people rushed together, and soon fire engines were clattering through the streets. But the big city swallows up such particular events. Five hundred steps farther along, the fire could no longer be heard and aroused no interest. In an illuminated palace people were dancing gaily, those coming from the theater moved slowly homeward, and in dark corners brazen nymphs, like silent misery, tried, as is their wont, to draw the attention of passersby.

Well, my good, dear Julie, everything must end; so too this long travelogue, which has certainly delivered one sheet for each year of my life. That it ends with a fire is a sign of my ardent love. But even though your superstitions will so incline you, there is no need to cry out "May good fortune stay with us this time!"—Where love is, even the unhappiest time is good.

$\mathscr{P}$RECIOUS JULIE!

Rehder left London for Harwich today and will be with you in two weeks. It will certainly please you to have a living witness of the comings and goings of your Lou, one who can be personally interrogated about the many nuances of things that, even with the best of intentions, cannot be captured in a letter. Meanwhile I have become reaccustomed to city life. Yesterday I dined at Prince Esterházy's, where we were kept in stitches by the secretary of a certain legation. He is a kind of amiable buffoon and, although himself of very ordinary stock, a superlative of superlatives (*tel le maître, tel le valet*).[1] I have often admired, even envied, the French talent for composing the most amusing tales out of the most banal events, which, if recounted by others, would immediately lose every bit of their piquancy.

No one better excels at this than Mr. Roth, who shows that this talent is no more than the result of the language best suited to it and the education to go with it. For although Mr. Roth is German, I think Swabian, he came to France as a two-year-old and was thus brought up as a Frenchman. It is language more than blood that makes the man, no matter that it was blood that first made the language.

By the way, I have to say that no matter how brilliant such engaging chatter may initially seem, it just burns up like a fuse and leaves no trace on the memory, making the pedantic German feel discomfited at having wasted his time. If only the Germanic elements in our language could be blessed with some French buoyancy, roundness, pleasing ambiguity, as well as precision and finish—qualities that also bring on a certain French audacity in social interactions—then German conversation would be more satisfying since it would include the useful alongside the enjoyable. But all that is left for us in society is the ability the French aptly call *l'esprit de l'escalier,* namely, a mind that waits until you've descended the stairs before letting you know what you should have said upstairs in the salon.

I cannot remember anything about this Frenchman's pyrotechnics except for the following anecdote. A diplomat at the time of Louis XIV who was considered quite an authority closed a treatise on the great privileges granted to foreign ambassadors with the words "Mais dès qu'un Ambassadeur est mort, il rentre aussitôt dans la vie privée."[2]

January 22nd, 1827

THE POOR DUKE of York has finally died after a long illness and is now lying in state with great splendor. I saw him this past October and found him already just a shadow of the robust and imposing man I used to see so often at Lady Lansdowne's or at his own house, where the six bottles of claret consumed after dinner only imperceptibly altered his appearance. I remember one such evening—it was already past midnight—when he led a few of the guests, including the Austrian ambassador, Count von Merveldt, Count Beroldingen, and me, into his impressive armory.[3] We tried to swing several Turkish sabers, but none of us could manage a firm enough grip, and thus it happened that both the duke and Count von Merveldt scratched themselves with an Indian weapon, a kind of straight sword, and drew blood. This led the count to speculate whether it was as efficient as a Damascus blade, and so he tried to slice through one of the wax candles on the table. The experiment turned out so badly that both candles along with their holders were knocked to the floor, and the flames went out. While we were feeling around in the darkness looking for the door, the duke's adjutant started to stammer pathetically: "By God, Sir, I remember. . . the sword is poisoned!" You can imagine how this unsettled the wounded men. Luckily, after closer interrogation, it was revealed that the colonel's assertion had more to do with claret than poison.

Given his many excellent qualities, the duke's passing is greatly lamented. The entire country is in mourning, wearing black gloves and crepe on their hats, something that is driving the clothiers to distraction. Every liveried retainer is in black, and letters are written only on paper with a broad black border. Meanwhile the Christmas pantomimes proceed apace in the theaters. It makes a strange impression when Harlequin and Brighella dash around the stage engaged in every possible frivolity and prank, while the audience, draped in raven black as if in a funeral procession, claps furiously and screams with laughter.

I just now received your letter from B——. Really, it has been a long time since you have written anything so amusing; indeed, I might say, so mordant. Those original B—— characters seem to have completely electrified you, and though I ought to be happy about it, I do feel a little bit jealous. But soon enough you will come back to your own personal eccentric. Like Caesar I can say with confidence, I do not fear the fat but only the lean,[4] and so as long as you assure me you are maintaining your pretty embonpoint, I will remain calm. Still let me tease you a bit more, even though I know you do not tolerate such joking *par distance*. Nonetheless, in order to satisfy my mood, I am sending you an extract from my journal as a pendant to your earlier African journey. For my poor diary may still be alive, but it is very emaciated, given that it often goes unfed for months at a time, and there is almost nothing piquant in the occasional bit of nourishment it receives. So do not expect anything amusing or satirical but rather something serious, for it is being imposed on you as punishment.

FROM MY JOURNAL

TODAY IN THE *Literary Gazette* I read a very thorough and convincing article demonstrating the agricultural advantages of large individual landholdings in England,* in comparison with the parceling out of property as is done in France, a practice also favored by economic theorists at home.[5] Here is a free translation of part of it:

> According to a calculation based on official documents, 27,440 square leagues of land are dedicated to agriculture. In England only 13,396; that is, not even half. Nonetheless

---

* Excepting cases of misuse.

the productivity of the land in England is one-seventh greater than in France. Since the quality of the soil is not significantly better in its totality, this clearly proves that agriculture is much better understood in England, and the reason lies in the great wealth of the large landowners, who are always ready to make sacrifices for ameliorations, new experiments, and the progress of science, which will subsequently prove advantageous to them or to others—an advantage that is lacking for small property owners who can never acquire sufficient working capital. But the next comparison is even more remarkable.

In England and Scotland there are 589,384 landowners and tenants. Add another third for Ireland, and assuming each of these families consists of five people, the total is still less than four million, that is, about one-fifth of the entire population of Great Britain.

In France, on the other hand, there are no fewer than 4,833,000 landowners and tenants.[6] If we also multiply this by five, it comes to an enormous 24,000,000, almost four-fifths of the nation engaged in agriculture. What can we conclude from this? That in England one-fifth of the population produces the same agricultural result as four-fifths do in France; that in England four-fifths remain for the factories, commerce, etc., and in France only one-fifth.

Can there be a better lesson for our levelers, who assert with such pathos that only a severe limitation on property size will produce the largest population and consequently the greatest prosperity for a nation? In claiming this, they echo like magpies the opposition newspapers' insistence that large landowners alone are responsible for the poverty of the lower classes, a view ridiculed by every informed person in England.

Here only the factory workers are afflicted with temporary poverty, and it is in the nature of things that when work comes to a standstill, these people, accustomed to having only one job for their entire lives, are unable and unwilling to take on another. This is the inevitable consequence of an industry that has made immeasurable progress, as it has here; the accidental and transitory suffering of a few thousand must be overlooked when compared with the power and wealth that England owes to this industry—an industry, it should be noted, that is based on a flourishing and protected agricultural system. Incidentally, the workers we are talking about are so spoiled by high earnings and good living that if they are deprived of the daily meat, white bread, beer, and tea that they normally consume in quantity, they start talking about starvation. I ask every open-minded foreigner traveling in England whether he does not find the general prosperity of the lower classes more remarkable than the often princely luxury of the wealthy few. Day laborers in England are almost always better off than the well-to-do bourgeoisie in Germany, and here it is worth citing a peculiar case reported by the public newspapers: last year, while in Manchester and Birmingham thousands were starving, factories were burning, and the military had to be called in, Parliament discovered that just six hours away, not a person could be found to work the harvest, even for triple pay.*

---

* The reader will find a similar discussion in another part of this text and may well find other passages that look like repetitions. Such things happen in a genuine series of letters, not just in a fictitious one assembled after the fact, and cannot always be deleted without damaging the coherency. We therefore ask the benevolent reader's generous indulgence.—*The Editor.* [Working conditions and property laws are discussed on pages 156, 384, and 397.—*Translator.*]

Still, when all is said and done, a fundamental reason for England's prosperity is surely the extraordinary reverence for property that is manifest both in the laws themselves and in their administration. And it is landed property that is the most dangerous for the state to violate, for the nation regards it as such a sacred right that the procedures commonly undertaken by continental powers for the good of their subjects, including the utilization of the property of one class to improve the economic situation of another, are absolutely unfeasible in England. Yet in England the result is security for the high-ranking as well as the humble classes. And prosperity follows.

Perhaps someday even our country will recognize how little the state benefitted when it rejected this principle and instead regulated the property of landowners in accordance with the demands of peasants, appointing expensive commissions that, by fiat, take land from the former and give it to the latter. But the peasantry gains no real benefit since both sides spend nearly the equivalent of what it is worth just to pay off the judges!

This is how the forced,* so-called regulation of rural conditions is configured in too many places, even though it was initially set up with good intentions. If as a despotic measure, it had been carried out quickly, it might have had a salutary effect. But instead it is now mired in conventions, unforeseeable difficulties, and judicial appeals, and like a toxic upas tree,[7] has inexorably drained the life out of the surrounding land and poisoned everything around it.

So, even if the lawmakers were well intentioned, the rule was nonetheless a high-handed usurpation of power over private property. A defective root and a poorly tended plant nearly always yield insidious fruits.

---

* The regulation is certainly forced because if one of the two parties submits a claim, the other must follow. Since the peasant can only receive and the landowner only give, it is self-evident that the claimant would always be the peasant. In later periods, however, when so many communities realized that the advantages gained through regulation did not stand in a proper relationship to the expenses incurred by the gentlemen regulators, they often chose to retain the traditional arrangements. Even when a procedure had already begun, many would have happily reversed it, but there is no escape for a fly once the spider has caught it in her web.

The government might simply have made voluntary separation easier and tried to encourage it without force. [This is a reference to the *Gemeinheitsteilung* (division of the commons) that had been introduced in Prussia.—*Translator.*] There was once much good will in this direction, and no system could have been more beneficial. The humanity of our century, which is growing more and more general, would have joyfully played into the government's hands. Landowners and tenants might have remained friends and been more deeply joined through mutual advantage. Instead we are now caught up in endless class conflicts that have artificially turned us into enemies who want only an abrupt separation of interests, an outcome most damaging to the state. Each side has now broken free of these patriarchal measures and, driven by the crassest egoism, entrenches itself. But what a curse if similar discontents should be transferred to *political* interests that could once again rally these demoralized and impoverished parties to further antagonism!

In Saxony, where we have a comparable wish to reform, it is very much to be hoped that the experiences of our neighbors will help us avoid an unjust path and, above all, help us to a quick conclusion. We are forewarned not to entrust this to a whole army of hungry lawyers and corrupt economists (fused together into one monstrous body with far-reaching fingers). Instead such regulations should be administered through special commissions of delegates drawn from the interested parties themselves, along with a carefully chosen public official and a tested lawyer. And their decisions cannot be appealed.

The current political circumstances make us fear, however, that the whole present generation is to be sacrificed for the sake of better conditions in the future. This is exactly the same principle that was applied at home to regulate rural conditions. Although fate may often compel such a solution, it is always perilous for a state to allow it.—*The Editor.*

Let me now turn to a review of Lady Morgan's *Salvator Rosa* in the same publication.[8] I was particularly moved by one passage, and with good reason. It is the inventive description of her hero and goes more or less as follows:

> With a thirst for praise, which scarcely any applause could satisfy, Salvator united a quickness of perception that rendered him suspicious of pleasing, even at the moment he was most successful. A gaping mouth, a closing lid, a languid look, or an impatient hem! threw him into utter confusion, and deprived him of all presence of mind, of all power of concealing his mortification.
>
> Abandoned by the idle and the great, whom his delightful talents had so long contributed to amuse, he voluntarily excluded himself from the few true and staunch friends who clung to him in his adversity. . . . Shutting himself up equally from all he loved and all he despised, he awaited with gloomy and unyielding firmness the completion of his destiny.
>
> His reference to this journey is curious, as being illustrative of those high imaginations, and lofty and lonely feelings, in which lay all the secret of his peculiar genius: while his pantings after solitude, his vain repinings, exhibit the struggles of a mind divided between a natural love of repose, and a factitious ambition for the world's notice, and the *éclat* of fame—no unusual contrast in those who, being highly gifted and highly organized, are placed by nature above their species in all the splendid endowments of intellect; and who are, by the same nature, again drawn down to its level through their social and sympathetic affections.
>
> His fine but fatal organization, which rendered him so susceptible of impressions, whether of good or evil, and which left him at times no shelter against "horrible imaginings," or against those real inflictions, calumny and slander, plunged him too frequently into fits of listless melancholy, when, disabused of all illusion, he saw the species to which he belonged in all the nakedness of its inherent infirmity.

Yes, this portrayal has been drawn from the very soul, and it applies to any man born with such a disposition, a man who can only feel comfortable in the world if circumstances place him very, very high above it or allow him to live in total obscurity.

The ideas of others have taken me this far. Now let me close my journal for today with a few of my own observations about a subject that touches the heart even more deeply, a question that must be of interest to everyone, even if they are just as far from being professional philosophers as I am: What is conscience?

Conscience undoubtedly has a dual nature as well as a dual origin. One flows from our highest strength, the other from our greatest weakness; one from the spirit of God that dwells within us, the other from our sense of fear. To attain serenity, which requires the greatest possible clarity, a person must distinguish between the two natures of conscience. Even after having escaped the primal instinct of emotion, we must still apply "the sweat of our brow" if we are to achieve anything lasting—even the capacity to reason. We are constructed of countless parts, and only when they are in perfect balance can we as human beings, both spiritual and sensate, be completely happy. It is a common error to want to develop one side more than the other: for some this may mean religion, for others a strict rationality, and for the child of the world just the mind and the senses. But when everything is in proper harmony—enjoyed and so to speak artistically unified—then we have the most perfect life on this earth, the authentic truth.

This is the perspective from which we must view what we call conscience and distinguish the True from the False.

I understand the True to include the infallible exhortation of the Holy Spirit within us, which holds us back from evil in general as well as from the entirely one-sided, inconsequential, and negative. This needs no further explanation. The False, however, arises only from convention, habit, and authority, from the sophistries and excessive anxiety that all spring from *fear*. Here it is those of a delicate, easily excitable nature dominated by the cerebral system who are most easily led astray, because in them the intellect and imagination—if I may put it this way— are stronger than the heart, and the analytical mind too easily nullifies the full intensity of the senses. However it is so difficult to follow such subtle ramifications and arcane interactions that we often mistake the reaction of a sophistical mind for a primary emotion.

It is obvious that the variations and complexities of right and wrong must be considered relative when applied to individual human actions. There is no alternative but for each person to apply all his strength of mind to truly understanding what he considers to be right and wrong and then to apply this standard to his actions calmly, not worrying about his so-called conscience, that inner unease and doubt that conflicting circumstances can generate. The qualms of conscience cannot be totally repressed since the lessons we learn about right or wrong in childhood and earliest youth—whether reasonable or absurd—always make an irresistible impression on our minds.*

Here are just a few illustrative examples. When any man of gentle spirit, raised in the fear of God and love of mankind, becomes a soldier and must take a human life in cold blood for the first time, he will scarcely be able to do so without a noticeable pang of conscience. At least that is how it was in my case. Yet it is his duty and can be quite well justified from a higher, albeit worldly, perspective, at least as long as humanity has progressed no further than it has today.

Similarly when, after a lengthy struggle, a man renounces the religion of his ancestors, the doctrine preached to him daily in his youth, and takes up another in the pure conviction that it is a better one, he will usually feel an irrepressible if muted anxiety. This is no more than the totally absurd fear of ghosts among all those who were earlier imprinted with a *belief* in such phantoms! They have a ghost conscience they cannot get rid of. Moreover for sensitive characters the mere suspicion that others consider us guilty of a wicked act is enough for us to be overcome by a bad conscience, often revealing itself in the customary signs of embarrassment, blushing, and turning pale. It can even lead to madness. For example, a man believed to have killed someone, or one who actually did so but in total innocence, can find his whole life robbed of happiness and tranquility. Indeed, we have read about a Brahmin whose caste equates the murder of an animal with that of a human being, so that he took his own life in despair when an English natural scientist

---

* Conscience can also be both right and wrong at the same time; in other words, an unavoidable act may be thoroughly flawed from one perspective although it was chosen as the lesser of two evils. No reasonable moralist can claim that such a choice would not be imperative under certain circumstances. For instance, we may choose to sacrifice a significant part of our moral dignity by telling a white lie, if we would wickedly betray our parents and friends by not telling it.—*The Editor.*

explained to him that by drinking a glass of water, he was killing thousands of invisible creatures. *Il n'y a qu'un pas du sublime au ridicule.*[9]

In his biography of the overly conscientious Passeroni, Ugoni tells how once Passeroni was crossing the bridge of the Porta Orientale when he found a porter lying in a deep sleep on the broad stone balustrade.[10] It was clear that he could fall into the water if he were unexpectedly awoken. Seizing him by the arm, he managed to rouse the exhausted man and with difficulty led him to understand why he had awakened him. The porter responded cantankerously to these efforts, emitted a vulgar curse, and told him to go to the devil.

Passeroni, extremely distressed at having caused this fury, took a handful of coins and handed them to the irate man so he might drink to Passeroni's health. He then walked on, feeling quite contented. Yet before reaching the end of the bridge, it struck him that this gift might have an even direr consequence than the earlier awakening since it could easily lead the poor man to the sin of drunkenness. He immediately rushed back, luckily found the man at the same spot stretched out exactly as before, and asked him awkwardly to return whatever of the money he had given him that was not required for his most urgent needs. The porter, who thought he had been made a fool of, was more enraged than ever, so Passeroni came up with another solution. "Here, my friend," he said, "since you don't want to return the coins, then take this scudo and give me your solemn word that if you spend the other money on drink, you'll use this scudo for food to eat along with it."

The *facchino* was delighted to offer his promise, Passeroni's conscience was finally soothed, and he went home with a light heart.

I repeat: in order not to become either unhappy or ridiculous or resemble a bending reed, we must *train* our conscience as we do all other capacities of the soul: that is, maintain it in its purity and at the same time keep it within firm bounds. Because everything—even what is most noble—will otherwise degenerate. In general, the best guideline will always be Christ's simple words, "Do nothing to others (or yourself) that you would not have others do unto you."

However, as long as we are not yet all Christians—indeed, cannot be—exceptions must be tolerated, like the case of the soldier I mentioned, or the codes of honor that are essential for certain classes. The only solution is that when we *ourselves* make an exception, we must also allow *others* to do the same, sacrificing ourselves to them as well. In this way we may barely salvage charity, or at least that justice, which is called the *ius talionis*.[11]

But anyone for whom nature and circumstances have made it easy to remain on the accustomed path, to be good and loving and ethical from the very beginning—that person will have a happy, richly pleasurable life! But things do go bad from the first error, because as our philosopher-poet so correctly says:

> Das eben ist der Fluch des Bösen,
> Daß es fortwuchernd immer Böses muß begären![12]

And rebirth is still not attainable in this world. Indeed it may be the greatest charitable act of eternal love to have created death, since death can erase the script that has become illegible and confused, offering a fresh, blank page to the muddled soul so it might make a more felicitous attempt. But whoever has already been registered here as *holy* will be given a more blissful assignment! A loving justice does not punish the feeble in the way that mankind does, but it can only reward where reward is earned, where it is destined by past achievement. So do not bury your talent. Amen.

IT HAS TURNED very cold again, and the fireplace where the coal burns night and day is unfortunately not up to the task of warming a room the way our stoves do; however ugly, they seem extremely efficient to me right now.

To get my blood circulating, I have been particularly diligent about going out riding, and on my way back today I saw one of the many cosmoramas installed here, which offer a thoroughly enjoyable "Reise auf dem Zimmer," as it is called in Berlin.[13] I was given a more comfortable view of the interior of Reims Cathedral and the coronation of Charles X than would have been possible in the crowded church itself. But what tasteless costumes, from the king down to the lowest courtier! New and old mixed together in the most repugnant way. If you put on such comedies, you should at least try to make them as pretty as at Franconi's.[14]

Next to this the spine-tingling ruins of Palmyra were spread out in an endless desert of sand, while on the distant horizon a caravan was crossing in the incandescent heat.

The most convincing illusion was the great fire of Edinburgh. It was quite realistically ablaze. You saw the flames flaring up more and more strongly, then clouds of black smoke would rise, and the view of the whole landscape kept changing in relation to this varied illumination no differently than in an actual conflagration. Probably the owner's kitchen was behind the picture, and the same fire heating the imaginations of credulous spectators was simultaneously cooking a leg of mutton he had bought with their entry fees!

FOR THE PAST few days I have simply been vegetating too much to be able to write you. But this morning I was startled to see Rehder—who I thought would have been back home by now—stepping into my room! It seems he was semi-shipwrecked halfway to Hamburg and driven back by the gale, remaining for an entire night in mortal danger in the ice near Harwich. This frightened him so much that he wants nothing to do with the sea for the rest of his life. It is a dangerous time of year for ship travel so I am sending him via Calais and only writing you so you will not worry about him. Unfortunately he lost some of the things he was taking along for you.

This morning Hyde Park offered me a new spectacle. The large lake was frozen over and teemed with an immense and colorful crowd of skaters and others who take genuine, childlike joy in the icy pleasures that are so very rare here. Some years ago, during another cold spell, a curious wager was made. There is an infamous man named Hunt, who deals mostly in boot polish. His wares are loaded onto a large wagon that moves through the city streets all day long, drawn by four elegant horses that are usually driven as a four-in-hand by the gentleman's son. The same young Hunt wagered one hundred pounds sterling that he could drive this equipage at a gallop right across the lake in Hyde Park, and he won the bet brilliantly. The event was immortalized in a caricature, and sales of the boot polish, as is only fair, went up threefold (Figure 33).

It has become very musical in my house, for Miss Ayton, a singer recently engaged at the grand opera, has moved in. The thin walls allow me to hear her every morning gratis. Since she is said to be pretty, I will also try to see her—which may not happen gratis, the more so since

EXTRAORDINARY EXPLOIT.

On Tuesday the 17th of January 1826, Mr HENRY HUNT JUNr for a bet of 100 GUINEAS made with a Noble Lord of sporting celebrity drove his Father's Matchless Blacking Van with four blood horses upon the Ice over the Serpentine at the broadest part – he accomplished the hazardous task in the grandest style without the smallest accident. – The plate represents his return to the North Bank from which he had set out amid the acclamations of the multitude. Vide Morng Chronicle, Jany 18th

J. Limbird 143 Strand

Madame Vestris visits her often. I do not mean to imply anything wicked by this, dear Julie, only that in England no one gets to see anything without offering a good tip.

By the way, I have not been feeling well for the last few days. The city air does not suit me and forces me into a regime like the one your *chanson* describes, since I am really not eating much more

qu'un bouillon
d'un rognon
de Papillon.[15]

33
Extraordinary Exploit
(*Hunt's Wager on the
Frozen Serpentine*).

Cobham Hall, February 2nd, 1827

LORD DARNLEY, WHOSE wife I met in London, invited me to spend a few days with him at his country estate, which I was especially happy to do because this is Cobham Hall, which Repton

COBHAM HALL.
SEAT OF THE EARL OF DARNLEY.

34

Cobham Hall.

wrote about, describing the improvements he worked on together with the owner for almost forty years (Figure 34).[16] As a matter of fact, it is a high tribute to both of them, although after everything I myself heard and saw, it seems likely that the excellent taste of the owners deserves the most credit; indeed they sometimes even clashed with Repton, who for one thing did not always take adequate care to protect old trees. Still, a sheltered resting spot with a marvelous vista, Repton's Seat, has been erected as an expression of gratitude to the man who has done so much for landscape gardening.[17] His son, who visited us at home,[18] had told Lady Darnley a great deal about Muskau, and since she is almost my equal in parkomania, we were able to find a very attractive point of contact, and soon after my arrival were taking a serious walk together through the flower gardens, which—more tasteful than splendid—are decorated with a few graceful marble statues by Canova.

The master of the house suffers from gout, and so I did not see him until I came down to dinner, where I found a large party, including Lord Melville, who was just returned from reviewing the battleships on the Thames.

Lord Darnley, lying on a sofa in the middle of the room and covered with a Scottish cloak, embarrassed me a bit by his salutation: "You don't know me," he said, "and yet we saw each other many times thirty years ago."

Since I was still running around in children's togs at that time, I had to ask him for a more detailed explanation, though I was not at all pleased to hear my age spelled out so precisely in front of the whole party (for you know that I still profess to look no older than thirty). Otherwise

I could not help but admire Lord Darnley's memory because he spoke of the time when he and the Duke of Portland visited my parents in the country, and he summoned up every detail so exactly that he even refreshed *my* recollections of otherwise long-forgotten things. His narrative confirmed to me in the most entertaining way how many eccentric characters there were in those days, and how merrily people used to indulge in all sorts of amusements.

For instance, he mentioned a baron who believed just as fervently in apparitions as he did in the Gospel, and thus considered Cagliostro to be a kind of second Messiah. One day when this baron was iceskating alone on one of the lakes near our house, the entire party disguised themselves in bed sheets and other paraphernalia borrowed from the theater wardrobe room and presented the terrified Illuminatus with the spectacle of ghosts appearing on the ice in broad daylight![19] Seized by mortal agony, he sank to his knees (however awkward this may have been in skates) and with a volubility that still made the venerable lord laugh after so many years, he began to pray, uttering abracadabras and various incantations from Faust's *Höllenzwang*,[20] alternating with the quavering singing of hymns. While this was going on, one of the ghosts, who had been changing his size from tall to short with the help of a pole hidden under his sheet, unfortunately slipped and, divested of his disguise, slid right up to the knees of the praying baron. The latter was much too firm a believer for an incident like this to release him from his spectral vision. On the contrary, his horror was intensified to such an extent that he leapt up, crashed back down because of his footwear (forgotten in his fright), then quickly picked himself up once more and, accompanied by the loud jubilation of the ghosts, disappeared like the wind, skating off with an agility never witnessed in him before.

Even later, when people confessed to the farce, he refused to be convinced that they had been pulling his leg, and during the rest of his stay at Muskau, no power on earth could ever get him near the Scary Lake again.

You know I cannot escape my tendency to reflect, something that even on the happiest occasions may plunge me into melancholy. This is what happened now, as Lord Darnley conjured up the image of bygone times, praised the amiability of my grandfather, and described the mischievousness of my mother and what a wild child I had been.[21] *Hélas, ils sont passés ces jours de fête.*[22] The amiable man has already been moldering in his grave for a long time; the mischievous woman is old and no longer mischievous; and her wild lad, too, has become more than tame. Indeed he is no longer all that far away from the days about which people say "I take no pleasure in them."[23] As for the zany young Englishman who had played a ghost on the ice, he was lying before me as an old man, plagued by gout, stretched out helplessly on his sofa, and telling stories—often interrupted by painful sighs—about the jolly pranks of his youth, while the poor fool whom he had frightened so long ago has himself been a ghost for some time already, and would certainly instill not a little fear in Lord Darnley were he to repay him with a posthumous visit.

"O world, O world!" as Napoleon said.*

---

* I must explain this exclamation. After the defeat at Aspern, Napoleon was in a very precarious position as he and a few companions headed back to the island of Lobau in a rickety boat. Next to him was the still-very-young General Chernyshyov, who records how the emperor sat deep in thought, spoke to nobody, and only occasionally burst out in an undertone: "*O monde, o monde!*" He may well have been silently adding "*tu m'échappes,*" as actually happened a few years later.—*The Editor.* [*Tu m'échappes*: you are escaping me.—*Translator.*]

AMONG THE MOST exquisite works in Lord Darnley's splendid picture gallery are a famous Venus by Titian, the *Death of Regulus* by Salvator Rosa,[24] a large painting by Rubens that is often reproduced in copper, and a magnificent Guido. In the latter two paintings it is true that the main role is played by a rather unpleasant object, namely, a severed head. In the first, it is that of Cyrus; in the second, of John.[25] But Guido's Herodias is another of those poetic, heavenly beauties animated by genius and combining the loveliest womanliness with the deepest tragic expression, figures that make an indelible impression and are almost never encountered in reality. A lady of your acquaintance corresponds to this ideal, Countess Alopaeus in Berlin. When I knew her she was the most beautiful and richly endowed woman I had ever seen.* Ideal proportions and the most perfect equilibrium reigned in her appearance and her heart so that the most heterogeneous things were equally becoming to her. She had the majesty of a queen when performing official duties; the most delicate, charming approach to the world when presiding over her salon; and the most naïve, touching kindheartedness and gaiety when in the intimate circle of her family. But whatever the guise, it was rendered yet more meaningful by a never fully hidden trace of pensive melancholy, paired with that genuinely female tenderness that instills a woman with irresistible charm in the eyes of men. Her resemblance to Guido's picture was striking. Two attendants in Herodias's retinue, also very pretty, provide a superb contrast. They are perfect ladies-in-waiting with apparently no interest in anything beyond their court and their service, and the emptiness of their beauty grants them a certain sensual charm that allows us to feel more comfortable, allows our minds to recover bit by bit from the deeper, more shattering imprint of the central figure. One of them wears a vacuous smile and is watching the face of her mistress, ready to fulfill a request; the other gazes with indifference at the martyr's head on the platter as if it were a pudding.

I must once and for all describe life in an English country house, or at least the fabric on which each person embroiders whatever particular features he or she may choose. I can do this because the arrangement is essentially consistent everywhere here and has not changed since my earlier visit. This life certainly embodies the most enjoyable side of English customs because it amounts to unbridled freedom to do what you like. Nearly all the tedious ceremonies we observe at home, so exhausting for the host and the guests alike, are banished here. Nonetheless it is just as luxurious as in the city, although as I have already pointed out, this is made easier by the custom of having only invited guests and only for short stays.[26] One can readily forgive the ostentation underlying such arrangements, given the improved hospitality that results.

In order to make the best use of space, strangers are generally assigned no more than one commodious bedroom on the second floor, hardly ever several rooms. And the English rarely enter this chamber except to sleep and dress twice a day, the latter de rigueur even without company and in the strictest domesticity because all meals are eaten collectively. Whoever has something to write usually does so in the library, which is also where people quite unabashedly arrange for a rendezvous in order to escape the larger group or avoid particular individuals. You can often manage to spend hours there chatting undisturbed with the young ladies, who are always quite literarily inclined. Many a marriage or seduction of the already married is instigated

---

* And still is.—*The Editor.*

here between the *Corpus Juris* on the one side and Boufflers' *Works* on the other,[27] while a popular novel lies open in the middle as a binding medium.

Ten or eleven is the time for breakfast, at which you are allowed to appear in extremely informal attire. The meal is always like the one in the inn that I described before, but of course even more rich and ample in private homes, and the ladies do the honors gracefully. If you do not arrive until after the others have already left, your needs are attended to by a manservant, who in the best houses is on the job until one o'clock or later so that even the last straggler will not go away hungry. It goes without saying that half a dozen newspapers must be lying on the table so everyone can read exactly what he wishes.

The gentlemen now go out hunting or pursue other business, as does the host, who does not trouble himself further about the guests (a genuine good deed!), and only half an hour before the evening dinner do people reassemble in elegant dress in the drawing room.

I have already described how meals tend to go. There is just one curious custom I have not yet mentioned that, however scabrous, I must describe to you now for the sake of completeness. Namely, once the ladies have withdrawn, the men—in a very uninhibited way and directly next to the table—let nature take its course, a remnant of the barbarism that runs totally contrary to our concepts of decorum. I was particularly struck by this today when an old admiral—dressed in his official uniform, no doubt because of the presence of Lord Melville—devoted a good half of a quarter hour to this exercise, during which time we imagined we were hearing, as if from a rain spout, the last, lingering traces of a thundershower.

England is the true land of contrasts—from the heights to the depths at every moment. Thus despite all the other luxuries to be found in the best houses, coachmen and grooms often serve at table (at least in the country) and are sometimes accompanied by of the smell of horses. At the second breakfast or "luncheon," which takes place a few hours after the first and is as a rule consumed only by the ladies (who *faire la petite bouche*[28] at dinner and therefore heartily eat their fill at luncheon), you are offered no napkins, a used tablecloth, and often quite-unappetizing leftovers from the previous day.

That as parenthesis. I will now return to the order of the day. Once the gentlemen have consumed sufficient drink and satisfied the rest of their needs with such patriarchal simplicity, they once again go off in search of tea, coffee, and the fair sex, with whom they linger for a few hours, although without much amalgamation. Today, for example, when I looked up to monitor the situation, I found the company distributed as follows: The ailing master of the house was lying on the sofa and slightly dozing; five other ladies and gentlemen were busy reading a diversity of books and documents (I was leafing through a portfolio of park views); another gentleman had been playing for a quarter hour with a long-suffering dog; and two aged members of Parliament were engaged in a heated debate about the Corn Bill. The rest of the company could be found in the darkened room next door where a pretty girl was playing the piano, accompanying another who was singing deafening, soulful ballads and provoking even the amiable lady of the house to join me in hearty laughter.

I cannot help remarking that Lord and Lady Darnley are extraordinarily enlightened and unpretentious and thus among the most pleasant of all people of rank here. A member of the moderate opposition, which is concerned only about what's best for this country, he is totally unselfish and a genuine patriot, the finest label a cultured man can have. She is goodness, cordiality, and modesty personified.

After midnight, and usually after you've served yourself a light supper of fruits and cold dishes, everyone retires. To this end a quantity of small candlesticks is on hand atop a side table, and each person lights one to illuminate his way upstairs, since most of the servants, who have to get up early, have long since gone to bed. It is not the custom for servants to sit forever in the anteroom, and except at designated times when their assistance is expected, you rarely see them and simply wait on yourself.

Welcoming me in my room was a splendid old Chinese four-poster, spacious enough to sleep a sultan with six wives. But being alone, with a remote fireplace that offered no heat, I froze like an icicle until my own warmth finally enfolded me.

February 5th, 1827

I MUST SAY, just between us, that however pleasant and uninhibited life may be in a strange house, it is still too inhibiting, too unhomey, and above all too dependent for my taste. Overly proud and comfort loving as I am, I cannot be properly *à mon aise*. I only feel completely serene when I am within my own four walls and, to a lesser extent, when traveling in a carriage or staying at an inn. This may not be in the best taste, but at least it is mine! And since so many people have no taste at all, I am still quite content with my inferior version.

So as not to wear out my welcome here, I will tomorrow make my enormous bed available to someone else, perhaps a more corpulent mortal, in order to hurry on to the spa town of Brighton, which is extraordinarily fashionable right now.

Before departing, however, I spent today riding with Lord Darnley's accommodating son through the entire estate, which is less striking for its extraordinary beauty than for its success in never displaying any flaws. Still, some of the views from shady dells onto the distant Thames or the harbor at Gravesend and its towering masts are splendid. But nothing surpasses the incomparable artistry with which the borderlines of the woods have been drawn inside the park in a masterful imitation of nature. In many respects I would recommend Cobham Hall as a better object of study than any park I have described, although it is not the equal of many in size or extravagant layouts and structures. Rather its character is more modest and, especially in the long run, more valuable to any friend of Nature. It also offers more variety with its hills, valleys, and enclosed woodlands.

I just now said goodbye to Lady Darnley in her own room, a little sanctuary that I found furnished with the most enchanting disorder and abundance, the walls lined with small mirrored consoles crowded with elegant curiosities, and magnificent camellias in an array of baskets distributed on the floor so they seemed to be growing right out of it.

Allow me, dear Julie, to take my leave of you as well, here among these flowers, and ask you to grant this letter an equally long answer so that it will not occur to your conscience that I love you (at least in writing) far more than you do me.

The friend of your heart,
Lou

Brighton, February 7th, 1827

MOST BELOVED!

Yesterday I covered the sixty miles here with great speed and in the most delicious lassitude, without even looking up, because from time to time one must travel like a genteel Englishman.

It seems that the prevailing temperature is better in Brighton than in the rest of this foggy country, at least to judge by the brilliant sunshine that woke me this morning at nine. Shortly thereafter I went out for a walk, first down the Marine Parade that runs a long way by the sea. Then I toured the large, tidy, and very cheerful town, which, with its broad streets, is like the newest parts of London. Next I visited various London acquaintances. Since my horses had been sent ahead in good time, I went riding and found myself looking in vain for a glimpse of trees. The countryside is completely barren, nothing but dunes covered with short grass. The only picturesque elements are the sea and sky, though together they prepared the most beautiful sunset to welcome me. The majestic star was so veiled in a rosy, transparent mist that it no longer emitted rays, but instead looked like a solid nugget of gold, intensely radiant and slowly melting as it touched the water and spread across the blue sea. Finally the ocean swallowed the fiery orb, the burning colors faded, first from red to violet, then gradually to whitish grey. And in the twilight the roaring waves, driven by the evening wind, whistled against the level shore as if in triumph over the now-submerged sun.

A renowned old statesman watched this lovely spectacle along with me and was not at all indifferent to it. He was Lord Harrowby,[1] an engaging man whose manners are as fine and gentle as his experience of the world and business is great.

February 8th, 1827

HERE THERE ARE absolutely no public meeting rooms, no lists of spa visitors or the like. Brighton is only *called* a spa town in our sense of the term. It mainly serves Londoners who, lacking their own country estates, are seeking distraction and healthier air, or those who find it too expensive to maintain a London household during the winter when the Season has moved here. The king made Brighton especially fashionable because he was once very fond of it and built a quixotic Oriental palace.[2] Seen from the nearby heights with all its cupolas and their elaborate domes and minarets, it looks exactly like a well-arrayed chess game (Figure 35). But inside it is furnished magnificently, if fantastically. Although it cost an outrageous sum, its owner supposedly grew tired of it a long time ago and has now and then shown an inclination to tear it down, which would not be a regrettable loss.

35

The Pavilion at Brighton.

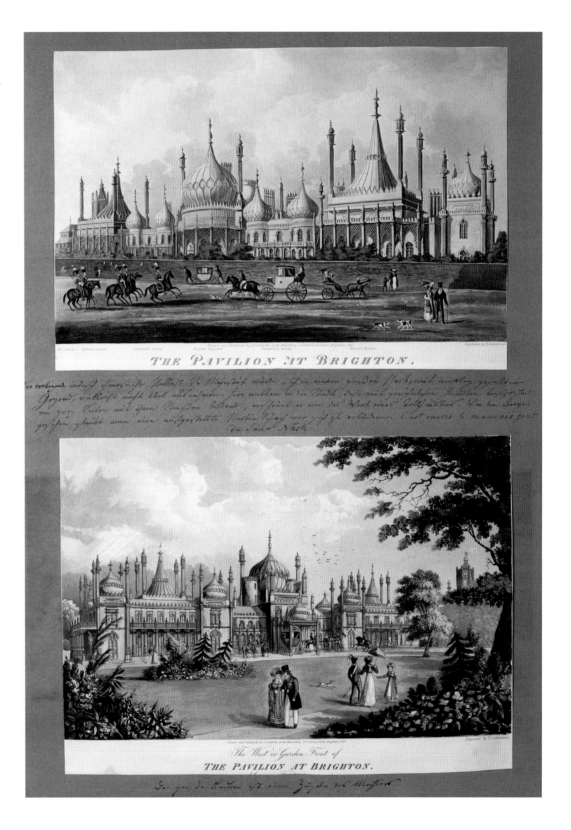

THE PAVILION AT BRIGHTON.

The West or Garden Front of
THE PAVILION AT BRIGHTON.

Only in the gardens of this palace have I seen any full-grown trees, but the promenades beside the sea are lovely even without them, especially the large Chain Pier or *jetée,* which extends one thousand feet into the water. From there you can embark on steam ships for Boulogne and Le Havre.[3]

Not far away an Indian has built Oriental baths where you can enjoy a Turkish massage, something supposedly quite invigorating and healthy, and very popular with genteel society, especially the ladies. I found the interior furnished in a European manner. The treatment is like that in Russian steam baths but less convenient, because you sit in a cool room on an elevated seat, enclosed in a kind of palanquin made of flannel, and the hot, herb-infused steam rises through the floor and fills the small space. The flannel wall has several sleeves hanging down on the outside, and the masseur inserts his hands and arms into them and gently kneads the bather's body. He then moves his thumb many times with a firm and steady pressure down over your limbs, back-bone, ribs, and stomach, which seems to be good for your physical state. Meanwhile you sweat as heavily and for as long as you wish, until finally the flannel tent is removed and you are doused in lukewarm water. Such sudden exposure to the chill of the room I find very unhealthy. Much more worthy of imitation is the way the drying towels are kept warm. They are laid out in a dresser fitted with tin-lined compartments, and steam heat keeps them at the same temperature all day long.

February 9th, 1827

THE SUN HAS disappeared again, and once more such a chill has arrived that I am writing to you in gloves to preserve my white hands (which I, like Lord Byron, think so highly of). I also confess this because I am not at all of the opinion that one must be considered a fop just for trying to retain the little bit of prettiness the dear Lord has granted him. And hands chapped from frost have always been anathema to me. This reminds me how once, many years ago in Strasbourg, I found myself quite early in the boudoir of a beautiful woman along with Field Marshal Wittgenstein (at that time still a general), who, singing the praises of Napoleon, also mentioned his temperance and added in an almost contemptuous tone, "A hero cannot be a gourmand."

The lovely lady (who was quite taken with me) knew that I was not altogether insensitive to sumptuous eating and drinking and took malicious pleasure in teasing me by asking the general to repeat his maxim. Although I have never been tempted to consider myself a hero (perhaps with the exception of a small novelistic episode here and there), I still felt myself blushing, one of those stupid habits I have never been able to break, and alas, still cannot, even when there is absolutely no good reason for it.

Annoyed with myself, I said in a fit of pique, "It's lucky for the lovers of a good table, General, that there are some brilliant exceptions to the rule you've established. Just remember the Round Table and then Alexander, who burned down Persepolis after an overly lavish meal, yet remains a hero. And gluttony did not hinder Frederick the Great from achieving the highest fame as both warrior and monarch. By the way, you who are battling the French so gloriously shouldn't be attacking good cuisine, since that nation, no matter how great its generals, has achieved longer-lasting and perhaps more enduring fame for its cooks."

This last observation was remarkably prophetic. How surprised the general, a Napoleon enthusiast, would have been, had I been able to tell him that in a short while he himself would confront that great non-gourmand and suffer one of the last successful swipes of the ailing lion's claws.[4]

You may be thinking, my good Julie, that this anecdote is like an *à propos* by our friend H——.[5] On the contrary, let me invoke the finery and excellent grooming of Alcibiades and Poniatowski as further proof that, given the appropriate talent, neither a predisposition to *bonne chère* nor a bit of *fatuité*[6] is an impediment to heroism.

I was interrupted here by a visit from Count Flahaut, one of the most likeable and worthy men from Napoleon's time. He carried the memories of prerevolutionary times into the emperor's court and still today maintains a reputation for perfect integrity and loyalty, a rare thing! He invited me to dinner the day after tomorrow. Our conversation delayed me, and now it is too late to go riding, and since I am not in the mood to visit the club, I will put on a second dressing gown, dream about you and Muskau, read through your letters again, and patiently shiver in my room until I retire. With nothing but an open fire in my breezy and richly fenestrated premises, it is impossible to get the temperature above forty-six degrees.[7] Thus, for now, au revoir.

February 10th, 1827

IT WAS ONLY fair that today I compensated myself for yesterday's house arrest by roaming around the area for many hours, all the more needed since in the evening I had to suffer through a large subscription ball.

The environs here are certainly peculiar because in four hours of riding, I did not see a single, full-grown tree. But the many hills, the city in the distance, several smaller towns nearby, the sea and its ships, as well as the frequently changing light—all this was enough to enliven the landscape; even the contrast with the abundant woodlands to be found elsewhere in England was not without its charm. The sun finally retired incognito, the heavens turned completely clear, and the moon rose cloudless and luminous above the waters. I turned my horse from the hills down to the sea and rode back the five or six miles I had traveled from Brighton, right along the edge of the waves on the sandy beach. The tide was just starting to rise, and my horse made an occasional leap to the side whenever a breaker, crowned with white foam, rolled under him and then retreated again, as if the sea were playing with us.

There is nothing I love more than riding alone in the moonlight along a deserted seashore, just me with the rippling and whooshing and rushing of the waves, so close to the mysterious depths, so eerie. Even horses resist being kept near the water, and as soon as you loosen the reins, they instinctively head for solid ground at double the speed.

How different from this poetic scene was the prosaic ball—so far from meeting my expectations that I was amazed! A narrow staircase led up to the premises, where you stepped directly, with no anteroom, into a badly lit and pathetically furnished hall with woolen ropes set up all around it to form a gallery separating the dancers from the spectators. A platform for the musicians had been draped so clumsily with such badly laundered fabric that it looked as if someone had hung sheets out to dry. Imagine, then, a second room adjacent, with benches running all along the walls and a large tea table in the center. Crowded into both rooms were the guests, legions of them, dressed from head to toe in nothing but jet black, gloves included. They were in mourning,[8] and danced with such a melancholy air and no trace of animation or enjoyment that you felt sorry for them in their listlessness and sense of futility. This will give you a true idea of the Brighton Almack's (what the modish balls are called here).[9] The whole setup is ludicrous enough. In London these Almack's are the pinnacle of fashion in the Season, which lasts from April into

June. Five or six of the most genteel ladies, who are called "Patronesses" (Princess Lieven is one of them), dispense the vouchers. The granting of these is a great favor, and they are very difficult to attain for those who do not belong to the absolutely most refined or modern world. Hence for months on end intrigues are hatched and the Lady Patronesses are flattered in the most ignoble ways by people hoping to be admitted. If a person is never seen at an Almack's, he or she is viewed as hopelessly unfashionable (I might even say disgraced), the greatest possible misfortune in the English world which so longs to be *fashionable*. This is confirmed by a recent novel on the subject depicting the goings-on of London society very faithfully.[10] It appeared in its third edition two months ago already. Yet upon closer examination it reveals more about the antechamber than the salon and seems written by someone who, as the Abbé de Voisenon said, *a écouté aux portes*.[11]

How poorly the English are informed about outsiders is clear from a passage in this book describing a foreign ambassador's English-born wife making great fun of Londoners, who, although familiar with other countries, nonetheless grant a higher rank to a German prince than to her own husband the baron, a title she claims is far more distinguished.

"But the word 'prince,'" she adds, "recognized as meaningless by everyone on the Continent, bedazzles my foolish countrymen."

"*C'est bien vrai*," a Frenchman chimes in, "*un duc cirait mes bottes à Naples, et à Petersbourg un prince russe me rasait tous les matins.*"

Since the English usually make mistakes when quoting foreign languages, I suspect that here, too, a small error has crept in and the passage should probably read "*un prince russe me rossait tous les matins.*"* [12]

Such a fashionable novel, however, has had a burlesque effect on the middle ranks, who are always groping blindly after fashion and therefore constantly fearful of betraying their ignorance of London high society. This tends to make them particularly ridiculous.

I witnessed a very amusing episode just a few weeks after the book appeared. I had been invited along with several other foreigners to dine at the home of the director of the East India Company, the former governor of Mauritius.[13] The other guests included a German prince, already long known to the family, as well as—apropos for the farce—a German baron. As people were about to go to the table, the prince approached the lady of the house to escort her as usual, and he was not a little amazed when she turned her back on him with a slight curtsy and took the arm of the very pleasantly surprised baron. An irrepressible laugh on my part almost offended the good prince, who could not fathom such irregular behavior on the part of the hostess. But

---

* It is only natural that the English, who worry so little about anything beyond their shores, should find it difficult to distinguish properly between German, Russian, and French princes and therefore rank them either too high or too low. In fact, in England and France there are no princes other than those of royal blood. If Englishmen or Frenchmen bear such titles, they are foreign ones, and in old families of the French nobility, they are attached to the younger sons. For example, the prince de Polignac carries the Roman title "prince" as the second son, whereas the eldest is the duc de Polignac.

In Germany, with the exception of one man of outstanding merit, there have been no princes who were not descended from old families with high rank, with all the appropriate rights and privileges, and hence a prince there occupies the first echelon directly after the ruling houses. In Russia, on the other hand, the title of prince is essentially nothing at all, because in that country rank, rights, and prestige come only through service. And the title is not worth much more in Italy. The English get this all mixed up and seldom know what respect is actually due a foreigner. [The exceptional man is likely Gebhard Leberecht von Blücher.—*Translator*.]

since I understood what had happened, I was quickly able to give him a proper explanation, and the prince, no longer concerned about rank, gave his arm to the prettiest lady in the party. As for me, I managed to place myself on the other side of Lady Farquhar, so I could be guaranteed an amusing conversation at dinner. The soup was barely finished when I remarked to her, with an engaging expression, how very much her tact and refined knowledge of social and, indeed, foreign relations had surprised me.

"Ah," she replied, "after such a long time as a governor's wife, one gets to know the greater world."

"Certainly," I chimed in, "especially in Mauritius, where everything is black and white."

"You see," she continued, leaning toward my ear, "we know very well that a foreign prince doesn't mean much, but a baron is owed all the honor one can grant him."

"Brilliantly differentiated!" I exclaimed, "but with an Italian you must be careful again, for there *barone* means 'rascal.'"

"Is that possible?" she said, startled. "What a strange title."

"Yes, madame, on the Continent titles are portentous things, and even if you were an Egyptian sphinx (she was at least that gauche), you would never get to the bottom of this enigma!"

"May I help you to some fish?" she said perplexed and uncertain about how to respond.

"With great pleasure," I answered, and found the turbot, although lacking a title, excellent!

Returning to the ball: the strangest thing about it is that a voucher for Almack's, which many of the English seek out as if it were a matter of life or death, must be purchased at a cost of ten shillings since this Almack's is nothing but a ball for money. *Quelle folie que la mode!*[14] Sometimes you have to believe that the earth is the true madhouse of our solar system.

Here in Brighton you find nothing but a miniature imitation of London. The Lady Patronesses of this Almack's are now . . . .
. . . .

When I entered, I saw no one I knew and therefore asked the first available gentleman I found to point out the Marchioness of Queensberry. I did not know her, but she had arranged for my ticket through the *entremise* of Countess Flahaut so I needed to present myself. I found her to be a very endearing, home-loving woman, who had never left England. She introduced me to her daughters, three genuine English *Aalheiten,** and to a Lady Minto, who spoke very good German. This, too, is stylish now, and the young ladies are agonizing tremendously over it.

Later I finally found a man I knew, who introduced me to several very pretty young girls. One among them stood out, a certain Miss Wyndham, a niece of Lord Egremont. She was raised in Germany and is more German than English, which could only be an advantage in my eyes. She was by far the loveliest and most graceful woman at the ball, so I nearly danced again, although I have always danced badly, and vanity has denied me that so-called pleasure for many years. I could probably have attempted it here since God knows there is no other place where people leap around more awkwardly; indeed anyone waltzing in step is a true rarity. But it seems ludicrous, just as I am about to approach the *Schwabenalter,*[15] for me to join the

---

* See *Reineke Fuchs.* This can also be translated as "ladyships."—*The Editor.* [In Goethe's *Reineke Fuchs* there is a goose named Alheit, explained as short for "Adelheit," a noble though perhaps excessively talkative personality. See *Goethes "Reineke Fuchs,"* ed. Alexander Bieling (Berlin, 1882), 25.—*Translator.*]

worshippers of the tarantella once again. *Il est vrai que la fortune m'a souvent envoyé promener, mais danser—c'est trop fort!*[16]

The marchioness then told me about one of her relatives who was present. Chief of a Highland clan, with a name as long as a Spaniard's, he was a descendant of the kings of the Scottish isles and as proud as Holofernes of his thousand-year-old nobility.[17] He wanted to make my acquaintance, and I could only congratulate myself on making his, since I found the man to be exactly like the Highland figures portrayed in Walter Scott's novels. A true Scotsman, devoted heart and soul to his ancestors and ancient customs and filled with deep disdain for the English, he was fiery, good-natured, honest, and brave, yet childishly vain, and in that respect just as easy to wound as to win over. It was therefore not hard to gain his favor, and since I was rather bored anyway, we sat down in the empty tearoom on one of the wooden benches covered with poor fabric. There I listened for an hour while he told me about his magnificent properties, the battles of his ancestors, and his own travels and exploits. This good man, who was already fifty or older, continually returned to the topic of his Scottish costume, which he described to me in full detail, at the same time mentioning with appreciation his stay in Berlin and how when he was there in 1800, his costume had attracted so much attention from everyone at the reviewing of the troops that, even before he had been presented to His Majesty, the king had invited him to dine in Potsdam. This, he assured me, was an honor granted only to the country's own noblemen and to foreigners of the utmost eminence. I wanted to say something here, but he quickly interrupted and insisted that there was more. On that day he was wearing just half-Scottish dress along with English pantaloons; the next day, however, he appeared at maneuvers with bare thighs and a suit studded with silver. The king and his entire court marveled at him, and a quarter hour later came another invitation to the table, something that amazed all the Englishmen present. The queen herself spent a long time in conversation with him, and immediately afterward an adjutant arrived to invite him the following day to a soirée and the Italian opera in Berlin.[18]

He went on: "I asked whether I could come with naked thighs. 'Don't hesitate for a moment,' the officer responded with a laugh." My worthy Scotsman continued with obvious pride: "And that evening was my triumph, for I arrived in the gala attire of red encrusted in gold. So I was invited three times in a row, something that has never happened to any peer of the land. And each time I looked more and more splendid. But now," he added, "I became extremely worried that a fourth invitation might arrive, because I didn't yet have a more impressive costume. Fortunately the fourth invitation never came."

He told this ludicrous story with such childlike ardor that it grew somehow quite touching. I was naturally full of admiration and attentiveness, and so I told him how strange it was that as a child, precisely in the year 1800, I had found myself with my father in a box at the Berlin opera just next to the royal box, and I remembered as if it were yesterday how there, for the first time in my life, I saw a Scotsman without trousers, and how I had been astonished at this marvel of splendor and beauty.

"Then I was the man, I was the man!" my old Scotsman exclaimed, entirely beside himself, and from that moment on I had captured his heart. He offered me a fervent invitation to Scotland, asked for my card, and requested the honor of introducing me to the Dukes of Atholl and Hamilton in London. He would do me the Scottish honors and "wait just a minute, on the . . . hmm . . . right! On the 26th I will give a ball, and in your honor I will don the traditional Scottish costume that is studded with gold, no . . . I think instead the one with silver. It's not as opulent, but more elegant."* I did not fail to display lively interest, regretted that urgent business in London meant I could not stay here for such a long time, but vowed to do my best to return on that very day so as not to miss such an interesting spectacle. At that very moment Lady Queensberry arrived with her daughters and, since I had heard enough for the time being, I called out to her that Mr. MacDonell, Duke of Clanronald and Glengarry, was not exactly a new acquaintance of mine, since I had already seen him more than twenty years ago when I was a lad. In response to her "how so?" my indefatigable friend launched into the story of the threefold escalation, and I slipped quietly away and went home.

February 11th, 1827

THIS MORNING I went to church in an attempt at piety, but failed. Everything was too sober and unaesthetic. What I like is a holy service that is artistic and appealing to the senses. If only we would follow Nature, still the best teacher of religion as well as the best model for government constitutions (since she rules constitutionally)! Her sublime spectacles instill us with the most devout emotions, do they not? Those paintings of sunrise and sunset, the music of the raging storm and roaring sea, the sculpture of rocks and mountains? So, dear people, do not try to be cleverer than the dear Lord, but rather imitate him as best you can.

Of course such sermons, delivered by me, would fall on deaf ears, except for yours, dear Julie; for you have long listened along with me to the heavenly song of the spheres, a melody that resounds forever in the magnificence of eternal creation. There it continues as long as people do not stuff the cotton of positivism in their ears so as not to hear it.**

---

* In Berlin we were recently lucky enough to admire a young Scotsman—the son of Sir Walter Scott, in fact—in his national costume. He appeared at a festivity with one of his countrymen, who in ordinary black dress looked extremely gaunt and pale, not unlike Lord Ruthven the vampire. On the following morning the party was described in a caustic *chanson,* which ended as follows:

> *enfin parut*
> *Lord Ruthwen et jeune Scott,*
> *L'un sans cul, et l'autre sans culottes.—The Editor.*

["finally appeared / Lord Ruthwen and young Scott / The one without (his) ass, the other without (his) pants." The allusion to the *sans-culottes* of the French Revolution is clear.—*Translator.*]

** My dear departed friend was obsessed by a kind of idée fixe that a New Church was soon to arise. How sad that he did not live to see what is now taking shape, for I just read the following heartening announcement in the *Allgemeine Zeitung:*

To the Unknown

I hear that harsh words have been printed in these pages about me and the New Church. Attack me, my dear ones, but listen to this word of warning about sin! Once again it approaches us, raising the shroud more and more, a glory that the human tongue cannot express and the human spirit can barely sense. If we scarcely comprehend that *all* may become new, then how did we so abruptly comprehend a new *All?* Be careful not to become hot-headed and insult the banner or assault the vanguard until we can discern the multitudes drawing closer and identify the mighty who lead them. Dear brother, consider how you would feel if, with invective still upon your lips, you were to recognize Him? He comes at an hour you cannot know.

This is a lot to take in. Not only is all that was old new, but there is indeed a new All! Truly, no reasonable person can ask for more. Only a rogue gives more than he has.—*The Editor.*

The sermon I heard was utterly fossilized and vacuous, even though it had been worked out ahead of time and delivered from a written text. Preachers could be far more effective if they abandoned the old routine of choosing topics only from the Bible and instead drew from the life of their locality and society in general; if they addressed themselves not to dogma but to the poetry of religion that dwells within each of us; and if they taught morality not just as a set of commandments but as something beautiful and useful; indeed something truly essential to the happiness of each individual and all society. If only there was effort given to instructing the common man from the pulpit, training him to *think* instead of *believe,* then there would soon be less vice in him. He would begin to feel a genuine interest in the church and a need for sermons as part of his education, whereas he now usually attends them for the least edifying reasons or without any thought at all. The laws of the land, not just the Ten Commandments, should be explained from the pulpit, and the congregation should also be made familiar with the reasons underlying them because, as Christ says, how many of them sin without knowing what they do.*

The most practical approach to adopting a general moral code is surely to ask oneself whether an action, if performed by everyone, would be harmful and therefore bad for human society, or beneficial and therefore good. If people became accustomed to applying this measure, and if they were given a vivid demonstration of the inevitable repercussions of their own actions *upon themselves,* then in a few decades we would witness an improvement not just in morality but also in culture and industry. Meanwhile the priestly wisdom we have become used to—one that places faith, authority, and dogma above all else—has left everything unchanged for centuries and often made matters worse.

In fact, one might well follow the example of France, where famous villains are pardoned so they can be employed by the police force; or choose some of our instructors from among those led to conversion by their personal experience of sin and its evil consequences; in other words, those best informed on the subject (such as the late Werner).[19] As the example of many saints verifies, a penitent is not only firmer in his conviction and understanding but also generally more zealous in his proselytizing. There is greater rejoicing in heaven over a repentant sinner than over ten righteous men.[20]

But in a well-organized society it is crucial, in my assessment, that all clergymen, whatever their affiliation, receive a fixed salary, financed either by the state or the congregation. To be paid in cash for each genuine blessing or conventional ceremony is an indecent practice that undermines every illusion and ounce of respect for the cleric and, if he has any sensitivity, debases him in his own eyes as well. It is truly horrible to see a poor man from the countryside stick two pennies behind the altar for the body of Christ he has just enjoyed, or press coins into the reverend's hand at a baptism as if it were beer money. Yet when you hear the preacher himself ranting and scolding from his pulpit about the offerings getting smaller and smaller and, uttering dire warnings, condemning any withholding of his income as a sign of diminished piety, then you cannot but be acutely aware of what so many clergymen are really after and what they consider their actual profession to be. Soldiers naturally love war and clerics likewise religion—in both cases

---

* Indeed it would be just as desirable for our laws to be made more comprehensible. If, instead of hundreds of different provincial and local rules, we had just *one* code of law for the entire monarchy, then what is right in one village would no longer be wrong ten miles away, and Prussian jurists could finally become workers in bronze instead of mere tinkers.—*The Editor.*

because of the benefits. Patriots, however, love war only as a way to attain freedom; philosophers love religion only because of its beauty and truth.

That is the difference.

However as the author of *Zillah* so rightly said, "Establishments are much more durable than opinions: the ritual survives the faith; the temple outlasts the religion that founded it; and when a priesthood, endowed with large revenues, has become interwoven with the institutions of a country, they may remain and flourish long after their creed has fallen into discredit."[21]

The afternoon was more gratifying. I climbed the hills surrounding the town and finally crawled up to the base of a windmill so I could see a full panorama of Brighton. A gale was spinning the sails around their axis with such force that the entire structure pitched like a ship. The miller's lad who had shown me the way up now brought out a telescope from a flour bin. Unfortunately, despite its soft resting place, it was broken. But I was already content with the beautiful, sweeping vista animated by several hundred fishing boats fighting against the wind. Then with the sinking sun, I hurried back to my social duties.

The guests at Count Flahaut's were few but interesting, due first to the hosts themselves, then to a lady renowned for her beauty, and finally to a gentleman once known for his prominence in Parisian society, namely, Monsieur de Montrond, who played an influential role there in his youth and was simultaneously embroiled in politics. He now spends much of every year in England, probably not without political intentions, and is one of those men, rarer by the day, who live in great style without anyone really knowing how they manage it; who acquire considerable and widespread authority without anyone knowing where it comes from; and who are always suspected of harboring something special, even mysterious, without anyone knowing why. This man is at least very likeable when he wants to be. He narrates with great skill and has forgotten nothing about his varied and active life, which thereby adds zest to his conversation. The French character is the best suited to such magnificent adventurers, who are always admirable for their consummate understanding of human nature, even if they mostly use it to dupe others. Their social graces blaze the way, and their less than generous hearts and economic savvy (if I may put it this way) help them care for what they have achieved and keep a firm hold on it forever.

The suave man I am talking about can also gamble in a charming manner and jokingly claims like Fox that he knows no greater pleasure than losing, except of course for winning.

There was much discussion of Napoleon, who was remembered with reverence by our host as he is by all who have lived close to him. One thing I heard astounded me. We were told how, during the first hour of the retreat from Waterloo—which proceeded (in complete contradiction to the usual account) only slowly and without any hurry under the protection of a battalion of his *Garde*—the emperor was so exhausted by the immense effort of the Hundred Days and the following events that he fell asleep atop his horse two or three times and would have fallen off if Count Flahaut himself had not held him up. The count assured us, however, that aside from this physical exhaustion, Napoleon showed not the slightest sign of any emotional distress.

February 14th, 1827

MY VERY ORIGINAL HIGHLANDER—who I have since heard is a real madcap and has already killed two or three men in duels—visited me this morning and brought me a printed copy of his genealogy, containing the entire history of his clan. He complained indignantly that another man of the same name was contesting him for the rank of chieftain, and he made an effort to show me how the papers he had brought along proved him to be the genuine one, also saying that "a trial by ordeal between the two of us would quickly decide it for the best."[22] He then pointed out his coat-of-arms to me, a bloody hand on a blue field, and explained its origin as follows:

Two brothers were engaged in a military campaign against one of the Scottish islands, and they agreed that he whose flesh and blood should first touch the ground there (a Scottish expression) would become its overlord. They put every effort into their oars until they encountered large rocks blocking their ships from further advance, at which point both the brothers and their warriors plunged into the water and began swimming to reach the island. When the eldest saw that his younger brother was getting ahead of him, he drew his short sword, laid his left hand on a protruding rock, severed it at the wrist with one stroke, gripped the fingers and threw it, bleeding, past his brother and onto the shore, crying out "God is my witness that my flesh and blood touched the land first." And so he became king, and his descendants were the absolute rulers of the island for ten generations.[23]

I found the story of the bloody hand not unpoetic and an apt image of those brutish yet vibrant times. I did not fail to tell him a pendant from the *Nibelungenlied* concerning my own progenitors, likely just as fabled, and we parted the best of friends over the spirits of our ancestors.[24]

There are several private balls occurring here daily, and in quarters so small that no respectable German would dare invite twelve people, whereas here a few hundred are packed together like negro slaves. It is worse than in London, and the space for the quadrille suggests only a mathematical possibility of dance-like motion. Yet a ball without these throngs would be very poorly regarded, and a guest who arrived to find the stairs empty would probably drive off. This very odd pretense reminded me vividly of Potier's no-longer-young man who ordered a pair of pants from his tailor that were supposed to be "extraordinarily tight" and, as the master clothier was about to depart, called him back once more with the words: "Do you hear me? Extraordinarily tight. If I can get in, I won't take them."[25] A dandy could say much the same about the rout here: "If I can get in, I won't go."[26]

Once you are finally inside, however, it must be admitted that nowhere else can you see more pretty girls, nor find yourself *bon gré, mal gré* pressed up against them. These days they have mostly had at least a few years education in France and therefore distinguish themselves through improved dress and deportment. And a large number of them speak German. You can receive as many invitations to this type of soirée as you want, but you can just as well show up uninvited as a total stranger, because if you do not stay too long you will never encounter the hosts, and in any case, they will certainly not know half the people present. At one o'clock in the morning, an elegant cold supper is always served along with copious amounts of champagne. The setting for this is usually the servants' room below, and since the table can barely accommodate twenty diners at the same time, brigades of people push their way up and down the narrow staircase. If you are able to find a seat, you can rest, and many people take advantage of this with little regard for those coming after them. There is also scarcely room for the ladies. Yet as soon as a dish or bottle is emptied, the serving staff is diligent about replacing it with a fresh one from the side of the table inaccessible to the guests.

In order to observe all this properly, I tarried in one of the better houses until four in the morning. I found that near the end, when three-quarters of the guests had left, the party was at its most pleasant—all the more so since the daughters of that particular family were exceptionally pretty and charming. On the other hand, there were some thoroughly infamous eccentrics there, among them a fat lady of at least fifty-five, wearing a velvety black fur trimmed in white and a turban with swaying ostrich feathers. Whenever she could find enough room, she waltzed around in a frenzy like a bacchante, with an energy her three quite-attractive daughters tried in vain to emulate. I realized the source of this Herculean stamina when I learned that this very rich lady had acquired her fortune through a successful cattle business.[27]

The music at all these balls consists of nothing but a piano and a horn; yet both musicians manage to coax such a noise out of their instruments that all conversation must be abandoned in their vicinity.

February 16th, 1827

YESTERDAY I READ that "strong passions increase with distance." Mine for you must be very strong indeed—and tender *friendship* is always the most enduring in any case—for I love you more than ever. This is totally understandable. If you love someone truly, then in their absence you only recall their good and adorable qualities, whereas the sometimes-annoying minor flaws everyone possesses disappear entirely from memory. Thus love increases at a distance quite naturally. And you? What do you think about this? How many more flaws of mine must you cover with the mantle of Christian love!

Tomorrow I am traveling quickly to London in order to deliver this letter by hand to our ambassador since the last ones were so long in transit. Some curious people probably got hold of them—we will not be rid of the infamy of censors opening letters any time soon.[28] In two days I will be back here and will feel quite content to have missed three or four balls. Before leaving today, I took another long, solitary walk, this time not alone but accompanied by one of the many elegant young ladies I have gotten to know here. In England unmarried women, once they have been launched into the world, are granted a tremendous amount of freedom. The young girl in question was only seventeen years old but already polished in Paris.

When I got home I found to my considerable surprise a letter from the unfortunate Rehder, who has been forced back to Harwich once again and is beseeching me for money and assistance. I only now learned that—against my wishes—he in fact did not take the prescribed route via Calais. These wanderings of the Garden Odysseus are just as ludicrous as they are unpleasant, and you will certainly have long since believed that the fish must have made a meal of our adventurer *malgré lui*. I still remember vividly how twelve years ago, also around this time of year, when I wanted to embark for Hamburg, I was luckily dissuaded by my old French manservant because, as he so oddly phrased it: "*Dans ces temps-ci, il y a toujours quelques équinoxes dangereuses, qui peuvent devenir funestes.*"[29] And he was right: the vessel was shipwrecked and several lives were lost.

London, February 17th, 1827

ALL HONOR TO Sir Temple! Because he conveyed your letter, it only took ten days to arrive, whereas those that go via our diplomatic channels are in transit for three weeks. Give him my sincere thanks. I laughed heartily at all the news that H—— reports with such wit.[30] Her portrayals of the little *Kriminalrat*, called *le rat criminel* by the satirists, the *renvoyé extraordinaire*, and the *diplomate à la fourchette* are splendid,[31] as is her account of the cheery house, court, state, and body servant who is busy both night and day and whose success should not surprise you. It is undeniable that there is a kind of parochialism in the world that almost always succeeds and a kind of intellect that never does. Mine is of the second type—a fantastic, image-making mind that restructures its own dreamworld every day and thus always remains a stranger in the real one. You think that I have scarcely paid attention to happiness when it presented itself, at best taking it playfully by the fingers instead of holding it in a serious embrace; that I have never valued the present until it stood like a tableau in the far distance; that the past would often be an image of regret and the future an image of yearning, but the present as elusive as a cloud! Marvelous. Your explanation is delightful. And nobody, I must admit, is better at emphatic moralizing than you are. If only it could be of some help to me! But say, even if you could convince a lame man it would be far better for him not to walk with a limp, still, when the wretched soul put one foot in front of the other, would he not limp just like before? *Naturam expellas furca, etc.*[32] Only in vain do you tell your stomach to digest better, your wit to be sharper, your reason to be more effective. With few modifications everything goes on the same until death.

You wrote me about the decisions of the ministries concerning a certain matter. These, too, are the same old thing, however civil. But is it not strange that our lower-level officials are as conspicuous for their imperious, rude, and even derisive manner as their superiors (with a single exception) are noteworthy for their refined and genteel manner? And yet the latter thereby achieve the appearance of the most bitter irony, do they not? You can submit that to our Goethian Academy of Dilettantes as next year's prize question.[33]

Apropos, who is the very clever minister H—— mentions? Ah ha, I can guess. But the ministers are already so clever ex officio that it is hard to know which one she means. On the other hand, I guessed immediately who the "over-the-hill" one was as well as the pitiful, now temporarily horizontal one. His illness truly distresses me, because when healthy he stands very straight and tall, in my opinion towering above resentment and envy, thanks to the dignity of his character as well as his business acumen. In fact, there are a few public servants in our country who constantly tempt one to cry out, along with Bürger's Lenore, "Bist lebend, Liebster, oder tot?"[34]

May heaven preserve us both in mind and body, and may it above all preserve your tender friendship, so essential to my well-being.

Your faithful Lou

Brighton, February 19th, 1827

P RECIOUS JULIE!

"To make the best of my time," as the ever-practical English put it, I visited three theaters in a row yesterday before leaving town. In the first play the main character was an Irish servant.

His master, just at the point of hiring him, is contemplating the abduction of a lovely lady friend and so asks his prospective employee whether he will be resolute in doing everything demanded of him. "Oh, everything!" exclaims the delighted O'Higgy, "everything you want— I'll steal a cow in the morning and make beefsteaks out of it for your dinner." And later on he observes "Two heads are always better than one; and even if the second is just a calf's head, you can make a meal of it, if you're hungry."

From all the comedies and novels I have seen thus far, the Irish must be a peculiar folk with an originality altogether different from the English. When you come across them begging on the streets of London, you recognize them immediately because of what I might call their Gasconesque manner and dialect. As a modern writer has quite drolly but also realistically observed:

> An English beggar cries out the same words over and over in a sluggish tone: "Give a poor man a halfpenny, give a poor man a halfpenny!" What an orator his Irish colleague is in contrast! "Oh, Your Worship, give us a penny, just a nice little penny, Your Honor, and glory and God's blessing be upon your children and your children's children! Give us the little penny and may heaven reward you with a long life, a gentle death, and a merciful judgment!" Who can resist such a plea, at once moving and funny?

In the second theater, we were regaled by a pantomime of a quadrille performed by birds, as well as one performed by a tea service. In the latter, the teakettle, milk jug, and a cup executed a *pas de trois,* while spoons, knives, and forks danced around them as walk-ons. The birds in the first performance were very hard to tell apart, and I would advise that Mephistopheles arrange something similar at the S——ian Court Theater, where perhaps parrots could also be given speaking parts. This would add more variety to the ingenious narrative, and a teakettle and accessories might also be good additions to the cast.

The Indian jugglers who practiced their artistry on the third stage performed something entirely new to me. They did the usual ball trick, but juggled short burning torches instead, making for a highly unusual kind of fireworks: a kaleidoscopic sequence of flaming geometric shapes—wheels, serpents, triangles, stars, flowers, etc.—executed with remarkable self-assurance and not a moment's hesitation.

The flood of fantastic nonsense in these pantomimes seems to have pursued me into the night, as I slept in my carriage between London and Brighton, and experienced the most bizarre visions. One dream set me astride my beautiful white horse, but this time I could barely control him. He continued to resist me, and just when I had finally subdued him, he shook his head with such furious force that it broke off at the neck and flew twenty feet away, while I plunged down a deep ravine riding his headless body. Next I was sitting on a bench in my own park watching a horrific hurricane as it uprooted all the old trees far and wide and piled them up like bundles of twigs. Finally I quarreled with you, dear Julie, and in despair went to join the army. I forgot you (something possible only in my sleep) and soon found myself young and radiant again in this new life, full of vigor and no less cocky. It was a day of battle: the cannons roared like magnificent thunder and were accompanied by superb military music, which inspired us all; in the midst of cartridge fire we went on, privileged by the dream, to breakfast with total composure on truffle pâté and champagne. Then a dull cannonball ricocheted slowly toward us and, before I could leap aside, ripped the head off the man seated on the ground next to me and took off both my legs as well, so that I collapsed groaning in blood and horror.

When I returned to my senses, there was a gale roaring around me and the sea howled in my ears. I believed I was in the middle of an ocean voyage, but then the carriage stopped in front of the inn on the Marine Parade in Brighton. Perhaps I will dream the next installment tomorrow.

The fantasies we construct in life are just as confused, are they not? Castles in the air, whether for good or evil, are nothing but castles in the air. Some endure for just a few minutes, others for years, others for decades, but in the end they all collapse—they only *looked* real! No one is imbued with a greater tendency to be an architect of such castles than I. At the slightest incentive, I can fabricate a gleaming palace or a miserable hut, a grave, or a dungeon. But *you,* dear Julie, are always at my side, sharing my good fortune, decorating the hut, weeping over the grave, or comforting me in my shackles. Right now I am drifting somewhere in between with no secure abode. But all the same, my spiritual disposition remains airy and cheerful, although it is three o'clock in the morning and my body is sleepy. So let me kiss your hand and say goodnight. I do, however, ask that you look in the book of dreams to see what my visions might mean.

You are familiar with my cherished embrace of superstition, a penchant from which no insipid argument can ever dissuade me; for instance, when a person of strong mind shrugs off anything he has not experienced personally, or when an unctuous cleric says "There is a strange inconsistency in the way people refuse to believe in religion (by which he always means his church and its statutes) and yet will otherwise accept all manner of unreasonable things with complete gullibility!"

"Oh, dear pastor," I reply, "what unreasonable things do you mean?"

"Well, the belief in hidden sympathetic attraction, for instance, or dreams or the influence of the stars."

"But most venerable sir, I find absolutely no inconsistency there! Every thinking being must admit that nature is brimming with mysteries, with telluric and cosmic influences and relationships, some of which used to be considered fables but have now been discovered to be true, and others that we may so far only sense but not quite identify. It is therefore not at all unreasonable to form hypotheses about these things and, more or less, to believe in them. I don't challenge your miracles or symbols, but there are certain things in your teachings that seem incomprehensible to our reason, mind, and heart. For example, a God who is more passionate and partisan than the frailest of men; or the infinite agonies imposed by eternal love for finite sins; or arbitrary forgiveness and damnation meted out as mere predestination; and so forth. These things can only be possible if two and two make five, and no superstition can match the insanity of such beliefs."

Apropos, I just realized that I forgot to thank you for the lovely New Year's wishes. That swan swimming amid hedges of roses looks so like you, its costume as perfectly fresh and white as yours and its appearance just as poised and elegant. Do you know how I interpret this greeting? Here is what it says to me: Julie is your Fortuna and someday will once again make you a bed of roses, though only after the two of us have been repeatedly scratched and bloodied by the thorns. When she finally sings her swan song, may the melody transport her friend to a peaceful rest as well.

February 22nd, 1827

I HAVE JUST come home from a grand Almack's "fancy ball," where everyone has to appear in fantastic costume or in uniform, not the most decorous mélange. As you can imagine, my friend from Glasgow did not fail to show up in his magnificent Scottish dress. In fact, it is a very handsome outfit—grand, picturesque, and manly. The only part I do not like are the shoes with their huge buckles. His sword is of exactly the same shape as our student rapiers, and a dagger, pistols, and ammunition pouches form part of the attire. The weapons are set with precious stones, and on his colorful cap is an eagle's feather, the mark of a chieftain.

I escorted two ladies to the ball. The first, Mrs. Clifton, is a cheerful and clever woman of about thirty-five, still quite pretty, who loves the world (which loves her in return) and tends to an invalid husband in the most attentive manner—the best kind of faithfulness. She is pleasant to look at and of good character; in short, she is very suitable to have as a friend in this realm. The second lady, her bosom friend, is a young, very appealing widow; less distinguished, admittedly, but a sweet, amicable creature, who is much pleased if you compare her teeth to pearls and her blue eyes to violets.

There was altogether nothing to be ashamed of in the attire or appearance of my ladies, but along with all the rest, they were eclipsed by the young Miss Fremantle, the "beauty of Brighton." Truly one of the loveliest girls I have ever seen, she is a sylph who must have smuggled in her marvelous foot and her gracefulness from some other land. Meanwhile she is just sixteen years old and as wild and nimble as quicksilver, as inexhaustible a dancer as she is a prankster. I was lucky enough today to win her good favor through a surprise gift—a cornet of especially well-made bonbon crackers,[1] which she had taken extravagant delight in distributing at previous balls. Due to the excesses she had perpetrated, however, these same bonbons were now strictly frowned upon by the mamas and were no longer available at supper as they used to be. I had prudently procured some from the confectioner ahead of time and now handed them to her quite unexpectedly. I doubt whether the gift of a million thalers could bring me as much delight as I gave her with this trifle. The dear thing was jubilant and immediately deployed her artillery units, which were all the more successful because the enemy believed itself safe. Every explosion sent her into spasms of hilarity, and every time I came near her she sent me a smile with her blazing eyes, sweet and friendly as an angel. The poor child! This perfect innocence, this expression of supreme happiness touched me deeply, for alas, soon, just like all the rest, she will be disappointed!

Many of the other girls were also beautiful, but they had been drilled too carefully. Some of them were dripping with jewels and precious objects, but none came close to the petite Fremantle, whose assets in *charm* and *grace* could not overcome her lack of *financial* assets in the eyes of these ugly, egotistical *men.*[2]

February 24th, 1827

I SPENT YESTERDAY evening at Mrs. FitzHerbert's, a worthy and engaging woman who, I have been assured, was once married to the king but is now without influence in that realm, although she is still universally loved and revered, of excellent manners and without any pretentions. While there I heard some interesting details about Lord Liverpool's catastrophe. Here was a man who at one moment ruled half the world with strength and wisdom, and then one hour later turned into an imbecile because someone failed to perform a bloodletting. The same thing led his predecessor, Lord Castlereagh, to commit suicide. There is truly something too fragile about the human spirit!

Also present were the two daughters of the well-known Sher——, both of them witty and singularly pretty. The eldest is bold like her father, something not so suited to a lady; the younger is of a gentleness that whispers "still waters run deep!"

You see nothing but *beau monde* in this house. Otherwise there is not much exclusive society here, or else they are living in total seclusion so as not to collide with the everyday folk, whom they call "nobodies" and shun as the Brahmins do pariahs. Although allowed by my circumstances to penetrate this sanctuary, I do not disdain the others. As a foreigner, and even more as someone independently minded, I can seek pleasure wherever I wish and often find it in less lofty spots. Indeed, even the vulgarity and ludicrous antics of the nouveaux riches are occasionally delightful, and far more burlesque in England than elsewhere because their residences, wealth, and extravagance—in a word, their entire surroundings—are really the equal of the great and the good; it is only that the arrivistes traipse around unabashedly.

Here a long pause inserted itself in my correspondence. Forgive me. I ate my solitary midday meal—a snipe stood in front of me and a *mouton qui rêve* next to me.[3] You can guess the identity of the latter. Do not worry about the place at my left, for the fire is flickering on the right, and I know only too well how much you fear that.

I am going to spend the evening at Count Flahaut's again, one of the Brahmins. Have I already described him to you? He is a not insignificant person. Combining French charm with English solidity, he speaks both languages with equal fluency. Although no longer young,[4] he is still handsome, and his appearance is elevated by a very noble demeanor. Simple and courteous, cheerful without malice, his conversation is pleasing and satisfying, even though at any given moment he may be less than brilliant. His wife, Lady Keith, is neither beautiful nor ugly. She has spirit, *l'usage du grand monde, et quelque fois de la politesse,*[5] no small talent for music, and ten thousand pounds a year. Given all that, I do not need to add that this is a pleasant house.

February 25th, 1827

THERE IS A custom at these balls that is very advantageous for the gentlemen, namely, once a dance has ended, each takes his partner on his arm and strolls around with her until the music starts again, which offers many men enough time to overcome their timidity. From our point of view, nothing is lacking except the large halls and secluded, empty rooms that make our gatherings even more charming. Here a walk means descending the stairs to the dining room and then climbing back up again; the throng itself affords considerable privacy, however, because no one pays attention to anyone else.

Since I am pestered on all sides to dance, but am not inclined (a German who does not waltz seems incomprehensible to them), I have declared myself bound by a vow and have allowed people to suppose it to be of the tender sort. The ladies find it difficult to reconcile this pretext with the conviction that I am only here in search of a wife, something they have fixed rigidly in their minds. Nevertheless, I have accrued a certain amount of homage, which gives some piquancy to the everyday sameness, although thank God there is nothing here that even slightly ruffles my feathers, a very cozy position to be in! It was far worse for the unfortunate Englishman who threw himself from the jetty today in despair over an unhappy love affair, while only yesterday he was dancing as if stung by a tarantula. The poor man must have felt like one of the turkeys that the Parisians encourage to perform ballet dances by placing them on a metal floor over a roaring fire. The spectators watching their desperate hopping believe them to be quite jolly, whereas the pathetic birds are being slowly cooked.

I have often complained that there is no vegetation in Brighton, yet almost nowhere have I seen spectacles more diverse than the sun setting into the sea and the cloud formations that accompany it here. Even today, which brought rain without cease, the weather cleared up in the evening, and above the water's surface, a dark mountain range arose on the horizon and little by little grew denser. Then, as the sun touched the highest peak and broke through the black masses in fissures of flaming gold, I thought I was watching Vesuvius again, streaked with ribbons of lava.

After having witnessed the queen of heaven so splendidly bedded down, I roamed amid the barren dunes until it was fully dark, gliding along like a shadow over hill and dale on my fast steed, both of us sped on by our fantasies—he probably by the enticing vision of oats and hay.

*March 14th, 1827**

I CANNOT CALL these eternal balls, concerts, dinners, and promenades boring, exactly, but they are certainly time killing. Meanwhile some poor dying man has moved in below me, and I am becoming overly melancholic as a result of his moaning and groaning, which penetrates up through the thin floor every night and in such glaring contrast to the frivolity and distraction of this place. I cannot help him, so tomorrow I will return to London.

I have received both your letters, and I profoundly regret hearing that you still have not found a cook or doctor for your spa.[6] You must certainly do everything you can to acquire these two important chemists (who are destined by nature to play into each other's hands) as quickly as possible. And they must be of the highest quality.

You know the story of the famous French doctor, who, the first time he was called to a house, would always start by going to the kitchen and embracing the cook to thank him for the new patient.

When Louis XIV grew increasingly sickly and did not trust his own doctors, he consulted our Asclepius, who proposed to the premier *homme de bouche* that the king be served fewer and

---

* The report of the preceding days has been suppressed.—*The Editor.*

simpler meals. "Allons donc, Monsieur," replied the heroic cook, embracing the physician, "mon métier est de faire manger le Roi—le votre de le purger. Faisons chacun le notre."[7]

Before leaving Brighton I had to attend another musical soirée, one of the hardest tests faced by foreigners in England. Every mother with a grown daughter, on whose behalf she has had to pay enormous sums to a music master, wants the satisfaction of having her offspring's youthful talent admired. The result is a squawking and pounding both right and left, so that you feel sore and weak; and even when an Englishwoman *can* sing, she almost never possesses either technique or voice. The gentlemen are far more pleasant dilettantes, for their songs at least offer the pleasure of a droll farce. The matador among all such society singers here is a certain Captain H——. This gentleman has no voice but that of a hoarse bulldog, no concept of singing but that of a peasant in church, and no better ear than that of a mole.

Nonetheless, however poorly endowed, he found nothing more pleasing than being heard; indeed the renowned David Garrick stepped on the stage with more timidity than the captain did. The most eccentric aspect, however, was the style of his performance. He would sit down at the piano, promptly strike just one note with his forefinger (the note upon which, in his opinion, the aria should begin), and then intone like a thunderstorm, although always one or two notes lower than the one he had struck. From there he proceeded to work his way through the entire song without any pause or halt, and without any further accompaniment, but with the strangest facial distortions. A thing like this must be seen to be believed, and this in a company of at least fifty people!

He generally chose Italian songs, although he has no knowledge whatever of that language, so that his stentorian voice often bellowed out words that would have sent all the ladies scattering had they understood their meaning. Nobody was at all bashful about laughing at him (it was almost impossible *not* to). But I never noticed that this had the slightest impact on his ecstatic self-satisfaction. Indeed, once he got going, it was really difficult to get him away from the piano so other less-amusing talents could have their turn.

At this final concert I saw two others who were noteworthy in a different way. They were an already-elderly couple who, *un beau matin*, had turned black, but I mean black, like ink. It is odd that a white person who turns black is enough to awaken horror, whereas this is not at all true with a negro. Even odder is the reason they turned black: there is supposedly a new medicine that works specifically against epilepsy and cramps, and contains primarily zinc and silver. If a patient is exposed even briefly to sunlight while using it, he will turn black, and forever. Such a misfortune happened to these poor people, and in this case the adage is more than ever true: "the remedy is worse than the disease!"

London, March 17th, 1827

I AM BACK on Albemarle Street again after a long absence, and yesterday morning I paid no fewer than twenty-two visits, attended a club dinner,* then a ball given by the previously

---

* In the club dining room, where you can eat only from the menu, there is a board where anyone can sign himself up for a special meal called the "house dinner," which is offered at a fixed price and taken in company. You pick the day you prefer, and as soon as twelve people have signed up, the subscription is closed.

These dinners take place in a special room, are highly sought after, and offer the opportunity of making new acquaintances.

mentioned lady Napoleonist,[8] and closed the day with a soirée at Mrs. Hope's, a very fashionable and pretty woman who looks far less sharp-cornered than her Anastasius or the antique furniture surrounding her.[9]

Today I visited two Chinese ladies "in another quarter," who lead an active social life and receive a lot of company, and in a very original way, too, for one must pay to be admitted.

Starting already with the staircase, everything is done as in China itself, and when you finally enter and see the ladies reposing beneath the glow of paper lanterns, with feet barely five inches long stretched out before them, you can actually embrace the illusion of having arrived in Canton. The ladies profess to be highborn, as evidenced by their tiny feet, something the lower classes do not have. How could they work, after all, given that women with miniature feet have so little centripetal force that without a cane they can barely hobble from one ottoman to another?

I am otherwise a passionate lover of the small female foot, but these were simply *too small* for my taste and, when naked, repulsive to look at, since their tininess is achieved by forcing the toes to bend under during childhood, so that they grow right into the sole, a vogue almost as irrational as our corsets, although it may do less damage to health.

I bought a new pair of shoes from the Chinese princesses, which they first had to try on right before my eyes, and I am sending these to you along with this letter, as well as several other examples of chinoiserie, some beautiful silk tapestries, a few paintings (including a portrait of the emperor and empress), etc. The good creatures sell *everything* you ask for and seem, without impairing their dignity, to have brought along a veritable warehouse, because the minute a thing has been carried off, it is immediately replaced. Although they have been in London for a long time already, they have not managed to learn a single word of English. I found their language very ponderous and their facial features, to a European's taste, more than ugly.

March 18th, 1827

THE ITALIAN OPERA has also started now and is, except for the French comedy, the only spectacle with any pretense to refinement. No one can appear there in anything but finery, so the sight is quite brilliant, even in the parterre. But the opera itself was bad, both orchestra and singers, and so was the ballet. The lighting in this theater is arranged more for people to be seen than to see, because a chandelier hangs down in front of every box, unpleasantly dazzling the eyes and obscuring the actors. Since the opera lasts until one o'clock, there is adequate time to visit it without having to forego other parties, which is good because the hustle and bustle has now started, and one seldom gets home before three or four in the morning. Anybody wishing to spend a lot of time in society—something not done by the exclusives but which a foreigner finds amusing—can easily obtain a dozen invitations every evening.

For this reason the fashionable world is dormant until two in the afternoon. Park time is between four and six, when ladies by the thousands don their morning clothes and are slowly driven around in their elegant equipages, while the gentlemen skirmish among them on their handsome horses, fluttering from flower to flower and displaying all the grace that the dear Lord has granted them. Of course nearly all Englishmen look good on horseback, and they ride much better and more naturally than all of our grooms, who are very good at sitting like a clothespin on a laundry line when they are on a horse that has been trained skillfully enough to decrease his speed through every kind of gait.

The broad expanse of the park lawn is likewise teeming with riders, who move across it with more speed than on the racetrack. By the way, they are intermixed with many ladies, who handle their mounts just as skillfully and steadily as the men.

But a moment ago Miss Sally was led up and is already pawing impatiently at the macadamized pavement. This letter is long enough anyway, so a thousand greetings to everyone inclined to remember me and the most cordial farewell to you.

Your friend, Lou

*M*OST BELOVED AND BEST!

It would be too boring for you, dear Julie, if I were to send you a daily list of all the social events I attend. I will only mention them when something strikes me as noteworthy, and perhaps later, if I feel inclined and adroit enough, I will close with a somewhat more general aperçu.

Overall, the technical aspects of social life are very well managed here. By this I mean the arrangements for catering to one's comfort and entertainment. Particularly distinguished in this respect is the house of the Duke of Devonshire, who is a sovereign of fashion and elegance. In London only a few high-ranking people have what we on the Continent call a *Palast*; it is only in the countryside that English palaces, luxury, and grandness are fully realized. The Duke of Devonshire is one of these exceptions as his *palais* is in the city and features a large number of significant art treasures, displayed with a great deal of taste and extravagance. The company there is always the most select, although, as everywhere else, too numerous; yet given the quantity of rooms, the throng is not particularly irritating, being less like the crowds on a market day. Concerts at the duke's house are especially lovely: only the premier talents currently in town are engaged, and exemplary order prevails amid the profusion. Also very much to be recommended here and in other houses as well are the incessant buffets and suppers (ideal given the flood of people). In a separate room, you find a long table richly laden with the most exquisite refreshments of every kind. It is set up so that only *one* side of it is accessible to the guests, and behind it stand uniformed serving girls in white dresses and black aprons who fill every request, while having adequate space to take care of their duties conveniently. At their backs, through a door that connects to the offices, everything necessary can be brought in without being impeded by the jumble of the company. This does away with the extremely unpleasant procession of servants who must otherwise push their way through a salon as they balance huge presentation platters, thus always being in danger of spilling the cold or warm contents of their load onto three or four guests. Later, in another room that communicates with the kitchen, a supper is served in the same way by male waiters, affording exemplary, prompt, and orderly service with a far smaller staff.

Here I must express my admiration because really, as far as good food goes, the most delicious in the world is to be found in the great private houses of London. The best French cooks and best Italian waiters have congregated in this city for the very legitimate reason that they are paid more. There are cooks here who earn a salary of twelve hundred pounds a year. *Dem Verdienste seine Kronen*![1]

It occasionally happens that a ball does not start until two o'clock, after the concert and supper, so you drive home in the morning sunshine. It is a lifestyle that suits me very well, for as you know, my tastes have always been similar to those of Minerva's bird.[2] Sometimes I even make use of such a "night morning" to go directly from the ball for a ride in the park, since, thank God, it is already visibly spring here, and above the high garden walls, the green leaves of lilacs and a few almond blossoms are starting to gleam through the dark web of swelling branches.

March 26th, 1827

I BEGAN THE day with an excursion to Deptford to see Captain Parry's ship, the *Hecla*, which is supposed to set sail for the North Pole very soon.[3] Whether he will reach it is another question. If only Parry does not suffer the same fate as poor Count Zambeccari, who to this day has not returned from his last trip in a hot-air balloon.[4]

Captain Parry did the honors of his vessel with great civility. His demeanor is exactly that of a candid, prudent, and bold seafarer, which is his reputation. On the deck of the ship were a few strangely shaped boats that were also intended to serve as sledges. The ship itself has heating vents and double walls packed with cork to better preserve warmth. The provisions consist of the strongest extracts, so that a whole steer, reduced to its quintessence, can be stuffed in your coat pocket, just as if one had the chefs d'oeuvre of all English literature in a *single* stereotyped volume.[5] All the officers seemed to be men of top quality. I found Lieutenant Ross, who has accompanied Parry on all his voyages, especially fine and engaging. The ship was teeming with visitors who were constantly climbing up the rope ladders, and you had to appreciate the cheerfulness with which the ship's crew approached such enormous dangers, all purely for the sake of science and to satisfy a lofty curiosity.

A major in the Horse Guards invited me to take my midday meal with him and his fellow cavalry members in their barracks. The so-called mess is a very worthwhile practice of the English military, whereby each regiment has its own common table to which every officer contributes a certain amount of money, whether or not he avails himself of its offerings. This gives him the right to dine there daily and, for a specified fee, to bring a guest as well. A committee takes care of the financial arrangements and purchases all necessities. The officers take turns presiding at meals, from the colonel down to the youngest lieutenant, and whoever happens to be serving in that capacity is invested with all due authority. The deportment of the officers, at least from what I have seen here among the Guards, is admirable and far more gentlemanly than is normal on the Continent. Although the strictest subordination prevails in the line of duty, outside that context the gentlemen regard one another as complete equals, such that a foreigner finds it impossible to distinguish their rank on the basis of conduct alone. The table itself is splendidly laid, with no lack of elegant silver or champagne, claret, or any other requisites of luxury. It was nevertheless not an excessive feast, and the conversation remained, for all its joviality, within the bounds of propriety. The whole affair did not last very long, which left me enough time to pay a few courtesy visits at the opera—always a convenient place for such social rounds.

March 28th, 1827

AT MOST EVENING parties you find that fairly serious gambling is a major part of the agenda, and the ladies are the most passionate about it. The crush around the écarté table, by now half out of fashion in Paris, never thins out, and the white arms of the English beauties are shown to their best advantage against table covers of black velvet embroidered in gold. But you must sometimes beware of those feminine hands, *car les vieilles surtout trichent impitoyablement.*[6] In the very top circles here you can meet a few old maids who make a real profession of gaming and, while keeping perfectly straight faces, will carry off fifty pounds in a flash. They also host their own very singular gaming parties, which have an extraordinary resemblance to gambling dens.

Nowhere but in English society can an aficionado of the "middle ages" find more well-preserved women of the "fat, fair, and forty" variety (Figure 36).[7] Even more advanced years make a claim for themselves. The Marchioness of Salisbury, who is almost eighty, is still regarded as the lady most often seen on the London scene. You can be sure of meeting her every evening, and in addition she goes out riding each and every morning. Indeed, when in the country, she occasionally participates in foxhunts while tied onto her horse and with opera glasses attached to her whip, since she is almost blind. A huntsman rides in front of her, and she follows him confidently over fences and ditches. Recently the marchioness fell down a long flight of stairs, but just three days later, when she appeared at a ball, she looked perfectly normal aside from a few large beauty spots atop her bright red rouge. She is fond of receiving morning visitors and can be found seated on her sofa, surrounded by a few parrots and four dogs, holding a small braided whip to keep the animals in order. She participates in the conversation with as much gaiety as the youngest person present. Attendance at her gatherings is always high, although the company is a bit motley.

The Marchioness of Hertford, not much younger, must still be deemed a beautiful woman; she has the demeanor of a monarch and covers herself in diamonds at every opportunity. She does the honors of her house better than most of the "exclusive" younger beauties.

The elderly Lady Londonderry is in the same league and still goes by the sentimental name Lady Emily Londonderry. She is very well-known on the Continent, especially since the Congress at Aachen, where she appeared with her husband's diamond garter on her forehead, while he wore a bagwig set with rubies.[8]

The ROYAL TOAST.   FAT, FAIR, and FORTY.

Published by W.S. Fores Mar. 20.d 1766 at his Caracature Warehouse N.º3 Piccadilly

36

The Royal Toast—
Fat, Fair, and Forty.

This class of society yields even greater burlesques. The top rank is claimed by a certain countess, originally nurtured in the world of commerce and now a grand *pazza per la musica*.[9] She regularly goes into raptures over the latest and most fashionable soprano, whom she then introduces to every pleasure of the capital as though she were a bosom friend. In a very good English novel, she appeared recently under the German name *Geigenklang*,[10] and the portrait is quite true to life. She is very rich, hosts good concerts, and through unswerving persistence and the distribution of sundry favors, has made herself passably fashionable. But it is not possible to display in the stylish world a less appropriate *tournure*,[11] which reeks of the bourgeoisie from thirty paces away—as an extremist might say.

I do not quite understand why the English satirist gave her the name *Geigenklang*, since it is undeniable that of all the instruments she worships, she has—by dint of her constitution, complexion, waistline, and voice—similarity only with the drum.

I closed my day with reading and whist at the club, where the composition of my party was quite unusual. It included the Portuguese ambassador, who looks strikingly like Napoleon; an erstwhile minister from Naples, cast up by his failed attempts at revolution; the French gentleman whom I described to you at Brighton; and my own humble German self, who proved victorious this time, winning eight rubbers and two monkeys.

"What's a monkey?" you cry.

Fashion has given idiosyncratic names to the different game tokens: the one for twenty-five pounds sterling is called a pony, and the one for fifty pounds is a monkey.[12]

April 3rd, 1827

YOU ARE ALREADY used to me leading you from a palace to a cottage and from a decorated salon into more beautiful nature. So follow me today to my dentist, the famous Mr. Cartwright.

His expertise earns this gentleman ten thousand pounds a year, and he wields it in the most grandiose manner. To start with, he himself will go to no one except the king; everyone else, gentleman or lady, must come to him. But this is still not enough. You must also make an appointment between eight and fourteen days in advance and request an audience. Then you receive a card with the following message: "Mr. Cartwright will have the pleasure of receiving N—— N—— on such-and-such a day at such-and-such an hour." Appearing at the specified time, you are led into an elegant room, where a piano, engravings, various books, and other entertainments are provided to help you pass the time—a necessary measure, since you usually have to wait another hour or two. When I arrived I found the room already occupied by the Duchess of Montrose and Lady Melville and her daughters; each was summoned sequentially, so that my turn came only after an hour. Once you finally get this far, however, satisfaction awaits, for I have never met another man of his profession so skillful and scientific, so totally without charlatanism, something hardly to be expected given the difficulty of access. In addition he has established prices and does not overcharge, really *c'est un grand seigneur dentiste*.[13]

In the evening, after having sought some suitable entertainment at four or five places, I finally arrived at Lady Charleville's, where I was captivated by a conversation with a certain Captain P——, a half-German who had just returned from the Orient and gave a very absorbing account of his travels. Among much else he told me the following anecdote about Lady Hester Stanhope, a niece of Pitt's, who left England ten years ago, became a Turk, and settled in Syria.

Now much revered as a prophet among the Arabs, she lives with all the prestige and magnificence of a native-born princess and only rarely grants Europeans an audience. After a lot of effort and careful scheming, Captain P—— was finally admitted to her presence. The first thing she did was demand that he give his word of honor never to write anything about her. As soon as he swore this oath (by which, thank God, I am not bound),[14] she became very cheerful and talkative and revealed herself just as unaffected as she was witty. She made no secret of the fact that she had abandoned the Christian faith, but immediately confided that she was now awaiting the true Son of God, for whom *she herself* was destined to prepare the way. Next she showed the Captain a magnificent Arabian mare of the most noble lineage, with a strange bony outgrowth on its back in a form very similar to a saddle. "This horse," she said, with an expression the captain still speculates may have betrayed either madness or a desire to pull his leg, "this horse was saddled by God for his son, and woe to any mortal whose foot dares to mount it! But under my care and protection, it awaits its true master."[15]

In the course of their discussion, she also confided *en passant* that Adam was still alive, although she could not betray his whereabouts or give any further details. Captain P—— replied that he did not doubt it, for *the old Adam* was also very well-known to him. (Note that P—— studied at a German university, where no doubt he got to know the old Adam!)[16]

The mistress of the house, Lady Charleville, the same one whose boundless admiration for Napoleon I have already mentioned, heard all of this and assured the captain that Lady Hester had indeed been out to tease him. Knowing her extremely well, and long an intimate friend, she declared that there had never been a woman with a more lucid, determined, and clever mind.

In any case, for someone with a personality such as this, Lady Hester made a profitable exchange between Occident and Orient. There she *reigns*, as free as a bird in the air, whereas in the midst of our "civilization" she might never have escaped the *slavery* that may forever prevail on the dark side of all civilized societies.

April 4th, 1827

SIR ALEXANDER JOHNSTON, also a great Orientalist, though in a different sense, had invited me to dine, and he too added piquancy to the meal through his wit and learning. He has already brought many important things to light in his area of expertise, although you and I, dear Julie, are so uninformed on the subject that I will not bore you with further details. One thing might interest you, however. He told of a cashmere shawl that belonged to Tipu Sahib. It was ten yards long, woven with gold and all possible colors, and valued at one thousand pounds sterling—an item to set fire to the female imagination.

In the evening I saw another enchantingly beautiful painting—a Titian portrait of Venus dressed in nothing but her charms, voluptuously reclining on soft cushions. A sweet dream seemed to flash through her like a spasm, and she covered herself with her small hands like the goddess surprised in her bath.[17]

Never in my life have I seen anything more beautiful than this heavenly creature. She was illuminated most advantageously by a blazing fire, its harsh glare gently muted by a half-lowered curtain. Behind this her lovely limbs appeared white as snow, and not the slightest blemish could be seen on her luscious, supple body, which was engulfed by an abundance of brown locks revealing only a hidden shimmer of the rosebuds of her virginal breasts. The most delicate hand, the sweetest foot—not ever disfigured by a narrow shoe; lips made for kissing; a yearning, pale face with Grecian features that, even with eyes closed, were thrillingly enlivened by a smile of painful sweetness—the most arousing ideal of female beauty imaginable.

I was lost in looking—then, oh heaven!—I believed I saw the dark eyes open and gently gaze at me. I lost my senses and did not awaken until four in the afternoon.

So, good morning or good evening, whichever you prefer.

April 6th, 1827

YOU PROBABLY CANNOT make any sense of my last painting. It is a puzzle, and until you solve it, let's talk of something else.[18]

Tell me, why is it that everything refracted through art inspires nothing but *pure* pleasure, whereas everything real has at least *one* defect? We look at Laocoön's agony in marble with undisturbed enjoyment, whereas such a scene in nature would arouse only horror. A fish market in Holland, rendered with fidelity by a skilled artist, delights us in its deceptiveness, and the more we follow the details, the more our satisfaction increases; yet we rush past the *real* market holding our noses and averting our eyes. The joys and sorrows of a hero portrayed by a poet touch us with a similar pleasure, whereas *real* sufferings, our own or those of others, cause pain; even *real* joys leave much to be desired. And when *happiness* is achieved—if that is indeed possible—it must always be accompanied by the bitter thought that it cannot last. All this may explain why Schiller says "Ernst ist das Leben, heiter ist die Kunst."[19] It is thus art alone, the mere figment of our imagination, which can actually bestow true happiness. And so, good Julie, let us always rejoice that an active and creative imagination is alive in us, and occasionally offers us pleasures that reality cannot.

Shall I undertake such a harmless celebration this very moment and fly across the sea to you? For we have been apart far too long!

Ah, how beautiful everything seems! It is spring; the scent of violets is magically sweet after the storm; swallows are whooshing through the air, and good little wagtails are sashaying merrily beside the lake. Just now the sun in all its majesty emerges from behind the last black cloud, and with its luminous script inscribes obscure characters on the distant mountains. The old lindens that surround us gleam like emeralds; brightly colored butterflies test their delicate wings for the first time and flit drunkenly across the carpet of grass. Bees circle industriously around a thousand blossoms, and green beetles glitter in the sunlight. Soon a splendid rainbow stretches across the blue sky above the castle in the west and drops beyond it into the black forest of pines. Now a cheerful table covered in a white cloth and set with brightly polished silver is brought out and placed among the flowers. Awaiting the guests are the ripe fruits of the greenhouse, hyacinth-colored sherry in a crystal bottle, and iced champagne frosted with mist. And look, who is slowly approaching through the purple lilacs with such gravitas?

"Oh, it's you, dear Julie," I cry out, enraptured, rush toward you, and . . . .
. . . .

Hélas, mon chancelier vous dira le reste![20]

This is how the imagination can paint a picture. But what puts me out of sorts with reality is that I have once more gone a long time without a letter from you, and I need one to fortify my nerves. So I am sitting here in desolation with only myself for company! But do not think I have a doppelgänger—it is simply the mirror reflecting my image, for I am now in the process of getting dressed for a couple of "Russian steam balls," as the ones here ought to be called.[21]

April 7th, 1827

HAVING BEEN INVITED to the lord mayor's grand dinner I rode into the city today to pay him a visit in advance. This is a fairly alarming undertaking on a fidgety horse, and at one point I got into such a throng that I was forced to swerve onto the sidewalk. The English rabble immediately took this as a violation of its rights, and without any regard for the fact that I was there only by necessity, they began to curse and some of them to strike my horse. A terrible colossus pushing a cart even held up his fist and challenged me to box with him. Since I felt no inclination at all to take him up on it—although I have had a few boxing lessons—I was saved by a small gap that opened up and I quickly got myself away. The relentless throngs in this city and the grim apathy of the faces that stream tirelessly past you have something profoundly gloomy about them, and every distraction can be a danger to anyone on a horse or in a carriage.

As I passed the insurance company building I was impressed by the bold inscriptions on the three different offices:

Sea   Fire   Life.

It would be difficult to explain to a savage how you can insure your life! I wanted to enquire whether I could possibly insure your letters, which must be at the bottom of the sea, given that they are so long overdue. But since they are invaluable, it would not be possible.

At noon I dined with Count Münster, a marvelous representative of Germany on this island. He has done his best to maintain the simplicity of our customs in his own household.

Everyone knows him as an excellent statesman, but his domestic talents are also very admirable. For instance, while here in England, he is quite brilliantly painting and designing embellishments for his family seat near the Harz Mountains, and his wife transfers his drawings onto glass with such artistry that in a few years the colorful windows of their castle chapel will be resplendent with her own creations.[22] Meanwhile this German housewife is not only an artist of a purely modern aesthetic, but just like the knights' ladies of old that she draws with her brush, she knows how to brew an excellent beer. She recently honored me with a sample, which I drank up with all the gratitude of a guest at Walhalla.

In the evening a large fete at Lord Hertford's, with concert, ball, French *comédie*, and more, brought together the fashionable as well as the *half*-fashionable world* in a magnificent and very tastefully furnished house. The peculiar thing is that all the rooms, one after the other, are decorated in flesh-colored stucco and gold, with black bronzes, very large mirrors, and silk drapes in crimson and white, a sameness that creates a very grandiose effect. Only the main hall (extraordinarily large for London) is white and gold, the floor carpeted in a scarlet textile, and with furniture and curtains of the same color. The company, or better the *throng,* was no more animated than usual, and the whole affair magnificently boring.

---

* Just as there are quarter-, half-, three-quarter–, and full-blooded horses in England, there are similar, even subtler divisions within the fashionable set.—*The Editor.*

Another house worth seeing belongs to the great banker Thomas Hope, particularly because of his beautiful collection of paintings. Here you can also admire the triumph of more modern sculpture, Thorvaldsen's *Jason*, and a number of valuable antiques.[23] Hanging gardens have been installed along one of the ledges on the house, and although the plants have only three feet of earth they nonetheless grow very luxuriously. But the mistress of the gardens is far from being a Semiramis, although she possesses no fewer treasures and perhaps even more pride—in this case money pride, because there is no opportunity for another kind.

Sometimes I could not help comparing her to her far wealthier rival Madame Rothschild and feeling amazed that the Jewish queen of money stood so far above the Christian one in warmhearted graciousness and outward propriety.

April 8th, 1827

WHAT ADDS SUBSTANTIALLY to the dullness of English society (at home, that is, because when abroad they are courteous enough) is their arrogant avoidance of speaking to strangers, and if anyone addresses *them* in such circumstances, it almost qualifies as an insult. They sometimes make fun of themselves about this, yet without behaving any differently when the opportunity arises. An anecdote: a lady saw someone fall into the water and implored the dandy accompanying her, who was known to be a good swimmer, to please go to the poor man's rescue. Her friend held up his lorgnette in the phlegmatic manner required by today's fashion, peered earnestly at the drowning man, whose head at that moment surfaced for the last time, and turning calmly to his companion responded, "It is impossible, Madam, I was never introduced to this gentleman."

I got to know a man of entirely different customs this evening, the Persian chargé d'affaires, an Asian of very pleasant manners, whose splendid costume and black beard were marred in my eyes only by his pointed cap of Persian sheepskin.

He speaks fine English and made quite perceptive remarks about Europe. Among other things he said that, although in a great many areas we are in fact further advanced, in Persia all opinions are more firmly held, and accordingly each person is content with his fate, whereas here we are in a constant ferment, a state of eternal dissatisfaction felt by the masses as well as individuals. Indeed he had to confess that he suspected he had already become infected and would find it difficult to slip back into the accustomed track when he returns to Persia. There, whenever things are going badly, one comforts oneself by exclaiming "Whose dog am I, then, to want to be happy?"

This certainly gives the followers of the Ideal—a secret society to which I, alas, also belong![24]—much to think about.

A ball at Mrs. Hope's was truly magnificent, *mais c'est toujours la même chose*.[25] At the party beforehand, I was introduced to the Duke of Gloucester, something I mention only to note that the royal princes here observe a more polite etiquette than at many Continental courts, because the prince, who was playing whist when I arrived, stood up from his party and only returned to his seat after a short conversation with me.

But allow me to go back for just a moment to the beginning of the day.

The gardens in this region are already in full bloom, the weather is beautiful, and my morning ride thus took me a good twenty miles from the city. The rich variety I encounter on these outings, beginning already in the suburbs, is far superior to the environs of other major capitals, which here and there may offer some natural beauty, but never so captivating a mixture of nature and refined cultivation, at least not to such a degree.

I would happily have ridden on and on, and when I finally turned back it was of necessity and with a heavy heart. The meadows around me were so lush that they only looked green in the distance. Up close they shimmered in blue, yellow, red, and lilac like a tapestry from Tournai. Cows were wading up to their bellies amid the colorful flowers or resting in the shade of colossal vaults of foliage that allowed no sunbeam to pass. It was gorgeous, and more richly embellished with the plain fare of our dear Lord than all the luxury that art could ever achieve. After an hour I reached a hill where the impressive ruins of a church stood in the center of a little garden. From behind a blanketing of clouds, the sun threw its rays across the entire sky like an immense fan, its hub resting directly over the metropolis, that vast Babylon stretching out interminably before me with its thousand towers and hundred thousand sins, its fog and smoke, its treasures and miseries. There was nothing to be done! I had to forsake this springtime of swelling buds and green meadows and head back to the macadamized morass, with its eternal sameness of dinners and parties!

Say farewell to me for now. The next letter will describe what became of Daniel in the lion's den.

Your faithful friend Lou

LETTER 15

London, April 15th, 1827

EAREST FRIEND,

Finally the long-awaited letter has appeared, in fact, two at once! Why were they so long in transit? *Quien sabe?* as the South Americans say. The official reader was probably being lazy and let them lie around too long before deftly resealing them.[1]

But how tender and sweet your poem is, dear Julie—I am discovering a brand-new talent in you. Yes, may God grant that "all your tears turn to flowers, to adorn and delight us with their fragrance," and grant that this loving prophesy may soon be fulfilled! Yet such a price is too high, even for the fairest flowers meant for me. It should not be *your* tears that bring them to blossom.

What you say of H——, "that he feels miserable, because he is arrogant only through pride, and liberal only through depravity," is striking and, alas, characterizes all too many liberals.

I wrote you about the matter in question, that you ought to think only of yourself; and you reply, "*I* am yourself."—You good thing! Yes, we will remain *one* self wherever we are; and were there guardian spirits, *ours* would perform in unison. Yet we seem to have no guardian spirits beyond our own moral fortitude!

Does everything really look so melancholy in Muskau? You write that it is stormy and the waters are threatening destruction. But two weeks have passed since that letter was written, and it will be a month before this one reaches you. I therefore hope that you are reading it in the midst of greenery with everything blooming around you, fanned by a zephyr and not a howling gale. I told my old Berndt that there were horrible storms in Muskau. "Yes, yes," he replied, "those were the ones from Brighton." Had you known that, dear Julia, you would certainly have found them more enjoyable, being the latest news from your friend. Ah, to be able to sail along with them!

Please convey my most profound thanks to our honored premier. How much more popular our entire class would be if we emulated him! How much less discontent would prevail in the world if all ministers were as noble-minded and just as he! If only he could be free of the many burdens that weigh on him just when he needs to soar.

Here everything is the same, and a brilliant fete at Lord Hertford's this evening concluded the pre-Easter festivities. Most fashionable people will now go for another short stay in the country and not begin the actual Season for another two weeks. I, too, am going back to Brighton for a few days, but will first attend the lord mayor's dinner.[2]

April 16th, 1827

THE DINNER TOOK place today in Guildhall, and now that I am over the strain of it, I am extremely glad to have been there (Figure 37). It lasted a full six hours and was served to six hundred people. All the tables were aligned parallel along the length of the hall, except for one placed crosswise on a raised platform at the top. That was where the most distinguished people and the lord mayor himself were seated. The view from there was imposing: the immense hall and lofty columns running around it; the endless rows of tables; colossal mirrors behind them continuing them into infinity. The lighting turned night into day, and high up on a balcony at the end of the room opposite us, two musical groups played an assortment of national favorites during the toasts, each preceeded by a fanfare. The lord mayor delivered, at a careful count, twenty-six longer and shorter speeches. A foreign diplomat also ventured to give one, but with minimal success. He would have ground to a complete halt without the generosity of the listeners, who called out "Hear, hear!" whenever he faltered, allowing him time to collect himself.

A master of ceremonies draped with silver chains stood behind the lord mayor's chair and called out at every toast: "My lords and gentlemen, fill your glasses!" The costumes of the lady mayoress and all her ladies were abominable, as was their demeanor. I was seated next to an American, the niece of a former president of the United States, as she told me, but I cannot remember which one. I presume that neither her red hair nor albino complexion is very common among her female compatriots; if so, that country's fair sex would not be so highly praised. Still, her conversation was really quite witty, occasionally with a whimsy worthy of Washington Irving.

The ball began at midnight and was supposedly quite odd, given that every Tom, Dick, and Harry showed up.[3] I, however, was so exhausted after sitting through the six-hour meal in full uniform that I quickly sought out my carriage and drove home, so at least once I could make it to bed before twelve o'clock.

Brighton, April 17th, 1827

ALREADY IN THIS morning's paper we were able to read the diplomat's speech that I mentioned yesterday. Interestingly it appeared as it was *supposed* to have been, not as it *was* delivered. This kind of thing probably happens quite often.

Right after breakfast, I drove here with Count Danneskiold-Samsøe, a very jolly Dane, and spent the evening at Lady Keith's, where I found many of the earlier spa visitors, including Lady Greville, whom you will remember from Paris where the Duke of Wellington was her admirer.

Apropos of the duke, are you reading the newspapers? Here a tremendous crisis has arisen in the political world. The other ministers were so offended by Canning's appointment as prime minister that only three remain, the other seven having resigned. If their party does not prevail, the government will be hard-pressed to do without several of them, such as Lord Melville. This has also meant a significant loss for the Duke of Wellington. As a ministerial publication put it today with the usual exaggeration of local party spirit, he who was everything is "now politically dead." Yet there is something grand about sacrificing all personal considerations to one's own opinion. The caricatures raining down on the defeated are now and then quite funny. Lord Eldon, old and not very beloved, comes in for particularly rough treatment, as does the Earl of Westmorland,[4] a strange old man, who possesses the most egregious

The Lord Mayor's Dinner.

aristocratic pride. He looks like a mummy and, in spite of his eighty years, is seen every day racing across St James's Park on a fast-trotting horse with the speed of a bird. This moment was also chosen for a caricature with a malicious inscription: "The flying privy" (Figure 38). He had, you see, been holder of the privy seal, something he has just let slip, and it falls on the public below, who are turning away with expressions of disgust; the second meaning of the word is easy to guess.

Brighton, April 20th, 1827

TODAY I LEARNED how dangerous the fogs can be here. This is something I had scarcely been willing to believe until now, since London fogs seem to result only in comical scenes.

An acquaintance had loaned me one of his hunters, because mine were left behind in the metropolis, and I decided this time to ride in a new direction toward a side of the dunes I did not yet know, called the Devil's Dyke. I had already gone several miles over hill and dale on the smooth turf when suddenly the air began to darken and, in a few minutes, I could not see ten steps in front of me. It continued like this, and there was no hope of the weather brightening up. An hour or so passed as I rode in one direction and then another, searching for a path. My light clothing was already soaked through, the air was icy cold, and if night had overtaken me my prospects would have been extremely unpleasant. In such distress and totally unacquainted with the country, it luckily occurred to me to let the old horse, one that had participated in so many local foxhunts, follow his own lead. After a few paces, he sensed he was free and immediately turned around in a short volt and set off at a rather animated gallop directly down the hill we had been standing on. Despite the half darkness around me, I took great care not to disturb him, even when he crashed his way through a field of tall, prickly broom and furze in a series of hare-like leaps. A few insignificant ditches and low hedges barely impeded him, and after a good half hour of laborious running, the trusty creature brought me happily to the gates of Brighton, though from a completely different side from where I had exited. I felt very glad to have gotten off so lightly, and determined that from then on, I would be more careful in this land of fog.

I generally spend my evenings at Lady Keith's or Mrs. Fitzherbert's, where I play écarté and whist with the men or loo with the young ladies.[5] These small circles are much more pleasant than the large parties in the metropolis where everything is understood, *everything except how to be sociable*. For instance, artists are trotted out as mere fashionable objects and paid a fee;[6] the idea of living among them, of drawing pleasure from their conversation, is unknown. True cultural refinement is mostly political in nature, and the spirit of political partisanship, like the fashionable spirit of caste, imposes itself on patterns of social interaction. From this arises an overall sense of disjunction. Given the deeply unsocial inclination of the English, this can only make a foreigner's sojourn here unpleasant in the long run, unless he finds his way into the most intimate family circles or adopts a lively interest in politics.

In this regard, the happiest and the most respectable class in England is, without a doubt, *the prosperous middle class*, whose political engagement is limited to the healthy promotion of their own interests, and who tend to share fairly similar views. This unfashionable class is the only one that is truly hospitable and without arrogance. They do not seek out foreigners, but if any come their way they treat them with kindness and sympathy. They love their own country passionately, but without an excess of personal interest; without hope of sinecures; and without intrigue. These people can sometimes be ludicrous, but they are always deserving of respect, and their national egotism is kept within reasonable bounds.

What used to be said of France can now be said of England: *les deux bouts du fruit sont gâtés,*[7] both the aristocracy and the mob. The aristocracy occupies an admirably splendid position, of course, but without great moderation, *without great concessions to reason and the times,* they may lose hold of it before even another half century has passed. I once said this to Prince Esterházy, and he just laughed at me. But we shall see.

In closing I will excerpt a few passages from the local newspapers, to give you an idea of the freedom of the press.

1. "Every ship in England ought to hoist celebratory flags, because Lord Melville was an incubus weighing heavily on the service. Now deserving officers may have a chance. Under Lord Melville they had none."

2. "We hear from a good source that the great captain (Lord Wellington) took extraordinary pains to get back into the cabinet, but in vain. This spoiled child of fortune should not have assumed that his resignation would embarrass the government for even a moment. We believe, by the way, that he is not the only ex-minister who already bitterly regrets his folly and arrogance."

3. "The ministerial septemvirate (seven resigned, as I told you) who tried to force their way to higher stations owe a great debt of gratitude to Mr. Hume's new Penalty Act, for according to the old law, servants who tried to extort higher wages from their masters were quite rightly sent to the treadmill."

4. "It is claimed that a great septemvir (Lord Wellington) offered to return to service, but only on condition that he be made directing minister, grand constable, and archbishop of Canterbury."

Our ministers would be astonished if our blotting-paper journals treated them so roughly.[8]

Tomorrow I return to town, for the English call London "the town" just as the Romans used to call Rome "the city."

London, April 22nd, 1827

I ARRIVED JUST in time to attend a large *dîner* at Canning's, the new prime minister, to which I had received an invitation while still in Brighton.

This excellent man is just as engaging doing the honors of his house as he is when capturing his listeners' hearts in Parliament. An aesthete and statesman by turns, he lacks nothing but good health; or at least to me he seemed to be suffering greatly. Mrs. Canning is likewise very intelligent. It is claimed that she runs the house's newspaper department; that is, she must read the papers in order to pass on the necessary excerpts to her husband, and she is not above writing a political article herself on occasion.

A concert at Countess San Antonio's was very well attended. Galli and Madame Pasta, who just recently arrived and will greatly enhance the opera, both sang. The rooms were crammed full of people, and several young men lay on the carpet at the feet of their ladies, their heads resting comfortably against the cushions of the sofas on which the fair ones were seated. This Turkish fashion is really very handy, and I am quite surprised that Clanwilliam hasn't introduced it in Berlin so he can deposit himself at the feet of one of the ladies-in-waiting. Such behavior on the part of the English envoy would have certainly been judged very *charmant*, as the Berliners like to say.

April 25th, 1827

TODAY I WENT to the theater again after a long absence. My timing was fortunate, for Liston gave a sidesplittingly funny performance in a little farce set in Paris at the time of Louis XV. A rich English merchant, plagued by melancholy, has gone there for some distraction. He has been settled at his inn for only a few days when the minister of police is announced and immediately enters, very well dressed in the costume of the time. He informs the astonished citizen that they are on the track of a notorious gang of thieves, who suspect that the merchant is carrying a lot of money and intend to break into his room that very night to rob and murder him. The policeman explains how everything depends on the merchant's behavior: if he draws any attention, if he appears less sanguine than normal or betrays anxiety, this might hasten the robbers' plan, in which case his life would be in danger and the police could not be responsible, since it is still not known whether people from the inn are part of the plot. He must therefore go to bed at ten o'clock as usual, and take his chances.

Mr. Jackson, more dead than alive on hearing this news, wants to leave at once. But the minister gravely refuses to allow it, insisting it would do no good anyway, for the robbers would quickly discover his new residence, and he would then become their prey with even more certainty. "Just remain calm," concludes Mr. de Sartines, "all will be well if *you* just maintain *your* composure."

It is easy to imagine the ridiculous scenes resulting from the elderly merchant's dreadful fear and his repeated attempts to hide it behind a mask of joviality. Meanwhile his servant, a true Englishman and always thirsty, finds some wine in a cupboard and drinks it down. But it is antimonial wine,[9] and soon he gets violently sick, which convinces his master that instead of a shooting or stabbing, the plan is to poison him. At this moment the innkeeper's wife appears with a cup of chocolate. Beside himself, Liston grabs her by the throat and forces her to drink the brew herself, which she does quite willingly, though feeling amazed by the strangeness of English customs.

Liston's miming during this scene is exceedingly comical, as is the way he breaks into convulsive laughter when he remembers his promise and tries to make a joke out of what has happened. Finally ten o'clock arrives, and after many burlesque interludes Mr. Jackson, wearing his velvet breeches and armed with a sword and pistols, goes to bed and draws the curtains tight. Unfortunately the daughter of the establishment is engaged in a love affair, and before the stranger took up lodging there, she had arranged for a rendezvous in this very room. Hoping to avoid discovery, she now glides in softly, cautiously puts out the light, and goes to the window to receive her *amant*. The moment he leaps into the room and begins to speak, strange sounds of terror come from the bed. First one pistol falls out with a clatter, then another, the curtains open, and Liston attempts a feeble thrust with his sword. But this, too, drops from his quivering hand, whereupon he bolts from the bed in his comical attire and kneels down before the girl (who is as terrified as he is) to plead heartbreakingly for his life. The lover, meanwhile, speedily conceals himself behind the bed. Then the doors open, and the minister of police enters with torches to inform the trembling Jackson that the band of robbers has been captured. "But," he adds looking at the couple before him and smiling, "my compliments to you, for knowing how to make such good use of your time."

April 26th, 1827

THIS MORNING I visited a very odd place, a church called the Areopagus, where a clergyman, the Reverend Mr. Taylor, preaches *against* Christianity and allows anyone to debate him publicly.[10] The only thing he has retained from the Anglo-Christian church is that here, too, you have to pay a shilling for your seat! Mr. Taylor is learned and not a bad orator, but he is as fanatically passionate about destroying Christianity as so many others are about defending it. The things he says are extraordinarily powerful, not infrequently true, often distorted, occasionally humorous, and sometimes thoroughly indecent. The place was packed full of listeners from every class. In a nation where the level of religious education is so low, it is easy to comprehend how such an anti-apostle can draw large crowds. At home, where we have already advanced down the reasonable path of gradual reform, this kind of undertaking would fill some people with holy horror, be of no use to others, and quite rightly scandalize everyone. And anyway, our police make it impossible.

The first Almack's ball took place this evening, and after everything I had heard about this famous social gathering, I was actually curious to see it. Never have my expectations been more disappointed. It was not much better than at Brighton. A large, bare hall with bad floorboards; ropes deployed to cordon off a space rather like a horse corral in an Arab camp; a couple of adjoining rooms, small and barren, where miserable refreshments were served; a company including ever so many nobodies who somehow managed to smuggle their way in, despite the immense difficulty of getting tickets; and bad deportment and dress—all these were endemic. The whole thing was, in a nutshell, like a party in a tavern. The most you could say was that the music and lighting were good. Yet Almack's is the absolute apex of the English world of fashion.

Originally this overstated simplicity was quite deliberate, a wish to counter the pomp of the rich *parvenus* with something cheaper, while at the same time making the venue inaccessible to those same people through the device of the Lady Patronesses, without whose approval no one could attend. But money and bad company (in the aristocratic sense) forced their way in, and the only feature remaining is the unsuitable appearance of the place, which is not much different from a room at a riflemen's ball in our larger towns. It makes for a ludicrous contrast with all the otherwise-typical grandeur and luxury of England.

May 1st, 1827

YESTERDAY MORNING AT Esterházy's, I found the Prince of Schwarzenberg. A few months ago, coming from the coronation in Moscow,[11] he passed through here on his way to Brazil, and he has just now returned. How fast and easy are even the longest journeys these days! Of all the places he saw, he preferred the island of Madeira for its natural beauty. It took him just eight days from there to London, which makes me yearn to embark on the same excursion as soon as the Season is over.

From four o'clock in the afternoon until ten at night I sat in the House of Commons—crushed, in horrible heat, extremely uncomfortable, and yet with such focused attention, so rapt, that the six hours passed in the blink of an eye. There is, in fact, something grand about a representative assembly such as this! The simplicity of its appearance; the evident dignity and experience of the participants; the vast power it wields beyond its doors; and the unostentatious, even familial relations that prevail within!

Moreover today's debate happened to be especially interesting. As you know, most of the former ministers have resigned, including the most influential men in England—in fact, even the most famous commander in Europe since the deaths of Napoleon and Blücher.[12] Canning, the leader of the liberal faction, defeated that government and, despite all its efforts, became leader of the new one, the composition of which was left entirely to him, as is customary in England. But the full might of the indignant ultra-aristocracy and their entourage still weighs on him heavily. Indeed, one of Canning's most eminent friends, also a commoner, was among those who resigned to join his adversaries. This man (Mr. Peel) opened the attack today with a speech that was long and deft, although too repetitive. It would be far too much for me to encumber our correspondence with the details of the political questions, but allow me to give you an idea of the tactics: how, on one side, the most skillful member of the new opposition went immediately on the offensive, and, after that, how several more obscure combatants were set loose to strike at random. In contrast, the old opposition of the Whigs, who now mightily support the liberal government, took the opposite tack, deploying their small arms first, which proved more expedient, and only later bringing in the heavy artillery, their major warrior, Brougham. He tried to disarm his adversaries with a magnificent speech that rushed on like the clear waters of a river. At times he tortured them with sarcasm, at others he aimed higher, all the while moving his listeners profoundly. Here is an example of his rhetoric:

> Not in order to gain places, not to acquire riches, indeed not even to see the Catholics of our land given back their natural and human rights (a benefaction for which I have been appealing to God and the nation in vain for these past twenty-five years), not for all this have I affiliated myself with the new government, no; but only because, wherever I turn my gaze, toward Europe's civilized states or America's vast continent, toward the east or west, I see the dawn of *freedom* everywhere. Yes, it is for this alone that I have affiliated myself with them, in order to follow the man who is both worthy and willing to be their champion!

The speaker concluded by solemnly declaring his impartiality because he would never, under any circumstances, take a position in a government of this realm.*

I had already heard and admired Brougham before. Probably no one has ever spoken with greater facility, continuing for hours in an unbroken, lucid stream of words; with a beautiful, clear voice; capturing one's attention without ever stumbling or ruminating; without repeating himself, misspeaking, or using one word for another—the flaws that often spoil Peel's orations. Brougham speaks the way a practiced reader delivers from a printed text. Yet in spite of all this, what you observe in him is no more than an extraordinary talent, a scathing wit, and a rare

---

* We now see that this was just a figure of speech.—*The Editor.* [In 1830, Brougham became Lord Chancellor, a position he held for four years.—*Translator.*]

presence of mind. To my way of thinking, he possesses but a fraction of the heartwarming power of *genius* that radiates from Canning.

Only now did Canning stand up, the hero of the day. If the previous speaker was like an adept and elegant boxer, then Canning was the consummate gladiator of antiquity. He proceeded with nobility, refinement, and candidness; then suddenly there came a scintillating moment when he erupted like a bolt of lightning, grand and captivating. Throughout he seemed somewhat weakened and fatigued, as if his energy were sapped by his recent afflictions as well as by the glut of work, yet in hindsight this may have garnered him even more in emotional power.

Canning's speech was in every respect the most dignified and also the most gripping for the impartial listener; the day's crowning achievement! I will never forget the impression it made on me, nor will I forget the famous speech he gave several weeks ago about the affairs in Portugal.[13] Both times I felt deeply that the highest power we can wield over our fellow creatures, the most dazzling radiance with which we can surround ourselves (casting in shadow even the gleam of the successful warrior, causing it to fade like phosphorescence in the sun) is the divine gift of oratory! Only a great master of this art can transport the hearts and minds of a whole nation into that state of magnetic somnambulism where they feel nothing but blind surrender, where the spellbinder's magic wand reigns with equal power over fury and gentleness, over war and peace, over tears and laughter.

The opening of the House of Lords the following day was just as noteworthy as the House of Commons had been the day before, although no great talent emerged to equal Brougham or, above all, Canning.

Lord Ellenborough (who, by the way, has the most beautiful wife in England*) rose first and said, in the main, that the departing ministers were accused of having resigned as part of a clandestine alliance, and that they were therefore guilty of the great injustice of trying to undermine the king's constitutional prerogative to replace his ministers however he saw fit. Lord Ellenborough went on to insist that, first and foremost, they justify themselves in a satisfactory manner *in order to save their honor*. Here I saw the great Wellington in an awkward dilemma. He is no orator, and now he was having to defend himself, *bon gré mal gré*, like an accused man before his judges. He was very agitated. This senate of his own country, composed of nothing but *individuals* who perhaps meant nothing to him, presented a greater challenge in its *collectivity* than Napoleon with all his hundred thousands. That such a thing is even possible is the great effect of wise institutions! Still it was touching to see the hero of the century in such a subordinate position. He stammered a lot, interrupted himself, got his words tangled up, but finally—with the help of his party who, whenever he stumbled, broke into applause and loud cheers so he could get back on track (just like during the ambassador's speech at the lord mayor's dinner)—he managed more or less to prove that no "conspiracy" had existed. He occasionally made very strong statements, perhaps stronger than he wanted, because he was not fully in control of his material. Among other things, he uttered the following words, which struck me deeply: "I am a soldier and no orator. I lack all of the talents needed to play a role in this lofty assembly. Although I have

---

* The young prince introduced earlier in this letter as a "fast traveler" carried her off to the Continent with equal speed some time later. [Lady Ellenborough ran off with Felix, Prince of Schwarzenberg (1800–1852), with whom she had two children before he abandoned her in Paris. —*Translator*.]

been accused of it, *I would have to be more than mad* to ever entertain the insane idea of becoming prime minister."*

Each of the lords who had resigned now spoke one after another in *his own* defense as best he could. Old Lord Eldon tried using tears, something he always has on hand for great occasions, but today he failed to garner an emotional response. Then the new lord and minister (Lord Goderich, formerly Mr. Robinson) responded for himself and the prime minister, since the latter, being just a commoner, cannot appear in the House of Lords, even though he now rules England and has become so famous under the name Mr. Canning to ever dream of exchanging it for the title of "lord."

The beginning of the new peer's otherwise good speech aroused general laughter because, out of habit, he addressed the lords and the speaker of the lower house as "sir" instead of "my lords." He was himself so disconcerted by this that he slapped himself on the forehead and remained speechless for quite a while until, encouraged by many friendly calls of "hear, hear!" he was able to regain his composure.

As usual Lord Holland distinguished himself through his acuity and talent for arresting statements; Lord King through his many witticisms, occasionally in poor taste; and Lord Lansdowne through his calm, proper discourse, more sensible than brilliant. Of them all, Lord Grey spoke with the most evident decorum, something that English orators scorn excessively or cannot really master. Here, however, you rarely find the indecorousness that is common in the lower chamber, which resembles a filthy coffeehouse, and where many of the people's representatives behave bizarrely, lying stretched out full-length on the benches with their hats on their heads or discussing a lot of nonsense during their colleagues' speeches. In contrast, the premises and behavior in the upper house are very proper.

If I had to give an overall impression of these days, I would say that it was both uplifting and melancholy—the first, because I felt transposed into the mind of an Englishman; the second, because I have the heart of a German!

This double senate of the English people, whatever its human failings, is something extraordinarily magnificent; and when you look at its workings from up close, you begin to understand why the English *nation* is still the first on the planet.

May 3rd, 1827

FOR THE SAKE of variety, follow me today away from the solemnity of parliament to the theater. A spectacular play is being put on, and staging here tends to be more dramatic and convincing than anywhere. I will describe just the scenery of two of the acts.

---

* This statement was often cited later, even in the lower house. But the following very recent exchange, which I owe to the engaging lady to whom it was addressed, may be less well-known. In November of the current year, 1830, the prime minister was talking to Princess C—— and the Duchess of D—— about several characteristics of the English and French nations and their respective advantages. "Ce qui est beau en Angleterre," said the duke with considerable self-assurance, "c'est que ni le rang, ni les richesses, ni la faveur sauraient élever un Anglais aux premières places. Le génie seul les obtient, et les conserve chez nous." The ladies cast down their eyes, and eight days later the Duke of Wellington was no longer *en place.*—*The Editor.* ["What is lovely about England is that neither rank, nor riches, nor favor can elevate an Englishman to the highest positions. Here these are won and retained through genius alone." The Duke of Wellington served as prime minister from January 22, 1828, until November 16, 1830, and again briefly in 1834.—*Translator.*]

In the wild mountains of Spain, a Moorish castle rises amid rock cliffs in the far distance. It is nighttime, but the moon shines brightly in a blue sky and its pale glow blends with the brilliantly illuminated windows of the castle and a chapel. At several points, a long road can be seen winding its way down through the mountains, over a series of arched bridges, and finally to the stage. Some robbers creep out of the bushes and conceal themselves furtively beside the road; you learn from their conversation that they are expecting to make a major haul. Their handsome young captain is recognizable by his imposing dignity and splendid costume in the style of the Italian banditti.

Now the gates of the faraway castle open, a drawbridge is lowered, and a state carriage drawn by six mules heads down the mountains. You lose sight of it occasionally behind the peaks, although each time it reappears it has increased in size. (This illusion is managed very dexterously with mechanical figures in various magnitudes). The carriage finally arrives on the stage at a fast trot, whereupon the concealed bandits fire several shots and the coachman is killed. The plundering of the carriage then proceeds amid great turmoil and clamor. During this tumult the curtain falls.

The second act begins with the same set, yet it awakens entirely different feelings. The lights in the castle are extinguished and the moon has gone behind a cloud. In the dim light, you can barely make out the carriage with its doors wrenched open and the murdered driver stretched out on the box. Looming out of a stony ditch is the ashen face of a fallen robber, and the handsome captain, near death, leans against a tree trunk as the young Gil Blas tries in vain to stop his soul from taking flight.[14] The effect of this tableau—half-alive, half-dead—is truly poignant.

My morning visits today were useful because they provided me with three new tickets for the next Almack's. I even persuaded one of the stern and dreaded Patronesses to give me a ticket for an obscure little miss I know—a huge favor! But I still devoted a lot of time to scheming and pleading before I got it. This miss and her entourage nearly kissed my hands as if they had all won the lottery. *Je crois qu'après cela, il y a peu de choses qu'elle me refuserait.*[15]

Apart from Almack's, the best way to engage English ladies is through politics. For the past few days, whether at dinner, the opera, indeed even at the balls, from every set of lovely lips you hear only one topic: Canning and Wellington. Even Lord Ellenborough complained that his wife was pestering him about it in the middle of the night. She woke him with a start by suddenly crying out in her sleep, "Will the prime minister stand or fall?"

So, if I learn nothing else while here, I will at least master politics, not to mention cabriolet driving. The latter you can learn perfectly, winding at full tilt through carriages and carts, whereas before you would have halted for minutes at a time. After a lengthy sojourn in such a cosmopolitan city, one really does become a little less small-minded, gaining a broader perspective and an ability to see more *en bloc*.

May 10th, 1827

THE ETERNAL MONOTONY of the Season goes on and on. My evening was filled quite pleasantly by a soirée at Lady Cowper's, one of the gentlest of the Patronesses; another at Lady Jersey's, among the most beautiful and distinguished women in England. But, preceding these, an Indian melodrama! The play was set on an island, whose inhabitants were endowed with the splendid gift of flight. Masses of gorgeous girls came sailing in like flocks of cranes. Only when insistently courted did they lower their wings; and if pressed too forcefully, these graceful, polychrome butterflies spread their wings and were gone in the wink of an eye. All this without anyone spotting the thin cords that lifted them up.

Several interesting people were present at a dinner and subsequent soirée at Prince Polignac's, among others the governor of Odessa, one of the most charming Russians I know, and Sir Thomas Lawrence, the famous painter. It is said that he regularly loses at the billiard table all of the enormous sums his art earns him, because he mistakenly fancies himself a master at the game. He is an attractive-looking man, and there is something medieval in his features that is strikingly reminiscent of paintings of the Venetian school.

I was more attracted by the Portuguese eyes of the Marquise of Palmela, for Portuguese and Spanish eyes surpass all others.

Prince Polignac's niece told me that her uncle, who is still youthful and pleasant in appearance, has a thoroughly *white* head of hair; he had observed his own locks turning gray in the course of just a few weeks when he was not yet twenty-five years old, the result of the fearful torment he experienced while being incarcerated in French Revolutionary prisons. He may well find the present era far more gratifying, but unfortunately the Restoration cannot restore his black hair!* This subject has special interest for me, dear Julie, because my own hair is unfortunately starting to take on our national colors of black and white, no doubt from excessive patriotism![16]

The local Season is hard to endure for a foreigner eager to experience the full spectrum of the domestic world. More than forty invitations lie on my table, five or six for each day. Every host wants to be paid a morning visit, and to be polite, one must make these in person. *C'est la mer à boire,*[17] and yet when I am out driving in the evenings, I pass dozens of houses that are unknown to me, and at each I am confronted by the same barricade of carriages, which I barely manage to force my way past.

I recently attended an especially magnificent ball at which a few royal princes were also present; nowadays vanity compels the hosts of such gatherings to announce the regal presence already on the invitation with the ludicrous catchphrase "To meet His Royal Highness," etc. The entire garden had been canopied, transforming it into huge rooms draped in white and pink muslin, decorated with enormous mirrors and fifty bronze chandeliers, the entire expanse perfumed by flowers from every clime. The Duchess of Clarence honored the fete with her presence, and everyone crowded around to see her, for she is one of those rare princesses whose personality commands much more respect than her rank. Her infinite kindheartedness and amiability have won her a popularity in England that we Germans can be proud of, all the more so since she will likely be queen of this land someday.[18]

The person who put on this glittering ball is anything but fashionable, a quality that has acquired the strangest nuances in England, where everyone, fashionable or not, seems to be engaged in a competition to "out-refine" the others with their parties.

On the following day the Countess of Listowel gave another ball,[19] and this time I had to get out and walk when I was still a thousand steps from the house, since there was no way to get

---

* My deceased friend could scarcely have guessed how much harm this badly organized head was still destined to deliver to the world! Of course, good will arise from it someday, as from all evil; but those fruits are not for us to reap.—*The Editor.* [By 1831, when Pückler was editing his letters, he could condemn Polignac's unconstitutional behavior as prime minister.—*Translator.*]

closer given the crush of carriages. The various equipages that had tried to blaze a path by force were hopelessly entangled, and the terrible curses of their drivers ricocheted around them. Here the conservatory walls were covered with tapestries of different-colored mosses, and the floor was thickly overlain with a new-mown lawn in which flowers seemed to be growing with abandon; these were illuminated from their stems, which doubled the splendor of their colors. The walkways were marked by multihued lamps that sparkled in the grass like jewels, and vibrant arabesques had been applied to the moss on the walls. Beyond lay a beautiful, transparent landscape of moonlight and water.

May 15th, 1827

RIDING OUT THIS morning with several ladies, the question arose as to which way we should go to best enjoy the delightful spring air. Then we saw a balloon floating high in the sky, and our objective was clear. My inexhaustible companions followed their airborne beacon for more than ten miles, as if we were in a steeplechase, until it finally disappeared from sight.

Midday I spent at a large diplomatic dinner with several of the new ministers in attendance, and in the evening I went to a ball in a German household that exhibited a solid and tasteful magnificence that was equal to the best of the English. Indeed, given the engaging qualities of the host, Prince Esterházy, it surpassed most of them.

Soon my journal will resemble the travel accounts of the late Bernoulli, who tells of nothing but invitations, midday feasts, and evening entertainments! But Julie, you must take things as they come. Think of this daybook as an embroidered garment with some details more extravagant than others. The durable fabric represents my unshakable love for you and the wish that you might share in my far-off life. But these embroideries are but poor copies of my experiences and will therefore vary in color, sometimes vibrant, sometimes pale. Indeed, they may perhaps fade away altogether in the gloomy atmosphere of the city, which can never offer pictures as sweet as those of splendid nature!

May 21st, 1827

FOR THE TIME being I must hold to my subject and mention a breakfast at Chiswick at the Duke of Devonshire's. It was one of those English fêtes that are particularly charming because they are set in the country, partly in the house and partly in the loveliest of gardens; and although they are called *déjeuners,* they do not begin until three o'clock and never end before midnight. Prince Borghese, at one time Napoleon's brother-in-law, was present. He was among those men I once saw basking in the luster conferred by that earthly sun, a glow that dimmed just as quickly as did the emperor's radiance.

The greatest adornment of this breakfast was the pretty Lady Ellenborough. She arrived in a small carriage drawn by two ponies no bigger than Kamchatka dogs, and she drove them herself. One felt suddenly tempted to unhitch the doves from Venus's chariot and replace them with ponies.

Equipages of all kinds are badly treated here. At yesterday's Almack's, such a brawl arose among the coaches that a number of ladies had to wait for hours before the chaos was straightened out. At such times the drivers behave like madmen as they try to force their way through, while the police pay no attention. The moment these heroic charioteers spy the tiniest opening, they drive their horses into it as if animal and carriage were an iron wedge, and they give no consideration to the preservation of either. One of the horses of good Lady Sligo got its hind legs so tangled in the front wheel of the neighboring carriage that it was impossible to disengage them, and a turn of the wheel would have crushed its bones. Even so, the other coachman could hardly be convinced to halt. Finally the crowd drew back a bit and the two horses were unharnessed. Yet even then it was difficult to extricate them. The whole time, the poor trapped beast whinnied more loudly than Nero, the lion at the Exeter Change.[20] Meanwhile a nearby cabriolet was smashed to smithereens, driving its shafts through the window of another coach, which, judging from the hue and cry of several female voices, must have already been fully laden. Many other carriages were damaged as well.

After this description, dear one, you in your timidity will probably never entrust yourself to a carriage in London. It was certainly safer at the time of Queen Elizabeth, when everyone, even the delicate ladies of the court, rode to balls on horseback.

May 27th, 1827

I HAD THE honor of dining at the Duke of Clarence's, where Princess Augusta, the Duchess of Kent along with her daughter,[21] and the Duchess of Gloucester were present. The duke makes for a very affable host and always graciously recalls the various times and places he has seen me before. There is a lot of Englishness about him, in the best sense, and he possesses the national love of domesticity. Today he was celebrating Princess Carolath's birthday, and his toast brought many blushes to gentle Emilie's cheeks, in spite of the familiarity she enjoys here as a relative of the charming duchess.[22]

Among the other guests I must mention the admiral, Sir George Cockburn, who conducted Napoleon to St Helena. After dinner he told me much about the emperor's talent for winning over anyone he chose. The admiral also admired the candor with which Napoleon spoke about himself, as if he were some other historical figure, and how he openly confessed that the Russians had completely outwitted him in Moscow. He said that every day, up to the very end, he had continued to feel there was hope for peace, and then it was too late. "C'était sans doute une grande faute,"[23] he added without emotion.

The Duke's daughters are *d'un beau sang* and all extraordinarily pretty, though each in a different way.[24] Among the sons, the one who stands out is Colonel Fitzclarence,* whose travels overland from India through Egypt and then to England you have read with so much interest.[25] He has also written about the German Landwehr, although he is by no means a partisan. One seldom meets a young officer of such multifaceted culture and refinement. I have known him for some time already and have been very pleased with his friendliness toward me.

His eldest sister is married to Sir Sidney, and she told me that the family possesses an uninterrupted series of ancestor portraits dating back to the time of Lord Leicester, and has even retained a lock of hair from each of their forebears. The documents are also said to include a complete list of every guest attending the Kenilworth feast, along with some very remarkable household accounts from that period. Walter Scott, I believe, made use of these papers.[26]

In the evening Pasta warbled beautifully at Countess San Antonio's, and two or three balls rounded out the day.

---

* Now Lord Munster. [This title was granted him in 1831.—*Translator*.]

I ENJOYED A hearty laugh this morning at the expense of a young lord who hasn't gained much from his sojourn in Paris, and whose handsome horse drew more attention in the park than he did.

"Quel beau cheval vous avez là," I said.

"Oui," he replied, with his English accent, "C'est une belle bête, je l'ai fait moi-même, et pour cela je lui suis beaucoup attaché."[27]

Clearly what he meant was that he had raised it himself. Is this not the perfect pendant to the deaf Russian officer in B——, to whom the king once called out, on the occasion of a sturgeon being brought to the table, "Ce poisson est bien fréquent chez vous," to which the Russian rose and responded with a deep bow, "Oui, Sire, je l'ai été pendant quinze ans."[28]

Rex Judaeorum[29] gave a magnificent dinner and told me that the dessert alone cost one hundred pounds sterling. I sat next to a very witty lady, the Duke of Wellington's friend Mrs. Arbuthnot, who has a very fine and *not*-English physiognomy. You can imagine what an impassioned politician she was! There is no doubt that I annoyed her a lot; first of all, I am a Canningite, and second, I hate politics during meals. There was a lot of splendor on display. The table service was vermeil and silver, replaced for dessert by a service entirely of gold. In the adjoining room, beneath a portrait of Prince Metternich (a gift from the sitter), there was a large box, also of gold, probably a copy of the Ark of the Covenant. The meal was followed by a concert in which Mr. Moscheles played as *enchantingly* as his young wife looked (she was standing next to him). It was two o'clock by the time I arrived at the Duke of Northumberland's rout, a small party to which only one thousand people—yes, believe it or not, one thousand—had been invited. In an immense picture gallery, where the temperature was 99.5 degrees Fahrenheit, grand music was being performed, but you could scarcely hear it over the clamor and crush. The smell of perspiration was, like that in the Black Hole of Calcutta, nearly unbearable. Does it really make sense to call nations that amuse themselves in *this* way civilized?

LADY LONDONDERRY, RICH in coal mines, has a complexion that contrasts beautifully with the darkness of that ore, and her slightly disheveled manner is thoroughly her own (Figure 39). She toured me through her bazaar this morning, not at all an ordinary one, for it contains jewels worth three hundred thousand Reichsthalers or thereabouts. What a pretty picture of refinement!—the whole boudoir filled with pleasant fragrances, flowers, and rarities; the *clair-obscur* of red draperies; and the marchioness herself stretched out on her chaise longue in a dress of yellow gauze, *plongée dans une douce langueur*.[30] Diamonds, pearls, pens and ink, books, letters, toys, and seals were lying in front of her along with a half-completed purse. Among the seals were two inscriptions, quite piquant in their contrasts. The first was a pair of lovely lines by Lord Byron:

> Love will find its way
> Where wolves would fear to stray.[31]

The second reflects an authentically French philosophy: *Tout lasse, tout casse, tout passe.*[32]

THE MOST NOBLE FRANCES ANNE,
MARCHIONESS OF LONDONDERRY.

Throughout the house one sees nothing but portraits in every size of Emperor Alexander, who paid court to the marchioness in Vienna, and his omnipresent likeness testifies to his gratitude. While serving there as ambassador, her husband made the fullest use of his English prerogative. Once he boxed with a coachman. Another time he presented the archduchess and, if I am not mistaken, even the empress herself, to his wife rather than the other way around. And he ran into the kitchen to stab his cook for having offended the marchioness. In short, the weather was bad and good in Vienna, or more likely there were storms and hail.

Just think of the disappointment for the poor lady, who ruled on the Continent for such a long time yet now finds herself irredeemably unfashionable, in spite of her diamonds, rank, and pretty looks. But the Fashion Aristocracy is more difficult to enter here than the topmost ranks of the Freemasons and indeed is more capricious than that venerable group—although both, like the dear Lord, create things out of nothingness!

I dined at Lord Darnley's where I found, among others, the once-prominent Lord Bloomfield (one of the king's favorites from the era of his youthful escapades) and the Archbishop of York, a majestic old gentleman who started out as a private tutor and achieved his lofty rank through the patronage of his pupils. Nothing is uglier—or at the same time more comical—than the informal dress of English archbishops. A short schoolmaster's wig, badly powdered, a black French coat, and, *in front,* a small lady's apron of black silk to cover the "inexpressibles,"* quite like what miners tend to wear in the *back.* Lord Darnley laughed uproariously when I asked him, amazed, *si ce tablier faisait allusion au vœu de chasteté.*[33] I had temporarily forgotten that English archbishops, otherwise so genuinely Catholic, have reserved for themselves the right to marry. It is nonetheless true that their wives are treated like mistresses, because they are not allowed to take their husbands' names.

We were very well fed with venison and delicious fruit from Cobham, and after dinner we attended a concert that truly diverged from the norm. It was an enterprise undertaken by several distinguished aristocrats, lovers of the bygone music of Handel, Mozart, and the Italians, whose compositions are the only ones performed here.

It has been a long time since I have enjoyed anything so much! What is modern warbling, after all, compared to the sublimity of this old church music? I felt transported back to my childhood years, a sensation that strengthens the soul for days on end and grants it lighter wings. The singing was absolutely superb, often heavenly in its simplicity; it is incredible what power God has granted the human voice when used correctly, how easily and confidently it rings forth. In Handel's choruses you are appalled to feel the night spreading over Egypt; to hear the tumult of the pharaoh's armies and the pounding of the sea as it entombs them beneath its waves.[34]

I could not listen to the fiddling at a ball after enjoying such divine tones, so I took myself home at midnight, quite happily abandoning Almack's and another gala of the fashionable world. I want to carry the echo of that music of the spheres into my dreams and let its wings transport me on a blissful nighttime journey with you, my Julie. Are you ready? Now we fly. . . .

---

* "Inexpressibles" is the name for this article of clothing in England, where a woman of good society may often abandon her husband and children to run off with a lover, but is always too decorous to bear hearing the word "breeches" spoken aloud. [This euphemism was widely used in the nineteenth century to refer to men's formfitting trousers or breeches.—*Translator.*]

MY OLD BERNDT awakened me very early this morning, something he does only when there is a letter from you. On less important occasions, he always lets me rest, even when I have made a point the evening before that he must get me up. His excuse is always "You were sleeping so soundly!"

It is lucky that I am not so vain as to become giddy from being praised, since otherwise you would make a real fool of me. Ah, I know myself only too well, the hundred flaws that your love mainly disregards. The little demon you are attacking does occasionally haunt me, 'tis true. Still, he is a relatively innocent one, often downright dumb, poor, and honest, the sort that in moral terms stands somewhere between an angel and a devil. In a word: an authentic, weak creature. But since you disapprove of this tiny demon, I will imitate Hoffmann and put him in a bottle, corking it with Solomon's seal.[35] From now on I will show you only my Moravian brethren side, for you know that I spent my youth among those men, "and if I feel the effects, I feel them only slightly."[36]

I will definitely put in an appearance at the costume ball you plan to give following the model of Brighton, yet I am sure nobody will recognize me, since I can only be there in spirit. I will simply plant a kiss on your forehead and then disappear like a premonition. So watch out!

YESTERDAY I TOOK another stroll away from the fashionable world and into the City, where I observed the tedious industry that produces all the frivolous luxuries of this society. Something new is invented here every day, including countless advertisements and ways of presenting them *en evidence*. It used to be enough to paste them up, but now they must be ambulatory. I saw one man wearing a cardboard hat three times normal height and emblazoned in huge letters: "Boots at 12 shillings a pair—recommended." Another was carrying a kind of flag with a picture of a washerwoman, and below this: "Only one sixpence a shirt." Boxes the size of small houses resembling Noah's ark were plastered with such promotions and being hauled slowly through the streets, each harnessed to a man or horse. They bore more falsehoods on their backs than Münchhausen ever managed to invent.

By the time I got to Mr. Rothschild's, I was very tired and accepted an invitation to dine with him at his counting house. During the meal we philosophized about religion. Rothschild is a very good-natured fellow and more accommodating than others of his class, as long as he does not think he is risking anything by it. He certainly cannot be blamed for that. To a certain extent he had the advantage in our discussion of faith, since his fellow believers are of a more ancient religious nobility than we Christians can claim. They are the true aristocrats in *this* subject, and have never been interested in innovation. I finally said, along with Goethe: "All viewpoints should be honored."[37] Then I took an extremely frail hackney carriage back to the West End (where there are neither Jews nor Christians but only fashionables and nobodies). There at Mrs. P——'s I heard Pasta sing again, and I played écarté at half stakes with the lady friend of Lord H——.

I finally got home at four and fell asleep in the rosy light of dawn, imagining myself in a forest on a bed of moss. A terrible scream woke me, and when I looked around, I saw a poor devil plummeting through the air diagonally from the top of an enormous tree and crashing down next to me. Groaning and pale as death, he picked himself up and wailed pitifully, "It's all over with me now!" I was about to go to his aid when a creature resembling an inkpot approached him and, cursing, repeatedly pounded the half-dead man with its stopper. I grabbed the attacker and pulled out the stopper, but as the ink poured forth, the pot metamorphosed into a Moor in a gleaming silver jacket and luxurious costume. He laughed and said that if I would just leave the man in peace, he would show me things I had never seen before. Now all sorts of magic began, conjurings that outstripped every Pinetti and Philadelphia. For instance, a large closet changed its contents every minute, and all the treasures of Golconda, with the most incredible rarities, appeared one after another. A portly man with four pretty daughters was watching intently, and I immediately recognized him as a gentleman named Rolls, who used to host balls in Brighton. There he was known as Double Rolls (because of his corpulence) while his daughters were dubbed Cut Rolls. Rolls remarked that all this was lasting far too long for his taste, and he was hungry. The offended magician gave us a furious look, and as his costume turned scarlet right before our eyes, he chanted

> Two is five and seven ten,
> Eyes, eat up! The mouth should see,
> Quickly change both front and back.
> *Fitzli Putzli very well.*[38]

This incantation had scarcely been uttered when a magnificent meal materialized, and poor Rolls eagerly stuck some fresh green peas in his eyes, which went down with no difficulty at all, while he held his lorgnette in front of his mouth and contemplated all the other marvelous things spread out on the table, devouring them in his imagination. He wanted to invite his wife and daughters to partake, but he had no other speech organ at his disposal than the one generally prohibited from making loud noises. The Cut Rolls almost died laughing at Papa's peculiar *propos*.[39] Last but not least, Rolls approached the magician to express his thanks. Although he was grotesquely twisted and walking on his hands, he still managed to reach his feet into a bowl of tutti-frutti while his new speech organ melodically declared "Delicious!"

Has anyone ever heard of such a crazy dream? It is due to the gloomy haze and the suffocating air of London—they are clouding my senses. So I am sending them off to be dispelled by the sunshine of home, and on their heavy wings I place a thousand loving greetings,

From your faithful friend, Lou

London, June 5th, 1827

WHILE PAYING A visit to Mrs. Hope today, I was able to study her husband's art collection in more detail; I found a very beautiful statue of Venus by Canova especially captivating. I saw it unfinished in Rome quite a few years ago, in the atelier of that delightful artist, and even then it impressed me more than any of his other works.[1]

Among the paintings I was most struck by Correggio's portrait of the infamous Cesare Borgia. What a sublime sinner! He stands boldly there in all his virile beauty, with spirit and greatness radiating from every feature of his face. Only in his eyes does a hideous tiger lurk.

The collection is especially rich in paintings of the Netherlandish school. Many are superbly true to life, something I am happy to admit often has greater charm for me than an idealization, however perfectly executed, if it fails to touch my soul.

I was thus drawn to the very respectable-looking old wife of a Dutch burgher. She is drinking down a glass of wine with great delight, while her husband, standing beside her wrapped in his cloak and holding the bottle, gazes down at her with good-natured amusement. Also noteworthy were some sixteenth-century officers in their handsome, sensible uniforms, enjoying themselves at a happy meal after their hard and bloody labors. There were others as well. Among the landscape painters I made the acquaintance of Hobbema, whose style is most like that of Ruisdael. Deceptively real fruit by van Huysum and van Os, houses by Vermeer (who is known for the careful rendering of every tile), several Wouwermans, Paul Potters, etc., etc. Nothing was missing from this abundant collection. Only the modern English pictures were poor.

I did not go out any more after this, but stayed quietly by myself to celebrate my good mother's birthday.

June 7th, 1827

AS AN EXAMPLE of everything that an English dandy requires, I am passing along the following advice from my fashionable washerwoman, who is employed by some of the most distinguished examples of this type. She is the only person who knows how to give the right stiffness to cravats or the proper folds to shirtfronts. Here are the weekly necessities: twenty shirts; twenty-four handkerchiefs; nine or ten pairs of summer trousers; thirty cravats (unless he wears black ones); a dozen vests; and stockings *à discrétion*. Even now I can see your domestic soul beginning to petrify. But, you see, a dandy cannot be expected to manage without changing clothes three or four times a day, for he needs to appear

1. at breakfast in a Chinese dressing gown and Indian slippers;
2. for his morning ride in a frock coat, boots, and spurs;
3. at dinner in a dress coat and shoes;
4. at the ball in pumps (a word describing shoes that are as light as paper and must be polished daily).

By six o'clock the park was so full of riders it was like a rout on horseback, but a pleasant one, with green turf instead of floorboards, the cool of evening in place of oppressive heat, and the effort of conveyance given over to the horse.

Earlier, when I called on Princess E——, I found three lovely young *ambassadrices en conférence, toutes les trois profondément occupées d'une queue,*[2] in short, whether or not it was necessary to wear one at the Queen of Württemberg's.

This evening at the ball given by the above mentioned Marchioness of Londonderry, I had my first glimpse here of the *polonaise* and the mazurka, both danced very badly. We ate in the sculpture gallery, where many of the statues had been topped and draped by the ladies' hats and shawls, something that really sparked one's artistic sensibilities! I came home at six in the morning and am writing to you while they close my shutters to prepare me an artificial night. The valets have it hard here. They only get short rests, or they sleep during the day like watchmen.

June 13th, 1827

AS I HAVE said, here one is invited to a royal prince's much as one might be asked elsewhere to share some delicacy with intimate friends. Yesterday it was dinner with the Duchess of Gloucester and today with the Duke of Sussex. The prince, although on thoroughly bad terms with the king,* has made himself very popular with the nation because of his liberal opinions, and certainly deserves this. Having spent considerable time on the Continent, he loves the German way of life and is entirely familiar with our language, as are most of his brothers. As soon as the ladies left us, cigars were brought out at his request and more than one was smoked, something I have not yet seen in England. Monsieur de Montrond told some very funny anecdotes with true French artistry. Major Keppel, the Persian traveler, was the most entertaining and shared a number of scabrous but piquant stories, things he could not publish, so I cannot pass them on to you either, which I very much regret.

Tomorrow I will drive to Ascot with young Captain Rose and will visit Windsor in order to bring a little variety back into my monotonous life. The races are supposed to be unusually brilliant, since the king will be there this time to watch his horses compete.

Windsor, June 14, 1827

WE QUICKLY TRAVELED twenty-five miles, partly through Windsor Park, with the castle, the ancient residence of so many kings, looming in the background. Finally we reached the broad and barren heath of Ascot, where the races are held. The place looked quite like an elaborate and

---

* One mustn't forget that the previous king, George IV, is meant here.—*The Editor.* [George IV, the Duke's elder brother, died in 1830.—*Translator.*]

festive military encampment. Endless rows of tents for horses and men; barricades of carriages along the racecourse, most of them filled with lovely ladies; platforms as high as houses in three or four stages, one above another, with the king's box at the finish line; and all this animated by twenty to thirty thousand people, many having already been here for five or six days. These are the main features of the scene. In one area is a market, and there—amid the other booths and tents, rather like an old Free Quarter[3]—you find various games of hazard, which are strictly forbidden elsewhere. But it is fair Venus more than Pluto who receives the most offerings here, since nowhere can intrigues be so discreetly initiated.[4]

The ladies in the carriages are daily provisioned with champagne and an excellent breakfast, which they then distribute with great hospitality. I ran into many old friends and made some new acquaintances too, including a very charming woman, Lady Garvagh, who invited Captain Rose and me for a meal at her cottage. Hence at six o'clock, when today's races were over, we drove to Titness Park, passing through a most beautiful area where the trees are so abundant that it looks like a cultivated forest in spite of the tilled fields. We got there before the family itself and found the house open, but without a servant or any other living creature to be found. There cannot be a more captivating place! It was like the enchanted dwelling of a fairy. If only you could have seen it! The house stood on a hill, half hidden beneath magnificent old trees. Its various projections, dating from different eras, were concealed by shrubs here and there, so there was no possibility of getting an impression of the whole. A gallery-like rose arbor bursting with hundreds of flowers led directly to the entrance hall, and passing through a few other rooms and then a corridor, we arrived in the dining room, where the table had already been handsomely laid. But there was still no one to be seen. From here the gardens extended before us, a true paradise, brilliantly illuminated by the evening sun. Verandas of varying shapes and sizes ran along the whole length of the house; some jutted forward, some retreated, and all were covered with different blossoming vines. These served as a border for the colorful flower garden that extended all across the hillside. A meadowy valley, deep and narrow, adjoined this, and behind the terrain rose again to a higher crest, its slopes appointed with ancient beeches. To the left, at the valley's end, the view was closed by water, and in the distance, over the tops of the trees, we could see the Round Tower of Windsor Castle, with its colossal royal flag rising into the blue sky. In this seclusion, the tower alone reminded us that we were in a place ruled not just by nature and a benevolent fairy, but that people, too, lived here with their joys, sorrows, and splendor. Looking down upon the peaceful cottages, the tower stood like a beacon of ambition, a temptation to greater and more treacherous pleasures. Whoever attains those pleasures must pay a heavy price, however, for peace and serenity dwell back in the valley of sweet tranquility!

My poetic ecstasy was soon interrupted by the lovely hostess, who was much entertained by our response to her enchanted palace. She immediately saw to it that we were shown to rooms where we could tidy up, something the day's dust and heat made necessary. We had an excellent dinner with iced champagne and delicious fruit, which kept us at the table until midnight. Still more hours were spent over coffee, tea, and music.

To be honest, we would gladly have left the music to the family! My digestion was seriously disturbed by the terrible struggle I had to endure—it was truly an agony—as I tried to suppress my laughter when the aged mother of our hostess finally sat down at the piano and gave us an aria from her youth, composed by Rousseau. Never in my life will I forget the refrain: *Je t'aimerai toujours.*[5] She put a trill on every repetition of the "ai," which at first sounded like the bleating of a lamb, then mimicked the cooing of a dove, and ended with the cadenza of a cock in full court-ship mode. The song went on interminably, and the young Captain Rose, who unfortunately succumbs to giggles just as readily as I do, sat up like a taut fiddle bow, squeezing his whole body tight with amazing force and making the strangest grimaces behind his huge moustache. As for me, I tried to boost my moral power by thinking constantly of *you*, dear Julie, and your exemplary restraint on such occasions. Meanwhile everyone was so gracious and friendly that I would have shed tears of blood rather than laugh at the songstress; but what can you do when your senses are so irresistibly provoked? Each time the dreaded passage approached was terrible, as I prayed God for the good old woman to intone "Je t'aimerai toujours" without any flourishes. But in vain. Scarcely had she begun the fateful "ai" when the merciless trill followed *immanquablement*. By the seventh verse I could not bear it anymore. For the first time Rousseau seemed truly immortal to me. I rained on the old lady's parade, as the students say! I grasped her hand before she could touch the keys once more, gave it a cordial shake, thanked her for her kindness, apologized for having burdened her for so long, shook the hand of the lovely daughter (for this is the custom here) and of the other family members, and in the blink of an eye, Captain Rose and I were safely back in the carriage, which had been ready and waiting for us an hour already. You can well imag-ine that we then indulged in laughter at our ease, the echo of that trilling delighting us all the way to Windsor. But awaiting me there was something unpleasantly sobering after such boisterous hilarity. Just as I was about to climb in bed, Berndt started to moan that *he* was being haunted by misfortune at every turn.

"Well, what's happened?"

"Oh, God, I wouldn't even mention it if I didn't have to, but I must."

"What the devil! Get on with it! What is it?"

And guess what? I had handed him a purse containing twenty-five pounds to be placed in the small chest in the carriage, but the confused old fellow had instead stuck it in the side pocket. Then, like Kotzebue's stupid *Landjunker*, he took it out again in the thick of the crowded booths to buy a glass of beer, paid with a sovereign (he claimed he had no change, but more likely he was swaggering a bit with the money bag), and then carefully put it back where it had been. It is hardly a surprise here in England that when he returned to the carriage, the purse was no longer to be found. What a blessing that I was still carrying some money myself and thus spared any momentary embarrassment.

Richmond, June 15th, 1827[6]

THIS MORNING WE visited Windsor Castle, which is only now being completed according to the original plans, and is already the largest and most magnificent residence of any European monarch. There was not enough time to see the interior, so I postponed that for another occasion. All I did today was call on the Duchess of Clarence, who lives in the big tower, and has a divine view from her lofty balcony. One of her servants was a handsome Greek boy, wearing his national costume of scarlet, blue, and gold, and with bare legs and feet. He survived the massacre at Chios by hiding in an oven.[7] Although he has already become a full-fledged Englishman, he retains something unusually noble and exotic in his bearing. At one o'clock we returned to the race-track, where I was served my meal by yet another beauty. When the races were over, we drove to Richmond where Captain Rose's regiment is garrisoned and spent a jolly, boisterous evening with the officer corps. The widespread prosperity allows for a far more luxurious life here. These gentlemen deny themselves nothing, and to us their mess often seems to rival a princely table at home.

Tomorrow the regiment of the Hussars and a regiment of Ulans will be mustered by the inspecting general, and I will stay to watch this before heading back to London.

June 16th, 1827

THE REGIMENT PERFORMED very well, with less affectation and perhaps less precision than our wonderfully trained three-year riders, but with more authentic military composure and deeply engrained self-assurance. They also executed their maneuvers more quickly due to the excellent horses, unmatched on the Continent. Since the last war, the English cavalry has improved enormously in handling the reins and in military riding, thanks to the Duke of Wellington's attention. The men kept their horses just as controlled as the best of ours do. Remarkable according to our views was the lack of ceremony, as fifty or sixty officers in civilian dress (including several generals)—some in top boots and informal jackets, others in frock coats and colorful cravats—took part in the review and swarmed around the inspecting general who, except for the members of the regiment being evaluated and his two adjutants, was the only man wearing a uniform. Even some supernumerary officers from the same regiment who were not in active service any longer were riding around in civilian dress and shoes, a sight that could easily boggle the mind of a Prussian general. In a word, people pay more attention to the *real* here; to the *form* at home. Here clothes actually *do not* make the man, and this simplicity is sometimes very impressive.

Rose told me that this regiment was originally established by the tailors' guild in London when the French were threatening to invade and in the beginning consisted of nothing but tailors. They have now evolved into very proficient and martial hussars and have fought with great distinction, particularly at Belle Alliance.

June 18th, 1827

I HAVE BEEN back in my accustomed track for two days now, making my debut with four balls and a dinner at Lord Carnarvon's. There I found the famous protector of the Greeks, Mr. Eynard, whose pretty wife exhibits as much enthusiasm for the Hellenes as he does. Yesterday I dined at Esterházy's, where I met a young Spaniard who I wished had been an actor, because then he could play Don Juan, a role to which he seemed perfectly suited. Finally, with my ears full of the dramatic tones of Pasta, who performs someplace or other every evening, I took myself off to bed.

Today was a concert at the great duke's,[8] where old Velluti, still resting on his laurels, crowed like a capon, but nonetheless sent everyone into raptures because he used to sing so well. I then went to one of the prettiest balls I have seen in London, given by a genteel Scottish lady. The main room was entirely hung with decorative paper lanterns, very tastefully grouped and imitating the shapes of all sorts of flowers.

At six o'clock, as we got into our carriages in the early morning sunshine, the ladies were looking extremely strange. No *fraîcheur* could stand such a test. Their complexions were changing like chameleons: some were looking very blue, others blotchy, most of them corpse-like, with drooping hairdos and glazed eyes. It was really quite repulsive to watch these roses that had bloomed by lamplight suddenly fade and lose their petals in the bright dawn. The fate of earthly beauty!

June 23rd, 1827

WHAT DO YOU say, dear Julie, to a breakfast for two thousand people? Such an event took place today in the horticultural gardens,⁹ which are vast enough to contain such a number with ease. Not to underplay the terrible crush in the food tents, especially where the fruit was displayed but not distributed until a specified time, when it was most indelicately devoured in the blink of an eye. One Providence pineapple weighed eleven pounds, and there were slightly smaller specimens in bright red and green, strawberries the size of small apples, and in general the most unusual and sumptuous selection of fruits. The whole festival was merry and had a pleasingly rural character.

The scene itself was so welcoming: smooth lawns dotted with beautifully groomed people, tents and gatherings among the shrubs, great masses of roses and flowers of every kind. I had driven there with our ambassador and returned home with him at seven in the evening. We had to laugh at the industriousness of an Irishman, who put on a great show of lighting our way to the carriage with a lantern that contained no candle since it was still bright out. This bit of fun earned him a few shillings from a cheered and indulgent company. At one point an English comrade called out to him, "You are shepherding really generous people!" "Oh," he responded, "if I didn't recognize them as such, I wouldn't go with them."

Also quite novel were the Tyrolean singers who have become very fashionable here. They address everyone with the familiar *du*, even the King, who speaks German with them; they are not intimidated by anybody. It is hilarious to watch as one goes right up to Prince Esterházy, whose patriotic support is mainly responsible for their being in vogue, extend a hand and exclaim, "Nun, was machst Du, Esterházy?"¹⁰ The petite woman in this group of weird and wonderful Tyrolean creatures came up to me today and said, "I've been looking at you for a long time, because you are so like my dear John that I want to give you a kiss." The offer was not particularly appetizing because the girl is ugly. But since she had also kissed His Royal Highness (a good caricature of that moment is currently available for sale), the impertinence has come to be viewed as flattering.

June 26th, 1827

THE DUKE OF Northumberland was generous enough to show me his lovely palace *en detail* this morning, and I finally saw what I have longed to see, a house in which lofty splendor and elegance reign; where everything, from the smallest to the largest, has been realized with the same care and perfection; where absolutely nothing is amiss. This ideal is truly achieved here, no trifle being neglected. There is not one skewed line, not a speck of dirt, nothing faded or out of fashion, nothing threadbare, nothing artificial; every piece of furniture, every door or window is, in its way, a masterpiece of craftsmanship. Achieving this extraordinary quality has naturally cost several hundred thousand pounds and certainly great effort, but it is perhaps unique of its kind (Figure 40).

There are likewise plenty of art treasures and curiosities of every kind. These are displayed very tastefully on terraced shelves in cabinets lined with purple velvet and backed by large, one-piece mirrors. The grand marble staircase with a gilded bronze balustrade is especially striking, and the handrail capping the balustrade is extraordinary. It is made of polished mahogany, and the joins in the wood—fashioned in some special way that is still a secret—are impossible to

NORTHUMBERLAND HOUSE

detect: not the tiniest trace of a joint can be found anywhere along the railing's entire length as it winds its way up through several curves. The whole thing seems to be, or perhaps really is, made of a single piece.

Another oddity is a disguised porte cochere in the house's exterior wall; it is opened only during fetes to accommodate the large crush of carriages and, when closed, vanishes into the facade. Although of iron, it is so completely masked by the roughcast of a stone composite and a false window that you cannot distinguish it from the rest of the house. I will save the paintings for another time.

In the evening, at the Duke of Clarence's I met Sir Gore Ouseley, an interesting man who was recently ambassador to Persia. His legation secretary was Mr. Morier, the author of the *Hajji Baba*. I must pass on a few illustrative anecdotes that I heard him tell about that country.

For a long time the present shah was kept in such subordination by his prime minister, Ebrahim Khan, who had placed him on the throne when he was still a child, that he ruled in name only.[11] Resistance was all the more impossible because, without exception, every governorship in the provinces and major towns of the realm was held by one of the minister's relatives or lackeys. Finally the shah decided to extricate himself from such servitude, no matter what the cost, and he chose a most energetic means, one that bears the authentic stamp of the Oriental character. In keeping with the ancient laws of Persia, there is a class of soldiers called the King's Guard who are sparsely disbursed throughout all major towns. These men follow no orders except those that come directly from the ruler himself and are endorsed with his own seal. Therefore this guard alone had remained independent of the all-controlling minister and was the throne's only reliable support. The king now sent out secret orders, in his own hand, to the leaders of these trusted men, directing them to assassinate every one of Ebrahim's relatives on a specified day, at a specified time. As the appointed hour approached, the shah held a Divan, a council of state, and tried to engage Ebrahim in an argument. But the prime minister was not to be ruffled and simply assumed his normal lofty tone, at which the shah ordered him to proceed immediately to the state prison. The minister responded with a smile that he would go, but the king ought to consider that he would be held accountable for this by every governor of his provinces. "Not anymore, friend Ebrahim," the king said cheerfully, "not anymore." Then, taking out his English pocket watch, he cast a ruinous glance at the dumbfounded minister and added coldly, "At this very minute the last man of your bloodline stopped breathing, and you will follow him." And so it happened.

The second anecdote demonstrates how the shah followed the principle of the French chanson that says "quand on a dépeuplé la terre, il faut la répeupler après."[12]

At his final audience with the shah, Sir Gore graciously asked the number of his children so that he might convey this information to his own monarch, should he enquire, which Gore expected him to do.

"One hundred and fifty-four sons," the shah replied.

"Might I ask His Majesty once more, how many children?"

Oriental etiquette prohibited him from uttering the word *girls*; in fact, the question itself was considered almost an insult. But the king, who regarded Gore with great benevolence, did not take it badly.

"Ah ha, I understand," he said laughing, and summoned his chief eunuch. "Musa! How many daughters do I have?"

"King of Kings," answered Musa, throwing himself full length on the floor, "five hundred and sixty."

When Sir Gore reported this to the dowager empress in Saint Petersburg, she simply exclaimed, "Ah, le monstre!"

June 29th, 1827

THE SEASON IS now (thank God!) coming to an end, and I am thinking of making a trip to the north of England and Scotland sometime soon. I have received several invitations from people there, but I would rather remain free to wander through the country *à ma guise*, as long as time and circumstances permit.

Today we had one of the most beautiful days since I have been in England, and in the evening, returning from the countryside where I had enjoyed an early dinner at Count Münster's, I saw—for the first time here—the horizon adorned with an Italian illumination of blue and lilac as brilliant as a painting by Claude.

Apropos of something else worthy of imitation, the countess has a very pretty flower table. The top is crystal-clear glass and below it is a deep tray filled with a layer of moist sand with a fine mesh stretched over it. Fresh flowers are placed close to each other in the interstices of the mesh, so that when you slide the tray back in, you have the most beautiful flower painting on which you can write and work. If you prefer to enjoy the refreshing fragrance, however, the glass top is constructed so that it can be opened or entirely removed.

Children's balls are this Season's order of the day, and I visited one of the prettiest of them at Lady Jersey's tonight. These refined northern children were all extravagantly dressed and many of them not ungraceful, but it pained me to observe how much they had already ceased to be children. Most of the poor creatures were as unnatural, listless, and self-centered as all of us larger folk around them. Italian peasant children would have been a hundred times more charming. Only at dinner were their unvarnished instincts more apparent, as the prospect of tasty indulgence restored nature to her rightful place. The prettiest and purest feelings were visible in the unaffected tenderness in their mothers' eyes, lifting the less-attractive woman to the tolerable, and elevating the beauties to a still-higher order of loveliness.

A second ball at Lady Scott Murray's had nothing to offer beyond the hundredth repetition of the usual stupid throng. Poor Prince Borghese, whose corpulence is unsuited to this kind of squeeze, fell into a faint, and leaning against the banister, gasped for air like a carp out of water. The pursuit of pleasure and happiness can take very odd turns in this world.

July 3rd, 1827

IN ORDER TO enjoy a solitary fish dinner, I took a long detour to Greenwich this afternoon. The view from the observatory is especially notable because it overlooks a vast sweep of landscape taken up almost entirely by London, which for years has been stretching its tentacles farther and farther, swallowing up one after another of the villages surrounding it. Admittedly space is needed for a population that will soon equal the kingdom of Saxony (ever since it has been circumcised in the Jewish manner).[13]

I went to the Ship Tavern, and since I was alone, handed my horse to the hostler; the grooming of horses is so excellent here that you can put even your best animal in the care of the hostler at any inn without a bit of worry. I was then shown to a very nice room with a bay window projecting over the Thames. Below me swam the various fish that I, the predator, would soon devour without mercy. The river was crowded with a hundred skiffs, music and song resounded from the passing steamboats, and above this colorful tableau the sun, bloodred in a light veil of fog, was sinking toward the horizon. Sitting at the window, I gave an extended audience to my thoughts until the arrival of sea eel, flounder, and sole, all in different preparations, summoned me to more material pleasures. The meal was nicely complemented by iced champagne and Lord Chesterfield's *Letters,* which I had brought along. After a brief siesta as nighttime arrived, I got back on my horse and slowly rode the seven miles home over well-watered roads and along an uninterrupted avenue of brilliantly shimmering gas lamps. I got there at the stroke of midnight, just as a black-draped coffin drove past me on the left, like a ghostly apparition.

July 5th, 1827

B——— GAVE ME your letter at Almack's, and I immediately hurried home with it. How happy your descriptions have made me, and I almost wept over the faithful old giants in our park calling to me through you: "Oh Master, don't you hear our treetops rustling, alive with thousands of birds?" Oh yes, I hear them in my spirit, and I will not experience true joy again until I am *there* once more, where my most faithful friend awaits and my botanical offspring prosper. I thank you very much for the five-leaf clover. Meanwhile the enclosed Viennese postilion's horse, after promising so much good luck, managed to lose his tail on the journey. I have gone ahead and replaced it with the clover leaf, a vegetal appendage that gives him the hybrid look of the Holy Alliance.

I was just interrupted by old Berndt, who came to ask if he could have the rest of the night off, promising to be back at eight in the morning. I gave my permission with a smile and inquired about the adventure he had in mind. "Oh," was the response, "I just wanted to watch a hanging and see how they're done here. At five o'clock five men are going to the gallows, all at the same time."

What dissonance those words brought into my comfy, indulgent life! What a contrast between the thousands exhausted with dance and glutted with merriment, who were heading home to a pleasant rest, and those unfortunate creatures who must face mortal agony on the way to an eternal one. Again I lamented with Napoleon, "O world, O world!"[14] Thus after a day squandered in frivolity, I had great trouble falling asleep, pursued by the thought that those wretches were just then being awakened to take their gruesome leave of the world and its joys; that they will not be lifted up to heaven in martyrdom to the good and the great, but instead demeaned in their guilt. We pity those who suffer in innocence, but to me the guilty are much more to be pitied.

My imagination, once it becomes excited, goes further than advisable. So now I saw profound sin in every vain pleasure, in every luxurious refinement that sneers at privation and misery. I often find myself in this frame of mind. I have more than once had a good meal turn bitter while observing the poor servants, born of the same Mother Nature, who were only present so they could pass the food like slaves; or when I thought of the needy who can barely afford their miserable evening meal after a long day of hard work. Meanwhile, as in the English caricature, we who are glutted with excess actually envy the beggar for *his hunger*! Yet in spite of all these good and just feelings (I am projecting my own views on others), do we not seek our excuse in acknowledging that we would be scandalized if that same servant were to play Tantalus and try to help himself from our table? Or if the poor man dared invite himself to our feast without a wedding garment?[15] God himself arranged it that some are supposed to enjoy and others do without; and so it remains. Every cry of delight is echoed elsewhere by one of despair, and just when someone dashes his head to pieces in a raging frenzy, another feels the greatest rapture of delight.

Therefore no one should fret about this too much, even if he cannot understand why things go better or worse for him than for others. Fortune loves this bitter irony. So pick the flowers while they bloom as a child would; share their fragrance with others while you can. And when it comes, confront your own pain bravely with a breast of iron.

July 7th, 1827

LET ME NOW return to my daily chronicle.

After dining with the epicurean Sir L——, I spent a very pleasant evening with a small group at the Duchess of Kent's. The court circles here, if they can be called that, have nothing in common with their counterparts on the Continent, where they once drove Count R—— to such distraction that when asked by the King of Bavaria how he was enjoying the current ball, he responded, "Oh, as soon as the court is gone, I think I'll be very happy."

From here I drove very late to another ball at Princess Lieven's, a lady whose fetes are always in keeping with her refinement. I happened into a conversation with another diplomat, which provided me with some interesting notes. He told me about a difficult mission he had undertaken to convince Marie Louise, the French empress, to let herself be removed from the midst of an army of at least twelve thousand select troops who remained loyal to Napoleon. Contrary to his every assumption, she offered almost no resistance and showed very little love for the emperor (something confirmed by what happened afterward). Only the five-year-old King of Rome refused to go along and had to be removed by force, just as earlier, directed by some heroic instinct, he had not wanted to join in the regency's cowardly departure from Paris. I will skip recounting the role that many another well-known figure played in this, but it strengthened my conviction that the French nation never displayed less dignity than at the time of Napoleon's abdication.[16]

July 10th, 1827

IT IS NOW turning more oppressively hot than I would have thought possible in this land of mist and fog. The grass in Hyde Park is the color of sand, and the trees are pale and withered; even the city squares, despite all the watering, do not look much better. The lawns are nonetheless constantly mowed and rolled as carefully as if they were still growing. With similar care and tending, we could certainly have more beautiful lawns in southern Germany, but it will never happen, for we are too content in our idleness.

London empties out more every day with this heat, and the Season is as good as over. Today, for the first time, I found myself without a single invitation and made use of my freedom to undertake a few excursions. Among other things, I visited the prisons of King's Bench and Newgate. The first is primarily intended for debtors and forms a completely isolated world in miniature, quite like a fairly sizeable town that happens to be surrounded by walls thirty feet

KINGS BENCH PRISON.

41

King's Bench Prison.

high (Figure 41). Nothing is lacking: there are food stalls, lending libraries, coffee houses; kiosks and craftsmen of every type; dwellings both decent and shabby; even public squares and girls of the night. There is a marketplace, too, where a very noisy game of ball was going on. Anyone with money lives well and comfortably within this precinct; the sole thing lacking is liberty. Even very reputable members of society, both ladies and gentlemen, are to be found in this small commune of a thousand inhabitants. Only the destitute are in a bad way, but for them every spot on earth is a prison! Lord Cochrane spent some time at King's Bench for spreading false rumors in order to manipulate the stock market.[17] The rich and respected Sir Francis Burdett, accused of libel, also tarried there a while. The prisoner who toured me around had been living there for twelve years already, and said, with the best of humor, that he had no hope of ever getting out. An old and very proper Frenchwoman expressed the same view; she did not want to tell her relatives about her situation, since she was quite content and not at all sure how things would go for her in France, very mindful *que le mieux est l'ennemi du bien*.[18]

In Newgate, the prison for criminals, everything looks much worse. Yet even there the treatment is very lenient and the cleanliness *exemplary*. Every morning the government gives each inmate half a tankard of thick gruel; at midday half a pound of meat one day, meat broth the next; and every day one pound of good bread. The prisoners are also allowed to purchase additional food and a half bottle of wine daily. During the daytime they may assemble in the separate courtyards attached to particular blocks of rooms or cells, where they can do whatever they like and associate freely with one another. There are rooms for those who want to work, but many just smoke and amuse themselves in the courtyards from morning till night. They must all gather for a religious service every morning at nine. Normally seven or eight men share a single room. Each receives a mattress and two blankets for sleeping; they also get as much coal as they need for cooking and, in the winter, for heating. Those who have been condemned to death are put in special, less comfortable cells that sleep three or four. Even these prisoners have their own courtyard for recreation during the day, however, and a special room for eating. I saw six young lads—the eldest was barely fourteen—playing and smoking very merrily. All were condemned to die, but since the judgment had not yet been confirmed, they were still mingling with the other inmates. Many believed they would eventually be pardoned and sent to Botany Bay for the rest of their lives.

Four older men in this compound were guilty of crimes too severe for any hope of pardon. They expected their lives to end in a matter of weeks, and yet they accepted their fate with better humor than the others. Three of them were playing dummy whist amid loud jokes and laughter, while the fourth sat on a window sill diligently studying a French grammar book. He was definitely a philosopher, without knowing it!

July 12, 1827

YESTERDAY EVENING I got my first look at Vauxhall, a public garden in the style of Tivoli in Paris, but far more grandiose and brilliant. The illumination is exceptionally magnificent, with thousands of lights in blazing colors. Particularly beautiful were the enormous "bouquets" of lamps that were hanging beneath the trees, the blossoms in red, blue, violet, and yellow, the leaves and stems in green. Then there were chandeliers of a colorful, very nuanced Turkish pattern and a music temple crowned by the royal arms and crest. Several triumphal arches were constructed not of boards as is common, but of seemingly transparent cast iron, which made them just as opulent yet infinitely more elegant.

The garden extended still further and offered various entertainments and expositions, the most remarkable today being the Battle of Waterloo. Vauxhall opens at seven, and there are different presentations everywhere. The opera starts at eight. This is followed elsewhere by tightrope walkers. Things are brought to a close at ten by the above mentioned Waterloo, a spectacle curious enough *an sich*; and in many scenes the illusion is truly overwhelming. An open part of the garden serves as the stage, with ancient horse chestnuts mingling with shrubbery. Between four of the chestnuts, their foliage so thick that the sky can barely filter through, a grandstand nearly forty feet tall had been erected with tiered seating for about twelve hundred onlookers. We got to our places in a fearful crush of people and not without some appreciable shoves on both sides. It was a warm and wonderfully soft night. The moon shone with extraordinary brilliance and illuminated a huge red curtain. This was painted with the arms of the United Kingdom and hung between two gigantic trees about fifty feet away. Behind the curtain the tops of other trees rose up as far as we could see.

After a momentary silence, the roar of a cannon thundered through the woods, and from the distance the military music of two guard regiments resounded in sublime harmony. The curtain swept open from the center, and we saw as if by daylight the shimmering ramparts of Hougoumont (not just a painted backdrop, but facades built of wood and covered with painted canvas in perfect imitation of actual buildings) standing on a gentle rise beneath towering trees. The music continued as the French guards in authentic uniform emerged from the woods, led by their bearded sappers. They formed a line as Napoleon, wearing a gray overcoat, rode past them *en revue*, astride his white horse and accompanied by several marshals. *Vive l'Empereur!* rang out in a thousand voices, the emperor touched his hat, galloped off, and the troops bivouacked in dense groups. After a little while you heard distant shots, the tableau grew more and more tumultuous, and the French marched off. Moments later Wellington appeared with his general staff, all very good representations of the actual personalities; he harangued his troops and rode slowly away. The man himself was in the audience and laughed heartily at his counterfeit. Now the sharpshooters initiated the battle; then whole columns advanced toward each other, attacking with bayonets; the French cuirassiers charged the Scotch Greys; and since about one thousand men and two hundred horses are involved and no gunpowder was spared, there were many moments when it was remarkably like an actual battle. The storming of Hougoumont, which was struck by cannonballs and went up in flames, was especially well done. For a while the dense smoke of a real fire enveloped the combatants, who in the general tumult could be seen only now and then in the flashes of small arms, while the foreground was occupied by the dead and dying. As the smoke dispersed, Hougoumont was still in flames, the English were victors, the French captives, and in the distance you could see Napoleon fleeing the scene on horseback followed by his four-horse carriage. Amid the distant thunder of cannon fire, the triumphant Wellington was greeted with loud cheers. The ridiculous part was how, in order to placate English hubris, Napoleon was made to race back and forth across the scene several times as he fled his pursuers, all to the great delight of the "plebs," whether in good or bad dress. Such is the fate of the lofty on this earth! The conqueror of the world, beneath whose feet the very ground once shook; for whom millions willingly shed their blood; whose nod was heeded by kings; has now been reduced to a children's game. All the fairy tales of his time have vanished like a dream. Jupiter is gone, and in his place only Scapin remains.[19]

Although past midnight, there was still enough time for me to take myself away from the strange scene of light and moonlight and go to a glittering ball at Lady Londonderry's, where I found beautiful women, extravagant refreshments, an opulent supper, and colossal boredom. I was in bed by five in the morning.

July 13th, 1827

I HAD OFTEN heard about a certain Mr. Deville in the City, a student of Gall's and an avid phrenologist, who, to enrich his own knowledge, offers his services every day of the week free of charge to anyone who wishes to consult him. He examines his visitors' skulls carefully and graciously informs them of the results.

Filled with curiosity I went to see him this morning, and in his reception room found a bizarre display of all kinds of skulls. There were quite a few men and women waiting there; some had brought their children to be examined with an eye to their further education; others, perhaps looking for a position or already employed, were seeking advice as to whether they would be successful. A pale-faced man of seeming modesty and earnestness took care of this business with evident good will and enjoyment. I waited until everyone else had left and then asked Mr. Deville if he would kindly consider my request, although it was too late for my education and I have no position, because I nonetheless wanted to hear his characterization of me so I might hold it up like a mirror for my own self-improvement. He looked at me attentively, perhaps first using Lavater's method to decide whether I was *de bonne foi* or just joking, and then politely asked me to be seated. He proceeded to feel my head for a good quarter hour, after which, in fragmented sentences, he laid out the following portrait. It will surprise you, who know me so well, just as much as it did me. I confess I was filled with amazement, for he could not possibly have met me or heard anything about me before. Given that I wrote everything down immediately, and because, as you can well imagine, the whole thing interests me a lot, I do not think I made any essential errors in my account.*

"It is very hard to win your friendship," he began, "and only those who devote themselves to you with the greatest loyalty can manage it. In such cases, however, you will repay them in kind with steadfast constancy.

"You are in every respect easily provoked and capable of great extremes, but the consequences are short-lived for you, whether it be a matter of fervent love, hatred, or other passions.

"You love the arts, and if you are or would like to be engaged in them, you can master them easily. I find the power of composition expressed particularly strongly on your skull. You are no imitator. Indeed, you want to create by yourself and often feel compelled to generate something new.

"You have a strong sense of harmony, order, and symmetry. Any servants or craftsmen you employ will find you very difficult to satisfy, because nothing can be sufficiently precise and accurate to win your approval.

"Strangely enough you love both domestic life and roving the world with equal intensity, although they are in conflict with one another.

"For this reason you bring as many things along on your travels as you can afford, hoping to recreate a domestic, homelike surrounding as readily as possible." (I found this observation so apt and detailed as to be particularly striking.)

"There is a similar contradiction in you between a sharp mind" (excuse me, but I have to repeat his words exactly) "and a significant penchant for fanciful enthusiasms. You must be deeply religious and yet likely do not subscribe to any positive form of religion; instead" (again, these are his very words) "you prefer to honor a first cause of all things from a moral perspective.

"You are very vain, but not in the way of thinking yourself great, but rather of wanting to be so. You do not feel comfortable for very long in the company of your superiors, those who are in any way above you, or even your equals. You feel truly at ease only when you are at least *some* way in a dominant position, either as a result of your status or in another respect. Your faculties

* I was about to omit this section, which is too confidential to interest many readers. But since it paints an unusually precise picture of the departed author, and since he refers to it more than once in other letters, I hope I shall be excused for including it. —*The Editor.*

are easily paralyzed by opposition, veiled satire, seeming coldness—especially when not overtly hostile but only vaguely expressed. As I said before, you are only able to be totally natural and cheerful when nothing injures your vanity and when the people around you also wish you well; to this your good nature, one of your stronger organs, makes you very susceptible.

"The latter quality, coupled with sharp judgment, also makes you a great admirer of truth and justice. The reverse appalls you, and you are always prepared to take the side of the oppressed with vigor and without personal interest. You readily confess your own wrongs and willingly rectify them. If touched by an unpleasant truth, you can be annoyed, but you are more inclined to be sympathetic to the person who spoke, or at least to feel genuine respect for him, as long as the intention was not hostile. For the same reason you do not value distinctions of birth all that highly, although your vanity is not entirely insensitive to them.

"You are easily carried away, but not particularly lighthearted. On the contrary, you possess too much cautiousness, which adds a tinge of bitterness to your life because you reflect on everything far too much, alternately filling your head with the strangest melancholy thoughts and unnecessarily lapsing into worry and anxiety over trifles; into mistrust of yourself, suspicion of others, or apathy. And you are concerned almost entirely with the *future,* little with the past, and even less with the present.

"You are always *striving,* covetous of accolades, and very sensitive about being ignored; all told, you have a lot of ambition of every variety, which you quickly change in the hope of achieving your goals immediately, for your imagination is stronger than your patience. This is why you have to find especially favorable circumstances in order to succeed.

"But you have traits that make you capable of achieving things beyond the norm, and even the organ of perseverance and steadfastness is strongly expressed in you, although it is hindered by so many conflicting organs that you require great excitement in order to find enough space for it.[20] Then the nobler powers emerge, and the minor ones subside.

"You value money and property very highly, as does everyone who wants to accomplish a lot, but only as a means, not as an end. You are indifferent to money in itself, and it is possible that you do not always handle it very economically.

"You want speedy and immediate satisfaction in all things, as if with a magic wand, yet the wish often dies before its fulfillment becomes possible. Sensuousness and pleasure in beauty have too great an influence on you, and since you already incline toward the imperious, domineering, and vain, there is a concentration of qualities here that you need to guard against so you do not fall into serious error. For all qualities are good in themselves; it is their misuse that spawns disaster. Even the organs that the father of our science so incorrectly called the organs of murder and stealing (now more properly termed tendencies to destruction and acquisition) are merely signs of vigor and covetousness that form a well-endowed skull when combined with good nature, conscience, and prudence; but without these intellectual qualities, they may easily lead to crime."[21]

He also said that the evaluation of a skull has nothing to do with the individual organs but with their combination, in that they modify themselves reciprocally in manifold ways; in fact, they sometimes completely neutralize each other. Hence only the *proportions of the whole* can give the actual key to a person's character. Here is the general rule he proposes for evaluating skulls: if you draw a straight line over the top from the middle of one ear to the other, you will find that some people have a larger mass in front than behind, and they are more commendable because the front part contains more of the intellectual faculties, the back part more of the

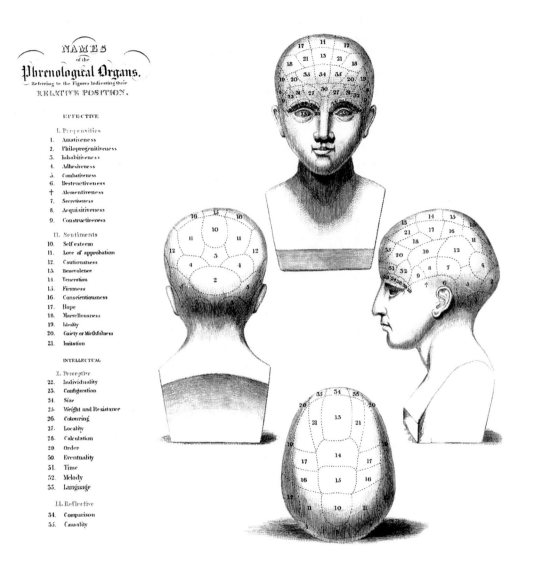

42

*Names of the
Phrenological Organs.*

bestial. He has collected the skulls of executed criminals, for instance, and they are all proof of this doctrine. In one of the most terrible cases, the back of the head occupied two-thirds of the whole skull. You notice a similar relationship in the busts of Nero and Caracalla. But where the opposite extreme exists, these overly intellectual people lack vigor. Here, as in all things, a proper balance is the most desirable (Figure 42).

Mr. Deville maintains that not only is it possible to significantly enlarge the prominent favorable organs by exercising those qualities related to them, but this process can also shrink others that are detrimental; and he asserts that this can happen at any time of life. He showed me the skull of a friend who undertook a very-sustained study of mathematics when he was sixty years old, and in just a few years the appropriate bump had become so prominent that it towered over all the others.[22]

At the end he gave me, as testimony to his delineation of my character, a record of the most prominent and collaboratively functioning organs of my skull, which provided a clear explanation of his judgment of me. I will not give you the entire list, for a man must always be prudent enough to withhold something about himself, just as one's most intimate female friend never divulges all her secret beauty techniques. And in so many ways you probably know me better than Deville does, since a more powerful talisman than phrenology stands at your disposal: true love. Still, just for fun I will cite the following:

Organ of wonder: weak, which is why the creditor in me is corrupted without my
    having to become a debtor.
Ideality: very strong, which is why I am never content with the moment.
Sense of numbers: weak, which is why it is so hard for me to keep my income and
    expenses in their proper relationship, and why I would never have written Adam
    Ries's *Computation Book.*
Sense of time: also weak, which is why I usually arrive too late, like a personification
    of *moutarde après dîner.*[23]
Organ of comparison: remarkable, again unfortunate for devout and blind obedience.

With so many flaws, the large bump of my organ of causality offers little comfort, since among other things this organ forces us to turn a jaundiced eye on the inadequacy of human existence. It achieves this by enabling us to analyze ourselves and our own minds impartially; to judge ourselves along with others as objects; and thereby to willfully abstract all this from the effects of education, fate, etc. Or put more precisely: the organ of causality wants to discover the cause of everything, investigate the connection between cause and effect, and always compel people to ask *why?* An annoying tendency that in normal life we call common sense.

Eventuality,[24] which might be called the capacity for reality, is unfortunately far weaker in me than the previous organ. It, too, is rather difficult to define, and since its size is so restricted in my case, I fear I am condemned to be the kind of poet who is allowed only in dreams to see and experience the things he cannot achieve in the world.

Eventuality is not the same as vigor, although when it is deficient, it hinders vigor's ability to remain focused on a single purpose, because without eventuality there emerges an absence of interest in, and attention to, what is happening, a lack of practical social consciousness. It has been observed that all great statesmen possess the organ for eventuality to a high degree, which connotes an intense desire to know everything about the workings of the world; to feel at ease in the whirl of business arising out of it, be ready to play an active role and spare no effort, and to find one's motives only in external reality, never in one's own imagination. Mr. Deville pointed out that eventuality was extremely predominant in the plaster cast of Canning's skull and even more in Napoleon's, although the other intellectual qualities were also very developed in both. In Napoleon's case, the animalistic qualities were equally powerful; in Canning's, fantasy and causality.*

---

* Consequently one of them perished on Saint Helena as a prisoner of Europe; the other died of sorrow over the intrigues of his enemies in his mourning fatherland.—*The Editor.* [See Pückler's lament over Canning's death on page 252.—*Translator.*]

I HAVE ALREADY paid several visits to the architect Mr. Nash, to whom I am indebted for so much that is instructive in my own art. It is said that he has "built up" a fortune of five hundred thousand pounds. He owns several magnificent country estates, and no artist in this town lives more comfortably.

I was especially impressed with his library. It takes the form of a long, wide gallery with twelve deep niches on each side and large portals at either end leading into two other spacious rooms. The gallery ceiling has a shallow arch and is partly illuminated from above by a string of elegant rosettes, their matte glass decorated with different figures painted in grisaille. There is also a semicircular window in the ceiling of each niche. High on the rear wall is a fresco painting after one in Raphael's loggia, and below this are casts of the best classical statues atop imitation-marble pedestals. The remaining space in each niche is occupied by bookcases, although these rise no higher than the pedestals. On the broad pillars between the niches are arabesques that are also copied from those in the Vatican and superbly executed in fresco.

A short distance in front of each niche in the central gallery is a table with open compartments containing portfolios of drawings, and on the tables are plaster casts of famous architectural monuments from antiquity. A broad passageway through the center is left open. Every inch of the walls and pillars not decorated with paintings is covered with matte stucco of a pale reddish hue, surrounded by narrow gilt moldings. All is executed with exquisite taste and refinement.

As I was driving from there to dinner, I saw a boat in the Thames filled with completely naked men like wild animals; occasionally one of them would jump into the water and swim a bit. I was amazed to find this kind of indecency in the middle of London, all the more so because only yesterday I read a newspaper report about an officer who saw a man and his son engaged in similar nude swimming right in front of the windows of his house, shouted at them to go away, and when they did not, unceremoniously aimed and fired a shot right through the father's body. The marksman testified in court that the swimmer had shamelessly exposed himself before the eyes of his wife, something he could not tolerate, and that he would do exactly the same thing if it were to happen again. It is typical that the jury acquitted him.

My midday meal at the Portuguese ambassador's almost ended like the famous feast of Prince Schwarzenberg in Paris.[25] One of Rundell and Bridge's beautiful silver chandeliers, gleaming like diamonds, got too close to a curtain, which immediately went up in flames.[26] The fire was quickly extinguished by the Spanish ambassador, however, something that—given the present political climate—might inspire a few clever quips in the newspapers.

Late at night I drove a couple of miles into town to see the steeple of St Giles. With its new, colossal clock face, rosy red and illuminated by many lamps, it beams in the night like a magnificent star.

At home I found your letter with its sweet reprimands about neglecting the personal for too many worldly matters. This might be the case from time to time, but please do not think that my heart is any the less filled with you. Sometimes a flower smells less fragrant, sometimes more; in fact, it can happen that not a single bloom is left on the rose, and then more will reappear and blossom again at their own pace. But the nature of the plant remains constant.

Despite the loveliness of Herder's prayer, here on earth it does not stand up. Although God's sun shines on both good and evil, his thunderbolt also strikes both. We must all protect ourselves as best we can.

You say that you find people annoying—oh God, how I agree! When two people have long shared every feeling and sincere thought with each other in such intimacy, then the banalities of an indifferent world can seem empty and tasteless at best.

I find your hypothesis about kindred spirits quite charming—that in another world they will merge into a *single* being—but this is not how I want to be united with you. A single being must love itself, after all, whereas two beings love each other *voluntarily*, and that alone has value! So let us always be close, and only become one through our reciprocal love and faithfulness as we are now, and may it remain so for as long as possible in this world.

That thought transports me back to the present with its torrent of activities, which yesterday carried me to the local art exhibition. The history paintings were not particularly enjoyable. A few portraits by Thomas Lawrence reflected, as always, both his genius and his arrogance, characteristics that compel him to finish certain areas and leave everything else just daubed on. You have to look from a distance, as if his paintings were stage sets, in order to find them decipherable. This is not the way Raphael and the heroes of art painted portraits. Among the genre pictures, on the other hand, I found much that was attractive.

First, the dead elephant. You see a wild, mountainous region in the interior of India; strange gigantic trees and a luxuriant tangle of undergrowth surround a dark lake with a deep forest in the background. A dead elephant lies stretched out on the shore in the foreground, and a crocodile, its wide-open jaws baring its terrifying teeth, is just climbing onto the corpse, chasing off a monstrous bird of prey and threatening the other crocodiles hurriedly swimming up from the lake to join in the feast. Vultures sway on the branches of trees, and a tiger's head appears in the bushes. On the other side you see even more powerful predators: three English hunters with rifles already aimed at the huge crocodile. Soon they will provoke yet more dreadful confusion amid this horrific gathering.

Another piece takes place in Africa. The setting is a seashore. Ships can be spied in the far distance; close by, crisscrossed by tropical vines, a palm grove slopes down to the clear water where a boat lies at anchor. Here a negro has been sleeping, but in what ghastly circumstances! A gigantic boa constrictor has emerged from the woods where its tail still reposes; but the front part of its body has already formed a loose ring around the recumbent man. It lifts its head and opens its jaws to hiss at the negro's comrades as they rush to his aid with their hatchets. The slave is staring at the boa with an expression of grisly horror on his face just as one of his rescuers manages to cut off part of the snake's body. This is a saving blow, because once any part of a boa's back muscle is severed, its entire body immediately loses its strength. The scene is a true rendition of something that actually happened in 1792.

Remaining in distant parts of the earth, we now go back much further in time. An absolutely splendid moonlit night glistens above the bay of Alexandria. Magnificent Egyptian monuments and temples stretch along the shore in varying levels of illumination, and beneath a vestibule of noble architecture in the foreground, we see Cleopatra surrounded by all the extravagance of Asia, as she steps aboard her golden ship and sets off to her Antony. The most beautiful girls and boys strew flowers beneath her feet, while a farewell song is played on golden harps by white-bearded ancients in purple robes seated on a rock at the water's edge.

Have you had enough, dear Julie? Well then, now look at the *traveled monkey* dressed like an exclusive, who has returned to his brothers and sisters in the secluded forest.[27] Stupefied, they gather around him: one tugs at his watch chain, another his starched collar. Finally Cocotte, jealous of such pomp, boxes him on the ear, which becomes the signal for a general plundering—and if this goes on for even one minute longer, then Balzer will be standing there *in naturalibus,* looking like my classical statues that you find so shocking.

With this I close my exhibition. My dear Julie, do confess that if you were the editor of the *Morgenblatt*, you could not have a more industrious correspondent. And whether I am sick or well, sad or happy, I always do my duty. Right now I am not at my best. I feel ill and have lost a lot of money at whist. It is remarkable, by the way, how quickly one gets used to regarding an English pound as a thaler. Although I am well aware of the difference and often do not like it very much, the feel of a pound here is just like that of a thaler at home, which often makes me laugh. I wish fate could reverse the equation and turn our thalers into pounds; I would certainly not bury mine.[28] Yet we have always made the most of what has been conferred on us, for when someone uses dead money in an attempt to beautify God's natural world, as I have, then he has invested well; and this is equally true when his efforts make people happy and contented, which I have done by employing them and you do more directly through your generous good deeds conferred on those in need.

Prudence has not been one of our strengths. If you exhibit more of it than I do, it is because you are a woman, for women must always remain on the defensive. Prudence is much more an art of defensiveness than aggression.

You can practice it yourself right now in the affairs of S——; I can readily imagine you taming the unruly and addressing them in dignified words of peace. Just look at your portrait here on the edge of the page—very à la Thomas Lawrence; you will surely discern much of that artistic propensity, which the Gallian read on my skull. My somewhat grumpy mood is to blame for the caricatures that surround your likeness.

Being in such a thoroughly dispirited mood, I am barely capable of thought; therefore let me send along some passages from a strange book that you will doubtless believe sprang from my own pen and the depths of my being.[29]

> It is impossible to calculate the importance that the circumstances of youth have on the shaping of one's character. It was in the somber woods of my native land, during my many solitary wanderings in nature, that my early affection for my own thoughts came into being. And as I became better known to my peers at school, this state of mind made it impossible for me to enter into any intimate friendship, except for those that I had already begun to discover *in myself.*
>
> In the daytime my joy was to wander alone in nature, in the evening to read Romantic fictions that I would relate to what I had seen. Whether I sat before the hearth engrossed in my book during the winter or lay stretched out beneath a tree in voluptuous indolence during the summer, my hours were always filled with the dim, luxuriant dreams that were perhaps the essence of that poetry *that I did not have the genius to embody.* Such a disposition is not suited to living with others. At one moment I would pursue something with restless activity, at the next I simply existed in idle reflection. Nothing was as I hoped, and finally my whole being was imbued with that

morbid and melancholy philosophy, which taught me, like Faust, that knowledge is nothing but useless stuff, hope nothing but deceit. And I, like he, was cursed by sensing the abiding presence of a hostile spirit, even in the pleasures of youth or the allurements of pleasure.

The experience of long and bitter years teaches me to look with suspicion on that far recollection of the past, and to doubt if this earth could indeed produce a living form to satisfy the visions of one who has dwelt among the boyish creations of fancy.

Elsewhere it is said of a highly regarded man, "He was one of Nature's macadamized achievements. His great fault was his equality; and you longed for a hill though it were to climb, or a stone though it were in your way. Love attaches itself to something prominent, even if that something be what others would hate. One can scarce feel extremes for mediocrity." *C'est vraiment une consolation!*[30]

And further: "Our senses may captivate us with beauty; but in absence we forget, or by reason we can conquer, so superficial an impression. Our vanity may enamour us with rank; but the affections of vanity are traced in sand; yet who can love *Genius* and not feel that the sentiments it excites partake of its own intenseness and immortality?"

July 18th, 1827

PLEASE BELIEVE ME, my best Julie, that although steeped in unpleasantness and near to being sick, I find these days of solitude where I am busy with nothing but you, my books, and my thoughts, far more satisfying—how can I put it?—far more complete than the bleak existence that calls itself the great world of fashion and society. Games are part of this, too; a way to kill time without consequence, but at least with the advantage that while engaged, you are not aware of wasting time as you are in other cases. Few people are capable of understanding such an attitude, and how fortunate for me that you can! But you indulge me too much, which leaves me not fully confident in your judgments. So polish the glass through which you see me. Apply cold reason to sponge away some (not all) of the rose-colored mist your love has blown onto its surface. And then, always with a jaunty eye on my confessed vanity, tell me the truth.

Now let me divulge a secret. Whenever I send you excerpts, you can never be sure who wrote them. Due to my famous organ of composition (as you can see, Deville still occupies my mind), immaculate transcription is almost impossible for me. Once in my hands, someone else's material gets altered and not necessarily improved. Since I am so versatile, however, I often appear inconsistent, and so my letters may contain numerous contradictions. All the same, I hope that a pure, humane spirit emerges in them, even a knightly one here and there, for every man owes a tribute to the circumstances surrounding his birth and life.[31]

Have we not already lived together in the *true* age of chivalry? Yes, of course—for how often does the captivating image of our ancestral castle appear in my imagination like a dim but treasured memory of our former abode in the wild Spessart? As it stares down menacingly from the rocks, surrounded by old oaks and firs, I see the lord of the castle with his horsemen riding along the narrow passage in the valley to meet the morning sun (as a knight, he was an early riser). You, good Julie, look out from the balcony, waving and fluttering your white handkerchief until not a single steel breastplate flashes in the sunlight, and nothing stirs but a timid deer peering out of the foliage, or a high-antlered stag surveying the landscape from a hilltop.

Another time, after successfully resolving a feud, we are sitting with our tankards as we once sat in Paris with champagne. You serve graciously, I quaff chivalrously, and our good parson reads to us of legends past. Then a dwarf's horn resounds from the tower to announce that a banner is being carried toward the castle gate. It is your erstwhile lover, returning from the Holy Land. *Gare à toi!**

July 19th, 1827

A FRIENDLY SUNBEAM lured me outside, but soon I exchanged the open air for the subterranean world. I visited the notorious tunnel: a miraculous, twelve hundred-foot-long passage beneath the Thames (Figure 43).[32] You likely read about it in the newspapers some weeks ago when the river broke in and flooded not only the entrance tower (100 feet deep and 30 feet wide), but also the completed section of the two-lane roadway (540 feet long). Like every major event here, whether fortunate or unfortunate, within a day or two a caricature appeared. This one shows the water pouring in and a fat man trying to save himself, crawling like a toad on all fours, terrified and screaming "Fire!" out of his gaping mouth. With the help of a diving bell it was possible to plug the hole in the riverbed, filling it with sacks of clay where the ground had collapsed. From now on the earth beneath the river will be reinforced to a thickness of fifteen feet by an admixture of clay, and it is claimed that no such accident can recur. Meanwhile one can again tour the tunnel quite comfortably, since almost all of the water has been pumped out by an enormous steam engine situated high up in the tower. This is a daunting undertaking, only feasible here, where people do not know what to do with their money.

I exited the tunnel and drove to Astley's Theatre, the local counterpart to Franconi's but superior to it. A horse called Pegasus, with strapped-on wings, performs wonderful stunts, and the drunken Russian courier who rides six to eight horses at once cannot be surpassed for agility and daring. The theatrical performance was a delicious parody of *Der Freischütz*.[33] Instead of casting bullets, Pierrot and Pantaloon make a pancake, to which Weber's music is an hilarious accompaniment. The spirits that appear are all of the kitchen, with Satan himself as the *chef de cuisine*. At the final moment of horror a ghostly bellows extinguishes every light except for one large candle that continues to catch fire again and again. Then a gigantic fist grabs poor Pierrot and lays him across the flame, whereupon a female cook—as big as the theater and in a devil's costume of black and red—covers both with a snuffer the size of a house. Meanwhile Pantaloon flies off on a rocket affixed to a certain spot discharging downward as he shrieks with pain.

All this nonsense provokes momentary laughter, of course, but it does not make a sad soul any happier. And you know that I have many reasons for distress, ones I cannot always forget. . . . .

---

* It is an historical fact that even the old German knights already had the bad habit of helping themselves to French clichés.—*The Editor*. ["*Gare à toi*": Watch out!—*Translator*.]

43

Cross Section of the Thames Tunnel.

We must be under an evil constellation right now; there are definitely lucky and unlucky currents in one's life, and to be aware of them would be a great help to the navigator. The star that you tell me was twinkling with such fire over your palace must have been hostile. Only *one* auspicious star still shines for me, and that is your love. If it went out, so would my life!

A change of scene seems more and more necessary, especially since I have almost entirely withdrawn from what little remains of society here. Till Eulenspiegel says, and very wisely, sunshine follows the rain—so go to meet it![34] And hearten me with your letters! Let them be cheerful and fortifying, because this means more to me than any news they might contain, whether good or bad. For me nothing is worse than to imagine you distressed and downcast and so far away. It is an art to suffer *joyfully*, like a martyr, and only possible when one suffers innocently or out of love for another. You, my precious Julie, have scarcely known any other woes. I cannot speak so well of myself.

July 23rd, 1827

HAYMARKET THEATRE IS now bursting with excellent actors and has become the rendez-vous of all the gay ladies who find themselves unoccupied at the end of the Season. I was sitting yesterday in my box, paying close attention to the play, when suddenly the most darling foot, encased in a pretty shoe and pearl-colored silk stockings, came to rest on the chair beside me. I looked around and saw a pair of splendid brown eyes smiling at me mischievously out of a Philine-like face half hidden beneath a large, Italian straw hat.[35] The rest of this petite person's finery consisted of a simple, dazzling white dress held together by a poppy red ribbon below her modestly covered breasts. She can scarcely have attained eighteen summers.

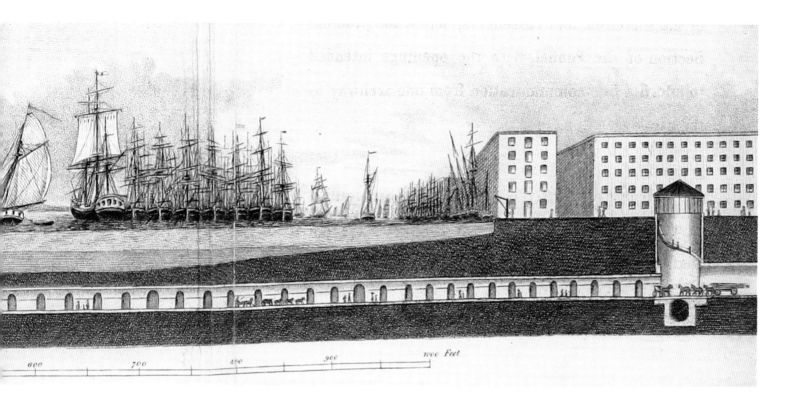

All the dandies here, as well as many young people in the fashionable world who are very much *not* dandies, tend to keep mistresses; they rent houses for them, move the young ladies in, and then while away their idle moments there, just as was once the case with the *petites maisons* in France. They quickly arrive at a domestic arrangement and are just as methodical in this relationship as in all others. Such women are seldom faithful in the long run, but those here are often superior in intelligence and social graces to their counterparts elsewhere.

The little one behind me seemed intent on establishing such an understanding, for she behaved not without refinement and knew how to create a kind of agreement between us. This owed just as much to her charming flirtatiousness as it did to her extreme reticence toward others who tried to approach her. All this without the two of us having exchanged a single word! And, for the sake of propriety, she was accompanied by a mother who served as her chaperone, though whether a real or a rented one, I cannot say. Such mothers are nowhere so congenial as in London!

These women, mostly young, go so cheerfully to meet a life of suffering. It is odd that they are not seduced into this lifestyle by men or love, but, as someone very knowledgeable assured me, almost always by others of their own sex. The situation is very much helped along by the inordinate luxury of all classes. Yet many of these creatures remain less mercenary and far more sentimental than their sisters across the Channel; in fact, their wretched profession notwithstanding, they do not lose sight of romance. In character and disposition they are, by the way, just as nuanced and varied as the different classes of society themselves, and their numbers in London are nearly equal to the entire population of Berlin.[36]

It is not too great a leap to take you from here to Bedlam, actually Bethlehem, which I visited this morning. Nowhere are madmen—the locked-up ones, in any event—better housed than here. In front of the palace gates there is a pleasure ground; and as for the interior, nothing can be cleaner or more efficiently set up. As I entered the first women's gallery guided by a very pretty young jailer, one of the madwomen, probably in her thirties, looked at me thoughtfully for a long time and then suddenly approached me saying, "You are a foreigner—I know you, Prince! Why didn't you put on your uniform to visit me? That would have been more proper. Ah, how handsome Charles looked in his!"

"The poor soul," said the jailer, who had become conscious of my discomfort. "She was seduced by a prince and now believes she sees one in every stranger. Sometimes she cries for days at a time and will not let anybody near her. Afterward she can be totally reasonable again for weeks. She was once very beautiful, but sorrow has robbed her of every charm."

Especially strange was a rich and well-educated young man who had the idée fixe that he was a Stuart and therefore possessed a legitimate claim to the throne. I talked to him for half an hour without managing to get him onto this subject, however, for he always broke off carefully, even shrewdly, and meanwhile spoke very engagingly on various topics—America, for instance, where he had traveled at length. There was not the slightest trace of madness in his manner or appearance. Finally, by repeatedly mentioning Walter Scott's novel about a pretender to the throne,[37] I succeeded in warming him up slightly and then said in a confidential tone, "I know that you yourself are a Stuart." He seemed alarmed and, laying a finger across his lips, whispered, "We cannot talk about that *here*. I am, indeed, but only with time can I expect justice to prevail. Soon, however, the light will shine brightly!" Since I knew where he was from and that his father was a rich landowner, I responded, "I'm going to Wales. Would you like to give me your father's address, so I can pass on your greetings?" "With great pleasure," he answered, "give me your notebook and I'll write it down." I gave it to him and he wrote down his real name, B—— G——. Pointing to it with a smile he said in my ear, "This is the name my father is known by there. Farewell!" And with a gracious wave of his hand, he released me.

Such a thing is truly awful! A single idée fixe makes the most charming man into an incurable fool, costs him his freedom, and condemns him for life to the society of the most common lunatics. What, then, is a hapless man when undone by physical maladies, and where, then, is freedom of the will?

A foreign "madman"—a German pedant and travel writer—joined me on my house tour. He was more amusing and fit right in at Bedlam. He could scarcely stop taking notes, addressed each of the inmates at length, and took great care to jot down their replies, despite the fact that they were often not particularly flattering to him. The minute he noticed my discussion with B—— G—— he rushed up and urgently begged me to tell him what the gentleman had written in my notebook. I gave him a short version of the story. "Oh excellent, very remarkable," he exclaimed, "perhaps really related to the Stuarts. B—— G——. I must look into this right away. It may be a state secret. Who knows? If he is in fact a relation, he has every excuse for his madness. Very remarkable. Rich material. I bid you farewell most humbly." With this he stumbled away so foolishly, looking so awkward and silly yet so satisfied with himself, that one almost expected him to be locked up before he made it to the exit!

Driving home I again encountered several funeral processions, admittedly no surprise in an abyss like London, where death is always hard at work. It is nonetheless a bad omen, even if a superstition so credulous is better suited to Bedlam than to a rational brain. In my case, however, there is a certain basis for it:

Once, when I was still very young, I was driving in an elegant curricle through the city of J——, where I was living at the time. A lengthy funeral procession came toward me, forcing me to stop; my horses became so shy and edgy that I had trouble controlling them. Their impatience finally infected me, so I broke through the procession and rashly called out, "To the devil with this old funerary pageantry. I won't be held up by it any longer."

I charged ahead and had scarcely gone fifty paces when a little boy darted out of a nearby shop and, like a moth to a flame, ran with such speed between the horses and the carriage, that it was impossible to stop before a wheel ran right over the poor lad. He lay on the pavement as lifeless as a bundle that had dropped unseen from a wagon. You can imagine my terror! I leapt down and picked him up as a mob formed around us. The wailing mother rushed over and pierced my heart with her laments, which likewise affected the onlookers, inspiring them to vengeance. I had to harangue the crowd to pacify the tumult, and finally, by relating what had happened, giving my name, and leaving some money for the mother, I managed (not easily) to get back in my carriage and extract myself from the brawl. I then found myself near the gate, which is approached by a rather steep hill. In my distraction I must not have been paying adequate attention to the reins, for one slipped out of my hand. The frantic horses bolted and, at an intersecting lane, collided with a hauler's cart with such energy that one of them was killed on the spot and my carriage dashed to pieces. I was hurled out with compelling force and temporarily dazed by the immensity of the shock. The next moment I found myself almost suffocating with my face pressed into the ground. I could feel a frantic animal raging above me, and I heard the thunder of blows that seemed to be hitting my head, although without causing much pain. In between I could hear the wails of many who were standing around me: "He's a dead man. Shoot the horse, now!" I then received a blow on the temple, and passed out completely.

When I opened my eyes again, I was lying on a mattress in the middle of a squalid room, an old woman was mopping the blood flowing from my head and face, and a surgeon, occupied with his instruments, was getting ready to trepan me. "Oh, let the poor gentleman die in peace," the woman exclaimed compassionately. Since I myself was absolutely convinced that, except for the bit of pain from my external wounds, no serious internal damage had been done, I fortunately opposed the operation. It would have been totally useless anyway, although the young man, an apprentice from the local clinic, was very eager to test his skill at an operation that, as he assured me, he had not yet had the opportunity to undertake by himself.

I immediately got to my feet to demonstrate my returning vigor, called for a carriage, and had someone bring me a mirror so I could clean up, although the face I saw was absolutely unrecognizable, given that most of its skin had been left on the road. Only later, when nature had replaced the old skin with new, did my coachman tell me the strange circumstances that had accompanied the event. He had been sitting next to me during the accident and was thrown sideways into a field, escaping with lesser injuries. The shaft of the two-wheeled curricle had smashed into the cart and shattered like a lance against a suit of armor; the light vehicle toppled over forward, with me in it. The remaining stump of the shaft had bored its way into the earth and jammed my head down, too. One horse lay on top of me, trapped in the harnesses and furiously attempting to get up. It kicked its rear hooves incessantly against the broken shaft, which served as my only protection, in that the shaft bore the blows that would otherwise have crushed my head ten times over. It was almost a quarter of an hour before anyone managed to free me and the horse.

Since that time I have not relished encountering funeral processions.

As a postscript to this memory from my past life I must add one comical note. The boy I ran over recovered completely, and six weeks after our mutual catastrophe, his mother brought him, all rosy cheeked and in his Sunday best, to see me at home. When I gave him a kiss and handed the mother a last gift, the poor woman's eyes flooded with tears of joy as she exclaimed, "Oh God, if only my son could be run over like that every day!"

July 28th, 1827

I HAD NOT been in the City for a long time and, as you know, like to spend a day there now and then, the way a gourmand sometimes likes to refresh his appetite with simple home cooking. So therefore I devoted the whole of yesterday to it.

Since, as a Teutonic knight, I am also a brewer, I first steered my cabriolet to one of the strangest and most interesting sights in London: Barclay's Brewery, a place of such colossal size as to look almost fantastic (Figure 44). Twelve to fifteen hundred barrels of beer—about twenty thousand quarts—are brewed here daily. Everything is done by machines, all set in motion by a single steam engine that also drives the liquid through copper pipes, which, I might add, may not yield the healthiest of beers. It is boiled in four vats, each holding three hundred barrels or more. The dry hops go in first and are constantly stirred by a machine so they will not burn. The stirring continues as the sweet wort is added in a steady stream. A special contraption cools the beer in hot weather by moving it through a series of tubes that resemble a pipe organ. A stream of cold water follows the same path, then beer again, and so on. Finally, the finished product flows into vats as high as a house—there are ninety-nine of them in gigantic sheds. Nothing can be as strange as having someone tap such a house-sized vat holding six hundred thousand quarts, in order to draw you a small glass of excellent dark ale that is as cold as ice. These vats are covered on top with a small hill of fresh sand, and they keep the beer cool and good for an entire year. Only then is it drawn off into small casks and sent to the buyer. The drawing off is done through pipes, like watering with a huge hose, and happens very quickly since the small casks stand ready in vaults under the room housing the large vats.

One hundred and fifty elephant-like cart horses are occupied daily with transporting the beer into the city. Two of them can haul half a ton.

The smoke of the entire factory is vented through a single, towering chimney, and from the elegant, zinc-covered platform of the main building, there is a very lovely panorama of London.

Next I visited the West India docks and warehouses, a facility so immense that even the most cold-blooded person must be overcome with awe at England's grandeur and power. What an amount of capital is piled up here in buildings, wares, and ships! It took me a full half hour to walk around the man-made basin, which is thirty-six feet deep and surrounded by warehouses and sheds, some of them five or six stories high. Several of these are built entirely of iron, with only the foundations made of stone. This kind of construction has been found to be danger-ous, however, since the iron sometimes expands and contracts unevenly due to changes in the weather. There was enough sugar in these vast depots to sweeten the entire basin and enough rum to make half of England drunk. The place employs twenty-five hundred workers and super-visors every day, and the value of the goods stored here is estimated at twenty million pounds sterling. This does not include the great quantities of backup equipment kept in a storehouse, so if anything is damaged or broken, the work is held up for no more than a few minutes.

92.—Entrance to Barclay's Brewery.

There were impressive numbers of machines and tools in use. I watched with delight as blocks of mahogany and other exotic woods, many bigger than the mightiest oak, were raised aloft like feathers and then lowered with great care onto the transport wagons as if they were exceptionally fragile. Everything is colossal here. On both sides of the basin, the ships are lined up one next to the other, most just now being freshly painted. There are two such basins, one for imports, the other for exports. I had to leave sooner than I wished, because at four o'clock the entry gate and all the warehouses close, with not a single thought given to whether someone might still be inside. If a man were to overstay, he would have to bivouac there until the following morning. The gatekeeper gravely assured me that if the king himself were inside, not a minute extra would be allowed. I thus made my escape as quickly as I could, in order to avoid such an awkward situation.

On my way home I passed a booth where a man was shouting about what was on view in the interior: a famous German dwarf with three dwarf children, a living skeleton, and, finally, the fattest girl ever seen. I paid my shilling for curiosity's sake, entered, and, after waiting fifteen minutes until five others joined me, the curtain was pulled aside only to present the most impertinent

44

Entrance to Barclay's Brewery.

charlatanry I have ever encountered. The living skeleton was a totally normal man, not much thinner than I am. The excuse peddled to explain this was that he had arrived from France as a skeleton but had become more and more corpulent due to good English beefsteaks. Next came "the fattest woman in Christendom," the perfect pendant to the skeleton, for she was no fatter than the Queen of Virginia Water.[38]

Finally the so-called dwarfs emerged and proved to be nothing but the little children of the impresario. They had been stuck into a kind of birdcage that hid their faces, allowing a clear view only of their legs and hands. The poor things were holding big bells and generated a terrible amount of noise. This closed the performance, an English fraud that no Frenchman could have executed with more burlesque or effrontery.

July 29th, 1827

EVER SINCE BECOMING Deville's pupil, I cannot stop my eyes from measuring the skulls of new acquaintances before getting to know them further. And today, like in Kotzebue's comedy, I was in top form as I examined an English servant before hiring him. I feel hopeful that the result will not be the same as in Kotzebue's play, because the line drawn from ear to ear seemed positive. This reminded me of the common proverb (and of how often these contain general truths), for I was struck by how fully this one corresponded to Deville's principle: "He has it behind the ears, beware of him!" All joking aside, I am completely convinced that with phrenology, as with magnetism, people are throwing the baby out with the bathwater when they think it is nothing but a chimera. There may be still more modifications to be discovered, but I have tested the accuracy of the principle so thoroughly on my own skull that I no longer find it ridiculous when parents take it into account in the rearing of their children, nor when grownups use it to facilitate their own self-knowledge. I, at least, have gained more understanding of myself in this way than might otherwise have been possible.

Since I spent the whole day busy with my own writing, I took advantage of the soft, bright moonlight to go out for a ride because, thank God, I do not need to bind myself slavishly to the clock. The night was thoroughly Italian, and lamps provided so much illumination that I could keep within their range as I rode for several hours through the city and suburbs. A marvelous view unfolded from Westminster Bridge. The many lights on the boats danced like will-o'-the-wisps across the surface of the Thames, and the numerous bridges stretched over the river from one mass of buildings to the other like broadly arched, twinkling garlands. Only Westminster Abbey was not illuminated, but there the pale glow of wistful Luna, long familiar with ruins and Gothic monuments, paid mystic court to the stone pinnacles and sculpted ornaments, delved ardently into the shadowy depths, and splashed silver across the elongated, glittering windows. Meanwhile the roof and tower of the lofty structure, starkly silent in black, colorless majesty, soared up above the glimmer and bustle of the city into the dark blue, starlit sky.

The streets remained relatively busy until midnight. I even saw a boy, eight years old at most, driving all alone in a child-sized carriage, pulled by a big dog trotting fearlessly alongside the last diligences and carriages. This kind of thing can be found only in England, where children are already independent by eight years of age and can be hanged at twelve.[39]

Well, dear Julie, I bid you good morning, for it is time to go to bed.

THE HEAT REMAINS oppressive, the ground is turning to ashes, and if it were not for the mac-adamized roads being continually drenched everywhere by an unbroken succession of enormous water wagons, the dust would make the city unbearable. But as it is, riding and driving are still pleasurable, and although the elegant period has passed, shopping is still very entertaining. It is one of the greatest temptations to buy more than one needs, and since right now I have little money, I allow my imagination to assist me with those things I would otherwise want to acquire for us. It is like that splendid Persian Harpagon,[40] about whom Malcolm told us the following:[41]

> A merchant, who had lately died at Isfahan and left a large sum of money, was so great a niggard that for many years he denied himself and his son, a young boy, every support except a crust of coarse bread. He was, however, one day tempted by the description a friend gave of the flavor of cheese to buy a small piece; but before he got home he began to reproach himself with extravagance, and instead of eating the cheese he put it into a bottle, and contented himself and obliged his child to do the same, with rubbing the crust against the bottle, enjoying the cheese in imagination.
>
> One day when he returned home later than usual, he found his son eating his crust, and rubbing it against the door. "What are you about, you fool?" was his exclamation. "It is dinner-time, father; you have the key, so I could not open the door; I was rubbing my bread against it, because I could not get to the bottle." "Cannot you go without cheese one day, you luxurious little rascal? You'll never be rich!" added the angry miser, as he kicked the poor boy for not being able to deny himself the ideal gratification.

In a similar way I, too, sometimes rub my crusts of bread against cupboard doors, for I gave up the idea of getting rich some time ago.

I once described Sir Lewis Moeller to you as a real eccentric. I was invited to a luxurious meal at his house today, an event so long in planning that one of the diplomatic guests had been summoned by courier—four weeks ago already—to come across the sea from Baden. This gentleman arrived punctually that very morning and seemed to have brought along an appetite both foreign and domestic. He had not forgotten to load himself down with various Continental delicacies to which everyone did the greatest possible justice, as they did to the numerous choice wines on offer. It takes a strong head to resist such feasts here, and the air makes copious food and strong drink more necessary than at home. A person who at first can scarcely drink English claret (that is, with brandy added) later finds a whole bottle of port quite accommodating, both to his health and the English fogs.

But if the major homage was to our sensory pleasures, the conversation itself was not without a pinch of salt. One of the officers present, who had served in the Burmese war, told us many interesting details about those regions; for instance, that the children are often breastfed for three years, quite in keeping with our theory of how to fatten up calves. And since smoking tobacco starts in earliest youth, the captain often saw young boys who would quit their mother's breast and then stick a burning cigar in their mouths for dessert. To me the most delectable story was an Irish bull. It was certainly extreme, since it concerns nothing less than a peasant who beheaded himself out of distraction. The facts are authentic, however. The *unerhörte Begebenheit* happened as follows:[42]

> When making their way home from mowing the fields, the peasants of Ulster customarily carry their colossal scythes on their shoulders, holding them pointed up in the air like rifles so the sharp blades hover just above their necks. The ends of the handles are sharpened to a point so they can be stuck into the ground. Two comrades were ambling home along a river when they caught sight of a large salmon, its head hidden in the roots of a tree and its tail stretched out in the stream.
>
> "Look, Paddy," exclaimed one of them, "that stupid salmon thinks we can't see him, because he can't see us. If only I had my pike, I'd give him a good poke."
>
> "Oh," said the other, sneaking up on the fish, "that should work with the scythe handle, too. Watch out!"
>
> He thrust and hit his target perfectly. But, alas, the scythe simultaneously cut off his head. It plopped into the water with a splash right before the eyes of his astonished friend, who for a long time could not grasp how Paddy's head had gotten there so quickly. Even today he claims there was something not quite right about the matter. In his opinion, an evil goblin must have been directing the movement of the blade.

I closed the day at the English opera, where the first act concluded with a mine collapsing and the main characters buried alive. In the final scene of the second act, however, they reappear in the bowels of the earth, three-quarters of the way to starvation, because, as they themselves explain, they have been languishing for three days already and now their last strength is fading away. Yet this in no way hinders the prima donna from singing a long aria, a *polonaise*, whereupon the chorus and trumpets chime in, "Ah, we are lost, all hope is gone." But, a miracle! The rocks collapse again, opening up a broad portal where daylight pours in. All lamentation, and with it all the miserable nonsense of the opus, comes to an end.

August 2nd, 1827

YESTERDAY'S FEASTING DREW my attention to an organ that Mr. Deville did not include in his list. This is the organ of gourmandizing, and it is found directly adjacent to the organ of murder, because both take greatest pleasure in destruction. I possess it in a significant degree and wish that all the other humps and dents on my skull produced such pleasing and innocent results. This organ not only confers the common delight in eating and drinking but also enables its owner to savor the true quality of wines and their bouquet, and to discern both the failings and the genius of a cook. This enjoyable organ only diminishes one's contentment if it is joined to a sentimental stomach, which is luckily not the case with me.

Today I visited an art exhibition where every picture in the gallery was stitched with a needle by one single person. The quality of the work was truly astonishing. The artist is a Miss Linwood, the most patient of all women. At a slight distance, the copies look like the originals, and how much they are appreciated can be judged by their enormous prices. One tapestry after Carlo Dolci had just been purchased for three thousand guineas; and a portrait of Napoleon as consul, widely divergent from the man he eventually became, is nonetheless said to offer an

45

Napoleon Bonaparte.

unusually good likeness from that time of his life and so was regarded with great reverence by the Frenchmen who were present (Figure 45).[43]

A few buildings farther along was a display of microscopes with a magnifying power of a million.[44] Anyone with a lively imagination could be driven mad by what they show. Nothing can be more atrocious, no one could invent a more dreadful, devilish thing than the hideously nasty aquatic insects that we swallow every day, invisible to the naked eye and even to less powerful magnifying glasses. They shoot around as fast as lightning in their swampy looking cesspool like the souls of the damned, and what is presumably their copulation resembles a brutal fight to the death.

Since I was now caught up in seeing things, and wanted to obliterate the appalling impression of this netherworld with more pleasant images, I managed to take in three different panoramas: Rio de Janeiro, Madrid, and Geneva.

The first is something totally different from the nature we know, a landscape both distinctive and paradisiacally lush. Madrid, with its treeless, sandy plain was a picture of inertia and inquisition, blistering heat brooding over the whole like an auto-da-fé. Geneva, in contrast, looked to me like a dear old acquaintance, and with an uplifted heart I gazed for a long time at that ever-constant and familiar friend, the majestic Mont Blanc.

August 8th, 1827

CANNING IS DEAD! A man in the fullness of his intellectual powers, who only a few weeks ago achieved the goal of his active life: to be the ruler of England and thus certainly the most influential man in Europe. Endowed with a fiery spirit that knew how to lead from strength; gifted with a soul capable of embracing the well-being of mankind from a still-higher perspective. Now *a single* blow has destroyed this proud edifice, and this intrepid man was forced to end his days as a criminal must—suddenly, tragically, amid the most terrible suffering, the victim of a merciless force of nature that tramples everything in its path, whether it be a new seedling, a mature blossom, a majestic oak, or a plant already twisted and broken.[45]

What will ensue from his death? It will be years before we know the answer. But it may hasten a denouement that threatens us in many ways, a situation that only a brilliant and enlightened statesman like Canning might have steered us through on an auspicious course toward unity. Perhaps the very party that now crows so indecently over his premature death will be the first to falter, for Lord Chesterfield was not wrong when he recently and prophetically declared, "But this I foresee, that before the end of this century, the trade of both king and priest will not be half so good a one as it has been."[46]

But what do I care about politics? If only I could always maintain my own equilibrium, I would be content, for Europe will take care of itself. In the end, cleverness and stupidity lead to the same end: the law of necessity.

Meanwhile Canning's death is the talk of the town, and the details of his sufferings are shocking. The sanctimonious, who abhorred him for his liberal views, have spread rumors that he converted during his final agony—what *they* call converted—whereas a friend who spent hours by his bedside could not praise enough the stoicism and serenity with which he bore his bitter fate; to his last conscious moment, he thought only of the welfare of England and the world, agonizing over how to present his case to the king one final time.

Since frivolity and seriousness always travel hand in hand on this earth, the attention paid his tragic death is being shared by an extremely bizarre novel, *Vivian Grey*,[47] notable for its often baroque but very witty and authentic portrayals of Continental manners. The description of the beginning of a ball at Ems can stand as a sample of how the English regard the idiosyncrasies of our mores:

> The company at the grand duke's fete was most select; that is to say, it consisted
> of everybody who was then at the baths: those who had been presented to His
> Highness having the privilege of introducing any number of their friends; and those

who had no friend to introduce them purchasing tickets at an enormous price from Cracowsky, the wily Polish intendant. The entertainment was imperial; no expense and no exertion were spared to make the hired lodging house look like an hereditary palace; and for a week previous to the great evening the whole of the neighboring town of Wiesbaden, the little capital of the duchy, had been put under contribution. What a harvest for Cracowsky! What a commission from the restaurateur for supplying the refreshments! What a percentage on hired mirrors and dingy hangings. The grand duke, covered with orders, received every one with the greatest condescension, and made to each of his guests a most flattering speech. His suite, in new uniforms, simultaneously bowed directly after the flattering speech was finished. Standing to the side, I next heard the following conversation:[48]

"Madame von Furstenburg, I feel the greatest pleasure in seeing you. My greatest pleasure is to be surrounded by my friends. Madame von Furstenburg, I trust that your amiable and delightful family are quite well." (The party passed on.) "Cravatischeff!" continued His Highness, inclining his head round to one of his aides-de-camp, "Cravatischeff! A very fine woman is Madame von Furstenburg. There are few women whom I more admire than Madame von Furstenburg."

"Prince Salvinski, I feel the greatest pleasure in seeing you. My greatest pleasure is to be surrounded by my friends. Poland honors no one more than Prince Salvinski."—"Cravatischeff! A remarkable bore is Prince Salvinski. There are few men of whom I have a greater terror than Prince Salvinski."

"Baron von Konigstein, I feel the greatest pleasure in seeing you. My greatest pleasure is to be surrounded by my friends. Baron von Konigstein, I have not yet forgotten the story of the fair Venetian."—"Cravatischeff! An uncommonly pleasant fellow is Baron von Konigstein. There are few men whose company I more enjoy than Baron von Konigstein's."

"Count von Altenburgh, I feel the greatest pleasure in seeing you. My greatest pleasure is to be surrounded by my friends. You will not forget to give me your opinion of my Austrian troop."—"Cravatischeff! A very good billiard player is Count von Altenburgh. There are few men whose play I would sooner bet on than Count von Altenburgh's."

"Lady Madeleine Trevor, I feel the greatest pleasure in seeing you. My greatest pleasure is to be surrounded by my friends. Miss Fane, your servant; Mr. St George, Mr. Grey."—"Cravatischeff! A most splendid woman is Lady Madeleine Trevor. There is no woman whom I more admire than Lady Madeleine Trevor! And Cravatischeff! Miss Fane, too! A remarkably fine girl is Miss Fane. There are few girls whom I more . . ."

Here the sound of the *polonaise* robbed me of the rest of the sentence, and I moved on to another scene.[49]

What do you think, Julie, caustic enough? Few accounts have amused me more, and my translation—very successful, do you not agree? There are few translations I like better than my own.

The writer's serious style is not bad, either.[50]

How fearful is the very life which we hold! We have our being beneath a cloud, and are a marvel even to ourselves. There is not a single thought that has its affixed limits. Like circles in the water, our researches weaken as they extend, and vanish at last into the immeasurable and unfathomable space of the vast unknown. We are like children in the dark; we tremble in a shadowy and terrible void, peopled with our fancies! Life is our real night, and the first gleam of the morning, which brings us certainty, is death.

Even more practical is what the celebrated Smollett wrote to a friend: "I am old enough to have seen and observed that we are all playthings of fortune; and that it depends on something as insignificant as the tossing up of a halfpenny, whether a man rises to affluence and honors, or continues to his dying day struggling with the difficulties and disgraces of life."[51]

August 15th, 1827

I GO EVERY day to look at the work being done in St James' Park and Green Park, once just cow pastures. Now, following the plans of Mr. Nash, they are being transformed into delightful gardens and expanses of water. I am learning a lot of technical things and admire the effective distribution and continuity of the work, the ingenious means of transport, the moveable railroad tracks, etc.

There is a characteristic dichotomy here. On the one hand, the laws protecting private property are so harsh that any individual who climbs over a wall to get into a private garden risks being hanged, or in any case severely punished, and if this happens at night, the owner is fully entitled to shoot him dead. On the other hand, wherever members of the public have even the semblance of a claim to access, they must be treated as carefully as a raw egg. Both these parks belong to the Crown, but they have been open to the public on Sundays since time immemorial, and now no one dares close them to the plebs even temporarily, irrespective of the radical changes and current projects that the king has ordered (admittedly at the nation's expense).[52] Instead a sign states the following:

> The public is most respectfully entreated, during the operations designed solely to increase their own gratification, not to damage the carts and tools of the workmen and to take the utmost possible care of the areas where the men are at work.

Yet very little attention is paid to this respectful request, and the carts the workmen leave in stacks at the end of the day are often appropriated by young boys, who wheel each other around and get up to all sorts of mischief. The girls seesaw on the long planks, and many idle scamps toss stones in the water directly next to where ladies are standing, treating them to an involuntary bath and requiring them to hurry home. This roughhousing is in fact quite particular to the English hoi polloi and provides the only excuse for the inhumanity that leads all the moneyed classes to lock up their delightful properties so aggressively. Though it is also possible that the inhumanity of the rich is what first provoked the malevolence of the poor.

Walking and riding in the environs are again very inviting diversions, since autumn is starting early. The burned grass once more flaunts a bright green, and the trees are holding their leaves more firmly and freshly than at home, although they begin to turn even earlier. But here winter

254   LETTERS OF A DEAD MAN

comes very late, or not at all, to cover them with its white mantle, so there is no pause in the mowing of the lawns and maintenance of the gardens and grounds. Indeed in the countryside, the most attention is lavished on these things during autumn and winter, when the Season moves there from the metropolis.

The fashionables have fled London, and with such a brouhaha that many of those who find themselves obliged to stay behind make a serious effort to go into hiding. In the west end of town, the streets are as empty as in an abandoned city. Only the common girls are evident, in the evenings pursuing every passerby in the most ill-mannered way and with the most shameless caresses. Not just English but also foreign women have adopted this repulsive practice. I was driven to desperation recently by an aged French female with pale lips and rouged cheeks, who, noticing that I was a foreigner, was so persistent that even the offer of the shilling she asked for did not rid me of her. *Encore un moment,* she kept calling, *je ne demande rien, c'est seulement pouri-parler français, pour avoir une conversation raisonnable, dont les Anglais ne sont pas capables.*[53] These creatures have become a real plague here.

In the current tranquility, I can now take at least as much time for myself as I want, work when I choose, and read the legion of newspapers at my leisure. The inanities they contain about foreign affairs are beyond belief. Today I found the following article:

> For a while the blessed Emperor Alexander's admiration for Napoleon was boundless. It is well-known that at the theatre in Erfurt, when Talma uttered the words "L'amitié d'un grand homme est un bienfait des dieux,"[54] Alexander leaned over to Napoleon and said, "Ces paroles ont été écrites pour moi."[55]

Perhaps less well-known is another anecdote, though we can vouch for its validity. One day Alexander told Duroc of his profound desire to own a pair of trousers once worn by his great confederate, the emperor Napoleon. Duroc sounded out his master about this admittedly unusual matter, and Napoleon laughed heartily. "Oh, absolutely," he cried, "donnez-lui tout ce qu'il veut, pourvu qu'il me reste une paire pour changer."[56] This is true, and we have also been assured that Alexander, who was very superstitious, never wore anything but Napoleon's trousers when riding to battle in the campaigns of 1812 and 1813. Englishmen believe such nonsense without thinking twice.

The day ended very pleasantly for me with the arrival of my friend Lottum, for whom I will now leave you and this tediously long, although relative to its length insubstantial, letter. And I close with the old assurance that I know you somehow find charmingly fresh: whether near or far, you are and will forever remain next to my heart.

Your faithful Lou

LETTER 17

London, August 20th, 1827

*D*EAR FAITHFUL ONE,

Today curiosity drew me back to the tunnel works, where I descended to the riverbed in a diving bell and watched for a good half hour while sacks filled with clay were stuffed into the breach to make it solid again. The lower we sank, the more comfortable I felt in the metal box, except for a rather sharp pain in my ears (some people's ears bleed, although this does no lasting damage to their health). There are thick glass windows at the top of the box and next to these two tubes that let fresh air in and stale air out. The bottom consists of a narrow plank where you can place your feet, two fixed benches at the sides, and a few miners' lamps providing the necessary light. The workmen have splendid waterproof boots that can withstand moisture for twenty-four hours, and I amused myself by jotting down the manufacturer's address in my *portefeuille* while sitting there among the fish "auf des Stromes tiefunsterstem Grunde."[1]

After successfully negotiating the waters, it was fire that nearly did me in this evening. While I was momentarily out of the room, a candle burned down and ignited the papers on my desk, and before I could put it out, many things of significance were destroyed. Copies of letters, prints, and drawings; the beginning of a novel (what a loss!); innumerable addresses; a section of my diary—all these fell victim to the flames. I had to smile when I saw that the receipts were left untouched, whereas the unpaid bills had been consumed down to the last vestige. That is what I call an obliging fire! The large packet of your letters is now scorched around the edges, giving them the mournful look of death announcements. Quite right, too, since letters between loved ones are always mournful for needing to be written at all. As witness and messenger of the conflagration, I am sending you back the Viennese postilion with a hundred thousand blessings; although he has become a negro, his life was saved and his clover leaf preserved.[2]

August 21st, 1827

LONDON IS SO vast and contains so much terra incognita that one is continually encountering something new and interesting, even with no guide other than chance. This morning, for instance, I came upon Lincoln's Inn Fields, a magnificent square with beautiful buildings, tall trees, and perfectly tended lawns about five miles from my lodgings. The most impressive building contains the College of Surgeons as well as a very interesting museum.[3] One of the gentlemen obligingly showed me around.

The first thing to capture my attention was a sweet little mermaid, a specimen that a few years ago had been exhibited in the city for a fee and then sold for a thousand pounds, whereupon it was discovered that she was nothing more than a Chinese contrivance made up of a small orangutan and a salmon. The actual existence of such beings thus remains as problematic as ever.

Next to her stood an authentic orangutan. This large male beast had lived here for a long time and even performed a number of domestic services in the house. Mr. Clift, as my guide was called, informed me of his conviction that orangutans were a distinct genus more closely related to humans than to apes. He said that for a long time he had carefully observed this particular individual (whom he referred to as Mr. Dyk) and found indisputable proof that his capacity for thinking and reflection went beyond instinct alone. For instance, after being given permission, Mr. Dyk would search through people's pockets just like other apes do, to see whether they contained anything edible. However, if he found something that did not suit his purposes, he would not throw it away or drop it, as his comrades did, but would always put it back very carefully. He was also sensitive to the slightest sign of displeasure, which could render him melancholic for days on end. And he had often been seen voluntarily helping the domestic servants when they were particularly overburdened.

There were exhibits of some almost unbelievable wounds. For instance, Mr. Clift showed me the front part of a male chest, preserved in spirits. The man had been so violently run through the middle and skewered by the shaft of a carriage drawn by runaway horses that he could only be pulled off it with the help of several people. The shaft had passed directly next to his heart and lungs, pushing them gently aside without doing them major damage, although it did break his ribs in front and behind. Once removed from the shaft, this man still had enough strength to climb up two flights of stairs to his bed. He proceeded to live another fourteen years in good health, although the surgeons kept an eye on him and the minute he was dead, took possession of his body in order to put it in their museum, along with the shaft, which the family had retained as a relic.

Also remarkable was a small, beautifully formed greyhound. It had been walled up in a cellar and was found there after many years in a perfectly desiccated state. Looking like it had been carved out of gray sandstone, it presented a touching picture of resignation, rolled up as if in sleep, with its little head expressing such wistfulness that you could not gaze at it without compassion. A cat, on the other hand, just as starved and dehydrated, appeared wild and diabolical. Thus does gentleness remain beautiful even in suffering, I thought. It was like a picture of good and evil, each in the same situation, yet the impressions were so dissimilar.

Finally I must mention the skeleton of the famous Frenchman who allowed himself to be exhibited here while he was still alive but already a skeleton, since his bones were almost entirely without flesh and covered with nothing but skin. His stomach was smaller than that of a newborn child, and the poor creature was condemned to a perpetual starvation diet, since he could not ingest more than a half cup of bouillon a day. He lived to be twenty, died here in London, and sold himself to the museum before his death.

On my trip home I got a lot of small change at the turnpike and, being in a strange mood, found it amusing to let a few coins drop quietly from the carriage every time I came across a poor, ragged person. Not a single one of them noticed; they all moved steadily on. This is just how Fortune does it! She drives continually through the world in her lucky chariot and blindfolded tosses out her gifts. Yet how rarely does one of us notice and bend down to pick them up. In fact, we are generally searching somewhere else at exactly that auspicious moment.

When I got to my room, I found a real gift of fate, and a very dear one—a long letter from you . . . .

Herr von S——, whom you mention as a recent visitor to the spa, is an old acquaintance of mine, a strange and eccentric character of whom we were all fond, but could not resist making fun of as well, and who was constantly encountering the most serious and ridiculous situations. You could see for yourself that he looks like a caricature and appears to be the creature least suited to being lucky in love. Still, as a young lieutenant he was madly infatuated with one of the most beautiful women of his time, the Baroness von B——, and one evening when her biting mockery had pushed him to the limit, he thrust his sword through his body right before her eyes. The blade pierced his lung, so that a candle held before the wound was extinguished by his breathing. In spite of this, our tragic fool healed, and the baroness (who was actually quite a gracious soul) was so touched by the proof of his devotion that she abandoned her cruelty and promised him a rendezvous. Among others, however, the deadly stabbing had aroused laughter, and somehow one of his comrades, a particularly devilish mischief maker, heard of the tryst and played the most hideous prank on the poor S—— by giving him some very powerful medicine a few hours before the appointed time. You can imagine the burlesque that resulted. Meanwhile it did the prankster no good at all, since two days later S—— killed him in a duel and was then forced to leave the Saxon military service. I have heard that he has now carved out a better life for himself under Alexander's flag.[4] I would have loved to see the old codger again, whose passions, like his tendency to become an object of comedy, must have receded somewhat!

Salt Hill, August 25th, 1827

I FINALLY GOT myself together and left the city with Lottum, who is going to accompany me for a few days, after which I will ride farther into the country by myself. The first rest stop is a charming inn not far from Windsor that looks like some distinguished person's villa.[5] Across its entire front stretches the sweetest verandah adorned with roses, every possible kind of climber, and hundreds of flowers in pots. The most carefully tended pleasure ground and flower garden stretch out below my windows, from which I have a splendid view of Windsor Castle, gigantic in the distance. Framed by two chestnut trees, it glows like a fairy palace in the evening sun. A long rain has painted everything emerald green, and the freshness of the countryside has the most beneficial influence on my spirits. Meanwhile, good Julie, I often talk about you with Lottum, whose company I find very pleasant. Tomorrow we intend to see a great many things, but this evening, since it became so late, we had to be satisfied with a walk in the fields and a good dinner with champagne, which, it goes without saying, we drank to your health.

August 26th, 1827

IN THE EARLY morning we drove to Stoke Park, an estate belonging to a grandson of William Penn, the famous Quaker.[6] In the house is a piece of the tree beneath which Penn concluded the treaty with the Indian chiefs, whereby Pennsylvania acquired its name. In a lovely parkland here, we saw more varieties of deer than Lottum or I had ever seen: black, white, striped, dappled, black with white blazes, and brown with white feet. Otherwise the park and garden, although quite pretty, offered nothing remarkable.

This was not at all the case at Lord Grenville's Dropmore, where we were captivated by the most wonderful trees and absolutely delightful flower gardens. There were, in fact, three or four gardens set in different spots and each truly unique in its display of flowers, some being set in beds on the lawn, but the most beautiful on gravel. Especially original and exceedingly effective was that each bed contained only a *single* type of flower, thus spreading an indescribable richness of saturated color over the whole picture. Countless geraniums of every possible type and hue, hundreds of different mallows and dahlias, along with many other blooms that we scarcely know or know only in isolated examples, formed large and imposing masses. At the same time, the colors were in general arrayed with such skill that everywhere your eye rested, it found true enjoyment.

A large part of the park, however, consisted of nothing but barren soil with some scraggly pines and heather, just like our woods. The grass looked scorched, yet the high level of cultivation gave the whole a thoroughly delightful appearance and strengthened my conviction that nearly every aspect of a terrain except the climate can be conquered with enough money and diligence.

After visiting yet another park boasting exceptionally lovely views, we drove to Windsor to look *en détail* at the new castle (which, as you will remember, I only saw from the outside on my last visit). Unfortunately, at almost exactly the same moment, the king and his retinue arrived in five phaetons drawn by ponies, so we had to wait more than an hour until he drove off again, and we were allowed to enter.

In the meantime we visited Eton College, an old educational establishment founded by Henry VI. Outwardly it is an extensive and beautiful Gothic building with an adjoining church. Inside it is more austere than our village schools. In the rooms where the most distinguished youths of England are educated, you see nothing but stark white walls and wooden benches incised with the names of pupils who have studied there (including famous men like Fox and Canning). In keeping with Henry VI's endowment, the King's Scholars get nothing but mutton to eat day after day.[7] What must the founder have been thinking!

The library is quite beautifully decorated and contains some interesting manuscripts.

When we got back from Eton, the king had departed, and his architect Mr. Wyattville, who is in charge of the new construction at the castle, was good enough to inform us about everything in detail and with the greatest courtesy. This structure is a colossal undertaking, the only one of its kind in England, and is being carried out not only with a great deal of money and technical expertise, but also with immense taste, even genius. The magnificence of the castle—which has already cost almost three million of our money and is not yet half finished—is definitely worthy of a king of England. Its position alone is hugely advantageous, for it rises atop a hill directly above the town and is thus splendid to look at from every side. The combination of historical interest, great antiquity, and astonishing grandeur and extent make it unique in the world.

The splendor of the interior is consistent with the exterior. For instance, each pane of glass in the colossal Gothic windows cost twelve pounds, and the velvet, silk, and gilding are dazzling. Adjacent to the king's apartments is a high terrace edged with greenhouses, although from outside you see only a stark and looming wall of the same earnest character as the rest. This terrace surrounds the most delightful flower garden and pleasure ground. The four large gateways in the castle courtyard are ingeniously contrived so that each serves as a frame for an exceptional view of the landscape. All the new additions are, as mentioned, so perfectly executed that they cannot be distinguished from the older sections, and it is hard to criticize the care with which the earlier style has been adhered to, even when it was not always that tasteful. I confess, however, that for me the adornments of the interior, in spite of their opulence, left a lot to be desired. In places they are far too ornate, and neither in keeping with the character of the whole nor pleasing in themselves.

August 28th, 1827

LOTTUM LEFT ME yesterday already, earlier than he had originally intended, and I was very sorry to see him go, since a companion with such a charming and friendly disposition doubles every pleasure. Therefore on the same day I drove to St Leonard's Hill with an acquaintance from the Horse Guards, who is stationed here. It is an estate belonging to Field Marshall Lord Harcourt,[8] and I had a letter of introduction from Esterházy.

Today the weather changed from overcast and occasional rain to splendid, with hardly a cloud in the sky. I could not have had a more beautiful day to see a more beautiful spot than St Leonard's Hill (Figure 46). Gigantic trees, refreshing woods full of variety, enchanting vistas both distant and near, a lovely house with the most inviting of all flower gardens, luxuriant vegetation, and a charming seclusion, from which you see, as if eavesdropping from behind a curtain, a panorama of infinite diversity spreading out mile after mile in the valley below you: there is nothing comparable to it anywhere in England. The owners are a very engaging elderly couple,

46

St Leonard's Hill with Windsor Castle.

the man eighty-five and the woman seventy-two, unfortunately without children and hardly any relatives, so that all this loveliness will fall to distant, indifferent people.[9] The old gentleman was well pleased by my enthusiasm for the area and invited me to come for a visit the following day, which I accepted with pleasure. As for today, I had already been invited by my acquaintance Captain Bulkeley to dine in the Guards' mess at Windsor, where I arrived at six o'clock and did not get away until midnight.

Quite early the next morning I was summoned by Lord Harcourt, who serves as the head ranger of the park at Windsor. He wanted to show it to me before the king arrived, because once the monarch has made his appearance, the private areas are hermetically sealed off, without exception, to everyone other than invited or immediate company. I arrived slightly late, the good old gentleman scolded me a bit, and I was immediately whisked into a landau drawn by four magnificent horses, in which we rolled speedily through the tall beech wood. In Windsor's immense park, which covers fifteen thousand acres, the king has had numerous roads built for his own use, leading to the most interesting points. We drove along one of these and after half an hour, arrived at the royal stables where the much-discussed giraffe is currently lodged. Here we discovered that the king had ordered his carriages only a moment before, and we found them already standing harnessed in the courtyard. There were seven of them, of every type, but all with very low wheels and constructed in the lightest possible way, like children's carriages. They were drawn by little ponies, most of different colors—the king's carriage by four, which he drives himself, the others by two each. Lord Harcourt looked upon these equipages with horror, because he feared that the king might suddenly arrive and feel ill at ease at the sight of unexpected strangers. The monarch is quite odd in this regard. He is extremely discomfited to see any unfamiliar face; indeed, to see anyone at all on his estate; and so, with the exception of the main roads leading through it, the park is totally secluded. In addition, the king's favorite spots are densely enclosed, and every day more large plantings are laid out to make them even more private and concealed. In those places where a curious glance might penetrate, three levels of fencing are placed on top of one another.

We thus made great haste so we could at least see the giraffe, which was led before us by the two Moors who had brought it over from Africa. Truly an outlandish animal! You know its form, but nothing can give you an idea of the beauty of its eyes. Imagine something between the most beautiful Arabian horse and the loveliest southern girl, with long, jet-black lashes and the most profound expression of benevolence combined with volcanic fire. This giraffe likes people, is extremely gentle, and has a pleasant disposition. It also has a good appetite, because every day it guzzles the milk of the three cows lounging nearby. Using its long, sky blue tongue like a proboscis, it purloined several things, including my umbrella, which it found so attractive that it did not want to relinquish it. Its gait was somewhat awkward, since it had spent too much time confined while on board ship. But the Africans assured us that it is very fast when in perfect condition. Apprehensive about the king, Lord Harcourt hurried us along, driving straight through a small, thickly planted area in the pleasure grounds of the Cottage, which we only glimpsed from afar, before conducting us to Virginia Water (Figure 47). This large, artificial, though very natural-looking lake is His Majesty's favorite spot, where he usually goes fishing every day. I was quite startled to find that the landscape took on an entirely different character here, one very rare in England, namely that of my own homeland. Forests of pine and fir were intermixed with oaks and alders, and beneath them were our heathers as well as our sand, where the spring plantings had

thoroughly withered. I could have given the king's gardeners some good advice about planting in sand, for I am convinced they do not really understand how to deal with such soil. On the lake itself was a frigate, rocking gently, and on the banks stood a number of charming follies, Chinese and American structures, etc., all in good taste and without excessive embellishment. The lord was driving us along at such speed that we could only see things very fleetingly and mostly in the distance. But I was nonetheless delighted to have been able to get at least a general idea of the whole.

Occasionally Harcourt climbed onto the seat of the carriage with great effort and stood up, supported by his wife and me, to see whether the king might not suddenly appear. He did not relax again until the doors of the holy of holies had finally closed behind us. On the way back we saw the king's hunters—beautiful animals, as you can imagine—along with a particular breed of very small, delicate hunting dog found only in England.

We returned with good appetites to dinner, where I met a few of the other guests. Our hostess Countess Harcourt is a very amiable woman and just as much a parkomaniac as I am. She herself, forty years ago, planted all the large, magnificent trees in front of the house, and in all that time, she has only had two of them removed. Now, looking under and between them, one can enjoy a variety of vistas, like numerous, individual tableaux. I become daily more convinced that wide-open vistas—essentially forbidden here—destroy all sense of illusion. Except on some very old estates, you find almost no houses or palaces in England that are not enclosed by tall trees repeatedly blocking the views to and from the buildings. The illustrations of these places

47

Virginia Water.

are deceptive, because the draftsmen, intent on showing the scope of the architecture, omit the surrounding trees. A convenience of this garden is a gigantic umbrella the size of a small tent. It is outfitted with an iron spike at the bottom that can be stuck in the lawn, so you can sit under it wherever you like, sheltered from the sun.

I was very happy that the friendly host invited me to return again tomorrow, when the ladies-in-waiting of the Queen of Württemberg are supposed to dine there. If they are pretty, it will in no way spoil our party. After dinner we took another walk in the park and visited a cottage set at the bottom of the valley. Surrounded on all sides by hills and woods, it forms a charming contrast to the splendid villa on high. Then Berndt and I rode home under romantic starlight.

August 29th, 1827

AT FOUR O'CLOCK, after paying an early visit in Windsor to Mrs. Chambre, whose pretty daughters you know from earlier letters, I went back to Lord Harcourt's, feeling renewed delight in the magnificent oak forest of his park. The loveliness of the whole is already announced by the sweetest gardener's house, tastefully constructed of unfinished tree trunks and branches, and overgrown with roses. I found a large party: several attendants of the Queen of Württemberg including her Mistress of the Robes, two additional ladies-in-waiting, and two squires, all German; the Marquis d'Harcourt, a Frenchman, his two sons and well-behaved daughter (a true Parisian); and in addition, an English cleric and another foreign nobleman.

Since the aging lord has no descendants, the French have very cleverly asserted their cousinship. They have been very well received, live in the valley cottage I described yesterday, and have every expectation of becoming heirs to this colossal fortune. Consequently, the little French girl is already seen as an excellent match.[10] But it was the Countess Harcourt who interested me most. She is an extremely likeable old woman, full of dignity and courtliness, along with a most graceful spirit. She has seen and experienced a great deal and knows how to talk about it in absorbing ways. She told me a lot about Lord Byron, who lived in her house for a long time when he was a boy, and was even then so irrepressible that he caused her untold problems. He was a defiant lad, who loved to do damage. She did not think he was bad but certainly naughty, for he always got a kind of pleasure out of inflicting pain, especially on females. Yet she herself had to confess that when he wanted to be loveable, there was hardly any woman who could resist him. "His wife," she continued, "admittedly a cold and vain yet learned fool, was also treated badly by Byron, who tormented her in truly ingenious ways, probably because she had initially refused him. For this he swore—already on his wedding day—to wreak never-ending vengeance on her."[11]

I did not altogether trust this account, however much respect I otherwise felt for the elderly countess, because a poetic soul like Lord Byron's is difficult to judge! In such a case, the normal standard can never be appropriate, yet I very much doubt that her comments were based on any other.

When you are pleased to be somewhere, you yourself are usually pleasing as well, and so I was strongly encouraged to stay on for a few days in this little paradise. But my restlessness, as you know only too well, is perfectly balanced by my lethargy. And since it is hard to move me from anywhere once I have settled down (witness my long and hapless sojourn in London), I find it hard to tarry once the interest of the moment is exhausted. I therefore gratefully declined the invitation and returned to Salt Hill.

THE TERRACE OF Windsor Castle serves as a pleasant promenade for the townspeople and it is often enlivened by the music of the guards. I went there this morning with the engaging Chambre daughters, and together we paid a visit to the castle's chatelaine, an aged, unmarried lady. No one could live more beautifully. Every window offered a view into another splendid landscape. The young ladies had distributed themselves in adjoining rooms when, to my considerable apprehension, the elderly maiden took me by the arm and whispered that she needed to show me a curiosity—admittedly old, but still very interesting—in her bedroom. The bedroom of an Englishwoman is generally a sacred place, open to none but her intimates. I was therefore not a little amazed by this offer, all the more so since, with no further ado, the venerable lady steered me directly to her bed. She then pulled open the curtains. *Que diable veut-elle faire?*[12] I said to myself, as she called my attention to a stone in the wall bearing a weathered inscription.

"That, my dear sir, was written at the hour of his death by a handsome young knight who languished here in prison and was strangled beneath this stone."

"My God, don't you dread sleeping here?" I responded. "What if the young knight should return as a ghost?"

"Never fear," the jovial old lady cried, "at my age one isn't so afraid any more, certainly not of young knights, living or dead."

We then strolled to the magnificent chapel for a religious service. The banners, swords, and coronets of the Knights of the Garter, arrayed proudly all around; the muted light falling through the colorful windows; the skillful carvings in stone and wood; the devout congregation: it all made for a lovely picture. There was only the occasional imperfection—for example, a ridiculous monument to Princess Charlotte, which showed the four minor figures with their backs to the viewer so that no other aspect is visible, whereas the princess appears twice: stretched out as a corpse and flying up to heaven as an angel.

Enveloped by the music and song, I squeezed quietly into a nook where I gave myself up to my fancies and, deeply immersed in the kingdom of sound, soon forgot everything around me. I imagined after some time that I was dead and standing before my own tomb, as a visitor to that Gothic chapel, dear Julie, which you and I wanted to build. In front of me, in the middle of the church across from the choir, a figure wrapped in abundant drapery was lying on a white marble sarcophagus with a lamb and wolf at his feet. A matching pedestal next to this remained unoccupied. I moved closer and read the inscriptions that were engraved in the stone and filled with gold. At the narrower side, beneath the head of the reclining figure, were the following words:

> In thy bosom, oh God!
> Rests the immortal part of his spirit,
> For the law of *eternal* life
> Is death and resurrection.

At the opposite end was written:

> His childhood was lacking its greatest blessing:
> A loving upbringing in a parental home.

His youth was stormy and vain and foolhardy,
But never estranged from Nature and God.

On the other side:

Serious was his manhood, and dismal.
It would have been shrouded in darkest night,
Had not a loving woman,
Like the sun with her clear, soothing beams,
Oft turned tenebrous night into cheerful day.

On the last side:

He was denied the long life of an old man.
What did he achieve and what create?
It blooms all around you.
Whatever else he strove for or attained of an earthly nature
Meant much to others yet little to him.

Now my thoughts focused on you and all those I hold dear, and I began to weep in pious distress about myself. Then, in perfect accord with a sudden end to the music, I awoke from my reverie and found actual tears running down my cheeks. I was almost ashamed to be seen.

August 31st, 1827

THE SERVICE IS good in England, 'tis true!

I had been invited to the Guard's officers for six o'clock and made myself late with my writing. Meals are served very punctually there, and the barracks are an hour from my inn (which is, as usual, also a post house), so I sent my servant racing down the stairs to fetch the horses. They were harnessed in less than a minute, and in fifteen, moving like the wind, I reached the table—at the stroke of six!

This military is on the whole far more socially adept than our own, simply because its members are far richer. Although the rituals of service are certainly observed, there is no trace of our pedantry and, when off duty, not the slightest distinction drawn between a colonel and the youngest lieutenant. Each man participates in the conversation with just as much ease as in other social settings. In the country all officers are in uniform at the table, whereas in London this holds true only for the barracks officer *du jour*. But after dinner everyone makes himself comfortable, and today I saw one of the young lieutenants sit down in his dressing gown and slippers for a game of whist with the colonel, who was still in uniform. The gentlemen have invited me, if I have no other engagement, to dine with them anytime I can as long as I am in the neighborhood, and they are extraordinarily friendly to me.

In the morning I visited Frogmore and spent a few more hours looking at the paintings at Windsor. There are many decent battle scenes by West in the throne room, depicting the deeds of Edward III and the Black Prince, with throngs of knights, snorting horses, antiquated costumes and equestrian trappings, lances, swords, and banners—very appropriate to the decoration of a royal hall. In another room I was struck by the extremely expressive portrait of a Duke of Savoy, the true ideal of a ruler. Luther and Erasmus by Holbein make good pendants, but also set a contrast. The fine and sarcastic face of Erasmus seems on the verge of uttering the words he wrote to the pope, who had criticized him for not keeping the fast: "Holy Father, my heart is Catholic, but my stomach is Protestant." The beauties of the court of Charles II, who adorn the whole adjoining wall, inspire immoderation of another kind.

Frogmore offers little worth seeing. The large lake is nothing but a frog swamp, though ringed by hedges of yews and roses. An entire encampment of light, moveable tents on the lawn looked quite nice.

September 3rd, 1827

I LET MYSELF be talked into devoting a few days to that special aspect of country life on offer at the beautiful Lady Garvagh's, a close relative of Canning's. At breakfast she told me she had been present three months earlier when Canning took leave of his mother, both of them in the best of health: "Adieu, dear Mother, we'll see each other again in August." Then in July his mother died quite suddenly, and her son followed her in early August. What a strange coincidence that they were, as agreed, reunited at the specified time!

Yesterday and the day before we went to the races at Egham, which are held on a large meadow surrounded by hills. I ran into many acquaintances, was introduced by the Duke of Clarence to the Queen of Württemberg, was lucky in my betting, and in the evening attended the picnic ball in the little town that, *tout comme chez nous,* has produced a lot of provincial behavior and quite ridiculous country dandies.

Nearly all of today was taken up with another outing and walk with the young ladies. English girls are tireless walkers through thick and thin, over hill and dale, such that it requires a certain amount of ambition to keep pace with them.

In the park of a nabob, we found an interesting curiosity: two dwarf elms imported from China. Barely two feet tall, they are a hundred years old and look completely scrubby and wizened, in keeping with their age. The secret of growing such trees is unknown in Europe.

Finally the mischievous lasses climbed over a fence at Windsor Park and disrupted the fiercely protected royal solitude with their jokes and laughter. This gave me the opportunity to see still more forbidden parts of the charming environs of Virginia Water, which the apprehensive Lord Harcourt had not dared enter. If we had been caught today, the company was such that we would surely have been treated graciously.

Windsor, September 5th, 1827

IN THE FOUR days of my stay we had all become such close friends that it was quite difficult to say good-bye. The ladies accompanied me for about an hour on foot until I climbed into my carriage. I picked a few forget-me-nots from beside the stream and passed them around with considerable sentiment as a silent farewell, first to the lovely Rosabelle who stood like a proud mistress among devoted slaves. She gently removed a flower from the bouquet and pressed it back into my hand. *Moquez-vous de moi, mais je le conserve encore.*[13]

At last, totally despondent, I drove off and instructed my post boy to take me to the Horse Guards barracks, where I arrived just in time for dinner. With the help of a lot of champagne and claret (for I was very thirsty after all the walking, dear Julie), I consoled myself as best I could over the abandoned beauties and then drove with Captain Bulkeley to a soirée at Mrs. Chambre's. Here, at about eleven o'clock and after tea, since the moon was shining so wonderfully, it was decided to grant the ladies their wish and take another stroll through the park, to see the imposing castle illuminated from a particularly advantageous spot. The walk was again a bit long but extremely rewarding. The deep blue meadow of the sky was speckled with flocks of sheep (which one of the officers rather unpoetically, although not unsuitably, compared to a curdled milk pudding), and the light from the radiant moon could not have been more magnificent. Soon, however, our pleasure was rudely interrupted by two gamekeepers bearing shotguns who threatened to arrest us—a party of twenty people, mostly ladies, and with at least seven uniformed guards officers!—for trespassing on prohibited footpaths and disturbing the peace. They finally settled for two of the officers, whom they immediately carted off. What a difference in customs! At home the officers would have deemed themselves dishonored by the harsh language of the watchmen and might have stabbed them to death on the spot. Here everything seemed quite in order, and no one put up the slightest resistance. The rest of us returned home, and the arrestees showed up about an hour later, having endured much rigmarole before being released. One of them, Captain T——, laughed heartily as he told us that the forest ranger had been very stern with him and said it was a scandal that officers, who were duty bound to prevent disorderly conduct, were quite prepared to engage in it themselves, etc.

"The man wasn't entirely wrong," he added, "but ladies' wishes must always be satisfied, after all."

Back at the inn I found my old Berndt, who wanted to receive my personal orders before his departure. Since I am very content with the Englishman—whom I have examined phrenologically[14]—I will not miss my countryman so very much. He is bringing you a large garden plan from me, on top of which I stretched out for an hour or so in my bedroom before I was finished with it, rather like Napoleon on top of his charts and maps of the world. *He,* however, sketched blood with his styluses, *I* nothing but water and meadows; *he* fortifications, *I* summer houses; *he* finally soldiers, and *I* just trees. In the end it may be all the same to God whether his children play with cannonballs or nuts; but for mortals the difference is significant, and in their opinion, the man who has people shot dead by the thousands is greater than the man who simply tends to their enjoyment.

A lengthy list will explain the plan to you. Be diligent in carrying out my suggestions, and when I am back, you can regale me with the realization of all the garden dreams that you find worthy.

My intention is to return now to London for a few days to see personally to my horses as they embark on their journey home. Only then will I set off on my longer tour of the country. My journal will no doubt become quite swollen for a considerable period before I am able to send it off to you again. But do not think that I will become dilatory in my reporting, for, as the brilliant prince says, "There are few things I would rather do than write to you."

Your Lou

LETTER 18

London, September 7th, 1827

$\mathscr{P}$RECIOUS FRIEND!

As you know, I am bad at remembering things like birthdays, but I do recall that tomorrow is the anniversary of that sad day when I left my poor Julie all alone in Bautzen! Now a whole year has rolled over the world, and we insects still crawl along in the same old track. But you and I are as fond of each other as ever, and that is the main thing! We will finally make our way through the difficulties that challenge us and come at last to a flowery meadow where the morning dew has spread its diamonds, and sunbeams dance over the sparkling droplets. Do not worry, one day we will round the Cape of Good Hope again.

I have not written you for the last few days because my routine activities involved nothing more than working and writing with Berndt, dining with Lottum at the Travellers Club, and going to bed alone. There was, however, another German *Graf* at our dinner yesterday, who has come here to buy horses. He appears wealthy and young enough to enjoy his fortune for a long time to come. He is also the true image of a good-natured country squire, certainly a most cheerful type of person. If only I were such a man!

As for your opinion about parks, I would say that they are never large enough, especially when properly rounded off. Here Windsor Park is the only one I have found satisfying as a whole, due mainly to its enormous size. It represents my own ideal: a lovely setting with areas where you can "live and move" exactly as you wish;[1] where you can hunt, fish, ride, or drive a carriage without ever feeling confined; where once past the entrance gates you never catch sight of a boundary; yet where a refined sensibility has incorporated all the complementary elements of the surrounding country, extending all the way to the furthest horizon. Concerning the natural terrain you are right, of course, that one must not throw the baby out with the bath water. It is often better to disguise the limitations of the land by cleverly designing paths and plantings than go to extraordinary lengths to alter the topography or acquire additional property.

My horses sailed off successfully today, although beautiful Hyperion acted up like mad, shattering the box that held him as well as the iron bars, halters, and straps as if they were made of glass. He missed falling into the water by a hair and will no doubt cause a lot more trouble along the way, although we tied him down like a wild beast. You cannot really blame these poor animals for being terrified when a huge crane grips them like the arm of a giant and swings them aloft in a broad arc from the quay to the ship. Some manage to endure it with the greatest serenity—even among horses there are Stoics!

Now there was nothing left to keep me in London, except that Lady Garvagh is here, and alone, and so attractive! It would be wrong to avoid such a friend, especially since I have no intention of falling in love with her. And is there not something terribly sweet about the *friendship* of a beautiful woman? I have found that many men spoil such relationships because the minute they get close to any female they are compelled to appear love struck, and this immediately puts the woman on the qui vive and prevents the gradual, easy familiarity and lack of self-consciousness that create the most receptive ground for whatever one wishes to sow. For my part, I am quite content with nothing more than a tender friendship, especially when I can see it in the gentle gaze of soulful blue eyes, hear it spoken by a mouth of crimson red, and feel it affirmed through the warm pressure of a perfectly proportioned, velvet hand. Add to this portrait the innocent expression of a dove; long, dark brown curls; a slender waist; and the most beautiful English complexion—there you have Lady Garvagh, as she lives and breathes.

Doncaster, September 16th, 1827

I COULD HAVE dated this from London, given how quickly I covered the 180 miles here in twenty hours, including enough time for brief visits to two famous Elizabethan houses and their parks. Hatfield, the first of them, belonged to the queen, who often stayed there. It is less magnificent than Burghley House, which her renowned minister Cecil had built for himself. Hatfield is constructed of brick; only the window framings, corners, and battlements are of sandstone. The proportions are superb, but the park and garden offer nothing of interest beyond very tall allées of oaks, supposedly planted by Elizabeth herself.

Even though the family was away, I was able to view Burghley House only from the outside, for nothing could convince the aged chatelaine to desecrate a Sunday by showing around a stranger. This was especially regrettable because it contains a very significant paintings collection. In the palace courtyard, which is bordered by gilded-iron grillwork, I admired a colossal chestnut tree with such a wide sweep of branches that there was enough space beneath them to break in a horse. The ancient park boasts many other arboreal wonders, although the water, like at Hatfield, is stagnant and swampy. The house is built of stone in a confused style: Gothic below, topped by chimneys that look like Corinthian capitals. The great statesman's taste in art must have been badly corrupted!

York, September 17th, 1827

THE DONCASTER RACES are the best attended in England, the racecourse being preferable to all others for its trappings, practicality, and ease of viewing. Watching a race here is more enjoyable than elsewhere, for it offers a less truncated spectacle. The entire course from beginning to end can be overlooked from the high, tower-like stands, which are very elegantly appointed. The horses run in a circle, the same spot serving as start and finish. The mass of people—beautiful women and fashionable society—was extraordinary. All the great nobility of the neighborhood drove up in full regalia, which fascinated me, for it was my first experience of this kind of pageantry, quite common here in the countryside, but very different from what you see in town. The Duke of Devonshire's equipage was the most distinguished of all. I will describe the procession so you can record it for Muskau. Six horses pulled his party's carriage, which had four seats and windows of glass. The harnesses and hammercloth were only moderately plush, and the coachman, in intermediate livery, was wearing a blond wig and boots. Twelve riders escorted them: four grooms rode horses of various colors with light saddles and bridles; four outriders were mounted on coach horses like those pulling the carriage and outfitted with harness reins and postilion saddles; finally there were four footmen in informal jackets, leather chaps, and jackboots, with embroidered saddlecloths, and holsters bearing the arms of the duke in brass. The order of the train was as follows: two grooms in front, then two outriders, next the carriage with its six handsome horses driven by the coachman on his box, and a postilion riding the lead saddle horse. A footman rode to the left of this postilion, another somewhat farther back on the right. Two more outriders followed behind the carriage, then two grooms, and at the end the last two footmen. Amid all this splendor, only one small outrider was dressed in full state livery of yellow, blue, black, and silver; he wore a powdered wig, and the duke's brightly embroidered arms gleamed on his left sleeve.

Today's Saint Leger race may cause many a sleepless night, for immense sums were lost. A small mare was considered so inferior that bets were going against her at fifteen to one, yet she came in first of all the twenty-six horses entered. An acquaintance of mine won nine thousand pounds and, had the horse lost, would have forfeited not even nine hundred. Another man saw nearly his entire fortune disappear. It is being widely claimed that he was deceived by the owner of one of the favorites, who bet very high amounts on his horse in public, while secretly betting much higher amounts against it and arranging for it to lose.

The hustle and bustle of the race and the thousands of equipages presented a stunning spectacle of English wealth. Immediately afterward I continued on with no specific destination in mind, and my carriage arrived at one in the morning here in York, England's second metropolis. I read throughout the journey, my lamp illuminating Madame de Maintenon's letters to the Princess des Ursins, a very entertaining book. Many passages are remarkable in their depiction of the time and its customs. Of course, the incognito queen understands life at court from the ground up, and her behavior is often strikingly reminiscent of a certain male friend of yours, especially her way of affecting persistent ignorance about whatever is going on and making light of her own influence. At the same time she displays great gentleness and wisdom, and such exceptional decorum in everything that one really finds her a much more likeable figure than what history has painted for us. It is, admittedly, always a bad idea to let an old woman govern, whether she wears a petticoat or pants; but it was easier then. People were obviously more like overgrown children and even waged war that way. In fact, they saw the dear Lord as nothing more than another Louis XIV raised to a higher power; yet *in articulo mortis*,[2] were, like true courtiers, quick to abandon their temporal king, taking no further notice of him as they dedicated themselves contritely and irrevocably to the mightier ruler they had previously neglected for being too distant. It is clear from old memoirs that people who managed well or at least tolerably at court, also died feeling more confident about how their savoir faire would serve them in heaven. Meanwhile those who found themselves in serious disfavor had to endure a far-more-difficult death and greater pangs of conscience. We can no longer conjure up a true idea of such a time, such a court, such a way of life, but it was probably not all that bad for people of our class. I reflected at length on these eternal fluctuations in the world until, touched by the aura of the invisible spirit that moves ceaselessly through the universe, and filled with tender longing, I called upon that magnificent evening star that has gazed on all this commotion for eons with such tolerance and unruffled composure.

SOME OF MY talents are truly regrettable. . . . .

. . . .

Now all that has been lost, for one always serves oneself badly. The same is true for much better things, such as a glorious tree in the distant wilds of America that every spring yields the most magnificent foliage and fragrant flowers, yet does so in vain, since it will never gladden the eyes or the spirit of a *single* living soul. But what amiable egotism it is for us to call such an existence pointless! I, too, must suffer this unfair condemnation, because those positive virtues of mine mentioned above remain similarly pointless. My entire person might be so as well, if I were not lucky enough to be of some use to my own servants, along with the odd innkeeper and post coachman, simply because I pay them every day. And to you, good Julie (at least so I flatter myself), I would be indispensible on other grounds.

So my life on this earth is not completely in vain, and since I harm no one—income without expenditures, so to speak—my accounts are still fairly well balanced.

I wandered around town all day today, starting at the York Minster, a cathedral that, in size and richness of decor, is quite comparable to the one in Milan. Its builder—that is, the person who initiated its construction—was Archbishop Scrope, a Shakespearean figure who was beheaded as a rebel in 1405 on the orders of Henry IV. He is buried in the church, and in the adjoining chapterhouse is a table covered with a four hundred-year-old tapestry that once belonged to him and is embroidered all over with his coat-of-arms. The tapestry is still in reasonably good condition. The cathedral windows are mostly of old stained glass (a great rarity in England), although here and there replaced by new ones. All the stonework is superb, executed with the refinement and delicacy of wood carving and depicting all kinds of foliage, animals, angels, and potentates. Of the two main windows at either end of the nave, one is at least seventy-five feet high and thirty-two wide.[3] The strange stone tracery of the opposing window represents the vessels of the human heart in bloodred glass. It is an amazing sight. Another large window at the side is remarkable because its glass has been painted in imitation of embroidery and needlework, so that it resembles the patterns of a colorful carpet with no identifiable image. In the choir is an ancient chair where several English kings were crowned. I sat down on it out of curiosity and found it very comfortable, for stone. It is no doubt still more pleasant when one is about to be crowned!

Next to the cathedral is a very pretty library in Gothic style, its organization particularly efficient. The cases and shelves are numbered, the first with Roman, the second with Arabic numerals. Every book has three numbers glued onto its spine so that it can be found in an instant: at the top is the number of the case, then that of the shelf, and at the bottom the book's unique number. These numerals do not deface the books at all, for they appear in the center of small labels that look like golden suns. An open spiral staircase in the corner leads to a gallery that runs around the room about midway up the shelves. All the volumes are covered by light cardboard, an excellent way to protect them from dust. These covers are folded at the ends and attached to the bookcase so they need be raised only a little when a book is removed. The books themselves are loosely sheathed in lavender paper and shelved very loosely. The alphabetical catalog is arranged as follows:

FORMAT	LETTER C	EDITION	SHELF	COMPARTMENT	NUMBER
8	Cosmo, &c.	Verona 1519	II	7	189–192
4	Cavendish	London 1802	I	5	52–55
Folio	Colley	London 1760	XI	3	1080–1082
12	Corneille	Paris 1820	X	6	920–930

This is especially suitable for a smallish book collection, and because I know from experience what a difficult business it is to organize a library and how many different approaches there are, I wanted to outline it for you. Another good arrangement is the presence of stands for books in regular or frequent use, so they will not be left lying around. These are in the form of a divided container with raised edges where volumes can be placed on both sides.

The library's Gothic windows, although modern, are good imitations of those in the church. The way the glass is set in continuous, overlapping circles of lead is exceedingly attractive. The fireplace and its surroundings are also in the form of a Gothic window, a novel idea of long ago.

I was not able to see any of the rare books or manuscripts, because the librarian was absent. But in one corner, I did find a curious picture of the grand procession at the Duke of Marlborough's funeral. It is almost unbelievable how changed the dresses and customs are since his time. The ancient verger who showed me around said he remembered seeing similar soldiers with long bagwigs when he was a boy.

About a quarter of an hour from the cathedral, on a hill bordering the town, are the romantic ruins of St Mary's Abbey, densely overgrown with trees and draped with ivy. Someone came up with the unfortunate idea of erecting a public building on the same hill, right beside the ruins. The foundations are already being dug and have turned up some of the most beautiful remains of the old abbey, as well preserved as if they were carved yesterday. I saw a number of magnificent capitals still in the ground, and there were some exquisite bas-reliefs to be seen in a neighboring house, where they had been moved during the excavations. We then crossed the river Ouse in a small boat and continued our walk along the top of the old city wall, a picturesque although near-impassable route. The surrounding countryside is exceedingly fresh and green, and the many Gothic towers and churches add variety to the vistas. After fifteen minutes we reached the Micklegate. Its ancient barbican was recently demolished, but the rest remains intact. Above the entrance, the colorful, gilded coats-of-arms of York and England gleamed in the sun with a chivalric luster.

Fifteen years ago a Roman tomb was discovered in a nearby field, and the owner of the land who found it now charges visitors to view it in his cellar. The vault of Roman brick is as fresh as can be, and anatomists have claimed that the skeleton in the stone coffin beneath it, which has turned dark brown over time, is that of a young woman. It says a lot that after two thousand years she still retains some of her beauty—magnificent teeth and an ideal phrenological skull, for example. I carefully examined its organs and found the most desirable attributes—indeed I deeply regretted meeting her two thousand years too late, since I might have married her! I'll certainly never find a better-organized cranium. She does not appear to have been wealthy, for just two glass phials were found in her stone coffin, although these are remarkable objects in themselves—perfectly preserved and of glass amazingly similar to our own, the likes of which have not been found before, so far as I know, anywhere but in Pompeii. The glass itself differs from ours only in its silvery sheen and, most strikingly, has no mark indicating that it was blown. We have not been able to conceal such marks in any of our uncut glass. The London museum has already offered the owner a large sum for these exceptional phials, but he finds it more profitable to charge strangers about a thaler for a look at the rarities.

Once we got back to the Micklegate, we continued with even more difficulty along the crumbling city wall until we reached, after a half hour's clambering, the beautiful ruin called Clifford's Tower. This ancient keep had a role in English history. Among other things, a thousand Jews but one were burned to death there;[4] today Rothschild would have rescued them. Finally, a hundred years ago, when the tower was being used as a gunpowder magazine, it exploded. Its remains have since been eaten away by Saturn, ancient and ravenous; yet time not only tears down, it also rebuilds. Thus the collapsed ruins were embraced once more by thick tresses of ivy, the nesting place of thousands of sparrows; and in the center of the high tower stands a stately nut tree, its crown already rising many feet above the roofless walls. The ruin stands on a hill supposedly first constructed by the Romans. Recently a man dug a shaft to a considerable depth in search of treasure, only to find that the base of the hill consisted almost entirely of the bones of men and horses. This is how the earth is everywhere—a vast grave and a vast cradle!

From ruins and death, I moved on to the living dead languishing at the foot of the tower: the poor prisoners in the county jail. From the outside their lodgings look palatial. But things are different inside, and I felt deep sympathy for the miserable devils who, merely *on suspicion*, must sit here in admittedly clean but still gruesomely cold, damp cells for the entire winter until the month of March, all the while enjoying the pleasant prospect of being hanged. If by some chance they are acquitted, they will get no compensation! In the courtyard where the debtors are allowed to walk around, two horses, a doe, and an ass were grazing alongside them. In all the rooms and cells I visited, I saw the same commendable order and cleanliness. But the strangest aspect of this prison is a kind of thieves' depository, elegantly arranged like the wardrobe room in a theater. A guard, quite befuddled with brandy, stammered out the following account:

"Here you see the wigs of the famous Granby. They disguised him so well he was not nabbed for ten years. Was hanged here in 1786. Here's the fencepost used to batter George Nayler to death two years ago on the road to Doncaster. Offender was hanged here last spring. That's Stephen's 'knockdown'—he used it to kill six people at once. Was also hanged here two years ago. The gigantic leg irons. Nothing else could restrain Kirkpatrick. He escaped from the sturdiest prisons seven times before. But these leg irons, I put them on him myself, they were a bit too heavy for him." (In fact, they were full-blown iron beams that a horse could hardly budge.) "He didn't wear them for long, because two months later, exactly on the first of May, a splendid day, he was dispatched to heaven. Here's the machine Cork used to make counterfeit guineas. Very distinguished gentleman. Hanged 1810."

"Please," I interrupted, "what kind of weapon is this gigantic wooden hammer?"

"Oh," the old fellow smirked, swaying a bit, "that's innocent, tee-hee, that's just my sugar hammer for when I make negus,[5] tee-hee, I just keep it here at the ready."

This depository is located directly next to the guard's own sitting room and appears to be an enthusiast's collection and solely a result of this man's zeal. How varied are the hobbyhorses of men!

I am afraid you are already tired from the lengthy promenade, dear Julie, but you need to follow me just a little bit further; indeed it is an arduous path that will lead us from the depths back up to the very heights. For I wanted to view from above the full amphitheater of my tour thus far, including the splendid York Minster, and for this I chose a most beautifully proportioned Gothic tower. It has elaborate, artistic openwork from top to bottom, and looking at it from a distance through my opera glasses, I had already seen behind the transparent tracery and discovered ladders leading to the top. I longed to climb them.

A sturdy march led us past an old city portal called the Nobles' Gate. It was walled up for fifty years but is now open again to provide access to the new cattle market,[6] itself elegantly and conveniently outfitted with three vaulted aisles for sheep, cattle, and horses. Finally we arrived at the tower, which adorns the oldest church in York.

It was not easy finding the verger, a man covered in soot who looked more like a coal miner than a church attendant, but who was full of goodwill. I asked whether it was possible to go to the top of the tower with its magnificent galleries.

"I don't know," was the response. "I've never been up there myself, though I've been verger for ten years already. There are only old ladders, and a piece is missing higher up. I'd say it's most likely not possible."

This fueled my spirit of adventure, and I immediately sped off to climb the worst, darkest, narrowest, and most decrepit winding staircase imaginable. Before long we reached the ladders, climbed straight up without pausing, and arrived at the first platform. Here, however, the verger and my hired servant thought better of going any farther. A final ladder, tall and very rickety, was missing the occasional rung and, at its top, for about six feet, had no rungs at all. This ascended to a square hole through which one reached the flat roof and the gallery. I did not want to go back having achieved nothing, so I scrambled farther, was quickly at the topmost rung, reached the edge of the opening with my hands, and with some effort succeeded in swinging myself up. The view was truly superb. And just as I had hoped, I achieved my main goal: to see the minster standing free in all its colossal majesty. Whereas from below the view is obstructed by buildings, from here it looms like a great warship surrounded by diminutive skiffs.

The wind, however, was making a fearful roar at this height, and everything around me was in such a state of decay that some of the stone candle brackets in the corners, indeed parts of the gallery itself, had fallen to pieces already, and the stones that remained were splintering like slate. Furthermore, the iron holding them together was so loose and rusted that the entire platform seemed to be swaying in the wind. I found the incessant gale more and more eerie, so I began my descent and found, as always, that going down was far more difficult than going up. I know that if one begins to feel what the English call "nervous," the best and only remedy is to resist discouraging thoughts. Thus, with my back to the ladder, I held firmly onto a beam, lowered myself into the depths, and hanging by my arms and with my legs stretched out like feelers, I diligently searched for the topmost rung . . . and was very glad when I finally gained a foothold. Arrived at the bottom, I was as black as the verger.

Meanwhile it was time for evening services in the minster, where *the greatest organ in England* and well-chosen music promised an interim of relaxation. I quickly made my way there, and for half an hour, engulfed by the power and delicacy of the organ—that tyrant of music, as Heinse calls it[7]—I dreamed away while its tones rolled and roared through the immense spaces, and the voices of lovely children, soft as the breath of spring, calmed my agitated spirit.[8]

Afterward, in the semi-twilight, I visited the town hall, where the lord mayor (only London and York have *lord* mayors) holds court three times a week, and where the trial sessions are held every three months. It is an old and handsome Gothic building. Next to it, newly rebuilt, are two rooms for the upper and lower advocates. In the upper advocates' room the coats-of-arms of all the lord mayors have been set in modern stained-glass windows, for here every tradesman has his own arms. The images alone identify each man's profession: the trader has a ship, the lumber merchant a wooden beam, the shoemaker a cobbler's last, etc. The mottos, however, I found too refined. Most fitting for the three I mentioned would be, for the first, the favorite song of Berlin's street urchins, "Oh fly, my little ship, oh fly!" For the second, "Don't look for the speck in someone else's eye while overlooking the beam in your own."[9] And finally, for the third, "Cobbler, stick to your last!"—though this would be too difficult for a lord mayor![10]

I have now achieved a proper balance, that is, my hands are just as tired from writing as my legs are from walking. It is time to treat my stomach to some work as well. If I were Walter Scott, I would give you the menu, but I do not dare. Instead I think it better to offer a word about my postprandial reading, served up once more by the famous Maintenon.

I was touched by how faithfully the poor woman depicts the sad monotony and bitter constraints of her situation, by how often—heartily, and with unmistakable honesty—she yearns to make her exit from this stage, which, she says, is worse than all others and *lasts from morning till night!* Amid all the splendor and power, she finds death the most desirable escape. It is easy to imagine, after such an endless void, after so many years of sacrificing every personal idiosyncrasy, how one's spirit could be inflicted with a fatal exhaustion and an overwhelming longing for release. This also helps explain why, in a time that was itself infantile, she succumbed to religious mania. If a woman of Madame de Maintenon's intellect had been born later, she would have granted Molinists and Jansenists no more than a contemptuous smile. But in her era it was different. She remains in her way a great woman, just as Louis XIV remains a great king in a minor time that cultivated the minor things, like court, society, etc., much better than we do, precisely because it was minor; a time that remains persistently appealing to poetic dispositions, for these delight in perfection, be it great or small.

September 20th, 1827

I CONTINUED WITH my gleanings this morning and visited the very old church of All Saints', where I found some excellent stained glass.[11] The *condition* of the windows was unfortunately poor, especially a Virgin and Child of such sweetness and beauty that Raphael himself would not have disowned it. In addition I went to the old church of St Mary's, which has a strange stone gate covered with delicate carvings of hieroglyphs and signs of the zodiac.[12] Since I had met the Archbishop of York in London, I wrote him a note yesterday and asked permission to visit him at his villa.[13] He responded very graciously, inviting me to stay a few days. Not feeling inclined, I accepted no more than a dinner invitation for today, and drove there at five o'clock.

I found a splendidly maintained, verdant pleasure ground and a stately Gothic building in an unusually attractive style (Figure 48).[14] The house is not especially large but extremely elegant. At each of the four corners of the flat roof is a colossal eagle with outstretched wings, and instead of heavy battlements, which would seem out of proportion on a building of this moderate scale,

BISHOPTHORPE PALACE,
YORKSHIRE
The Seat of the Archbishop of York

Drawn by J. P. Neale.   Engraved by Radclyffe.

there is a sort of openwork stone arcade serving as a gallery. It runs all around the roof, giving an artistic touch that both lightens and enriches the architecture.

That the interior was just as magnificent as the rest you may imagine, given that the resident is a man with forty thousand pounds of ecclesiastical revenue. The elderly archbishop, still a sprightly man, toured me all around, not omitting his kitchen gardens and hothouses. These are remarkably lovely, especially the gardens, which were adorned throughout with flowers and filled with all kinds of vegetables and fruits. Meanwhile they were as tidy as the most elegant interior room, something our gardeners are incapable of imagining. The hothouses were the same—not a trace of clutter or filth, no boards or tools lying around, no manure next to the walkways, and so forth. Along the walls on both sides, you saw the choicest fruit trees planted in symmetrical rows, including many currant bushes with their small branches removed. They grew as much as twelve feet up the walls and were festooned with clusters of berries the size of small grapes. There was also an abundance of magnificent pineapples and granadillas (a West Indian fruit in the form of a small melon, tasting like a pomegranate) and at each window a different variety of grape. Everything was dense with fruit. The trees against the walls outside were draped with nets that

48

Bishopthorpe Palace.

will eventually be covered with mats, so that ripe fruit can be picked until the end of January. One patch in the garden was still full of ripe strawberries, a special sort that the archbishop assured me would also bear outdoors until January. He pointed out a novel and especially tasty vegetable called Norman cress, which can be cut even in the snow.

A remarkable variety of plants were still in bloom all along the paths and around the vegetable beds. I know, of course, that the climate here is beneficial to gardeners, but they clearly have other advantages in the way they nurture flowers.

In the pleasure ground, I found larches that were not only gigantic but also had foliage as dark as spruces, and their drooping branches spread out a good twenty feet over the grass. I heard here for the first time that it is considered very beneficial to conifers if their branches can touch moist ground, because they are said to absorb a tremendous amount of nourishment that way.

The pleasant evening concluded with a dinner truly worthy of an archbishop. I was, however, struck once again by the peculiar relationship between distinguished English clergymen and their wives. I may have told you already that the wives do not assume their husbands' titles or names, but keep their own as if they were simply girlfriends. In the present case, the archbishop's wife, a lady in her own right, is from a respected family and very charming as well. She has ten sons and three daughters. Only one daughter was at dinner, a girl of about twenty. She had suffered a misfortune, especially rare among women: one of her legs had to be amputated after a fall from a horse. Clothing makes it much easier for a woman than a man to hide such a defect, however, and I did not notice any awkwardness in her gait until I was informed of it.

Scarborough, September 21st, 1827

I FORGOT TO tell you a funny story that was related yesterday at dinner, certainly the most notable example of distraction you have ever heard (apart from the self-decapitating Irishman).[15] Lord Seaford told how his uncle, the old Earl of Warwick, who was already famous for his absent-mindedness, traveled one evening from Warwick Castle to London on important business, settled it to his satisfaction the next day, and returned home that night. When he arrived back at Warwick, he fainted. Everyone was frightened and asked his valet whether his master had been sick already in London. "No," was the answer, "he was fine. But I believe, God forgive me, that the whole time he was away, he completely forgot to eat!" This was, in fact, the case, and a bowl of soup was immediately administered to His Lordship, quickly putting everything back in order.

I am writing you from a seaside resort that is considered very romantic, although I cannot confirm this because it was pitch black when I arrived. I anticipate the most beautiful view tomorrow morning, however, for I am installed on the fourth floor, the entire inn being fully occupied.

On my way here I visited Castle Howard, which belongs to Lord Carlisle. This is one of the English showplaces, though it did not appeal to me in the slightest. The castle was designed by Sir Vanbrugh, the architect from the time of Louis XIV who built Blenheim in the same bad French style. Blenheim, however, is impressive because of its mass, whereas Castle Howard is neither impressive nor charming. In fact, the entire park has something extremely sad, stiff, and desolate about it. On one hill, there is a large temple—the family burial vault. The coffins are distributed all around in cells, most of them still empty, so that the interior resembles a beehive, though admittedly quieter! The castle does house some beautiful paintings and antiques. The

so-called *Three Maries* by Annibale Carracci is especially famous (Figure 49). It shows the dead Christ and behind him, his mother Mary collapsed in a faint. His grandmother Mary rushes up with a gesture of lamentation, and Mary Magdalene inclines over the body in a posture of despair. The gradations from death to mere unconsciousness, the restrained sorrow of age and fervent despair of youth, are rendered with laudable veracity. Every limb of Christ's body looks truly dead; you can see that this motionless, cold, and stiff form has expired forever. Meanwhile the lovely Magdalene is full of movement and life, even her hair; everything is vital energy and abundance, aroused by the most bitter misery.[16]

49

The Dead Christ Mourned
("The Three Maries")

Opposite this hangs a self-portrait by Annibale, whose features are very striking; he looks more like a highwayman than an artist. What would have appealed most to you, dear Julie, was a collection of drawings from the time of Francis I that includes fifty to sixty portraits of all the ladies and gentlemen of the court. They are painted memoirs. One of the antiques I found amusing was a Capitoline goose in bronze, which you could almost hear squawking as it stretched out its wings and opened its beak.[17] A portrait of Henry VIII by Holbein, in excellent condition, is also worth mentioning. Otherwise nothing struck me particularly. The well-known St John by Domenichino is also here, allegedly the original, but unless I am wrong, the real one is in Germany.[18]

The park, planted in large, stiff masses, has a plethora of gateways. I passed through seven, believe it or not, before reaching the castle. And not far from the house, I saw a large stone bridge with five or six arches leading over a muddy pond, yet there is no way across! It serves only as a prospect. To make sure you are perfectly aware of this, not a single shrub has been planted next to or in front of it. Apparently the grounds have remained just as they were laid out 120 years ago, with all their allées, quincunxes, etc. Obelisks and pyramids have sprung up like mushrooms everywhere, and each view offers one of them as a fixed terminus. At least one pyramid is useful, for it serves as an inn!

September 22nd, 1827

IF PEOPLE OFTEN die of colds and consumption in England, it is due more to their habits than the climate. Walking on wet grass is their favorite pastime, and you can hardly bear the drafts in most public rooms because of the open windows; even when closed they are seldom airtight and never double, so the wind whistles right through them. The climate itself, however beneficial for the vegetation, is awful for the population. This morning at nine o'clock, I rode out on a hired horse in the most beautiful weather and under the clearest sky; but I had barely been gone an hour when a horrific cloudburst soaked me through and through. I finally reached a village, where in despair at not finding even a gateway for shelter, I noticed a room at ground level with its door open, leapt from my horse, went directly in, and found two ancient women cooking something over a fire. In England everything domestic is held so sacred that any man entering a strange room without taking care to announce himself first and ask for permission will arouse fear and indignation. Thus, even though the cause of my intrusion was streaming fairly obviously from my hat and clothes, I was not offered a very warm welcome by the old ladies, whose station can have been no higher than the wife of a cobbler or carpenter. However, nothing can capture the helpless outrage of my hostesses *malgré elles* when my hired steed, whose wisdom would have done honor to Nestor, made his own way in through the door and, before anyone could stop him, went to stand by the fireplace. Totally serene and proper and with a mischievously dumb look, he began drying his ears by the flames. The two old witches were apoplectic with fury, and I with laughter. I ought to have dragged the animal back outside, but I felt too sorry for my poor comrade, and the women did not dare lay a hand on him. They continued scolding and storming around, while I did my best to appease them with sweet words and a shilling. In the end we travelers remained contentedly inside, half by pleading, half by force, until we were somewhat dried out and the squall had passed.

The drying was of little help, for as we entered the romantic Forge Valley, the storm and rain began to rage anew. This time I surrendered to my fate, having no means of protection, and

THE CLIFF BRIDGE, AT SCARBOROUGH

consoled myself with the beauty of the surroundings: a luxuriant wood blanketed a deep, narrow valley, through which a frothy torrent was carving its path. A comfortable road ran alongside the stream, where I noticed a simple and attractive idea for enclosing a spring: nothing more than two large blocks of stone placed upright, with a third, still larger, laid over them crosswise, creating a portal through which the bubbling water can gush on its way.

    To fend off a cold, I took a bath in warm seawater as soon as I got home and then proceeded to the "sand" (the part of the beach that is uncovered at low tide), where I undertook a very peculiar outing. Large numbers of saddle horses and carriages stand there ready for hire, and you can ride for miles at the very edge of the waves over ground as soft as velvet. The old Castle of Scarborough on one side and a splendid iron bridge connecting two hills on the other heighten the picturesqueness of the scene (Figure 50). Afterward, in the glow of the evening sun, I rode up to the castle, an imposing ruin with a magnificent view. This is where Gaveston, Edward II's favorite (I described his grave in my first tour of the countryside) was captured by the Earl of Warwick, who immediately took him to his own castle to be executed.

50

Scarborough and Bridge.

At the top of the ruin is an iron container constructed like a woven basket, which functions as a beacon. A large barrel of tar is placed in it, set on fire, and left to burn on high, its flames blazing throughout the night. The castle stands on a cliff projecting far into the sea and rising perpendicularly to a height of a hundred and fifty or two hundred feet. Atop the cliff is a lovely meadow that stretches all around the castle.

September 23rd, 1827

TODAY'S EXCURSION TOOK me along the coast to Filey, a fishing village, where nature herself has built a celebrated bridge of rocks right into the water. The same hired nag that I rode yesterday—a mare—pulled me today in a fairly decent gig. The sea was a beautiful blue and dotted with sails. I hired a guide at Filey and hurried across the firm sand toward the bridge. We passed by many strangely shaped rocks and now and then saw fish lying in the full sun on their pointed tops, obviously stranded by the ebb tide and subsequently roasted alive. I found many hollows in the stones filled with innumerable small mussels that from a distance resembled balls of clay. The bridge itself is just a wide reef that extends about a half mile into the sea. The separate boulders are strange, tossed in a confusion of fantastic formations, and you must be very careful not to slide off their slippery edges. The tide was already coming in and had covered part of the reef. After taking a good look at everything, I scrambled rather arduously back up the rocky bank so I could return by the upper route, and then followed a pleasant meadow path that soon led me to the nearby inn where my gig was waiting.

Flamborough Head, September 24th, 1827, evening

DISTANCES ARE CALCULATED differently in England than at home.[19] Today my respectable equine matron brought me here quite comfortably, twenty-three miles, in two hours. As soon as I arrived, I hired another horse to go seven miles farther to the lighthouse and cavern for which Flamborough Head is known. The weather was gorgeous, though very windy, so this time I hoped to stay dry; I was very, very disappointed. I had just reached the cliffs when I encountered not only the obligatory cloudburst but also a violent storm as an extra bonus. At least it was a pleasant change this time, for the thunder and lightning were most impressive when viewed from the top of chalk cliffs rising perpendicularly above a raging sea. The customs officer who was accompanying me (these people are stationed next to the lighthouse) had very obligingly brought along an umbrella, since I was protected by no more than a light jacket. But the gale did not allow me to make use of it on the slippery and perilous path above the abyss. The sea has eroded and undermined the chalk cliffs so thoroughly that many tower-like pillars stand isolated in the waves, making their blinding whiteness even more dazzling against the black sky. They look like giant sea spirits wrapped in shrouds. There are also many large and small caves that you can enter at low tide without getting your shoes wet. But it was now high tide, and I was only able to reach the largest cave by taking advantage of a fishing boat that happened to be waiting there. Stimulated by the fresh breeze, I valiantly lent a hand in the rowing, which I attempted this morning for the very first time, and found the exercise so pleasant that I intend to repeat it as often as I can. Meanwhile the sea was so rough that I thought we were in danger and said this to the fisherman.

"Oh, sir! Do you think that just because I'm a humble fisherman, my life is less sweet to me than yours is to you? As far as the mouth of the cave, there is no danger, but we can't venture inside today."

I was only able to cast a few glances into the cavern's monstrous gateway, where the sea foam was churning in all directions and swirling up like smoke amid the howling waves. Afterward, because the fisherman assured me that no one could catch a cold from seawater, I dipped my wet limbs once more into the green salty flood, then mounted my horse and rode to the lighthouse. It was all the more interesting to me because I had only an imperfect notion of how these towers were constructed. At the top is a glass cap like in an orangery and in the middle are twenty-one lamps fastened around an iron pole that continually revolves at a slow pace, driven by a kind of clock mechanism. All the lamps are outfitted with large reflectors, heavily plated with silver on the inside and kept extremely clean and polished. In addition, seven of these are fronted by a piece of red glass made in Newcastle and almost the equal of old ruby glass. This has the function of altering the light from the tower, so that it appears in the distance sometimes as red, sometimes white, which means the ships can easily distinguish it from other lights. The lamps run on oil as pure as wine, and there is always a whole cellar stockpiled with barrels of it. Just in case, the entire apparatus exists in duplicate, so a damaged part can be replaced on the spot in case of an accident. The lamps are arranged in two tiers on top of each other, with twelve below and nine above. I noticed a special table where the lamps are polished, and it seemed very practical for avoiding any breakage of glass. The upper surface is of sheet iron, with many niches and holes next to each other where the glass can be inserted. On the lower surface is a coal fire. This serves a double purpose, for the sheets of glass can be placed there quickly and safely and will not break easily, since the sheet metal is always kept slightly warm.

I have found an opportunity to dispatch this letter to the embassy in London, which allows me to divide up my travel account. So I will close for now, always with the proviso—like Scheherazade—of beginning again tomorrow.

Therefore, *sans adieu.*

Your Lou

Whitby, September 25th, 1827

*P*RECIOUS JULIE,

I slept rather late after yesterday's fatiguing tour and did not leave Scarborough until two o'clock. Given the many mountains, the road to Whitby is difficult and the countryside peculiar. Not a shrub nor a house, not a wall nor a fence to be seen anywhere. Nothing but endlessly undulating hills, often in strange formations, like piles of waste deposited in a regular pattern. They are thickly overgrown with heather; up close you can see the most beautiful blossoms of purple and rosy red, but at a distance the same drab, reddish brown hue spreads over the whole landscape, promising grouse hunters, at least, a rich harvest. There is no variation in the view except for many white spots moving slowly back and forth. And what are these? Thousands of moorland sheep,[1] very shy, most with black faces and wool so coarse that poodles and Pomeranians seem soft and silky in comparison. An hour outside of Whitby, as you descend again from the barren hills, the landscape gradually improves and becomes very romantic near the town. Meanwhile English cleanliness and prettiness are less and less evident. Whitby looks like an old German *Stadt*—narrow streets, no *trottoirs*, and just as dirty, though with more congenial inhabitants.

It is unlikely that many strangers of any sort ever visit this wretched place, or perhaps I was taken for someone else. In any case, the people laid siege to me as if I were some weird and wonderful animal. I could not go anywhere without an escort of a hundred souls surging around me with great good nature, but also intrusively, even trying to examine me from head to toe. It made me think of a funny anecdote that the Duke of Leeds told me recently. He is known for his affability toward his subjects and tenants, and one day when he was out riding, one of them came up to him and asked if he might request a favor. Permission was granted, and the man confessed that his twelve-year-old son had been plaguing him day and night to be allowed to see the duke, and since his cottage was nearby, perhaps the duke might allow his son a glimpse of him. The duke gave his smiling consent, went to the cottage, and the delighted father fetched his inquisitive offspring. But the lad had scarcely dashed up when he came to a standstill before this elderly and rather plain gentleman, whose greatness and power he had so often heard proclaimed. The boy contemplated the duke for some time, touched him, and then suddenly asked, "Can you swim?"

"No, my good lad."

"Can you fly?"

"No, I cannot do that either."

"Then, I swear, I like father's drake better, for he can do both."

Whitby has a harbor surrounded by picturesque rocks, with a handsome granite breakwater extending far into the sea and giving you a splendid view of the town. Especially beautiful

Whitby Abbey, Yorkshire.

51

Whitby Abbey.

are the famous ruins of the abbey atop the steep rocky cliff (Figure 51). Founded in the sixth century by a king of Northumbria, the property now belongs to a private individual who does absolutely nothing to maintain it. His cattle graze in the crumbled remains of this noble monument of ancient grandeur, depositing so much filth and muck that you can hardly inspect it from up close. I ascended by the light of the young moon and was captivated by the romantic effect. Enormous columns rise into the air as lightly as slender fir trees; long rows of windows are still well preserved; and much of the exquisite ornamentation is as unscathed as if the first autumn wind were just now sweeping through the vaults. Yet other parts were utterly transformed by time, and many a hideous mask grimaced in the moonlight like death's head. Next to the abbey stands an even older church that is still in use.[2] It is surrounded by a burial ground containing thousands of gravestones thickly covered in moss.

I am staying in a rustic but excellent inn run by two sisters, whose eagerness to please arises not from self-interest, but from authentic good nature. When I asked for something to read, they brought me the chronicle of Whitby, and I leafed through it while a storm raged outside, the wind whistling as eerily as it does in our good palace of Muskau. The chronicle records a seventh-century appraisal of the land, in which Whitby and its properties, now worth perhaps a million pounds sterling, are estimated at sixty shillings—that is, three pounds sterling![3]

I also learned that this large and magnificent abbey had not been ravaged by fire or sword, but had succumbed to a quieter destructive force: when he broke with the pope, Henry VIII confiscated this monastery along with all the others and proceeded to sell everything down to the individual stones of the buildings. Luckily, after several houses in town had been built out of material taken from the abbey, the ancestor of the current owner purchased what remained, which has ever since been left untouched.

Guisborough—Evening

I HAD WRITTEN a letter to Lord Mulgrave, who owns a beautiful mansion and park as well as a large alum works along the coast near Whitby, asking if I might tour these places. He sent me not only a very polite response but also a groom on horseback to accompany me everywhere. This only intensified the bothersome crowds in the town, so an hour later the local magistrate paid me the compliment of sending along two associates, who were also secretaries of the museum, which they offered to show me. I was happy to accept, for the museum is noteworthy for its collection of fossils uncovered in the vicinity. Half the town had reassembled and followed us with an *arrière garde* of boisterous youths. A large crowd of dignitaries was also in attendance, as well as a bevy of inquisitive ladies, so I was obliged every other minute to turn my eyes from their alluring gazes in order to look at a crocodile, ancient whale's tooth, or petrified fish. The two secretaries divided up the curiosities: one presented the fish and amphibians; the other the quadrupeds, birds, and minerals. Both were so eager for me to not miss anything that when one embarked on a disquisition to delight me with something from *his* domain, the other would interrupt him. At first this was amusing, but it finally became arduous, for while A was holding me firmly by the left arm, declaring: "This is the famous little crocodile found petrified in the stomach of a boa constrictor, and here the yet more famous, six-yard long . . . ," B would grab me by the right arm, turn me around, and draw my attention to cloaks made of parrot feathers or the tattooed head of a New Zealander, whose skin had been pulled over his ears and tanned like leather. Meanwhile a few dilettantes pressed zealously forward to point out yet more curiosities. I would have needed Argus's hundred eyes to see everything at once. What interested me most was an Eskimo canoe complete with fishing apparatus that Parry had donated. Made of nothing but whalebone and sealskin, it was so light that you can scarcely imagine trusting yourself to it on the sea. Although rather long, it is barely *one foot* across at the widest point in the middle and closed like a box, even on the top, except for a single round hole in the center, where the Eskimo sits and keeps himself upright with a double oar in the shape of a balancing pole. A kind of spade from the South Sea Islands was so beautifully carved that no London artist could have done better. The petrifactions of all kinds, of both existing and antediluvian animals and plants, are extraordinarily numerous and beautiful, and the nearly complete petrified crocodile is certainly unique of its kind.

Another unusual thing was a conglomerate built up many years ago from the runoff of a nearby coal mine and preserved inside a square wooden gutter. It bore a continuous alteration of stripes, six black and one yellow, like a slice of Baumkuchen.[4] This came about because on

Drawn by J.Jackson R.A.   Engraved by J.C.Allen.

MULGRAVE CASTLE.

weekdays, when the mine was working, the runoff from the coal was black; but on Sundays, the day of rest, the water, which contains lot of ochre, flowed in its natural yellow color. This alternation continued with extreme regularity for seven weeks and, now polished, forms a very nice pattern.

The gentlemen insisted on bringing me back to my inn, along with my customary entourage. When I drove on from there, a formidable "Hurrah!" rang out, and several of the younger people of both sexes refused to abandon me until their lungs could no longer keep pace with the horses. I then proceeded slowly along the sandy beach toward the alum works with Lord Mulgrave's servant leading the way. I went for a while on foot and entertained myself by collecting the little stones that covered the shore, some of them dazzling in both color and form. After an hour we reached the mine, which is very romantically situated between steep cliffs next to the sea. I examined everything very closely, as you will see from my enclosed letter to the director of our own alum works.

In order to get from there to the quarries, I had to go back along a path that seemed made only for goats. The overseer had already alerted me to its difficulties. In places it was scarcely a foot wide, and on one side was a smoothly worked alum cliff two hundred feet high. Many such footpaths have been cut through these rocks as places for the workers to stand while they hew away at the exposed ore. This presents the strangest spectacle you can imagine. The men seem to be hanging onto the wall like swallows and must often be pulled up there by ropes. In the valley below, large railway carts stand ready to carry off all the ore that clatters down incessantly from the heights. It took me three hours to see everything, after which I drove to the house, where I was treated to a fine luncheon by Lord Mulgrave's sons (the earl himself was ill with gout). The young men then toured me through the beautiful park. Its loveliness is bestowed entirely by nature, and many miles of carefully planned roadways guide you to its rocks, brooks, and thickly wooded ravines.[5] At the house I looked from under high oaks and beeches across a gently sloping lawn, down to the nearby sea flecked with a hundred sails (Figure 52).

A major ornament of the park is the Old Castle, a ruin believed to have begun as a Roman fort, which then became the castle of the Saxon prince Wada. It was later given to an ancestor of the present family by King John as a reward for the murder of the young prince so movingly described by Shakespeare;[6] its origins are therefore both bloody and romantic, and the view from the weathered battlements is suitably wild and picturesque.

In the new palace, built fifty years ago in the Gothic style, I was struck by the portrait of a great-grandmother of the present earl. She must have been an enticing and eccentric woman, for she is shown in deep mourning, yet sits at a window with a smile on her face. The painting bears an inscription in antiquated English:

> Since the Count of Anglesey died with no remorse to confess,
> I admit I mourn him solely by the blackness of my dress.[7]

The youngest son—whose family name, Phipps, does not sound very pleasant to our ears[8]—told me that a strange event took place ten years ago on the slate cliffs that plunge into the sea nearby. Two girls were sitting on the slope with their backs to the sea, talking earnestly to one another. At that moment, a sharp piece of slate accidentally broke loose high above them and, reaching lightning speed as the fall increased its velocity, decapitated one of the girls so cleanly that her head rolled some distance onto the sand, while her body remained quietly seated. The parents still live in the village.

Ripon, September 27th, 1827

I SLEPT THROUGH the night in my carriage, ate breakfast in the flower garden of a pleasant inn, and then hurried to Studley Park, home to the famous ruins of Fountains Abbey, considered the largest and most beautiful in England (Figure 53). They far surpassed my expectations, as did the park. Therefore I want to describe everything to you in order.

The road leads first along a slope through a majestic forest, then makes an abrupt turn and enters a long, meadowed valley, perhaps three or four hundred feet wide, with a small river, interrupted by various natural waterfalls, flowing down its center. On one side of the valley is an impressive ridge of hills covered with mature ashes, beeches, and oak; on the other is a rugged wall of rock, swathed in vines and likewise crowned with ancient trees. The valley's end is terminated across its entire width by the abbey's ruins and lofty tower. You can easily imagine the vastness of these remains when you realize that the abbey buildings once covered fifteen acres of ground, and the ruins still cover four. The nave of the church, with most of its walls still standing, is 351 feet long; the large window across from the altar is 50 feet wide; and the tower, although partly

53
Fountains Abbey.

collapsed, is 166 feet tall. The architecture of the twelfth and thirteenth century, the best period, is as simple as it is sublime (Figure 54). A gate leads from the church to the vaulted double arcade of the west range, 300 feet long and 42 wide. A second gate leads to the cloister garden, which the present owners have transformed into a flower garden; surrounding this are other picturesque ruins, namely, those of the library, court, and chapter house. The vaulted ceiling of the latter, as in the refectory in Malbork,[9] is supported by a single pillar in the center. In the kitchen, on the other hand, one admires vaulting of such low profile as to be nearly flat. It is constructed with consummate skill and without any support at all. Next to this is the magnificent refectory, 108 feet long and 45 wide, rightly the highlight of an abbey infamous for its high living and debauchery.

You can still see many tombs in the church: one of Lord Mowbray in full chain mail, carved in stone; those of several abbots; and finally an empty stone casket in which Hotspur Percy is supposed to have been buried.[10] High above you is a well-preserved angel with the date 1283 distinctly legible below it. And at the top of the tower, floating in the air, you see a Latin inscription in gigantic Gothic letters that proclaims, beautifully and fittingly, "Honor and glory to God alone!"[11]

Curtains of ivy and creeping vines drape the entire ruin, while here and there the branches of majestic trees sway above the walls. The river meanders alongside and a few steps farther on

South Transept of Fountains Abbey, Yorkshire.

drives the old abbey mill wheel, which is still in use, as if to instruct us that when grandeur and majesty have passed away, the useful perseveres in its modest fashion.

About two hundred paces behind the abbey is the old dwelling of the owner, which was built in the sixteenth century out of fallen stones from the ruin (Figure 55).[12] This, too, is extremely picturesque, although of a far less noble style. Within its walled gardens are tall, pruned yew hedges and well-ordered flower beds, and the intermingling of the timeworn and nascent offers delightful scope to the imagination. The yews may well be the most ancient in England. One of them, thought to be about a thousand years old, is thirty feet in circumference at its thickest point. On a wall of the house are statues of two old knights, looted from the abbey, and between them is a modern inscription that probably alludes to these figures: *Sic transit Gloria mundi*.[13]

Fountains Abbey, too, owes its downfall to the dissolution of the monasteries under Henry VIII. Within half an hour of leaving it, you come to a magnificent and very finely tended pleasure ground, which is particularly attractive because of the alteration of hills and vales, gorgeous trees,

54

South Transept of Fountains Abbey.

South West View of Fountains Hall, near the Abbey, Yorkshire
Belonging to Miss Lawrence of Studley Royal.

55

*South West View of
Fountains Hall.*

and well-arranged groups of plantings. Its somewhat antiquated layout is otherwise excessively cluttered by too many summerhouses, temples, and leaden statues of no merit. In one of these temples, dedicated to the ancient gods, there is a bust of none other than Nero! It would be easy to fix these minor flaws, however, whereas the many beauties of the natural setting are almost never to be found in such bounteous combination. At the end of the game park is the house of the proprietress, who at sixty-seven is still an old maid despite an income of four hundred and fifty thousand pounds. I encountered her in the garden, and she invited me to lunch, which I accepted with pleasure, since my outing had made me quite hungry. I found six more old maids and a law-yer there, as well as a young officer of the Hussars who seemed to be the *coq en pâte*.[14]

But to return to the ruins (I mean the abbey, not the old maids), if I were to indulge my crit-ical vein, I might find fault with one thing: that in contrast to the ruins at Whitby, which are given too little care, these are *too well* maintained. Not a single loose stone lies on the ground, which is kept carefully mowed and as smooth as a carpet. And the flower beds in the old cloister garden are too modern. If this poetic edifice were mine, I would quickly employ whatever artificial

LETTERS OF A DEAD MAN

means I could to make it look wild and overgrown, because the greatest enchantment for the imagination resides in half-decayed grandeur.

When I got back to Ripon, I visited the old cathedral, another beautiful relic. There are elaborate carvings in the choir, and in a subterranean crypt is a kind of catacomb decked out with bones and skulls. Here, in keeping with my hobby, I spent considerable time in phrenological investigations. Among the remains was a skull so strikingly similar to mine that even the aged verger noticed it. Who might the old boy have been? Perhaps I myself in another guise? Nobody could inform me about the origins of this ossuary, but I was told about the truly French-looking skull of an emigrant priest that the verger himself had smuggled in. This head still appeared quite talkative and charming, as if he were about to say, "Monsieur, j'ai l'honneur de vous présenter mes respects, vous êtes trop poli de venir nous rendre visite. Nous avons si rarement l'occasion de causer ici!"[15] That it was a well-bred skull was apparent at first glance. My likeness, in contrast, looked meditative and taciturn. It would certainly be bizarre if, without knowing it, one found oneself standing in front of one's own bones like this!

Harrogate, September 28th, 1827

THIS SPA IS set up quite like ours and has a more convivial atmosphere than is generally found in English establishments. People congregate at tea, at the communal dining table, or while drinking the waters, and therefore get to know each other more easily. The place consists of two villages, both of them cheerful and attractive, and the surrounding area is beautiful and fertile. Unfortunately the weather right now is horrible, since the rain refuses to let up. Meanwhile the sulfur water I drank early this morning made me so sick that I have not been able to leave my room. In such a condition, the English vogue for having the sitting room on the ground floor and the bedroom always two or three stories up is awkward at best. It is twice as unbearable if you are availing yourself of waters that serve their purpose vigorously throughout the day.

September 29th, 1827

ALTHOUGH THESE WATERS still disagree with me, today I went to the end of the world. It is just a short promenade from here, since World's End is nothing but a nearby village with a pretty view into, I suppose, the beginning of the world. After all, given that the world is round, you can make any spot you like into the beginning or the end. At the communal table, I ran into an acquaintance and dined with him and seventy other people. Although the Season is more or less over, there are still about a thousand visitors here, mostly of the middle classes, since Harrogate is not one of the fashionable watering places, although to *me* it seems far more pleasant than the extremely fashionable Brighton.

My neighbor at dinner, an old general of eighty, was very entertaining. He had known Frederick the Great, Kaunitz, Emperor Joseph, Mirabeau, and even Napoleon in various capacities, and related interesting details about them all. Beyond this he had been governor of Surinam and Mauritius, had long served as a commander in India, and was now what we call a *General der Infanterie*, second to a field marshal. All this would mean a high rank at home. In England it grants very little status, something he himself commented on: "Here the aristocracy is everything. Without a family of good repute, without relatives in the upper nobility who can push him ahead, a man may attain a high rank in the army, but except in very special circumstances, he will never be someone of renown."

"I am a baronet," he added, "an empty hereditary title, yet it grants me more status and regard than my high military rank; and I am not called general or, as with you, *Euer Excellenz,* but Sir Charles." ("Sir" is the title of a baronet.)

After dinner the company gathered for tea, followed by a little ball.

Leeds, October 1st, 1827

I STAYED SO long in Harrogate mainly because I was waiting for letters from you, having given that address to Lottum. And today one appeared! I discovered it when I got back from my walk, and you can imagine how happy it made me! I fancied myself with you in Dresden, and I drank your health before the illuminated letters of your signature. It is in keeping with my natural eccentricity that, although I spent four years garrisoned in Dresden,[16] I saw neither Pillnitz nor Moritzburg. I thus found your description of the latter, with its portrait of the old *Landvogt,* particularly interesting.

You scold me for preferring to write rather than speak about certain things, and on the whole you are right. But this particular affair and all pleading are so contrary to my nature that I can only speak awkwardly and badly, and it is therefore always better for me to write. It makes failure not so unpleasant. But back to my journey.

The number of magnificent estates in England is almost beyond calculation. One must concentrate on the most important, such as Harewood Park, a lovely residence that I found about ten miles down the road from Harrogate (Figure 56). The grounds were laid out by Brown a hundred years ago on the kind of terrain I have always wanted for myself: namely, a natural wood with ravines, rocks, a forest stream with abundant water, and atop a hill, the ruins of an old castle, all set in the most fertile countryside with distant views of the Cumberland mountains. The great master made superb use of these elements, built a magnificent palace in a noble, classical style on one of the hills, and in the valley before it, expanded the small river into a broad lake, thus giving the palace a totally delightful view into the secluded park on one side and the far distance and verdant countryside on the other.

For me the scene was particularly animated, since just as I drove across the front of the house, its owner, Lord Harewood, was returning from a fox hunt and could be seen descending a slope and advancing across the meadow with his pack of a hundred hounds, his red-coated *piqueurs,* and a number of spirited horses. I could not avoid going to meet him and explaining my presence. I found a tall, handsome man who looked extraordinarily likeable, still young and vigorous in figure and manner, yet in years already a man of sixty-five (which one has to be told to believe). He welcomed me with the utmost courtesy, said he had already had the pleasure of seeing me several times in London (I didn't know what he was talking about), and begged my permission to personally show me around the park. However much I tried to decline, given his fatigue from the fox hunt (during which one generally rides twenty-five miles at a gallop and in the process makes fifty or sixty jumps over hedges and ditches), my resistance was in vain. The old man accompanied me uphill and down through most of his princely domain. Most interesting, being new to me, was the kennel. There I found a hundred and fifty dogs in two capacious, very clean rooms, each outfitted with a large bed sleeping seventy-five dogs, and each room with

HAREWOOD HOUSE.

its own enclosure in front. You could not detect the slightest offensive smell or notice the tiniest bit of filth. In each enclosure, there is a raised trough with running water, and a servant is present all day long, armed with a broom and constantly sluicing water over the ground. The dogs themselves are fully trained, docile, and never sully their beds or rooms. Feeding them properly is a real art. In order to maintain endurance, they must be lean and yet powerfully muscled. This is consistently the case; nowhere could you find prettier animals than these slim, obedient, spirited hounds. Half of them had just returned from the hunt and, although resting on their colossal communal bed, did not look at all tired. They wagged their tails and looked very friendly, while the other half bounded around in their enclosure.

The stables form a quadrangle about a thousand yards from the palace and were also very beautiful, housing about thirty choice horses. My carriage was there, the old gentleman having arranged for it to follow us, and now he gave the postilion detailed instructions about which route to follow through the park, in order for me to see its most beautiful spots. Only then did he head home, accompanied by two great water dogs and a jet-black pointer. He needed to change for dinner, since he was still in his scarlet foxhunting coat, a costume that looks to me like livery.

I forgot to mention that we first made a tour through the house, which is lavishly and beautifully furnished and adorned with family pictures by Van Dyck, Reynolds, and Lawrence, the best painters of England, although from three different centuries. There was one particular curiosity in the main room, namely, red draperies made of painted wood; they were carved some

57

View of Leeds.

time ago and with such skill that certainly Rauch himself would be astonished at the flow of the "fabric." Even though I was told what they were, the imitation of the silken cloth was so completely deceptive that I was dubious and only convinced myself by touching it. The fringes were of real gold, the exact opposite of our theater curtains of silk with wooden fringes. Also unusual were the handsome stucco ceilings throughout the house, for they were of the same design as the carpets, certainly a costly undertaking, since all the carpets must have been specially woven in imitation of the ceiling patterns.

The long drive through the park, a good hour in length, was a real treat. The road first took us along the lake with a majestic view of the house, and then through woodlands, following the river that forms many cascades and small lakes. The woods were exceedingly varied, sometimes dense and impenetrable to the eye, sometimes grove-like, then becoming open meadows with dark borders or young thickets sheltering fallow deer, and occasionally offering a narrow view of the distant mountains.

An aristocrat so well situated is a worthy representative of his class, and it is only natural that a man enjoying so many advantages would be as benevolent, estimable, and contented as this noble earl. I will always remember him with the same pleasure I feel when recalling his beautiful property.

The evening left an impression different but no less beautiful than the day. At dusk I reached Leeds, a large factory town spreading across several hills, with a thin cloud of smoke settled over its entire expanse (Figure 57). A hundred red fires flashed up through the haze, and as many chimneys were lined up among them, exhaling black smoke. In such a setting the colossal, five-story factories looked stunning. From every window two lights shone for the workers who toiled until deep in the night. To add a touch of the romantic to all this tumult of activity and industrial illumination, two ancient Gothic churches rose high above the houses, and in the blue dome of the heavens, the golden light of the moon poured down a majestic calm onto their spires, as if to temper the feverish labor below.

Leeds, with its hundred thousand inhabitants, has no representative in Parliament.[17] This is a result of its being a new town, although many a wretched village boasting two miserable dwellings sends two or more representatives—the positions filled, of course, by the owner and his minions. However glaring this injustice, English statesmen have not yet dared to abolish it, perhaps because they fear that any change in so complex an organization is too risky and should be undertaken only in the gravest emergency.[18]

Late evening

I HAVE ALREADY gotten used to many English customs, cold dinners among them. As an occasional novelty, they are quite healthy and, being typically English, almost always of excellent quality. Thus my solitary table was decked with the following provender, an offering that requires an English stomach to digest: a cold ham (carved partly into large slices), an imposing roast beef, a leg of mutton, a veal roast, a cold hare pie, a hazel grouse, three kinds of pickles, boiled cauli- flower, potatoes, butter, and cheese. It is obvious that this would be enough to feed a whole party of Germans!

October 2nd, 1827

THE FIRST THING I saw out my window this morning was the clever industriousness of a drug- gist who, not content with the customary display of innumerable Chinese tea tins, nodding dolls, and vases, had also placed a real automaton in his shop window: a stately Turk who was diligently grinding coffee. From here I continued my tour, going first to the city market hall, a handsome building with a glass roof. Next I went to the cloth hall, an enormous room filled with nothing but fabric of all sorts and colors; and finally to the largest cloth mill in town, which is powered by three steam engines. You see the process begin with the raw material (wool sorting) and end with the finished cloth; if you brought a tailor along, you could easily deliver your wool to the factory in the morning and in the evening emerge with a brand-new coat. Our Rehder actually accom- plished this feat and wore his "instant" coat for a long time, with particular fondness.

The various machines are absolutely ingenious, but the stench they produce, not to mention the unwholesome air and dust arising from many of the operations, must be very unhealthy for the poor workmen, who were all tinged dark blue like negroes. Yet the young man who showed me the factory said that the manufacture of cotton was, in fact, far unhealthier because of the fine dust, and that those workers seldom lived to be fifty, whereas here men had been known to reach sixty.

The Gothic churches that yesterday made such an impression from a distance were nothing remarkable on close inspection, and the town itself, enveloped in perpetual fog from the smoke pouring out day and night, is the most unpleasant place you can possibly imagine.

Rotherham—Evening

CONTINUING ON MY journey, I made my first stop in Temple Newsam, a mansion from the time of Elizabeth that belongs to the Dowager Marchioness of Hertford. The house has an idio- syncratic feature: instead of battlements, there is a stone gallery of letters running all around the roof quoting a sentence from the Bible.[19] The park is sad, and the furnishings of the house are old-fashioned, but without charm. I found nothing special in the picture gallery, either, though there were a few interesting portraits in other rooms: first the two Guises, uncles of Mary of Scotland; also General Monk, who looks strikingly like our old friend Thielemann; and Lord Darnley (Mary's husband), to whom this castle belonged and who hangs in the same room where he was born. I was suffering from a very bad headache, which is perhaps why I found a second park, Stainbrook Castle, both desolate and eerie, nor could I perceive any quality in the paintings there. After this the road led through an unbroken series of manufacturing areas, all of which looked like burning towns and villages. Rotherham itself, where I am now, is famous for its great ironworks, and I plan to see some of them tomorrow, if my indisposition abates.

October 3rd, 1827

UNFORTUNATELY, AFTER I had walked more than two miles to the largest ironworks, I found everything at a standstill, because yesterday the tall furnace had been damaged. Consequently there was little to see, so I went on to the cast-steel plant, a quarter of an hour away. But the steam engine had just gone out of commission, and work had stopped there as well. I therefore plodded on still farther to the thread and linen factory, and both my guide and I were astonished when there, too, we saw no signs of activity. This time it was the main machine's great spindle, which had broken just that morning. This last bit of bad luck ended my vain attempt at information gathering for today. The only thing worth mentioning, something I saw *en passant,* was a contraption on a tall furnace; instead of the usual wooden bridge leading up to it, there were iron rails, on which the coal cart, powered by a waterwheel, could move up and down by itself.

Sheffield—Evening

FROM ROTHERHAM I drove to Wentworth House. This estate, which belongs to Lord Fitzwilliam, is once again truly regal in its scale, splendor, and riches, but (as is generally true of most English parks) also sad and monotonous. The interminable tracts of barren grass, appointed with a few isolated trees and tame deer, eventually become unbearable. The tasteless custom of allowing these wastelands to come right up to one side of the house makes the buildings look as if they were haunted palaces inhabited by deer instead of people. This is all the more convincing given that you rarely see a human being outside the house, which is usually closed up anyway, so that you must wait at the door for a quarter of an hour, ringing away, until the lady chatelaine finally admits you and then agrees to play the cicerone and collect her gratuity.

Wentworth House abounds in beautiful statues and paintings. One of these is a magnificent canvas by Van Dyck, which portrays the builder of the castle, Lord Strafford, just after receiving his death sentence, when, holding the fatal notification in his hand, he dictated his last will to his secretary (Figure 58).[20] Another picture shows his son, a good-looking lad of sixteen in extremely becoming mourning clothes: black with ornate lace, fawn-colored boots, a tight-fitting collar; a jacket, costly sword, and sash *en bandoulière.*[21]

The picture of a racehorse, fully life-size and painted on a gray canvas with no frame, was standing in a niche and thoroughly deceived me into thinking it was alive (Figure 59).[22] This horse has won so much money that the profits allowed the previous lord to build a quadrangle of

*Thomas Wentworth,
First Earl of Strafford,
with Sir Philip Mainwaring.*

magnificent stables, the most complete I have ever seen in England. Sixty beautiful and exceptionally fine horses reside there, and there is also a riding school.

I was intrigued by an excellent portrait of the enterprising and vain Cardinal Wolsey and by another of the frivolous Duke of Buckingham. As the chatelaine was showing me the portrait of William Harvey, she said, "This is the man who *invented* the circulation of the blood." Who would not want to meet *that* man!

There were a few pretty sections in the flower gardens; one, a gallery, enclosed in wire mesh and running all along the colorful parterres. Inside were exotic birds, a clear brook flowing through, and evergreen shrubs where the feathered inhabitants could freely flit about. Several black swans floating on a small pond nearby have already reared four cygnets here and seem perfectly adapted to the climate. I was particularly struck by a common beech beside the pond, for its character had been completely altered by early pollarding. Though it was not very tall, its branches stretched great distances in every direction and covered an immense space, forming an orderly tent of leaves. I have never seen anything quite like it. There was also a pollarded hemlock, and this treatment lent it far more beauty than if it had been left to grow naturally.

I made good time to Sheffield, where thick smoke blocked the rays of the sun, making it look just like the moon. I admired the various knives and shears manufactured here, including a knife with a hundred and eighty blades and a useful pair of scissors that cut perfectly but are so small they can scarcely be seen with the naked eye, etc., etc. In the process I bought some needles and scissors for you, unburdened by superstition.[23] These will be enough to last you your whole life, along with a few other trifles of recent invention that I hope you will enjoy.

Nottingham, October 4th, 1827

I DROVE ON right through the night and in the moonlit distance saw Newstead Abbey, Lord Byron's now-neglected birthplace and family seat.[24] Aside from the Gothic church (an appointment of nearly every English town, some of them more beautiful than others), there is not much to see in Nottingham. The one exception is a curious *Petinet* factory,[25] where the machines do all the work *by themselves*, with only a solitary man standing at the ready should something go awry.

It is truly disorienting to watch the iron monsters begin operating with all their clamping and pricking, as if they were directed by invisible hands, and then to witness the most beautiful lacy fabric, stretched in a frame, emerge slowly from the top, tidy and complete, while below you can see the spindle wrapped with the raw thread continue its leisurely rotation. All this without the touch of a single human hand.

It was just time for the local fair, which had attracted a lot of curiosities, including a fine collection of wild animals. Two enormous Bengal tigers were so tame that they were sometimes let out onto the riding area where the menagerie was on display; indeed women and children were even allowed to enter their cage. No dogs could have been more docile, though I cannot imagine that our police would put up with such experiments. One remarkable animal, which as far as I know has not yet been seen in Europe, is the horned horse or *Neyl Glu*, from the Asiatic Tartaric regions of the Himalayas: handsome, fleet, and strangely constructed.[26] Also new to me was a lovely wild ass from Persia that supposedly runs faster than a horse, has greater endurance, and can go for weeks without food. As on the Pfaueninsel in Berlin, this animal collection included a giant and a dwarf.

London, October 6th, 1827

BEFORE LEAVING NOTTINGHAM I visited the nearby seat of Lord Middleton, whose country house is well worth seeing.[27] Those who fancy dahlias will see some in the garden here that are almost as big as sunflowers. A few greenhouses were also noteworthy, but otherwise the park had little to offer. In the house is an old painting showing the mansion and gardens as they were two hundred years ago. It invites closer scrutiny because it depicts the family strolling in the garden with a large company and attendants, all in the strangest costumes. The lord portrayed there is the one who is so often associated with the famous ghost story. Everyone should have such paintings made for their descendants, since the comparisons are always delightful and sometimes instructive.

I reached St Albans after dark and admired the famous abbey by moonlight and then soon by lamplight, for the verger was quickly awakened and insisted on giving me a tour (Figure 60). This imposing structure was built by the Saxons in the eighth century out of Roman bricks, which are totally indestructible. The nave must be one of the largest in existence, for it is over six hundred feet long.[28] It contains many magnificent carvings in stone and wood, and although it was difficult to see clearly in the dim glow of the lantern, the whole effect was truly romantic: the eerie half-light; our silhouetted, black figures in the center; and, intoning from the tower above, the midnight bell.

The romantic atmosphere intensified as we descended into the crypt, where we found a tin coffin that had been broken open. Inside it lay the skeleton of the Duke of Bedford, the regent who was poisoned by Cardinal Beaufort six hundred years ago.[29] With the passage of time, the bones have become as brown and smooth as polished mahogany, and curious antiquarians have already made off with some of them. Even the verger himself, an Irishman, nonchalantly picked up one of the leg bones and, swinging it in the air like a cudgel, mentioned how wonderfully hard the bone had become over time, remarking that it would make an excellent shillelagh. What would the proud duke have said, if he had known how such negligible people would someday be treating his poor remains.

60

St Albans Abbey.

The best proof of the solidity of construction in those days is the magnificent wooden ceiling, now more than one thousand years old, but as beautiful and well preserved as if there were no zeros following the one. Unfortunately the colorful windows, as well as the golden tomb of Saint Alban, were mostly destroyed at the time of Cromwell.

I got to London with enough time to rest for half the night, and my first task of the morning was to finish this letter to you, now swollen to the size of a parcel. I hope it will be on its way in a few hours. Until then, do keep yourself occupied, and welcome this letter with the same love and indulgence that you have shown its many predecessors.

Your faithful Lou

LETTER 20

London, November 1st, 1827

A FRENCHMAN SAYS, "L'illusion fut inventée pour le bonheur des mortels, elle leur fait presque autant de bien que l'espérance."[1] If this is true, then I will be allotted much happiness, for I am always full of hopes and illusions. Your letter destroyed a few of these, I admit. But be of good cheer—new ones will pop up again like mushrooms. More about that soon. However, I cannot write to the objectionable, ever-sleeping president from here, and besides, as a dandy might observe, the man is not fashionable enough. Besides, you are taking such excellent care of all these matters, it is only fair to leave them entirely in your hands. This is, of course, selfish of me, but in a forgivable way, since it has advantages for us both. . . . .[2]

A few days ago, I went on a short excursion to Brighton and on the way back made a detour to Arundel Castle, the seat of the Duke of Norfolk, a place I was curious about. It has certain similarities with Warwick Castle, but remains far inferior, even though at least some parts may be just as old. Here, too, there is an artificial mound and a keep at the eastern end. The view from the top of the dilapidated circular tower is said to be lovely, but today the vista was so obscured by fog that I could not see even the terraced gardens that encircle the castle, although I did enjoy the companionship of the dozen eagle owls (the largest kind of owl) that occupy the room of the tower's former keeper. One of these tame birds was already fifty years old, very friendly, and barked just like a dog whenever it wanted something. The English are fond of animals, an inclination I share, so in most large parks one finds immense swarms of ravens orbiting the main house, an attribute well suited to an ancient castle and the gigantic trees surrounding it, although their caws are hardly musical. This castle interior is nothing special. The numerous stained-glass windows are modern, and although I thought one of the family portraits noteworthy, it was only because of the strange costume. It shows Lord Surrey, who was executed during the reign of Henry VIII.

The library is small but magnificent, entirely paneled in cedar and decorated with beautiful carvings and paintings. It is deficient only in books, for it contains no more than a few hundred. There is also a large but simple room, the Baron's Hall, which boasts many colorful windows, none particularly successful.

All the rooms are packed full of old, worm-eaten furniture, and every possible effort is expended to keep it from collapsing. This is now the fashion everywhere in England: things that we would throw away as too rickety and outmoded fetch the highest prices here, and even new pieces are made in the style of old ones. I find this fitting in venerable palaces, as long as it is not detrimental to comfort; in modern structures, however, it is ludicrous.

People say that the oldest part of the castle was a fort already at the time of the Romans, which is why many ancient bricks are found in the walls. It went on to serve as a fortress and withstood numerous sieges. The newer part is in the same style and was built by the father of the current duke at a cost, I was told, of eight hundred thousand pounds.³ In Germany you could certainly produce its equal for three hundred thousand Reichsthalers. The gardens seemed varied and sizeable, and the park is said to be very extensive and picturesque, but the atrocious weather prevented me from seeing any of it. On the same evening, I drove to Petworth, where there is another important mansion. I am writing to you from the inn, where it took me just a few minutes to install myself, my traveling equipage and domestic routine having been perfected here in England.

*Petworth House, the 26th, 1827*⁴

COLONEL C——— CAME to see me this morning and reproached me for not having gone directly to his father-in-law, Lord Egremont, the owner of Petworth House. He invited me to spend at least a day with them in such a friendly manner that I could not refuse. Thus my luggage was transferred, and I was quickly installed. The palace is handsome and modern with a magnificent collection of paintings and antiquities, as well as a large park and famous stud farm.

Three of the pictures spoke to me in the strongest terms: an extraordinary, life-size portrait of King Henry VIII by Holbein, remarkable for the perfect detail of the ornaments and costume and the fresh, masterful coloring (Figure 61);⁵ a portrait of the immortal Newton who appears far less *intelligent* than he is *elegant*; and another of Maurice of Orange looking so like our poet Houwald that it could certainly pass for a portrait of him. The intermixing of sculpture and paintings that has become popular here is unflattering to both, however. Among the many curiosities is an ancestral relic, the large sword of Percy Hotspur.

As usual, the library also served as a salon, a very practical custom. Moreover it is arranged as you prefer, with only the most modern, valuable, and above all elegantly bound volumes on display; all the rest were consigned to a special room on an upper floor. The bookcases were painted white and several stools provided, so one could easily reach the higher shelves.

There was complete freedom in this house, making it twice as pleasant for me. One did not experience even the slightest constraint. A large crowd of guests was present, among them several charming ladies. The host himself is a learned connoisseur of art and also a very significant man on the turf, for his racehorses win more often than others. At the stud farm, I saw a stallion called Whalebone. He was more than thirty years old and required the support of several grooms just to walk, yet his foals sell for enormous sums while still in the womb. That is what I call a glorious old age! The principles of stud farming here are totally different from ours, but I will reserve that subject for another occasion; despite your general thirst for knowledge, I know it would not greatly interest you.

The Duchess of St Albans arrived here the following day, a woman whose fortunes have, against all odds, done nothing but improve. Her earliest recollections are of finding herself abandoned in an English village, where she was starving and freezing in an isolated barn. From there a band of gypsies took her in, and eventually she left them to join a company of traveling actors. She earned a considerable reputation in this profession through her good looks, constant good cheer, and idiosyncratic nature, and she gradually acquired a number of friends who were generous in their concern for her. She lived for some time in an untroubled union with the rich banker Coutts, who finally married her and at his death bequeathed her an income of seventy thousand pounds a year. Through this colossal inheritance, she subsequently became the wife of the Duke

61

King Henry VIII.

of St Albans, the third English duke of rank. It is an odd coincidence that the duke himself is the descendant of an actress, the well-known Nell Gwynn, and that, albeit a century or so earlier, her charms procured him his title in the same way his wife procured hers.[6]

She is a very good woman who is not shy of discussing her past—on the contrary, she mentions it too often, voluntarily entertaining us the whole evening with reenactments of various roles she has played. Most amusing of all, she has coached her very young husband (thirty years her junior) to act out the lovers' parts, a task he could not manage at all. This naturally kept wicked tongues wagging, all the more so because his lines were replete with the most piquant innuendos.

After a pleasant, three-day visit, I returned here and celebrated my birthday in profound isolation. It is clear that most of my melancholic spells are due to the month in which I first saw the light of day. The children of May are far more cheerful; I have never encountered a man born in springtime who was inclined to depression. I once came across a song called "Prognostica," which I am sorry not to have kept, since it forecast the destiny associated with every month of the year. All I remember is that a melancholy temperament is bestowed on anyone born in October. The maxim began like this:

If the month of October bears a son,
He'll become a critic, and a nasty one![7]

I take leave of you now for an important dinner at Prince Esterházy's, because I do not want to devote my whole day to solitude—I am too superstitious for that. Adieu.

November 4th, 1827

AS A KNIGHT of St Louis—the name day of my saint, or of the king of France[8]—I was present today at a great banquet given by Prince Polignac, and afterward I saw the continuation of *Don Juan* at Drury Lane. The first act takes place in hell, of course, where Don Juan has already seduced the Furies and, finally, even the devil's grandmother, for which he is emphatically banished by His Satanic Majesty. As he reaches the picturesque banks of the River Styx, which is roiling in flames, he finds the aged Charon arriving in his boat with the souls of three women from London. As the ferryman disembarks, Don Juan distracts him by asking to change a banknote (yes, paper money has already been introduced in the netherworld) and uses this opportunity to push off from the shore with the three women and escort them back to earth. Once in London, he has his customary adventures, duels, abductions, etc. The equestrian statue at Charing Cross invites him to tea. But then his creditors haul him off to King's Bench. He is liberated by a rich marriage and finally suffers the punishment equal to his sins: a wicked wife—something hell itself could not deliver! Madame Vestris performs the most wonderfully delightful and seductive Don Juan you can imagine, and it is abundantly clear that this young "man" is not lacking in experience.

Although the play was very amusing, I found the new novel on my table at home even more entertaining. It is set in the year 2200, admittedly not a new idea, and depicts England as once again Catholic and an absolute monarchy, where general education has made such progress that learning is the common property of the lowest classes.[9] Every craftsman works with great efficiency according to mathematical and chemical principles; lackeys and cooks with names like Abelard and Heloïse converse in the tones of the *Jenaer Literaturzeitung*. Among the higher classes, in contrast to the rhetorical flourishes of the plebs, it is fashionable to use the most vulgar language and, with the exception of reading and writing, conceal all manner of learning. A clever idea, and perhaps prophetic! The lifestyle of the novel's upper classes is also extremely primitive; only a few rude dishes make up their meals, fancy cooking being reserved for the servants' tables.

By the way, hot-air balloons are, of course, the normal means of transportation, and steam rules the entire world. Thanks to a new application of galvanism, a German professor invents a way to resurrect the dead, and the mummy of King Cheops, recently discovered in an unopened pyramid, is the first to be submitted to the experiment. Once the book is translated into German, you will learn how the living mummy is transported to England, and how abominably he behaves there. I often feel like that myself—bound hand and foot and fervently awaiting my reawakening.

November 5th, 1827

THIS MORNING THE city was blanketed in such a dense fog that I could only eat breakfast in my room with the aid of candlelight. There could be no thought of venturing out until nearly evening. I had been invited to dine at Lady Love's, and P—— was there as well. She is normally very hostile to him, I really don't know why, but today he really made a calamity of it with his typically thoughtless blundering. As you will remember, the lady has a rather red nose, and her detractors cite General Pillet's allegation concerning a certain habit among Englishwomen.[10] P—— was probably unaware of this, and while seated next to her at table, he observed her mixing something into her wine from another bottle—a dark liquid that appeared to be liquor. In his innocence (or malice), he jokingly enquired whether she had already become so much an Englishwoman that she was mixing her wine with cognac. Only when he saw her *entire* face turn bright red and noticed the embarrassment of those sitting nearby, did he discover his gaffe.[11] Her beverage was actually nothing more than *toast water*.[12] This reminded me of the ludicrously pedantic instructions delivered in one of our nation's guides to proper behavior:

> When going to a social gathering, be sure to inform yourself ahead of time with precise details about the people you are likely to meet: their relatives and relationships; their failings and faults as well as their exceptional qualities; so that, on the one hand, you will not utter something unwittingly that might touch a sore spot, and, on the other, you will be able to flatter in a manner at once natural, charming, and appropriate.

Laughably expressed and somewhat difficult to carry out, but not a bad rule!

There was a lot of talk about politics and about the splendid way the war began with the eradication of the Turkish fleet.[13] How inconsistent the English can sound! But since Napoleon's fall, nearly all the leading politicians no longer really know what they want. They are dissatisfied with the miserable results of the Congress and so far have nothing to inspire them further; they no longer feel a sense of purpose or force of will, and thus the fate of Europe now rests not on its leaders, but on chance.[14] Canning's appearance was only transitory, and look what his successors are made of! The destruction of the fleet of their most reliable and loyal ally, with no war declared, is the best evidence of the current malaise, although as an individual and friend of the Greeks, I am wholeheartedly pleased.

But amid all these political monstrosities, this widespread vacillation, still other strange things await us, perhaps combinations that we now think impossible. Canning himself is partly to blame, because his plans were never given the opportunity to mature, and any man of genius who achieves a high position is always a detriment to his successors, especially if they prove to be pygmies. The current ministers give the strong impression of wanting to lead England slowly into the same pit that Canning dug for others.

Meanwhile the storms forming on the borders of Asia may strike at the heart of Europe even more forcefully. I hope, however, that the god of thunder will be with *us*. I suspect that Prussia's future will be far greater and more dazzling than fate has granted thus far; just let it not lose sight of its motto: *Onward!*

Back at home I found your amusing letter, and I especially laughed at H——'s pointed witticisms, haplessly bottled up in Paris and of so little use in S——. For you are surely correct: *Rien de plus triste qu'un bon mot qui se perd dans l'oreille d'un sot.*[15] And he must often find himself in this trap.

November 20th, 1827

SINCE THERE IS now time to go to the theater, and the best actors are playing, I have devoted many of my evenings to this aesthetic diversion and yesterday, with renewed enjoyment, again saw Kemble's artistic rendering of Falstaff, which I wrote about earlier.[16] Here I can add that his costume of white and red was very recherché and of a studied elegance—albeit a little threadbare. Like the beautiful curls of his white hair and beard, it achieved a happy mixture of the distinguished and the comic, which I felt greatly heightened the effect.

All the costumes were excellent, but I must say it was inexcusably disruptive that the minute Henry IV went offstage with his splendid court, including a great many knights gleaming in steel and gold, two servants showed up in theatrical liveries, shoes, and red leggings to carry away the throne. It was just as hard to listen for a quarter of an hour while Lord Percy, with his back to the audience, addressed the king seated at the rear of the stage. In England, oddly enough, it is the most celebrated actors who affect this bad habit, whereas with us they succumb to the opposite error; for example, when the romantic male lead, during his most ardent declaration of love, turns his back on his beloved in order to flirt with the audience. Of course, it is difficult to hold to the proper mean, and the stage directions ought to make it easier for the performers.

German actors tend to make a kind of raging calf out of Percy's character, someone who behaves toward both his wife and king as if bitten by a mad dog. These people no longer have any idea when they should moderate and when they should intensify what the playwright has written. Young understands this perfectly and knows very well how to unite the stormy effervescence of youth with the dignity of a hero and decorum of a prince. He allows that fire to flare up like lightning bolts above a thundercloud, but not to degenerate into a hailstorm. I also find the ensemble acting better than on the German stage, and there is a lot of sound judgment in the scenic arrangements. To give you just one instance: think of the scene (we once saw this play together in Berlin, and comparisons make things more vivid) where the king receives Percy's messengers. You found it indecorous, because Falstaff was constantly forcing himself on the king and interrupting him with rude jokes. This only happens because our actors think more about their personalities than about their roles: Herr D—— feels himself, in comparison with Herr M——, to be "every inch a king," and each of them forgets the figure he is portraying. Shakespeare is better understood here and accordingly better represented. The king stands in the foreground with the ambassadors; the court is scattered around the stage; and halfway back on one side are the prince and Falstaff. The latter admittedly cracks his jokes as a half-privileged buffoon, but he delivers them in an undertone—more to the prince than the king—and when reprimanded, he immediately reverts to his properly respectful attitude, not fraternizing with the sovereign as if they were of the same rank.

In this way you can give in to the illusion of seeing a court before you; in our version, you think yourself still in Eastcheap. The actors here live in better society and therefore have more tact.

November 23rd, 1827

IT IS STRANGE enough that men tend to marvel at something far away in time or space, whereas they completely ignore the daily wonders near at hand. Yet we must still be living in the period of *One Thousand and One Nights*, for today I saw a creature that seems to surpass every phantasm of that era.

Listen to what this brute can do. First of all, its food is the cheapest imaginable, for it eats nothing but wood or coal; and when it is not actually working, it needs no food at all. It never tires and never sleeps. It succumbs to no diseases as long as it has been properly organized, and only refuses to work when, after a long, long time, its great age renders it useless. It performs equally in all climates and untiringly accepts any kind of job. Here it acts as a water pump; there a miner; here a sailor; there a cotton spinner, weaver, blacksmith, or miller. In fact, it performs each and every activity, and you can find it—a small creature—pulling ninety tons of commercial goods, or carriages packed with a whole regiment of soldiers, at a speed far surpassing that of the fastest stagecoaches, all the while marking its own rhythmic steps on a tablet attached to the front. Beyond this, it regulates all by itself the degree of warmth required for its well-being, miraculously oils its own internal joints when they need it, and removes any and all unhealthy vapors that might accidentally penetrate those parts of its system where they do not belong. Yet if it happens that something becomes so deranged within and assistance is required, it immediately rings a loud bell to warn its supervisor about the impending harm. Finally, despite its strength— nearly equal to that of six hundred horses—it is so obedient that a four-year old child can interrupt its activity at a moment's notice with no more than the pressure of one small finger.

Could anyone have come upon such a ministering spirit without benefit of Solomon's signet ring? And has ever a witch been burned at the stake whose magic was the equal of this?

Now, a new miracle. Simply magnetize five hundred pieces of gold with the firm conviction that they will be turned into such a lively machine, and after a few formalities it will be at your service! The spirit ascends in steam, but never vanishes. It remains your legitimate slave, approved by god and man. These are the miracles of *our* era, which must overshadow those of the heathen, or even of Christian times.

I spent the evening at the home of the Brownonian Lady Charlotte Bury, who has just completed another new novel called *Flirtation*.[17] We had a very frank discussion about it, for she is a clever and good woman, and the result of our conversation was quite unexpected. She urged me to write a book of my own and promised that afterward she would translate it herself. *Dieu m'en garde!* By the way, I am skeptical enough to know that, were I to write a book, the pious and proper Lady Bury would be unable to translate even two pages of it without thrusting it aside and crossing herself! Despite the occasional bits of my humor that would not appeal to her, I am delighted to accept her enthusiastic invitation, delivered today, to accompany her to Scotland this summer. It will be a triumphal procession. As the sister of one of the most important men in Scotland and aglow with her own literary radiance, she will be greeted with delight throughout that feudal land, where true hospitality is not just a fable, and one can still meet seigneurs and not just fashionables.[18] In my imagination I can already see her moving from one palace to the next, followed by an entourage of sansculottes, with Fame leading the way in fine English attire. I will attach myself to this company as a foreign knight and take note of all the good things that happen to us, the spiritual and physical, the romantic and prosaic. We will end our tour with a visit to the Great Bard, Sir Walter Scott; after having so often enjoyed the fantastic table he has laid for us, we will finally take a seat at his own.

I do not know whether I mentioned that I am staying in Albemarle Street at the house of a milliner, who has gathered around her a veritable garland of English, French, and Italian girls. Everything is propriety itself, yet many of their talents are of value. One of them, a French girl, is a superb cook and made it possible for me to entertain my friend Lottum in my own quarters today, a small recompense for the many courtesies he has paid me. There was dinner, a concert (it was droll enough, for the performers were all milliners), a little ball for the young ladies, lots of artificial flowers, many lights, a very few well-chosen friends—in short, a sort of fete champêtre in the middle of the funfair that is London. It was almost morning by the time the wild lasses went to bed, although the duenna chaperoned them faithfully to the end. I was highly praised, even though in their hearts, they no doubt much preferred my younger friend Lottum.

November 28th, 1827

A GREAT ACTOR, a true master of his art, and certainly of high standing! What knowledge and ability are required! And how much genius must he combine with physical grace and dexterity, how much creative power to overcome the most boring routine. Today, for the first time since I arrived, I saw *Macbeth*, perhaps the most sublime and accomplished of Shakespeare's tragedies. Macready, an actor only recently returned from America, played the leading part splendidly. He was particularly genuine and thrilling at certain moments. First in the night scene, when he emerged with the bloody dagger after the murder of Duncan and told his wife what had happened. He delivered the whole speech quietly (as the nature of the incident requires), like a whisper in the dark, and yet so distinctly and with such a dreadful expression that all the terrors of the crime were brought to penetrate the listener's very soul. The difficult scene with Banquo's ghost was equally successful:

> What man dare, I dare:
> Approach thou like the rugged Russian bear,
> The arm'd rhinoceros, or the Hyrcan tiger;
> Take any shape but that, and my firm nerves
> Shall never tremble. Or be alive again,

And dare me to the desert with thy sword;
If trembling I inhibit then, protest me
The baby of a girl. Hence, horrible shadow!
Unreal mockery, hence!

He performed this beautiful passage most appropriately. Instead of intensifying his delivery, he began at once with all the vehemence of furious despair and, overcome by horror, dropped his voice lower and lower, speaking the final words in a soft murmur. Then, uttering a muffled cry of mortal agony, he suddenly cast his mantle over his face and sank back half lifeless onto his seat. This achieved the greatest possible effect. One could not but shudder at the realization that our mightiest courage is no match for the horrors of another world. There was no trace of the stage hero who cares little about nature and plays only to the galleries, seeking triumph through ever-escalating sound and fury. Macready was also magnificent in the last act, where conscience and fear are exhausted in equal measure and a numb apathy has at last settled in. Then the final judgment descends upon the sinner in three quick, successive strokes: the death of the queen, the fulfillment of the witches' deceptive prophecy, and finally Macduff's shattering declaration that he is not of woman born.

What previously tormented Macbeth's soul and made him brood about his condition and struggle against the torment of his conscience now only flashes through him with a sudden shock, like a bolt of lightning. He is weary of himself and of existence, but struggles on, remarking with bitter scorn,

They have tied me to a stake; I cannot fly,
But bear-like I must fight the course.

At last he falls—a great criminal, yet a king and hero nonetheless.

The duel with Macduff, where untalented actors so easily fall short, was performed with equal mastery. Nothing was hurried, yet all the fire, all the final rage and despair, all the hideousness of the *end* found expression there.

I will never forget the ludicrous effect of this scene at the first performance of Spiker's translation of *Macbeth* in Berlin. The adversaries were in such a frenzy that, against their will, they ended up behind the scenes before they had finished the dialogue. Then the words "Hold, enough!" rang out from there (what went before was no longer audible). It sounded exactly as if the overwhelmed Macbeth were holding out his sword and trying to stop the fight by crying out, "That's enough—hold it, enough!"[19]

Lady Macbeth was played by a second-rate performer (unfortunately, there are no first-rate actresses left since the departure of Mrs. Siddons and Miss O'Neill).[20] Nevertheless, in her feeble delineation of the character, she was more to my liking than many self-professed great female thespians of our fatherland, whose affected recitals are no match for any of Shakespeare's characters. Not only am I in complete agreement with Tieck's well-known view of this role, but I would like to take it still further.[21] Few men understand how a woman's love can center *everything* on her beloved and, at least for a time, define virtue and vice exclusively in regard to *him*.

When Lady Macbeth is represented as a furious Megaera, who uses her husband only as an instrument of her own ambition, she not only lacks all inner truth, she no longer holds any interest. Such a woman would be incapable of feeling the profound and dreadful wretchedness expressed in the sleepwalking scene. It is only in the presence of her husband that she appears the stronger of the two; that she exhibits no fear or remorse and derides those emotions within him, all the while trying to stifle them within herself in order to give *him* courage.

She can hardly be called a character of gentle femininity, yet love for her husband, expressed in a womanly manner, is the primary motive behind her behavior. Just as the poet clearly portrays her hidden suffering in the night scene, so he also reveals that Macbeth, already long before, had unveiled those concealed ambitions in his own breast, ambitions he scarcely acknowledged to himself. And the witches, too, select Macbeth for themselves, the way maggots and worms attack only what has already grown morbid and hence ripe for their purpose. Thus Lady Macbeth knows what *he* most deeply desires, and *to satisfy him,* she invests him with the benefit of her wild passion. And, as is a woman's way, she quickly compels him to extremes that he himself had not intended. The more Macbeth resists, enacting his own semicomedy with her complicity, the more *her* zeal increases, and she presents herself—both to herself and to him—as crueler, more wicked than she really is. She provokes herself to extremes in order to inspire him to undaunted courage and decisiveness. For *him* she sacrifices everything that might stand between Macbeth and his wishes, and she also sacrifices *herself,* the serenity of her own conscience, indeed all her womanly thoughts and feelings for others. And she calls upon the infernal powers to aid and strengthen her. This is the only interpretation that, for me, renders her character dramatic and the rest of the play psychologically true. Otherwise we find nothing but a caricature, something Shakespeare's creative spirit is incapable of, for he always paints credible *human beings,* never unnatural monsters or imaginary devils. The two finally shove each other into the abyss. Alone, neither would have gone so far, but Macbeth's selfishness is greater, and therefore his end, like his torment, all the more painful.

It is a great advantage to this play when an actor of genius performs the role of Macbeth, not of the lady. I was heartily convinced of this today. When Lady Macbeth, through superior acting, becomes the principal character, you see the whole tragedy from a false perspective, and it loses most of its interest. Then we see nothing but a ferocious Amazon and a henpecked husband who lets his wife use him like a fool to further her own plans. No, the root of sin lies within *him* from the beginning; his wife simply assists. He is not a man possessed of nobility, who is then seduced by the witches into becoming a monster. That would be unnatural. Rather, as in *Romeo and Juliet,* in a *too receptive* mind, the passion of love is led from the innocence of its first budding through all the stages of delight and finally to despair and death. Here the subject of the play becomes selfish ambition and how, shaped by evil powers, this transforms itself in the person of Macbeth. Ostensible innocence and the fame of a celebrated hero evolve into the bloodthirstiness of a tiger. Finally he turns into a wild beast hounded to its death, and yet the man whose soul is gnawed by this poison is gifted with so many superior qualities that we feel sympathy for him in his evolving struggle. What an endless pleasure it would be to see such products of genius played by nothing but great actors, without a single subordinate role! But this could only be accomplished by *spirits,* of course, as in Hoffmann's ghostly *Don Juan.*[22]

You will perhaps find much in these views that is overwrought, but remember that great poets work like Nature herself. They address each of us in the guise of our own soul and can therefore accommodate many interpretations. They are so richly endowed that they can distribute their gifts among a thousand poor and give something different to every one of them.

Other aspects of the production were also commendable. For instance, the two murderers whom the king hires to kill Banquo are not, as on our stage, ragged bandits dressed in tatters, the likes of which would never be seen in a royal palace; in their company, the king in his splendid regalia, surrounded by his important retainers, looks quite ridiculous. Instead their appearance and behavior are respectable. They are villains but not riffraff. Everything about the old Scottish costumes is handsome and probably more true to the era and certainly more picturesque than what I have seen in German theaters. The apparition of Banquo, as well as the whole arrangement of the banquet, was infinitely better. In this scene, the Berlin director made a ludicrous blunder. When the king questions the murderers about Banquo's death, one of them answers, "My lord, his throat is cut."[23] This is an English idiom for someone being killed, much as when we say "he broke his neck" after a man falls from a horse, without exactly meaning that he broke his neck in two. But in Berlin the expression was taken literally, and a foul papier mâché head appeared at the banquet with its throat atrociously slit! The presentation of this monstrosity had so much the look of a puppet show that one could barely keep a straight face, even with the best of intentions. Here, however, the ghost's entrance was cleverly concealed by the guests thronging around the tables, so that only when the king is about to sit down do he and the audience suddenly recognize the apparition seated in his chair. Two bloody wounds disfigure the phantom's pale countenance (it is, of course, the same actor who played Banquo), but without the ludicrous addition of a slashed throat. Then, when he stares rigidly at the king amid the busy stir of the guests, nods to him, and slowly sinks into the earth, the effect is as deceptively real as it is horrible.

But in order to give a balanced account, I must mention one ridiculous thing that occurred here. After the murder of the king, when a knock is heard at the door, Lady Macbeth says to her husband,

> Hark! more knocking.
> Get on your nightgown, lest occasion call us,
> And show us to be watchers.

She is urging him to hurry off and put on a dressing gown so it will not be noticed that he is still fully clad. Now, "nightgown" does indeed mean *Schlafrock,* or dressing gown; but in fact, I could scarcely believe my eyes when Macready entered with a modern dressing gown of flowered chintz (perhaps the one he wears every day) thrown loosely over his steel armor, which peeped out with his every movement. In this charming costume, he then drew his sword to kill the chamberlains sleeping near the king.

I could not tell whether anyone else was bothered by this. Frankly, the low level of attention was an apt counterpart to the incessant noise and mischief. Indeed it is hard to imagine how such distinguished actors can emerge, given the ill-mannered, indifferent, and ignorant audiences they typically confront here. As I have pointed out, the English theater is not fashionable, and so-called good society is scarcely ever in attendance. The only advantage for the actors is that they are not spoiled. In Germany, they seem to have been totally corrupted by the opposite circumstances.

Der Freischütz was performed that same evening, following *Macbeth*. Weber, like Mozart, must tolerate being reworked with abridgments and additions by Mr. Bishop. This is truly deplorable; not only the music but even the plot is robbed of all its character. It is not Agathe's lover, but the king of marksmen who comes to the wolf's glen and sings Kaspar's beloved song. The devil, in long red robes, finally performs a ceremonial shawl dance, before he and Kaspar settle down in hell, a place appealingly represented by fiery cascades, scarlet backdrops, and skeletons piled on top of one another.

In the opera, the comparison with Germany turns out entirely to our advantage, however greatly we are outclassed in the performance of the tragedy. I wish it were the other way around.

December 2nd, 1827

I WROTE YOU recently that I was feeling better; ever since then, I have been unwell. One should be careful about making such declarations, as the old wives say, because, in Walter Scott's words, "to announce what is not yet certain brings misfortune." This has, in fact, often been my experience, although as far as my health is concerned, it is just as incomprehensible as everything else about me. Since I am in the process of citing others, let me copy a short passage for you from a popular English medical book. It provides information not only about us but about many others of our era.[24] Listen:

> Certain kinds of individuals, without being generally infirm, are nonetheless always —from cradle to grave—what one calls "nervous," that is, they may be sound and well-constructed by nature, as far as the basic structure of the machine goes; they may have a strong and solid bone structure; their muscles may be equally toned, their blood circulation and organs full of vigor. And yet in *one aspect* they must be called feeble, namely, in those organs that nature has appropriated to enhance the effects of the emotions and the senses. For these are so constituted that the slightest irritation can cause a lightning descent into disorder; at one moment they are pathologically excitable, at the next they lapse into a kind of stupor, never achieving the strength demanded by a regular fulfillment of their functions.

We cannot change this, but we can work against it by careful attention and willpower. Our medical friend continues in the same wise manner:

> A person suffering from a nervous illness is never done with complaining. He has hundreds of mental sufferings to confide to his friend, and every day he discovers new problems and tells his doctor about peculiar pains in his eyes, in various places on his head, about twinges, about buzzing in his ears. These spread from his head throughout his body, showing up in his belly, his back, his legs. Once he has stolen a half hour of his doctor's valuable time with a catalog of his illnesses—their cause, symptoms, and consequences—he will likely delay him further by inquiring about his diet (since he suddenly feels a bit hungry) or what he should wear if the weather is warm or cool.
> The late Dr. Baillie, when in the hurry of great business, when his day's work, as he was used to say, amounted to seventeen hours, was sometimes rather irritable and betrayed a want of temper in hearing the tiresome details of an unimportant story. After listening with torture to a prosing account from a lady, who ailed so little that she was going to the opera that evening, he had happily escaped from the room, when he was urgently requested to step upstairs again; it was to ask him whether,

on her return from the opera, she might eat some oysters. "Yes, ma'am," said Baillie, "shells and all."

It is strange that people suffering from nervous disorders are exceedingly apprehensive and regard every minor affliction as highly dangerous. The moment an actual, organic malady shows itself, however, they generally start to think of their condition as simple and inconsequential; and whereas they previously exhausted the doctor with a litany of all their symptoms, they now feel compelled to give him adequate information, so instead of detaining him, they seem just as happy as he is when the consultation comes to an end. It is the same with fear. I have seen many people who could be unsettled for hours by the opening of a window, who nonetheless listen with the greatest tranquility to the news of an inevitable and quickly approaching death. Will power can do wonders.

The dyspeptic ought to run away from, or determine to combat, the first menace of discontented feeling. Low spirits may be successfully resisted if the attempt be commenced sufficiently early. "I will be good," says the child who sees the rod ready to direct the will into the way of goodness; and "I will be cheerful" ought the dull and dyspeptic to say, who observes above him a cloud of hypochondric fancies ready to burst upon his devoted head, if he chooses the path that leads to afflictive feeling. It is easier, I shall be told, to preach than to practice—to prescribe than pursue. But of this I am certain, that before the habit becomes confirmed of yielding to their influence, a determined, and I would say, conscientious resolution of dispersing the coming mists of vaporish depression, may prove, to a very considerable extent, successful and effective. We would not be paradoxical or extravagant enough to assert that for a person to be in health, it is sufficient that he wills it. But without transgressing the moderation of truth, we may venture to give it as our opinion that a man often indolently bends under the burden of indisposition, which a spirited effort would, in the first instance, have shaken from his shoulders. If upon the approach of the malady, he had resolutely set his face against it, he would probably have arrested it in its threatened attack. The doctrine of irresistibility, in all its extent, is neither a true nor a wholesome doctrine; and the hypochondriac should reflect that in saying to gloom, "Henceforth be thou my good!" *he not only directs his destiny, but implicates others in his fatal choice.*

Melancholy has something in it poetical and sentimental, which constitutes a great portion of its charms: but stripped of its ornamental accompaniments and laid bare to a dissecting view, it will be found to consist, in a great measure, of pride, selfishness, and indolence. I cannot conceive of a more delightful spectacle than that of an individual whose constitutional cast is melancholic, warring against his temperament and determining to enter with hilarity into the scenes and circumstances of social life. In this case, we have all the interests of melancholy, without its objectionable parts.

Is that not beautiful and sensible? And will it not convert you as much as it has strengthened my own conversion? I hope that when the next hypochondriac impulse arrives, you will answer me: "Dear friend, please, not one word more. I *will* be cheerful."

You must be surprised that I am staying in London during this thankless season, but Lady Garvagh is still here, and anyway, I have settled down into a solitary life, interrupted only on occasion by the little flock of milliners in the house. The theater has begun to interest me as well, and the peacefulness of this still life refreshes me after the earlier hurly-burly. It is truly so quiet that, like the celebrated prisoner in the Bastille, I recently formed a liaison with a mouse—a delightful little creature, doubtless an enchanted lady, who sneaks out timidly as I work, looks over from a distance with her little eyes twinkling like stars, and becomes steadily tamer. She is enticed by bits of cake that are laid out for her, each day six inches farther away from her residence in the right corner of my chamber. Having just now polished off one of these with consummate grace, she is cavorting around the room with abandon. But what is that I hear? Incessant loud shouting in the street! My startled mouselet has already fled into her little hole.

"What's going on?" I ask. "What's this ghastly noise?"
"War has been declared—a special edition of the newspaper is being cried out on the streets."
"War with whom?"
"I don't know."

This is one of the branches of industry practiced by the poor devils in London. When they cannot come up with anything else, they cry out some great piece of news and sell an old paper to the curious for half a shilling. You grab it quickly, do not understand it clearly, look at the date, and laugh that you have been taken for a ride.

Unfortunately, as always when I am living alone, I have turned day into night so completely that I often do not have breakfast until four in the afternoon, eat my lunch at ten or eleven o'clock after the evening's theater, and go walking or riding at night. Not only does the weather tend to be better at night, but *mirabile dictu*, it is lighter outside! During the daytime there is so much fog blanketing the city that you cannot see any lights or street lamps, even if they are burning at noon. But at night, the lamps sparkle like jewels, and what's more, the moon shines as if this were Italy! Galloping home alone last night along a broad street, for some time I saw white and coal black clouds drifting with equal speed across the moon like fine, transparent veils, offering a strange and wildly enchanting spectacle. The air was completely still and warm, for after the recent cold, we are finally having genuine spring weather.

Besides Lottum and the supernumeraries at the clubs, I see few other people beyond Prince P——, whom people here accuse of great haughtiness and brusqueness, and about whom it is whispered that he is a true Bluebeard, who treats his poor wife very badly and locked her up for six years in a solitary castle in a forest, so that finally, wearied by her maltreatment, she agreed to divorce him. What, good Julie, do you say to the sorrowful fate of that woman, your best friend?[25]

Yet how strangely rumors and calumnies turn up in the world! How difficult it is to predict the unimaginably diverse consequences of human actions or the unexpected obstacles that may endanger our journey through life! Yes, in the moral as in the material world, weeds grow too often where wheat was sown, and flowers and fragrant herbs spring up where dung was spread.

I received your long letter and offer my heartiest thanks for it. Do not hold it against me that I rarely respond to each detail or acknowledge every point, a failing you so often reproach me with. In fact, not a single word is lost on me. Remember that one gives no other response to the rose for its precious fragrance than to inhale it with relish; to tear it apart would not increase the pleasure. And yet I regret that I am now lacking both the materials and frame of mind to deliver such roses in return. The wall before me is as bare as a sheet, and no shadow puppet silhouette is likely to appear on it.

Woolmers, December 11th, 1827

SIR GORE OUSELEY, former English ambassador to Persia, invited me to his country estate, and since it is so close by and promised some diversion, I drove there yesterday. Arriving late in darkness and rain, I had to dress at once to go to Hatfield House to attend one of the weekly balls that Lady Salisbury gives for the whole neighborhood whenever she resides in the country. Attending is therefore seen as a sort of social call, and no invitations are sent. Sir Gore took his whole crowd along, including his family and Lord Strangford, the well-known ambassador to Constantinople.

You will remember that on my earlier excursion to the North I saw Hatfield only from the outside *en passant*. I now found the interior, with its air of antiquity, just as imposing and respectable. You enter a hall hung with banners and armor, then climb a curious wooden staircase with figures of apes, dogs, monkeys, etc., and from there arrive in a long, somewhat-narrow gallery, where the dancing was in progress (Figure 62). The walls are of old oak *boiserie*, embellished with antiqued silver sconces, gothic chairs, and red window shades that roll up. This gallery, some 130 feet long, has a library at one end, and at the other a magnificent hall-like room, with metal ornaments hanging low from the coffered ceiling and a chimneypiece as tall as a house crowned by a bronze statue of King James. The walls are covered with white satin; the drapes, chairs, and sofas in crimson, velvet, and gold. The place was quite lovely, but the ball seemed rather dead, the company too rural, the refreshments by no means abundant, and the supper nothing but a meager buffet. By two o'clock everything was over, and I was very pleased to have survived it since, fatigued and filled with ennui, I longed for some rest.

The next morning I got up rather late and almost missed breakfast, which is taken rather early here. I delighted in the many Persian curiosities that decorate the rooms and was particularly struck by a splendid illuminated manuscript; the brilliant coloring of the miniatures surpasses even the best examples from the European Middle Ages, and the drawing is often more accurate as well. The book tells the story of Timur's family and is supposed to have cost two thousand pounds in Persia. It was a present from the shah. Other things as well: doors inlaid with precious metals; sofas and carpets of curious velvet fabrics embroidered with gold and silver; above all, a golden bowl covered with the most perfect, colorful enamel, as well as a number of beautifully worked bijoux—all this showed that the Persians, if behind us in many things, also far surpass us in others.

The weather had cleared a little and enticed me to a solitary walk. The park's major beauties are the noble trees, a little river, and a grove where the ground and trees are totally covered with vines and where, in dense shade, a remarkable spring bubbles up with great force, as if from the bowels of the earth, sending hundreds of gallons of water to the river every second. When I got back it was two o'clock, time for luncheon, after which Sir Gore brought out his Arabian horses for me. A few were quickly saddled, so we could go riding. The groom was incessantly occupied

62

*The Gallery at
Hatfield House.*

with dismounting and remounting, for he had to open the gates that everywhere obstructed our path. Such barriers are common in English parks and even more so in the open country, which makes riding inconvenient anywhere but on major roads.

In the evening, there was music, and the daughter of the house and Mrs. F—— proved to be excellent pianists. The audience was meanwhile totally uninhibited; they came and went, talked or listened to the music, did whatever they wished. Afterward, when the ladies retired to their rooms to dress, Sir Gore and Lord Strangford told us stories from the Orient— a subject I never tire of. Both are great partisans of the Turks, and Lord Strangford praised the sultan as a very enlightened man. He himself, he said, was perhaps the first of all Christian ambassadors to have had several private conferences with the Great Man, during which, however, a peculiar etiquette was observed. The sultan received him in the garden of the seraglio in the dress of an officer from his bodyguard, and—consistent with this role—always spoke of the sultan with the utmost reverence and in the third person; meanwhile Lord Strangford was not supposed to let on that he recognized him. The lord declared that the Turkish emperor was better informed about Russia than a great many European politicians, and therefore knew very well what he was undertaking.*

After dinner, which included some Oriental dishes, and at which I drank genuine Shirazi for the first time (not a pleasant wine, by the way—it tastes of goatskins), more music was performed and some little intellectual games played. These were not particularly successful, so at a decent hour everyone reached for a candlestick and headed for bed.

December 12th, 1827

FROM MY HOST's Arabian stock, I have purchased a raven–black horse, barely tamed from his wild state. To test him a bit more, we paid a visit this morning to Lady Cowper, who lives in the neighborhood. Panshanger Park and her mansion are well worth seeing, especially the picture gallery, which contains two Madonnas from Raphael's early period and an extremely handsome equestrian portrait of Marshal Turenne by Rembrandt. Lady Cowper received us in her boudoir, which leads directly into a flower garden, even now still lovely and beautifully maintained; on the opposite side were additional greenhouses and a dairy shaped like a temple, with bronze dolphins spouting cool water at its center. Panshanger is famous for having the largest oak in England. Two yards above the ground, its trunk still measures nineteen and a half feet in circumference and is at the same time very tall and slim, even though its branches extend some distance on all sides. We have larger oaks than this in Germany.

To reconnoiter the country yet further, we made a second visit to Hatfield and managed to inspect everything more carefully. The whole house, including kitchen and laundry, is heated by a *single* steam engine, a furnace commensurate with the magnificence of the establishment. The dowager marchioness, the sprightliest woman of her age in England, led us upstairs, downstairs, and into every corner. In the chapel, we found some superb old stained glass that had been buried in Cromwell's time to save it from the demented iconoclasts who destroyed church windows everywhere. In one of the rooms was a very good portrait of Charles XII, that veritable Don Quixote writ large, who—but for Poltava[26]—might have been a second Alexander.

Hatfield's present stables were formerly the mansion, and there Elizabeth was held prisoner during the reign of Mary I. On a gable across from Elizabeth's window, Queen Mary had a very tall pointed chimney built with an iron rod attached to it, and she let word get to her captive that the rod was intended as a mount for her head, or so the marchioness told us. The chimney is still standing and now thickly overgrown with ivy. Elizabeth, in order to revel in the way it all worked out, had the new palace built next to the old, so she could contemplate with composure the once-threatening maw of that chimney. The house is poor in works of art, and the park, rich only in large avenues of oaks and too many crows, is otherwise bleak and without water, with the exception of one slimy, green puddle near the house.

---

* If one may judge from the outcome, this opinion was not borne out.—*The Editor.* [The Russo-Turkish War of 1828–1829 was concluded with the Treaty of Adrianople, which forced many concessions from the Ottoman Empire, greatly strengthening Russia's position in Eastern Europe.—*Translator.*]

IN THE HOUSE of my current host, there is a peculiar picture gallery containing some curious portraits of Persians, the most interesting among them one of the shah and another of his son Abbas Mirza. The shah's yellow costume, covered with precious stones of every kind, and his enormous black beard, provide a rather good image of this Son of the Sky and Sun. His own son, however, surpasses him in the beauty of his features, but his costume is almost too simple and the pointed sheepskin cap unbecoming. The late Persian ambassador to England makes it a threesome. He was a very handsome man, who felt so much at ease with European manners and customs that the English describe him as a true Lovelace. Moreover, on his return, he is supposed to have been indiscreet and to have maliciously compromised several distinguished English ladies.

In the same gallery, a few costumed dolls offered us a faithful idea of the fair sex in Persia: long hair colored red or blue, arched and painted eyebrows, large eyes of languishing fire, and wearing enchanting gauze pantaloons with golden rings round the ankles. Lady Ouseley related many interesting details of the harem, which I will tell you in person, since I must reserve a few things for *then*.

Much about Persia seems especially inviting, other dimensions less so, including the scorpions and the insects. Once, when Lady Ouseley was reclining on a divan, a snake slithered from her neck down into her clothes, and she could only rid herself of it by quickly removing everything she was wearing. Such incidents are unlikely to happen in our temperate climate. May it thus be praised, along with all those who are content with it, among whom I hope the two of us will always count ourselves.

Your Lou

D EAR JULIA!

After writing a poem in the Woolmers guestbook, verses that teemed with Arabian steeds, Timur's glory, Cecil, Elizabeth, and the fair beauties of Tehran, etc., I took leave of my friendly hosts and returned to London.

On the very evening of my arrival, Lottum took me to a strange spectacle. In a suburb a good five miles away, we were led into a sort of barn—dirty, with no ceiling other than the coarse roof, moonlight peeking here and there through the timbers. In the middle was an area with a wooden floor about twelve feet square, enclosed by heavy wooden barriers and surrounded by a gallery full of common folk and dangerous-looking faces of both sexes. A narrow ladder led up to a second gallery intended for dignitaries at a cost of three shillings a seat. In strange contrast with this outward appearance was a crystal chandelier lit with thirty fat wax candles hanging from one of the crossbeams of the roof truss. A few fashionables were seated above the vulgar crowd; members of the latter, by the way, were continually offering and taking bets of twenty to fifty pounds. The subject of these wagers was a good-looking terrier, the illustrious Billy, pledged to bite a hundred rats to death in ten minutes (Figure 63). The arena was still empty as everyone anxiously awaited the contest. The delay was dreadful. In the lower gallery, large tankards of beer were passed from mouth to mouth, and cigar smoke swirled up in dense clouds. At last a burly man appeared carrying a sack resembling a bag of potatoes; in fact, it contained the one hundred live rats. All at once, he gave them their freedom by untying the knot and scattering them in every direction, and while they were scurrying about, he made a hasty retreat into a corner. At a given signal, Billy rushed in and set about his murderous business with unbelievable fury. As soon as one rat lay there lifeless, Billy's Knecht Ruprecht was on the spot to pick it up and put it in the sack.[1] Some may have been merely unconscious, old hands who feigned death from the get-go. In any case, Billy won in nine and a quarter minutes, according to the many watches that were pulled out, and the one hundred dead, or counted as dead, were once again safely back in the sack.[2]

This was the first act. In the second, Billy—invigorated by the approving cheers of his audience—went on to fight with a badger. Each of the combatants had a second who held him by the tail. Only one bite or one grip was allowed, then the combatants were pulled apart and immediately let loose again. Billy always had the advantage, and the poor badger's ears streamed with blood. In this skirmish, too, Billy was expected to seize the badger firmly in a certain number of minutes, I have forgotten how many. This he accomplished with equal brilliance and then retired, greatly exhausted.

63

Billy Killing Rats.

BILLY,

THE UNRIVALLED DOG PERFORMING HIS WONDERFUL MATCH OF KILLING 100 RATS IN FIVE MINUTES AND A HALF.

The spectacle ended with the bearbaiting, in which a bear mauled a few dogs while seeming to suffer little himself. It was evident throughout that the entrepreneurs were reluctant to expose their valuable animals to real harm, which is why I suspected from the beginning that even the conduct of the rats might conceal some degree of artistic talent!

Cockfights will be held here in a few months. I will send you a description.

December 21st, 1827

THERE ARE WITHOUT any doubt three natures in man: a botanical one, which is content to vegetate; an animal one, which destroys things; and an intellectual one, which creates. Many people are satisfied with the first; most lay claim to the second; and fewer to the third. I must unfortunately confess that my way of life here has me languishing in the first category, which often puts me in a bad mood, "but I can't help it."

You have probably already heard of the English Roscius. This new wunderkind displays prodigious talent at just ten years of age. Master Burke, as he is called, played to a full house at the Surrey Theatre. He performed five or six different roles and demonstrated familiarity with the stage as well as humor, aplomb, volubility, acuteness of memory, and suppleness of body— in short, he was astonishing. But most striking of all was his prologue, when he presented himself in his natural role as a ten-year-old lad. There was such profound truth in his genuine, childlike naiveté that it could only be the inspiration of genius, not the result of self-conscious reflection. He went on to play other roles, first an Italian music master, where he showed himself to be a true virtuoso of the violin. It was evident from this whole performance that he was a born musician, not merely in a few memorized skills, but in the good taste of his playing and unusual richness and beauty of his tone. Next he portrayed a pedantic scholar, after that a rough captain of a ship, and so on. He was excellent in every one and especially superb in pantomime, where so many founder. His final character was Napoleon, his only failure, and I must say it was this lapse that put the crown on my acclamation. It is a mark of true genius that in rendering the pitiful, inept, and foolish, the rendition appears foolish as well, and this role was the quintessence of tasteless silliness. It is no different in life. Turn Lessing into a fawning courtier or Napoleon into some lowly lieutenant, and you will see how badly they perform their parts.

In general, it is only a question of each man standing in his allotted place, and then he will manage to develop something excellent. My own genius, for instance, consists in what one might call a practical application of the imagination, which I can set like a clock. This allows me to be immediately at home in every actual situation, but it also serves as a provocation to fling myself into every conceivable abyss. If I suffer damage as a result, I can remedy that by inventing a bit of good fortune for myself. Is this proclivity the result of my physical constitution, or something gained from my own resources, inherited over a hundred generations? Did I, my spiritual self, experience a prior existence in some other connection, other forms; and does this spirit persist on its own or simply disappear again into the General Totality like one more bubble coughed up by the eternal fermentation of the cosmos?[3]

Is, as many would claim, the history of the world (what happens in time) just like nature (what happens in space) predetermined throughout its entire course according to the immutable laws of a guiding hand? And does it culminate like a drama in the so-called victory of good over evil? Or does the free power of the spirit dictate its own future, unconscious of what is to come and subject only to the conditions required for its own existence? That is the question! Meanwhile so much appears clear to me: By adopting the first hypothesis—however we want to express it—we become little more than artificial puppets. Only under the second premise can we truly be considered free spirits. I do not want to deny that there is something in me—an unconquerable, primal urge, like the most inward consciousness of self—that compels me to the second view. Perhaps it is the devil who makes me think this! Yet he does not lead me so far astray that I do not want, in all humility and with the most heartfelt love, to thank a God incomprehensible to us for our mysterious origin. But precisely because we were created by divine insemination, we must continue to live on, independently, in God. Hear what Angelus Silesius, the pious Catholic, has to say about this:

> Soll ich mein letztes End und ersten Anfang finden,
> So muß ich mich in Gott und Gott in mir ergründen
> Und werden das, was er, ich muß ein Schein im Schein,
> Ich muß ein Wort im Wort, ein Gott im Gotte sein.[4]

For this very reason, I also find it an intolerable tenet that man was formerly in a more exalted state, was in some way *better*, but has gradually deteriorated; such that now, just as gradually, he must work his way back through sin and misery to his original state of perfection. How much more commensurate it is with the laws of nature and existence, how much more in keeping with the premise of an eternal, supreme, all-prevailing love and justice, to assume that the human race (which I deem to be a true individual, a single entity) improves through its own energy, advancing from a necessarily imperfect beginning toward a state of increasing perfection, the seed of that energy planted by the generative love of the Supreme Being! The golden age of mankind, says the comte de Saint-Simon, is not behind us, but yet to come. Ours could be called the mystic age (more out of desire than capability). True mysticism is admittedly rare, but we must acknowledge that the worldly-wise gained great advantage by contriving to drape a cloak of titular mysticism over absurdity itself. Unfortunately most things belong behind this cloak—even, for example, original sin, or "hereditary sin,"[5] as our modern mystics like to call it.

A few years ago I found myself at a small and highly learned gathering consisting of just one lady and two gentlemen. We were arguing about original—hereditary—sin. The lady and I declared ourselves against it, the two gentlemen for it, although perhaps more for the sake of displaying their intellectual fireworks than out of conviction.

"Yes," our opponents finally said, "hereditary sin is certainly a fundamental truth; as with the new French charter, the path was laid by a thirst for knowledge. As this thirst was being satisfied, evil entered the world, something that was also necessary to our purification, to our *own* merit, the only truly commendable merit."

"When you put it like that," I responded, glancing toward my debating partner, "we can acquiesce, for it represents our own *meaning* expressed in other *words*, that is, a learning process, the necessary transition from bad to better through one's own experience and knowledge."

"Certainly," the lady chimed in, "except then you shouldn't call it 'hereditary sin.'"

"Gnädige Frau," answered one of our antagonists, "let's not quarrel about terminology; if you prefer, we'll call it 'hereditary nobility' from now on."

After all these ruminations, I learned today that even the most frivolous of sophisticated people are given to self-reflection. An Austrian of rank, who has been staying here for some time, passed on the following bit of practical philosophy, which, for the sake of its originality, I must put down as he said it:

> Nothing is really more foolish than to fret about the future. Look, when I arrived here, summer had started and the Season was over. Another man might have fretted at having such poor timing, but I thought, it'll pass soon enough. And I was right, it's already November. Meanwhile Esterházy took me to the country, where I had a grand time; and now there's just one bad month left, and then the place will be packed again, the balls and routs will start, and I won't want for things to be better! Wouldn't I have been a downright fool to have fretted for nothing? Aren't I right? You have to live in the world just like a harlot, and never think too much about the future.[6]

I can assume that this practical gentleman and I have very different natures, and that many a professional philosopher would look upon my ruminations with approximately the same amount of sympathy as I do his. Unfortunately it seems that, in the end, the result is the same with all of us: the only thing that remains uncertain is which of us is the greatest fool. Probably the one who considers himself the cleverest.

I HAVE RECEIVED some unpleasant news. The ship on which I sent the seeds and flowers I had bought for you sank just off Helgoland, and only a few of the crew were saved. Friend Lottum also lost many of his belongings. It is the only ship to have foundered in that stretch of water this year, and there is no doubt that its misfortune is due to the outrage of having departed on a Friday. You laugh, but there is something strange about this day, and I myself am suspicious of it, because among the inexplicable personifications that my imagination has involuntarily created for the days of the week, Friday is the only one that is pitch-black. It might interest you to know the colors of the others as a kind of mystical puzzle: Sunday is yellow, Monday blue, Tuesday brown, Wednesday and Saturday brick red, Thursday ash grey. At the same time, all of these day creatures have strangely spiritual bodies, namely, they are transparent and without any distinct form or outline.

But back to Friday. The secretary to the American legation here recently opined on this topic:

The superstition that Friday is an evil day is still, even now, more or less deeply ingrained in the minds of all our sailors. A few years ago, an enlightened merchant in Connecticut wanted to contribute whatever he could toward alleviating these worries that so often have very inconvenient consequences. He therefore arranged for a new ship to be built. The work began on a *Friday*. He had it launched on a *Friday*, gave it the name *Friday*, and on his orders it began its maiden voyage on a *Friday*. Unfortunately for the success of this well-intentioned experiment, not another word was ever heard of the ship or its crew.

I received your letter yesterday.

The fact that your jewel, as you lovingly call him, may be not only overlooked but even merrily tromped on by many in the world is quite natural, since only a few of his facets have been properly polished, and if one of these shinier surfaces does not happen to beam at a passerby, then he is *comme de raison* thought to be nothing but a common pebble; and if one of his sharp edges causes injury, he may be crushed underfoot. Every now and again he is valued by a connoisseur. And as for his possessor—by that person he is *over*valued.

Your account of the English family M—— in Berlin made me laugh. The models for such portraits are very common here in the fashionable world. Indeed the general appearance of the ladies is almost as bad, although long-established immeasurable wealth, old historical names, and austere reserve grant something imposing to this aristocratic society, particularly in the eyes of an insignificant, *north German* nobleman.

The little mishaps you told me about should not be taken to heart. What are they other than trivial cloudlets, *as long as the sun of the mind shines bright in our inner heaven!* By the way, you should seek out more distractions. Go visit W—— and H—— and L——. One should not see people only when one has need of them, for they will not believe they are loved and valued, but only that they are being used. Yet how good it would be if exactly these three could see into our hearts! They would learn to love us more than just through talking and visiting. As far as the park goes, I fear that you, like a dreadful tyrant, have murdered grand old creatures in cold blood. So lindens that were three hundred years old had to fall like involuntary martyrs, sacrificed for a more open view? It is, mind you, in keeping with the times; but from now on I instruct you to plant, and as much as you like, but not to remove anything that is already there. Later I will of course come myself and separate the wheat from the chaff.

December 31st, 1827

DOM MIGUEL OF Portugal has arrived here, and I was presented to him this morning. Only the *corps diplomatique* and a few foreigners were present. The young prince is not unattractive, even looks a bit like Napoleon, but was somewhat embarrassed in his behavior. He was wearing seven stars and likewise seven large ribbons over his coat. His complexion was like the olives of his fatherland, and the expression on his face was more melancholic than cheerful.

January 1st, 1828

MY BEST WISHES for this day and a most heartfelt kiss for the new beginning. Perhaps this is the good year that we have awaited for so long, as the Jews have the true Messiah. For me, at least, its inauguration was most cheerful. We spent yesterday at Sir Lewis Moeller's, who had invited five or six very pretty women and girls, and around midnight we drank a toast to the new year. As part of this, Lottum and I introduced the German fashion of kissing the ladies, which—after the requisite struggle—they enjoyed a great deal.

Then today I dined on Hanoverian venison (not to be had here) at Count Münster's country estate and heard how, as a kind of Christmas present, a blunderbuss (short musket) was fired through the large window of the parlor just as the countess was passing out Christmas gifts to her children. The shot penetrated the plate glass as if it were cardboard, making hundreds of little holes without shattering even one pane. Luckily the gifts had been placed well away from the window, so the shot did not reach them. No one can imagine who might have been responsible for such an infamous act!

Dom Miguel's presence has invigorated London. This evening there was a soirée at the Duke of Clarence's, and tomorrow there will be a great ball at Lady K——'s. The prince seems universally well liked, and now that he feels more at home here, he exhibits a certain dignity and refinement in his bearing, while at the same time it seems as if more than one ulterior motive may be lurking in the background of his great affability. For the Portuguese, by the way, etiquette is so strict that every morning, when he first catches sight of the prince, our good Marquis of Palmela must fall to his knees.

January 3rd, 1828

I WILL SKIP yesterday's party at Prince Esterházy's in order to tell you about today's pantomime, which Dom Miguel also graced with his presence. He suffered even more in the process than did the late Elector of Hesse in Berlin, who, when the opera's opening chorus wished the queen of the Amazons a long life, stood up to express his thanks.

Because Dom Miguel has been portrayed as a tyrannical extremist, the people here expected him to be a fearful monster. Instead they find him a totally charming and handsome young man and have moved from repugnance to love, welcoming the prince with enthusiasm. So it was today in the theater, and Dom Miguel stood up straight away with his Portuguese and

English retinue and bowed to express his profound gratitude. Shortly thereafter the curtain was lifted to a new round of boisterous applause at the beautiful scenery. Once more Dom Miguel arose and expressed his gratitude. The audience, although taken aback, overlooked his error and repeated their good-natured cries of "Long live Dom Miguel!" But then their favorite clown appeared on the stage as a huge orangutan with all the suppleness of Mazurier. The enthusiastic applause rang out stronger than ever, and Dom Miguel stood up and expressed his profound gratitude yet again. This time, however, his bow was met with nothing but loud laughter, and one of his English companions, Lord Mount Charles, grasped the infante unceremoniously by the arm and pulled him back down. The audience must have, involuntarily, continued to identify Dom Miguel with their favorite actor for some time after that!

January 6th, 1828

WE ARE ADRIFT in endless parties. One was given yesterday by the beautiful marchioness, and today the celebrated Princess Lieven gave hers, which lasted until six in the morning. No matter the hour, people persist in their efforts to keep the prince amused. It is no doubt pleasant to be so privileged that the highest and lowest, the smartest and dumbest, do their utmost to entertain and please you.

In the midst of this confusion, I received another letter from you by way of L—— and was delighted by the hundred thousandth affirmation of your love, an affirmation that I will not tire of hearing for the first million times, and after those million I will still exclaim, "L'appétit vient en mangeant!"[7] This is how it is with the parties here; no one gets tired of them. Even as our diplomats see more and more clouds gathering on the horizon, they go on dancing and dining, laughing and joking their way toward the threatening storm, while the great and the sublime mingle with the common and mundane as they do in Shakespeare's true-to-life tragedies.

Through all this *my* mood remains pleasantly stimulated, healthy, and vigorous. My *masculine* soul is in ascendancy right now, which always makes me feel steadier, freer, and less susceptible to external influences. (I have, of course, in addition to *your* soul—which belongs to me—another *feminine* one of my own). This is very appropriate for my sojourn here, because the English, like their flints, are cold, angular, and fitted with cutting edges; but it is therefore easy for steel to elicit exhilarating sparks from them, creating light through congenial antagonism.

But I am generally too lethargic, or better, too little aroused to want to play the steel blade with those around me. Yet I have always at least countered their pride with a greater version of my own, thereby winning some over, while estranging others. I find both of these acceptable, for the phrenologist said something absolutely true of me: that I was allotted an intellect driven to create. And such people, you know, only *love* whatever they find congenial, or whatever is subordinate and can be a useful instrument for playing their own melodies. To the rest, they remain opposed or aloof.

January 11th, 1828

THE LAST SOIRÉE for Dom Miguel took place today at the Dutch ambassador's.[8] This led to all sorts of interesting historical reflections, since Portugal and Holland, though only small countries, were nonetheless world powers in former times. One went the way of freedom, the other of slavery, yet in the end both became comparably insignificant, and their internal fortunes appear not all that different either. I want to leave this musing, however, and offer a few words of praise for the amiable ambassadress, whose Gallic lightheartedness has not yet taken on the depressing follies of English fashion. Her house is also among the few where one can drop by in the evening uninvited, in keeping with the Continental custom, and actually find a *conversation*. When Madame Falck was still unmarried and living in Tournai, my dear commander, the old Grand Duke of Saxe-Weimar, was living in her parents' house during the War of Liberation and was in the habit of referring playfully to the charming daughter as his favorite adjutant.[9] Given that I myself once occupied that same post, I have sought to assert a kind of comradeship, an honor I am loath to relinquish, because her husband is also not only very pleasant, but exceptional in his intellect and kindheartedness.

At midday I had a German dinner at Count Münster's, who again served up some Hanoverian game. Today it was a marvelous boar, with that royal sauce invented by George IV, a concoction described in the *Almanach des Gourmands* as follows: "avec une telle sauce on mangerait son père."[10] In addition to this delicacy we were offered an excellent rendition of an anecdote by Walter Scott. The latter met an Irish beggar on the street, who asked him for sixpence. Sir Walter could not find one, so handed him a shilling, adding jokingly: "Pay attention, now—you owe me sixpence!" "Oh, certainly!" the beggar exclaimed, "and may God let you live long enough for me to repay it."

Before going to bed, I reread your last letters. You understand my view of Macbeth's role exactly, and in just a few words you express yourself masterfully about it, as well as about the achievements of our actors. It is certainly odd, although indisputable, that the stage is degenerating almost everywhere. Certainly this must also be due to the excessive egotism of our mechanistic, unpoetic times.

Your comments are equally astute about the upper echelons of Berlin society and how its cleverness and even its knowledge are displayed with such pretension that no trace remains of the good-natured camaraderie that could grant either quality some true social charm. The beat of a warm heart is missing from that desiccated terrain, the people can do nothing about it, and if Lady Fancy does ever pay them a visit, she appears only as she did to the late Hoffmann—as nothing but a ghost or a horrific, articulated mannequin.[11] Unfortunately your friend, for whom things often fare no better, was also born in sandy soil; yet I believe his cradle was surrounded by the scent of minerals arising from deep shafts, the flaming breath of gnomes floating up from below, the dark solitariness of the forest pines above, and the whisper of the dryads from their thickly festooned branches. All these have invested this poor little fellow with a number of odd yet auspicious qualities.

The *par force* participants in the new *par force* hunt made me laugh very heartily.[12] They are the perfect counterpart to the volunteers in the Landwehr.[13] I myself am a sincere volunteer in the latter and love our king deeply,[14] so I serve him not just out of duty but also with pleasure. Therefore, once I am back home, I will gladly submit to the *douce violence* of participating in a *par force* hunt, for I feel great affection and respect for the most elegant and admirable prince who is its main proponent. This will definitely revive the art of field riding, otherwise nearly forgotten at home. And England teaches me daily that traditions like this involving danger and exertion have a very advantageous effect on the young; indeed on the whole culture of a nation.

January 14th, 1828

THIS MORNING I drove into the City with Count B—— and a son of the famous Madame Tallien in order to see India House, where many remarkable objects are stored. One is the Dream Book of Tipu Sahib, in which he daily recorded his dreams and their interpretation, and he, like Wallenstein, had these to thank for his death.[15] Tipu's armor, a section of his golden throne, and an odd barrel organ are also kept here. The organ is located in the belly of a life-size metal tiger, very nicely displayed in natural colors (Figure 64).[16] The tiger has pinned down an Englishman in a red uniform and is in the process of mauling him. When you turn the handle, you hear the lifelike screams and whimpers of a man suffering the agony of death, alternating with the spine-chilling roars and grunts of a tiger. It is revealing that this instrument pays tribute to Tipu, that fearful enemy of the English, who put tiger stripes on his coat-of-arms and liked to claim that he would rather be a tiger on the prowl for a single day than graze peacefully like a sheep for an entire century.

I am fascinated by Daniell's magnificent publication on the famous Temples at Ellora carved out of the hard cliffs.[17] The age of these splendid monuments is unknown. It is remarkable and entirely compatible with Merkel's hypothesis that the oldest cultures on the earth began

64

Tipu's Tiger.

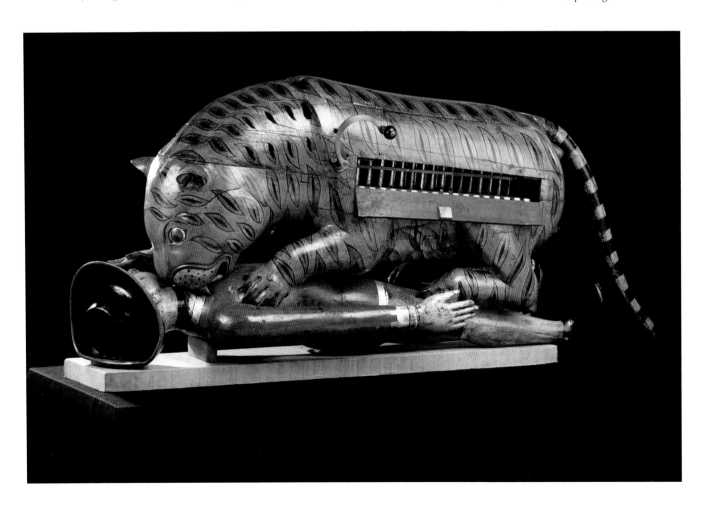

with the Negroes and that the statue of the god in the inner sanctum of the oldest Buddhist temple so obviously displays the distinctive features and wooly hair of a Negro.[18]

The greatest curiosities in this collection include a sizeable stone from the ruins at Persepolis, covered with still-undeciphered cuneiform inscriptions; large Chinese paintings; Chinese lanterns as tall as a house; a gigantic map of the city of Calcutta; beautiful Persian miniatures; and so forth.

After this we took a look at the warehouses, where you can buy every possible Indian product at an extremely good price provided that you send the item to the Continent immediately, in which case no tax is owed to the government. Shawls that would cost at least one hundred louis d'ors at home were to be had here in large quantity for no more than forty. The most beautiful I have ever seen, of a delicacy and luxuriance that would certainly cause a huge stir among our ladies at home, were available for one hundred fifty guineas. Meanwhile shawls are not at all fashionable in England and not particularly esteemed, so nearly all of them are sold abroad.

65

Patent Kite and Charvolant.

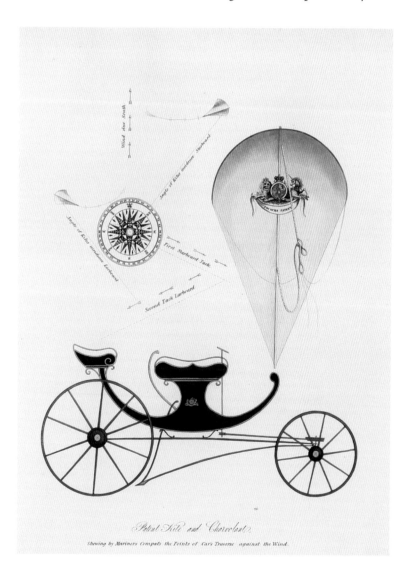

Patent Kite and Charvolant.
Shewing by Mariners Compass the Points of Car's Traverse against the Wind.

January 16th, 1828

THE NEWLY COMPLETED, steam-powered mail carriage covered five miles in a half hour during its test run in Regent's Park. But every minute, some part of it needs repair. I was one of the first people to try it out, but found the smell of oil on iron, which makes steamships so unpleasant, twice as unbearable here.

I also entrusted myself to another, even-stranger means of transportation. This one consists of nothing less than a carriage pulled by a kite—in fact, a paper kite constructed not very differently from those flown by children (Figure 65).[19] Indeed it was a schoolmaster who invented this vehicle, and he knows how to drive it so well that he makes good progress even in a light wind, and given a really favorable one and good terrain, he can cover a mile in just over a minute. The sensation is very pleasant, for you glide past the small irregularities of the ground as if lifted over them (Figure 66). The inventor proposes to cross the deserts of Africa by this means and has therefore added a place at the back of the chassis for a pony to stand the way a servant would, and then if the wind fails, he can be harnessed at the front. But what about forage? The schoolmaster is counting on the trade winds that blow regularly in those regions. The contraption is in any case

66

Charvolants Travelling in Various Directions with the Same Wind.

highly recommended for amusement in the countryside, so I am enclosing a detailed brochure with explanatory illustrations, and you can commission any likely enthusiasts among your own schoolmasters to undertake something similar.

I devoted the evening to a pantomime, its crazy ingenuity reinforced by such superb decorations and machinery that you had no difficulty imagining yourself transported to a time of fairy tales. Such delightful nonsense is marvelous. For instance, there was an immeasurable, reedy swamp in the kingdom of the frogs, its inhabitants portrayed by the most talented actors; and lastly a temple of glowworms, a boisterous fantasy with a wonderful radiance the equal of any Chinese fireworks.

Brighton, January 23rd, 1828

FASHION IS A great tyrant, and as much as I recognize this, I still allow myself (like everyone else) to be ruled by her. She led me back here again, a few days ago already, to the engaging Miss J——, the clever Lady L——, the charming F——, etc., etc.

Already tired of the balls and dinners, I am flirting with the sea again, the only poetic object in this prosaic part of the world. Just now, returning at the night's end from a rout at the furthest edge of town, I walked for a good half hour along the shore, accompanied by the spume and thunder of the incoming tide. The stars were still twinkling brightly; eternal peace was enthroned on high even as the roaring and seething raged wildly here below. Heaven and earth in their truest image! How splendid, how soothing, how fearful this world is, and how exhausting! A world that never began and will never end, whose extent has no limits. When faced with its endless, all-encompassing pursuits, even the imagination shrinks back and collapses, trembling to the ground. Oh, my dearest Julie, only *love* can find the way out of this labyrinth! Does Goethe not also say, "Glücklich allein ist die Seele, die liebt!"[20]

January 24th, 1828

WE WENT ON an excellent hunt today. The weather was unusually clear and sunny, and something like a hundred red coats had assembled. Such a spectacle is certainly of great interest: the many handsome horses, the elegantly dressed huntsmen, fifty to sixty hounds pursuing Reynard over hedge and ditch, the wild troop of riders at the rear, the quick alternation of forest and mountain and valley, the cries and cheering. It is almost like a miniature war.

The countryside here is very hilly, and at one point the chase went up a long incline, too steep for most of the horses to follow—even the best were moaning like a bellows in a blacksmith's shop. But once you reached the top, the view was truly magnificent. The entire scene could be taken in at a single glance, from the fox to the last straggler, all moving at full tilt. To the left lay a fertile valley stretching all the way to London, and to the right, the sea in its most beautiful summer brilliance.

We got the first fox; the second, however, reached Maleperduys ahead of us and so escaped his pursuers. Almost all these hunts are maintained by subscription. This pack, for instance, which consists of eighty hounds, three *piqueurs,* and nine horses, costs 1,050 pounds annually to maintain. There are twenty-five paying participants (anyone who wishes can also ride along free of charge), which comes to no more than forty-two pounds a year for each subscriber. The charges are not distributed equally, however. The rich give a lot, the poor very little, so that some contribute two hundred a year, others only ten. I believe it would be very good if we imitated this arrangement, especially for the poor.

To my spoiled eyes, the most striking aspect of these hunts is the pastors in their black garb who go flying over fences and ditches. Before the hunt—already in boots and spurs and holding a crop—they manage to officiate at some marriage, baptism, or burial, and then, the minute they leave the ceremony, they leap onto their steeds. There is a story about one of the most famous of these clerical foxhunters, who always carried along a tame fox in a bag and, if no other was found, would volunteer his own. The animal was so well trained that it would amuse the hounds for a while and then, when it became tired of the hunt, escape into its unassailable hiding place—none other than the altar of the parish church. Accessible through a hole in the wall, a comfortable bed awaited him beneath the steps. This is proper English religion!

February 6th, 1828

I CAME DOWN with a cold and then a high fever, which has kept me chained to my bed for fourteen days already and left me extraordinarily exhausted. It has not been entirely without danger, but the doctor assures me the worst is now over, so have no worries. It is odd how, when faced with a debilitating illness, one becomes so indifferent to the thought of death. It begins to appear like mere rest and slumber, and I very much hope that, when my certain end approaches, my bodily dissolution will advance at the same gradual pace. Being someone devoted to observation, I would like to be as cognizant as possible of my own self expiring; that is, observe my emotions and thoughts in a fully conscious state and savor existence until the very last. To me a *sudden* death seems to have something vulgar, even bestial about it; only a slow, self-conscious experience of death seems ennobling and truly human. I hope to die peacefully, for although I have not really achieved sanctity in life, I have nonetheless practiced charity and kindness, and I have loved mankind, if rather more collectively than individually. So not yet ripe for heaven, I very much wish—in accord with my theory of metempsychosis— to become a resident of this dear earth again every so often. The planet is beautiful and interesting enough to romp around on for a few thousand years in an ever-renewed human form. But if it turns out differently, that is all right with me too. It is certainly not possible to fall away altogether from God and the world. Nor are we likely to become more foolish and wicked, but rather more clever and good.

For me the worst part of death is the thought of *your* grief, and yet, would I be able to feel so benevolent and resigned about dying without the awareness of your love? It must be such a sweet feeling at the moment of death to know that we are leaving someone behind who will lovingly preserve our memory, and in this way, as long as those eyes are open to the light, we ourselves live on with and within that person. Is this merely egotism as well?

Since we are on the subject of dying, I must tell you something else. Do you remember a Scottish chieftain from my earlier sojourn in Brighton, a somewhat fantastic but sturdy and original man? Just now, at the peak of his manly powers, he has ceased to live. He had embarked with his two daughters on a steamboat, and shortly before they were to land, a boom struck him on the head with such force that he suffered a sudden attack of frenzy, sprang into the sea, and swam to shore, where he expired a few hours later. This finale has a tragic affinity with the story he told me with great pride. You will recall it was about one of his ancestors, a man who cut off his hand, threw it onto the shore, and swam after it.[21]

THE DOCTOR FINDS me very patient. God knows I have learned patience well enough! Adversity, to be fair, is a worthwhile school for the spirit; even though it is most often the result of our failings, it is also what helps them to reform. And we can unconditionally assert that if people acted reasonably and virtuously from the very beginning, they would know hardly any sorrow. But then their joy would be equally curtailed, so it would become difficult to put any value on earthly things. No more dinners at which one so gladly risks indigestion. No more fame pursued for the sake of contented vanity. No ventures into sweet and forbidden love. No luster and pomp with which to outdo others. In the end it would be—God forgive me my sin— nothing more than a stagnant, humdrum life, even if a life of seeming perfection. Motion and contrast are the essence of living. It would be a terrible misfortune if all of us suddenly became reasonable. Not that I think we are in much danger of this quite yet. As you see, I am so far unchanged despite my illness, and indeed I would not have shared these reflections with you at all, had this letter been sent off before I was thoroughly recovered.[22] Thus you can read it with peace of mind and rest assured that, until my last breath, I will enjoy everything the good Lord has granted us: whether it be a penny or a gold piece, a house of cards or a palace, soap bubbles or the display of rank and titles, whatever time and circumstances may bring, including death itself and whatever might follow after, either here or there. The serious virtues are fine when interspersed to add piquancy! For instance, I am thoroughly enjoying my momentary temperance. I feel unusually light and ethereal, more than usually elevated above the bestial. As for other deviances, they are out of the question now, and really, all of this has given me a foretaste of the future, the purer joys of old age. For in certain things (let us admit this openly), the wicked Frenchman is at least half correct when he says "C'est le vice qui nous quitte, et bien rarement nous qui quittons le vice."[23] Even the most sincere zealots found the most reliable road to virtue only in the knife, like the great Origen.[24]

I HAVE NEVER had a doctor who acted so kindly to the pharmacist! Two medicines every day; I subsist on nothing else. Since, unfortunately, I am seriously ill, I calmly swallow whatever is required. I very much miss having a nurse like you, however, and my wizened, dried-out landlady, who frequently and very obligingly offers her services, would be a poor substitute. Meanwhile I have been reading a lot and am in very good spirits. If I wanted to indulge in melancholic self-torment, I could. Besides the positive grounds for courting such a mood, I find negative ones to irritate me as well. For example, now while I have had to remain indoors, the weather has been at its best. But since I have put my spiritual clock on a totally different setting, I am in fact very grateful to see the friendly sun every day. Despite its splendor and majesty, it deigns to warm my chamber from early morning on, covering everything in gold throughout the day; and in the evenings, it bothers to paint weird and wonderful cloud pictures on the horizon of the sea, coloring them sometimes deep blue, sometimes fiery yellow or purple. To think this is all for me, a poor invalid bundled up by my large window. As if to bid me farewell, it appears each evening in such magnificence that for a long time afterward its memory lightens the dusky shadows of descending night, erasing the bleak and sinister impression that they otherwise inflict on solitary, suffering souls. And so all things have two sides to them. A fool can find despair in everything and a wise man pleasure and satisfaction.

February 10th, 1828

A LETTER FROM you brings me great joy, as you know, but how much more in my current circumstances! Judge for yourself with what jubilation yours was received today..................

....

F—— is very mistaken to refuse what is offered him. It would be madness for someone shipwrecked, swimming in the sea and already exhausted, to rebuff a fishing boat that offers to rescue him, just in order to wait for a three-decker. Certainly it is possible that such a comodious craft is about to approach from behind the cliff and will arrive under full sail at the very moment the fishing boat has carried the helpless man off to a humbler destination. But we are not omniscient; we must calculate our chances according to probability, not possibility.

So you are pleased with my gifts? Well, may God bless them! Little pleasures are as good as big ones, and we should learn how to engage in this kind of thing much more often. There are certainly a lot of inexpensive items available. But there can be no superstition involved—for example, about the scissors I sent. Good Julie, no pair of scissors yet invented could cut our friendship in two! They would have to be crab scissors and operate backward, cutting away the past. But I must scold you about something else. Why have I sent you so much beautiful colored blotting paper, if you are going to persist in the loathsome practice of strewing sand, something long since abandoned in England—along with scattering sand on the floorboards. Several grams of this ingredient flew in my face when I opened your letter. Do you, too, want to throw sand in my eyes, dear Julie, and is it possible that Jeremias bought you a newly pious sand shaker from Berlin?

I am very diligent and using my leisure time to bring some order to several volumes of the atlas of my life.[25] All day long I arrange, cut, write (for you know that there is some commentary under every picture), which is the only thing a poor, sick man can do to pass the time. In my imagination, I already see twenty folio volumes of this classic work arrayed in our library and the two of us, old and stooped, sitting in front of them, talking a little drivel, but nonetheless taking triumphant pleasure in former times. Meanwhile some tall, gangly youngsters are laughing surreptitiously behind our backs as they hurry to and fro, and when someone outside asks, "So what are those old folks doing?" they reply, "Oh, they're poring over their picture Bible—they no longer see or hear anything else." I would so love to experience this, and I keep thinking that it really will come to pass! But what may transpire in the interim, only God knows!

Bellows are playing a big role in the newspapers these days. A donkey, killed with upas poison as an experiment,[26] came back to life one hour after its death by someone continually forcing air into its lungs. In the future, Parliament will be given a huge bellows to provide it with a continuous supply of fresh air! Finally a proven measure against a sudden attack of suffocating asthma has been reported: you need do nothing more than hold the patient's nose closed and, using the bellows hanging by the fireplace, blow air into his mouth. There will soon be an even greater number of puffed-up people in England than before.*

MY ILLNESS HINDERED me from going to Scotland, for which I had prepared everything and received many invitations; now I will probably be kept in London by the expected arrival of W—— and the beginning of the Season. Today, for the first time, the doctor allowed me to venture outside, and I made my way to Stanmore Park, not far away, in order to fully enjoy the fresh air and the pleasure of a romantic walk. But I was not allowed entry into the garden, even though I sent my card in to the lady of the house. *We* are admittedly more liberal, but this exclusive habit of keeping people at bay also has its good aspects. It adds value not just to the forbidden thing itself but, if granted, to the privilege of finally gaining access.

Apropos, this makes me think of your new steward. It is to our advantage to keep him, but nonetheless I ask you to treat him a bit as the lady of Stanmore did me. Do not start out by being overly accommodating; thus, when he has earned it, there will be scope for you to become more so. Be friendly, but with dignity and tact regarding the *superior* position that you must maintain. Do not try to win him over through flattery and excessive courtesy, but rather through respectful confidence and solid advantages, which in the end never fail to make an impression, whatever people may say or think. Yet this does not mean you should pay less account to his ambition; on the contrary, keep it alive through prudent concessions and gratitude for any display of diligence, as well as through a gentle reprimand whenever you think it is needed, so that he will see that you have a sense of judgment. As an honorable man, he will doubtless soon be attending to our affairs with the same interest he devotes to his own. Finally, you do not want to burden him with too many details concerning his supervisory duties, or exercise too much control over every trifle, but you should take special care to support his authority over his subordinates, while maintaining yours over him. If ever you fear something important may be amiss, however, do not hesitate to demand a detailed explanation. In very important cases, where a delay is possible, you will of course consult me. Herewith does Polonius conclude his exhortations.

THE SHORT WALK was clearly premature, for it did me no good. Meanwhile the lovely weather has turned horrible. A snowstorm is whipping up the sea beneath my windows, making it foam and roar with rage, and its breakers are rearing up across the high jetty and right up to the houses.

---

* The invention of the bellows, or *Blasebalg* (blow-belly), is very simple. You bring a bellows and large bladder together from below, make a small hole at the upper end of the bladder, and by activating the bellows, let air—set to a specified temperature—flow in. Then a Parliament of Lilliputs could sit in the belly and deliberate, while all their emanations would exit continuously at the top, and the fresh air from below would be constantly renewed in exactly the same measure. This method of simultaneous heating and ventilating is the principle of Mr. Vallance and should be administered to the English government. Perhaps one could also combine it with an Aeolian harp as a way to rescue failing organs.

Yesterday, amid this thundering, I began writing my memoirs and have already filled eight pages, which I enclose with this letter. In addition, I have used the time to read through Lesage's historical atlas once more. I honestly cannot claim to have felt one bit of boredom during my long illness. In fact, the great tranquility and sense of detachment of such a period do my soul good. By the way, my body will soon be fully restored to health, too, and as soon as the skies clear a bit, I think I will venture back out among my fellow mortals.

Adelheid, to whom I sent your letter, sends her fondest greetings. When the king dies she may well, as intimate friend of the new queen, play a significant role here.[27] In public she is already treated as a *princesse du sang*. She is also beginning to sense her own importance, has amended her formerly shy demeanor very much to her advantage, and has learned to appear distinguished while remaining affable. The glow of fortune and favor changes a person just as the sun affects a plant stunted by the dark, causing it to lift its drooping head beneath the bright beams and, infused with their soothing warmth, open its fragrant blossoms to the light. We, good Julie, are for the time being still lying in the cellar, like hyacinth bulbs; but in the spring the gardener can move us to richer soil and into the sun, *if that is his will.*

February 20th, 1828

I CAME BACK to life, and behold! wherever I went, everything seemed strange. My acquaintances were almost all gone, and I was met with new faces on the esplanades and in the houses. The only thing unchanged was the barren landscape I found when I went riding, although there was a difference, for the green fields had all been fertilized—with oyster shells!

Miss Gibbings, a no-longer-young but charming and rich creature,[28] who would have been married long ago except that any suitor is required to take on her unpalatable parents, told me that the local newspapers had announced I was on my deathbed. The London *Morning Post,* meanwhile, reported me dancing at the Almack's ball, which seems a bit eerie. This good Miss Gibbings is still extremely grateful for the ticket I once procured for her to the aforementioned ball, so in gratitude she played and sang for me today, rather more than my still-weak nerves could endure. As soon as her fat mother came in, I took my leave, but shortly thereafter fell into the hands of two other Philomelas,[29] who are also staying on here.

Under such circumstances, as soon as my strength is fully back, I will head for London. And I can now send off this long epistle with a clear conscience and without fear of causing you worry.

The short meaning of the many words is always the same: the heartfelt love of your

Lou

London, February 28th, 1828

I WANT TO ADD a kind of postscript here about an acquaintance I made in Brighton, for the story is quite interesting. You have heard how one of the ancestors of the Thellussons left a will stipulating that his estate remain untouched for a hundred and fifty years, during which it would earn interest upon interest and only then pass to the youngest living member of the family.[1] That deadline will arrive in twenty years. Well, I ran into two members of the family: a forty-year-old man with very little money and his attractive, eight-year-old son, who, at the age of twenty-eight, is supposed to come into twelve million pounds sterling, that is, ninety-four million thalers. An act of Parliament has forbidden such wills in the future, but nothing could be done about this one, even though people very much wanted to bar it, because such a monstrous fortune grants unnatural power to a private individual. Meanwhile the boy should be wished the best of luck in his fair hopes. To have so much wealth is something grand, since we really cannot deny that money is the administrator of most things on this earth. If wisely used, a fortune that large could achieve marvels for the benefit of all mankind!

I was intrigued not only by this future young Croesus but also by a famous eccentric, Colonel C——, who spent a few days here. Lady M—— brought him to my attention and related the following:

When I was young, the elegant, middle-aged man you see there was already one of the capital's most successful dandies. He had lost all but a few thousand pounds of his fortune, however, when one day fate presented him with a map of America, and he suddenly had the idea of emigrating there. He looked at the map and quickly chose a spot on Lake Erie, sold all his possessions that same week, arranged for his servant to marry a pretty young girl, and set sail with the two of them. Safely arrived at his chosen spot in the middle of a primeval wood, he lived for a few days by hunting and slept under a canopy of leaves, and then—with the help of a few other backwoodsmen— quickly built himself a log cabin, where he still lives. Soon he had gained considerable influence over the various adventurers scattered about the territory, and this he used to encourage communal undertakings, while making himself useful by cooking and baking for everyone, supplanting the half-raw dishes they were otherwise condemned to eat. He fell in love, produced offspring, and watched a new generation arise, a generation entirely dependent on him. He now owns land equivalent to a small principality. He figures his annual revenues at ten thousand pounds sterling, and he returns to England every tenth year for *one Season*, during which he lives, as before, like a dandy and with all the *aisance* of a man of the world. Then he retreats to the woods for another ten years, once again exchanging his modern dress coat for a sheepskin.

My first visit in the metropolis was to Countess M——, who despite her forty years had managed, during my absence, to add another baby to her previous dozen. I dined there and admired a lovely gift from the king. It was made of silver, which is always more artistically wrought in England than anywhere else, thus often raising the cost of the workmanship over that of the material by a factor of ten. During the meal, the count offered a striking example of how justice is administered here.

A man I know had his handkerchief stolen on the street. He grabbed the thief and, being stronger, held him very firmly, not without treating him a bit roughly, and handed him over to an approaching policeman. The situation was clear, there were many witnesses, and, if the case had been presented to a jury, the delinquent would have either been hanged or transported to Botany Bay for many, many years, with no chance of rescue. The culprit's wife, however, called upon the gentleman and begged him on bended knee for mercy; and the thief himself, a not-uneducated man, wrote him the most moving letters, until—who can be surprised—he finally won the sympathy of the plaintiff, who then failed to appear at court on the appointed day. The guilty man was thus acquitted in accordance with English law.

This misplaced sympathy turned out badly for the gentleman, however. Fourteen days later, the same man who had stolen his handkerchief charged him with assault and violent attack on a public street, noting that there had been witnesses. The defendant retorted that it had happened only because the plaintiff had stolen his handkerchief. But since the delinquent had already been acquitted on that count, and no one can be brought to trial twice for the same offense, this objection was disregarded. In short, damages and costs included, the too-generous robbery victim had to pay the thief and the courts almost one hundred pounds.

The whole company found this kind of justice to be atrocious, but one old Englishman resolutely defended it, interrupting with great eagerness:

I believe that the anecdote we just heard serves as a graphic illustration of the wisdom of our laws. At their most fundamental, the laws themselves, like the judicial authorities, exist only to prevent crime. And punishment is meted out only to this end. Thus in the eyes of the law, the receiver of stolen goods is almost as guilty as the thief, and anyone who knowingly tries to help a criminal already subject to the law escape his punishment is no less detrimental to the community than the criminal himself. That man, who perhaps began his career with the stealing of a handkerchief and was supposed to have been removed from society for penance and reform, may, having been further emboldened, commit a far-greater theft, or perhaps even a murder. Who then should accept the blame for this? The gentleman you refer to was rightly punished for his *unlawful* pity. Whoever rashly and uninvited interferes with the wheels of a well-intentioned machine should not be surprised when it breaks his fingers.

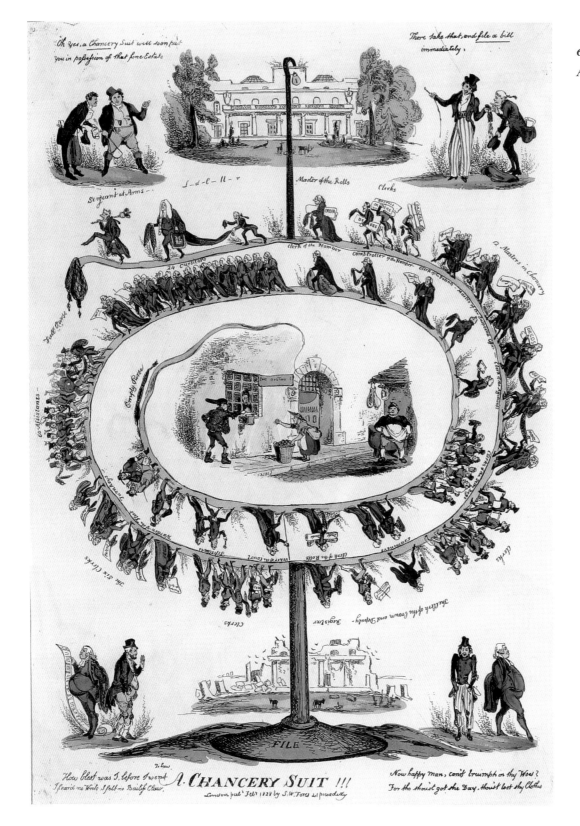

The English are, one must admit, very talented sophists when it comes to lauding their own practices. Yet Brougham, the greatest of them all, recently gave a speech lasting six hours that dealt with nothing but the *abuses* of the English judiciary. The most colossal at present seems to be the tremendous sum of fifty million pounds sterling that is lying there in the Court of Chancery with no actual owner. A case before this court has become proverbial for something that never ends, and there is a delicious caricature about it bearing the caption "A Chancery Suit!!!" (Figure 67). A dapperly dressed young man, bursting with health, is shown dropping pieces of gold into a hat being held out by a skeletal, undernourished lawyer, who is to plead his case for him. A very long procession of diverse figures holding various objects winds round and round, and below we see the young man again, now a ragged, frail beggar, humbly beseeching his lawyer—who in the meantime has become fat as a barrel—for a small handout. The lawyer refuses, of course, and haughtily turns away. Alas, it's just the same at home, except here in more corpulent proportions.

As with much that can seem scandalous to a foreigner, one must guard against jumping to conclusions, since apparent abuses and even obvious failings are often only the unavoidable shadows cast by far greater lights—bribes during Parliamentary elections, for example, and perhaps also the rotten boroughs or the acknowledged dependence of one part of Parliament on government patronage, and so forth.[2] It is a good question whether any administration could endure without such reprehensible expedients. That such things are theoretically not allowed (as they are in despotic states) is an advantage in itself, even though no government can actually do without them. This is rather like the preacher whose life does not always live up to his sermons. It must not be forgotten that human conduct at its best can only approach but never actually attain perfection, and for this reason one must be very careful about reforms, always remembering *que le mieux es l'ennemi du bien.*[3] Nonetheless, there are many indications that England is heading for reform; in fact, it can scarcely avoid it for other reasons. Whether this will prove an advantage is still very much in doubt; the necessity of reform may be proof that the country has outlived its greatness and entered into decline.

This evening I visited the Adelphi Theatre where a magician performed his tricks in an entirely new way under the title "Conversazione." He stood on the stage surrounded by many tables and machines and began a tale about his trip in a diligence, introducing various characters and anecdotes, singing a few songs, and inserting stunts, apparitions, and optical illusions along the way, whenever appropriate to his story. This is an excellent idea and lends greater interest to the usual sleights of hand. Just as remarkable as his confidence and agility as a magician were the dramatic quality of his acting and his prodigious memory. In closing, he filled glasses with varying levels of water and skillfully played several musical compositions on them, not only tunes in the harmonica style but also waltzes and the like, even lengthy trills, which were splendidly successful.

March 9th, 1828

THE SEASON IS already exercising its power. The streets swarm with elegant carriages, the shops display new treasures, all the theaters are filled, and all the prices have doubled or tripled. Mr. Peel, the minister, hosted a brilliant soirée this evening for the Duchess of Clarence. His house is adorned with many beautiful paintings, among them the famous *Chapeau de Paille* by Rubens.[4] Mr. Peel bought this small, half-length portrait for the equivalent of just fifteen thousand reichstalers.

England possesses unbelievable treasures of this sort. Yesterday, in the company of Princess Esterházy, I visited the small private collection of a certain Mr. Carr, a clergyman, containing no more than thirty paintings that nonetheless cost him twenty thousands pounds sterling.[5] But they were absolutely worth the price, for there are just as many masterpieces as there are pictures! This is the only proper way for a private individual with a small gallery to collect, not for the purpose of education but simply for pleasure. There is a Garofalo of such unearthly glory, of such holiness in the depths of its poetry that you believe you are looking at a picture not of this world but from Eden. Nearby is an enormous Claude that takes up almost half the wall. It is also of magnificent beauty, its economy of means as admirable as the remarkable effect the painter was able to achieve. In an adjoining room are yet more excellent landscapes by Domenichino and Annibale Carracci. The richness of the compositions, the intimacy and candor of feeling were imbued with such notable charm and variety of detail that I could have lost myself the whole day in these beguiling regions: in the mirrored surfaces of their waters; in the islands, groves, and cozy huts; in the deep blue of the mountain ranges and the tenebrous and ghostly forests. Only in the third room, however, do you come upon the crown jewel of the entire collection, a painting by Leonardo da Vinci composed of three figures—the Savior, Peter, and John—the ideals of youth, maturity, and old age, each of them manifesting a grace, truth, and perfection leaving nothing to be desired. Of all the heads of Christ I have ever seen depicted, this is the only one that fully satisfies me, and it expresses greatness and power just as compellingly as it does holiness and gentleness, at the same time expressing this eloquence through the most ideal beauty. Meanwhile the grouping of the figures is so pleasant to the eye, the coloring so radiant, each nuance of paint so fresh, the execution of the smallest detail so masterful that one feels a profound sense of gratification, which no other work of art can provide.* Since nothing lags so far behind the actual contemplation of such a masterpiece as its cold dissection in words, I will say no more, though I do wish that connoisseurs were better aware of Mr. Carr's outstanding collection.

Genre paintings are much easier to describe; for example, an exhibition of several works by General Lejeune depicting battles and skirmishes that he fought in and later painted. They are executed with much talent and good taste. The Battle of Borodino centers on the histrionic Murat, King of Naples, and his entourage, as he holds his position amid the musket fire, self-satisfied and adorned with feathers, ringlets, and embroidery. The king is giving the French and Saxon cuirassiers the order to begin their murderous attack and seize a battery of forty guns, a command that cost the lives of many (including my dearest friend H———), and he is about to place himself at their head. Who could have prophesied that he would soon be shamefully attacked by a mob and finally executed for his crimes?

Profoundly moving, though perhaps too lurid a subject for art, is a painting of the Battle of Marengo in which an Austrian field officer is shown with his lower body torn viciously open by enemy fire, so that his intestines are lying on the ground (Figures 68 and 69). In order to escape his hellish pain, the poor wretch has beseeched a French gendarme for a pistol, which he puts in his mouth with a gesture of despair, while the man who provided it shudders and turns away.

---

* A learned antiquarian once told me that in former eras artists tended to paint on a chalk ground and used varnishes in preparing their colors, which is why such works remain permanently fresh and brilliant. Strange that no one tries to master this technique any longer.—*The Editor.*

68

Battle of Marengo.

69

Battle of Marengo, detail
of lower left corner.

LETTERS OF A DEAD MAN

Another painting depicts a French detachment being attacked by Spanish guerillas. You see a romantic mountain pass in Catalonia, remarkable for the colossal stone statues of six bulls, their construction ascribed to Hannibal. At their feet lie the skeletons of two or three French cuirassiers, still in their armor, who met their death here a month earlier. General Lejeune was the only member of the entire detachment to escape murder, and this was due to a near miracle: the weapons aimed at him failed three times in succession, at which point El Empecinado, superstitiously wary that destiny must somehow be involved, ordered his men to hold their fire. You can see General Lejeune in the painting, stripped naked, with one of the murderers grasping his hair and another kicking his body, as the rest aim their guns at him. Meanwhile, amid the surrounding corpses and debris, his servants and a soldier lie close by breathing their last, having already been run through repeatedly by pikes and swords.

The Battle of the Nile also conveys a very romantic effect, as the Mamluks, in half-crazed flight, spur their magnificent Arabian horses off a precipice into a river.[6] Only a few reach the opposite shore (Figure 70).

70

Battle of the Nile.

March 13th, 1828

I FORGOT TO tell you that about two weeks ago, the recently completed and elegant Brunswick Theater collapsed during the rehearsal of a new play, and a large number of people lost their lives (Figure 71). I went to see the ruins yesterday and found, still lying under the rubble, the carcasses of two cart horses that had been struck down in the street next to the building. It was a fearful sight. A single box seat somehow remained intact, and there the actor Farren was able to save himself by cold-bloodedly remaining on the spot and watching, unharmed, as the entire horrible catastrophe took place—a truly genuine tragedy that no one had anticipated.[7] Now, in the frenzy of the Season, it has already been forgotten. Despite everything, this boisterous life offers less substance than one would think, and what it does offer fades away in the eternal hurly-burly.

THE FALLING OF THE NEW BRUNSWICK THEATRE.

71

Brunswick Theater Fire.

A diversion in the midst of all this was a family dinner at the great Rothschild's, a man people have compared with the sultan, who is said to be sovereign of all believers, whereas Rothschild is the creditor of all sovereigns.[8] There is something truly original about him. Today he was especially jovial and asked that someone go fetch his new Austrian consular uniform, which, he said, his friend Metternich had sent him from Vienna. He showed it to us and even let himself be persuaded to try it on in front of a mirror, and then strutted around, quite like a virtuoso who, once started, cannot be stopped. He therefore had a few other splendid examples of court dress brought out and changed costume several times, as if on stage. This bit of child-like behavior in such a moneyed hero almost reminded me of the time a foreign ambassador happened upon Henri IV playing a horse for his small son. It was certainly amusing to watch this otherwise sober and business-like man mimicking, with the most varied pirouettes and bows, the light and gracious airs of a courtier, and how, not at all disconcerted by our laughter, he assured us with great conviction and joviality that if he so wanted, Nathan Mayer Rothschild could play any role and, with the help of six to eight more glasses of wine, cut just as good a figure at court as anyone.

LETTERS OF A DEAD MAN

An acquaintance I made the following day drew my interest for very different reasons. This was General Mina. You have certainly seen a number of his portraits, all showing him with a large mustache and wild features, quite like a fearsome bandit. Imagine, then, my amazement, when I found the hero of Spain to be nothing but a gentle, simple, and modest man, without the slightest hint of a military demeanor. On the contrary, he is more like a tenant farmer or schoolteacher with an open, friendly face, and he blushes like a girl at the sound of praise. Yet afterward, when he became more animated in discussion, I did notice a change in his features and an enigmatic spark in his eyes that revealed what kind of person he really was. On the whole, he is still very well preserved and could pass for barely forty; although his short hair has gone completely white, this does not make him appear at all elderly, however, but merely as though he were powdered. He remarked that he had never enjoyed those luxurious locks so generously bestowed on him by some, and he often had to laugh at the caricatures he saw in shop windows.

There were two other notable Spaniards in the party. The first was Argüelles, minister under the constitutional government and one of the foremost popular speakers in Spain, a man of engaging appearance and fine manners. The second, General Valdés, was the commander of Cadiz during the final siege and took the much-loved Ferdinand aboard his ship and delivered him to his French internment (Ferdinand was also an admiral; in fact, the oldest in the navy). As Valdés tells it, the king showered him with adulation both before and during the voyage, repeatedly expressing his gratitude for the good treatment he received in Cadiz and making many promises about the future; yet a sad fate awaited poor Valdés, who continued:

> As soon as the king left my ship, his behavior suddenly changed. Finally confident that he was safe, he quickly cast a piercing gaze of triumph and long suppressed fury at me. I recognized this look and made an immediate decision. Without reflecting any further or bidding him farewell, I sprang back onto my ship, ordered it to reverse course at once, and rushed under full sail back to Cadiz. This probably saved my life. But my exile here in poverty and misery, far from my unhappy native country, is perhaps even worse than death for a sixty-year-old man accustomed to greatness and riches!

Today I will take you to the theater again, this time in the company of the renowned Lord Lauderdale, an old acquaintance of mine, who now, after an eventful career, preserves himself—rather like a pickle—by washing daily in vinegar baths. Formerly he only pickled others with his verbal sallies, just as sour and biting as the so-called *Confiseur* of the *Elegante Zeitung* once delivered in print.[9] We spoke about the old days, and when we got to Drury Lane, he began reciting some wild but lovely verses by Moore. He no doubt wanted to draw a connection with his own past and offer a comment without being overly precise, although the poet has these words issuing from the mouth of a fallen angel's beloved. The verses go approximately like this (in one of my typical doggerel translations):

> Oh! What would love be, if not always the same
> Through joy and through torment, through poverty and wealth,
> Through glory and shame, through youth and old age,
> Why, beloved, would I ask about vice or about virtue.
> I only know that I love you, even if your heart were black,
> For I am *yours*—and your joys and sorrows are *mine*.[10]

Not a bad motto for Desdemona, who awaited us, although the Moor rewards such selfless love so heinously. Before I move on to the performance of *Othello* itself, let me make a few general remarks.

There is a never-ending argument in Germany about whether Shakespeare should be presented in a literal or free translation, or even in a free adaptation. I myself would choose the loose translation, provided that it be allowed complete spontaneity of movement within the spirit of the German language, even though here and there a pun or witticism may be lost. To alter the course of the play significantly, however; to omit scenes entirely; to provide Shakespeare with utterly foreign words and ideas can only mutilate him, even in the hands of the greatest poet. It is said that Shakespeare is better to read than watch and, especially in literal translation, cannot be performed without taking us back to the very infancy of the dramatic arts. At the same time, it is claimed that theatrical productions during Shakespeare's time were essentially fairy tales written in dialogue and acted out in costume. I am not interested in evaluating the accuracy of these statements, but I do know that the productions of *Romeo and Juliet*, *Macbeth*, *Hamlet*, and *Othello* on today's English stage—all performed with very few omissions and including most of what is presumed shocking, even the obligatory king's trumpeter—all of them left me feeling completely satisfied and content. Neither reading nor hearing them read (even by Tieck, the best reader I know) could begin to evoke the same depth of response in me. Indeed I confess that only since seeing Shakespeare's plays here have I grasped the full extent of his gigantic stature. To be sure, exceptional ensemble acting is required, as are brilliant actors in the main roles, and these are completely lacking in Germany. As Clauren would say, the Macbeths in Berlin and the Macbeths in England are as unlike each other as Shakespeare himself is unlike his excellent commentator Franz Horn. The premier actors such as Kean, Kemble, Young, and so forth, are, as I have already mentioned, men of extreme refinement, who to some extent associate with the very best of society and have dedicated their lives to studying their national poet. Only rarely do they perform other roles, and they are not required—like our artful beasts of burden—to switch back and forth between a tragic hero for one of Iffland's privy councilors and a Talbot for Herr von Langsalm.[11] Nor are they forced to appear today in *Othello* and tomorrow in *Der Wollmarkt*.[12]

It is truly odd that these artists actually have to perform for an audience so crude, ignorant, and ill-mannered! But perhaps it has a salutary effect on the players. Just as the genuinely virtuous must love virtue for its own sake, so the actors here must love art for its sake alone and be relatively unconcerned with how they themselves are received. In the end, this is the surest way for them to achieve universal acclaim. Meanwhile one must also admit that, despite the widespread roughness, there is actually a healthier spirit lurking in the English theater public than in the indolent, overly refined audiences of our major German cities. Yes, even amid the vulgar *foule* here, there abides an invisible congregation of the initiated, who guarantee that the sacred fire within the artists can never be fully extinguished. This is not so evident in official critiques, but it has a powerful effect in the realm of society.

Many Germans, myself included, do not like to hear it said that other nations surpass us in something. But I must nonetheless agree that, just as we have no dramatic poet of Shakespeare's caliber, likewise we have no actor capable of bringing his characters to life in their full significance. It is true that this has not always been the case, and I still retain impressions from my earliest youth of Fleck and Mrs. Unzelmann that I have never seen the like of since on our stage. Schröder and Ekhof may have stood even higher, and I recall with great pleasure the enthusiastic description of them given me by old Archenholz, who had also seen Garrick and judged Schröder to be at least his equal.

It should be apparent to any sensible person that, in order to be a fair judge of foreign actors, one must to an extent imagine oneself transfigured into their nationality. One must become accustomed to certain mannerisms and turns of phrase that seem strange, however well we understand them. At first these occasions have a more or less disturbing effect. I have known only a single artist who, in this respect, was, I might say, organized in a completely cosmopolitan manner: the inimitable, perhaps unequaled, and certainly unsurpassed Miss O'Neill (see Figure 107). Her acting spoke to us with nothing but intelligence and soul; nationality, time, and outward appearance vanished from our minds, swept away in a rapturous delight that carried everything else along with it.

But back to the present. We saw *Othello*, where the interplay among the three greatest dramatic artists in England granted me one of my most pleasurable evenings, and accordingly induced this somewhat-long outpouring of mine. Yet it also left me feeling the painful absence of the above mentioned heroine. Had she been there today, I would have witnessed the culmination of all theatrical performances.

Kean, Young, and Kemble, as I said, comprise the ruling triumvirate of the English stage. The first is clearly the most intellectually brilliant, the second sparkling and reliable, the third—although less distinguished in the loftiest tragedies—is nonetheless always dignified and smart. It was only in this production of *Othello* that the three could be seen performing together in the same tragedy. My, that was a rare pleasure! Next to Shylock, Othello is Kean's greatest role. It is amazing what deep human understanding he invests in portraying the jealousy from its initial slumbering through its gradual awakening to the final explosion in a raging frenzy, and also how convincingly he captures the southern nature of the Moor, the so peculiar individuality of this kind of man. However noble the Moor's essence, something bestial emerges on occasion and makes us shudder, even as it presents us with a sharper view of his monstrous suffering. Through the simplicity of his performance *at the beginning*, the absence of all boasting about his great deeds of the past, and his profound love for the woman of his choice, he wins the hearts of the spectators, just as he won Desdemona's. The ugly Moor is forgotten in the presence of the consummate hero until, goaded by the lacerating anguish of jealousy, a concealed and gruesome nature slowly emerges before our eyes, so that by the end we think that what we have before us is no longer a man, but a raging tiger. Here I reinforced my conviction that a great poet, even more than a mediocre one, needs superb actors in order to be fully understood and appreciated. In Berlin, for example, the strangling scene came across as not only ridiculous but truly indecent, whereas here the blood really froze to ice in one's veins. Even the rowdy English audience went silent for a long time as if struck by lightning. Yes, I confess that a few times during the tragedy I found Othello's long torment so painful—doled out to him drop by drop with such devilish calm by the satanic Iago—and my terror at what I knew was still to come grew so inexorably large, that I involuntarily turned my face away as I would from an unbearable, heart-wrenching sight. Young's portrayal of Iago is a perfect masterpiece, and only through *his* acting did this character become fully clear to me. And here I am compelled, just this once, to contradict what I said earlier about Iago: perhaps contrary to Shakespeare's customary practice, he is not grounded in nature, but is rather a dazzling fantasy of the poet's, but realized with such admirable consistency! He is the devil incarnate, a creature fed on gall and bitterness, who, incapable of pleasure or joy, looks upon evil as his element and finds his sole gratification in philosophizing about himself, contemplating and clarifying his own atrocities. Only a very weak thread binds him to humanity—the desire to avenge himself against the Moor—who, Iago believes, "twixt my sheets . . . has done my office." Even this seems just a pretext, an excuse that he utters to himself with his last breath of moral feeling, whereas his genuine delight in misfortune and misery is always the primary motive. Yet this monster never becomes completely revolting. His intellectual superiority, his courage, his constancy, and finally his steadfastness in adversity never allow this consummate villain to sink fully into vulgar wickedness. In contrast to Kotzebue's figures of virtue, Iago remains a hero. This is the sense in which Young plays the character throughout, his bearing dark and sullen yet noble; no smile crosses his lips, and his jests therefore lose nothing for being dry. Confident in his power, he treats everyone with a calm superiority, albeit with well-defined nuance. Toward his wife he is rough and imperious, to Roderigo authoritative and moody, to Cassio respectful and friendly, and in the case of the Moor, reverent and guileless, although always earnest and dignified. In his own way, Kemble plays the role of Cassio almost as superbly and like a man "framed to make women false," as Shakespeare describes him. Young, cheerful, reckless; of noble bearing, good-natured character, and refined manners. Unfortunately Desdemona was performed only indifferently. Still the touching contrast between her gentle, long-suffering womanliness and the Moor's fiery passion was not entirely lost.

Kean played Othello in the costume of a Moorish king from the Bible, in sandals and a long silk cassock, which is patently absurd. But his splendid acting makes you quickly forget the dress.

Your faithful Lou

London, March 24th, 1828

BELOVED FRIEND!
Among the *aristocratic* soirées are the concerts hosted by Lord L——,[1] one of the most liberal members of the opposition. You frequently find this anomaly here, when a certain general liberalism goes hand in hand with a self-interested arrogance and pride in one's noble birth, instances in which a man is haughty in his own house and yet has the reputation of being thoroughly unassuming in public life.

Especially amusing parties are also given by a duchess who has held the title for such a short time that the exclusives still count her among the plebeians. One of these affairs took place today; on the second floor there was an excellent concert and on the third, a ball. Meanwhile on the ground floor, there was nothing but eating. At the dinner beforehand, the servants, following the example of another fashionable duke, were wearing white kid gloves; this rather ruined the festivities for me, because I could not stop thinking about the lazaretto and scabies!

Yesterday's midday meal at the Duke of Somerset's, a widely cultivated man, was much more rewarding from an intellectual point of view. At table the well-known parliamentary speaker H—— told us some startling things. For example, he said that he had recently sat on a government commission investigating possible collusion between criminals and the police, about which there have been so many complaints. It was revealed that there is a London society organized like a regular agency with bureau clerks, etc., which runs larcenies and counterfeiting on a grand scale, supports those who get caught, provides massive assistance to prosecutors and defendants alike, and for all this receives a fixed share of the profits. At its head are not only a number of respected figures, including members of Parliament, but even a well-known peer in the House of Lords! The evidence was apparently indisputable, but the ministry decided that in order to avoid a horrible scandal, it was better to let the matter drop. This shows that, even in free countries, things happen that we would not dream of at home.

Next, a natural scientist gave us a lecture about frogs, an account that in its own way seemed just as surprising to me as the preceding one. Not every expression in a scientific report like this one should be taken too literally, of course. In any case, he said that frogs are the most libidinous of all creatures, and nature has given them special encouragement by endowing them with the faculty of propagating through their forefeet alone.[2] If a male does not find any females in a given pond, he will position himself on top of a carp, affix his forefeet over its eyes, and often remain there for so long that the fish goes blind—a process this biologist jokingly called "blind love" and claimed to have observed personally!

I HAVE JUST returned from the king's levee, which this time was very well attended.[3] Due to his gout, the monarch had to remain seated, but otherwise looked very well. The Duke of Wellington, intent on expressing his gratitude for having been elevated to the position of prime minister, dropped to both knees instead of lowering only one to the ground, as is the custom here. He was probably doubling his thanks on account of his doubled capacity as prime minister and commander in chief. This is how he is represented in caricatures, with the left half of his body dressed as courtier, the right as field marshal, and laughing with both eyes. Except for the *grandes entrées*, almost anybody is allowed into the levees—gentlemen as well as ladies, as long as they appear in the prescribed attire. A lover of caricature can find no richer source material in England, because the unfamiliar dress and the equally unfamiliar splendor raise the level of national embarrassment and awkwardness to the burlesque. Our own obliging and better-experienced ladies of the court would find themselves in a state of utter disbelief.

As soon as I changed my clothes, I went riding in the most beautiful spring weather through the ever-unpopulated Regent's Park, where hundreds of almond trees are in bloom, and I had a look at the new zoo that's been laid out there, a model of its type and very worthy of emulation. There is nothing overstated about it, and it boasts a tidiness that can be realized only in England. Here I saw a rare animal, one of the most beautiful creatures in existence: a tiger cat, a truly splendid paragon of elegance among the quadrupeds.

After this, there was a grand meal awaiting me at the Marquess of Thomond's, an Irish peer. There I made the acquaintance of the most uncompromising Tory in England, the Duke of Newcastle. I must confess, he did not look like a genius, and the entire party was so stiffly English that I was heartily pleased to be seated next to the Princess Polignac, whose cheerful Ultra chatter delighted me today as if it were not only pleasant but the most stimulating and intelligent in the world!

I finished the evening with a ball at the Marquis of Beresford's. It was given in honor of Dom Miguel's sister, the Marquesa de Loulé, who seemed not a little bored, since she speaks only Portuguese and could therefore talk to almost no one but the host.

The marquis himself, an imposing-looking warrior, is the butt of unjust factionalist criticism.[4] Not only does he have a likeable manner, he is also a man of vigorous character, strong as a lion and wise as serpents,[5] someone many governments besides Portugal could make good use of. He considers Dom Miguel's claim to the Portuguese throne to be better founded than that of his brother,[6] and argues that in order to be fair in judging the Portuguese, one must apply an entirely different standard than the one we are accustomed to using. Among other things, he said that Dom Miguel's education had been intentionally neglected—he still could not write at the age of twenty-three—and that one cannot expect too much from such a prince. Yet in spite of this, he is distinguished by many brilliant personal qualities, and one should not believe everything one reads in the newspapers! At least this last point cannot be doubted by anyone.

April 7th, 1828

IT WAS A great relief today to dine in the country, finally unconstrained, at Holly Lodge, the favorite estate of the Duchess of St Albans. The house stands on the slope of a hill and in front of it, amid bright green grass, was a magnificent star of crocuses and early tulips in full bloom, decoratively arrayed around a marble fountain. Far off above the trees at the bottom of the valley, the gigantic city loomed tenebrously through a veil of fog like a fata morgana of the New Jerusalem. The meal was excellent, as always, and afterward we were delightfully entertained with singing and a concert in the lush greenhouse overflowing with flowers and fruit. During dinner I sat next to a great-granddaughter of Charles II's, a relation of the duke's; indeed the majority of the foremost half dozen English dukes are proud to be descendants of mistresses of Charles II, and have therefore incorporated the royal coat-of-arms into their own.[7]

It is still quite cold, yet everywhere leaves and blossoms are emerging with a vengeance, a sight that would delight me at home, but here makes my heart ache so much I can sometimes barely endure it. Nonetheless I do not want to sit down again on the old, golden seat of thorns; I prefer instead the freedom to search out a smooth and comfortable everyday stool somewhere else.

Wrotham Park, April 9, 1828

I HAVE BEEN here since yesterday, along with many other guests, at the estate of a very fashionable lady. The house is as tasteful and sumptuous as you can imagine, but too genteel and pretentious to be truly pleasant, at least for me. What is more, a certain Luttrell is present, a brash joker. This very debonair company feels obliged to admire his every word, and they feign a liking for him merely from fear of his evil tongue. I loathe such intellectual swashbucklers like poison, especially when they lack all grace and combine a foul appearance with nothing but gall and bite. They appear among us like venomous insects, and we, in our pitiful weakness, abet their feasting on the blood of others, so they will not draw any of our own.

I found the inanimate objects much more congenial than the people, especially the custom of perfuming each room by filling every kind of vase and receptacle with fresh flowers. Among the paintings, I admired a Murillo of Joseph leading the infant Jesus, a beautiful child in whom you can sense, half hidden, a future greatness. The god-like nature of the savior, wonderfully expressed, still slumbers in his expectant, upward gaze. Joseph appears as a modest man in the full vigor of middle age, betraying more dignity of character than of station. The landscape is wild and original, and, at the top, sweet cherubs' heads eavesdrop amid the dark clouds. The owner told me that he paid 2,500 for this picture.[8]

In the garden I was very taken with the palm house, made almost entirely of glass and so light and transparent that it looks like an ice palace. But what I find repugnant is the prevailing enthusiasm for old, deformed tree trunks that one finds embedded in many spots in the mown lawns, partly covered with clematis vines or decked out with flowers in concealed pots. Whole ruins of this sort are being built, which—along with other things—reveal the decline of good taste in English gardens.

For me, country life here is in certain respects too social. If you want to read, for instance, you go to the library, where you are seldom by yourself; and if you need to compose a letter, you write it just as publicly at a large, shared desk, after which it is stuck into an open box that a servant carries to the post every morning. To do all this alone in your room is simply not customary and thus invokes displeasure and disapproval. Many a foreigner would prefer to eat breakfast in his own quarters, but this is impossible unless he can plead illness.

Despite all the liberty and the absence of pointless deference, a person used to our customs will eventually feel constrained here, a discomfort aggravated by always having to speak in a foreign tongue.

I LEFT WROTHAM Park this morning just as a spring storm was departing. I joyfully inhaled the fragrant air and gazed with delight at the sparkling green and swelling buds—a sight one can never weary of. Springtime compensates the northerly regions for all the inconveniences of their winters; in the south, this awakening of young nature is far less coquettish.

At midday I was once again at lunch with the Duchess of St Albans at her country house, where a pleasant surprise awaited me. Having arrived late, I was seated between my hostess and a tall, very simple, but affable-looking man of a certain age, although his broad Scots dialect was anything but pleasant. He would scarcely have drawn my attention, if it had not dawned on me after a few minutes that I was sitting next to the Great Unknown.[9] It was not long before a number of dry witticisms escaped his mouth, along with several anecdotes related in an unpretentious manner that were, without appearing brilliant, nonetheless always striking. His eyes glowed whenever he grew animated, and they were so bright and congenial, they conveyed so much genuine goodness and naturalness that one could not but grow fond of him. Toward the end of the meal, he and Sir Francis Burdett took turns telling ghost stories, half spine-chilling, half jocular, which provoked me to repeat your famous *histoire à clef*, embellishing its denouement a bit. This met with great success. Would it not be amusing if you were to discover it in the prolific Scotsman's next novel! He then recited the lines of a strange old inscription he had recently discovered in the churchyard of Melrose Abbey:

> The earth goes on the earth, glittering in gold,
> The earth goes to the earth sooner than it would,
> The earth builds on the earth castles and towers,
> The earth says to the earth: All this is ours.

Certainly true! For we were, are, and will be earth, and we may well belong to the earth alone.

A small concert concluded the evening; the great bard's very pretty daughter—a healthy Highlands beauty—participated, and Miss Steevens sang nothing but Scottish ballads. I did not reach London until deep in the night and, thanks to the kindness of my hostess, enriched my Memory Album with a sketch that is an extremely good likeness of Sir Walter Scott. Since none of the engravings I know resemble him at all, I will send an exact copy along with this letter.

THE TURBULENCE OF these days has in any case been very routine; my only agreeable memory is of a dinner at the Spanish ambassador's, where after the meal, a fiery and beautiful Spanish woman sang boleros in a way that aroused an entirely new feeling for music in me. To judge by this and the dancing of a fandango I once witnessed, Spanish society must be very different from ours and far more piquant!

72

Henriette Sontag.

Yesterday I was invited to meet the Dukes of Clarence and Sussex, but I declined in order to meet Miss Henriette Sontag at our friend Bülow's, for I had not yet seen her. Both young and old alike are now lying at her feet. She is truly enchanting, an alluring creature and very seductive for all who are either new in the world or have nothing to think of but their own pleasure (Figure 72). It is impossible to imagine a more ingenious and yet effective, more innate flirtatiousness, one might say—so childlike, so delightful, and yet the devil is somehow mixed up in it. She seemed to find my own weak points rather quickly and, with absolutely no affectation, managed to raise only appropriate and comfortable topics. And the sounds of home tumbled from her pretty lips like pearls and diamonds into the stream of conversation, and the loveliest blue eyes shone like a springtime sun behind a light veil of clouds. "Tomorrow Kean will be playing *Richard III*," she said casually at the end. "The Duke of Devonshire has offered me his box. Would you perhaps like to accompany me?"

That such an invitation supersedes any other goes without saying.

April 28th, 1828

I HAVE NEVER seen or heard less of a performance than I did today, though I must confess that none has ever seemed shorter. Yes, in spite of the presence of a *gouvernante* and a visit from Mr. Kemble between acts, there was scarcely a pause in our conversation, which was made ever more interesting by the many reminiscences of home. For my part, the excitement persisted throughout the fashionable ball that followed at Lady Tankerville's, for I was far less filled with ennui than I usually am at these otherwise-stilted fêtes. Forgive me for writing so few words to you today, but Helios is now getting up, and I am just going to bed.

April 30th, 1828

EVERYTHING HERE IS of a colossal size; even my tailor's workshop looks like a factory. You enter to enquire about the fate of a tailcoat you ordered and find yourself surrounded by hundreds of bales of cloth and textiles and just as many workers. An obliging secretary appears and with great formality asks for the day of the order. As soon as you give it, a quick gesture brings the delivery of two large volumes, which he studies for a moment. "Sir," comes the answer at last, "tomorrow at twenty minutes past eleven your coat will be ready enough to be tried on in the dressing room." There are many of these rooms decorated with large wall mirrors and cheval glasses. They are continually occupied by people being fitted, and here the millionaire tailor himself makes ten alterations without ever expressing ill humor.

Justice having been done to my tailcoat, I continue my walk and come to a butcher's shop, where not only is the raw meat arranged into the most beautiful garlands, pyramids, and other fanciful forms, but decorative trays of ice give off a delightful coolness. In addition there is a playbill hanging behind each ham, and the most popular newspapers are lying on the highly polished tables.

A few shops farther along, competing with the butcher, is a vendor of sea monsters who, like King Fish in the fairy tale, sits between marble and fountain. He will not easily match the success of his famous colleague Crockford, however, an ingenious man who knew how to catch above-average fish; that is, he made his way up from the ranks of poor fisherman to become the scourge and at the same time the favorite of the rich and genteel world.[10] He is a gambler who has won millions, money he has used to build a gaming palace in the style of Parisian salons, but with an Asiatic splendor that almost surpasses that of royalty. And now the prevailing taste is once again imitating the period of Louis XIV, with all its decor of tasteless flourishes, excessive gilding, heaped up mélanges of stucco and painting, etc.—a very logical change in fashion, since English aristocrats are looking more and more like those of that era.

Crockford's cook is the renowned Ude, both in theory and practice the foremost chef in Europe. Not only are the food and service of the utmost perfection, but there is betting at high stakes, whereby it often happens that some individual gambles away twenty thousand pounds or more on a single evening. Set up as a club, it is very difficult to gain entry to, and although the game of hazard is illegal in England, most of the ministers are members. Indeed one of the directors of this gaming establishment is the prime minster, the Duke of Wellington!

May 2nd, 1828

YESTERDAY, THE FIRST of May, the month of delight, was celebrated by the Duchess of St Albans with a very pleasant country fete at her beautiful villa. A maypole decorated with many ribbons and flower garlands had been set up in the middle of the bowling green, and gaily adorned country folk in old-English attire circled it in dance. Guests strolled around in the house and garden just as they wished. Many shot bows and arrows, others danced beneath tents or played all sorts of games, went swinging and spinning, or gossiped in the dark shadows of *bosquets* until five o'clock, when a few blasts of a trumpet announced a splendid breakfast, at which every delicacy and extravagant morsel that luxury can offer was presented in abundance.

Many servants had been dressed in fancy costumes as gardeners, and fresh flower garlands hung on every bush, making it all indescribably wonderful. It was, in addition, such a beautiful day that I was able for the first time to get a view of the whole of London in the distance, utterly free of fog and only slightly dusky from smoke.

At the onset of darkness, the effect of the flower garlands was revived. Colorful lamps were judiciously distributed on all the trees or half hidden in the maze of shrubbery. It was already past midnight when breakfast ended.

This was all very appealing, yet they were just lifeless objects. To my eyes, a small rose on the bosom of the lovely Henriette far outshone every garland and illumination. I had given her the rose in the morning, and I noticed at the concert in Devonshire House that it was the only decoration on her black dress. The concert ended with a ball, and here too our German beauty outwaltzed and outsparkled all her rivals with a modest aplomb that seemed oblivious to her conquests. There has never been a mischief maker so well aware of how to appear childlike; such coquettishness is certainly a woman's greatest charm and the most captivating.

May 3rd, 1827

IN MAY I am, like the birds, most attuned to love, and should not be blamed if I cannot listen to a warbling nightingale these days without a pounding heart.

"I have only Saturday left," she said to me yesterday, "and after that I will probably not be free again for over a month. So tomorrow is in every respect *my* day, when I can live just as I wish, and then be a poor slave for a long, long time!"

I timidly suggested that she come with me for a meal in the country and that we ride there together early in the morning. I recommended my horse as a phoenix of gentleness and, so as not to tire her too much, I would drive her back in the evening. After many entreaties, she finally accepted.

Oh, Nature, oh the joys of the countryside!* How lovely you are, how doubled your charms when in such company! We were supposed to visit the Greenwich Observatory, but we stuck to the two blue stars that were close by, sparkling a hundred thousand times more magnetically than all the worlds of the Milky Way. I thank the dear Lord from deep in my heart that we did not have to travel to Sirius and Jupiter with Dr. Nürnberger to find ecstasy, or attend to the Venus *in the sky*, but rather lost ourselves for many hours in the undisturbed enjoyment of her pleasures on earth.[11]

Due to the perversities of the world and an inconvenient arrival, we had to carry out this plan somewhat secretly. The horses were sent on ahead, and I rode after them on a nag, while Henriette and the good governess traveled to the rendezvous in a rented carriage.

The yellow coach took a long time to arrive, and I was not a little worried that something had happened. In fact, something had, but the dear lass kept her word honorably. When I finally saw the old box cart moving slowly toward us, I galloped up, lifted the lovely girl onto her palfrey, and off we flew (she rides as boldly as a man) into the sweet fragrance of the May air like a pair of merry little birds, billing and cooing. We rode until it grew dark, roaming everywhere, lingering over this and that, and we dined by candlelight in that hidden little room above the river that is already known to you, its windows open to the glow of the stars. The carriage did not arrive for the homeward journey until eleven o'clock at night.

Heaven made this creature out of very special material! What variety and grace in her every nuance! Whether timid or trusting, cross or good-natured, sulky, devoted, indifferent, gentle, mocking, measured, or wild—in Schiller's words, "she captures the soul with the power of heaven."[12] And what self-possession combined with the greatest tenderness, what a steady little head when she wants, and how much kindheartedness and thereby how much pert craftiness!

She was created to please men, but women all love her too. Certainly a fortunate, singular nature. But dear Julie, it is surely time that I end this. For you may well think me foolish, in love, or both at once. *En vérité, pour cette fois-ci je n'en répondrai pas.*[13]

May 8th, 1828

FOR A WEEK my ears have been ringing from three to four concerts each evening—or better, each night, as one more appropriately calls it here. These have suddenly become all the rage, from the highest and most-exclusive circles right down to the nobodies. The ladies Pasta, Caradori, Sontag, Brambilla; the gentlemen Zucchelli, Pellegrini, and Curioni sing the same arias and duets over and over, yet people never tire of hearing them. They often sing negligently, doubtless

---

* How unlike what I once heard an obliging prince, no stranger to irony, declare to his royal household: "Just spare me your damnable rural pleasures and domestic joys!"—*The Editor.* [A reference to himself?—*Translator.*]

exhausted by the eternal sameness, yet no one seems to care. Few have a musical ear, and most are inspired only by fashion; those who occupy the last seat in the crowd can rarely distinguish a bassist from a prima donna, though they fall into raptures nonetheless. This situation is very lucrative for the artists, of course. Miss Sontag, for instance, at *every* party where she allows herself to be heard—often three or four in a *single* evening—receives at least forty pounds and sometimes one hundred. She is rivaled by Miss Pasta, whose singing I find sweeter, more superb, more tragic. The others, although commendable, are of the second rank.

In addition to these, Moscheles, Pixis, the Bohrer brothers—*enfin*, a whole herd of virtuosos—can be found here. They are all flying toward English gold like moths to a flame, yet somehow they avoid getting burned. On the contrary, at least in the case of the women, they manage to ignite new fires right and left, and these are sometimes even more profitable than their artistry.

As a rule, the concerts at Prince Leopold's are the most pleasant, since the large space renders the unbearable crush more avoidable. This prince is not as popular as he deserves, because the English cannot quite forgive him for being a foreigner.

May 9th, 1828

WHILE OUT RIDING in a lovely area with M——, I came by chance upon Strawberry Hill, the house built by Horace Walpole that he mentions so often in his letters, which has remained unaltered and is rarely inhabited. It was the first attempt at modern Gothic in England, totally in the clinquant taste of its time: stonework imitated in wood, a great deal that glitters without being gold. Yet it also contains several genuine artistic treasures and a number of curiosities. Among the former is a splendid, jewel-studded prayer book full of drawings by Raphael and his pupils; among those of his pupils are a drawing of Cardinal Wolsey's hat, a very expressive portrait of Walpole's blind and witty lover Madame du Deffand, and a picture of the famous Lady Montagu in Turkish costume.

One can find anything in this country. Today I even discovered an elegant Englishman, who in his house is trying to imitate German customs, the German way with servants, and the German tone of social interaction. This is Earl S——, who lived in our country for a long time in somewhat straitened circumstances and then suddenly inherited an immense fortune. Only his servants' crimson liveries, with inexpressibles and stockings of canary yellow, were in accordance with English taste. Otherwise everything in the house was German, even the dinner hour was adjusted to ours. The prolonged meal was exceedingly annoying. It put me on pins and needles, because someone was waiting for me at a place that is now dearer to me than anywhere else.

Despite my bad humor and somewhat against my will, my Austrian neighbor managed to get a smile out of me. He was drinking an immense amount, and when I offered him yet more, he answered, "No, no more wine, otherwise I'll go overboard and *fange an zu stänkern*."[14] Your Viennese dialect is better than mine, so I do not need to explain the meaning of this phrase.

May 16th, 1828

I SPENT A few days in the country and went to the Epsom races. The scene was very lively. All the roads were packed with fast-moving equipages, and in the middle of the field next to where the races take place was a tall, green hill, so thickly covered with a thousand unharnessed wagons and a colorful throng of riders and pedestrians that no public festival has ever looked more picturesque. And this pretty scene was framed by a truly lovely, well-cultivated landscape, a sky full of black clouds, a lot of rain, and glimpses of the sun—all the more intense for being so rare.

I came back yesterday so as not to miss a party today at the king's, for such an invitation is viewed as a true *bonne fortune*. The usual notion of a court does not apply here, yet nowhere else is the ideal of a fashionable house more perfectly achieved. Every comfort, every elegance available to the private individual is joined with royal splendor in the most tasteful and distinctive way. And there is no title that the monarch is prouder of than being the first gentleman of his country.

May 30th, 1828

THE ETERNAL SOCIAL whirl leaves very little time to spare, and once you become involved, there is no reasonable way to escape, even when the enjoyment begins to wane. Yet I still manage to find the occasional moment for more solitary and lasting enjoyment.

For instance, I recently saw a collection of excellent paintings made up of nothing but portraits of notable individuals from England's past. It was striking how closely most of them seemed to correspond in their features and bearing to the historical image we have of them. Moreover the renowned Lord Burghley had an astounding resemblance to the great state chancellor of Prussia,[15] although his headdress, which looked like a granny's cap, quite skewed his appearance. James I looked delightfully true to character, as did his ambassador, that eccentric knight who makes such strange statements about himself in his memoirs, claiming that he was liked by men and women everywhere, and that his essence was unlike any other because of the lovely natural fragrance emanating from him and everything connected to him.[16]

Another gallery contained modern watercolors, a technique in which the English are especially adept and achieve an astonishing glow and depth of color. A few Scottish landscapes were particularly outstanding; for example, a sunset in the highlands with a truthfulness that is the equal of a Claude Lorrain, or a twilit scene of Loch Lomond, a poem redolent of romanticism.

There was still enough time for an extended ride, during which—trusting myself to chance, as always—I came upon one of those delightful parks that can only be achieved in the English climate. The gardens with their indescribably brilliant display of flowers lay in a narrow, verdant, meadowed valley full of tall trees, where three silvery, clear springs emerge to form brooks that meander off in all directions, winding in soft murmurs among thickets of blooming rhododendrons and azaleas.

My joy in such things is always tempered by my regret that you cannot share it with me. Your refined taste would scoop up a thousand new ideas here, which you could then use later to yield still-lovelier things, as far as our locality and means allow, through the skillful composition of floral colors or the selection of graceful forms and enhanced light effects, something that can be immensely improved by appropriately opening or blocking vistas.

These pleasant memories of the morning had to sustain me through the rest of the day: namely, a dinner at Lady P——'s, the greatest female gourmand in London; two balls given by the English and foreign diplomatic corps; and a concert at Lord Grosvenor's. It is true that the concert was held in a gallery full of excellent pictures, but on such an occasion, these can be no more enjoyed than any other piece of wallpaper.

June 6th, 1828

FOR ME, ONE of the most distinguished houses belongs to the noble Scotsman, the Earl of W——, a direct descendent of Macduff. Still displayed in his armory is a tree branch, *allegedly from Birnam Wood*. This relic is likely as credible as the others.[17] Whoever believes in it will be blessed!

The family is highly cultivated, and the Scottish mind certainly more akin to the German than the English. From the charming daughters, I learned a new technique for preserving one's favorite members of the bird family with results more faithful and durable than the stuffed variety. You pluck the feathers and glue them, along with the beak and legs, in a natural shape on sturdy vellum or varnished wood; this creates a bas-relief that is extremely lifelike and will not deteriorate.

Charles X once spent a while at Lord W——'s in Scotland, and he left behind an old chamberlain, who, funnily enough, is called Bonneau, like the one in the *Pucelle*.[18] He is from that near-extinct race of servants, men of total discretion who today are encountered only on the stage, if at all. As such, having fulfilled his role in the house for twenty-five years, he is allowed—contrary to the English custom of prohibiting the servants the slightest approach beyond what is required for their duties—to put in a word every now and then. I have found nothing more entertaining than this old Frenchman's stories of the court and society. His world actually came to a close at a time we can now hardly even imagine. That this singular old fellow is only a chamberlain makes no difference. Being so observant, he probably saw more of the great world than many men of high rank.

When I was visiting at Lady W——'s this morning, a large shipment of exotica arrived from one of her sons traveling in South America. There was a live lion marmoset, with a head and mane like the king of beasts and a body hardly the size of a rat. Instead of giving off the nasty odor of apes, this one smelled of cinnamon and musk, perfuming the whole room like a scented candle, quite the same as the above mentioned knight. An unusually representative collection of hummingbirds displayed colors that are only seen painted on the sky by the sun as it rises or sets; the same was true for the rich collection of butterflies, which included several entirely new specimens. I saw here for the first time the so-called stick bug that appears to be in transition from plant to animal. It is about six inches long and can hardly be distinguished from a leafless elm twig, with branchlets forming its feet. Only the head, with its antennae hidden at the top, reveals it to be fauna and not flora.

At midday I dined at Lady Farquhar's, where an odd event occurred. Her husband used to be governor of Mauritius,[19] and there she purchased from a black woman the supposed fortune-telling book of the Empress Josephine. The empress had owned it since before her embarkation for France, and she is said to have read in it of her future greatness and fall. Lady Farquhar brought it out at tea and invited the party to pose questions to be answered according to the method stipulated in the book. Listen to the answers it gave, which are truly remarkable! Frau von Rothschild went first, and she asked whether her wishes would be fulfilled.[20] She received the response "Don't tire fate with wishes; whoever has achieved so much must be satisfied." Next Mr. Spring-Rice, a well-known member of Parliament and one of the most zealous advocates of Catholic emancipation (a topic currently of the greatest interest to absolutely everyone here, whether for or against it), asked whether tomorrow, when the question is to be decided in the House of Lords, it would be passed. Here I must interject that it is already known that it will *not* be passed, but it is at the same time generally believed that with the next Parliament the desired outcome *must* be achieved. And this was exactly the book's laconic answer, namely, "You will have no success, *this time.*" A young American woman was then encouraged to ask whether she would soon be married, to which the answer was "Not in this part of the world." Now it was my turn, and I asked whether what was moving my heart so deeply at the moment would turn out happily for me. "Drop this inclination," responded the magic book, "for you will see it is neither true nor lasting." Whether this was an allusion to my own feelings or to those of someone else toward me remains obscure, as with all oracles.

The other guests, who naturally had no idea about the actual meaning of my question, poked a lot of fun at the rebuff I had received and insisted that I try again. So I asked, "Will fate be good to me in my more serious plans?" "Seek," was the answer, "and you shall find; persevere, and you shall achieve."

Without trying, I made a very pleasant acquaintance that same evening when the Duchess of Clarence introduced me to her mother, the Duchess of Meiningen, an engaging woman of authentic German character, whose unaffected naturalness remains undiminished by her age or her rank—perhaps the surest sign of a pure and beautiful mind. This worthy mother of such a highly revered daughter must be a very welcome figure to the English, who are extremely attached to their future queen, and the greatest enthusiasm was apparent on all sides. It is only a pity that on such occasions English ladies, whether of high or low rank, are generally so incapable of graceful demeanor or clever conversation that they fail to make the overall spectacle attractive. A drawing room and a presentation at court are just as ludicrous here as the levee of a *Bürgermeister* from one of our former Free Imperial Cities. The pride and wealth of the aristocracy disappear in the awkward embarrassment of these ladies, who are not so much *adorned* as they are *loaded down* with diamonds and finery. When young Englishwomen are informally attired and moving uninhibitedly within the accustomed surroundings of their own homes, they often appear to great advantage, but elaborately bejeweled or at large gatherings almost never. An unconquerable, graceless timidity suddenly paralyzes them and their intellectual qualities so completely that stimulating conversation becomes a huge challenge.

For this reason, I consider them the most pleasant and comfortable wives of all European women, as well as the least able to present themselves fittingly or engage in society. It should be obvious in this judgment that my praise far outweighs the criticism!

June 16th, 1828

TODAY I ATTENDED an interesting breakfast given by a pigeon club, a designation that in no way means that the members go out of their way to be as gentle and guileless as doves; on the contrary, the club is made up of the wildest young men in England, and the only role doves play, like all other poor, miserable creatures, is to be shot dead.[21] The setting was a large, grassy area surrounded by a wall. On one side stood a row of tents, and in the largest of these was a table with a never-ending array of fresh dishes, iced champagne, and Mosel wine, all continually replenished from one until six o'clock. About a hundred marksmen and a few guests were present, and they alternately shot, ate, and drank throughout the whole afternoon. The pigeons were lined up in a row in boxes, always eight at a time. Strings attached to the boxes run up to the shooting stand and are set up so that when someone pulls on one, the box opens and the bird flies out. Whoever shot last pulls for the next man, but stands behind him, so the marksman cannot see which box will open and is therefore unprepared for whichever pigeon will emerge. If a shooter brings a bird down within the enclosure, it is counted as his. If it falls outside, it is judged a miss. Every marksman has a double-barreled gun and is allowed to use both barrels.

The two most famous marksmen in England are Captain Ross and Mr. Osbaldeston. They once shot for a wager of a thousand pounds sterling, and the result is still undecided to this day. Neither one of them ever missed, and Captain Ross's pigeons failed to get even twelve feet up, scarcely fluttered, and almost always fell to the earth like stones at the very moment of the shot. I have never seen such inconceivably good shooting. One of the club's very pretty little pointers retrieved each bird, always carrying out its duty like a machine, flawlessly and without haste. Finally the entire group shot for the annual prize, a golden vase worth two hundred pounds sterling. Captain Ross won it.

I did not get away from this merry breakfast until seven o'clock, when I went to a theater called Sadler's Wells, previously unknown to me. It is a good three or four miles from my rooms, and I went there in a hackney coach. At about one in the morning, when I wanted to return home, there was no carriage to be hired in that remote corner, and every house was shut tight as well. This was all the more unpleasant, since I really had no idea in which part of the city I was. After wandering around the streets in vain for half an hour, hoping to turn up a coach, and already resigned to going home on foot with the help of a night watchman, a diligence came by, luckily heading my way, and I therefore found myself back with the household gods at about two o'clock.

Sadler's Wells is idiosyncratic in that the stage can be submerged in actual water, and the actors often splash around in this element for hours at a time like aquatic animals.[22] By the way, nothing outdoes the nonsense of the melodramas performed there, nor, for that matter, the horrible singing that accompanies them.

June 20th, 1828

I WENT TO another fancy ball, but it left me with nothing but a gloomy impression. I noticed a pale man there shrouded in a simple black domino, and on his face was an unspeakable trace of the most bitter mental anguish. He did not stay long, and when I asked L—— about him, he told me the following details.

> This pitiful mortal, Colonel S——, could serve as the hero of a spine-chilling novel. If you can say that anyone was born under an unlucky star, this is the man. He lost his great wealth early through the fraudulent bankruptcy of a friend. Good fortune has approached him a hundred times since then, only to mock him at the decisive moment with the disappearance of all hope; and almost always everything foundered on the most insignificant trivialities—a delayed letter, a simple confusion, an indisposition that brought calamity—things that appeared to be his own fault, but were really only a web woven by derisive, malevolent spirits.

"For a long time now," L—— continued,

> he has stopped doing anything to change his situation, has looked for no way to improve his fate, since he is already convinced in advance, through long, gruesome

experience, that *he* can succeed in *nothing*. I've known him since we were young. Although he's as harmless as a child, a large part of the world considers him to be wicked, to be false and scheming, although he is one of the most upright of men. Yes, people avoid and shun him, although there's never been a heart that beat more ardently for the welfare of others. The young woman he adored committed suicide because of his supposed infidelity. For outrageous reasons, he himself was long a suspect in his brother's murder, because—having offered his own life in the latter's defense—he was discovered next to him, bleeding. Sentenced to be hanged, he was saved from an ignominious death only by the king's pardon; the proofs of his innocence did not follow until later. Finally a woman who lured him into marriage, through a fraud that had been scandalously long in preparation, ran off with another man and yet knew how to manage it, so the world attached almost all the blame to him alone. Time has thus crushed every bit of his self-confidence; his every hope in fate or mankind has died. He lives among us as no more than an apathetic, solitary ghost—a heartrending example that there are creatures who, at least in this life, seem to have been sold to the devil already before birth. Because whoever has once been struck by the curse of misfortune is not only faced with enemies at every step, but is robbed of the trust and finally the hearts of his friends, until at last the poor soul, always and everywhere trodden underfoot, rejected, and ill-treated, sinks to the ground, lays down his wounded, weary head, and dies; and his last sigh seems to the pitiless crowd a sign of arrogance and an insufferable note of discord.

Woe to the unlucky! Threefold woes to them! Because for them there are no virtues, no wisdom, no providence, no joy. For them there is only one good and that is death!

June 25th, 1828

YET ON THE whole, there is, in fact, something pleasant about dealing with so many invitations every day and, if you are not happy in one place, being able to seek out more suitable company. Something new, piquant, or interesting is always to be found. Such as yesterday at Prince Lieven's, where I made the acquaintance of a second Ninon de Lenclos. Certainly no one considers Lady A—— to be older than forty, although she is approaching eighty. Nothing about her appears forced or unnatural, yet everything—*taille*, dress, liveliness of manner, grace, and suppleness of limbs (as much as this can be noticed at a ball)—everything about her is utterly young, and in her face there is scarcely a wrinkle. She has never let herself worry and has led a merry life ever since her youth; she has twice run away from her husbands and therefore avoided England for a long time, spending her large fortune in Paris. All in all a delightful woman, more French than English in her behavior, and entirely *du grand monde*. She has studied the art of the toilette seriously and has made some astute inventions. I would be happy to share whatever I have been able to overhear with you and with all of my beautiful lady friends.

On the next day, the Duke of Somerset gave a *déjeuner champêtre* at his villa. There he demonstrated that it is possible to do something new at such fetes. His whole house was hung with beautiful *haute-lisses* and colorful Chinese tapestries; a lot of furniture, sofas, armchairs, chaises longues, mirrors, etc., were distributed all over the garden as well as in numerous salons and small rooms. In addition, small encampments of tents in white and pink muslin were set up and looked splendid in the emerald green of the pleasure grounds.

In the evening, there was, as usual, an illumination, mostly of individual lamps imaginatively hidden in the trees and bushes, looking like so many glowing fruits and fireflies in order to lure both lovers and solitary wanderers. But even those who prefer noise to more serene joys could find satisfaction, for a large number of the party was dancing in a big tent approached by a path of radiantly illuminated archways of rose garlands. An excellent concert rang out from there, performed by the top virtuosi and singers of the Italian opera. Italian weather, too, blessed this festival from beginning to end, which was fortunate, since the smallest teasing climate sprite could have destroyed it. This is why it should be recognized as an act of daring to undertake such an event *in England*, and yet exactly these kinds of *fetes* are more frequent and more beautiful here than anywhere else, just as the least-productive ground is often the most richly cultivated.

I have now got things managed to the extent that I can leave England in four weeks at the latest, so as to spend some time touring through Wales and especially Ireland, which, according to so much I have heard, interests me far more than Scotland. But I am sorry that first illness and then the distractions of the big city have denied me a look at the north country. I must record this omission in my book of sins, which, unfortunately, already contains too many of the same sort under the heading "Indolence," an abhorrent enemy of mankind! That French marshal from the era of Louis XIV, a time so unfavorable for *parvenus*, was certainly right when, asked by some friends how he had managed to climb up from the rank of common soldier to the highest level of his station, he responded, "Only by *never putting off until tomorrow what I could do today*." Indecision falls under the same heading, for it is also the archenemy of many and much hated by the even better-known Marshal Suvorov, who, in keeping with his immoderate nature, would immediately withdraw his support from anyone who answered a question with the statement "I don't know."

Non mi ricordo is much better,[23] and in keeping with my principles, I will respond thus to all the aforementioned sins, once they have been committed. We must repeat to ourselves daily: the past is dead, only the future is alive.

May it, dear Julie, always be favorable to us.

Your faithful Lou

Cobham Hall, June 30th, 1828

BELOVED FRIEND,

After sending off my letter to you and then going on a country excursion with a few ladies, I drove to a gathering at the Duke of Clarence's, where this time there was such a genuine English crush that it was impossible for me and several others to gain entry. Having achieved nothing after half an hour, we were forced to leave, hoping to recoup our losses at another ball. There the crowd in the first room was so thick that several gentlemen donned their hats just so they could free up their arms! Jewel-bedecked ladies were pressed on all sides with such torturous force that they fell (or leaned) into faints. All you heard were screams, moans, curses, and sighs, although some people just laughed. However bestial, I must confess that I was among those who could only chuckle at the very idea that such a thing could be called society. In fact, I had never before experienced anything so awful.

Early the next morning, I rode to Cobham Hall to spend a few days there on the occasion of Lord Darnley's birthday, which we celebrated today in a rural and unpretentious way. Except for me, it was just the family, augmented by the presence of the eldest son and his lovely and charming wife, who reside in Ireland. Domesticity was the order of the day. We ate early, so that toward evening we could enjoy our supper in the open air. Lord Darnley hosted all his paid laborers, about one hundred in number, and the meal transpired with the greatest propriety. We sat in the pleasure ground next to an iron fence, and tables were laid for people on the mown grass. First tea and cakes were distributed to about fifty young girls from the Lancasterian school that Lady Darnley had established in the park.[1] They were children of six to fourteen, all dressed alike and some quite pretty. After them came the workers, who sat down at a long table richly decked with mammoth platters of roast meat, vegetables, and pudding. Each man brought along his own cutlery and earthenware mug. The house staff served, did the honors, and poured the beer out of large garden watering cans. The village musicians played their music far better than ours manage to do and were also much better dressed; the workmen, on the other hand, did not look as good, nor were they as tidy as our Wends in their Sunday best. The only outsiders invited were the inhabitants of the village and immediate vicinity who work for Lord Darnley. The health of all the lord's family members was drunk very formally with nine repeated hurrahs, after which our old coachman Child (now in Lord Darnley's service), who is a kind of English *improvisatore*, climbed onto the midsection of the table and made a highly comical speech in verse. I myself made an appearance in it when he wished me "to have always plenty of gold and never to become old." Given that this is a double impossibility, it had the ring of satire.

Until it got dark, the little girls danced and skipped tirelessly around on the grass with a great deal of gravitas but little coordination, as if they were puppets; this continued with or without the music. Our party in the pleasure ground was finally infected by the enthusiasm for dancing, and since it was impossible to turn down my partner, the sixty-year-old Lady Darnley, I myself was compelled to break my vow.

July 4th, 1828

IT HAS BEEN a long time since I have enjoyed myself so much. During the day I make excursions in the beautiful countryside or drive around in Lady Darnley's one-horse phaeton through the meadows and high forest of the park, where there are no roads or paths. And in the evening, I, like everyone, participate only as much as I wish in the social gathering. Yesterday after dinner, all nine of us sat together for a couple of hours in the library and read without a single interruption—each, it goes without saying, attending to his or her own book. Finally we had to laugh at the peripatetic silence, mindful of the Englishman in Paris who declared that *parler c'était gâter la conversation.*[2]

On the first day, I visited the above mentioned Lancasterian school, where a single person instructs the sixty girls, who come here for four hours each day from the surrounding areas belonging to Lord Darnley. After this I rode to Rochester to see the ruins of the old castle, a beautiful remnant of antiquity. Whatever was not destroyed by violence is still standing as solid as a rock since the time of William the Conqueror, more than eight hundred years ago. Especially fine are the remains of the refectory, with its colossal pillars connected by richly decorated Saxon arches. The stone ornaments were all carved in Normandy and sent here by sea. I climbed to the highest point of the ruin, where I found a splendid view of the confluence of the Medway and Thames rivers, the town of Rochester, Chatham with its dockyards, and a richly cultivated countryside (Figure 73).

At dinner our company was increased by Mr. and Mrs. P——, Mr. M——, and a nephew of Lord Darnley's. Mrs. P—— told a good anecdote about the actor Kemble, who while on tour in the provinces was appearing in a play where a camel was required to arrive on the scene. Kemble spoke to the stage designer to tell him that there happened to be an actual camel in the town and suggested that he take a look at it, so as to make his artificial animal as true to life as possible. The man appeared very irked by this and responded that he was sorry the gentlemen from London believed people in the provinces to be so ignorant; as for his part, he flattered himself that, without any further inspection, he would produce a more natural camel for the evening performance than any that might be walking around town.

On the following day, I went on another excursion, this time in the company of the ladies, and then after luncheon we took a trip on the water in Lord Darnley's elegant yacht. I drove the four-in-hand that brought everyone as far as the Thames.[3] I have had so little practice in this recently that, against my will, the two leading horses ended up with their heads almost inside a fast-moving diligence that was passing by at a crossroads. This gave rise to a few screams of terror from both carriages, the one behind and the one in front of me, and quite scandalized old Child, who considers me his pupil. Thus on a single day, like the great Corsican,[4] I lost all my luster in the fine art of guiding the reins; from the throne, this is called ruling; from the coach-box, driving. I had to abdicate my throne in the carriage, because the ladies insisted that as long

as I continued to occupy that position, their lives were in danger. This chagrined me so much that the minute I boarded the yacht, I climbed up the rope ladder and remained in the crow's nest, where, at my leisure and fanned by a mild zephyr, I was able to admire the ever-changing view and philosophize over my profound fall from grace.

73

View of Rochester, Stroud, and Chatham.

July 5th, 1828

TODAY I DILIGENTLY helped clear a few new vistas through the brush, to which everyone lent a hand, and I also devised a road through the park, which they want to name in my honor. Afterward I bid a fond farewell to this excellent family—a model for the nobility of any country—and headed back to London, provided with various letters of introduction for Ireland.

July 8th, 1828

BECAUSE I STILL have much to send you before my departure, including my horses, carriage, and some birds (you are going to receive an entire shipment of the rarest examples of these), I have been very busy the last few days with all sorts of purchases. In the process, I happened upon an exhibition of industrial production, where there were a lot of interesting things to see; for example, a machine that by itself, so to speak, draws a perspectival view of everything in its field of vision; or a pianoforte that, in addition to serving its normal purpose, also plays an extra hundred pieces all by itself, and you can accompany them on the keys with your own fantasias. There was a very convenient domestic telegraph system,[5] which dispenses with more than half one's servants and almost all their onerous presence; also a washing machine requiring only *one* woman to tackle the largest pile of laundry; an extremely elegant butter churn to make your own butter at breakfast in the space of two minutes; and still more novelties of this kind.

From here I drove to the largest plant nursery in the vicinity of London, which I have been wanting to see for a long time. The multifarious needs of the many wealthy people here produce private undertakings on a scale that you never come across anywhere else. For instance, in this garden I found a collection of greenhouses in every size. Some of them had narrow lead tubes affixed along the framework of the glass roof, about three on each side. Small holes had been drilled in these tubes at points relative to their distance from the floor. The simple turn of a faucet fills the tubes with river water, and at once a heavy shower falls throughout the whole structure, just like natural rain, but you can have this downpour continue as long as you like. Laborious watering becomes almost unnecessary; the sprinkling has a much more powerful and uniform effect and is given a boost only where excessively dense leaves may hinder the rain from penetrating.

There was a simple device to protect against large hailstones: at the ridge of the glass roof and on both sidewalls, iron points have been attached on which there are rolled-up pieces of canvas, two feet above the glass. When hail arrives, an efficient gadget stretches the canvas taut by means of pulled cords, so that it forms a second roof, and all the hail bounces off without ever touching the glass.

I will not go into detail about the innumerable varieties of pineapples, roses, etc., but will only remark that the vegetable department contained 435 kinds of lettuce, 261 of peas, and 240 of potatoes, and almost all the plants in the garden precinct were represented on a comparable scale.

On my way back, I met the Tyroleans who were taking a day off, and I asked the girl, my old acquaintance, if all of them had been satisfied with their stay here. She assured me enthusiastically that their saint must have led them to this place, because after only a few months, they had already earned seven thousand pounds cash just from singing the same twelve songs. Prince Esterházy has made this type of yodeling fashionable, and fashion is everything here. In fact, the ladies Sontag and Pasta, however great their talent, have only this to thank for their success in London: they became fashionable. It is well-known that Weber never did, and he got nowhere; the two Bohrers fared no better, nor did Kiesewetter and several others of great merit.

Since we are on the subject of fashion, and I am about to depart England, this seems the moment to write at greater length about the nature of society here, something more striking to a stranger in this promised land than fog, steam engines, or stagecoaches. I should begin with a caveat: a generalized account like this can only outline the most prominent aspects of such a complex subject, and the criticism directed at the whole necessarily ignores the hundreds of counterexamples reflecting all that is praiseworthy in English society.[6]

England now finds itself in a period similar to that of France thirty years before the revolution, albeit with an entirely different zeitgeist. However, the same thing will happen here unless England undertakes a succession of radical reforms. Very similar, fundamental evils are present here, as they were there. On one side, the sense of superiority, abuse of power, stony arrogance, and exercise of frivolity among the magnates; on the other, the selfishness and greed now so common as to have imprinted itself upon the national character throughout the lower orders. Religion no longer resides in the heart and mind, but has instead become moribund and formulaic. The English church, in spite of an unrefined *spirit* of Catholicism, has fewer ceremonies but the same degree of intolerance and the same priestly hierarchy, which—in addition to its bigotry and pride—also has the advantage of owning half the property in the country.*

As anyone who has the opportunity to study the high life in England can see, these circumstances have also corrupted what we prefer to call their "society." It is fascinating to observe how, as a result of the differences in the original rooting medium, the same plant has developed differently in France than on John Bull's territory. In France, the tenor of society grew more out of chivalry and its poetry, together with the natural vanity, lightheartedness, and true delight in sociability of the French character. In England, on the other hand, it grew out of a brutal feudal system, the commercial success that followed, the inherent bad temper of the population, and an abiding, if ossified, self-love.

People living abroad tend to form a more-or-less republican (as opposed to monarchal) notion of English society. This principle is indeed very noticeable in the nation's public sphere and becoming ever more so. This also holds for their type of English domestic life, where selfishness surprisingly dominates. Grown children and their parents quickly become strangers to each other, and what *we* call family life is here applicable only to a husband, wife, and small children, as long as the offspring live in direct dependence on their father. When they grow older, republican coolness and estrangement set in between the generations. An English poet once went so far as to claim that the affection grandfathers feel for their grandchildren exists only because they regard their grown *sons* as nothing but greedy and antagonistic heirs, whereas they can embrace their grandchildren as the future enemies of their enemies. The very *thought* could only emerge from an English brain!

On the other hand, one finds absolutely no trace of republican principles in relationships outside the family, no matter the level of society. Here everything is to the utmost degree ultra-aristocratic; it is like the caste system of India. The so-called Great World of English high society might have developed very differently had there been a court, in the Continental sense, to set the tone and direction from the uppermost stratum. But no such thing exists here. English kings all live as private individuals, and most officials at court are only nominal appointments; they meet rarely and then only on important occasions.

Since it is necessary to have a stable center in society from which the brightest light and highest authority may continually radiate, and since it was not being provided by the court, the

---

* It is extremely striking that English writers torment themselves trying to scrutinize the immense taxes on the poor, the increasingly perverse and threatening condition of the working classes in Great Britain, and how all this might be remedied. Some have even recommended systematic exportation of the destitute, much the way cotton fabric and steel products are sent off with the support of government premiums. Yet the remedy is obvious: nothing more than the repeal of tithing. Because tithes rise along with increased cultivation, vast stretches of land are left fallow in England—land we at home would deem good—because nobody wants to hand over his money and sweat to the priests.—*The Editor*. [The situation was slightly improved by the Tithe Commutation Act of 1836, which followed the Tithe War of 1830–1836 in Ireland.—*Translator*.]

wealthy aristocracy felt called upon to take up the role. But despite all its power and wealth, it was incapable of fulfilling this responsibility. The English nobility, however proud, cannot make special claims for its antiquity or purity of blood. If such things can be assigned any value, the English can hardly measure themselves against the French and absolutely not against the higher and mainly intact German nobility. The English aristocracy dazzles us only by its old historical names, wisely retained, that run throughout the country's history like theatrical masks,[7] providing a disguise to hide behind for new families and the offspring of very humble people or mistresses. Admittedly England's nobility has the most solid advantages over other countries because of its actual wealth, and even more because of its share in the legislative power granted by the constitution. But it seeks to authenticate and justify its prideful place in society *not on those grounds, but precisely on the higher extraction of its flaunted nobility of the blood.* The pretense is therefore doubly ludicrous.

The aristocracy instinctively recognized this charade, and thus through tacit agreement, the true monarch they placed on their throne was not nobility as such, nor was it wealth (money was equally concentrated in industry, and the supreme authority could not possibly be transferred *there*). No, indeed, an entirely new power had to be crowned: fashion. Only in England could such a goddess reign quite personally, even—if I may put it that way—as a merciless despot, although a few adept usurpers of both sexes always stand in for her earthly manifestation.

The spirit of caste has evolved to an unprecedented level here, descending from this goddess and penetrating nearly every social tier. It is enough to have enjoyed a familiar visit within a lower circle to find yourself denied access to the next step up the ladder or at best to receive an icy reception. And no Brahmin can shrink from a pariah with more vehemence than an acknowledged exclusive shrinks from a nobody. Just like English fields, every type of society is separated from the next by thorny hedges. Each has its own manners and expressions, its "cant," as one calls it here, and above all an utter contempt for everyone ranked lower. It is clear at first glance that the separate coteries within such a society become extremely provincial, a characteristic that distinguishes London very much from its Parisian counterpart.

Although the aristocracy *as such* does not occupy the pinnacle of this odd structure, it nonetheless wields enormous influence, for it is indeed difficult to become fashionable without being of noble lineage. Just being elegant or merely rich is a far cry from being fashionable. Although laughable, it is thus true to say that George IV is highly fashionable, whereas his predecessor was not in the slightest. Nor are his brothers, which is much to their credit, since no truly distinguished man would be frivolous enough to maintain himself in this category for long. Nevertheless it is difficult to say just what guarantees high status in this scheme. One finds the most unlikely characters achieving positions of influence, and in a country like England, political motives cannot be discounted. But I believe that in the end—just as in the rest of the world—it is caprice and above all females that have the greatest effect.

On the whole, the fashionable English, without managing to abandon their inherited proclivity for ponderousness and pedantry, yearn to emulate the immoral frivolity and haughtiness of the ancien régime. Meanwhile the French are doing exactly the opposite and, by exchanging those attitudes for good old English gravitas, are daily acquiring a more dignified purpose in life.

London exclusives of today are little more than bad reproductions of former Regency *roués* or courtiers of Louis XV. They are selfish, flippant, immeasurably vain, and utterly lacking in heart. Both the French and the English, however, share a haughty scorn for everything; and they fall to their knees in the dust before one idol—the French in former times before their king, and the English before whichever new monarch assumes the throne of fashion. But what a contrast in the final consequences! In France, the loss of morality and probity was replaced by an exquisite courtesy; the lack of good nature compensated for with intellect and charm; the impertinence of superiority made bearable by elegance and agreeable manners. Overbearing vanity was to a certain extent justified in France, or at least excused, by the splendor of an impressive court, an elegant and dignified self-presentation, the perfected art of social interaction, winning *aisance*, and a conversation that captivated through wit and facility.

What can an English dandy offer compared with this? *His* highest triumph is to adopt the most wooden manners and get away with being as uncouth as possible—yes, even crafting his civilities so they veer close to insults and employing this skill to gain celebrity. Instead of noble *aisance*, the dandy does away with every constraint of decorum; he subverts his relationships with women so as to make *them* appear the aggressors and he alone the injured. As soon as close acquaintances cease to impress him as fashionable, he treats them—occasionally on a whim—as if he no longer knows them. He "cuts them," as the technical term has it. The dandy masters the unspeakable jargon and affectations of his set, and he always knows what "the latest thing" is. These are the qualities that make up the young lion of the fashionable world. If, in addition, he has an especially pretty mistress, and has succeeded in seducing some foolish woman silly enough to abandon her husband and children for him and sacrifice herself to fashion, then he has burnished his halo all the more. If he also wastes a lot of money in the process, if he is young and has a name in the peerage book, then he will have at least a transient role to play and all the elements of a modern Richelieu. That his conversation consists of nothing but parochial jokes and slanders whispered into a woman's ear at large gatherings, as if no one else were in the room; that he can only speak to men about gambling and sport; that he is totally ignorant of anything beyond the routine of a few modish clichés; that his awkward *tournure* is no better than the slack posture of a country lad stretched out by the hearth; and that his grace is that of a bear taught to dance in some foreign country—none of this robs a single jewel from his crown.

Even worse is that however haughty and coarse his external behavior, the ideal of modishness requires that his internal morality be even more degraded. It is notorious how much cheating goes on in the many games that constitute the daily fare in this Great World and how, with much practice, it has acquired a kind of almost-sculptural definition. Even more striking is the fact that no one attempts to disguise the crass selfishness of such transactions. People flaunt it openly, as if it were the only reasonable course, whereas being good-natured is ridiculed as the epitome of vulgarity. This is no longer true in any other country; elsewhere the people holding such views are at least ashamed of them. "We are a selfish people, I confess," says a popular fashion setter, "and I do believe that what in other countries is called *amor patriae* is amongst us nothing but a huge conglomeration of love of ourselves; but I am glad of it; I like selfishness; there's good sense in it." He continues, not satirically but earnestly and eagerly, "Good nature is quite *mauvais ton* in London, and really it is a bad style to take up and will never do."[8]

Admittedly, if you want to examine every human feeling, you will perhaps always discover some degree of selfishness at its core. But for this exact reason, you find that a noble sense of shame leads other nationalities to throw a veil over their egoism, much as the brutish often seek to conceal things such as the sexual instinct that are natural and genuine.

Here, however, people are little ashamed of their self-infatuation. A distinguished English-man once explained to me how a good foxhunter must never be disconcerted while in pursuit of his prey; even if he saw his own father lying on the ground after missing a jump, the huntsman would unhesitatingly urge his horse to vault over or even onto him, if necessary, and leave the man to his own fate until the hunt was ended.*

Meanwhile our model dandy has no originality, even in his negative qualities, but is instead an anxious slave to fashion, no matter its level of trivia. In short, he is the abject satellite of anyone who may outrank him. If virtue and modesty were suddenly to become fashionable, the dandy would be the first to adopt these attributes, and he would do so impeccably, however difficult it might be for him. Lacking any independence and without a single thought of his own, he is much like that clay figure in the story of the *Galgenmännchen* who manages to deceive people into thinking him human until he is discovered to have no soul, at which point he dissolves into muck.[9]

Anyone who reads the best of the recent English novels—for example, those by the author of *Pelham*[10]—can acquire an accurate sense of fashionable society, provided, *nota bene*, he does not forget to subtract those qualities that English self-love unjustifiably ascribes to itself: grace to its *roués*; seductive manners and skill at winsome conversation to its dandies. I spent some time not only with the rulers of the Mountain of Fools, who command the summit of fashion, but also with the colonizers of the middle heights, not to say with those unfortunates at the foot of the slope, who gaze longingly toward the unattainable peak. But seldom did I find any trace of that art of social interaction, that perfect and satisfying equilibrium of all social talents, as far removed from constraint as from abandon, which speaks with equal congeniality to the mind and heart and continually excites but is never tiring—that art for so long mastered solely by the French.

Instead what I observed throughout the fashionable world was an increase in true vulgarity, a crass immorality, an undisguised arrogance, and an uncouth disregard of good-heartedness—all of it striving for the luster of an empty refinement. In this respect, the fashionable are even more unpalatable than the most avowed nobodies with their awkward, comical affectations. It has been said that vice and poverty make for the most revolting combination, but since I have been in England, vice and crassness seem to me a much more nauseating blend.

But now let me move from generalities to a few fleeting sketches of some gentlemen of this region. We first meet a nobleman who is hard of hearing and speaks with difficulty. A tall, blond figure (what Napoleon's soldiers called, in a mean but fitting expression, *un grand flandrin*).[11] His face has the cut of a Spanish merino sheep and is only good-looking to the extent possible for someone without refined features or an intelligent expression. His unimpressive eyes reflect only *one* big idea, namely what he thinks about himself.

"Take a look at this man," I said to my recently disembarked friend, "he's no dandy and any-way no longer young enough for it, yet nevertheless he enjoys a still higher potency, for he is right now the sultan of fashion in England."

"Impossible," my friend exclaimed, "you're joking."

---

* Certainly the new Parisian society called "Aide-toi, le ciel t'aidera" has never gone so far in praxis.
—*The Editor.* ["Help yourself and heaven will help you," was the name of this Jacobin society, founded in August 1827.—*Translator.*]

"Not in the slightest," I answered, "and despite what you see, this happy mortal does possess a few characteristics appropriate to his role that should not be scorned."

"And they are?" H—— interrupted.

"Well, first of all, he is one of the wealthiest and most distinguished noblemen in the land, for whom at least fifty thousand Irishmen must suffer starvation, although he rarely graces them with his presence. Furthermore he is still unmarried and in both body and mind the most suitable of mediocrities, the sort that neither awakens envy nor gives offense. He is generous to those around him, likes to give parties, is convivial, lets himself be dominated by the ladies with such patience and pleasure that he would willingly lay down his life for them. In addition, he owns the best palace in London as well as the most beautiful country house and, to be fair, has better taste when it comes to furnishings, equipage, and fetes than many others. But what redounds most to his honor, he is a very upstanding man."

To some extent, what I have just said may appear to contradict what I identified as the main characteristics of the fashionables, but the exception does not make a rule, and one must also keep in mind that the admirers of dazzling scoundrels also appreciate a dupe in their midst. Even with all these advantages, it would have been difficult for this man to achieve such heights had a great foreign talent not singled him out and by this means elevated herself just as high on the throne. This lady's proud and manly spirit, which she conceals beneath the most charming affability *when she chooses*, is combined with all the diplomatic cunning of her rank, enabling her to place her foot on the neck of English supremacy. The court has gathered around her ever since and blindly submits to her rule.[12] Yet she has not managed to imbue it either with her wit and sense of tact or her aristocratic manner, not to say that off-putting civility toward everyone not among the chosen, the *ne plus ultra* of what the exclusives are striving for. The distance that exists between her and her co-sovereign in these respects is thus almost burlesque. Yet the two now reign side-by-side on Olympus.

Even the immortal gods have to endure some opposition, and we have a giant in this role—a certain marquis. With equal wealth, more intellect and taste, more dignified manners, and more spirited if ugly features than the duke, his reputation is also superior. Some perhaps avoid him because of his character, it is true, though others seek him out all the more eagerly. He, too, is a strict observer of that wise principle governing the self-serving English fashion world, namely, that one must make it very difficult for anyone to gain access to one's intimate circle. Nonetheless, he is more popular than the coryphaei I named first.[13] At his grand *assemblées*, even the King of the Jews might appear,[14] to whom H——'s doors are always barred and those of Sontag secretly and with acute diplomacy left open. One finds many other *dei minorum gentium* there as well,[15] such as actresses who have become duchesses and ladies, figures rarely glimpsed in those circles par excellence.

The young heir to a famous name and a large estate also displayed his ambition to become prominent among the fashionables, but in his case, the excellent life lessons conveyed in his progenitor's letters fell on arid soil.[16] And since circumstances have otherwise been unfavorable to him, so far he has had to be satisfied with inferior sovereign rights and only a measured appreciation of his handsome carriages, horses, and the charms of his celebrated mistress.

There is a foreign ambassador who also possesses much influence and would doubtless have achieved still more if the only prerequisites were an excellent demeanor, a gemütlich amiability, high rank, the finest taste, and (despite an assumed English *tournure*) the complete absence of that ponderousness and pedantry that English fashionables can never seem to shake off. But precisely because he stands at too far a remove from the English—both through his foreign affability, which consistently manages to triumph over his Anglomania, and his German warmheartedness—he arouses their envy more than their admiration. And although most people seek him out simply because he is in vogue, he is nonetheless something of a strange lodestar for them, someone they now and again treat with hostility and cannot finally accept with the same warmth as they do their own Jupiter Ammon; nor do they wish to subjugate themselves to him as blindly as to their own Lady Autocrat and her *autorité sans réplique*. The ambassador's lovely wife could have easily played that lady's role, since she surpasses her in charm and in youth, and the odds might have remained equal for a time. But she was too innocent in her good nature, too natural and warmhearted to win a definitive victory. Thus however high her position within the realm of fashion, her rival has, at least for the time being, barred her from the topmost rank. But none of this will make her any less endearing.[17]

Among the female corulers of the first category, I must mention a few others who cannot be ignored if one hopes to be admitted to the inner sanctum. At the top is a countess, no longer quite young but still lovely, one of the few Englishwomen who can be credited with a perfectly pleasant and truly distinguished *tournure*. Given her natural attributes, she would certainly have succeeded in any other country, but here she was unable to disguise the imprint of caste, which is so pitiless and destructive of all beauty and human kindness. She has often been attacked in hateful ways in the malicious game of social one-upmanship, although she is too superior and charming to have been damaged by this.

I know a Scottish viscountess, for example, who thrived in the shadow of the foreign lady sovereign. Twelve years ago, I watched her clamber up rather humbly beneath the wings of her protectress, though since that time she has acquired all the arrogance, not to say coarseness, of her Olympian compatriots. Of the impertinent civility I mentioned above, she understood how to acquire only the first part. And, were it not for her control over her husband, as well as a large, independent fortune with its accompanying political influence, her lofty patroness would hardly have granted her the place she now occupies; even in a female ministry with its many ambassadorial objectives, one may now and again have need of some odd characters. When I first visited England all those years ago, this lady was quite pretty and already then in diplomatic fetters, but of a different sort. Now her entire life is dominated by nothing but fashion and politics.

A third lady serves as the benevolent governess of the others; I believe she also lays claim to the title of a German *Reichsgräfin*, which, although not highly regarded in England, will naturally acquire a different sheen when possessed by an Englishwoman. This family title was attained in the same honorable manner through which the first dukes of England were awarded theirs: a German emperor took a fancy to an ancestress of the family, etc., etc. Her granddaughter, however, scarcely enjoys the same good fortune, although she still shows traces of the Austrian lower lip and a slightly elongated face.[18] She has a cultivated mind and is certainly the most good-natured of the Lady Patronesses, not at all on the offensive. She often seems fonder of gracing the domestic fireside than enjoying her high position as a countess among the Almack's royals.

Another countess can be construed as her opposite. A Frenchwoman by birth, who emigrated to England when she was a child, she has long since been nationalized, though certainly not to her advantage. She is, however, better made for society than the women I have described thus far. Thoroughly urbane, she is no longer young but well preserved, with expressive, fiery eyes topped by lovely, thick eyebrows, which have drawn much attention. The *chronique scandaleuse* claims that, in the counsel of the fashion ladies' directorate, she skillfully assumed a role not unlike that of the *tâteur* in the old French regiments, the officer chosen to test the valor of each new recruit. She is said to have played exactly this part by judging all newcomers on the basis of their prospects for becoming fashionable.

Two women remain, and then the tally of the elect will be more or less complete. In fact, the second of them does not actually belong there anymore, but is floating freely in the ether like a comet in a planetary system. Both are marquesses, both pass for pretty, both are rich, one also has some sense (altogether lacking in the other). It is therefore quite possible that the first would feel somewhat insulted to find herself listed with the second, if she were ever to lay eyes on my modest account of their rankings.

It is truly a shame that this woman has such a high opinion of herself and, as one of the most ardent extremists, is completely steeped in politics. When she holds court in her ancient palace, which once belonged to Queen Elizabeth, she actually seems to find herself under the *douce illusion* that she *is* Elizabeth. Politics had at that time created some tension between her and the absolute dictatress, and consequently also with her rival's male satellite, the tall and lanky H——. On the other hand, her house was frequented by two other important figures from among the fashionables (who, by the way, had thrown themselves politically at the feet of the hero of Waterloo).[19] Since one of these figures is the most extreme sort of dandy and the other the number one *bel esprit* of high society, I should probably grant them passing attention as well.

As long as England's fashion was in its age of innocence, Continental manners provided the template; now, however, the English have achieved a kind of autonomy, and their conventions are looked upon as a model for other countries. It is thus no longer possible for a dandy to rule primarily through his attire (as was the case with the celebrated Brummel, who tyrannized town and country for years solely by this means). On the contrary, the superior exclusive today affects a certain inattention to his dress, which is nearly always the same, and far from following every fashion or inventing one for himself, his costume is distinguished mostly by tidiness and refinement. To be sure, there is more than this to being a man of fashion nowadays. Among other things, one must have the reputation—as used to be true in France—of being a heartless seducer of women. And one must also be a *dangerous* man. But a gentleman of undistinguished appearance and hopelessly clumsy manners, no matter how hard he tries, will never be in a position to emulate the brilliant rapport and enchanting ease of the French in former times. Instead he must, like Tartuffe, know how to put himself forward as a hypocrite, both sweet and poisonous, and utter false words in the subdued tones currently in fashion and forge his dark way to unscrupulous deeds. (False play and the duping of novices are part of every kind of sport, after all, leading so many young Englishmen to reap suicide and despair rather than the amusement they had hoped for.) Or if duplicity fails him, he must conspire to spoil the reputations and fortunes of those who stand in his way, or at the very least, rob them of their influence among the exclusives.

Anyone familiar with the dark side of England will know I am not exaggerating, and will not be surprised that the fashion hero I mentioned, a young man of good family but with no fortune of his own, who is nothing but an adroit swindler, regards himself as well characterized and flattered by the name "sweet mischief." So far the marquise seems drawn only to the sugary, entertaining aspect, which mostly consists of sweetly whispered slander; perhaps she will get to know the mischief a bit later.

The *bel esprit*—his caustic power so feared that he is literally courted the way savages court the devil in order to keep him from biting—has one of the most disgusting exteriors I have ever come across. He is certainly more than fifty years old and looks exactly like a Seville orange preserved in gall. A gray and greenish old sinner, he cannot eat his supper until he has robbed two or three men of their good names and offered clever but malicious remarks to just as many others. Yet his words are received with loud acclaim and convulsive laughter by everyone in his vicinity, even though many feel a shiver go up and down their spine at the prospect of being given the same treatment as soon as their backs are turned. But the man is simply Fashion. His comments are oracular, his wit *must* be exquisite since modish society has granted him the franchise, and where Fashion speaks, the free Englishman becomes a slave. Moreover a vulgar man no doubt concedes that in matters witty and artistic, his own judgment is not competent. He therefore prefers blindly to applaud a *bon mot* whenever he sees others laughing, just as he celebrates every opinion issuing from a prestigious mouth. This is why the Tyrolean street tootlers managed all winter long to transport the local public to the third heaven for a pretty sum of money, which the green butcher family gleefully pocketed.

I almost forgot one additional lady whom I must describe in just a few words, a truly charming *petite maitresse*, whose great wealth allows her slightly empty but ever-so-pretty little head to be adorned by the most beautiful and colorful jewels to be found in England. If you see her in the morning reclining *languissant* on her chaise longue, you find her surrounded by countless baubles in a hundred elegant containers, all charmingly laid out. Yet they are not enough to keep a faltering conversation in gear. A friend of the family, usually with a vacuous smile hovering on his lips, brings little to the discussion. And her bosom friend, a long-nosed, nimble dwarf, is more amiable when silent than when speaking. The picture is often complemented by the display of two adorable dolls in the cutest fanciful outfits, who prattle away with consummate charm. Yet despite all her languishing and pale, transparent complexion, the poor marquise, like all narrow souls, can sometimes turn downright nasty, especially when her vanity has been pricked. What annoys her incessantly is her inability to become entirely *la mode*; she is neither fish nor fowl, as one says. This amphibian condition of hers is not only quite unpleasant but also seemingly incurable, for no matter what she may try—playing the role of a Gurli,[20] parading as a paragon of virtue, or giving herself a new luster by spending some time in Paris—"it will never do."

I have already written you about the celebrated Almack's and the unrivaled power of the Lady Patronesses. But it remains to describe two of their most masterful acts. One time these ladies proclaimed in their charming way that no one arriving after midnight would be admitted to a ball. A few minutes later the Duke of Wellington came from a session of Parliament, believing an exception would be made for him. *Pas du tout.* The hero of Waterloo could not conquer this fortress and had to fall back in defeat! Another time the Lady Patronesses issued a decree that only those gentlemen who had bow legs would be permitted to appear at Almack's in long trousers; breeches were required for everyone else, a bold stipulation in England, where the very name of that article of clothing is otherwise taboo.[21] The fear of the ladies' new tribunal was so great that at first even this edict was observed. But later a reaction ensued. A large number of men appeared at the door wearing the prohibited trousers and demanded entry, claiming themselves guilty of having bow legs and, in the event they were not believed, inviting the Lady Patronesses to give closer inspection. The ladies have turned a blind eye to this element of male attire ever since.*

July 10th, 1828

I AM ALL the happier to be setting off on my trip away and departing from here, since something unpleasant and unexpected just happened that makes me, for the moment, more conspicuous than I would wish.

I think I have already written you about a niece of Napoleon's whom I first saw at the Duke of Devonshire's, where she was engaged in a very lively discussion with Lord Brougham just as I was introduced to her.[22] She has a good figure, an extraordinarily bright complexion, Napoleon's classical nose, large expressive eyes, and all the vivacity of the French mixed, as a bonus, with a touch of Italian fire. In addition, there is an eccentricity to her whole demeanor, something I love dearly when it is natural, although I must admit that here it seemed not entirely free of design. Meanwhile I was impressed by her name. You know of my respect for the exalted emperor, that latter-day Prometheus whom Europe bound to a rock on the other side of the equator, that giant who was finally slain by a million pygmies, to their eventual detriment, *because they did not have the strength to tame this mighty spirit so that he might perform a service for them.*

Mainly in order to talk about him, I approached this handsome, somewhat mannish woman and cultivated her acquaintance more than I otherwise might have done, not because she was unstylish, but because her particular constellation of female attributes are not the ones I prefer. Still, by the time she departed for Ireland, we had become quite well acquainted, though after that I thought no more about her. Then a few weeks ago she returned, divorced from her husband, an Englishman, whom she had only married, eccentrically enough, so she could travel with him to Saint Helena, a plan that was later frustrated.

Her Frenchness and lively conversation along with all these other details drew me to her again, and I saw her even more often than before. Last week she asked if I would get her a ticket to a *déjeuner champêtre* in the Horticultural Society garden, a fete the Lady Patronesses also take seriously, and when I brought her the ticket she insisted that I accompany her. I responded very amiably that gossip could easily start in this provincial society, and if the two of us went together to this event, we would be at risk of seeing it reported in a newspaper article the next day. Instead of answering, she broke down in tears and said that it made no difference, everything was all the same to her anyway, since tomorrow she would no longer be of this world. At this she pulled a little bottle of opium or prussic acid from her bosom and assured me that she was determined to empty it before nightfall; until then she wanted to anesthetize herself as much as possible.

---

* It might be useful to note that since this letter was written, English high society has been modified. The noble and more practical way of thinking of the present king and his charming and excellent queen have broken the fool's scepter of those days, and people are beginning to adopt a more worthy standard for measuring merit and grace. But the coryphaei of the past must acquiesce in this or else be satisfied in the future with their own self-admiration, and instead of being the *exclusives* become the *excluded.—The Editor.* [King William IV and Queen Adelaide reigned 1830–1837.—*Translator.*]

Amazed by such an unexpected confession, I tried to calm the sobbing woman as best I could, tossed the flask of poison out the window, and expressed my hope that the cheerful fete, the society, the fresh air, the acclaim that would be bestowed upon her pretty dress would quickly vanquish this foolish and overly excited mood. Although I had no knowledge of her intimacies, it was not hard to guess that there must be an unhappy love affair in play, the only reason women tend to want to take their lives, and since I have endured similar pain, I confess that I felt very sorry for her and took her words, however exaggerated, as more than mere affectation.

In the meantime, my carriage had arrived and we got in, while I repeated that she was forcing herself to the diversion of this *déjeuner* because she could no longer bear the torment of being alone. During our drive she told me everything, which I will skip, since it was that old song about the sorrows and joys of love that people sing in every generation, just as certainly as the nightingale and siskin sing theirs.

While I was comforting my lovely friend as much as I was able, I found myself reflecting on how strangely fate can turn, and how much more strangely it is handled and judged by us. Sitting next to me was a niece of Napoleon, the former ruler of nearly the whole civilized world, a woman whose aunts and uncles once occupied the most ancient thrones of Europe and have now, due to the most outrageous events, been cast down among the commoners. Yet none of this had made the slightest impression on the individual seated next to me. It caused her no distress—whereas the unfaithfulness of a silly English dandy had aroused her despair and carried her to the brink of ending her life!!! With true indignation I beseeched her to consider the family she belonged to, to think of the sublime example that her uncle had given her and the world of a life endured in true unhappiness. In a typically female way, however, she paid no attention to this tirade and responded: "Ah, if only I had the choice now, *j'aimerais cent fois mieux être la maitresse heureuse de mon amant que reine d'Angleterre et des Indes.*"[23]

In spite of all this, the fete and the company, as well as the few glasses of champagne that I urged on her at breakfast, seemed to alleviate her despair, and I brought her back at six o'clock (fairly sure that no second bottle of opium would be fetched) in order to prepare my own *toilette* for a large dinner at our ambassador's house, something I did not want to miss. Just imagine my fright when a few days later Rothschild, with his nicely acquired English phlegm, told me:

"Lady Wyse drowned herself this morning in the Serpentine, was fished out by a passing servant and then, accompanied by a huge crowd, brought back to her residence, already several hours before the likes of us had even gotten up."

"My God, is she dead?" I cried.

"I don't think so," Rothschild answered, "if I heard correctly, she is supposed to have revived."[24]

I rushed immediately to see her, but found all the shutters closed, and a servant said no one but the doctor was to be admitted, that his mistress was deathly ill. This is taking folly a bit too far, I thought to myself, and the niece, such a poor imitation of her immortal relative, is an apt illustration of a fundamental truth: how much easier and weaker it is to cast off an unbearable sorrow through suicide than to endure it boldly unto one's last breath! Yet I felt strong compassion for the poor woman and was almost happy that my imminent departure would spare me another meeting with her after such a catastrophe, since I could neither help her nor condone her behavior. For the same reason that she had visited the Horticultural Gardens—namely to find distraction from unpleasant thoughts—I went to a large gathering today at the Marquise H——'s. After passing through only a few rooms, I happened upon the Duke of C——, a prince who, although he has no pretensions to being a liberal, is nonetheless very fond of publicity.

He had barely caught sight of me when he called out from a distance, "Oh, P——,[25] what the devil kind of mischief have you been up to? It's already in the newspapers that Lady Wyse drowned herself because of you!"

"Because of me, Your Royal Highness? What a fable!"

"Don't deny it, I saw you myself with her in the carriage *solus cum sola.* The entire world has been informed about it, and I have also already written to the king in Berlin."

"Well, well, just what I really needed—to be blamed for a sin that's not mine," I responded sullenly. "By the way, are you aware that it's only *the English* who are catastrophic for the Napoleonic line. The patriarch himself left the ignominy of his death as an eternal bequest to the English nation, and in recompense it seems his poor niece will doom no more than a single English dandy to the powers of the underworld. But since Nemesis never fails to involve herself in world history and minor human relationships alike, it is quite possible that a latter-day Bonaparte will take vengeance on your nation for his imperial ancestor's shameful end. Indeed, perhaps someday an English dandy will shoot himself in Paris over the beautiful eyes of one of Napoleon's descendants. We Germans, however, remain content to admire the emperor and his heirs only from afar; as with the sun, it was not healthy to stay too close to his radiance in the heat of midday, although by now that sun has set."*

With that I took my leave and, once at home, gave immediate orders to speed up my departure. I hope by tomorrow I will be in a position to begin my journey to more distant and open regions and leave behind cooped-up city life for once and for all!

Somewhere Lord Byron says about himself that only in solitude is his soul released to its full sphere of activity. I now see that this truth applies to lesser mortals as well, for it is the same with me. In the aggravations of society, I feel only half of my soul and am appalled at the thought of having to be amiable! On the other hand, as you know, it is in solitude that I am least alone, and it is there that I least feel the absence, dear friend, of your companionship.

Although you are so far away, my spirit hovers over your waking and your dreaming, and across the sea and the mountains my heart feels the loving beat of your own.

Lou

---

* We might have had misgivings about allowing the foregoing to remain in the text if the essentials of the matter had not already been publicized in various tabloids in much greater, if partly incorrect, detail.—*The Editor.*

Cheltenham, July 12th, 1828

M Y PRECIOUS JULIE,

I left London at two in the morning, this time really sick and in a very foul mood, in harmony with the weather, which, utterly *à l'anglaise*, was raging like a storm at sea, the rain pouring down in buckets. But after the sky cleared up around eight o'clock and the gentle, swift roll of the carriage allowed me to slumber a little, I found everything refreshed and sparkling like emeralds, while through the open carriage window a magnificent fragrance wafted in from the flowery meadows. And then, within a few moments, your morose friend, so burdened by worry, became an innocent child once again, taking delight in God and the beauty of the world.

Traveling in England is, in truth, most delectable—if only I could see *you* take joy in it, I would feel my own doubled in your company! Although it continued to rain off and on, which I am little aware of in the closed carriage, the day with its balmy air was nonetheless very pleasant. Our road passed first through a part of the countryside that was bursting with luxuriant vegetation like the loveliest park. Next we were presented with fields of grain as far as the eye could see, and without hedges—a rarity in England. The last was almost a match for the rich plains of Lombardy. I drove by several large estates, but left them unvisited because of the uncertain weather and time constraints. In any case, after my lengthy hunts for parks and gardens through half of England, it is no longer easy for me to discover one offering something new. In Cirencester I visited a beautiful and very old Gothic church with a few reasonably well-preserved stained-glass windows and strange, old baroque carvings. It is a shame that all Gothic churches in England, without exception, have been disfigured by tasteless, modern gravestones and monuments.

Late in the evening I arrived in Cheltenham, an enchanting spa town of an elegance not found on the Continent. My mood was already cheerful and comfortable because of the copious gas lighting and new-looking, villa-like houses, each surrounded by a little flower garden. This is always my favorite time of arrival, when the daylight is in competition with artificial illumination. I entered the inn, which could almost be called sumptuous, and went to my room preceded by two servants who lit my way, first up a snow-white staircase of stone adorned by a balustrade of gilded bronze, and then across bright gleaming carpets. There in my own chamber I surrendered *con amore* to the sense of comfort that one finds in such perfection only in England. Indeed this country is ideally suited to a misanthrope like myself, because everything unconnected with the world of society, everything one can simply *pay* for, is not only excellent and complete but can be enjoyed in isolation, without anyone else needing to bother about it.*

---

* At least *you* know that this frame of mind is not rooted in selfishness.

It would be the sweetest pleasure to travel here with you, free of cares and duties. How much I miss you everywhere. And I must love you deeply, my dear, because, whenever things go badly for me, I am always comforted by the thought that you escaped at least *that* moment; and on the other hand, whenever I see or feel something that makes me happy, I must always—as if it were a *reproach*—experience a pang of regret for enjoying it all without you!

One can certainly find a larger and more varied provision of life's pleasures in England than we could ever discover at home. It is not in vain that wise institutions have long prevailed here, and what is most comforting and heartening to a philanthropist is the frequent evidence of greater well-being and more dignified living conditions. What *we* call affluence is here considered to be the bare essentials and is manifest across all classes. From this arises a striving for refinement even in the smallest details, a meticulous elegance and immaculateness—in a nutshell, an aspiration for the beautiful and the useful, something still totally unknown to our lower classes.

I think I already wrote you from Birmingham that just when I was there, the opposition papers in London reported how the local factory workers were suffering from a famine. In reality this meant that instead of having three or four daily meals with tea, cold meat, bread and butter, and beefsteaks or roasts, the people were having to get by with only one or two meals a day and nothing but meat and potatoes. It was harvest time, however, and the lack of workers was so severe that almost any price was being paid to hire them. Nonetheless I was assured that factory workers would rather demolish their machines—indeed actually die of hunger—before they would pick up a scythe or bind a sheaf. This is how spoiled and stubborn the common people of England have become from their life of luxury and the certainty of employment (should they seriously wish it). Such stories make it clear to what extent the frequent articles on this subject in the newspapers should actually be trusted.[1]

July 13th, 1828

THIS MORNING I visited some of the public promenades and found they did not meet my expectations. I also tried the mineral waters, which are similar to those of Karlsbad, but made me feel overly heated. The local doctors say, as do ours, that one must drink the water very early in the day or it loses a lot of its power. But the funny thing is that in their view *early* begins at ten o'clock, exactly when it ends with us.

Unfortunately the weather is disagreeable, having turned cold and stormy following what was, for England, a rather long period of intense heat. It is not so bad for traveling however. At least I feel far more cheerful than in London, and I am deeply looking forward to the beautiful landscape of Wales, where I am now heading. So please stay with me, if only in thought, and let our spirits glide hand in hand over land and sea, looking down together from the mountains and enjoying the quiet tranquility of the valleys; in forms as infinitely varied as infinity is boundless, spirits rejoice across all worlds at the glory of God's magnificent nature.

I will lead you first to the seven sources of the Thames, which emerge one hour's drive from Cheltenham. I undertook this excursion in a fly (a kind of small landau, drawn by just one horse), sitting on its roof in order to watch the lovely views from an elevated position. After a long ascent, you finally arrive at a secluded mountain meadow where you see, beneath a few alders, a marshy group of tiny springs forming an insignificant little brook that trickles off as far as the eye can follow. This is the modest beginning of the proud Thames. My mood turned quite poetic when

I thought of how, not many hours before and just a few miles away, I had seen this same water covered with a thousand ships, and how every year that glorious river, despite the shortness of its course, probably bears more ships, more treasures, and more people on its back than any of its colossal kin; and how the capital of the world stands on its banks and rules the four parts of the earth through an omnipotent network of trade. With reverent amazement, I looked at the burbling droplets and compared them first to Napoleon, born in obscurity in Ajaccio, who was soon setting all the thrones of the world atremble. Then I compared these watery pearls to an avalanche that, set loose by the foot of a sparrow, can bury a village in five minutes; or with Rothschild, whose father sold ribbons, yet without whom no European power seems able to wage war today.

My carriage driver, who was also a certified Cheltenham cicerone, took me from there to a peak called Lackington Hill, which boasts a celebrated view and the bonus of a friendly inn catering to visitors. Hidden in the shelter of a rose arbor overlooking a rich plain,* I let my gaze roam seventy miles into the distant landscape dotted with towns and villages, with the cathedral of Gloucester the most imposing prospect among them. Two mountain ranges rise in turn behind it, those of Malvern and Wales. As lovely as it all was, the distant blue mountains fading into the haze only made me feel a yearning for home. How happily I would have flown to your side beneath Fortunatus's wishing hat!

Until then black clouds had been chasing each other across the sky, and just as I left the view behind, the sun teasingly appeared and lit my way through a beech wood to the charming country estate of Mr. Todd. It is laid out in the form of a cheerful village in the midst of a shady forest—nothing but huts, thatched roofs, and moss houses. In the center, on a green expanse of lawn, is the town's venerated linden with a three-tiered bench for exactly that many generations. There is a sundial on a weathered trunk not far away and, at the edge of the hill looking toward the valley, a rustic seat with heather covering its arching roof, the ribbing prettily interlaced with roots. Often on special occasions, the entire place is decorated with evergreens and flowers and, in the evenings, brightly lit with lamps. In the adjoining park, which boasts many lovely spots, the ruins of a Roman villa were discovered by chance just eight years ago when a tree suddenly sank into the ground. A few of the baths are still in good condition, as are two mosaic floors, although these are of rather coarse workmanship and in no way comparable to the ones excavated at Pompeii. The walls are still partly covered with red and blue stucco two inches thick, and the brick heating pipes are of unmatched quality and durability. About a quarter of an hour away, you can clearly follow the old Roman road, part of which is still in use. It is distinguished from English roads primarily by being completely straight, like a North German thoroughfare. One hopes the Romans had better taste than to border their roads, as we do, with endless lines of Lombardy poplars, thereby doubling the monotony and imposing real torture on a poor traveler. What a contrast with an English country road that winds its way in gentle curves around the hills, avoiding deep valleys and protecting ancient trees, so much preferable to the idée fixe of an unwavering line that forces its way, at six times the cost, through thick and thin, over peaks and into chasms.

Returning to Cheltenham, I passed through a large village where I visited my first so-called tea garden. It is remarkable how a small space is divided here into a hundred tiny niches, benches, and picturesque, often-enchanting seats amid flowers and trees. The charm of the

---

* It is one of the great beauties of England that next to most dwellings, even in the winter, you come upon luxuriant bowers and climbing tendrils of damask roses.

setting contrasts strongly with the stolid crowd that seems only to populate the scene rather than enliven it.

Since it was still fairly early when I got back to town, I made use of the beautiful evening to visit a few other mineral springs, and it became apparent to me that the one I happened on this morning was a minor example. These establishments are dazzling, often ornamented with marble, but more often with flowers, greenhouses, and beautiful plantings. As soon as something becomes fashionable in England, it generates intense financial speculation, and this is so much the case here that in just fifteen years, the price of an acre of land close to town rose from forty to one thousand guineas. The places intended for public enjoyment are, I believe rightly, laid out very differently from the gardens and parks belonging to private individuals. Shade, broad promenades, and public areas are more the objective than are vistas or the sense of a magnificent, integrated landscape. I like the way they plant allées. A strip of ground five feet wide is double-dug along either side of the path and then thickly planted with a mixture of trees and shrubs. The most successful trees are allowed to attain their full height, while the others are kept trimmed into irregular, low undergrowth. The crowns of the high trees and the bushes provide a more handsome frame for the views, rendering the whole fuller and more lush; this also has the advantage that the wall of foliage can be allowed to grow thickly from top to bottom if the surrounding countryside is uninteresting.

Worcester, July 14th, 1828

YESTERDAY, *entre la poire et le fromage,*[2] I received a visit, already declined twice, from the local master of ceremonies, one of those gentlemen who do the *honneurs* of the spa and exercise significant authority over the visitors to English watering spots, greeting strangers with an otherwise very un-English torrent of words and obliging helpfulness and seeking to attend to their entertainment. As a rule such an Englishman is playing a nasty game vividly reminiscent of the character Martin in the fable, who wants to imitate the caresses of a lapdog.[3] I could not get rid of this one until he had slurped up a few bottles of my claret and tasted every dessert the house had on offer. He finally took his leave, but not before extracting my promise to honor tomorrow's ball with my presence. Since I am not feeling particularly interested in society and making new acquaintances, I stood him up and left Cheltenham early in the morning.

The landscape continued to be altogether delightful, covered by meadowlands and groups of trees in deep green, with increasingly clear views of the mountains crowning the horizon. At almost every stage we passed a considerable town, never lacking its towering Gothic church. I found the setting of Tewkesbury especially charming. Although nothing could be more peaceful or idyllic than these flourishing plains, they were all blood-soaked battlegrounds during England's countless civil wars, and this has provided the singularly inappropriate names they have borne since: Bloody Meadow, Murder Field, Field of Bones, etc.

I am now writing you from Worcester, the county town, which does not offer anything very remarkable beyond its splendid cathedral. The few ancient stained-glass windows still remaining have been augmented with new glass that stands out harshly against the soft, glowing colors of the old. King John is buried in the middle of the nave, his effigy carved in stone atop his stone tomb. This is the earliest grave monument of an English king in Great Britain. The coffin was opened a few years ago, and the skeleton found still well preserved and dressed exactly like the figure on the lid of the sarcophagus. When the air touched the clothes, however, they turned into dust; the sword had already been consumed by rust, so only its handle was recognizable. Another notable monument commemorates a Templar. It bears a Norman inscription from the year 1220: "Ici aist syr guilleaume de harcourt fys robert de harcourt et de Isabel de camvile."[4] The figure of the knight (in an entirely different costume, I might add, than that of Graf Brühl's Templar in Berlin) is superbly carved and lies there with a naturalness and abandon that would befit a classical statue. The clothing consists of boots or stockings, however you want to call them, made of *cotte de mailles* and fitted with golden spurs; the knees are exposed, and above them the chain mail continues to cover the entire body and head, with only the face left bare. Over this the figure is wearing a long, red robe that hangs down in folds to a point below the calves, and lying on top is a long sword in a red scabbard on a black bandolier. The family crest—not the Templars' cross—has been carved onto a narrow pointed shield on his left arm; this is found only on the tomb. The entire figure is painted, as you will have gleaned from my description, and the colors are renewed from time to time.

The last and greatest object of interest shown to the foreign visitor is the monument to Prince Arthur.[5] Its elaborately interlaced stone tracery truly rivals the most skilled wood carving. On one side of the chapel are five rows of small portrait figures carved one above the other in the following order: at the bottom, abbesses; above them, bishops; over these, kings; then saints; and at the very top, angels. *Quant à moi, qui ne suis encore ni saint, ni ange, souffrez, que je vous quitte pour mon diner.*[6]

Llangollen, July 15th, 1828

IF I HAD the privilege of being the Wandering Jew (who must at least have money *ad libitum*), I would definitely spend a large part of my immortality on the road, particularly on English roads. It is so delightful for someone who feels and thinks as I do. First of all, there is no human soul to disturb and inconvenience me; I am, wherever I pay well, number one (always a pleasant feeling for domineering types) and have nothing but friendly faces and people to associate with, all zealously in my service. Continuous motion undertaken without fatigue keeps the body healthy; and the beauty of unbounded nature in its constant variety has the same fortifying effect on the mind. I am also, I confess, partly in accord with Dr. Johnson, who maintained that the greatest human happiness was to drive briskly over a good English road in a good English post chaise with a pretty woman.[7] For me, too, one of the most pleasant of experiences is rolling along in a comfortable carriage and stretching out at my leisure, while my eyes relish the ever-changing pictures that pass by like a *laterna magica*. Once they are gone, these images continue to excite my fantasy in ways sometimes serious, sometimes felicitous, sometimes tragic or comic. Then with great enjoyment I embroider the proffered sketches in my imagination. And what gigantic, ingenious, and uncanny forms they then assume, often with lightning speed—billowing up and down like cloud pictures before my mind's eye! If, however, my fantasy is feeling sluggish, I find it just as congenial to read and sleep in a carriage. My packing is not racking, to speak like the Capuchin;[8] in fact my luggage is so well organized (through long experience) that I can instantly get whatever I want with no trouble and without making my servants' lives too miserable. Sometimes, if the weather is good and the country beautiful, I will go for miles on foot. *Enfin*, here alone I attain perfect freedom. And as a final point,

I must not underestimate the pleasure of spending a tranquil hour writing about all this to the dear friend of my heart.

But back to the subject! I traveled all through the night, after having witnessed another bizarre drama in the evening sky: from the top of a peak I thought I saw a colossal range of black mountains with an immense lake at its foot. It took some time before I could convince myself that what I had in front of me was only an optical illusion made up of fog and various layers of clouds. The sky above was a pale, unnuanced gray, yet lying against this was an entirely black mass of clouds in the form of the wildest crags; the upper contour, boldly drawn, rose and fell repeatedly, while the base of the range was severed by a band of fog in a perfectly horizontal line. This fog seemed to form a silvery white body of water vanishing into the distance on either side; and since the green of the foreground, a sunny wooded meadowland beginning right at my feet, flowed directly to it, the illusion truly was extraordinary! Only little by little, as I descended, did the magical image disappear.

In contrast, the most beautiful reality awaited me this morning in Wales. It was as if my reverie of the clouds had heralded the magnificence of the Vale of Llangollen, a region that for my taste far surpasses all the beauties of the Rhineland. It is particularly original in the unusual shape of its peaks and the precipitous slopes of its mountains. A torrential river, the Dee, winds through the meadowed valley in a thousand fantastic bends, shaded by thick broad-leafed trees. On both sides high mountains rise up abruptly, some crowned with ancient ruins or grotesque, isolated groups of rock; others are topped by modern country houses or occasionally by little factory towns where dense smoke swirls up from towering chimneys. The vegetation is uniformly prolific, and hill and dale are covered with lofty trees in the manifold shades of green that contribute so immeasurably to the charm and picturesqueness of a landscape.

Arising from this luxuriant nature to even more grandiose effect, is a single, long, black mountain wall—barren except for a covering of thick, dark heather—that parallels the road for some time. This road—a splendid, two-hundred-mile thoroughfare as smooth as a parquet floor all the way from London to Holyhead—here cuts across the face of the left-hand mountain range approximately halfway up its slope and follows all its bends, so that while you are traveling along at a brisk trot or gallop, the view is completely transformed almost every minute, and without changing your position you overlook the valley variously, now seeing it before you, now to the side, now behind. At one spot an aqueduct of twenty-five slender arches, a work that would have made the Romans proud, leads right through the middle of the valley and over the Dee, allowing a second river to flow 120 feet above the first. After a few hours, the little mountain town of Llangollen, justly celebrated and much visited for the charm of its setting, affords an exquisite resting place.

The loveliest view is from the churchyard next to the inn; a half hour ago I clambered up and stood on a gravestone there, delighting with profound and blissful piety at the beauty of the vista. Below me a terraced garden was in full bloom with vines, honeysuckle, roses, and hundreds of bright flowers descending all the way down to the edge of the foaming river as if to go bathing. On the right, my gaze followed the rippling, busily murmuring waves between thick overhanging bushes; in front of me, the forest rose in two tiers divided by flat meadows dotted with grazing cattle; and high above, on top of all this, rose the bare, conical peak of what was perhaps once a volcano, now capped, like coping on a wall, by the gloomy ruins of the age-old Castell Dinas Bran, or Crow Castle. To the left, the stone houses of the small town are scattered in the valley, and here, next to a picturesque bridge, the river forms an impressive waterfall. Right behind, three huge mountain colossi present themselves majestically, like giant watchmen, and obstruct the view of the more-distant secrets of this wonderful region.

Now let me turn from the romantic pleasures to sensual ones—perhaps less refined but nonetheless in no way to be scoffed at—and retreat inward, that is, back to my room, where my appetite, made ravenous by the mountain air, was granted a not-insignificant feeling of well-being. For there I found, arrayed on a beautifully flowered tablecloth of Irish damask: steaming coffee, fresh guinea-fowl eggs, deep yellow mountain butter, thick cream, toast, muffins,* and finally, two freshly caught trout with dainty red spots—a breakfast equal to any that might be served to the highland heroes of Walter Scott, that great painter of human needs. I am already devouring an egg. Adieu!

Bangor, evening

THE RAIN HAS accompanied me steadily since London, save for short intervals, and today remained as faithful as ever, although the weather now seems inclined to improve. Meanwhile I have all sorts of things to tell you and an interesting day to describe. Just in time, before I left Llangollen, I remembered the two celebrated spinsters (certainly the most celebrated in Europe), who have been making their home in these mountains for more than half a century, and about whom I heard stories even as a child and then again in London. You must have heard about them from your father as well. If not, here is their story (Figure 74).

Fifty-six years ago, two distinguished, young, pretty, and fashionable ladies in London— Lady Eleanor Butler and the daughter of the recently deceased Lord Ponsonby—took it into their little heads to hate men, love and live only for each other, and from that moment on, dwell as two hermits in a single hermitage.[9] Their decision was immediately carried out, and ever since then these two ladies have not slept even a single night away from their cottage. However no respectable person travels to Wales without having obtained a letter or other introduction to them. Word has it that the outside world and its scandals provoke their curiosity just as much now as when they once lived in it. Several ladies had asked me to pass on their compliments, but I had forgotten to request a letter and therefore simply sent my card, having decided that if they refused my visit, as people led me to fear, I would storm their cottage. But here rank opened the doors readily, and I received an immediate and gracious invitation to a second breakfast.

In a quarter hour, I reached the most charming spot, and driving through a fine pleasure ground, arrived at a small, tasteful, Gothic house set directly across from Crow Castle, toward which many vistas had been cut through the tall trees. I got out and was received by both ladies just as I reached the stairs. Fortunately I had already been appropriately prepared for their eccentricities; otherwise I would have found it difficult to maintain my composure.

Imagine two ladies, the eldest of whom, Lady Eleanor, is a small, sprightly maiden now beginning to feel her years a little. She has just turned eighty-three. The other, however, is a tall, imposing figure and still thinks of herself as quite youthful, since the pretty child is only seventy-four. Both had their still-abundant hair powdered and combed back very simply, and

---

* A kind of light roll with a crispy crust, eaten hot with butter.—*The Editor.*

\text{}

74

The Ladies of Llangollen.

each was wearing a man's hat, a man's necktie and waistcoat, but a short *jupon* instead of inexpressibles,* together with boots. The whole was covered by a coat of blue cloth of a very particular cut, somewhere between a male overcoat and a female riding habit. On top of this Lady Eleanor wore, first, the *grand cordon* of the Order of St Louis across her chest; second, the same order around her neck; third, ditto once again the small cross of the same in a buttonhole; and as a crowning glory, a silver lily of nearly natural size, as a star. All of these, she said, were gifts of the Bourbon family.

Up to this point the entire ensemble was, in fact, extremely ludicrous. Yet now just imagine both ladies, again with the comfortable *aisance* and manners of the great world of the ancien régime, being gracious and entertaining with absolutely no affectation. They speak French at least as well as any distinguished English lady of my acquaintance, and at the same time with that essentially polite, natural, and, I would say, ingenuously cheerful essence of the good society of earlier days. In our own earnest, industrial century of business life, such qualities appear headed for the grave, and thus I found them truly touching in these good-natured old women. I could not help feeling a keen sense of empathy for the continuous and yet so natural and tender consideration with which the younger treated her older and already slightly more infirm friend, immediately and solicitously anticipating her every need. The essence of this behavior resides in its manner, in seemingly insignificant gestures that are nonetheless always noticeable to a sensitive man.

I began by telling them that I considered myself lucky to be able to extend the compliments that my grandfather, who had had the honor of visiting them fifty years before, had asked me to convey to the lovely hermits.[10] They had, it is true, lost their loveliness, but by no means their good memory, for they remembered Graf Callenberg very well, and even brought out an old keepsake from him. And they expressed amazement that such a "young" man should already be dead! Not only were these venerable ladies of great interest, but so too was their small house; indeed here and there it contained real treasures. There is hardly any noteworthy person of the last half century who has not sent them a portrait or some other curiosity or antique as a memento. This collection; a well-stocked library; the delightful setting; an equable, untroubled life; and the profound friendship and mutuality between the two—these are the sum of their life's possessions; and judging from their robust old age and cheerful spirits, they have not chosen so badly.

Incessant rain had accompanied my visit with the good elderly ladies, and now the journey continued under the same deluge, first as I passed by the ruins of an old abbey and then by the former palace of Owain Glyndwr,[11] whom you will remember from Shakespeare and my recitations at Muskau. The variety of the scenery is extraordinary; at times you are surrounded by a real jumble of mountains of every form; then you overlook the countryside in the far distance as if you were back on the plain; then you are once again hemmed in by a dark, narrow forest road. Farther along the river quietly turns a tranquil mill wheel and then abruptly thunders over boulders into a chasm, forming a magnificent waterfall to the depths below.

At exactly this spot, opposite the cascade of Pont-y-Glyn, I encountered a very elegant English hackney coach (the much-improved version of the Viennese original) drawn by four pretty horses, with a still-prettier English girl inside, accompanied by an older but also not-bad-looking woman. We all stopped to admire the waterfall, and while our carriages were standing

---

* See footnote on page 216; a "jupon" is an underskirt.—*Translator*.

across from each other, I noticed the curious girl stealing a look at me, and I laughed. This startled the shy creature, who flushed all over and yet, in her youthful gaiety, suddenly could not stop laughing at the pantomime that I, hidden from her companion, addressed to her from my carriage. The battle she was having with herself over this made the scene even more comical. At that moment my eye fell on a bunch of beautiful flowers I had just collected, and on a page ripped out of my portfolio, I wrote the following words: "Prince Muskau conveys his respectful greetings to the unknown ladies and begs permission to send them two newly picked bouquets of mountain flowers. As a return gift he requests the names of the amiable travelers, whom his lucky star allowed him to meet near the Pont-y-Glyn." I sent my valet to deliver this. I could see from behind the lowered blind that it was received with satirical laughter by the older lady and with blushes by the younger. The answer read: "Very grateful, but the unknown ladies must remain incognito . . . perhaps we will see each other again in London."

The sign for departure was given, and we hurried away toward very different parts of the world, exchanging nothing but a couple of diffident glances. Was that not the beginning of a charming little *aventure*? If I were still a man who could give in to his fancies, I would have immediately turned around and followed the girl until . . . But no more of this! Yet she was in my thoughts for a long time, because she was too pretty to be so quickly forgotten. I enquired about her at the next station, but no one claimed to know her. So I tarried alone with the remainder of my flowers and sulked a while, until new subjects once again claimed my full attention. Because, in fact, the Vale of Llangollen is only the prologue to the true epic: the higher mountains of Wales.

After leaving the waterfall and traveling about a half hour across a negligible plateau interrupted only by a few hills, you enter all at once, not far from Cernioge Mawr Inn, the holy of holies. The view is completely overwhelming! All around, enormous black rocks form the most sublime amphitheater, its serrated and tattered peaks appearing to swim in the clouds. Eight hundred feet below, at the bottom of a sheer wall of rock, the river forges its difficult path, plunging down from precipice to precipice. In front of us was a view of mountain ranges undulating one over the other in a seemingly endless perspective. I was so delighted that I let out a loud shout. Also beyond praise is the splendid road that, never climbing or sinking too abruptly, allows one to enjoy the *belles horreurs* of this mountainous world with ease. Where it is not protected by rocks, the road is edged by low walls, and small recesses have been built at regular intervals where the stones for repair work are stacked up, looking far more orderly than the open piles of stones along our major roads.

The mountains of Wales have a peculiar character that is difficult to compare with any other. They are about the same height as the Riesengebirge, but they appear far more grandiose in their form, are more plentiful in peaks, which are more effectively clustered. The vegetation is also more diverse, although in general there are fewer trees, and there are rivers and lakes, which the Riesengebirge lack. On the other hand, these mountains do not host the majestic, impenetrable forests of Rübezâhl's native home, and in some places cultivation has already transgressed the middle course that to my mind is essential to a perfect landscape. Yet the higher region, from Capel Curig until a few miles from Bangor, is as wild and precipitous as you could ever hope for, with broad stretches of red and yellow blooming heather. Ferns and other plants that do not thrive in our harsher climate crown the rocks, in place of the trees that no longer grow at this altitude. But the principle variation in this picture resides in the colossal, wild, and bizarre shapes of the mountains themselves, some of which really look more like clouds than solid masses. Among them is Tryfan Mountain, its top ridge covered with such oddly shaped basalt columns that every traveler

is convinced they are human figures who have just made their ascent and now look out over the wide vista (Figure 75). But they are just the mountain spirits that Merlin exiled there for all eternity.

75

Tryfan Mountain.

I found it tasteful that all the houses on the main road are so entirely in keeping with the region. Built of undressed, reddish stone in a simple, heavy architectural style, they have roofs of slate, and the latticework of their iron gates imitates the intersecting rays of two suns. The postboy showed me the ruined remains of an old Druid castle where, according to my book, Caratacus withdrew after his defeat at the Battle of Caer Caradoc. (The Welsh language itself sounds like the cawing of crows. Almost all names start with *c*, which is pronounced with a guttural crackle that no foreign throat can duplicate.) This ruin has now been converted into two or three inhabited huts, and its original outline is not even marked. What I found more noteworthy was a rock not far away in the shape of a bishop with crook and miter, as if he were just emerging from a cave in order to preach Christianity to the astonished heathens. Why is it that when nature indulges in such play, the effect is nearly always sublime, yet when art tries to imitate it, the result looks ludicrous?

The many children in the mountains are a minor annoyance because they shadow the carriage, appearing and vanishing like ghosts, and beg with inconceivable persistence. Fatigued by their pushiness, I firmly decided to give nothing more to any of them, because otherwise you can count on never being left alone. But the perseverance of one little girl managed to overcome all my resolutions. She ran along next to my carriage at a fast trot for at least five miles, up hill and down dale, only occasionally taking a shortcut along a footpath, but never letting me out of her sight; and all the time she was uttering the same plaintive cry, like that of a seagull. This finally became so unbearable that I surrendered and, for a shilling, purchased my peace from the inexhaustible sprinter. But the ominous cry kept resounding in my ear, like the ticktock of a clock that you get accustomed to hearing, and I could not get rid of it for the whole day.

July 16th, 1828

I SLEPT EXTREMELY well and am now sitting in an inn beside the sea, resting from my trip and delighting in the ships cutting through the clear waters in all directions. On the land side, there is a castle of black marble towering over the crowns of ancient oaks,[12] and there I will begin my excursions. I am setting up my headquarters in this guesthouse, where I find myself very well looked after. Here I also encountered, quite unexpectedly, an entertaining countryman. You know the witty A——, who is so thin and yet possesses such impressive calves, so elegantly dressed and yet so thrifty, so good-natured and yet so sarcastic, who appears so English and yet so German.[13] To be brief, A—— breakfasted with me for a second time, with undiminished appetite, and during this told of the most amusing things. He came from S——, about which he recounted more or less the following:

Jest and Earnest

You know dear friend, that in Vienna anyone who can eat and, *nota bene*, pay for a roast chicken is granted the title *Euer Gnaden* (Your Grace), whereas in S——, on the contrary, anyone wearing a full-length coat is, *in dubio*, dubbed *Herr Rat* (Mr. Councilior) or better still, *Herr Geheimer Rat* (Mr. Privy Councilior)—never mind whether he is a real councilior or not (i.e., if he's just an ostensible, phantasmagorical one), a half (that is, retired), a whole (namely, fully paid), or a completely unpaid one, a titular zero. The attributes and functions of this mysterious councilior creature are strangely various. Sometimes the title is worn by a disabled statesman in the *Residenz*, who has just been decorated with the golden griffin as a gesture of great respect for his decrepitude and in reward for a happily achieved special birthday; or by a provincial governor, not very active but all the more enamored of himself, whose services during the visit of a foreign sovereign finally earn him honors and medals. He might be the sprightly mainstay of the financial world, or even that rara avis, an influential man close to the throne who is nonetheless modest and highly meritorious; or yet again he might be nothing but a vegetating *Exzellenz*, whose only occupation is going from house to house, dishing up antiquated jokes and contorted wordplays that for a half century have had the privilege of delighting the *crème de la bonne société* in the capital. But then again he may be a person of brilliance, someone delightful as poet and man, who only sets foot on the straight path. Further along the title falls on an admittedly less brilliant, but all the more comprehensive genius, who, although dedicated to Themis, is equally well informed about the stars—both heavenly and theatrical. Finally this Proteus may even transform himself into a cameralist,[14] a famous sheep breeder and economist who manures his fields, and later into a doctor, who manures the churchyard. He can also be found in the invincible

Landwehr, and neither the postal service,* the lottery, nor even the water closet itself can exist without him. The court philosopher, court theologian, court Jacobean— all in the end shake hands as privy counciliors, for this they are, were, or will be. In short, no country seems better counseled and none more privily. For such is the modesty of these innumerable counciliors, that they often keep nothing as private as their own talent.

Yet what a joy it is to see the candid, even touching, bonhomie with which they bestow titles and honor on each other, each one jacking up the rating of the next to a still higher level, while, it goes without saying, expecting the same in grateful return. The various additions and convolutions that the poor word *geboren* must endure as a result of these pretensions pose a mystical enigma to any foreigner attempting to learn the German language.[15] Without venturing any deeper into this labyrinth, I will simply mention that even the beggar on the street is no longer satisfied with just being "born," and it is already the case that *edelgeboren* is an appreciable insult to the lower functionaries, just as those of higher but not noble status take offense at the designation *wohlgeboren*.[16] For myself, I always wrote to my tailor here as *Hochwohlgeborener Herr*.[17] He was, mind you, a very eminent figure, a descendant of our noted friend Robinson Crusoe, who himself attained an important place in world history thanks to the bold and matchless cut of his uniforms. He was thus in every way a tailor deserving of *at least* a life peerage.**

So that this arbitrary distribution and assumption of titles will cause no embarrassment, things have been arranged so conveniently here that, even given the enormous addiction to rank, there is no binding *order of rank*, whether determined by the court, birth, or national opinions and habits that have more or less become law. Sometimes it is birth, more often one's position, sometimes merit, sometimes patronage, and sometimes simply compelling impertinence that grants priority, as chance and circumstances decree. This gives rise to particular anomalies that an old nobleman like me—a Baron Thunder-ten-tronckh, *qui ne saurait compter le nombre de ses ânes*,[18] as General P—— said—cannot get his mind around. Thus there is no end of complaints, worries, and distress in society, except for a certain merry and excellent old lady who alone knows how to maintain the first rank almost everywhere; and because she unites a fine mind with great physical strength and personal bravery— and by means of these unified characteristics, sometimes with wit, sometimes with god-like crassness, sometimes even (when nothing else will do the trick) with a sturdy shove—on every occasion behaves as, and remains, the leading presence at court and at other festivities. I know on good authority that the Countess Kakerlack felt herself discriminated against by a cabal at one of the courts (for there are several

---

* In that *Reich*, by the way, the entire postal service should be converted to special delivery, and many are sorry that it is not driving an even greater part of the machinery of state, in order to give fresh impetus to the gridlock caused by the jubilee.—*The Editor.*

** This artist, by the way, boasted traits that would do honor to many an industrial nobleman of our time. For example, he only bills his clients every five years and is the generous creditor of all Isolanis of the army. *Avis aux lecteurs!* ["Readers take note!"—*Translator.*]

here), and on the advice of her friend the Starosta von Pückling, she appealed directly to the just and fair sovereign with an official request that her place in the ranking be determined. This was immediately done, and she was positioned directly after the Princess Bona who occupies the first spot (for once owing to the merits of her late husband). The *Groß-Würdenträger*,[19] Prince Weise, brought her this order himself but said, "Dearest Countess, you really must cede your position to the Baroness Stolz, for what can you with your slender figure achieve against *her*? A single thrust of her elbow and you are lame for all eternity! So always let *her* go first, because you know that the police themselves are afraid of her, ever since the notorious invitation she issued them a few years ago."[20]

Everything must yield to force, and this also demonstrates how difficult it is simply to grant priority to merit without generally established rules. After all, merit is so relative! If a general or a minister is great, who is to say that the excellent cook or the engaging opera performer does not possess great merit as well? This has always been acknowledged, as history teaches us, even by monarchs and states. In England, for example, where rank is normally granted only by aristocratic titles (certainly the most reliable means and the most appropriate to a monarchy),* the great field marshal and prime minister Wellington must come after the small, admittedly known, but not-at-all-famous Duke of St Albans. Why? Because this young man is the elder duke, which is to say that the services of his ancestress, the actress Nell Gwynn, mistress of Charles II, are of an earlier date and consequently have priority over the much later service provided by the Duke of Wellington.

Things are different in our capital. As a rule we are too accustomed to bad food to rate a good cook very highly, and most of us have recently become too virtuous to have mistresses. No one particularly talks about the value of service anymore either.** Nowadays the real source of rank and esteem here comes just from *serving* in the state or the court, no matter in which one or how. *Beati possidentes*[21]—because here, too, the sound German proverb applies: When God gives someone a job, he also gives him the mind for it! Bureaucracy has taken the place of aristocracy and may soon become just as hereditary.[22] It is already the case that the government can no longer dismiss any of its functionaries until they have been found guilty. Civil service positions are viewed by all who hold them as their most firmly established *property*, and it is no surprise that functionaries everywhere praise this arrangement to the skies. Yet it is strange that all states with a *free* constitution—namely, where it is an accepted principle that the *nation* is the most important thing, not some privileged class, including its own bureaucrats—nevertheless follow an entirely different

---

* NB, when the nobility is composed accordingly, that is, when it is a true national nobility, as is partly the case in England, or also as Grävell describes it in his *Regent*.—*The Editor.*

** Here my late friend is referring only to certain functionaries who love mediocrity above everything else, and for good reason. If I am correct about the place he is describing, it is unmatched in the way its highest office dispenses gracious appreciation for service. The entire nation recently witnessed a gratifying example in the sensitive honoring of a revered statesman who, having achieved the highest station, also demonstrated that he fully deserved it. If there is anyone who still doubts this, it can only be the man himself.—*The Editor.*

system.* Meanwhile the nonserving middle class is happy to go unnoticed. They enjoy their prosperity *con amore* and add spice to life by filing the occasional lawsuit, to which the judiciary offers every imaginable encouragement. The merchant too, whether of Christian or pre-Christian faith, finds his account and, if he knows how to get it, effective patronage as well. Indeed having a great deal of money is almost as valuable as being a *Wirklicher Geheimer Rat*;[23] and if wealthy bankers keep their house in order, they are counted among the privileged classes and even occasionally elevated to the nobility.

Thus many manage very well. The situation is miserable only for the poor nobility, especially the old nobility (insofar as they have not entered the safer harbor of bureaucracy). Without money or their own land; with their aristocratic titles being infinitely multiplied and their family estates infinitely divided; without any share in legislation beyond what would be granted them in an institution where they were placed for a bit of education after starting secondary school; having long ago been stripped of their former benefactors and sinecures;** being treated very shabbily by the authorities, indeed often not only ridiculed and persecuted but faced with hostility because of their poorly justified pretensions, the nobility have, as a *corporation*, lost all prestige in the eyes of the people. Almost the only useful capacity they have left is to be their own nursery for the propagation of chamberlains at the various courts in the capital—still, of course, an enviable destiny.

This last truth is fittingly recognized by many, and a lot of witty remarks have been made about it, especially by the person leading the charge, a celebrated authoress once involved at length in a sort of mutual novel-writing race with her husband, a competition that used to result in two or three such creations, composed of two or three volumes each, being offered to a delighted public every year at the Leipzig book fair.[24] The most remarkable part of this is that the husband's works seemed to betray

---

* If I did not know for certain that my friend wrote this in 1828, I would consider it a reminiscence of the first speech of President Jackson, who wants all civil servants of the United States government (with few exceptions) to make room for others every five years, just as the president does. *Eheu iam satis!* [That's enough!—*Translator.*] What would our governing councilors say to such a thing? Entire general commissions could literally be struck down in one blow! For who knows whether or not, when it came time for the fifth-year housecleaning, anyone would think it worth the effort, or rather the money, to keep them on.—*The Editor.* [In his first annual message to Congress, on December 8, 1829, Andrew Jackson proposed limiting government appointments to a length of four years.—*Translator.*]

** To strip away, to regulate, to separate—what country squire, what rural landowner, in that enlightened country knows the actual meaning of these words! The concept behind the law was good and liberal, although the knot was severed quite violently. But how is it being implemented? A book could, and should, be written about this. The implementation of this business is precisely in the style of a certain Herr von Wanze who, disguised as a tenant farmer at the parish fair in A., instructed a well-to-do peasant about the game of faro: "*You* put down your money," he said, "*I* deal the cards to the right and left. What falls to the left, I win; what falls to the right, you lose."—*The Editor.* [The law referred to here is the Edict of Regulation of 1811, which dealt with the end of peasant tithing and a peasant's obligation to render services to a landowner, and to the subsequent Prussian agricultural reforms between 1812 and 1850. Because it created private property that could be held by people of any class, it was beneficial to many, although at first only to the local lords and large landowners. This topic is discussed by the Editor in a lengthy footnote on page 156.—*Translator.*]

the effusively delicate style of a *woman*, whereas those of the wife seemed to exhibit a somewhat-more-ponderous, *male* know-it-allness—a leaden quality that even the alchemical hand of a kind and ingenious prince could not transform into gold. In the meantime, the writings of both, particularly those of the husband, have lost their vogue. The noble, heroic knights of the north, charming to look at and naively childlike, who duel so tenderly and with clear blue eyes press the kiss of peace onto the dying lips of the friend they have just stabbed; and their wonderful steeds, who gallop over rocky peaks and swim through oceans following their masters—all have finally given way, in spite of these marvelous talents, to the bare-legged Highlanders of Walter Scott.

The poetic squires of the bedchamber and learned tea parties of the gracious lady were already abandoned as a bit desiccated some time ago. It is also known, as we have read in the Devil's memoirs,[25] that it was at such a tea party that Ahasuerus, after his restless wanderings, at last found some peace and fell blissfully asleep. Since then the heavy tomes of this renowned authoress have atrophied into thin storybooks, sweet ephemera that admittedly last no more than a day, but in recompense circulate exclusively at courts and in chambers; among princes, ladies-in-waiting, and maids of honor; chamberlains, squires of the bedchamber, and even lackeys of the bedchamber (for nothing attached to a court should be held in low esteem). Even *haunted* chambers were recently reported, but the ghosts that appeared in them were so dull, so like emaciated, fawning courtiers, and with such a strong family resemblance, that they were slightly reminiscent of goose bumps, but without giving rise to them. Certainly the most piquant of all was the story that satirized society in the capital: poor Viola plays a suspicious role, and a genteel lady appears, who supposedly sold her to a high-ranking person for a considerable sum. This story was justly regarded as a moral one, for every good-hearted person who read it was rightly moved to loathe slander and rash condemnations. Malicious readers, however, took a different kind of pleasure in it—and so the whole thing was not without value. It could even be called a master-piece if you compare it to all the Italianizing and hyper-Germanicizing "medieval" tales full of virtue and wretchedness, Christianity and bawdiness, etc., now being gen-erated in such number by our insatiable journals and almanacs; indeed about some of these we cannot even agree with Schiller, that "when crime becomes sick, virtue sits down to the feast."[26] Neither of these extremes is actually reached here; instead one simply suffers from beginning to end from the mental equivalent of the nausea cure. After taking ineffectual aim in every possible direction, the whole thing finally burns up in the powder pan without exploding, and the unhappy reader, far from ready to sit down for a meal, is disgusted by all manner of food for a long time.*

---

* For the sake of fairness it must be admitted that there are many exceptions to this account. Goethe, for instance, is not above describing "a man of forty years" as a minor; Tieck takes pity on us with *an absolutely real novella*; L. Schefer manages to touch our hearts and souls with strange, intersecting bolts of lightning; Kruse makes a crime story charming; or some Therese, Friederike, etc., unveils the otherwise impenetrable secrets of the female heart (not to mention, in the service of brevity, the contributions of other major storytellers). Such examples make it clear that a number of craftsmen could deliver fine and complete merchandise—if the entire factory weren't already ruined by mechanistic templates.—*The Editor.*

But to return to the learned and engaging lady, who was just now our topic of discussion: While I was sojourning there, I observed a strange swarm of insects—called, in the great world, a coterie—frolicking in the winter sun of her courtly literary radiance. As far as I know, such hordes still maintain the principle (and everyone must have principles nowadays!) that a different blood flows in the veins of the nobility, and if a common tree can be improved, it is only through grafting—for instance, through the illegitimate children of great lords. The noble class, they instruct us, remains above all pure and sequestered; it does not degrade itself through industry or through speculations beneficial to the public weal, something that a certain Frau von Tonne, in a very substantial work, identifies as a main reason for the decline of the country's aristocracy. The nobility, however, is still permitted a bit of dabbling in literature and the fine arts (for money, too, even bourgeois money), since artistic types are allotted an intermediate station between the nobility and the bourgeoisie. On the other hand, a constitutional high nobility and a representative government are by no means to the taste of this group, for the very natural reason that under such dire conditions, their own nobility—whose true venerableness they alone know, and whose encumbered landholdings are splintered into a thousand undetectable, microscopic plots—would be condemned to the horror of taking a seat in the Chamber of Commons (where else?). Who, then, can hold it against them if they prefer the prince's chamber to such a fate, especially since they can become masters there. But God forbid! With luck, they will remain only titular, and not real *privy* counciliors and *lords* of the bedchambers.

(To be continued another time.)

Evening

I COULD NOT bear staying in my room any longer; the castle outside my windows was too powerful an attraction.[27] Therefore, as soon as A—— departed, I climbed on a scrawny mountain pony and rode in good spirits toward this remarkable structure. It was built by a man who is literally *steinreich,* because his stone quarries, located an hour farther into the mountains, bring him forty thousand pounds annually.[28] He laid out an extensive park at the most favorable spot beside the sea and had the odd but masterfully executed idea of constructing all the buildings in the Old Saxon style. In England this kind of architecture is incorrectly ascribed to the Anglo-Saxons; in fact, it stems from the emperors of German Saxony, and certainly none of these many monuments is any older.[29] Even the high wall that encircles the park, easily over four miles in length, has a strange appearance. Irregularly shaped, pointed pieces of slate three to four feet high have been affixed upright along its top, a very effective measure. At every entrance, a tower-like fortress with a portcullis threatens the intruder (an apt symbol of the illiberality of the modern Englishmen, who lock up their gardens and their properties more securely than we do our living rooms). Next the visitor must cross a drawbridge before entering the shadowed gateway of the imposing castle. The massive structure is made of black, roughly worked marble from the Isle of Anglesey, which harmonizes wonderfully with the majestic character of the region. Everything down to the smallest detail, including the servants' rooms and even more-modest areas, has been carefully rendered in a pure *Old Saxon style*. In the refectory I found a picture of William the Conqueror's castle in Rochester, a structure I have already described to you. What in those days could be undertaken only by a great monarch can now be produced as a kind of toy, but more beautiful, more expensive, and on an even larger scale. And this by a simple country gentleman, whose father may have started out in the cheese trade. How times change!

The castle's ground plan, which the obliging architect showed me,[30] revealed some *domestic* details which I will share with you, because nearly all large English country houses are arranged in a similar way. Like so many other things, they demonstrate the efficiency of English practices. The servants never linger in the anteroom, here called the hall, a place that, like the overture to an opera, always tries to suggest the character of the whole. It is usually decorated with paintings or statues and, like the elegant staircase and all the other rooms, serves only as a congenial area for family and guests, who sometimes prefer waiting on themselves to having some attendant spirit dogging their footsteps. The servants are therefore all gathered in a large room some distance away (usually on the ground floor), where they also eat together—men and women at the same time, without exception—and where all the bells of the house are also located. These are numbered and hang in a row on the wall so the source of the ring can be seen immediately; in addition, a kind of pendulum attached to each one continues to move for ten minutes after the bell has gone quiet, in order to remind the dawdlers of their duty!* The female staff members also have a large assembly room, where they sew, knit, and spin during tranquil interludes. Next to this is a place for washing the glass and china, which is the responsibility of the women. Each of them, like the male servants, has a private bedroom on the top floor. Only the housekeeper and the butler have their own rooms downstairs. Immediately adjacent to the housekeeper's quarters is a room for preparing coffee and a larder containing everything necessary for breakfast—her special charge and an important meal in England. On the other side, connected to a small courtyard, is her laundry. It consists of three rooms: the first for washing, the second for ironing, the third—with a notably high ceiling and heated by steam in bad weather—for drying. Next to the butler's quarters is his pantry, a spacious, fireproof room with cupboards running all around it for storing the silver (which he also polishes here) as well as the glassware and china required for meals, which is promptly washed by the female servants and immediately put away again. An enclosed staircase leads from the pantry to the beer and wine cellar, likewise under the butler's purview.

A very romantic road brought me first through the park, then along the edge of a beautifully wooded mountain stream, and in an hour to the slate quarry that lies in the mountains six miles from the castle. From what I have already told you about the income it generates, you can imagine what a significant enterprise this is. Five or six high terraces of great extent climb up the slopes, and all teem with men and machines; with processions of a hundred wagons attached to each other and speedily rolling off on iron railways; with cranes lifting huge loads, water conduits, and so forth. Just a cursory survey took quite a long time. In order to reach a more remote part of the quarry where the rocks were just then being blasted with gunpowder, something I wanted to observe, I had to stretch out flat on one of the small rail wagons that transport the slate

---

* Depending on whether they swing for a longer or shorter time, these pendulums can also be used by a discriminating servant as a thermometer or hygrometer of the patience of their respective masters and mistresses.—*The Editor.*

and let myself be pulled by means of a winch through a pitch-black passageway hewn out of the rock, which was four hundred paces long and no more than four feet high. It was a nasty sensation to be dragged at great speed and in Egyptian darkness through this narrow gorge lined with a thousand irregular projections that, at least near the entrance, are clearly visible. Strangers tend to decline the opportunity. Despite the soothing assurances of the guide who rides in front, you cannot rid yourself of the thought that if you did somehow knock against one of those jagged points, you would arrive at the other side without your head. After making it through this passage, I still had to walk along the edge of a precipice, on a path just two feet wide and without railings, until after going through a second low grotto, I finally arrived at the long-awaited and fearsomely magnificent spot.

It was as if you were already in the underworld! The blasted walls of slate, several hundred feet high and smooth as glass, revealed barely enough of the blue sky to distinguish midday from dusk. The ground on which we were standing was likewise of blasted rock, and in the middle was a deep fissure, six to eight feet wide, already worked lower down. Some of the stoneworkers' children, in order to win a few pennies, were amusing themselves by making daredevil leaps across this gap. Miners, looking like black birds, were hanging all over the rock walls, striking them with their long iron picks, and throwing down blocks of slate with a rumbling crash. But now the whole mountain seemed to totter, loud shouts of warning reverberated from various sides, and the powder mine exploded. High above, a huge slab of rock broke loose in unhurried majesty and plunged with tremendous force into the depths. And while dust and flakes of small rock particles darkened the air like thick smoke, the thunder resounded in a wild echo all around us. These operations, near daily necessities at various places in the quarry, are so dangerous that, according to the overseer's own testimony, it is expected that an average of 150 men will be injured and 7 to 8 killed in the mine each year. It is like a battlefield. A hospital has been set up exclusively to take in the wounded, and on my way here, I encountered without knowing it the corpse of a worker who had passed away the day before yesterday. Initially I thought the procession was a wedding, because the people were so formally dressed and adorned with flowers, so I nearly leapt back in horror when, in response to my question about where the groom was, one of the attendants pointed silently at the coffin following behind. According to the overseer, half of the accidents are due to the apathy of the workers; although always given a warning, they are as a rule too careless to react quickly or move far enough away before an explosion. And since the slate often breaks off in flat, razor-sharp pieces, an insignificant fragment that is flung a great distance can shear off the hand, leg, or even the head of the man it hits. The latter, I was told, actually happened once.

Since we were not standing very far from the blast zone, I took the hint and made another turn to the left through the hellish passageway in order to have a look at more peaceful operations. There was much of interest. For instance, paper cannot be cut more delicately or quickly than the hunks of slate are here, and no block of pine can split more easily and neatly than these stone slabs. With a single, nearly effortless blow of the chisel, they divide into sheets three to four feet in diameter resembling the thinnest cardboard. The unfinished stone comes down to the processors from the quarries via authentic, Parisian *montagnes russes*,[31] and the power generated by the loaded cars rolling downhill serves to carry the empty ones back up again. Here the rails are not concave, as is usual, but rather convex, with corresponding wheels on the wagons.

TODAY PASSED WITH rest, writing, and reading, and therefore I have little of substance to report. But before I go to bed, I must keep to the dear habit of chatting with you a bit. Just now I was thinking of home and our honored friend Lottum, who is currently traveling around again but recently sent me a whole notebook of his earlier observations. Shall I share one specimen with you? All right, listen:

Observations of a devout soul from Sandomir or Sandomich*

1. When the Saxon mail coach drivers had drunk a lot of schnapps at my expense, among other things.

    How much better it is at home than anywhere abroad! One really has many strange experiences. For instance, it is certainly peculiar (and yet, after repeated experience, I can no longer doubt it) that when the horses here are tired and lazy (which happens all too often, unfortunately), it is enough for *the mail coach driver* to drink some schnapps, and suddenly the *horses* become bright and spirited again. Nature's wisdom and hidden powers are unfathomable! This phenomenon is perhaps explained by the well-known fact that wine begins to ferment in the casks just as the vines blossom.** At the last stop before Torgau, my companion from Potsdam, the Lieutenant of the Guards Count S—— (to whom the Kingdom of Grace has yet to be revealed and who therefore still gets perpetually and pointlessly agitated by mundane matters) got into an argument with our driver, becoming so angry that he threatened him with his walking stick and called him a Saxon dog. "Oh, Jesis, no, most gratchius Sir Lieutenant," the coachman responded quite foolishly, "yer wrong there, we's bin Prussian dogs fur more'en tin years awreddy." Obviously the people here are still totally lacking in our national culture and refinement.

2. After my providential accident on July 6, 1827.

    For four weeks I have not been able to write! Today, grateful and deeply moved, I finally take up my pen again to record a remarkable stroke of Providence! As I was traveling to M—— last month, I was knocked over quite violently—just like the stranger in *The Small Towners*[32]—right in front of the toll house and broke my right arm. My initial shout, I am ashamed to confess, was a nasty curse! But quickly thereafter came my expression of gratitude—fervent gratitude to the Creator—that I had

---

* The inhabitants themselves are unable to say which ending is correct. [Pückler's German-speaking readers would have understood this as a droll allusion to the Berlin dialect, which fails to distinguish between accusative and dative—between *mich* (me) and *mir* (to me), for example—and to the city's location on the sandy plains of Brandenburg, dubbed "the sandpit of the Holy Roman Empire" in the eighteenth century. The driver's words a few lines later are in the Berlin dialect.—*Translator.*]

** NB. We must remember to ask our learned Professor Blindemann what he thinks of this interpretation.

only broken my arm and not my neck! On such occasions one recognizes the *inscrutable ways* of Providence and its protective hand, always there at the right moment. Was my life not hanging by a thread? And was God not offering me vivid proof that he alone will close my eyes forever or choose to spare my young life? Indeed since nothing is impossible for God, I may still be destined for greatness. Yes, you philosophers, I feel it profoundly and joyfully: faith alone makes us blissful.

3.   When I nearly drowned in the Elbe near Torgau.

It is clear, as a wise Greek once remarked, that no one should enter the water until he has learned to swim. I was rash enough to go swimming yesterday without having acquired this skill (for I have always avoided rebellious *Turnen* and any physical exercise of the kind).[33] And because I got a cramp in my calf and somewhat lost my composure, I might well have been a goner by now were it not for a man whom Providence sent to rescue me *at exactly that moment*. How could I be blind to so many examples of this special protection!

Even so, the entire Elbe has since become distasteful to me. Yet I struggle against this reprehensible feeling, since we must remember how useful this river is for so many of our comrades.* Although the observation is not a new one, I think it is still worth noting that you almost always find a river adjacent to every large city. But Providence, so wise and gracious, has arranged all things to our advantage, and we human beings recognize it only too rarely! Yes, Nature has taken care of us like a generous mother! She gave the bee its sting, the beaver its tail, the lion its strength, the ass its patience; but to mankind she gave lofty understanding and, when this and our elusive rationality are insufficient, divine revelation. Oh, how thankful I am when I consider this rightly and reflect on the many spiritual and physical advantages I have over so many of my fellow creatures—May I never forget! Amen.

4.   When I finally had to pay the Jew Abraham my already twice-postponed bill, plus a lot more.

I have been troubled by doubt as to whether or not the Jews really will survive until the end of the world, whether they will continue to live on the earth as they do now—cursed, scattered, and oppressed—and therefore be forced to continue swindling us so incessantly.

But is not the very doubt already a sin, since so much scripture attests to the truth of it? Besides, the conversion of these unfortunate lost souls is proceeding once again from our own country, where enlightenment has always prevailed. Yet alas, here a new fearful doubt bears down on me! Will all peoples of the earth be called Christians someday? This has been proclaimed, it is true. But in my learned studies, I recently saw a calculation that showed, to my horror, that among the earth's population of eight hundred million, so far only a few more than two

---

*   For the Commissioners of Elbe Shipping, too, who have just concluded their work so nobly and have all received medals for their labors. I wonder whether God will bestow a medal on me also?

hundred million call themselves by the true name. One hopes the worthy Bible societies will not tire of doing their part. The English cannot be taking this very seriously, since they have scarcely made a single convert in India. Perhaps, as usual, they see it only as a political matter.*

I recently read, by the way, about a missionary in India who was met with the following impertinent response from a Hindu: "I will not let you convert me to

---

* To add a serious word to this jest, I would like to ask: who does not honor the benevolent motives that gave rise to Bible societies and missionaries? But are these the correct means to an end, even when they are not scandalously misused, as is unfortunately too often the case? In most instances, the result tells us the opposite. It should be remembered that God himself delivered Christianity as the *second* covenant; the *first* was based entirely upon *earthly* interests and despotic power.

If I were not afraid of sounding too facetious, I would be tempted to say that we ought to begin by converting the savages into Jews before we try to make them Christians. This would also dovetail nicely with our commercial interests, an important lever. Haggling might civilize them much more quickly than Paul's epistles to the Corinthians could.

It seems worth a try, given human nature; and one way or another the results would be telling. Wanting to make Christians of people who are so little civilized, like the still mostly bestial inhabitants of Africa, seems just as unreasonable to me as sending European linguists to teach the apes. At this level of culture, the only practical course is to serve self-interest and to exercise the benevolent use of force. Assuming it is our job and our right to lift those less fortunate than ourselves up to our level of civilization, with or without their consent, even conversions by the sword may be preferable to the attempts of the Bible societies, provided that they are managed without cruelty and on the basis of truly good intentions.** [Here the Editor has added a footnote to his footnote.—*Translator.*]

The other way to have an effect on the savages, namely by appealing to their own, immediate interests, can only be achieved through trade. This seems the most just and mild of all, but it too would have to be accompanied by a certain force to produce quick and lasting results. Yet the worst part of introducing Christianity too precipitously is, without any doubt, that once savages collide with Christians—whether as governments, corporations, or individuals—they quickly become aware that Christians continually violate nearly every aspect of their own doctrine of love, both among themselves and with their converts, whose simple understanding, not yet rectified by higher culture, can make neither head nor tail of this. Moreover, since savages, like children, focus mainly on the myth of the new doctrine, we cannot really blame them much when the liberals or free-thinkers among them cry out: "Fable for fable, murder for murder, slave trafficking for slave trafficking— what's the difference?"

If the Christian powers had *seriously* abolished the slave trade and at the same time destroyed the robbers' lairs that—to Europe's shame—still exist on the coasts of Africa; if the English, instead of sending one lone traveler after another to be murdered by the natives or die from the climate (and who, on top of everything else, make laughingstocks of themselves with their English-Christian arrogance and no means to sustain it), were to send a respectable expedition into the interior, made up of men already toughened by previous residence on the coast, a group that with dignity and benevolent power could give trade a more humane orientation; and if they tried to destroy the obstacles in their way, even if partly through the force of arms— then certainly a large part of Africa would be more civilized than can possibly be achieved through centuries of missions and Bible shipments. Some may respond: What's the good of all that? Others will ask: Who gives us the right to meddle uninvited in the affairs of strangers? The answers to these questions would take us too far. As for me, I confess to sharing the Jesuit's basic tenet: a noble purpose, a plan conceived with the utmost advantage to others, which is also invested with the power to carry it out, sanctifies, from the superior perspective of humanity, whatever means may be honestly applied to fulfill it, as long as they involve nothing more than undisguised coercion. Treachery and dishonesty can never lead to good.—*The Editor.*

** It cannot be denied that the most successful conversions of the heathens were those carried out by Charlemagne and the Spanish; it is only a pity that the Spanish forced a new paganism on people who were actually better Christians than they were themselves.

Christianity until you have let me convert you to Hinduism—because *I* believe in the truth of my religion, *you* in the truth of yours. What is right for one is also fair to the other—some fables and abuses may exist in both, but the spirit is likely to be from the same family." These are downright appalling views!* I myself, without wanting to brag about it, managed to convince an old Jew in my hometown, whose trade was no longer going well, to be baptized; for this he still receives a pension from me. I also tried to do my bit toward the spiritual transformation of a *real* Indian, who after many wonderful turns of fortune had been cast up on our hyperborean shores, where even the Moravians toiled at length to convert him, though in vain. He listened to me patiently, and I confess that I was swept away by the importance of the circumstances and awed by my own eloquence. But what was the end result? He looked at me with a smile, took my alms, shook his head like a nodding Chinese doll, and left me standing there without another word!

P.S. Just now, to my horror, I received news that the Jew I converted has died, and on his deathbed, overcome with pangs of conscience (can anyone think this possible!), he became a Jew again.

5. When I returned from Madame R——'s burial

A few days ago a very strange thing happened. It has been just ten years since a pretty and, more importantly, pious young woman was hired to work in a local *Konditorei*. Although she was exposed to many temptations in her sweet occupation (for not all young people who frequent pastry shops are as well behaved as I), she listened to no one and found joy only in devoutness. She never missed a prayer meeting at President S——'s or at any other place where she could gain admission, and above all she went to church at least once every Sunday. But one Sunday (it was St Martin's day, I believe), she forgot her obligation and stayed home, absorbed with worldly finery. Then Nemesis approached in the form of a young man, someone to whom she had long been secretly inclined and who on that fateful day must have advanced greatly in her favor, because a short time later they were married. At first they lived very happily and had several children. But little by little, amid the distractions of conjugal life, her piety declined significantly. The unfortunate woman seemed to grow too fond of her worldly duties as wife and mother, and began even to prefer these to the pleasure of her prayer meetings and the reading of scripture. Alas, the consequences of her carelessness showed themselves soon enough. Her husband endured a series of misfortunes—all undeserved, I am assured; some of her children died; the family fell into poverty; and finally, as a result,

* In his recent account of his voyage around the world, Otto von Kotzebue gives us a gripping picture of the wicked practices of the English missionaries in Tahiti and the Sandwich Islands. He tells how, when they were trying to convince King Kamehameha—who, to the misfortune of his newly created kingdom, died too soon—to accept the Christian religion, he responded by pointing to the statues of his cult and saying: "These are our gods, whom I worship; whether I do right or wrong, I do not know; but I follow my faith, which cannot be wicked, as it commands me never to do wrong."—*The Editor.* [Quoted from the English translation by H. E. Lloyd, *A Voyage of Discovery into the South Sea and Beering's* [sic] *Straits* (London, 1821), 1:312.—*Translator.*]

the husband sank into the most profound melancholy. Then last Sunday, exactly on the tenth anniversary of the above mentioned day when the unhappy girl first failed to attend church, her husband, overcome by an attack of madness, gruesomely murdered her and then took his own life!

Here one sees how punishment that is both divine and just will slowly yet surely find its quarry. I will refrain from any severe remarks, but anyone who does not learn a lesson from this cautionary example, does not realize how culpable and dangerous it is to be careless and neglect, even once, regular attendance at church—I pity him! He can grasp this only through suffering, and may he do so in this life!

6. When I got my last *Korb* in D——.[34]

I am very unlucky in love, something that is difficult to comprehend; but so it is that yet again one of my best-laid plans has come to nothing.

I had loved Miss M—— for a long time already, with all the ardor of my impetuous nature. It is true, I dared not tell her, but my eyes (fastened languishingly on her for hours on end) spoke too clearly to be misunderstood. Even so, I was unable to elicit more than a mocking smile from the object of my adoration until, finally, an opportunity arrived: her eighteenth birthday. I decided to besiege her heart with an exquisite act of gallantry, something I could allow myself all the more readily and in good conscience, because I harbored only the most upright intentions. I pondered my choices at length. Roses and all botanical gifts such as fruit are so ordinary; finery was out because it might suggest that I considered her vain; nor did I want to offer something costly for fear of implying she was acquisitive; I dared not choose a book of devout songs or a devotional pamphlet so as not to profane the holy for worldly ends. No, it could only be something full of feeling that at the same time made a delicate allusion to our circumstances.

Suddenly, like a bolt of lightning in a dark night, I was struck by the thought that the season for fresh herring was approaching. The very word "herring" electrified me, and with my customary acuteness I saw instantly all that might transpire. Immediately I sent a courier to Berlin, where all that is new first appears, in hopes of obtaining the aforementioned creatures of God before the annual advertisement in the two blotting-paper news rags. Everything went as I wished, and after only a few days, a pair of these fish lay before me. I arranged them not on a bed of parsley but on a few tender leaves of Clauren's *Forget-me-not* (which never fade), and I reflected again on all that their mute language (the herrings, I mean) would be capable of expressing.[35]

Is it too far-fetched to assert that herrings are reminiscent of Hymenaios, and that the two obviously have an etymological relationship, since they both begin with a large *H* and also include a small *n*? But what I particularly wished to suggest was that they made up a *couple*. The blue color, reminiscent of the sky, stood for our mutual gentleness, and the salty brine for the acuteness of our intellects and Attic wit. The nonwilting leaves seemed to cry out "forget-me-not!" while alluding to the undiminished bliss we would feel when we finally possessed each other for the first time! But what to my mind crowned the whole thing was the charming play of words within the word itself: herring—here, ring! How could I possibly express my love and my honorable intentions more clearly and at the same time more delicately (in every sense of the term, since freshly salted herrings are indeed a delicacy in Prussia and Saxony). But in order to be absolutely sure of being properly understood, I placed on top a tastefully painted rose that I had cut out of Chinese rice paper, and among its leaves, with a bashful hand, I concealed the first small progeny of my muse:

> Who is so happy at the bottom,
> Who becomes healthy in the blue waters,
> The Herring.
>
> The waters are your blue eyes,
> Oh, let me dive into them
> As a herring.
>
> Oh, hear then my pleading,
> Let it, Loveliest, oh, let it happen—
> Give—here, ring!

Who could believe that *in spite of this,* all was in vain! Her mother answered me in simple prose, open and brief, that her daughter was sorry to say she had always borne an idiosyncratic aversion to herring, so much so that she had been unable to watch the last plays of the celebrated Willibald Alexis, once she learned that the author was actually named Häring. She was therefore respectfully sending my fish back in the accompanying *basket*, along with the poetry and many thanks for the good intentions.

Fortunately piety helps a truly devout spirit recover from anything. Still, I had to read the Bible for at least two hours before I regained my patience and composure. And even though the whale that swallowed Jonah—the subject of my reading today—was very large, it nonetheless kept fleeing my mind before the sad fate of my brace of herring.

In my anger, alas not yet entirely conquered, I must now say something to the two blotting-paper rags as well. Not only should they strive to spell better in their advertisements, they should also pay a bit more attention to the content. I will say nothing about the humiliating *Wurstbälle*, Wisotzky's, or *Jungfernstechen*.[36] But I must mention the collection of national curiosities shown me by a Berlin friend, which included some pages from these newspapers with the following two death notices submitted by a most unfortunate father, as well as an earlier announcement about a concert.

1. "Today the dear Lord, on his trip through Teltow, took unto himself my youngest son Fritz by his teeth."
2. (One month later): "Today the dear Lord took unto himself, *again,* my daughter Agnese to eternal salvation."

3. "On Monday there will be a concert in the theater here. The proceeds are intended to establish a *support fund for our countrymen who have died* in the service of their fatherland."

Now I ask, is this not making death laughable? That is a grievous sin, even if done unintentionally.

So that from the hand of our friend Lottum.

But the night is growing paler—already the new day is dawning. I will therefore say, as in Moore's song: It is already *day,* therefore good *night.*[37] Tomorrow morning an acquaintance will take this long letter with him to London—I am sending it to you via our embassy—and I close it with a heartfelt kiss which, well sealed, I hope will pass unchallenged through the Prussian customs.

Your faithful Lou

Caernarfon, July 19th, 1828

ℬELOVED FRIEND,

I have just returned dead tired from climbing the great Snowdon, the highest mountain in England, Scotland, and Wales,[1] which admittedly is not saying much. Grant me my rest until tomorrow, when I will offer a true account of my *fata*. In the meanwhile, good night.

July 20th, 1828

AFTER HAVING HANDED Mr. S—— the packet for you and entrusting it to his special care, I left Bangor as fast as four post horses could carry me. On my way, I saw a few ironworks, but I'll forego a description, since I did not notice anything new in them. I felt somewhat ill when I got to the inn in Caernarfon, where the daughter of the absent innkeeper, a picture-pretty girl with long black hair, did the honors with great charm.

The next morning at nine o'clock and in rather promising weather, I got into a *char-à-banc* drawn by two native horses and driven by a small lad who understood not a single word of English. He drove like mad at a hunting gallop over the narrow byways of the rocky countryside. All my shouting was in vain and seemed to be interpreted by him as the reverse of what I intended, so that we covered the nine miles to Llanberis Lake, over hill and dale, in less than half an hour. I can still hardly comprehend how the wagon and horses endured it.[2]

Near the fishermen's huts, which are quite scattered and isolated here, a gentler means of transportation awaited me—a pleasant boat, which I boarded along with two sprightly mountaineers (Figure 76). Snowdon now rose before us but had unfortunately put its nightcap on, as the locals say, while the surrounding mountains of lesser altitude sparkled in the brightest sunshine. It is only about four thousand feet high, but appears far more impressive, because it rises directly to its full height from the shore of the lake, whereas other mountains of this category tend to lift their peaks from an already elevated base. It is a three-mile crossing to the small inn at the foot of Snowdon, and since the wind was blowing strongly, our progress was very slow and rough. The water of the lake is inky black, the mountains bare and strewn with rocks, varied only by the occasional green alpine slope. Here and there you see a few low trees near the base, but the whole is wild and gloomy. Not far from the small Church of Llanberis is the so-called Sacred Well, inhabited by a solitary, gigantic trout that has been exhibited to strangers for centuries. It is often unwilling to be lured out, and people regard it as a lucky omen if you catch a quick glimpse of it. As an enemy of all oracles, I left the fish unvisited. I was also told of a strange Amazon woman, endowed with the strength of a giant, who led the life of a wild man here for a long while; and of huge bees so

76

*View of Snowdon
and Lake of Llanberis.*

greatly treasured by the Welsh that they imagine them to have originated in paradise. Many excel-lent salmon are caught in the lake, and in quite a novel manner: the fish are set upon by small dogs that have been specially trained to fetch them from the mud where they occasionally hide.

At the inn I quickly procured a guide and a pony and hurried on my way, still hoping that the threatening clouds would break up after noon. Unfortunately the opposite occurred. It became darker and darker, and in less than half an hour's climb—a feat I accomplished ahead of my pony, which the guide was leading by the bridle—the mountains, valleys, and we our-selves were enveloped by a single dark cloak, and a heavy rain poured down on us, quickly rendering my umbrella useless. We finally escaped into the ruins of an old castle, and after struggling up a dilapidated spiral staircase, I arrived at the remains of a balcony, where I found some shelter under the ivy. Everything around me looked profoundly melancholic. The crum-bling walls, the wind roaring plaintively through them, the monotonous fall of the rain, and my so-unpleasantly-dashed hopes left me in utter gloom. I thought with a sigh how nothing, not even the smallest thing, works out for me the way I want; how everything I undertake assumes the appearance of being untimely and eccentric, so that everywhere—as now—what others accomplish in the sunshine, I am forced to endure through rain and storm. Impatiently I left the old ruins and headed on up the mountain. But now the weather became so dreadful and the intensifying storm so perilous that we had to seek shelter again, this time in a dilapidated hut. In its smoky interior, an old woman was spinning in silence, and a few half-naked children were lying on the floor chewing dry crusts of bread. My entrance seemed scarcely noticed by the whole family; at least nothing disturbed their activities. The children stared at me briefly without any curiosity and then fell back into the apathy of their misery. I sat down on a round table, the only piece of furniture in the house, and granted a further audience to my thoughts, which were not particularly pleasant. Meanwhile the storm was raging more and more wickedly, and my guide implored me to turn back. That would doubtless have been the most reasonable thing to do, all the more so since we had not yet covered a third of our route. But since I had already long planned to drink a champagne toast to your health, dear Julie, on the summit of Snowdon, and to this end had brought a bottle with me from Caernarfon, it seemed a bad omen to give it all up. So with the cheerfulness that a firm decision always conveys on both large and small occasions, I said to the guide with a laugh, "And even if it should rain down stones instead of water, I will not turn around until I have seen Snowdon's peak," and with this, I mounted my pony. I left a gift for the old woman, but she received it with little interest. The path grew extremely difficult, passing continually over loose, flat stones washed by the rain or across extremely slippery grass. I admired how sure-footedly my small, industrious animal, shod with nothing but smooth, unstudded English horseshoes, advanced across this terrain.

Meanwhile it soon became so bitterly cold that I, now thoroughly drenched, could no longer continue riding. I am so unused to climbing these days that I was almost overcome with exhaustion, but then—just like the knight in Spieß's *Twelve Sleeping Virgins* who hears the encouraging little bells[3]—I heard the impelling "ma-ma" bleatings of the mountain sheep that graze by the hundreds here on the meager patches of grass. And thus, with constant thoughts of my dear little lamb at home,[4] I pressed on vigorously until, after an hour, I had recovered entirely and felt fresher than when I first set out. There were still no vistas to offer compensation because, enveloped by clouds, I could barely see twenty paces in front of me; in this mysterious clair-obscur, I approached the longed-for summit by a narrow ridge of rock. The spot is marked by a tall wooden pillar rising from a pile of stones.

Here a young man emerged out of the fog, and it was as if I were meeting the apparition of my doppelgänger, for he looked exactly like me—that is, like the me from sixteen years ago while I was wandering around the Swiss Alps. He was carrying, as I then, a light knapsack and an alpenstock, and wore a sturdy, classic mountaineering outfit; all of this, mind you, contrasted sharply with my London promenading boots, stiff cravat, and narrow frock coat, just as much as his youthful freshness outshone my complexion, sallow from city life. He looked like a young scion of nature, and I like a *ci-devant jeune homme*.[5] He had ascended from the other side of the mountain and paused only long enough to ask the distance to the inn and condition of the path. As soon as I told him, he hurried off, singing and warbling his way down the rocks, and quickly disappeared from sight. Meanwhile I scratched my name alongside a thousand others onto a large rock and then, taking out the cow's horn that the innkeeper had given me as a drinking vessel, ordered my guide to remove the cork from the champagne bottle. It must have been unusually compressed, because the cork soared above the nearby pillar. Therefore, in good conscience and without having to borrow anything from the Baron of Münchhausen, you can affirm that, as I drank to your health on the nineteenth of July,[6] the champagne cork sailed some four thousand feet above sea level. The moment the horn was filled and foaming over, I called out into the gloom in a stentorian voice: "Long live Julie, with nine times nine!" (in the English manner). Three times I emptied the animal cup, and really, although thirsty and exhausted as I had reason to be, champagne had never tasted better. But when I finished the libation, I prayed with all my heart. These were not vacuous phrases, but profound sentiments, including the fervent wish that God grant you a good life here on earth and do the same for me as well—if possible. And lo! Just then a dainty lamb clambered toward me out of the veil of clouds, the mists separated, and for a moment the gilded earth lay before us in the flashing rays of the sun. Yet too soon the curtain closed again—an image of my destiny! Only now and then does the beautiful and desirable, the *gilded* earth, appear before me like a will-o'-the-wisp; but when I try to catch it, everything disappears as in a dream.

Since there was no hope that today's weather would clear up permanently in these high regions, we had to turn back. I was now so invigorated that I not only felt no more fatigue but even experienced that sensation—unknown to me for years—in which walking and running, instead of being an effort, are in themselves an elastic pleasure. So like the youthful version of myself, whom I had just met, I bounded down so rapidly over the rocks and the wet, rush-covered slopes that in just a few minutes, I covered the part of the trail that had cost me an hour and a half to ascend. And here I finally emerged again from the enveloping clouds. If the view was less magnificent than at the summit, it nonetheless gave me enormous pleasure. I would guess I was still some three and a half thousand feet above the Irish Sea, which spread out endlessly before me. I had a clear view, like on a relief, of the Isle of Anglesey resting against its shore, and within the many intersecting ravines all around me I counted about twenty smaller lakes—many dark, many so brightly lit by the sun that the eye could barely endure their mirror-like sheen. By this time my guide had descended too, and since I could now assess the terrain perfectly well myself, and the evening was lovely and I felt no fatigue, I let him and his sensible little horse follow the straight road back home together, for I had decided to seek my own solitary path by way of the most beautiful spots—and it is just as well I did, for I can recall no more captivating walk since I was in Switzerland (Figure 77).

I followed a gorge along the wild pass of Llanberis, famous from the wars between the English and the Welsh. It was from here that the Welsh, under their great Prince Llewelyn, often watched the destruction of foreign invaders, perhaps from the exact spot where I was standing. The precipitous rock walls, which at many points fell off almost vertically toward the pass, provide a good drill for countering dizziness. I gradually ascended several rather-alarming pinnacles of this sort and found that the slight *frisson* instilled by the danger provided yet another pleasure. As Madame de Staël says, the feeling of danger is pleasing. I was not entirely alone, in fact. The mountain sheep, far smaller than what we are used to and as wild and nimble as chamois, were often startled by me the way deer are, and in their flight plunged down over precipices where no one could easily follow. The wool of these creatures is the coarsest there is, yet their flesh is the most tender and flavorful. Even the gourmands of London rate it very highly and maintain that anyone who hasn't eaten sheep from Snowdon has absolutely no concept of how delicious roast mutton can be.

At another point I almost collided with a large bird of prey floating slowly with wings outspread. It had fixed its gaze so keenly on the depths and so little reckoned on making my acquaintance on this inaccessible path that I was almost able to grab it with my hands. Then it noticed me and shot away like an arrow, although it was not at all distracted from the object of its investigations far below. After a while, as the sun sank behind the towering mountains, I could still see

the bird hovering like a point in the blue ether. Now I tried to descend in the straightest possible line to the hut where I had rested earlier. Not far from it a girl was milking her cows, and I greatly appreciated their fresh milk. There I also met up with my guide and, gratefully, spent the remainder of my journey wrapped in my cloak and resting quite comfortably atop the sure-footed pony. Back at the inn I changed my clothes—a precaution that should never be neglected in mountain travel—and embarked anew on the lake, now magnificently aglow in the red of evening. The air had become mild and soft, fish were leaping joyfully out of the water, and herons were circling the reedy banks in graceful arcs, while here and there a fire flared up in the mountains and the hollow thunder of blasted rocks resounded from the distant quarries.

The sickle moon had long been hanging in the dark sky when raven-haired Hebe welcomed me back to Caernarfon.

July 21st, 1828

I WAS STILL a little tired today from the preceding twenty-four hours and therefore contented myself with a walk to the celebrated Caernarfon Castle built by Edward I, the conqueror of Wales. Destroyed by Cromwell, it is now one of the most beautiful ruins in England (Figure 78).

77

View of Snowdon and Lliwedd.

CARNARVON CASTLE

I only regret that it is so close to the city and not standing solitary in the mountains. The external walls, although dilapidated, still form an unbroken line encompassing about three acres of land. The space inside, overgrown with grass and covered with rubble and thistles, is nearly eight hundred yards long and surrounded by seven slender and sturdily built towers of varying shapes and sizes. One of these is still accessible, and I climbed 140 steps up a ramshackle staircase to a platform with an imposing view of the sea, mountains, and town. As I was descending, I was shown the ruins of a vaulted room where, according to tradition, Edward II, the first Prince of Wales, was born. The story is that the Welsh, recalling their oppression under English overlords during intermittent periods of partial conquest, had told King Edward I that they would only obey a governor who was a prince of their own nation. At once, in the middle of winter, the king had his wife Eleanor brought in secret to this castle to await the birth of her child. After a boy was delivered, the king summoned the nobles and highest-ranking men of the land and solemnly asked them if they would submit to the reign of a young prince who was born in Wales and could not speak a word of English. When, joyful and astonished, they answered in the affirmative, he presented them with his own newborn son, crying out in broken Welsh "eich dyn," which means "this is your man!"—words that were later corrupted into "ich dien" in the motto of the English coat-of-arms.[7]

A carved likeness of Edward with a crown on his head and a drawn dagger in his right hand still hangs above the large main gate, as if after six centuries he remains ready to guard the stone remnants of his castle. And he would be justified in lamenting its desecration, for on a green space in the midst of the ruins, a camel and a monkey in a red braided coat were performing their tricks, cheered along by a crowd of ragged onlookers unconscious of the pathetic contrast they made with the solemn remains of the past that surrounded them.

The prince was born in the so-called Eagle Tower, a name that comes not from him but from four colossal eagles that once crowned its pinnacles, just one of which survives. The tower is thought to be Roman, because Caernarfon stands on the site of the old Segontium, which . . . But now I am straying too far afield. I was well on my way to adopting the tone of a professional travel writer who is convinced of his right to bore you while instructing you, even though he has only acquired the information by tedious perusal of local books and pamphlets. I do not make this claim, you know; I allow my pen to wander, unconcerned about where it may lead.

Not long ago the Marquess of Anglesey had a public seaside bath built here. It is kept regulated by a steam engine and very elegantly equipped. I took advantage of it on my way back from the castle and, in the recreation rooms, noticed a metal billiards table mounted on stone. You could not ask for anything more accurate; I forgot to ask if the steam engine also keeps track of the games. This would not be far-fetched in a country where, just recently, someone seriously suggested installing steam waiters in the coffee houses, and where things would not be much different if a forty-horsepower steam engine were sitting on the throne.

Dear Julie, a traveler must be allowed to speak often and at length about weather and food! The novels of the Famous Though Once Unknown or Once Famously Unknown owe much of their charm to masterful depictions of this kind, do they not?[8] Whose mouth does not water at the sight of Dalgetty, the soldier of fortune, at table; and who does not find him even more invincible there than in battle? I assure you, all joking aside, that when, with my sensitive nerves, I had lost my appetite as a result of some small bout of indigestion, a complete recovery was achieved after just two hours of reading the Unknown. Today, however, I needed no such stimulus. When I saw, steaming on the table, the excellent fish fresh from the sea, bordering the legendary mountain mutton, it was enough for me to fall on them ravenously. A dip in a sea bath and the ascent of Mount Snowdon have a greater effect than does Walter Scott.

My black-haired girl waited on me herself today, as I was the only guest in the house. Finally impatient at watching me return again and again to the mutton, she sullenly remarked that when I was not running about, all I did was eat. She herself is far more ethereal in nature and has already, since I arrived, finished half the novels in my portable library. Every time I see her, she presents me with another volume that she has devoured and ardently begs for another. To refuse her would require a harder heart. Thus our two appetites—mine for the real, hers for the ideal—have joined both mutually and most innocently.

July 22nd, 1828

TODAY A LARGE packet arrived, having followed me from Bangor, and I hoped it contained news from you, but in vain. I did laugh heartily over a letter from Lottum, who writes in despair about how horribly things have been going for him. He had allowed excerpts to be published from his "Observations" (the first part of which I sent you),[9] and a certain party, feeling wounded and excessively vulnerable, thought he detected malice in it. The offended person immediately composed a furious article against him that appeared in the *Lamm Zeitung*,[10] and poor Lottum, who knows what these people are like, is now afraid he will fail his examination. Since the philippic is not long and, meanwhile, is a good characterization of the times, and since I am also taking the day off, I will copy out the main contents for you, albeit with abridgments.

"On the Observations of a Good-Natured Soul from Sandomir."

An address by Mr. von Frömmel,[11] Adjutant of his Highness, Prince of ——.
Delivered in the noble and pious conventicle of both sexes at A——, 33 Heilige Geiststraße,
on the 4th of May 1828; and here specially printed from the Collections for True Christians.

My devout, high, and highly wellborn brothers and sisters!

Our Savior says rightly: there are many wolves in sheep's clothing! And without any doubt, such a one is at hand: the anonymous composer of the "Observations, etc." It is not hard to discern a pernicious snake beneath the mask of sanctimony and simplicity that borders on silliness, a snake hissing with scorn and ridicule, the very same beast that once seduced our pious mother Eve and has ever since sprayed its venom on our holy religion, plotting to undermine both church and throne. We, however, do not wish to follow our unfortunate and too-gullible progenitress, but would rather vanquish all the devil's acolytes with fire and sword, wherever we may find them.

Yes, my brothers and sisters, *you* know it: the devil exists. He lives not within us, something claimed by the unbelieving mob, as the devil of our passions, vanity, hatred, and sin. No. When he lets himself be seen, he appears *in person,* creeping around on the earth like a roaring lion with a goat's horn, a horse's tail, and a pestilential stench. Whoever does not believe *this* of the devil does not believe in Jesus . . . *
But why am I so agitated—there are no fancy thinkers here, no wise men of the world; here we are all just simple Lambs of Christ, *one* flock and *one* shepherd.

Yet a warning is called for, and today I sound the alarm! Until now we have read only fragments of these poisonous "Observations" and do not know exactly where the author intends to go with them. But there can be no doubt that they are aimed at us, and praise God, we have already seen enough to condemn him as an atheist! Is it not obvious that he is wantonly ridiculing the all-powerful Providence?

We therefore hope, we pray faithfully and fervently, that omnipotent power will undertake its own vengeance and give this self-satisfied soul a foretaste of what

---

* Anyone who still doubts this can be assured that we *ourselves* have already encountered the devil. Yes, he appeared in a far more scandalous way to one of the most commendable members of our holy society, a distinguished lady, whom we will identify only by the name *Sexaginta.* It happened when she was standing alongside the worthy Herr Lieutenant Graf von N—— before a devout conventicle and had just delivered a victorious speech, successfully moving the congregation to ban, unanimously and henceforth, any resort to heathen expressions such as "the *god* Amor" or "the *goddess* Venus" and instead, whenever the subject was unavoidable, to refer to those impure demons—mindful of our Christian *duty*—only as "the *idol* Amor," "the *idol* Venus," etc. This must have touched Satan most acutely. Desperate for revenge, he now sought to corrupt the dove-like woman. Appearing before her with despicable cunning in the figure of that self same lieutenant, he tried to bewitch her with dissembling words. But piety prevailed, and soon he had to reveal himself, in all his ignominy. Thus do the righteous always triumph! But thereafter Sexaginta knew that there are things not dreamed of by our so-called wise men and, with more piety than the poet, she could declare: The devil is no empty illusion!— *A note from the editor of the Lamm Zeitung.* [Sexaginta is an invented name meaning "sixty," and the number six, especially when repeated three times, is associated with the devil, so this may be a hint that the lady is the wife or perhaps grandmother of the devil. Exactly whom Pückler is referring to in this aside remains a mystery, but he appears to be taking revenge on someone's excessive piety. —*Translator.*]

awaits him in the eternal flames. And may the *all-loving* God resolve this quickly and horribly, lest a pure lamb from our flock be led astray by this unclean one and suffer a shameful fall. Certainly, my friends, a fiend, a vampire, an atheist wrote those words. Nothing is sacred to him and with insidious phrases, this blasphemer attacks not only eternal Providence but even our Redeemer! He is despicable!

> The sweet lamb that died for him
> Does not touch his unrepentant heart!
> Therefore, Oh my Lord, swiftly
> Judge this depraved soul.*

Oh my brothers and sisters! The fate of such a person on Judgment Day will be dreadful. We can be absolutely sure that when the dead rise up and his worldly ear hears once again, he will discern the thunder of the trumpets announcing his eternal damnation. There will be no pity! There will be wailing and the gnashing of teeth. We should take this example and be likewise merciless!

We can scarcely believe—after all our Christian efforts in our so truly, I say with pride, truly Christian city, where every effort is made to destroy the poison of tolerance and loathsome independent thinking—that there are still those among us who, untroubled by authority, dare to follow their own path to the truth: freethinkers and heathens, who are popping up again only because the authorities (headed by our otherwise-active censors) persist in being too lenient about this greatest of crimes, lack of religious faith. For how can the miserable worm known as man think to impose *his* thoughts on the divine; think to counter God's *own*, special revelation with his deficient reason, which he possesses only from God. Such nonsense! It might have been beneficial if a moderate Inquisition had been introduced along with the new prayer book, so as to protect the orthodox believers, those true Christians, those privileged favorites of God, who, without pondering or interpreting, unhesitatingly believe whatever their prince or church commands. Only such people can be of true value to the state and the church. Away with the rest! May they be damned like all unbaptized children of the Jews and heathens!

Oh, if only our annals could be purged forever of that shameless time when a philosopher (and not even an ideological but a practical one) sat on a German throne! And, my fellow Christians, can you believe this?—he was called "the Great"![12] Now the mildest thing that we, returned to the realm of grace and piety amid tears of blood, can say about him is: May God have mercy on his poor soul! However, the devout and their holy legion face a long fight before the seed sown by this (great!!!) man is crushed underfoot, before the last trace of that miserable rationality he worshipped is exterminated. But do not despair, my brothers in Christ; nothing is impossible for a noble zeal such as ours, and assorted earthly rewards already await you now in the sublime wellsprings from which we draw each day. Even greater glory is to come in the palace of the Lord. Just guard against reasoning in any form; do not

---

* From an old hymnal.

believe in your own investigations but only in what has been prescribed for you, and guard especially against toleration! Love your Savior, not only above all else but also solely and alone. Whoever is not for him is against him—have no compassion for such a person. Persecute him relentlessly and openly; if this is impossible, then undermine him with secret slander and malevolent defamation. Yes, do not shy away from the crudest of lies, provided that you can spread them safely in secret, for here the end sanctifies all means.

Ah! If only we were always moved by the true spirit of communion and our fervor never abated. Solely because they are neither hot nor cold, have those philosophers preached about tolerance, that heathen virtue. We have seen what happened when the insane hoax of freedom took hold of the mob, and collective anarchy threatened to bring down the throne, the Church, our old nobility, and everything venerable. Therefore, away with that noxious idea of tolerating people who think differently! It is true that Christ said, "Bless those who curse you" and "When someone slaps you on one cheek, turn the other one as well." But I have my own thoughts about this. It is crucial that such passages be understood differently, for how can we reconcile them with the essential laws of our station? Does not the honor of our rank and our uniform require us without hesitation to stick a knife into anyone who dares lay violent hands on us? Indeed I do not know whether even I, the prince's favorite, could let myself be seen at court or in the very highest places after publically receiving a slap on the face. Thus our Savior likely intended that a brief qualification accompany this dictum, namely that it was *for the common people,* since they are certainly to be commended if, when struck upon one cheek, they do not give in to bitterness, but immediately offer the other one. We ought to consider, too, that when Christ became man, he sought out not just a noble but a royal line. And who can prove that the disciples were really of such common origin as people think and not perhaps old Jewish noblemen who had simply come down in the world? The whole thing is shrouded in so much historical darkness. And did Christ not say elsewhere, "My mission is not to bring peace, but rather the sword!" These two utterances would appear contradictory if we did not accept that toleration is required of only *one* class and combat of the *other*. But is this not the age-old destiny of the nobility? Formerly with weapons, nowadays with word and pen! For this purpose, my brothers and sisters, fight against the godless! Gird on the sword of the times and fight for the Redeemer with the Bible and Jakob Böhme, with chamberlain's key and seneschal's baton, with prayer book and surplice. Believe me, my dear comrades, we already reap the fruits of our holy zeal; we already begin to claim unshakable ground. More and more people submit to our secret influence. And our firm cohesion, the support we extend to our own for their deserving labor in the vineyards of the Lord, the many favors from on high that we dispense, but above all the unrelenting devoutness that everyone recognizes in us—all these keep even the bold in check and cast scores of the timid at our feet.

But when an Antichrist dares to encroach upon us—and anyone who tries this is such a one—I call out once more: Keep watch, do battle, annihilate, and do not rest until your victim has fallen! It is all for the sake of love, a last attempt to teach a poor lost soul to know Jesus Christ. Amen!

This noble congregation in Christ will perhaps find their hearts agreeably touched when I report that in the current month we have once again been so lucky as to lead seven and one-half condemned souls to the only true faith, at a cost of no more than one hundred Reichstalers cash and three meetings. We keep records of these activities and prefer, for the sake of brevity, to list children under twelve as half souls.* So may heaven continue to bless our pious efforts and the selfless fervor with which the newly converted are drawn to the lap of Jesus. Amen!

I have another announcement: next Sunday evening, again at eight o'clock in the same room at Miss S——'s, there will be a meeting, held behind closed doors and in the dark, so that no external objects can distract us from giving free rein to the sacred, sweet shudders of devoted love. We are hoping for a large turnout, especially on the part of the gentler sex, to whom our conventicle already owes so much. . . .

I had gotten this far in my reading when the little Elisa appeared with my breakfast and bid me a mischievously friendly good morning "after my long sleep." She had just come from church, was very conscious of her pretty attire, and was waiting on a foreigner—all things that put a woman in a softhearted mood. She therefore seemed almost embarrassed when I told her I would be departing tomorrow morning, but she was consoled by my promise to leave my library behind and come back again in a week with just as many books.

In the afternoon, with her as my guide, I visited the city promenades, one of which is very romantically laid out atop a large cliff. From here we saw Snowdon in almost perfect clarity, not one tiny cloud was spoiling its purity, and I could not help feeling a bit by aggravated at having missed going there on the right day.

After this idyllic walk, tender mutton once again closed the day, and I regret having nothing more interesting to tell you. But wait—a rather strange anecdote has just occurred to me, something the innkeeper told me today: In 1820, on the night of August 5th, the local ferry sank and of twenty-six people aboard, only one man was saved. Exactly thirty-seven years before, the ferry had met the same fate and then, too, only one man of sixty-nine people survived. But what makes it extraordinary is that the name of the survivor, in both cases, was Hugh Williams.

Bangor, July 22nd, 1828 [13]

BANGOR IS ALSO a bathing resort, which is to say, anyone is free to jump into the sea. The man-made arrangements, however, have been reduced to the private bathtub of an old woman who lives in a miserable hut on the shore and will heat up some seawater in pots on top of her stove if you make a reservation one hour in advance. She herself tends unceremoniously to the stranger's bathing needs, undressing him, drying him off, and dressing him again, if he has not brought his own servant along for this purpose. After I, having entered quite accidentally, had

---

* I believe that this custom of dividing souls, a triumph of political chemistry, arose at the Congress of Vienna where the King of D——k, assured by a celebrated diplomat "que S. M. avait gagné tous les coeurs," quite appropriately responded, "Oui, mais pas une âme! Pas même la moitié d'une âme."—*The Editor*. [His Majesty has won every heart.—Yes, but not a soul! Not even half a soul!—*Translator*.]

taken such a bath just for its rarity, I hired a small gondola to transport me to Beaumaris, across the inlet that separates the Isle of Anglesey and Wales, where there is another castle built by Edward I and destroyed by Cromwell. At one time it was even larger than Caernarfon, and it still covers five acres, although it is less picturesque as a ruin, having lost all its towers. To get a good look at it, you must walk on top of narrow, dilapidated, and very high walls that are wholly unprotected. The young boy in charge of the keys ran along them like a squirrel, it is true, but the town barber, who had offered himself as a guide when I debarked and had brought me this far, abandoned me after the first step. This ruin is in a park belonging to Mr. Bulkeley, who very inappropriately had a tennis court built inside the walls. The view from his residence is highly touted, but is far surpassed by another view about one and one-half hours away, from a simple but charming cottage called Craig-y-Don on an estate that is a true gem, one of the few blessed spots that leave almost nothing to be desired. It is situated close to the sea amid bluffs covered densely with thickets. Not too large, decorated like a boudoir, and surrounded by the freshest green grass and flowers in a warm fusion of all colors, the whole house—together with its thatched roof and veranda draped with Old Blush roses and blue convolvulus—peeks out between woodland and rocks, forming an indescribably delightful contrast with its sublime surroundings. Labyrinthine footpaths wind off in all directions through the shady, cool groves, multiplying the spectacular treasury of vistas offered by the site. Below you is the deep blue inlet, the spume from its breakers gnawing at the foot of the pointed rocks on which you stand, while farther off the surface teems with a hundred fishing boats and other vessels. Most prominent among them are the estate owner's cutter, lying at anchor, and two steamboats, one of which you spy in the distance trailing a broad black cloud, while from the other, very close by, a slender, white column wafts straight up into the air. On your right, you see a bay cutting deep into the land and creating an archipelago of small islands of every shape and type; some are covered with vegetation, others are barren and polished smooth by the waves; huts have been built on some, others jut up like pointed towers. If you now turn your gaze back to the inlet and follow it farther along the same shore until it gradually begins to narrow, you are astonished to find your view blocked by a stupendous chain bridge, a gigantic structure that people here rightly call the eighth wonder of the world and that, in defiance of nature, has joined together two parts of land separated by the ocean's flow.[14] Soon I will have a chance to give you a more precise description of it; from here it looks like something woven in the air by spiders (Figure 79).

After you have you tarried a while at this fantastic sight of *human accomplishment,* you see, just opposite you, the most varied and grand spectacles *of nature:* the entire chain of the Welsh mountains, here rising straight out of the water. Clearly visible and near enough to clearly distinguish woods, villages, and ravines, the peaks spread out to a length of nearly fifty miles. The mountains are arranged in groups of every shade and nuance; many are still muffled in clouds, many gleam openly in the sun; others stretch their blue summits all the way above the clouds; and in the folds of the slopes, you can see villages, towns, white churches, handsome country houses, and castles, while sparkling rays of light play upon the green meadows. In need of a rest, you finally turn your gaze toward the north, now at your left, and nothing more distracts you, nothing but the broad ocean blending into the heavens. For a brief time you follow the wooded shoreline of Anglesey as it retreats to one side, with tall nut trees and oaks suspending their broad branches above the sea. And then you are alone with the sky and water, convinced that all you

79

Menai Suspension Bridge.

can see are the sails of a three-decker in the foggy distance, or perhaps a cloud painting fantastic figures just for you.

After a pleasurable hour here, I rode toward the great bridge, urging the pony I had hired in Beaumaris to give its best effort. The finest view is from below, about a hundred paces away from the span, on the sandy bank next to some fishermen's huts. The longer you look, the more you are amazed, as if the whole thing were really just a dream, a kind of filigree held aloft by a fairy—indeed one's fancy cannot contain all the images. And when a diligence drawn by four horses drove quickly across the arch, one hundred feet high and six hundred feet long, half hidden by the webbing of chains from which the bridge is suspended, you would have thought you were seeing some larks fluttering in a net. The human figures looked no different as they sat perched everywhere in the chains giving them their first coat of oil paint, for the entire structure had only recently been completed. People familiar with the Berlin City Palace will get a vivid idea of the enormous dimensions of this bridge when they hear that the palace would fit very comfortably under the main arch between the water and the road surface; and yet the chains hold the roadbed so firmly that even at top speed—which is permissible—and carrying the heaviest load, you sense no movement at all. The bridge is divided at the top into three roads, one for driving over, the other for driving back, and the center for pedestrians. The thick planks rest on an iron grid, so if they are damaged or broken, there is no cause for alarm, since they can easily be taken up and replaced. Every three years, all the ironwork will get a new coat of paint to prevent rust. The architect, who has earned himself long-lasting fame here, is named Telford.

Sur ce, n'ayant plus rien à dire, I close my report and wish you, my dear Julie, all the happiness and blessings you deserve, c'est beaucoup dire.[15]

Ever your most faithful Lou

CHÈRE ET BONNE,

One small disadvantage of this otherwise richly endowed landscape is the effect of the tides. For a significant part of the day, the ebb dries out a large stretch of the Menai, the name of the strait here, leaving behind nothing but sludgy sand. The unimaginably tenacious flies that go hunting by the thousands, swarming like bees and attacking people as well as cattle, are probably a result of this. You may drive your horse as fast as it can go, but in vain. As soon as you stop, the swarm, balled into a clump like a Macedonian phalanx, flies along with you and the warriors distribute themselves over their prey, succumbing only if you beat them to death. Even retreating into a house does not always help. On a few of my walks I have discovered that these flies, once they have adopted you, will wait patiently outside until you reemerge. The only recourse is to seek out a spot where the wind is blowing too strongly for them to tolerate it. The cows grazing on the hilly shores are quite aware of this, for you always see them standing alone in breezy places, ruminating peacefully. Today I observed one of these animals for a long time as it stood on an isolated point of rock, its contour sharply delineated against the sky, unmoving but for the gentle working of its jaw and occasional sweep of its tail. How beautifully a skilled craftsman could reproduce this sight, I thought, elevating the animal to a colossal Apis and equipping it with a mechanism to imitate its simple movements. And what an acquisition that would be for a German-English park at home—for instance, in Kassel where it might stand opposite the Hercules, or even in Wörlitz, where it could graze on the fire-spewing mountain.[1] Certainly a commendable idea; you really must try to make good use of it.

Do you still remember when Count L—— was showing Clemens Brentano and the brilliant and engaging Schinkel the view from his hunting lodge, from where one looks out over a charming but flat wooded landscape, and how, turning to the two men, the count asked them, somewhat naively, what might be done to make a really significant improvement?[2] Brentano fell into deep contemplation and after some time, responded slowly, his curious eyes cast earnestly on his attentive patron: "How would it be, Count, to construct a mountain range out of planks and have it painted blue?" In spite of the new Berlin Horticultural Society, such things, even if not so flagrant, still happen in our beloved fatherland every day.

Dear Julie, will you come with me now to Plas Newydd, Marquess Anglesey's park on the Isle of Anglesey? Your imaginary horses are quickly harnessed.

Passing by the giant bridge again, we follow the main road toward Ireland for a short time until we see in the distance the lofty column erected by a grateful fatherland for General Paget (at that time Lord Uxbridge; now Marquess of Anglesey and Lord Lieutenant of Ireland), as

80

Cromlechs at Plas Newydd.

recompense for the leg that he left behind at Waterloo![3] A half hour farther along we arrive at the park gate of Plas Newydd, most remarkable for some cromlechs whose actual significance is unknown, although they are thought to be tombs of the Druids (Figure 80). They consist of mammoth stones, usually only three or four in number, arranged to form a kind of rough gateway. Some are so colossal that it is scarcely conceivable how anyone could have lifted them without the most complicated mechanical equipment. Of course, a great deal is possible when human strength is inspired by unbounded will or fanaticism. Did I not read once that a ship's captain, when sailing along the Japanese coast, saw along the range of mountains running parallel to his course two enormously large junks, not much smaller than our frigates, being transported *overland* by thousands of men?

The local cromlechs, which are not the largest known, probably gave rise to the idea of building a druidic cottage with a beautiful view of Snowdon.[4] What materialized, however, is a strange, cluttered chaos of ancient and modern objects. Light enters the structure and illuminates the small, dark spaces quite cleverly by means of mirrored doors, which in different rooms also serve to capture the most advantageous parts of the landscape, making these appear as if they were framed beneath glass. In addition, in the window of the main room, there is a large peep-show box, a camera obscura, and a new kind of kaleidoscope. The kaleidoscope is not filled like the old ones were, but instead creates endless variations on whatever object one aims it at. Flowers, especially through the infinitely shifting brilliance of their refracted colors, create a wonderful effect. If you would like such a device, I can easily have one sent from London. They cost eight guineas. The house and rest of the estate offer nothing worth mentioning and are rarely visited by the owner, whose main residence is in England.

July 23rd, 1828

TODAY I RECEIVED, with great delight, a long letter from you. . . . .

I am glad that you did not misinterpret Lottum's joke and do not consider him to be a godless, wicked person like Mr. Von Frömmel does.[5] First and foremost, he is just making fun of the blind faith of those who transform the inexpressible—the essence of all things that we can only intuit but not comprehend—into an odd amalgam of human overlord, schoolmaster, and ancillary guardian spirit; who believe themselves to be controlled by this guide like children by leading strings;[6] and who unfailingly assume that whatever they perceive as relating to them must be an act of God focused on their own insignificant selves. If they fail at something, for instance, or win the lottery, *then* they recognize the finger of God *indisputably* at work; if they avoid some danger, they thank God, as if some *foreign* power had caused the danger, and God had merely served as a concerned guardian who rushed to intervene. They ought to consider that the rescue and danger come from the same source; where there is pleasure, there is also pain; where living, also dying. The whole is simply life in this world; it cannot be bestowed and regulated according to caprice, but follows immutable laws.

The petty-minded views that Lottum criticizes drag the idea of omnipotence down to the level of our own decrepitude. We should give thanks to eternal love for all of existence, even if we do so wordlessly. And perhaps no prayer offered by man can be more worthy of the deity than this rapturously mute gratitude. But how childish it is to take all those everyday, *external* events—things like strokes of luck or misfortune, wealth, poverty, death, etc., that are subject to the laws of nature or that we ourselves bring about according to the measure of our powers—and ascribe them to some omnipotent force, to some special and heaven-knows-how-useless nurturing of our precious selves.

Furthermore he is making fun of those Christians who are absolutely *not* Christians and, he says, these are not the so-called atheists (altogether a meaningless designation), nor the real fanatics, but rather that unholy race of modern, sanctimonious frauds, who are either weaklings with overexcited nerves* or hypocrites of the most godless sort, further removed from the sublime purity of Jesus than the Dalai Lama. *They* are the real Pharisees, the money changers in the

---

* Somewhere Jean Paul makes a superb observation about such people: "I have somewhat often compared this cursed exaltation of souls, merely from low motives, with the English horsetails, which also always stand pointing to heaven only because their sinews have been cut." [Translation from *Titan: A Romance*, trans. Charles T. Brooks (Boston: Ticknor and Fields, 1863), 1:389–90.—*Translator.*]

temple, whom Christ would still drive out today. It is they who, were he to appear again under another name, would be the first to cry out "crucify him!"*

In most of this I have to agree with Lottum, although regarding his initial premise, every opinion must remain no more than an hypothesis, for the truth of everything must be very different from what we can begin to fathom. If it were intended that we could or should know it, then the creator of our existence would have revealed this to us; revealed it so unambiguously that we would know it just as surely as we know that we feel, think, and are. Whatever we need is revealed to us *in our hearts*, something that the greatest minds on earth have expressed from time immemorial.

I have no doubt whatsoever that there is no need for the human race to stand still like a machine with no will of its own or to revolve in endless circles; rather it must stride on and move beyond itself until someday it reaches the end of its life cycle and achieves its highest level of perfection. *My* hypothesis would be only that the earth, like a ship that has been launched and stands under the protection and dictates of immutable natural laws, is now entrusted to its own crew. Henceforth, through our own moral strength or weakness, we construct our life (as far as this is dependent on our own capacities, apart from those natural laws) as we do our history, in things both big and small. We need not assume, for instance, that some special power intervened to send Napoleon a hard winter in Russia in order to bring him down; rather, Napoleon was toppled by the flawed principle that guided him, which was destined to fail eventually for one reason or another. In his case, the natural event occurred by chance, yet still within the necessary sequence of the laws to which it was subject, even though these laws are unknown to us.

This is exactly why the dear Lord will, as a rule, allow things to go well for the good, diligent, thrifty, wise, etc., and grant many of their wishes. But things will not go so favorably for the foolish and evil who go to battle with the world. It is very likely that if a man leaves his hand lying in ice, the Lord will let it freeze, and if he holds it in the fire, he will let it burn—unless he's the fireproof Spaniard.[7] Occasionally the Lord will allot the fate of drowning to those who travel by ship; there is no chance that he will allow those who have never left the land to perish in the sea.

For this reason it is rightly said, God helps those who help themselves. The truth is that God has helped us from the very beginning. The master's work is completed and, as far as it was intended, perfect—it needs no extraordinary assistance or improvement from above. Any further development has been placed in our own hands. We can be good and evil, wise and foolish—not perhaps always the way we as *individuals* might freely choose to be, but as we have been formed by those in the *human race* who preceded us. Virtue and sin, prudence and folly are, after all, just words given meaning by *human society,* and without that society, the meaning would be

---

* It is a serious error to think that this is nothing but material for ridicule and a bit of righteous indignation. The confederacy of the *pious* is not without danger for the *liberal minded.* The Jesuit host is in ferment here and, finding Catholicism too *enlightened,* is seeking affinities among the Protestants. The latter are guided by the same principles that grant the Jesuits their power. The same esprit de corps holds sway among them; both have developed a regulated organization and instead of the ax, they successfully use what is often ten times more vicious: wicked slander, which, like so many instruments of darkness, a secret society can easily employ without detection. Germany will suffer much more from such "saints" than from the *Studiosi* dreaming of freedom on the Wartburg! [On October 18, 1817, the three-hundredth anniversary of Martin Luther's posting of his ninety-five theses, German students organized a festival at the Wartburg to protest the suppression of liberal ideas by reactionary policies. A period of persecution of students and professors ensued.—*Translator.*]

completely lost. It is obvious that the concept of good and evil depends on our relationships with others; a person who never saw a fellow creature could never behave, or even feel or think, in a way that was good or evil. Each of us is capable of such, and this is the bedrock of our higher, spiritual nature. But it can only become active in the presence of our fellow creatures, just as fire can only come into being, or be perceptible, where there is something to burn.

The concept of wisdom and folly, on the other hand, emerges earlier within each individual, because a single human being, in conflict with so-called inanimate nature, can choose foolishly to harm himself or wisely make use of what has been given him and be cognizant of these choices. In every respect then, to be "good" means nothing but to love others and submit to the laws of the community; to be "evil," however, means a refusal to heed those laws, to pay little or no attention to the well-being of others, and, in our own actions, consider only our own immediate gratification. To be "wise," then, means knowing only how to preserve our *own* advantage in the most skillful way, whereas being "foolish" means neglecting or miscalculating this same advantage.

Thus we can readily see that "good" and "wise," just as "evil" and "foolish" in their turn, must be understood in the highest degree as being almost synonymous. Because, as a rule, whoever is good will be pleasing to his fellow creatures, and therefore be loved by them, and by this means, will wisely gain the truest advantage for himself; whoever is evil, on the other hand, will be engaged in perpetual strife, ultimately fail, and consequently suffer harm. But once the moral principle has developed further, the virtuous individual will come to establish his own law, one that he adheres to without worrying about advantage, danger, or the opinion of others. Rather, as I have said, the foundation of this law will always rest on a regard for the well-being of one's fellow creatures and the resulting duty to follow the path one has chosen. And then, with the inner conviction that this duty has been fulfilled, the person of spirit will achieve a greater sense of satisfaction than all worldly goods could ever provide. It therefore follows that, in every respect and at every level of culture, it is the greatest wisdom to be good and the greatest folly to be evil.

But here, of course, given life's confusion, many nuances emerge. In the realm of worldly, external things, a certain amount of wisdom may let someone achieve the *appearance* of the good, but not the reality. You can deceive others and even make them believe you are acting for their benefit and deserve their esteem and gratitude when, in fact, you are only using them to your own advantage and causing them the most bitter harm. Folly too often yields the contrary effect—that is, leading others to wrongly suspect evil and bad intentions, when the opposite is the case. What naturally ensues from this is the truth—substantiated by considerable and often-painful experience—that in *worldly affairs*, an individual will incur more harm by being foolish than by being evil and bad: the external consequences of the latter can be kept in check by wisdom, even averted altogether; but nothing can hold off the consequences of folly, which continually works *against itself.*

The need for and the development of positive religion may largely be due to this realization and to the inadequacies of the secular penal codes that follow from it.[8] Here especially we find the doctrine of future punishment and reward by an omniscient power for whom wisdom is insufficient and from whom the foolish expect compassion and recompense. Because truly, the good and the wise require no further reward—they already find their rich and exalted reward within themselves. Who would not happily give up everything in order to enjoy the blessedness of being perfectly good! There could come a time when all state religions and churches will be carried to their graves; but poetry and love—whose bloom is the *true* religion, just as virtue is their fruit—must rule the human spirit for all eternity in their holy trinity: the worship of God as the origin of all existence, the admiration of nature as his lofty work, and the love of humanity as our brethren. This alone is *Christ's* teaching—never expressed more purely, ardently, simply, and yet profoundly, although in keeping with the forms and assumptions of his own time. And for this reason he has become the seed *from which springs the fruit of all time*, the true mediator, whose teachings, as we must hope, will become Christianity in reality and not just in name. . . .

(There is a gap in the letters here; they begin again on the 28th.—*The Editor.*)

Capel Curig, late evening, July 28th

SINCE THE WEATHER cleared up and the friends I was expecting did not arrive, I hurried to take advantage of the sun's first rays to make my way more deeply into the mountains. Thus at about seven in the evening, with no servant, I headed off toward the mountain pass leading to Capel Curig in an Irish car pulled by a single horse, carrying nothing but my light portmanteau containing a few linens and a change of clothes. These cars consist of an open box resting on four horizontal ribs standing on two wheels; each is fitted with two opposed benches where four passengers can fit quite comfortably. You climb on from the rear, since the door is situated between the wheels. The whole is very light and convenient.

The moment was exceptionally favorable. Nearly a week of steady rain had swollen the waterfalls, rivers, and streams so that they were at their loveliest; trees and grass had donned their most luscious green, and the air had become as pure and transparent as crystal. I admired the masses of colorful alpine flowers and heathers growing in profusion in the rocky crevices and regretted knowing so little about botany that I could do no more than enjoy the look of them. I soon reached more serious zones where there could be little talk of flowers and none at all of trees. At the waterfall of Idwal, I got out to look at a small lake not ill suited to serve as the entrance to Hades.

The dreary desolation and wildness of the deep rocky cauldron is truly horrific. I had read that it was possible to get to Capel Curig in a straight line from here by way of the Tryfan (the mountain with the basalt columns I wrote you about) and its surrounding rocks, but the passage was described as very difficult, if also extremely beautiful. Since a shepherd was just then coming down out of the mountains, I felt greatly tempted to try this route with the guide that chance had so obligingly provided. I had the postilion explain my wishes to him, but he thought it was already too late and the descent on the other side too dangerous to attempt at night. After further urging, however, he said that the moon would soon be shining, and if I followed him briskly enough, we could probably cover the distance in two hours, although there were some precarious spots to be negotiated. Having been reassured by my strength on Snowdon, this did not frighten me, so I settled the transaction, instructing the postilion to wait one hour for me as a precaution, in the event I might be forced to turn back, and if not to continue on the road to Capel Curig.

From the very beginning, we had to clamber up steeply over marshy ground between the enormous boulders that were strewn all around. It was probably about seven thirty, and there was no trace of a path. Tryfan lifted its grotesque peaks before us like a crenellated wall (see Figure 75), and nowhere could we make out how we might get across it. Here the mountain sheep did us a real favor as they scrambled ahead of us, repeatedly showing my often faltering guide the most passable course. After a quarter hour's exhausting climb and many dizzying glimpses into the depths (to which one soon grows indifferent), we arrived at a small plateau consisting of just a bog, which we waded through, sinking up to our knees in the quagmire. From here there was a beautiful view of the sea, the Isle of Man, and—dimly resting on the horizon—Ireland. A completely different terrain awaited us just beyond the bog: a dreaded, compact wall of stones, lying on a diagonal, that required us to clamber along on our hands and feet. The sun, already hidden behind a high mountain to the side of us, was spreading a dark red, fiery glow on the wall to which we clung and over the entire wild landscape, one of the most marvelous effects of sunlight I have ever seen. It was like a stage set of hell.

Next we crossed a swollen mountain stream on a natural bridge of collapsed blocks of stone, and then continued over completely barren rocks until we finally reached the high ridge that had been rising in front of us for so long, where I expected all of our difficulties to end. I was therefore not a little perturbed to be faced with yet another deeply plunging ravine, into which we had to descend and then climb back out of; the only shorter route was along the top edge of the ridge's half-moon curve, where no human foot could find purchase. By now we had lost our earlier view of the sea and were instead looking inland, where the full expanse of the Welsh mountains lay before us in ranks, peak after peak, solitary, silent, and mighty! The barren valley below was filled with nothing but giant boulders hurled down in a disorderly jumble. The revolution that was once played out here with rocks in place of balls must truly have been a spectacle for the gods! Meanwhile, lost in thought and marveling at this chaos, I heard a shrill cry repeated over and over, and looking up, saw two majestic eagles with outstretched wings soaring above us, a rarity in these mountains. "Welcome, my faithful heraldic birds," I cried out, "here where there are no duplicitous human hearts but only grim rocks, do you, like the roc bird, want to carry me off to a valley of diamonds, or are you bringing me news from my dear and faraway home?"[9] These creatures seemed to respond to me with their continuous calls, but unfortunately I am not well enough versed in bird language, and so they left, circling higher and higher until they disappeared between the columns of Tryfan. I interpret the repeated attentions of these birds of prey as a good omen.

It was extremely awkward that conversation with my guide was no more successful than with the eagles, for he knew not a word of English. We therefore had to make ourselves understood through signs and by this means descended for a while with relative ease until he pointed to the place where we had to turn our steps next: the *evil passage*. This consisted of a perpendicular wall that descended at least six hundred feet and, rising above it, a slope almost as steep, washed by rain and strewn with small, loose stones, across which we were supposed to make our way for about fifteen hundred paces. Earlier I would have considered this undertaking unfeasible but, forced by necessity, I found it very easy after my first apprehensive steps. It looked treacherous, to be sure, but the many stones and damp soft ground offered a firmer footing than expected. When such feats are described, even without exaggeration, they always sound more perilous than they really are. It is true that just *one* false step would bring inescapable disaster, but that is why you are careful not to take one. You would also drown in the water if you stopped swimming. Really, whoever can walk and is levelheaded can manage such a thing without danger.

Now dusk began to fall, the mountains were becoming hazier, and below us were the lakes near Capel Curig and Beddgelert,[10] sending up their mist like a couple of bubbling tureens. We had reached the highest point and hurried down as best we could to Capel Curig. Once more we waded through a bog and scrambled over rocks until we reached the part of the path that looked the least difficult but was the most tiring—a smooth and firm alpine pasture, very steep and with a rocky subsoil that at many points broke through the surface in broad sheets. Over much of this sloping ground, we slid more than walked and the strain on our knees finally became so painful that both my guide and I fell down several times in the dimness, although without doing ourselves any harm. The circle of lofty mountains had been hiding the moon, but now it rose large and bloodred above their wavy silhouette. We soon lost sight of it again, and only when we were close to the shore where our inn stands did we see it once more, now golden yellow, small and clear, mirrored in the still waters of the lake. The last part of our route followed a level road and, in comparison with the earlier path, was so effortless that I could have fallen asleep while walking. It was as if my steps were involuntary, driven on by some mechanism, like a child's windup toy that runs around on the table without stopping. We had completed our tour in one and three-quarter hours. Very proud of this accomplishment, I arrived in Capel Curig, where the innkeeper could hardly believe we had covered the course in such a short time and at night. I have grown so soft in the last few years that I was starting to think of myself as almost old, but to my joy, today's experience proved that I only need some inducement to feel freshly invigorated in mind and body. And in fact, whenever circumstances have presented me with both danger and adversity, it has always proved highly beneficial.

My postboy had not yet arrived with the carriage, and I therefore had to make use of the stout innkeeper's wardrobe for a needed change of clothes. I must look pretty bizarre in them. While my own garments dry before the fire, I am alternately writing to you and consuming my evening tea. Tomorrow I am supposed to rise from the feathers at four o'clock in order to seek out—guess what!—the rock of Merlin the wizard, the spot where he prophesied future events for King Vortigern and where his wondrous treasures—the golden throne and diamond sword— still lie buried in hidden caves.[11] This might offer a new and much more secure speculation for the mining entrepreneurs in London and Elberfeld!

Beddgelert, July 29th, early

ADMIRE MERLIN'S VALLEYS with me, dear Julie. They are, in fact, *enchanting*—although it is his rocky crag, Dinas Emrys, that I will remember! But let me tell you about them in order.

First, although I did not go to bed until one o'clock, I got up promptly at four in the morning. In ten minutes I was ready to travel, because once you do away with servants and luxuries, everything happens much more quickly and easily. The good weather had already transformed itself into the customary mist of these mountains, and my umbrella, which I used yesterday only as a walking stick, served me well as a shelter in the open carriage. So did that veteran of my battles against the French, my fifteen-year-old cloak—an esteemed relic that I was once forced to toss from a high-flying balloon along with a lot of other ballast to avoid ending my aerial journey in the water.[12]

At the beginning, the road was rather bleak and uninteresting, but then we got to the foot of Snowdon, where, above the low-hanging cloud that was sprinkling on us, the mountain magnanimously revealed its peak. It looks especially majestic as it rises almost perpendicularly out of the deep valley of Gwynant, which begins here. This abundantly watered valley combines the most luxurious vegetation with the most sublime views, with the highest mountains in Wales grouped around it in a myriad of forms and colors. The course of the river flowing through it forms two lakes that are not particularly wide and therefore all the deeper, for the valley is narrow throughout, something that emphasizes even more the immensity of the giants surrounding it. In the most sumptuous region of the valley, a merchant from Chester has a park that he has not unjustly named Elysium. On a bright meadow above the river, atop a high, thickly wooded mountain ridge, its dark green interrupted by many strangely shaped rocks that protrude almost competitively, stands the unassuming, pleasant villa. It looks over the lake stretching out far below, and behind, in total isolation, Merlin's enchanted rock seems to close off the valley, which at this point makes an abrupt bend.

Dinas Emrys will always be doubly fixed in my memory: first, for its romantic beauty, and second, because I literally hung from it, suspended between life and death. Although no higher than four or five hundred feet, it is nonetheless considered accessible only from one side. I had brought along a small boy as my guide, but once he reached the spot, he seemed unsure of himself. The path he took through the oak thicket looked suspicious to me from the very beginning, due to its extraordinary steepness; but he calmed my fears in broken English, and I could do nothing but follow the little chamois as best I could. Merlin seemed to be angry with us; a fierce wind came up, and the sun, after shining on us for a moment, settled down behind black clouds, and the long wet grass hanging over the blocks of stone made climbing very dangerous. This did not seem to disturb the barefoot little boy much, but it bothered my limbs, still somewhat stiff from yesterday. The higher we climbed, the steeper the rocks became; often we could only swing ourselves up with the help of the bushes growing from the crevices while doing our best to avoid looking back. Finally I noticed that the lad himself had become altogether uncertain and, crawling on his belly, was looking around anxiously, first in one direction, then another. We now wriggled our way left and right through a few crevices until we were suddenly standing at the peak of a smooth, high wall with hardly enough space to set a foot down, while above us was nothing but a similar wall of stone with just a few tufts of grass growing on it. It led to the summit, which it seemed to surround.

It was a disheartening sight, and the child started to cry while I considered with a pounding heart what might be done. I confess that I would have been happy to turn back and leave Merlin's rock to the witches and gnomes if I had thought it possible to descend by the way we'd come up without becoming dizzy or even to locate the same path again. But in front of us there was no prospect of advancing any farther other than by scaling the wall on the off chance of success. The boy, being lighter and more nimble, had to go first; I followed hard on his heels, and holding on to tufts of grass as our only support, our hands and feet digging like claws in every tiny crack—thus hanging between heaven and earth—with luck we reached the breakneck pinnacle. I was totally exhausted and almost faint when I made it to the top. A bolder man may mock me, but when a tuft of grass or root seemed to shift in my hand and threaten to break away before I could swing myself up, I understood the meaning of *terror*. Then, as I lay panting on the grass, I caught sight of a large black lizard stretched out opposite me, looking my way with apparent scorn, as if it were the spiteful enchanter himself in his dressing gown. But I was happy to let it do as it liked and was feeling in very good spirits at having gotten off so easily. I did, however, threaten the little imp who had, after all, led me into danger like a teasing mountain goblin, and I promised him every possible horror if he did not scout out the right way back. During his absence I took a look at the rest of the area, as it is called here, the demolished walls, where:

Prophetic Merlin sat, when to the British King
The changes long to come, auspiciously he told.[13]

I rooted around in the piles of stones, I crept into the tumbledown vaults, but the treasures remained hidden from me, just as from other good people. Clearly the right moment has not yet arrived. But as recompense the triumphant boy appeared, extolling the beauty of the route he had finally found. If it was not in fact quite as smooth and easy as the pathway to sin, it was at least accessible, unlike the previous one. Merlin's disfavor continued to hound us, however. A downpour of torrential rain forced me to use the fireplace here in Beddgelert as a drying facility again. The really charming inn where I am staying is completely tucked away beneath tall trees, with a green, freshly mown meadow just in front of my window. Behind this a monstrous mountain flaunts itself, covered from top to bottom with crimson heather that glows like the rosy dawn in spite of the streaming rain and overcast sky. While my midday meal is being prepared (for today, like Suvorov, I am eating my dinner at eight in the morning), a harpist—humble relic of the Welsh bards—is playing original tunes on his age-old instrument. He is blind, as is the dog standing on his hind legs beside him, tirelessly entreating a coin for his master and a piece of bread for himself. *Beddgelert* means "Gellert's grave," for in the Welsh language, bed and grave are poetically expressed by the same word. Your sharp wit has certainly already guessed that this is not a reference to the German writer. In fact, not at all, since it refers to the resting place of a hound.[14] But the story is so touching that I will relate it to you as soon as my breakfast-dinner has been cleared away, for my anxiety on that cursed rock has made me desperately hungry.

Après dîner

HERE IS THE promised tale.

Llywelyn the Great, Prince of Wales, had a favorite dog named Gelert, a terror for wolves but his master's joy. When Llywelyn married a young and beautiful wife, the hound, as was proper, was removed to the background, but remained, though less loved, devotedly loyal to his master, with an unwavering, canine-like faithfulness (*car les hommes ne sont pas si bêtes!*).[15] Llywelyn's most fervent wish was granted and a beloved son crowned his marital bliss. The infant now had to follow his overjoyed father everywhere he went, and his cradle was placed next to the prince's own bed. When the princess was indisposed on one occasion and thus unable to accompany her husband on a hunting expedition in the rugged mountains, he insisted that his son, attended by a wet nurse, go with him. They spent the night in a miserable hut and leaving early the next day for the hunt, Llywelyn entrusted his boy for just those few hours to the care of the wet nurse and his loyal Gelert. Given the profound peace then prevailing in the land, he had no worry that his son would be in any danger. The wet nurse, beguiled by the same feeling of security, took quick advantage of her freedom to visit her lover nearby, so only the dog kept to his duty with strict obedience. Thus he became the boy's savior, because a wolf, sensing the isolation of the building, had approached with stealth and was already appraising the sleeping child as his defenseless prey when Gelert sprang forward and after a long fight, in which he was seriously wounded, overcame and killed his foe. Drenched in blood, he placed himself at the foot of the cradle, alternately licking the infant's delicate little hands and his own wounds. At this moment Llwelyn returned with his hunting spear still in his hand, entered the room, and was horrified by the sight of his son covered in blood and the hound bent over the cradle. Deluded by his dismay and fury, thinking in a rage that the dog had murdered his son, he plunged the barbed lance into Gelert's faithful breast. With his eyes turned plaintively to his master, wagging his tail adoringly in a final gesture of submissiveness, the poor animal departed with a heartrending howl of pain. Hardly had his last sigh died away when Llywelyn caught sight of the dead wolf stretched out on the floor and of his son smiling gently in his cradle. According to legend, faithful Gelert's final cry haunted the distressed prince day and night forever after. He had a monument built in the dog's memory, and today there is still an old Gothic church on the site, where, for a very long time, the prince performed acts of severe penance. He even sought to build a new castle nearby on Merlin's rock, but was never able to carry it out, for whatever went up in the day sank back into the earth at night. Neither then nor since has the jealous enchanter allowed anyone to defile his abode.

The sun is shining again, for here April lasts the whole year, *et je pars. Adieu.*

Caernarfon, July 30th, 1828

DURING MY DINNER in Beddgelert, I kept the harpist playing diligently and amused myself like a child with the musician's dog; standing on two legs had become so much second nature to him that he would have served better than a plucked chicken to represent Platonic man.[16] His earnest expression and total *aisance* of pose were somehow so comical that you only had to imagine him dressed in a petticoat with a snuffbox in his paw to swear he was a blind old lady. Just as this dog resembles the heroic Gelert, so may the modern Welsh be seen to resemble their ancestors. Lacking the energy and industriousness of the English, still less animated by the fire of the Irish, they vegetate somewhere between the two, poor and isolated. But the simplicity of the mountains remains with them, and they are not so coarse nor do they cheat so unashamedly as the Swiss. The aphorism *point d'argent, point de Suisse* does not yet apply.[17] On the contrary, people live so frugally here that bankrupt Englishmen often spend their last days in Wales, where they are free to hunt, have the use of a pony, and find good food and lodging for fifty guineas a year.

The region around Beddgelert is the final stretch of the gorgeous valley I described to you, which is enlivened at this moment by hundreds of waterfalls that plummet down, white and frothy as milk, in every mountain gorge. A half hour behind the village, the rocks are so close together that there is scarcely room left for the river and road to run alongside each other. Here the Devil's Bridge arches up and closes the valley, or rather the ravine into which it empties.[18] From this point on you are approaching the sea again, and for quite a while the landscape takes on a cheerful character. In two hours, I reached the valley of Tan-y-Bwlch, so popular with tourists. Its main attraction is a lovely park spread out across two rugged mountains covered with tall trees; coursing between them is a torrential stream that forms a variety of cascades. The walkway in this park is superbly laid out, leading in suitable gradations and diversions to various viewpoints, from which you first glimpse an island in the distant sea, then a nearby precipice with a frothing waterfall, next a faraway peak, and later a solitary outcropping of rock beneath the darkness of primeval oaks. I wandered for more than an hour along these paths, although I was amazed to find the whole neglected to such a degree that most everywhere I had to wade through high grass and force my way through overgrown plantings. The house seemed dilapidated as well. I later learned that the owner had lost his fortune gambling in London![19]

Since I feared losing too much time, I gave up the idea of visiting Ffestiniog and its renowned waterfalls, hired a fresh sociable* and horse from the innkeeper, and made my way to Tremadog, a very rewarding ten-mile journey, although the road was the worst I have yet come across in Great Britain. For a few miles, it actually led through the sea, or at least through a part of it that a rich individual, Mr. Madocks, has blocked off with a monstrous embankment, thereby reclaiming a fertile parcel of terrain the size of a knight's estate. From this embankment, which is twenty feet high and two miles long, the view is magnificent. The drained basin forms a nearly perfect semi-circle, enclosed like an amphitheater by the mountain walls. Here the industrious artistry of man has drawn back the veil from the sea's bed, so that a plow rather than a ship might ply its furrows across the broad expanse. But to the left, the immeasurable ocean still conceals the secrets of its unfathomed depths with surging mountains of water. From this perspective, the coast ends nearby at a bold, rocky promontory, on top of which you can see the ruins of old Harlech Castle, with its five collapsed towers leaning out over the water (Figure 81). In front, however, at the end of the embankment, a pleasing and tranquil valley opens up, nestled among high mountains and with a small but lively harbor, where the village of Tremadog snuggles against the cliffs.

By the way, Julie, dear heart, it is unlikely that you would decide to ride over this embankment, because its structure is suitable only for pedestrians. It is, as I mentioned, twenty feet high and consists of a steep, roughly stacked heap of sharp, angular stones, and the top is only three yards wide, without anything resembling a railing. On one side the breakers assault it furiously, and if your horses were to spook, you would inevitably be skewered by the jagged tips of slate. Only mountain horses can move safely on such roadways, since they seem able to gauge the danger and are used to it. And yet you seldom see a carriage here. The only thing leading across the embankment is a railway for rock carts, which makes it significantly more difficult for other vehicles to cross.

Tremadog itself stands on a seabed reclaimed somewhat earlier through a similar operation. At close range it is striking how much this area—dry land for only a few centuries—resembles the sandy regions of northern Germany, themselves partly freed from the sea for hardly more than a thousand years. As if like soil produces like character, the little town and its inhabitants seem totally related to the dour features of that country: bleak, neglected, and dirty, the people shabbily dressed, the inn no better than in Silesia and equally unclean. And just for good measure, the post horses were out to pasture, meaning I had to wait an hour and a half for them, and when they finally arrived, their appearance, the poor condition of their harnesses, as well as the driver's attire, held true to the pattern. But this applies only to the area reclaimed from the sea. A half hour farther along, when you reach the surrounding heights, the scenery reverts to a lovely, fertile landscape. It has admittedly lost the wild and gigantic character of the earlier stretch, but after my long sojourn amid the masses of rock, this sight did me good, especially because the landscape was now illuminated by an evening light of the utmost brilliance and clarity. The sun cast such a golden glow on the emerald meadows, the wooded hills were so peacefully settled around a crystal-bright stream as if at rest, and scattered huts were perched so invitingly on their shady slopes that you immediately felt you could stay there forever! I had gone ahead of the carriage on foot, and resting on soft moss under a tall nut tree, I joyfully abandoned myself to daydreams. The evening light twinkled effervescently like sparks through the thick foliage, and a hundred tiny, teeming insects played in its rosy beams, while in the treetops, the soft wind murmured in

---

* A kind of four-seated, light *calèche* without a roof.

Pl.34

HARLECH CASTLE in MERIONETH-SHIRE.

melodies that an accustomed listener comprehends with sweet delight. Then the carriage arrived. **81**
Once more I cast a yearning glance at the deep blue sea; once more I drank in the fragrance of the *Harlech Castle.*
mountain flowers; and then the horses carried this dawdler quickly down to the lowlands.

From this point on we were in a well-cultivated region, and everything that was romantic about the road came to a complete end until the towers of Caernarfon Castle emerged from the twilight above the treetops. I am thinking of resting here a few days, since from four o'clock this morning until ten tonight I covered seventy-four miles, partly in a carriage and partly on foot.

August 1st, 1828

EARLY TODAY I received some letters from you that made me sad! Of course you are right: it was a harsh trial of fate that disrupted the most serene happiness, the most perfect concord, which, like a storm stirring up a tranquil sea, tore apart the two souls that fit together better than any in the world (moreover, while both went on pursuing their own, particular interests). Indeed, for a time, it nearly destroyed their spirits, condemning one to restless wandering, the other to comfortless solitude, and both to grief, worry, pain, and longing! But was the storm not inevitable for those sea dwellers? Would totally motionless air not be more damaging to them? So let us not mourn too much, nor *regret* what is past, which is always futile. Let us simply strive onward to something better and, even in the worst moments, not lose our way. How often are imaginary evils the most difficult to bear! What searing pains are aroused by wounded vanity, what tormented shame is inflicted by false notions of honor! I am not faring any better, and often I wish I could adopt Falstaff's philosophy. Meanwhile nature has bestowed another gift on me, which I happily convey to you. I find the *good* side in every situation, quickly and almost instinctively, and I enjoy it with a freshness of emotion, with a child's Christmas Day joy in trifles that I will certainly never outgrow. Where, over time, will good not significantly outweigh evil? This conviction is the bedrock of my piety. God's gifts are infinite, and one might even say it is irresponsible of us not to be happy. If we look back at our past lives, we can see how much is within our own power and how easily we could have turned almost every evil into a good. As I have said to you before and often: we make our own destiny. We have not, of course, made ourselves, and a vast unknown lurks there; but to rack our brains over it would lead to nothing. All of us, with renewed courage and without exception, must simply do our best to take the outward things of this world *lightly*, because the things of this world, good or bad, weigh very little. There is no better defense, although we should not therefore sit with our hands in our laps.

Your womanly error, good Julie, is that when times are bad you rely solely on the dear Lord, but with a frail kind of devoutness, trusting in a deus ex machina. If such help fails to materialize, however, there is no escape from destruction. Yet pious *hope* and hearty action work well together. And there is no doubt that the first of these makes the second much easier. Because if the kind of piety as generally known in the world—that secure confidence in special earthly protection from above, that appeal for goodness or against evil—is nothing but self-deception, it is nonetheless benevolent. Indeed it is perhaps grounded in our very nature, given that we are subject to so many illusions, which, if we truly believe in them, become individual truths for us. It seems that wherever reality is no longer sufficient, we have in our nature the capacity to *create* an *imaginary* reality that we make for ourselves as a helpful prop. Thus a pious faith in special protection, even though no more than a form of superstition, can provide courage. If you go into battle convinced that a talisman has made you invulnerable, you no longer pay attention to the bullets. Even more effective is our enthusiasm for the ideas that elevate our egos to a commanding position above the material world. We have often seen religious fanatics who, when so inspired, have overcome the most unbearable physical pain with truly miraculous power. Similarly, those who suffer and are oppressed generate blissful hope for future happiness, and this rewards them even here.

All this results from the powerful instinct for individual self-preservation in its broadest sense—an instinct that avails itself of the abovementioned capacity of our nature wherever required. Finally, in the case of *weak* characters, this can lead to deathbed conversions—admittedly useless *an sich* but nonetheless comforting to such souls. In the end, each of us must pay tribute to this need in one form or another. That is, each makes his own earthly God, and this is also an ever-repeated incarnation of God. Certainly the concept of the all-loving father is in general the most beautiful of these constructs, and as humans, we can take it no higher. One must admit that the mere idea of the lofty principle of all things being spiritualized—one might say, evaporated—into the incomprehensible, the unutterable, no longer warms the sensitive human heart, aware of its own weakness, with the same intensity.

It often seems to me, by the way, that what really constitutes man and nature can be traced back to just two primary elements: love and fear, which we might also call the divine and the earthly. All thoughts, feelings, passions, and actions arise from these, either from one or a mixture of the two principles. Love is the *divine* cause of all things; fear seems to be their *earthly* advocate. The saying "you should love and fear God" must be interpreted like this, or it makes no sense, because unmixed love, being the very opposite of egotism, *cannot* fear; indeed, when it truly fills our soul, it becomes one with God and the universe, and we do have moments when we sense this.

If I apply this same standard to all human actions, I find it confirmed everywhere. Love creates; fear preserves and destroys. Throughout the whole of nature, I see how the principle of self-preservation (or fear, since they are one and the same), is founded on what we, in our *human* moral code, would have to call evil, that is, the destruction of another's individuality. One species always survives by destroying the other; life comes into being only through death, to all eternity of appearance, which remains, in this way, a unity in perpetual change.[20]

It is also worth acknowledging that this fear, so essential to each of us in our earthly existence, is so undervalued by the divine in us that we hold *cowardice* to be the most *contemptible* of crimes. On the other hand, nothing conquers fear better than a great idea that springs from the kingdom of love. A person inspired in this way carries others along with him, and entire peoples are willingly swept along as well, although nothing of this world can remain entirely free of some admixture of the baser principle. Thus fear *comes into being* in time and space; love simply *is* and knows no time or space. Love is never ending and blessed, fear dies an eternal death. Love is God, fear is the devil—and we all know that more than half the world belongs to him.

Kinmel Park, August 2nd, 1828

YESTERDAY, WHEN I returned to Bangor, I made the acquaintance of the owner of Penrhyn Castle (the black Saxon palace I described to you),[21] a man who shares my passionate affinity for architecture.[22] Work on the structure has been going on for seven years already, at an annual cost of twenty thousand pounds, and it may well take four more years to bring it to completion. Meanwhile this rich man is living with his family in an extremely plain cottage he has rented not far away, and he associates with only a few people. Still he goes once a week to feast his eyes on his fairy castle, even though he will probably never bring himself to inhabit it, accustomed as he is to such a simple life. He seemed very happy to show and explain everything to me, and my own pleasure was no less due to *his* enthusiasm, which was quite becoming in this otherwise cold man.

Responding to an invitation received a while ago in London that has since been insistently renewed, I drove here early this morning. At first the road leads through a fertile meadowland between the bay and the foot of the mountains, where sometimes a ravine suddenly opens and torrential streams hurry off to the sea. At Penmaenmawr, however, the roadway has been blasted out of the rocks and narrows to a difficult pass, plunging perpendicularly on the left, at times even overhanging the five-hundred-foot drop to the waves. An indispensable walled parapet safeguards the carriages. I sat on the upper deck, a place I often occupy when the weather is good, and from here I was totally free to enjoy the wide vista of the sea. The wind kept up its whistling in every possible tone, and I barely managed to hang on to my cloak. In an hour I reached Conwy,

View of the Suspension Bridge, Erected at Conway, North Wales, Looking towards the Castle.

*Conwy Castle and
Suspension Bridge.*

its situation among the most captivating I have ever seen. The fortified castle is the largest of all those built by Edward I and destroyed by Cromwell. Due as much to the surroundings as to its own particular beauty, it is also the most romantic (Figure 82).

Although the outer ramparts are in ruins, they remain standing with all their thirty-two towers. The whole of the newer town, a strange but not unpicturesque mix of old and new, is located within the periphery of these walls. The castle rises on the rocky banks of the Conwy River, across which a chain bridge with pillars in the form of Gothic towers was recently built, adding yet more to the magnificence and strangeness of the scene. The surrounding country-side is splendid, with wooded hills opposite the ruins and even higher ones towering up behind. Many country houses adorn the slopes, among them an enchanting villa bearing the seductive name Contentment, which has just been offered for sale.

Within the castle you can still see the royal chambers, as well as the imposing ruins of the banquet hall containing two fireplaces as tall as houses.[23] In the queen's closet one can admire a rather well preserved and beautifully worked private altar as well as a magnificent oriel window. In the town are also some remarkable old buildings, with wonderful carvings in wood that look like fantastic hieroglyphs. According to the inscription on a tombstone in the church, one of these houses was built in the fourteenth century by a certain Hookes, his father's forty-first son, a rare occurrence in Christendom! A large baby in swaddling clothes, borne by a stork, was therefore carved in old oak and installed as a wall decoration everywhere possible.

Conwy is also commendable from a gastronomic point of view. There is an extremely tasty local fish with firm yet tender flesh called plaice, a most appropriate name, as if it were calling out "A place for me. I'm better than the rest of you!" I wish I could grant it the place of honor at my table more often.

I left Conwy in good time by way of the suspension bridge, which serves as a venerable fulcrum for the ruined castle.[24] The immense chains vanish so fabulously into the rock-solid towers that you would hardly notice the bridge's newness, except for the unfortunate tollhouse built just opposite in the form of a diminutive castle, a clown-like version of the large one. The closer you get to St Asaph, the gentler the look of the countryside. In a semicircular bay that you can scarcely see across, the placid sea washes against fields and meadows, frequently intermingled with towns and villages. All the local landowners seem to subscribe to the Gothic taste. This mania has been taken so far that even a tavern by the side of the road was outfitted with portcullises, embrasures, and *créneaux,* although apart from the hens and geese, there was no garrison to defend. Don Quixote would have fit right in here. Indeed the host would do well to embellish his signboard with an image of that hapless knight, with his couched lance and a barber's basin for a helmet.

Farther ahead a mountain ridge appeared, looking as if it were entirely covered by a Gothic town. From a distance, the effect was so striking that I let myself be tempted to get out of the carriage and scramble up the arduous path. It was both comical and annoying to discover that the hub of this frivolity was just a small, undistinguished house. The rest of it was no more than walls built on the mountain and its slopes in imitation of towers, roofs, and enormous battlements half hidden in the woods. From up close it became clear they served only to enclose a lot of fruit and vegetable gardens. I was told that some lucky devil, a shopkeeper, having gotten rich entirely by chance, had built this harmless robber's citadel only two years earlier—a true satire on the prevailing taste!

Toward evening I arrived at the house of my good colonel, a true Englishman in the best sense.[25] He and his engaging family received me in the friendliest manner. These esteemed and well-to-do landowners (at home they would be considered very rich) make up the most truly respectable class of Englishmen: they are not in London anxiously pursuing fashion, but endeavor to win the affection of their neighbors and subordinates; their hospitality is not just a form of ostentation, nor are their manners exclusive or exotic; they find satisfaction in a civilized domesticity, a dignified affluence supplemented by strict integrity. In the great world of London, they may well play an insignificant role, but in humanity at large, they definitely play a venerable one. Yet in England the dominance of the aristocracy, their arrogance, and the prevalence of fashion itself, are so overwhelming that even families such as this one would likely feel less flattered to read my words of praise than if I listed them among those who set the tone. It is hard to believe the extent of this weakness among the most worthy people here without having experienced it and having seen how all classes are infected by it in the most ludicrous ways. But I have written you enough on this topic from the very foyer of European aristocracy, and I do not want to repeat myself. In any case, it is high time to close this letter, since I am already worried that our correspondence might be straining your patience—for even if the heart does not tire, the head responds otherwise. Nevertheless, I know I can rely on your indulgence.

Your eternally faithful and devoted Lou

Kinmel Park, August 4th, 1828

M Y MOST PRECIOUS friend,

I am feeling most content with my situation. One lives comfortably, the food is excellent, the company warmhearted, and—as always in the countryside here—the sense of freedom complete. Yesterday I went for a very pleasant ride on one of my host's indefatigable horses and covered some twenty miles, for these fine mounts and good roads make the distances disappear.

I must tell you about everything. First I rode to the small town of St Asaph in order to visit the cathedral. It is adorned with a large window of modern stained glass containing many very well-executed coats of arms, with no misguided attempt to represent objects in a manner unsuited to an art form that requires dazzling masses of color without any blurry nuances. To better orient myself, I climbed the tower and from there noticed a church-like building on the summit of a high mountain about twelve miles away. I asked the verger what it was, and he responded in awkward English, "That is the tabernacle of the king, and anyone is allowed to live there if he is willing to go for seven years without washing or cutting his nails or trimming his beard. After the seventh year, he has the right to go to London, where the king must provide for him and make him into a gentleman." The man earnestly believed this mad fairy tale and swore it was true. *Voilà ce que c'est la foi.*[1] When I enquired afterward about the actual history of this structure, I learned only that one of the county's districts had built it to mark the jubilee of the previous king's reign, and the sanctuary had stood empty ever since. But it seems that elsewhere some buffoon advertised in the newspapers an offer of a considerable sum to anyone who could live under those same conditions in a cave belonging to him. The common people proceeded to associate that unlikely ordeal with the tabernacle of good King George III.

I climbed back down the tower, and now you can watch me galloping along the foot of some gentle slopes until I reach a solitary, rocky hill and the ruins of Denbigh Castle. The dilapidated houses and huts of the wretched little village cling to the hillside all around, and you reach the top after a toilsome climb through narrow lanes (Figure 83). The gentleman who graciously showed me the way and did the honors of the ruins with great charm later revealed himself to be the town surgeon. The local dignitaries have set a kind of performance space most romantically inside the compound, along with a very pretty little flower garden from which there is an excellent view. The remainder of the rambling castle, on the other hand, offers only an abandoned labyrinth of walls and grassy areas where thistles grow rampant. Nonetheless, every three years a large national festival—the congress of the Welsh bards—is held at this spot, and like the former Minnesingers of Germany, all the harpists of Wales congregate for a competition. The victor wins a golden cup, and a communal chorus of a hundred harps echoes his praises throughout

83
Denbigh Castle.

the ruins. The next meeting is supposed to take place in three months, and the Duke of Sussex is expected to attend.

Continuing on along a ravine, I came to an absolutely beautiful valley. The deep night of the forest enveloped me; rocks greeted me like old friends, stretching their mossy heads out of the branches; the wild river foamed, skipping and dancing through the woodland flowers; and secluded meadows flashed furtively at me, gleaming with all the golden freshness of the mountains. After wandering around the area for several hours, I climbed to the top on an arduous footpath in order to discover my actual location. I was standing right over the bay, and behind lay the broad, calm sea, which the gentle mountain slopes before me seemed to bring closer than it really was. With considerable effort I discovered the house of Kinmel Park among the groups of trees on the plain, and I went toward it at a quick trot, arriving in good time to dress for my midday meal.

August 5th, 1828

THIS MORNING, SINCE everyone else was still sleeping, I took a walk around the park and garden with the delightful young Fanny, who showed me her dairy and aviary. She is the youngest daughter of the house and has not yet come out.*

---

* In the case of young girls in England, "to come out" means to enter the world. Parents let many daughters wait for this happiness until they are twenty or even older. Before then they learn about the world only

I have already written you that a dairy is one of the main adornments of every park here, usually taking the form of an elegant pavilion that stands alone, quite removed from the cowsheds, and is decorated with fountains, marble walls, and valuable porcelain bowls, large and small, which are filled with all kinds of the most beautiful milk and other dairy products. There is no better spot than this to refresh yourself after a tiring walk. It goes without saying that there will be a little flower garden, something the English like to add to any building. In *this* one, the splendid colors of the mineral kingdom compete with those of the flowers, for the owner has a share in an important copper works in Anglesey, and hence little mountains of this ore— shimmering in iridescent flashes of gold, red, blue, and green—provide a magnificent bed for rare wintergreen and other plants.

The aviary, normally dedicated to golden pheasants and exotic birds, was here of a solely economic sort and intended exclusively for hens, geese, peacocks, doves, and ducks. But it was nonetheless a very pleasant sight due to its extraordinary cleanliness and functionality. All you German wives and housekeepers, listen and be amazed! The yards—which are equipped with the finest watering arrangements—as well as the individual rooms, dovecotes, and brooding pens are all scrubbed twice a day; and the straw beds for the hens are so pretty, the staves on which they perch so smooth and clean; the duck ponds bordered by rectangular stones such clear basins; and the large-grained barley and the boiled rice (like Parisian *riz au lait*) so appetizing that you might think you have entered a birds' paradise. And in this paradise there are no clipped wings; all the birds are free. A small grove of tall trees stands immediately adjacent to their quarters, an utterly charming pleasure ground. As we approached, most of the feathered inhabitants were still swaying contentedly on the upper branches. But hardly had they caught sight of the little, rosy-cheeked Fanny, coming toward them like a beneficent fairy with delicious tidbits in her apron, than they hurtled down in a blustery cloud and settled at her feet, pecking and exulting. I felt touched by a kind of idyllic warmth, and turned toward home to recuperate from the flash of my ardor before settling down to breakfast. But there were still the children's gardens to be seen, a *Haus der Laune*,[2] and God knows what else. In brief, we arrived too late and were scolded. Miss Fanny exclaimed, with true English pathos:

> *We do but row—*
> *And we are steered by fate.*[3]

In other words: *Der Mensch denkt, Gott lenkt.*[4] And yes indeed, I thought, the little philosopher was only too right! Things never turn out the way you think they will, even regarding such insignificant events as taking a walk with a pretty girl while her parents wait for you at breakfast.

The afternoon saw me back on my horse again. I blazed my own trails in the wildest mountain areas of the interior, repeatedly fording the torrential stream and often reveling in the most beautiful and surprising vistas. Now and then I would come upon country girls alone at work. They are strikingly pretty in their quaint costumes, which accentuate their figures and reveal their bosoms very openly; at the same time, they are as timid as roe deer and as chaste as vestal virgins. Everything exhibits the character of the mountains—my horse, too! Never tiring,

---

through novels, and their lives often proceed accordingly, wherever domesticity and virtue (for such a thing does sometimes exist in England) have not provided a solid foundation.—*The Editor.*

like a machine made of steel and iron, he gallops up and down the rocky slopes and springs with undisturbed composure over the hedgerows that repeatedly bar my way. He exhausts me long before feeling any fatigue himself. This is the right way to go riding—to venture many miles away through regions you have never seen, not knowing where you will end up, and then having to find your way back along a different route. Today I at last came to a park where wooden statues, painted white, contrasted strangely with the solemnity of nature. There were no human beings to be seen, just hundreds of rabbits, either sticking their heads out of the holes that riddle the mountainside or racing across my path. There was much evidence that the owner was an eccentric, the most noticeable being a dark spruce wood completely surrounded by a ring of brilliantly colored mallows. I finally emerged onto a high, barren plateau and exited as I had entered, through a self-closing portcullis. The same solitude reigned overall, and soon the enchanted castle was far behind me.

Bangor, August 8th, 1828

I WAS SUPPOSED to stay at Kinmel Park for several weeks, but you know my restlessness. I am soon oppressed by uniformity, even when it is good. I therefore took leave of my pleasant friends; paid a visit to another landowner who had invited me, but only for a few hours; watched a sunset from Conwy's ruins, ate a plaice, and returned to my main quarters, which I am about to leave forever. Unfortunately I do not feel very well; my chest seems somewhat affected by the strains of recent days and often hurts quite severely, *mais n'importe*.

Craig-y-Don, August 9th, 1828, early

DO YOU REMEMBER this name? It is the comely villa that I described to you, whose engaging owner I have come to know.[5] I could not resist his congenial invitation to spend my last night in Wales with him. Yesterday evening, because of my chest pains, I was only able to take short walks in the delightful gardens with his son; an attempt at a substantial hill nearby did not agree with me at all, so that afterward I had to amuse myself with the newspapers until supper. In the lengthy mishmash of the press, there was one item I must quote for you. The article was about the king's address to Parliament, in which the following sentence appears: "The Speaker is *commanded* to congratulate the masses on their universal prosperity." The reporter remarks on the insolence of making such blatant fun of these impoverished people, although he goes on to note how it is well established that no one should ever expect honesty in such matters, because if a king or politician were ever so insane as to speak the truth, he would have to replace the conventional salutation "My lords and gentlemen" with "My knaves and dupes."

Our host is a member of a yacht club and a passionate lover of the sea. Therefore our *dîner* would have satisfied each and every Catholic during Lent, for it consisted solely of fish in a variety of excellent preparations. An oyster bed just below the windows also contributed its slippery occupants, still moistened by the seawater. And the cows grazing in front of the house provided for many a delicate dessert, while delicious fruits came from the hothouses adjoining the salon.

Are you not content to think that, in England, hundreds of thousands comfortably enjoy such luxury in their peaceful homes; that they are kings in the bosom of domesticity and live placidly in the quiet assurance that their property is inviolable? These happy people are never pestered by stern communiqués from those impertinent authorities who seek to control everything—even in living rooms and bedrooms—and who believe they have done the state a great service when they manage to burden their poor subjects with many thousand thalers of unnecessary postage each year. Nor are they content to stand *above* the governed, but rather they place themselves in *opposition* to them, uniting as best they can both judge and party in one person. Here, in a word, *fortunate* souls are free from assaults on their purses, free from degradation of their persons, free from the pointless torment of bureaucrats who wish to impose their power, free from the government's insatiable sucking leeches; and, at the same time, as unlimited masters of their own property, they need follow only the laws that they themselves helped legislate! When you consider this, I say, you must admit that England is a blessed land, if not a perfect one. Thus no one can much blame the English when, fully aware of the contrast between their country and others, they persist in treating *foreigners* as *strangers,* despite all apparent politeness and civility. Their fully justified self-assurance is so all-consuming that they instinctively view us as an inferior race, just as we, for example, in spite of our German warmheartedness, would find it difficult to swear eternal friendship to a Sandwich Islander. In a few centuries these roles may well be reversed, but unfortunately we are not there yet!*

Holyhead, August 9th, 1828, evening

I HAD A terrible night—a high fever, bad weather, and rough roads. The latter was because I left the main route in order to visit the renowned Parys Mines on Anglesey (Figure 84). This island is the very opposite of Wales, almost completely flat, not a tree, not even bushes or hedges, but just field after field in rows. The copper mines on the coast are interesting, however. Colonel Hughes had already announced my arrival, so I was greeted by canon volleys echoing wildly in the many shafts where the ore is mined. Wherever daylight enters them, these caverns sparkle with color. I collected several beautiful pieces of the ore for myself. After extraction the stones are pounded into small segments and, as with alum, deposited in heaps, set on fire, and left to burn for nine months. Some of the smoke is collected and forms sulfur. For the uninitiated this is a remarkable phenomenon. During the nine months of burning, all the sulfur is driven out simply through the power of elective affinity activated by the fire.[6] The pure copper, previously distributed throughout the stone, is reduced to a compact little lump in its center, such that when the burned stones are smashed, the copper simply emerges like the kernel in a nutshell. After the burning, again as with alum, the ore is leached or washed, and the water collected in sumps. The powder deposited in these sumps contains 25 to 40 percent copper, and the residual water is so strongly impregnated that an iron key submerged in it will take on a lovely, reddish gold copper color in a manner of seconds. Next the ore is repeatedly smelted and at last refined, then formed into square blocks of one hundred pounds each, to be sold or milled into panels for sheathing vessels.

---

* Nothing is more ridiculous than the repeated declamation of German writers about the poverty reigning in England, where there are, according to them, only a few immensely wealthy people and thousands who are destitute. In fact, it is the extraordinary number of well-to-do people of the *middle class,* and the ease with which the poorest, if they are willing to *work seriously,* can acquire not only necessities but even luxuries, that make England independent and happy. One must absolutely not parrot the opposition newspapers.

During the founding, which makes for a pretty spectacle, a curious thing happens: the molten ore flows into a sand mold that is divided into eight or ten compartments, like a feeding trough intended for several animals. The divisions between molds do not quite reach the height of the sidewalls, so when the plug is removed and the red-hot ore streams in at one end, it must fill the first compartment before flooding into the second, and so forth. The curious aspect of this is that all of the really pure copper contained in the furnace remains in the first compartment, while the others fill up with nothing but slag, which can only be used for road construction. The explanation for this phenomenon is as follows: the ore contains iron in a magnetized state, and this holds the copper together and forces it to flow out first. Since experience has determined with reasonable accuracy how much pure copper ought to be contained in a given amount of material put in the furnace, the size of the first compartment is designed to collect exactly that amount. The inspector, a clever man, informed me half in Welsh and half in English that he had first invented this far more efficient art of founding and had taken out a patent on it. The advantage it offers is certainly evident, because without the divisions between the molds, the copper—even though it flowed out first—would afterward spread through the entire mass and be hard to remove. The Russians, who nowadays miss nothing in the field of industry, have already sent a traveler here to learn the entire process, which in any case has not been kept secret; most factory owners have generally become very liberal in this regard.

While I stood there by the smelting furnace, an officer appeared with a message from Colonel Hughes's brother, who is also a colonel and in command of a Hussar regiment stationed nearby, inviting me for the remainder of the day and the night. But I felt too exhausted and unwell to endure the hazardous business of an officers' *diner* in England, where—at least in the provinces—the wine is poured out in Old English quantities. I was also hoping to sail to Ireland with the packet boat tonight, so I politely declined the invitation and took the road to Holyhead, where I arrived at ten o'clock. But, as typical of my luck with the sea, there was such a violent gale that the packet went off without passengers. I am content, however, to rest for a day in a very comfortable inn.

August 10th, 1828

HOWEVER WEAKENED BY illness I may be, an excursion to the newly built lighthouse four miles away gave me enormous pleasure. Although the Isle of Anglesey appears to be very flat, the exceedingly picturesque, jagged cliffs along the coast of the Irish Sea rise to a significant height above the constant surge of the tides, and a solitary lighthouse stands on its own rocky foundation at a certain distance from the shore. These cliffs, wild beyond all describing, do not just plunge vertically several hundred feet into the sea, they actually undercut the edge as they drop; and they do not look like nature's creations, but rather as if they had been blasted with powder. Across a dense carpet of yellow broom and crimson heather, you reach the edge of the precipice, and there you climb down four or five hundred steps cut roughly into the rock until you reach a footbridge suspended on ropes; then, clinging to the webbing at the sides, you essentially swing yourself over the abyss that separates the two cliffs. Thousands of seagulls, which breed here, wheeled around us on all sides, ceaselessly calling out their melancholy lament into the gale. The young ones had just recently fledged, and it seemed as if the adults were making use of the tempestuous weather to train them. You cannot imagine anything more graceful than these flying lessons. It was easy to recognize the younger birds from their gray color and still uncertain swoops, whereas the older ones would hang for minutes at a time, almost without moving a wing, held aloft by the wind alone as if fossilized in the air. Once in a while the younger birds sought rest in the crevices, but their strict parents quickly forced them to renew their efforts.

The lighthouse is exactly like the one on the east coast of England at Flamborough Head, only without the revolving red lights. Here, too, the neatness of the oil cellars and the extraordinary immaculateness of the lamps are worthy of admiration. In addition, I noticed an ingenious kind of storm window that can be opened with no effort and no danger of its breaking, even during the most powerful winds, and a vertical stone staircase like a jagged saw, which saves a lot of room. But neither of these features can be fully visualized without a drawing.

Dublin, August 11th, 1828

A NASTY SEA voyage is beyond enduring! For ten hours I was thrown around, sick to death. The heat, the revolting stench of the steam boiler, the nausea of all the others on board—it was a ghastly night, a true Carl von Carlsberg picture of human misery.[7] On a longer voyage, one finally gets hardened, and sundry pleasures compensate for the privations; but short crossings that reveal only the dark side of the sea are truly repugnant to me. Thank God it is over, and once more I feel solid ground beneath my feet, although it sometimes seems as if Ireland itself is pitching a bit.

THIS KINGDOM IS more like Germany than England. The almost overly refined industry and culture in all things disappears here, along with, unfortunately, English cleanliness. Although Dublin is adorned with magnificent palaces and broad, nicely aligned roadways, the buildings and streets have a dirty look. The lower orders go around in rags, and the people you meet from a more-cultivated class lack the polish of the English, whereas the quantity of splendid uniforms, which you never see on the streets of London, remind you of the Continent. The environs of the city, too, lack the habitual English lushness: the ground is neglected, the grass and trees sparse. But the grander features of the landscape—the bay, the distant mountains of Wicklow, the foothills of Howth, the amphitheater-like masses of buildings, the quays, the harbor—they are all beautiful. At least this is one's first impression.

By the way, although lodging at the best inn in the city, I am less comfortable than in the tiny town of Bangor. This building, for all its size, seems silent and abandoned, whereas I recall how in Bangor, just during the course of one meal, I watched thirteen carriages arrive, and all of them had to be turned away. The influx of foreigners is so enormous on the major roads of England that waiters in the inns are not hired for money but must themselves *pay the innkeeper* up to five hundred pounds a year for their jobs. The tips they receive amply compensate for this substantial outlay. In Ireland, on the other hand, the Continental custom prevails.

As soon as I had freshened up a little, I took a walk through the city, passing by two rather tasteless monuments. One represents William of Orange on horseback, dressed in a Roman costume; both the man and his mount are misshapen. The horse has a bit in its mouth and a halter on its head, but there is no trace of reins, although the king's hand is extended exactly as if he were holding them. Is this supposed to mean that William needed no reins to ride John Bull? The other monument is a colossal statue of Nelson, standing atop a tall pillar and dressed in modern uniform. A cable hanging behind him looks rather like a tail. Furthermore the pose is ignoble and the figure too elevated to be clearly seen.[8] Later I came to a large, round building with a crowd of people standing guard at the entryway. In answer to my query, I learned that this was the site of the annual exposition of flowers and fruit. Some of the flowers were already being carried away as I entered, but I still managed to see many remarkably beautiful specimens. In the middle of these blooms, which formed a kind of temple, was a space set aside for the different fruits. There twelve judges, earnest and business-like, sat and consumed, smacking their lips with relish as they prepared to award the prizes. This had apparently taken them some time already, because the peelings of melons, pears, and apples; the remnants of pineapples; the pits of peaches, plums, and apricots were forming into mountains on the tables nearby, and although the flowers were all gradually removed by the owners, it appeared that none of the fruit would find its way from the Temple of Pomona to the exit.

August 12th, 1828

SINCE I DID not know what else to do (all the prominent inhabitants of this city are in the country), I visited a lot of showplaces. First the castle where the viceroy resides when he is here; its shabby staterooms, with coarse wooden floors, have little attractive about them. Prettier is a modern Gothic chapel, its exterior deceptively imitating something of great antiquity. Inside it is

adorned with splendid stained glass from Italy, painted in the fifteenth century and richly ornamented with wood carvings by no means inferior to earlier examples. The whole church is heated
through a system of vents, and a carpeted passageway, warmed in the same way, connects it to the
apartments of the lord lieutenant.

A student acted as my cicerone through the rambling and beautiful university buildings.
While they are on the grounds, these guides are required to wear a black cape over their usual
dress and a tall, odd cap with tassels three-quarters of a yard long, giving them a rather grotesque
appearance. This dress is more strictly adhered to than used to be true of pigtails and powder
among Saxon staff officers.

The young man took me into the museum and showed me a model of the burning glass with
which Archimedes set the Roman fleet on fire! Also Ossian's harp,* a stuffed Indian chieftain
with tomahawk and spear, and a few column fragments from the Giant's Causeway, which could
not be more accurately crafted and ring like English glass. I will spare you the rest.

In the large hall where the exams are held (the student informed me of the room's purpose
with a slight shudder), there is a Spanish organ seized from the Great Armada. More interesting
are the portraits of Jonathan Swift and Edmund Burke, whose physiognomies match their well-
known characteristics. The one exhibits an expression just as sharp and mischievous as it is dignified; the other's features are intelligent and powerful, almost coarse, yet benevolent and honest,
invoking the thunderous speaker who fought candidly for his opinions, sparing none, and who
never simply disguised his own interests with an artificial enthusiasm for the opposing view.

After I had seen the courts of justice and customhouse, in addition to other magnificent
palaces, and was ready to go home, I found myself tempted by a flyer for a Peristrephic Panorama
of the Battle of Navarino. This is a very entertaining spectacle and gives such a clear idea of the
untoward event that one can almost feel comforted for not having been there. You enter a small
theater and soon see a curtain go up, behind which there are paintings that depict the particular
events of the battle in their entire sequence. The canvas does not hang down flat, but is stretched
in a retreating half circle and slowly pulled sideways across rollers so that the pictures almost
imperceptibly change one after the other, and you move from scene to scene without any intervals. Meanwhile a voice explicates the details, and the illusion is increased still more by the
distant thunder of cannon, military music, and the roar of battle. At times the panorama-like
painting and gentle swaying of the area depicting the waves and ships caused the imitation to
become almost real.

The first scene shows the Bay of Navarino with the entire Ottoman fleet in battle order. At
the opposite end of the bay, you see Old Navarino and its fortress on top of a high cliff; to the side
among date palms is the village of Pylos, and in the foreground the town of Navarino itself as well
as Ibrahim's camp, where the eye is drawn by handsome groups of horses and by lovely Greek girls
who have been taken prisoner and are being fondled by the soldiers. In the far distance, just on
the horizon, the allied fleet appears as if enveloped by haze. Now this picture slowly disappears;
you see just the open sea rippling past, and then the entrance to the Bay of Navarino gradually
emerges. You discover armed men on the rocks and finally catch sight of the allied fleet forcing its
entry. By means of an optical trick, everything appears life-size, and viewers are placed so that they

---

* Probably donated by Macpherson himself.—*The Editor.*

themselves seem to occupy the Turkish position in the bay. Then we see the admiral's ship *Asia* speeding toward us under full sail. Codrington can be observed on the deck in conversation with the captain; the other ships follow in extending lines and with swelling sails, as if ready to attack —a beautiful sight! Next you see, one after another, the various engagements of different ships, the explosion of a fireship, and several Turkish frigates sent to the bottom of the sea. The finale shows the struggle of the *Asia* with the Egyptian admiral's ship on one side and the Turk's on the other. As is well-known, both sank after doggedly defending themselves and burning for several hours.

Following the battle came some views of Constantinople that offered a very vivid picture of Asiatic hustle and bustle.

In the evening, I went to the theater, a pretty place with an audience less coarse than in London. The actors were not bad, although none surpassed mediocrity. Nearly all the boxes in the lower tier were filled with uniforms intermingled with ladies, an elegant picture. But I understand that here, too, higher society rarely attends the theater.

August 13th, 1828

TODAY, HAVING HAD an adequate tour of the city, I began my rides in the environs, which turn out to be much more beautiful than expected, given that my initial approach brought me via the least favorable side. The road has captivating views, first onto the bay, which is intersected by a three-mile-long seawall and closed by the two pillar-like lighthouses of Dublin and Howth;[9] then onto the wooded mountains of Wicklow, some like sugarloaves rising high above the others. Finally, after leading me through an allée of ancient elms along a canal, the road brought me to Phoenix Park, the prater of Dublin and in no way inferior to that in Vienna: neither in size nor turf lovely for riding; nor in the long allées for driving a carriage; nor in its shady walks (Figure 85). A large though badly proportioned obelisk has been erected here in honor of the Duke of Wellington, and, also on the park grounds, the lord lieutenant has a pretty summer palace enclosed by gardens. On the whole I found the park rather empty, whereas on my way back the streets of the city were, by contrast, all the more bustling with doings and dealings. The filth, poverty, and ragged clothes of the commoners are often past belief, yet these people always seem in good spirits and, on the open street, display occasional fits of merriment that border on madness. Usually whiskey is to blame. Thus I saw a half-naked lad at the marketplace dancing the national dance for so long and with such exertion that, as exhausted as a Muslim Dervish, he fainted dead away amid the cheers of the crowd.

Moreover the streets are filled with young beggars, who, buzzing like flies, incessantly offer their services. Despite their glaring poverty, however, you can totally rely on their honesty; and as oppressed as they might seem by misery, however emaciated and starved, you nonetheless detect no melancholy in their guileless, friendly faces. These are the best-behaved and most easily satisfied street urchins in the world. Such a lad dashes along for hours like a regular runner next to your horse, holds it when you dismount, takes care of every errand, and is not only content with the few pennies you give him, but full of gratitude, which he expresses with Irish hyperbole. The Irishman seems more patient than his neighbors, although somewhat demeaned by prolonged slavery. For example, I watched as a young man, having posted a playbill incorrectly, was manhandled on the open street by the theater director, who arrived on the scene and slapped him in the face. Any Englishman would have immediately made reprisals, but this youth put up no resistance at all.

85
*View of Dublin
from Phoenix Park,
with Obelisk.*

VIEW of DUBLIN from PHOENIX PARK.   VUE DE DUBLIN DU PARC DE PHOENIX.

I spent the evening in the family circle of an old acquaintance, a brother of the lord lieutenant, who had just arrived in the city for a short stay. We reminisced about old times, when
I saw a lot of him in London. He has a particular talent for imitating the late Kemble, whom he
also resembles. It was as if I were hearing Coriolanus and Zanga again.[10]

August 14th, 1828

ANOTHER FRIEND FROM even earlier days visited me this morning to offer me his country
house for my sojourn. This was Mr. W——, someone I had once been able to do a favor for in
Vienna. He had just left when it was announced that Lady B—— (an Irish peeress and one of the
prettiest women in this country, whose company I had cultivated intensely during the previous
Season in the metropolis) was waiting right outside in her carriage and wished to speak to me.
Since I was still in total dishabille, I told the steward—a true simpleton whose Irish blunders
provide me with daily amusement—that I was not dressed, as he could see, but would be ready
right away. He duly delivered the message about the state of my attire, but added—on his own
initiative—that my lady might best come up. Imagine my amazement when he returned and
told me that Lady B—— had laughed heartily and asked him to tell me she was very pleased to
wait, but making morning visits to gentlemen in their chambers was not the custom in Ireland.
This response encapsulates the warm and cheerful, open-minded, and congenial character of

Irishwomen, something I had already grown fond of. A prudish Englishwoman would have driven off indignantly and perhaps ruined a young man's reputation over such a misunderstanding, for in English society it is possible to give offense in ways that would have the opposite effect elsewhere. Furthermore, when an influential person here reports such an episode, the words "it is said" become a two-edged sword. "He has a bad character"* is enough to close a hundred doors to a stranger. An Englishman is much more guided by hearsay than people think. He will always attach himself to a faction and see things accordingly.

This afternoon I went to dine with a friend, and the journey to his villa provided a very pleasant outing. It began at Phoenix Park and then followed the course of the Liffey, the river that flows through Dublin, where its beautiful quays and bridges of stone and iron add so much charm to the city. Here, however, it looks rural and romantic, draped with leaves of coltsfoot a foot wide and enclosed by gentle hills and green trees. I came across an invalid begging for alms and asked him the distance to W—— and whether the road continued to be so lovely. "Oh," he called out with the patriotism of the Irish, "a long life to Your Honor! Keep going on without hesitation— you have never seen anything more beautiful in this world!"

Indeed, the entrance to W—— Park, about a quarter hour farther on, is the most charming of its type imaginable. A natural setting, already very beautiful in itself, has been modified by art to the fullest extent possible and, without obscuring any of its free character, has resulted in a captivating variety of vegetation. Colorful wildflowers and bushes, the softest grass, and colossal trees covered with vines crowd the narrow rocky valley, through which the path winds beside a woodland stream. The water continually forms little cascades as it flows along, sometimes hiding itself beneath a thicket, resting like molten silver in a green basin, or rushing out from under arches of rock that nature has erected as triumphal gateways for the benevolent river god of the dell. But as soon as you ascend from these depths, the magic suddenly disappears, for the rest in no way lives up to your eager anticipation. Dried-out grass, stunted trees, and motionless, stagnant water surround a small Gothic castle that looks like a bad stage set. Yet there are interesting things to be found within, including some paintings of value and the best and most cordial host you could wish for. And I must mention a curious *pavillon rustique* built at a suitable spot in the pleasure ground. It is hexagonal; the three rear sides are closed and attractively covered with rough tree branches laid out in rosettes of various types. The other three sides are open to the outside—two with windows and in the last, the door. The floor consists of a mosaic of small river stones; the ceiling is covered with shells and the roof with a thatch of wheat still bearing full heads of grain.

August 15th, 1828

DESPITE THE FACT that my chest continues to hurt and the doctor occasionally makes concerned faces, I am continuing with my excursions, for they alone give me true pleasure. I feel better in unvarnished nature than among humans wearing masks.

---

* It is highly *characteristic* that in England, where appearance counts so much, "his character" means not the sum of a person's intellectual and moral qualities but exclusively his *reputation*, what people say about him. In German we would call this *sein Titel*, although only in its second meaning.—*The Editor*. [The secondary meaning of *sein Titel* (his title) refers to one's standing in society.—*Translator*.]

From among the mountains about four or five miles distant, I had already gazed with longing at one called the Three Rocks, with three upright, isolated projections at its peak. Convinced that the view from there must be very beautiful, I set off earlier than usual so as to reach the summit in good time. Passing through various villages, I repeatedly inquired about the best route, but I could never get a straight answer. Finally, in a house at the foot of the mountain, I was assured that it was only possible to go up *on foot*, not on horseback. Given the condition of my chest, this was unfeasible. But having become familiar with what people here consider impossible, I proceeded to ride in the direction indicated, all the more confident because I could rely totally on my sturdy little mare, since Irish horses climb over walls and rocks like cats. For a while I followed a tolerably cleared footpath and then, when this ended, the dry bed of a mountain stream. Eventually, after about three-quarters of an hour and without any particular trouble, I reached the top and found myself on a large, barren plateau. About a thousand yards in front of me, I saw the three rocks stretching out their rounded summits like witches' stones. The whole area, however, appeared to be nothing but a wide, impassable bog. I tested it gingerly and soon found that there was a dense substratum about eight to ten inches beneath the mud. After a little while I reached completely solid ground and was standing at the highest point. Now at last the longed-for vista lay before me: Ireland like a map, with Dublin like a smoking lime kiln in the verdant plain, for not even *one* building was visible through the coal smoke. I could see the bay with its lighthouses; the foothills of Howth in bold outline; and, on the other side, the mountains of Wicklow extending to the horizon, all aglow in the sunshine. Thus I felt greatly rewarded for my slight fatigue.

The scene was all the more enlivened by the appealing young woman I discovered in this wilderness engaged in the modest business of haying. The natural grace of Irish peasant women—often true beauties—is just as surprising as their dress or, better, their lack of dress. For although it was downright cold in these mountains, the entire outfit of the woman before me consisted of nothing more than a broad, very coarse straw hat and, *literally*, two or three rags of the coarsest haircloth held together by a rope under her breasts, beneath which the loveliest white limbs were more than half on display. Her conversation was like what I have observed in others: cheerful, teasing, and even witty, while being entirely uninhibited and to a certain extent free and easy, although one would be very mistaken to consider her wanton. On the contrary, Irish females of this class are almost universally very proper and indeed strikingly oblivious. The few individuals who stray from the path of virtue are rarely motivated by self-interest, an attribute perceived as both unnatural and ignoble.

After working my way down another side of the mountain while leading my horse along as best I could, I reached a big road. Here I happened upon a park gate standing open (in this, too, Ireland resembles the Continent, where the owners of large estates, from kings to country noblemen, enhance their own pleasure through the public's enjoyment). So I rode in, but quickly gave up my exploration when I saw, standing at a crossroads, two giant-sized Capuchins complete with cross and cowl, cut out of painted boards and each holding out a book inscribed in outsized letters: "Path to the Pheasant House" and "Path to the Abbey." Such poor taste is very rare here.

Back in the city I was hailed by a London dandy—I had not recognized him—who laughed heartily about meeting in "such a horrid place." He went on making satirical remarks about Dublin society and finally revealed to me that, through his family's good name, he had just been granted a directorship here that brings him more than two thousand pounds per annum with nothing to do except spend a portion of each year in this objectionable spot pro forma. Younger sons of the aristocracy are provided with these sinecures everywhere in England, often much more generous than his. Here too I think that the pitcher cannot go to the well forever without breaking, although it must be admitted that compared with the despotism of other countries, these lapses in the English statutes will remain no more than sunspots. I exclude Ireland, of course, which gets treated like an orphan in almost every respect, yet must nonetheless make the largest contribution to the greatness and power of the English nobility with no advantage in return, even though England has so many.

August 18th, 1828

YOUR LETTERS ARE still so gloomy, good Julia. . . . .

You do see, then, that this melancholy is caused less by what really happens than by your own perspective, and as you are getting on in years, you are becoming more worried and hypochondriac. But of course this, above all, is an unavoidable curse. One is no longer what one was, and yet we all persist in believing we can still help ourselves by mustering our strength, when in fact that strength is no longer present. There is just as little chance that we can become and look young again! I am beginning to sense this myself, but only in cases where the chains of the world are put upon me. When alone with my God and nature, then even life's darkest horizon cannot shadow my inner sun.

Today Lady B—— and I had breakfast in the country at the home of a very celebrated young woman. The man of the house professed to have a migraine, so I had to take a long walk through the grounds alone with the ladies. But when we got to the garden gate leading to the loveliest area of woodland, it was locked, with no key to be found, because, as the old gardener assured us, his gracious lady's personal maid had already gone in and taken the key. A servant jumped over the wall to go search for the guilty party, but to no avail. So I had a ladder fetched and was able to help the laughing women climb over, which they managed very clumsily, though they looked adorable. After a quarter hour we discovered the unfortunate maid, who, believing herself to be safe, was not alone . . . and you can imagine in whose company. A mute domestic scene ensued, and I, too compassionate to laugh, felt deeply sorry that my ladder had caused such unhappiness.

I refused an invitation to dinner and hurried back to the city to visit Lady Morgan (Figure 105). I had brought along a letter of introduction to her, and she had earlier sent me a charming invitation that I had not been able to accept. I was most eager to make her acquaintance, since I esteem her so highly as a writer, but she turned out to be very different than I had imagined. She is a small, frivolous, quick-witted woman who appears to be between thirty and forty years old, not pretty, not ugly (though not without pretensions to the former), with truly lovely, expressive eyes. She knows nothing of false modesty and embarrassment; her manners are not the finest, affecting an *aisance* and facility with the world of high society, yet lacking a sense of repose and naturalness. She possesses the authentic English weakness of boasting about her distinguished acquaintances and wanting to be considered very refined, to a degree inappropriate for a woman of such an excellent mind; and she is absolutely unaware of how much she thus undervalues herself.

It is not hard to get to know her, by the way, because right from the start—with more animation than good taste—she is very open about herself and at every opportunity makes a point of bringing up her liberality as well as her unbelief—the latter something from the out-dated school of Helvétius and Condillac. In her writings, she is far more cautious and dignified than in her conversation, although her tongue is just as satirically biting and nimble as her pen, and just as unscrupulous about adhering to the truth. Given all this, you can imagine that two hours flowed by very enjoyably. I was sufficiently adept to voice some well-timed pleasantries, and she treated me with a great deal of courtesy, first because of my distinguished title, and then because she had seen frequent references in the London *Morning Post* to my dancing at Almack's or attending the sundry fetes of the tone setters. This seemed so important to her that she mentioned it repeatedly.

August 20th, 1828

YESTERDAY EVENING I was supposed to attend a soiree at Lord C——'s, the head of a new family but one of the oldest wits in Dublin. I had been invited by Lady Morgan, a friend of his, but was unable to get there because of a tragicomic incident. I had ridden to the country in order to pay a visit to the H—— von L—— at his residence (which, *entre nous,* was no more worth the trouble than he and his family were), and it was already late when I departed on my return trip. To save time I headed off across country, à la Seydlitz.[11] Everything went splendidly until dusk began to fall, and I came to a broad ditch encircled by a wide meadow. The bank in front of me was significantly higher than the opposite one, but notwithstanding I sprang successfully into the walled enclosure. But when I tried to get out on the other side, my horse refused, and every effort to make it behave was in vain. I dismounted in order to lead it, then got back on to try a jump at another spot, applying both force and kindness—all without success. Finally it made a clumsy attempt and fell with me into the mucky water, only barely managing to scramble out again below the inner, lower bank. All hope of escaping that bewitched place was now lost; I was caught as if in a mousetrap and, what's more, it had turned very dark. Finally, both overheated and drenched, I decided to leave the horse behind, get over the fatal ditch on foot—*tant bien que mal*—and seek out a dwelling and some help. Luckily the moon lent a hand, emerging from the clouds to serve as my most-needed lantern. A half hour later, after a truly difficult trek across fields of high, wet grass, I arrived at a miserable hut where everyone was already asleep. I felt my way in (for the houses are all unlocked here), a couple of pigs grunted under my feet, and immediately afterward, so did the master of the house lying nearby. With some difficulty, I got him to understand my request by clinking some silver coins next to his ears. This universally understood ring woke him quickly, and he leapt up, fetched a companion, and back we went to my *Didone abbandonata.*[12] The Irishmen knew what to do. They dismantled a ruined bridge nearby, laid it across the ditch, and I found myself back on the road with my liberated horse. I got home very late, in such a state and so in need of rest, that I was not at all unhappy to hear that Lady Morgan, who had come to pick me up, had driven off, much annoyed, an hour before.

The next morning, I conveyed my apologies, and she graciously forgave me but allowed that I had forfeited *much,* because every genteel and fashionable person in town had attended the soiree. I assured her that my only regret was the loss of *her* company, but I hoped this would be recouped once I returned from my "Sentimental Journey" to the county of Wicklow,[13] which my romantic German soul fervently longed for, and that I planned to set off on horseback early the following day. After this our conversation became very jovial—to her delight—and finally so silly that she cried out *"Finissez!"*[14] When you come back I'll receive you just like an older sister." I responded, laughing, "I cannot accept that—*je craindrai le sort d'Abufar."*[15] Vis-à-vis Lady Morgan, this was a rather tasteless joke.

You will receive the next installment from amid the rocks and mountains. Adieu, and may heaven lift your spirits and may every word of my letters call out to you: true love until death.

Your Lou

LETTER 29

The Inn at Avoca, August 22nd, 1828

$\mathscr{B}$ELOVED JULIA!

I left Dublin around noon, all by myself. Comfortably ensconced on my trusty horse, I left my carriage and attendants behind in the city and sent a small portmanteau containing my most necessary effects on ahead with the diligence. Unfortunately there must have been some sort of confusion, because although I waited all day and night in Bray, only twenty miles from Dublin, the coach never arrived, so in order not to have to travel back or wait still longer, I bought myself a Scottish cloak along with some linens in Bray and set off on my tour entirely in student style. I had supper with a young clergyman of good family, whose orthodoxy in religious matters made me laugh, since his conversation was otherwise so frivolous. But such is the nature of piety among the English—it is a *party matter* of its own and at the same time, a question of decorum. In just this way, they persistently follow their party in political affairs, through thick and thin, whether reasonable or not, and always with tenacity, because it is *their* party. And just as they will slavishly submit to a custom because it is *their* custom, so too do they approach religion: with no poetry whatsoever and from exactly the same perspective. They go to church on Sundays as unfailingly as they dress every day before sitting down to a meal, and they condemn anyone who neglects the church almost as firmly as they do someone who eats fish with a knife.*

Accompanied by the young theologian, who was traveling along my same route for a while, I left Bray already at five o'clock the next morning. In an exceptionally beautiful area, we passed Killruddery, the residence of the Earl of Meath. The mansion, recently constructed according to the architectural taste of Queen Elizabeth's time, would need to be considerably more massive to make a good impression. The park is long, narrow, and not particularly extensive; the gardens in the old French style are much praised, but when we tried to visit them, we were turned away very impolitely, no doubt due to our unassuming attire. This is common in England, though rare in Ireland, and did not leave us with a very charitable view of the owner's benevolence. In his anger, my companion, a follower of the *grace efficace*[1]—i.e., firmly convinced that God has predestined his favorites for heaven and those he finds less pleasing for hell—was convinced that the owner of Killruddery was one of the latter. "It's a disgrace for an Irishman!" he cried indignantly, and it took some effort to persuade him of the duty of tolerance.

---

* In England the commoners put broad knives into their mouths just like forks, whereas the cultured classes consider this a true sin against the Holy Ghost and cross themselves inwardly when they see, for example, a German ambassador eating this way. For them it is enough to spoil the reputation of a whole nation.

A second park, Bellevue, which belongs to a worthy old gentleman, opened its gates more readily to us. Here there is a deep abyss called the Glen of the Downs, with two extinct volcanoes rising behind it like pointed cones. A retreat has been built above this, a small pavilion, seemingly suspended in air and prettily covered with blooming red heather. The very lifelike stuffed tiger lying in the entry hall was less well-conceived.

My traveling chaplain left me, and I rode on alone to the valley of Dunran, where, in a narrow, romantic pass, there is a rock between eighty and one hundred feet high that looks roughly like the outline of a man. It is therefore called "the Giant" by the locals, who tell a number of fanciful tales about it. Not far away are the ruins of a castle so overgrown with ivy that you have to be standing very close to it before you can distinguish it from the surrounding trees. At the end of the valley, the path winds its way across some meadows toward a significant hill with an astonishing view. Here, feeling almost homesick, I gazed at the mountains of Wales in the blue haze above the sea.

After refreshing myself a bit with milk and bread at a country inn, I continued on my way to the Devil's Glen, which justly bears this name. A Gothic castle marks the wild scene, its smoke-blackened walls towering out of the woods. Then you dip sideways into a valley with walls that gradually rise higher and higher and draw closer and closer together, while in the dark thicket the whistling of the wind grows more fierce and the roaring of the stream more and more dreadful. Advancing with difficulty over the slippery ground and ceaselessly molested by the overhanging branches, you suddenly find the path closed by a magnificent cascade that plunges over high ledges like a white, agitated monster and disappears into the depths below (Figure 86). If it is not the devil himself, then it is at least Kühleborn.

What a very pleasant change to find this spine-chilling ravine followed by the idyllic valley of Rosanna, where I ate my midday meal beneath the shade of tall ash trees. Here I came upon two regular tourists armed with a mountain ax and herbarium. They had been living in the valley for weeks already and, with the punctuality of a London coffeehouse, had their clean tablecloth removed from the dirty table before dessert. They then sat there for an hour with a miserable sour wine instead of claret and roasted apples instead of ripe fruit.

At seven o'clock I got back on my horse and galloped for ten miles along the main road until, still ahead of sunset, I reached the exquisitely beautiful Avondale. In this paradise there is a unity of every possible charm: a wood that appears endless, two magnificent rivers, picturesque rocks in a multitude of shapes, the greenest meadows, deciduous and evergreen trees, and shrubs of all kinds in amazing abundance—a nature that never stops changing with every step and never seems to lose its power. Because I passed through the last part of the valley by moonlight, I would have had difficulty finding my way if not for a young gentleman who was returning from the hunt and who—with true Irish helpfulness—accompanied me on foot for at least three miles over the most difficult terrain. The night was extremely clear and mild, the sky as blue as during the day, and the moon as lustrous as a jewel. Although I missed the distant views, I may have gained more from the magical glow permeating the air, the darker contours of the rocks looming more fantastically, the hush more crowded with thoughts, and the sweetly eerie loneliness of the night.

At ten o'clock I reached today's goal, Avoca Inn, where, if your requirements are modest, you can find quite reasonable accommodations and very friendly service. In the dining room, I met another tourist from London, a jolly and interesting young man who was fully in harmony

86

*Waterfall in the
Devil's Glen.*

with my delight over this charming area and with whom I then spent an hour at tea chatting amiably before sitting down to write to you. But now good night, because one must get up early when traveling in the mountains, and therefore must not retire all that late to bed.

Roundwood, August 23rd, 1828

YESTERDAY I RODE thirty-eight miles, today forty-two, and my chest feels none the worse for it. Enjoying oneself does a lot of good, and I have seen so many different things that these few days seem like several weeks.

I slept well, although the broken window of my room had simply been plugged with a pillow. The night's modest lodging was followed by a better breakfast, and I also found that my horse had been excellently cared for. I rode like the Arabs, either at a gallop or a walk, since this is the least fatiguing and you cover the most distance. My first excursion was to the famous spot known as the Meeting of the Waters, where the two rivers Avonmore and Avonbeg join together, having chosen the most picturesque setting possible to celebrate their marriage (Figure 87). Atop a cliff on the other side is Castle Howard with its many towers and battlements. Unfortunately these have all been built only recently and from close-up are not impressive. The entire household was still asleep, so a servant—in his shirt—showed me the paintings, among which is a splendid portrait of Mary Stuart, certainly a striking likeness and clearly dating from her lifetime. The attractive, genuinely French face with its fine nose, charming mouth, and soulful fiery eyes bears an inimitable expression: not exactly accommodating, although instilling courage; not lacking womanly dignity, but evoking a feeling of familiarity already at first glance. All this convinces you that *this* is just how she must have looked, and how, despite her high rank, she quickly inspired every man who drew close to assume the role of a lover. Her hands are lovely, and everything about her attire—although in the Baroque style—is so harmonious that you quickly realize she was just as conversant with the art of the *toilette* as her fellow countrywomen are today.

A well-maintained road leads from here to the entire vale of the Avoca and the park of Ballyarthur. This valley is peculiar in that the hills on both sides are covered so thickly and impenetrably with beeches that there is no space between them, and it really looks as if you could ride uphill across the treetops. I left the road here and followed a footpath through the thicket that led me to a very beautiful vista, where the towers of Arklow appear at the end of the long ravine as if set in a frame. But a half hour later the path ended abruptly at a ha-ha, which my horse absolutely refused to jump across. Since the grass below was soft and the descending wall on my side, I resorted of necessity to a new method. Namely, I blindfolded the stubborn beast and then nudged him backward over the wall. The fall startled him a little but, as I had foreseen, did him no harm whatever, and he proceeded to graze peacefully in his blindfold while awaiting my arrival. This maneuver saved me at least five miles.

The new park where I now found myself—for this whole part of the county is a continuous expanse of nature beautified by art—used to belong to Shelton Abbey, another modern "Gothicry" that is supposed to represent an old monastery. The master and mistress have not lived here for years, and a negro who was working in the garden showed me through the rooms, which contained a few interesting old genre paintings. The hero in one picture is a great-grandfather of the family: the scene is Italy, and the costumes, like the manners represented, are extremely odd, even offensive. From here the accommodating negro led me

MEETING of THE WATERS, COUNTY of WICKLOW.

In the distance is seen the Vale of Avondale & Wooden Bridge, to the right on a rising Ground the Seat of Captain Mills, and in the fore Ground a Stone Bridge with the junction of the Rivers Avon and Avoca.

diagonally across the meadows, through a rather deep ford (he displayed no fear of the ice-cold river), and all the way to the town of Arklow, from where I returned along the main road for my midday meal in the Avoca Inn. Along the way I ascended another mountain promontory and from there looked into three different valleys, each with a character completely divergent from the others—an extraordinary sight.

I had hardly taken my seat at the table in Avoca when I was told that a gentleman wished to speak to me. A young man, whom I had never laid eyes on, entered and handed me a pocketbook that I recognized with considerable astonishment as my own. Besides other important papers that I always carry with me on a journey, it contained all my travel money. Without my noticing, it had fallen out of my breast pocket, God knows how, in the pavilion at Bellevue, and I therefore had every reason to be grateful for such an honest and obliging finder. In England there would

87

Meeting of the Waters.

have been scarcely any chance of seeing my pocketbook again, even if a *gentleman* had found it, for he would just have let it lie there or . . . kept it.

I must take this opportunity to mention what the well-known term "gentleman" actually implies, since its connotation provides an usually apt characterization of the English. A gentleman is neither a nobleman nor a noble man but, strictly speaking,* nothing more than a man whose wealth and meticulous knowledge of the customs of good society renders him *independent*. Any man who serves or works for the public in some way or other—with the exception of higher public servants and, for instance, writers and artists of the first rank—is not a gentleman, or at best half a one. Only recently I was astonished to hear a prominent man say of himself, "I cannot understand how the Duke of B—— could have commissioned me to relay a challenge to Count M——; he should have chosen a *gentleman* to do it—such things are none of my business."[2] This is someone known to all horse lovers both here and abroad, someone who is wealthy and on familiar terms with many a duke and lord, and in general enjoys a high reputation, but who nonetheless auctions off horses on a weekly basis at a large establishment, during which he is to an extent engaged with the public.

A truly *poor* man, who is not in a position to incur any debts, can in no circumstances be a gentleman, because he is the most dependent of all. A rich scoundrel, on the other hand, if he has been properly brought up and knows how to manage his reputation reasonably well,** can pass for a perfect gentleman. Still-finer nuances are evident in the exclusive society of London. There, for instance, anyone who behaves with ladies in a timid and courteous way, instead of acting familiar and treating them with a certain *nonchalance* and little deference, will arouse the suspicion that he is not a gentleman. But should that unlucky man ask for a second helping of soup at a *dîner* or appear in evening dress at a large breakfast that begins at three in the afternoon and ends at midnight, though he may be a prince and a millionaire, he is definitely no gentleman.

However, back from the dictates of Babylon to the freedom of the mountains. The countryside I was now riding through was strikingly like the flatter areas of Switzerland, rising gradually and continuously until I found myself across from the highest mountains of Wicklow, their peaks—again like Snowdon—veiled in clouds. The valley of Glenmalure has a character of forlorn sublimity, and the gloomy weather harmonized with it perfectly. At its center, like a haunted castle, stands a large, abandoned, and dilapidated barrack. There is not a tree or bush to be seen, and the slopes of the high mountains are covered with nothing but crumbled rocks. Only underground is there life in this valley, and even this is a life that brings about death. For there are some large lead mines here, and their unhealthy vapors can be detected in the pallid faces of the workers. I was enveloped in black overalls and conducted into the mineshafts—a dismal, horrific journey! The tunnels were as cold as ice; deep darkness reigned, and a piercing wind blew against us, smelling of the grave. Water dripped with a hollow, rhythmic sound from a ceiling low enough to double us over, and the unbearable jolts of the cart, which a man was slowly pulling along over the uneven ground, completed the image of a terrible existence! The ailing condition of my chest did not allow me to stay there for long, and so I abandoned the site without any further investigation and was happy "as I once more greeted the rosy light."[3]

---

* Because in general terms, of course, every man who looks respectable is called a gentleman.—*The Editor.*

** This is not about morality but only about scandal.—*The Editor.*

To cross over one of the colossal mountains that close the valley, I followed a fine, newly constructed military road—the government's bad conscience makes it especially concerned about Ireland! The view from the top—distant and magnificent and yet of a very different character from what I had seen before—was greatly augmented by a most cheerful radiance as the sun sent out its beams from behind black clouds. Nothing else gives distant objects this much clarity or a more transfiguring light. The rays were spread out in broad bands like a halo over the many intersecting mountain ranges, and the two sugar loafs stood towering over everything else, deep blue against the bright horizon. The road descending the mountain is laid out in such gradual, serpentine lines that I could gallop down in comfort. It was nonetheless well into evening by the time I entered the last of the valleys to be visited today, that of the Seven Churches.[4] Here, more than a thousand years ago (so the story goes), there was a large city with seven churches that were destroyed by the Danes. One fine gate is still standing, complete but for the missing keystone, which time has replaced with a thick trunk of ivy that now holds the whole arch together. These seven ruins are, according to popular belief, all that is left of the sacred establishments that give the valley its name. Only one indisputably exhibits the appropriate character, however, and is remarkable for having one of the tallest of those mysterious towers without doors or windows that you come upon amid the ruins of many Irish monasteries, their actual purpose not yet rediscovered. Farther along, resting on lower ground in devout silence, are two dark lakes made famous by the adventures of Saint Kevin. Here the cliffs are unusually steep and in many spots formed like stairways. In one there is a deep, narrow fissure that looks exactly as if it had been cut by a violent blow. Legend tells how the young giant Fionn mac Cumhaill, when his comrades feared he was still too weak to make war alongside them, proved his strength by splitting this rock with his sword, thereby putting an end to any doubt. In addition it was discovered that a black hole in the face of a cliff overlooking the water on the other side of the lake was Saint Kevin's cave. There the holy man hid away from the amorous pursuit of the king's beautiful daughter, Cathelin, and lived for a long time on roots and herbs in the most profound solitude. But at a fateful moment, the lovely young woman, driven by her passion to wander the countryside, discovered the fugitive and, in the black of night, surprised him on his bed of moss. With sweet kisses she awakened the ungallant saint, who, seeing his virtue being lost, made a quick decision and threw Cathelin off the ledge into the cold waters of the lake, where she gave up both her love and her life. Afterward this man of God felt a stirring of human pity, and he put a magic spell on the waters, so that no one would lose their life there ever again, a charm that is still in force, according to the testimony of my guide.

This cicerone was a comely and as usual half-naked youth of eleven, and his clothing—a specimen of Irish *toilette*—is worth mentioning. He was wearing the evening attire of a grown man, which, in addition to various transparent spots, was missing one and a half sleeves as well as one coattail, while the other trailed behind him on the ground like the tail of a comet. Scarf, vest, and shirt were simply discarded as pointless. On the other hand, the tattered remains of a pair of red plush trousers looked quite splendid, although farther down only bare legs and feet peeked out. To watch this figure scrambling over the rocks like a squirrel and hear him at the same time singing pieces by Tommy Moore* and Walter Scott was certainly remarkable. As he was leading

---

* This is how the Irish prefer to call him, proud that he is their fellow countryman.—*The Editor.*

me to the cave where the passage was a bit slippery, he called out: "Oh, this is easy going. I also brought Walter Scott here, and he managed to climb up the worst of it with his lame foot." He could not stop talking about this and quickly recited four verses that either Scott or Moore (I cannot remember which) had composed in the cave. The people here, so perfectly suited to the wild, ruin-covered landscape, are essential to the romantic appeal of this whole place.

In order to get a night's rest at a tolerable inn, I had to ride on by the light of the moon for ten more miles across a peat bog, the customary habitat of all sorts of ghosts, although those who honored me with their presence were no more than a few solitary will-o'-the-wisps gliding by.

When I arrived at the village, both inns were already full of tourists, and it was only with great difficulty that I managed to have a small anteroom arranged, where I will sleep on straw. The tea, butter, toast, and eggs are excellent, however, and my hunger adds spice to the meal. I cannot tell you how pleasant I am finding this life! Even with all the privations, I still feel a hundred times more *à mon aise* than when I am encumbered with a thousand unnecessary conveniences. I am as free as a bird, and it is a great delight. Incidentally, honor where honor is due: Few men would, after such fatiguing activities, religiously return every evening to write such a lengthy report of the day's events. As long as it makes you happy, I am rewarded a hundredfold.

Bray, August 24th, 1828

YOU WILL RECALL that when he examined my skull in Paris, Gall claimed that I had a very prominent organ of theosophy.[5] Yet in spite of this many think me an evil heretic. But Gall was right, provided that being religious consists of love and the sincere pursuit of truth. In just such a joyful and pious mood, I greeted the chilly morning with prayerful gratitude, soothed by a sense of inner happiness that broke through the nasty, damp fog surrounding me—for the weather was truly awful. The road, too, was bleak and cheerless. But patience! The evening brought sun and beauty.

At first there was nothing but barren heath and peat bog as far as the eye could see, and a gale whistled sporadically across the land, driving clouds of misty fog that drenched me like a heavy rain whenever I entered their realm. Only a few feeble glimpses of sunlight offered momentary hope until around noontime when the clouds parted, and just as I arrived at the mountain peak above the magnificent lake and valley of Luggala, the sun transformed the lowlands before me into splendid gold, while leaving the tops of the mountains veiled.

This valley also belongs to a wealthy landowner, who has made it into a captivating park.[6] Since the layout is unusual, I will try to give you a clear description. It is shaped almost like a regular elongated basin, the first half filled with water right up to the edge of the mountains. The second part is a level meadow dotted with groups of trees and crossed by a stream meandering along a serpentine course. At the center, backed up against a solitary rock, you see an elegant shooting lodge. The mountains surrounding the valley are very high and steep, all rising from the level plain in smooth, unbroken contours. To the left are naked rocks of imposing shape, only here and there overgrown with red and yellow heather. The other three sides, however, are covered thickly with a variety of plants, the foliage extending all the way down into the lake. As the stream flows across a glistening green bed of grass and into the lake, it forms a wide waterfall. This, to be sure, is a lovely patch of earth—solitary and secluded, the woods full of game, the lake full of fish, and nature full of poetry.

Since the hunting season has not yet begun, the master and mistress were absent, so my breakfast was seen to by the steward's wife, a still-pretty although somewhat faded woman with lovely white hands and manners above her station (she probably receives an allowance here). Her lively young son toured me around the valley. We were accompanied by a handsome greyhound that glided over the ground as lightly as a windblown leaf and occasionally celebrated his freedom in boisterous gambols. We clambered about four hundred feet up a cleft in the rock (not without some pain in my ailing chest, *car je ne vaux plus rien à pied*),[7] and from there you can overlook the entire valley. Across the way you see a strange freak of nature, a monstrous face shaped entirely in stone that looks down darkly and sullenly over the lake. The eyebrows and beard are formed with particular clarity by moss and heather, and the thick cheeks as well as the deeply set eyes are remarkably well imitated by cracks in the rocks. The mouth is open, but if you walk a bit farther, it closes without otherwise altering any features. To possess such an animated mountain spirit is truly a special prerogative. But this one, as I said, is staring quite peevishly into the depths, and his gaping mouth seems to be shouting down at the lake: "You human riffraff! Leave my valley, my fish, my woods, my rocks, and trees in peace, or I will bury all you pygmies under the rubble." But it does no good; the call of the spirits lost its power when the spirit of mankind awoke. Rübezahl's countenance remains trapped in stone, and his voice fades away in the blustery wind, which irreverently buffets his bushy eyebrows and curls the waves of the lake toward him as if in ridicule.

Ten miles of uninteresting countryside lay between this walk and my arrival at the gates of Powerscourt Park, one of the largest and most beautiful in Ireland. But it was Sunday and the owner being a sanctimonious type, the entrance was locked. In his mind, a godly man who chooses to leave his dwelling on this day should do so only to visit a dank church, certainly not to enjoy himself in God's own splendid temple. Since Lord Powerscourt was not in favor of encouraging this sin, he had forbidden the opening of the gates during his current absence. You know how wary I am after my earlier *aventure* in England,[8] so I made no attempt to gain entry by means of a gift but continued on outside the wall, occasionally casting a stolen and wistful glance at the great waterfall and enchanting setting. Dear God, I thought, how varied are the ways in which you are worshipped! Some roast their neighbor in your honor, others transform you into Apis, some believe you more biased and unjust than the devil himself, and others find their greatest satisfaction in spoiling your beautiful gift of life by denying it to everyone, including themselves. Oh Lord Powerscourt, you will not read these lines, but it would be good if you did and took them to heart! Many a poor man who sweats for a week in order to pay you his rent would be elated to find himself in your lovely park on a Sunday, and he would bless the kindness of the lord who does not in fact deny him everything, including a glimpse of his majesty. And in the end this would please you, too, but you are probably not even around and only convey your pious commands from a distance. You are perhaps, like so many of your colleagues, one of those absentees who make use of voracious and pitiless functionaries to strip the lower orders of their last rag and rob them of their last potato in order to enrich mistresses and charlatans in London, Paris, or Italy.* Then, I suppose, your religion cannot do more than hold Sundays sacred, along with the ceremonies of your priests.

---

* This is not at all an exaggeration. I have examined reliable reports of such things here and have seen misery of a kind unheard of during the period of serfdom in Germany. Its equal cannot be found even in countries practicing slavery.

From here to Bray there is an impressive display of lush, cultivated land strewn with the country houses and gardens of rich city dwellers. The road passes close by the foot of the great Sugar Loaf, with its whitish gray, rocky cone stripped of all vegetation. I could spy some travelers who had just made the climb and were now walking around on its summit like chess figures, and I envied them the sublime view, for the day was splendid and the sky had turned completely clear. Toward evening, at a solitary spot next to the brook, I lay down among the wild flowers and, giving thanks to God, daydreamed my way into this gorgeous world, while like a knight errant, I allowed my gentle steed to graze next to me. I thought a lot about you and past times; I conjured up the living and brought the dead back from the grave. And as if in a mirror, I looked over my own life that has faded away—at times with a pang of melancholy, at times with a cheerful smile. In reviewing all the follies and vanities of this world, every error and blunder, I found *one* pure silver thread that is still strong enough to endure: a feeling of childlike love and a great receptivity to the joys that God's goodness makes attainable by every one of us.

I got back to Bray in good time and found that my portmanteau had finally arrived. Much of what it contained was, after my lengthy privation, not to be scoffed at; among other things, it provided me with the most interesting table companion—Lord Byron. I was just looking at two portraits of him, both of them drawings that I received as gifts and have now inserted into *The Giacour* and *Don Juan*. Like Napoleon, he looked thin, wild, and afflicted while he still had aspirations, but fat and simpering once he had achieved them. Yet the features in these two very different faces are animated by the same spirit profoundly shaken by fate, a spirit that feels more deeply and yet is at the same time mocking, contemptuous, arrogant.

I always have to laugh at the English who judge this man—their second greatest poet (for after Shakespeare he certainly merits the palm)—with such pathetic philistinism just because he ridiculed their pedantry and was not interested in bowing to their small-minded customs or in sharing their cold superstition; because their insipidness revolted him, and he deplored their arrogance and their hypocrisy. Many cross themselves when they mention his name, and even the women—although their cheeks glow with enthusiasm when they read him—take a vehement stand in public against their secret favorite. They often side with his common soul of a wife,[9] who was never worthy of untying her husband's shoelaces and yet with mean-spirited revenge found it easy to destroy him in English society!* Since this hero belongs to all of Europe, it was fitting that our appreciative countrymen and our patriarch, through profound and enduring words, erected a German triumphal arch in Byron's honor to counter the column of infamy that the English made for him.[10]

If only I could call out a farewell to you in his immortal words—not a final, nor I hope a long one, but equally heartfelt! Think of me thus.

Your faithful, Lou

---

* That we also have this relationship to thank for the destruction of Byron's memoirs is likewise a bitter misfortune, and it is hard to comprehend how his noble friend Thomas Moore justifies to himself such disloyalty to the poet and such a theft from the public.—*The Editor.* [Moore, who was Byron's friend, confidant, and publisher, acquiesced to Lady Byron's wishes and burned rather than published the poet's private journal that had been entrusted to him.—*Translator.*]

Dublin, August 29th, 1828

Ｄ EAR AND GOOD ONE!

I spent the past few days in bed with aches and a fever and was incapable of answering your letters until today. What the sagacious Varnhagen has written about me is certainly flattering, although the enthusiasm my little creations inspire in him arises out of his poetic soul alone, which can conjure up an *authentic* ideal out of something that is just *taking shape.*[1] But do not ask me to return before it is possible. And believe me, wherever a person is *not,* he is generally desired, but once he is *there,* many are quickly fed up with him.

Today I went riding again for the first time in order to visit the fair in Donnybrook, not far from Dublin, which is viewed as a kind of carnival (Figure 88). Nothing could be more Irish! Everywhere the enormous poverty, filth, and raucousness were matched by the delight and merriment aroused by the cheapest entertainments. The food and drink being consumed with great jubilation compelled me to avert my eyes in distaste, and I have to admit that the heat and dust, the throng and stench, soon drove me away. But none of this troubles the natives. Several hundred tents had been set up, all tattered (like most of the people) and decked out not with banners but with colorful rags. Many sported no more than a plain cross or hoop; one even posted a dead, half-putrid cat as a sign! Meanwhile the lowest sort of clowns pursued their disagreeable trade in shoddy, worn-out finery on plank stages, dancing and grimacing to the point of exhaustion in the terrible heat. A third of the public was lying down or staggering around drunk; the others were eating, shrieking, or brawling. Many of the women were riding two or three to a donkey, forcing their way with difficulty through the *foule* as they contentedly smoked their cigars and bantered with their sweethearts. The most ludicrous sight of all was two beggars on horseback, something I thought was a native practice only on the Rio de la Plata.[2] They rode bareback and used a piece of string to guide the horse; with its wretched appearance, it seemed a willing participant in their begging.

As I left the fair, an amorous couple, extremely drunk, took the same road, and I was thoroughly amused by their behavior. Both were dreadfully ugly but treated each other with great tenderness and many tokens of regard. The lover even displayed a bit of chivalry. Nothing could be more gallant, and at the same time more commendable, than his repeated efforts to protect the fair maid from falling off, although he had no little difficulty maintaining his own balance. From his gracious demonstrations and her merry laughter, one could see that he was doing everything in his power to keep her well entertained. Meanwhile, despite these exalted circumstances, her responses were delivered with a coquettishness and tender familiarity that would have been delightful in a prettier woman. In truth I must also testify that there was not a trace of English

Drawn on Stone by A.Murphy

Printed by M.H. & J.W. Allen

A VIEW OF DONNYBROOK FAIR.

88

*A View of
Donnybrook Fair.*

brutality in their behavior. They were more like the French, although along with their Gallic gaiety, they displayed greater humor and good nature, two authentic parts of the Irish national character that are always redoubled by poteen (the best kind of whisky, though illicitly distilled).

Do not rebuke me for the disreputable pictures I paint for you. These people are closer to nature than the overly made-up wax dolls that attend our salons.

Bray, August 30th, 1828

I HAVE RETURNED here today to visit Powerscourt Park, which I was barred from last weekend. It would not be easy for nature to unite greater resources than she has bestowed here with a liberal hand, and these gifts have been deployed with intelligence. The first major section is called the Dargle, a very deep and narrow ravine overgrown by tall trees, with a torrential river roaring along the bottom (Figure 89). The road leads up on the right side, and from here one's eyes plunge far into the green abyss, from which the water may suddenly sparkle forth or a bold group of

rocks emerge. Three fairly large mountains loom over the ravine and, although at a considerable distance, appear to be close at hand, since you cannot see their foothills. This evening a thoroughly Italian sun tinted them a deep rose red, which contrasted magnificently with the luscious green of the oaks.

Later, near a rocky crag called Lover's Leap, the ravine opens onto a multitude of valleys formed by low ranges of hills and then enclosed at a certain distance by the highest mountains of the region. Amid this landscape, the house appears on a gentle slope at the edge of the woods, beautifully surrounded by beds of flowers (Figure 90). From here to the large waterfall five miles away, the road leads through constantly changing vistas that resemble open country more than a park. Finally you reach a wood, and before you can actually see the cascading water, you can hear it rumbling in the distance. It is only sizeable after a rainstorm, but then magnificent (Figure 91). The high rock walls are thickly covered with shrubs on both sides, and the cascade pours forth from this colorful foliage to arrive at a basin embraced by a fragrant meadow. Adjoining this are ancient oaks, and beneath their shade stands a house nicely suited to the

90

A View of Powerscourt.

character of the site. Here refreshments are offered, making it a popular objective for country outings. Green pathways lead farther into the wilderness of the mountains, but since it was already dark, I had to think about my return route. On the way to Powerscourt, I covered most of the considerable distance at a gallop and, so as not to be held up unnecessarily, hoisted the raggedy, twelve-year-old boy who was my guide up onto the horse behind me, untroubled by the amazement of the passersby, who were evidently bemused by this bizarre cavalcade. After dark, however, I was forced to ride slowly on the stony road, until the orange-colored moon rose above the mountains, where it seemed to sway in the nighttime mist like a huge paper lantern. I did not get back to the Bray inn until eleven o'clock, tired and hungry.

August 31st, 1828

MY COUNTRY SOJOURN is so pleasant that I spent today, Sunday, in the same place. Life at these inns offers a good opportunity to observe the middle classes, since everyone behaves

without pretension and more or less believes himself to be alone. I have already mentioned that English travelers of this class (I am including under this rubric the inhabitants of all three kingdoms who have adopted the *English* manner), when not away from the inn, tend to spend the day together in a communal space called a coffee room. In the evening this room is lit by lamps, and individual candles are brought only on request to the gentlemen seated at small, separate tables. It has often surprised me, in a country where luxury and refinement in the necessities of life are so widespread, that even in the best inns of the provinces (and for the most part in London as well) tallow candles are burned everywhere. Wax candles are an extraordinary luxury, and anyone who asks for one is treated with double courtesy, although double charges are *continuously* chalked up as well.

There is something amusing about the astonishing uniformity of behavior, as if everyone had been turned out by *a single* factory. This is especially obvious at meals. Placed at separate tables, with no one taking the slightest notice of anyone else, they all nevertheless seem to have the same manners as well as the same gastronomical preferences. No one likes soup, which is not

91

*Powerscourt Park
with Waterfall.*

to be had without placing a special order ahead of time. (This is the reason my old Saxon servant left me, maintaining he could no longer live amid such barbarism—without soup!) Usually a large roast is carried from one person to the next and each carves off what he wants; potatoes and other vegetables—all boiled—are placed on every table, along with a *plat-de-ménage* full of sauces and spices. Beer is poured at the same time, and this generally concludes the main meal. Only the extravagant begin with a fish course.

But now comes the essential second station: the tablecloth is removed, clean cutlery is set, wine and a fresh glass are brought, along with a couple of miserable apples or pears and some rock-hard sea biscuits, and only now does each diner seem to settle down in full comfort. His face assumes an expression of contentment, and apparently lost in deep meditation, he leans back with a fixed, unfocused gaze and from time to time indulges reflectively in a sip of wine, only now and then breaking the deathly quiet with a laborious crunch into a stony biscuit. When the wine has been consumed, a third station follows: digestion. Here all movement ceases; the satiated diner falls into a kind of compelling stupor, distinguished from actual sleep only by his open eyes. After about thirty minutes to an hour, he suddenly jumps up and cries out as if possessed, "Waiter! My slippers!" and seizing a candle, walks solemnly out of the room to meet his slippers and his repose. To watch this farce enacted by five or six people at once amuses me more than a puppet show, and I must add that, except for the slippers, the scene is presented in much the same way even by the more distinguished performers in the top clubs of the metropolis.

I have almost never seen Englishmen read during a meal, and I do not know whether this is because it is viewed as unseemly or even godless—something like singing or dancing on a Sunday. But perhaps it is just another dietary rule that has over time become a law, and no intellectual animation compels anyone to violate it.

Englishmen who are not members of the aristocracy or very rich almost always travel without a servant, by means of a mail or stagecoach, and the inns are set up for this. The man who waits on the visitors and polishes their boots is commonly named Boots. So it is Boots who brings you your slippers, helps you remove your traveling clothes, and then takes his leave after enquiring not at what time you would like coffee, as he would in Germany, but when he can bring you boiling water for shaving. He appears punctually with this amenity, and also returns your things all nicely cleaned. The traveler usually dresses quickly, takes care of a few necessary items of business, and then hurries off again to his beloved coffee room, where all the ingredients for breakfast are richly arrayed at his table. He seems to bring along more animation to this meal than the later one, and more appetite too, I believe, for the vats of tea, the masses of bread and butter, eggs, and cold meats he devours awaken a mute envy in the breast (or better, the stomach) of the less capable foreigner. And here he is not only permitted to read, but indeed through custom (the Englishman's gospel), *invited* to do so. With each cup of tea, he unfurls a newspaper printed on a sheet of paper the size of a tablecloth. Not a speech, not a crime, not a single murderous tale fabricated by the London accident maker is skipped over.* Like someone who would rather die of indigestion than leave untouched something that he had already paid for, so too does the methodical Englishman think that once having begun his newspaper,

---

* In the absence of any real murder stories or terrifying accidents, newspaper editorial boards pay poetic talents to invent such things for the ever-inquisitive public. These artists are known as accident makers.
—*The Editor.*

he must not neglect a single word. This is also why his breakfast lasts for several hours, and his sixth or seventh cup of tea is drunk cold. I have seen this glorious meal drag on until it merges into *dîner*, and you will scarcely believe me when I say that it can carry on all the way to a light supper at midnight without the company ever leaving the table.

On this occasion there were several people gathered together, and I really must note that in such cases, an entirely different picture emerges. Rather than allowing them to sink into lethargic meditation, the wine often makes them altogether too talkative. Something like this happened today. Five or six travelers were living it up, and after they had gone over the top, fell into a violent argument that, after a lengthy clamor, ended bizarrely when all of them pounced on the waiter and threw him out the door. At this point the innkeeper was obliged to intervene and beseech them to pardon the innocent victim. Not one of the men eating alone at the other tables took the slightest notice of this disruption, but instead stared straight ahead as placidly as before. But shortly thereafter one of them, who had begun his *dîner* quite late, volunteered a new scene. He was dissatisfied with his mutton and ordered the waiter to tell the cook that she was "a damned bitch." Such a slander caused the Irishwoman to lose control, and despite the attempts of her companions to restrain her at the door to the dining room, she tore herself free and descended on the offender, hands on her hips, and unleashed such a deluge of Irish epithets that he, blanching before this virago of a cook, retired from the field of battle. Once again hollering "*my slippers!*" as loudly as ever, he abandoned his sally and hurried off to his room on the third floor, for as you know, like in a dovecote, the bedchambers here are always just under the roof.

Once when the late Grand Duke of Weimar was in England, he felt the urge to travel by stagecoach alone and incognito, so he might become familiar with this life. He enjoyed it very much, but on the following morning was not a little amazed when the local Boots, *nonchalamment*, brought him his clothes and greeted him with the words: "I hope Your Royal Highness slept well!" Thinking he might have misunderstood, he continued his journey seated on the upper deck. The next morning, the same form of address. Now he inquired more specifically and discovered that there was a card with his actual name and rank attached to the inside of his cloak, thereby betraying his identity. What doubtless struck him the most, however, was that no one paid much attention to whether a German sovereign sat on top of the coach.

Commoners in England take little note of rank and none at all of foreign rank. Only the middle class is slavish in this regard; they love parading around with foreign noblemen, since they cannot get near their own haughty aristocrats. However, at the bottom of his heart, even the lowliest English lord considers himself superior to the King of France.

By the way, for anyone who is interested in something beyond just moving from place to place or who is not flattered by excessive reverence on the part of innkeepers and waiters, this kind of traveling is certainly preferable to the normal way of undertaking a Grand Tour. The reduced level of comfort is so counterbalanced by things instructive and pleasant that you gain a hundredfold through the trade-off.

Dublin, September 1st, 1828

THIS TIME I returned from Bray via Kingstown, following a rough but very romantic route along the coast. Innumerable beggars stood beside the road, but they were not lacking in industry, for an old woman among them was diligently collecting some white sand that had fallen through the planks of a loaded wagon. Why could we not open the treasures of our Sand-Golconda to the poor creature for just one hour![3] Instead I made her happy with a few of the pence I always carry in my coat pocket to scatter like grain among the chickens, for here everyone begs.

Kingstown is a small town composed mainly of country houses belonging to the rich; the lord lieutenant sometimes resides here as well. A harbor has been under construction since the king's visit to Ireland and work on it continues to this day.[4] It is a significant project, given the shallowness of Dublin Bay, but at the moment serves primarily as a means of providing work for the poor. The many ingenious inventions being used here are instructive and interesting: the four sets of rails running side by side, whereby a *single* horse can pull the most enormous loads; the chain winches that pick up colossal blocks as if they were small bricks and then set them into the levee walls; and so on. A number of large ships were anchored in the unfinished harbor, which already affords adequate depth and safety. I was struck by one that was completely black, unrigged, and hulking there like a solitary ghost. It must have been eerie on board, for I was told it contained prisoners intended for Botany Bay; the transport that was to carry them away had already arrived. For the convicts this deportation is not such a harsh punishment (apart from the seasickness) and converts at least two-thirds of them back into useful citizens. Every government could, depending on its resources, create its own Botany Bay. But it will probably be a long time before the principle of retribution is eliminated from the law or, for that matter, from religion.

A monument has been erected at the entrance to the harbor to mark the king's memorable visit to Ireland (memorable, that is, for being such a disappointment).[5] It was designed and executed in the same poor taste that curses almost every public construction in Great Britain. A short, ridiculous stick of an obelisk has been set atop four balls on the edge of a natural rock in such a way that you are sure the next gust of wind will topple it into the sea. And you cannot stop yourself from wishing for this to happen—the sooner the better. The royal crown is clapped on the top like the lid of a mug, and the whole thing is so small and pathetic, set against the grandiose dimensions of the harbor and surrounding buildings, that it is easy to see it as the caprice of a private citizen, but certainly not as a national monument. Perhaps the architect was a *mauvais plaisant* and meant it satirically. Only as an epigram can it be praised!

The road from here to Dublin is quite superb and always busy with carriages and riders. I was amazed to find it was not watered, something that makes the roads around London so pleasant. Probably this happens here only when the lord lieutenant is around. Today the dust from the disorderly crowds was almost unbearable, and all the trees looked as if they were coated in chalk.

Just as I arrived in Dublin the Catholic Association was meeting, and I therefore stopped in front of their building.[6] Unfortunately neither Shiel nor O'Connell was present, so the gathering held absolutely no attraction for me. The heat and the nasty odor soon drove me off (*car l'humanité catholique pue autant qu'une autre*).[7]

In the evening I found much more amusement in the performances of some other charlatans: a company of so-called English riders who make their home here.[8] Mr. Adam, in his way the best of them all, directs the academy, which deserves this title more than many. It was a pleasure to watch twenty elegantly dressed young people, almost all of them equally agile. Through the artful confusion, variety, complexity, and startling rapidity of their movements, they often attained a level of chaotic dissonance that dazzled the eye, only to be resolved a moment later in the most graceful harmony.

Still more delightful were two inimitable clowns whose limbs could mimic the movements of any puppet. Moreover one of them was supported by a spotted donkey that put even the noble steeds to shame with the precision of its tricks; the other clown managed to achieve, by means of a peculiar instrument of his own invention, such truly crazy music that the unheard-of tones themselves provoked irrepressible laughter. The spectacle closed with a pas de deux performed by the two clowns, who danced with their hands as well as their feet. But their feet made the *pas* in the air, while their bodies moved around on their hands. It was as if the human form vanished, and the whole scene, as uncanny as a tale of Hoffmann, appeared to the *bewildert** spectator like the dance of two insane sea anemones.

(Here a few pages of correspondence are missing.)

Following that last performance, I will take his example and say goodnight and farewell for a few days, since this letter is departing with tomorrow morning's post.

Your most faithful Lou

---

* *Bewildert* is a term adopted from the English, and I am taking the liberty of using it to enrich the German language.

Bermingham House, in the west of Ireland, September 5th, 1828

GOOD JULIA!

You make me laugh with your gratitude for my diligence. Do you not know that nothing can give me greater pleasure than writing to you? Already after my first words I feel *at home;* comfort and strength fill me once more. Just as I have always felt better after consulting a doctor, even before taking any medicine, I also need only to sit at my desk, lift my pen, and write the words "dear Julia" for my soul to feel invigorated. You are the best of physicians, because you nourish me not with medicine but with honey. *Gare aux flatteurs! Vous me gâtez.*[1]

Do you remember the young clergyman from Bray, a good-hearted person who, though he meant no harm by it, nevertheless made the dear Lord into the greatest of tyrants?[2] Well, he begged me so fervently to accompany him to Connacht where he was going to see his father—a man he said was as hospitable as he was well-to-do—that I relented, and here I am. This wild part of Ireland, never visited by foreigners and only rarely by natives, has such a bad reputation that there is a proverb "Go to hell and Connacht." Thus I might well have given a bit more thought to the matter, but what tends to put off others only attracts me; these are the situations I find most profitable, and this time everything seems greatly promising, at least with regard to the unexpected.

Yesterday evening after *dîner*, we got into my carriage and left the metropolis. The distance we were supposed to cover was exactly 101 miles. In England this would have been quickly accomplished, but here the condition of the mail coaches is not the same, and it took us twenty-four hours.

The local landscape is remarkably similar to the Wendish areas of Lower Lusatia, where once my unlucky star also cast me up. However it lacks our abundant forests, which here—save for a few scrawny pines—are things of the past. Instead bogs and peat moors stretch out interminably, and the thousand-year-old wood of oaks found buried in their depths is sold at a high price for decorative furniture; even snuffboxes and ladies' jewelry are made of it. The rest of the ground is either sandy or wet. On the dry soil the fields are infertile, whereas bog farming, something fully understood here, thrives superbly. First you level the bog by cutting the uplifted terrain into turf bricks; only then do you begin the burning and cultivation of crops. All the bogs seem extraordinarily deep, and buckwheat, potatoes, and oats are most commonly planted. The huts of the inhabitants are wretched beyond all description, and the appearance of the entire flat area is exceedingly poor until you get close to my friend's estate, where nature becomes more congenial. Here your eye is caught by the blue mountains on the horizon, the setting of many fairy tales and marvels.

Captain Bermingham, my host, is one of the notables of his county, but his house is no finer than that of a moderately affluent German nobleman. English elegance and English luxury do not exist here. Wax candles are as unknown as claret and champagne. People drink sherry and port, but above all whiskey punch, and although the coffee is detestable, the ordinary fare is quite nourishing and hearty. The house itself is not excessively clean, and the small domestic staff—admittedly worthy of respect for their enthusiasm, dedication, and years of service—have a somewhat unwashed and coarse appearance.

From the windows of my room, I can unravel all the secrets of the domestic economy, which is too modest to construe its manure piles as a grand vista, something we do in northern Germany. The rain (unfortunately it is raining) runs merrily in under the windows to form a few romantic waterfalls from the sill to the floor, where the old carpet drinks up the flood. The furniture is a bit rickety, but I have enough tables (a matter of great concern, given all my things), and the bed appears commodious and adequately firm. Excellent peat is burning, or rather glowing, in my fireplace, and besides providing warmth, it also, like Vesuvius when it erupts, covers every object with a fine coat of ash. Although none of this is dazzling, how greatly are such trifles counterbalanced by the *patriarchal hospitality* and *cheerful, unaffected friendliness of the family*! They must regard my visit as a favor to them, for they all seem obliged to me as if I were performing some significant service.

September 6th, 1828

I LIKE MY host a lot. He is seventy-two and still as hale and hearty as though he were fifty. He must have been very handsome once, and his manliness is proven by his twelve sons and seven daughters, all by the same wife, whom I have not seen, for she is currently unwell. Some of his offspring have long been married, and the old man now watches grandchildren of twelve playing with his own youngest daughter of fourteen. A large part of the family is here at the moment, which makes my stay somewhat noisy. This is augmented by the musical talents of his daughters, who can be heard daily on an instrument that is horribly tuned, a fact that does not seem to trouble them in the slightest.* As a rule the men talk only of riding and the hunt, and are otherwise fairly ignorant. Today, for instance, a country squire from the neighborhood spent a long time puzzling over a map of Europe in a hapless search for the United States. Finally his brother-in-law suggested he try his luck with a map of the world. The old gentleman was attempting to find the free states of America because he wanted to show me where, during the American wars, he had laid the foundation stone of Halifax and B——town, the latter named after him. In those days he commanded seven hundred men, and he enjoys thinking back on his youth and importance. His scrupulous chivalry and constant readiness to sacrifice his own comfort for others reflect the education of a long-vanished era and actually reveal his age more certainly than his appearance does.

Our entertainments for the next few days have been arranged as follows: Tomorrow we will visit a church; the next day we will go to the town of Galway to watch the horse races, during which the poor animals not only run five miles but have to leap over various walls in the process. They are ridden by gentlemen. That evening there is a ball, where I have been promised a look at

---

* I have often noticed that the love of music is merely a thing of fashion in all of England. There is no nation in Europe that pays more for music, while understanding and enjoying it less.

all the beauties of the neighborhood. To be honest, although very touched by the kindness shown me, I am a bit apprehensive about staying too long with this family. But these warmhearted people would be deeply hurt if I revealed any of my misgivings. *Je m'exécute donc de bonne grace.*[3]

September 7th, 1828

THE MANNERS HERE are so old-fashioned that every day the head of the household proposes a toast to my health; and as we have no napkins at our meals, we must resort to handkerchiefs or the edge of the tablecloth.

We spent four hours this morning in the nearby town of Tuam, where we visited the church and watched while four priests were ordained by the archbishop. The English Protestant service is very different from ours, being an odd mix of Catholic ceremony and reformed simplicity. Pictures are not tolerated on the walls but are allowed in the windows. The attire of the priests—even of the archbishop—is just a white surplice. On the other hand, the archbishop's seat, standing resplendently across from the chancel, is built like a throne, upholstered in purple velvet, and embellished by an archbishop's crown. The sermon is read and lasts a very long time. The most tiring part, however, both before and after, is the endless recitation of antiquated, often totally contradictory prayers, their refrains sometimes repeated in song by the choir. These lead you through a true course of instruction in English history. Henry VIII's ecclesiastical revolution, Elizabeth's politics, and Cromwell's puritanical exaggerations join hands in confusion. Meanwhile certain beloved catchphrases are reiterated every minute, and many of them are more characteristic of groveling slaves prostrating themselves in the dust before a tyrant of the south than they are in harmony with Christian *dignity.* Oddly enough, the text for the day was the Gospel story about evil spirits being cast into a herd of swine, and after this had been analyzed for an hour, the four priests were ordained. The old archbishop, who has a reputation for being strictly orthodox, is very dignified and has a beautiful, sonorous voice. In contrast, the behavior of the younger theologians was disgustingly hypocritical and displeased me enormously. They continuously rubbed their eyes with a handkerchief, holding it up full of contrition as if they were dissolving in tears, and issued their responses in strangled voices. In short, the Moravians could not have outperformed them. Certainly there was no grace there of any kind.

One of the strangest customs is that while entering and leaving everyone says a prayer, but does so by turning into a corner or toward the wall as though engaged in something improper that should remain unseen.

I have to say it straight out: I do not understand how a thinking person can be edified by this kind of church service. And yet how beautiful and sublime it could be! If only the sectarian spirit could be outlawed and the ridiculous part of these pointless ceremonies eliminated, there would be no call for an abstract cult intent on such a complete denial of the senses—an impossibility for sensuous beings! Why should we not honor the Supreme Being by applying the best of those strengths—which he has granted—for the fulfillment of such a goal? Why not avail ourselves of every kind of art at its highest level of achievement and dedicate to God the most magnificent things of which mankind is capable? Of course I am imagining here a congregation far removed from both slavish servility and arrogant conceit; one that seeks only to praise the greatness of the father of all, the wonders of his world and eternal love; a congregation that does not bring the hatred of intolerance inside the walls dedicated to him; and whose tenets demand only *that* measure of faith made possible by the revelation of a person's own heart. What looms in my fantasy is the disappearance of separate churches for Jews and fifty kinds of Christians* and, in their place, true temples of God and mankind. Their gates would be open at all times to anyone in need of physical and spiritual consolation from the holy and heavenly, whether oppressed by the things of this world or filled with the happiness and well-being of a grateful heart.

Galway, September 8th, 1828

WE ARRIVED AT the racecourse very late and saw little of today's competitions. I find the life of common folk here quite peculiar, and in many respects they can truly be compared to savages: the absolute lack of proper dress among ordinary people, even on festival days like today; their total inability to withstand spirits (the "water of death") as long as they still have a penny in their pocket; their wild quarrels that break out at every moment; the customary battles with the shillelagh, a dreadful wooden cudgel that every man keeps hidden beneath his rags; and the terrifying war cries let loose on such occasions, in which hundreds often take part at the drop of a hat, and which carry on until several men are lying wounded or dead on the battlefield (some insult or offense initiates the thirst for revenge, which can preoccupy an entire community for years and be passed along to subsequent generations); and then there is the unaffected jauntiness that approaches life one day at a time; the harmless, carefree attitude and good-natured hospitality ever ready to share the last morsel; the congenial response to any stranger who approaches; and the natural ease of their conversation—all are the characteristics of a half-civilized people!

Hundreds of drunks accompanied our carriage as we drove from the racecourse to the town, and more than ten times they fell into brawling. Given the hordes of guests, we barely managed to find some miserable accommodations, although the midday meal was good and very substantial.

In earlier times the Spanish undertook extensive building in Galway, and a few descendants of those old families still exist, as do a number of very notable houses from that period. It struck me as characteristic that in this city of forty thousand there is not a single bookstore or lending library to be found. The suburbs, like all the villages we passed through, were like nothing I have seen before. Pigsties are palaces by comparison, and I often saw many groups of children as naked as God made them, blissfully wallowing with the ducks in the mucky lanes (for the fertility of the Irish seems equal to their misery).

Athenry, September 10th, 1828, early

I AM WRITING you this morning from the house of one of the most engaging women I have ever met. She is, in fact, an African who claims to be born a Miss Hardenberg. *Que dites vous de cela?*⁴ But more of that later. First you must accompany me back to the racetrack, where the running and jumping have just begun—an odd drama of its kind and quite appropriate for a

---

* Caraccioli already lamented that in England there were sixty Christian sects and only one kind of sauce— melted butter! [This comment was ascribed to Caraccioli by Claude Adrien Helvétius in *De l'homme,* published 1773.—*Translator.*]

half-savage nation. I confess that it far exceeded my expectations and kept me in a state of tremendous suspense, yet, as you will see, one must leave one's compassion and humanity at home.

The racetrack is laid out in an oval circle, and the course begins at the left, with the goal opposite it, on the right. Between these, at two opposing points of the circular line—that is, points lying in the middle between the start and the finish line—are walls of blasted fieldstone built without mortar, five feet high and two feet long. The track, which each race circles one and one-half times, is two English miles in length. Thus you see that the first wall must be jumped twice in each race, the second wall only once.* Many horses compete, but in order to be victorious, the same horse must win two races, which means that it must often repeat the race three, four, even five times, if a different horse comes in first each time. Today there were four races, so that in less than two hours, counting the intervals, the winner had to run hard for twelve miles and jump over a high wall twelve times, something so fatiguing that almost no one at home would believe a horse capable of enduring it. The riding was done by six gentlemen dressed like very elegant jockeys in colorful silk jackets and caps, leather leg coverings, and top boots. The son of my host had loaned me an excellent hunter, and therefore, by crossing the track, I could follow along very well and be present at every jump.

On such occasions everyone fixes on a special favorite. Mine, and everyone else's, was an extraordinarily beautiful dark sorrel called Gamecock ridden by a gentleman in yellow, a handsome young man of distinguished family and a superb rider. The horse I liked second best was called Rosina, a dark brown mare ridden by one of Captain Bermingham's cousins (a poor rider) in sky blue. The third-best horse, in my opinion, was Killarney, a strong but rather unattractive gelding ridden by a young man who betrayed more innate talent than perfected horsemanship. He was dressed in crimson. The fourth gentleman, perhaps the most skillful of all the riders, but somewhat feeble, rode a not particularly distinctive brown horse and was himself attired in brown. The remaining two men deserve no comment, since they took themselves out of the race right at the beginning. Namely, they both fell at the first jump, one of them injuring himself badly on the head, the other escaping with a lesser contusion but likewise unable to ride. Gamecock, starting off in a fury and scarcely controllable by his rider, flew rather than leapt over the walls in great bounds and easily won the first race. He was followed by the empty-saddled Rosina; having thrown her rider, she completed the remaining jumps on her own and with utter grace. Gamecock was now so decisively the favorite that the odds for him were five to one. But it ended very differently, and tragically. In the second race this magnificent horse had once again left the other two far behind and had executed the first two jumps in the most brilliant way. Then at the third jump he stepped on a stone that had been dislodged by one of the clumsier horses before him and fell. *The stone was still there because it was forbidden to remove it from the track.* The horse fell so violently that he went head over heels with the rider. Both were still lying motionless when the other competitors approached and, without paying the slightest attention, successfully managed their jumps. A few seconds later Gamecock picked himself up, but the rider did not

---

* To clarify this description, just think of a compressed circle marked with the four points of the compass. In the west is a post where the horses start. In the north is a wall they must jump. Then they pass the goalpost to the east for the first time, without stopping, and find another wall to the south. Once they have this behind them, they pass the starting point for the second time, jump the northern wall once more, and only then reach the finish line, after having run three miles and jumped three times over walls.

regain consciousness, and a surgeon who was present declared the case to be hopeless. The man's breastbone and skull had both been shattered. His old father, who was standing nearby when the accident happened, fainted to the ground, and his sister threw herself with heartbreaking wails onto the quivering but unconscious body of her brother, whose mouth was filled with foam. The overall response, however, was slight. After the poor young man had been repeatedly bled and was lying on the grass immersed in his own blood, he was carried off, and the race began anew as if nothing had happened. The man in brown had come in first in the previous race and now hoped to begin the decisive and final course. It was what the English call a hard race. Both horses and riders performed splendidly, running and jumping almost in rank and file. In the end Killarney won by only a quarter of a head, so the race had to be run again. This last contest was, of course, the most interesting, since one of the two *had* to win the whole event; this provided an opportunity for large bets, which at the beginning stood at par. Twice the victory seemed decided and then ended in the opposite way. At the first jump the two horses were next to each other, but before they got to the second, you could see that the brown was losing energy, and Killarney was gaining so much terrain that he arrived at his second jump more than a hundred strides in front of the other. But here, against all expectations, he balked, because the rider did not have him adequately under control. Before he could be made to obey, the brown reached him and made the leap successfully and now, exerting his every strength, got so far ahead that victory seemed a sure thing. The bets stood at ten to one. Nevertheless, the last wall still threatened, and in fact proved ruinous. The already weary horse, having expended the last of his strength in the sprint, willingly attempted the leap but could no longer accomplish it. Breaking the wall halfway down, punctured and bleeding, the horse rolled over and over, burying the rider under his weight in such a way that he could not remount. While this was happening, Killarney's rider finally conquered his unruly animal and, cheered on by the crowd, completed both remaining jumps and proceeded at a walk toward the goal, fully at his leisure and without rivals. He was so exhausted, however, that he could scarcely speak.

During the intervals I was introduced to several ladies and gentlemen, all of whom very hospitably invited me to their country houses. But I preferred to follow the son of my host, who promised to show me the fairest of the fair, if I would let him be my guide and not balk at riding ten miles in the dark. On the way he told me that the woman in question was the daughter of the former Dutch governor of——, a Mrs. L——, currently staying in the isolated village of Athenry because of its healthy air, since she suffers from chest problems due to the climate. We did not arrive until ten and surprised her at tea in her miserable little cottage.

I would like to describe this adorable creature to you so that you imagine her right before your eyes, since I am convinced that you too would love her at first sight. But I feel description is inadequate, for everything about her is heart and soul, and *that* cannot be described! She was dressed very simply, entirely in black, with her dress closed up to the neck, yet still outlining an extremely lovely figure. She was slim and extraordinarily youthful, full of gentle poise, and yet animated, even fiery, in her movements. Her complexion is brown, pure, and clear, with a soft, marblelike smoothness. I have never seen dark eyes more beautiful and sparkling or white teeth more dazzling. Her mouth, too, with its smile of angelic, childlike innocence, was enchanting.

Her refined, informal decorum and the effortless grace of her conversation, both cheerful and witty, were of that deliciously innate sort that would prove just as pleasing in Paris as Beijing, or in a village as in a city. The widest experience could not bestow greater finesse, and no girl of fifteen could blush more sweetly or banter more delightedly. Nevertheless her life had been a simple one and her unfading youth not so much of the body as the soul, for she was the mother of four children, rather close to her thirties, and now barely recovered from a lung disease that had threatened her life. But the fire of her movements, the lightning-quick animation of her conversation, were youthful and fresh, not only captivating in themselves but imparting an irresistible charm to the inner gentleness of her being. You felt that this creature had been born beneath a warmer and more joyful sun, in a place more verdant than our misty lands. She expressed a most melancholy yearning for her native country, and pain spread momentarily across her features when she declared that she would probably never again breathe its balmy, fragrant air.

I was too absorbed by the sight of her to think of physical nourishment, but she, with all the gracious industry of a housewife, set about as best she could to provide some food for us in her little cottage. A table was set in the same room, so that the frugal meal would not interrupt our conversation, and it was long past midnight when we finally said goodnight and went off in search of our beds. Not until I was lying in mine did I learn that, given the impossibility of finding a bed among the few miserable huts in the hamlet, the good-hearted and unassuming woman had ceded her own to me and was sharing a bed with her eldest daughter. You can imagine my emotions as I finally fell asleep after hearing this report!

Mrs. L——, whose name struck me so deeply, could tell me little about her family. When she was twelve she married Mr. L——, who was then a captain in the English army, in——. Immediately thereafter her father died, and she sailed with her husband to Ireland, where she has since remained. Although she knew of some relatives in Germany, they had not corresponded until three years ago, when she received a formal letter from a cousin in A——, declaring that her father's brother had died, making her his sole heir. This African child of nature was so indifferent to her situation that she had left the letter (which was written in Dutch) unanswered until now. Also, as she explained, she could only partly decipher it, since by this time she had nearly forgotten the language. "I don't know the man, after all," she added to excuse herself, "and I've left the whole inheritance issue for my husband to settle."

The spa town of Athenry (the springs are the same type as those in Salzbrunn in Silesia) is one of Ireland's idiosyncrasies. I have already told you that no Polish village could look more miserable. The huts are clustered on top of a barren hill rising out of a peat bog, without a tree or shrub. There is no inn and no convenience of any kind, and the huts are inhabited only by ragged beggars, with the exception of the handful of spa visitors, who carry everything they need along with them. Their provisions, down to the smallest bit of food, must be brought over from Galway, twelve miles away. It was once different, and you feel sad when you look at the proud ruins of a better time at the far end of this wretched spot. The wealthy abbey that used to stand here is now overgrown with ivy, and the vaulted arches that protected the sanctuary have collapsed, exposing the altars and tombstones to the sky. Farther along you can see the ten-foot-thick walls of the palace of King John, who held his court of justice here when he came to Ireland.

I visited this ruin with a very large retinue, and I do not exaggerate when I assure you that more than two hundred half-naked individuals from across the region, a third of them children, had gathered idly around my carriage by early morning and now surrounded me begging amid shouts of *vivat*! as they faithfully accompanied me, every single one of them, through the ruins and over the rubble and brambles. The strangest compliments would sound forth from the crowd, even "long live the king!" Upon returning I tossed them a couple of handfuls of copper, and soon half of them, including both young and old, were beating each other senseless in the filthy road, while the rest ran straight to the tavern to drink up their pittance.

That is Ireland! Neglected or oppressed by the government, degraded by the stupid intolerance of the English priesthood, abandoned by the rich landowners, and stigmatized by poverty and the poison of whisky. It is the home of naked, miserable wretches.

Even among the educated classes of the provinces, the level of ignorance seems unparalleled, at least judging from our notions of education. I hesitate to report what happened this morning at breakfast, when the phenomenon of magnetism was mentioned, and no one knew the slightest thing about it. You can be sure that I volunteered instruction on the subject to Mrs. L——, and her vivacity was immediately ignited. But this provincialism was still more pronounced at Bermingham House, where among a party of twenty people, not a soul had heard that such places as Karlsbad and Prague existed. That they were situated in Bohemia offered no clarification, since it also went unrecognized. Indeed, *everything* beyond Great Britain and Paris was effectively a Bohemian village to them.[5] "So where are *you* actually from, then?" I was asked. "From Brobdingnag,"[6] I replied jokingly. "Oh, is that on the sea? Do they have whiskey there, too?" And more: once when I was out riding with my host's son, we encountered some asses, and he asked me very earnestly whether this kind of animal was also to be found where I came from? "Ah, far too many of them," I responded with a sigh.

Bermingham House, September 12th, 1828

YESTERDAY WE RETURNED here, tearing ourselves away from the lovely African who promised to follow us soon, and today I took advantage of the leisure time to ride to Castle Hackett at the foot of an isolated hill, which, in the opinion of the locals, is a favorite spot for fairies—"the good people," as they are called here. No people are more poetic or endowed with a richer imagination. The old man who oversees the castle woodlands and has the reputation of being fully informed about the good people told us the story about losing his son, all in the tone of a romance. "I knew already," he said, "four days beforehand, that he would die, because when I was walking home in the twilight that evening, I saw *them* storming along across the plain in a wild chase, their red garments fluttering in the wind. And as they approached, the lakes froze into ice, walls and trees bent to the ground before them, and they rode across the tops of the thicket as if over a field of grass. The queen thundered in front on a white, stag-like horse, and next to her I saw, with a shudder, my son. She was smiling and sweet-talking him, while he, as if feverish, gazed at her yearningly. They all disappeared in the vicinity of Castle Hackett, and I knew he was doomed! On that same day he took to his bed, and on the third day I carried him to his grave. There was no handsomer, no better young man in Connemara—that is why the queen chose him."

The old man seemed so candid and so firmly convinced of the truth of his tale that it would only have been mortifying for him if anyone were to utter the slightest doubt. When we inquired about further particulars, he answered most willingly; but I will reserve for your next masked ball the pleasure of describing the queen's dress in exquisite detail.

At the foot of this eerie hill is a pretty country estate, and the hill itself is covered to its very top with young, vigorous plantings. On the rocky peak stands an artificial ruin of loose, piled-up stones that can only be climbed with great difficulty and, given how easily the stones are dislodged, not without danger. But the view is worth the effort. On two sides the eye wanders unimpeded across the immeasurable plain; on the other two sides the horizon terminates with the Corrib (a thirty-mile-long lake) and behind it the hills of County Clare, and then the gloomy, romantic forms of the mountains of Connemara. Midway along its length, the lake curves like a river into the interior of the mountains and is gradually lost to sight in a narrow mountain pass between the highest peaks, which form a kind of gate to receive it. Exactly at this moment the sun began to set, and nature, who often repays my love for her, unveiled a wonderful spectacle. Black clouds hung over the mountain, and the entire sky was overcast. But just now the sun emerged from behind the dark veil and filled the entire mountain gorge with the radiance of an otherworldly light. The lake sparkled beneath it like molten bronze, while the mountains looked transparent in a steel blue shimmer like the glitter of diamonds. Across this scene of light and fire, fluffy pink clouds moved slowly over the mountains like grazing lambs, while in the distance, on either side of the unfolding sky, torrential rain poured down like a curtain, closing off the view to the rest of the world. This is the magnificence that nature has reserved for herself alone; even Claude's brush could not imitate it.

On the way home my young companion talked incessantly about Mrs. L——, and it was clear to me that for some time he had been circling around her like a moth to a flame, and not without repercussions. At one point he remarked, "I never noticed, with all her vivaciousness, a single instance of moodiness or impatience in her—no woman has ever had a better 'temper.'" This word, like "gentle," is untranslatable. Only a nation capable of inventing the word "comfort," could also think up "good temper"; because "good temper" is to the spiritual what "comfort" is to the material. It is a contented condition of the soul and the greatest happiness, both for those who possess it and for those who enjoy it in others. In its perfect form it is perhaps found only in females, because by nature it is more acquiescent than active. Yet it must be strictly distinguished from mere apathy, which is either boring or annoying, if not infuriating, whereas good temper sets everything at ease. It is a truly gentle, loving, and cheerful principle, as mild and soothing as a cloudless day in May. With gentleness in his character, comfort in his house, and good temper in his wife, a man's earthly delights are taken care of. Good temper, in the highest degree, is among the rarest of qualities, the consequence of a perfect harmony, an equilibrium of intellectual powers, the most complete *health of the soul.* For this reason it cannot coexist with distinctive or pronounced individual qualities, because where a single strength stands out, there can be no equilibrium. Thus one can be thrilling, can inspire passionate love, admiration, and respect, but lack a good temper; however only by possessing a good temper can one ultimately become *completely* worthy of love. To perceive harmony in all things has a beneficial effect on the mind; the soul is always gladdened by it, often without knowing why, no matter which of the senses conveys the feeling. Therefore those people gifted with good temper provide us with lasting enjoyment, without ever exciting envy or awakening fierce sentiments in others. We are fortified by their tranquillity, invigorated by their steady good cheer. We find comfort in their acquiescence; we feel our anger disappear in the face of their loving patience; and we become, in the end, better and happier because of the harmony achieved by their spiritual timbre.

You will say, dear Julie, how many *words* to describe just *two*! And yet I have only imperfectly expressed what good temper is.

THE BEAUTIFUL VIEW yesterday evening tempted me today to see from nearby what I had only beheld from afar. My obliging friend quickly arranged for an equipage, a small *char-à-banc* that we drove with two post-horses tandem—that is, with one harnessed in front of the other. We decided to take a look at Lough Corrib and Cong's dripstone caves and, in order to make the best of it, not to return until nightfall. We reached Cong, which was about twenty miles away, after four hours at a brisk trot and a few small mishaps with the frail vehicle. There we stopped at the wretched inn to have the breakfast we had brought with us—lobster prepared in the Irish manner.* Since no knives or forks were to be had, we consumed it like the Chinese, with small sticks of wood, and then immediately made our way to the caves, accompanied as usual by a half-naked retinue. Each and every one of them was looking for some kind of service to perform; if you bent down for a stone, ten of them scrambled to pick it up and asked for a tip; if there was a door to be opened, twenty of them rushed at it. Later, when I had distributed all my small coins, one more supplicant arrived and claimed to have shown me some trivial thing, I cannot remember what, and so I had to turn him away claiming my purse was empty. "Oh!" he cried, "A gentleman's purse can never be empty!" Not a bad response, for it harbored a malicious ambiguity in the form of a compliment. It meant: You look too much like a gentleman not to have any money; but if you are so ungenerous as not to give me any, then you are no longer a gentleman; and if you really have nothing, you are even less a one. The crowd understood this and laughed, until I bought myself free.

But back to the cave—the Pigeon Hole—an extraordinary natural phenomenon. It lies in the middle of a field on a bleak, treeless plain punctuated by oddly shaped pieces of limestone, while the patches of ground between these outcroppings are being painstakingly maintained as meadows and fields. The limestone is as smooth as if it had been polished, and the stones look half-worked, as if brought here and placed in orderly piles for some colossal building project. In this rocky field, about a quarter of an hour from Lough Corrib, the cave opens like a wide, dark well, in which thirty to forty rough steps have been cut into the rock. These lead down to the river, which flows *underground* here, channeling its way through bizarrely shaped arches of rock, then stepping into the light only to turn a millwheel before burying itself a second time in the belly of the earth. It reemerges later as a wide, deep, crystal-clear river that pours into the waters of the lake.

Not far from the cave where we now stood lives a *Donna del Lago,*[7] who pays four pounds a year to the owner of the land for the right to show strangers the Pigeon Hole. She is perfectly suited to be the guardian of such an entry to the underworld, and the whole scene could not be more "in character," as the English say. We had already clambered down the steps in the dark and could hear, without yet seeing, the roaring river, when a gigantic, haggard old woman descended, enveloped in a scarlet cloak; her white hair was long and streaming and she was holding a blazing firebrand in each hand—the living image of Scott's Meg Merrilies.[8] It was a remarkable sight as her torches swept back and forth, throwing a dazzling glow over the waves and up onto the high vaulting with its jagged stalactites, as well as illuminating us pale, ragged creatures below. Now the ancient crone, declaiming in words that rang like an incantation, threw flaming bundles of straw into the water. As they floated swiftly away, they exposed yet more unseen grottoes and

---

* An excellent dish! The recipe will be delivered in person.

grotesque forms until finally, after a hundred meanders, they disappeared in the distance like little candles. Scrambling over the slippery rocks, we followed their beams as far as we could, and now and then in the ice-cold water we came upon large trout, said to possess the distinction that not one of them has ever been caught, no matter what bait was offered. The locals naturally consider them to be enchanted.

When you turn back from the darkness to the spot where the light of day is filtering down as if into a shaft, you see ivy and other creeping plants hanging over the rocks in the most picturesque festoons and garlands. Here the wild pigeons assemble in large numbers for their nightly rest—hence the cave's name. The local superstition prohibits any hunter from disturbing them in this place, so they are as fearless as if they were in a dovecote.

From these somber regions where everything is confined, we now walked to the wide, ocean-like lake, where everything seems to lose itself in boundlessness. The majestic waters of the Corrib fill a massive basin nearly sixty miles long and fourteen across at its broadest point. It is a remarkable coincidence that the lake has the same number of islands as there are days in a year. (This, anyway, is what the natives claim; I did not count). It is bounded on two sides by the high mountains of Connemara; on the other its waters almost merge with the plain. Our approach, facing the mountains, was therefore incomparably more beautiful than our return. Navigation on these waters is said to be very dangerous because of the many rocks and islands, as well as the sudden squalls that often erupt; indeed there were recent newspaper reports about a vessel that went down while carrying butchers and their sheep to market, men and animals alike falling victim to the angry water sprites. We ourselves enjoyed a very calm though not-always-clear day, and when we reached shore again, I let my companion go on ahead to make the necessary arrangements, while, as the sun was setting, I toured the ruins of an abbey at the lake's edge, admiring the lovely architectural and sculptural remains.

Ireland is teeming with the vestiges of ancient castles and monasteries, more than any other part of Europe, although these ruins are not on the same scale as, for example, in England. Most of the *old* ruins (many are *new*, unfortunately) now serve as graveyards, a poetic notion that is, I believe, peculiar to these people. They never erect tasteless modern monuments, as one finds in English churches, but are content with a simple mound of earth or at most a stone atop the grave, something that heightens rather than profanes the affecting aura of earthly transience. But this impression is frequently rendered gruesome by the lack of consideration shown by subsequent gravediggers, who often summarily toss aside the skeletons of those already buried simply to free up space for new arrivals. Hence the ruins are cluttered with skulls and bones, most often in unruly piles, but sometimes arranged in pyramids and other formations by children at play. I climbed over such rocks and bones and worked my way to a dilapidated room on the upper floor, where I reveled in the exoticism of this romantic scene: To my left the wall had collapsed, opening up a view of the lovely landscape surrounding the lake, the foreground a pale green with the mountain range in the distance, and to one side the castle and the towering trees of MacNamara Park, named after the family living here. In front of me was a window, still well preserved, with a superbly carved frame like Alençon lace, and above it, inaccessible from the freestanding wall, clusters of inky blue blackberries were hanging on rampant, luxuriant vines. In the intact wall to the right was a low niche within easy reach, which probably once housed the figure of a saint. Now a solitary skull resides there, its empty eye sockets directed at the beautiful view, as if the freshness of life and the radiance of the scene could bring joy even to the dead! As I continued on in the same direction, I discovered very close to the ground a barred window I had overlooked before; this illuminated a vast cellar housing an immense pile of bones in diverse arrangements. The sunny landscape above; the dark heaps of bones below, where childhood toyed with death—it was at once a glimpse of life and the grave, symbolizing the joys of the one and the indifferent repose of the other. But like messengers from a lovelier world, the comforting rays of the setting sun bathed the living and the dead in a warm, golden light.

Our return journey in the pitch of night, accompanied by incessant rain, was difficult and unpleasant. Once again we broke a spring in our carriage and suffered sundry other mishaps. And yet when we finally reached Bermingham after midnight, we found—to my true horror—the old captain and his entire family still up, waiting to dine with us. I feel embarrassed by the lavish attention and enormous good-heartedness of these people, and I must constantly admire how such ardent hospitality is never marred by any trace of ostentation.

So that my letter will not be too heavy and cost too much postage (for I usually have to pay a few pounds just to get these voluminous packets to the English border), I will close now, even before my departure from Bermingham. At least you know I am in good hands and being looked after by people who have *hearts* like yours, even though they cannot match your mind and refinement. May heaven bless and keep you!

Your most faithful Lou

LETTER 32

Bermingham, September 14th, 1828

BELOVED FRIEND!

All your preaching is of no use, good Julie! Your rhetoric is superb, your reasons may be valid, but I am simply of the opposite *belief*. And, as you realize, belief is a thing that not only moves mountains but constructs its own, beyond which it simply cannot see. Therefore no conversion, from whatever point of view, will ever be effective unless one's belief has already been shaken. Until then you may speak with the wisdom of Plato and act with the purity of Jesus, but you will dislodge no one from their belief, something generally indifferent to reason or good sense.* Anyone who seeks to change people before they are prepared to expose themselves to the grindstone of world history and acquire a new facet will be seen as a fool and sent packing, or assailed and crucified as a martyr. History teaches us this on every page. What applies universally applies also to the individual, so *parlez-moi raison, si vous l'osez.*[1] But let me say one thing in earnest. Anyone who is born with too free a spirit and pays scant attention to common opinion if it is simply *common*, will remain that way his whole life long. The consequences of this kind of thinking, and the animosities it engenders, will only become painful—and eventually dangerous—when one grows weak and ceases to be independent. As long as one hold's one's ground and looks boldly in the eye of the antagonists, their critiques remain ineffectual. But as soon as one begins to fear instead of scorn the opinions of others, the hordes will notice and set off in single-minded pursuit of their quarry. For the *world* there is no better lesson than this: *bouche riante et front d'airain, et vous passez partout.*[2] We Germans are almost always too serious, and also too timid, and are only capable of controlling our defects momentarily; moreover, in so doing, we typically overshoot the mark. This is the main reason we love seclusion so much and prefer our own fancy to the company of others, however trustworthy. We are sovereign rulers of the realm of the air, to quote Madame de Staël.[3] We feel no affection for the larger world as it is and have just as little understanding of how to gain its affection for ourselves. Therefore we prefer seclusion and, with it, freedom!

Today we experienced a strange fulfillment of prophecy. Yesterday, while we were taking a walk, Miss Kitty, the most charming of my host's daughters, had some gypsies tell her fortune. I listened as the woman claimed, among many other ordinary things, that Kitty should be on guard, because shots would be fired through her windows within twenty-four hours and she would not be staying in Bermingham much longer after that. We found this prophecy somewhat alarming and therefore reported it when we got home, but were only laughed at and teased about it. Quite early the next morning, however, there was real alarm when two shots were heard, and

---

* At most one might convert in name, but not in deed.

Miss Kitty, half dressed and almost faint with terror, dashed down the stairs just as everyone rushed over to find out what had happened. It turned out that two of Kitty's younger brothers, who were visiting at Mrs. M——'s, had returned unexpectedly that morning in order to pick up their sister and take her back with them, and they—completely unaware of the gypsy's prediction—had played the silly joke of setting off two firecrackers in front of her window, but did it so clumsily that a few panes of glass were damaged.[4] They received a serious dressing-down and then the three of them departed. Thus everything happened exactly as the old woman had read in the lines of her hand, heaven knows how.

September 15th, 1828

I WAS A bit of a hypochondriac yesterday, my soul felt dull—but I took my medicine, it worked, and my soul has been cured. I am cheerful again and thus feeling much more benevolent toward my fellow man; virtuous, too, *faute d'occasion de pécher,*[5] and merry, in that I laugh at myself for want of finding anything more amusing.

Meanwhile the scene here has changed. The beautiful African arrived, and we have already taken a group ride, ten people strong, during which the elderly captain, with the passion of a young man, showed us his bog cultivation and irrigation systems. He was no less enchanted by his potato beds than I was by my female companion. In the most desolate region he gestured toward a flourishing field of tubers and called out enthusiastically, "Isn't that a magnificent sight?" It certainly never entered his head that we could be thinking of other things and were only agreeing with him out of politeness. Afterward I recruited a few peasants for my colonization plan. They were all keen to emigrate, but unfortunately did not have a single penny to spend on the scheme. It is, by the way, easy to promise them that everything will be better than here, where a person lives on less than a half acre and cannot find work, however willing he is to labor away from home. Those who are best off live in huts that our peasants would not think good enough to serve as stalls. I visited one and found the walls constructed of rough fieldstones, the holes stuffed with moss, and a roof of poles covered half with straw, half with turf. The floor consisted of bare earth, and there was no ceiling beneath the semitransparent roof. Chimneys, too, seem useless luxuries here; the smoke drifted unhindered from the freestanding hearth through the unglazed windows. To the right a low partition divided off the sleeping area of the family, who all repose together; another to the left separates off the pig and cow. This tiny house stood in the middle of a field without any garden or other convenience—and everyone called it an *excellent* abode.

Although it was still summer the hands of our pretty guest were nearly frozen by the time we got home. They had turned completely white and numb, and we had to rub them for more than a quarter of an hour before life and blood returned. *C'est le sang africain.*[6] She only feels thoroughly comfortable before the sweltering heat of a peat fire, where the rest of us are half roasted, and only then does she recover her childlike exuberance, which sometimes infects me as well. She really seems to have her eye on me a bit, and it is hard to resist her affectionate teasing. When she pushes aside her raven black hair and looks at you so piercingly with her fiery, dark blue eyes, she seems able to read your mind. And then she mischievously lowers her gaze as if she has understood only too well the silent language of the eyes meeting hers, and a few moments later, in charming confusion, a tender, fleeting glance touches your heart with an electric spark. So it is difficult to maintain one's composure and play along when, in the next instant, her nimble and ingenious spirit ripples with laughter over the tragicomical face she claims you are making, or yet another foolishness that has come into her little head. Yes, dear Julia, it is a seductive game, I well realize—but the poison is sweet!

September 16th, 1828

MY FRIEND JAMES is starting to get a bit jealous and no longer talks to me as much about the charms of Mrs. L—— and her good temper. Currently I am teaching her how to shoot a pistol. The first time she fired, she recoiled with such childlike shock that she nearly fainted, then fell into my arms and began to sob. James came up at this critical moment and seemed anything but edified by it. I quickly handed him the pistol and proposed a small wager as an entertainment for our friend, while she recovered from her fright. But poor James could not hit a thing, whereas I, with practiced accuracy, outlined a fairly legible *H* on the target—for her name is Henriette, or Harriet, as she is called here. As she grew accustomed to firing, she shot quite well and embarrassed the young men, all of whom performed rather inexpertly.

Afterward we went for a ride, she and I, with Miss Kitty and one of her brothers. The two of us went on ahead a little and talked about English literature. She mentioned a lovely, well-known song by Moore, in which the poet declares himself one moment for blue and the next for black eyes, and teasingly asked me which of the two I preferred.

"Oh," I exclaimed, "blue ones beneath black hair, for this unites the sweet gentleness of the one with the sparkling southern ardor of the other."

"Oh, nonsense!" she laughed, "You've forgotten the song entirely. The poet gives preference to *those* eyes, no matter what their color, *that look at him most tenderly . . .*"

"Well, then," I responded "all I wish is that you are of the same opinion."

"How so?" she asked, confused.

"That you would love the eyes that look at you with the most tenderness." With this I gripped her hand and was about to whisper still more to her, when she—laughing and jesting like the little minx that she is—cried out for no reason to Miss Kitty, claiming that her horse was about to bolt!

When later, just for a moment, I found myself alone with her again, she drew in a deep breath and said in a quiet voice, "Now I declare you are a great rogue and never more I'll be alone with you."[7]

O Africa! Your daughters, I clearly see, understand coquettishness just as well as do the fair beauties of Europe.

In the evening we had a lot of fun with Henrietta's fifteen-year-old daughter, also a pretty, fresh-looking creature, though not the equal of her mother. In this instance the cross with English blood was not advantageous, and Prometheus's fire was hidden again in the sand.

We looked through her "album" or "sketchbook," where—among the lines she had transcribed from various tomes—we found the following Irish poem that she had clearly practiced with great innocence but that now caused her to suffer. It goes like this:[8]

And pray, how was the devil dressed?
Oh! He was in his Sundays best,
His coat was black, and his breeches steelblue

And a hole behind, that his tail went through.
And over the hill and over the dale
He rambled far over the plain,
And backward and forward he switched his tail
As a gentleman switches his cane.*

Everyone, even the girl herself, had to laugh heartily over the switching devil—for these were innocent children of nature, and there was not a prude among them ready to be offended, no newly pious lady eager to uncover godless mockery. Any female member of a conventicle would of course have turned her eyes to heaven and left the room—either in order to enjoy a rendezvous with her lover in the *Tier*garten or to ruin the reputation of a good friend, for *such* things are blameless![9]

September 17th, 1828

MR. L—— ARRIVED today. How strangely the goods of this world are distributed! The loveliest, sweetest woman becomes the booty of the most disgusting man, someone incapable of reciprocating or appreciating the richness of her nature! He is an ugly old pedant, steeped in gall, the exact opposite of his wife in every way. His conversation was enough to spoil the cheerfulness, indeed I would say the innocence, of our life up to then. He is a fierce Orangeman (orange being, by the way, his natural coloring!), and it was to be expected that a character of his type would take the side of injustice and partisan fury, but based on what principles! I will give you the essence of his conversation, since it offers a taste of just how intense the partisan spirit has become here and how blatantly it is expressed.

"I have served my king for thirty years in nearly every part of the world and am in need of rest," he said. "Yet my most ardent wish, for which I pray to God daily, is that I live to see a proper rebellion in Ireland. If I were to reenlist that very day and lose my life because of it, I would welcome the sacrifice so long as the blood of five million Catholics flowed along with mine. Rebellion!— that's where I want them to go, where I await them, and where they must be guided, so we can be rid of them once and for all. There will be no peace in Ireland without *the total annihilation* of this race, and nothing will accomplish it but an open rebellion and an English army to put it down!"

Do you not think that such a malicious fool should be locked up—and his wife given to another man? *Qu'en dites-vous,*[10] Julia?

The young sons of my host were just as shocked as I was and manfully challenged his diabolical principles. This infuriated the lunatic Orangeman even more until finally everything went quiet and several got up from the table to escape this repugnant discussion.

September 18th, 1828

LUCKILY MR. L——'s visit lasted only one day, and we are again just among ourselves. This new-won freedom was immediately celebrated with a twenty-mile excursion to Mount Bellew, the beautiful property of a country squire. We did not return until late at night, and I was granted

---

* Mrs. Sexaginta will be able to judge whether the dress is correctly described. [This name may be an allusion to the devil's wife or grandmother, see page 416, footnote.—*Translator.*]

the company of Henrietta in my carriage, for she could not bear the cold air—*mais honi soit qui mal y pense.*[11] The park at Mount Bellew offers a true course of study in how best to lay out large bodies of water, for it is generally a challenge to grant them appropriate prominence as well as naturalness. You must turn to nature for the details, but the main point is that you never allow the entire mass of water to be overlooked at one time. And the water itself must disappear from view little by little, preferably in several places at once, in order to allow adequate scope for the imagination—the true art of every landscape design.[12]

The owner, who is rich, also possesses a sizeable art collection, including some excellent paintings. Among others there is a winter landscape by Ruisdael, the only one I remember seeing by this master. The cold, foggy air and crunch of the snow were so faithfully represented that you almost felt yourself shivering—or at the least you gazed at the flickering fireplace beneath the picture with a doubled sense of coziness. A beautiful *Miraculous Draft of Fishes*, indisputably a Rubens, was distinguished by an unusual feature: Peter, in a green robe, is wearing a *scarlet* wig, yet this does not damage the overall impression. Indeed the effect is that of a halo, distributing light all around. It seems to be a clever trick by the painter, perhaps undertaken in response to a joke, *pour prouver la difficulté vaincue.*[13] A very painstaking landscape on panel by an unknown hand was previously in the private collection of Charles I, whose cipher and name, surmounted by the crown, are branded into the verso and still clearly visible. But what I regarded as the jewel of the entire collection was a painting by Rembrandt, which is supposedly the portrait of an Asiatic Jew, but at the same time represents the epitome of the type. The reality of those eyes with their scorching gaze was almost frightening, while the eerie and yet sublime effect of the whole was increased by the inky blackness of the rest of the picture. The head with its glowing eyes and satanic laughing mouth look out chillingly from an Egyptian night.*

After breakfast a number of hunters and racers were brought out, and we performed riding exercises for the ladies. These hunters are perhaps not as fast as the best English ones, but they are unsurpassed at jumping, to which they are encouraged from their youth. They approach a wall with the utmost composure and leap over by touching down on it with their forefeet and hind feet the way dogs do. If there is a ditch on the other side, they leap over this too by giving themselves a fresh élan at the top of the wall. With such a well-trained horse, you normally allow minimal play in the reins and simply do your absolute best to interfere as little as possible, keeping a consistent light check on the bridle and otherwise turning everything over to your mount.

I do not know if such equestrian details will be very edifying for you, but since these letters are simultaneously my journal (how would I find time for another one?), you will have to be entertained by whatever may be interesting for you, or me.

Galway, September 19th, 1828, evening

YOU KNOW THAT my decisions are typically impulsive—you have often called them my pistol shots. Well, I have just executed such a one. I was afraid of the softening effect of Capua and of becoming enslaved to Africa (*j'aime à effleurer les choses, mais pas les approfondir*).[14] Therefore

---

*   If one of the Rothschilds looked like this, he would definitely become king and Solomon's throne would no longer be unoccupied.

I *fled*, feigning the receipt of some important news as a pretext. You may well imagine my emotion at having to tear myself away from such warmhearted male friends and captivating female friends, but I kept my resolve. I chose not to wait for the post-horses to be fetched from the nearby town but leaving all other arrangements to my manservant, I rode to Tuam with James, mounted for the last time on Doctor, his excellent hunter. I think my friend was happy to accompany me. From Tuam I had wanted to travel on with the mail, but this was not its day. The only available conveyance to Galway was an inferior letter-post cart, nothing but an open, two-wheeled wagon pulled by a single horse, with room for just two passengers besides the driver. Nevertheless I hesitated only briefly before giving James's hand a final shake, then leapt bravely into the frail vehicle, and *clopin-clopant*, the old nag rattled off down the street. The other passenger was a young, sprightly man in rather elegant attire, with whom I quickly entered into an interesting conversation about the sights of his country and the character of his countrymen. He himself was immediate proof of their cordiality and obliging nature. I was very lightly dressed and at the same time warm from my ride, so I found the cold wind extremely uncomfortable and offered the driver a tip for letting me use his cloak. On closer view, however, the thing was so horribly filthy and disgusting that I could not persuade myself to put it on. The young man immediately took off his impressive, very ample traveler's overcoat and almost forced me to wrap myself in it, while assuring me with the utmost zeal that he *never* caught cold and, if necessary, could sleep the whole night immersed in water; and further, that he had worn the overcoat only because he did not know where else to put it. Because of this friendly assistance, we quickly became better acquainted, and amid our chatter on many topics, the time passed much more swiftly than I could have hoped. The distance was twenty-eight miles, the road very bumpy, the equipage the very worst, the seat uncomfortable, the landscape monotonous and bleak. Not a hill, not a tree, only a network of walls stretched across the land. Every field is enclosed in this way, the walls built of fieldstones without mortar, yet constructed such that, unless brutally knocked down, they hold up well. Admittedly there were also many ruins of old castles to be seen in this region, but on such a flat, barren plain, without the interruption of *a single* shrub, they produced no romantic effect.

Yet everywhere we looked we found the ragged, potato-eating population uniformly cheerful. There was constant begging, of course, but it was done with laughter, good-natured wit, and droll expressions, without any pushiness, and with no rancor if nothing came of it. The great poverty of these people makes their equally great honesty very striking. Perhaps one arises from the other, for with luxury comes covetousness, and a poor man often gets along without a necessity more easily than a rich man does without something superfluous.

We saw a lot of laborers sitting along the main road on the piles of rocks that they were breaking up, and as their work progressed, their seats became accordingly elevated. My traveling companion said, "Those are conquerors—all they do is destroy, and yet they rise higher through that destruction." Just then our driver sounded his horn, the signal of the mail coach, for which, as at home, everything has to make way. The tone came out with such difficulty, however, and sounded so pitiful, that we all laughed. A pretty boy of about twelve, also sitting and hammering atop his pile of rocks, seemed the very image of happiness and joy, although almost naked. He shouted with gleeful mischief to the exasperated driver, "Oh ho, friend! Your trumpet must have the sniffles, for it's as hoarse as my old grandmother. Cure it quickly with a glass of poteen, or it'll drop dead from consumption before you reach Galway." At this all the workers burst into a chorus of laughter. "You see," my companion exclaimed, "those are our people. To starve and laugh—such is their fate. Can you believe that with so many workers and so little work, not one of them earns enough to eat his fill? Yet despite this, each man will find something extra to give to his priest, and if you go into his hut, he'll share his last potato with you, and make a joke about it too."

We were now nearing the hills of Galway, with the sun setting magnificently behind them. I can never watch this drama without emotion. It captivates me and leaves behind a feeling of tranquility and security. I am convinced that *this language*, through which God himself speaks to us, cannot lie, even though what is revealed may be no more than a patchwork, understood differently by each individual and only too often distorted by cunning and self-interest.

We got out at the same inn I had come to know during the horse races, and to compensate my young friend for his civility, I invited him to have supper with me. It was quite late when we parted, probably forever, but this is exactly the kind of acquaintanceship I love. It allows no time for dissembling: unaware of his interlocutor's relationships, each values just the man in him. Whatever one gains in the good opinion of the other, he owes only to himself.

September 20th, 1828, early

I HAD HOPED that my carriage would have arrived during the night, but it is still not here, so I am using my time to take a more careful look at this age-old city. I have been usefully assisted by the fragments of a very early chronicle I happened to discover in a spice shop where I was enquiring about the crossbones. Namely, in an out-of-the-way part of town, I came upon an ancient house and noticed over the door a skull atop two crossbones carved with considerable skill out of black marble. This house is called the Cross Bones, and here is its tragic history:[15]

In the fifteenth century, James Lynch, a man of old family and great wealth, was chosen mayor of Galway for life. In those days the powerful influence of this title was almost equal to that of a sovereign. Lynch was especially respected and admired for his unshakable love of justice, but also for his gentle manners and lack of haughtiness. His son Edward was even more beloved, and indeed was the idol of the citizens and their lovely wives. According to the chronicle, he was one of the most outstanding young men of his time. To perfect beauty and the noblest physical presence, he joined that invariably cheerful humor, that unfailingly serene familiarity that subjugates while seeming to flatter, and that obliging grace of manners that effortlessly conquers all hearts simply through the charm of its own nature. Furthermore his often-proven love of his native land; his generosity, romantic courage, and an education rare for the period (including the mastery of all military exercises) added *permanence* to the deep respect he commanded on first encounter.

But so much light was not without its shadows. Red-hot passions, arrogance, jealousy of any competition, and a wild, unbounded penchant for the fair sex made every one of this youth's good traits into just as many perils. His stern father, though proud of having such a son and heir, often had cause for bitter reproaches and serious apprehension about the future. Yet even he seemed unable to resist such amiability in a young man who was as quick to repent as to err, and who was consistent in both love and deference to his father. Thus once the father's anger abated, Edward's failings seemed to him, as to everyone else, nothing more than minor spots on the sun. And before long he was further reassured by his son's passionate and tender fondness for Anna Blake, the daughter of his best friend. This girl was attractive in every respect, and he confidently looked forward to their union as the fulfillment of his most ardent wishes. But the dark powers of fate had decided otherwise!

While young Lynch was encountering difficulties—more than he was used to—in touching the heart of his newly beloved, his father found it necessary to undertake a business trip to Cádiz. The aristocracy of Galway, like that of other significant port cities in the Middle Ages, had always considered large-scale trade a worthy activity for a nobleman. Indeed Galway was so powerful and widely known that, as the chronicle relates, an Arab merchant with long experience traveling from the Orient to trade along these coasts once asked in which part of Galway Ireland was located! So the mayor placed the rudder of state in secure hands for the period of his absence, prepared everything for a lengthy trip, and blessing his son with an overflowing heart and wishing him all progress in his present quest, sailed off to his destination in good spirits.

Wherever he went, his undertakings were crowned with success. A significant part of this was due to the services of a Spanish merchant named Gomez, who kindled the most intense gratitude in the noble heart of the mayor of Galway. Gomez also had a son who, like Edward Lynch, was the idol of his family and the darling of his city. Yet in character as in appearance, the two were very different. Both were handsome, but Edward more in the way of Apollo, and Gonzalvo more in that of Saint John. The one looked like a rock crowned with flowers, the other like a fragrant hill of roses threatened by a storm. The first was adorned with pagan virtues, the second with Christian humility. Gonzalvo's dashing figure revealed more softness than vigor; his soulful, dark blue eyes expressed more yearning and love than audacity and pride. A gentle melancholy overshadowed his face and a hint of suffering flickered around his full lips, lips only rarely touched by the play of a half-bashful smile, the way a gentle wave glides over coral and pearls. His heart, too, lay in accord with his affect: loving and tolerant, of a solemn and wistful serenity. Always more inwardly than outwardly focused, he preferred solitude to the noise and crush of people, yet attached himself with the most profound sincerity to those who offered him goodwill and friendship. Thus in the depths of his nature he was warmed by a fire, which, like a volcano too deeply buried to erupt, simply confers greater fertility on the soil above it, clothing it more beautifully than any other spot with delicate green and glowing floral colors.

Seductive and easy to seduce—was it any wonder that such a young man would automatically capture the palm even from the hand of Edward Lynch? But Edward's father foresaw none of this. Full of gratitude toward his friend and delight in his promising son, he decided to offer his daughter to old Gomez as a wife for Gonzalvo. The proposal was too flattering to be refused. The fathers quickly came to an agreement, and it was determined that Gonzalvo would immediately accompany his patron to Ireland's shores, and if the young pair's affections went according to plan, they would be wed at the same time as Edward and Anna Blake, and after that return to Spain. The nineteen-year-old Gonzalvo joyfully followed his father's venerable friend. His young romantic spirit, quietly captivated, was already savoring the spectacle of foreign lands, the marvels of the sea, and the new life of an unknown people he was about to make his own. And already his warm heart embraced the girl, whose charms her father had perhaps described with less than total impartiality.

Every moment of the long voyage, lengthier and more dangerous in those days, strengthened the familiarity and mutual affection of the travelers, and when they finally caught sight of Galway Harbor, old Lynch believed not only that God had granted him a second son, but he confidently reckoned that the unfailing gentleness of this engaging young man would have the most beneficial influence on the wilder and darker attributes of his own Edward.

And it seemed that this hope was to be fulfilled in every way. Edward found in Gonzalvo everything he himself lacked, and felt his own nature being made complete. In addition, given what his father had told him, he already looked upon him as a brother. Accordingly their friendship soon acquired the appearance of the most profound and enduring affection.

But in only a matter of months this harmony was marred by an unpleasantness that began to surface in Edward's soul. Gonzalvo had by then married Edward's sister, and yet he had postponed his trip home indefinitely. Everyone treated him with great affection, everyone was eager to show him love and attention. Edward, however, was not so happy; neglected for the first time, he could not hide from himself that he had found a dangerous rival in Gonzalvo's widespread popularity. What unsettled him far more, however, and wounded his heart just as badly, inflecting a restless and unbearable agony on his vanity, was the growing perception that Anna—whom he considered to be *his*, though she still hesitated to acknowledge it—*his* Anna had become increasingly cold ever since the handsome stranger had arrived. In fact, had he not himself already seen how she, in unguarded moments, let her eyes rest soulfully on Gonzalvo's appealing features, and how her once-pale cheeks would then blush the softest pink? And if his gaze happened to meet hers at such moments, the pink hue immediately turned a feverish red. Yes, certainly, her entire behavior had changed! Erratic, moody, restless, at one moment gripped by the deepest melancholy, only to abandon herself wildly to boisterous hilarity at the next, she retained only the outward appearance of the sensible, clear-headed, and reliably congenial girl she once was. To the penetrating eye of jealousy, every move betrayed a deep passion that had her in its grip, and who other than Gonzalvo could have fired it? It was he alone whose comings and goings altered the chords of her heartstrings.

A wise man once said: Love is, for the most part, more closely related to hate than to affection. The truth of this assertion played out in Edward's breast. From now on his only pleasure lay in hurting his beloved, for he felt that she alone was the guilty one. At every opportunity he sought, out of pride, to humiliate her, to wound her, to inundate her with insulting accusations. Finally the wretched creature, conscious of her secret passion, was overwhelmed by shame and indignation and burst into a flood of tears. This sight offered Edward his only refreshment, such as may be granted to the damned in the midst of their sufferings. Yet no reconciliation followed, as can sometimes happen with lovers. In fact, each incident only intensified his fury, pushing him to the brink of despair. And he now saw the flames kindled in Gonsalvo, a man incapable of deceit, and it was the same fire that burned in Anna's eyes. Thus when Edward found his sister already neglected and himself betrayed, as he thought, by a serpent he had cherished in his own breast, his whole being was reduced to that level of human frailty where only the All-Knowing can distinguish between madness and sanity.

On the same night that suspicion finally drove the restless Edward from his bed, the lovers had arranged a secret rendezvous, perhaps their first. According to Edward's later testimony, he was hidden behind a pillar when he saw Gonsalvo, wrapped in a cloak, creeping stealthily away from the Blake house, having exited from a side door that led to Anna's rooms. Struck with terrible certainty, hell took possession of his soul. His eyes stared rigidly from their sockets, the furies gnawed at his breast, his pulse seemed about to burst with the pounding of blood, and just as someone dying of thirst craves a drink of water, so did his entire being crave the blood of vengeance. Like a raging tiger he rushed toward the unlucky youth, who, recognizing him, tried in vain to flee. But in a few moments Edward reached him, and with the speed of lightning this madman buried his dagger a hundred times in Gonsalvo's twitching body, his satanic rage tearing to pieces the charms that had robbed him of his beloved and his peaceful life. Only when the moon emerged from behind a black cloud to illuminate the grisly scene, when a mutilated body lay before him with no more than a vestige of his murdered friend's features remaining, when a stream of coagulating blood already covered him, the corpse, and the earth all around, only then did he awake with frightful horror, as if from an infernal dream. Yet the deed had been done, and the judgment began.

Driven by the instinct for self-preservation he ran, like Cain, fleeing into the nearby woods. Later he could not recall how long he wandered there. Fear, despair, love, repentance, and finally madness pursued him like ghastly companions and robbed him of consciousness, suppressing for a while the horrors of what had happened to him. Nature, whether by fainting or death, heals the unbearable sufferings of both soul and body.

In the city, meanwhile, the murder had already been discovered, and the gruesome end of the gentle youth, a stranger who had entrusted himself to their hospitality, was received by all classes with grief and indignation. A dagger, steeped in blood, was found next to the Spaniard's velvet beret, and not far away lay a hat ornamented with colorful feathers and a jeweled clasp; fresh tracks of a man heading in the direction of the woods were also discovered. The hat was immediately recognized as that of young Lynch, and since he was nowhere to be found, people began to fear for his life as well, believing that *he had been murdered along with his friend*. The stunned father mounted his horse, accompanied by throngs calling for vengeance, and swore that nothing would be allowed to save the murderer, even if he had to hang him from the gallows himself.

Try to imagine: first the joyful shouts, next the shudder of the crowd and the father's emotions, when, at daybreak, Edward Lynch was found collapsed beneath a tree, alive and covered with blood but apparently unwounded. And imagine then,

Edward clasping his father's knee, condemning *himself* as the murderer of Gonzalvo and urgently demanding punishment.

He was brought back in shackles and, during a plenary session of the magistrates, condemned to death by his own father. But the people were reluctant to lose their darling. Like the waves of a storm-tossed sea, they filled the marketplace and the streets, forgetting the son's guilt in the face of the father's cruel justice. With fury they demanded that the prison be opened and the criminal pardoned. During the following night the guards were redoubled, yet even so they had difficulty keeping the rebellious mob at bay. Toward morning, however, the mayor was told that resistance would soon be futile, because some of the soldiers had gone over to the side of the people, and only the foreign mercenaries were holding fast. Everyone cried furiously for the prisoner's immediate release.

Then his steadfast father made a decision that many will consider inhuman, yet his awesome strength of mind is certainly among the rarest examples of stoic determination. Accompanied by a priest, he made his way through a secret passageway to his son's prison cell. The youth sank down at his feet, his desire for life rekindled by the sympathy of his fellow citizens. Hesitantly he inquired whether his father brought mercy and forgiveness, to which the old man answered with a steady voice, "No, my son. In this world there is no more mercy for you. Your life is irrevocably forfeited to the law, and at sunrise you must die! For twenty-two years I have prayed for your earthly happiness, but that is over. Direct your thoughts toward eternity; and if there is still hope there, then let us together implore the Almighty to grant you mercy in the hereafter. I hope that my son, although unable to live in a way worthy of his father, will at least know how to die in a way worthy of him." These words reawakened the noble pride of this once-intrepid youth, and after a short prayer he yielded to his father's pitiless will.

Just as the people, along with most of the soldiers, were about to storm the building, their threats growing ever wilder, James Lynch appeared to the astonished crowd in a high arched window of the prison, his son at his side with a rope around his neck. "I have sworn," he called out, "that Gonzalvo's murderer would die, even if I were myself forced to act as his executioner. Providence takes me at my word, and now, you deluded people, learn from the unhappiest of fathers that nothing must stand in the way of the law; even the bonds of nature must be undone before it." While speaking these words, he fastened the noose onto an iron bolt that projected from the wall and quickly pushed his son out, finishing the horrifying deed. He did not move from his place until the last convulsions of the pitiful victim signaled the certainty of his death.

As if struck by lightning, the once tumultuous crowd watched this horrible spectacle in deathly stillness and then crept off, numbed and silent, to their dwellings. From that moment on, the mayor of Galway renounced all offices and activities and was never again seen outside his immediate family, nor did he leave his house until carried to his grave. Anna Blake died in a convent. In the course of time both families disappeared from the earth, yet the crossbones and death's head still mark the spot where this dreadful thing once occurred.

MY CARRIAGE FINALLY arrived at ten o'clock, and I immediately left Galway. As long as the landscape remained monotonous, I passed my time reading. Around Gort the countryside grows more interesting again, and not far away there is a river that disappears several times into the earth, like the one at Cong. One of the deepest basins it forms is called by the locals the Punch Bowl. (To fill such a bowl, one needs a bigger barrel than the Heidelberg Tun.)[16] Now we are beginning to approach the mountains of Clare, and nature is donning ever-more-picturesque attire. A lovely park belonging to Lord Gort surprised me in its magnificence.[17] It adjoins a broad lake dotted with thirteen beautifully wooded islands, a stretch of water nowhere visible in its totality; with the mountains as a backdrop, the effect is superb. One of the miserable post-horses shared my pleasure so intensely that he could not be moved from the spot. The postilion reassured me that it was only *this* place that the horse loved, and if we could just get him away from *here,* he would move like the devil himself. But after many vain attempts to drive him from his stupor, we finally had to unhitch him, since he had begun to kick and was tearing his decrepit harness to bits.

In comparison with the Irish postal service, the former Saxon arrangements can still be considered excellent. Here the horses attached to tattered harnesses at the front of your carriage—bleeding skeletons, starving and well beyond old age—are blatant displays of dismal treatment. But if you were to ask the postilion, himself dressed in rags, whether he believed that such beasts could manage to pull this heavy carriage and its baggage even one mile, not to mention a stage of twelve or fifteen, he would answer very seriously that no better equipage could be found in all of England, and he would promise to have you at your destination in no time at all. But one hardly covers twenty paces before something breaks down; one horse becomes unmanageable; the other collapses to the ground exhausted. This does not disconcert the driver in the slightest, who is always ready with the perfect excuse until the bitter end. Then, when nothing further can be done, he declares himself hexed.

This is how it went today. We would probably have had to spend the night in the Gort Park had the castle not very hospitably sent out some assistance and an extra team of horses. Nonetheless our stopover lasted so long that I did not get to Limerick until ten at night. James Lynch has made my letter too thick; I must send it off before it becomes *impayable.*[18] It is likely that you will not hear from me again for at least fourteen days, since I am planning to plunge into the wildest of regions, where foreign feet have rarely trod. Pray then for a successful trip and, above all, continue to love me with the same tenderness.

Your faithful Lou

Limerick, September 22nd, 1828

DEAR DISTANT ONE,

Limerick is Ireland's third city and the kind I love—old and venerable; adorned with Gothic churches and moss-covered castle ruins; with dark, narrow streets and curious buildings from various periods; with a wide river flowing through the entire length of town, spanned by many old-fashioned bridges; finally with bustling marketplaces and pleasant environs. For me a city like this has something in common with a natural wood that offers deep shade as well as lanes lined with trees of varying shapes, sometimes high, sometimes low, and often forming a leafy canopy like a Gothic church. In contrast, modern planned cities are more like an over-trimmed French garden. They are in any case less appealing to my romantic taste.

I was not feeling entirely well and therefore, after a short walk through the streets, returned to my inn. Waiting for me was a Catholic sexton who announced that the minute my arrival became known, the bells had been rung for me. For this he requested ten shillings. I sent him packing. Shortly thereafter a Protestant called on me. I asked what he wanted. "Simply to warn *Your Royal Highness* about the imposition of the Catholics, who accost strangers in a shameful way, and I ask Your Highness to give them nothing." (Here people are very generous with titles as soon as someone arrives with the special mail coach and four horses.) "At the same time I would take the liberty of requesting a small donation to the Protestant poorhouse." "Go to the devil, Protestants and Catholics," I exclaimed indignantly, and slammed my door shut. But there was already another, formal deputation of Catholics awaiting me. This consisted of the French consul (an Irishman), plus a relative and namesake of O'Connell's, and yet a few more, who wanted to harangue me and even grant me the Order of the Liberator. I had the greatest difficulty escaping both them and an invitation to lunch at their club, and finally did succumb to the pressure and allowed two of them to accompany me through the city so they could point out its noteworthy sights.

Hence I good-naturedly let myself be brought first to the cathedral, a very old building, in style more like a fortress than a church—just as solidly and roughly constructed, but imposing in its massiveness.[1] In the interior I admired five-hundred-year old seats, beautifully carved out of bogwood, which time has turned as black as ebony. The lavish ornamentation consists of exquisite arabesques and peculiar masks, different on each seat. The grave of the Thomonds, kings of Ulster and Limerick, although mutilated and otherwise violated by modern accretions, is nonetheless interesting. Their descendants are still alive today, and the head of the family bears the title Marquess of Thomond, a name you will have found mentioned occasionally in my letters from London, since the man who possesses it hosted good dinners! Everywhere in Ireland you find very old families who are proud of never having sullied their name through a mésalliance, something the English and French aristocracy have done so often for monetary reasons that you find no pure pedigrees there, no *stiftsfähiges Blut,*[2] as we call it in German. Although not always flattering for the bride, the great people of France jokingly call such marriages *mettre du fumier sur ses terres,*[3] and many an English lord likewise has his *fumier* to thank for the current splendor of his family.

We left the church in order to visit the large rock near the Shannon upon which the Irish and English signed the Treaty of Limerick after the Battle of the Boyne, although the English have not held to it very rigorously.[4] By this time a huge crowd had gathered around us, swelling like an avalanche and pursuing us with as much deference as enthusiasm. Then suddenly they called out, "Long live Napoleon and Marshal——!"

"My God," I asked, "who do they think I am? As an unassuming stranger, I can't comprehend why people here seem to be doing me so much honor."

O'Connell responded, "Wasn't your father the Prince of ——?"

"Anything but," I assured him. "My father was, it's true, a somewhat elderly nobleman, but not remotely that famous."

"Then you must forgive us," Mr. O'Connell continued, unconvinced. "To tell you the truth, you are thought to be a natural son of Napoleon, since his great fondness for your mother is well-known."

"You're joking," I said laughingly. "I'm at least ten years too old to be the son of the great emperor and the beautiful princess."

But he shook his head, and I, surrounded by repeated shouts of "*viva,*" finally reached my lodgings. I shut myself in tight and have not left again all day. The patient crowd, however, took up its post outside my windows and did not disperse until nightfall.

Tralee, September 23rd, 1828

THIS MORNING I was again greeted with the cry "Long life to Napoleon and to Your Honor!" And while my carriage with my manservant inside was driving off accompanied by further shouts and cheers, I snuck out the back door along with an errand boy who was carrying my overnight bag and took my seat in the diligence bound for the Lake of Killarney. My people have been told to wait for me in Cashel, where I plan to meet up with them in fourteen days.

Now that I was simply attired, it no longer occurred to anyone to burden me with homage and, provoked by this *manifest* farce, I could not stop philosophizing about how all ambition also leads to a *hidden* farce. Certainly this is the most shadow-like of life's dreams. Love is occasionally gratifying, knowledge calming, art pleasing; but ambition—ambition gives only the tortured enjoyment of a hunger that nothing can satisfy, or resembles the pursuit of a phantom that will never be attained.

After a quarter hour I was comfortably ensconced in my diligence. Besides the passengers on the upper deck, the company consisted of three women—one fat and jovial, another very thin, and a third quite pretty and well proportioned. Accompanying us was a schoolmasterly gentleman with a long face and an even longer nose. I was seated in the back between the two slender ladies and talked to the chatty, corpulent one. Just as I was letting down a window, she told me that she had recently traveled in the very same coach and had become almost nauseous because the *sickly* woman seated opposite her would not allow the windows to be opened. *She*, however, would not be deterred and after a quarter hour succeeded in convincing the lady that one inch be allowed, a quarter hour later another inch, then again another, until finally she maneuvered the whole window open.

"Excellent," I said, "for that is exactly how women get everything—first *one* inch and then as many as there are to be had. A French priest tells a very edifying story about this." (Here the man with the nose made a face like a satyr.) "But how differently *men* act in the same situations!" I continued. "In his handbook for travelers, an English writer proposes that if someone in the mail coach insists on keeping all the windows closed, you should not engage in any negotiations but immediately, as if through clumsiness, bash in a window, then beg the person's pardon and calmly enjoy the coolness of the breeze."

The ruins of Adare now drew our attention, interrupting the conversation, and somewhat later the Shannon afforded us an imposing sight. In many spots it is like an American river, more than nine miles wide, its banks splendidly covered in vegetation. In Listowel, a small place where we stopped for our midday meal, a hundred beggars gathered around the coach as usual. What seemed new to me, however, were the little wooden bowls on long sticks that they extended into the carriage like collection plates, the better to retrieve the pence they were soliciting. On the side of the road another beggar had built himself a sentry box of loose stones, where he seemed to be permanently bivouacked.

I must close, since the mail coach is setting off again in a few hours, and I am in need of rest. More tomorrow.

Killarney, September 24th, 1828

TODAY I SAW twelve rainbows, one after the other—a bad omen for the weather, but I am taking it as a good one for myself. It promises me a colorful trip.

My previous companions dropped off one by one like ripe fruit, and when we arrived in Killarney I found myself alone with an Irish gentleman from the north, a manufacturer. The incessant flow of English tourists has conferred an almost English elegance—and almost English prices—on the inns in this pleasant town. We immediately enquired about boats and the best way to view the lake but were told it was impossible to sail in such stormy weather, that no craft could "live" on the lake today, as the boatsmen put it. Meanwhile, an English dandy who had attached himself to us during breakfast ridiculed these claims. Since I, as you know, also give little credence to impossibilities, we outvoted the unenthusiastic manufacturer and embarked, *malgré vent et marée*,[5] near Ross Castle, an old ruin not far from Killarney (Figure 92).

We had an excellent vessel, an ancient and characteristically hoary helmsman, and four industrious oarsmen. However it was as if the sky was torn apart—in some places nothing but blue, in others gray with gray shadows, but mostly pitch-black—and clouds of every form were tumbling around, from time to time tinted by a rainbow or illuminated by a weak sunbeam. The high mountains could barely be seen through the gloomy veil, while on the water everything was night. The inky waves heaved vigorously against one another, and here and there dazzling white foam rippled along their crests. Because the swells were towering up like the ocean, I felt a small touch of seasickness. The manufacturer turned pale with fear, but the young Englishman, proud of his amphibious nature, laughed at the two of us. In the meantime the storm was making

92

Lake of Killarney.

such a racket that we could barely hear each other, and when I asked the old helmsman where we were heading, he answered, "To the abbey, provided we get there!" This did not sound very encouraging, and our boat (the only one on the lake, since even the fishermen had not dared go out) was bobbing up and down so dreadfully and making no progress despite every effort of the rowers. Hence the manufacturer, beginning to think of his wife, child, and factory, peremptorily demanded that we turn back, having no intention of sacrificing his life on a pleasure trip. Meanwhile the dandy, on the verge of laughter, assured us that he was a member of the yacht club and had suffered much worse. He then promised the rowers—who themselves would have much preferred to be at home—more and more money to persevere. As for me, I followed the maxim of General Yermolov, "neither too rash nor too timid," and, heavily wrapped in my cloak, kept to myself and calmly awaited the outcome. It seemed, by the way, that I was the only person enjoying the beauty of the scene, since one of my companions was hampered by fear, the other by his own self-satisfaction. We fought against the current of the waves for a while longer as we were

LETTERS OF A DEAD MAN

tossed about like seabirds in the storm and darkness. Finally we were set upon by such powerful gusts of wind emanating from a ravine opposite that even the yacht-club member became apprehensive and acceded to the helmsman's request to row back with the wind and put up at an island until the storm had abated, which he said usually occurs around noon.

And so it happened. After we had camped for a few hours on Innisfallen Island, a charming place with ruins and lovely groves of trees, we were ready to continue our journey in a more leisurely fashion. All the islands in this lake, down to the most diminutive (only a few yards long and called Mouse) are thickly overgrown with arbutus and other evergreens that thrive here in the wild and are resplendent both winter and summer with their brightly colored flowers and fruits. Many of these small islands present shapes that are just as peculiar as their names are idiosyncratic. They are mostly linked to O'Donoghue. Here the surf breaks against the rocky hooves of O'Donoghue's white horse; there is his library; next his pigeon house or flower garden, etc. But perhaps you do not know about the origin of Killarney Lake? Well then, just listen.[6]

O'Donoghue was the most powerful chieftain of a clan that inhabited a large and wealthy city on the spot now submerged beneath the waves of the lake. Everything was abundant there except water, and legend has it that even the one small well in the city had been donated by a powerful wizard, who called it into being one day at the request of a beautiful young virgin, but with the strict warning that it must be covered every evening without fail with the large silver lid he would leave behind for that purpose. Its strange shape and ornamentation seemed to confirm the wonder of the legend, and the ancient custom was never neglected.

O'Donoghue, however, a powerful and intrepid warrior (perhaps, like Talbot, an unbeliever as well), simply made fun of this fairy tale, as he called it. Then one day at a wild banquet, when he was overheated by excessive consumption of wine, he commanded—to the horror of everyone present—that the silver well cover be brought to his house, where it would make an excellent bathtub, he flippantly claimed. All objections were in vain. O'Donoghue was accustomed to being obeyed, and when the frightened servants finally dragged the heavy vessel to him, lamenting all the way, he laughed and told them not to worry. "The cool of the night will do the water good, and tomorrow you will all find it fresher!" But those who were standing closest to the silver cover turned away from it in horror, for it seemed to them that the intricate, complex characters engraved on it were weaving in and out of each other like a tangle of snakes, and a spine-chilling, mournful sound seemed to arise from it, as once emanated from the Colossus at Thebes.[7] Fraught with worry, everyone retired to bed. Only one man fled into the nearby mountains, and when dawn broke and he looked back into the valley, he rubbed his eyes in vain, thinking he must be dreaming. The city and the land had completely disappeared; the rich fields were no longer there, for the small fountain, rising ever more copiously out of a cleft in the earth, had given birth to a vast lake. It happened as O'Donoghue had prophesied: in a single night the water had cooled everyone, and his new tub had provided him with a final bath!

The fishermen assured us that even now, on days when the water is bright and clear, many people can see palaces and towers shimmering as if through glass at the deepest point in the lake. And when storms approach, there have been sightings of O'Donoghue's gigantic figure riding over the waves on a snorting white horse or gliding across the water in a ghostly gondola with the speed of a falcon.

One of our crew was furtively pointed out to me by the others as someone who, they whispered, had encountered him. This was a man of about fifty, with long black hair driven across his temple by the wind and a serious, quiet, yet visionary look. You can imagine that I quickly struck up a conversation and tried to win his confidence, since I know that these people, whenever they presuppose skepticism and ridicule, become stubbornly silent. At first he was reserved, but soon he became impassioned and swore by Saint Patrick and the Virgin that what he was about to relate was the absolute truth. According to his testimony he encountered O'Donoghue just as twilight was falling, shortly before the outbreak of the most terrible storm he had ever experienced. He had been kept from fishing, rain having poured down in torrents all day long; it was piercingly cold, and without his whiskey bottle he could hardly have endured it. There had also been no living creature anywhere on the lake for some time already, and then suddenly a boat, as if fallen from the heavens, sailed toward him. Its oars were moving with the speed of lightning, yet there was not a single oarsman to be seen. At the rear a gigantic man dressed in scarlet and gold sat motionless, a three-cornered hat with a broad strip of braid on his head. And so the ghost ship approached. Paddy stared at the apparition with a fixed gaze, but when the tall figure came almost opposite him, with two eyes as black as coal burning into him from out of the red cloak, he dropped his whiskey bottle and passed out, only regaining consciousness under the rough caresses of his better half. She railed at him in a fury, blamed it all on the whiskey, and denounced him as the worst kind of drunkard. But Paddy knew better!

Is it not strange that the costume I just described is so like that of our German devil of the previous century, who is now so popular again? But Paddy had certainly never heard of *Der Freischütz*.[8] It almost seems as if hell, too, has its own fashion magazine. I found it very amusing to see the old man's anxious remorse after telling this story. He rebuked himself loudly several times, crossed himself, and continually insisted that O'Donoghue, although terrifying, had looked like a true gentleman, because, he added, glancing around timidly, "he always was, is, and will forever be a perfect gentleman."

The younger members of the crew were not quite so superstitious and seemed to have half a mind to tease the ghost witness a little, although his sincerity and his anger also impressed them. One of the men was the perfect model of a young Hercules. Amazingly hale and hearty, he played constant pranks while doing the work of three.

Now we landed near Muckross Abbey, which is located in the park of Mr. Herbert but is nonetheless richly provided with skulls and skeletons (Figure 93). The ruins are extensive and full of interesting features. In the monastery courtyard, for instance, stands what must be one of the largest yews in the world, for it does not just tower over all the buildings, but its branches are like a tent overshadowing and darkening the entire courtyard. On the upper story I noticed a fireplace, where two trunks of ivy, one on each side, formed the most beautiful and orderly decoration, while higher up the foliage was so dense that the chimney looked like a tree.

Here our guide related a curious instance of the unlimited power Catholic priests have over the local commoners. Two families, the Moynihans and the O'Donoghues, had been engaged in a perpetual feud for a half century. Thus, whenever they happened to meet in adequate numbers, a shillelagh battle immediately broke out, and many lives were lost. Ever since the establishment of the Catholic Association, however, it was in the priests' interest to foster peace and harmony among their flocks, so they decreed a punishment for all parties involved in the previous year's brawl: the Moynihans were to march twelve miles to the north and offer a prayer of repentance; the O'Donoghues were to do the same to the south; all those who had

To the Honb.le and Rev.d Rob.t Ponsonby Tottenham
This VIEW of PART of MUCRASS ABBEY, GREAT LAKE of KILLARNEY IRELAND

participated as onlookers had to make six-mile pilgrimages to other spots. In the event of another brawl, the punishment would be doubled. All this was carried out with religious exactitude, and there had been no more feuding.

On a thickly wooded shore an hour farther along that side of the lake, we came to O'Sullivan's Cascade, which was swollen from the rain and appeared doubly bounteous. The lushness of the trees and vines that hung picturesquely over it, as well as the cave from which, with dry feet, you could watch the foaming water plunging down before you, made the scene even more extraordinary. Splendid, solitary paths lead from here over the mountain's crest to a village in the midst of a dense forest, completely isolated from the rest of the world. But since the sun continued to do battle with the clouds, and we were feeling sufficiently exhausted and drenched from both the sky and the lake, whose waves had inundated us more than once, we decided to end our tour for the day and return to Lady Kenmare's welcoming villa.

93

Muckross Abbey.

Because we still had about four miles to cover on the water, the handsome young man—whose face, by the way, despite his athletic build, bore a remarkable similarity to that of the famous Mademoiselle Sontag—offered us a wager of three shillings that he could bring us home in half an hour. The old ghost witness did not want to strain himself with such an effort, so the young Sunday's-child assured us that he would take his oar.[9] We accepted the bet and, from then on, flew like an arrow across the lake. I have never seen a greater demonstration of strength and endurance, accompanied all the while by singing, tomfoolery, and jokes. In spite of this, the oarsmen won their bet by just half a minute, but they received double payment from us, which they all, with great merriment, promised to drink away that same night. Last but not least, they carried on an amusing conversation with the echo from the walls of Ross Castle, their wording carefully planned so that the response always had a facetious meaning, for example, "Shall we have tonight a good bed?" Answer: "Bad"—and so on.

September 25th, 1828

UNFORTUNATELY TWO ENGLISHMEN whom I know arrived today and immediately attached themselves to us, which ended my treasured incognito, for though I am no "großer Herr,"[10] I take just as much pleasure in it as if I were. Incognito you always escape some embarrassment and gain a bit more freedom, however insignificant you may be. Since I could not alter the situation this time, I was at least able to spend half of today's tour on land with my worthy manufacturer, sending the three Englishmen off together on the same boat as yesterday, which we had immediately chartered again for today.

My pony bore the high-sounding name Knight of the Gap, but he was a degenerate cavalier and could only be set into motion with whip and spurs. Before we reached the large ravine from which he takes his name, we had a very beautiful view of the mountain range from a hill rising in the plain. Mountains, water, and trees were so happily distributed as to create an exceptionally agreeable harmony; in contrast, the ravine seemed all the more ruggedly uniform—in the manner of Wales, but less overwhelming. At one point an immense boulder had broken away several years ago and plunged into the middle of the road, splitting it into two halves. Someone had the idea of excavating the rocks to make a hermitage, but his commitment to this new dwelling lasted just three months, which is why the natives (who express themselves so energetically) call it the madman's rock. A few thousand paces farther on, we found an old woman cowering beside the road. The sight of her surpassed anything ever conjured up in a fairy tale; I have never seen anything more abhorrent. I was told that she was already one hundred and ten years old and had outlived every one of her children and grandchildren. Although intellectually she had become entirely bestial, she was still in tolerable possession of all her senses. Yet her form no longer looked animal or human, but only like a corpse that had been exhumed and revived. As we rode by she emitted a pathetic whimper and then seemed satisfied when we threw a few coins her way, although in her apathy she did not reach for them but collapsed back into a torpor. Every furrow on her greenish face was filled with black filth, her eyes appeared to be festering, her lips were a whitish blue—*enfin,* Fanferluche would look like an angel in comparison.

We met up with our boat again at Brandon Castle, a ruin made habitable, which boasts a high tower and a few neglected areas of park, including some stretches of water through which our guides carried us on their backs (the horses having been sent back here).[11] The boat arrived at the appointed time, sailing out from behind a concealing point of land just as we reached the shore, and its crew, in addition to the Englishmen, included the best bugler in Killarney. Such artists blow a kind of alp horn with great skill, creating magnificent echoes at various spots. Along the way we passed the arch of a bridge, where boats are occasionally wrecked when the waters are high. Our bugler told us that he himself had already capsized twice there and the last time nearly drowned. Therefore today he wanted to be set ashore so he could climb along the rocks past the point of the alarming passage. But the old helmsman would not allow it; in his opinion, if the foreign gentlemen were willing to remain in the boat, then it was appropriate that he stay as well and drown along with them! In fact, we made it through without incident.

There are nearly always some eagles nesting on top of the so-called Eagle's Nest, a handsome rock of imposing shape. Not far from there is Coleman's Leap, with two rocks towering out of the water at some distance from each other, on which you can clearly see the indentations of footprints about three or four inches deep. Such leaps and footprints occur in nearly all mountains.

Our boat was packed with victuals for a brilliant dinner (the English rarely overlook such things), and when we spied a cottage under lofty chestnuts in a most romantic setting, we decided to land there and take our midday meal. And we would have had a most pleasant one if the dandy had not ruined it with his affectation, lack of appreciation for the natural beauty of the surroundings, and ill-natured mockery of the admittedly less-refined yet perhaps more-estimable Irishman, to whom he gave the derisive nickname Liston (who shines especially brightly in stupid roles). He had the poor devil playing such a burlesque part without knowing it that now and then I had to laugh against my will. Nonetheless I found the whole thing totally inappropriate and in bad taste. It is also possible that the Irishman was only pretending to be a fool and was actually the sharpest one of them all. While the others were laughing, he applied himself to eating and drinking with such untiring perseverance that little was left for them. I cannot deny that I provided him with good assistance in this; in particular I found the juicy, freshly-caught salmon roasted over the fire on arbutus sticks to be an absolutely superb national dish.

We headed slowly back under the silvery glow of the moon, while the bugler's horn awakened echo after echo from its sleep. The night was entrancing, and as my thoughts glided from one thing to the next, I fell into a frame of mind where I too could have seen ghosts! The men next to me seemed like nothing more than marionettes; only nature, the mellowness and magnificence surrounding me, seemed real. How is it, I wondered to myself, that your heart is affectionate yet lacks companionability, that people in general matter so little to you? Is your soul too small for the intellectual world, too closely related to plants and animals? Or did you already outgrow things of this world in a previous existence and now feel uneasy in your restricted guise? Then, as the melancholic sound of the bugler's horn pulsed again with its soft tones across the waves of the quiet lake and, like the voice of invisible spirits, filled my imagination with words from an unknown language, I felt like Goethe's fisherman and imagined myself drifting gently into the deep to seek out O'Donoghue in his coral grotto.

Before we landed a peculiar ceremony took place. The boat's crew—headed by the young "Sontag," who, due to an unusually generous tip he had received from me, persisted in calling me "his gentleman"—now asked permission to put ashore at a small island and christen it after me, something that could only be done by moonlight. For this I had to place myself atop a projecting rock, while the six boatswains, leaning on their oars, formed a circle around me. Then the old man solemnly recited an incantation in a kind of rhythm that, given the night and the wild surroundings, sounded downright eerie. Next young Sontag broke off a large arbutus branch and handed first me and then each gentleman in the boat a cluster of leaves, which we attached to our hats; he divided the rest among his comrades and now inquired with great respect and gravity, what name the island should, with O'Donoghue's permission, bear in the future. "Julie," I said in a loud voice, after which this name was repeated three times—albeit not with a very correct pronunciation—accompanied by a thundering hurrah. Now a third man, the poet of the group, delivered a short speech in verse to O'Donoghue. He grasped a water-filled bottle and threw it with all his might against a rock protruding out of the water, so that the glass shattered into a thousand atoms. Finally a second bottle, this time filled with whiskey, was drunk to my health, and Julie Island was given another threefold hurrah. The boatmen assumed that this strange sounding name was my own, and after that they addressed me only as Master Julie, which I heard with great wistfulness.

Your domains have thus been increased by an island on one of the romantic lakes of Killarney. It is only sad that the next party to land at this same spot will take it back from you again, since it is likely that christenings take place here as often as godparents present themselves. The actual child—the whiskey bottle—is always close at hand, after all. Still, for the moment I am enclosing an arbutus leaf in this letter; it is from the selfsame branch that hung resplendently from my hat, so that you will retain undisputed possession of at least something from your island.

Glengarriff, September 26th, 1828

EXCELLENT JULIE, IT is truly an effort to write to you today, and I deserve a reward for it, since I am extraordinarily tired and, like my father Napoleon, had to drink coffee incessantly in order to stay awake.*

I left Killarney at nine in the morning in a rattletrap of a cart and followed the new main road that leads along the middle and upper lakes to the Bay of Kenmare. This route unfolds more beauties than you find on the lakes themselves, which suffer from having a picturesque view on one side only; in the other direction, you generally see just a flat plain. Here, however, on the road leading through the woods on the mountainside, every turn creates a picture more beautiful for being more enclosed. In general I find that vistas looked at from water level are always deficient, because the foreground, an essential, is lacking.

Near a pretty cascade not far from the road, yet in the most appealing wilderness, a merchant has built himself a country villa with a garden and a park. The cost must have come to at least five or six thousand pounds, perhaps a lot more, yet the land itself can be held by the family of the current tenant for only ninety-nine years.[12] At that point it and everything that has been built on it (which must be fully maintained in structurally sound condition) reverts to the landowners, the lords of Kenmare. No German would be inclined to spend his fortune on beautification and improvements under such conditions. In England, however, where almost every piece

---

* The maître d'hôtel who recently published his memoirs of Napoleon's life absolved the emperor of this charge with some indignation. These memoirs are certainly the most flattering to the great man, for they prove *qu'il est resté héros, même pour son valet de chambre!—The Editor.* ["That he remained a hero, even to his manservant." There were many tales about Napoleon's obsessive love of coffee.—*Translator.*]

of property belongs to the government, the church, or the powerful aristocracy, there is only very seldom the opportunity to acquire a freehold. On the other hand, industry, which the wise government encourages in its proper relationship in addition to agriculture, has likewise enriched the merchant and the middle classes. Accordingly such contracts are commonplace and eliminate nearly all the disadvantages of excessive land ownership while doing nothing to diminish its great benefit to the state.

We were ascending more and more steeply and soon found ourselves on the barren heights, for you rarely find plants more than midway up the taller mountains here. It is not like Switzerland, where the luxurious vegetation extends almost to the snow zones. But it would be inappropriate to try to apply Swiss standards to Ireland, since the two countries offer romantic spectacles of entirely different types. Both awaken admiration and astonishment at the sublimity of nature, however, even though much in Switzerland appears still more colossal. The road was constructed in such twists and turns that within half an hour we found ourselves directly above the cottage I mentioned before. Its soft, gray, thatched roof lying so far below us looked like a tiny mouse sunning itself in the green grass. Yes, the sun had finally, after a long struggle, established itself as the absolute lord of the heavens. Eight miles from Killarney you reach the road's highest point and a solitary inn. There you stand before the broad ravine that shelters the largest part of the three lakes in its lap, able to encompass it all in a single glance.

From that point the road descends again, leading through treeless but boldly shaped mountains down to the sea. When I got to Kenmare it was market day, and I could barely force my one-horse cart through the throngs of people, particularly because of the many drunkards unwilling to get out of my way or perhaps unable to do so. As a result, one of them fell and hit his head so hard on the pavement that he lost consciousness and had to be carried off, a common occurrence. Irish skulls seem to be of firmer stuff than those of other nationalities, probably because they are accustomed from a young age to the blows of the shillelagh. While eating my midday meal at the inn, I was able to observe a number of such bouts. They generally begin with a screaming and yelling crowd that gets more and more densely packed, until all at once a hundred shillelaghs whiz into the air, and then you hear the blows, mainly applied to the head, thudding and crackling like distant rifle shots until one side emerges victorious. Finding myself here at the source, I purchased, with the innkeeper's assistance, one of the handsomest examples of this weapon, still warm from the fray. It is as hard as iron and, so as not to fail in its purpose, additionally loaded at the end with lead.

The celebrated O'Connell is now living about thirty miles from here in his solitary stronghold in the most desolate part of Ireland. Since I have wanted to meet him for some time, I sent a messenger on with the necessary request, and decided, while awaiting his response, to make an excursion to Glengarriff Bay, setting off immediately after my meal. From this point onward it is impossible to drive a carriage; the only way to continue is on mountain ponies or on foot. Such a pony carried my luggage, while the guide and I walked next to him; if one of us got tired, the good little pony had to carry him too. The sun soon set, but the moon was shining very brightly. The region was not without interest, but the road was atrocious and often led through bogs and roaring streams with neither bridge nor stepping-stones. After six to eight miles it became arduous beyond imagination; we had to clamber almost perpendicularly up a tall mountain, treading on nothing but loose and pointed scree on which one repeatedly slipped backward half the distance just ascended. The descent on the other side was almost worse, especially when

94

Glengarriff Bay.

a looming mountain blocked out the moon. I was so tired that I could not go on and therefore mounted the pony. This animal demonstrated true human understanding. Going uphill he helped himself with his nose (and even his teeth, I think), as if it were a fifth leg, whereas going down he continually twisted his body around like a spider. If he came to a bog where there was not even a small bridge but just a few rocks tossed here and there, he crept ahead with the slowness of a sloth, always making a preliminary test with one foot to see if the stone could support him and his burden. The whole scene was extremely strange. By the bright moonlight you could see a great distance all around, but there was nothing, absolutely nothing but rows of rocks and more rocks of every shape and kind, cast by the moonlight in even more gigantic, fantastic forms, thrusting up sharply against the sky. There was no living thing to be seen, not even a bush, but only our shadows drifting slowly along beside us. Not a sound could be heard except our voices and occasionally the distant rush of a mountain stream or, less often, the melancholic intoning of a shepherd's horn, music that holds the freely roaming cattle together in these immeasurable wastelands of rocks, moss, and heather. We did see a cow once; it was lying in the middle of the road but on our approach bounded off in a rush across the rocks like a black ghost, and vanished in the darkness. (These creatures, like the mountain sheep in Wales, have acquired the skittishness of wild animals.)

About an hour before Glengarriff Bay, the landscape becomes just as luxuriant and parklike as it was previously bleak and wild. Here the rocks, in the strangest of shapes, jut out of Hesperidean thickets of arbutus, Portuguese laurel, and other delightful, sweetly fragrant shrubs. Many of these rocks loom like palaces, as smooth as marble, without any cracks or uneven spots; others form pointed pyramids or long, continuous walls. A few solitary lights were shining in the bottom of the valley, and a gentle breeze swayed the crowns of tall oaks, ashes, and birches, intermixed with lovely holly, its bright red berries visible even in the moonlight (Figure 94). But already the magnificent bay was shimmering nearby, its surface interwoven with pulsating moonbeams, and I really believed I was in paradise when I soon reached its banks and found myself happily at the door of the most pleasant-looking inn. Yet however cheerful its outward appearance, it was mournful inside. The innkeeper and his wife, very respectable people, came to meet me attired in deep black. In answer to my question, they explained that the wife's sister, the loveliest girl in Kerry, just eighteen years old and up to now the picture of health, had died just yesterday from brain fever or, more likely, from the ignorance of the village doctor. But, the poor woman went on tearfully, the eight days of illness had aged her to forty, so that no one recognized the corpse of this radiant girl or those fair features that, so recently, had been the pride of her parents and made her the idol of all the young men in the neighborhood.

She rests next to my room, dear Julie, separated from me by nothing more than a wooden wall. The table on which I am writing to you stands just four paces from her. Such is the world! Life and death, joy and sorrow join hands everywhere.

Kenmare, September 27th, 1828

I WAS UP and about at six o'clock, and by seven was in the splendid park of Colonel White, brother of Lord Bantry, whose family owns all the land around the bays of Bantry and Glengarriff, perhaps the most beautiful place in all of Ireland.[13] These estates are princely in extent, although less significant from a pecuniary point of view, since most of the terrain consists of rocks and uncultivated mountains that pay their annuities only in romantic beauties and magnificent views. Mr. White's park is certainly one of the most successful creations of its type, and owes its existence to the persistence and good taste of its owner. Admittedly he found the most rewarding spot on earth for his endeavor, but it seldom happens that art and nature join together so graciously. Suffice it to say that the artistry draws attention to itself through perfect harmony alone, and otherwise disappears entirely into nature. Thus no tree or bush appears to have been planted intentionally; the vistas are incorporated with wise economy and open only gradually, as if by necessity. Every path is laid out in such a way that there seems absolutely no other direction it could take without being forced. The most splendid effects of forest and plantings are achieved by skilled arrangement—through the contrast of masses, through felling some trees and thinning others, through clearing out some branches and keeping others low—such that the view deep into the forest gloom draws your eye, sometimes over, sometimes under the boughs. Every possible variation in the realm of the beautiful is elicited, yet without anywhere laying this beauty bare but instead always keeping it veiled enough to allow room for the play of the imagination. Because a perfect park—in other words an area idealized by art—should, like a good book, *awaken* just as many new thoughts and feelings as it expresses.

The residence, scenically veiled by trees in isolation or in groups, is not visible until you reach the hill opposite, when suddenly it emerges out of the wooded mass, covered with ivy, wild grapes, and roses. It too was constructed by the owner according to his own plans, and its style is not so much Gothic as a curiously antiquated picturesqueness, conceived with a fine sense of tact in a manner totally in keeping with the surrounding landscape. The execution is also outstanding, for it imitates the genuinely antique to the point of deception. Not only are the embellishments applied sparingly and appropriately and the whole kept so comfortable and practical, but that which is ostensibly the oldest part has been given the appearance of neglect and abandonment. This is so successful that I, at least, utterly confirmed the builder's intention by believing that the buildings had just recently been made habitable, thinking them to be the remains of an old abbey, modernized only as much as our needs require. At the back of the residence are greenhouses and an extremely tidy enclosed flower garden, both connected to the interior rooms, so you live continually amid flowers, tropical plants, and ripening fruits without having to leave the house. The climate, too, is the most favorable you could want for vegetation—moist and so warm that, as in England, not only azaleas, rhododendrons, and all sorts of evergreens can overwinter outside, but also camellias, if they are planted in an advantageous location. Dates, pomegranates, magnolias, tulip trees, etc., achieve their greatest beauty, and only the dates are ever covered. The setting boasts scenic panoramas, extraordinary variety, and yet a totality beautifully contained by the horizon of colossal mountains. The bays of Bantry and Glengarriff look like a miniature sea with its shores pushing across and over one another without ever presenting you with the vast emptiness of the great ocean. Inland, however, the undulating line of mountains seems almost endless.

The smaller bay of Glengarriff, which stretches out in front of the residence, is nine miles in circumference; the larger bay is fifty. Another Sugar Loaf pokes out from among the mountains lying directly opposite the park, and from its base a narrow line of foothills extends into the middle of the bay, its tip picturesquely marked by an abandoned fort. The park itself continues along one whole side of the bay and at its narrow end borders on the bay of Bantry, where the palace of Lord Bantry forms the major vantage point on the opposite shore.[14] Only half completed and planted no more than forty years ago, the entire estate was created out of nothing. Such a work deserves a crown, and the worthy man who did it with only limited resources but enormous talent and matching perseverance, should be held up as a model to the Irish landowners who squander their riches abroad! I also heard with real satisfaction that factional hatred is unknown in his and Lord Bantry's domains. Both men are Protestants and all their tenants Catholics, yet despite this, the authority of these two gentlemen is boundless and voluntarily recognized. Indeed White lives among them like a patriarch, something I learned from the commoners themselves, and he arbitrates all their disagreements, so that not a single penny needs to be handed over to unscrupulous lawyers in these remote mountains.

You may take for granted that I would want to meet such an estimable man, and therefore it was truly auspicious that I ran into him in the park, where he was supervising the work of his laborers. Our conversation quickly took what was, for me, a highly instructive direction. I did not reject an invitation to breakfast with him and his family, and I discovered that his wife was a fleeting acquaintance of mine from the hustle and bustle of London. She responded warmheartedly to seeing me again so unexpectedly and introduced me to her two daughters, aged seventeen and eighteen, who have not yet been brought out. As I recently wrote, although horses (*sans comparaison*) are brought out too early in England, already racing when they are still two year olds, the poor young girls have to wait until they are almost elderly before being untied from their leading strings and launched into the wicked world.[15]

The family bestowed every possible courtesy and kindness on me, and since the ladies saw that I was so passionately drawn to nature, they pressed me urgently to stop over a few days in order to visit some remarkable sites with them, specifically the famous waterfall and the view from Hungry Hill. It was not possible for me to stay any longer, since I was expected at O'Connell's, but I will certainly take advantage of such a friendly invitation when I continue my trip to Cork. *Such* society is not the kind I shy away from.

For the time being I was satisfied with taking an extended walk accompanied by the entire family—first along the bay to get a general view of the park and palace, then to a wooded area situated in the direction of my return trip, where Lord Bantry has a shooting lodge.[16] This setting seems invented for a romantic novel! Whatever can be achieved by utter seclusion, the most beautiful vegetation, the freshest green meadows embraced by mountains and cliffs; valleys, sometimes enclosed by steep walls a thousand feet high; thickly forested ravines; a river rushing over boulders, with picturesque bridges formed of branches and tree trunks; groves shot through with glistening sunlight, where the translucent ripples of cool water refresh thousands of wild-flowers; deer that have become tame, nesting eagles, and brightly colored songbirds—in short, everything made dear to a poetic heart by the sweetest tranquility, all the components nature can provide, are joined together in rich measure, such that two souls tuned to the same pitch can enjoy every rapture the earth has to offer.

With melancholy regret I abandoned this captivating reverie evoked by our dear mother earth, tearing myself away just as we came to the rustic gate where my guide and pony awaited me. The moment I said farewell to my new friends and left the charming valley behind, the skies became overcast and, as I reentered the gruesome, rock-strewn area that I described to you yester-day, the landscape took on the color most fitting to my mood. Still weary from the slow ride of the previous day, I would have liked to walk; but the ground was wet, and when I asked for my high overshoes, it was discovered that the guide had lost one of them, a domestic mishap important enough to mention here because, as the saying goes, "without Bacchus, Venus freezes."[17] A romantic spot is far better appreciated with dry feet than wet. I therefore decided to send the man back so that, at least for the days to come, my mournful galosh might be reunited with its faithful companion of so many years; but for today I resolved to go the whole way on foot, through thick or thin.

A gentle rain started to fall, and one mountain after another became veiled in clouds. Filled with melancholic yearning for my *Paradise Lost*, I strode on toward that region where the earth, like a skeleton, allows only its bones to be revealed. Meanwhile the rain was growing more intense, and the occasional gust of wind announced the imminent arrival of a serious storm. From here I had to climb the high mountain that rises midway through the first half of my jour-ney, encountering torrents of water that were already shooting down every mountain furrow in little cascades. Since I rarely enjoy the luxury of such a drenching bath in the open air, I waded around in the liquid element, adopting to a certain extent the blithely satisfied mind of a duck. My nimble imagination is, as you know, quite capable of this kind of thing. But as the weather got darker and wilder, my mood also took on a more sinister aspect, I might even say a mocking and, in a *modern* sense, a diabolical one. Enfolded by the superstition of the mountains, I could no longer resist, and became preoccupied with thoughts of Rübezahl, the Bohemian huntsman, the fairies, and the Evil One, complete with magic incantations and apparitions, so that every-thing felt more and more spooky until finally I heard myself wondering out loud, "Why should the devil not appear to *me* just as he does to other decent people?" With these words I reached the summit of the steep mountain. The storm had reached its highest pitch, the gale howled fright-fully, water poured down from the heavens in sheets, and the deep rock basin below me looked as if it were hidden behind black drapes, emerging intermittently before disappearing again in the rolling mists and deepening twilight. Then I remembered the incantation, according to which, by calling one's own name three times and laughing loudly in a church at midnight, one will invoke an apparition that is supposedly impossible to endure. What happens in a church at midnight, I thought, might also be made to happen here in the pandemonium of the elements, in the terrible mountain ravine as night is falling. And so, bracing myself firmly against the wind, opening the umbrella like a cloak above my head (I had previously employed it only as a walking stick), and looking down fixedly into the deep basin, I was overcome by ghostly shudders. But I followed the rules and loudly cried out my full name in a strange, shrill voice:* "——." Then, as if astonished, "Who calls me?"

Muffled, half-stifled laughter.

I called my name again, louder this time: "——!" Deeply unsettled, *"Who* calls me?"

Wild laughter.

With a thundering voice I called my name for the third time: "——!" and, full of horror, cried "Who *calls* me?"

There was a momentary silence. Then laughter—soft, yet bright and triumphant, which the echo mockingly repeated.

Until now I had enacted the comedy alone; but every time I cried "who calls me?" it seemed as if weak bolts of lightning from elsewhere flashed across the basin below me. I could explain this only by the wind gusts that shivered the silk top of the umbrella, which I held very close to my face in the gale, thereby generating a lightning-like effect on the eye. But just as the last laugh died away, the umbrella suddenly turned inside out, nearly knocking me over, and certainly giving me the impression that I was being seized from behind by a gigantic fist. It was admittedly—doubtlessly—just a sudden gust of wind. Nonetheless, after my initial fright I turned slowly around . . . and saw . . . in fact . . . nothing! But wait! Is something moving there in the corner? By heaven, it is . . . I was not a little astonished when I saw—at a distance of twenty paces, about as far as I was able to distinguish anything in the darkness and rain—a figure covered from head to foot in black. It wore a scarlet cap on its head and was walking toward me nonchalantly and—I was not mistaken—with a limp . . .

Now, dear Julie, *est-ce le diable ou moi, qui écrira le reste?*[18]—or do you think I am just having fun, telling you a fairy tale? *Point du tout—Dichtung und Wahrheit* is my motto.[19] But to close my letter here is at least proper. I trust the next one will be awaited impatiently. So, until then, *adieu.*

Utterly your Lou

---

* Anyone can insert their own name here, if they would like to attempt the incantation themselves.
—*The Editor.*

Kenmare, September 28th, 1828

BELOVED FRIEND!

So, you ask, was it the devil, or not? *Ma foi, je n'en sais rien.*[1] In any case, on the occasion described, he had adopted a very commendable if dangerous form, that of a pretty young girl. Barefoot and shivering with cold, she wore the red cap of Kerry on her head and was wrapped up in a long, dark blue cape, turned almost black by the rain. Just as she was about to walk past me, I stopped her and asked about her limp and why she was wandering alone in this weather. "Oh," she said, in a half-comprehensible patois and pointed to her bandaged foot, "I'm only going to the next village. I was late and fell down in this loathsome weather and hurt myself badly!" Meanwhile she looked utterly mischievous and unbridled (there really was something quite spooky about her) and displayed so much of her beautiful plump leg that my mood changed once again, and I think the devil was somehow mixed up in it. From then on we shared the difficulties of the road, helped each other along, and when we finally reached the valley, found better weather, a shelter where we could recover, and a restorative drink of fresh milk.

Fortified again, I continued on through the night, and when I arrived in Kenmare, I had covered the eighteen miles in a little over six hours. But I was totally exhausted, and as soon as I entered my bedroom, I spoke the words of Wallenstein with considerable pathos, "I think to make a long sleep of it!"[2]

Derrynane Abbey, September 29th, 1828

AND SO IT happened. Indeed, there was more than enough time to sleep, because the weather was terrible, and I waited until three in the afternoon for it to improve, unfortunately in vain. The messenger I had sent to Mr. O'Connell appeared back at the inn the previous evening; he had no response, but did have a broken collarbone. I had recklessly paid him in advance, and once he felt the money in his pocket, he found whiskey irresistible, as a result of which he and his horse tumbled off a rock during the night! He resolved the problem quite reasonably, however, by dispatching a good friend of his to make the delivery, and thus when I woke up this morning, I was happy to find a very charming invitation from the Great Agitator.

As I said, I did not set out until three o'clock and then had to ride for seven hours, in the heaviest downpour and with the wind in my face, through a desolate wasteland, without even the shelter of a single tree; after the first half hour not a thread of my clothing was dry. Nevertheless almost nothing would incline me to miss this arduous day in the book of my life.

95

Blackwater Bridge.

The beginning was certainly onerous, for it took a long time to obtain a horse, since the one I had ridden to Glengarriff had sprained a foot. Finally an old black cart horse was found for me, as well as a little, cat-like mount for a guide. I was also having trouble with my personal effects. The fugitive galosh was still at large, and my umbrella had already come apart at the seams up on the witches' mountain. I replaced the galosh with one of the innkeeper's large slippers; the umbrella I bound together as best I could and then held it in front of me like a shield. Thus, wearing a cloth cap covered with a piece of oilcloth on my head, I galloped off to new adventures, not unlike Don Quixote and, what is more, provided with a veritable Sancho Panza.

Within a quarter mile from town, a destructive burst of wind brought a pitiful end to the umbrella—once the pride of New Bond Street and subsequently my companion through so many hardships. All of its ribs came loose, leaving me holding nothing but a shredded piece of taffeta and a bunch of whalebone. I handed the remains to my guide and from then on jauntily exposed myself to the mercy of the weather, accepting with the best of attitudes what could not be changed. As long as we hugged the shore of Kenmare Bay, we rode as fast as we could, since the road was entirely passable. But soon it grew difficult. The entry into the more rugged section of the mountains was marked by the Blackwater Bridge, more than a hundred feet high and very picturesque (Figure 95). Here was a ravine studded with oaks—the last trees I have seen since. I noticed that my traveling bag, which the guide had tied onto his horse in front of him, was itself starting to get drenched. I therefore asked the man to see if he could possibly get a rug or mat from one of the nearby huts to spread over it. I soon enough regretted this impetuous request because he, too, must have been held captive there by whiskey; in any case I did not see him again, although I repeatedly paused to wait until near the end of my journey, which later put me in a very awkward position.

The road, which was gradually worsening, led mostly along the sea, now being magnificently churned up by the gale. At times the track passed over desolate flat moors, here and there along ravines and deep gorges, elsewhere through broad, chaotic areas where the rocks were so fantastically tossed every which way that you might easily imagine it was here the giants stormed the heavens. From time to time shapes resembling men and animals would appear like a petrified version of the play of cloud shapes. One wall of rock struck me as particularly attractive: in the middle of the general unruliness, its cracks were distributed in perfectly regular squares, dividing it up like a chessboard. Three sorts of heather—yellow, bright red, and purple—were growing in the crevices and marking the sharp lines in an astonishing way.

Only rarely would I come across a solitary, ragged wanderer, and then I could not stop myself from thinking how easy it would be for someone to attack and rob me in this remote country without anybody taking the slightest notice. For, in fact, all of my travel funds are stowed in the breast pocket of my jacket: like the wise Greek, I carry *omnia mea* along with me.[3] But far removed from any predatory thoughts, the poor, good-natured people always greeted me respectfully, even though my dress was anything but imposing and in England would not have identified me as a gentleman.

I was often uncertain which half-invisible path I should follow, but luckily, by keeping close to the sea, none that I chose was entirely wrong although probably not always the shortest. Meanwhile time went by. And whenever, at long intervals, I came upon a human being and asked, "How much farther to Mr. O'Connell's?" the purpose of my visit drew a "God bless Your Honor!" in tribute, although the distance cited seemed more prone to increase than decrease. It became clear to me only later that I had wasted a lot of time by missing a shortcut of several miles.

It was finally starting to get dark when I reached a part of the coast that is beyond compare. Foreign travelers have probably never before been cast up in this desolate corner of the earth, which belongs more to owls and seagulls than to humans, and it is very difficult to give a satisfactory description of its awesome wildness: the tortuous, coal black cliffs fractured by deep caverns, where the sea crashes thunderously before spraying its towers of white foam back out again; later, when some of the foam has dried at different spots and looks like thick tufts of wool, it is caught up and hurled to the very tops of the mountains by the wind. More: seabirds circling restlessly, the resonance of their plaintive cries piercing the gale; the incessant howling and pounding of the undermining waves, which would suddenly reach right up to my horse's hooves and then hiss back down again; the dismal isolation, remote from all possible assistance; and on top of it all the incessant rain and approach of night on an unknown and indeterminate path—I was really starting to feel worried . . . seriously . . . not half in jest as on the previous day. This quest for the romantic will probably turn out just as badly as it did for the famous knight,[4] I thought apprehensively, and hurried my tired horse along as best I could. It stumbled repeatedly over the loose rocks, and only with great difficulty did I finally urge it into a labored trot. My worry increased when I remembered from O'Connell's letter that the actual entrance to his property lay on the Killarney side, and carriages could only get all the way there over the water, but that the road from Kenmare was the most difficult, and I ought therefore to take along a reliable guide so as to avoid an accident. Then, as often happens when you concentrate on one train of thought, something else occurred to me: a sentence that I recently read in one of Croker's folktales, "There is no better place than the coast of Iveragh to be drowned in the sea, or, if you prefer, to break your neck on land."[5] I was still pondering this when suddenly my horse stumbled and, shying away from something, turned back in a single bound, a maneuver I would not have believed the old mare had in her. I was in a narrow ravine, but there was still enough light to see several steps in front of me, and I could not conceive of what had caused the panicked alarm in my horse. With great resistance and only under the encouragement of the shillelagh I had purchased, we finally began to move forward again. But after only a few steps I was astonished to see that the road, not bad at this point, simply ended in the sea. Then the reins almost slid from my hands as a frothing wave, chased by the gale, headed toward me like a monster and sprayed its white foam deep into the narrow channel. I had no idea what to do! Steep, impassable cliffs stared at me from all sides, the sea thundered in front of me . . . the only way out was to reverse my course. But if I was lost, as I had to assume, then even if I rode back, I could not count on meeting up with my guide, and then where would I spend the night? With the exception of O'Connell's undiscoverable castle in the rocks, there was no chance of finding any trace of shelter for twenty miles. I was already feverish from the cold and wet, and it was obvious that my constitution would not endure the bivouac of such a night. Clearly I had good reason to be distraught. In any case what help was all this pondering? I had to turn back, that was apparent, and as quickly as possible. My horse had come to the same conclusion, because it carried me away almost at a gallop, as if endowed with new powers.

But—can you believe it?—once again a black figure was destined to rescue me from my predicament. *Vous direz que c'en est trop—mais ce n'est pas ma faute. Le vrai souvent n'est pas vraisemblable.*[6] In short, I saw a black figure glide like an indistinct phantom down the path and disappear behind the rocks. My calls, my pleas, my promises were in vain. Was it a smuggler (they are said to be especially active along this coast) or a superstitious peasant who took me, most pitiful *revenant*,[7] for a ghost? Whatever the case, he did not seem inclined to venture out, and I was close to despairing of help when, suddenly, his head peeked out from a cleft in the rock right next to me. I was soon able to reassure him, and he explained the puzzle of the roadway ending in the sea. It had been designed for use only at low tide, he said. "Right now the high tide is already half in, and in another quarter of an hour, passage will be impossible. For a decent gratuity, however, I will still try to bring you across, but we mustn't lose a moment." With these words he took a single leap and landed behind me on the horse, and we sped as quickly as we could against the incoming, ever-rising tide. I was in a very peculiar state of mind as we now appeared to be actually *submerging* ourselves in the stormy sea and were forced to blaze an arduous trail through the white waves and rocks that seemed to rise up like ghosts in the dim twilight.

We also had enormous trouble with the horse, yet the man in black knew the terrain so perfectly that, although we were bathed almost to our arms in salt water, we reached the opposite shore intact. Unfortunately, the terrified beast shied again, this time at a projecting rock, and broke both rotten girths right through the middle, damage that could not be repaired there. Now, after all the troubles I had endured, I faced the agreeable prospect of having to ride the final six miles balanced precariously atop a loose saddle. The black man had, it is true, given me excellent instructions about the continuation of my journey, but it soon grew so dark that you could no longer see any landmark. It seemed to me that the road led across a broad moor and was initially quite level. After a half hour of jerky trotting, with my knees locked together as firmly as possible so as not to lose the saddle, I noticed that the road was turning back to the right again into the higher mountains, because the climb grew steadier. Then I encountered a woman spending the night with her pigs or goats. The road forked here, and I asked her which of the two branches I ought to take to get to Derrynane. "Oh, both lead there," she said, "but the one on the left is two miles shorter." Naturally that's the one I took, but I was soon persuaded, to my detriment, that it was passable only to goats. I cursed the old witch and her duplicity, while the horse exhausted itself in vain trying to clamber through the blocks of stone. Half stumbling, half falling, it finally threw me and my saddle off, and since it was impossible to keep the saddle balanced on its back as I walked alongside, I was finally forced to heft it onto my own shoulders and lead the horse as well. So far I had managed to remain in fairly good humor, but now, although the spirit was still willing, the flesh was beginning to weaken. The man by the sea had said, "Six more miles and you're there." Yet after I had ridden hard for half an hour, the woman I asked insisted it was still six miles to Derrynane by the shortest route. I began to fear that this ghostly mountain castle might be altogether inaccessible, and that one goblin was just passing me off to another. Totally despondent I sat down on a rock, shuddering from fever and frost in equal measure. Then, like the comforting voice of the angel in the wilderness, a shout rang out from my guide, and soon I heard the hoofbeats of his horse. He had taken a completely different path through the interior mountains, one that avoided the passage by the sea, and had fortunately learned from the woman which direction I had gone.

Treasuring my current feeling of safety, I forgot all my grumbling, loaded the saddle and wet cloak onto my guardian angel, gave him my stripped horse, and mounted his, urging it on to its top speed. We really did have five more miles to ride and, as the guide told me, the way led through a narrow mountain pass hemmed in by precipices. But I cannot report anything further about the road we covered, for the darkness was so intense that it was a struggle just to follow the blurry shadow of the man in front of me. I could easily tell from the horse's repeated stumbling that we were on uneven ground. I sensed that we were ceaselessly moving steeply up or down and forded two deep mountain streams, but that was all. Every so often I would not so much see as intuit a sheer wall of rock at my side, or the even deeper black below me would betray the proximity of an abrupt slope. The whole adventure reminded me so vividly of the novels of Miss Ann Radcliffe that I almost took myself to be one of her heroes, just about to discover Udolpho's mysteries.[8]

Finally!—finally a bright glow broke through the darkness, the road grew more level, a few traces of hedge became visible, and in a few minutes we came to a halt before an old building standing on the rocky shore and emanating rays of friendly, golden light through the night (Figure 96). The clock in the tower struck eleven, and I confess that I got a sinking feeling about my *dîner* when I saw no sign of life except for a man in his dressing gown at an upper window. Soon, however, there was more noise from the house, an elegant servant appeared holding silver candlesticks and opened a door for me at the side, where I was amazed to see a party of fifteen to twenty people sitting at a long table enjoying wine and dessert. A tall, handsome man with an amiable demeanor came toward me, apologized for having no longer expected me at this hour, regretted that my trip had been in such horrible weather, introduced me provisionally to his family (who made up more than half of the guests) and then led me to my bedroom. This was the great O'Connell. I was quickly restored by a short change of clothes, while preparations were made downstairs to provide me with my supper, not to be spurned after such a journey.

When I got back to the dining room, I found most of the party still gathered there. The food was excellent, and it would be ungrateful not to praise Mr. O'Connell's well-aged wine, which

DARRYNANE ABBEY.

The Residence of Daniel O'Connell Esq.ʳ M.P.

96

Derrynane Abbey, Residence of Daniel O'Connell.

was, in truth, superb. After the ladies had left us he sat down next to me, and it was inevitable that Ireland became the subject of our conversation.

"Have you already seen a lot of its curiosities?" he asked. "Have you been north yet to admire the Giant's Causeway?"

"Oh, no," I responded with a smile, "before visiting Ireland's Giant's Causeway, I wanted to see Ireland's giants." And with that I raised a glass of his excellent claret in a heartfelt toast to him and his lofty undertakings.

Daniel O'Connell, although a man of the people, is truly no ordinary man (Figure 97). His power in Ireland is so great that at this moment he could doubtless say the word, and the flag of rebellion would be planted from one end of the island to the other, were he not much too sharp-sighted, much too confident of attaining his goal in a less-damaging way. It is certainly remarkable how he has managed, in full view of the government and via legal channels, to make ingenious use of the moment and the mood of the nation to acquire this power, which, without benefit of an

97
Daniel O'Connell.

Daniel O'Connell.

army or weaponry, nonetheless equals that of a king, and indeed, in many ways, surpasses it. For example, how would it ever have been possible for His Majesty George IV to convince forty thousand of his loyal Irishmen to abstain from drinking whiskey for three days, as O'Connell managed to do for the memorable County Clare election.[9] Enthusiasm reached such a high pitch that the people themselves established a penalty for drunkenness. This consisted of the delinquent being thrown into the river at a shallow spot, held there, and repeatedly dunked for two hours.

On the next day I had more opportunities to observe O'Connell, and on the whole he exceeded my expectations. His external appearance is attractive, and the expression of wise benevolence on his face, paired with determination and intelligence, is extremely winning. He has perhaps more power of persuasion than exceptional eloquence, and one often notices too much intention and affectation in his words. But in spite of this, you cannot help but see the strength of his arguments, take pleasure in his martial demeanor, and laugh often at his wit. There is no doubt that he looks much more like one of Napoleon's generals than he does a Dublin lawyer. This similarity is all the more striking in that he speaks excellent French, for he was educated at the Jesuit colleges of Douai and Saint-Omer. His family is old and was likely very important here in earlier days. His friends even claim that he is a descendant of the former kings of Kerry, which definitely increases his reputation among the populace. He told me himself, not entirely without pretension, that one of his cousins is comte O'Connell and a *cordon rouge* in France,[10] the other a baron, general, and imperial chamberlain in Austria, but that he himself was the head of the family. As far as I could tell, those family members present revered him with near-religious zeal. He is presently about fifty years old and very well preserved, although he wears a blond wig.[11]

He had, by the way, quite a tumultuous youth. For one thing, a duel he fought ten years ago brought him considerable fame. The Protestants, to whom his talents were already proving dangerous, had put forward a certain D'Esterre as his opponent, a thug and adventurer by profession, who rode through the streets of Dublin holding a hunting whip, in order to place it on the shoulders of the King of Kerry, as he said. The natural consequence was a meeting the next morning, where O'Connell placed his bullet in D'Esterre's heart, while the latter's shot punctured nothing but his opponent's hat. This was his first victory over the Orangemen; many victories of more importance have followed and, I trust, will continue.

To me his ambition seemed boundless, and if he succeeds with the emancipation, which I do not doubt, he will by no means take this as an end to his career but will likely only then *begin* it. In any case, the evils of Ireland, and of the whole constitution of Great Britain, lie too deep to be erased simply by the emancipation of the Catholics. But for me to rehearse this now would require a major digression. To return, then, to O'Connell, I must mention that nature has also blessed him with a splendid voice (a valuable gift for the leader of a party), along with good lungs and a strong constitution. His mind is sharp and quick, and his knowledge—also outside his own field—not insignificant. In addition, his manners are winning and popular, although there is a bit of the theatrical in them, and from time to time, given the high opinion he quite obviously has of himself, a bit of what the English call vulgarity. But where could you find a picture without any shadows?

Another interesting man was present, likewise a leader of the Catholics (though one working in silence), the same man I had glimpsed in his dressing gown as I arrived. This was Father L'Estrange, a Catholic friar who is also O'Connell's confessor. *He* can be considered the actual founder of the Catholic Association, which, so ridiculed in England, has nonetheless succeeded in achieving unlimited authority over the populace. Indeed there are similarities with the medieval hierarchy of the Middle Ages that underwrote slavery and darkness, except that the present society is dedicated to liberty and light. Essentially all this has been managed with nothing but *negative* machinations—by means of deft activity in secret, and through the gradual organization and education of the people to a specific purpose.* It is yet another eruption of that *second* great revolution beginning to be accomplished by purely intellectual means, with no element of physical force and with weapons that, although irresistible, are only the soapbox and the press. L'Estrange is a person of philosophical mind and unshakable calm. His manners are those of an accomplished man of the world, who has traveled throughout Europe for many different transactions, has a fundamental knowledge of human nature, and, for all his gentleness, cannot always conceal a sharp measure of cunning. I would be inclined to call him the ideal of a well-intentioned Jesuit.

Since O'Connell was busy, I went for an early walk with the friar to a desolate island, and we strode with dry feet over the smooth sand laid bare by the ebb tide. Here are the actual ruins of Derrynane Abbey, to which O'Connell's house is just an appendix. It is expected to be restored by the family one day, probably only when other aspirations have been fulfilled.

When we got back, we found O'Connell on the castle terrace, surrounded like a chieftain by his vassals and other locals, who were picking up their orders or awaiting his dispensation of justice. Since he is a lawyer and solicitor, this is all the easier for him; in any case, no one would dare appeal his decisions, for here O'Connell and the pope are equally infallible. Lawsuits are hence nonexistent in his realm, not only among his own tenants but, I believe, throughout the surrounding area as well. I was afterward astounded to find both O'Connell and L'Estrange entirely without bigotry as far as religion is concerned; indeed their views are rather more philosophical and tolerant, without forsaking a *wish* to remain believing Catholics! Right then I would have been happy to conjure up a few of those furious *imbéciles* among the English Protestants (such as Mr. L——, for instance), who shout the Catholics down for being irrational and bigoted, while they alone (in the true sense of the word) cling in isolation to the fanatic belief of *their* political-religious party and remain resolute in keeping their pointed ears forever closed to reason and humanity.

A rabbit hunt was supposed to take place sometime today (for Mr. O'Connell keeps a small pack of hounds). This would have provided a very picturesque spectacle in the mountains and along the broad, barren slopes, but bad weather prevented it from happening. I, for one, found great pleasure in the repose and interesting company, to whom I am indebted for many a correction.

Kenmare, September 30th, 1828

WITH AUTHENTIC IRISH hospitality I was urged to stay on another week, for a great festival was being prepared and many guests were expected. But I did not think I ought to take this entirely *à la lettre,* and meanwhile I was pining too much for Glengarriff to remain here any longer than necessary. I therefore said farewell to the family this morning, expressing my most sincere gratitude for their welcome. Mr. O'Connell, who accompanied me to the border of his estate, rode a

---

* All Catholic children in Ireland are carefully instructed and can at least read, whereas Protestant children are often extremely ignorant. In general, the moral reputation of the Catholic clergy in *Ireland* is thoroughly exemplary, as was that of the persecuted reformers in France. It appears that the *oppressed* church always becomes the most virtuous, and the reasons are easy to discover.—*The Editor.*

large, beautiful white horse, on which he looked even more soldierly than before. The road was rough and, though entirely cleared of vegetation, provided many sublime vistas, some landward, toward the cliffs, some toward the sea, dotted with rocks and islands, several of which are steep and totally isolated, like tall, pointed mountains rising out of the water. Mr. O'Connell gestured toward one of these and related how, some years before, he had had an ox shipped there and released so it could fatten up on the excellent, undisturbed grass. After only a few days, however, the animal had taken such determined possession of the island that it became infuriated if anyone attempted to land, attacking and chasing off even the fishermen hoping to spread their nets on the shore. It was often seen making the rounds of its domain in a wild run, like Jupiter in the guise of a bull, with raised tail and eyes spitting fire, reconnoitering to see whether anyone had dared to approach. The emancipated ox finally became so dangerous that it had to be shot. To me this seemed a fine satire on the love of liberty, which, once it gains sway, tends to degenerate into a lust for power. It was inevitable that this spontaneous association of ideas evoked comical images in my mind.

Later we came to some strange ruins, part of the so-called Danish forts along this coast, probably not built by the Danes but as a defense *against* them. They are over a thousand years old, and the lower walls, although constructed without mortar, are nonetheless solid and very well preserved. O'Connell stopped next to the remains of a bridge destroyed by a swollen mountain stream to bid me his last farewell. I could not help telling this champion of the rights of his fellow countrymen how much I hoped that, when next I saw him, he and his supporters would have succeeded in destroying the fortress of English intolerance, just as the torrent, in forcing its own path, had broken down the decayed walls of the bridge. And so we parted.*

I returned in large part by the same road I followed in coming here, and so I do not have much new to report except that, in spite of the good weather, I found it twice as exhausting—probably because I was under less strain. Not far from Kenmare I met several transports carrying stones, lumber, beer, and butter, everything loaded on the backs of horses. The Irish are very ingenious about modes of transport. I have already described their excellent cars, with which one horse can *comfortably* move five or six people.[12] Their carts for transporting hay, wood, etc., are equally effective, with a single horse doing the same work that requires three at home. It is the equilibrium in which the load is balanced, so to speak, that makes all this possible. For instance, a cart may be piled so high with long timbers that you can hardly see the horse, because it is entirely enveloped by the wood projecting several yards behind the wagon and in front of the horse. Yet this method achieves such a perfect distribution of weight on both ends that the timbers are resting on a *single* point, and therefore the horse has relatively little to *pull.* Uphill and down, the driver helps a bit by lifting or pushing down on the ends, which because of their balance respond to the slightest pressure. Similarly, five or six heavy oak planks laid across a flat saddle on a horse's back can be carried with little effort like a balancing pole, although if the same weight were in a different configuration, such as a crate, the horse would sink beneath the burden. They also have an ingenious contraption for transporting stones: containers like wooden boxes hang over the saddle and are attached to a thick pad of straw atop the horse's back.

The cheerfulness and friendly courtesy of the people I met was very gratifying. I am not familiar with any nation whose lower classes appear more lacking in egoism and, without the

---

* This wish expressed by my late friend is now already at least partly fulfilled, and the future promises so much more!—*The Editor.*

slightest trace of self-interest, more grateful for the slightest word of kindness that a gentleman might grant them. I truly know of no country where I would rather be a large landowner than here. Things I have done elsewhere that reaped only ingratitude and were met with obstructions of every sort would here win me ten or twelve thousand devoted subordinates. And what is more, I would have achieved an infinitely greater outcome, more quickly and at less cost, since anything that can be accomplished by man and nature is achievable here. In general, despite all their rough edges, these people combine the decency and poetic good nature of the Germans with the vivacity and quick-wittedness of the French; and they possess, as a bonus, all the naturalness and submissiveness of the Italians. It is quite right to say that they have others to thank for their failings, but only themselves to thank for their virtues. In this context I must relate an otherwise insignificant event that I omitted earlier, but that well illustrates a national characteristic.

While I was traveling from Killarney to Kenmare four days ago, I repeatedly encountered people driving home cattle they had bought at a nearby market town. The men were usually riding, without bridles, colts they had just acquired also, and since man and beast had not gotten to know one another yet, the animals were difficult to control. Several times this forced us to a standstill. I finally got bored, and on the third or fourth encounter of this type, I shouted brusquely at the people that I did not have time to spend half the day on the road because of their incompetence, and I ordered my coachman—a bit rashly—to drive on ahead. Immediately two of the colts spun to the left and galloped off, bearing their riders past the front of the carriage, and the entire herd of cattle took fright, split up, and headed for the mountains. I regretted my impulsiveness and had my driver stop at once. There were altogether four or five drovers whom I had put to flight, all hale and hearty young fellows, and the trick I had played on them was exceedingly unpleasant, since it was clear it would take them at least a half hour to round up their scattered cattle. If any Germans, English, or French were ever treated in such a reckless way by a traveler in a miserable one-horse carriage driven by a ragged coachman, they would certainly shower him with well-deserved abuse, and might even try to detain him to compensate for whatever damages ensued. The behavior of these good people was entirely different, being at once witty and respectful. "Oh, murther, murther!"* cried one, while his unruly colt made another attempt to leap up the mountain, nearly throwing him off. "God bless Your Honor, but every gentleman in England and Ireland gets out of the way of livestock! Oh, for God's sake stop now, Your Honor, stop!" By then I had stopped, and when the poor devils had managed with enormous effort to catch those cattle that had run off the farthest, they again approached my carriage, caps in hand, to thank me for my *benevolence* and proclaim "long life to Your Honor!" They then went off merrily with their fugitives, and I continued on my way. I had to admit that their behavior was more praiseworthy than mine, and I rectified this as best I could by means of a sizeable gratuity.

October 1st, 1828, early morning

ALTHOUGH PAINFULLY TIRED, I could not fall asleep last night and therefore asked the innkeeper if he might have some sort of book for me. I was brought an early English translation of Werther's sufferings.[13] You know how profoundly I admire our prince of poets, and you will

---

* "Murder, murder!"—a favorite curse of the Irish.

therefore hardly believe me when I tell you that I have never read this famous volume. Many may find the reason very childish, namely, that when I first held a copy of it, the passage right at the beginning where Charlotte "wipes the little boy's snotty nose"[14] filled me with such revulsion that I could not read any further, and this unpleasant impression has stayed with me ever since. Now, however, I settled down to a serious perusal and found it bizarre to be reading *Werther* for the first time in a foreign language and in the middle of the wildest mountains of Ireland. But to be honest, even here I could not conjure a proper taste for the antiquated sufferings—the excess of bread and butter, the provincial and outdated manners, even the ideas that were then new but are now platitudes (like the beautiful melodies of Mozart reduced to street ditties). Finally there was the involuntary recollection of Potier's delicious parody. It was impossible to achieve the proper "spirit of communion," as Dr. von Frömmel terms it.[15] All joking aside, I realized that the book was destined to cause a furor in those days, because the state of mind that brings on Werther's ruin is essentially *German*, and German gemütlichkeit was just then starting to make headway in a Europe overtaken by materialism. Of course, Wilhelm Meister marched right through those lands, as Faust did later, with even greater, though very different strides! We, I believe, have outgrown the Werther period, whereas we are only now approaching Faust; and no era, as long as there are human beings, will ever outgrow *him*.

As with Shakespeare, the entirety of the human heart is reflected in the tragedy of Faust. The main character personifies nothing less than the eternal, mysterious longing of mankind, restlessly striving for an unknown something that is here unattainable. Thus the play could never be definitively concluded, even if it were extended through many more acts. Meanwhile the nobler human mind steps onto its vertiginous path, like the bridge of the Koran,[16] and is at every moment closer to the abyss than the bovine man who grazes calmly and securely on the plain.

A cousin of Mr. O'Connell's, who holds *par force* hunts on the lake of Killarney,[17] had promised me one for tomorrow. But I feel true apathy about reexperiencing *something already seen, as long as novel things still await me*, and dogs and hunters will certainly not much change the scene I already know. In contrast, engaging people and many new things await me in Glengarriff, so I gave that priority, rode back over the devil's mountain, this time in daylight, and in an hour I was here, settled in a pretty little room, with all the splendor of the bay spread out before my window.

Prior to leaving Kenmare, my vanity was severely tested. The Irish naïveté of the innkeeper's daughter had so much appealed to me every time I returned to her father's establishment that I tended to talk only to her and thereby earned her favor. She had never been out of her mountains and was remarkably unacquainted with the world. I jokingly asked her whether she wanted to accompany me to Cork.

"Oh, no," she cried, "I would be afraid to go so far with you! Just tell me who you really are! That you're a Jew, I already know."

"What? Are you crazy? What makes you think I'm a Jew?"

"You can't deny it; don't you have a long, black beard around your chin and five or six golden rings on your fingers? And don't you wash yourself for an hour every morning, while performing ceremonies that I've never seen a Christian perform? It is true, so just confess it: you're a Jew, aren't you?"

My protestations got me nowhere, she stuck to her analysis. But finally she said with good humor that if I absolutely refused to admit to being one, she at least hoped I would become as rich as a Jew (an English expression). This I reinforced with a Christian amen!

I HAVE JUST returned from a sixteen-mile outing with Colonel White. We went to Hungry Hill, a sublime rocky peak at the end of Bantry Bay, notable for its waterfall and for Thomas O'Rourke's journey to the moon on the back of an eagle, which started here.[18] This amusing fairy tale, recounted frequently in prose and verse, has been translated more than once in Germany too, where you may have come across it. The hero of the story—the chronically drunk *garde-chasse* of Lord Bantry—is still living, and Mr. White introduced me to him at the inn when we returned. He is now proud of his fame and, when I saw him, seemed ready to undertake another lunar expedition.

The intense rains of these past days have been very advantageous for the waterfalls. In dry weather the cascades at Hungry Hill disappear almost entirely, but after heavy downpours they surpass those at Staubbach and Terni, at least for several hours. Hungry Hill, a nearly bald, gigantic mass of rock, is about two thousand feet high. Landward it forms two steep ledges, and on the plateau between these there is a lake, naturally invisible from below, so that the whole thing looks like the continuous line of two colossal terraces. The upper one consists of extremely barren rock, divided in the middle by a deep vertical channel that has been incised as if by art. Hundreds of goats are usually grazing on the slope of the lower terrace, which, although not appearing particularly rough, is covered with heather and coarse grass.

The flood of water plunges from the topmost peak of the mountain through the cleft and into the lake on the plateau; then, once this fills up, the deluge roars down to the valley meadow in four separate cataracts, forming such enormous arcs that the goats continue to graze calmly on the slopes beneath the cataracts, while the lower meadows are transformed into a temporary lake. Because neither the separation of the upper and lower falls nor the lake lying between them is visible from below, the whole seems to be *one* immense torrent, its effect surpassing all description. Colonel White assured me that, when the water was at its highest, he had seen the liquid arcs flung out so far that, in his own words, a regiment could have marched beneath them without getting wet and the deafening noise approximated the thunder of nearby cannon fire.

The marvelous battle between the great O'Sullivan and O'Donovan, a scene from Ireland's fabled history, took place in one of the neighboring ravines, and people still point to the remains of an ancient arbutus trunk, from which, according to legend, O'Donovan was hanged. In fact, money and valuables were recently discovered buried deep in the earth not far away.

In these mountains the eagles, which build their aeries on wholly inaccessible rocks, play an important role in folktales. They are extraordinarily large and strong, and it has been established that they occasionally carry off children. Some time ago one of these predators abducted a three-year-old boy and, probably because he became too heavy, deposited him on a rocky ledge scarcely injured, or anyway still alive. Someone immediately climbed up and saved this new Ganymede as corpus delicti, and he is now in the best of health. A similar event occurred just a few months ago, when an eagle picked up a tiny girl right before her father's eyes and vanished into the rocks; no one has found any trace of the poor child yet.

October 3rd, 1828

COLONEL WHITE IS just as much a parkomaniac as I am, but not entirely as much of a gourmet, *et sa cave s'en ressent un peu.*[19] Nevertheless the hunting parties on land and in the water provide his table with many delicacies. The red partridges, among others, are excellent, and the park's oyster beds supply especially delicious, plate-sized specimens. In addition the bay is swarming with fish and seals. This morning a seal was sitting on a projecting rock directly across from my window and seemed to be listening with great delight and engaging in dance-like movements to the music of a bagpiper, whose tunes resonated from the nearby inn. Supposedly these animals are so passionately fond of music that when there are boat parties on the bay, twenty or thirty of them will follow behind the musicians. They can also be lured in this fashion by hunters, but how cruel to make them the victims of their taste for art!

Unfortunately it rained all day today, so I was forced to stay indoors. In the morning I attended the *daily* private worship service of the family, the female contingent seeming somewhat sanctimonious, though genuinely pious. We all sat in a circle, and the mother read one passage from the English prayer book,[20] the eldest daughter the next, and so on back and forth in imitation of a preacher and sexton in church. After this the daughter, who has something reserved and visionary about her, began a very long, unusual prayer that lasted a good quarter of an hour, during which the rest of us (I, of course, as well) had to turn modestly toward the wall, fall to our knees in front of our chairs, and bury our faces in our hands. The mother sighed and moaned, the father seemed a bit *ennuyé,* and the youngest daughter (a delightful girl, who is a good deal more sophisticated than the eldest) lapsed occasionally into absentmindedness, whereas the son preferred to absent himself altogether. As for myself—for whom every inwardly directed thought at any time of day is a prayer to God—I felt I could look around a little without being impious.

After the party had stood up again, brushed off knees and tugged at clothes (for the religious fervor of the English does not forget itself all that easily), the mother read a story from one of the Gospels. The lesson this time was the meal at which, if I am not wrong, six thousand people were sated on two fish and three loaves of bread, and a lot of food was left over.

Happily our midday meal was not apportioned with equal frugality, and its divine gifts were seasoned with extremely merry conversation. I did, however, commit one involuntary offense. When speaking in jest about the comet that is expected to appear in 1832 and come closer to the earth or the earth's orbit than any previously recorded, I remarked that according to Lalande's calculation, a comet approaching within fifty thousand miles of the earth would necessarily have such a power of attraction that it would draw the waves of the ocean over the top of Chimborazo.

"If the one of 1832 comes that close to us," I added, "then we will at least all drown at the same time."

"Excuse me, that is absolutely impossible," answered Mrs. White very earnestly, "for that would be a second Flood, and you seem to have forgotten that it is promised us in the Bible that there is not to be a second Flood, but that the earth will be destroyed for the last time by fire." (*Il faut avouer que la faveur n'est pas grande.*)[21] "That this destruction may not be far off, however," she continued with a sigh, "I myself believe. For the most informed of our holy men are all agreed that we are probably now in the seventh kingdom of the Revelation of St John, in which the end of the world is prophesied, and where our Savior will come to judge us."

How peculiar these devout people are! The mother and daughter lapsed into such a violent and bitter argument over these remarks that I, unworthy layman, had to do what I could to lead them to reconciliation. The quarrel arose over whether, during the prophesied catastrophe, the people were to be judged immediately and then burned, or first burned and then judged. The daughter asked indignantly (and I promise you I am not embroidering) whether our Savior, when he came, was supposed to postpone his judgment until the world was burned? She insisted that it was clearly written in the Scriptures: he would come to judge the *quick* and the dead, which was not possible if everyone had already been burned beforehand. Thus it was clear that the world could only be burned after all had been judged. With equal indignation the mother declared this to be utter nonsense. People must necessarily die first before they can be saved or damned, and the quoted passage, when it spoke of the quick and the dead, referred first to those who would still be alive when the fire began, and then to those who would have been lying in their graves for a long time already. She stuck to her position: *first* burned and *then* judged!

Both of them now wanted to hear *my* opinion, each hoping to be reinforced through my joining the battle. I dared to answer that I was not very well versed in these details, and that to me their argument seemed quite like the one that took place at Madame du Deffand's about whether Dionysius had walked one or six miles without his head, about which Mrs. du Deffand famously declared, "*dans ces sortes de choses, il n'y a que le premier pas qui coûte.*"[22] I added that, when it came to the teachings of Christ, I had always tried to abide by the rules concerning the fulfillment of one's duty: to trust in God and practice gentleness and brotherly love, although only rarely did I manage to meet my own expectations. Nevertheless I was indifferent to whether we would first be judged and then burned, or first burned and then judged. Whatever God did, in any case, would be done well. But I did have to admit that I considered myself to be just as much in God's hands, and just as close to his power, during my earthly life as after my mortal end, and even after the end of the little terra that we call the world. In my opinion the Last Judgment would endure forever, like the World Spirit. This explanation brought the antagonists to a happy reconciliation, in that they became united in turning *against me*. But I was finally able to beat a dexterous retreat without losing their favor entirely.

Toward evening, amid localized rain, twilight, and sunset, we had another magnificent run of light effects. *Our* waterfall in the park was so swollen that it allowed itself to thunder a bit, and the grasses and shrubs were charmingly illuminated with bright sunbeams. We strolled around until dark, watched the lofty Sugarloaf shift gradually from dark blue to pink, and took delight in the lucid mirror of the sea, the fish jumping on its surface, and the peaceful play of the otters. Then the cruel fishing lights in the bay brought the festival to a close with a universal war dance.

Here everything is beautiful, even the air, which is famously salubrious.* There are also no insects to plague you, since the bay is of such enormous depth that the low tide almost nowhere exposes the ground, and the constant, gentle breeze of the valley cannot make things easy for them either. The climate is almost always the same, neither too warm nor too cold, and the vegetation so luxurious that the greater part of the barren mountains, as well as the rocks in their interstices, would be clothed with the loveliest of forests if only there were *more* of *one* thing and *fewer* of *another*—namely, planters and goats. The former do not have the money to spend, nor the inclination to spend it *here*; the latter do not let anything sprout that is not protected by double walls. At one time most of these mountains were supposedly covered with high forest, but the English, always thinking of making as much money out of Ireland as possible, cut everything

---

* It has so far not been taxed.—*The Editor.*

down for charcoal and to use in their forges. The forges have since been shut down, although in many places you can still find some ruined remains. For my taste another advantage of this region is its isolation. A carriage can scarcely get here, and, with the exception of a few curious travelers such as myself, no one attempts to conquer the difficulties of access. The good-natured residents do not huddle together in villages, but are dispersed throughout the mountains, where they lead patriarchal lives unspoiled by the tumult of the city. They are also not so alarmingly poor as in other parts of the country. The needs of these people are few: they are allowed to take from the bogs as much peat as they want for their fires and whatever grass they require for their cattle, and the sea provides more than enough fish to nourish them. For a landowner equipped with a passion to create, a limitless field of opportunity presents itself here. If I were a capitalist, *this* is where I would settle.

My friendly host is going to see that this letter is sent quickly on its way. It has been written in a happy state of mind, and may the heavens grant that it will find you in a similar mood. Always remember the motto of my ancestress: *Coeur content, grand talent!*[23]

Your faithfully devoted Lou

Glengarriff, October 4th, 1828

D EAR JULIE!

I am leaving tomorrow, and with considerable regret. But I will take along a sweet memory, one of the few *thoroughly* happy images from my wanderings.

On my walk this morning I came across such luxurious heather hanging down from the rocks that a single plant measured ten feet in height.[1] The gardener who accompanied me pointed out yet another curiosity. In a secluded spot, not far from the fetchingly rustic dairy, bees had constructed large honeycombs in the open air, simply suspending them from blackberry branches in the thicket. The weight of the honey was enough to bend the bush to the ground, and the bees were still working vigorously as I watched. The top of the dairy is covered with soil on which red heather has taken root, and the roof has been cut into six points from underneath, which looks quite attractive. A clear stream flows through at the center, and along its banks Egyptian lotuses flourish and even survive the winters.[2]

In the afternoon I went riding with Colonel White to look at an eagles' aerie. First we passed the area where Lord Bantry's handsome hunting lodge stands, then forded the swollen river three times, and after several hours reached a wild wasteland where two solitary huts rest at the foot of a vertical wall of rock. The eagles were nesting about five hundred feet above these huts in a crevice overgrown with ivy. When eaglets are present, the adults can be seen attentively alighting with fowl, hare, lambs, etc., to supply the domestic table. But there is a surprising instinct that teaches them never to plunder anything from the two families living below them, thus honoring the reciprocal rules of hospitality they themselves have been shown. I am distraught that these sovereigns of the rocks have not yet been considerate enough to reveal themselves to me; both were absent again today.

We returned by way of the caverns of Sugarloaf. There is a Wild Huntsman here, and no mere mortal's tallyho may ring out anywhere near his hunting preserve, or he will descend with his entire wild army and carry off the foolhardy offender in a whirling vortex. In spite of all this, he is totally different from his German counterpart. The feral huntsman is an elfin king, as small as Tom Thumb, dressed splendidly in emerald green and accompanied by a retinue mounted on horses no larger than rats, which gallop with the speed of the wind over rocks and sea. Sugarloaf itself is the great assembly point for all Irish fairies. The caverns, full of seashells and fantastic stone formations that prick the curiosity of the visitor, are places where no native, for all the treasures of the earth, would ever spend the night. And when the weather is clear, you can see a singular freak of nature: extending from the summit of the mountain—or better, the rock—down to these caves are two winding but parallel grooves that from a distance look exactly like wagon ruts. What could these be but the tracks of the fairy queen's carriage? Of course many an old mountain dweller has seen her at sunrise or sunset, driving up there in otherworldly pomp to adorn the annual festival with her presence. Certainly these old men would be ready to back up the truth of their claim with any oath whatever, for they *believe* it; and this is what makes the fairy tales of the region so seductively charming that you cannot help but find them contagious.

Colonel White, once a passionate huntsman, has intimate knowledge of every mountain in the district from its foot to its peak, and along the way he told me such interesting stories that if I were to echo them all faithfully, my letter would never end. In these parts the hunt is still associated with *dangers,* and not trifling ones, either! Many a man has lost his life because of them. There are three kinds. First, to be in the midst of the rocks and overwhelmed by one of those wintry fogs that often occur here, almost instantly engulfing the wanderer in black night and icy cold. If he cannot find his way out, his only alternative is to freeze to death (these fogs often persist in the ravines for whole days and nights) or fall headlong from an invisible precipice. If the fairies wish him well, then he will happily reemerge into the light somewhere. But woe to anyone who has incurred their disfavor! His friends will surely find him the following morning dashed to pieces or dead from exposure.

The second peril is of a totally different type. Not even the smallest bush interrupts the sublime uniformity of the boundless mountain plateaus as they merge into the horizon like the sea. Here are extensive bogs that the game birds, particularly grouse (a kind of partridge common in the British Isles), have chosen as their favorite abode. These bogs are full of small knolls formed by the heather and spaced not far from each other, like so many molehills. Only by leaping from one of these hummocks to the next can you cross the bog. If, in the heat of the chase, you miss one and do not find another close by, you are sure to sink into the bottomless morass. The only means of survival is to spread out your arms quickly or hold yourself up with your gun braced horizontally, until finally help arrives or you succeed in catching hold of the next hillock.

Worse and more dangerous than all this, however, is being attacked by one of the quite savage mountain bulls. Mr. White has often found himself in this predicament, although by various means he has always successfully escaped. Sometimes he or one of his companions managed to shoot the bull before it came too close; another time he escaped into a bog where the furious animal could not follow, although it did lay veritable siege to him for more than an hour.

But the story of the last attack is what I find especially remarkable, for it proves that a man endowed with strength, courage, and agility can single-handedly resist any living creature. Colonel White was accompanied only by a friend and by a local man leading the dog and equipped with a long white staff, which is common here. The Colonel's friend shot a grouse, and at that very moment, they saw a bull charging toward them in a fury at a distance of about eighty paces. White shouted to his friend to quickly reload the gun while he took the first shot. He was just raising the gun to his shoulder when the tracker called out, "If you both promise to give me an extra glass of whiskey, I'll deal with the bull myself." Meanwhile White fired his gun but missed, his friend was not yet done loading, and he hardly had time to yell to the man, "You can have a dozen bottles!" when they saw this mountain hero running directly at the bull, just as fast as the animal was charging. In a flash the two were confronting one another, and with the greatest dexterity, the young man grabbed one of the horns of the bull, whose head was now touching the ground, swung himself one step to the side, and then, during his adversary's leap, repeated the same step back with lightning speed, grabbing the bull's tail with both hands—all this without dropping his staff. The whole incident transpired at the speed of thought. And now began the strangest race that has ever been seen. The bull used everything in his power to shake off the burden hanging onto his tail, but in vain. He ran about in a frenzy, up- and downhill, over rocks and forest streams; but like a goblin, his chaperone swung with him over every obstacle, sailing through the air when he was not running at the end of the bull's tail. In a short while, exhausted from fear and exertion, the beast finally sank down, utterly drained and feeble, at the foot of a broad grassy slope, just below where the astonished Mr. White and his friend were bracing themselves for the outcome. But the real punishment had only begun, for *that* was the day when this creature was forever cured of his wild temper. Now the shepherd made use of his staff, which was filled with lead and topped by an iron point. He had very prudently retained this as a corrective device, and using it with great fervor, he really tanned the hide of the stubborn bull, forcing the beast to drag himself back uphill, where finally, panting heavily and with his tongue hanging far out of his mouth, he sank down once more, right at the feet of Mr. White. In this state of total incapacity, they left him. The young peasant, described by White as a marvel of strength and agility, seemed for his part not in the least tired from the chase, nor vain about his deeds. Instead he calmly continued his search for the discarded sack of gunpowder and the dog's leash and wasted no words on recent events beyond winking with amusement at the colonel and reminding him, "Now, master, don't forget the bottles!"

A proper hunt with the hounds must be magnificent in these rocks! Sometimes storming over a peak or along a slope, or with fox and hounds leaping over chasms, or with everything vanishing at once into a mountain ravine like a shadow picture. Once Colonel White saw such a hunt on Hungry Hill, where the entire pack ran under the waterfall, their howling and barking blending wildly with the roar of the cataract, until finally Reynard met with the same fate as had already befallen three or four of the hounds: he slipped off the smooth rock, plunged down several hundred feet, and landed, amid jubilant cheers, directly at the feet of the huntsmen, where they were comfortably observing the spectacle from a projecting rock in a basin-shaped meadow below. There all Reynard's slyness and all his troubles found their end.

Shall I tell you more?

Well, fine! Witches again! Saddle my pony for me, and then farewell to the land of the fairy tales and the waves still baring their white teeth that have gnawed at these rocks for millennia.

Sit behind me, Julie! Climb on behind the saddle, like an Irish lass, and follow me quickly through the air and back to O'Connell's wilderness at Iveragh. This is truly the land of eagles and vultures, of storm-tossed surf and shattered cliffs! Yet there is a place on Ballinskelligs Bay, not far from O'Connell's castle-abbey, where many a dance was danced and many a marriage celebrated in olden days. For the lonely spot was tranquil and lovely with its velvet meadows; high walls of rock protected it from the storm; and at low tide sand as smooth as satin sloped down to the water. In the clear moonlight the sea, like the rest of creation, seemed to be slumbering, and its gentle waves, touched by the breath of a zephyr, only now and then stirred and rippled as if in a dream.

It was on such a night that the piper Maurice Adair coaxed the most inviting tones from his instrument, and the young people of Iveragh, merrier than ever, celebrated the festival of their saint with dance and cheer. Maurice was a handsome and sprightly fellow, although he was blind. The poor creature had never seen the sunlight, so day and night were both the same to him. Yet his imagination was filled with obscure images of beauty and heartrending charms whenever he heard the sweet voices of young girls, touched a soft swanlike neck, or sensed a rosy breath, like the fragrance of flowers, wafting against his cheek. Maurice was in love, yet so far had not found an object for it; and his longing could only be expressed in the captivating melodies that poured forth in unaccompanied songs or in the sounds of his bagpipe.* But Maurice's music could achieve still more. He had one particular tone in his instrument called "the wondrous sound," which was generally believed to have been originally installed by an elf. This was a sound like Hüon's horn,[3] and certainly of the same origin, which no one could hear without being overcome by a passionate and irresistible desire to dance. Although many a young girl attending her first ball in the city has no need for such a stimulant herself, she would nonetheless give a lot to be in possession of that tone so she could rouse the lethargic dandies, who tend to sneak off one after the other, or merely recline on the sofa indulging in *dolce far niente* instead of spinning her around in the cotillion. On this moonlit meadow, however, the lively peasant lads required no such extrinsic, compelling incentive. Their own pleasure was sufficient stimulation, and Maurice played tirelessly, taking delight in his lusty thoughts about what the others were enjoying in reality, and thus perhaps less profoundly. Yet finally he began to long for some reality of his own, and since it is in the nature of musicians to be both amorous and thirsty—with Irish musicians possessing a double measure of each craving—Maurice did not neglect diligent use of the hot whiskey punch to refresh the pleasures of his imagination. Soon he felt that his head was spinning even faster than the whirling couples themselves; indeed all of Iveragh was rocking beneath his feet.

"Oh, another glass, Kitty! And a kiss to go with it," he cried out with a stammer.

But Kitty, worried that the dance might end if the whiskey tore the bagpipe from the piper's hands, staunchly denied him his drink. Maurice repeated his demand ever more vehemently, but Kitty remained inflexible.

"Anyone who drinks so much doesn't need any kissing," she said, "and beyond that, you have to play so *we* can dance, and already you can hardly move your fingers."

"I can't move my fingers?" Maurice exclaimed indignantly. "Well then, you and all the rest will dance until you're exhausted and yearning for a drop of water, just like I now yearn for a glass of the blessed whiskey punch!"

At this he squeezed the bagpipe angrily, and it emitted, loud and bellowing, *the wondrous sound*. In the blink of an eye, young and old were whirling around in a raucous tumult. But look! Now the sleeping sea awoke, and out of it crawled crabs and prawns to execute a delicate minuet on the smooth sand. A sea spider waltzed up, performing uncanny steps with its long legs; codfish and turbot, haddock and plaice balanced on their tails with every grace at their command. Seals tried out the newest *Galloppwalzer*, and oysters opened their shells and glided around with all the propriety of a Parisian lady, arms akimbo, delicately lifting the hem of her evening gown. These new dancers were welcomed with astonishment into the swirl, while Maurice, blowing without cease and taking no notice at all, twirled around amid them, full of malicious glee. Then the waters parted once more, and the most beautiful of the mermaids emerged in a voluptuously

---

* The Irish know how to elicit much more complex qualities from their bagpipes than do the Wends, Poles, and others.—*The Editor.*

captivating dance. Her face was as fresh as an early morning, her long hair flowed over her snow-white breasts like transparent waves, her lips blushed redder than the ocean's fiery coral, her teeth were more dazzling than its most precious pearls. Her silvery garment seemed woven from the froth of the waves and adorned with exotic flowers of the sea, their burning colors shimmering more richly than the brightest jewels of India.

It was obvious that underwater ladies, just like the land-bound variety, take a lot of trouble with their grooming, especially when they are out to make a conquest. According to eyewitnesses, no one had ever seen a more alluring and coquettish outfit, which succeeded in exposing and, much better, hinting at her beauty. Poor Maurice saw nothing of this, and yet it was he alone whom the Queen of the Sea was seeking, because only a few moments later in the confusion of the dance, her arms softly embraced him and a melodic voice called to him in dulcet tones:

> Mein Reich ist das Meer,
> Und prachtvoll mein Schloß.
> Komm, Maurice Adair,
> Komm, schwing dich aufs Roß.
> Das Seepferd, horch! schnaubet,
> Und harret auf Dich,
> Der das Herz mir geraubet,
> Nun herrscht über mich!
> So komm denn und eile,
> Geschmückt ist der Saal—
> Nicht länger mehr weile
> Und sei mein Gemahl![4]
> [*My realm is the sea,*
> *And my castle magnificent.*
> *Come, Maurice Adair,*
> *Come, swing up on this steed.*
> *Listen! The sea horse snorts*
> *And awaits you,*
> *You, who have stolen my heart*
> *And now reign over me!*
> *So come along then, and hurry,*
> *The chamber is adorned—*
> *Tarry no longer*
> *And be my spouse!*]

It seems that Maurice responded to this urgent invitation with equal fervor, because although his elderly mother (who had been leaping around in a frenzy for half an hour, not only losing both her wooden shoes but also a number of essential bits of clothing) called out to him pitifully with her last breath, "For God's sake, don't marry a *fish!*"—and although she added the final argument that, if he did, she would never again be able to eat dried cod in melted butter without fearing that she was perhaps consuming her own grandchild, in the end it was all in vain! "She half dragged him, he half sank down,"⁵ and as *the wondrous sound* died away and all the exhausted dancers gasped for air, the two were already engulfed by a towering wave that had been standing behind them the whole time (probably the queen's own personal steed). Borne along by the wind came the last sound ever heard from Maurice the Piper, a soft "fare-well, mother!"

And my letter will close with this, dear Julie. I do not yet know from where I will send you the next one, but when you think of me, tell yourself that I have never felt better or happier.

Your eternally faithful Lou

DEAR PRECIOUS ONE,

Parting was difficult for me—although you, who want me to be somewhere else altogether, will certainly say that I had already stayed too long—and so I tore myself away from the good people and their romantic country estate. It was Sunday, and the elderly lady, despite her evident cordiality, could not resist reproaching me, "But how is it possible that a *good* person like you can start a journey on a *Sunday*!"

You know that ever since the days of James I—when this idolization of Sunday began and then quickly became a raging partisan issue—the English Protestants have almost universally branded it as a true day of death. Dancing, music, and song are taboo, and the most pious of all even drape their canary cages to stifle every chirp during these holy hours. No bread can be baked, and no useful work performed. Yet it is clear that drinking and other vices flourish more luxuriantly than on weekdays, for the streets are never as full of drunks as they are on Sundays, and according to the police, certain "houses" are never so full of visitors! Many of the English consider dancing on Sunday to be a greater sin than stealing. I once read in a *printed* history of Whitby that its once-rich abbey had to be destroyed because the monks not only indulged in every vice, including rape and murder, but that the abbot himself had allowed the construction of the monastery and other *work* to be continued on the Sabbath, a criminal offense.

This mania also infected the good Mrs. White, which made urgency an unconvincing ground for the sin I was about to commit. In order to soothe her, I first accompanied the entire family to the other side of the bay to attend church in Bantry, which was not much of a detour for me, and I took this opportunity to relate the strange apparition seen by a son of my former host, Captain B——, who joined the Catholic church because of it. He was, as he told me, just as avid a Protestant as he was an Orangeman, and one day he went into the Catholic church in Dublin more to make fun of the ceremonies taking place there than for any other reason. Yet against his will he found himself touched by the beautiful music, and then, look!—when he cast a glance back at the high altar, the Redeemer himself was standing there in the flesh with his angelic eyes gently fixed on the poor mortal. Then, waving his hand with a friendly smile and all the while holding him in a steady gaze, he floated slowly up to the cupola, where he vanished, borne aloft by angels. From that moment on the younger B—— saw himself as one of God's chosen, and a few days later he joined *another* church uniquely able to assure him salvation (for the orthodox English Protestant church also believes it controls this franchise). My devout friends expressed their opinions on *this* conversion with philosophical deliberation. "Is it possible?" they cried. "What crass superstition! It must certainly have been a feverish delirium, or the man is a hypocrite and had other reasons; either he is mad, or he invented this fairy tale for his own advantage."

Oh people, people, how correct Christ was when he said that you see the mote in the eye of another, but not the beam in your own. Of course, it is like this for all of us, more or less, and I certainly do not exclude yours truly from the general rule.

We finally parted, not without emotion on both parts. I was then picked up by a mountain cart harnessed to a horse far from dazzling in its appearance. The young ladies were very taken with my eccentric mode of travel. This day's journey was to be thirty miles long, and it began at a slow pace. After a while the miserable horse became unruly while climbing uphill, compelling me to get out of the carriage more than once so as not to end up buried in some abyss. At a certain point the stubborn animal declined to take another step unless led by the bridle, and the coachman did this for some time, trotting heartily alongside until he could sustain it no longer. Heaven knows what would have become of us if we had not met a man on horseback, who agreed to harness his horse in place of ours. By this means I finally reached Macroom late in the evening. I noticed nothing remarkable along the way except for the so-called glen, a long and deep pass through the rocks. Here, at the time of the Whiteboys conspiracy,[1] Lord Bantry and Colonel White barely escaped ambush by some of these men, who were occupying the heights. The Whiteboys had made their arrangements carefully and during the night loosened a huge boulder, which they then set rolling down into the middle of the road just as the troops were marching past. The cavalry detachment sent out against them was not only taken by surprise and halted in its advance, but also found itself cut off from behind and thus in a desperate situation. Many were killed, but the two gentlemen I named were riding excellent hunters and fortunately escaped with the help of mounts that managed to find a way along the near-impassable terrain of precipitous rocky slopes, a continuous hail of bullets raining down upon them as they went. Colonel White was in the end slightly injured in the arm; Lord Bantry escaped entirely unscathed.

In this thoroughly wild area, not far away, is a large lake with a brush-covered island in its center. Here is a sacred chapel, which is the object of annual pilgrimages. Given the lateness of the hour, I was unable to examine it closely.

Macroom is a pleasant spot with a beautiful palace belonging to the uncle of the captivating African (her husband's uncle, in fact). She had given me a letter of introduction so as not to lose any more time, but I made no use of it.

Cork, October 6th, 1828

I LEFT MACROOM very early in a jingle, a kind of covered diligence with two horses. It was raining and blowing again; it seems, dear Julie, I am no longer "on the sunny side of life," as the Irish so charmingly put it.

With me in the carriage were three women and one large, five-year-old rascal, who made a great nuisance of himself and was horribly spoiled by his quite comely and energetic mamma. Although he fed heartily on a large roll of bread and an equally large piece of cake, filling up the coach with crumbs and scraps, his nasty temper nonetheless welled up at every opportunity. The shrieks he emitted; the stomping of his feet, which repeatedly knocked against my own; the mother's attempts to mollify him; her appeals for assistance from her husband, who was seated on the top deck; her continual requests to make a brief stop, because the poor little mite was sick from the motion, or because he needed a drink or whatever else; and last but not least the noxious air, which became so pervasive that it drove her at last to open the windows, hermetically sealed until then at her insistence, for fear that the little one, despite his fur wrap, might manage to catch cold. It was a genuine ordeal! The young woman seemed just as apprehensive about herself as about her child, for every time the carriage tilted slightly to one side, she began to scream and cling to me, clasping me firmly around the neck with both hands. This was the more bearable of my sufferings, and it therefore amused me to increase her fear a little bit from time to time. During the intermissions she told me with patriotic fervor about the curiosities of the region, pointing out the beautiful ruins and explaining their history. Finally she showed me a pointed, tower-like stone standing isolated in the middle of a field and related how a Danish king had thrown it there from across the sea in order to prove his strength. Her husband, too, had to get down from the imperial to admire this stone, whereupon she mockingly rebuked him for being, like all the men of today, nothing but a miserable weakling compared to those giants of the past. At the same time she handed the boy over to him, so he could ride at his father's side. The poor man made a long face, tugged his nightcap over his ears, and meekly followed orders.

The country now became very fertile and full of rich, open farmland, here and there appointed with stately country mansions. Cork itself is in an extremely picturesque setting in a deep valley next to the sea. It has an ancient look made all the more quaint by the many houses clad all over in a scale-like armor of slate. The two new prisons are magnificent structures, one belonging to the city and the other to the county. The first is in a classical style; the second in the Gothic, and resembles a large fortress.

After finishing breakfast and taking care of several domestic details, I rented a so-called whaleboat (narrow and pointed at both ends and therefore safer and faster than others) and sailed under a good wind on the bay, called the "River of Cork,"[2] to Cobh, where I intended to take my midday meal. This bay is here about a quarter of an hour wide, and the part you see as you approach Cork from the sea has to be one of the most beautiful entrées in the world! Both shores consist of very high hills covered with palaces, villas, country houses, parks, and gardens. Rising to unequal height on each side, they form the most luxuriant, ever-changing frame. Bit by bit the city emerges in the center of this painting, capped by the imposing mass of a military barracks, set on the highest hill and closing the horizon. This is the view from out on the water, and it changes constantly as you move toward Cobh, since the bends of the canal shift the landscape and draw parts of it forward in different ways. One of these vistas terminates with uncommon beauty in a Gothic castle built by the city on a broad, projecting rock (Figure 98).[3] The virtue of its superb location confers significance on the structure and, if I may put it this way, makes it seem as if it belongs there, whereas similar buildings elsewhere so often strike one as an unpleasant hors d'oeuvre. Although I believe we are superior to the English in architectural design of the nobler sort, we nonetheless pay much too little attention to the settings of our buildings and their surrounding landscape. Yet this is exactly what should determine the choice of a style.

The castle here looks as if it were meant for some ancient hero of the sea, for the only entrance is from the water. A colossal gate with a coat of arms arches over the shadowed entryway, and there the incoming tide came right up to the foot of the stairway. I thought of Folko with the vulture's wings just returning from a successful marine battle, and I brought the sea to life with visions from Fouqué's *Magic Ring*.[4]

BLACK ROCK CASTLE, NEAR CORK.

98

Blackrock Castle.

Next, under a good wind, we sailed by Passage, a fishing village, and Monkstown, named after the ruins of a monastery in the forest above. Here the rain, which had paused for a while, began again, but this time it gave me the opportunity to view a magnificent natural scene. Near the island of Haulbowline, we turned into the narrow passage toward Cobh's harbor, which afforded a very lovely view (Figure 99). On the left of the approach is an elevated coastline with houses and gardens, and on the right you see the island I mentioned, with a fort, a stretch of marine buildings, and storehouses for the materials required by a maritime power. In front of us, in the bay itself, many battleships and frigates of the royal fleet lay at anchor along with a second ship for deportees,[5] and behind all this the city of Cobh climbed up the hill in orderly stages. Just as this came into view, the setting sun emerged from beneath the rain clouds at a fiery yellow spot in the sky behind us, while in front of us a rainbow, more complete and deeply colored than I remember ever having seen, arched over the entrance to the bay, arising out of the sea, and sinking back into it like a gateway of flowers meant to join heaven and earth. Within its gigantic semicircle the sea and the ships, now cast into shadow by a mountain off our stern, appeared utterly black, while in contrast the evening light poured such a splendid glow over the higher amphitheater of Cobh that the seagulls floating in it glimmered like bright silver, and every window

W. H. Bartlett.   Heath

COVE HARBOUR, CORK, LOOKING TOWARD ROSTELLAN.

sparkled like glittering gold where the town gradually ascended the hill. This indescribably beautiful sight lay under the same illumination the whole time we were heading in, and then shortly
before we landed the rainbow doubled, its two arcs burning in colors of equal beauty. As a finale,
when we had scarcely set foot on the shore, both arcs vanished almost in an instant.

    I now settled down happily at the window of the small inn, hoping to break my fast with
an excellent meal of the most delicate fresh fish. It never got beyond *fasting*, however, for there
was not a single fish nor oyster or mussel to be had. You come across this more often than you
would think in the small fishing villages along the coast, for everything available is immediately sent off to be sold in the big cities. In this respect, my goal went unfulfilled, and I had to be
content with the normal fare in English inns: the immortal mutton chops. Yet I did not let this
ruin my mood. During my meager repast I read a few old newspapers—I had not seen any in a
long time—and resumed my trip back after darkness had already settled in. The only conveyance I could find was an open car with straw seats, and as the wind was blowing cold and hard,
I found it necessary to wrap myself tight in my cloak. We kept close to the sea at a considerable
elevation, while the numerous lights of the ships and marine buildings below us were like a daz-
zlingly festive illumination. Five flames danced like will-o'-the-wisps on the black ships of the

99
Cobh Harbor.

deportees, and a cannon shot fired from the guard ship thundered with a muffled tone through the still of the night.

As this view disappeared, I turned my attention for the first time to the brilliant, star-filled skies. Who can gaze for very long into the sublime magnificence of these flickering, celestial bodies without being infused with the deepest and sweetest emotions? These are the signs through which God has forever spoken most lucidly to the human soul. And yet I had not given a thought to those heavenly lights as long as the earthly ones sparkled. But this is how it goes—not until the earth abandons us, do we seek out heaven. The earth, being closer to us, always asserts its authority. Just as the peasant is kept more in check by the local official than by the king, or the soldier is more afraid of his lieutenant than of the commanding general, or the courtier pays more heed to the favorite than to the monarch, and finally the pious man . . . but then one should not go on philosophizing in this way, dear Julie, for I need not say once again *qu'il ne faut pas prendre le valet pour le roi.*[6]

October 7th, 1828

FROM WHAT I see in the newspapers, the political skies are getting more and more cloudy. Oh, if only I were there in those regions so different from ours! I would fight in the ranks of what was once the *arrière-garde* of civilization but has become the avant-garde, so that it turns around now, sword in hand, to carry enlightenment to the barbarians—indeed, while spreading enlightenment, it is itself always learning more, and soon may take over the leadership of the whole, aging continent. This war can, indeed *must*, have incalculable consequences.[7] It is no longer the usual Turkish war, for all signs proclaim it the beginning of a new world epoch, and, although European interests are hardly ready to condone a major crisis, these will nonetheless prove to be the initial strokes of magnetism (the Russian cannons make up the *baquet*) destined to bring clairvoyance to the Orient, which has slumbered for so many centuries as if in a frozen grave.[8] How relentless the effect and countereffect will be, and what secrets the magnetized will reveal to the magnetizer!

In Europe, however, the culture and politics of our era are moving in such a way that the last act of this drama can only end with a commercial campaign against England, that proud country, its monarchy of universal trade demanding a heavier tribute from us than all the military pressure we suffered in the bygone days of Napoleon. It is clear from that hero's Continental System that he had grasped what Europe actually needed.[9] But he was like an overly authoritative physician, who temporarily binds a patient's hands and feet so that, *bon gré, mal gré,* he can pour what he sees as beneficial medicine down the sufferer's throat. It was therefore only natural that the patient broke free as quickly as possible and threw the physician out the door. Whether or not the convalescent will feel the need to begin the treatment again voluntarily is a separate question.

England has lit the way for us in civilization, thereby becoming greatest and most powerful; but for exactly this reason, in accordance with the immutable laws of nature (which permit no individual perfection), it also contains the seeds of premature decay. Furthermore, it harbors irreconcilable elements, both old and new, and of equal authority. These are at war with each other and must sooner or later drag this empire down from the heights, where it still shines so resplendently. Then, in the course of things, after having dwelt on the mount for so long, it will serve others as a footstool to climb to the next level, because everything of this earth has its appointed time. Indeed, perhaps this has happened already. Once the culminating point has been reached, the retreat will inevitably begin, and it may be that the epoch of Waterloo and the fall of Napoleon have signaled that very moment for England.

It is nonetheless odd that the mightiest fountainhead of freedom and enlightenment has issued from those same islands where we will eventually have to do battle against foreign despotism. Yet such apparent thanklessness is the rule almost everywhere in history. A certain amount of reflection explains and justifies it.

Mitchelstown, October 9th, 1828, morning

I LEFT CORK yesterday at four o'clock in the afternoon, seated in the mail coach next to the driver and occasionally taking over the four horses myself. The landscape was picturesque until an hour from the town but then became rather uninteresting, and soon it began to grow dark. After a few stops most of the passengers left us, and I went to sit inside the carriage, where I was blessed with a three-hour tête-à-tête with a lady—unfortunately she was seventy years old and a Puritan, although not, it seemed, a purist. This unpleasant company, along with the panegyrics that a previous traveling companion delivered on the newly constructed Gothic castle in Mitchelstown, persuaded me to leave the mail coach in the middle of the night and wait here until morning. I was awakened at seven o'clock in order to study this much-praised marvel of construction; however I found myself extremely disappointed, as were some other strangers who'd been drawn here for the same purpose. We were, it is true, shown a large and expensive pile of stone, which had cost its owner fifty thousand pounds to erect. But a major ingredient had been forgotten in the process—namely, good taste. The building is, first of all, too tall for its breadth; its style exhibits nothing but confusion without variety; its contour is awkward; and it manages to make an absolutely *diminutive* impression despite its *enormous* mass. It stood bleakly on the lawn without a single picturesque interruption, exactly what castles in the Gothic or related manner most require. Neither did the unattractive park possess a pretty group of trees or a view worth mentioning.[10]

I have wasted so many words on this inadequate edifice, because it has a certain stature in Ireland on account of the reputation of its owner and great cost of its construction. How infinitely superior is the estate of my worthy Colonel White, which was created for perhaps one-eighth the cost and yet remains almost unknown. The interior decoration of the castle resembled its exterior: in five minutes we had our fill, and although we were told of a lovely view from the top of the tower, no key could be found, so we all returned quite sullenly to the inn. Here during breakfast one of the strangers told me all sorts of interesting things about this region and its inhabitants.

Lord Kingston, he said, lived through some exceptional adventures, some on his own and some within his family. As one of the most zealous of the Orangemen, he is now more feared than loved. When his father was just twelve, he was married to the ten-year-old heiress of what now constitutes his entire family fortune.[11] The tutor and governess were given instructions to keep the young couple under careful surveillance, and especially to keep them from any tête-à-tête. But "somehow or other," as my Irishman phrased it, they did manage to get together once three years later, the present lord being the result of this little escapade. They subsequently had several more children, one of whom, by the way, was a son I knew in Vienna. He was an extraordinarily handsome man and famous for his *bonnes fortunes*; at the time he was the professed lover of the

Duchess of——, whom he treated very unconventionally. Once, when he had invited me to breakfast in the hotel where they both were living, I found the duchess alone; he only appeared later in his dressing gown and slippers, coming from his or her bedroom—I do not know which.

The lord's youngest child was one of the most captivating girls in Ireland.[12] She was just sixteen years old when a cousin on her mother's side, a married man named FitzGerald, who also had the reputation of being an irresistible seducer of women, fell in love with her. In her case he confirmed his reputation so brilliantly that he was able to convince her, the beloved daughter of the mightiest earl, not only to sacrifice her virginity but to accompany him to England as his mistress. He lived with her there for almost a year, first in secret. Then he had the effrontery to take her to one of the most frequented seaside resorts, where she was of course discovered and abducted for a second time, now on her father's orders, and brought to a place of safe custody in northern England. FitzGerald, perhaps prompted by the resistance of the family, decided, no matter what the cost, to get her back in his power; and since he believed she had been returned to her father's estates, he headed back to Ireland without delay, thoroughly altering his appearance by a disguise. There he lodged at the same inn where we just breakfasted, and tried to spy out where his beloved was sequestered. His occasional enquiries, his mysterious behavior, and the unlucky happenstance that a previous acquaintance of his mentioned an astonishing similarity between the stranger and the notorious FitzGerald—all these things awakened the suspicions of the innkeeper, who immediately set out to inform Lord Kingston. The earl received this message with what appeared to be great equanimity and simply advised the informer to practice the utmost discretion. He then enquired at what hour this particular stranger usually got up, and when hearing that it was never before eight o'clock, he gave the innkeeper a present and sent him off, adding that he would investigate the affair himself the following morning at six o'clock and requesting that the innkeeper wait for him *alone*. Morning arrived, and punctually along with it came the earl. Without further ado he and the innkeeper climbed the steps and demanded of the stranger's servant that the door to his master's room be opened. When the man refused, the earl himself broke down the door with a powerful kick, and went to the bed where FitzGerald, startled by the noise, was just sitting up. Lord Kingston looked at him steadily, and as soon as he felt sure of his identity, pulled a pistol out of his pocket and very calmly blew out the brains of this modern Don Juan. The corpse sank back onto the bed without a sound.

The aftermath demonstrates how in England a distinguished and powerful man can readily elude the law, as long as there is no one even grander willing to call him to account. Lord Kingston was, it is true, brought to trial, but since he took care to come to an arrangement with the only two witnesses—both of whom he sent off—he was acquitted, there being no plaintiff and no evidence. In this country no one already acquitted of a crime can be tried again for the same offense, so in spite of the utterly flagrant murder, all risk of punishment was over from this moment on. The young girl supposedly disappeared or died shortly thereafter.[13] Lord Kingston outlived her by many years, and even in his old age was infamous for having the most beautiful mistresses, one at each of his residences. The final consequence of these irregularities was a separation from his wife, leading to extremely bitter disputes and litigation that continued until his death. Meanwhile his eldest son, the present earl, had, against his father's will, gotten married in Sicily while he was still a minor.[14] He already had three children with his young wife, and was completely severed from his native country. When he suddenly received an extremely loving invitation from the aged lord, promising to forgive and forget all that had happened, he was persuaded to return to England with his entire family. Scarcely had he arrived, however, when, through his father's influence, his marriage was declared invalid and annulled, the young mother sent home, and the children declared illegitimate in England. Contrary to expectations, the son appears to have acceded to his father's views without much bother. Not long afterward, he too married a rich heiress and, after the old earl's death, brought an even more acrimonious lawsuit against his mother than had his father, in order to gain immediate possession of the property she had denied him. This he was unable to achieve, however, just as she was later unable to disinherit him.

What a portrait of the genteel folk of the eighteenth century!

Cashel, late evening

MY GARRULOUS FRIEND traveled on to Cashel with me. The weather was tolerable—in other words it did not rain—and in such wet country that was enough to cause the good fellow next to me to call out repeatedly, "What a delightful day! What lovely weather!" I preferred to go part of the way on foot, whereby a tall, predictably tattered, eighteen-year-old lad served as my guide. He was walking with great difficulty, wearing what looked like slippers, and appeared to have injured feet. But when I asked him about it, he answered, "Oh, no, I've only put on shoes, because I want to become a soldier, so I must accustom myself to wearing them. It's so hard to walk in these things that I can barely make any progress!"

In keeping with my habit of scorning no information but gleaning, even from the most common sort of people, a few useful morsels, I enquired with my guide about the current state of affairs in the province.

"Yes," he said, "here it's still calm, but in Tipperary, where we will soon arrive, and especially farther north, they know how to stand up to the Orangemen. O'Connell and the association have organized us properly there, like troops. I am one of them, too, and have my uniform at home. If you saw me in it, you would hardly recognize me. Three weeks ago we were all there to be reviewed, more than four thousand men altogether. We wore green jackets—everyone must acquire one as best he can—with the inscription 'King George and O'Connell' on the sleeve. We've chosen our own officers, they drill us, and we can already march and turn sharply like the Redcoats. Admittedly we had no weapons, but . . . they can be found somehow—as long as O'Connell wants it. We had flags, and anyone who abandoned them or got drunk, we threw into the water until he was sober. This did not happen often. We are called simply O'Connell's militia."

The government has subsequently, and wisely, outlawed this military review, and my prospective citizen-soldier was furious with Lord K——, who saw to it that every one of his tenants present at the review was arrested (these tenants are small leaseholders, who in Ireland are practically serfs). "But" he added, "the tyrant we'd rather see dead than alive will have to pay for every hour they sit in prison. If only they weren't such tame sheep here in Cork! In Tipperary they would have put a stop to him long ago. O'Connell never comes through here, even if it's the shortest route, because he can't bear the sight of Lord K——'s face."

This is how the party spirit operates everywhere, and how well informed the destitute are about their affairs!

The trip to Cahir was of little interest. True, the road leads between two mountain ranges, the Galtee and the Knockmealdown Mountains, but since the broad plain that separates them boasts only a few trees and little variety, the vistas are without charm. My traveling companion pointed out the highest peak of the Galtees, where the most renowned sportsman* of the area is buried along with his hound and his shotgun. Not far from there are stalactite-filled subterranean caverns, supposedly of unfathomable extent. These are only visited during the hottest time of year, however, because at other seasons they are full of water.

In Cahir there is a very beautiful park belonging to Lord Glengall, who was so wickedly mistreated by the London caricaturists last year. It is announced by the imposing ruins of a castle of King John's, where Lord Glengall's flag now flies atop its dilapidated tower.[15] At the other end of the park you find the contrast to this ruin, namely a cottage *orné,* where the owner lives when he is here.[16] The location of this cottage is so charming and well chosen that it merits a fuller description. The whole park, beginning with the town and castle, consists of a very long and relatively narrow valley, with a river winding through meadowland, where groups of trees and small woods alternate with each other delightfully, and a path leads along either side of the water. The mountain ranges that close the valley are thickly covered with forests cut through by additional paths. Toward the end of the park, which is about an hour long, the valley opens up and reveals a lovely vista of the higher Galtee Mountains. But before arriving there you find, exactly in the middle of the basin, a long hill standing isolated in the meadowland. Atop this stands the cottage, more than two-thirds of it concealed by the woods covering the entire hill. Within these thickets are the pleasure ground, all the gardens, and lush, flower-lined walkways, along which the valley's loveliest vistas unfold on both sides. On the high mountains in the distance, you can see several ruins of castles and monasteries, but close by there is nothing but peace, rural stillness, and cheerful floral embellishments, *even in winter.*

When I returned to the inn for my supper, the host told me a great piece of news: the carriage and servants of a foreign prince had been waiting for him in Cashel for the last two weeks, but the prince had undertaken a secret journey—to O'Connell, it was said—and consequently the entire neighborhood was in an uproar and filled with curiosity. Many thought he had been sent to O'Connell with secret commissions from the king of France; several, however, had already seen him themselves in Limerick and insisted that he was a son of Napoleon.

While the innkeeper was uttering this and even more such nonsense, without suspecting that he was speaking to the *personage* himself, who had just arrived on a cart, he also informed me that a second cart (the only way to get around here) had just been readied to carry me farther on my way. So I set off and soon had the opportunity to undertake new philosophical speculations on the wonderful power of habit among draft horses. The one pulling me was a pliant and benevolent animal, but as soon as it reached the place where it had been given water for the past fifteen years, it suddenly came to a stop. Even fire could not induce it to take a single step until it had been given its drink. Once that had happened, however, no further urging was required, although the same maneuver was repeated later when we met the return cart, since this always occasions a stop for the exchange of news. As if suddenly gone lame, it halted instantly; then, as soon as the two coachmen had shaken hands, it moved off abruptly of its own accord. Truly, this reveals the great secret of educating man and beast: habit, *voilà tout.* The Chinese are an example of this, and I remember how once in London the well-known ambassador of a great nation

---

* "Sportsman" is just as untranslatable as "gentleman." In no way does it mean just "huntsman," but rather a man who pursues, with passion and skill, all or even just several enjoyments of this type. Boxing, horse racing, duck shooting, fox hunting, cock fighting, etc., all are sport.—*The Editor.*

expounded at length on how the political system of the Chinese nation was actually the best and most effective, because nothing ever changed there. *C'est plus commode pour ceux qui règnent, il n'y a pas de doute.*[17]

I reached Cashel at seven o'clock, beforehand passing the Suir, a river called the Flower of Ireland, since the most fertile fields and most beautiful country estates lie along its banks. At the inn I ran into some terrible trouble, because one of the liberal clubs was just having a meeting followed by dinner.* I hardly had time to enter my room, when the president *in propria persona* arrived along with his deputation and invited me to join them at table. I implored him to excuse me from the meal, pleading exhaustion from the trip and a bad headache, but promised to appear at dessert, because I was curious to observe their goings-on from close-up. The club had a quite reasonable aspiration to thank for its existence, given that it was composed of Catholics as well as Protestants, all of whom had resolved to work for the reconciliation of both sides and to collaborate simultaneously on achieving emancipation. When I entered I found about eighty to a hundred people seated at a long table, and they stood up while the president led me to its head. I made a small, grateful speech, after which they drank to my health, a gesture which I reciprocated. Innumerable other toasts followed, always accompanied by speeches. The eloquence of the speakers was not, however, very distinguished, and the same commonplaces were repeated over and over in different words. So after half an hour I took advantage of a propitious moment to excuse myself. Now please allow me the same courtesy, since I am very tired. I have not heard anything from you in a long time and will not find your letters again until Dublin. Just stay healthy, that is the main thing for you—and do not stop loving me, that is the main thing for me.

Your most faithful Lou

---

* Nothing even remotely ceremonial happens in England without *dinner*, whether the occasion be religious, political, literary, or of some other nature, from a royal banquet to the last meal before an execution.—*The Editor*.

Cashel, October 10th, 1828

$\mathcal{B}$ELOVED GOOD ONE,

The Rock of Cashel, with its renowned, splendid ruins, is one of the great "lions"* of Ireland and was recommended to me by Walter Scott himself as the site most worth visiting in all of Ireland, next to Holy Cross Abbey (Figure 100). It is an isolated hill standing in the middle of a plain. Strangely enough, along the crest of one of the distant mountains, you can see a missing piece the very size of this rock, as if it had been bitten off and deposited below. According to legend, the devil took this bite in a fury over a soul that had escaped his clutches while being transported to hell. Then as he was flying over Cashel, he spat it out. Later M. C'Omack, king and archbishop of Cashel, built his castle and a chapel there;[1] both structures are still remarkably well preserved (Figure 101). Connected to them are the church and abbey—added in the twelfth century, I believe, by Donal O'Brien.[2] The whole forms the most magnificent ruin, where all the details of old Saxon architecture can be studied with great interest. This has been made considerably easier thanks to the efforts of the current archbishop's son-in-law, Dr. Cotton,[3] who several months ago had Mac Carthaigh's chapel completely cleared of rubble, dirt, and a few layers of whitewash, and at considerable expense thus made it possible to visit the entire ruin. Nothing could be more strangely exotic, I might say more barbarically exquisite, than this baroque, fantastic, often brilliantly executed ornamentation. Many of the sarcophagi and monuments found in the rubble and below ground present interesting puzzles. You might be tempted to believe that the dreadful, grotesque faces, rather like Indian gods, must belong to an earlier, pre-Christian, idolatrous age, except you know that paganism gave way to Christianity only very slowly, and with great resistance—and the retreat is still not over today! For instance, I myself possess a bell that one of my ancestors carried off from the prisons of the Inquisition, on which the Virgin is surrounded not by angels but by monkeys, some of them playing the violin, while others perform somersaults in the clouds.

I looked at everything very thoroughly and was still atop the highest accessible tower as the sun set over the Devil's Bite. The archbishop had been good enough to send his librarian to show me the ruins, and I learned from him that the well-known and often-quoted psalter, written in the Irish language and listed in every travel guide as the enduring object of note in Cashel,

---

* "Lion" is a fashionable term and means "the first," "most famous," or "whatever is in vogue." The contrasting more common term is "tiger." Thus the young dandies of the capital in their cabriolets are called *lions,* but the little lads standing at the back, *tigers.* The swells of the lower social orders are also identified with the latter term. *C'est tout bête, comme vous voyez.*—*The Editor.* [It's all pretty asinine, as you can see.—*Translator.*]

is nothing but a fable. Or at least it was never here. This did not interest me very much, but I became truly stricken when I heard that the Catholics who sought to acquire the property were considering restoring and enlarging the church. May heaven protect the holy ruins from these devout characters!

On the open square in front of the church is an extremely old, mutilated statue of St Patrick, standing on a granite pedestal. At one time the coronation chair, supposedly brought here from Portugal, stood next to him; it was then sent to Scone for the coronation of the Scottish King Fergus, and from there carried off by Edward I to Westminster, where it is still seen today.[4] At the foot of the Rock of Cashel are the equally worthwhile ruins of Hore Abbey, which was once, so people say, connected to the castle by a subterranean passage. Especially noteworthy are the lovely proportions and perfect ornamentation of a large window illuminating the chapel.

October 11th, 1828

ONE OF THE gentlemen I met yesterday, Captain S——, a man of distinguished family and courteous manners, offered me his horses for a visit to the ruins of Athassel Priory and the park and castle of the wealthy Earl of Landaff. The excellent hunters carried us quickly to our destination, but the sites did not live up to expectation. The abbey is, to be sure, a beautiful and extensive ruin, yet its location in a bog, in the middle of a plowed field without a tree or shrub, is too unfavorable for a picturesque effect. Lord Landaff's park is likewise of unusual size, 2,800 acres in extent, but not in any way outstanding. The tree growth is not the best, water is essentially lacking, and I found the modern Gothic castle, painted pale blue, atrocious.[5] The owner, in his seventies, is still handsome and interesting, and often resides on his own property, something of great merit in Ireland. We came across this man, who knows how to shine in the wider world thanks to manners polished abroad, standing in the rain, wearing rubber boots and a waterproof coat as he directed his workers like a true country farmer. I liked this very much, and you can easily guess why.[6]

On the way back Captain S—— related several interesting details about the outrageous oppression the Catholics are suffering here, a circumstance that, taking local conditions into account, is harsher than the slavery imposed on the Greeks by the Turks. Catholics are not allowed, for instance, to call their places of worship churches but only chapels, and no bells are allowed. These things, insignificant in themselves, are nonetheless degrading in their intention. It is well-known that no Catholic is allowed to sit in Parliament or become a general in the army, a minister to the king, a judge, etc.* Their priests, whose titles are not recognized by law, cannot perform marriages if one party is Protestant. But the worst is that Catholics must pay monstrous sums to the Protestant clerics, while in addition supporting their own, of whom the state takes no notice. This is a major reason for their abysmal poverty. How intolerable this must seem in a country where more than two-thirds of the overall population are zealous devotees of the Catholic religion! In the south this ratio is even more lopsided. In the county of Tipperary there are approximately four hundred thousand Catholics and only ten thousand Protestants, yet in spite of this the Protestant clergy costs the residents annually the following sums: 1) the archbishop, twenty-five thousand pounds sterling; 2) the dean, four thousand; 3) for about fifty parishes, an average of fifteen hundred pounds each—expenditures that are almost all borne by the Catholics alone. Most holders of these sinecures do not even live in Ireland, but instead install some poor devil (one of the notorious curates) and pay him forty or fifty pounds annually to perform their duties, something that is readily dealt with, since there are congregations that number no more than ten members. Indeed, in one parish, there is *not a single Protestant to be found*, and no church, either, but just an old ruin, where every year the *farce* of a sermon is enacted, delivered to empty

101

Cormac's Chapel, Cashel Cathedral.

---

* This has been successfully challenged, as we know.—*The Editor.* [O'Connell was elected to Parliament in 1828 and a new Catholic Relief Bill was passed in February 1829, a great victory for Catholic emancipation in Ireland.—*Translator.*]

walls, and a *Catholic* is hired to perform the role of verger! Meanwhile, year in, year out, the priest is traipsing through the streets of London and Paris leading the most unspiritual of lives! Just recently I read in an English newspaper that an English priest in Boulogne had lost a lot of money gambling, gotten into a brawl over it, and shot his opponent in a duel. This necessitated that he leave the area immediately and retreat to his benefice. Even the higher-ranking clergy, who have to be present at least some of the time in the appropriate bishop's or archbishop's diocese, allow none of their ill-gotten lucre (under such circumstances it really must be called this) to be given to the poor, because most of these holy men are saving what they can in order to enrich their own families.[7] To this end the English church has even legalized a kind of fraud—just the way nobles who possess the right of conferment sell positions, often quite publically—in that benefices are handed out free of charge only where they serve political or family interests. For example, people making use of church property are permitted to enter into a new lease on that same property in advance and before the deadline, settling the terms once and for all with a lump-sum payment to the benefice holder. Naturally, if the priest were to die shortly thereafter, his successor would lose whatever would have been due *him*. Can anyone wonder why such institutions have repeatedly driven the unhappy population to despair and revolt? But the result each time is that their chains are only cinched more tightly and more blood is drawn from their lacerated flesh. Wherever you see a handsome estate with fertile fields and inquire about the owner, the answer is usually "This is forfeited land," which is to say land that used to belong to Catholics, but now belongs to Protestants. O'Connell told me that until recently there was a law proclaiming that no Catholic could possess his own land in Ireland, and if a Protestant was able to prove in court that a certain piece of land was still being held by a Catholic, then the judge was to grant the property to *him,* namely the plaintiff. Sham purchases were the only solution; nevertheless, according to O'Connell, property worth millions was moved into Protestant hands by this means. Is it not remarkable that Protestants, who in a barbaric era broke from the Catholic Church exactly because of its greed and intolerance, are now in the most enlightened age persisting in the same error? Comparatively, therefore, they have placed themselves under a heavier burden of guilt than they themselves once had to endure! So one would like to ask, will this monstrosity of religion,* this spawn of despotism and hypocrisy, which for so long the world has had to feed with blood and tears, never be destroyed by a more enlightened generation? If it happens, then people will no doubt harbor the same sense of pity looking back at us today as we feel looking on the darkness of the Middle Ages.

In the afternoon I visited the Catholic dean, an extremely amiable man who had lived on the Continent for some time and was the late pope's chaplain. His conversation, just as frank as it was enlightened, astonished me, because we are always inclined to think Catholics are necessarily superstitious. One thing he said was "Believe me, this land is consecrated to misfortune. There are hardly any Christians left here. Both Catholics and Protestants have one and the same religion—that of hatred!"

Somewhat later Captain S—— brought me the latest newspaper, in which my visit to the meeting I have already described, the words I uttered there, and the other speeches, along with all the charlatanism typical of England, filled three or four pages. To give you a sample of this genre and simultaneously flaunt my own eloquence, I will translate the beginning of the article,

---

* It need not be mentioned that the discussion here can only be about false and pseudoreligion.—*The Editor.*

where I am praised in exactly the manner that the snake-oil huckster eulogizes his pills or the horse trader ascribes qualities to his nags that they never possessed. Listen:

As soon as we heard of the arrival of ——, the president and a delegation went to his room, in order to invite him to honor our banquet with his presence. Shortly thereafter the man entered the room. His appearance is commanding and graceful. He has a mustache, and his face, although very pale, is exceedingly pleasing and expressive. He took his seat at the upper end of the table and, bowing to the assembled party, spoke clearly and with proper emphasis, but in a somewhat foreign accent, the following words: "Gentlemen! Although ill and very tired, I am nonetheless too flattered by your gracious invitation not to accept it with thanks and express to you personally what heartfelt interest I take in your efforts on behalf of your fatherland. May God bless this beautiful and richly endowed part of the earth, which offers every sensitive stranger such a multitude of pleasures, but where I especially want to acknowledge, with deep gratitude, the kindheartedness and hospitality I have enjoyed at every turn. May heaven bless this sorely afflicted land, as well as every true Irishman, be he Catholic or Protestant, who, aloof from party loyalties, hopes for nothing but the welfare of the fatherland—a welfare that can only be achieved through peace, tolerance, and 'civil and religious liberty' (the great slogan of the association). Gentlemen! Fill your glasses and allow me to offer a toast to you. Long live the king, and *Erin go Bragh!*"

(This is the old Irish motto that appears on the medal of the Order of Liberators and means "Hail Erin!").

The President: "Gentlemen! Please concur with my sentiments and hear what I am now privileged to deliver: Should he ever return to us, may our illustrious guest, to whose health we now fill our glasses, find us blessed by equal laws and equal privileges and in possession of the general and internal peace that is the single aspiration of our union. Three times three."

The Prince: "I reiterate my thanks to you for the honor that you have just now shown me by drinking my health. Nothing could make me happier than to witness the fulfillment of our mutual wishes, in this country I love like my own native land and only leave with heartfelt regret, etc."

Now dear Julie, how would you evaluate my performance? Can I not string together platitudes as well as the next man when the occasion arises? I did not get too close to the truth at any moment, by the way. But what is *not* a platitude, even if repeated at the close of all my letters, is the assurance of my tender love for you, with which I now am and will eternally be,

Your friend Lou

$\mathcal{M}$OST PRECIOUS FRIEND,

Why do I get such pleasure from writing to you? Certainly because I believe it gives *you* pleasure to hear from me when I am far away—but also because *you* understand me and no one else does! This in itself would be enough to bind me to you forever, because in the midst of the world, I live only with you as if we were secluded on a desert island. Thousands of other creatures swarm around me, it is true, but it is only you I can talk to. If I attempt it with others, my inclination to always tell the truth can often cost me dearly! Or I may cause offense in some other way—because my nature is no more capable of attaining worldly wisdom than the swan in winter, who waddles awkwardly on the frozen lake outside your window incapable of running a race with the ice skaters gliding by. Yet his time will come, and with proudly curving neck, he will part the waters or soar alone and majestic through the blue ether. Then is he finally himself.

But back to Cashel. Today I used my good friend's horses, which stand ready for me daily, to make a second excursion of about six miles to the ruins of Holy Cross, a worthy rival to the Devil's Rock. At first we amused ourselves by riding across the fields and leaping over a few walls. Then we arrived at the top of a hill from where the Rock (as the name is abbreviated here) can be seen at its most impressive: the wreath of distant blue mountains encircling the single rock that rises from the fertile plain; at its summit the castle, abbey, and cathedral forming a single great entity, silent and magnificent, proclaiming the history of successive ages; and finally the town at its foot, so destitute, and yet the seat of two archbishops (one Protestant, one Catholic). All this speaks its own mute language about the present day and awakens in me many contradictory emotions.

Holy Cross is of an utterly different character. Cashel stands in solitary grandeur, nothing but rocks and stone, totally barren and black; only here and there do you see a forlorn ivy vine creep timidly along a crevice. Holy Cross, by contrast, is in the valley on the banks of the Suir, buried in a leafy wood and embraced and entwined with such rampant ivy that you can hardly see its walls (Figure 102). Even the tall cross, the last one still remaining in the abbey,* is so ardently clasped that the vines seem to be protecting it from all contact with the profane. In the interior you see a number of splendid vaulted ceilings; an elegant monument atop the tomb of Donnell O'Brien, the king of Limerick who built the abbey at the beginning of the twelfth century; and a beautifully carved stone baldachin, under which the bodies of the previous abbots were placed (Figure 103). Everything is so well preserved that with just a little restoration it could

---

* A piece from the True Cross preserved here gave the monastery its name; for this reason every building was decorated with a tall stone cross, although only one has survived.—*The Editor.*

Holy Cross Abbey.

be made to look like new. And the view from the tower is very pleasant. Here you are close to the Devil's Bite, whose grotesque form proved too striking not to be employed in Irish legend. These people always have a fairy tale ready for every rarity of nature.

We hurried back more quickly than I liked, because the Catholic dean had invited me to a dinner, and I could not be late, for I was to meet the archbishop and sixteen other clerics there. No other layperson would be present. The dinner was a tribute to a chaplain of the Roman pope.

"You have probably never attended a meal where the guests were nothing but clergymen?" the archbishop said to me.

"Oh, but I have, my lord," I answered. "And what's more, I myself was recently a kind of bishop."

"How is that possible," he cried out in amazement. I explained to him that I . . . .
. . . .
"So," I continued, "we are a group of eighteen clerics, just among ourselves, and I can assure you that I make no distinction between Catholics and Protestants; in both I see only Christians."

After this we discussed religious topics freely and impartially; nowhere did I detect the slightest hint of bigotry or any annoying affectation of the holier-than-thou variety. During dessert several good voices joined in singing national songs, some less than devout! When the man sitting next to me noticed a touch of surprise on my part, he spoke in my ear, "Here we forget the foreign prince, archbishop, and clergy. Here at dinner we are all gentlemen and enjoy life."

This man was the undisputed descendent of one of Ireland's ancient royal families, and although this no longer conferred any distinction on him, he was not a little proud of it. "I have a strange dwelling for a priest," he said to me. "If you visit Ireland again, perhaps you will grant me the honor of welcoming you there as a guest. It is located directly below the Devil's Bite, and there is no more beautiful vista than mine in all of Ireland."

Later he remarked that to be Catholic in this kingdom could easily be considered a certificate of nobility, since only *new* families were Protestant. The Catholics are of necessity old, having made no new converts since the Reformation.

The melodies were strikingly like those of the Wends, and in fact I found many similar connections between the two peoples. Both love and distill only pure whiskey; both subsist almost solely on potatoes; the national music of both knows nothing but the bagpipe; both adore passionate singing and dancing, yet their melodies are always melancholic; both are oppressed by a foreign nation and speak a gradually dying tongue that is rich and poetic, yet without a written literature; both honor the descendants of their ancient princes and maintain that whatever has not been altogether relinquished is not yet entirely lost; both are superstitious and shrewd, and have a tendency to exaggerate their stories; both are revolutionary when possible, but somewhat groveling in the face of a determined power; both *like* dressing in tatters, even when they could clothe themselves better; and both are nonetheless capable of great exertion in their wretched lives, although they much prefer sloth. And yet both are equally fertile, which a Wendish proverb refers to as "the roast of the poor."[1] Other, better qualities are possessed by the Irish alone.

I took advantage of the acquaintances I made today to instruct myself further on the current proportion of Catholics to Protestants here, whereby I found everything I had heard before completely confirmed and learned a few more details as well. One of these is the official list of

103

Holy Cross Abbey, Interior.

a part of the present parishes and townships in the diocese of Cashel, and it is too remarkable not to send to you, even though the material is rather dry and seems almost too pedantic for our correspondence.

Thurles	has	12,000	Catholics and	250	Protestants
Cashel		11,000		700	
Clonoulty		5,142		82	
Cappawhite		2,800		76	
Killenaule		7,040		514	
Boherlahan		5,000		25	
Fethard		7,600		400	
Kilcummin		2,400		—	
Moycarkey[2]		7,000		80	
Golden		4,000		120	
Annacarty		4,000		12	
Donaskeigh		5,700		90	
New Inn		4,500		30	

In these thirteen districts there are 78,182 Catholics and 2,379 Protestants (including the military).

Each district has just one Catholic priest but often four or five Protestant clergymen, so that on average a Protestant congregation consists of barely twenty people. Kilcummin is the place I mentioned where no Protestant congregation exists at all, and the church service—which according to law has to take place at least once a year—is performed by a Catholic verger inside the ruin. In another district with the name Tullamaine, where there is likewise not a single Protestant, the same farce takes place. Nonetheless, the absent holders of these sinecures must be given their tithes and other fees down to the very last penny, and nothing is more mercilessly collected than the revenues of the church! No compassion exists here, certainly not concerning Catholics. Anyone who cannot pay the rent for his church-owned lands or his tithe to the Protestant cleric will be powerless to halt the sale of his cow and pig (it's been ages already since he had furniture, beds, or the like), while he himself, along with his wife and perhaps a dozen children (*car rien n'engendre comme les pommes de terre et la misère*[3]), are thrown out onto the street. There he is handed over to the grace of God, who feeds the birds and adorns the lilies of the field.[4] What an excellent thing, a state religion! As long as this kind of thing persists, as long as no one is allowed—as people are in the United States—to worship God however they like, *without thereby suffering reversals in their civic life*—then the age of barbarism has not yet ended. Someday *the law alone* must rule in the polity, as it does in nature. Religion will continue to offer comfort in adversity and an increase in happiness, but it shall not be allowed to rule. Only the law ought to wield irrevocable force; beyond that, liberty should reign everywhere. The civilized part of humanity can insist on this, to the degree it has already attained and indeed paid for it with so much blood and misery. What madness to dictate to people what will become of them after their death or what they should believe about it! It is bad enough that here on earth the best institutions, even the wisest laws, remain inadequate. In the unforeseeable future may each individual at least be allowed to shape himself according to his own discretion. Yet great, clever, and good men have felt entitled to practice spiritual despotism! That is human infirmity. One person can be noble in eleven things and prove an idiot in the twelfth. For example, a splendid warrior who vanquished the Aggressor of the World in battles that astonished all of Europe was secretly afraid that he was going to give birth to a young elephant.[5] This led to many a difficult moment for his adjutants. And whereas Cardinal Richelieu established the ideal of a wise minister, all he really cared about was to be a great poet; he suffered agonies writing miserable tragedies that became nothing but wastepaper when he died.[6] Louis le Grand, who could be called the absolute king par excellence, was so unbelievably foolish as to exclaim in all earnestness after the battle of Malplaquet, "Et Dieu a-t-il donc oublié ce que j'ai fait pour lui?"[7] Cromwell, who was not only a visionary but also the boldest and slyest of imposters, piled up murder on murder, ruin on ruin. Yet he soothed his conscience after inquiring of a priest and being assured that no matter what one had done before, one ecstatic moment of grace would ensure salvation. "Then I am saved," the protector cried out joyfully, "because I know for certain that at least *once* I felt I was in a state of grace!" This is how people are, and therefore I will never be impressed by temporal authority unless it corresponds to my own carefully considered opinions. Indeed if *all* of mankind were suddenly brought to the opposite view, I still would not change my own. Thank God, we are all individual minds and not a flock of sheep condemned to follow the bellwether. So then, what is universal opinion? Is it simply a perpetual sequence of errors, since it changes from century to century, as if dependent on time and place alone? If you are born in Constantinople, you swear by Mohammed; in the rest of Europe by Christ or Moses; in India by Brahma. In earlier days, if you came into the world as one of Augustus's subjects, you were a heathen; in the Middle Ages you accepted the rule of force as law; whereas today you demand freedom of the press* as something you cannot live without. And you yourself, in your short life, what do you think and what are you as a child? As a young boy? As an old man? Herder was certainly right when he said, "No two drops of water are alike, and yet you want to confer one faith on all people?" Or put differently, no atom remains unchanged, and you want to tell mankind to stand still?

Before the archbishop retired for the evening, he spoke to me with great courtesy: "You are, as you told us, a bishop, and consequently you owe obedience to the archbishop. I am therefore invoking my authority and commanding you to dine here again tomorrow with your colleague the bishop of Limerick and me. We are expecting him today, and I will permit no excuses."

Embracing the jest, I responded that I had to concede, and happily, since it would not be proper to resist the authority of the church. "And," I added, "since Your Grace and the dean are so adept at sweetening one's duty, I submit with all the more pleasure." ("Your Grace" is the title given to Protestant archbishops in England, and out of courtesy polite people grant it to Catholics as well, although according to English law they are not entitled to any rank whatsoever).

I spent the evening in the company of the ——, a Catholic, and I must say that I have only rarely found Protestant clergymen to be as candid and sincere. We quickly agreed that a person

---

* An unusually well-cultivated Moor who had lived in England for a long time said to Captain L——, "I would never want to serve a monarch as powerless as the king of England. What a different feeling it gives me to serve a master whose omnipotence is God's image on earth, and who with a nod can cause thousands of heads to fly off like chaff in the wind." *Il ne faut donc pas disputer des gouts.—The Editor.* ["You cannot argue with taste."—*Translator.*]

must accept from the very outset what the church dictates, and do so with blind faith and without indulging in the slightest scrutiny. If this is impossible, one must form one's own religious views on the basis of individual thoughts and feelings—which can rightly be called the philosopher's religion. The —— spoke French, in which he was most fluent, and I therefore quote him in his own words:

"Heureusement, on peut en quelque sorte combiner l'un et l'autre, car au bout du compte, il faut une religion positive au peuple."

"Et dites surtout," I responded, "qu'il en faut une aux rois et aux prêtres—car aux uns, elle fournit le 'par la grâce de Dieu' et aux autres de la puissance, des honneurs et des richesses—le peuple se contenterait peut-être de bonnes lois et d'un gouvernement libre."

"Ah!" he interrupted me, "vous pensez comme Voltaire:

> Nos prêtres ne sont pas ce qu'un vain peuple pense.
> Notre crédulité fait toute leur science.

"Ma foi," lui dis-je, "si tous les prêtres vous ressemblaient, je penserais bien autrement."[8]

October 13th, 1828, evening

UNFORTUNATELY I WAS unable to keep my word with my friendly Amphitryon. A migraine forced me to spend the whole day in bed. The archbishop sent me a message that he would like to cure me, and if I would only bring along my firm faith, he was sure to drive out my headache devil with a well-targeted exorcism. I was forced to counter that this devil was one of the most invincible, that he respected nobody besides nature herself, and that nature sends him out and calls him back whenever she feels like it, which almost never happens short of twenty-four hours of suffering. I must therefore, dear Julie, also take leave of you this evening with a poverty of words.

October 14th, 1828

APRÈS LA PLUIE le soleil![9] The present day has compensated me for yesterday. Already at seven o'clock I was on horseback and on my way to have breakfast at Captain S——'s country house, where the rendezvous for today's hare hunt had been set. I found six or seven robust country squires assembled there, men who do not think much and accordingly lead all the more cheerful and carefree lives. After the obligatory ingestion of the most heterogeneous items—coffee, tea, whiskey, wine, eggs, beefsteaks, honey, lamb kidneys, cakes, bread and butter, all mixed up together—the company boarded two large carriages and set their course toward the Galtee Mountains, where hounds and horses were awaiting us at a distance of about eight miles. The weather was lovely and the route very pleasant, passing along a ridge with a full view of the fertile plain, which is enclosed by mountains and richly varied by the host of estates and ruins strewn across it. As usual, however, I alone profited from these beauties, the huntsmen having nothing but hunting and hares in their heads.

Someone pointed out a place to me where an extraordinary phenomenon of nature occurred ten years ago. A high-lying bog, probably driven up by subterranean springs, tore loose from the ground and wandered off in a mass sixteen feet high and three to four acres in extent. It moved in a continuous zigzag depending on the objects it encountered, and thus covered nine miles before reaching the nearby river, in which it slowly dissolved, causing the river to overflow its banks. The pace of this march was about two miles per hour, but it destroyed everything in its path. At its touch houses were immediately leveled to the ground, trees ripped out by the roots, fields churned up, and low areas filled with bog. A vast crowd of people gathered near the end of its run, but they could offer not the slightest resistance to this magisterially destructive natural event.

When we arrived at the rendezvous for the hunt, we found the horses, but no hounds. A number of gentlemen had assembled, however, and instead of chasing after hares, we now traversed all the fields in a long, stretched-out line in an attempt to locate the hounds. You cannot imagine the kind of riding that took place. Most fields are enclosed by walls that are three to five feet high and constructed of fieldstones, either loosely piled up or properly mortared with lime; others are bordered by so-called ditches, firm earthen walls of lime and fieldstone five to seven feet high that come to a point on top and are flanked by a trench on one side or sometimes both. None of this, however, poses the slightest hindrance to the riders maintaining their line. I believe I have already described how remarkably the local horses can jump. But one must also admire their intelligence in knowing instantly how to distinguish a loose wall from a solid one, or a recently built, soft embankment from one hardened with time; springing over the loose ones with a single bound ("clearing them," as the technical term goes), and taking it easier with the firm ones, touching down once on the top. The horses accomplish all this equally well when at full tilt, walking along calmly, or approaching in a short sprint. Although some of the gentlemen fell, they were simply laughed at, because here anyone who does not immediately break his neck at such a moment can only count on ridicule, not condolence. Others dismounted before the most difficult jumps, and their well-trained horses leapt over ahead of them with empty saddles and trailing bridles to graze peacefully while awaiting their riders. I can assure you that I repeatedly expected I would have to follow this example, but Captain S——, who was well acquainted with the excellent horse I was riding and was always at my side, continually encouraged me to trust the creature, so that at the end of the day I had acquired a considerable reputation among the fox hunters. It is certainly true that only in Ireland do you see what horses are capable of; the English cannot match them at all in this. Anywhere a man could go, my horse found a way to jump, sidle, or clamber in some manner or other. It even worked its way through marshes where it sank up to its belly, moving with determination and without the slightest haste; an animal that was excessively feisty and edgy would certainly not have been able to extricate itself, however powerful it might be. Such a charger is invaluable in battle, but must be trained from earliest youth and be of an excellent bloodline. Experience teaches us that, even in animals, training over a period of centuries can transform acquired characteristics into what seem inborn traits or second nature. In England I saw bird dogs on their first hunt who pointed as fixedly at their prey, without any guidance at all, as if they had been trained with a "coral necklace."[10]

Even ten years ago the prices fetched by these superb horses were extremely modest, but ever since the English began buying them up for their own hunts, this has completely changed, and an Irish hunter of the quality of my mount today will bring no less than one hundred and fifty to two hundred guineas. If passion comes into play, the price can go up to four or five hundred. At the Galway races I saw a white thoroughbred stallion, a famous hunter that had been purchased at such a price by Lord Cl——. This horse had won every steeplechase he had run, was as light as he was powerful, as swift as the wind, could be managed by a child, and so far had never met a wall too high nor a ditch too wide to jump over.

We finally found the hounds—their handlers had gotten totally drunk—and we did not end our hunt until nightfall. It had become miserably cold, and as we returned to Captain S——'s country house, the flickering fire in the hearth and a table already laid in front of it gleamed most pleasantly through the windows. A true hunters' and bachelors' feast ensued, with no attempt at elegance or pomp. Glasses, plates, and cutlery in every form and from every period had been cobbled together. One man drank his wine from a liqueur glass, another out of a champagne flute, the thirstiest from a beer mug; this one ate with some great-grandfather's knife and fork, that one with the new, green-handled cutlery a servant must have bought the day before at the Cashel marketplace. Vast amounts of food and drink were hauled in by an elderly maid and a plump-fisted groom; each man served himself, and there were just as many hounds as guests in the room. The plain cooking, by the way, was not at all to be sneezed at, and neither was the wine nor the genuine poteen illicitly distilled in the mountains, something I tasted here for the first time in its totally unadulterated state. In order to sweeten a pudding, two large lumps of sugar are held over it and rubbed together, just the way savages make fire by rubbing pieces of wood together until they start to burn. You can take it for granted that there was an enormous amount of drinking.

Although eventually a number of us were capable of little more than stammering, no one behaved indecently, and those few overcome by the wine increased the merriment with many a worthy *bon mot* or amusing story. One of these fellows, who had lived in England for a considerable time, claimed to have been an eyewitness to George III's last appearance in Parliament, a story he narrated as follows: Before the late king (we Germans would say *hochselig*,[11] because we allow the deceased to smuggle in an itsy-bitsy title, even into heaven) had been completely and forever overwhelmed by the mental illness that rendered him incapable of participation in the business of state, it came time for the opening of Parliament. Meanwhile the king—who admittedly had experienced some disturbing attacks, though he still had many *lucida intervalla*—insisted on opening Parliament in person and reading the customary speech himself, which always begins with the words "My lords, and gentlemen of the House of Commons!" The king seemed fully rational, and the ministers, although not a little concerned, had to comply with his very firmly expressed intention. You can imagine their horror when the king, after looking long, fixedly, and confusedly at the company, began clearly and with great pathos in the following way, "My lords and woodcocks, with their tails cocked up . . ." But from that point on he read his speech with utter decorum and no further sign of instability. "This contrast," the narrator added, "was unbelievably comical. The faces of the members of Parliament who did not know whether they could trust their ears or had been dreaming, the suppressed laughter of some and the amazement of others, who were riveted to the spot with mouths agape, provided an intensely amusing drama for those looking on. Once His Majesty had been safely driven home, all such performances were forbidden, and he was not shown to the public again until after his death."

The enormous courtesy, I could even say enthusiasm, with which I have been received here, I owe entirely to my visit with the "man of the people."[12] I, being no more than curious, am now believed to have God knows what kind of rapport with him. My riding through a village is enough to raise a hurrah. And in Cashel, where my inn is on the marketplace, the square is filled early every day with people who greet me with the same cry when I step out the door. Indeed many of them crowd around me, ask to shake my hand, and are delighted when they manage to do so (in a desperately rough way).

We did not get up from the table until very late, at which point another gentleman and I were packed into the host's car in order to return to Cashel in the ice-cold fog. Everyone hurried outside in order to be helpful. One pulled felt gloves onto my hands; another wrapped me in a fur; a third tied a foulard around my neck. Everyone wanted to do me at least *one* small service, and with many a "God bless His Highness," I was finally released. The gentleman next to me, Mr. O'R——, was of all the company the wittiest and most inebriated. Imbued with the same good opinion of me as the others, he too was continually trying to assist me, by which he just made a bad thing worse. One moment he opened my fur wrap, instead of buttoning it closed; the next he ripped off my scarf while attempting to tie it tighter; and then he fell into my lap while trying to make more room for me. His poetic gemütlichkeit was distinctively revealed as we approached the Rock of Cashel. It was horribly cold, and the cloudless sky was twinkling and shimmering like so many diamonds, although on the ground between the road and the rock, a dense fog had settled. It enveloped the whole surrounding area as well, but without rising any higher than the foot of the ruin. Since the base of the hill was invisible, the ruin looked as if it were built on a cloud suspended in the deep blue air just under the stars. I had been admiring this drama for some time in silence, when my neighbor, whom I thought to be asleep, suddenly exclaimed, "Ah! There is my glorious rock! Look, how grand! And above all, sacred! The place where all my ancestors repose and where I too shall lie in peace!"

After a pause he tried, in a fit of ecstasy, to stand up, and were it not for me, would no doubt have fallen out of the carriage. Once he had regained his footing, he took off his hat in a sweeping gesture and, with a touching yet burlesque devoutness, exclaimed with tears in his eyes, "God bless almighty God, and glory to Him!" Despite the nonsense, which was surely redoubled by the power of his inebriation (may God bless God), I was nonetheless gripped by the intensity of his *emotion*. In this, at least, I agreed with all my heart and soul.

October 15th, 1828

LORD H——, WHOM I knew in London and who has a beautiful estate here in the vicinity, invited me to spend a few days with him. I was not able to accept, but did dine there this afternoon. The well-maintained pleasure ground and the excavations being made for a lake reminded me too vividly of the castle where you, my dear one, are now dwelling, so that I could not look on it without emotion. When will we see each other again? When will we once more breakfast at home beneath the three lindens, where the swans so trustingly took their food from our hands and tame doves picked up the crumbs, while little Coco, amazed and jealous, glared at those pushy birds with his clever eyes—a bucolic image, before which a hardened man of the world might shrug scornfully, but which in all its simplicity touches *us* to the heart!

Lord H—— is one of those distinguished Irishmen who maintain some of their revenues in their native land and occasionally even reside there, but who nonetheless have such a poor understanding of their own interests as to create an adversarial relationship with the local population, rather than acting as their leader. The result is inevitable. The Earl of Landaff, also a Protestant, is beloved; Lord H—— is hated, although in my eyes he does not deserve it at all. I have heard, it is true, quite a few tales of the cruelties he has inflicted on Catholics, and I myself was a witness to his impassioned sentiments in this regard. But I believe that here, as so often in the world, *a mere alteration of one's views would also alter all other circumstances.* This is a primary rule of pragmatism, and the effect is certain, because objects are just so much stuff; everything depends on how the individual understands and shapes them. How many a situation changes from black to rosy pink, once you find the willpower to remove your dark glasses or don your rose-colored ones? With which glasses will *you* read my letter? I can hear the answer from here and kiss you for it.

May heaven protect you and maintain these sentiments.

Your faithfully devoted Lou

B——, October 17th, 1828

DEAREST JULIE,

Since yesterday I find myself ensconced in a pretty little Gothic castle at the foot of the mountains. From one window I see fertile fields, from the other I gaze on woods, a lake, and rocks. My host is Mr. O'R——'s brother, who also possesses, in addition to the castle, a very pretty wife whom I am courting just a bit, because the gentlemen do too much hunting and drinking for my taste. By rights the family property would have come down to my droll friend, but since he was always a bit of a rake and seemed already in his youth too ready to capitulate to whiskey punch and the good life, his father (who had the right to dispose of the estate) bequeathed it to his youngest son instead. The two brothers nonetheless remain very close, and in his gentle good nature my friend detects no trace of wormwood in the wine he drinks at his younger brother's house. For his part the younger acknowledges the inequity and makes sure his kindhearted and amusing elder sibling is reliably drunk every evening and wants for nothing. Such a relationship is a tribute to them both, even more so because, when the father died, the lawyers concluded that the will could easily have been contested. Certainly they both acted with equal benevolence and good sense and so kept the oyster for themselves—not, as in the caricature, leaving it to be consumed by the lawyers, so that nothing remains to feed on but the two shells.[1]

We spent the whole day walking along splendid mountain paths, while others went snipe shooting. In the evening *we sat at the table until two o'clock in the morning.* Right after dessert was served, the ladies took their leave in accordance with established custom, and now the real wine drinking began. Then, very late, coffee was brought to the table, followed by a stimulating *souper* made up of all sorts of "devils,"* raw oysters, and pickles. This formed the prelude to the poteen punch, which several of the gentlemen consumed in the amount of twelve to sixteen large tumblers, while O'R——'s inexhaustible wit and tomfoolery kept the whole party roaring with laughter. What is more, everyone was required to sing a song. Even I had to offer a German one, which of course no one understood, although everyone was politely enthusiastic. At two in the morning I retired, but all the others stayed on, and their noise and laughter kept me awake for a long time, since my room is unfortunately directly above.

---

* These are, as my departed friend often boasted, especially well prepared in Ireland, and consist of poultry that is grilled and served either dry with cayenne pepper or with a fiery sauce in a stew. This for any possible gourmands among the readers.—*The Editor.*

104

*Fitzpatrick,
the Blind Irish Piper.*

KEARNS FITZPATRICK, the *CELEBRATED IRISH PIPER.*

October 18th, 1828

YOU ARE PROBABLY amazed at the somewhat rough and ready life I am leading here, and to be honest, I am surprised by it myself; but it is "genuine," that is to say, completely natural to these people and not at all affected—something that for me holds a kind of charm. In addition, the lady of the house is truly adorable, as vivacious and gracious as a Frenchwoman, with a little foot as soft as cassimere,² which I have often kissed when paying her a little evening visit, while the others were still at table. I allowed myself to behave this way on the pretext that the unaccustomed punch had gone slightly to my head.

This morning we hunted hares, which again occasioned many a bold jump; and in the evening the most celebrated piper of Ireland performed for us, a certain Kearns Fitzpatrick, known as the King of the Pipers, who even "His Gracious Majesty King George the Fourth" has honored with his acclamation (Figure 104). In fact, the melodies this blind man coaxes from his strange instrument are often just as surprising as they are pleasant, and like his highly cultivated manners, his skill is worthy of a virtuoso. These pipers, who are almost all blind, originated in ancient times and are now beginning to disappear, for whatever is old must fade and pass away.

October 19th, 1828

IN THE COURSE of the day, we came upon two people in the woods, who looked very suspicious. My companion told me unabashedly that they were well-known robbers, who partly through cunning, partly through the fear they instill, have always managed to remain at large—one more sign of how inadequate this government is and how entirely corrupt the general tenor of society is (two things, unfortunately, characteristic of Ireland). Both men looked extremely striking and convincingly Irish. They call themselves farmers, because they have leased part of a potato plot. One of them, a slim, handsome man of about forty with a wild but imposing physiognomy, presented a highly picturesque image, even in his rags. Complete disregard of danger was stamped on his noble forehead, indifference to shame played scornfully around his impudent mouth. His history confirmed the language of his features. He was wearing three or four military medals that he had earned in Spain and France. Once, because of his repeated demonstrations of bravery, he had been advanced to the rank of noncommissioned officer, but due to some dissolute escapades, he was demoted again. Then he served for a second time, distinguished himself as before, but was discharged once more on the same grounds, though without anyone managing to convict him of a major crime. He is now strongly suspected of being the leader of a band of robbers, who are causing a lot of trouble in the Galtee Mountains and have already committed various murders.

His companion was the complete opposite in appearance. For an Irish farmer he was unusually well dressed—that is to say, he was not wearing anything tattered. He was sixty years old, short and stocky, and a bit like a Quaker in his conduct. In the feigned innocence of his features, however, lurked such a high degree of cunning and ruthless determination that he seemed considerably more dreadful than the other. Two years ago this man was charged with passing false banknotes and was as good as convicted, when an adroit shyster he trusted managed to rescue him from the gallows in return for the promise of a rich reward. Shedding tears of gratitude, he stuck fifty pounds into his savior's hand and, amid sobs, requested the normal receipt. This was provided, and the lawyer, pleased with this successful outcome, filled his wallet with the notes. How profound was his annoyance when, after closer inspection, he saw that Paddy had paid him with forged banknotes, just like those that had condemned him to the gallows. When the Irish go bad (and it is amazing that not all of them do), they are the most dangerous of all, because their salient characteristics—courage, recklessness, and shrewdness—are the perfect attributes for those who would take risks and succeed.

At supper, while we were consuming our oysters—which are excellent on the west and south coasts of Ireland—a gentleman from the area, who has an oyster farm of his own on his property, told us a few details about their natural history and how they are handled, all of which was quite new to me. I am going to tell you about this, even at the risk of boring you. What you need to know first is that three-year-old oysters are the best to eat, because only then, when they are fully grown, do they attain the proper size and succulence; later they become tough. This clever oyster-economist has oyster beds of every age and, according to the composition of the seabed, of varying tastes and "flavors." In those spots where the oysters reproduce in their natural state, left undisturbed by art, they never attain the peak of perfection. This can be improved as follows: you harvest the young ones when they are no bigger than a four-groschen coin and sow them like seeds at a spot not too far from shore, where the seabed is soft mud and a maximum of fourteen feet deep. After three years you harvest them again, and then sow others from the mother bed. Naturally you have several such mud banks in operation, so that every year you can empty out one that has matured. It seems oysters must be very old before they reproduce, since no new oysters had appeared in the artificial colonies I just described. The way they reproduce is curious, another example of the infinite diversity of nature. Oysters are probably hermaphrodites, since no sexual distinction can be discerned in them, so propagation happens when fifteen or sixteen little oysters develop like warts on the outside of a shell and then fall off once they have reached the proper consistency. The production of these sixteen offspring puts such a strain on the old mamma oyster that there is scarcely anything to be found but a little muddy water if you open her shell afterward; and as soon as the little ones have detached themselves, she digs herself into the mud to a depth of six or seven inches and stays there for a whole year, until she has recovered enough to think about procreation again. Hence you can comfortably harvest the young oysters during this period without coming too close to the old ones, who are buried below, peaceably sleeping or dreaming! Oyster harvesting happens with the help of a device similar to those used to haul up mud from the rivers; and they are distributed by being cast onto a piece of canvas and then, as I said, sown like grain. Very old mothers finally become infertile, because their shells attain such a thickness that love can no longer penetrate—just like the human heart!

Cashel, Oct. 20th, 1828

WE DROVE BACK here in the afternoon after several days spent with much merriment but little intellectual exercise. In order to keep my mental capacities from dozing off entirely, I will try to entertain you with a folktale that I was told by an old woman in Holycross.[3]

Johnny Curtin was a poor schoolboy and, according to one dark legend, the progeny of a lineage that in olden days was high and mighty, but whose luster had since faded. Their riches vanished, the family's descendants sank lower and lower, and no longer certain of their own origins, they had for many years been forced to take up a profitable trade that would at least keep them securely if not richly fed. But death carried off Johnny's mother and father before he was grown, and now a helpless orphan, he depended on the generosity of a relative to sustain him—a farmer living not far from the ruins of Holy Cross Abbey—and there he was spending his school holidays. Johnny was a diligent and eager pupil, and his cousin good-natured enough to manage without him when he needed the time to learn whatever was to be learned at school.

Learning and knowledge broaden our lives, but also give rise to many a worry and not a few imaginary evils unknown to simpler folk. Johnny knew the history of his country. He knew that its ancient greatness had faded almost everywhere, and that the princes of the realm had been forced to yield to strangers, who, springing up like mushrooms, drained the nourishment from the nobler plants until the inexorable movement of time finally transformed everything. Those whose ancestors had once been kings were branded as no better than slaves. He saw himself thus, and the few joys that were possible for someone in his position were too often clouded by these diminishing, self-punishing thoughts.

In such a mood, this dreamy young man's solitary walks often drew him to those proud remains of faded centuries that are scattered over the fields of Tipperary like gravestones. He spent quite a few summer nights in the weather-beaten cathedral, enthroned in all its stark sublimity on Cashel Rock; in the midday sun he roamed through the boggy meadows, where the remains of Athassel Priory have sunk deeper and deeper over the last eight centuries; or he rested in the town of Golden, in the shadow of a robber baron's castle, with its ten-foot-thick walls that defy time today as they defied countless enemies for so long. But what he treasured most were the magnificent, ivy-covered ruins of Holy Cross Abbey, where even now a stranger can admire the well-preserved grave of the great O'Brien, king of Limerick, and where Johnny's parents were also sleeping in an unassuming corner. In his imagination the place was filled with figures of wonder, first among them the spirits of his great ancestors, who had found their resting places here, as he had so often heard. It is possible this assumption was correct, because in keeping with the poetic ways of his people, the preferred burial place of both high and low was not the grounds of the humble chapel, where the oppressed Catholics now hold their barely tolerated services, but rather the noble ruins of their older churches and monasteries. This is why you see the ground overrun with upright tombstones, intermixed with piles of bones and skulls carelessly dug up to make space for the new arrivals. Here, sitting in a window niche, Johnny dreamed away hour after hour, until the sun sank over the majestic Galtee Mountains, those dark giants that alone had survived unchanged through every century and every catastrophe.

One evening when he was feeling more deeply moved than usual, as he stared into the past with longing and into the future with despair, and when it seemed that the spirits of the departed were close by and murmuring more and more audibly, he sank into a deep slumber, his eyes still wet with tears of melancholy. He did not know how long he slept, or whether he actually experienced the scene that appeared before him; perhaps he merely dreamed it. This puzzle could never be solved. In any case he believed that he awakened in the middle of the night and saw every space in the enormous church, down to the most distant corner, illuminated by a celestial light that joined the clarity of day to the silvery glow of the moon and rosy shimmer of the sunset. In front of him stood a female figure enveloped in a snow-white garment like a swirling cloud, and from the cloud two eyes sparkled like stars on a December night. Then a voice called to him. Johnny could never adequately describe its tone, but its magical melody seemed to invigorate every sinew, calm every fear, and send a feeling of optimism and courage pouring like fire through every vein. It spoke to him in friendly sounds that faded softly away:

"My son! Do you know where you are?"

"Where I am? Certainly, in Holy Cross," Johnny responded, rubbing his eyes.

"Do you also know that in the misty days of old, your forefathers used to rule here, and all the land that your eyes survey so often from yonder tower was once their property?"

"Ha! I suspected as much—oh, why couldn't they have protected it better, so that today their grandson wouldn't have to beg for his sour bread in poverty and misery, dependent on the mercy of strangers?"

"Johnny!" the voice continued, "Leave the past in peace. It will depend on you alone to combine courage and intelligence and become as great as our forebears were. Your lucky star has brought you on exactly this night inside the walls of the monastery, where I, who used to have dominion in this place, am now allowed to appear just once every hundred years. Know then that a vast treasure belonging to our family is buried here, and if you unearth it, it will make you richer than a king. But John Curtin!—Pay close attention to what I say, because I came today for your salvation, if you know how to make use of it; but you will never see me on this earth again. You know the hill above the abbey, the blessed spot where the fragment of the holy cross descended at the sweet chiming of the church bell, and where the good old woman met her son as he was returning from Jerusalem. You know the ancient yew that stands there alone, close to the path, on a knoll of earth and stone. There you should dig, six feet away from the tree in a straight line with the abbey towers, and six feet deep. The deed must be completed in the dead of night and—be very mindful of this—*without a single word* being spoken, or woe to those who undertake it!"

At this point a bright thunderbolt seemed to flash through the church and a hoarse laugh struck his ears. Johnny jumped with a start, as if from a dream, but an impenetrable darkness surrounded him, while an irresistible desire to sleep swept over him once more. When he awoke, he was not a little amazed to find himself on his straw mattress at Dick Cassidy's, his cousin's, without any memory of how he had gotten home. Had it really been just a dream? Was it all nothing but an illusion of his overheated fantasy?

It must have been, because, to give the truth its due, it cannot be concealed that Johnny, before strolling to his favorite ruin, had spent the middle of the day with a close comrade and had not gone easy on the whiskey punch. In fact Bridget, the housemaid, insisted that when Johnny came home so late, she immediately noticed how powerful the poteen spirit was in him, and how in some people *that* spirit, once encountered, may reappear in the strangest ways. This is what Johnny told himself; but despite all logic, his steps carried him repeatedly to the place where the abbey stood, and whenever he saw the solitary yew tree, even from a distance, his heart beat faster, the blood shot into his cheeks, and images of future grandeur fluttered before his inward eye with ever-increasing color and radiance. The demon of covetousness had taken possession of his soul.

He finally decided to take his relative, a thoughtful and sensible man, into his confidence and leave the matter to his discretion. Contrary to his expectations, Dick gave the revelation much more credence than Johnny had hoped; greed and superstition caught up the older man as well, propelling the two of them into action. They agreed that the attempt needed to be made as soon as possible, and the treasure, once they had excavated it, would be evenly divided between them.

After a good supper and more than one glass of "blessed whiskey" to stimulate the heart, Dick and Johnny set off. They had to pass close below the walls of Holy Cross, and the wind, which was beginning to turn blustery, shook the branches of the old ash trees so eerily, murmured with such hollow gloominess through the thick tangle of ivy, and threw such huge stones down from the walls onto their path that both of them grew increasingly despondent. But they pulled themselves together, and hurrying quickly over the bridge across the Suir, they directed their steps as fast as they could toward the designated tree. As soon as they reached it, Dick wasted no time; he threw off his jacket, carefully measured the six feet from the knoll to the abbey's tower, and began to dig with the utmost zeal. Johnny followed his example in silence, and after about an hour, accompanied by fleeting inward prayers and many signs of the cross, Dick's spade hit against something hard. Shoveling the loose earth aside, they found a broad, flat stone lying before them. For a long time they toiled in vain to budge it, and only after unbelievable effort did they finally succeed in lifting it ever so slightly, and then, with the help of iron crowbars they had had the foresight to bring along, turning it right over. They could now see a narrow staircase, and emboldened by the newly formed conviction that the apparition had not deceived them, they lit their lanterns and climbed slowly down, one after the other, filled with confidence, though seized by the occasional shudder. The steps led into a long gallery with a heavy iron door at the far end. This seemed to bar any further advancement, but approaching more closely, they found a golden key sticking out of the lock, and the door opened with ease. Now they walked intrepidly into the hallway, where they soon saw another gate, and just above it, at about chest height, their eyes were drawn to an open grate. Johnny held the lantern up so Dick could look through, but hardly had he cast a glance inside than he cried out full of joy, "Hurrah! By Noonan's ghost! We are made men!"

The last word was still hanging on his lips when the vaulting collapsed with a terrible, thunderous crash, a screeching wind blew the lantern to the ground, and Johnny, falling flat on his face in unspeakable horror, lost his memory and consciousness. When he came to again, he was lying beneath the ancient yew, and on the tower of the abbey a high flame was playing like a gigantic will-o'-the-wisp, and a black figure seemed to be dancing gleefully in it. From very close by came the same hoarse laughter that he thought he had heard in the ruin, but now it rang out more loudly. Pale with terror, he turned to look for his cousin, and found Dick lying beside him, harshly illuminated by the flames, his neck twisted violently, his blue, swollen features dreadfully distorted, and his glassy eyes staring fixedly at him.

Beloved Julie, I fear that the materialistic nature of life these days has made me a little brutish, and this has colored my story. In fact, it resembles a dream born of indigestion. After a bit of fasting, I will perhaps manage a better one for you.

Meanwhile I bid you a good night and more pleasant dreams than poor Johnny's.

October 21st, 1828

I HAD SO often taken advantage of the hospitality of the excellent country squires here that I felt bound by good conscience to reciprocate, so I invited them all to a small celebration before my departure. In the morning I offered them a cockfight (for one must run with the pack), then a concert by the great piper, a ride on their own horses, and finally a grand banquet, excellent meat, and a good fire. During our ride we came to a spot where a magistrate named Baker was shot dead three years ago. This man was a character, just exactly like the prefects in Iffland's plays, but unfortunately without a noble soul to thwart him. On the day before his death, as he was finally releasing a man whom he had kept in chains for six weeks on feigned suspicion of revolutionary activity, he publically declared, "Last month I sent you a message demanding that you come speak to me. You didn't come, and so I gave you this small lesson in the hope that you will be more compliant in the future. If you're not, then in six weeks you will hang, depend on it!"

At the time the county was still under martial law as a result of some limited uprising, and the authorities had enjoyed almost unlimited power for so long that they were able to get away with *anything*. The motive behind Baker's murder was such that you can hardly feel sympathy for him. He owed five hundred pounds to a dairy farmer, partly for goods already delivered, partly for a loan, and he had promised to pay the amount as soon as the man's daughter married, the sum being intended to make up her dowry. After a few years the time came for the girl to be wed, and the farmer humbly requested his money. But Baker put him off with a series of excuses, and the dairyman could get nothing more than vague assurances, so he finally threatened him with legal action and even traveled to Cork to talk over the case with a lawyer. Taking advantage of the man's absence, Baker showed up at his house the very next day followed by a detachment of soldiers and, dissembling, asked his wife, then pregnant with her seventh child, whether she knew of any concealed weapons in the house, because a very serious charge had been brought against her husband. She cheerfully assured him that there was nothing of that sort, that her husband would never be involved in such activities, as the magistrate himself, an old acquaintance, must know better than anyone.

"Be careful what you say," Baker cried, "because if we find something, and you have denied it, then the law will condemn you without mercy to be deported for life."

The woman stuck by her statement. "Well then, it's at your own peril. Soldiers," he ordered, "make the most careful possible search of the house and barn and bring me a report of what you have found!"

They found nothing. But when a second search was done under Baker's own leadership, someone turned up a loaded pistol that had supposedly been hidden beneath some straw, although it has always been assumed that Baker himself had slipped it under there. The woman was immediately dragged off, and since she was considered already convicted by means of the corpus delicti, she was condemned to deportation after a short trial. Her husband returned a few days later and moved heaven and earth to win her freedom. He pleaded in vain that at least they send *him* to Botany Bay in place of his unhappy wife, the pregnant mother of six children. He also offered Baker the five hundred pounds as a gift. But the magistrate was merciless, reminding the desolate husband with a sneer that he would of course need the money for the dowry of his daughter, who, he added, could now keep house for him—if he still had a house to be kept after the search he had initiated. He further declared that he did not need to worry about his wife's traveling expenses, for these were covered by the generosity of the state. The law took its course, the poor woman was deported and is perhaps now in Port Jackson. But her husband, brother, and two other men were infuriated, and they avenged her tragic fate a short time later by gruesomely murdering Baker: attacking him in the open country, chasing him as if he were wild game, and finally killing him slowly with several shots. They were all apprehended and hanged.

In those days such horror stories were a daily occurrence in this unhappy land, and similar ones are taking place *even now*. But that such a contrast exists between England and Ireland, both under the same government, and has persisted for so long, is truly distressing for every person possessed of humanity. All the more so when you consider that it results from nothing but uncontrolled bigotry and the obsession to rob, plunder, and retain the spoils of six million victims.

I will say nothing about my banquet. It was like the others and lasted more than too long. I will only mention two anecdotes, borrowed from the realms of Venus and Bacchus, because they seem noteworthy and exemplary of the customs here. I beg your forgiveness in advance if the first one seems a bit coarse, but it is impossible to participate, as you do, in so many feasts in the provinces without hearing something risqué, at least once in a while. The whole thing is, by the way, a criminal case to be argued in public, and to that extent suitable for incorporation in an intimate letter.

One of the guests was being teased about his love affairs, and somebody reckoned he might very well be capable of imitating his cousin R——. When I asked what was meant, I was told that last year the gentleman in question broke his neck while on a foxhunt, which certainly rescued the virtue of many a young woman and perhaps saved him from the much worse death he once nearly suffered. The matter caused quite a sensation and may remain unrivaled in our annals of criminality:

Mr. R——, already well-known for his multiple adventures, had long been pursuing the pretty daughter of a tenant farmer without succeeding in luring her to a rendezvous or otherwise meeting her alone. He finally encountered her not far from her father's house, just as she was going to the well with two water jugs hanging from her shoulders. She was holding them with both hands, as the country girls tend to do here, and after bantering with her for a while and playing all kinds of tender little pranks, he suddenly took advantage of her defenseless position. *Enfin,* he succeeded, certainly at least half by force, in obtaining everything that she had to give. In English law, something like this is not judged according to the principle of the Empress Catherine or Queen Elizabeth, but is viewed as an act of criminal violence, and the delinquent, if he is found guilty through the testimony of witnesses, is hanged without further ado.[4] Mr. R——'s dismay was therefore not incidental when, still consoling the sobbing girl, he straightened up and found that the girl's younger sister, who had also come to fetch water, was standing right behind her and had watched the entire thing. Oh, for shame!" she cried in outrage, "that I had to witness this, sister! Mother and father are going to hear about it right away!" As this threat was delivered poor Maria was more dead than alive, but her lover, with rare composure and singular gumption, knew how to give things an entirely unexpected turn. Seemingly furious, he drew his knife and rushed toward the younger girl, as if he wanted right then to seal her mouth forever. Half fainting with terror, she sank down at his feet, powerless and begging for mercy, and thereby met with the same fate as had just befallen her sister. Both kept totally mum about it, but nature forced them to confess some time later, because both became pregnant and gave birth, one to a boy, the other to a girl. The parents began legal proceedings, and the case was clear-cut; moreover the youngest girl was just thirteen years old, and it was assumed Mr. R—— was lost. But against all expectation, the sympathetic jury (*que tant de valeur sans doute avait désarmé*[5]) found him not guilty, because the doctor of the municipality, whose expert opinion had been solicited, obligingly declared that the attested event *was not possible. Voilà une belle occasion de disputer pour les jurisconsultes et les médecins.*[6] The cynics maintain that before this trial Mr. R—— had been a danger to women, but that afterward he became irresistible.

Now to the second story.

About ten years ago Lord L——, who at the time was considered nearly invincible when faced with a battery of whiskey-punch glasses, hosted a great *dîner,* the main purpose of which was unbridled drinking, a fashion that is now, relatively speaking, in decline. But it used to be very common for a merry party to lock itself up in a room with a barrel of wine and not leave until the last drop had been consumed. In his memoirs Barrington speaks of one such party, which took place in a hunting lodge where just the day before, the walls had been covered with plaster that had not had time to dry. The revelers locked themselves up as usual, along with a barrel of claret newly arrived from France. The next morning those participants who had stumbled into the walls awoke from their inebriation and found themselves so firmly identified with the plaster that they had to be cut free, some suffering a loss of hair, others of their clothing.

Lord L—— hosted a dinner party of a similar sort, the large group soon becoming exceedingly merry and loud. Once their eyes had become blurry and their tongues less articulate, Lord L—— heard someone at the lower end of the table calling out repeatedly, "Oh, Sergeant Scully!

That won't do! Fair play, Mr. Scully!" This man Scully was a sergeant in the estate owners' militia under the command of Lord L—— and otherwise a well-known and determined drinker. So Lord L——, who thought Scully was refusing to refill his own glass, became highly indignant and called out loudly across the table: "Shame on you, Scully! To need such prompting! *Allons, fill your glass right now! Ireland forever!"

Here several pitiful voices arose, "Oh, my lord, Your Majesty is entirely in error. Sergeant Scully has *two* glasses standing in front of him, while we only received one. We don't want to put up with such cheating any longer!"

Since then it has become an Irish proverb that when anyone does something excessive or doubles his advantage, it's known as taking Sergeant Scully as an example.

Because no one could think of any more anecdotes to relate, all sorts of tricks and tours de force were performed, one of which I had never seen. Although just an easily repeated experiment with a rooster, it is nonetheless rather odd. The wildest and nastiest bird of this kind becomes immediately motionless and, for as long as you want, remains lying on a table in a death-like stillness, beak stretched out in front and eyes not budging one instant from a white line that has been drawn before him. You do nothing more than draw a straight line in chalk on the table, grasp the rooster with both hands, and force his beak to trace the line. Then you press him down onto the table, and he will stay there, without moving, until someone picks him up again. This experiment can only be done by candlelight, however.

Voilà de grandes bagatelles, mais à la guerre comme à la guerre.[7]

October 22nd, 1828

I HAD SUMMONED Fitzpatrick the piper for yesterday's party, and since he stayed on in town today, I took advantage of the opportunity to have him play *privatim* for me in my room during breakfast this morning and thereby got a closer look at his instrument. It is, as you know, peculiar to Ireland and betrays a strange mixture of old and new.[8] It weds the original, simple bagpipe with the flute, oboe, and some individual tones of the organ and bassoon, all together producing a rather full and exotic concert. The small, elegant bellows that are connected to it are fastened to the right arm by means of a silk strap, and the wind tube that communicates between them and the bag lies across the body, while the hands play on an upright pipe equipped with holes like a flageolet, which forms the end of the instrument and is connected with five or six shorter ones that resemble a colossal Papageno flute. While playing, the right arm constantly pumps in and out to keep the bag filled with air. The opening of a valve brings forth a deep, humming tone that continues *unisono* during the rest of the piece, with an effect similar to the sustaining pedal of a piano. By agitating his whole body as well as the pipe described above, Fitzpatrick brought forth sounds that no other instrument can produce. The whole picture, in which you have to envision the handsome old man with a full head of white curls, is really very quaint—tragi-comic, so to say. The decoration of his bagpipe was especially luxurious: the pipes were made of ebony with silver fittings, the strap was richly embroidered, and the bag surrounded by fire red silk with silver fringes.

I had him play the oldest Irish melodies for me, wild compositions that usually start out sad and melancholic, like the songs of the Slavic peoples, but then finally end either with a jig, the national dance of Ireland, or with war-like music. One of these melodies presented a very deceptive facsimile of a foxhunt, and I thought another had been borrowed from the "Hunters' Chorus" of *Der Freischütz*,[9] but it was five hundred years older. Great minds think alike in every era.

After some time the piper suddenly stopped playing and said with a smile and a great deal of charm, "You must already know, sir, that an Irish bagpipe doesn't have good tone when sober—it requires the evening or the still of the night, merry company, and the sweet fragrance of a steaming whiskey punch. So please allow me to excuse myself now."

I rewarded the good old man generously, and he will always be in my mind as a true representative of the Irish national character.

Now along with Fitzpatrick, I take leave of you, dearest Julie, in order to head back to Dublin after this long tour, and it is from there I intend to send off my next letter.

Your faithful Lou

Dublin, October 24th, 1828

𝒢OOD, PRECIOUS FRIEND,

When one has for so long led a half-wild life, the tameness of the city seems altogether strange. I can now almost appreciate the homesickness of the American Indians and understand how the most cultured among them will finally retreat into their forests once more. Freedom is too great a lure!

Yesterday afternoon I left Cashel, taking Captain S——'s brother along in my carriage. While the daylight lasted, we saw about twenty different ruins, some nearby, some far off. One of the most beautiful of these stands at the foot of the isolated Killough Hill, called the garden of Ireland because, according to legend, every plant native to Ireland grows there. The reason for this fertility is that Killough Hill was once the summer residence of the Queen of the Fairies, whose gardens were resplendent, and the otherworldly, magnetized soil still retains a portion of its enchanting powers. The above mentioned ruin has one of those puzzling round towers, slender and generally without any access, although in a few you do see a doorway partway up, but not at the base. From a distance this one looked like an enormous kingpin, standing isolated among the nine.[1] No more romantic sentry box could have been found for the sentinels of the fairy hill. The weather was extraordinarily mild and lovely and the light of the full moon so brilliant that I could comfortably read in the carriage. In spite of this we slept through a good part of the night.

In Dublin I found a letter from you. A thousand thanks for all the kindness and love that it contains. As for your friend's situation, do not worry too much about it. Tell her she should do whatever is necessary to postpone the inevitable evil for as long as possible, always enduring what she must with serenity. This, at least, is *my* philosophy. I found your quotation from de Sévigné very amusing. Without a doubt her letters are remarkable!—to repeat the same bland vacuities in volume after volume, yet with new, unexpected turns, and in a way that is entertaining and sometimes enchanting; to depict court, city, and country with equal grace, and to adopt a somewhat-affected love for the most insignificant person as the major theme of the whole, yet without actually becoming tiring—these were certainly challenges that no one else could have overcome. She is anything but romantic and was not extraordinarily prominent during her lifetime, but she was unquestionably the most well-bred ideal *du ton le plus parfait*.[2] She certainly possessed good temper too, instilled by nature and refined and enhanced by art. In any case, art is apparent everywhere, and her letters—which she knew were being read by many with enthusiasm—were probably intended as much for society as for her daughter; they were polished, you might say, because the admirable ease of her style discloses far more attentiveness than the effusiveness of the moment would allow.[3] It has always been the case that what looks the easiest is the most difficult to achieve. Her depiction of the manners of her time contributes to the current interest in her letters, but I doubt that similar ones written today would have the same success. We have become too serious and intellectual for such things. *Les jolis riens ne suffisent plus.*[4] The mind wants to be provoked, intensely provoked. Wherever a giant like Lord Byron appears, the lesser figures, however endearing, all disappear.

I was just reading Byron's works (for I never go anywhere without them), and I came upon a scene that is similar to some I have experienced often these past days myself. And how sublime was his expression of my feelings! Allow me to translate a fragment for you as best I can, in a poetic prose and as literally as possible:

> The sky is changed!—and such a change! Oh night,
> And storm, and darkness, ye are wondrous strong,
> Yet lovely in your strength, as is the light
> Of a dark eye in woman! Far along,
> From peak to peak, the rattling crags among
> Leaps the live thunder! Not from one lone cloud,
> But every mountain now hath found a tongue,
> And Jura answers, through her misty shroud,
> Back to the joyous Alps, who call to her aloud!
>
> And this is in the night:—Most glorious night!
> Thou wert not sent for slumber! let me be
> A sharer in thy fierce and far delight,—
> A portion of the tempest and of thee!
> How the lit lake shines, a phosphoric sea,
> And the big rain comes dancing to the earth!
> And now again 'tis black,—and now, the glee
> Of the loud hills shakes with its mountain-mirth,
> As if they did rejoice o'er a young earthquake's birth.[5]

Is that not beautiful and poetically felt? What a shame that we have no good translations of his writings. Only Goethe, perhaps, would be capable of offering a satisfactory version—if he were not himself busy creating equally magnificent works of even greater lightness and loveliness.

October 25th, 1828

YESTERDAY I PAID a visit to the lord lieutenant in Phoenix Park (see Figure 85),[6] and he invited me to return today to dinner, where I found a quite scintillating company. He is beloved in Ireland, because he aligns himself with no party but nevertheless seems to desire emancipation. His feats as a general are well-known, no one has a more dignified presence, and I have never seen a more skillfully made artificial leg than his! The marquis, though no longer young, still cuts a very fine figure, and the leg, like the foot, could be mistaken for real ones. Only when he is walking do you notice a bit of awkwardness. In general I know few Englishmen who have a *tournure* equal to that of the current Lord Lieutenant of Ireland. When he is residing in the city, a very strict etiquette is maintained, as though at a small court; but when he is in the country he views himself as a private individual. A lord lieutenant's power and prestige are rather great, since he represents the king, although the ministry may curtail him when it sees fit. He is allowed, among other things, to confer the title of baronet, and in earlier times it happened that innkeepers and even less qualified men were granted this honor. The responsibilities of this position gain him no permanent increase in rank, although he can readily build up his own earnings, since a lord lieutenant's pay is fifty thousand pounds per annum, and he is allotted a royal residence free of charge for as long as he administers his office. The current lord, however, does not seem to be economizing much, since I found his establishment superbly appointed. He is also surrounded by a number of interesting people, who join very good manners with great intelligence and seem to be adherents of the political party of moderation and reason. Under such circumstances one can almost take for granted that Lord Anglesey will not stay here long, and I heard some allusions to this eventuality. Since he suffers badly from the painful illness of tic douloureux, I recommended h—— to him, which has proven so effective against it, and I presented his private physician with the book that discusses it.[7] The marquis said with a smile, "It is unlikely that I will be denied a leave of absence" and looked meaningfully at his private secretary. This confirmed my assumption, but it would be a great tragedy for Ireland, which for the first time is enjoying the blessing of a governor who views the absurd religious quarrels with a philosophical eye.

Before leaving for Phoenix Park, I attended a church service in the Catholic chapel, a beautiful building. The interior space is a large oval with an Ionic colonnade running around it, a beautiful dome, and, at the end of the room, an excellent relief in the ceiling vault behind the altar, depicting the Redeemer's Ascension. The body and expression of the Savior are particularly commendable, and you feel this is exactly how they must have looked, although the artist created them solely out of his imagination. The Catholics, of course, maintain that they possess actual portraits of Christ. Indeed in southern Germany I once saw an advertisement for a collection of *authentic* representations of God Almighty.

Standing entirely alone is the main altar, beautiful and simple in form. It was made in Italy out of white marble, with darker marble for its top slab and base. The front facade is divided into three sections: in the middle field is the image of a monstrance in ormolu; on the two other fields are bas-reliefs of worshipping angels. On the top, in the center of the altar, is a magnificent temple made of precious stones and gold, in which the actual monstrance is kept, and next to this are two equally magnificent gold candlesticks. On both sides of the altar, angels with folded wings support small tables of bronze, where the host and wine are placed. Every detail has been executed in the best of taste, and the most noble simplicity reigns overall. A heavy chain of silver hangs down from the ceiling and bears an antique lamp of the same metal, which is continually burning.

It is certainly one of the finest Catholic practices that some churches remain open day and night for anyone who feels in need of prayer. In Italy I almost never retired without first visiting such a church and observing the wonderful effect created when, in the still of the night, the reddish glow of the eternal flame so sparingly and preternaturally illuminated the high vaulting. I always found a few solitary figures kneeling before one of the altars, fully engrossed in their god and themselves, unaware of all else. Leaning against the central column in one of these churches was an enormous statue of St Christopher, his head pressed against the vaults. His shoulder bore the heavy burden of the little Christ Child, and the staff in his hand was a full-grown tree trunk, covered with fresh, green boughs replaced each month. From high above, the light of a hanging lamp surrounded the infant with a halo and cast down scattered beams onto the pious giant as if blessing him.

When I compare the Catholic service here with the English Protestant version, I must give unconditional preference to the former. There may be a few too many ceremonies, some even touching on the burlesque (for example, the swinging of the censers, the incessant changing of vestments, etc.), yet this cult has a kind of ancient grandeur that is impressive and satisfying. The music was excellent, the singers very good as well as invisible (which greatly increased the effect). Some Protestants call this a corruption of the senses, but I do not see why the ear-piercing shrieks of an unmusical Lutheran congregation are thought more pious than listening to good music performed by people who have learned how to perform it.* My observation of the contents of the sermon likewise weighed in favor of the Catholic cult. Whereas I observed the English Protestant congregation in Tuam being entertained with nothing but miracles, swine, and evil spirits, here the lesson was purely moral and practical. The speaker's main topic was envy, and one of his most striking remarks was "If you would like to know whether you are free of this vice, one so destructive of human kindness and so debasing to the individual, then look very carefully into your heart and ask whether you have never discovered an uncomfortable feeling in yourself in response to the steadily rising prosperity of another, or if you did not feel a quiet sense of satisfaction at the news that something had either gone awry for a habitually lucky person, or some kind of accident had befallen another. This is a serious question, and most all of you will benefit from posing it."

I also admire the way each person here reads quietly in a prayer book, while magnificent music lifts the spirit far beyond mundane trivialities; this seems far preferable to the loud recitation and open reading of prayers in the other church. During this time of hushed devotion, one takes little notice of the ceremonies, changes of vestment, and incense burning that occupy the priests at the altar; these seem instead like household activities of no particular significance. But even this last little drawback reminds you that what you always see in the Catholic Church is something *entire* and, given its longevity and continuity, something venerable. In the English Protestant church, on the other hand, you see only an unfinished patchwork. These two churches, along with the German one (but only in the sense of our Krug and Paulus), could be compared to three individuals who find themselves at a beautiful spot offering many pleasures and a great deal of useful instruction, but separated by a high wall from God's magnificent sun and unspoiled nature. The first of the three is satisfied with the glow of the jewels and candlelight and never looks longingly through the few cracks in the wall that allow a hint of daylight to enter. The other two, however, grow restless; they feel there must be something better and more beautiful on the other side and, regardless of the consequences, finally decide to climb over the wall. Fully provided with everything they think they need, they begin the grand undertaking, and after enduring great danger and much discomfort, they finally reach the top. Here, it is true, they discover the shining orb of the sun, but find it frequently hidden by clouds, and in addition the lovely green

---

* The introduction of the new liturgy in Prussia did a great deal for the improvement—I might almost say, humanization—of music in the churches, and the influence on the congregations everywhere has been very beneficial.—*The Editor.* [King Friedrich Wilhelm III had long attempted to unify the two branches of the Protestant church in Prussia, and the disputed introduction of a new liturgy in 1821 was part of this. —*Translator.*]

of the meadows below is often invaded by weeds and thorny shrubs, where wild, dangerous animals skulk. But so far there is nothing to discourage the second of the three, nor to dissuade him from his resolve; his inner spiritual voice conquers all fear and every doubt. Cheerfully he lowers himself into the new world and, wanting to be completely unhindered, leaves behind everything he brought along and quickly vanishes into the sacred grove with a light step. The third, however, still sitting on the wall between heaven and earth, living off the food he has carried with him and gloating over the baubles and tawdry finery he brought along, is unable to tear himself away, although the rays of the sun now falling unhindered on his false trinkets have already made them less luminous. Like the animal in the fable, he vacillates between the two bundles of hay, without knowing which he ought to choose.[8] He can no longer go back, but lacks the courage to go forward. Still, for as long as they last, the fleshpots of Egypt will sustain him.*

October 27th, 1828

IF I DID not engage in *allotria*,[9] that is, talk about things having nothing to do with my travels and my stay here, my life in the world would render my letters downright vacuous. I could easily draw up a lithographic plate for my reports with a few spaces to fill in *ad libitum*, such as: "Got up late and feeling morose. Paid some visits: walked, rode or drove. Dined at Lord ——'s, or Mr. ——'s; good or bad. Conversation: commonplaces. In the evening a boring party, rout, ball, or even amateur concert. NB: My ears are still hurting from it!" In London one could add for every event: "I was soon crushed by the throng and the heat was worse than on the top bench of a Russian steam bath. Physical exertion for today = 5 degrees (a fox hunt counts as 20), intellectual proceeds = 0. Result: *diem perdidi*."[10]

Here it is not quite so appalling. At this time of year you become no more exhausted than in a large German city, but there are still too many invitations without any reasonable way of turning them down. I might well cry out along with the English poet, "How different are the emotions of the sojourners in the world that they find great and merry, from the feelings of those who, not sharing in the merriment, find it unbearably melancholic and tedious."

October 28th, 1828

I HAVE JUST returned from a rather provincial but not unpretentious *dîner* in the country. There were some amusing moments, but a little laughter must always be purchased with an equal measure of boredom. The banquet took place at the home of two very lean and ugly misses, who are, however, said to be very rich. If this is true, then they must also be very miserly, because the meal was a true mystification for a gourmet, and the house and park just as inferior. My lucky star had me sitting alongside Lord Plunket, a renowned political figure who has steered his party to the side of the noble and the good and has always remained faithful to the cause of emancipation. I was very happy to find him in such agreement with the opinions I was concocting on the spot. But one of his statements struck me for its naiveté. I remarked that, according to everything

---

* Need I tell you what I mean by the fleshpots of Egypt?—The teachings of Christ, made so rewarding and certainly more nourishing here than the fleshpots of Egypt in former times.

I had seen here, even emancipation would not offer much help, for the real evil stemmed from the fact that most of the land and all the riches of the countryside belonged to a nobility whose chief interest would always oblige them to live in England, and furthermore that the problem was rooted even more in the sums that the poor Irish Catholics had to forfeit every year to the Protestant clergy. As long as this remained true, conditions could not be expected to become stable and prosperous.

"Yes," he responded, "but it's impossible to change *that*. Without those resources the English clergy would lose all their standing."

"How can that be," I said laughing, "isn't it conceivable that virtue, gentle teachings, and pious enthusiasm in office, even with only a moderate income, would bring the most distinguished cleric more esteem than worldly extravagance could? Or are annual revenues of twenty thousand pounds absolutely necessary to make a bishop or archbishop appear decently in society?"

"My dear sir," answered Lord Plunket, "such a thing may exist and maintain itself abroad, but will never do in old England, where above all money and *much money* is required to obtain respectability and consideration."[11]

Of course, the aristocracy did not come into "consideration" in this remark, but it is true that without money it, too, would quickly amount to nothing, although in England it has, with no little arrogance, ranked noble birth above mere wealth.

Lady Morgan, who was also present, entertained the company with her great wit, and afterward told me an amusing anecdote about our hostesses. "Only one of these two," she said (I no longer recall if it was the taller or the shorter one),

possesses a large fortune; the other has scarcely a third as much. But many years ago already the sisters traveled to London in hopes of finding a husband for each. A foreign ambassador heard about the good match, perhaps by way of a secret commission from the ladies themselves, and as rumor has it, he unhesitatingly made his bid. It was accepted with astonishment, but also with great delight, for he had unexpectedly chosen the *poorer* of the two sisters; indeed he had more than once declared himself utterly overcome by her charms. His infatuation was unfortunately based on inaccurate information. He learned the truth in the nick of time and, outraged over this perilous mistaken identity, wrote the two ladies immediately to explain that he had erred in his feelings and, after careful consideration, was now convinced he would find his good fortune not with the tall one, as he had earlier believed, but with the short one, whose hand he therefore and forthwith most humbly requested. After a lengthy struggle, feminine pride conquered its usual counterpart, and both ladies rejected this lofty alliance. Since that time they still travel to London each winter, host dinner parties, outdo Parisian fashion magazines in their dress, and speak at length about country estates and bank obligations; one hammers at the piano, while the other sings without a voice—and both remain single to this day.

It is really quite strange that nowhere else do you come across even half so many old maids as in England, and very often they are rich. The main reasons for this are two: excess of vanity regarding their money, leading to the belief that no level of greatness or rank is good enough for them, and an extravagant upbringing in the manner of a romance novel. These girls want to be loved completely and only for themselves. (This is something that a French girl, for example, does not care a whit about, because she rightly thinks that this feeling will grow during marriage if the right ingredients are present, and if they are absent, it will not *endure* anyway, even if the prospective husband believes himself to feel such devotion). Incidentally Englishmen, like Turks, try to constrain the intellects of their daughters and wives as much as possible in order to preserve them as part of their own property, and nine times out of ten they are entirely successful. A stranger like me is useful to an Englishwoman, but only as a diversion and a plaything. He will always instill an element of fear and nervousness in her. It is extremely rare that a foreigner is granted the same trust bestowed on a countryman, since there is no question that Englishwomen consider all of us to be half atheists or crass worshippers of Baal, although sometimes they find the business of conversion amusing. I am not speaking here of the London exclusives—they produce the same result you get when you mix all colors together: finally not a single one remains.

October 29th, 1828

THE BEAUTIFUL WEATHER lured me outside, so I rode around the whole day and saw two noteworthy castles, Malahide and Howth. Both are unusual in that each has remained the property of just one family for nine hundred years, something that, as far as I know, cannot be claimed about a single residence of the high aristocracy in England. Malahide is, in addition, historically significant, because it belongs to the Talbots, and even the armor of the famous commander, with the mark of a partisan's thrust on the breast, is still preserved here. One half of the castle is ancient; the other was destroyed by Cromwell and afterward rebuilt in the style of the original. In the first section I was shown chairs that are five hundred years old and a room in which the richly carved black oak of the *boiserie*, ceiling, and floor all date back seven hundred years. The new part contains many interesting paintings. A portrait of the Duchess of Portsmouth was so charming that I would have envied Charles II, even in his grave, for having managed to elevate her to the rank of duchess, but then I suddenly recalled the homily of the Catholic priest. An old painting of Mary Stuart, although shown at an advanced age, corroborated for me the image of this unfortunate and beautiful queen that I had seen in County Wicklow. I also looked with considerable interest at a scene at the court in Madrid, including a portrait of the king sitting gravely in scarlet robes; another of Charles I as Prince of Wales, dancing a minuet rather *légèrement* with the infanta; and one of the seductive Buckingham, splendidly dressed and earnestly entertaining a pretty lady-in-waiting.

Howth Castle, which belongs to the St Lawrence family and is the residence of Lord Howth (who is no absentee landlord, but generously expends his income locally), has been more modernized over the course of time, although not very successfully, since a Greek portal looks peculiar next to the small Gothic windows and high battlements in trefoil form. Here, too, the sword and armor of a famous ancestor with a fabled name have been preserved. This was Sir Armoricus Tristram, who in the year 1000 engaged the Danes in a battle somewhere close by, during which, I believe, he also lost his life.[12] The antiquated stalls were full of splendid hunters, and Lord Howth's hounds are just as highly praised.

On my return I went to the theater, where Ducrow, the English Franconi, has refined the art of the equilibrist with his wondrous representation of flexible statues. This is a true artistic treat and far preferable to the so-called tableaux. When the curtain rises, you see a motionless statue standing atop a tall pedestal in the middle of the stage. This is Ducrow, and it is hard to grasp how tricot can adhere so closely at every point on the body and imitate marble so successfully, interrupted only here and there by a bluish vein. I also think that his bare skin was for the most part painted, and that he had availed himself of the tricot only for those areas where the rules of etiquette do not allow nudity. In any case he appeared first as the *resting* Hercules, where the lion's pelt spared him embarrassment. Then, with great skill and precision, the mime gradually abandoned his position and moved into another, from gradation to gradation, advancing to increasing demonstrations of strength. But then, in the peak moments (when the most famous statues were being mimicked), he would suddenly harden himself into lifeless marble. Helmet, sword, and shield were now handed to him, transforming him in the blink of an eye into the wrathful Achilles, Ajax, or some other Greek or Trojan hero. Then it was the Blade Sharpener's turn,[13] the Discobolus, etc., every one equally successful and convincing. He closed with the different positions of the Gladiator, the final one being the masterful representation of the dying figure. This man must provide an excellent model for painters and sculptors, since his physique is perfect, and he assumes any position with ease. It also occurred to me how much our frivolous dancing could be ennobled if we introduced something like what I have just described, instead of our preposterous hopping and leaping. It almost pained me when I later watched the same artist (for he thoroughly deserves this title) first as a Chinese magician riding nine horses simultaneously in the arena, then as a Russian courier driving twelve at once, and finally going to bed with a pony that was dressed as an old woman.

Following that last performance, I will take his example and say goodnight and farewell for a few days, since this letter is departing with tomorrow morning's post.

Your most faithful Lou

Dublin, October 30th, 1828[1]

M OST EXCELLENT JULIE,

Oh, what reproaches! But three letters all at once—that makes everything right again. For a start I now have nearly my fill of news from home, and I hardly know how to express my gratitude to you . . . .
. . . .

You are undoubtedly correct that an ally such as you would have been a great benefit to me. Schoolmistress Prose would have been better at keeping Poetry under control, and the never-aging elfin lad—inclined to swing on a flower and play with colorful soap bubbles—would, reined in by a wise mentor, have sought out some earthly fruit more substantial than these many-hued orbs, and he might even have succeeded. *Mais tout ce qui est—est pour le mieux.*[2] Let us never forget this axiom. Voltaire was wrong to make a joke of it, and Pangloss was certainly right. This conviction alone consoles us—and as for me, I confess it to be the essence of my religion.

Your letter number one is wisdom and goodness itself, but, good Julie, with regard to the first of these, I fear that I am a hopeless case. I remain too much—how can I explain it?—a man of *feeling,* and such people never become wise, are never clever in the ways of the world. Hence goodness has all the greater effect on me—with the exception of *your* benevolence, which I have already received in such full measure that not a single drop more could find space in my heart. You must be satisfied once and for all with this overflowing heart—your poor friend can give you no more! How can you still harbor fears that my two years of absence will have changed my feelings toward you? That I will no longer find in you what I once did? Do you know what the English call that kind of thing? *Nonsense.* You should need no further assurance from such a tireless correspondent as I. There is nothing I would more ardently wish for than to see you again, yet you somehow forget that . . . .
. . . .

How often have I said I am unsuited to the world! Both my defects and my merits, even the inquiring spirit you claim to find in me, are just so many stumbling blocks in my path. To be cerebral, somewhat poetic, good-natured, and genuine tends to make a person ungainly and disgruntled in everyday society. An English writer has described those whose emotions and affections paralyze their sense of judgment, and I, like them, never discover until too late how I might have behaved more wisely. "An artless disposition," the Englishman continues, "is badly suited to engage in a contest with the cunning and cold egoism of the world." I know a famous man, a hundred times my superior, who is experiencing much the same difficulty and continually regrets having been transformed from a poet into a statesman. "I should have ended my life as I began it," he said, "wandering unknown around the world and rejoicing undisturbed in the magnificence of God's creation—or far away from other people, shut up in my room, alone with my books, my imagination, and my faithful dog."*

October 31st, 1828

TODAY I SPENT a very pleasant evening at Lady Morgan's (Figure 105). The company was small but witty and enlivened by the presence of two very pretty friends of the hostess, who sang in the best Italian manner.[3] I spoke at length with Lady Morgan about many topics, and she has enough spirit and emotion to be constantly vivacious and interesting as an interlocutor. In my earlier letter I was insufficiently appreciative of her. Or at least I did not then know her most attractive quality: that she possesses two such pretty bosom friends.

At one point the conversation turned to her writings, and she asked me how I liked *Salvator Rosa*.[4]

"I haven't read it," I responded, "because," I added, excusing myself *tant bien que mal*, "I love your fictional works so much that I have not wanted to read anything historical by the most ingenious female writer of novels."

"Oh, it's also only a novel," she exclaimed, "so in that regard you can go ahead and read it without any pangs of conscience."

"Very well," I thought, "probably just like her travel descriptions," but I took care not to say it.

"Ah," she said afterward, "believe me, it is only ennui that drives all my writings. The lot of mankind in this world is so miserable that I try to forget it this way." (Probably the lord lieutenant had not invited her, or some other great man had disappointed her somehow, for she was hopelessly melancholic). "What a terrible puzzle the world is!" she continued. "Is there a God or not? And if he is all-powerful, and turns out to be wicked! How dreadful!"

"But for heaven's sake," I said, "how can an intelligent woman like you, please don't take offense, talk such nonsense?"

"Ah, I am already well aware of everything you might say on this topic," she continued, "but no one can offer me certainty."

This kind of vagueness in a mind with such acute powers of observation was almost incomprehensible to me, even for a woman (*ne vous en fâchez point*, Julie).[5] Lady Morgan's husband, formerly a physician and now a philosopher and unrecognized writer—what is known in French as *un bon homme*[6]—as well as a gourmand and a bit of a pompous ass, gave me a book he had written, containing a thoroughly materialistic philosophical system.[7] It did, however, include a few worthy thoughts and is better than I would have expected from the author. It took me half the night to read it. The untenable nature of the whole made me think that either Lady Morgan had produced a good portion of it herself, or at least that these undigested views had rendered her so muddled and doubtful that she had come to imagine "the dear Lord might be sinister after all!" Famous people are also human beings, heaven knows!—both scholars and statesmen—and with

---

* We almost feel we should apologize for not having suppressed this and other similar passages. Yet those who have read this far must feel somewhat engaged by the author, whether favorably or unfavorably, and in either case his candor about himself cannot be entirely unwelcome to those who appreciate what is distinctive. Anyone interested only in facts can, after all, skip these reflections.—*The Editor.*

almost every new acquaintance of this kind, I am reminded of Oxenstierna's comment when his then-young son, who was about to travel to the congress in Münster, expressed some reservations about what role he would play, faced with such wise and great men. "Ah, my son," the father said with a smile, "go in peace and see for yourself what *mere mortals* are ruling the world!"[8]

November 1st, 1828

THE CATHOLICS ARE paying court to me here. Today the archbishop sent a lady to me with the message that, as I was so fond of their church music, I should come to the chapel, where there would be a full complement of voices in the choir, and he himself would be officiating. There I heard some splendid vocal music (here female singers are also permitted), accompanied only by individual tones from the mighty organ. This music of the spheres was a true pleasure, filling the soul with sweet delight and carrying everyday cares off on the wings of melody, while the entire congregation remained reverently on their knees.

Eventually, dear Julie, you will believe that I am about to imitate the Duke of C—— and become a Catholic.[9] Well, in fact, the sentiments that would tempt one to such a step seem not utterly groundless. Protestantism, as practiced by many, is hardly more rational and far less poetic and beautiful when it comes to the senses. But I still believe that a new Luther or even a new Christ is *imminent* and will help us all over the wall, when there will be no more need to look back. Until that day, however, many will perhaps find, at least, more consistency in the Catholic cult! It is not just a semi-idolatry but a full-fledged one, and its ladder of divinely made creatures finishes with the saints—adoring, engaged, and of both sexes, those saints who stand near to us and know so well our human wishes, sentiments, and passions! . . . .

. . . . . Whenever the priests and choirboys swing the censers; when every moment finds the bishop enveloped in yet another embroidered cope, collar, or stole; when he stands stiffly before the high altar, runs forward, then back again, then lowers his face to the ground; and finally when he turns around with the monstrance, like a windsock, keeping his eyes fixed on it as if on a microscope, I am fully prepared to hear an account of seven thousand men who were not only sated by three fish and four loaves of bread but had just as many baskets of crumbs and bones left over, or to be told of the Last Judgment and of Christ taking his place beside God the Father and damning to eternal torment all those who did not believe in him.

But when a modestly clad, prudent man speaks to me of tolerance, virtue, eternal truth, and love, yet goes on to tell the same kind of fables; when he attributes such enormities, tales that offend all sound judgment, to the God of righteousness and love and to his most noble spokesman on earth, claiming all this as something holy and divine—then I turn away with revulsion from what seems either hypocrisy or folly. A sanctimonious hypocrite may wish to tell me that God cannot be measured by common sense. To which I retort: but *your* God is a human being. The only true and genuine revelation of God that we can experience, that no one can doubt, springs from our own reason and intellect, and from the knowledge we abstract from our recognition of external realities. Of course each person is by his very nature destined to continue educating himself by these means. And Christianity itself, just as Mosaic law before it, was a consequence of this onward march of civilization, as were later (to continue this line of thinking) the Reformation and its second act, the French Revolution. This more general progress has at last brought freedom of thought and of the press, as well as everything that now emanates more calmly but all the more certainly from that final upheaval. Thus on every side we perceive the same incremental acquisition of civilization, and no one can know where it may end. But whatever level it achieves, it can and should always be nothing but human and be carried forward by human means alone.

November 2nd, 1828

MY LAST AND longest visit this morning was with the sweet girls I met at Lady Morgan's. I brought them some Italian music, which they sang like nightingales in their entirely natural and unpretentious way. Their father[10] is a highly esteemed physician and, like most of the important doctors here, a baronet or "sir," a title that in England does not signal nobility, although as is true among our lower nobility, some very ancient and respected families bear it, along with sundry Toms, Dicks, and Harrys.[11] A baronet is usually addressed not by his family name but by his given name, such as Sir Charles, Sir Anthony—much as in Vienna one tends to say Graf Tinterle, Fürst Muckerle, etc. This medical knight was granted his title for designing some very good public baths, and he is an interesting man as well. His wife strikes me as even more intellectually stimulating; she is superior to her celebrated female relation in tact and judgment,[12] and possesses great talent as a mimic that she deploys hilariously, occasionally even at the expense of her own family. The daughters, although very different, are also extremely witty, the one in a gentle, the other in a wild manner (my reason for referring to her as "Lady Morgan's wild Irish girl").[13] All three exhibit a characteristic Irishness* and have, in fact, never been out of the country.

That evening Lady Morgan told me that the poor and often totally corrupted translations of her works caused her great annoyance. For instance, in her letters from Italy, she says of the Genoese, "They bought the scorn of all Europe."[14] "Scorn" was, however, misread as "corn," and gaily translated, "Gênes dans ce temps achetait tout le blé de l'Europe."[15] This is a good counterpart to the "Nation der *Haid-Schnuken.*"[16]

November 3rd, 1828

I GOT UP early, and when I stepped to the window, my eyes were granted once again an authentic Irish scene, right in the middle of the streets of the capital city, something only seen in this country. An old woman was sitting across the way selling apples and contentedly puffing away at her cigar. Nearer to my building a man dressed in rags was performing all kinds of tricks, assisted by his monkey. A regular circle four to five people deep had gathered around him, and with each new prank shouts of glee erupted, combined with such hurly-burly, clamor, and gesticulation, you would have thought a quarrel was going on and somebody was soon to get a thrashing. Yet as each new episode commenced, a deathly quiet descended. At this point the liveliest female member of the group, no longer satisfied with just watching, felt compelled to act. With uncontrollable

---

* This "Irishness" is rarely encountered in the fashionable world here, since the tyrannical requirements of English education are universal in the three isles, which, as you will also notice, is why I often unite the Irish and English under one name. I should actually call them British.

joviality she springs into the magic circle, grabs hold of the startled monkey, and outperforms him in pranks, leaps, and grimaces of every kind. This is rewarded with redoubled laughter and cheers from the delighted crowd. The frenzy to get into the act is contagious, and many join the first actress, the previous order of play moves quickly into chaos, and the original performer, worried about his monkey's safety or not wanting him to be led astray by bad example, flees the scene. His precipitous escape results in the entire horde dashing after him shouting and cursing, each wanting to be the one on his heels. Suddenly a number of shillelaghs appear, brought out of the sheaths where they had rested during the merriment. As others take the artist's side, he manages to escape, and before you can turn around, the pursuit concludes in a universal skirmish among the mob.

A *garçon-dîner* that I attended later at Lord S——'s ended my day almost as raucously, if not so peevishly, and kept me awake until the middle of the night.[17] *Voilà tout ce que j'ai à vous conter d'aujourd'hui.*[18]

November 16th, 1828

I CONTINUE TO spend my time with the little nightingale angels, see Lady Morgan quite often, and avoid the rest of society as much as I can. The girls are keeping a burlesque journal, in which they are composing and illustrating (with the most extravagant drawings) a highly amusing chronicle of our daily *fata*. Afterward we sing, gossip, or perform tableaux, for which their mother, with her theatrical talent, drapes us beautifully in the most heterogeneous of things. You would have smiled today had you seen how the "wild Irish girl" gave herself a charcoal mustache and side-whiskers, put on one of her father's overcoats, and appeared as a caricature of me, handkerchief and cane in her hand, paying court to her sister in, as she said, my particular style. These girls have an inexhaustible, authentically Irish (not at all English) grace and sense of fun. Luckily I am allowed to spend every evening here, which is making my sojourn in Dublin much more pleasant than I had dared hope. This departs somewhat from the normal rules of etiquette in these countries; in England it could only happen on special request, since visits are not permitted past noon. At midnight, of course, I am always harshly maligned for having stayed much too long, but afterward the incorrigible one is invariably forgiven.

After the tableaux I magnetized the eldest girl, who often suffers from headaches. As you know, I have often been successful with these cures and have absolutely no doubt about the relationship between magnetism and electricity: when I touched the hem of her dress with my fingertips or stroked the farthest ends of her silken locks, crackling sparks seemed to spray out of them. This eldest one, afflicted with eighteen years of age, has brown eyes and hair of an entirely strange appearance and texture that partakes of a fiery element without being red. A dewy glow rests in her eyes, and from time to time the true reddish light of a fire comes over them, too, but remains merely a glow, not the blazing flash that often lights up the eyes of the little wild one. With that creature everything is flames, and emerging from beneath her girlish blushes is the determination and audacity of a young boy. Impetuous and carried away by the present, she sometimes lets herself get caught up in an excess of vivacity, but because of her adorable disposition and her inimitable grace, this only enhances the rarity of her charm.

When my carriage was announced today, I exclaimed with a sigh, "Ah! que cette voiture vient mal à propos!"

"Eh! bien," she exclaimed, standing there still in her male costume, like a real little hussar, "envoyez-la au diable!"[19]

An extremely stern and disapproving glance from her mama and her sister's look of fright immediately caused a scarlet hue to spread over every part of the little face still visible behind the mustache. As she cast down her eyes in shame she was so irresistibly pretty that I . . . what? Good Julie, you may complete the sentence for yourself—and with that, good night.

November 17th, 1828

LADY MORGAN RECEIVED me early today in her author's boudoir, where she—in an elegant costume, wielding a pen of mother-of-pearl and gold, and not without a flirtatious air—was busy with her writing. She was working on a new book, for which she had invented an extremely good title: "Memoirs about myself and for myself." She asked me whether "about myself" or "for myself" should come first. I decided for the former since it was more logical, given that she first had to write before she could have written for herself. This devolved into a playful argument in which she reproached me for my German pedantry and insisted that *bonnet blanc* and *blanc bonnet* had always been the same, which I laughingly conceded.[20] The motto she had chosen was: *Je n'enseigne pas, je raconte* (Montaigne).[21] She read me a few passages, which I found superb. With a pen in her hand, this otherwise rather superficial-seeming woman becomes an altogether different creature. You could say true pearls drop from the mother-of-pearl pen, while the mother remains behind, a cold shell.

She told me she was going to Paris for the winter and would like to travel from there to Germany, but was very afraid of the Austrian police. I advised her to choose Berlin.

"Won't I be persecuted there as well?" she enquired animatedly.

"God forbid!" I consoled her, "in Berlin people worship talent. My only recommendation is that you bring along at least one of your pretty young friends, who is fond of dancing and good at it, so that you will both be invited to the balls at court and can get to know the likeable young military men, which is worth the effort; and you might otherwise not have the opportunity."

At this point her husband entered and asked me if I could not arrange for his philosophical book to be translated in Germany, so that he could fly in on his own wings rather than merely as his wife's aide-de-camp. I promised everything he wished, although I did point out that, at present, a new prayer book would be better received than a new philosophical system, of which we already had enough.

In the evening I took a box at the equestrian theater for the young ladies, who are not allowed to go out very often, and I accompanied them there. Their naïve delight at the artistry of the horse tamers was enchanting to watch. The little sixteen-year-old never took her eyes off Ducrow's breakneck maneuvers and, trembling with anxiety and excitement, kept her tiny hands clenched the entire time. The elder girl, quietly blushing, contemplated the beautiful figures and dashing poses of the nimble riders.

There was a gorgeous child in the company, just seven years old, who was already dancing on her horse and playing a host of roles with uncommon grace. Especially captivating was her impersonation of Napoleon, for which she did extremely amusing imitations of the Emperor's gruff manners, always reaping thunderous applause. Since my young friends wanted to see this child up close, I went into the theater building, where the angel had just taken off her costume and was standing naked in front of the mirror like a cupid come to life. She was finished for the day, so as soon as she was dressed, I picked up *l'enfant prodige* (as she is called on the posters) in my arms and brought her in triumph to the box. After the initial round of hugs, the little one became the most attentive of us all in watching the show, even though one might have expected her to have more than her daily fill of it. Only the bag of sweets I presented to her proved a brief distraction, and we all had to laugh heartily at her droll naïveté when, sitting on Miss Sydney's lap, she tossed half of the bonbons down the front of that lady's bosom and then, despite Sydney's resistance, reached for them with her velvety little hands, exclaiming, "Let me! These are my favorite bonbons." Miss Sydney, who had gone quite red, finally set her down a bit hastily, so that the poor child stuck herself on a protruding pin and drew blood. We were afraid she would cry, but the petite Napoleon only got angry, struck the offender as hard as she could, and cried out indignantly: "Fie, for shame! You stung me like a bee!" And with that she vaulted onto the lap of the other sister, rested her little arms on the box railing, and watched the Siege of Saragossa with the same attentiveness as before.

During the entr'acte Lady Clarke told her that I was Napoleon's son, alluding to the ridiculous case of mistaken identity in Limerick that I had told her about. The child turned and fixed her gaze on me for a while, then exclaimed with the most earnest grandeur, "Oh! I have played your father many a time and have always won the most enthusiastic applause." Thus ingenuous, comical, and unabashed, the dear little creature conquered us all, and we regretted that the end of the performance was approaching, when we would have to deliver her back. She would not allow anyone but me to carry her down, since I had carried her up, and when we arrived behind the scenes, the whole place was full of horses, and I became quite worried about how I was supposed to push my way through. But she spoke out with great animation while tapping impatiently on my arm, "Really now, are you afraid? Just go on, I'll keep the horses in order." And with this she delivered right and left little slaps on the noses of her old acquaintances, who obediently gave way until we had passed. "Now put me down," she said, and hardly had her feet touched the ground than she flew like a young hare across the back of the stage and quickly vanished in the tumult.

Children are certainly the most charming creatures when they have not been crippled by a bad upbringing. Seldom does one encounter so much naturalness on the stage, and even less often in the loftier theater of the fashionable world.

November 18th, 1828

I FORGOT TO tell you that I met O'Connell again here. I have already heard him speak a few times at the Catholic Association, the current Irish parliament, which I visited today for the second time. I was received with applause as a sympathetic foreigner, and Mr. O'Connell immediately made room for me between himself and Lord C——. The room is not particularly large and just as dirty as the English House of Commons, but here every man keeps his hat on, except when he is speaking. These orators are likewise good and bad, but their manners are occasionally more disreputable here. Although I had to hold out for five hours in the suffocating heat, the debates were so interesting that I scarcely noticed my discomfort. O'Connell was, without a doubt, the best speaker. Idolized by the majority, he was nonetheless pressed hard by many, and he defended himself with moderation and fluency. He attacked the ministers and the English government mercilessly—in language that was too strong, in my opinion. A great deal of intrigue was evident, as was the unshakable loyalty of each party to its own. Predetermined notions are the rule, just as elsewhere in such bodies, and therefore the discussion rarely goes further than mere shadowboxing. But at least the leaders have made a close study of their craft. The three most prominent speakers are O'Connell, Shiel, and Lawless; Mr. Fin and Mr. Ford also speak well, and with a great deal of personal decorum. Shiel is a man of the world, with even greater naturalness and *aisance* in society than O'Connell, but as an orator he struck me as much too affected, too artificial, and premeditated in what he said. His "delivery," as the English put it, is extravagantly theatrical, yet devoid of any true emotion. I am not surprised that, in spite of his not-insignificant talent, he is so much less popular than O'Connell. Both men are very vain, but O'Connell's vanity comes across as more forthright, more assured, and even more contented, whereas Shiel is awkward, chafing, and gloomy. Therefore, as far as his own party goes, the one man is dipped in honey, so to speak, the other in gall. And Shiel, although fighting for the same objectives, is visibly jealous of his colleague, whom he mistakenly believes he can disregard. Mr. L——, on the other hand, is the Don Quixote of the association. His handsome head and white hair, his wild but noble manner, and his magnificent voice lead you to expect something extraordinary whenever he makes his appearance; but the earnest opening of his speech quickly dissolves into the most unbelievable extravagances, and often descends to utter nonsense as he attacks friend and foe alike with equal spleen. He is thus little respected and often ridiculed when he lapses into rages like King Lear, unmindful of his audience and all that goes on around him. Still, where necessary, the dominant party often uses him as a loud troublemaker. Today he lost his bearings so completely and with such uncontrollable momentum, that he suddenly planted the flag of deism in the middle of the Catholic,

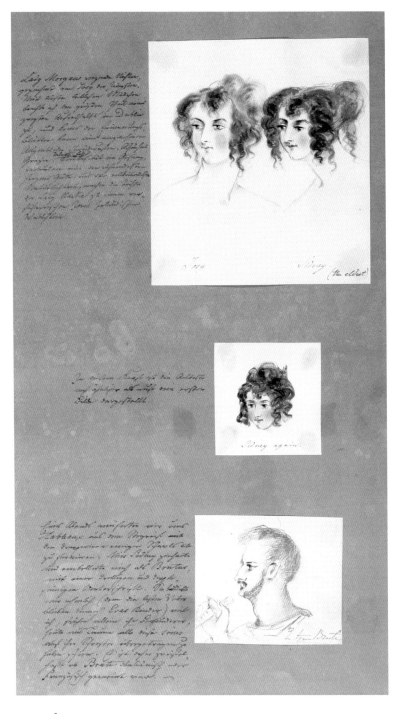

106

Josephine and Sydney Clark, Sydney, and *Pückler as Brutus.*

arch-Catholic association. This was perhaps only so he could give O'Connell the opportunity of indignantly calling him to order and then delivering a pious tirade. For on a speaker's platform as atop a barrel, on the throne as in a puppet show, puffery is part of the trade.

In the evening I relaxed in the usual place. Tableaux were once again on the agenda, and I had to appear seriatim as Brutus, an Oriental Jew, Francis I, and Saladin. As a student from Alcalá Miss Josephine was a seductive little rascal, and her elder sister, as a slave from the seraglio, was a welcome companion for Saladin. And as Walter Scott's beautiful Rebecca,[22] she was also not a bad pairing with the Oriental Jew. Their mother contrived all these metamorphoses using nothing but four candles, two mirrors, a few shawls, some colorful pieces of fabric, a wine cork blackened in a flame, a pot of rouge, and various hairpieces. Yet Talma himself could not have draped Brutus to more advantage, nor altered a physiognomy more beguilingly than did the skillful contrivances of Lady Clarke. Finally, caricatures were drawn, and at my request each sister attempted a portrait of the other. Both were great successes and now hang in the gallery of my life's pictures (Figure 106).[23]

November 19th, 1828

TODAY I WAS compelled to undertake something unpleasant that I had put off for ages, and I used my "Grand Method" to overcome the aversion. You will laugh when I tell you what it is, but it helps *me* in matters both large and small. Most people are occasionally reckless, or more often fickle, and since I am no better, I have invented my own strategy for such situations, something that helps me make a *contrived* decision and then hold to it with a determination I might otherwise lack. A person occasionally needs some kind of external setup for such a thing.* What I do is give *myself,* with great solemnity, my *word of honor* that I will do, or leave undone, this or that. I am, of course, very cautious about employing this tactic and reflect on it carefully before coming to a determination; but once I have, even if it appears I have made a mistake or been too hasty, I hold to it *firmly,* even though it might lead to certain doom! Finding myself bound by such an immutable pledge, I am left with a sense of well-being and serenity. If I permitted myself to recant, I would lose all self-respect. And faced with such an alternative, what thinking person would not unhesitatingly prefer death? Because *dying* is just a necessity of nature and consequently not something evil. It only seems so in the context of our worldly existence; our instinct for self-preservation requires that we fear death. But reason, which is eternal, sees death in its true form as nothing but a transition from one state to another. To be convinced of one's very own, unconquerable weakness, however, is an emotion whose barbs must, at the very least, endlessly embitter this life. Thus, in the case of conflict, it is preferable to call it a day with an inward victory than to continue vegetating in a hospital for lost souls.

I am by no means subordinating myself by making this pledge; in fact, I remain independent because of it. As I said, so long as my conviction is not yet firm, the mysterious formula will not be *spoken*. But once it has been, for the good of my soul, no change of perspective, *nothing* short of physical impossibility will allow me to break my resolve. I am sure you realize that

---

* Even religion and morality are not always sufficient, given the convoluted state of human affairs. Proof: the conventional laws of honor, which are often at odds with both religion and morality, nonetheless prevail among the best of men.

while I am creating this *reliable support* for myself in the *most extreme* cases, I am simultaneously gaining a formidable weapon of *attack*, should I ever need it. However insignificant this resource might seem to some, I find it most satisfying that out of nothing or scarcely more than nothing, a person can create such things for himself, simply by an act of will, which truly in this case can be called omnipotent!

Whether you, good Julie, will find this reasoning foolhardy and reprehensible, I hesitate to guarantee. Indeed it was not made for a woman, and a *really* strong mind might have just as little need of it. But each person must sort himself out according to his own nature, and just as no one has yet discovered the secret of making a reed grow like an oak, or a cabbage like a pineapple, so too, as the common but worthy proverb says, human beings must fit under their own blankets.[24] Happy is he who does not believe himself capable of more than he can actually accomplish! Incidentally, without taking it so tragically, my "Grand Method" also works admirably with trivialities. For example: in the serene fulfillment of unbearably boring social duties; in conquering laziness in order to dispose finally and decisively of a long-postponed task; in imposing a benevolent abstemiousness on myself so as to have all the more enjoyment afterward; and in confronting the many other similar occasions that life—sometimes exalted, but more often childish—offers us.

In the afternoon, to chase away my gloomy thoughts, I went riding deep into the countryside toward the mountains. After about twelve miles, I entered an entirely bleak tract with an endless sea of peat bogs spreading out in all directions. You would have thought you were a hundred miles from a major town. The landscape was not wild, and not as desolate as sand dunes, but eerily empty, lonely, and monotonous. A single, miserable hut stood in ruins and without inhabitants; a white footpath meandered toward it like a giant worm winding its way laboriously through the brown heather. Everything had been dusted with snow, and the wind on the barren heights was icy cold. In spite of all this, I was so attracted to the melancholy of the scene that I only turned my horse homeward of necessity. Closer to Dublin I found an oddly whimsical structure atop an isolated mountain peak, a house that had been built in imitation of a rock. It was in fact so deceptive that you took it for the real thing until you were standing right before its entryway. The moon was shining by the time I got back to the inn, and my face was smarting from the freezing air. I had invited Father L'Estrange to dine with me, *car j'aime les prêtres, comme Voltaire la Bible, malgré tout ce que j'en dis.*[25]

I also found a letter from you, but I must protest that you included too few details! Remember that every trifle from home is precious to me. Whether my favorite horse is healthy, whether my sweet girlfriend (the parakeet) still calls my name from time to time, whether your domestic tyrant Fancy is more or less charming, whether the parrots are in good spirits, the new plantings vigorously growing, the spa guests cheerful—all these things have, from a distance of a few hundred miles, significant interest. But in order to learn something about them, I can see that I have to surprise you, even if it is only for the length of a single day. You know that I hate scenes and solemnities, also noisy receptions as well as all leave-takings—therefore one fine day you will find me ensconced in your breakfast room, where I intend to greet you with jokes and teasing, as if this long journey had only been a dream. And all of life, alas! Is it anything else? To be completely serious, we ought to take all such things with the utmost ease and detachment. Let an English dandy serve as a model for you: His best friend and regiment comrade was going to India, and as he was about to bid an emotional farewell, he was moved to grasp both his friend's hands and shake them, perhaps for the last time. But the *incroyable*,[26] half repulsing him, extended nothing beyond the tips of his fingers as he lisped with a smile, "An odd and highly tiresome English custom to pump each other's bodies by moving their handles up and down!"

Your portrait did not make me as happy as it should have. The features are much too hard and need first to be softened before I can accept them as stand-ins for the original—whose image lives within my heart with so much vividness that it needs no other to refresh it.

Your eternally faithful Lou

*B*ELOVED FRIEND!

I have seen quite a bit of B—— H—— here, a man whose acquaintance has become of great interest to me. He is, although a cleric, one of the few independent thinkers who are capable of shaking off the tyranny of outdated views and well-worn habits, and seeing only by the light of reason, or rather, heavenly revelation. He is also of the opinion that a religious crisis is not far off. Just today he said:

> For the most part, religious systems remain the most monstrous and strange amalgams of the sublime and the ridiculous, of eternal truth and blind ignorance, of genuine philosophy and patent idolatry. The more we *learn,* that is, the more science teaches us through established facts to understand the nature that is both outside and within us, the milder and more ethical our customs as well as our governments become. *Religions follow more slowly!* This is true even of the Christian church. Although it was one of the most consequential steps ever to result from profound thought and a deep understanding of the heart's purity, its ecclesiastical history reveals on almost every page how it has since drenched the world in blood a hundred times and repeatedly generated and then suppressed the most lunatic ideas. Philosophy and science have meanwhile supplied their mitigating effects, without requiring any such sacrifices or transgressions. The question is whether Newton's discovery of the secrets of the heavens, or the inventors of the compass and the printing press, have not been more beneficial to mankind and the advance of civilization than were the many founders of religions who demanded allegiance to their banner *alone.* Indeed there may come a time when religion and poetry will be regarded as sisters, and it will be considered just as preposterous to have a state religion as a state poetry. If I were a Turk I would say to myself: it is certainly difficult to liberate oneself from the prejudices of childhood and the superstitions of one's early teachings, such that, with unshakable confidence, one can acknowledge the conviction of millions to be folly. Yet in spite of this, once I have grasped it, I do not wish to remain a Turk. As a Christian, however, I declare: I will abide by the *pure doctrine,* which my reason can revere. But I will have the courage to discard the unpoetic clutter of fairy tales as well as all the distortions and misrepresentations of earlier days, and even more the bloody and hateful paganism of more recent adherents, despite the two hundred million people who, on someone else's authority, profoundly embrace these beliefs

as holy. Luther acted from this same principle when he took his first steps toward reform; but the light that he purified is very much *in need of cleansing again.* Let honor be granted to that man of the church who, great enough to be called to this service, will carry it out fearlessly in the face of the great hullabaloo that will be raised against him; for history has taught us all too clearly that he can expect nothing else.

Has it not always been only the few who recognized the better and the true, and always the many who persecuted them? Did truth stand with the fanatical mob that offered the poisoned cup to Socrates, crucified Christ, or burned Hus at the stake? Not until centuries later did this Christian horde adopt the view of the martyred and harden themselves in orthodoxy *for* the very thing they had earlier been *against.* The need for religion is certainly one of the strongest desires in mankind, especially when laws and institutions are still in their infancy. And those unable to fashion their own belief must adopt the *form* of it from others. Since few people can manage the first, the majority always fall among the latter. This readily explains how the power of the church and the priesthood necessarily developed, and how humanity was guided like a child in leading strings for hundreds, even thousands of years. But if religion is to succeed, knowledge must be suppressed in favor of *belief,* and where inquiry is *free,* one fraud after the other must finally disappear, albeit slowly, until light illuminates even the remotest corners of understanding. And as soon as that goal is reached, moral constraints will come to an end, and everyone will demand an unlimited arena for the exercise of his beliefs, as he does for the exercise of his judgment. Indeed absolute sultans, fat dervishes, and arrogant satraps will sink to the bottom like the dead lees in a noble wine! But at the dawning of such an age, how pathetic will be those who think they can stop the sun from rising by turning their backs on it or block its radiance by holding up an antiquated, worm-eaten parasol that is incapable of withstanding even moonlight. For a while they will be able to fish in these muddy waters, but they will not be able to halt the daytime star. On the contrary their intransigence, just as passionate as it is feeble, is the most reliable harbinger of the new age.

I must agree with B——— H——— in much of what he said; but whether his sanguine hopes may be realized so soon, or at all, is another question. That Jesuitical dogmas will no longer rule the world, and that freedom of the press will perform unimagined miracles—of this I am perfectly convinced. But people will still be people, and as a result I fear that force and deception will always prevail over reason.

In the late morning I visited the law courts with Father L'Estrange in order to watch the military O'Connell plead in a long and curly powdered wig, black robe, and bands; after that I went to the association to watch the Great Agitator once more in a completely different guise. Today's meeting was very stormy. Mr. L——— spoke as if totally confused, and he attacked even O'Connell with vehemence, almost causing him to lose his habitual dignity. O'Connell managed to make a commendable reply, but went overboard in trawling for witticisms, which were not always in the best of taste. Later on, ten members started speaking at the same time. The secretary called for order, but did not have enough authority to command obedience. In short, the scene became somewhat unruly, until finally a handsome young man in outré dress and with an enormous beard (he is the dandy of the association, just as L—— is their Don Quixote) leapt onto a table and gave a fulminating speech that was received with great applause. Thus was peace restored!

I took my midday meal at Lady Morgan's. She had invited me with a note similar to the dozen or so I have received from her during my sojourn here, all of which share certain characteristics—I have never in my life known a lady to write billets with worse calligraphy or a more negligent style. It reveals the renowned author's intent to manifest the greatest possible *insouciance,* the most complete *abandon* of the most common of lives. It is just like the great solo dancers in Paris, who feign a pigeon-toed walk during the pantomime sections of their ballet performances, so as not to betray that they are professional dancers. At table Lady Morgan and her already mentioned aide-de-camp, C—— Cl——,[1] assumed responsibility for all the obligatory wit, and Mr. Shiel, too, presented himself as a very amiable man of the world. But what I found most amusing was the evening performance of proverbs by Lady Morgan and her sister, both of whom extemporized quite brilliantly in French. Among others, they presented "love me, love my dog" as follows:

Cast of characters: Lady Morgan, an aging coquette; Lady Clarke, an Irish fortune hunter; her eldest daughter, the French chamber maid; and the youngest daughter, a captain of the Guards, the old lady's lover.

First you see Lady Morgan at her *toilette* with the maid. Confidential advice concerning various ludicrous secrets of the *toilette.* Lamentation on the coquette's part about incipient wrinkles. Eventually reassurances from the abigail that, nonetheless, no one is more beautiful in the evening light.[2] As evidence, various admirers are listed and love stories of former times are related. *La comtesse convient de ses conquêtes,*[3] and with much humor makes a picture of her triumphs. "Chut!" cries the chambermaid, "j'entends le capitaine."[4] This man, an exclusive, arrives quite boisterously holding a small dog in his arms, and after delivering a few tender compliments explains that, as he is obliged to return to his regiment, he wants to leave Fidèle with her, so that the beautiful countess will never forget to remain *fidèle* to him. Burlesque protestations, sobs, embraces, farewell. Scarcely has the captain left than an Irishman appears bearing a marriage contract, stipulating that the countess should make her entire fortune over to him. As a connoisseur of women, he treats her brusquely and yet ardently, so that after a weak defensive maneuver and a small scene, both finally agree. Meanwhile the Irishman notices the strange dog and, taken aback, asks where it has come from. With some embarrassment a few excuses are stammered out. O'Connor MacFarlane now plays the jealous man overcome with fury. The women try in vain to calm him—he rages and insists on the immediate removal of the interloper. The countess tries to faint, but all in vain. Even the maid, who earlier in the negotiations over the marriage contract already received a full purse behind her mistress's back, takes the side of the Bramarbas, who, restraining his lady with one hand, finally gets hold of the small unhappy creature with the other and throws it out the door. But alas! At that very moment the captain comes back with the collar he had forgotten, and Fidèle flies into his arms. The terrified women take flight, the men measure each other with their eyes, O'Connor MacFarlane utters dire threats, but the captain draws his sword, and the Bramarbas leaps out the window.

The meager skeleton is made highly entertaining by hilarity, whimsy, and wit. The imperfection of the costumes increased the piquancy, for the ladies were men only about halfway down; the other half stayed female. They simply donned jackets and vests over their dresses and put hats on their heads. Their swords were riding crops and Fidèle a muff.

107

Eliza O'Neill.

Miss O'Neill

Afterward Lady Morgan told me many interesting details about the renowned Miss O'Neill, whom, as you know, I consider the greatest dramatic talent I have ever seen (Figure 107). She said that this artist, who from the very beginning evidenced the most sublime genius, remained totally neglected here at the theater where she had long performed. Indeed, she was held in low regard! Moreover she was so poor that she returned home after an exhausting performance to eat a bowl of potatoes and sleep in a miserable bed shared with her three siblings. Lady Morgan visited her one time and found the poor girl mending her only two pairs of old stockings, which she washed every day so as to appear neat and clean on the stage. After that Lady Morgan supplied her with sundry articles of clothing and even attended somewhat to dressing her, which no one had bothered to do for any of her previous stage appearances. From that time on, the applause improved, though it remained meager. Then one of the managers of the London theaters came to Dublin and, being a fine judge of acting, engaged her immediately for the metropolis. Her first appearance there caused a furor, and she rose in a flash from an unknown and penniless young actress to the leading star in England's theatrical firmament, bathing the entire country with her radiance.

I still recall her London performances with rapture. Since then I have never been able to bear the role of Juliet played by any other actress, including the best of our own. They all seem nothing but style, affectation, and unnaturalness. One needs to see for oneself how, in those few hours, the entire life of Shakespeare's Juliet can be so authentically played out before the audience. At first you behold only the playful and uninhibited innocence of childhood. Then, as love is awakened, a new sun seems to rise; all her movements become more voluptuous, her expression more radiant, as the maiden abandons herself to her beloved with all the fire of the south. Thus she unfurls the sweetest, richest blossom. But sorrow and misfortune quickly ripen the noble fruit before our eyes. Dignity, supreme tenderness for her spouse, and the firmest resolve in affliction now take the place of her passion, of the pleasure-seeking spirit. And how well despair was represented in the end, when everything was lost! How dreadfully, how heartrendingly, how genuinely, *yet always beautifully*, did she add intensity, even to the last moment. Confident in what she was doing, she sometimes let herself venture to the extreme boundary of her acting abilities, something no one else could have dared, lest they plummet into the ridiculous. In her case, however, it was exactly *these* effects that worked like an electric shock. Her madness and death as Belvidera* bore such a fearsome physical truth that she was almost impossible to watch; and it was no more than the agony of the soul made overwhelmingly manifest through the body that was so powerful, even devastating, for the spectator. I still remember how, for a long time after that evening, I could no longer indulge in any sensory impressions,** and even the next morning I awoke weeping burning tears over Belvidera's fate. I was admittedly very young, but many others shared my feelings, and it was striking that the Germans as well as the French and Italians were equally enthusiastic in their judgment, since differing national characteristics usually retard our appreciation of an actor. *She*, however, had no trace of affectation; hers was simply the most genuine and noble image of humanity, and spoke directly to the heart. You could not really

---

* A character in *Venice Preserved*, by Otway.—*The Editor.*

** This is how I explain the miracle of the loaves and fishes better than Paulus does (I mean the member of the church council).—*The Editor.* [The theologian Heinrich Paulus was known for his natural explanations of biblical miracles.—*Translator.*]

call her beautiful; however her appearance was dignified, her shoulders splendid, her hair lovely. Her face possessed that indefinable tragic expression that at first glance stirs you to the depths of your soul. You believe you can read the trace of every passion in her features, although an ethereal tranquility is spread over them like a mask of ice over a volcano.

The Dubliners were blind to so much genius and talent. But when, in the following year, the celebrated, indeed idolized, Miss O'Neill returned from London for a few guest roles, the magic she radiated was so enormous that not only did the entire public get caught up in a kind of frenzied intoxication, but many ladies had to be carried out of the theater unconscious. One woman was truly driven *mad* while witnessing Belvidera's insanity and ultimately died in a lunatic asylum.* Really, such episodes make the enthusiasms of the multitude almost disgusting!

This great actress always distinguished herself by the thorough goodness of her character. She never ceased supporting her family all by herself, even through direst poverty. Her first appearance had been in a small private theater in the provinces.⁵ It was on the verge of closing, but one festive performance was still to be given by the best local amateurs, with the proceeds going to the poor people of the region. A letter was sent to Miss O'Neill in England asking her if she might help celebrate this final performance by her presence, since it was here that she had first tested her strengths, now renowned in all three kingdoms. Any condition she might stipulate would be met. Miss O'Neill responded that she was tremendously flattered and honored by the request, and rather than accepting any remuneration for herself, she would joyfully pay tribute to the cradle of her minor talent. But only under the condition that she be allowed to add *her* contribution for her poor countrymen, would she appear on the appointed day. Eyewitnesses assured me that they had never seen a more perfect performance of Shakespeare's immortal masterpiece. Never had Miss O'Neill been better supported, and never had she so outdone herself. It was a peculiar twist of fate that on that same day a rich young baronet fell in love with her, and shortly thereafter they were married. He thus stole her away from the public, but who can damn him for that! Miss O'Neill now has several children and is said to be as charming as ever. She lives happily on her husband's estate, but has never again set foot on a public or private stage.

(The conclusion of this letter, which, according to the beginning of the following one, contained the description of a few public festivals and events has been lost.)

---

* Doubtless as a sacrifice to Nemesis for the earlier obtuseness of the others.—*The Editor.*

Dublin, December 7, 1828

EAR JULIE,

The descriptions of public dinners and of the inane perfidiousness of Sir Charles M——
are now at an end, and so I will take you to breakfast at the post office, where our host was the
director, Sir Edward Lees, a very cultivated and charming man. He first led us, together with a
group of elegant ladies, through the various offices, *pour nous faire gagner de l'appétit.*[1] In one of
these, called the dead-letter office, a strange incident occurred during our visit. All letters with
illegible addresses, or those whose recipients cannot be ascertained, come to this office. After
fourteen days they are opened and, if they contain nothing important, burned. To me this seems
a rather barbaric practice, since a heart could easily be broken on the basis of what might seem
insignificant to a postal worker. But so it is, and we found three people industriously engaged in
the process. Several of us were curious, picked up a few of the doomed letters, and were leafing
through them, when the clerk I was standing next to came to a rather heavy missive, on which
there was no address at all, but just the postmark of a provincial Irish town. How great was his—
and our—surprise, when he opened it and found no writing, but instead 2,700 pounds in genuine
banknotes! This, at least, we all recognized as important. The order was immediately given to
write to the town in question in order to clarify the matter.

When I went to visit my nightingales in the evening, I found they had fled, and only their
father was at home, so I conversed with him *faute de mieux* about a range of scientific topics. He
showed me a variety of newly invented instruments, among them one that gives a very exact
reading of the power of the lungs and is therefore supposedly invaluable in understanding
consumptive diseases. Sir Arthur told me that a distinguished local official had been suffering
from incurable pulmonary consumption, and had a year ago been given up as hopeless by all the
physicians in Dublin. Facing what he saw as his imminent demise, he was in the process of relin-
quishing his post and undertaking a journey to Montpellier, hoping if at all possible to postpone
his death for at least a few months. Finally Sir Arthur was consulted and had the idea of trying
out his new machine, which had just then arrived from London. He could hardly believe his
eyes when the experiment revealed the lungs of the sick man to be putting out two degrees more
power than his own, which were in very good condition. It was then realized that the problem
was a disease of the *liver,* which bore all the symptoms of the last stages of consumption, and
within four months the patient was completely cured and able to retain the lucrative post he had
been about to sacrifice.

Another very compact machine served for bloodletting and scarification, and as a stomach
pump, ear syringe, and enema syringe—all at the same time. You have to admit that the idea of

consolidation can hardly be taken further! The remaining instruments of martyrdom I will not describe, *tant pis pour l'humanité, qu'il en faut tant!*[2] More attractive was a barometer in the shape of a lady, who takes hold of her umbrella when bad weather threatens, opens it during a heavy rain, and employs it as a walking stick when the forecast is positive. To use a lady as a continuously changing prophet of the weather! *Quelle insolence.*

December 8th, 1828

THIS MORNING SIR Arthur showed me the bank where he has a position.[3] The premises are handsome and once served as the meeting place of both houses of the Irish Parliament, which so many people now wish could be restored. The part most worth seeing is where the banknotes are printed. The entire operation is driven by a magnificent steam engine. Next to this is a second, smaller engine that fills the boilers with water and the furnaces with coal, so there is almost nothing left to be done by human beings. The printer's inks are prepared in the first room; in the adjoining, larger rooms the banknotes are rapidly given their various ornaments and markings. Just *one* man is occupied at each printing press, and as he lays the blank sheets under the press one after the other, the quantity of printed notes is marked down in a closed box beside it. Then on a small chest in the next room, another machine numbers the notes from one to one hundred thousand, as if with invisible hands. The worker engaged here has nothing else to do but dab the emerging numbers with printer's ink and lay the notes in the proper order. The machine does everything else on its own.

Every note that finds its way back to the bank after distribution is immediately torn up and stored for seven years before being burned. During this last operation, the paper and specially composed printer's inks form a residue of indigo, copper, and paper that looks like metal and sparkles with all the colors of the rainbow. Naturally it requires several hundred pounds of notes to make a half ounce of this substance, from which I took a lovely sample for myself.

Afterward we climbed up onto the lead roofs of this vast structure, which formed a world in miniature, and from there, by going up and down staircases like the *diable boiteux*,[4] we were able to see into various other buildings. Finally we got so lost that, not having Ariadne's thread, we barely managed to extricate ourselves, and for this reason I arrived late at a grand *dîner* at Sir Edward Lees's, a faux pas that the English take more lightly than we do.

December 9th, 1828

LORD HOWTH HAD invited me to a stag hunt, from which I have just returned both contented and exhausted in equal degrees. My lessons in Cashel came in very handy today, because Lord Howth is one of the best and most determined riders in England. I had been given a very good horse, and in spite of the fact that I fell twice—which also happened once to Lord Howth—I followed on his heels so well that I believe I did our cavalry proud. In the end, more than two-thirds of the fifty red coats went missing. One officer seemed especially remarkable, for he had only one arm, yet was always in the front line, and his magnificent horse never refused or missed a single jump.

Although this kind of hunt can occasionally be a pleasant pastime, it is incomprehensible to me how anyone can devote six months every year, three times every week, to a mindless diversion, and do so with such unstinting passion. Moreover stag hunting in England is much less

Vue de L'interieur du GYMNASE 26. St James's Street.

Designed & Drawn on Stone by R. Seymour.   Printed by W. Day.59 (3 Queen S.^t

pleasant than elsewhere, since the stags are tame, having been trained to it like racehorses. Shut up in a box, they are brought to the hunting rendezvous and then released. Once they are given a head start, the hunt begins, and before it ends the hounds are called off and the stags put back in their box. Is this not appallingly prosaic? And it is hardly offset by the added attraction that you can break your neck over a wide ditch or batter your head against a high wall!

December 10th, 1828

FOR THE PAST few weeks I have been making regular visits to the gymnastic academy, a diversion that has become very fashionable in Great Britain and Ireland (Figure 108). These exercises are certainly invaluable for the education of the young—it is *Turnen* raised to a much higher power, and *without* politics.[5] Consider the various means now on offer for physical as well as spiritual education; how even the most deformed people, harnessed in splints of iron, are transformed into Apollos; how noses and ears are created; and how every day in the newspapers you find praise for educational establishments that promise to create the most rigorous scholars in just three years!* One might wish to be a child again in order to get a piece of it for oneself. It seems that the law of gravity works in the moral as well as the physical realm, and civilization

---

* The Prussian Landwehr system also produced perfect infantrymen and cavalrymen in just two years.
—*The Editor.*

(the march of the intellect) accelerates with the speed of a falling cannonball. Only a few more political revolutions in Europe, the total perfecting of steam power for soul and body, and God knows what we might achieve—even without discovering how to manage hot-air balloons! But to get back to the gymnasium: *its* usefulness is not in doubt. It strengthens the physique so much and endows the body with such agility that a person's well-being is improved by a factor of two or three. This is true even in the literal sense, for I saw a young man who, after three months of steady exercise, had increased the size of his chest by seven inches; and during the same period the muscles of his arms and thighs bulged out at three times their former volume and were as hard as iron. But older people too, even men of sixty, although they cannot achieve the same benefits, are still capable of significantly increasing their strength through moderate training in gymnastics. Every day I found several men of about that age who had only recently begun instruction, but were already competing very well with their younger peers. A certain amount of stamina is required, however, for the older you are, the more painful and exhausting it is at first. Many ache all over for months, as if they had been broken on the wheel or stricken with rheumatism. A Frenchman is now directing the establishment, after his predecessor sacrificed himself *pro patria* two years ago. That man, Beaujeu, had wished to show two ladies how easy it was to perform exercise number seven, for the institute also trains female gymnasts. But the bar broke when he fell, and so did his spine. He died a few hours later. With an enthusiasm worthy of a greater subject, he forced out the doleful words, "Voilà le coup de grâce pour la gymnastique en Irlande!"[6] But his fear was unwarranted, for gentlemen and ladies are more disposed to gymnastics than ever.

December 14th, 1828

BECAUSE I HAVE been unwell for several days and could not go out, I have nothing interesting to report. Therefore I'll make do with a few random thoughts engendered by my solitude. Do leave them unread if you find them boring.

Parlor Philosophy

What constitutes good and bad fortune? Since the former has not often come my way, I have frequently asked myself this question. Fortune is neither blind nor accidental; rather it is necessary and logically consistent like everything else in the world, although its causes are not *always* dependent on us. But we would all benefit from considering the extent to which we do bring it on ourselves. Fortunate and unfortunate circumstances confront everyone in the course of a lifetime, and how deft we are at taking advantage of them or avoiding them altogether is normally what grants us a reputation for being lucky or unlucky. It cannot be denied that certain people, including some of the most powerful and intelligent among us, come to naught as a result of what we call chance. Indeed, we are possessed of a certain intuition that can give us a sense of dark foreboding that we are going to fail. This feeling can beset us whether our confidence is high or, seemingly, at its most insecure. Sometimes I am tempted to believe that fortune, either good or ill, is nothing more than a subjective attribute we bring with us into the world like health, physical strength, a better organized brain, etc., and that circumstances are magnetically compelled to submit to its power. Like all attributes, fortune too can be cultivated or left undisturbed, increased or diminished. Volition plays a large role here, which accounts for the expressions "nothing ventured, nothing gained" and "boldness is part of luck." Notice also that luck, like the other faculties, tends to diminish over time, that is to say, along with physical vitality. This is not always the consequence of weaker or less adept intellectual standards, but instead seems to be a mysterious capacity *an sich*. As long as it is young and strong, it keeps a firm hold on fortune; later it loses control. Gambling offers good opportunities for studying this, which is the only poetic aspect of that dangerous and often seductive passion, since nothing gives a truer picture of life than the lofty game of hazard; nothing provides a better means of helping the observer plumb his own character or that of others. All the rules that obtain in the struggle of life also obtain here, and insight along with strength of character will be certain to prevail or, at least, muster a successful defense. But if insight is paired with a tendency to good fortune, then the result is a gaming Napoleon, a winner at the faro table! I am not speaking of the cheating scoundrels who improve on luck, although here, too, the comparison holds. For how often do we encounter people who use fraud to manipulate fortune? (These are, incidentally, the least fortunate of all speculators.) They are busy carrying water in a sieve or gathering empty nutshells. For what is pleasure without security? And how can external fortune help us, when our inner equilibrium is missing?

———

There are people endowed with extraordinary intellectual capabilities who still do not know how to use their skills to get on in the world. Unless fate has positioned them well from the very beginning, they never know how to arrive at the proper spot through their own resources, because an imagination that is too feminine, too susceptible to outside influences, prevents them from seeing the truth as it is, forcing them to dwell forever among capricious phantoms. Such people begin their plans with fervor and dexterity, it is true. Yet the steed of their poetic imagination rushes on ahead into the realm of dreams, unhesitatingly carrying them with dazzling assurance to their goal. The slow tedium of the actual road becomes intolerable, and so they let one project after another fall by the wayside before it reaches maturity. Like everything in the world, however, there is a positive side to this state of mind. It may prevent someone from making a fortune, but it nonetheless offers immeasurable comfort in adversity and an irrepressible elasticity of spirit, because the imagination will never exhaust its supply of delightful fancies. A whole city of castles in the air is always at the disposal of these mortals, and in hopeful anticipation they enjoy countless, ever-changing realities. Such people can often serve as a superb resource for the more prudent and practical, as long as the latter can manage to arouse the enthusiasm of the former. Then, compelled by a positive inclination, their reasoning achieves a staying power that their own interests cannot inspire; and their zeal is more enduring when focused on others than on themselves. The principle is the same as I stated above. If they are placed on the mountaintop at the outset, they can accomplish great things, for the varied and splendid material, along with the requisite enthusiasm, is already a given. There is no need to initiate something new, uncertain, or vague, or to use their artistic ingenuity to improve, elevate, or adorn what lies beneath them. These heights are their true station, and from here their brilliant gaze, supported by thousands of heads and hands and strengthened by an internal poetic eye, will penetrate far beyond those of more ordinary beings.

But at the foot of the mountain, as on its slopes, the horizon is obscured, and their sharp gaze is useless. Their indolent limbs will not undertake the strenuous climb. Nor can they resist the flickering apparitions that appear along the way, enticing them from their path.

They therefore live and die on the mountain without ever attaining its summit, never realizing their own strength. In such cases the well-known saying can be reversed: *Tel qui brille au premier rang, s'éclipse au second.*[7]

————

However lovely and splendid the words "morality" and "virtue" may sound, their practical benefit to human society depends entirely on being universally recognized as useful. The sinner is like a savage who chops down the whole tree in order to get a single, often-sour piece of fruit, whereas the virtuous person acts like a prudent gardener and waits for all the sweet fruits to ripen before picking them, happy knowing that the tree will produce subsequent crops. Whoever actually grasps this is likely endowed with the most unwavering virtue. The more people realize what is beneficial to them, the more useful and tolerant of others they will become, and a benevolent circle will arise from this interaction, namely, enlightened individuals will build a better constitution and government and, in turn, further enlighten the population. If it ever happened that such a rational, elevated form of education would free us from the chimeras of these darker times, would consign religious compulsion to its place among the absurdities while allowing a clear perception of love and virtue as requirements, both internal and external—for society's happy existence, and if this conviction would instill in us the habit of sustaining these through wise and well-founded political institutions, then Paradise would be found.

Absent this inner conviction, however, mere penal laws—whether for here or the hereafter; all the worldly politics of clever scoundrels; all prophets, divine revelations, heaven, hell, and priests will scarcely get us that far. Indeed, as long as these are hanging on the spokes, the wheel of the enlightenment will turn only slowly.* This is why so many are working mightily to oppose such an outcome; indeed, even the Protestants are protesting *backward,* and many would even like to establish a new continental barrier against foreign beams of light.[8]

In any case, no one can be blamed for promoting his own agenda. To demand, for example, that an English archbishop with fifty thousand pounds a year be enlightened is just as preposterous as expecting the shah of Persia to willfully transform himself into a constitutional monarch. Few individuals will voluntarily reject a luxurious sinecure requiring nothing more of them than scattering a bit of dust in people's eyes or playing the despot who commands millions according to his mood. It is the business of *society* to arrange things so that *none of us,* whether or not our intentions are good, can achieve such privileges.

————

When I was a child I fretted over the fate of Hannibal or lapsed into despair over the battle of Poltava. Today I was wailing over Columbus! We owe a debt of gratitude to Washington Irving, the witty American, for this history.[9] It is a handsome tribute to the great navigator and comes from the very land that he presented to the civilized world, one that seems destined to be the final stage in the cycle of human perfectibility. What a man, this sublime, patient sufferer! Columbus was someone too great for his time, for forty years considered nothing but a fool. Throughout the rest of his life, he endured the enmity of his peers and ultimately succumbed

* It is worth noting that morality was at its worst during the period when belief in eternal damnation was most intense, and the number of serious crimes was a thousand times what it is now.—*The Editor.*

in misery and woe. But such is the world, and we would be foolish to dwell on a single instance. Let us recognize that, for nature in her wisdom, the individual counts for nothing, the species for everything. We live for and through mankind, where everything finds its recompense. This should reassure any reasonable person. Every seed sprouts, whether or not for the hand that planted it, and not even one, whether bad or good, is lost to mankind.

What then is the purpose of everything?—It is this *life* in which we constantly participate, eternally old and eternally new. Thus I assert: whatever *is* can only be perfect and necessary, otherwise it would not exist. What happens *must* happen, not because it has been preordained by caprice as the fatalists assume, but rather because the chain of consequences must necessarily issue from a chain of causes. In relative terms and in the particular circumstances of life in the universe, this unshakable chain of causality vanishes from our sight and makes room for a thousand uncertain connections, without which the entire game of life would suddenly collapse. The similarity to works of art is great, for this is their prototype. Lear, a hero conceived by a true poet, stirs us profoundly on the stage, perhaps more so than he would in reality. And yet we know that everything we are seeing and hearing is an illusion. The expression "the theater of the world" has a deeper meaning than we normally grant it, and everything that lives is in reality acting out *a divine comedy.*

We require a certain element of illusion. It is our proper element, a necessity of our mortal existence. We long for the past, revel in images of the future, and are unaware of the present. Of course, the one genuine truth—that of the mind—constitutes the invisible core on which the colorful faux fruit of life must develop. Hence Goethe's profound formulation: *Wahrheit und Dichtung—Geist und Erscheinung.*[10]

———

I find it bitterly exasperating to hear people lamenting the wretchedness of this life and calling the world a vale of tears. Not only does this show an appalling ingratitude (humanly speaking), but it is also a true sin against the Holy Ghost. Is it not obvious that enjoyment and well-being are the norm throughout the world, whereas suffering, evil, and deformity are merely its dark side? Is life not an endless feast for the unjaundiced eye, its splendor something that fills one's heart with adoration and bliss? Were life no more than the daily sight of the sun and the radiance of the stars, the green of the trees and the luster of a thousand blossoms, the jubilant songs of birds, and the exuberant abundance and delight of all creatures—would this not be enough for rejoicing? But how much more wondrous are the inexhaustible treasures to be unfolded by our own minds; what troves are opened by love, art, science, by the history and observation of our own race, and—most profoundly—by the pious beholding of God and his universe! Truly, if we were less fortunate, we would be more grateful; too often we must suffer in order to become aware of this. We could call the grateful disposition our sixth sense, through which we recognize happiness. Anyone truly convinced of this will nonetheless complain from time to time like other thoughtless children. But he will come to his senses more quickly, because the profound feeling of happiness—*of being alive*—reposes within his heart like a rosy background, through which even the darkest figures that fate may inscribe there shimmer softly, like blood in the arteries.

———

Paradoxes of my Friend B——— H———

Yes, the spirit prevails in us, and we in it, and it is eternal and prevails through all worlds. But what we call our *soul* is something we create here for ourselves. The seemingly binary creature within us—one part inclined to follow the impulse of the senses, while the other reflects and restrains the first—arises quite naturally out of our double nature and out of human purpose, since we must live as individuals, but also as integral members of society. The gift of speech is essential to our social existence, which would never have evolved without it. In isolation an individual is no more than an animal endowed with a superior intellect, with no more soul than a beast. Consider it in the following way. As soon as a man begins to live communally and the exchange of perceptions becomes possible through *language,* he quickly realizes that the individual must subordinate himself to the whole, that is, to the society of which he is a member, and to which he must make sacrifices to sustain its existence. And here, you might say, is the essential origin of the soul and morality. The sense of one's own weakness and ignorance also gives birth to religion, to the need for other people and for love. Self-interest and humanity now engage in that perpetual antagonism we call, for some reason I do not understand, the enigma of life; to me, given my expressed views, nothing appears more logical or more natural. Mankind's task, then, is to establish the proper balance between these two poles. The more this is achieved, the greater the feeling of well-being for the individual, the family, and the state. It is the extremes that are harmful. The egoist thinks he alone matters, but he will be defeated by the power of the majority. That altruism which starves itself to feed others—a motive branded either noble or foolish by those who admire or alternatively ridicule every sacrifice offered them—can never become universal and therefore a model to be imitated. That is to say, altruism can never become a *duty.* Martyrs who let themselves be roasted for the sacred number three, or let the nails of one hand grow through the other in honor of Brahma, belong in the same category—albeit at its lowest level.[11] They are called either saints or madmen depending on their times, but in every case they remain exceptions to the rule. I do not deny that a principled renunciation of oneself for the benefit of others can be something beautiful and sublime. By no means. Such an example—one that is both beautiful and beneficial to mankind—places society over the desires of the individual. This disposition certainly occurs, as does its all-too-frequent opposite, namely those who attend to themselves alone, descend into ruthlessness, and become callous criminals who wage perpetual war against society. Meanwhile, since we are intrinsically more connected to ourselves than to society (something necessary for our existence, the natural law of self-preservation being the strongest), egoists are more abundant than humanitarians, and there are more sinners than saints. The sinners are the genuine brutes, the saints no more than a refined version (a lesson, by the way, for all governments preferring to rule in the dark). Given that the rough substratum remains even in the most refined of people, just as when a piece of highly polished marble breaks off to reveal the coarse grain underneath, so must humanitarianism accept that it has risen out of egoism. Indeed it is really no more than a form of egoism extended to embrace all of mankind.

Hence, wherever this egoism develops in an extreme way—whether for the benefit of one or many—those mortals called great men and conquerors will compel our admiration, even if we disapprove of their behavior. Indeed experience teaches us that those who disregard the welfare of others and afflict their fellow creatures with the most monstrous earthly sorrows are nonetheless highly esteemed by the very people whose suffering they have caused. Overwhelming *power* abetted by fortune commands respect. This demonstrates once again that necessity and fear are at the root of society and thus remain its mightiest levers. In the end, *power* makes the deepest impression. Alexander and Caesar loom larger than Horatius Cocles and Regulus (assuming that the tales of the latter two were not merely fables).[12] Selflessness, friendship, compassion, and generosity develop only later, and then only as rare blossoms of a subtle and refined fragrance, much as in philosophy, where the highest power is manifested only in the ideal of the good, and self-sacrifice becomes the greatest pleasure for the individual.

Another compelling proof that what we call morality arises only from socialized living is the fact that we still recognize no such principle among other creatures. If we could, to scientific ends, unhesitatingly pull down a star for inspection, we would; and we would not make much fuss over an angel in our control, once we had nothing to fear from him. It is obvious that we are total egoists in our treatment of animals (and even still of Negroes), and it will require a higher level of culture for us to stop torturing them or letting them suffer for no reason at all. What is more, *people among themselves* will suspend their moral principles the moment an acknowledged authority partially suspends the social contract. Once war is declared, the most virtuous soldier murders his fellow man ex officio, even if he is in compulsory service to a despot he regards as the scum of the earth. Or the pope, by virtue of the religion of love, may release us from all feelings of loyalty, justice, or humanity. Thus the pious man is suddenly free to burn, ravage, murder, and lie—all of it *con amore*—so he dies for the glory of God, contented and blessed in the fulfillment of his duty!

People rightly say that the animal destined to live only for itself knows no virtue and therefore has no soul. Yet in household pets, despite their limited intelligence, we can still observe the trace of a visible morality, a clear feeling for what is right and wrong, developing little by little. This is the result of their training and a kind of sociability acquired through their acquaintance with human beings. We can see unselfish love in them, can observe them making sacrifices without the motive of fear. In short, they begin to move along the same path as people do. Their souls begin to emerge, and if animals had the faculty of speech, it is possible they would progress as far as we have. However, since their physical powers are superior to ours, the first use they would likely make of their newly evolved souls would be to seek *our* annihilation.

It would be best if we could, without speculation or effusiveness, look at ourselves and see just what we are, and why. This is the only means to true and lasting enlightenment and, consequently, to true happiness. German philosophy has chosen too poetic a path, and seems less like a warm hearth than a rocket that soars up to the heavens with a thousand flickering sparks as if to dwell among the stars, but soon turns to nothing and vanishes. From Kant to Hegel, how many eccentric systems of this kind have twinkled for a moment only to fade away, or are cut up to proliferate in separate pieces like an earthworm. It is difficult to gauge whether they have bestowed as much practical benefit on society as those little-valued French philosophers who adhered to whatever was closest at hand and for starters used their scalpels to excise the central nerve of clerical superstition, the boa constrictor that has done nothing but sidle around feebly ever since. In fact, through his teachings the philosopher should also have an effect on *life*. The greatest of all wise men was just as practical as he was generally intelligible, and those who elucidate matters in this way rank higher in history than do the marvelous, pyrotechnical specialists mentioned above.

The true and only object of philosophy is the investigation of truth, or in any case, such truth as *can be investigated*, since only this can bear fruit. To seek the inscrutable comes to little more than threshing straw. In my opinion, the most viable means of arriving at a discoverable truth is the same as it was in Aristotle's time, through experiment and knowledge. We may at some point be able to say that, the law being what it is, experience *must* confirm our conclusions. But it was only by way of experiment that such a law was discovered in the first place. Therefore, because he already *knew* the immutable law, Lalande could specify the relationships of certain stars to one another a priori, even though careful observation seemed to establish the opposite. On the other hand, without Newton's falling apple, that is to say, without sustained observation of natural phenomena and the truths thus *discovered*, the secrets of the heavens would still be a book with seven seals.

If philosophy is now to investigate truths, then it must do so for the sake of human beings. Its main charge will always be the history of mankind, in the broadest sense, and whatever benefits may result from this study. Only thus will we succeed in moving from what happened and what is to a recognition of causes, of why things are one way and not another; and by working backward from fact to fact, we may approach the fundamental laws governing our existence, and hence discover the basis for what follows. Even though the cause of all existence must remain inscrutable, it would be sufficient to establish clearly and distinctly what our powers originally were, what they have since become, and what direction we should pursue in their further development. Here we see that continued progress depends on freedom, on the unrestricted exchange of ideas. In this regard, the art of printing was the most providential of inventions. It was a vibrant birth, for the human spirit was already sufficiently mature to use this immeasurable resource for great purposes. And since then it has made possible the colossal and ultimately irresistible power of public opinion. By this I do not mean the delusions of the many, but the opinions of the best, which, with the ability to reach everyone, must finally overcome those delusions.

Without printing there would have been no Luther. And has Christianity made any headway since then? Did it moderate its practices, make people more compassionate, more ethical, more charitable during the Thirty Years' War, or during the reign of the English Queen Mary, when pregnant women were burned at the stake, their babies delivered into the flames, or—*horribile dictu!*—during the Inquisition? I see few signs of it. Freedom of the press was the great step that eventually brought us closer to universal enlightenment. It has given momentum to events, so that we now

experience more in a single decade than our ancestors did in a century. The accumulation of knowledge that will inevitably be disseminated in this way is the one thing
that will prove truly beneficial to mankind. In every period there have been extraordinary perhaps inimitable individuals, whose influence nonetheless all but vanished,
whose brilliance, like that of a meteor, radiated momentarily only to fade quickly
away. Consider the supreme example of Christ, who, as our Gibbon has so clearly
shown, appeared under the most favorable circumstances. How many millions have
called themselves after him, and how many of these are truly Christians? He, the
most liberal and open-minded of men, has served for almost two thousand years as a
shield against despotism, persecution, and lies, and has lent his exalted name to a new
form of heathenism.

Therefore, I say, only the *whole accumulation of knowledge*, the intelligence that
pervades an entire nation, is capable of founding lasting and robust institutions for
the betterment of the individual and society. This is what the world now strives to
accomplish; politics in its highest form is the religion of our day. This is what provokes our enthusiasm, and if there are to be further crusades, they will be driven by
this alone. Today the idea of representational government is more electrifying than
that of a reigning church, and even the warrior's fame begins to pale when set against
the profile of the great citizen.

Prove all things; hold fast to that which is good.[13]
But now, enough chatter. In the mountains I would not have bored you with so much of
this, but in the gloomy walls of a city, I feel like Faust in his study. Meanwhile a little fiery air is
already prepared. I will spread out my cloak and starting tomorrow, once again a fresh wind will
fill my sails. But everywhere, in the dungeon or under the blue sky, I am and remain eternally,[14]

Your faithful, ardently devoted Lou

P.S. This is my last letter from Dublin. I have had my carriage packed and sent on to S——, and
discharged my Englishmen. Now, with one honest Irish servant, I will travel romantically under
my nom de guerre to Paris by way of Bath. I will neither make too much haste nor delay myself
unduly. The most difficult thing, parting from my friends, is already done, and nothing more
detains me.

Holyhead, December 15th, 1828

PRECIOUS AND CONSTANT ONE!

You have often called me childish, and there are no words of praise I value more highly. Yes, thank heaven, dear Julie, we will both remain children as long as we breathe, even if covered with a hundred wrinkles. But children like to play, are occasionally inconsistent, and always chase after pleasure. That is essential. So judge me as such, and do not expect more of me or reproach me for my purposeless wandering. Good heavens! Didn't Parry, who *had* an objective, sail to the North Pole three times *in vain*? Didn't Napoleon pile up victory on victory for twenty years, only to end up withering away on Saint Helena because he had achieved his goal so successfully? And what is our purpose, anyway? No one can actually specify it. The ostensible purpose is only part of the goal, often no more than the means of attaining it; and even our real objective is frequently modified in the pursuit. So it was with me. But everyone has *secondary* objectives as well, which often supplant the primary goal because they are more palatable. So it was with me again. In the end I am content—and what more can one ask for?

Neptune must be especially fond of me, for every time he has me in his power, he keeps me there as long as he can. The wind was directly against us and blowing with the fiercest possible vehemence. My good fortune seems to abandon me on the water and in high mountains, for I have almost never had favorable breezes on the sea, and the sky is very, very rarely clear once I have climbed a few thousand feet closer to it.

I left Dublin in a post chaise yesterday evening, around eleven on a beautiful moonlit night. The air was balmy and as mild as in summer. I thought back a bit over the preceding two years and let everything pass in review.[1] I was not displeased with the results. I have, it is true, made a mistake here and there, but I find that in general, I have become steadier and clearer. I have learned some things, not impaired my physical machine in the process, and finally pasted a number of interesting memory pictures into the atlas of my life. Compared to my decrepit state of mind when I left you, my good spirits and love of life are ten times stronger. And as these are more valuable than external things, I found, in the wake of my reflections, that I was looking forward to the unknown future with great cheer. I also felt content in the present, which at that moment was dominated by the excessive pace set by the half-drunk mail coach driver. In the pale moonlight we rushed *hop, hop, hop, dahin im sausenden Gallop* along a high embankment by the sea,[2] finally arriving at an elegant inn at Howth, where I spent the night. An enormous Newfoundland kept me company at tea and also breakfasted with me the next morning. Completely white with a black muzzle, this handsome animal looked very much like a polar bear that, temporarily distracted as in *The Bear and the Pascha*,[3] had mistakenly donned the head of a brown cousin. I wanted to buy him, but the innkeeper was not at all interested in selling.

During the night, I had a strange dream. I found myself enmeshed in political affairs, and as a result I was being stalked and my life threatened in every way. The first time that I barely escaped death was on a great hunting party in the middle of an incredibly thick forest, where I was attacked by four or five disguised huntsmen who fired their rifles at me, but missed. Next someone tried to poison me. I had already swallowed a green powder (presented to me as medicine), when the Duke of Wellington entered and said calmly that I should not worry, for himself had been given the same substance; here was the antidote. I swallowed the antidote, and it began to take effect. (Here the dream was probably anticipating my next day's condition on the sea). Soon I felt better than ever, and moreover all my other affairs went according to plan. But when I had departed and was nearing my goal, robbers attacked, pulled me out of my carriage, and dragged me through brambles and ruins to a narrow, towering wall. As we hurried along its top, the wall, crumbling from age, seemed to sway beneath our feet. Our march appeared endless, and I was tormented not only by fear but also, like the robbers, by a gnawing hunger. They finally yelled at me in fury, insisting that I get them something to eat or else they would slaughter me themselves. At that anxious moment, I thought I heard a soft voice calling to me, "show them the door over there." I looked up and saw a high, monastic building, overgrown with ivy, with dark fir trees huddled against it; there were no windows or doors except for a closed porte cochere of bronze so tall that a house could pass under it. Pulling myself together quickly, I called out to the robbers, "You fools, why are you demanding food from me, when a huge storeroom is right in front of you!"

"Where?" the captain bellowed.

"Open this door," I responded scornfully. As if the entire band had just caught sight of it, they all now raced toward it, the captain in the lead. But before he got there, the immense portal opened slowly and silently by itself to reveal a strange sight. We were looking into a deep, seemingly endless hall; the roof arched over us in the dizzying heights. Everything was magnificently decorated with brilliant gold and finely crafted bas-reliefs and paintings, all of which seemed full of movement and life. But stretched out along the wall on either side was an interminable row of grim-looking wooden figures dressed in gold and steel and mounted on stuffed horses. Their faces had been crudely painted, and their swords and lances were drawn. In the center was an enormous black steed bearing a rider who, encased in black iron from tip to toe, was three times as large and formidable as the others. Suddenly inspired I call out, "Ha, Rüdiger! It's you! Most venerable ancestor, save me!"

In the high vaults, the words reverberated a hundred times like thunder, and both the wooden figures and their stuffed horses seemed to roll their eyes in a ghastly way. Everyone shuddered. Then suddenly the giant flung his terrible battle sword like a lightning bolt into the air; his steed had already closed in on us in terrifying bounds, when the resounding chimes of a bell rang out, and the giant stood once again rock-like and still before us. We, however, overcome with horror, all fled at once, as quickly as our legs could carry us. To my shame, I must confess I did not stay behind. I had gotten as far as some old walls, but fear turned my bones to lead. Then I saw a side door and was just trying to get through it when a shrill voice screamed in my ear, "Half past seven!" I was sinking to the ground in dread, but a strong hand seized me, and dazed, I opened my eyes. My Irish servant stood before me and announced that if I did not get up soon, the steamboat would sail without me. You see, Julie, when I embark on a journey, these little adventures continue to arise, even if only in my sleep.

On the boat, I found people still occupied with loading a handsome carriage, packed with even more superfluous comforts than those I carry along when I travel. The *valet de chambre* and servants were diligently engaged with all this, while a small man of about twenty, with a head of carefully crimped blond curls, sauntered back and forth on the deck, dressed elegantly in black. He displayed all the indolence of an English fashionable and took no notice of his belongings or the labors of his people. As I later learned, he had just come into an inheritance in Ireland of twenty thousand pounds a year, and was beginning to spread it around. He was now rushing off to Naples and seemed in such good spirits that even seasickness was unlikely to disturb his mood. While we were talking, I silently reflected on the two of us and thought, *voilà le commencement et la fin!*[4] One the world sends forth, saying to him, *savor me*. The other the world sends home, saying to him, *digest me*. May heaven preserve my good stomach for this! Yet these melancholic views were only a result of my qualms due to the steam boiler and seasickness, and on further reflection I rejoiced at the sight of this young man—so full of hope—as if I were the one relishing the illusions of youth.

I think that I will continue by mail coach this evening, and I hope that a good dinner will put an end to this *methodus per nauseam* that still afflicts me in the aftermath of the transit.[5]

Shrewsbury, December 16th, evening

I DID NOT feel quite as recovered as I had expected. The dinner was by no means good; in fact, it was really foul, and the consequences of the sea gave me a migraine that was still with me when I departed at midnight. Luckily there were just two of us in the comfortable, four-seated coach, so that each of us could occupy one whole side. I thus slept reasonably well, and the air in combination with the gentle motion had such a beneficial effect that, when I awoke at seven o'clock, my headache was mostly gone. The Holyhead Mail must cover ten miles in an hour, including all stops, which means that it moves mostly at a gallop, not a walk.* We were already here in time for breakfast, and I stayed behind to see the city. First I visited the castle, an ancient building made of red sandstone blocks, but somewhat modernized inside. The view from the old keep, where there is now a little summer cottage, is very lovely, extending over the river and across a verdant, fertile landscape. Nearby is the city prison, where I saw the poor devils working the treadmill. They were all dressed in yellow cloth, similar to Saxon mail-coach drivers, whose sluggish indifference could well benefit from a similar activity. From this newfangled reform school, I wandered back eight hundred years to the remains of the old abbey, of which nothing but the beautiful church survives. Although it is still in use, its stained-glass windows were destroyed—as everywhere in England—by Cromwell's mad fanatics. Here they have been extraordinarily well restored with newly painted glass. The founder of this abbey, Roger Montgomery, who was 1st Earl of Shrewsbury and one of William the Conqueror's commanders, is buried in the church under a handsome monument. Nearby lies a Templar, just like the one in Worcester except not painted in color. Both lie stretched out on the stone with crossed

---

* Our express coaches will only begin to equal the English ones if the post is released from official controls and a similar competition established to attract travelers. Neither is to be expected.

109

High Street, Shrewsbury.

legs, a position that seems to have been peculiar to the tombs of Templars. In order to atone for his sins, the Earl of Shrewsbury not only built and endowed the abbey but also died there as a monk. Thus did suppleness of mind discover a spiritual bridle and bit to harness the raw power of the knights.

The town is remarkable for the large number of old private residences, all of the strangest design and construction (Figure 109). I stopped in the street many times in order to sketch a few of them on my writing tablet, which inevitably drew a crowd of people who watched me in amazement and not infrequently interrupted me. The English should not be so surprised then, if the same thing happens to them in Turkey or Egypt.

Hereford, December 17th, 1828

IT IS UNDENIABLE that, after a period of deprivation, there is great pleasure in rediscovering English comfort. Change is the very soul of life and gives each thing in its turn renewed value. The good inns, the substantial breakfasts and dinners, the spacious and carefully warmed beds, the polite and deft waiters—all these I found very pleasant after the deprivations of Ireland. And they quickly reconciled me to the higher prices. I left Shrewsbury at ten in the morning, once again with the mail coach, and reached Hereford at eight in the evening. Since it was not cold, I sat outside, ceding my place in the coach to my servant. Two or three inconsequential men and a good-looking, bright lad of eleven made up my society on the upper deck, where there was intense discussion of politics. The boy was the son of a well-to-do landowner and was traveling alone, returning home for Christmas from his school about a hundred miles away. This practice of instilling self-reliance in such young children certainly increases their independence and self-assurance later in life, something the English most definitely can boast of beyond other nationalities, particularly the Germans. The restless elation and sprightliness of the boy as he got closer and closer to his father's house both touched and delighted me. There was something so natural and heartfelt in it that I was spontaneously reminded of my own childhood years—that invaluable and at the time undervalued happiness, which we only appreciate in hindsight!

Monmouth, December 18th, 1828

GOOD JULIE, TODAY I relived one of those romantic days I have missed for so long, those days full of a diversity of images that delight us like the fairy tales of our youthful years. I owe this to the famous scenery on the River Wye, which even in winter can claim to be among the most beautiful spots in England. Very early, before leaving Hereford, I visited the cathedral and found that, apart from its handsome porch, if offers little worth seeing. Because of this, I nearly missed the mail, which in England waits for nobody and was already moving at a full trot, so I literally caught it in flight. I only made use of the coach for the thirteen miles to Ross, which we covered with extraordinary speed, although *with four blind horses.* There I hired a boat, sent it five miles ahead to the ancient Goodrich Castle, and made my own way on foot. The path led me first to a churchyard situated at a considerable height, which had a splendid view; then through a luxuriant region reminiscent of Lake Lugano; and finally on toward the ruin. There I found the small boat, two oarsmen, and my Irishman already waiting at the river. The current was quite strong at that spot, but I had to get across in order to reach the hill crowned by the old fortress (Figure 110).

Climbing up the slippery turf was fairly arduous, and as I stepped through the high gateway, a gust of wind took the cap from my head, as if the ghost of the hill wanted to instill me with more respect for the shades of the long-deceased knights. But there was no way to increase the awe I felt as I wandered through the dark corridors and spacious courtyards, and climbed up the decaying stairways. In summer and autumn the River Wye is never free of travelers, but in winter the locals are not equipped for visitors, since it is unlikely that any sensible Englishman would ever undertake the trip then, so the whole day long there was not a guide to be found anywhere, nor any kind of assistance for tourists. Also missing was the ladder required to reach the truncated steps to the main tower; it had already been moved to its winter quarters. With the help of the boatmen and my servant, however, I set up a Jacob's ladder and swung myself up from their backs. From the ramparts you look over an immense stretch of countryside, and the robber knights—if there were any here—would have been able to see travelers coming from miles away. After I had dutifully crawled over the whole place and climbed down the hill on the other side, I had a comfortable breakfast in the boat as it carried us briskly down the river. The weather was beautiful and the sun shining brightly—a rare occurrence at this time of year—and the air was as warm as on a pleasant April day at home. The trees were bare of leaves, admittedly,

110

*Goodrich Castle
on the Wye.*

but since their branches were unusually thick and interspersed with many evergreens, and the grass shined far greener and more vividly than in summer, the seasonal loss to the landscape was much less than one might expect. The soil is exceptionally fertile, and the soft hills are covered from top to bottom with vegetation. There are few fields, mostly meadows between the thickets, and at every moment another tower, village, or castle appears in prospects constantly varied by the river's repeated bends. For a while we floated past the borders of three counties: Monmouth on the right, Hereford on the left, and Gloucester in front of us. At a picturesque spot across from an ironworks, its flames visible even by daylight, there is a country estate, half in the style of our times, half of a dusky antiquity. This is the cradle of Henry V, who spent his childhood here under the care of the Countess of Salisbury.[6] Below, deeper in the valley, the simple church, where he was baptized and his nurse lies buried, is still standing. Agincourt and Falstaff, the Middle Ages and Shakespeare, came to life in my imagination, until *nature herself, even older and greater than they*, soon overwhelmed everything else. For now our small boat was gliding into a rocky area, where the frothing river and its bold environs took on a most imposing character. The precipitous sandstone cliffs, weather-beaten and crumbling, are of gigantic proportions, jutting up out of oak forests and festooned with hundreds of ivy vines. The storms of millennia have eroded the soft stone and modeled it into fantastic shapes that look like works of art made by human hands. Castles and towers, amphitheaters and walls, battlements and obelisks mock the wanderer, who imagines himself transported into a ruined city of demons. Often during storms, some of these formations tear loose and plummet down with a devastating roar, ricocheting from rock to rock before plunging into the river's unfathomable depths. I was shown the remnant of one of these boulders, along with the monument to a poor Portuguese man who was buried by its fall.

This bizarre rock formation stretches for almost eight miles, up to one hour from Monmouth, where it terminates in an isolated colossus known as the Druid's Head. Seen from a certain perspective, it shows the ancient profile of a handsome old man seemingly sunk in a deep sleep. Just as we moved past, the moon climbed higher and gave him a haunting expression. For how long, I wondered, have these eyes been closed in sleep; how often has the moon shone on his pale face; and what might his eyes, if they were ever open, have seen in those faraway times? At that moment I had no doubt, for faith had overtaken me and made me blessed. Saint Augustine was right when he said, "I *believe* it, because it is *childish* and *impossible!*"[7] Yes, that is how it was; the dead stone had taken on more life than all the living figures around me.

For a short while, the passage led narrowly between banks thickly wooded from the water to their summits. Then a large and bare rocky plateau became visible; it is called King Arthur's Plain, because the fabled hero is supposed to have set up an encampment here.[8] A half-hour later we arrived in Monmouth, a small, ancient town where Henry V was born. His tall statue is displayed on the roof of the town hall;[9] but all that remains of the castle where he first glimpsed the light of day is a single, ornate Gothic window and a courtyard in which turkeys, geese, and ducks are being fattened, a birthplace more suited to Falstaff.

I went into a bookshop to purchase a written guide, and there I unexpectedly made the acquaintance of a very nice family. It consisted of the old bookseller, his wife, and two pretty daughters, the most innocent country girls I have ever met. I entered as they were having their evening tea, and the father, a good-natured but—for an Englishman—unusually garrulous chatterbox, took me captive and presented me with the oddest set of questions about the Continent and politics. The daughters, no doubt out of experience, felt sorry for me and tried to dissuade him, but I let him have his way and with good grace surrendered myself for a half hour, thereby earning the entire family's affection to such a degree that they all invited me most insistently to stay on for a few days in this beautiful area and lodge with them. When I finally left, they would accept no payment for the book, and I was forced *bon gré mal gré* to keep it as a gift. Such simple conquests make me happy, because they can come only from the heart.

Chepstow, December 19th, 1828

I HAD GOTTEN dressed early and was about to depart after a quick breakfast when I noticed, not without an unpleasant sense of surprise, that I was missing my purse and notebook, both of which I always carry with me. I clearly remembered having set them down yesterday evening in the coffee room, where I was completely alone while I ate and wrote to you. I used some passages from my notebook for the letter, and I used the purse to pay the boatmen. Doubtless I had left both objects lying there, and the waiter had helped himself to them. I sent for him at once, recapitulated the above facts, and asked—while looking at him very sharply—if he really had not found anything. The man turned pale and embarrassed, and stammered that he had seen nothing but a single sheet of paper with writing on it, which, he thought, was still lying under the table. I looked, and it was still there as he described. All this seemed more and more suspicious to me, so I approached the host, an exceptionally tall and extremely repugnant-looking fellow, and made some complaints that also contained a few threats. But he answered curtly that he knew his people; in thirty years there had not been a single theft at his inn; and thus my claim struck him as highly remarkable. He would, of course, if I so wished, send for a magistrate to take the sworn testimony of his entire staff and search through the whole establishment. "But then," he added with a sneer, "do not forget that all of *your* belongings, too, will be examined down to the smallest trifle, and if nothing is found on any of us, you will have to bear the costs and pay me compensation." *Qu'allais-je faire dans cette galère*, I thought, and realized that the best thing to do would be to get over the loss of the ten pounds and go away.[10] I therefore took some fresh bills from my valise, paid the quite reasonable bill, and because of the slight nick above the eye of His Majesty George IV, thought I recognized one of my own sovereigns among those I received in change. Convinced that the innkeeper and waiter were in cahoots, I boarded the mail coach, shook the dust off my feet, and felt like a man who had just escaped from a den of thieves.

But in order to render a service to future travelers, I had the coach stop as soon as we had turned the corner and went on foot to the bookseller's to tell of my misfortune. Everyone was astonished and regretful, and the daughters soon began whispering with their mother, made signs to each other, and then took their father aside. After a brief deliberation, the youngest came up to me bashfully and blushing to ask whether the loss had caused me a "temporary embarrassment," and whether I would accept the loan of five pounds, which I could repay when I returned? While saying this, she tried to put the note in my hand. This kindness touched me profoundly. There was something so tender and selfless about it that I might well have felt less gratitude for a far greater gesture made under other circumstances. You can imagine how cordially I thanked them. Certainly, I said, if I had the slightest need of it, I would not be too proud to accept such a well-intentioned loan; but since this was by no means the case, I would call upon their generosity in a different way and request permission to take a kiss from each of the two pretty girls of Monmouth back to the Continent with me. This happened amid a lot of laughter and good-natured surrender, after which I returned to my carriage laden with this extra cargo.

Since I traveled by water yesterday, today I choose to go by land, taking the road that follows the river to Chepstow. The countryside is still of the same type: fertile, with dark woods and green meadows, but here frequently enlivened by smelting furnaces, tinworks, and ironworks, their flickering flames of yellow, red, blue, and greenish hues flaring up out of towering chimneys. These occasionally assume the shape of huge, glowing flowers whenever the fire and smoke, weighed down by the atmosphere, linger for a while in a thick, immobile mass. I got down from the coach in order to visit one of the tinworks. It was not driven in the usual way by a steam engine, but by an enormous waterwheel the size of a house, which in turn set three or four smaller wheels in motion. The big one had the power of eighty horses, and the raging speed with which it turned, the horrifying noise it emitted at the moment it started moving, the furnaces around it showering sparks, and amid them the glowing iron and black, half-naked figures wildly brandishing hammers and clubs and tossing around the red-hot pieces of hissing metal—it was the very image of Vulcan's forge.

From an original Drawing by E. Dayes
Engraved by F. Jukes

To John Meyrick Esq.r of Peterborough House Fulham.
THIS VIEW of TINTERN ABBEY on the RIVER WYE

Plate 8th

The process starts with forged iron bars or rods one-half inch thick and eight feet long being held under a mechanical blade, which cuts them into foot lengths with such graceful ease that they appear as soft as butter. The severed piece is immediately thrown to another worker, who thrusts it into a blazing fire, where it begins glowing within just a few minutes. He takes it back out with a pair of tongs and throws it one station farther, onto the sandy ground. Here a third man picks it up and pushes it under a roller, which transforms it, after several quick passes, into a sheet four times as large and correspondingly thinner. This sheet now follows the same path back into the fire again, where it is once again rolled out, and so forth, until it is as thin as paper. Only now are the sheets cut into their intended shapes and then beaten and cleaned, which again involves fire as well as other ingredients. Next they go on to a second building, where they are washed in vitriol and sand, and afterward dipped into tin that is kept liquefied with fat. Finally women clean them with bran and polish them so beautifully that you can see your reflection. Such a factory is like a world in miniature. You see the high and low side by side;

111

Tintern Abbey.

LETTER 44

625

the difficult passage from one level to the next; and how, eventually, what is coarse becomes the most refined.

Halfway along the route the cheerful landscape changed, as it did yesterday, into severer rocks. And there, in the center of a deep basin surrounded by variously shaped hills, we could see the famous ruins of Tintern Abbey standing directly above the silvery stream (Figure 111). You can hardly imagine a more advantageous location or conceive of a large monastery with more imposing ancient remains; indeed the entrance itself is like a striking stage set. Most of the large church has survived; it is missing only a few columns and the roof. The buildings have been maintained to exactly the degree that old ruins should be—namely, the debris that would disturb a picturesque and congenial visit has been cleared away, yet nothing has been restored, nor has any of the care taken been allowed to become obvious. A lovely, smooth carpet of grass covers the ground, and large-leaved plants grow rampantly over the stone. Fallen ornaments have been partly used to create a kind of artistic disorder, and a perfect double allée of thick ivy stems (I cannot call it anything else) climbs up the columns and forms a marvelous, lofty canopy of foliage (Figure 112). To make the ruin more secure, a new entry gate with iron fittings has been crafted in the style of the original, and when it is suddenly opened in front of you, the most astonishing impression results. Unexpectedly you find yourself standing in that allée of ivy-clad columns, and you see them recede in perspective until they come together three hundred feet ahead of you, terminating in a magnificent window eighty feet high and thirty feet wide; and behind the window's entwined stone traceries, you catch sight of a thickly wooded peak, with steep, rocky crags emerging here and there. High up the wind wafts through the garlands of ivy, and clouds scud across the deep blue sky. When you get to the middle of the church, where you perceive its crossing, you find that the transept windows—almost as large as the rose window— offer similarly beautiful and yet very different views, all of it in keeping with the wild sublimity that so befits the abbey. The church is surrounded by a luxuriant orchard, which must be captivating in the spring when the old, dark walls rise up out of the sea of fragrant blossoms. I heard that a Vandal leader, a lord lieutenant of the county, had the pious intention of restoring the church, but luckily heaven embraced him before he was able to accomplish the task!

From Tintern Abbey, the road climbs steadily until high above the river, without ever quite losing sight of the water. After about three or four miles, at Moss Cottage, the Duke of Beaufort's villa, the landscape is at its most beautiful.[11] Here charming paths have been laid out through wild woods and evergreen thickets, leading at times along the edge of deep walls of rock or then through dark, natural caverns before emerging onto open plateaus. The paths wind through myriad turns to the summit of the mountain called Wyndcliff, where you can enjoy one of the grandest and most sublime vistas in England.

The rather precipitous slope below you drops about eight hundred feet, at some places down to isolated, projecting rocks; at others to a steep, green, brush-covered expanse. The Wye runs along the foot of the slope for several miles into the distance, and your eye can follow the river's course from where it gushes forth on the left out of a wooded mountain gorge, draws nearer in a wide arc, then flows around a green, garden-like peninsula, which forms a hill decked with *bosquets*; to the right the frothy course runs past an enormous wall of rock that nearly reaches your standpoint; and finally, near the ruins of Chepstow Castle, which stretch out like a dilapidated city, the river empties into the Bristol Channel. There everything fades into the distant horizon of the misty ocean.

112

Tintern Abbey.

THE CASTLE AND NEW BRIDGE OF CHEPSTOW.

Beyond the river, a sharp crest of hills stretches across nearly all the country you overlook. It is thickly covered with woods, and out of this mass of trees, a continuous wall of rock emerges, picturesquely festooned with ivy. Beyond the ridge, you see water again—the Severn, five miles wide, teeming with a hundred white sails; and on its opposing banks, you can make out two more rows of blue hills arrayed one above the other and abounding in lush growth and rich farmland. This configuration presents an ideal vista, and I know of none more beautiful. Infinite in its detail and boundless in dimension, the main features of this landscape are so prominent and overwhelming that the sensation of emptiness and disorientation generally provoked by such an extensive panorama is totally absent. Piercefield Park, which occupies the ridge of hills and rock from Wyndcliff to Chepstow, is undoubtedly one of the most splendid in England, at least as far as its situation goes. It possesses all that nature can offer: lofty woods, magnificent rocks, the most fertile soil, a mild climate favorable to every type of vegetation, a rapidly flowing river, the nearby sea, solitude, and, from the midst of its tranquility, a view over the varied landscape I have described. Moreover, all this is enhanced by the sight of ruins so sublime that only a painter's brush could invent them: the remains of Chepstow Castle, suspended above the river and covering more than six acres of land (Figure 113). The side facing the town borders the park, although it does not belong to it.

We have Cromwell to thank for almost all the ruined castles in England, just as we have Henry VIII to thank for the derelict churches and monasteries. The former were ravaged by fire and sword, whereas the latter were simply *dissolved* and abandoned to the gnawing tooth of time and human self-interest. Both forces were successful to the same degree, and thus each of the two great men created an effect that was unintended but aptly mirrors the reputation each left behind: that is to say, a picturesque one. I roamed through the park on foot and had the carriage follow by road, not reaching the ruin until it was nearly twilight. This only increased the magnificent impression it made on me. The castle, still well preserved in parts, has four extensive courtyards as well as a chapel. The interior is adorned with tall nut trees and yews, orchards, and beautiful lawns; wild vines and all kinds of creepers cover the walls. A woman lives with her family in the most intact section of the fortress. She pays the owner, the Duke of Beaufort, an annual fee for permission to show the ruins to strangers, each of whom must pay a shilling for the tour. You see *qu'en Angleterre on fait flèche de tout bois*,[12] and an English nobleman with an income of sixty thousand pounds a year neither disdains a widow's pennies nor shies away from obliging strangers to make regular contributions. Alas, there are certainly a number of little German sovereigns who do things no differently.

Just as satisfied with my day as I was tired of the climbing, and soaked with the rain that had begun again during the last hour, I hurried back to the inn and into informal attire for supper. Then I felt something odd in the pocket of my dressing gown. Startled, I pulled it out and, shamefaced, saw my presumed-stolen purse and notebook! Only then did I recall having tucked both into this unaccustomed spot out of concern that I might later forget and leave them behind on the table. This at least should be a lesson to me never to condemn too quickly on the basis of appearances and the embarrassment of the accused; because for those with sensitive nerves and an active sense of honor, the mere thought that others might harbor such suspicions can easily arouse the same symptoms as the consciousness of guilt does in those who have sinned. It will reassure you of the goodness in my heart to know that I immediately dispatched a letter to my friend the bookseller to exculpate the innkeeper and the waiter, and as reparation I also enclosed two pounds for the latter, requesting that it be delivered to him along with my sincere apologies. Having done what I could to redress the wrong, my meal undeniably tasted better.

Your faithful Lou

Bristol, December 20th, 1828

GOOD JULIE!

I hope you are following me on the map, which will make my letters more comprehensible to you, even though it will not bring you here to enjoy the lovely views; but I am at least bringing them all back to you in faithful copies in my Memory Albums.

Early this morning I visited the magnificent Chepstow Castle once more, and this time my guide was a blooming young girl who provided a graceful contrast to the scorched towers, the horrific prison of the regicide Marten, and the murky dungeon, into which we descended along many steps. I then visited a church with an especially refined Old Saxon portal and a very beautifully worked baptismal font in the same style. Here poor Marten lies buried. He was one of Charles I's judges and was held captive in the castle for forty years,[1] without, it is said, ever entirely losing his good humor. After the first few years his confinement seems to have gotten more lenient, and as time went on he was housed in better and better circumstances, for Charles II was not cruel. At any rate, the girl showed me three rooms this morning, the lowest of which was certainly a ghastly hole, and in her role as cicerone she explained, "This is where Marten was put at first, when he was still wicked; when he later became more introspective, he was moved one floor higher; and finally, when he became *religious*, he got the room at the top with the beautiful view."

At two o'clock I left for Bristol in a very full stagecoach; despite the heavy rain, it was only with great effort that I got myself a seat on the box. We crossed the river on a handsome bridge, which also provides the best spot for viewing the castle. The ruins, rising directly above cliffs that descend perpendicularly to the Wye, are extraordinarily picturesque.[2] For a considerable time we had a view of Piercefield Park and its walls of rock on the other side of the river. I said to the stagecoach owner, who was also the coachman, that the proprietor of that lovely park must be an extremely happy man! "Not at all," he replied. "The poor devil is deeply in debt, has a large family, and would like very much to find a good buyer for Piercefield. Three months ago everything was properly arranged with a rich merchant from Liverpool, who had planned for the estate to go to his youngest son. But before the transaction was complete, the son secretly married an actress, for which his father disinherited him, and the sale was canceled." Truly this must have provoked some serious meditations on morality!

Meanwhile the weather was getting more and more atrocious and finally exploded into a huge tempest. Although we had the wind at our backs, the crossing of the Bristol Channel was nonetheless highly unpleasant. The four horses, along with all of the luggage and the passengers, were packed pell-mell into a boat so small and crowded you could hardly move. The position next to the horses was truly dangerous, since they sometimes shied at the sails, especially when these were shifted. During one such occasion, a gentleman fell directly beneath their hooves, as did the carton he was sitting on. Luckily the good-natured animals did not kick him, but only trod on him a little. The boat, driven sharply along by the gale, was listing acutely, and the waves sprayed ceaselessly, drenching us from head to toe. When we finally landed, the debarkation was just as arduous as it was filthy, and during it, to my intense displeasure, I lost part of my set of Lord Byron's works. I was told that there were often accidents on this crossing due to the frequent storms, the shallow waters, and the many rocks. Indeed, only six months ago, the mail ship foundered, and a number of people lost their lives. This time we were unable to reach the usual landing place and therefore disembarked on the shore, proceeding on foot along the beach of red- and white-striped marble until we arrived at an inn. Here we got into another stagecoach packed with twenty people and drove (not as quickly as with the mail) to Bristol. For today I saw nothing of this city's muchvaunted setting, except the bright gas streetlights and well-stocked, colorful shops.

Bath, December 21st, 1828, evening

WHEN I SEARCH my memory for what makes the Wye so beautiful and superior to so many other rivers, I find it is foremost the assertive delineation of its banks, which never flatten out into vague lines or exhibit a nondescript diverseness with no real character. Furthermore, the river is almost always bordered by forests, rocks, or meadows enlivened with buildings, and only seldom by fields or cultivated land (which, however useful, are not picturesque). The many radical bends create a constant shifting of the banks as well, and thus a hundred different beauties emerge from the same run of features, just as when we turn our voices in one direction and then another to call forth multiple echoes. By the way, this is the main reason that landscape gardeners prefer curved paths to straight ones. Painters had this idea; but always in search of their imaginary line of beauty, they took their brushes and made convoluted corkscrews out of it, not understanding that the purpose of such a path is to achieve a *varied view of the landscape.*

Since the landscape features along the Wye are almost always few and of large dimension, they constitute their own manner of beautiful *painting,* for paintings require a limiting boundary (Figure 114). Nature creates on a scale that we cannot judge in its total effect, so its *loftiest harmony* is necessarily lost to us. The ideal of art is to form just a part of this into a whole that we can comprehend. To my mind, this is the same principle that underlies landscape gardening. Yet nature herself often provides us a perfect model for this end—a landscape microcosm. It is rare to find such a concentrated sampling of these model landscapes within a short distance, but on this journey, every bend of the river presents a new artistic delight. Somewhere Pope sings about this region:

> Pleas'd Vaga echoes thro' her winding bounds,
> And rapid Severn hoarse applause resounds.[3]

The German language, for all its richness, is somewhat ungainly when it comes to translating, especially from English, because as a composite of so many languages, English is marked by a singular ease in expressing foreign thoughts.[4] To me the lines above seem almost untranslatable. As often as I have tried, the thought lost its grace, although perhaps my own awkwardness was at fault.

Drawn, Etched & Engraved by J.M.W. Turner Esqr R.A.

That two of the world's most beautiful ruins are on the River Wye is no small asset, and it has never been more clear to me than here that prophets are not honored in their own country.[5] Otherwise why would so many thousands of the English travel enormous distances so they can be overcome with enthusiasm about beauties much inferior to those on offer at home? And another question: why is it that ruins move the human spirit so much more than the most perfectly completed architectural monuments? It almost seems as if these works of man only achieved their state of perfection once nature had amended them. And yet it is good for us to finally intervene again, just when nature is about to erase *each and every* trace. A superb and *well-preserved* ruin is therefore the most beautiful of structures.[6]

I have already mentioned that the environs of Bristol have an excellent and deserved reputation, for they are unmatched in their richness, luxurious vegetation, and productivity, and few can surpass them in picturesque beauty. It is like the Promised Land. Everything you see here—and I must add in my capacity as *gourmand,* everything you taste—has attained perfection.

Bristol, a city of one hundred thousand residents, lies in a deep valley. Clifton climbs up the hill directly above it in a series of terraces, and seems to be simply another part of the same town.

114

*Junction of
Severn and Wye.*

It is easy to imagine why this location creates extraordinary effects. Three weathered Gothic churches tower above the confused turmoil of houses clustered in the old capital in the valley. Like proud vestiges of former hegemonies, both feudal and priestly (for these two hostile brothers went hand in hand), they seem conscious of their past greatness and unwilling to bow their venerable heads before the rampant growth of modernity. This is especially so with Radcliffe Church, a thoroughly wonderful structure, though unfortunately built of sandstone, which has suffered so much with the passage of time that all the decorations are eaten away. The organ was playing as I entered, and although I moved with all due reverence and decorum to a corner, where I could discreetly overlook the interior, the ungenerous Anglo-Protestant cult sought to deny me this. The preacher sent over an old woman to let me know that I had to *sit down*. Since it is not so easy to disturb the faithful in a Catholic church, even when you barge in thoughtlessly only to see the highlights and pay no attention to the ritual, I justifiably wondered why Anglo-Protestant piety considered itself so weak as to be blown aside with a single breath. Later someone explained the puzzle to me: I would have had to *pay* for my seat, and the *half shilling* was the actual pious motive. I had already seen enough, however, and left the mummery* without paying.

Back at the inn, I quickly had a post chaise hitched up, took my seat on the box (not as the highest place of honor, like the emperor of China, but as the best spot for a view), and began my excursions through the neighborhood. First I visited the city's warm baths; they are on the banks of the Severn at the threshold of a blissful valley that recalls the Plauenscher Grund near Dresden, except that the rocks are higher and the expanse of water much grander. Here we encountered the mayor in his official equipage, more magnificent than the transports of our kings on the Continent. It made a strange contrast with the desolate rocky landscape. Just as he passed us, the postilion was showing me a distant, crumbling tower called Cook's Folly, which had been the *ruin* of its former owner, also a mayor and a merchant, who now lives in a *ruin* of his own. He began building a Gothic castle in this most marvelous setting, but was never able to complete it, although in its present condition it may well be an even greater adornment to the region.

Ascending once again from the rocky valley, we came to a broad plateau that serves locally as a racecourse, and from here we passed through luxuriant countryside to Lord Clifford's park, with its beautiful entrée.[7] You drive along the side of a high hill for more than half an hour, through a winding allée of primeval oaks that have been planted far enough apart for them to stretch out completely in all directions without touching. Below their branches, the most spectacular panoramas materialize as if in a picture gallery, with discrete views of the fertile Bristol valley framed like paintings beneath nearly every tree. To the right, beyond the meadow on the ascending slope, you see the dark hem of a pleasure ground, where plantings of laurel, arbutus, and other evergreens border the road, until the house and flower garden suddenly emerge in decorative splendor at a bend!

At the end of the park are green foothills, and after a short drive along their narrow crest, you come to a beautiful view of the sea. Far below us, a small Russian flotilla lay at anchor. It had been en route to the Mediterranean when it barely escaped being shipwrecked here in last week's storms. According to the English, this was entirely the fault of the crew's ignorance. I later met

---

* The English Protestants call the Catholic ritual "popish mummery," but their own deserves exactly the same name.—*The Editor.*

OAK COTTAGE. DIAMOND COTTAGE JESSAMINE COTTAGE.

DOUBLE COTTAGE. ROSE COTTAGE. DIAL COTTAGE

CIRCULAR COTTAGE. SWEET BRIAR COTTAGE VINE COTTAGE

BLAISE HAMLET

the captain and five other officers, and to my amazement they spoke *no* foreign language, just Russian, which meant that our conversation had to be limited to signs. Otherwise they seemed to be courteous and civilized people.

Not far from the park is an interesting establishment called "the cottages."[8] Here the owner, Mr. Harford, has sought to realize the ideal of a small village. A beautiful green space in the midst of a wood is ringed by a meandering path with nine dwellings distributed along it, all of different design and diverse materials: one is sheathed in fieldstone, another in ashlar; this one in brick, that one in wood; one is roofed with thatch, another with shingles, the next with slate, and so on (Figure 115). Different trees have been planted around each cottage, and each is wreathed in various types of clematis, climbing roses, honeysuckles, and vines. The dwellings are separate, yet together form a whole. Each has its own garden, and they share a common well, which stands in the middle of the green and is shaded by several groups of old trees. The gardens, bordered by pretty little fences, create a fresh garland of vegetables and flowers around the village. But what crowns the entire settlement is that all the families here are poor, and the generous owner allows them to live in the houses free of charge. Misfortune could not be granted a more charming or suitable spot; this utter seclusion and tranquility is redolent of nothing but a peaceful obliviousness of the world.

In the distance, just opposite the wood, a modern Gothic castle rises imposingly above ancient oaks. I wanted to visit it and the surrounding park as well, but was not admitted. Whenever a main road skirts an English park, a section of the wall is replaced by a ha-ha or a see-through iron grid, allowing the curious passerby to cast a humble glance at the forbidden splendor. This exhausts the liberality of the English landowner, however. Given that today was also a Sunday, I gave up all hope of convincing the sullen porter to make an exception; on his brow I could clearly read the reverse of Dante's infernal inscription: *Voi che venite di entrare—lasciate ogni speranza!*[9]

My return route took me through the hillside town of Clifton, from which you see Bristol lying below, as if in an abyss. The scene was further embellished by the gaily colored attire worn by the many churchgoers of both sexes whom I encountered in every lane. In stark contrast was a large house painted entirely black with white windows, looking like an immense catafalque. I was told it was the city hospital, and a gentleman offered to show it to me. The interior was far more attractive than the exterior. Its spaciousness, friendly rooms, and perfect cleanliness must make it a very comforting abode for the sick. And nowhere did I sense the slightest bad odor, except for the pharmacy, which smelled of pills and rhubarb. The right side of the building was occupied by male, the left by female patients, with the lower level of each reserved for those needing a doctor, and the upper level for those needing a surgeon. The operating room was especially elegant and equipped with several water faucets along the walls with marble basins under them so that, on all sides, any blood could be washed away immediately. In the center was a mahogany cot with morocco leather cushions for those who were to go under the knife. In fact, everything had been made as inviting as possible for the discriminating.

However beneficial the skill of surgeons may be, it tends to make them a bit insensitive, and the one accompanying me was no exception. For instance, I noticed a woman in one room who had completely covered herself with a sheet, and I asked him quietly what was wrong with her. "Oh," he answered at full volume, "she has an aneurism; as soon as it bursts, she will die." From the twitches and soft moans issuing from under the sheet, I could easily imagine how grievously this remark affected her, and I regretted my question. When we came to the male patients, I saw a man lying as white as snow and as still as a marble statue, and since this time we were still quite far away, I inquired again into the nature of his illness.

"I don't know myself," he exclaimed, "but I'll ask him right now."

"For heaven's sake, no," I pleaded.

But he was already off, felt the motionless man's hand, and came back laughing: "That one is cured, for he is dead."

Toward evening I drove to Bath in one of the small carriages that only go back and forth between there and Bristol. I was alone and slept the entire way. When I awoke from my siesta, I saw in the moonlight an extensive, brightly illuminated palace on a bare hill, and in answer to a question, learned that this is the charitable endowment of a mere private citizen, intended for fifty poor widows who live here in easy circumstances—indeed, in luxury. Soon many more rows of lamps gleamed on the horizon, and in a few minutes we were rolling over the pavement of Bath.

Bath, December 22nd, 1828

SINCE THE DAY I wrote you with the important news that the sun was shining, I have not caught a glimpse of its benevolent face! Yet despite fog and rain, I spent the entire day walking around this wonderful town, which, originally built at the bottom of a deep and narrow basin, has gradually crept its way up to the higher verges. The magnificence of the palaces, gardens, streets, terraces, and half-moon squares called "crescents," all of which gleam at you from the slopes, is an impressive reflection of English prosperity. Although nature is also beautiful here, Bath has nonetheless been abandoned by *fashion*, which has given itself over with feverish rage to the nondescript, treeless, and ultraprosaic Bristol. This does not mean that Bath has been forsaken by spa visitors, and the forty thousand well-to-do residents alone make it lively; but the elegant world is no longer to be seen. The formerly renowned "King of Bath," the erstwhile "far-famed Nash," has lost even more of his halo than his peers have.[10] The man currently serving in Nash's position goes about modestly on foot, whereas Nash never went anywhere in public with fewer than six horses and a retinue of servants; and nowadays no Duchess of Queensbury will find herself dismissed from a ball for being inappropriately dressed.[11]

The Abbey Church made a great impression on me. It was splendidly illuminated the first time I saw it, which, frankly, very much increased the distinctive look of its interior. As I have often noted, all old churches in England are disfigured by modern monuments placed here and there, but in this case, they are so plentiful, and situated with such an original kind of symmetry that the sharp contrast generated by the simple yet exalted architecture produces an entirely new genre of picturesque effect. Imagine the interior of a magnificent, soaring Gothic church with the most perfect proportions, brightly lit, and divided down the middle by a red curtain. The visible half is an entirely empty space without chair, bench, or altar. The floor, however, is a mosaic of inscribed tombstones; and the walls, marked up to a certain height by a horizontal line, are covered with busts, statues, tablets, and monuments of every type, some of polished black or white marble, some of porphyry, granite, or other colorful stone, leaving no space between. The whole looks like a museum installed by an art lover, who has adorned the walls with all sorts of different objects. As far up as the line running along the top of these monuments, everything was bathed in the most brilliant light; while on high, beneath the tracery of the vaulting, the brightness gradually faded to a dim twilight. The sexton and I were alone in this space when an even greater light seemed to radiate from behind the red curtain, and the muted singing of the congregation could now be heard, issuing as if from an invisible sanctuary.

Many interesting people are buried here, one of them being Quin, the famous wit for whom Garrick commissioned a marble bust and supplied a poetic inscription. The figure on the monument to Waller is missing his nose, and people say that James II himself chopped it off with his sword in a fit of bigotry when he visited the church shortly after his coronation.[12]

December 23rd, 1828

HAVE YOU EVER heard of the eccentric fellow Beckford, a sort of Lord Byron in prose, who built the most magnificent palace in England, surrounded its park with a wall twelve feet high, and for the same number of years allowed absolutely no one access? Well, this man suddenly put that wonder house, Fonthill Abbey (Figures 116 and 117),[13] and all its contents up for auction* and

---

* The auction lasted for several months, and no one had ever seen a similar occasion that boasted such a rich collection of costly and tasteful rarities.—*The Editor.*

Drawn by J. Martin.   Engraved by T. Higham.

VIEW OF THE WEST, & NORTH FRONTS.

116

Fonthill Abbey.

moved to Bath, where he continues to live a solitary life. (The Abbey's tower, which had been constructed night after night by nothing but torchlight, collapsed after only a short while.)[14]

In the middle of a field not far from Bath, Beckford has built another odd tower, the roof being an exact copy in miniature of the temple in Athens known as the Lantern of Diogenes (the Monument of Lysicrates).[15] I drove there today and could easily imagine that the much-vaunted view must indeed be remarkable. I was not admitted, however, and was obliged to turn back with nothing but a picture of it in my imagination. The tower, very tall and still unfinished, stands like a ghost in the boundless solitude of a high plateau (Figure 118). The owner is said to have had assets of three million pounds once, and is still very rich. I was told that he is rarely seen nowadays, but when he occasionally goes out riding, it happens like this: An ancient, gray-haired butler precedes him, followed by two grooms with long stock whips. Beckford comes

next, surrounded by five or six dogs. The retinue closes with another two grooms carrying whips.
Whenever one of the dogs proves disobedient, the whole caravan stops, and punishment is
immediately meted out with a whip. This course of education continues throughout the entire
outing until they return home. Some time ago Mr. Beckford wrote an admittedly bizarre but
nonetheless ingenious novel in French, which was translated into English and received with great
acclaim. Here, too, a lofty tower plays a major role, and in the end the devil conquers all.[16]

     One more amusing anecdote about this Beckford. While he was living at Fonthill, a
neighbor of his, a lord, was so plagued by curiosity about the estate that one night he had a ladder brought to the high wall of the park and used it to climb inside. He was quickly discovered,
however, and brought before the owner, who, after hearing the interloper's name, welcomed him
very graciously and, contrary to all expectations, gave him a personal tour the following morning, subsequently wined and dined him, and only then withdrew, taking the most courteous
leave of his lordship. The latter, fully satisfied with the success of his venture, was ready to head
home, but found all the gates locked and no one there to open them. He therefore had to return to
the house and ask for assistance. When he did so, he was told that Mr. Beckford requested he exit
by the same way he had entered, and that the ladder would still be leaning at the same spot. The
lord's response was quite caustic, but it did no good; he was compelled to rediscover the site of

118

Beckford's Tower.

his illicit entry and climb the ladder again. Cursing the malicious misanthrope, he departed from the forbidden paradise, cured forever of his curiosity about the place.

Once Fonthill had been sold, Mr. Beckford lived for a while as a recluse in a suburb of London. Nearby was a nursery belonging to a market gardener famous for his cultivation of flowers. Mr. Beckford went for walks there every day and paid fifty guineas a week for permission to cut as many of the flowers as he wished during his promenades.

In the evening I went to the theater, which I found to be a truly attractive building. Inside it, alas, was a dreadful play. They were performing *Rienzi*, a wretched modern tragedy that, given the hyperbole and the awkwardness of the actors, aroused neither tears nor laughter but only distaste and ennui. I therefore soon left Melpomene's defiled temple and visited my friend the verger of the Abbey Church to ask permission to visit it by moonlight. The minute he opened it for me, I sent him off, and feeling the *frissons* of the night and the specter of death wafting around me, wandered for a long time like a solitary shadow beneath the compound columns and the tombs, lifting my thoughts to the more serious tragedy of life.

December 24th, 1828

THE WEATHER IS still so bad and has cast such a veil over every distant object that I cannot make any excursions and must restrict myself to the city. Given the number and variety of its prospects, however, it is well suited to provide the most interesting walks. I always start with my favorite place of tombs, the Abbey Church, and I end there, too—just like human life, which rises and finishes with death. The architect who built this magnificent edifice went far beyond what is customary, both in decoration and proportion. For instance, on the exterior, ascending the turrets beside the main portal all the way to the roof, are two Jacob's ladders with angels climbing up until the little figures disappear from view behind the pediments.[17] These industrious sky walkers are a great delight to look at and were conceived, in my opinion, in the spirit of a fanciful architecture that perfectly understood how to combine the most childish things with the most sublime, the most refined embellishments with the most overwhelming scale, as it strove to portray all of nature—the giants of the forest, flowers, rocks, precious gems (the stained-glass windows), and people and animals, of course—to evoke the sacred atmosphere of the *hereafter* with the greatest possible success. To me this has always been the truly romantic—that is, truly German—architectural style, one that emerged from our own distinct character. But we have become estranged from it, I think, for it belongs to more impassioned times. We can still admire and love its individual monuments, but anything we would create in that idiom would inevitably bear the mundane stamp of imitation. Nowadays steam engines and constitutions outdo all of the arts. To each era, its own.

Being fond of contrasts, I went this evening from one temple of profound significance to a second one that was in a certain way just as lavishly appointed and brightly illuminated: the city market, where all kinds of provisions are sold in covered galleries. Everything here is inviting and elegant, a resource for composing thousands of Flemish still lifes and a pleasurable sight for the epicurean, who can marvel here at *his* kind of natural beauties. Never have my astonished eyes seen more enormous chunks of beef, juicy red and quivering in golden fat; never plumper poultry, looking as if it were stuffed with eiderdown; never more glorious vegetables; more lusciously yellow butter; more succulent fruits; more appetizing fish! Everything was glorified by the glow of a hundred lamps and decked out with laurel and red-berried holly. Instead of a single German Christmas table, there were a *hundred* of them, with the saleswomen serving as excellent caricatures of gingerbread dolls, while we customers stood in nicely for the curious and marveling children. It would have been a challenge for the most brilliant soirée to have entertained me better. As I gazed at a solemn sheep holding a tallow candle in each foot to illuminate itself, or at a suspended chicken with a red wax taper planted in its backside, at a calf's head with a lantern between its teeth, next to a large gander lit up by two tall candles, or at an oxtail pierced by a gas tube that terminated pretentiously in a tuft of flame—I found myself making the most delicious comparisons with a similar gathering in my own country and found the resemblances to be even more striking than the portraits by the famous painters W—— and S——.[18]

Life is much less expensive here than in other English cities, especially in the so-called boarding houses, where two to three Guineas a week gets you excellent food and accommodations along with pleasant company. A carriage is unnecessary, since sedan chairs are the norm.

December 25th, 1828

EIGHT AND "FORTY" hours" have finally placated the heavens,[19] and today was what the English call "a glorious day," namely, one in which the sun occasionally steps out from behind the clouds. You will doubtless guess that I did not waste it. I climbed a nearby hill from where you can overlook the entire city and almost every house. The Abbey Church lies in the center like a nucleus, the streets ascend upward on all sides like rays of light, and far below at the deepest point, the silvery ribbon of the Avon winds its way along. From the hilltop I continued on a lovely walk to Prior Park, an extensive and once-splendid property. It was built by a prideful lord but is now owned by a humble Quaker, who has left the mansion empty and, true to his convictions, lives in the old stable.

Thus passed the morning. In the twilight, and then by moonlight, I undertook a second walk to the other side of the city and, in the stillness of the bright night, found the view even more superb. The sky shimmered in a pale green, and to the right were stacked masses of black, deeply serrated clouds. In contrast, the softly rounded profile of the mountains rising opposite drew a sharply delineated line against the clear heavens. The whole valley was filled with a single blue haze, through which I could see thousands of flickering gas lights, without being able to discern the houses themselves. It looked like a misty sea, reflecting the sparkle of countless stars and redoubling their intensity.

I concluded the day with a hot bath in the main bathing establishment and found the accommodations all very convenient, clean, and inexpensive; the service, too, was prompt and unobtrusive.

December 26th, 1828

I HAD A laughable mishap last night, thanks to my bad habit of reading in bed: my hair caught fire without my noticing, and I had to wrap my head in the blankets to put it out. The damage done was horrible, for one entire half of my hair has been destroyed, so that I had to have my entire head shaved almost bald. Luckily *my* strength at least does not reside in my hair.

A letter from you consoled me upon awakening. Your fable about the nightingale is splendid. If L—— had considered that and said to himself when he was twenty, "remain dead to the world until you are thirty-five," how brilliantly and happily (*nota bene*: according to the world's standards, that is) he could now enter it![20] I, too, in those years, and even now, have often laid blame on the world and others. But looked at in the light,* this is just as foolish as it is unjust. The world is and remains simply the world, and to blame it for all the evil that comes our way is to be like the child who wants to punish the fire because she burned her finger in it. Therefore L—— ought to regret nothing, because if he had vegetated for fifteen years like a groundhog, he would not have had the experience of that time, and consequently would not have known it. It is still the case *que tout est pour le mieux dans le meilleur des mondes.*[21]

In the profound hope that you, too, will always recognize this, I take my leave of you most tenderly for now, and am as always

Your faithful Lou

---

* It appears that the conflagration on my head has been unusually enlightening.

Salisbury, December 27th, 1828

BELOVED FRIEND,

I left Bath for Salisbury yesterday evening at seven o'clock, again with the mail, and found myself alone in the carriage with a widow, who, in the depths of mourning, had already acquired another lover! He joined us just outside the city gates as a blind passenger (no Amor, however, just a real John Bull).[1] When he was not talking about farming, he entertained us with those grisly tales of which the English are so fond, and that fill their newspaper columns every day. One of them concerned two young workers in a textile mill in Exeter who were joking and chasing each other around eight days ago, when they fell into a seething mass many degrees hotter than boiling water. Although they fell in headfirst, both managed to leap out in an instant but then ran frantically against the wall in front of them, where they died in convulsions. According to eyewitness testimony, the spectacle was dreadful beyond description, because the monstrous heat immediately consumed every bit of exposed flesh, and thus the men bolted from the vat with *living* death's heads on their shoulders. Maybe the narrator of these awful accounts was simply an accident maker,[2] for the horror stories never stopped, and he later claimed that the Holyhead Mail, the same one I had come with, had been washed away a few days later in a cloudburst, and the horses, driver, and one of the passengers drowned. If true, I am very happy to have chosen a more convenient time to make use of it.

After a few hours the amorous couple left me at a place where the widow owns an inn (probably the true reason for John Bull's affection), and I was all alone. Before long, however, a very pretty young woman, whom we caught up with in the darkness, asked if she could be taken along to Salisbury, since she would otherwise have to spend the night in the nearest village. I happily granted her permission and even promised the driver to assume the payment, whereupon I learned from the grateful creature that she was a hatmaker and had stayed a little too late at her parents' house for Christmas, but had counted on the mail coach passing through. Our conversation was more pleasant than my recent encounter with the seventy-year-old Puritan, so the time passed very quickly until we reached the city at midnight. There I was given a good supper, but only a smoky, cold bedroom for the night.

December 28th, 1828

I WAS AWAKENED very early by the dreary splashing of a gentle, steady rain, so I am still (it's already noon) sitting at breakfast reading. A good book is truly an electrostatic generator! It can make one's thoughts burst like fireworks, although like fireworks they are quickly extinguished;

and if you attempt to capture the sparks on the page with pen and ink, you discover that the pleasure is already over. As with a dream, it seems hardly worth the effort.

The book that magnetized me today is an ingenious amalgamation of the essentials of history, geography, and astronomy, admirably arranged for self-instruction. Such small encyclopedias are a great convenience of our time. Admittedly, real utility comes only with the study of details; nonetheless, walls must be erected before rooms can be decorated. In any case, *self*-instruction is the most successful approach; at least this has always been true for me. Yet it is certain that many people are incapable of truly learning anything. The study of history, for example, never makes its eternal truths clear to them and remains no more than a chronicle for their excellent memories to count off on their fingers. Every other field of knowledge is acquired in the same mechanical way and can be nothing but a reference work. Yet exactly this is typically considered to be fundamental knowledge. Indeed most professional examiners demand nothing more, and the farces that often result would give rise to delicious anecdotes, if anyone scrutinized them. I know of a young man who, in the diplomatic examination recently introduced at a certain *Residenz*, was posed the following question: "How much does a cubic foot of wood weigh?" Too bad he did not answer, "How much does a gold coin weigh?" or "How much brain does an imbecile have?" Another, from the military realm, was asked: "What was the most noteworthy of sieges?" Without faltering he responded (he was a foreigner, nationalized in Germany), "The siege of Jericho, because the walls were blown down by trumpets."

You could make conundrums of such things, and I almost believe that these boring pastimes originated with such interrogations.[3] Many clerics are again asking, "Do you believe in the Devil?" One cynical hoaxer, who was not all that afraid of being rebuffed, recently answered, "Samiel, hilf!"[4]

Evening

THE SKY CLEARED a little around three, and since I had been waiting only for that, I climbed into the gig I had reserved in advance and drove the aged hunter at a gallop to Stonehenge, the great Druidic temple, burial ground, or sacrificial altar. The countryside around Salisbury is very fertile, but devoid of trees and in no way picturesque. Even the prodigious Stonehenge stands on an open, elevated plain. The inscrutable monument rose before me under a cloudless sky, and just as the fiery ball of the sun touched the horizon, I approached the first Druidic stone, now tinted a rosy hue by the sinking rays. No wonder the popular mind attributes demonic power to this monument, for such a structure could hardly be replicated, even today, with all the tools of modern engineering. How, then, was it possible for a near-savage people to lift up such massive pieces of rock and transport them thirty miles (for there is no quarry any nearer). The whole thing forms an irregular circle of cromlechs (two erect stones with a third laid across the top), some still upright, some knocked over and sunk halfway back into the ground. Several of these stones are twenty-five feet in length and ten in breadth, genuine boulders, leading many people to assume that Stonehenge is nothing but a freak of nature. But this could never be credible to any eyewitness.

I was not the only onlooker. Every so often I caught sight of a solitary stranger, who, taking no notice of me, had been walking among the stones for a quarter hour, counting. He seemed to be regarding something with much impatience, and I therefore took the liberty of disturbing him

NORTH WEST VIEW OF

Salisbury Cathedral

with a question about his peculiar behavior. He immediately and politely responded that he had been told no one could count the stones correctly; that a different number came out every time; and that it was a trick of Satan, who had built this work and was toying with the curious. He said he had confirmed this story seven times in the last two hours, and would certainly go mad if he continued. I therefore advised him to desist and go home; it was getting dark, and Satan might subject him to a much worse prank. He fixed his rather sinister eyes on me, glanced around as if looking for someone, and then sarcastically exclaimed, "Good-bye, sir!" Then he set off like Schlemihl without his shadow (the sun had, admittedly, set), taking seven-league strides across the meadow until he suddenly disappeared below the hill. I myself now hurried to head back and was soon moving at a trot toward the high tower of Salisbury Cathedral, already fading in the twilight (Figure 119). I had scarcely covered a mile when the high, rickety gig imploded, and the driver and I were rudely thrown onto the turf. The old horse ran at an increased tempo toward the main road and the city, trailing the detached shafts of the cart and whinnying lustily. While we were struggling to pick ourselves up, we heard the clatter of horses' hooves behind us. It was the stranger, who galloped past on a handsome black steed and, smiling, called out to me, "The

Devil sends his best greetings, most honored Sir! Au revoir!" And with this he thundered away like a whirlwind. This taunt was truly galling. "Oh, you ill-timed jester," I yelled after him, "better to offer us help instead of your twaddle!" But only the echo of hoof beats answered us through the descending darkness. My driver ran after the fleeing nag for a mile, but soon returned empty-handed. There was nothing to be done and not even a hut along our path, so we had no choice but to cover the remaining six miles on foot. Never did a road seem more tedious to me, and the miraculous tales the driver told along the way about his horse—twenty years ago the leader of the Salisbury Hunters—offered little compensation.

December 29th, 1828

I MADE VERY good use of the daylight hours today, but in the evening, probably the painful aftermath of yesterday's nighttime escapade, I had a bad headache. Meanwhile, since it is only of a rheumatic nature, I am paying no attention. I have immersed my feet in mustard, salt, and hot water, and now begin.

Salisbury's widely celebrated cathedral prides itself on having the highest tower in Europe. At four hundred and ten feet, it is five feet taller than Strasbourg Cathedral, if I am not wrong, and is in any case far more beautiful.[5] Its exterior is distinguished in particular by a striking appearance of newness and neatness, as well as by an utter perfection in every detail. It owes this to two major repairs, the first under the supervision of Christopher Wren, the second of Wyatt.[6] The siting of this church is likewise singular, since it stands alone like a model on a beautifully tended square of short grass, with the bishop's palace and the cloisters on one side, and tall lindens on the other. The tower is topped by an obelisk-like spire with a cross, onto which, slightly ominously, a weather vane has been attached. This tasteless custom desecrates most Gothic churches in England. The tower is twenty-five inches out of plumb, although this is not noticeable except from inside, where you can see the soft curvature of the pillars that serve as its supports. The interior of this exalted temple is hugely impressive and has been further enhanced by Wyatt's genius (Figure 120). It was a brilliant idea to remove the strange old monuments from the walls and corners and place them on their own between the magnificent double allée of columns, nearly vertiginous in its slender, uninterrupted height. Nothing can look more beautiful than this long row of Gothic sarcophagi, on which the huge figures of knights and religious notables lie outstretched in their eternal sleep, while the stained-glass windows flood the stone, metal armor, and heraldic devices with all the glowing colors of the rainbow. Among the Templars and other knights buried here is Richard Langschwert,[7] who came to England with the Conqueror. Next to him is a giant figure in alabaster, Henry VII's sword-bearer, who fell at Bosworth Field and is depicted here with the two long swords, one in each hand, that he always carried into battle.

The cloisters are also very beautiful. Long, elaborate galleries lead in a rectangle around the chapter house, which is supported by a single column in the center, like the refectory at Malbork. The bas-reliefs that surround the room in broad bands seem to be of very fine workmanship, although they were largely destroyed during Cromwell's time. In the middle stands a half-rotten oak table from the thirteenth century, where, according to plausible reports, the workers building the church were paid each evening in the amount of one penny per day. It is very difficult to scale the tower. You have to climb up the second half on narrow ladders, like in the tower of St Stephen's in Vienna, finally arriving at a small door in the roof, thirty feet below the ball at the top. This is the door from which, once a week, a man ascends to oil the weather vane atop the spire. It seems inconceivable that the seventy-year-old, whose job it is, actually manages such a dangerous feat. As I said, the narrow peak of the spire extends another thirty feet beyond this opening, and there is nothing to climb on except for some iron brackets attached to the exterior. The old man has to go out *backward* through the small porthole, and then, because of a rain canopy, must bend his upper body a long way out and grope his way to the first bracket above him without at first being able to see it. When he has finally gotten hold of it, he swings himself up, now hanging with his feet suspended in the air, seeking to gain purchase on the rain canopy, from which he then clambers, bracket by bracket, to the top. Certainly it would be easy to introduce a more convenient and less dangerous procedure, but he has been performing this task since childhood and does not want it any other way. He has even undertaken this perilous course at night, and he is delighted that strangers—even sailors, accustomed to climbing everything—almost never dare follow him.

When we got back to the first gallery that leads around the tower, the guide showed me a hawk, hovering no more than twenty to thirty feet above us. "For many years now," he said, "a pair of hawks has nested in the tower and fed on the bishop's pigeons. I often see one or the other of them poised above the cross before swooping down suddenly on the birds below. Sometimes they drop a pigeon onto the roof of the church or gallery, and if so they never retrieve it, leaving their lost quarry to rot, which it would if I didn't carry it away."

The bishop's palace and garden were spread out picturesquely below us, and all the chimneys were smoking cheerfully, for "His Lordship" had just arrived, though he was already preparing to depart again for a spa. My guide told me that Sir Bishop was seen in the church only two or three times a year and sermons were something His Loftiness never did. Further, his sacred duty consisted solely in using up fifteen thousand pounds a year with as much good taste as the dear Lord had granted him, the actual work being adequately performed by subordinates. Such a beautiful arrangement is the only thing we on the Continent lack in order to be entirely happy, the only thing in England worth imitating! On the way back, I walked around for a while in the dusky church past the splendid monuments and ancient knights, resurrected from their tombs

120

The Choir of Salisbury Cathedral.

by my imagination. For we too, good Julie, have witnessed all this before and now look with amazement at our own ancient images, just as descendants a thousand years from now will marvel at the current ones.

I took the trouble of arranging for a sturdier carriage than the one I hired yesterday and then traveled quite restfully to Wilton, the beautiful house of the Earl of Pembroke (Figure 121). There is a valuable collection of classical sculpture here, very tastefully arranged by the deceased earl, who was a great lover of art. It is displayed along a wide gallery that runs around the inner courtyard and communicates with every one of the apartments on the first floor of the house, thus receiving its ample light from just one side. This is therefore a most interesting place to walk, both in winter and summer, and can be reached from any room in a few steps. The windows are fitted with the colorful coats-of-arms of every family allied by marriage with the Pembrokes—a rich assembly, including even the royal arms of England. Arranged in the large hall are suits of armor belonging to the old, heroic warriors of the family and their most notable prisoners, such as the Grand Constable Montmorency, a French prince of noble blood, and so on. Certainly these ageing reminders of a high and mighty aristocracy have their poetic side.

The chatelaine who led me around seemed to have crawled out of one of those colossal suits of armor herself, because she was fully six feet tall and adorned with a mustache that the old constable would not have felt ashamed to wear. And although no one could be better versed in the history of the Middle Ages, she bungled the names of Roman emperors and Greek philosophers in a barbaric manner, meanwhile delivering a few risqué but accurate portrayals without diffidence and with the droll vocabulary of a connoisseur.

One of the adjoining rooms is also filled with family portraits, but these attain their glory more through Holbein and Van Dyck than the individuals they depict. With the passage of time, artistic nobility will usually outshine nobility of birth, *comme de raison*. The house contains yet more significant paintings, but what I found to be the most striking was a highly detailed *Entombment* executed in watercolor by Albrecht Dürer.[8]

The library doors open onto the countess' garden, which has been laid out in the old French style and is closed by a small and elaborately ornamented temple that boasts one particular feature of note: it was built by Holbein.[9] But in no way does this make it any more tasteful. Rather the opposite, as it is an ugly, overly ornate monument. The garden is all the sweeter, and it is a credit to Englishwomen of rank that most of them are distinguished by their superior artistic skill in this arena. It would be quite erroneous to imagine that just any English gardener could be capable of laying out masterpieces of garden decoration like the many described in earlier letters. They owe their existence solely to the female proprietors, with their artistic understanding and devoted engagement in domestic life.[10]

Since it is absolutely forbidden to grant entry to any stranger without written permission of the owner, I would never have managed to visit this house had I not resorted to a harmless ploy. I announced myself to the courtly chatelaine as a Russian relative of the family, with a name that she could neither read nor pronounce. (The lord of the mansion will likely forgive me, if he ever hears of it.) It is simply too inconvenient to travel four miles and be turned back, having accomplished nothing. I therefore blame my white lie on the inconsiderateness of English custom. At home no one is so cruel and no Englishman ever meets with such illiberality.

On the other side of the city is another interesting estate: Longford, the property of the Earl of Radnor, which consists of an extensive park and a very old castle of a peculiar

triangular form, with tremendously bulky towers and walls that resemble mosaics. Here, in unimpressive, low-ceilinged, and badly furnished rooms, I found one of the most precious collections of paintings and choice portraits by the greatest masters; there are so many of these in English private homes, hidden treasures that no one sees and no one knows about. Here two by Claude Lorrain—a sunrise and sunset—outdid all the rest.[11] The morning picture shows us Aeneas with his retinue landing on the happy shores of Italy, and one envies the newcomers for the landscape paradise that stretches out before them. In the evening scene, the setting sun brushes gold over the magnificent ruins of overgrown temples and palaces that are surrounded by a solitary, wild countryside. These are said to be allegorical portrayals of the rise and fall of the Roman Empire. Water, clouds, sky, trees; the diaphanous, quivering, sun-filled atmosphere—as always with Claude, it is nature herself that you see as if newly created. It is truly hard to comprehend how a man can still be a cook and a color-grinder at the age of thirty-five, and at forty-five present the world with such unsurpassed masterpieces! The beautiful head of a Magdalene by Guido, her tearful eyes and ardent, slightly parted rosy lips seeming to invite a thousand kisses rather than contrition; a *Santa Famiglia* by Andrea del Sarto, glowing in all the magnificence of its colorful palette; these and many more masterpieces by other celebrated artists kept me here for several hours. A portrait of Count Egmont would have been ill suited as a title frontispiece for the tragedy by Goethe, since the jolly visionary appears as a rather corpulent forty-year-old with a bald head and a strictly ordinary face. Egmont's friend from Orange, whose portrait was hanging nearby, bore an altogether different and more intelligent countenance. Between these two, mounted on his horse, was the sinister Alba, who luxuriated in cruelty.

In addition to the paintings and a few antiquities, the castle houses another rare treasure: a chair or throne of steel. Given to the city of Augsburg by Emperor Rudolf II, it was *stolen* by the Swedes under Gustavus Adolphus and then *bought* in Stockholm by an ancestor of the Earl of Radnor. The craftsmanship is so admirable that all the delicate pieces of our own day—whether from Birmingham, the Berlin ironworks or elsewhere—dwindle into miserable baubles, if not veritable junk, when compared with this work of art! You believe you have a masterpiece by Benvenuto Cellini in front of you, and do not know what you should admire more—the splendid execution and grace of detail or the tasteful and artistic disposition of the whole.

London, December 31st, 1828

I HAD TO sacrifice yesterday to my mortal enemy, the migraine. Today I drove to the metropolis through incessant rain, and tomorrow morning I will continue on to France. The landscape offered little that was attractive, but the conversation on the coach's upper deck was all the more animated. It revolved almost all day long around a famous boxing match, in which a Yankee supposedly cheated a John Bull by bribing the lead boxer and thus winning ten thousand pounds. Such cheating has become commonplace in English sports from the lowest to the highest classes, much as foul play used to be at the time of the Count of Gramont. Many boast of it almost openly, and I have never found that these men—seen to be those "in the know"—suffered any social consequences. Au contraire, they were considered all the wittier, and only occasionally was I warned with a smile to be wary of them. Certain of the high aristocracy are notorious in this regard. For example, I know that the father of one such nobleman, responding to a concern that his son might be cheated by a "blackleg" (swindler), declared, "In this affair I am far more afraid for the blacklegs than for my son!" Different countries, different customs! Also symptomatic of the English perspective, although at a lower level, was our coachman, who lost two hundred pounds on that same unfortunate boxing match. He only laughed about it, letting us understand that he would in due course find himself another dupe and recover his losses with interest! How far will the march of intellect have to proceed on the Continent before the stagecoach drivers of the Prince of Thurn and Taxis, or the express coach drivers of Mr. von Nagler, begin to make such wagers with their passengers?

A few hours before Windsor, we passed through a landscape quite rare in England, one consisting of nothing but sand and pines. A magnificent palace with park and garden has been erected here: the New Military College, an establishment endowed with all the luxury of a princely estate.[12] The pines made me feel at home, but the building did not. While I was still gazing tenderly at the former, *car à toute âme bien née la patrie est chère*,[13] we caught sight of a fox, grey with age, coming toward us over the heather at a gallop, its tail dragging behind. The gambling coachman saw it first and cried:

"By God, a fox, a fox!"

"No, it's a dog," another insisted.

"I bet you five pounds to four it is a fox," answered the driver.

"Done!" the doubter exclaimed, and almost immediately had to pay up, because it was undeniably a fox, although of extraordinary size. Now several hunting dogs appeared, and the odd red coat was glimpsed in the pine thicket, but the scent had been lost. Everybody in the mail coach called out, pointing to where the fox had gone, yet they could not make themselves understood. The mail's time schedule is very strict, and any unnecessary delay is taboo, but here a national calamity was in play: the pack and hunters had *lost the fox*! So the driver stopped, and several men sprang down to offer directions to the growing entourage. We only headed off again once we saw the entire hunt back in full swing, at which we waved our hats and shouted tallyho! As soon as our consciences were thoroughly assuaged, and the fox had been consigned to its inevitable fate on the plain, the coachman whipped his horses to make up for lost time, and we sped off at a hurtling gallop, as if the Wild Huntsman himself were in pursuit.

But the clock has struck twelve, and I nearly forgot to follow our well-established custom of congratulating you, being that

> Ein neues Jahr beginnt,
> Schon Sand auf Sandkorn rinnt!
> Wird's Glück bedeuten,
> Oder Unheil bereiten?

In a daydream I see a picture of the enigma of my life:

> Die Wolken zieh'n, die Stürme sausen,
> Der Donner rollt, die Fluten brausen,
> Gefahrvoll ist das Schiff zu schauen,
> Wer mag dem falschen Meere trauen!

> Doch hinter jenem schwarzen Schleier
> Erhellt die Nacht ein goldner Blick—
> Ist es der Mond in sanfter Feier,
> Oder der Sonne Abschiedsblick?[14]

Dover, January 1st, 1829

THE BOX OF the mail coach has become my throne, and from here I occasionally take command and skillfully manage the reins of four swift steeds. I then survey the countryside with pride and hurry *forward* at speed (something not all rulers can boast of). And yet sometimes I wish I had wings, so I could be back with you even more quickly.

I did nothing in London all day Monday, except look for a worthy wife for Francis, in accord with your command. But purebred Blenheim spaniels are desperately rare. Those I found were unsuitable—the ears either too long or too short; the legs too bandy or too splayed; the coat too colorful or not adequately speckled; the temper too snappy or too lethargic. In short, I had to abandon the hunt.

When I arrived in Canterbury, all the towers were flying New Year's flags. I celebrated the day even more splendidly in the proudest and most beautiful of all English cathedrals. This romantic building, begun by the Saxons, continued by the Normans, and now intelligently restored, is actually made up of *three* quite distinct but interconnected churches, with many irregular side chapels, staircases leading up and down, stone floors covered in black-and-white grids, and a forest of columns, all in harmonious confusion. The yellowish color of the sandstone works to great advantage, especially in the Norman parts of the church, where it alternates with the black marble of the columns. Here the bronze effigy of the Black Prince lies atop his stone sarcophagus. His half-decayed gloves as well as his sword and shield from Poitiers hang above him.

A good many other monuments adorn the church as well, including those of Henry IV and Thomas Becket, who was murdered in one of the side chapels. Many of the old stained-glass windows are largely intact and their colors extraordinarily beautiful. Some of them simply display patterns and arabesques, like transparent velvet tapestries; others look like jewelry pieced together out of precious stones of every hue. Very few depict historical subjects. What gives this superb cathedral a special advantage over the others in England is that here there is no disruptive screen across the nave, allowing you to look down its full length, four or five hundred feet, in a single glance. The organ is concealed in the arch of an upper gallery, and when it resounds, the effect is magical. My timing was so fortunate that in half darkness, just as I was about to leave, the singers and musicians held a practice session, and heavenly choirs—beautiful and invisible— filled the cathedral along with the last rays of the sun, glowing through the sapphire blue and ruby red of the windows.

The Archbishop of Canterbury is primate of England and the only subject in Great Britain who bears the dignity of a prince without having royal blood—although as far as I know, this holds solely in his own see, not in London. This Protestant cleric has an annual income of sixty thousand pounds, and he may marry, which I believe is the only thing that distinguishes him from the princes of the Catholic Church.

Calais, January 2nd, 1829

FINALLY, I AM back in my beloved France! However unfavorable the first contrast may appear, I nonetheless welcome the half-native soil, the purer air, the more informal, friendly, and familiar manners. It almost feels as if I am returning after a lengthy prison term.

We were awakened in Dover at five o'clock, climbed into the packet boat in total darkness, strolled back and forth for a half hour with no sign of setting sail, and then suddenly the rumor went around that the boiler was damaged. The most timid escaped at once to the dock; the rest yelled for the captain, but he was nowhere to be found. He finally sent someone to inform us that it would not be safe to sail, and our things would be transferred to a French steamer departing at eight. I made use of this interval to watch the dawn from the fort that crowns the chalk cliffs high above the town. The English—since they have the money to carry out any useful plan—have blasted a tunnel through the rock in place of an exposed path. It forms a kind of funnel in which two spiral staircases lead up 240 feet. The view from the top was exceedingly picturesque, and the sun rose out of the sea and over the broad vista into a nearly cloudless sky. Meanwhile, as I was indulging myself in ecstasy, I nearly missed the departure of the ship, which sailed the very moment I boarded. In two and a half hours, the wind had hurled us across. This time I found the seasickness bearable and followed it with an excellent *dîner* in Calais, such as no English inn could offer. I was now completely restored, given that the Hotel Bourbon is admittedly, as far as its cuisine goes, one of the best in France.

When we had taken care of the universally hated nuisance of passports and police and were hurrying to the city center, I witnessed a ridiculous scene that vaulted me immediately to France. (Excuse the impending *naturalia,* because *quod natura non sunt turpia*—the superintendent will translate for you.[15]) Well then, my companion, an Englishman, stepped aside into a dirty side court for a reason easily surmised and had scarcely begun his business there, when a very well-dressed young lady burst out the door! An Englishwoman in this situation would have been appalled and taken to her heels at top speed, her hands in front of her face, as soon as she caught sight of the peril. In this case, however, the girl was highly incensed and went straight for the intruder, shouting at him with that uniquely French volubility, "Comment, monsieur, quelle insolence de p—— dans notre maison! Est-ce que la rue n'est pas assez grande pour cela! Vous êtes un grand polisson! Maman, Maman, voilà un monsieur qui p—— dans notre maison!"

The fury of the petite virago and the confusion of the startled Englishman were picturesque, but the true climax occurred when *Maman*, a dignified matron, appeared in response to the summons and likewise positioned herself close to the unfortunate man, crossed her arms, measured him from top to toe with a penetrating gaze and—without paying the slightest attention to the state of his attire—asked with an earnest expression, but laced with irony, "Eh bien, monsieur, est-ce que vous ne finirez point? Monsieur, permettez-moi de vous dire qu'on ne p—— pas ainsi chez les personnes, on p—— dans la rue, monsieur."

Here the daughter interrupted, almost in tears, "Vraiment je crois, qu'il se moque de nous, Maman! Insolent, il ne bouge pas."[16] I do not know what happened after this. Laughing heartily, I left the Englishman to his fate, and as I did so, the poor, flabbergasted sinner was still staring at the two ladies and awkwardly stammering out his apologies.

January 3, 1829

MY FIRST MORNING walk in France was luscious. This constant sunshine, the cloudless sky that I had not seen for so long, and finally once again a town where the houses and rooflines stand out sharply against the clear air, not obscured by fog or coal smoke. I gaped with real wonder and felt at home again. Then I walked to the harbor to bid my last farewell to the sea. It lay there before me, glassy and blue, boundless in all directions, except where the English coast was betrayed by a mountain range of black clouds, probably the compacted fog of that island. For at least a quarter hour, I followed the *jetée* (a kind of wooden dam) leading out into the sea, and found myself totally alone at its end. The only living thing was a waterfowl swimming smartly around in the silvery water, often plunging suddenly and then, after several minutes, reappearing not far away. This diversion continued for some time. Indeed the creature's behavior was so agile and merry that it was easy to imagine it was parading its skills just for me. While I was engaged in such fantasies, I heard behind me the footsteps and conversation of an English family, and so the two of us—the bird and I—quickly fled.

On the city ramparts, I came upon a French housemaid with two extremely pretty English children dressed elegantly in poppy red cashmere and white. The youngest was clinging firmly to a tree and steadfastly refusing, with that English love of liberty, to go home. The poor Frenchwoman verbally mangled every English cajolery and threat she could possibly muster, but all to no avail. "Mon darling, come *allons*," she cried plaintively. "I won't," was the laconic response. The stubborn little so-and-so interested me so much that I obligingly went over to the tree to try my luck with her. I had more success, for after a few English jokes, she followed me happily, and I led her in triumph to the bonne. Just as I was about to go off, the little demon grabbed hold of my coat with all her strength and said, laughing aloud, "No, no, you shan't go now. You forced me away from the tree, and I shall force you to remain with us." And indeed, she kept a grip on me until, amid lots of teasing and wrangling, we arrived at her parents' door. "Now I have done with you," the little one cried, and she let me loose and ran jubilantly into the house. "Oh, you little flirt!" I called after her—"A French education won't have much to add in your case!"

Back in town, I visited the famous Brummell. I see you searching in vain through the *Dictionaire historique* and *des Contemporains,* without being able to find this renowned name. Did he distinguish himself in a revolution or a counterrevolution? Is he a warrior, a statesman? *Vous n'y êtes pas.*[17] He is much more and much less, however you see him. In a word, he is one of the most celebrated and, in his time, most influential dandies that London has ever known. He once ruled a whole generation through the cut of his coat, and leather breeches went out of fashion because everyone despaired of matching the perfection of his. But when he finally, for good reason, turned his back on his native land, he left it one last gift: the immortal secret of starched cravats! This enigma had so plagued the *élégants* of the metropolis that—according to the *Literary Gazette*—two of them took their own lives in despair, and a young duke died wretchedly of a broken heart. That duke's malady had begun earlier, however, when on a festive occasion he timidly asked Brummell for his opinion of the coat he was then wearing, at which Brummell gave it barely a glance and responded with astonishment, "Do you call this thing a coat?"—an irreparable wound to the duke's honor.

Although dress no longer sets the tone in London, it is only the vehicle that has changed, not the thing itself. The influence that Brummell managed to wield there for so many years— *without* the benefit of fortune or high birth, *without* a handsome figure or superior mind, but only through sublime impudence, a measure of droll originality, a delight in sociability, and a talent for costume—provides an excellent measure of that society. In my earlier letters, I have described the people who now occupy Brummell's place (although they have far less influence), and you will perhaps agree that *he* was superior to them in brilliance as well as in his greater innocence of manners. His was a more open foolishness, one achieving a unity that was both more original and more harmless. It compares to current foolishness more or less the way Holberg's humor and morality compare to Kotzebue's.[18]

Only the power of fashion can be blamed that people found it clever when Brummell, asked by a country squire, "Do you like green peas?" answered, "I once ate one." But more delectable were his quarrels with the Prince of Wales, whom he first drew into the realm of fashion, only to twist its scepter out of his hand.[19] Later he was even successful in carrying out his resolution "to cut the prince," as follows: Brummell, who enjoyed the prince's highest favor, finally treated him with such little respect that it caused a breach. This happened one day after lunch, when he forgot himself so thoroughly as to call out to the prince, "Pray, George, will you ring the bell for me!" The prince, deeply offended by the indiscreet laughter of the party as well as by the impertinent familiarity of the adventurer, stood up and making a show of his equanimity, rang it. But when the servant entered, he pointed his finger at Brummell: "This person wants his carriage." Brummell did not lose his composure but responded with a laugh, "Capital, Georgy! By God, I'd completely forgotten that the beautiful duchess was waiting for me! I will take the joke seriously and depart. So good-bye to Your Royal Highness."

He was never received at that royal residence again, which did almost more damage to the prince in the fashionable world of the day than it did Brummell, who knew very well how to twist the thing around into a story about how *he* had broken with the prince. To his intimate friends he said, "That fellow first ruined me in champagne, won my money afterward, and now thinks he can cut me!" A few days later, chance had it that Brummell ran into the prince and a few famous gentlemen of fashion in New Bond Street. The prince acted as if he did not see him. But Brummell approached with all his particular *aisance* and *effronterie,* and with that impertinent condescension of which he was master, shook the hand of Colonel P——, a man of society and at the same time a coryphaeus of the elegant world. Then, holding up his quizzing glass and focusing it on the prince, Brummell whispered to the colonel in a voice overheard by all, "Who the devil, colonel, is your fat old friend, the one you were just talking to?"[20] With this he abandoned the party to their consternation, mounted his horse, and rode off laughing.

These anecdotes were related to me by a completely reliable source, an eyewitness. I am less certain about the truth of something else I heard: how earlier, at a *dîner* where the drinking had already been excessive, the prince, half drunk, responded to a sarcastic remark of Brummell's, who was seated next to him, by throwing a glass of wine in his face. Unable to reply to the princely personage in kind, Brummell immediately reached for his own glass and poured it on his neighbor's jacket, calling out capriciously, "The prince has commanded that it should continue to the left!"

For a long time after this Brummell continued to reign in London and dim the luster of his lofty antagonist. Indeed it was then that his genius soared, for he managed to deliver a most sensitive nudge to the prince, who was celebrated for tying his cravat into an inimitable knot. As a rejoinder to this, Brummell invented the use of starch and isinglass for cravats. From this memorable moment onward, his victory was unquestioned, and for years dandies tortured themselves in vain, trying to wear their cravats as he did. In the end it was gambling that accomplished what the prince had failed to do, namely, drove Brummell out of exclusive society. He lost all his worldly means and was forced to flee. But on his desk he left a sealed package for his native country, and once opened, it was found to contain only the following words, written in large letters, "My friends! Starch is the thing."

And just as great men live on in their works, even when they themselves are long gone, so too does Brummell's starch still remain visible at the neck of every fashionable gentleman, proclaiming the inventor's great genius. Since then he has lived in Calais, out of reach of the authority of his creditors, and every migratory bird from the modish world whose path leads through this town is duty bound to pay tribute to the former patriarch with a visit or an invitation to dinner.

I did this myself, although under an assumed name.[21] Unfortunately another stranger had preempted me with regard to the dinner, and therefore I cannot even judge how a coat should actually look, or whether the long sojourn in Calais along with advancing age has made the dress of the erstwhile King of Fashion less classical—because my visit found him still at his second *toilette* (three of them are necessary each morning), in a flowered dressing gown, a velvet cap with gold tassels on his head, and Turkish slippers on his feet. He was giving himself a shave, after which he carefully cleaned his remaining teeth with a little piece of the popular red root. The furnishings surrounding him were fairly elegant, some even opulent, although significantly faded; I cannot deny that I found his whole demeanor consistent with the rest. Although depressed by his current situation, he displayed a considerable fund of humor and good nature. His manners were those of proper society, simple and natural and of greater urbanity than current dandies manage to exhibit. Smiling, he showed me his Parisian wig, which he praised highly and much to the detriment of English versions, while referring to himself as the once-young man who divides his time between Paris and London. He seemed curious about me and solicited information concerning the state of affairs in London society, but without giving offense or betraying a lack of good breeding. It was clear he wanted to prove that he remained very well informed about everything happening in the English world of fashion and politics. "Je suis au fait de tout," he exclaimed, "mais à quoi cela me sert-il? On me laisse mourir de faim ici. J'espère pourtant que mon ancien ami, le Duc de W——, enverra un beau jour le consul d'ici à la Chine, et qu'ensuite il me nommera à sa place. Alors, je suis sauvé."[22] And really, it is only proper for the English nation to do something for the man who invented starched cravats! How many men did I see with heavily endowed London sinecures who had done *far less* for their native land.

After I had said goodbye and was going down the stairs, he opened the door and called after me, "J'espère que vous trouverez votre chemin, mon Suisse n'est pas là, je crains." And I thought, "Alas! point d'argent, point de Suisse."[23]

So you will not be left too long without news, I am sending this letter off from here. Perhaps I myself will follow it soon. But I do want to stay in Paris for fourteen days, and will take care of all your commissions there. In the meantime think of me always with constant love.

Your faithful Lou

Paris, January 5th, 1829

*M*Y PRECIOUS AND beloved friend!
I could not write yesterday, because the diligence takes two days and a night from Calais to Paris and only stops once every twelve hours for a half-hour meal. The journey is not very pleasant. The countryside looks quite dead, miserable, and dirty, as does the capital, when compared with the hubbub, sparkle, and neatness of England. And in such close proximity, the contrast is doubly striking. You note the grotesque machine you are sitting in and the poorly harnessed cart horses dragging you along, and when you then recall the lightweight grace of English mail coaches; the handsome teams of horses, with their harnesses of shiny brass and polished leather, you feel as if you have dreamed yourself a thousand miles away. Although the bad roads, the shabby and dirty towns, awaken the same feeling, there are four respects in which people's lives are obviously better here: climate, food and wine, affordability, and sociability. *Mais commençons par le commencement.*[1]

After exchanging my incognito passport at the town hall for another provisional one, valid only as far as Paris, and in the process almost failing to remember my new name when asked for it, I approached the wonderful vehicle that the French call a diligence. This monstrosity was as long as a house and consisted of four distinct but amalgamated sections: the berlin in the middle,[2] a coach with a luggage basket at the back, a coupé in front, and, attached to this, the cabriolet where the driver sits. I took my seat next to the *conducteur*, an old soldier from the Napoleonic Guard who was dressed like a lowly cart driver in a blue smock, with an embroidered cap of the same fabric on his head. The postilion looked even more bizarre, truly half wild. He too was wearing a smock, the enormous boots beneath it caked with dung, but he also had an apron of black sheepskin hanging down on both sides over his thighs. He was managing six horses that he had harnessed himself, three and three, and they were pulling a load of some six thousand pounds on a badly maintained road. The whole route from Calais to Paris is altogether one of the sorriest and least interesting to be found anywhere, and I would therefore have spent most of my time reading, if the driver's conversation had not provided even better entertainment. His and the guardsmen's heroic deeds provided inexhaustible material. For example, he assured me without any hesitation, "that the thirty thousand men" (of whom, as he put it, he was one at the time) "would have been more than enough to conquer all the nations of the earth, and that the presence of the others had only ruined the whole operation."

He sighed every time he thought of his emperor. "But it's his fault," he exclaimed. "Damnation, he would still be emperor if, during the Hundred Days, he had simply recruited young men who wanted to get rich, instead of those old *maréchaux* who were already too wealthy, and all of them afraid of their wives. Weren't they, every one of them, big and fat like monsters? Ah . . . let's talk about a young colonel instead, like the one we had! He would surely have taken care of them nicely. But after all, the emperor should have died at Waterloo, like our colonel. Let me tell you, sir: that brave soldier had been shot three times, once in the leg and twice in the chest, and yet—carried by two grenadiers—he still led us into battle. Nonetheless, when it was clear that all was in vain and everything was over for us, he said, 'Comrades! I have done what I could, but we've reached this point. Since I am no longer of use to the emperor, what's the point of living any longer? So goodbye, my comrades, long live the emperor!' And then he takes out his pistol and shoots himself in the mouth. I swear that's how the emperor should have died, too."

Here we were interrupted by a pretty girl who ran out of a drab house and straight for the carriage, calling up to us (for we were sitting at least eight yards above the ground), "Ah, ça, monsieur le conducteur! Oubliez-vous les crêpes?"

"Oh ho! Es-tu là, mon enfant?"[3]

At this he speedily clambered down what was basically a breakneck henhouse ladder, told the postilion to wait, and disappeared into the house. After a few minutes he reemerged with a parcel, deposited himself contentedly next to me, and unwrapped a stack of steaming German blintzes—confections, he told me, he had gotten to know in Germany and grown so fond of that he had introduced them to his native land. You see, then, my conquests do repay the effort. With characteristic French civility, he offered that we share his *goûter,* as he called it, and patriotism compelled me to accept with pleasure! I was also forced to admit that no farmer in Germany could do a better job of preparing what is, after all, our own national dish. We ate them to the health of Napoleon, wherever he may be!

This *conducteur,* although clearly a man of considerable strength, was constantly struggling with a strange mechanism next to his seat. It was approximately the shape of a pump, and he was constantly adjusting it, screwing it, turning it forward and backward, or pumping it with all his might. In answer to my question, I learned that it was a newly invented piece of machinery, which serves superbly—without a brake shoe—to slow the diligence down during descents and increase its speed on ascents. Extremely proud of the contraption, he never called it anything other than his "*mécanique,*"[4] and treated it with just as much love as respect. Unfortunately this technical marvel fell to pieces on the first day, and thus we had to slog along at an even slower pace, the poor warrior enduring much teasing from the passengers regarding his defective *mécanique,* just as he did about the name of his immense vehicle, *l'Hirondelle,*[5] a title that appears to have been bestowed on it with the most bitter irony!

It was comical to hear the poor devil explaining the accident to the postilion at every new relay station. The dialogue, with few modifications, went like this:

"Mon enfant, il faut que tu saches que je n'ai plus de mécanique."

"Comment, sacré diable, plus de mécanique?"

"Ma mécanique fait encore un peu, vois-tu, mais c'est bien peu de chose, le principal brancheron est au diable."

"Ah, diable!"[6]

It is simply not possible to be more uncomfortably seated or to progress at a slower pace than what I experienced in my lofty cabriolet. And although I had done without my most familiar amenities for a considerable period, my mood and my health had never been better. I was continuously cheerful and contented, because I felt completely free. O the great blessing of freedom!

We do not treasure you nearly enough! If only each of us could see exactly what our individual happiness requires and categorically elect what accords best with this objective, heartily discarding the rest. (After all, no one can have everything in the world simultaneously.) How many blunders would be spared, how much petty ambition eradicated, how much true cheerfulness engendered! We would all discover an abundance of well-being, instead of torturing ourselves with disgruntled unhappiness to the grave.

I will not tire you with further details of our uneventful journey. It resembled the melodrama *One O'Clock*, and was just as boring, because after we left Calais in the morning, we stopped at one o'clock to eat, and then had our supper at one o'clock in the morning.[7] On the second day, breakfast and *dîner* were again amalgamated at one o'clock in Beauvais. There the pretty girl who served us and a friend of Bolívar's, who told us much about the altruism of the Liberator, caused us to regret our hurried departure. Later, again at one o'clock in the morning, we had to fight for our luggage at the customhouse in Paris. Afterward my servant loaded mine onto a handcart, which a man pulled along in front of us, at the same time showing us the way through the dark and filthy streets to the Hôtel St-Maurice. I am now writing you from a frugal little room that I chose for myself, where the cold wind whooshes through every door and window, and the blazing fire in the hearth warms me up on just one side. The silken wall coverings, along with the dirt shrouding them; the plentiful mirrors; the large pieces of wood stacked by the fireplace, as well as the tile parquet—all this vividly reminds me that I am in France and not in England anymore.

I am going to rest here for a few days and make my purchases. I will then hurry into your arms without, if possible, seeing a *single* acquaintance, for that would delay me too much. So do not expect to hear anything new from me about old Paris. All I can offer will be a few scattered journal entries.

January 6th, 1829

IN ORDER TO put up some resistance to the brutal cold, which I find most severe in France and Italy, where they make no provisions against it, I had to have weather stripping stuffed into all the chinks in my small quarters this morning. Then I rushed out to take every foreigner's first walk— to the boulevards, the Palais Royal, the Tuileries, etc. I was of course very curious to see what might have transpired in these parts over the past seven years. On the boulevards, everything is as it was. At the Palais Royal, the Duke of Orléans, in every respect a distinguished prince, has begun to replace the disgraceful wooden galleries and other nooks with new stone buildings and an elegant glass corridor. All of this, when it is done, will make the *palais* among the most renowned anywhere; it is already the most unusual and striking, perhaps only for the rarity of its circumstances: A royal prince inhabits the same house as several hundred ladies of the night, along with an equal number of shopkeepers, and obtains sufficient revenue from these tenants and from the gambling and taverns to cover his *menus plaisirs* with money to spare![8] No nobleman in England would conceive of such a thing in his own residence, but were it to happen, he would at least make certain to keep everything much cleaner. For it must be admitted that these idols of Venus and Mercury are surrounded by filth, however showy the display.

Nearly all of the buildings begun under Napoleon in the area near the Palais des Tuileries and along the Rue de Rivoli bordering it are still in the same condition in which he left them. In fact, Paris forfeited a lot by losing an imperial dynasty that in twenty years would have transformed the city into true magnificence; and the luxury of beauty would have finally, of necessity, been followed by cleanliness. Instead, scaffolding still awaits the projected statue in the Place de Louis XV;[9] at the Place de L'Etoile, the Arc de Triomphe is, like the Tower of Babel, pulled down and reerected by turns;[10] the Temple de la Victoire,[11] now infinitely more suitable for the victorious church, is also unfinished; and as for the Pont de Louis XVI, one might better wish that nothing had been done, since the ridiculously theatrical statues, at least two times too big for the bridge, seem about to crush the pillars on which they are balanced and look more like bad *acteurs de province* than the French heroes they are supposed to represent.

Since cooks are also considered among the heroes of France—first on account of their unsurpassed skill, and second on account of their sense of honor (just remember Peregrine Pickle's cook,[12] or Vatel, who stabbed himself to death because the fish had not arrived),[13]—I now turn to the subject of Parisian restaurateurs. From what I can tell, judging from the visits I paid today to the most admired among them, they all seem to have degenerated a bit. It is true that their already overlong menus have been transformed into elegantly bound books, yet the quality of the dishes and wines has decreased correspondingly. After this sad experience, I hurried to the once renowned Rocher de Cancale. Not only has Baleine swum back to the infinite sea, but whoever may seek refuge on the Cancalean rocks will find nothing but sand.[14] *Sic transit gloria mundi!*

On the other hand, I must bestow high praise on the Théâtre de Madame, where I later spent the evening. Léontine Fay is a most delightful actress, and no better ensemble can be found anywhere. Since I had just come from England, I was all the more *frappé* at the naturalness of her masterful performance in *Malvina*.[15] She played a Frenchwoman raised in England, this nuance being managed without detriment to the rest of her character. The artistic performance was in no way an imitation of Mademoiselle Mars, and yet it captured the natural in a way that was just as true and subtle, although differently portrayed. In the second piece, a farce, a provincial uncle hastily abandons his small town, where he is on the verge of being accepted as a member of the League of Virtue.[16] He goes to Paris to see his nephew, about whom he has received the most distressing reports, hoping to cure him of his dissolute lifestyle, but instead is himself lured by the young man's friends into every possible frivolity. This play was performed with all the comic finesse and caprice that make these French trifles so delightful and amusing in Paris, but so empty and insipid in German translation.

Right at the beginning, just after Mademoiselle Minette has employed her coquettishness to convince old Martin to give her a kiss, her lover, the waiter, steps in carrying a pig's head and then stops speechless, letting the dish slide slowly out of his hands as he cries, "N'y-a-t'il pas de quoi perdre la tête!"[17] However ridiculous this is, you would have to be very stoical not to laugh heartily, given the superb, natural acting. What follows is just as delectable. Martin, terrified at having been caught in such an adventure, takes comfort in the thought that he is unknown there, and in his confusion accepts an invitation to lunch from Dorval, newly arrived on the scene. This is served on stage a bit later, and at first Martin is quite moderate. Eventually, however, the truffles and other delicacies tempt him, and he finds it absolutely necessary to moisten them with a little champagne. Having taken care of this requirement, he resolves, moralizing all the while, to drink a glass to virtue. *Hélas! Il n'y a que le premier pas qui coûte.*[18] A second glass is drunk to *piété,* a third to *miséricorde,* and before the guests finally rise, we hear Martin, drunk and jubilant, joining in the toast: *Vivent les femmes et le vin!*[19] Now comes the gambling. At first he agrees only to one game of piquet, during which he sings a few droll couplets, ending with the refrain

"L'amour s'envole, mais le piquet dure."[20] In short, Martin is enticed from piquet to écarté, and finally to hazard, loses an enormous sum, and at last, to make the confusion complete, learns that he had been betrayed from the very beginning: his nephew had been testing *him* all along, rather than vice versa, and unfortunately found him much too lightweight. He then willingly agrees to everything asked of him, provided that it be kept completely secret, and the drama ends with the arrival of an old friend, who has come on the express mail coach to inform him that yesterday, in his hometown, amid widespread applause, Martin was elected president of the League of Virtue.

January 7th, 1829

IN SPITE OF the weather stripping and a burning stack of wood in the fireplace, nonetheless I continue to feel bitterly frozen in my entresol. In addition, a persistent clair-obscure prevails, so that I see the letters before me only as if through a veil. The small windows and tall buildings across the way do not allow otherwise, so I must beg your forgiveness if my writing is even more illegible than usual. You will of course have noted that the shockingly expensive postage in England has taught me to write with greater care and density, so that now a Lavater of calligraphy would be able to analyze a large part of my character in my letters to you—and I mean just by looking at, not reading, them. And so it goes, as with life itself, where many an undertaking begins with the good intention of imposing limits, indeed restrictions, of all kinds. These hold for a while, but soon the lines begin to spread out involuntarily, and before you know it, through the invisible power of habit, they are back to their former proportions!

I have already told you that the restaurateur's menus have been transformed into books as thick as a finger and richly bound in morocco and gold. An English officer, whom I found today in the Café Anglais, was so impressed by this that he repeatedly requested *la charte* instead of *la carte* from the astonished waiter.[21] Perhaps he was of the opinion that in liberal France, something similar would have been adopted for cafés, too. Although the French rarely pay attention to foreigners' linguistic muddles, this red flag seemed to be greeted with smiles. Still, I was thinking how happy many would be if we turned it around and gave the French cards instead of charters to play with again.

I was in for a big surprise this evening at the French opera. When I last left, it was a kind of madhouse, where a few maniacs screamed and swooned, as if they were being skewered. Now I found sweet songs, the best Italian technique, and lovely voices combined with very good acting. Rossini, having tamed the opera like a second Orpheus, has become the true benefactor of musical ears, and natives as well as foreigners are profoundly indebted to him for their salvation.

Although it is less fashionable to do so, I now unquestionably prefer this pageant to the Italian opera, since it unites almost everything you could wish for in the theater—not only the good singing and acting, but also magnificent, fresh decorations and the best ballet in the world. If the lyrics were also masterpieces, I would not know what else to ask for, although one can be quite content with them as they are, as with the *Muette de Portici* I saw today.[22] Mademoiselle Noblet is noble as the mute girl, her performance full of grace and animation without any exaggeration; and the elder Nourrit is an excellent Masaniello, although he did appear to be screaming excessively from time to time. The costumes were exemplary, but the fire-spitting Vesuvius went wrong, for the clouds of smoke sank to the ground instead of rising up out of it. At least that was not the experience I enjoyed when I witnessed an actual Vesuvian eruption.

SOMEWHERE A FRENCH writer claims that we are like children, but because of our weaknesses, not our happiness. This, thank God, I can in no way say of myself, for I am like a child for both reasons, despite having attained more than three dozen years. Thus I am having an exceptionally good time here in the loneliness of the great city and can imagine, just like a young man would, that I have just entered the world, and all this is still new to me. In the morning I look at the sights, stroll through a museum, or go "shopping" (this means to meander around in shops and buy the new bagatelles that luxury is continually inventing in Paris and London). I have already collected a hundred little gifts for you, and my cramped quarters are scarcely capable of holding them; yet I have spent even less than eight pounds, for in England it is *costliness* that is expensive; here only *cheapness* is seductive. I must sometimes laugh when I see a canny French shopkeeper who thinks he has soundly cheated one of those stiff islanders, who himself departs agog at having bought something for a sixth of what it would have cost in London.

At midday I continue my scientific study of the restaurateurs and, in the evening, of the theaters, although I will not have time to complete either survey.

During my shopping today, I noticed a poster in the Palais Royal advertising the marvelous exhibition about Prince Poniatowski's death in Leipzig. I do not like to miss such things of national interest and therefore, to see this marvel, I climbed up a miserable, dark staircase, where I entered an even darker, windowless room, to find a raggedly dressed man sitting next to a half-extinguished lamp. In front of him was a large table covered with a grimy tablecloth. As soon as I came in, he hurriedly lit three other lamps, but they did not burn properly, and he began to rant loudly and vehemently. I thought the show was already beginning and asked, since I had not been paying attention, what he had said. "Oh, nothing," was the answer. "I'm just talking to my lamps, which are not burning brightly enough." After the conversation with the lamps had finally achieved its purpose, the tablecloth was pulled aside to reveal a work of art that resembled a Nuremberg toy with small, movable figures. But the owner's exposition amply compensated for the entrance fee. He began in a nasal, singing tone as follows: "*Voilà* the famous Prince Poniatowski turning gracefully toward the officers of his corps and exclaiming, 'When one has lost everything, when one has given up all hope, life is a disgrace and death a duty.' Notice, gentlemen" (he consistently addressed me in the plural) "how the prince's white horse turns around as nimbly as a real horse. Look—zap to the right—zap to the left—but look at him, as he leaps, rears, rushes headlong into the river, and then disappears."

This happened by means of a string under the table that pulled the figure first right and left, then forward, and then, by moving a sliding panel painted to look like water, the little prince fell into a drawer.

"So, *voilà*!—a drowned Prince Poniatowski. He is dead. That was part one. Now, gentlemen, you will soon see the most astonishing thing ever exhibited in France. The innumerable little soldiers you see before you" (there were about sixty or seventy of them), "are all dressed in actual costumes: uniforms, ammunition pouches, weapons—everything can easily be taken off and put back on. The cannons function like real cannons and are admired by all the officers of the army corps of engineers who come here."

In order to demonstrate this visually, the first tiny cannon was lifted off the gun carriage and the sword belt removed from the first soldier, which was intended as sufficient proof of his claim.

"So! Now, gentlemen, you are going to see this little army maneuvering as if on the battle-field. Each soldier and each horse will make its own separate and fitting movements, just look."

Next, to the sound of a drum beaten by a small boy under the table, all the little dolls—none of which had budged in the first act, probably out of respect for Prince Poniatowski—began repeating the same two continuous, rhythmic movements: the soldiers raised and then lowered their arms, the horses reared and kicked, while the commentator recited the French account of the affair with increasing pathos. This closed act 2. I could not conceive of it getting any better, a few more spectators had appeared by then, and since I did not want to go on enduring the awful stench of the two extinguished lamps, I escaped from the battlefield and all its wonders. It was nonetheless tragic to see such miserable treatment of a hero once so valiant and self-sacrificing!

At the opera I was very pleased with *Comte Ory*,[23] sung by the young Nourrit. The connoisseurs may cry out against Rossini as much as they like, but the fact is that here again the ear delights in streams of *melody*, sometimes melting in tones of love, thundering in a storm, exulting at a knightly banquet, or soaring to heaven in solemn prayer. It is a bit strange that the knight's prayer, which is presented as pure hypocrisy in this more-than-frivolous opera, is the same one that Rossini composed earlier for the coronation of Charles X. Madame Cinti sang the role of the countess extremely well, Mademoiselle Javoureck displayed very lovely legs as the countess' page, and the bass was excellent too.

The ballet, it seems to me, has declined somewhat. Albert and Paul are not getting any lighter on their feet as the years pass, and except for the ladies Noblet and Taglioni, not one of the female dancers was distinguished.

During the opera today, I noticed that the same actor who plays one of the leading roles in the *Muette* was performing an insignificant part among the brigade of knights. This kind of thing happens often here and is a practice well worth imitating. A truly excellent unity can only be created when the best performers also participate in the *ensemble*, whether their roles be large or small.

In general, much more is done to support the *ensemble* in France than in Germany, where the illusion often collapses because of trifles that are neglected by the lethargic managers or actors. The late Hoffmann[24] (not the one who allocates souls but the one who moves souls) used to say that, of all dreadful moments he had experienced in the theater, none was more uncanny than what once happened on the Berlin stage. Iffland, playing a privy councilior, had been behaving in a completely prosaic manner, until he suddenly exited not though the door in a human fashion, but through the wall, as if he were the Evil One and consisted of nothing but air.

January 10th, 1829

IT IS A special delight to find the museum, after all the required restitutions, still so abundant in riches![25] Denon's new galleries now offer a worthy location for the majority of the sculptures; it is only a shame that the old spaces were not set up in a similar style. Little would be lost by demolishing the ceiling paintings; they are not very worthy in themselves, and paintings generally look quite bad when associated with statues. Sculpture and painting should really never be combined.

Without dwelling on the avowed masterpieces, let me mention a few works of art that I found especially appealing and do not recall having seen before. First a beautiful Venus, discovered only a few years ago on Milos and presented to the king by the duc de Rivière.[26] She is portrayed as a victrix, and in the opinion of archaeologists she was originally either presenting the apple or holding the shield of Mars with both hands, although this remains hypothetical, since her arms are missing. But how lovely her body is, naked from the waist up! What life, what tender softness and enticing form! The triumphant, proud expression of her face is genuinely womanly, yet also nobly divine.

Second. A female figure shrouded in loose robes (called *Image de la Providence* in the catalog), a splendid, ideal woman, gentleness and kindness in her countenance, heavenly tranquility in her whole figure. The drapery is of the highest grace and perfection.[27]

Third. Cupid and Psyche from the Villa Borghese. Psyche is on her knees begging Cupid's forgiveness, and his sweet smile shows that her request is already inwardly granted. The layman, at least, is certainly captivated by the voluptuous forms and the loveliest of facial expressions! The group is in remarkable condition; only one hand of the god of love seems to have been restored.

Fourth. A sleeping nymph.[28] The ancients, who knew how to portray everything from the most striking point of view, often decorated their sarcophagi with such figures as emblems of death. Here the sleep is profound and yet the pose almost ravishing, with the captivating limbs only half concealed by beautiful drapery. She is more suggestive of new, young life than of the death already transpired.*

Fifth. A gypsy (allegedly), remarkable for the integration of stone and bronze.[29] The figure is of bronze; the Lacedaemonian cloak of stone. The head is in fact modern, but with a highly appealing, mischievous expression that is perfectly suited to an authentic *zingarella*, just as you find in Italy.

Sixth. A magnificent statue of a praying figure. The head and neck of white marble have the severe, ideal beauty of the best classical art, and the drapery, of the hardest porphyry, could not fall more lightly and freely if it were composed of velvet and silk.

Seventh. A colossal Melpomene gives her name to one of the new galleries, and below her an elegant bronze railing surrounds Professor Belloni's exquisitely successful imitations of ancient mosaics. The technique is extremely interesting, and I am amazed not to see it more often in the houses of the wealthy.

Eighth. A bust of the young Augustus. A handsome, mild, intelligent head with a different expression, but the same general features as in the statue portraying him at a more advanced age. By then the force of circumstances and the influence of various parties had compelled the emperor to commit innumerable atrocities, and yet in the end his inborn, gentler nature regained the upper hand.

Ninth. His great general, Agrippa. I have never seen a more distinctive physiognomy in a more noble form! It is strange that the brow and the upper part of the eyes betray a close similarity to Alexander von Humboldt, a man who, within an entirely different sphere, can also be counted among the great. Elsewhere in the general's face, however, the resemblance entirely disappears. The more I looked at this iron head, the more convinced I became that the mild Augustus needed exactly such a man in order to achieve mastery of the world.

Tenth. For me, the last and also the most interesting was a bust of Alexander, which, according to Denon, is the only authentic one that exists (Figure 122).[30] It is a real study for the

---

* This is how all of us should contemplate, represent, and approach death. Only a faulty understanding of Christianity, and perhaps its Jewish substrate (unlikely a gold ground), made death so gloomy and, with coarse sensuality and lacking even the slightest bit of poetry, chose putrefaction and skeletons as its emblems. —*The Editor.*

physiognomists and phrenologists, because these ancient artists gave the same careful attention to shaping every part in exact accord with nature's model. This head really has all the truth of a portrait. The features are far from idealized and not even particularly handsome, yet the remarkable proportions and expression correspond perfectly with the history of this great man. The sometimes careless abandon of the character is very nicely suggested by the graceful inclination of the neck toward the left and the voluptuous outline of the mouth; the brow and lower jaw are strikingly like Napoleon's, just as the whole, full shape of his skull, both back and front (animal and intellectual) is completely developed, as with Napoleon (Figure 123).* [31] The forehead is not too high (no evidence of an ideologist), but instead compact and strong as metal. The features are in general quite regular and well formed, but as mentioned cannot be called ideally handsome. The area of the nose and eyes expresses an acuteness of mind—augmented, if I may express it this way, by a sublime astuteness—paired with a most determined courage and thoughtful congeniality of the soul. It was all this that made Alexander into a unique historical presence: the young, poetic hero who was as invincible as engaging. Had Charles XII or Napoleon been endowed with the same complement of attributes, neither would have come to ruin in Russia. The one would not now be looked upon as a Don Quixote nor the other as a tyrant, calculating strongman, and rationalist. Overall, this sculpture presents a highly attractive being: imposing, yet inspiring courage, love, and trust in the viewer. Bathed in the aura of these features, you feel comfortable and secure, and realize that at all times and in every condition of life, such a man must have aroused admiration and enthusiasm, sweeping everyone along in his wake.

* As Napoleon said of himself, "carré, autant de base que de hauteur."—*The Editor.* [Square, below and above.—*Translator.*]

122

Portrait of Alexander the Great, called the "Azara Herm."

123

*Napoleon and
His Son.*

NAPOLÉON ET SON FILS.

I should also mention a delightful bas-relief and an unusual altar. The bas-relief is also from the Borghese collection, which, like so much else, France owes to Napoleon. It shows Vulcan forging the shield of Aeneas with the Cyclops grouped around him, all delightfully depicted with the faces of Silenus and his fauns.[32] But it is the sweet little Cupid who is most charming: half hidden behind a door, he is whisking away the cap of one of the Cyclops. Everything in this appealing composition is full of life, whimsy, and movement, and the truth of the forms and precision of the detail are masterful.

The altar, dedicated to a dozen gods at once, resembles a Christian baptismal font. Twelve magnificent busts in high relief surround the edge of the basin like a lovely wreath; the workmanship is exquisite; and the state of preservation leaves little to be desired. The gods are arrayed singly in the following order: Jupiter, Minerva, Apollo, Juno, Neptune, Vulcan, Mercury, Vesta, Ceres, Diana; lastly Mars and Venus are united by Cupid. I am surprised that this elegant composition has not been replicated on a smaller scale in alabaster, porcelain, or crystal for the ladies' bazaars, like the well-known doves and other *objets d'art*. Nothing could be better suited to that purpose, and yet there was not a plaster cast to be found, not even at Jacquet's (the successor to Getti, *mouleur du Musée*),[33] just as there were no casts of most of the works I have mentioned, simply because they are not the most famous, although some that are better known are not nearly so attractive. People really are too much *comme les moutons de Panurge*—they simply follow authority and allow that alone to determine their tastes.[34]

The forced restitutions would be less evident in the picture galleries if their places were not occupied by a proliferation of works from the more recent French school. I must admit that, with very few exceptions, these often look like mere caricatures to me. The theatrical distortion, the stagey propriety that even David's figures sometimes make a show of, and the persistently exaggerated passions seem sophomoric compared with the Italians' noble fidelity to nature; even the engaging gemütlichkeit of the German and Netherlandish schools is altogether absent. Of all the prominent new artists, I liked Girodet the least; certainly nobody with sound artistic taste can look at his *Deluge* without revulsion.[35] Horace Vernet, too, excels only in genre pieces, although Gérard's *Entry of Henri IV* seems to me a picture whose fame will endure.

The many Rubenses and Le Sueurs brought here from the Palais du Luxembourg to fill the gaps are wholly inadequate substitutes for the missing Raphaels, Leonardo da Vincis, and van Eycks.[36] In short, everything both new and old that has arrived since the Restoration makes an unfavorable impression, including the inferior busts of painters that have been installed among the columns at certain intervals in the galleries and would never be well suited to a room of paintings, even if they were of higher quality. As always, however, the splendid long gallery still provides the most pleasant walk in winter, and the liberality that allows it to be always open and accessible cannot be sufficiently lauded.

When I think how even more deplorable the state of painting is in England, and how nothing great is on offer in Italy or Germany either,* I tend to worry that this art form will soon go the

---

* But what about the commendable exception of Munich, where a truly great artist has found an even greater protector of the arts?—*The Editor.* [This is probably a reference to Ludwig I of Bavaria, an enthusiastic patron of the arts, who brought the painter Peter von Cornelius to Munich and appointed him director of the Academy of Fine Arts.—*Translator.*]

way of stained glass—indeed, that its most profound secrets may be lost already. The richness, power, truth, and life of the old masters, like their technical mastery of color, where are these still to be found? Thorvaldsen, Rauch, Dannecker, and Canova may rival antiquity, but who among the painters can be ranked even with the second-tier artists of the golden age? Only the above mentioned genre pieces show success, although they too will never approach the Netherlanders in the faithful rendering of nature.

The colossal sphinx from Drovetti's collection, intended for the main court of the Louvre, is now standing in a side courtyard.[37] It is of pinkish granite, and the sculpture is as grandiose as its mass is stupendous. It is intact except for the nose, which has just recently been replaced with one of white plaster, still without its final *couche* or coloration. The sight of it made me laugh involuntarily, and thinking of the peculiar chain of circumstances that finally brought this giant here, I exclaimed to myself, "You huge, white-nosed, Egyptian smart aleck![38] What do you think you're doing here, after three thousand years, in the new Babylon, where no sphinx harbors a riddle anymore, and discretion was never much at home anyway?"

In the evening I chose the Porte Saint-Martin from among the theaters on offer and went to see *Faust*, which has been drawing the curious public for eighty or ninety performances already.[39] The culminating point in this melodrama is a waltz that Mephistopheles dances with Martha, and indeed no waltz can be performed more diabolically! In the still-pretty dancer you can clearly see the hellish fire at work, sometimes terrifying her, sometimes filling her veins with the rapture of love, and *both* these emotions generating nothing but voluptuous movements in the French version of Martha, something that southern dancers understand even better. This waltz never fails to elicit the most boisterous applause—which it deserves—since the pantomime is thoroughly expressive, appealing, even at moments almost gripping, rather like a ghost story with intermingled jokes. And Mephistopheles, although ugly, nonetheless has distinguished manners, something always missing in our *German* devils.

The most striking part of the scenery was the Blocksberg with all its atrocities, a staging that left the wonders of the wolf's glen far behind.[40] Illuminated by horrid lights of every color, flashing from behind black firs and timber felled by the wind, it was swarming with animate skeletons, florescent dragons, frightful monstrosities—headless or lacerated—bleeding bodies, hideous witches, huge smoldering eyes peering out through the branches, man-sized toads, snakes bloated with poison, half-decayed corpses, and many other charming sights of this ilk. In the last act, however, the scenic display went too far by having the audacity to display heaven and hell at the same time! Heaven, which naturally occupied the upper part of the stage, admittedly sparkled in a luminous light blue; but this was unflattering both to the complexion of Gretchen's soul and to the angels pirouetting around her. They all looked more like the corpses of the Blocksberg than the blessed of the firmaments! In contrast, the devils dancing directly under the wooden floor of heaven were of a much more successful coloration, their red cheeks merited by the zeal with which they tore the Faust puppet to shreds until the curtain fell. (It is actually nice to see grown-ups act like such children!)

The theater itself is tastefully decorated—cheerful painting and gilding on a white satin ground—and the colorful flowers, birds, and butterflies are pleasant to look at. The interior of the boxes is light blue, and the railing pretends to be in red velvet. Beside the annoying cries of the soft-drink sellers, who call out the words *orgeat, limonade, glace,* in abbreviations very strange for a German ear, there was also a Jew wandering around with a supply of opera glasses that he was *renting* for ten sous a pair for the duration of the performance. I do not recall having noticed this practice before, and it provides a very convenient service if you have not brought your own along.

This letter will probably get to you by sleigh, because ever since I arrived, the climate has been totally Russian, though unfortunately without Russian stoves. May heaven grant you a better temperature in B——.

Your faithful Lou

Paris, January 20th, 1829[1]

DEAR JULIE!

It is certainly a lovely thing that on any day in Paris you may avail yourself of a walk in the Louvre and freely wander through the rooms of the gods and among creations of genius simply to escape from the rain or snow. For this general munificence, *vive le Roi!*

After spending my morning in the splendid galleries and visiting the new Egyptian Museum (which I will tell you about later), I happened upon an interesting companion at dinner in the person of a *géneral de l'Empire,* whose conversation I found preferable to the theater. He related a good many anecdotes from his own experience, imparting a more vivid picture and often a more penetrating view of those days than it is possible to convey in memoirs (where no one discloses the unvarnished truth *entirely*). It would take too long to relate much of this to you, and anyway, too much of the invigorating color of his language would have to be sacrificed, so I shall wait to deliver most of it in person. Just a few passages as an example.

It cannot be denied, said my interlocutor, that within Napoleon's family there have been many disreputable relationships that betrayed something *roture* or plebian (which does not at all imply ignoble birth, but rather an inadequate and undignified education). This is particularly so in the intense hatred and sordid mutual intrigues that prevailed between the family of Napoleon and that of the Empress Josephine, who in the end became their victim. At first Napoleon always took his wife's side, and for this his mother, Madame Letizia, often rebuked him to his face, saying he was a tyrant and calling him Tiberius, Nero, and other less classical names. By the way, the general said that madam often told him how even as a small child Napoleon had aspired to be the sole ruler, never caring about anyone but himself and those closest to him. He tyrannized his brothers from the very beginning, with the exception of Lucien, who never let the slightest offense go unavenged. Madame Letizia declared that she was therefore astonished how each of the brothers had managed to retain his character throughout those years. The general claimed that madam was convinced Napoleon would come to a bad end and made no secret of the fact that she was saving up for that catastrophe. Lucien shared this conviction, and as early as 1811 he remarked to the general, "L'ambition de cet homme est insatiable, et vous vivrez peut-être, pour voir sa carcasse et toute sa famille jetées dans les égouts de Paris."[2]

After he left military service, the general held a post (he did not tell me which) in the court of the Empress Mother. In any event, at Napoleon's coronation, madam gave him the task of monitoring the number of fauteuils, chairs, and taborets set up for the imperial family, and of surreptitiously reporting his findings to her as soon as she appeared. The general, at the time rather unaccustomed to court etiquette, wondered about this strange assignment, but carried it out promptly and reported that he had counted only two fauteuils, one chair, and so and so many taborets. "Ah ha, that is what I thought," Madame Mère cried, red with fury; "the chair is meant for me—but their plans are flawed!" Striding quickly up to the portentous chair, she asked the attending chamberlain, her lips trembling, to point out her seat. He gestured with a deep bow toward the chair—the taborets had already been occupied by the queens and sisters. Taking hold of the chair, ramming it against the chamberlain's feet so hard that he nearly cried out with pain, the indignant Corsican then charged into the room where the emperor and Josephine were waiting, and the most indecent scene ensued. In the strongest terms, the empress mother explained that if she were not given a fauteuil immediately, she would leave the hall, but not before loudly declaring the reason for her behavior. Napoleon, although furious, had to put a good face on it and ducked the charge by letting all the blame fall on poor Count Ségur, whom he identified as solely responsible for this gaffe. "And soon," the general added, "one saw the worthy count, totally alarmed, arrive carrying a fauteuil for *sa Majesté l'Impératrice mère*." This was characteristic, and that the guilt lay with the emperor and not Josephine was demonstrated when the exact same thing happened at his marriage to Maria Louise, but by then his mother was too humbled and intimidated and had lost the courage to resist.

Napoleon was raised to be a bigot; and although he was too perceptive to remain that way or was perhaps never seriously bigoted, the force of habit, as is true for us all, had nonetheless influenced him so strongly that he never entirely escaped the effect of those first impressions. It even happened occasionally, when he was suddenly taken aback by something, that he would involuntarily make the sign of the cross, a gesture that, coming from a man like the emperor, struck the skeptical children of the Revolution as highly disconcerting.*

And finally a charming aspect of Charles IV's character. He is thought to have been incapable of kindhearted consideration, yet those who knew him personally were aware that this prince was exceptionally liberal and beneficent, if also extremely weak and uninformed. He was much more worthy as a person than a king.

When Napoleon's brother Lucien went to Spain to take up the post of ambassador of the republic, the general, my informant, accompanied him as secretary to the legation. The previous ambassador had flaunted all the crassness of republican manners, thus scandalizing the most etiquette-bound and formal court in the world. Needless to say, people feared even greater arrogance from the brother of the French head of state. But Lucien had the good sense to do exactly the opposite, even appearing in shoes and a bagwig, and fulfilling all his ceremonial and courtly duties with such punctuality that everyone at court was sent into raptures of delight and

---

* My friend also wrote *me* about the conversation with his dinner companion and included an amusing detail that, though warranting no place in a letter to a lady, can perhaps be hazarded here in a footnote, since it captures so well the tone both of the important people of the day and their ruler—although I warn the ladies in advance! Once while the narrator and several other military men were present, Napoleon playfully reproached Marshal Masséna for being unable to live without women. "I cannot comprehend this weak creature," the emperor said. "The whole time that I was commander in Italy, I never let a woman get too close to me, so as not to be distracted from more important matters. Mais j'ai ma saison comme les chiens," he added, "et j'attends jusque là." The general insisted that ever since, if anyone at court noticed a particular inclination to jealousy on the part of Empress Josephine, the courtiers would smile at each other and exclaim, "Ah, l'Empereur est dans sa saison."—*The Editor.* ["But I have my season like dogs do . . . and I wait until then." . . . . "Ah, the Emperor is in his season!"—*Translator*]

gratitude. Lucien did not just become extremely popular, he became the *true darling* of the entire royal family. He returned this friendship sincerely, often passing on grave warnings to the king and the Prince of the Peace about his brother's disloyalty and insatiable ambition, and speaking unreservedly about him at every opportunity.[3] Yet the old king's confidence in his *grand ami*, as he called Napoleon, remained unshakable until the last moment.

Before his departure, Lucien crowned his popularity with a magnificent celebration, the likes of which Spain had never seen; it supposedly cost about four hundred thousand francs. The highest-ranking members of the court and many grandees honored it with their presence, as did the entire royal family, who seemed barely able to express their feelings of obligation to the ambassador. A few days later, all the members of the legation received magnificent presents. Only the ambassador came away empty-handed, which, given the informal republican atmosphere in the embassy palace, caused quite a few jokes to be exchanged at his expense.

Meanwhile the final audience had taken place, and Lucien's departure was scheduled for the next day. At the point when all hope of a gift had been abandoned, an officer of the Walloon Guards, with escort, arrived at the hotel and delivered a large crate to the embassy secretary; it contained a painting—a keepsake from the king to Napoleon's brother. Informed of this, Lucien remarked that it was doubtless the *Venus* by Titian, which he had praised many times in the king's presence, and it was certainly a work of great value, although he was quite concerned about transporting it and had to admit he would have preferred something else. Nonetheless the officer was thanked with great civility, and as Lucien dismissed him, he pressed him to accept his own precious breast pin. Subsequently the ambassador ordered that the picture be removed from the crate, taken out of the frame, which was to be left behind, and rolled up so that it could be packed on the top deck of a carriage. The secretary proceeded to do as he had been asked; but as the cloth wrapping was removed, he found not the beautiful face of the lauded Venus but—smiling at him cheerfully—the less-than-lovely countenance of the king. Feeling a certain schadenfreude about the amusing revelation, he was just about to hurry to the ambassador and deliver a jocular report, when the unwrapping was completed, and an even greater surprise stopped him in his tracks: the entire painting was bordered like a miniature with large diamonds, stones that Lucien later sold in France for four million francs. This was indeed a truly regal surprise, and the ambassador was quite correct in changing his initial instructions about leaving the frame behind.

In Badajoz, according to the general, Lucien became very closely acquainted with the queen of Portugal, who had given him a political rendezvous there, and he speculated that Dom Miguel might well be the issue.[4] It is certainly true, as I wrote you already from London, that the prince looks remarkably like Napoleon.

January 13th, 1829

TODAY MY INSPECTION of theaters brought me to the Gaîté, and I will admit I had a very good time there.[5] However genteelly the French may protest, their real national stage now consists of such small melodramas and burlesques. In fact, these may be partly responsible for the public's remarkable shift to the Romantic, for people have become heartily tired of the *meager* fare of the . . . *pathos tragique, qui longtemps ennuya en termes magnifiques.*[6]

When I failed to give you a theater report recently, it was because I had been bored at the Théâtre Français in a truly objectionable way. Mademoiselle Mars was not performing, and the stage—which once boasted the greatness of Talma and Fleury—had sunk to the depths of wretchedness. I will give you a short account of both productions, one from the national and one from the suburban theater,[7] and although the latter case concerns no more than a melodrama and is consequently a matter of coarsely applied colors, frivolity, and *coups de théâtre,* I nonetheless leave it to you to determine whether the classical or melodramatic should be given preference. I will begin with the melodrama at the Gaîté, noting in advance that the actors were skilled, the costumes appropriate, the decorations as well as all aspects of the scenery very good, and the ensemble (as in nearly all Parisian theaters, with the exception of the Théâtre Français) excellent.

The play opens with dancing and merriment.[8] Sailors and factory hands are at a celebration in the garden of their boss, Mr. Vanrick, a man of significant independent means, who, when he arrived from the New World six years ago, became the benefactor of the Dutch territorial city in which he settled. Because of this he aroused the government's envy, and the primary judicial officer is now his deadly foe, a result of various indignities on the officer's part that drew the people's affection to the newcomer. During the festivities, Vanrick himself appears along with his sweet daughter Ysel, who is escorted by young Frédérick, son of the baron de Stéeven. They are met with jubilant cheers. Vanrick distributes presents to the most deserving and asks his daughter and the baron's son to lead the children to the banquet being prepared next door. He stays behind and confesses in a pensive monologue that all the happiness, honor, and love surrounding him cannot take away the curse that haunts him. In fact, they make it more dreadful. He abandons himself to the most profound anguish, though its cause is not disclosed.

His elderly servant enters, and in a short discussion, we learn that this man alone knows everything, but that he nonetheless considers his master's fears to be chimerical and tries to calm him with the assurance that his secret is absolutely safe and its discovery next to impossible. The daughter now returns with her nurse and asks her father for permission to go fetch some of her young friends for the celebration. A tender scene follows, in which the father feasts his eyes on the marvelous, blooming charms of his daughter and then sends her off with a solemn embrace, a gesture that only the old servant comprehends. At the door, she encounters Frédérick's father, richly attired and accompanied by his entourage. Vanrick receives him with great reverence, almost to the point of repelling his friendliness, until the baron concludes his praiseful accolades and respectful avowals by saying that, despite his standing as one of the richest and most eminent noblemen in the country, he has come on his son's behalf to ask for the hand of Vanrick's daughter. Greatly agitated, Vanrick explains that such a union would be impossible, and though the baron makes it clear that the young couple are already in agreement about this and bound together with the most profound affection, his pleas are in vain. "That's the last thing I need in my wretchedness!" Vanrick calls out, almost in despair, just as the door is thrown open and his daughter, holding her nurse's hand, dashes in breathless, followed by a beaming young troublemaker, who, disconcerted at the sight of the baron and Vanrick, pauses for a moment but then quickly pulls himself together and, with the presence of mind of a man of the world, attempts to excuse his behavior. The baron asks scornfully who he might be, and he responds with a proud demeanor, "My name is Knight Vandeck. I am first secretary of the grand pensionary of Holland, Count d'Assenfeld, who has just arrived here in order to review the state of affairs in the province."

"Is the count here already?" asks the baron, with increased politeness. "If so, I must hurry to welcome him, because he has granted me the honor of staying at my residence; I am baron de Stéeven and this is Mr. Vanrick, the father of the young lady who ..."

Vandeck interrupts by bowing and approaching Vanrick to apologize again, but when he catches sight of his face, he stops speechless. Quickly gaining control of himself, however, he attributes his confusion to the awkwardness of his position, and hurries off after uttering a few commonplace remarks. At the doorway, unnoticed by the others, he turns around once more, casts an attentive glance at Vanrick, who is preoccupied with his daughter. Vandeck then leaves the house, uttering the words "by heaven, it is he!"

The scene changes.

We are looking at a sumptuous room as Count Assefeldt is ushered in by the baron. Following some discussion about the state of the province, the baron mentions Vanrick and his service to the country, adding that just today he asked him, on his son's behalf, for his daughter's hand in marriage, convinced that Vanrick's virtue, influence, wealth, and dignified character would make him the equal of any nobleman. During this speech, we see the secretary Vandeck smiling derisively, and he now steps forward to announce the arrival of the city authorities. They have come to show their respect for the grand pensionary, and the audience quickly learns that their leader is Vandeck's uncle, Vanrick's aforementioned enemy. In the report that Vandeck now makes to Count Assefeldt, he publically accuses Vanrick of being nothing but a shrewd trouble-maker who, from behind the mask of a factory manager, attempts to mislead the people. He says his case is supported by the enigma surrounding the identity of Vanrick's family, the utter uncer-tainty about his origins, and the obscurity of his intentions, finally intimating that the man may well be serving as a spy in the pay of a foreign power. Count Assefeldt remains cool but benevo-lent, and urges a united response and collective diligence for the general good. He dismisses the authorities as well as the baron, and then turns sternly to his secretary, emphatically admonish-ing him for the impropriety of his conduct that morning, about which the baron had complained. The knight, with sullen resentment, begs his pardon, but adds that his admittedly reprehensible conduct has nonetheless led to a remarkable discovery, namely, the true identity of the revered Mr. Vanrick.

"So, who is he?" the count asks expectantly.

"The executioner of Amsterdam!"

Astonished, the count presses his hands together, and the knight continues his explanation.

"As a seven-year-old child," he says, "in unwitting play, I made off with a costly diamond ring of my mother's. The hunt for it lasted a long time but was unsuccessful, and afterward, in order to cure me forever of such a bad habit, my mother came up with the strange scheme of summoning the executioner, along with his heir and official successor, his eldest son, to appear in their dread-ful vestments, both holding broad swords in their hands. The young one grabbed me and shouted at me, brandishing his sword, predicting that the cold iron would bring my death if I ever again abandoned myself to the abominable crime of stealing. A benevolent swoon then freed me from further dread, but I never forgot the young man's countenance, so horrible it was for me. Even after twenty years, I recognized it today at first glance—and not without an inward shudder."

The count remains incredulous, stressing the improbability that a memory from one's ear-liest youth could be so reliable after twenty years, and asks his secretary to maintain the deepest silence, at least for the time being.

Here we are taken back to Vanrick's house, where he is talking to Ysel. She confesses her love for Frédérick and, before departing, urgently implores her father's consent. In the next scene, Vanrick confides everything to his aged servant, who encourages him at length and makes it seem so plausible that the secret will never be uncovered that he admits he has never before felt more reassured and safe. Shedding tears of paternal love, Vanrick sends for the young couple so he can extend his most sincere blessing. Everyone's happiness seems complete, and the old baron, who has also arrived, shares their delight. He invites father and daughter to a fete he is hosting that day for Count Assefeldt, an ideal opportunity to introduce his future daughter-in-law and Vanrick to the grand pensionary and ask for his favor.

They all exit, and the stage is transformed into a picture gallery, where a large party is gathered in a magnificent adjoining hall glimpsed behind a colonnade. In the foreground, the count is still talking to the government officials, who respectfully make room as baron de Stéeven arrives to present the Vanrick family, loudly proclaiming them benefactors of the province. The count, politely bowing to the daughter, says with a certain gravity, "Such a virtue is an asset to *anyone*," and fixing his gaze on the father, he adds, "no matter what class he is from," at which he quickly turns his back on him.

Vanrick anxiously betrays his perplexity, while Vandeck, standing to the side, never takes his eyes off him. Ysel asks apprehensively whether her father is unwell, since he has so suddenly turned pale. "Nothing, nothing," he stammers, "I'll be along in a minute." He lays her hand in Frédérick's, who leads her hesitantly from the hall. Everyone exits except for Vanrick, who, horribly stunned, pauses and places his hand on his forehead. Meanwhile Vandeck has withdrawn into a corner as if lying in wait like a tiger for its prey. Suddenly the knight steps forward, presses his hat onto his head, and striking Vanrick on the shoulder, calls out in a loud voice, "You shameless creature! The first magistrate of Holland forbids you to sit down at table in his presence."

This scene is gripping. The unhappy man, entirely beside himself, sinks to his knees and cries, "Have mercy!" But Vandeck has already disappeared, leaving Vanrick shattered. "Righteous God," he cries with the pain of despair, "has the sign of Cain been burned into my brow, so that even strangers can read my disgrace?" Now his daughter, who never let him out of her sight, hurries back from the hall and implores him to tell her the reason for his incomprehensible outburst. But before any others arrive, he sweeps her away with him. "Let us flee, my daughter," he whispers in her ear, "only flight and the cover of night can hide us from mortal eyes." The two plunge out the door, and the curtain falls.

According to Dutch law, the post of Amsterdam executioner was inherited, and the son who was the designated successor could not evade it, unless he was a cripple. The family members were considered bondsmen of the state, and an escape was punished as a felony. Thus Vanrick had to bear the double burden of the infamy of his trade and the crime of having escaped from it. Enjoying exceptional luck in all his enterprises, he amassed a large fortune abroad and, returning for the first time after a long absence, had hoped to spend the last years of his life in his native country, unrecognized. Yet the consciousness of his misery* had never allowed him a moment's peace.

We learn these details during a discussion between Vanrick and his ancient servant in the shuttered house where he is preparing for their flight. His daughter enters in tears and begs her

---

* Conscience?

father to explain. The scene, which is heart-wrenching, ends with his confession, although he does not have the strength to utter it in words but must write it down. Ysel grasps the sheet of paper with trembling hand, unfolds it slowly, and after reading the frightful text cries out in a tone of anguish, "Father!" Then, slumping down in a swoon, she stammers out "executioner!" and collapses unconscious to the floor. Her father cannot endure the sight and disappears through the door. When she revives in the arms of the loyal servant, she gestures to be left alone, prays, then throws herself onto a chair, buries her head in both hands, and weeps bitter tears. A loud noise at the window startles her. Astonished, she sees a man enveloped in a red cloak, who bounds into the room. It is Vandeck. She is about to call for help, but he asks reverently for a brief hearing for her father's sake. A fiery declaration of love follows: Vandeck volunteers to flee with her, keep her and her father safe forever if she will be his; but if she refuses, he threatens every possible kind of ruination. Since her rebuff is as cold as it is dignified, he ends by telling her with uncontrolled fury that he knows very well who actually stands between them, but that Frédérick will not be able to escape him either, and his death, within just a few hours, will be *her* fault. The frightened girl calls for help, and Vanrick's servants and factory workers break down the door. But Vandeck draws his sword and manages to battle his way outside, using his cloak as a shield.

Now we see a gallery in the baron's palace. It is a night scene, sparsely illuminated by a solitary lamp. Frédérick paces restlessly back and forth, considering what he should do. He cannot understand the sudden flight of Vanrick and his daughter, and his thoughts become mired in hypotheses. Meanwhile a light hand knocks on his door. He opens it, bewildered, and Ysel's nurse enters in disguise with a message from her mistress, beseeching Frédérick to come down to the garden; a terrible fate is compelling his beloved to abandon all caution in order to speak with him once more. With increasing astonishment, he accepts the invitation, which he finds as disconcerting as it is endearing.

The scenery changes and beautiful moonlight shows us a carefully maintained Dutch garden with boxwood figures and flower beds. Here Ysel, dressed for travel, anxiously awaits her bridegroom. Frédérick enters, and amid many tears and mysterious words, she says her very last goodbyes to him. She then declares that the main purpose of this rendezvous is to warn him about Vandeck, who has vowed to kill him. Frédérick now thinks that Vandeck is the reason for their separation—perhaps he has even won the family's favor! He heaps reproaches on the unfortunate Ysel, and when his fury is at its peak, Vandeck emerges from behind a hedge and, drawing his sword, calls to him mockingly: "Give Ysel up, or fight for her like a knight!" Ysel and her nurse cry for help, while the young men battle to the death. The baron and Count Assefeldt, in their nightclothes, rush in with servants and torches, just as Vandeck, mortally wounded, sinks to the ground. Cursing himself and his murderer, he explains with his dying breath that he had been treacherously ambushed by Frédérick. "But," he concludes, "Vanrick will avenge me on my murderer—*Vanrick Polder*, the executioner of Amsterdam!" Frédérick and the baron recoil in horror, Ysel lies unconscious in the arms of her nurse, and Vandeck dies. Here the curtain falls for the second time.

Several days seem to have passed. The scene is a courtroom, its doors besieged by the populace. Frédérick is interrogated for the last time and is convicted of the murder, at which the judges, presided over by Vandeck's uncle, unanimously condemn him to death. Although Count Assefeldt, who is present, is profoundly distressed, he cannot halt the course of the law. The incensed crowd manages to break down the doors with the intent of liberating Frédérick, but the count calms the mutineers with a dignified address, which he closes by declaring that the law must stand above everything else, but that all hope is not yet lost, since the general proconsul could exercise the right of pardon. Having already been informed of the outcome of the ruling, he has sent baron de Stéeven ahead to the proconsul in The Hague.

Vanrick's enemy, however, makes use of the uproar to arrange for the execution to be moved forward, and brashly counters the count's appeal by claiming his duty as magistrate, which is his to discharge. Here Vanrick, or rather Polder, joins in, and on his knees begs the count for mercy toward the unfortunate and, according to his daughter's statement, innocent Frédérick. The count, however, regrets that under the circumstances the daughter's testimony can have no validity against the clear accusation of a dying man; that Frédérick is guilty of Vandeck's death, however it may have happened; and finally, that the count's own authority does not extend far enough to obstruct the course of the law. Everything now depends on the primary magistrate, the uncle of the murdered man, who is standing here before them. With a diabolical laugh, this man fixes his gaze on the frightened supplicant, and as Polder prostrates himself, says in a friendly tone, "Now then, dear Polder, you appear as if summoned here! I understand that you have not yet performed your masterstroke, and I hereby requisition you, in the name of the government and in the absence of anyone else who could carry out your task, for the imminent execution."

Vanrick Polder, struck dumb with horror and rage, at first stares at his inhuman enemy for a long time in silence, until he erupts with blistering words that at moments attain an almost tragic grandeur, finally crying out, "I have never yet spilled the blood of my fellow man, and I will never do so. But if I had to, then it would be yours, you monster!" Then, as if suddenly inspired and transformed, he adds after a pause, "Forgive me! Grief robbed me of my senses. It is to be—I will obey the command. Allow me a short time to prepare." Astonished and appalled, they both watch him leave and then follow in silence.

We now find Frédérick in his cell, where Count Assefeldt has just entered to ask the condemned man if there is anything he might still do for him. Frédérick would only like to know whether a quickly performed marriage to Ysel, and her appointment as the heir to his name and fortune, could be valid in the present circumstances. "Certainly," the count responds, "but her true name and class must be clearly and correctly recorded in the document." Frédérick shudders, but remains true to his resolve. The count leaves to go fetch Ysel, who is led in, a picture of inconsolable anguish.

(At this point I must comment that in France, the actors take care that they look the way their emotional state would dictate in such circumstances, rather than appearing with bright red, chubby cheeks even as they are suffering mortal fear and despair, or even dying in this glowing condition, as I have so often seen in Germany.)

Frédérick and Ysel present an authentic picture of the most extreme suffering. He asks her to swear to carry out a request for his own peace of mind. His word, she cries out fervently, is her command, and she falls tearfully to her knees, begging his forgiveness. Helping her up, he says, "What do I have to forgive you for? I have you alone to thank for the little bit of happiness I have enjoyed, Ysel! In a few minutes you will become my wife, in a few hours my widow. Forget, then, the past altogether, and live a new and happier life!"

The sad ceremony takes place in the presence of the count. Soon an orderly enters bringing a letter from the old baron. "Praise God," the count exclaims, hoping for a pardon from the proconsul. But as he reads, his face becomes mask-like. "The unhappy young man is now lost!" he says with a deep sigh. For the baron has written that he was unable to locate the proconsul in

The Hague and although he will continue the search, does not yet know where he may find him. He therefore requests a delay, which the count is unfortunately not in a position to grant without the consent of Vandeck's uncle—an impossible hope. A guard appears, and Frédérick is led off.

The scene changes to an open landscape with busy canals in the background. Crowds are gathering to watch the execution; they are uttering wild threats against the cruel judge, which finally degenerate into rebellion. The gallows are stormed and smashed to pieces, soldiers move in, the theater is filled with tumult and fighting. Vandeck's uncle, in the front lines of the military, manages to reestablish order and commands that since the scaffold has been destroyed, the balcony of a nearby house should be set up for the execution. To one side of the stage, you can hear the men at work on this, while Count Assefeldt mixes his pleas for an extension with serious threats—all to no avail. The procession appears. Frédérick in the middle in fetters, and Polder, in the red robe of his office, holding in his hand the broad, unsheathed sword, move across the stage at the rear. Soldiers with bayonets at the ready struggle against the indignant crowd. Slowly the procession disappears, until only the count, profoundly grieved, remains behind with just one servant. As in the *Jungfrau von Orleans*,[9] the servant, who has climbed up a small hill, reports what is happening to the count, who has turned away in horror. At last the scout calls down from above, "Now the young baron is kneeling . . . they are blindfolding him . . . the executioner is approaching him . . . Oh my God . . ." A muffled thump is heard offstage, like that of a sword falling onto a block. The count covers his face and steps back shuddering, as Polder, deathly pale and wrapped in his cloak, is led across the stage, supported by two citizens, while a loud roar rings out from behind the scene.

"Good heavens! What have you done?" cries the count.

"Here, see what I've done," Polder answers in a weak voice, and opening his cloak he holds out the bound stump of his right arm, from which he himself has just cut off the hand. "My young friend can now be sure of at least a few more hours," he adds, his voice weak.

The people stream past mute and stupefied, but Vandeck's enraged uncle is with them, and he orders that the irresponsible executioner be thrown at once into the deepest dungeon. While he is still speaking, however, an anxious clamor rings out in the distance. You hear the gallop of hooves and see baron de Stéeven dismount his lathered horse, hold the proconsul's pardon high in the air, and cry loudly "Mercy! Mercy!" before collapsing exhausted into the arms of the bystanders. Count Assefeldt unfolds the sheet of paper, reads Frédérick's reprieve aloud, and simultaneously notifies the first magistrate of the immediate suspension of his duties. Deeply moved, he embraces the freed man, and the curtain falls.

I am well aware of the long litany that aesthetes can offer here about horrible circumstances, *coups de theater*, improbabilities, etc. But it must be remembered, I repeat, that we are talking only about a melodrama, from which no great demands should be made. And in any case, I am convinced that no impartial mind could watch this performance without feeling deeply engaged.

Let us now move on to the Théâtre Français, which I can dispatch much more succinctly, given how well-known the plays are. Following a Greco-French tragedy, in which the classical costumes attempted in vain to transform the French into Greeks, the old provincial hero Joanny struggled in vain to construct a weak copy of the god-like Talma, and Duchesnois (who has become inadmissibly ugly) raised her hands in vain at the end of every sentence in a lachrymose, antiquated, and stilted manner (also trembling quite *à la Talma*), and the rest reeled off performances of truly dismal mediocrity, until the *Mercure galant* was finally staged in conclusion.[10] The threadbare, embroidered silk clothes, as well as the clumsiness with which the modern actors wore them, suggested the days of yore in which the action is set. The ladies, on the other hand, made it easy for themselves by dressing according to today's latest fashion. The comedy, having absolutely no plot, is nothing but an occasional piece of its era, and to perform it today is almost absurd. At its high point, an old man appears and breaks off his relationship with his young fiancée shortly before the wedding. Then, when confronted by her brother as she and her best friend look on, he explains bluntly, "C'est tout simple, j'ai peur d'être cocu."[11] He goes on to recite a few hundred verses that orchestrate this theme in the most *lurid* light.

The play closes by posing a riddle, and when no one can solve it, the author himself does. What is it about? Breaking wind! "Oh," cries the young lady, "one must have a good nose to guess that." And with this classic joke, the curtain falls. To me this poor example of breaking wind seemed, in truth, the last gasp of the Théâtre Français!

Considering that all genres are good except the boring genre, the contents of this last play were better suited to a crooked back alley in the provinces. What seems even more remarkable is that it is now necessary to put on melodramas (which is what they are in content, although absent the music) in this exalted, classical national theater. It is these alone that attract an audience, as evident in the only moneymaking play of the moment, *The Spy*.[12]

Thus one theater after another plants the Romantic flag more or less successfully, while the tragedies and dramas appearing daily à la Shakespeare, as the French say, toss all the revered unities into disarray. And this without even the slightest pangs of conscience on the part of author or audience! The Revolution has given the French a new lease on life in every respect. Their poetry, too, is newly reborn, and Germany, perennially envious, calls out to them joyfully "Glück auf!"[13]

January 14th, 1829

TODAY I VISITED some new buildings, including the Bourse (Figure 124),[14] which is surrounded by a stately colonnade. It is imposing in size and overall impression, although the tall and narrow arched windows behind the columns look very unsightly. Modern needs often harmonize quite poorly with the classical style. The interior is overwhelming as well, and the deceptiveness of the painted ceiling in the main hall is perfect. You would swear you were looking at bas-reliefs, albeit bad ones.

Today I noticed for the first time that significant improvements have been made on the boulevards through the removal of several buildings, and the Portes St-Denis and St-Martin look much better now than they used to. Louis XIV deserves these monuments, if only for his embellishment of the capital, because whatever you see in Paris that is beautiful or grand was begun, in fact, by Louis XIV or Napoleon. Fortunately the allées have been carefully protected, unlike on Unter den Linden or the Dönhoffplatz in Berlin, where the great trees were felled in order to plant tiny, branchless sticks in their place.

The many *Dames Blanches* and omnibuses—carriages holding twenty to thirty people—are a strange sight, continuously traversing the boulevards from one end to the other and accommodating every tired pedestrian at fixed and very cheap prices.[15] When someone raises a hand, the conductor, who is seated at the back, rings a bell and the driver stops. A folding stair is lowered and a few seconds later the forward movement continues. Just three unhappy horses pull

LA BOURSE.

these weighty vehicles, and when the streets are slippery, as they are now, I often saw all three fall down next to one another.

People say that England is hell for horses, but if metempsychosis turns out to be true, I would nonetheless always ask to return as an English horse rather than a French one. The way these unhappy animals are treated here can be truly outrageous! It would be desirable if the police would protect them, as they do in England. I remember once witnessing a poor cabriolet horse in London being similarly mistreated by his driver. "Come along," said the Englishman who was accompanying me. "If you have an hour, you can see this man quickly punished." Very nonchalantly, he hailed the coach. We climbed in, and he ordered the driver to take us to the police station. There he presented his charge that the coachman had tormented and abused his horse unnecessarily. I testified to this, and the fellow had to pay a rather significant financial penalty on the spot, after which he was obliged to drive us back. You can easily imagine his good humor.

Such omnibuses are being used in other parts of the city too, and the longest route costs only a few sous. It is highly entertaining to take this kind of ride in the evening, even without any objective, because of the strange characters you come across, and the bizarre conversations you overhear. You often feel that you are witnessing a performance at the Variétés and rediscovering faithful renditions of originals by Brunet and Odry (Figure 125).[16]

You know how much I enjoy being among people and observing them in this way, and that I am particularly fond of watching the middle classes. These days they are the only ones who are still somewhat idiosyncratic, and they are also the happiest; for truly, the coin has been flipped. Through

125

*View of the Boulevards
of Paris with the New
Carriages.*

custom and circumstance, the advantage is now held by the middle classes down to the artisans. The higher classes, accustomed as they are to their rights and pretensions, find themselves condemned to ongoing opposition and humiliation. As long as the funds are there, things go along reasonably well. But ostentation (the original sin of the rich—or might that be avarice?) renders their money far less pleasurable than it would be for those on lower rungs of the ladder. However, if their social rank is not supported by wealth, their fellow citizens consider them to be, with the exception of criminals, the most deplorable of all, and just barely above those who are actually starving.

Therefore everyone should, I repeat, properly assess his position in the world and sacrifice nothing to ambition or vanity, for no period in history has been less favorable to these attributes. (Here I exclude the aspiration to perform *true service,* which finds its reward in, and only in, the works themselves.) We genteel folk are now effortlessly led to the wisdom of self-denial and practical philosophies of every type—thank heaven for that!

Pondering all this as I rode along in the *Dame Blanche,* I arrived at Franconi's theater, which even a blind man can find just by following the smell of horses. What is being staged here is in

abominable taste, mind you; indeed, an audience that never saw anything else would themselves eventually become half brutish. In contrast with the senseless dramas, however, the individual balancing acts are often quite worth watching. I especially liked the rope dancer called Diavolo, who certainly surpasses all of his rivals, just as Vestris once did his.[17] A more beautiful form and greater agility, stability, and perfected grace of this kind are almost unimaginable. He is the winged Mercury who has once again assumed human form; the air seems to be his true element and the rope a mere ornament that he drapes around himself like a garland. At a towering height you see him in the wildest swoop while he lies free and unbound on the rope, at one moment wafting by close to the boxes with the classical dignity of the ancient world, and immediately thereafter, head down and legs pointed up, executing an *entrechat* like a marionette in the clouds of the theater's heavens. That he can spin himself backward and forward like a wheel, with the speed of a clock mechanism; stretch out untethered along the length of a rope; or swing back and forth on it while hanging from just one foot goes without saying. He earns his name with his deeds: *Diavolo non può meglio.*[18]

AS AN ADDENDUM to my letter of yesterday, I have bought you a *Dame Blanche* filled with
... bonbons! And I have also included, as a belated Christmas gift for Mademoiselle Helmine,
a bronze pendulum clock with a running fountain at its base and a functioning telegraph at its
top. Tell her that she can make very good use of the latter to engage in public conversations that
only the initiated will be able to understand. Paris has an inexhaustible supply of such baubles,
although they are primarily aimed at foreigners, since the French rarely buy them, finding them
(not entirely unjustifiably) *de mauvais goût.*

Today, in order to be done with the theaters, I went to three in a row. First, in the Théâtre
Français, two acts from the fairly recent, extremely wretched tragedy *Isabelle de Bavière.*[19] Again
I found my earlier impressions confirmed; not only were the performers mediocrity itself (with
the exception of Joanny, who was not bad in the role of Charles VI, even though he cannot be
compared to Talma), but neither did the costumes, scenery, and all the other paraphernalia rise
to the level of the lowest theater on the boulevards. The people of Paris, among others, were
represented by seven men and two women, and the *Pairs de France* were portrayed by three
or four extras shrouded in real rags, with gold paper crowns on their heads, like in a puppet
show.[20] The hall was empty and the cold almost unbearable. So I drove quickly to the Théâtre de
l'Ambigu-Comique, where I found a pretty new building with very fresh scenery. As an entr'acte
they put on a kind of ballet that was a fair parody of our territorial army and at least not boring.
I have been surprised, by the way, that the French do not respond to the Prussian army horns as
the Burgundians do to the alpine horns of the Swiss, which they hate because, as the Chronicle
claims, "*à Grandson les avoient trop ouis!*"[21]

My evening closed with the Italian Lyric Theater.[22] Here you find the most select audience,
for it is the fashionable stage. The theater is very nicely decorated, the lighting brilliant, and the
singing up to one's expectations. It is still odd, however, that even a cast consisting entirely of
Italians never sings *abroad* the way it does in Italy, never achieves that delicious whole. Their fire
seems to cool in an alien region, and their humor dries up. They know they will be applauded,
of course, but they will no longer be part of a family with their public; the buffo (like the lead
singer) will be only half understood and probably only half appreciated musically as well. In Italy
the opera is part of nature and, I might add, a necessity; in Germany, England, and France it is
merely an artistic treat and a way of passing time.

Madame Malibran García does not, it seems to me, equal Sontag in this role (*La Cenerentola*
was being performed),[23] but she does have a style of her own that is more and more attractive the
longer one hears it; and I have no doubt that she also has roles in which the palm would accrue to
her before all others. She is married to an American, and her singing style seems very American
to me—that is, free, bold, and republican—whereas Pasta sweeps you away despotically like an
aristocrat or even an autocrat, and Sontag warbles mellifluously and *mezza voce* as if in some heavenly realm. The tenor Bordogni had the difficult task of singing without a voice and, given these
conditions, he did what he could. Zucchelli was, as always, excellent, and Santini his worthy rival.
Nearly without exception, the acting and singing had more life, power, and grace than on any
other stage outside of Italy.

When I got back to my hotel, I was surprised by one of those Parisian amenities that truly
brings dishonor to a city. Although my hotel is a respectable one and situated in the busiest part

of town, I thought I had stumbled into a sewer, for they had just begun dredging out certain cess-pits, something that pollutes the buildings here twice a year.

I have already burned a dozen pastilles, but without any significant result.[24]

January 24th, 1829

I WAS SEATED in a cabriolet quite early this morning in order to take a longer tour than usual and visit some old friends. First I had the driver go to Notre Dame, and on the way, as we came to the Pont Neuf, found myself regretting that the statue of Henri IV had been placed there. It is set so inappropriately on the naked base intended for the obelisk that Napoleon planned to erect here, and for which the site had certainly been chosen with great astuteness. Instead, the dimin-utive statue has a background of massive buildings closing around it in a colossal triangle, and the prancing horse looks at a distance like a hopping insect.[25] While I was still pursuing this train of thought and wondering what would have come of Paris if Napoleon had continued to rule, my driver suddenly called out "*Voilà* la morgue." I asked him to stop (for I love lugubrious emotions) and entered the mortuary, which I had never seen before, and where, as you know, the bodies of all the unidentified dead are kept. Behind a wooden grille, you see a small, clean room with eight wooden litters, all painted black and arranged in rank and file, the top ends turned to the wall, the lower ends pointed at the viewer. On these the dead are laid out naked, while their clothing and effects hang on the white wall behind them, making it easier for people to identify their rela-tives. Just one corpse was lying there today, an old man whose physiognomy was very much that of a French national. With rings in his ears and on his fingers, he looked quite cheerful, smiling deceptively with open eyes like a wax figure, and with an expression suggesting that he had been on the verge of offering his neighbor a pinch of snuff when death hurried him away. His clothes were good—*superbes*, as a ragged fellow next to me said, eyeing them wistfully. There were no signs of violence to be seen on the body. Death had likely struck the old man in some distant part of the city, and his relatives were not yet aware of it, because destitution seems to have played no role here. One of the custodians told me a strange fact, namely, that suicide by drowning—which is now *the* fashionable method in Paris—is two-thirds less common in winter than summer. However ludicrous it may sound, the reason must be that the water is too cold in the winter (the Seine is only very rarely frozen over). But just as trifles and everyday things have considerably more sway over life's significant events than we may imagine, so too do they seem to exercise their power even in death, and despair itself remains somehow vulnerable and a prisoner of the sensual.

You will remember the three portals of Notre Dame, with their oak doors embellished with magnificent floral designs and arabesques in bronze, and how they present such a curious sight, as does the whole facade, so interesting in its details. But like the ancient temple in Jerusalem, Notre Dame is disfigured by booths and vendors installed everywhere, even inside the church. A new coat of paint has rendered the interior, so unrelated to the exterior, even less noteworthy.

Continuing my tour, I got out for a few moments at the Panthéon. It is a shame that the location and surroundings of this temple are so very disadvantageous. I have always found the interior almost too simple and unembellished, which does not suit the style; and the new ceiling by Girodet is almost invisible without opera glasses.[26] The opening of the cupola is too small and high to allow anything of the painting to be seen clearly. I spied a loose piece of carpet hanging on one pillar, and on enquiring learned that it was the work of the unfortunate Marie Antoinette

LETTER 48

685

and had been donated to the church by Madame Letizia. Above the side altar was an inscription, "Autel privilégié"[27]—that is, indulgences dispensed here!

The associations this sight awakened in me brought the nearby menagerie to mind, and I drove to the Jardin des Plantes, where it had grown too cold for the animals. All of them, both living and dead, were locked away, and I could only visit one large polar bear. As I entered, he showed no sign of being disturbed and continued sweeping his compound with enormous patience and calm, like a day laborer. After using his forepaws as a broom, he brought straw and dry snow into his den and made a soft bed out of them, and there he finally stretched out with a contented grumble. His neighbor Martin, the brown bear who once ate a sentry, is also still apparently feeling fine, but he was not visible today.

On the way back I visited a third church, St Eustache, which is grander in its interior than Notre Dame or the Panthéon, and is enlivened by some colorful windows and paintings. In fact, on the occasion of some festival or other, a kind of exhibition of paintings had been set up there, although with little evidence of artistic taste. The music was more pleasant; it included several trombones to stirring effect. Why is such a sublime instrument not used more often in church music?

As I drove across the Place des Victoires, I heaved a great sigh toward the heavens in acknowledgment of the emptiness of fame and its monuments. On this square, as you will remember, there was a statue of Desaix, something he was truly owed by France. Now tossed out, his place has been taken by Louis XIV in Roman armor, with that long, curly wig on his head and a steed like a large, wooden hobbyhorse. I managed to console myself about the sorry homilies this sight awakened in me by indulging, at the Salon des Frères Provençaux, in the more sensory experience of good truffles and the pleasures of a less-than-commendable novel. Indeed I needed a whole bottle of champagne before I could finally cry out with Solomon, "All is vanity!"[28] and then add to that, "Therefore enjoy the moment, without thinking about it too much!" In this good mood, I crossed through the Palais Royal for the last time, where so many colorful baubles and new inventions twinkled at me from the brightly lit stalls that I almost mistook the full moon for a new kind of toy, since it seemed so small and egg yolk colored against the crystal-clear night sky, as if hanging from one of the chimneys across from me. I would not have been remotely surprised if the man in the moon or Mademoiselle Garnerin had climbed out of it, only to vanish into one of Very's chimneys. But since nothing changed, I went on to the Variétés, *pour y finir ma digestion en riant,*[29] my way lit by the heavenly body that far outshone the dim oil lamps. My hopes were perfectly fulfilled, because although the small theater had lost Potier, it had not lost its ability to incite laughter. And to please the eye, it has gained an adorable little actress, Mademoiselle Valerie, and a renewed exterior. Among other happy innovations, the curtain, no longer the usual painted drapery, is now made of real fabric, dark blue and hanging in folds, which looks very good with the crimson, white, and gold of the room. It is also not rolled up stiffly as elsewhere, but pulled back gracefully from both sides at the beginning of a performance. Large theaters should imitate this.

January 16th, 1829

IT USED TO be that "anas" were fashionable. Now it is the "amas," and the change is for the better, because the former automatically make you think of an ass and the second of love. The first referred to great men, of course, and the second only to the love of science and art, yet somehow the Egyptian darkness that tends to reign in these places also grants Amor the occasional bit of room to maneuver.[30]

I dedicated my entire morning to these amas, beginning with the "georama," the ama of geography (Figure 126).[31] Here you suddenly find yourself in the center of the globe, which Dr. Nürnberger has not yet reached with his projected shaft, but where the alternate hypothesis of a sea of light in the earth's interior is readily confirmed. It is so bright here that the entire crust of the earth is made transparent, and from inside the space, you can even make out the *political* boundaries of different countries. Unfortunately you have the North Pole above you, and such a desperately cold draft of air was coming through it today that the small iron stove, at the South Pole down below, was absolutely incapable of spreading any of its warmth. This decreased my curiosity a great deal, which is why I can only tell you that no globe makes geography as vivid as the georama does, and it would be desirable if all Lancasterian schools would similarly be placed

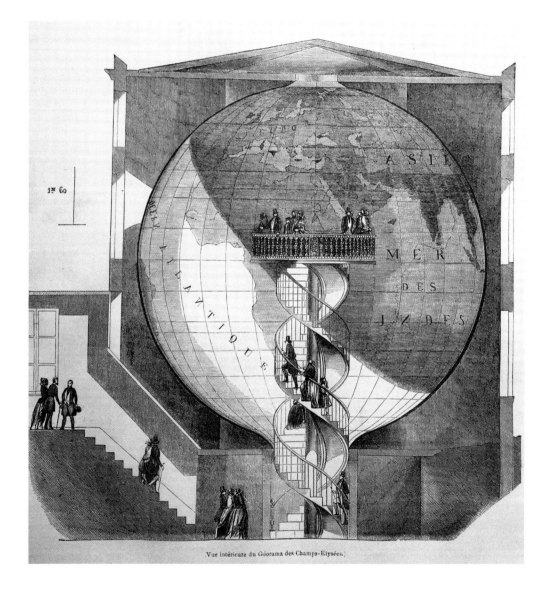

Vue intérieure du Géorama des Champs-Elysées.

126

The Georama in Paris.

in the belly of such an earth, where people could, in a larger group, keep each other warm. The lakes are, as in reality, limpid and of a very pretty blue; the volcanoes resemble small, glowing points; and your eye easily follows the black mountain ranges. It struck me as odd that the great lakes in China bore the distorted outlines of Chinese faces, exactly like the grotesque images of their gods. The largest of these, with no effort of the imagination, looked like a flying dragon, just as one sees them so often depicted on Chinese vases and on the breastplates of mandarins. I am quite proud of myself for this last discovery, and who knows whether it will not somehow illuminate Chinese mythology. In contrast, what caused me some indignation was that the new (and now already old) discoveries at the North Pole, in Africa, and in the Himalayas went unmentioned, and the whole display seemed somewhat in decline.[32] Instead of what one usually finds in Parisian shows of this kind, namely, pretty females in the ticket booth enticing you in, a terrifying specter resembling the leper from Aoste took your money.[33]

A half hour farther down the boulevards, another diorama presented views of Saint Gotthard and Venice. The region on the Italian side of the mountains, which I have seen *in natura,* was beautifully depicted; but since there was no change in the lighting—unlike in the (far-superior) diorama in London—it offered much less variety and enjoyment. Venice was badly painted and illuminated by such a yellowish glow that it looked as if it had contracted jaundice—perhaps out of anger at the French, who first destroyed its political existence and then abandoned it.

At the "neorama," you find yourself transported into the middle of St Peter's;[34] the illusion is worse than mediocre, however, and the motionless crowd is annoying in the face of such pretense of making a perfect imitation. Only sleeping or dead figures should be used as *staffage* in this kind of picture. It is supposed to represent the festival of Saint Peter, and the pope, cardinals with their retinue, and papal guards fill the church. But they are so badly painted that His Holiness the pope looked like a dressing gown thrown down before the old Jupiter-like statue of Peter.[35]

Skipping over the well-known panoramas and "cosmoramas," I finally bring you to the "uranorama" in the new Passage Vivienne. This is a very ingenious mechanism that illustrates the course of the planets in our solar system. I must admit that I have never before had such a clear understanding of the seasons, cycles of the moon, and so on as I did after the hour I spent here. I will tell you more about it in person. In fact, if you would like to spend twelve hundred francs on it, you can obtain a miniature copy of the whole machine, something that no respectable library should be without.

So I started the day in the middle of the earth, next admired the various splendors of its surface, and ended up, after a brief visit to all the planets, in the sun. The only thing missing was a final ama that would show me the seventh heaven and the houris. Then my journey would have been complete, and I would have seen more in a single morning than the Egyptian dervish during the five seconds he spent with his head in a water bucket.

It is definitely for the best if I now lower the curtain on my activities. When it is raised again in your presence, I will be the figure who emerges and walks toward you. Because tomorrow I will hurry home, faster than any letter can travel. Only after my strength of mind has been restored will I turn to my erstwhile plans—of dreaming away a winter among the orange and oleander blossoms of Granada, roaming beneath African palms, and even gazing at the aging wonders of Egypt from atop its pyramids. Until then, no more letters.

Your most faithful friend Lou

SECOND PREFACE BY THE EDITOR[1]

everal months ago my publisher began pressing me to send him the two last first parts of the *Letters of a Dead Man*, yet it was almost impossible to fulfill his request, because so much remained obscure or entirely incomprehensible in the confused and often-incomplete manuscripts. In my distress, I was haunted by a strange thought: what if it were possible to speak with the dead man? And then, despite how preposterous, even crazy, it may seem, such a discussion actually took place. Once faced with facts, all theories must fall silent. What follows is a brief explanation of the miracle by which this came to pass.

I had been longing more than ever for a chance to see my deceased friend again, so I might gladden him with tidings of the favorable judgment that had fallen on his pages from the peak of Parnassus, like a revitalizing manna of resurrection.[2] To this end, I first attempted some cabalistic conjurations, and then one evening a physician friend explained how I might achieve the same objective in a faster and more Christian manner. The reader can probably guess what he suggested. Yes, he sent me an extraordinary book, that recent revelation, *The Seeress of Prevorst.*[3]

Imagine how, in the face of such temptation, the last bit of common sense readily vanished, and an extraterrestrial spark ignited in my heart like a powerful bolt of lightning. "Oh, you noble benefactors of humanity," I exclaimed with devout triumph, "the realm of the spirit is accessible once more! And even if the first visionary died while practicing her profession, why should she not be succeeded by another? What once occurred can occur again. Indeed, unless hope deceives me, her successor has already been found!"

This declaration, dear reader, had a solid foundation, for there was a young woman living not far away who was renowned for the preternatural sensitivity of her nervous system. She had once lived as a pious nun in the B—— Cloister at B——, where a strange fate befell her. Whatever genuine female characteristics she possessed, she was also known for her virile decisiveness in the face of various persecutions. It was even rumored that she had been poisoned more than once, but had been saved each time by resort to a stomach pump. Due to these enigmatic occurrences, she had acquired the lugubrious name of *Nonnerich,*[4] although her actual name was Theresel, and her birthplace, Bohemia. Following the dissolution of the monasteries, she retired to the house of a maternal friend and, following that woman's death, in her boundless love of humanity, devoted her life in quiet solitude to the mysteries of a fervent pietism and the performance of good works.

Since this gifted creature had attained a state of voluntary magnetic ecstasy so often, there could be no doubt that superior results would be attained from a scientific application of the art; and given what was known of her temperament, she would almost certainly consent. I wasted not a moment and wrote to my friend Dr. Upsilon,[5] a learned and good-natured man (likewise unburdened by inconvenient scruples where such experiments are concerned), requesting his help in realizing the great project I had in mind. He was, as I had expected, immediately enthusiastic. "You can count on me," he responded, "and even if I should lose my head, and Theresel her life, she will nonetheless, *bon gré mal gré*, achieve the highest level of clairvoyance and in no way fall short of her great predecessor.

Heaven blessed our undertaking in the most dramatic way, far exceeding our wildest expectations. Before six weeks had passed, Theresel was able to look right through herself and others, up and down, right and left, both spiritually and corporally; indeed spirits of every kind, size, and color were passing in and out of her as if she were a tavern. They may not have been of the most brilliant variety—we were unlucky in this point, it is true. But we mortals harbor the undue expectation that every spirit will possess a spirited mind, something just as unlikely as supposing that all humans are humane. There are, after all, foolish devils—why should there not be foolish spirits!

Anyway, the long-awaited moment finally arrived, the goal of all my efforts was achieved, and as the prophetess reached the first stage of intense excitement, I placed my request on her— *stomach*—declaring the ardent hope of all my different souls and spirits: to see once again the departed friend of my heart. She reflected for a while and then said, "How much you are demanding, my dear! You know that L—— can only appear on horseback."

"*What?*" I exclaimed, "*à cheval* like Napoleon?"

"In no other way, my friend. These are the immutable laws of the intermediate realm. Don't forget that among L——'s many flaws, he was a too-passionate equestrian. Just as my soul mate, the Seeress of Prevorst, found the old leading dancers at balls still spinning around in a never-ending performance, so it is with L——, who can only appear on horseback. It will be frightful, I can tell you, so be brave. Still, you requested it, and so I have summoned him. Listen! He is already here!"

Although I was not unaccustomed to trafficking with the other world, a small shudder passed through my bones as I heard a *tap—tap—tap* outside the door. And then, like the commander in *Don Giovanni*, a dusky, horrifying figure, with a dreadful, nodding head, rode slowly into the room.

It appeared that my friend, as retribution for his vain insistence on riding the most handsome of mounts, had been assigned an emaciated horse of the Apocalypse, a pallid monster with nostrils emitting steel blue vapors and eyes rolling like pinwheels. That this creature, with the gargantuan dimensions of a Trojan horse, managed to find space in our little room was a miracle in itself. The most adamant unbeliever would at that point have trusted his senses.

"Oh, beloved friend!" I exclaimed, trembling and beside myself with joy and alarm. "Is it really you? Yes, now I recognize the dear, old features, and by all the spirits of the intermediate realm, you are better preserved than I expected! I have so much to discuss with you, so much to tell you, so much to learn. But first of all listen to this: The only part of you that has remained on earth—the innocent letters you left behind—they have found more favor than you ever hoped for in all your dreams. And if I were to express myself in a slightly Oriental fashion, which is more suited to your exotic appearance, I would say that the finest steel has created a brilliant ruby out of an unprepossessing stone; that the sun's powerful rays have transformed a bit of glass into a powerful lens; in a word, to speak plainly . . ."

At this I reached into my pocket for the piece of paper I had placed there and, as if standing on the tribunal of the French Chamber of Deputies, I read aloud the rest of my speech to the astonished spirit, along with volume 59 of the *Jahrbücher für wissenschaftliche Kritik*.* The ghostly presence (who was a soft ash gray and thus, according to the law of uniformity in the intermediate realm, already half beatified) went slightly pale at the first mention of the Solomonic name,[6] blushed, and then listened attentively without saying a word, apparently caught up in his own thoughts. When I concluded, he breathed a contented sigh and, smiling, lisped (just as in life), "Fortune never shone on me while I walked the earth, but here in the intermediate realm, I was meant to find salvation. Were I still wandering the earth right now, I would feel like the Turk who, lost in the crowd, suddenly sees one of the sultan's ambassadors coming to enrobe him with the honorary fur and name him a pasha of several horsetails.[7] Don't laugh at my vanity, dear Hermann,[8] for it is only right for me to be proud of Jupiter's praise. Indeed, it would be presumptuous to allow my modesty to prevail, for it would imply that my judgment is more correct than his!

"If, however, I am allowed to reply with a few humble words to what you just read aloud, I must first of all express my amazement that an eighty-year-old is still capable of responding with such vitality and amiability to my mischievous banter, the mere prattle of a worldling's childlike joy in nature.[9] How far superior is he who hovers on high in his poetic splendor, comprehending every human condition like a physician who examines hearts and kidneys without having to dissect them or rely on personal experience. (When I entered the underworld, Rhadamanthus read my heart no more accurately.[10]) And when the benevolent master suggests, delicately, that a number of the essays in that curious book might be by another hand, he is essentially correct. For it seems that the author and editor were indeed the same person, that the entire work is the product of a single hand (although this can be only *mystically* possible, since you are still alive and I am dead). We know, however, that one personality can have many parts, and if the left knows not what the right is doing, it can also happen that the left does something that the right does not want to know about at all.

"You, my faithful editor, won't come away empty-handed, and you deserve credit for admitting 'openly, if not candidly,' how certain circumstances made it necessary to convert the end into the beginning and cast a salutary clair-obscure over the entire opus in order to give it an epic veneer, as our Solomon says.[11] Thus, alongside the fortunate author, you may take your place as a deft editor, both in this and the intermediate realm. And the two of us will be granted absolution, even if, here and there, we did mix poetry (or, more modestly, fiction) and truth."[12]

The dead man, clearly a talkative type, seemed intent on continuing, but was silenced by the resounding din of a bell—a warning sign, as we both realized, for it was time for him to perform his hourly punishment: three-by-three volts around the room in nine different gaits.[13] It was terrible to watch the progress of his infernal mount, something beyond a Spanish walk,[14] as it seemed to rob him of his last breath. But we shuddered even more as the beast's tail arced like a

---

* Oh, vanity! [The allusion is again to Goethe's review, see page 722, note 2. —*Translator.*]

comet on an elliptical path, sweeping several lovely porcelain cups (all authentic Old Saxon) onto the floor, where they shattered without making the slightest sound. Not only can the Prevorst spirits make immaterial sounds audible, they can also make any sound *inaudible*, if they find it unpleasant or improper, a convenient privilege of intermediate regions.

At last my friend stopped moving, and as he gasped for breath and dried the sweat from his brow, I took the opportunity to speak to him again. "I have yet more good news to relate. You should know that another weighty voice among German critics has resounded in your praise. This man has offered his own fame as a foil for yours, and many others have followed his example, including a certain *Freimütiger* who seems to know you fairly well,[15] though he has obviously confused you with someone else, for he ascertained that, despite your liberality, you still possessed pride in your noble birth. (Confess it, most honored *intermediate* spirit, he is not entirely wrong.) At the same time, he disclosed his own theory that nobility should really *be* and not just *seem* to be—which is asking a lot! For to say that the aristocracy should not just *seem* but really *be* noble would be impossible, even inconceivable—at least in Sandomir. Yet to *be* without any *seeming* at all—an invisible existence, as it were, a new light without a flame—*voilà qui est difficile*! Oh, God! Another French cliché just escaped my lips, one too harsh for the sensitive German ear! *Pardon.* It won't happen again.*

"Even more flattering than the *Freimütiger* is the acknowledgment appearing in the well-appointed picture gallery of that engaging German humorist. This man manages to bring tears to your eyes, while compelling a smile from your lips to catch the tears as they fall.[16]

"And just so you lack for nothing, some obscure reproaches were delivered by the Pharisees as well. Indeed one poor soul was *resurrected* in order to fling his bombast at the dead man here before us. This, however, only made his friends and enemies wish that he would rest in peace rather than cause the public to yawn. And there's still more: you were even associated with the Great Unknown himself,[17] in that many people nowadays cannot conceive how a minister without his advisors, a general without his staff, a monarch without his ministers, could ever create something *on his own*. So they have assigned your little book, just as they did that great one's immortal novels, to a whole company of famous and lesser-known authors of both sexes, and feeling now and then quite petulant (for the truth is painful), they attacked innocent parties, or just snapped at the air. Thus, dear deceased friend, great good fortune has joined light and shadow in order to . . ."

Here Theresel interrupted me and peevishly gripped my arm. "*Mon cher*, don't forget that all genres are good, except for the boring kind, the only point on which I do *not* agree with my friend from Prevorst. That's enough for now. You must all depart. The time is approaching for the spirit to dismount and pass the night with me. As you know, the immediate surroundings of a chosen one can accelerate his salvation by centuries; thus it behooves me not to delay this work of Christian compassion a single moment longer, no matter how weakened I become in the process. What does my wretched body matter in the face of such a lofty destiny—that I might have a redeeming effect on the world of spirits!"

---

* By the way, a certain German purist, whom I heartily revere, would have expressed himself far more *correctly* at the end of his critique had he deigned to use the English word "scandal," instead of the not-even-entirely-German *Skandal*, which was inappropriate and harsh. [The "purist" was Ludwig Börne, who was critical of the extensive use of French in the *Letters.*—*Translator.*]

Awestruck, we—the living—stepped back, while my friend smiled sarcastically, almost like a black spirit, and said, blowing me a kiss in farewell, "Au revoir, mon ami." Then he disappeared, just as I grasped the door handle behind Theresel's bed curtains. His steed, however, spun up the chimney like the delightful aroma of *essence de bouquet.*

Back on the street, I looked at my watch, still half dazed, and, *oh, horrors*! All the clocks in the town were striking five when I entered the house of the seeress, yet now it was just three o'clock. I shuddered as I suddenly realized that time had gone *backward*!

I need hardly mention that, after this first encounter, I not only saw my friend repeatedly and obtained whatever information I wanted from him, but I began to enjoy the traffic with spirits as much as my assistant, Dr. Upsilon, did. Day after day, friend and foe were summoned before us, and we were often able to release some poor spirit who had spent centuries running around for want of the four pennies he needed to do a good deed. If I wished to tell you more—the information that was revealed to us, the puzzles solved, the astonishing historical revelations, the confidences imparted by Moses and the prophets, the Man in the Iron Mask, Sebastian of Portugal, the False Waldemar, Cagliostro, and the Count of Saint Germain—we would be here forever.[18] It is true that Theresel, who begged for mercy, was unable to endure it. She died a miserable death and now rests in the same graveyard as her famous predecessor. But those who sacrifice themselves are as blessed as those who are sacrificed for the general weal. To the survivors, anyway, both fates are equal.

But Dr. Upsilon and I made our own sacrifice and paid our debt. For each experiment took us further back in time, so that, unlike those who circumnavigate the globe and lose one whole day, we lost several years, although it often seemed as if we had lost as many centuries.*

---

* If anyone finds these details ridiculous and beyond belief, we would be flattered, for these exact qualities are the surest sign of authenticity. For details, see the compelling introduction to the *The Seeress of Prevorst.*

POSTSCRIPT

Before bidding farewell to my gracious readers, I must humbly apologize on behalf of my publisher, first, for the outrageous number of misprints that swarm like mosquitoes after sunset in the earlier parts of this work—we hope they will not be reborn in the present offering; and second, for the extremely odd illustrations that were included (some as *lithographs*).[1] One can look at hundreds of reproductions and see no difference between any two of them, yet by imperceptible steps, they span the distance from the Apollo Belvedere to a spread-eagled frog. The grotesque plates in the *Letters of a Dead Man* fall near the bottom of the scale. But art, especially of the trifling sort, prostitutes itself on every street corner, and therefore one needs only to *want* some improvement in order to find it. Hence I suspect Mr. F. G. Franckh of having a secret agenda up his sleeve—perhaps some mystical intent, or a mordant satire, maybe even a dangerous cabal!—in which case I wash my hands of it![2]

The most egregious of the misprints were identified, although not even half had been noticed in the initial perusal. Especially misleading are the many notes by the *author* that are identified as notes by the *editor*, and occasionally the reverse has happened as well. This might lead an inattentive reader to think that author and editor were one and the same, and here I must object, since I am not at all of a mind to count myself among the dead. I hope that at least a plurality of readers allow me to go on with my life, "die süße Gewohnheit des Daseins."[3]

In closing I would like to note that although the following letters are from the years 1826, 1827, and 1828, and thus may seem somewhat outdated, the sympathetic reader will find much in them that is reminiscent of the more recent epistles.[4] Furthermore, we have taken care to retain only what is still true and pertinent, and to delete all that is no longer of interest for the present.

S——, March 1st, 1831.

Notes

NOTES TO THE FIRST PREFACE BY THE EDITOR

1 This is the first of several misleading claims made in the First Preface by the Editor, for the letters were not only significantly altered by rearranging, cutting, and adding but were prepared specifically with publication in mind (something denied by the Editor in the following sentence). In addition, the supposedly deceased author was, in fact, very much alive, and indeed was the very Editor commenting here and in the footnotes.

2 The First Preface by the Editor accompanied the second half of the letters (nos. 25–48), which were published first as parts three and four of the original edition. Parts one and two appeared the following year. "Certain circumstances" likely refers to the more careful editing required of the earlier letters that describe Pückler's search for a bride. The second, more obscure preface (Second Preface by the Editor) is included here as an appendix.

3 "In the manner of Minellius." Minellius was a Dutch grammarian who edited Latin texts and supplied them with footnotes, usually with helpful translations. The practice became so popular that this expression became a common description for such notes.

NOTES TO LETTER 1

1 "Let us never love, or love just a little, / it is dangerous to love so much." This and the following quotation are from a letter to Sévigné from her cousin Comte de Bussy, dated May 10, 1675.

2 "Pour moi, j'aime encore mieux le mal que le remède, et je trouve plus doux d'avoir bien de la peine à quitter les gens que j'aime, que de les aimer médiocrement."

3 "M——" is Muskau, not spelled out in the original to conceal the writer's identity. Hereafter, it will be identified by name in this translation.

4 "You've doubtless cooked up all sorts of bitter brews, just as I have."

5 In *Gulliver's Travels*, the inhabitants of Brobdingnag are over seventy feet tall and those of Lilliput are less than six inches tall.

6 From 1813 to 1814, Pückler served as an aide-de-camp to Karl August, Grand Duke of Saxe-Weimar-Eisenach, in the Grand Alliance against Napoleon. Karl August had a passionate interest in the arts and sciences, and his court was renowned for its intellectual brilliance. One of his first acts as a young grand duke was to summon Goethe to Weimar in 1776, thus helping to establish the literary beacon to which Pückler alludes.

7 Weimar's Park on the Ilm was designed by Goethe beginning in 1776 in the style of an English landscape garden.

8 Pückler gained enormous notoriety in 1816 for his balloon trip from Berlin to Potsdam, where he crash-landed atop an enormous pine tree, an adventure that he relates with considerable humor in *Tutti Frutti*, trans. Edmund Spencer (New York: Harper, 1834), 121–25.

9 Karl Bernhard of Saxe-Weimar-Eisenach, seventh son of the grand duke, made a trip to the United States in 1825–1826. His two-volume book about his travels (*Reise Sr. Hoheit des Herzogs Bernhard zu Sachsen-Weimar-Eisenach durch Nord-Amerika in den Jahren 1825 und 1826*) appeared in Weimar in 1828, as did an English translation published in Philadelphia. He did not go to South America, and there are no remarks by Goethe.

10 Louise of Hesse-Darmstadt.

11 "The Baron de J—— takes the liberty of introducing the late [i.e., deceased] Captain de M——, once in the service of various members of the Confederation of the Rhine."

12 Scott continued to publish anonymously, although his authorship was an open secret.

13 *Manfred* is a dramatic poem published in 1817 that was influenced by Goethe's *Faust*. Byron claimed never to have read *Faust*, although a friend read it aloud to him in English translation.

14 Pückler writes: "Es ist doch schön von einem großen Herrn, / Mit einem armen Teufel so human zu sprechen," slightly altering the closing lines of the "Prologue in Heaven" from part 1 of *Faust*, "Es ist gar hübsch von einem großen Herrn, / So menschlich mit dem Teufel selbst zu sprechen."

15 Karl Friedrich of Saxe-Weimar-Eisenach would succeed his father Karl August as Grand Duke of Weimar in 1828.

16 The Grand Duchess Maria Pavlovna, wife of Karl Friedrich, was the daughter of Emperor Paul I of Russia and the sister of Emperor Alexander I of Russia. The latter died in 1825 at the age of forty-seven.

17 Catherine Pavlovna, daughter of Emperor Paul I and sister-in-law of the grand duke, married King Wilhelm I of Württemberg in 1816.

18 The cochineal is a scale insect from the genus *Opuntia* that lives on cactuses and is the source of carmine, a crimson-colored dye, which was used in the original recipe for Fürst-Pückler-Eis, an ice cream named after Pückler.

19 *Granby* (1826) by Thomas Henry Lister was one of the popular "silver fork" novels that focused on the lifestyle of Britain's upper classes.

NOTES TO LETTER 2

1 A reference to Matthew 22:1–14, the Parable of the Wedding Feast.

2 "In the French manner"—that is, without bidding farewell.

3 The following description—as well as other passages in *Letters of a Dead Man* (for instance, the story of the will of Peter Thellusson; page 339)—were the inspiration behind "The Domain of Arnheim," a story by Edgar Allen Poe. See Linda Parshall, "Hirschfeld, Pückler, Poe: The Literary Modeling of Nature," in "Pückler and America," ed. Sonja Duempelmann, *Bulletin of the German Historical Institute*, supplement 4 (2007): 149–69.

4 The exceptional windows by Dirck Crabeth are in the Sint Janskerk, a sixteenth-century Gothic structure. It was badly damaged by fire from a lightning strike in 1552; the windows date from 1555–1571.

5 "Farewell ducks, canals, rabble!" Voltaire was known for this ironic farewell to Holland, though he put canals at the top of the list.

6 Pückler included this picture in his first Memory Album; see pages xliii–xliv. The inscription in his hand begins: "The steamship that I took from Rotterdam to London. The crossing was rough and all passengers without exception were seasick."

1 "Really? You couldn't sleep? I slept perfectly, very comfortably; I lay very warmly ensconced between two sailors, and I feel marvelous." "Madame, it is easy to see that you are not afraid of the sea." The lady's malapropisms include "comfortable" with an *m* as in English, but more important is her confusion of *matelas* (mattress) and *matelot* (sailor).

2 When Pückler went to London in 1814 in the retinue of Tsar Alexander I and Frederick William III, king of Prussia, he rented a suite at the luxurious Clarendon Hotel on Bond Street and stayed for almost a year.

3 The steeple is on All Souls Church, Langham Place, on the north end of Regent Street.

4 "What gives, your honor?" "Was it *you* that just rang?" The accent is from the Berlin area.

5 Gas street lighting was introduced in London in 1814 and was brought to Berlin in 1826 by an English firm.

6 Wine from an estate on the Rhine near Johannisberg belonging to Prince Metternich.

7 There were regular publications containing information about mail, mail coaches, routes, charges, and the like.

8 The first Exchange was destroyed by the Great Fire of London in 1666; Pückler saw the second Exchange designed by Edward Jarman. Charles II laid its foundation stone in 1667. It opened in 1669 and was destroyed by fire in 1838.

9 "Marvel at nothing," a phrase best known from Horace's *Epistles*.

10 This was the popular name for the Exeter Exchange, located on the Strand in London. The famous menagerie remained on its upper floors from 1773 until 1829.

11 Likely King Frederick I, who died in 1816.

12 There was a student revolt in Leipzig in 1768, which Goethe describes in his autobiography *Dichtung und Wahrheit*, calling it the *Musenkrieg* (battle of the muses).

13 This imaginative narrative conflates two different Montagus.

14 Franz Grillparzer was made famous by his play *Die Ahnfrau* (The Ancestress). First performed in 1817, it is a complex tragedy of mistaken identities, a ghostly ancestress, thwarted love, and many deaths.

15 The novel *Frankenstein* by Mary Shelley, published anonymously in 1818, was immediately popular and reached a wide audience through many melodramatic theater productions and translations. "The Vampyre" (1819), a short story by John William Polidori, was initially attributed to Byron, who denied authorship; it was followed by other stories, a novel, and then a French play, which was first performed in English in London in 1820.

16 The "Great Vine," which was planted as a cutting by Capability Brown in 1768, is still producing five hundred to seven hundred pounds of grapes per year. The greenhouses at Hampton Court Palace have been continually expanded in order to house it.

17 Since 1865, the cartoons (full-scale preparatory designs for the tapestries) have been in the Victoria and Albert Museum, London, on loan from the Royal Collection.

18 For three weeks in 1520, there was a meeting on the Champ du Drap d'Or near Calais between Henry VIII of England and Francis I of France. Its purpose was to strengthen ties between the rulers and to display each court's wealth and magnificence. Both sides established enormous encampments with pavilions and tents covered with cloth of gold, hence the name.

1 By "models," Pückler probably means plaster casts. Such casts, usually of ancient sculpture, were an important part of the collection of most major European museums at the time.

2 Count Gusztáv Batthyány. The magnates were a group of about one hundred wealthy, landowning families in Hungary.

3 "Done" was the equivalent of saying "The bet is on!"

4 Probably the Tharp family of Chippenham Park.

5 A niece of Beau Brummell (then in exile).

6 Sometimes called "nodding Mandarins" and popular already in the eighteenth century, these were small porcelain figures with mobile, grotesque heads that nodded.

7 "Fost" is Pückler's rendering of a bad English pronunciation of *Faust*.

8 Girls used to bet their gloves instead of hard currency. Kid gloves from Paris were recognized as the best; see page 32.

9 The town is Saffron Walden, and the Gothic spire belongs to the church of St Mary the Virgin.

10 Pantalone is a character in Italian comedy—an old, rich lecher who lusts after and pesters women (generally without success).

11 The history of the land tenure system in England is extremely complex; unsurprisingly, Pückler's account contains some errors and misunderstandings.

1 In Smollett's *The Adventures of Peregrine Pickle* (1751), a comic view of mid-eighteenth-century society, an outrageously unappetizing meal "in old Roman taste" is described in chapter forty-eight, beginning with a soup: "The Frenchman having swallowed the first spoonful, made a full pause, his throat swelled, as if an egg had stuck in his gullet, his eyes rolled, and his mouth underwent a series of involuntary contractions and dilatations."

2 A common term in the nineteenth century for a fashionable evening gathering.

3 "Those who are absent are at fault."

4 "One must be brave."

5 "The Bavarian Girl's Song," which was first sung by Vestris in 1827 in a farce by Peake called *The £100 Note*, became one of her most popular performances. The lyrics in English and German were set to the music of the song "Ach du lieber Augustin."

6 In the nineteenth century, benefit performances were often staged, with the proceeds going to a single member of a company.

7 "While never missing a bite."

8 "Oh, that doesn't matter. His brother has a child every year, so it works out the same for the family." "For the family, yes . . . but not for him. His brother eats and he digests."

9 Pückler seems to have done his own rhymed translation of an unidentified poem, here loosely translated back into English:

Is the sad cheek dim,
The eye no longer bright,
And does the solemn realm draw near
Where youth so quickly flees!
Yet your cheek still smiles,
Your eye still knows tears,
Your heart still beats as warm and free
As in life's greenest May.
So do not think that only youth
And beauty grant blessings—

Time teaches the soul lovelier virtues
In years of faithful tenderness.
And even when the night above
Enfolds your breast in darkness,
Your head, upheld by the hand of love,
Will be granted eternal rest.
Oh, thus the evening star still twinkles
Gentle and warm from on high
When the sun's light is gone,
And you will not miss the glow of day.

10 Braham, the famous Jewish tenor, was just ten years older than Pückler. He would have been about fifty-two when Pückler saw him for the second time. The German equivalent of the expression "wandering Jew" is "ewiger Jude" ("eternal Jew"), which explains Pückler's comment about Braham's apparent failure to age.

11 "As if nothing were happening."

NOTES TO LETTER 6

1 Pückler's account of the scenes and dialogue is very close to the earliest printed version of the script, *The Tragical Comedy, or Comical Tragedy, of Punch and Judy*, published by John Payne Collier with illustrations by George Cruikshank (London, 1828). This was clearly his source, and a copy of the whole booklet was placed in his Memory Album (III, 13), although he no doubt studied it only after he had returned to Muskau and was embellishing his letters for publication. The two Punch and Judy illustrations included in the 1831 edition of the *Letters of a Dead Man*, which Pückler claims to be sketching in the margin of his epistle, were in fact "borrowed" from the Collier publication (see Figure 14).

2 "he is never in doubt about anything."

3 "Marlborough is off to war," a popular folk song about the 1709 Battle of Malpalquet.

4 "Eia popeia" is a nonsense phrase often heard in German lullabies, children's songs, and other poetry.

5 Solomon was said to have had seven hundred wives and three hundred concubines.

6 A curative or stimulant paste made with pitch, comparable to a mustard plaster. It caused the skin to redden.

7 "I could not bear it."

8 A French term used repeatedly by Pückler to describe the ease, informality, casualness, and freedom of movement assumed by the fashionables.

9 "In the style of Joachim Murat" (1767–1815), one of Napoleon's cavalry generals in Italy and Egypt. A marshal of France and king of Naples, he married Napoleon's sister Caroline in 1808. He was known for his long, curly hair.

10 "A true lord." Probably Esterházy.

11 "You will not find the portrait a good likeness [of his parsimony] . . . but the diamonds [represent it well]."

12 Alleyne FitzHerbert, 1st Baron St Helens. Ségur makes repeated mention of "Fitz-Herbert" in his memoirs.

13 Gallstones, kidney stones, or both.

14 "Tant bien que mal": for better or worse; "gêne": constraint.

15 "Sweet idleness": literally, "sweet doing nothing."

16 "And all the stars would pale before my own."

17 George IV. A levee was a monarch's ceremonial reception of visitors on rising from bed in the morning.

18 "That was no doubt very catholic."

19 "He has the heart of a t[iger?] and the face of an a[ss?]."

20 An exhibition of the Burmese imperial state carriage, part of the booty from the first Anglo-Burmese War of 1824–1826, was first displayed in London in November 1824.

21 A poecilorama was a panoramic viewing device with windows through which one could watch a moving scene that generally depicted changing natural phenomena. Pückler saw this one when it was quite new, since it opened at the Egyptian Hall in 1826.

22 A clever pun, since *At Home* was the title of Mathew's most famous one-man performance piece.

23 *Pächter Feldkümmel von Tippelskirchen (Tenant Feldkümmel from Tippelskirchen)* is the title of a Shrovetide play from ca. 1811 by August von Kotzebue in which the plump hero (whose name means "creeping thyme") makes a fool of himself.

NOTES TO LETTER 7

1 Lady Charleville was the "distinguished lady"; she reappears in Letter 13 and is finally named in Letter 14.

2 From Jean Racine, *Britannicus*, act 1, scene 1: "Quand les ambassadeurs de tant de rois divers / Vinrent le reconnaître au nom de l'univers."

3 "Stabs of a sword, pricks of a pin"—that is, major blows and petty annoyances.

4 "I bequeath the shame of my death to England." Pückler omits a few words from the original. According to the *Correspondance de Napoléon Ier*, vol. 32, *Oeuvres de Napoléon Ier à Sainte-Héléne* (Paris: Plon, 1870), 388, Napoleon wrote: "Je lègue l'opprobre de ma mort à la maison régnante d'Angleterre" (I bequeath the shame of my death to the ruling house of England).

5 Her brother was George Campbell, 6th Duke of Argyll (1768–1839). After the death of her first husband, she married Edward John Bury, her son's tutor.

6 "Brownonian" has been explained in several unconvincing ways: as an allusion to Lady Morgan's novel *The Wild Irish Girl* (1806), in which brown, the color of the fields, stands for a connection to the land; as a reference to Capability Brown; or as an allusion to the Scottish doctor John Brown and his "Brunonian" theory of medicine (in German, *Brownianismus*), which holds that disease is due to either an excess or a deficiency of excitation.

7 Likely Henry Colburn. The first one thousand copies of *Waverley* appeared anonymously in 1814 under the imprint of Archibald Constable (1774–1827) and sold out in two days. By the time of Pückler's visit, the bank crisis of 1825 had led in January 1826 to the failure of Constable's business. Colburn's survived, as did that of Robert Cadell (1788–1849), a partner of Constable's, who brought out a new edition of *Waverley* in 1827 and in 1828 secured the copyright for all of Scott's novels.

8 There were insurrections in Portugal in 1820. Brazil—having declared its independence in 1822—experienced a succession crisis following the March 1826 death of John VI of Portugal, whose son Pedro I, Emperor of Brazil, was himself briefly king of Portugal (Pedro IV; March–May 1826) before abdicating in favor of his seven-year-old daughter. This was Maria II, who served as regent from 1826 to 1828, when she was replaced by Pedro's brother Dom Miguel, whom Pückler met several times in London. In December 1826, Canning asked Parliament to approve sending five thousand British troops to Lisbon to stem the unrest.

9 During the so-called resurrection times (ca. 1750–1832), it was common in England

for thieves, sometimes termed "resurrection men" or "body snatchers," to dig bodies out of graves and sell them to the highest bidders, usually surgeons, medical schools, and anatomists.

10 Pückler brought Jacob Heinrich Rehder, his head gardener at Muskau, to England for five weeks. They visited many landscape parks together, went to the theater, and enjoyed other diversions. Rehder was devoted to Muskau and stayed on, as did his successor Eduard Petzold, long after Pückler had moved to Branitz.

11 In *Faust*, part 1, the *Erdgeist* (earth spirit) is a supernatural presence conjured up by Faust.

12 *Scheren* (to shear) has a second meaning in German: to trouble or to bother someone.

13 The lord chancellor's seat in the House of Lords is a large, square sack of wool covered with scarlet; the term also refers to the office of the lord chancellor. This was a sign of the enormous value of the wool trade in England.

14 *Arme Ritter* is the German name for a quick, inexpensive meal made by frying leftover bread.

15 Kenwood House, in Hampstead, London.

16 "Who are you, sir? What are you looking for here?"

17 The Duke of Devonshire.

18 *Honigmonate*: honey months. Probably an allusion to a popular novel, *Die Honigmonathe*, by Caroline Auguste Fischer, that was first published in 1802.

19 Alexander von Humboldt lived in Paris for many years before returning to Berlin in May 1827 to become adviser to Friedrich Wilhelm III, king of Prussia. Pückler's comment anticipates this, but the news of his appointment was probably known earlier.

20 Friedrich Wilhelm III fractured his leg on December 14, 1826.

21 "Even worse is that I am sometimes too sensitive and sometimes not sensitive enough to the opinions and behavior of others."

NOTES TO LETTER 8

1 Bentley Priory.

2 From Horace's *Epistles*, book 1, epistle 6, where he claims that the only way to happiness is to "marvel at nothing."

3 A small bowl used to wash the dregs out of tea and coffee cups.

4 A special preparation of pig's ears.

5 Here Pückler gives the temperature as fourteen degrees on the Réaumur scale, which is about eighteen degrees Celsius.

6 Repton's designs for the Ashridge gardens are discussed and illustrated in a book that he published with his son John Adey Repton: *Fragments on the Theory and Practice of Landscape Gardening* (London: Printed by T. Bensley and Son, 1816), fragment 27. Pückler had a copy in his library.

7 Pückler includes much of this description and its humorous comment in his 1834 *Hints on Landscape Gardening*, praising an unnamed "travel writer" as the source.

8 Ballerino was the tame crane that accompanied Pückler when he was gardening at Muskau.

NOTES TO LETTER 9

1 The German *Zauberwort* (magic word), a term with magical power, would become a central metaphor of the Romantic era due to Eichendorff's famous poem "Wünschelrute" (Divining Rod) of 1835 (not published until 1838).

2 Warwick Castle was begun in the eleventh century, rebuilt in the twelfth, and expanded and altered thereafter. "Guy's Tower"—named after Guy de Beauchamp, 10th Earl of Warwick (ca. 1272–1315)—dates to the fourteenth century. It was not Beauchamp but Richard Neville, 16th Earl of Warwick (1428–1471), who became known as the "Kingmaker."

3 This kind of elaborate marquetry, named after André Charles Boulle (1642–1732), is called "boulle" or "buhl" in English.

4 The portrait that Pückler admired, which was a seventeenth-century copy, still hangs in the Red Drawing Room at Warwick Castle; Figure 25 shows the painting in situ, and includes the unavoidable shadow of a lighting fixture on the lower edge. The 1518 original in the Louvre—long attributed to Raphael and thought to portray Joanna of Aragon—has recently been ascribed to Giulio Romano, and its sitter has been identified as Isabel de Requesens, wife of Romón de Cardona, viceroy of Naples.

5 Probably Frederick William III (reigned 1797–1840), who attempted to restore dignity to the rather depraved court that he inherited from his father.

6 Pückler paraphrases Machiavelli: "And in fact there is no sure way to hold onto cities except to destroy them. Any man who becomes master of a city accustomed to freedom, and does not destroy it, may expect to be destroyed by it. Because such a city, when it rebels, can always call on the name of liberty and its ancient ordinances, which no passage of time or bestowal of gifts can ever cause to be forgotten.... If one does not divide or disperse the inhabitants, they will never forget that name or those ordinances." Niccolò Machiavelli, *The Prince*, 2nd ed., trans. and ed. Robert M. Adams (New York: Norton, 1992), 15.

7 The portrait of Elizabeth I is no longer ascribed to Holbein.

8 Friedrich Schiller's play *Mary Stuart*, which was first performed in Weimar in 1800, relates the final days of Mary, Queen of Scots.

9 Edward, Prince of Wales "the Black Prince" (1330–1376), known during his lifetime as Edward of Woodstock, was a hero of the Hundred Years War with France.

10 An ancient Roman marble vase, discovered at Hadrian's Villa in Tivoli ca. 1771. It was sold to Sir William Hamilton, who gave it to his nephew George Greville, 2nd Earl of Warwick.

11 Guy of Warwick supposedly withdrew to a hermitage on this site. In the fifteenth century, a chantry was established here, but scarcely anything remains. The house Pückler saw dates from the mid-eighteenth century.

12 Not a cathedral, in fact, but the Collegiate Church of St Mary. This parish church, which has some similarities to a cathedral, is the resting place of the earls of Warwick. The chapel is called the Beauchamp Chapel since it was originally built for Richard de Beauchamp's tomb.

13 "Vernon" is a misspelling of Varney, the villain in *Kenilworth*, a novel by Sir Walter Scott. Pückler likewise errs on the location of the murder, which happens at Cumnor Place in Berkshire.

14 A reference to Berlin's horticultural society, the Verein zur Beförderung des Gartenbaues.

NOTES TO LETTER 10

1 This Swiss bridge may be a reference to the famous Teufelsbrücke (Devil's Bridge) in Switzerland.

2 The eighteenth-century statue atop an obelisk in Hawkstone Park is of Sir Rowland

Hill, lord mayor of London in 1549, during the reign of Edward VI (not Henry III).

3 The grounds were designed by Capability Brown, who created the lake by damming the River Glyme. The park itself covers two thousand acres. Pückler writes that the lake covers "eight hundred Morgen," which is nearly double its actual size.

4 Rosamond is a character in Scott's *Woodstock, or the Cavalier,* published in 1826.

5 The Blenheim Palace collection was auctioned off in July and August 1866 in 936 lots. See W. Roberts, *Memorials of Christie's: A Record of Art Sales from 1766 to 1896* (London: G. Bell, 1897), in which many of the paintings Pückler describes can be identified.

6 Raphael's Ansidei Madonna, which did not impress Pückler, was one of the most important paintings in the collection. In 1885, George Spencer-Churchill, 8th Duke of Marlborough, sold it to the National Gallery, London, for three times more than the gallery had paid for any previous painting.

7 The notorious Lady Castlemaine was the longtime mistress of both King Charles II and John Churchill, the 1st Duke of Marlborough, her second cousin. There are innumerable stories related to her, one of which concerns Churchill leaping out a window to escape detection by the king.

8 "He remains calm under fire."

9 The Sheldonian Theatre was a circular building designed by Christopher Wren for the University of Oxford. Intended for graduation and degree-granting ceremonies, it was erected ca. 1665.

10 *Der Katholik* (The Catholic) was a periodical published in Mainz and Strassburg. The passage Pückler quotes from the June 1824 issue was singled out for scorn in Johann Jacob Fezer, *Deutschland und Rom seit der Reformation Dr. Luthers* (Frankfurt, 1830), 2:332–33.

11 This painting by an unknown artist was presented to the University of Oxford in 1683 by Elias Ashmole; it formed part of the founding collection of the Ashmolean Museum, Oxford. Many figures and locations are identified in trompe l'oeil labels on the panel.

12 "How the troops of the Emperor defeated the French in the year 1525."

13 The portrait of John Tradescant the Elder, now in the Ashmolean Museum, is attributed to Cornelis de Neve (1609–1678). Already in 1634, visitors were allowed to see Tradescant's collection of curiosities (Musaeum Tradescantianum) in Vauxhall, London. His botanical and collecting interests were continued by his son John the Younger, upon whose death the library and museum went to Elias Ashmole, who gave them to the University of Oxford, where they formed the core of the Ashmolean Museum, the first English museum to be opened to the public.

14 The dodo, a flightless bird unique to the island of Mauritius, was driven to extinction in the seventeenth century. A stuffed dodo remained in the Ashmolean Museum, but it slowly decayed and in 1755 was destroyed, except for its head and a foot.

15 Known as the Alfred Jewel, this ornament is inscribed "Aelfred mec heht gewyrcan" (Alfred had me made).

16 This painting is no longer ascribed to Giulio Romano, but is thought to be an early seventeenth-century copy of Raphael's fresco. There is also debate on the identity of the youthful figure in white, with many scholars doubting that it portrays the Duke of Urbino.

17 A late seventeenth- or early eighteenth-century copy of Raphael's *Portrait of Bindo Altoviti*, of which the original is now in the National Gallery of Art, Washington, D.C.

18 The portrait of Charles XII by Georg Engelhard Schröder (Pückler writes "Schröter") is now in the collection of the University of Oxford.

19 Thomas Hudson (Pückler writes "Hodson").

20 *Das Wilde Heer* (The Wild Hunt) is an ancient folk myth from northern Europe that tells of a phantasmal group of huntsmen and their hounds engaged in a mad pursuit across the skies.

21 Now known as the Radcliffe Camera (1737–1749), it was built after a design by James Gibbs with funds left for the purpose by John Radcliffe, physician to William III and Mary II of England.

22 The earliest printed bible is Gutenberg's so-called Forty-two-line Bible, which dates from the early 1450s; the Johann Fust Bible was the fourth to be printed and the first with a printer's mark and date (1462).

23 A German game; literally, "little rooms for rent."

24 "Never use your fists."

25 *Hahnenschlag* was a game in which a person tried to behead a cock, often while blindfolded, as in blindman's bluff.

26 A machine named after the 4th Earl of Orrery that models the relative movements of the planets and moons in the solar system.

27 Frideswide (ca. 680–727) was the patron saint of Oxford.

28 "But we will continue tomorrow."

29 "But let us return to our sheep; that is, continue our discussion of parks." The popular idiom about sheep means "let us return to the subject at hand." It originated in the fifteenth-century *La farce de maître Pierre Pathelin.*

30 "Louis the Inevitable" and "Louis Two-times-nine/Two-times-new" were unflattering puns about Louis XVIII, the Bourbon king who had been twice expelled from France.

31 The so-called Chandos portrait was presumed to have been painted by the actor Richard Burbage (Pückler writes "Barnage"). Once called the Stowe portrait, it was in 1856 the first acquisition of the National Portrait Gallery, London, where today it is attributed to John Taylor. Many of the pictures Pückler saw were auctioned off in 1848; see Henry Rumsey Forster, *The Stowe Catalogue: Priced and Annotated* (London: D. Bogue, 1848), which also contains a lengthy description of Stowe itself.

32 Phrenology was one of Pückler's favorite topics. See especially pages 232–36.

33 *Saint Catherine Reading a Book* and *Saint Barbara with a Book in Her Left Hand.*

34 This portrait was sold in the 1848 Stowe sale. In January 2000, it fetched $772,500 at a Christie's auction in New York. It depicts Charles de la Vieuville; it was not Charles but rather his son Vincent who died at Newbury.

35 The portrait of Duc Henri de Guise is listed in the catalogue of the Sotheby's sale of the Stowe Collection in 1848; see Forster, *The Stowe Catalogue.*

36 Likely a copy of the portrait of Oliver Cromwell by Robert Walker, now in the National Portrait Gallery, London.

37 Wycombe Abbey.

38 In this case, it is a version of a harlequinade.

39 An allusion to Louis Angely's popular comedy *Sieben Mädchen in Uniform* (1825).

1 "Like master, like man"—that is, good masters have good servants.

2 "But as soon as an ambassador is dead, he returns at once to private life."

3 Both Merveldt and Beroldingen were envoys in London during the time of Pückler's first visit.

4 An allusion to Shakespeare's *Julius Caesar,* act 1, scene 2.

5 The article originally appeared in French in the *Revue encyclopédique* 32 (1826): 51–63, and was later reprinted in more than one English publication. With the exception of one error (see note six below), Pückler's German translation of the excerpt is correct.

6 In fact, Pückler wrote "483,300," omitting the final zero and ruining the math.

7 *Antiaris toxicaria,* a tree native to Africa and Asia-Polynesia, has long been used as poison for arrows and darts in Malaysia and elsewhere.

8 Lady Morgan's two-volume biography, *The Life and Times of Salvator Rosa,* was published in London in 1824. Pückler translated an excerpt quoted in the review; the original passages from the book are quoted here (1:310, 22, 146).

9 "It is but one step from the sublime to the ridiculous."

10 "Porta Orientale": one of the entry gates of Milan, now called the Porta Venezia. Camillo Ugoni tells this anecdote in his *Della letteratura italiana nella seconda metà del Sicolo XVIII* (Brescia, 1820).

11 "The law of retribution" (as in retributive justice) or, alternately, "an eye for an eye."

12 Slightly misquoted from Friedrich Schiller, *Die Piccolomini,* act 5, scene 1: "Das eben ist der Fluch der bösen Tat / Daß sie fortzeugend immer Böses muß gebären." In Coleridge's translation (*The Piccolommini, or the First Part of Wallenstein,* act 3, scene 1), the lines are rendered as "This is the curse of every evil deed, / That, propagating still, it brings forth evil."

13 Cosmoramas were perspective pictures, sometimes with movable parts. Usually of exotic places, they were painted on long, curved canvases and viewed under special lighting through optical devices. "Travel in your room" was the name that Karl Wilhelm Gropius gave to his similar

and very popular diorama productions in a Berlin theater (designed by Schinkel), where large silkscreen paintings were slowly unrolled before the audience to give the impression of movement.

14 Antonio Franconi, a well-known circus performer, had two theaters in Paris, one of which Pückler visits (683).

15 "than a bouillon / made of the kidney / of a butterfly."

16 Cobham Hall is likely where Pückler met the young Charles Dickens, who ridicules him as "Count Smorltork" in *The Pickwick Papers.* Dickens was a friend of Lord Darnley's, and he set part of *The Pickwick Papers* at Cobham Hall.

17 Designed by Repton's sons John and George, it was dismantled in 1972 after being damaged; it has been reconstructed.

18 In 1822, Pückler invited John Adey Repton to consult on his plans for Muskau Park.

19 "Illuminatus": a member of the Illuminati, a secret society founded in 1776 in Bavaria.

20 *Höllenzwang,* which is loosely translated as "the coercion of hell," is the title of numerous handbooks of sorcery and magic. The most famous was ascribed to Johann Georg Faust, the historical figure behind the Faust legends.

21 Pückler's maternal grandfather was Hermann von Callenberg.

22 "Alas, those festive days are gone."

23 From Ecclesiastes 12:1: "Remember now thy Creator in the days of thy youth, while the evil days come not, nor the years draw nigh when thou shalt say, I have no pleasure in them."

24 The history of this painting—considered to be one of Rosa's greatest compositions and now in the Virginia Museum of Fine Arts, Richmond—is outlined in Lady Morgan, *The Life and Times of Salvator Rosa.*

25 Peter Paul Rubens, *Head of Cyrus Brought to Queen Tomyris,* ca. 1622–1623, was acquired by the Museum of Fine Arts, Boston, in 1941.

26 See page 53.

27 *Corpus Juris* (body of law) is a reference to the entire body of law of a country or jurisdiction. "Boufflers" is likely Stanislas de Boufflers (1738–1815), a writer and diplomat known for his witty light verse and picaresque tales.

28 "Pretend to have a small mouth (appetite)."

1 Dudley Ryder, 1st Earl of Harrowby, who would have been about sixty-five years old.

2 The Royal Pavilion at Brighton was built by King George IV of England. Construction began in 1787, when he was Prince of Wales, and continued until 1822. The building still stands today.

3 There were daily ships to Dieppe, but not to Le Havre or Boulogne. The Royal Suspension Chain Pier was built in 1823 and destroyed by a storm in 1896.

4 General Wittgenstein (promoted to field marshal in 1823) fought in the Napoleonic Wars until he was severely wounded at Bar-sur-Aube in February 1814.

5 In this context, an *à propos* is an occasional poem, composed for a particular occasion such as a wedding or a funeral.

6 Sumptuousness, eating and drinking; foppishness.

7 Pückler writes 8 degrees Celsius, which is 46.4 degrees Fahrenheit.

8 The Duke of York died on January 15, 1827.

9 The name is derived from the original Almack's Assembly Rooms in London, a social club founded by William Almack (died 1781) in 1765.

10 Marianne Spencer Hudson's *Almack's: A Novel* was first published in 1826.

11 "Was listening at the door."

12 "That is quite true ... a duke used to polish my boots in Naples, and in Saint Petersburg a Russian prince shaved me every morning." The wordplay in Pückler's response involves a change of verb: "a Russian prince spanked me every morning." The original passage is slightly different: "Madame, à Petersbourg j'ai été rasé par un prince; à Naples il y a des princes qui vous demanderont l'aumône dans les rues" (Madam, in Saint Petersburg I was shaved by a prince; in Naples there are princes begging for alms in the streets). Hudson, *Almack's,* 2:150–51.

13 Robert Townsend Farquhar was governor of Mauritius from 1810 to 1823. Pückler's table companion at dinner was Farquhar's wife, Maria Frances Geslip.

14 "What folly is fashion!"

15 The phrase Pückler uses, "an der Grenze des Schwabenalters" (verging on the Swabian age), alludes to the adage, "Die Schwaben werden erst mit 40 gescheit" (Swabians only become sensible when they turn forty).

16 "It is true that fortune has often sent me walking, but dancing—that's too much!"

17 This is MacDonell, who appears again on pages 176–77 and 183.

18 The royal couple was Frederick William III, king of Prussia, and his first wife Louise.

19 After many years of self-indulgence and three failed marriages, the dramatist Zacharias Werner traveled to Rome and converted to Catholicism, becoming a priest in 1814.

20 Luke 15:7: "I say unto you, that likewise joy shall be in heaven over one sinner that repenteth, more than over ninety and nine just persons, which need no repentance."

21 Horace Smith, *Zillah: A Tale of the Holy City*, 2nd ed. (London: H. Colburn, 1828), 1:296. Pückler's German translation of this passage is quite close to the original, although for "fallen into discredit" he uses the stronger "zum Gespött geworden" (become a mockery). This is a case of Pückler adding something to the published letters that was not part of the actual correspondence; *Zillah*, a very popular novel, was first published in 1828. Edgar Allen Poe incorporated whole sections of it into his 1832 spoof, "A Tale of Jerusalem."

22 There was a lengthy feud between the two Scottish families bearing similar names; see *Vindication of the "Clanronald of Glengary" against the Attacks Made Upon Them in the Inverness Journal and Some Recent Printed Performances, with Remarks as to the Descent of the Family Who Style Themselves "of Clanronald,"* by John Riddell (Edinburgh: W. and C. Tait, 1821); and the chapter "Macdonell of Glengarry, Chief of Glengarry," in John Bernard Burke, *Vicissitudes of Families, and Other Essays,* 5th ed. (London: Longman, Green, Longman, and Roberts, 1861), 54–65.

23 This story is told in a number of variations and contexts, and the bloody hand appears as a device in the heraldry of several Irish and Scottish families. It is often associated with the O'Neills (O'Neals) and the Rileys.

24 Pückler claimed that his own family was descended from Rüdiger von Bechelaren, a figure in the *Nibelungenlied*. See pages xxxii; xxxvii, note 3; and 240.

25 Lines from one of Potier's celebrated vaudeville routines, which Pückler quotes in French: "Entendez vous?—extraordinairement collant; si j'y entre, je ne le prends pas."

26 Pückler writes this line in French as well: "Si j'y entre je n'y vais pas."

27 The reference to cattle implies that the woman was bovine—that is, unrefined, excessively boisterous, and stupid.

28 Pückler alludes again to ongoing censorship of the mail on page 199, but he is jesting in both instances, since postal censorship was usually active only during times of war (although in England the government's right to censor certain mail was not officially abolished until 1847).

29 "During this time of year there are always some dangerous equinoxes that can become fatal."

30 This could be Hilmina (Wilhelmine), Lucie's ward.

31 *Kriminalrat*, the German title for a counselor for criminal affairs or detective superintendent includes a pun on "rat," the same rodent in French as in English. This is followed by more wordplays: *renvoyé* (someone fired from a job) replaces *envoyé* (envoy), and "diplomat of the fork" probably plays on the second meaning of *diplomate* (a sponge-cake dessert).

32 From Horace: *Naturam expellas furca, tamen usque recurrit.* (You may drive nature out with a pitchfork, she will nevertheless come back.)

33 The Königlich-Preußische Akademie der Wissenschaften (Royal Prussian Academy of Sciences) began holding annual competitions in the mid-eighteenth century to reward new ideas in the sciences and humanities. The dilettante comment alludes to the Berlin Mittwochsgesellschaft (Wednesday Society) that used to assemble on Goethe's birthday for a celebration.

34 "Are you alive, dearest, or dead?" An allusion to the ballad "Lenore" by Gottfried August Bürger. The exact quotation is "Bist untreu, Wilhelm, oder tot?" (Are you unfaithful, Wilhelm, or dead?)

NOTES TO LETTER 13

1 These are comparable to today's Christmas crackers, consisting of a cardboard tube, colorfully wrapped, with mottos, trinkets, and other delights inside. Two people pull on either end until the cracker splits, emitting a bang like that of a cap gun.

2 Pückler makes a pun involving *Anmut* (loveliness, charm) and *Armut* (neediness, poverty).

3 "Mouton qui rêve": a dozing sheep. Probably someone dumb and inattentive.

4 He was exactly Pückler's age.

5 "Is familiar with high society, and sometimes with good manners."

6 The spa at Muskau, called the Hermannsbad, was primarily Lucie's project. She began work on it in 1822 in the hope it would bring them financial security. It failed to do so.

7 "Well, Monsieur, my business is to make the king eat; yours is to purge him. Let's each take care of his own." This remark has been attributed to Benoist, a head cook to Louis XIV.

8 On page 95, Pückler visits "a distinguished lady" who talks of nothing but Napoleon; this is Lady Charleville.

9 Mrs. Hope was wife of the English art and antiquities collector Thomas Hope, who was sometimes called Anastasius after his popular novel of that title.

NOTES TO LETTER 14

1 "Give the crowns to those who earn them." A line from Friedrich Schiller's 1785 "An die Freude" (Ode to Joy), which is best known for its incorporation into Beethoven's Ninth Symphony (1824).

2 Pückler is implying that he is a night owl with his reference to the Roman goddess Minerva. An owl, a symbol of wisdom, was her attribute.

3 Parry had made previous expeditions to the Artic, but this was one of the earliest attempts to reach the North Pole. Though unsuccessful, he reached a northerly latitude that set the record for the next forty-nine years. He departed for Norway on April 4, 1827.

4 In fact, Zambeccari died in September 1812 shortly after takeoff, when his balloon was blown into a tree and became engulfed by flames.

5 Stereotyping was a method of printing from a cast mold (as opposed to movable type), which made cheap editions possible. It was introduced by the French printer Firmin Didot in 1798.

6 "Because especially the old ladies cheat mercilessly."

7 The alliterative expression has been attributed to the Prince Regent (later George IV) as descriptive of when a woman was at her most seductive. This was understood as a reference to his beloved

"wife" Mrs. FitzHerbert, who, only thirty at the time, is portrayed in the famous caricature by S. W. Fores in 1786.

8   Pückler met Lady Londenderry and her husband, Lord Castlereagh, at the Congress of Aachen in 1818. Lord Castlereagh, a member of the Knights of the Garter, was an important but finally unpopular figure who lapsed into depression and committed suicide in 1822.

9   This woman who is "mad about music" is the Countess San Antonio.

10 "Sound of a violin." A Madame de Geigenklang is featured in *Almack's Revisited; or, Herbert Milton,* a novel by Charles White that was first published anonymously in 1828. This is likely another example of Pückler adding material to the *Letters of a Dead Man* when he was editing them for publication.

11 Pückler often uses the French term to imply demeanor, bearing, deportment, or general appearance.

12 The slang terms that were applied to English money, not just game tokens, included a "pony" (twenty-five pounds) and a "monkey" (five hundred pounds; Pückler was mistaken in saying fifty).

13 "He is a great gentleman among dentists."

14 In fact, Pückler himself visited Lady Stanhope, spending eight days in her mountain castle, Daer-Dschuhn near Beirut, in 1838 (both wearing Turkish dress!); see Ludmilla Assing, *Fürst Hermann von Pückler-Muskau: eine Biographie* (Hamburg: Hoffmann and Campe, 1873–1874), 2:94–101; and Lady Hester Stanhope, *Memoirs of the Lady Hester Stanhope,* 2nd ed. (London: H. Colburn, 1846), vol. 3.

15 When Pückler visited her, he too was shown the sacred steed on which the New Messiah would ride into Jerusalem.

16 This evokes a proverbial expression, based on a passage in Luther's catechisms in which the sins of "old Adam" are said to be cleansed by baptism.

17 This begins as a description of the *Venus of Urbino* (now in the Galleria delgi Uffizi, Florence), but as Pückler continues, it merges into something more personal; this is clear in the original letter to Lucie, which was heavily redacted for publication. There—with excessive frankness and detail, for which he later apologizes— Pückler describes an encounter with a London prostitute, specifically comparing the seventeen-year-old beauty to this painting. Bowman offers an English translation of the original passage in *Fortune Hunter,* 94–95. Not surprisingly, Sarah Austin expunged this entire episode from her translation.

18 Pückler is hinting at the hidden meaning in his description of the Titian *Venus.*

19 "Life is serious, art is joyful." This is the closing sentence of the prologue to Schiller's *Wallenstein I.*

20 "Alas, my chancellor will tell you the rest." Except for the "alas," these were the words delivered by the French king in opening a session of the Parliament of Paris under the ancien régime.

21 A pun on "Russian steam baths."

22 The family seat referred to is Castle Derneburg.

23 Hope was an early patron of Thorvaldsen; he commissioned the *Jason* (now in the Thorvaldsen Museum, Copenhagen) from him in 1803.

24 Pückler was a Freemason.

25 "But it is always the same thing."

NOTES TO LETTER 15

1   See pages 178 and 703, note 27.

2   The event still takes place annually in Guildhall.

3   The expression Pückler uses for "every Tom, Dick, and Harry" is "Krethi und Plethi"—that is, Kerethites (Cretans) and Pelethites (Philistines), the motley group that King David used for his palace guard. 2 Samuel 15:18.

4   John Fane, 10th Earl of Westmorland, served under five prime ministers as lord privy seal, the officer originally responsible for the monarch's personal ("privy") seal.

5   Ecarté, whist, and loo (also called "lanterloo") were popular card games.

6   Under the term "Künstler" (artists), Pückler and his peers included writers, poets, painters, musicians, and the like.

7   "The fruit is rotten at both ends."

8   A reference to the cheap paper and illiberal attitude of Prussian publications.

9   A wine containing tartar emetic (antimony potassium tartrate), a drug that induces vomiting.

10 Pückler's visit was timely, because Robert Taylor was arrested and imprisoned later in 1827 and was forced to sell his church building.

11 The coronation of Tsar Nicholas I took place on September 3, 1826.

12 "The most famous commander in Europe" was Wellington.

13 See pages 98 and 699, note 8.

14 This may well have been the five-act, farcical opera *The Youthful Days of Gil Blas* by John Hamilton Reynolds, which was first performed in 1822 at the Theatre Royal, English Opera House.

15 "I believe that after this, there is little she would refuse me."

16 The colors of Prussia. Pückler had already started dyeing his hair by the time he left for England.

17 "It is like having to drink up the ocean."

18 She became Queen Adelaide (1830–1837), queen consort of the United Kingdom and Hanover.

19 A note in the *Morning Post* of May 12, 1827, seems to describe this party. See Bowman, *Fortune Hunter,* 80.

20 See page 42 and Figures 5 and 8.

21 The daughter is the future Queen Victoria, who was just eight years old when Pückler saw her at this dinner.

22 Princess Carolath, "Emilie," is Pückler's stepdaughter Adelheid, who was related to the Duchess of Clarence.

23 "That was doubtless an enormous error."

24 Among his children "of good stock" were two legitimate offspring as well as the five sons and five daughters he had with his mistress.

25 See George Augustus Frederick Fitzclarence, Earl of Munster, *Journal of a Route across India, through Egypt to England, in the Latter End of the Year 1817, and the Beginning of 1818* (London: J. Murray, 1819).

26 Kenilworth, the residence of Robert Dudley, Earl of Leicester, was the site of a spectacular festival that he organized to celebrate the three-week visit of Queen Elizabeth in 1575. Most of Scott's novel *Kenilworth* (1821) takes place there.

27 "What a beautiful horse you have there." "Yes, it's a beautiful animal; I made it myself, and for that reason I am very attached to it."

28 "This fish is very common in your country." "Yes, sire, I was one myself for fifteen years."

29 "The king of the Jews." The allusion is to Baron Rothschild.

30 "Immersed in a sweet languor."

31 These lines are from "The Giaour" by Lord Byron; the exact passage is "love will find its way / Through paths where wolves would fear to prey."

32 A French proverb: "Everything tires, everything breaks, everything ends."

33 "If this apron was an allusion to the vow of chastity."

34 Handel's oratorio *Israel in Egypt* premiered in London in 1739.

35 An allusion to the novella *Der goldne Topf* (The Golden Pot) by E. T. A. Hoffmann.

36 At the age of seven, Pückler was sent away to a Moravian school in Uhyst, about twenty miles southwest of Muskau, where he stayed for five unhappy years. Although he claims to have been little affected by his experience with "those men," he was certainly mistreated by them, perhaps even abused, and it is easy to imagine that his lifelong animosity toward excessive religiosity was first nurtured here. See page xxvii.

37 This quotes something Goethe said when Pückler visited him in Weimar; see page 23.

38 "Zwei wird fünf und sieben zehn / Augen eßt! Der Mund soll seh'n, / Vorn und hinten wechselt schnell. / *Fitzli Putzli verywell.*" This was a magic charm used for sleights of hand and card tricks.

39 "Utterances." Clearly an off-color linguistic pun, "pro-po" suggests in German "by way of his backside."

NOTES TO LETTER 16

1 Antonio Canova, *Hope Venus*, 1818–1820, now in the Leeds Art Gallery.

2 "Lady Ambassadors engaged in a colloquy, all three profoundly occupied with the train of a dress."

3 "Eine alte Freiheit." In the middle ages, a part of a city or encampment could be deemed "free"—that is, open to normally forbidden activities and professions, such as gambling and prostitution.

4 Venus, the goddess of love, trumps Pluto, the god of riches.

5 "I will always love you."

6 This letter is erroneously dated June 13.

7 In 1822, the Ottomans put down a rebellion on this Greek island, killing or enslaving a large percentage of the population.

8 Probably Wellington.

9 Kew Gardens.

10 "So, what's up, Esterházy?"

11 Fath Ali Shah Qajar, "Baba Khan" (1772–1834) ruled Persia from 1797 to 1834. He ascended the throne after his uncle, Mohammad Khan Qajar, was assassinated. His grand vizier, Ebrahim Khan Kalantar, had served the Zand and Qajar rulers for some fifteen years.

12 "When one has depopulated the earth, it is necessary to repopulate it again."

13 Most of Lusatia, the region where Muskau was located, had been part of German Saxony, but it was divided at the Congress of Vienna in 1815, with Lower Lusatia awarded to Prussia. Although he felt an affinity with Prussia, the consequent lessening of his sovereign rights was a significant blow to Pückler.

14 See page 163.

15 In the Parable of the Royal Wedding Feast, the one who comes to the feast without the proper attire (i.e., humility, acceptance, etc.) is cast out. Matthew 22:1–14.

16 Marie Louise of Austria was Napoleon's second wife and bore him his only son, Napoleon (given the title King of Rome), in March 1811. She was appointed regent in 1813 and again in 1814, when she had to be persuaded to leave Paris as the Allies were advancing. The boy, later Duke of Reichstadt, was first named Emperor Napoleon II when his father abdicated in his favor on April 4, 1814, and again after the Battle of Waterloo, although this was never officially acknowledged. He was raised from 1815 in Austria. Meanwhile, the empress had fallen in love with the Count von Neipperg (an enemy of Napoleon), and when she was recognized as Duchess of Parma by the Congress of Vienna, she retreated there with her lover. She had three children with Niepperg, but married him only after Napoleon's death.

17 Cochrane was accused of being part of a conspiracy that used rumors to send stock prices up, at which point he sold certain shares. Sentenced to the King's Bench Prison for one year, he was finally cleared of the charges near the end of his life.

18 "The best is the enemy of the good": a quote from Voltaire's poem "La Bégueule" (1772).

19 The roguish Scapin is a scheming, social-climbing valet in Molière's farce *Les fouberies de Scapin* (1671).

20 Gall held that the brain was divided into twenty-seven separate "organs," each related to a human faculty.

21 Many of the names for the various organs were changed more than once. The older terminology can be found in Franz Joseph Gall, *On the Functions of the Brain and of Each of Its Parts,* vol. 4, *Organology* (Boston: Marsh, Capen, and Lyon, 1835), translated from the French by Winslow Lewis.

22 Sarah Austin seems to have known Deville personally, for she adds a note: "The individual in question is Dr. Herschel, of whose head Mr. Deville possesses two casts corresponding to the description above. Mr. Deville bears testimony to the accuracy in the main of the above report, though the language is, he says, considerably more ornate than that which he is likely to have used." Pückler, *Tour in England, Ireland, and France,* 161.

23 "Mustard after the meal."

24 Gall initially named this "memory of things," then "sense of things." Spurzheim renamed it "eventuality."

25 Karl Philipp, Prince of Schwarzenberg, handled the negotiations involving Napoleon's marriage to Marie Louise of Austria. In July 1810, at the enormous ball he gave in his palace to honor the bride, a catastrophic fire broke out and many of the guests were killed.

26 Rundell and Bridge were the royal goldsmiths from 1797 to 1843.

27 The painting from 1827 by Sir Edwin Landseer is now in the Guildhall Art Gallery, City of London. Its subject is The Monkey Who Had Seen the World, from John Gay's *Fables* (also known as *Fifty-One Fables in Verse*), 1727.

28 An allusion to Matthew 25:14–30 and Luke 19:12–27.

29 The first of the following paragraphs translates Pückler's loose paraphrases from Edward George Bulwer-Lytton, *Falkland* (London: H. Colburn, 1827). The subsequent excerpts are quoted in Bulwer-Lytton's own words, since in these cases Pückler stayed close to the original. (As he himself points out a paragraph later, he often paraphrases and rewrites!)

30 "That is truly a consolation!"

31 A reference to Pückler's claim of medieval ancestry. See pages xxxii; xxxvii, note 3; and 177.

32 The Thames Tunnel, originally intended for horse-drawn carriages, was built between 1825 and 1843. Progress was slow, as only eight to twelve feet were completed a week, and to help cover costs, sightseers

were charged a shilling to view the work in progress. The tunnel flooded several times, first on May 18, 1827, and work was stopped altogether between 1828 and 1836.

33 An opera by Carl Maria von Weber.

34 Till Eulenspiegel is a fabled German peasant-prankster.

35 Philine is a character in Goethe's *Wilhelm Meisters Lehrjahre* (1795–1796). An enchanting actress, carefree and uncomplicated, she seeks the attention of the hero.

36 An exaggeration. Officially there were 29,773 prostitutes in London in 1827 and 31,965 in 1828. The population of Berlin was approximately 200,000; that of London, 1,350,000.

37 Scott's *Waverley* (1814) and *Redgauntlet* (1824) feature Charles Edward Stuart, pretender to the throne.

38 Perhaps an allusion to King George IV's last mistress, Lady Elizabeth Conyngham, who was featured in a number of contemporary cartoons. Virginia Water is in the park of Windsor Castle, the royal residence where she lived until the king's death in 1830.

39 The Children Act of 1908 banned the hanging of children younger than sixteen.

40 Harpagon is the name of the central figure in Molière's comedy *The Miser*, first performed in 1668.

41 Pückler's retelling of this anecdote is very close to the original in John Malcolm's *Sketches of Persia* (1827), quoted here from the 1888 New York edition (1:178–79).

42 An allusion to Goethe, who famously defined a novella as based on an "unerhörte Begebenheit" (unprecedented incident).

43 Mary Linwood was famous for her embroidered pictures; her portrait of Napoleon is now in the Victoria and Albert Museum, London.

44 Modern light microscopes can magnify fifteen hundred times. Only electron microscopes can magnify over one million times.

45 Canning and several other dignitaries became ill after enduring the freezing temperatures at the Duke of York's funeral on January 20, 1827; Canning never fully recovered. Already in bad health when he became prime minister on April 10, 1827, he held that office for just 119 days.

46 Philip Dormer Stanhope, Earl of Chesterfield, *The Letters of the Earl of Chesterfield to his Son*, ed. Charles Strachey, 2 vols. (New York: Putnam's Sons, 1901), 2:222 (letter of April 13, 1752). Pückler translates the quotation into French.

47 *Vivian Grey: A Romance of Youth*, by Benjamin Disraeli (1804–1881), appeared in 1826–1827. The quoted passages are from book 5, chapter 12. Pückler is proud of his German translation (see his comment just after the quoted passages), and it is indeed very close to the original quoted here.

48 Pückler has added this line.

49 Pückler has added this sentence and the preceding sentence fragment.

50 In fact, the following quotation is not by Disraeli but from Bulwer-Lytton, *Falkland*. Once more, Pückler hews very close to the original quoted here. (See page 705, note 29.)

51 Published in *The Literary Gazette and Journal of the Belles Lettres* (April 14, 1827): 231.

52 The parks were remodeled in 1826–1827, in a project commissioned by the Prince Regent (later George IV) and overseen by the architect and landscaper John Nash.

53 "Just another minute, I'm not asking for anything—just to speak French, to have a reasonable conversation, something the English are not capable of."

54 "A great man's friendship is a gift of the gods": a quote from Voltaire's *Oedipe* (1718), act 1, scene 1.

55 "Those words were written for me."

56 "Give him whatever he wants, provided there's still a pair left for me to change into."

NOTES TO LETTER 17

1 "In the nethermost depths of the stream." A slightly altered quotation from a line in Friedrich Schiller's famous ballad "Der Taucher" (The Diver) of 1797.

2 See page 228.

3 The Hunterian Museum.

4 Alexander I of Russia.

5 Pückler was likely staying at the Castle Inn, one of the best-known inns in the area and prized for its view of Windsor Castle.

6 John Penn.

7 King's scholars were non–fee-paying students.

8 William Harcourt.

9 Pückler proved to be correct; St Leonard's Hill passed to the field marshal's French relatives. Mary Harcourt was in her late seventies, slightly older than Pückler thought.

10 Marie-Augusta d'Harcourt, born in 1813, was about fourteen.

11 Byron's relationship with his wife, Anna Isabella, Baroness Byron (1792–1860), was a rocky one, and they separated shortly after their first wedding anniversary.

12 "What in the devil does she intend?"

13 "Make fun of me, if you want, but I have kept it."

14 On page 248, Pückler reported examining the skull of a potential servant before hiring him.

NOTES TO LETTER 18

1 An allusion to Acts 17:28: "For in him we live, and move, and have our being."

2 "At the moment of death."

3 The west window dates from 1338. The great east window, completed in 1408, is the largest medieval stained-glass window that exists. The present building dates from 1220 to 1472. Scrope is buried there but did not "initiate its construction."

4 In 1190, the members of the York Jewish community took refuge in what was then a wooden keep, but it was burned down by a mob and nearly all the refugees (estimated at one hundred fifty people, not the thousand cited by Pückler) died from the flames or the massacre that followed. The stone tower was built in its place in the thirteenth century. Parts of it were damaged and rebuilt over the centuries, before it was finally gutted by an explosion in 1684.

5 A beverage made of wine and hot water, with sugar, nutmeg, and lemon.

6 This seems to be a mistake, as the four main gates (called "bars") are Bootham Bar, Monk Bar, Walmgate Bar, and Micklegate Bar; the minor gates are known as Victoria Bar and Fishergate Bar. Pückler may be referring to the latter, which was reopened in 1827 to provide access to a nearby cattle market.

7 Wilhelm Heinse uses this expression in his novel *Ardinghello und die glückseligen Inseln* (1787).

8 The great organ admired by Pückler was destroyed in the fire of 1829.

9 Matthew 7:3: "And why beholdest thou the mote that is in thy brother's eye, but considerest not the beam that is in thine own eye?"

10 The motto derives from a well-known proverb concerning the Greek painter Apelles, who cautioned a cobbler to stick

to what he knew, a "last" being a foot-shaped wooden block used in shoemaking.

11 The parish church of All Saints on North Street contains some of the most important displays of medieval stained glass in the British Isles.

12 Pückler may have meant St Margaret's Church, which had signs of the zodiac on its Romanesque doorway.

13 Archbishop Edward Venables-Vernon, who lived to be ninety, was seventy years old at the time of Pückler's visit.

14 Bishopthorpe Palace has been the residence of the archbishops of York for over seven centuries.

15 See pages 249–50.

16 Annibale Carracci, *The Dead Christ Mourned ("The Three Maries")*, ca. 1604, is now in the National Gallery, London.

17 The squawking of the Capitoline geese, according to legend, warned the Romans of the approach of the Gauls in the fourth century BC. See Livy, *History of Rome* 5.46–47.

18 The Castle Howard painting is now in the collection of the Bob Jones University Museum and Gallery, Greenville, South Carolina.

19 Pückler gives distances sometimes in German miles, sometimes in English. In this translation, miles are always given according to the English measure.

NOTES TO LETTER 19

1 Pückler calls these black-faced sheep *Heidschnucken*, a type of German moorland sheep.

2 The Church of Saint Mary.

3 The figure of sixty shillings is the same as that recorded in the Domesday Book, a survey covering much of England and Wales that was completed in 1086.

4 "Tree cake." Assembled out of many layers, it looks like a series of tree rings when sliced.

5 In 1793, Humphry Repton produced one of his Red Books for the park at Mulgrave; the book remains in the castle library.

6 William Shakespeare, *King John*, act 4, scene 1. There are numerous speculations about the tragic end of Prince Arthur; one identifies his murderer as Peter de Maulay and claims that King John rewarded him with the heiress of Doncaster, Isabella de Turnham, who brought him the barony of Mulgrave.

7 The sitter is Catherine Sedley, Countess of Dorchester, and the inscription is in French. See *Letters Written during the Years 1686, 1687, 1688, and Addressed to John Ellis, Esq., Secretary to the Commissioners of His Majesty's Revenue in Ireland,* ed. Lord Dover [George Agar Ellis] (London: H. Colburn and R. Bentley, 1831), 1:23–24, where she is described as "a coarse, vulgar woman, with some humour," and where the following account is given: "At Mulgrave Castle, in Yorkshire, the seat of Lord Mulgrave, (who is descended from her only daughter by Lord Anglesey) is a curious portrait of her. She is represented in widow's weeds for Lord Anglesey, and upon the picture are the following lines in gold letters:—'Puisque le Comte d'Anglesey mourut sans remords, / j'avoue que mon deuil n'est qu'en dehors.'"

8 Pückler spells the Mulgrave family name "Fips," which in German means a swat on the nose.

9 Malbork Castle contained a summer and a winter refectory; in both, the enormous vaulted ceiling was supported by a single slim granite pillar.

10 Although several medieval Percys were buried at Fountains Abbey, Sir Henry Percy, known as "Hotspur," was not.

11 "Soli Deo Honor et Gloria." The inscription was added by Abbot Marmaduke Huby (1495–1526), who had the new tower built in the late fifteenth century.

12 Fountains Hall, built 1598–1604.

13 Pückler nodded here, for the inscription is on a sundial above the entrance portal, between two niches containing statues of Mars (left) and Saturn (right).

14 The idiomatic equivalent of "[happy as] a cow in clover."

15 "Sir, I have the honor of presenting you my respects, you are too kind to come visit us. We so rarely have an opportunity to chat with anyone here!"

16 Pückler gave up his study of law in 1802 and became a lieutenant in the Saxon Garde du Corps regiment in Dresden.

17 Pückler wrote "10,000," omitting a zero. In the first census of 1801, Leeds had thirty thousand residents; by 1851, it had over one hundred thousand.

18 The Reform Act of 1832 finally succeeded in correcting many of the problems in the English electoral system.

19 The inscription on the balustrade, not from the Bible, was first cut in stone in 1628; the metal letters, added in 1788, read "ALL GLORY AND PRAISE BE GIVEN TO GOD THE FATHER THE SON AND HOLY GHOST ON HIGH PEACE ON EARTH GOOD WILL TOWARDS MEN HONOUR AND TRUE ALLEGIANCE TO OUR GRACIOUS KING LOVING AFFECTION AMONGST HIS SUBJECTS HEALTH AND PLENTY BE WITHIN THIS HOUSE."

20 *Thomas Wentworth, First Earl of Strafford, with Sir Philip Mainwaring*, 1639–1640. There are numerous copies, but the original (still in the Wentworth Woodhouse estate) is the property of Lady Juliet Tadgell. Current scholarship does not accept that this painting depicts Strafford's final testament but rather suggests that it is part of a tradition of portraits of important men and their secretaries.

21 Diagonally across shoulder and breast. The son was William Wentworth, 2nd Earl of Strafford. Pückler may be referring to a portrait by Van Dyck of William and his sisters Anne and Arabella.

22 George Stubbs, *Whistlejacket*, ca. 1762, is now in the National Gallery, London.

23 There is an old superstition that a gift of knives, needles, or scissors will destroy a friendship. In fact, Lucie reacts negatively to this gift. See page 335.

24 Byron's ancestral home, although he was actually born in London.

25 A kind of knitted lace. Nottingham was a lace-making center.

26 Pückler must mean the gnu, which was often called a horned horse, but was, in fact, an antelope from Africa, not Asia.

27 His house was Wollaton Hall.

28 At 276 feet, the nave is the second longest in England. Pückler was likely referring to the entire length of its interior, which at over 500 feet is also extraordinary.

29 Pückler has confused John of Lancaster, 1st Duke of Bedford, with Humphrey, Duke of Gloucester. Both men were brothers of Henry V and served as regents to the child king Henry VI, as did Henry Beaufort (Henry V's half uncle). But it was Gloucester, the one buried at St Albans, who was rumored to have died by poisoning.

NOTES TO LETTER 20

1 "Illusion was invented for the happiness of mortals; it does them almost as much good as hope."

2   Pückler includes numerous tantalizing elisions, but since Lucie's letters to him were all burned, we often cannot understand his allusions.

3   Charles Howard, 11th Duke of Norfolk, who restored Arundel Castle, was the cousin, not the father, of Bernard, 12th Duke of Norfolk, who resided there at the time of Pückler's visit.

4   The dates and places named in this and the preceding letter are contradictory. According to Pückler, the previous letter (headed "London, Nov 1st") was written at an inn near Petworth. The heading of the present letter is "Petworth House, the 26th," and thus it is out of sequence and not compatible with Pückler's comments about his birthday, which was October 30. This seems to be one of the few moments where he nodded while transforming his letters for publication.

5   The Petworth portrait is thought to be a studio copy of a lost work.

6   In the seventeenth century, the actress Nell Gwynn was mistress to Charles II, who acknowledged her son Charles Beauclerk, 1st Earl of Burford, as his illegitimate child and created the title of Duke of St Albans for him in 1684.

7   "Ein Junge, geboren im Monat Oktober, / Wird ein Kritiker, und das ein recht grober!"

8   Pückler's second name was Ludwig, but the name day (one of them) for Saint Louis is August 25.

9   *The Mummy! A Tale of the Twenty-Second Century,* a science fiction novel by Jane C. Webb Loudon (1806–1858), was published anonymously in three volumes in London in 1827.

10 Pillet's book, *Views of England,* includes a chapter (36) entitled "Habitual Intoxication Common among Females."

11 Pückler here disguises a faux pas of his own. During dinner at Ashburnham House, the residence of the Prince and Princess Lieven, he made this unfortunate joke to the hostess, damaging their relationship for some time to come. See Bowman, *Fortune Hunter,* 136–37.

12 A popular health drink in the eighteenth and nineteenth centuries made by pouring boiling water over toasted bread.

13 At the Battle of Navarino on October 20, 1827, the Ottoman and Egyptian armada was destroyed by a combined naval force from Britain, France, and Russia. The

sultan would not admit defeat, however, and what followed was the Russo-Turkish War of 1828–1829, which the Editor refers to on page 319, footnote.

14 The Congress of Vienna (1814–1815) redrew the political map of Europe after the French Revolution and the Napoleonic Wars.

15 "Nothing is sadder than a witty remark that is lost on the ear of a fool."

16 See pages 86–88 and Figure 16.

17 On Brownonian, see page 96, note 6.

18 Lady Bury's brother was George Campbell, Duke of Argyll, the lord keeper of the Great Seal of Scotland at the time of Pückler's visit.

19 Macbeth means the opposite: "Yet I will try the last. Before my body / I throw my warlike shield. Lay on, Macduff, / And damn'd be him that first cries, 'Hold, enough!'"

20 The inferior performer was Sarah West.

21 Ludwig Tieck, who edited and completed August Wilhelm von Schlegel's translation of Shakespeare's plays, was the first to see Lady Macbeth as a tender, loving wife rather than as a monster.

22 In the story "Don Juan" by E. T. A. Hoffmann, the narrator is watching a performance of Mozart's *Don Giovanni* when the actress playing the heroine Donna Anna miraculously appears in his box.

23 Pückler renders this in his unidiomatic English as "Depend upon, he has had his throat cut."

24 The following six paragraphs are not from a single source, as Pückler states, but from at least three. I have not been able to identify the source of the first two passages ascribed to a "medical friend" nor that of the fourth paragraph. The third, with the anecdote about Dr. Baillie, is quoted here from William Macmichael, *The Gold-Headed Cane,* 2nd ed. (London: J. Murray, 1828), 243–44. Pückler's source for this quotation seems to have been "Diary for the Month of May," *The London Magazine,* n.s., 8, no. 30 (1827): 168, since the same introductory words appear there. The final two paragraphs are quoted from David Uwins, *A Treatise on Diseases which are Either Directly or Indirectly Connected with Indigestion* (London: Underwood, 1827). Pückler adds the italics and omits a short poem.

25 Here, Pückler is referring to himself ironically as Prince P—— and to his own wife Lucie as Julie's "best friend." There were, indeed, troubling rumors circulating about

him and his fortune hunting, a situation that, combined with his dwindling funds, would soon force him to abandon his quest.

26 King Charles XII of Sweden invaded Russia in 1708 hoping to bring the Great Northern War to an end; he was defeated at the Battle of Poltava by Peter I of Russia.

NOTES TO LETTER 21

1   In German tradition, Knecht Ruprecht is a helper of Santa Claus.

2   The illustration, taken from Pückler's Memory Album II, 103, was included in the first edition of the *Briefe.*

3   Pückler is alluding to metempsychosis, also known as the reincarnation or the transmigration of the soul, which he calls *his* theory in a subsequent letter (page 333). Ephraim Lessing focused attention on the subject in the late eighteenth century, and the debate attracted many German thinkers, including Goethe, Heine, and Krug, who is named on page 582.

4   "If I am to find my final end and first beginning, / Then I must ground myself in God, and God in me / And become what He is: I must be a light in the light, / I must be a word in the Word, a God in God." Translation from Angelus Roland Pietsch, "The Spiritual Vision: Meister Eckhart, Jacob Boehme, and Angelus Silesius," *Studies in Comparative Religion* 13, nos. 3–4 (1979): 11.

5   The German expression for original sin is "hereditary sin," which Pückler invokes in a play on words in the following paragraph.

6   Pückler renders this phonetically in a broad Austrian dialect, an amusing touch that I have not attempted to emulate.

7   "Appetite comes with eating"—that is, the more you have, the more you want.

8   Baron Falck.

9   In 1813–1814, Pückler served as an aide-de-camp to Karl August, Grand Duke von Saxe-Weimar. See page 19, note 6.

10 "With such a sauce, one would eat one's own father."

11 Ghosts haunt many of E. T. A. Hoffmann's stories. In "The Sandman," the hero falls passionately in love with a strange but lovely young woman who is finally revealed to be an automaton, like an artist's articulated mannequin. The revelation drives the hero mad and ultimately to suicide.

12 Hunting "par force" meant to hunt with hounds, long considered the noblest form

of hunting; it was certainly the most expensive. Pückler is making a pun on the French "par force," meaning "by force."

13 A Prussian edict of 1813 called up all men between the ages of eighteen and forty-five to serve in the Landwehr, or territorial army.

14 Frederick William III.

15 In Schiller's *Wallenstein,* the hero foresees his own death in a dream.

16 Tipu's Tiger (in the Victoria and Albert Museum, London, since 1880) was first displayed in 1808 at the East India Company's museum.

17 Thomas Daniell, *Hindoo Excavations in the Mountain of Ellora near Aurungabad in the Decan* (London, 1803).

18 Pückler is referring to Garlieb Merkel, "Ueber die früheste Welt-Cultur," *Neues Museum der teutschen Provinzen Russlands* 1, no. 1 (1824): 51–66.

19 The schoolteacher George Pocock patented his invention of the *charvolant,* a kite-drawn carriage, in 1824.

20 "Only the soul that loves is happy": a quote from *Egmont,* act 3, scene 2.

21 Pückler tells this story on pages 176–77.

22 Pückler edited these letters after the fact, which leads to occasional anomalies such as his use of the past perfect here and subsequent use of the present tense to discuss his ongoing ill health.

23 "It is vice that abandons us, and only very rarely we who abandon vice": a variation on a maxim by François de La Rochefoucauld, published in *Maximes (Réflexions ou sentences et maxims morales)* (Paris: Claude Barbin, 1665): "Quand les vices nous quittent, nous nous flattons de la créance que c'est nous qui les quittons" (When our vices abandon us, we flatter ourselves by believing that we have abandoned them).

24 Origen (ca. 185–254), one of the fathers of the church, was said to have castrated himself because of a passage in Matthew (19:12) suggesting that self-made eunuchs could enter the kingdom of heaven.

25 The four Memory Albums. See page xliv.

26 A highly toxic poison from the upas tree (*Antiaris toxicaria*), native to southeast Asia.

27 In 1830, upon the death of King George IV, his younger brother, the Duke of Clarence, assumed the throne as William IV. William's wife Adelaide of Saxe-Meiningen, a relative of Pückler's step-daughter Adelheid, became Queen Adelaide.

28 Miss Gibbings was only about twenty-eight years old at this time!

29 In Greek mythology, a princess named Philomela is transformed into a nightingale.

NOTES TO LETTER 22

1 This was the famous will of Peter Thellusson, who died in 1797 and whose family fought the terms of the bequest, leading the House of Lords in 1800 to ban any such *future* arrangements. The Thellusson heirs, however, had to wait to receive their inheritance until 1859, by which time the fortune had not vanished entirely (as in Dickens's *Bleak House,* based on this case), but was only scarcely larger than the original estate due to the cost of legal challenges by the heirs, although it had been speculated that it would grow to over fourteen million pounds. The Thellusson will also inspired Edgar Allen Poe; see page 26, note 3.

2 In the United Kingdom, rotten boroughs were constituencies with very small populations that nevertheless had representatives in Parliament who wielded unwarranted power. The Reform Act of 1832 was a first step toward a more balanced system.

3 "That the best is the enemy of the good": an aphorism known especially from Voltaire's poem "La Bégueule."

4 The painting, *Portrait of Susanna Lunden (?) (Le Chapeau de Paille),* is now in the National Gallery, London, which bought Peel's entire collection of seventy-seven paintings in 1871.

5 Carr bequeathed his collection of thirty-five paintings to the National Gallery, London, upon his death in 1831. Of the items in the bequest, those Pückler discusses are Garofalo, *Saint Augustine with the Holy Family and Saint Catherine of Alexandria (The Vision of Saint Augustine),* ca. 1520; Claude, *Landscape with David at the Cave of Adullam,* 1658; landscapes by Domenichino and Annibale Carracci (some have been reattributed); and Bernardino Luini, *Christ Among the Doctors,* ca. 1515–1530, which was formerly ascribed to Leonardo da Vinci.

6 The battle between the French army and local Mamluk forces took place in Egypt on July 21, 1798. Napoleon called it the Battle of the Pyramids. In the 1806 painting by Lejeune (Figure 70), the pyramids are visible on the horizon.

7 Percy Farren, an actor and manager of the Brunswick Theater, published a letter and a book about the catastrophe (*A Full and Accurate Account of the Destruction of the Brunswick Theatre* [London: J. Robins, 1828]).

8 This is a pun in German: one man is "der Herrscher aller Gläubigen" and the other "der Gläubiger aller Herrscher." *Gläubiger* has two meanings: "believers" and "creditors."

9 *Confiseur* (French for "confectioner") was the nom de plume of the infamously rude letter editor of the *Elegant Newspaper* (*Zeitung für die elegante Welt*), published in Leipzig between 1801 and 1857.

10 The lines are based on Thomas Moore's "Come, rest in this bosom," as follows: "Oh! what was love made for, if 'tis not the same / Through joy and through torment, through glory and shame? / I know not, I ask not, if guilt's in that heart? / I but know that I love thee, whatever thou art." In his own translation, Pückler adds poverty, wealth, youth, and old age to the things love survives, making the verse more appropriate to his own circumstances.

11 The "Talbot" is likely John Talbot, 1st Earl of Shrewsbury, who figures in Shakespeare's *Henry VI, Part 1.* Herr von Langsalm is a character in the 1804 farce *Der Wirrwarr, oder der Muthwillige* (The Confusion, or the Wag) by August von Kotzebue.

12 *Der Wollmarkt oder das Hotel de Wibourg* (The Wool Market, or the Hotel de Wibourg) was a lightweight comedy by Heinrich Clauren.

NOTES TO LETTER 23

1 Likely Lansdowne, who was known for his liberal views.

2 Most frogs reproduce through amplexus, in which a male grasps a female from above with his front legs and stays attached to her while she ejects eggs and he fertilizes them, all externally.

3 The king was George IV. Pückler distinguishes between the levee, the ceremonial reception of visitors as the monarch rises in the morning, and the more exclusive *grande entrée,* generally restricted to noble visitors with special privileges.

4 Beresford lost one-quarter of his men in a successful battle against the French at La Albuera in 1811, for which he was harshly

criticized in Britain, most caustically by William Napier in his *History of War in the Peninsula and in the South of France,* 6 vols. (1828–1850), particularly in vol. 2 (1829).

5 A variation on Matthew 10:16: "Be ye therefore wise as serpents."

6 See page 699, note 8 (Letter 7), on Dom Miguel's brother Don Pedro and the crises in Portugal.

7 Charles II, "the Merrie Monarch," had more than twelve illegitimate children, most of whom were granted titles. Charles Beauclerk, for example, became the first Duke of St Albans.

8 This picture from the Wrotham estate, *Saint Joseph and the Christ Child,* was sold at Christie's on December 14, 1990, for £2.42 million to Bruno Meissner of Zurich.

9 Ironic nickname of Sir Walter Scott, who was widely known as the author of his anonymously published works.

10 William Crockford was the son of a fishmonger who first worked in his father's shop and then went on to establish Crockford's, one of the most famous gaming clubs in Europe, where the English aristocracy (Pückler's "above-average fish") lost enormous sums of money.

11 Joseph Emil Nürnberger's book *Astronomische Reiseberichte; oder, Skizzen der Topographie des Himmels und planetarischen Metempsychose* (Astronomical Travels; or, Sketches on the Topography of the Heavens and Planetary Metempsychosis) was not published until 1837, but individual "travel reports" had been appearing regularly in the *Dresdner Abendzeitung.*

12 "Da ergreifts ihm die Seele mit Himmelsgewalt": a quote from Schiller's poem "Der Taucher" (The Diver).

13 "In truth, this time, I will make no reply."

14 "Begin to use harsh, abusive language"—that is, be spoiling for a fight.

15 Hardenberg.

16 The Duke of Buckingham.

17 Macduff and Birnam Wood figure in Shakespeare's *Macbeth.*

18 Bonneau is the king's councilor in Voltaire's *La Pucelle* (The Maid of Orleans).

19 From 1810 to 1823, Robert Townsend Farquhar was the first governor of Mauritius, an island in the Indian Ocean taken over by the English during the Napoleonic Wars.

20 Hannah Barent-Cohen Rothschild was the wife of Nathan Rothschild, who had the title Freiherr von Rothschild.

21 There were two types of pigeon clubs in nineteenth-century England, those whose members were fanciers and breeders of doves (Charles Darwin was a member of such a club), and those whose members were interested in shooting the birds (the trapshooting type that Pückler describes).

22 Its location near the New River allowed Sadler's Wells to build a water tank that covered the entire stage; this "aquatic theater" was launched in 1804.

23 "I do not remember."

NOTES TO LETTER 24

1 A type of school started by Joseph Lancaster (1778–1838), in which advanced students taught those who were less advanced. Popular in England from 1798 to 1830, the schools following this model were superseded by others that grouped students by age and employed lecturers.

2 "To talk is to ruin the conversation." It is not clear what Pückler means by peripatetic silence, since the adjective refers to an ancient Greek school of teaching. Perhaps he simply means "philosophical."

3 "Four-in-hand": a carriage drawn by four horses with the reins connected, enabling a single driver to control them.

4 Napoleon.

5 More than one kind of "domestic telegraph" was invented in the early nineteenth century, both in Britain and America. Circular dials showing the alphabet were connected mechanically via rods and wires to stations elsewhere in the house.

6 Here, Pückler begins a diatribe against certain aspects of English high society. We should remember that this was written at the nadir of his London sojourn, when he was forced to admit the failure of his matrimonial hopes and depart in defeat. It is notable, however, that he could easily have changed the tone, given that he edited his words heavily before publication. Also, since the letters appeared in inverted chronology—making this letter the last one—it is striking that he chose to conclude with such a scathing, personally directed attack. For even though he disguises most of his targets by using initials instead of full names, many of his English readers (and he knew by this time that his first volume

had won considerable attention in Britain) would have recognized themselves or their friends. Sarah Austin certainly recognized the risk, for she eliminated nearly 40 percent of the diatribe—even for her an enormous reduction in Pückler's unflattering remarks about her country. Although she regularly modulated his prose, eliminating or softening words or sentences and sometimes making mollifying additions of her own, this case is exceptional. See pages xli–xlii, for a fuller discussion.

7 The improvisatory plays of the sixteenth-century Italian commedia dell'arte relied on a set of stock character types, each of whom appeared wearing the appropriate mask. The practice spread throughout European theaters, especially for farces.

8 The somewhat awkward language is Pückler's own English rendition.

9 Age-old superstitions surround the *Galgenmännchen* (mandrake) as a temperamental bringer of good luck.

10 Edward Bulwer-Lytton's *Pelham; or, Adventures of a Gentleman* was a very popular novel, a kind of murder mystery set among the English aristocracy. It established the author's reputation as a witty dandy. Pückler was quite up-to-date, for the book was first published in 1828.

11 A tall, ungainly man.

12 The powerful London hostess was likely Princess Lieven, with whom Pückler had a falling-out.

13 The leaders of the chorus in ancient Greek drama; hence, the highest authorities.

14 Baron Rothschild.

15 "Gods of lesser extraction."

16 The man being satirized is probably George Stanhope, 6th Earl of Chesterfield (1805–1866), a British politician, racehorse owner, and celebrated dandy. His father, Philip Stanhope, 5th Earl of Chesterfield (1755–1815), was the godson of Philip Stanhope, 4th Earl of Chesterfield, who from 1737 to 1768 wrote over four hundred letters to his illegitimate son, also named Philip (1732–1768). These *Letters to His Son* were published (against the writer's wishes) by his son's widow, Eugenia Peters Stanhope, in four volumes in 1774 and quickly gained notoriety.

17 This paragraph appears to be a tongue-in-cheek description of Pückler himself and his "lovely wife" Lucie. In this case, the

criticism is of English society and *not* of the foreign "ambassador."

18 Members of the Habsburg dynasty were known for having an extended lower jaw, colloquially known as the "Habsburg lip" or "Austrian lip."

19 Wellington.

20 A naive but crafty figure in Kotzebue's *Indianer in England* (1790).

21 See page 216, footnote, on this article of clothing.

22 Letizia Bonaparte.

23 "I would prefer one hundred times more to be the happy mistress of my lover than the Queen of England and India."

24 Letizia Bonaparte, daughter of Lucien Bonaparte, was rescued from the Serpentine by a Captain Hodgson, who became her lover and the father of her three children. She died in her late sixties. The story involving Pückler did indeed hit the papers, not only the *London Sphynx* of June 25, 1828, but also the London *Times* and *New York Times*. Bowman devotes a chapter to this incident in *The Fortune Hunter*.

25 Pückler.

NOTES TO LETTER 25

1 Pückler's views on the treatment of the lower classes in England become more conflicted as he traveled through Wales and Ireland. See page xxxii.

2 "Between the pear and the cheese"—that is, during dessert.

3 Likely from Aesop's "The Ass and the Lapdog."

4 "Here lies Sir Guillaume de Harcourt, son of Robert Harcourt and of Isabel de Camvile."

5 The tomb itself is quite plain, but it stands at the center of an elaborate memorial chapel known as Prince Arthur's Chantry, a celebrated example of Tudor architecture.

6 "As for me, who is not yet a saint, nor an angel, please allow me to leave you now and go have my supper." Pückler often uses French with Lucie when he wants to convey a more intimate tone.

7 Pückler is referring to a passage in Boswell's *The Life of Samuel Johnson*: "'If,' said he, 'I had no duties, and no reference to futurity, I would spend my life in driving briskly in a post-chaise with a pretty woman; but she should be one who could understand me, and would add something

to the conversation.'" James Boswell, *The Life of Samuel Johnson, LL. D.*, ed. William Wallace (Edinburgh: W. P. Nimmo, 1873), 337.

8 "Meine Packerei ist keine Plackerei" means "my packing is not drudgery"; the second meaning comes from the addition of a single letter. The monk reference alerts the reader to this homophonic wordplay, for in scene 8 of Schiller's *Wallensteins Lager* (*Wallenstein's Camp*), a Capuchin monk speaks at some length in similar puns.

9 Pückler makes a pun here that cannot be captured in English, since the word for hermit, *Einsiedler*, implies a single person (a "one settler") and he makes these women into *Zweisiedler* ("two settlers") living in an *Einsiedelei* (hermitage), a home for a solitary person.

10 Pückler's maternal grandfather was Graf Hermann von Callenberg (1744–1795).

11 A Welsh national hero and self-styled Prince of Wales who, with his name anglicized as Owen Glendower, leads the revolt against the king in Shakespeare's *Henry IV, Part I*.

12 Penrhyn Castle, which Pückler describes at length on pages 399–400, is built of a dark limestone called Anglesey marble.

13 "A——" is likely Pückler himself, and "S——" is Berlin (Sandomir). The Editor (also Pückler) nods by referring to the author as "my late friend" and "my friend" in two of his footnotes.

14 "Cameralism" is the name given to the science of government taught in German universities in the seventeenth and eighteenth centuries that was concerned with public policy and economics.

15 "Geboren": born.

16 "Edelgeboren": nobly born; "wohlgeboren": wellborn (higher and more prestigious than *edelgeboren*).

17 "Hochwohlgeboren": highly wellborn.

18 "Who would not know how to count the number of his asses." Voltaire's *Candide* (1759) begins at the castle of the Baron Thunder-ten-tronckh, a man with a pretentious name and an inflated ego.

19 *Großwürdenträger* is a term for a high dignitary, but it can also be a pun meaning "large dignity bearer."

20 These names are mostly puns: Kakerlack (cockroach); Starosta von Pückling ("Starosta" is a Polish title given to an official or unofficial leader, and von Pückling is likely a

playful reference to Pückler himself); Bona (good); Weise (wise); and Stolz (proud).

21 "Blessed are those who have."

22 One of many allusions to the situation in Berlin during the Restoration that would have been immediately understood by a contemporary reader as critical of the fact that the office of chancellor was abolished following Hardenberg's death.

23 "Wirklicher Geheimer Rat": real privy councilior. *Geheimer Rat* or *Geheimrat* was a title awarded to long-time public servants. In seventeenth-century Prussia, the term *wirklicher* (real or actual) was added as a sign of high distinction for members of the privy council and, later, the government. Pückler is also playing with the implication that only some privy councilors are "real."

24 Likely Elise and Leopold von Hohenhausen.

25 A reference to Wilhelm Hauff, *Mitteilungen aus den Memoiren des Satan* (Stuttgart: Franckh, 1826).

26 Pückler writes, "wenn sich das Laster besp . . . , die Tugend zu Tische setze," slightly misquoting from Schiller's poem "Shakespeares Schatten" (Shakespeare's Shadow): "wenn sich das Laster erbricht, setzt sich die Tugend zu Tisch."

27 Penrhyn Castle.

28 *Steinreich* is a pun in German; translated literally, it means "stone-rich," but it is used metaphorically to imply "stinking rich" or "rolling in money." The Penrhyn quarry in north Wales, the largest such quarry in the world by the late nineteenth century, was known for its dark slate. At the time of Pückler's visit, its owner (who was also the owner of Penrhyn Castle) was George Hay Dawkins-Pennant.

29 Penrhyn, a country house in the form of a castle, was built for Dawkins-Pennant from 1820 to 1840 in the Norman style. The term *Anglo-Saxon* has come to have various meanings, but it is the correct term for the Germanic tribes who invaded Britain in the fifth century and ruled until the Norman conquest of 1066. There are few remains of Anglo-Saxon architecture in Britain, but many significant examples of Norman buildings.

30 This fantasy castle by architect Thomas Hopper was still not completed when Pückler saw it.

31 *Russian mountain* is the French term for a roller coaster. The gravity railroads used in mining were based on a similar principle; the history goes back to the ice slides built in seventeenth-century Russia.

32 An allusion to the comic play *Die deutschen Kleinstädter*, published in 1803 by August von Kotzebue.

33 The first *Turnverein* (gymnastics club) was introduced in Germany in 1807 by Friedrich Ludwig Jahn, who was convinced that it could restore the spirits and the national pride of young Germans humiliated by Napoleon, while also helping to train them to fight. The gymnastics movement spread rapidly, but Jahn's ideology came under suspicion, and—after the Wartburgfest of 1817 and the murder of August von Kotzebue by a radical gymnast in 1819—Jahn was arrested and barred from teaching gymnastics again. The movement itself was banned from 1820 to 1842 (the so-called *Turnsperre*).

34 This title and the story involve a German pun; *Korb* usually means "basket," but in the expression "to get one's last *Korb*," it means a rejection or brush-off.

35 The "leaves" are pages taken from a popular literary annual, *Vergißmeinnicht* (Forget-me-not), published from 1808 to 1834 by the sentimental writer known as Heinrich Clauren.

36 *Wurstbälle* (sausage balls) were dances put on by Berlin innkeepers during the regular ball season. Wisotzky's was the name of a Berlin tavern in the Stallschreibergasse. *Jungfernstechen* (poke the girl) was a game in which blindfolded players tried to strike dolls with a broom handle. Berlin barkeepers sometimes organized such competitive games.

37 Thomas Moore's poem "Rondeau" includes the lines: "'Good night! Good night!'—And is it so? / And must I from my Rosa go? / Oh Rosa, say 'Good night!' once more, / And I'll repeat it o'er and o'er, / Till the first glance of dawning light / Shall find us saying, still, 'Good night.'"

NOTES TO LETTER 26

1 Snowdon, with an elevation of 3,560 feet, is the highest mountain in Wales, but not in the British Isles. Ben Nevis in Scotland tops it at 4,409 feet.

2 The town of Llanberis lies on Llyn Padarn (Pückler's "Llanberis Lake").

3 *Die zwölf schlafenden Jungfrauen*, a Gothic novel published in 1795.

4 One of Pückler's affectionate nicknames for Lucie was "Schnucke," a small German moorland sheep.

5 "Ci-devant jeune homme": a once-young man.

6 Pückler nodded here, writing "seventeenth."

7 The German phrase *ich dien* (I serve) still appears on the Prince of Wales's heraldic badge. Pückler's proposed etymology continues to be cited, but it is probably legendary, as is another claim that the Black Prince (the eldest son of Edward III) took the German motto from John I of Bohemia after killing him in battle at Cressy in 1346.

8 The allusion is to Sir Walter Scott, who published his novels anonymously.

9 See page 402 ff.

10 This "Lamb Gazette" is a periodical that Pückler invented, along with the article he pretends to quote, in order to indulge in a biting satire on the extremes of Prussian orthodoxy.

11 Pückler's name for the author is a play on *fromm* (pious) and *Frömmler* (a sanctimonious hypocrite). The address given is on "Holy Ghost Street."

12 Frederick II of Prussia.

13 This date is the same as on the last letter, no doubt a typesetting error.

14 The Menai Suspension Bridge, completed in 1826, was one of the first modern suspension bridges in the world and is still the only connection between Anglesey and the mainland. The inlet is the Menai Strait.

15 "With that, having nothing more to say … which is saying a lot."

NOTES TO LETTER 27

1 In the elaborate baroque gardens of Wilhelmshöhe Park in Kassel, there is an enormous copper version of the Farnese Hercules. The statue, itself over twenty-seven feet tall, tops a monument soaring to over two hundred feet. At Wörlitz, one of the earliest and largest landscape parks in Germany, Duke Leopold III of Anhalt-Dessau had an artificial volcano built on an island in the lake, and fireworks were often staged there to look like volcanic eruptions. Pückler is being ironic, for he despised such garden features.

2 "Count L——": likely a tongue-in-cheek self-reference. Pückler did not acquire the title of prince until 1822.

3 Paget's leg was shattered at the Battle of Waterloo and had to be amputated. It was buried in a garden near the battle-field; the burial place became a kind of shrine, and, in 1816–1817, the town of Llanfairpwllgwyngyll, near his Anglesey estate, took up a public subscription to erect an enormous column in his honor. A bronze statue was added on top of the column in 1860. One of the artificial legs designed for him is still extant.

4 This may be the gardener's cottage, which was improved in 1819 and thereafter known as Druid Lodge.

5 Frömmel is the supposed author of the inflammatory anti-Lottum article quoted on pages 416–19.

6 Leading strings were narrow strips of fabric attached to children's clothing in seventeenth- and eighteenth-century Europe; these strings helped support children as they learned to walk, while also serving as a kind of leash to keep them from wandering off.

7 Probably an allusion to the commander in "Don Juan."

8 Revealed (or positive) religions are based on the idea of revelation and contain elements beyond understanding and reason, as opposed to (the one) natural religion, deriving from a person's own reason. There was much debate on this topic; see Hegel ("The Positivity of the Christian Religion") and Lessing ("On the Origin of Revealed Religion"). Pückler would have enjoyed Lord Byron's celebrated comment: "I do not believe in revealed religion—I will have nothing to do with your immortality; we are miserable enough in this life, without speculating on another."

9 The roc is an enormous, legendary bird, known especially from Marco Polo and from the *Arabian Nights*. A Pückler coat-of-arms sported an eagle.

10 Llynnau Mymbyr—actually two long, connected lakes—lies near the village of Capel Curig. More distant lakes in the direction of Beddgelert may have been visible as well.

11 In Arthurian legend, Dinas Emrys, a wooded hill with the ruins of a fort, is associated with the wizard Merlin and the warlord Vortigern.

12 In 1816, when Pückler was an officer in the wars of independence, he went on a balloon trip that started in Berlin and ended atop a tall spruce near Potsdam. He was forced to throw this cloak, a roast pheasant, and two bottles of champagne overboard to avoid an even more disastrous crash landing.

13 From a passage describing the River Conway in Michael Drayton, *Poly-Olbion; or, A Chorographicall Description of Tracts, Rivers, Mountaines, Forests, and Other Parks of this Renowned isle of Great Britaine . . .* (London: Printed by H[umphrey] L[owns] for Mathew Lownes, 1612).

14 Pückler adds a second "l" to the name of the legendary hound, so that it matches that of the German poet Christian Fürchtegott Gellert.

15 "For people are not so stupid." There is also a pun, since the French *bête* (stupid) also means "beast," hence "bestial."

16 A reference to Plato, who defined man as a "featherless biped." Diogenes is said to have declared a plucked chicken to be "Plato's man."

17 "No money, no Swiss." A proverbial expression alluding to Swiss mercenaries who, if paid, will serve anyone.

18 Pückler may be referring to the Pont-aber-glas-lyn, not the nearby bridge also called Pontarfynach, which is near Aberystwyth.

19 Most of the house, known as "Plas Tan y Bwlch" (the mansion beneath the pass), dated from the nineteenth century, although the original structure was from the seventeenth century. Built by the Oakeley family, who owned a huge slate quarry, it belonged at the time of Pückler's visit to William Griffith Oakeley.

20 Pückler's meaning here is not clear, but he appears to be referring to the proposition of eternal life and the idea of reincarnation.

21 The owner was George Hay Dawkins-Pennant. See pages 399–400 where Pückler describes it at length without naming it. See also Figure 12.

22 Pückler uses the adjective *wahlverwandt*, which German readers of his day would likely have associated with Goethe's 1809 novel *Die Wahlverwandtschaften* (Elective Affinities). Also see page 445, note 6.

23 What Pückler calls a banquet hall is known as the Great Hall; it is 125 feet long and 38 feet wide.

24 The Conwy Suspension Bridge was built by Thomas Telford in 1826. Part of the castle had to be demolished to anchor the bridge's suspension cables in the rock. The supporting towers were designed to match the castle's turrets, a style similar to that of Telford's Menai Suspension Bridge (page 420 and Figure 79).

25 The owner of Kinmel Park was William Lewis Hughes.

NOTES TO LETTER 28

1 "Look at what faith can do."

2 "A house of caprice." The most well-known building of this type was a small, temple-like garden folly built by Maria Theresa in the English park at Laxenburg, near Vienna, and destroyed by French soldiers in 1809.

3 Pückler's own English rendering of Samuel Butler's *Hudibras*, part 1, canto 1: "For whatsoe'er we perpetrate, / We do but row, we're steer'd by Fate."

4 "Man proposes, God disposes"—a proverbial expression in German, just as in English.

5 Owen Williams was the owner; his son was Thomas Peers.

6 The term "elective affinity" described a tendency of some chemicals to combine with others in certain circumstances. Goethe used this phrase metaphorically in his 1811 novel *Die Wahlverwandtschaften* (Elective Affinities) to describe a compelling mutual attraction within human relationships. Pückler also uses *wahlverwandt* in Letter 27; see page 713, note 22.

7 The reference is to C. G. Salzmann's *Carl von Carlsberg; oder, Über das menschliche Elend* (Carl von Carlsberg; or, Concerning Human Suffering), a six-volume novel published in 1783–1787.

8 The 13-foot-tall statue rose atop a 121-foot-tall column known as Nelson's Pillar, which stood in the middle of a busy street and was much criticized before being destroyed by a bomb in 1966.

9 The Great South Wall (also called South Bull Wall, or Southbull Wall), nearly four miles long with the Poolbeg Lighthouse at its end, was begun in the early eighteenth century. The Bailey Lighthouse, Howth, is situated high on a rocky cliff on the north side of the bay.

10 The actor John Philip Kemble was famous for his portrayals of the legendary hero in Shakespeare's *Coriolanus* and of the Moorish priest Zanga in Edward Young's *The Revenge: A Tragedy*.

11 The great cavalry general Seydlitz was known for his cross-country attacks.

12 "Dido Abandoned": the name of an opera libretto by Pietro Metastasio that was put to music by a number of composers.

13 An allusion to Laurence Sterne's novel *A Sentimental Journey Through France and Italy*, published in 1768.

14 "Finissez": stop.

15 "I will fear sharing the fate of Abufar." This quote alludes to the 1795 play *Abufar; ou, La famille arabe* (Abufar; or, The Arab Family) by Ducis, which involves an incestuous love affair between a young man and his sister.

NOTES TO LETTER 29

1 Efficacious or irresistible grace, a Calvinist doctrine that God's grace saves the elect.

2 "A prominent man" is likely Richard Tattersall.

3 "Wie ich wieder begrüßte das rosige Licht," a free rendition of lines from "Der Taucher," a poem by Schiller that was set to music by Franz Schubert.

4 The ruins of seven churches are in Glendalough, County Wicklow, Ireland, where Saint Cóemgen (Kevin) founded a monastery in the sixth century.

5 See page 232 ff. where Pückler's head is examined at length by one of Gall's disciples, though theosophy is not mentioned.

6 Peter La Touche, from a family of Dublin bankers, inherited this land and built Luggala, his hunting lodge, on Lough Tay.

7 "For I am no longer worth much on foot."

8 Pückler is referring to his successful attempt to visit the gardens of Chiswick House. The porter who allowed him in and received a tip for his trouble was later summarily fired by the owner, the Duke of Devonshire. Pückler relates the anecdote on page 99.

9 After a brief and stormy marriage, Anne Noel separated from Byron, who she feared was going mad and whom she accused of having incestuous relations with his half sister and having committed homosexual acts, both of which were illegal in England.

10 A reference to Goethe, who was a great admirer of Byron and who wrote a number of essays about him beginning in 1817.

NOTES TO LETTER 30

1 Lucie had read some of Pückler's letters aloud to the Varnhagens, who were deeply impressed. See pages xxiv–xxv. For details, see Assing, *Fürst Hermann von Pückler-Muskau*, 1:239–40.

2 There were reports that horses were so numerous in Buenos Aires that even beggars rode them.

3 Golconda, long associated with troves of diamonds, is here compared to Muskau and its abundant sand.

4 George IV visited Ireland for eighteen days in August and September 1821, sailing back to England from Dun Laoghaire, renamed Kingstown in his honor.

5 The self-indulgent George IV spent his time enjoying himself at Phoenix Park with his mistress Lady Conyngham and accepting the accolades of the Irish, who were enthusiastic because they believed he would support the cause of Catholic emancipation. He disappointed them. The story is told in great and entertaining detail in William Howitt, ed., *Cassell's Illustrated History of England* (London: Casser, Petter, Calpin, 1863), 7:43–57.

6 The Catholic Association was founded by O'Connell in 1823 with the goal of fighting for Catholic emancipation.

7 "For Catholic humanity stinks just as much as any other."

8 Trick-riding exhibitions, essentially the beginnings of the modern circus, were already popular in the late eighteenth century.

NOTES TO LETTER 31

1 "Beware of flatterers. You are spoiling me."

2 Pückler is referring to the theologian who condemned the impolite, unwelcoming park owner (see page 457).

3 "So I am acquiescing with good grace."

4 "What do you say to that?" Lucie's maiden name was Hardenberg.

5 "Das sind böhmishe Dörfer für mich" is a German expression meaning, in effect, "terra incognita."

6 A fictional land inhabited by giants in Jonathan Swift's *Gulliver's Travels*.

7 *Donna del Lago* (Lady of the Lake) is the title of an 1819 opera by Gioachino Rossini, the first of several based on a poem by Sir Walter Scott.

8 A character in Sir Walter Scott's novel *Guy Mannering*.

NOTES TO LETTER 32

1 "Talk sense to me, if you dare."

2 "With a smile on your face and a steely brow, you will go very far."

3 In her *De l'Allemagne* (1810/1813), Madame de Staël credits Jean Paul Richter for her widely quoted remark that "the empire of the seas belonged to the English, that of the land to the French, and that of the air to the Germans." She precedes this analysis with the claim that "it is imagination more than understanding that characterizes the Germans." Quoted from Madame de Staël, *Germany,* ed. O. W. Wight (New York: Derby, 1861), 1:35.

4 The noisemakers that they used were *Schlüsselbüchsen*, which were made of large keys with hollow shafts. Children would transform these keys by making a hole in them, then packing the hole with gun powder and setting them off.

5 "For want of any occasion to sin."

6 "It is the African blood."

7 Pückler renders this in his slightly faulty English.

8 Pückler quotes the lines in English, but his rendering does not match any of the published versions of the poem. Alternately titled "The Devil's Walk" or "The Devil's Thoughts," the verse was written by Robert Southey and Samuel Taylor Coleridge. It first appeared in print in 1799. See *The Complete Poetical Works of Samuel Taylor Coleridge*, ed. Ernest Hartley Coleridge (Oxford: Clarendon Press, 1912), 1:319–20.

9 "*Tiergarten*": zoo (literally, "animal park"), but the added italics indicate that it is likely also a pun.

10 "What do you think of that?"

11 "But shame be to him who thinks evil of it." The motto of the English Order of the Garter.

12 The water feature referred to is probably what is now known as Mountbellew Lake, once part of the Bellew estate.

13 "To demonstrate his virtuosity."

14 "I like to touch things lightly, but not venture into their depths." The prosperous city

of Capua in southern Italy was proverbial for its luxury and the debilitating effect it supposedly had on Hannibal and his troops.

15 According to local tradition, the mayor of Galway, James Lynch fitz Stephen, hanged his son as a murderer in 1493. Today, the place of execution is marked by a plaque and the so-called Lynch Memorial Window.

16 The Tun is an enormous wine vat in the cellars of Heidelberg Castle; the current vat, dating from 1751, holds 220,000 liters (58,100 gallons).

17 Lough Cutra Castle and Estate.

18 A pun on the French *impayable* ("invaluable" or "priceless") and English "unpayable."

NOTES TO LETTER 33

1 St Mary's Cathedral was founded in 1168. The seats that Pückler describes are in the choir: twenty-one elaborately carved misericords dating from the fifteenth century.

2 "Blood that is entitled to a church benefice"—that is, a pure ancestry reaching back many generations to a family member who had been elected a canon.

3 "Spreading manure on his lands."

4 Fought in 1690 between two claimants to the English throne—the Catholic King James and the Protestant King William—the battle was won by William, thus helping to ensure the continuation of Protestant supremacy in Ireland. It ended with the siege of Limerick and the signing of the Treaty of Limerick in 1691.

5 "In spite of wind and tide."

6 Pückler's tale is one of many versions of the story about the origins of the Lakes of Killarney and the O'Donoghue clan.

7 Of the two massive stone statues (also called the Colossi of Memnon) depicting Pharaoh Amenhotep III, one was said to emit mysterious sounds.

8 An opera by Weber in which a major figure is the satanic Samiel, the Black Huntsman.

9 In German, a *Sonntagskind* (Sunday's child) is a child born under a lucky star. Here, there is a pun alluding to the young man's resemblance to Pückler's adored Henriette Sontag.

10 "Great gentleman." Pückler was one, of course. He would have enjoyed the irony even more had he known that one of his biographies would bear the title *Ein großer*

Herr—namely, Gerhard F. Hering, *Ein großer Herr: das Leben des Fürsten Pückler* (Düsseldorf: E. Diederichs, 1968).

11 Only the foundations remain of Brandon Castle in Warwickshire, England. The tower described here belongs to a place known as Lord Brandon's Cottage, a nineteenth-century structure that served its owner, Lord Brandon, as a hunting lodge. Pückler was severely criticized for his carelessness in describing this site by John Windele, who faults him for misconstruing the cottage and tower as "ruins," since both were modern, the tower being a folly in an old Irish style. "Prince Puckler Moskua [*sic*], as if writing from a somewhat failing memory, speaks of having met his boat at Brandon castle.... Our traveler should have remembered, that one note on the spot is worth a cartload of recollections." John Windele, *Historical and Descriptive Notices of the City of Cork and Its Vicinity* (Cork, 1839), 365–66.

12 Pückler discusses the English property laws in some detail on pages 59–60.

13 Colonel Simon White built Glengarriff Castle. Bantry House, located across the bay and dating from around 1700, belonged to his brother Richard White; the extensive gardens were developed by his son, while still Viscount Berehaven.

14 Bantry House.

15 Pückler discusses the ritual of "coming out" on page 442.

16 Glengarriff Lodge.

17 Adapted from Terence, *The Eunuch*, act 4, line 5: "sine Cerere et Baccho friget Venus" (without food and wine, love grows cold).

18 "Who will write the rest? The devil or me?"

19 "Not at all—Poetry and Truth is my motto." *Poetry and Truth* is the title of Goethe's autobiography.

NOTES TO LETTER 34

1 "Really, I have no idea."

2 "Ich denke einen langen Schlaf zu tun": from Schiller's *Wallensteins Tod* (The Death of Wallenstein), act 5, scene 5.

3 The "wise Greek" is Bias of Priene. Fleeing his homeland without any belongings, he recognized that he was carrying everything he owned. *Omnia mea mecum porto* (All that's mine I carry with me) became a Latin proverb.

4 Don Quixote.

5 From "The Wonderful Tune," in Thomas Croker, *Fairy Legends and Traditions of the South of Ireland*, 2nd ed. (London: J. Murray, 1838), 197: "Beyond all other places Iveragh is the place for stormy coast and steep mountains: as proper a spot it is as any in Ireland to get yourself drowned, or your neck broken on the land, should you prefer that."

6 "You will say that this is too much—but it's not my fault. Reality is often unrealistic."

7 A pun on the French *revenant*, which can mean someone who is returning, as Pückler is turning back, but also one who returns from the dead.

8 A reference to the fourth and most popular gothic romance by Ann Radcliffe, *The Mysteries of Udolpho* (1794).

9 The Catholic Association put up O'Connell, its president, as a candidate for parliament in the special County Clare election of 1828. Thousands of farmers heeded the call to vote and abstain from drinking. It is said that the only intoxicated participant was O'Connell's own coachman, an Englishman and a Protestant.

10 A chevalier of the Order of Saint Louis.

11 O'Connell was supposedly challenged by a political rival to remove his wig, which he did, revealing himself to be totally bald. Pückler, who dyed his own hair, must have been particularly sympathetic.

12 These cars are described on page 428.

13 The title of Goethe's novella *Die Leiden des jungen Werthers* is most often translated as "The Sorrows of Young Werther," although *Leiden* is correctly rendered as "sufferings." The first English translation, *The Sorrows of Werter* [*sic*]: *A German Story,* was based on the French translation and appeared in 1779. The first English edition based on the German original was entitled *Werter and Charlotte: A German Story* and appeared in 1786. An English translation in which the hero's name is spelled correctly did not appear until 1854.

14 Pückler is misremembering, for it is Werther who is tender toward the lad, *kissing* his *Rotznäschen*.

15 A reference to the "Observations" of the so-called Mr. Frömmel, which Pückler "quotes" on pages 416–19.

16 The As-Sirāt, a narrow bridge—"finer than a hair and sharper than the edge of a sword"—spans the fires of hell and must be crossed in order to enter paradise.

17 Explained on page 708, note 12 (Letter 21).

18 The titular narrator of Thomas Croker's 1825 fairy tale "Daniel O'Rourke" lived at the bottom of Hungry Hill. He tells of how he got tipsy one night and had some amazing adventures, including this trip to the moon. The Grimm brothers published a German translation (*Irische Elfenmärchen*) in 1826.

19 "And his wine cellar shows some signs of this."

20 The Book of Common Prayer.

21 "Admittedly this is no great improvement."

22 "In such cases it is only the first step that matters." The reference is to Saint Denis (also called Dionysius), the patron saint of France, who was martyred by being beheaded, after which he is said to have walked six miles carrying his head and preaching a sermon the whole way.

23 "It takes talent to have a contented heart."

NOTES TO LETTER 35

1 *Erica erigena* (Irish heath), a species native to western Ireland, Portugal, and northwestern Spain, grows to an extraordinary size.

2 Likely *Nymphaae alba*, the European white water lily. It is similar to *Nymphaea lotus,* the Egyptian white lotus native to East Africa and Southeast Asia.

3 Hüon is a character in Wieland's romantic epic *Oberon* (1780). His magic horn causes those who hear it to dance.

4 This seems to be Pückler's own composition.

5 "Halb zog sie ihn, halb sank er hin," from Goethe's ballad "Der Fischer." The next and final line is "Und ward nicht mehr gesehen" (And was never seen again).

NOTES TO LETTER 36

1 The Whiteboys were members of an agrarian secret society in Ireland, dating from the 1760s, that used violence—including opening up common land and protesting tithes and rents—to defend tenants' rights against landowners.

2 Cork is on the River Lee, which flows into Cork Harbor.

3 Blackrock Castle.

4 *Der Zauberring*, 1813.

5 A ship like the one Pückler saw in Dublin Bay that takes convicts to Australia.

6 "That one must not confuse the valet with the king."

7   The Russo-Turkish War of 1828–1829 was bound up with the Greek War of Independence (1821–1832). It was aimed at limiting Turkish dominance in the Mediterranean and liberating Greece. As Pückler was writing, the battles were taking place in present-day Bulgaria.

8   A magnetic stroke, which played a role in the theory of animal magnetism, was achieved via the *baquet* (French for "tub"), the name given by Franz Anton Mesmer to the vessel used in his experiments. Up to ten people sat around the *baquet* and held onto iron stalks, which descended into the charged water and supposedly transmitted electricity. In fact, it seems that the real purpose was to focus the energy of Mesmer's animal magnetism.

9   Although Napoleon decided not to invade England (impossible once Trafalgar had destroyed the French naval forces), he established a trade barrier known as the Continental System or Continental Blockade to prevent the importation of goods from Britain to the Continent.

10 Pückler seems to have viewed it from just one side.

11 Robert King, 2nd Earl of Kingston, was born in 1754, and his wife, Caroline FitzGerald, in approximately the same year. They were married in 1769, when they would both have been fourteen or fifteen years old.

12 Mary Elizabeth King (b. ca. 1780). The scandal touched Mary Wollstonecraft, who had served briefly as governess at Mitchelstown Castle. The story has been told many times, most recently in Lyndall Gordon, *Vindication: A Life of Mary Wollstonecraft* (New York: Harper Collins, 2006), chap. 5.

13 Mary Elizabeth moved to Wales under a false name, and married George Galbraith Meares in 1805. She died in 1819.

14 George King, 3rd Earl of Kingston.

15 The ruin is Cahir Castle; it is not, in fact, associated with King John.

16 "Cottage orné": a small, thatched structure with elaborate rustic elements typical of the picturesque style in England. Now known as the Swiss Cottage and open to the public, it was built in 1812 by the 1st Earl of Glengall after a design by John Nash.

17 "It is more comfortable for the rulers, no doubt about it."

NOTES TO LETTER 37

1   The spellings, names, and history of the structures on the rock are varied and often obscure. Pückler's M. C'Omack is probably the name McCormick, coming from Saint Cormac (Cormac Mac-Cuilennáin [d. 908]), the first bishop of Cashel. He is sometimes credited with erecting Cormac's Chapel which was, in fact, built ca. 1130 by Cormac Mac Carthaigh, king of Munster.

2   St Patrick's Cathedral was built between 1235 and 1270 on the site of an earlier cathedral founded by O'Brien.

3   Henry Cotton.

4   "King Edward's Chair" was commissioned to contain the Stone of Scone, a block of sandstone that was used for hundreds of years during the coronations of Scottish kings. Edward captured the chair from the Scots in 1296 and moved it to Westminster Abbey, where it still serves as the throne during English coronations.

5   Thomastown Castle.

6   Pückler was personally very engaged in the development of his own park at Muskau. See his *Hints on Landscape Gardening*.

7   "Ill-gotten lucre." The German term is Sündengeld, "sin money," a pun that cannot be duplicated in English.

NOTES TO LETTER 38

1   "Den Braten der armen Leute." I have not been able to find this proverb. It resembles "children are the wealth of the poor," but the tone of this passage recalls Jonathan Swift's hyperbolically bitter suggestion that the destitute Irish could help themselves by selling their young children as food for the wealthy. Jonathan Swift, *A Modest Proposal for Preventing the Children of Poor People from Being a Burthen to Their Parents or Country, and for Making Them Beneficial to the Publick* (Dublin: Printed by S. Harding, 1729). Thanks to Rolf-Bernhard Essig for this reference.

2   Pückler writes Mickarky for Moycarkey, Doniskeath for Donaskeigh, New Irin for New Inn, and, in the following paragraph, Tollamane for Tullamaine.

3   "For nothing breeds as well as potatoes and misery."

4   An allusion to the Sermon on the Mount, Matthew 6:25–29.

5   This refers to Blücher, a great Prussian commander who was already elderly when he led his army against Napoleon. At one point, the stress led him to hallucinate that he was pregnant with an elephant.

6   Richelieu is said to have been anxious to achieve literary fame, though the extent of his authorship of plays such as *Les Thuileries, La grande pastorale, Mirame,* or even of his memoirs, is not clear.

7   "And has God then forgotten what I have done for him?" The Battle of Malplaquet (September 11, 1709) was a turning point in the War of the Spanish Succession, with many casualties on both sides. The Allies, under the Duke of Marlborough, were the victors, but they lost nearly twice as many men as the French.

8   "Fortunately one can in some way combine the one with the other, for in the final analysis, people need a positive religion."

"And above all," I added, "the kings and priests need one—because it confers divine right on the former and power, honors, and wealth on the latter. The people would perhaps be content with good laws and a free government."

"Ah, you're thinking like Voltaire: 'These priests are not what the vile rabble think them, / Their knowledge springs from our credulity.'"

"Indeed," I said to him, "if all priests were like you, I would see things quite differently."

The Voltaire couplet is from the first act of *Oedipus*; the English translation is taken from *The Dramatic Works of Mr. De Voltaire*, trans. Rev. Mr. [Thomas] Francklin (London: Printed for J. Newbery, 1761), 1:79.

9   "After the rain, the sun!"

10 A dog-training collar that is ringed with egg-shaped balls bearing inlaid spines. It can easily damage a dog's neck and is now banned.

11 This is a play on words, since *selig* means "blessed" and is also used for "late," in the sense of "deceased." *Hochselig* literally means "highly blessed," and is the adjective used for deceased or "late" royalty or other people of importance.

12 O'Connell.

NOTES TO LETTER 39

1   A well-known caricature entitled *A Sharp Between Two Flats* (1791) shows two litigants, each holding an oyster shell, and between them, a lawyer holding the oyster. A couplet at the bottom reads, "A pearly

shell for him and thee, / The oyster is the lawyer's fee."

2 Pückler uses the word "zephyr," another term for cassimere (kerseymere), a very fine, soft, lightweight wool cloth.

3 What follows is Pückler's version of the Irish tale "Scath-a-Legaune," one of the many examples of Irish folklore collected and published in Croker, *Fairy Legends and Traditions of the South of Ireland*. Some of the stories—but not this one—were translated into German and published by the brothers Grimm in 1826.

4 Pückler is referring to Empress Catherine II of Russia and Queen Elizabeth I of England, both of whom were known for the lax morals at their courts.

5 "No doubt disarmed by so much valor."

6 "*Voilà*, a good occasion for a dispute between lawyers and doctors."

7 "*Voilà*, great bagatelles. But war is war."

8 Irish bagpipes are also known as Uilleann pipes, from the Gaelic word *uille* (elbow), because of the elbow's role in pumping the bellows. This and other characteristics distinguish Irish pipes from Scottish and other pipes. The air is blown from the bellows into the bag, from where it is fed into the reeds of the melody chanter and as many as three drones.

9 An opera by Weber.

NOTES TO LETTER 40

1 An allusion to the game of skittles or ninepins, in which the "kingpin" is the largest.

2 "Of the most elegant style."

3 Pückler could be speaking of his own carefully edited and rewritten letters here.

4 "Pretty nothings no longer suffice."

5 The lines are from *Childe Harold's Pilgrimage*, canto 3, stanzas 92 and 93.

6 General Paget, 1st Marquess of Anglesey.

7 This painful facial neuralgia is still very hard to treat. Pückler's suggested treatment, "h——" is likely "homeopathy," because the person who in 1835 finally cured Paget of the disorder was Samuel Hahnemann, a German physician who founded this system of alternative medicine and published a number of articles and books about it.

8 An ancient philosophical paradox, often referred to as "Buridan's ass,"

because it came to be associated with the fourteenth-century French philosopher Jean Buridan.

9 In German, *Allotria treiben* means to "fool around" or "engage in monkey business." The word *allotria* derives from Greek and Latin, however, in which it signifies strange, peripheral, or irrelevant things, which is more Pückler's meaning here.

10 "A lost day."

11 Pückler has written part of this exchange in his own sketchy English.

12 This version of the story is slightly mangled.

13 This sculpture is known as the Arrotino and survives in many copies.

NOTES TO LETTER 41

1 This was Pückler's forty-third birthday.

2 "But everything that is, is for the best": a paraphrase of the famous argument made by Pangloss in Voltaire's *Candide*, which is usually quoted as "tout est pour le mieux dans le meilleur des mondes possibles" (all is for the best in the best of all possible worlds). A parody of Leibniz, the claim is finally rejected for the more practical notion—certainly of personal resonance for Pückler—that we must cultivate our own garden.

3 Pückler disguises the identity of the singers, but it becomes clear that they are Sydney and Josephine, the daughters of Lady Morgan's sister, Olivia Clarke.

4 Pückler discusses this novel by Lady Morgan on page 157.

5 "Do not be angry at this, Julie."

6 "A kind-hearted man."

7 Thomas Morgan published two books: *Sketches of the Philosophy of Life* (London, 1818); and *Sketches of the Philosophy of Morals* (London: H. Colburn, 1822), a response to criticisms of the first volume.

8 Pückler's paraphrase of words written by Oxenstierna to his son, who was involved in negotiating the Peace of Westphalia in Münster: "An nescis, mi fili, quantilla prudentia mundus regatur?" (Do you not know, my son, with what little wisdom the world is governed?)

9 Likely Ferdinand Friedrich, Duke of Anhalt-Köthen (spelled Cöthen in the nineteenth century), who converted to

Catholicism in 1825, a change he tried unsuccessfully to impose on the residents of his duchy.

10 Sir Arthur Clarke was a physician and author of several medical treatises.

11 Pückler writes "Krethi und Plethi" (see page 704, note 3) which has accrued the meaning of "average Joe" or "lowlifes" in German.

12 Lady Olivia Clarke was the sister of Lady Morgan, the "celebrated female relation" alluded to here.

13 *The Wild Irish Girl* (1806) was Lady Morgan's best-known novel.

14 The English is Pückler's rendering.

15 "At this time Genoa was buying all the wheat in Europe." In England, "corn" usually means wheat or, less often, another type of grain.

16 "Nation of *Haid-Schnuken*" alludes to some translation error that must have involved Pückler. A *Heidschnucke* (modern spelling) is a moorland sheep from northern Germany, and one of Pückler's various pet names for Lucie, *Schnucke*, derives from it.

17 "Garçon-dîner": men's dinner.

18 "That is all I have to tell you today."

19 "Oh, what a bad time for this carriage to arrive!" "Well, then . . . send it to the devil!"

20 "Hat white . . . white hat": a French idiom for "the same difference" or "six of one, half a dozen of the other."

21 "I do not teach, I narrate." Lady Morgan's memoirs were published the following year as *The Book of the Boudoir*, 2 vols. (London: H. Colburn, 1829); the Montaigne quotation appears on the title page.

22 A character in Scott's novel *Ivanhoe* (1820).

23 Pückler is referring to his Memory Albums, where he affixed, with commentary, a double portrait of the girls, a portrait of Sydney, and one of himself as Brutus (Figure 106).

24 The English equivalent of this idiom is "to live within your means."

25 "For I love priests, as Voltaire does the Bible, in spite of everything I say about them."

26 During the late eighteenth century, the extravagantly stylish, dandified men of the wealthy classes, often nouveaux riches, were known as *incroyables* ("incredibles"); their female counterparts were called *merveilleuses* ("marvelous women").

NOTES TO LETTER 42

1. Earlier (page 593), her husband (Thomas Charles Morgan) is identified as her aide-de-camp, although the initials here do not conform with his. It should be remembered that in the original Pückler consistently disguises Lady Morgan as "Lady M——" as well.

2. "Abigail": an English term for a lady's maid, from the 1610 play *The Scornful Lady*, by Francis Beaumont and John Fletcher.

3. "The countess confesses to her conquests."

4. "Hush! I hear the captain."

5. She debuted at the Drogheda Theater in her birthplace, Drogheda, Ireland, where her father was an actor and theater manager.

NOTES TO LETTER 43

1. "To help increase our appetites."

2. "All the worse for humanity, which needs so many of them."

3. Sir Arthur Clarke was physician to the Bank of Ireland.

4. "Limping devil": an allusion to *Le diable boiteux* (1707), a popular farce by Alain-René Lesage, in which a demon removes the roofs of houses to reveal everything going on inside.

5. *Turnen* (gymnastics) alludes to the "father of gymnastics," Friedrich Ludwig Jahn, who put an emphasis on German nationalism in the struggle against Napoleon. See page 712, note 33.

6. "This is the finishing stroke for gymnastics in Ireland!"

7. "One may shine in the first rank, but be eclipsed in the second": an inversion from Voltaire's *La Henriade*, chant 1, line 31, "Tel brille au second rang qui s'éclipse au premier."

8. A reference to the trade barrier of the Continental System. See page 544 and 716, note 9 (Letter 36).

9. Washington Irving's *The Life and Voyages of Christopher Columbus*, a mixture of history and fiction, appeared in 1828 and was an enormous success; a German translation was published the same year. Pückler was quite up-to-date in his reading.

10. "Truth and poetry—spirit and appearance": an allusion to Goethe's autobiography, *Dichtung und Wahrheit*, usually translated as *Poetry and Truth*. Pückler reverses the two words, as Goethe himself sometimes did.

11. There are accounts of extreme ascetics who kept their fists clenched until their uncut curving fingernails punctured their flesh and even protruded through the back of the hand—but not through the opposite hand, as implied here.

12. Many historians have suspected that the stories involving these two heroes were more legendary than real.

13. 1 Thessalonians 5:21.

14. Pückler is alluding to a scene in Faust's study where Mephistopheles utters the lines "We spread this cloak—that's all we need. / But on this somewhat daring flight / Be sure to keep your luggage light. / A little fiery air, which I plan to prepare, / Will raise us swiftly off the earth; / Without ballast we'll go up fast—/ Congratulations, friend, on your rebirth!" *Goethe's Faust*, trans. Walter Kaufmann (New York: Anchor, 1961), 209, lines 2065–72. The "fiery air" (*Feuerluft*) probably refers to the gas used in balloon flights, namely hot air or hydrogen.

NOTES TO LETTER 44

1. His first letter is dated September 8, 1826, so he has been gone for two years and three months.

2. "Chop, chop, chop, off in a charging gallop": an imprecise quotation from "Leonore," a ballad by Gottfried August Bürger ("Und als sie saßen, hopp hopp hopp! / Gings fort im sausenden Galopp").

3. Pückler writes *Bär und Bassa*, using the title given to Augustin-Eugène Scribe and Xavier Saintine's popular French vaudeville *L'ours et le pacha* in the German translation by Carl Blum (*Vaudevilles für deutsche Bühnen und gesellige Zirkel* [Berlin: Duncker und Humblot, 1824]).

4. "*Voilà*, the beginning and the end."

5. "Methodus per nauseam": an early method of treating sick people by inducing nausea.

6. Courtfield was the manor house in Welsh Bicknor, Herefordshire, where Henry V was entrusted to the care of Sir John Montacute, 3rd Earl of Salisbury, and his wife, Maud.

7. Although the passage Pückler refers to is often attributed to Augustine, it is, in fact, from Tertullian, who said, "Credo quia absurdum est" (I believe because it is absurd). Augustine said, "Credo ut intelligam" (I believe in order to understand).

8. Also called Doward Hills or the Great Doward.

9. The statue is now mounted on the front of the building (known as Shire Hall), not on the roof.

10. "What the hell am I doing here?" A loose translation of a repeated line in Molière's *Les Fourberies de Scapin*, act 2, scene 7: "Que diable allait-il faire dans cette galère?" (What the devil was he doing in that galley?)

11. This was a small, picturesque summerhouse built by the Duke of Beaufort to accommodate visitors to the area.

12. "In England people make arrows out of any kind of wood"—that is, they use any possible means to an end.

NOTES TO LETTER 45

1. More like twelve years: Charles I was beheaded in 1649 Marten surrendered as a regicide in 1659, and was found guilty of participating in the king's death in 1660. He first went into exile in the north of England, but Charles II had him brought to Chepstow Castle in 1668, where he lived until his death in 1680.

2. The Old Wye Bridge, Chepstow, was built out of cast iron in 1816. See Figure 113.

3. From *Moral Essays*, epistle 3, "Of the Use of Riches," lines 251–52. Vaga was the Roman name for the Wye.

4. Sarah Austin added her own quotable footnote here: "Few persons will agree with this position of the Author. If it be true, how doubly discreditable to English translators is the comparison of their performances with such translations as Voss's Homer, Schleiermacher's Plato, Schlegel's Shakespeare and Calderon, &c. For any approach to these wonderful transfusions, where are we to look? At the abortive attempts at presenting to England any idea of Goethe?"

5. A reference to John 4:44: "a prophet hath no honor in his own country."

6. Ruins were greatly appreciated in this period for their aesthetic power. Hirschfeld discusses them at length in *Theorie der Gartenkunst, 1779–1785*, 5 vols., ed. and trans. Linda B. Parshall (Philadelphia: University of Pennsylvania Press, 2001), and Diderot wrote quite famously of his own emotional reaction to them in his 1767 review of Hubert Robert's salon debut: "The ideas ruins evoke in me

are grand. Everything comes to nothing, everything perishes, everything passes, only the world remains, only time endures. How old is this world! I walk between two eternities." Denis Diderot, "Salon of 1767," in *Diderot on Art*, ed. and trans. John Goodman (New Haven and London: Yale University Press, 1995), 2:198–99.

7 Ugbrooke Park, with gardens laid out by Capability Brown.

8 Known as Blaise Hamlet, this is a complex of small cottages around a green, built ca. 1811 by John Harford for his retired employees.

9 "You who seek to enter here, abandon all hope." Pückler has modified the well-known line from Dante's *Inferno*, canto 3, line 9: "Lasciate ogni speranza, voi ch'entrate" (Abandon all hope, ye who enter here).

10 Richard "Beau" Nash.

11 The story goes that when Nash saw the Duchess of Queensberry wearing an apron of costly point lace, he tore it off, claiming that only servants donned white aprons. The famous report is from Goldsmith: "I have known him on a ball night strip even the Duchess of Q[ueensbury], and throw her apron at one of the hinder benches among the ladies' women; observing that none but *Abigails* appeared in white aprons. This from another would be an insult, in him it was considered as a just reprimand; and the good-natured duchess acquiesced in his censure." Oliver Goldsmith, *The Life of Richard Nash, Esq.: Late Master of the Ceremonies at Bath*, 2nd ed. (London: Printed for J. Newbery, 1762), 37.

12 Waller's armored figure appears on the impressive tomb monument he had built for his first wife, Jane Reynell. The story about James II appears to be apocryphal.

13 See the Annotated Index of Places for a detailed history.

14 In fact, the three-hundred-foot-tall tower collapsed four times, the first time in 1796 and the last time in 1825, three years after Beckford had sold the abbey and moved to Bath. Other parts of the building, including the kitchen, also collapsed, and the entire structure was later demolished.

15 Beckford's Tower, originally called Lansdown Tower, was built in 1827. See Figure 118.

16 Beckford wrote *Vathek*, a gothic novel, in French in 1782; its first publication was in an English translation by Samuel

Henley of a supposedly anonymous Arabic source (*An Arabian Tale, From an Unpublished Manuscript* [London: Printed for J. Johnson, 1786]). Beckford's French version appeared in 1787. At the end of the novel, the character Vathek, who earlier built a soaring tower (fifteen hundred steps high), descends into hell, where he is doomed to suffer endlessly.

17 Towering carvings of angels ascending and descending Jacob's ladder appear on either side of the main window on the west facade of Bath Abbey.

18 We can identify these artists as Wach and Schadow, thanks to handwritten glosses that Varnhagen inserted at places in his copy of the first edition of *Letters of a Dead Man*.

19 A reference to the Forty Hours' Devotion, a Catholic devotion in which prayer is continued for forty hours before the Blessed Sacrament.

20 "L——": Ludwig or Lou, a facetious self-reference.

21 An ironic reference to Voltaire's *Candide* (see page 41, note 2).

NOTES TO LETTER 46

1 The term "blind passenger" refers to a traveler who is not seen—that is, one who keeps himself hidden and, therefore, does not pay his fare.

2 Some English newspapers paid for invented stories that fed the readership's appetite for scandal. The Editor comments on this on page 472, footnote.

3 Pückler meant the kind of riddle involving word play, but he spelled it "Cannondrum's," either an unclear pun or another example of his weak English.

4 "Samiel, help!" This cry summons Samiel, the devil-like Black Huntsman in Carl Maria von Weber's extremely popular 1821 opera *Der Freischütz*.

5 The tower of Salisbury Cathedral (404 feet) is the tallest in Great Britain, but the tower at Strasbourg Cathedral in France, at 466 feet, is still taller; it ranked as the tallest building in the world from 1647 to 1874.

6 In 1688 and 1790, respectively.

7 Pückler writes the name Richard Langschwert ("Longsword" in English), but likely means William Longespée, 3rd Earl of Salisbury, whose tomb is indeed there.

8 Now ascribed to a South German hand.

9 The so-called Holbein Porch, once the entrance porch and supposedly designed by Holbein, was moved to the garden in the early nineteenth century by James Wyatt.

10 The much-admired, idyllic gardens of Wilton House had a long history, with major changes dating from the eighteenth century. That Pückler gives such great credit to a woman's touch is remarkable.

11 These celebrated paintings, both in private collections, are now called *Coast Scene with the Landing of Aeneas* (1650) and *Pastoral Landscape with the Arch of Titus* (1644). See Martin Sonnabend and Jon Whiteley, *Claude Lorrain: The Enchanted Landscape* (Oxford: Ashmolean Museum, 2011), cat. nos. 5 and 6.

12 Designed by James Wyatt in 1807–1812, it is now called the Royal Military Academy Sandhurst.

13 "For one's own homeland is dear to any noble soul."

14 These verses seem to be Pückler's own compositions. "A new year is beginning, / Already sand runs onto grains of sand! / Will it mean happiness, / Or will it bring misery?" And then: "The clouds fly by, the gales roar / The thunder rumbles, the floodwaters boom / The ship seems in peril / Who trusts the deceitful sea! / Yet behind yonder black veil / A golden gaze lights up the night—/ Is it the moon in gentle celebration, / Or the farewell glance of the sun?"

15 "What is natural cannot be bad": a proverbial Latin expression inspired by Servius's commentary on Virgil's *Georgics* (3:96).

16 The exchange is: "What! Sir, what insolence to p—— on our property! Isn't the street big enough for you! You are a great scoundrel! Mommy, Mommy, look, there's a man p—— on our property!"

"So, sir, are you ever going to finish? Sir, permit me to tell you that one does not p—— on private property, one p—— in the street, sir."

"Really, I think he's making fun of us, Mommy. Intolerable, he won't budge."

17 "You are quite wrong."

18 Ludvig Holberg, an important Danish writer and historian, was best known for his comedies, which influenced the prolific and controversial German writer August von Kotzebue.

19 The future George IV.

20 "Quizzing glass": Pückler uses an English term for monocle. He has rendered most of these exchanges in his own slightly awkward English.

21 Brummell discovered the identity of his visitor and was clearly infuriated over what Pückler had written: "The author of the pretended tour is a Russian prince, Mouska Pouska, the greatest imposter that ever existed; no dentist, that was always supposed to excel in fabrication, could possibly equal his misrepresentations about English society." Letter dated January 1, 1836, in William Jesse, *The Life of George Brummell, Esq., Commonly Called Beau Brummell* (London: Saunders and Otley, 1844), 2:292.

22 "I'm up on everything, but what good does it do me? I'm being left here to die of hunger. But I hope that some fine day my old friend, the Duke of W——, will send the local consul to China and appoint me in his place. Then I will be saved."

23 "I hope you find your way. My Swiss [man] isn't here, I fear." Pückler comments "Alas!—no money, no Swiss." See page 713, note 17, about this proverbial expression.

NOTES TO LETTER 47

1 "But let us begin at the beginning."

2 "Berlin": a fast, comfortable, closed carriage with a thoroughbrace suspension between two perches.

3 "Well, really, Mister Conductor, are you forgetting your pancakes?"
"What a surprise! You're still here, my child?"

4 "Equipment": Pückler clearly hears an unintended, off-color double entendre here; see page 720, note 6.

5 The swallow, a small swift bird.

6 "You should know, my boy, that I no longer have the use of my equipment."
"What? Damnation! No longer any equipment?"
"My equipment is still working a little, you see, but it's hardly enough, the main shaft is shot to hell."
"Oh, the devil!"

7 *One O'Clock* was the popular *Ein Uhr oder Der Zauberbund um Mitternacht* (1822) by Eduard von Lannoy. It was based on a musical romance by Matthew Lewis, *One O'Clock, or The Knight and the Wood Daemon* (1811), which played to considerable success at the English Opera House.

8 "Menus plaisirs": small pleasures.

9 During the Revolution, the statue of Louis XV was torn down and the square was renamed Place de la Révolution; it was called Place de la Concorde from 1795 to 1799, then a series of other names until reverting to Concorde in 1830.

10 Although this was commissioned in 1806, it took years to build, as work was halted altogether during the Restoration and only begun again under King Louis-Philippe in 1833–1836.

11 The Church of the Madeleine. Its foundations were built shortly before the Revolution, but they were razed and the design changed to that of a classical temple under Napoleon, who wanted a "Temple de la Gloire de la Grande Armée." It was completed in stages: the nave was covered in 1831, and it was consecrated as a church in 1842.

12 Cooks, banquets, and food figure in Smollett's *The Adventures of Peregrine Pickle* (1751).

13 The story goes that François Vatel, a famous seventeenth-century maître d'hôtel, had ordered seafood for an enormous banquet in honor of Louis XIV. When the delivery failed to arrive on time, he ran himself through with his sword, a death regarded as a national tragedy.

14 "Rocher de Cancale": rock of Cancale. This was the name of a famous Parisian restaurant opened in 1804 by Baleine (a name meaning "whale"). Cancale is a town in Brittany famous for its oysters. Pückler makes puns on both names.

15 The Théâtre du Gymnase Marie Bell, established in Paris in 1820, was renamed the Théâtre de Madame four years later due to the patronage of the Duchesse de Berry. It reverted to its original name in 1830. There, Léontine Fay first acted the role of Malvina in Eugène Scribe's *Malvina, ou un marriage d'inclination* on December 8, 1828, less than one month before Pückler saw her perform.

16 Although the *Tugendbund,* a secret, quasi-Masonic society founded in Prussia in 1808, was disbanded after just two years, its goals of social justice, education, and patriotism attracted many important military men, civil servants, and scholars. It was particularly dedicated to freeing Germany from Napoleon's influence. Pückler uses an analogous term, *Tugendverein,* which alludes to the 1808 group but also seems to be a more generic reference to an association of virtuous men.

17 "There's no reason to lose one's head over this!"

18 "Alas, it is only the first step that matters." See page 715, note 22.

19 "Long live women and wine!"

20 "Love flies away, but piquet endures."

21 "Carte": menu; "charte": charter. The Charter of 1814, granted by Louis XVIII of France before he was restored as monarch, was followed by the so-called Charter of 1815 prepared for Napoleon when he returned from exile but was never fully applied.

22 *The Mute Girl of Portici* was one of Daniel Auber's most popular works and is regarded as the earliest French grand opera. It was first produced in Paris in 1828, so Pückler was very up-to-date.

23 By Rossini, first performed on August 20, 1828, in Paris.

24 Pückler means his late friend, E. T. A. Hoffmann. The allocator of souls is probably Johann Gottfried Hoffmann, who was involved in the Congress of Vienna's decision to transfer part of Pückler's property to Prussia.

25 The Louvre was forced by the Congress of Vienna to repatriate several thousand works of art that the French had looted under the direction of Napoleon and his museum director, Denon.

26 The *Venus de Milo* was discovered in 1820.

27 *Juno, called "Providence."*

28 Likely *Sleeping Ariadne,* a Roman version from the Villa Borghese gardens.

29 *La Zingarella,* by Nicolas Cordier.

30 This portrait of Alexander the Great, also called the Azara Herm, is a second-century Roman copy of a Greek original from 330 BC.

31 In this print, the Azara Herm—which was given to Napoleon by Joseph Nicolas Azara, the Spanish ambassador to the Holy See—looks down from the mantelpiece.

32 *The Forges of Vulcan,* first century AD.

33 The museum's cast maker.

34 "Like the sheep of Panurge"—that is, people who will blindly follow others regardless of the consequences. In the *Pantagruel* of Rabelais, Panurge buys a sheep, believes he has been overcharged, and in revenge tosses it into the sea, whereupon the rest of the herd go after him to their deaths.

35 The *Scene of a Deluge* was acquired by the Louvre in 1818.

36 The Louvre was, indeed, relatively empty after many of the pieces looted by Napoleon had been returned, but the void was filled when the Borghese antiquities were purchased and works were brought from Versailles, the Palais du Luxembourg, and elsewhere in France.

37 Probably the Great Sphinx of Tanis, which was acquired by the Louvre in 1826.

38 There is a pun here in German, for *Naseweis* means "smart-aleck," but *Nase* alone means "nose" and *weiss* means "white."

39 This was *Faust: Drame en trois actes,* by Antony Béraud and Jean-Toussaint Merle, with music by Alexandre Piccini and choreography by Eugene Coralli. It opened at the Théâtre de la Porte Saint-Martin on October 29, 1828.

40 The Blocksberg, the tallest peak in the Harz Mountains of Germany and long associated with witches and devils, appears in Goethe's *Faust.* The wolf's glen is a setting in Weber's *Der Freischutz.*

NOTES TO LETTER 48

1 Several of the dates in this final letter are out of order.

2 "The ambition of this man is insatiable, and you will perhaps live to see his carcass and his entire family thrown into the sewers of Paris."

3 "Prince of the Peace": Manuel Godoy, the prime minister of Spain under Charles IV, was often called the Principe de la Paz.

4 There was talk that Dom Miguel (Miguel I of Portugal) was an illegitimate child resulting from one of his mother's alleged affairs, although Lucien is not the father generally named.

5 The Théâtre de la Gaîté was a popular theater founded in Paris in 1759. It was known especially for its melodramas, which often included music and tomfoolery.

6 "Tragic pathos, which bored for so long in magnificent language."

7 The Théâtre de la Gaîté and several other popular "boulevard theaters," were located on the boulevard du Temple, which forms the eastern boundary of the third arrondissement.

8 The play described here is *Polder; ou, Le bourreau d'Amsterdam,* by René-Charles Guilbert de Pixérécourt and Victor Henri-Joseph Brahain Ducange. It was first produced at the Théâtre de la Gaîté on October 15, 1828.

9 *The Maid of Orleans*, a play by Schiller about Joan of Arc.

10 This play by Edmé Boursault was also known as *Comédie sans titre* (play without a title) and ridiculed social pretensions.

11 "It's very simple, I'm afraid of being cuckolded."

12 *L'Espion*, by Léon Halévy, premiered in Paris on October 26, 1828.

13 "Good luck!"

14 The stock exchange was designed by Alexandre-Théodore Brongniart, who undertook the project in 1807 at Napoleon's request. It was not completed until 1825, after the architect's death, and was renamed the Palais Brongniart in his honor.

15 The first public omnibus lines were inaugurated in Paris in 1828. The name *Dames blanches* (white ladies) was borrowed from a comic opera by Eugène Scribe (1825) and was one of several fanciful names given to these public carriages.

16 The Théâtre des Variétés was an essentially vaudeville theater founded in 1807 by the actress and director Marguerite Brunet; Brunet and Odry were well-known comedic actors at this theater.

17 The Portuguese acrobat "Il Diavolo Antonio" was well-known in England and on the Continent.

18 "The Devil can't do any better."

19 By Lamothe-Langon, first performed in Paris in 1829.

20 "The peers of France." To be a peer in France was a very high distinction. The peerage was abolished during the Revolution, reinstated in 1814, and abolished for good in 1848.

21 Old French: "They had heard too much at Grandson." The 1476 Battle of Grandson, on Lake Neuchâtel, was a humiliating rout for Charles the Bold, Duke of Burgundy. It began with the frightening din of Swiss battle horns.

22 Théâtre-Lyrique Italien, also known as the Opéra-Italien.

23 *La Cenerentola* (Cinderella) is an opera by Rossini.

24 A pastille is a tablet containing aromatic substances that is burned to fumigate or deodorize the air.

25 In 1792, a statue of Henry IV was melted down to make cannons. Events dashed Napoleon's ambition to replace it with a two hundred-foot-tall obelisk. The present statue was erected in 1818; the bronze for it came from melting down a statue of Napoleon that had stood atop the Vendôme Column.

26 It is likely that Pückler means Antoine-Jean Gros, who painted the frescoes in the dome of the Panthéon.

27 "Privileged altar."

28 From Ecclesiastes 1:2 and 1:14.

29 "In order to finish my digestion there in laughter."

30 Pückler indulges here in an extended wordplay: "ana" is a collection of information about a given subject; "ama" (more correctly "–orama," as in "panorama") is a suffix added to compound nouns to denote either a display or spectacle or the space where such a scene is viewed. The French homophones are *âne:* ass, and *amant:* lover. Egyptian darkness, a biblical reference (Exodus 10:21–22), here suggests that certain spectators may have taken liberties in the dimly lit halls where these tableaux were viewed.

31 The first georama was patented in Paris in 1822 and 1825 by Charles Delanglard and opened to the public in 1825. See Giuliana Bruno, *Atlas of Emotions: Journeys in Art, Architecture, and Film* (London: Verso, 2002), 161; and Stephan Oettermann, *Das Panorama: Die Geschichte eines Massenmediums* (Frankfurt: Syndikat, 1980), 73–74.

32 In fact, the georama was not as successful as had been hoped, and it was dismantled in 1832 after Delanglard's death. A new one was installed in the gardens of the Champs-Elysées in 1844.

33 *Le lépreux de la cité d'Aoste* is a dialogue by Xavier de Maistre published in 1811.

34 "Neorama": a panorama representing the inside of a building.

35 The statue *Saint Peter Enthroned* has been attributed to a thirteenth-century sculptor, but many still date it to the fifth century and consider it to be a representation of Jupiter.

NOTES TO THE SECOND PREFACE BY THE EDITOR

1 The Second Preface originally introduced the first half of the letters, since they were published second. I have relegated it to the end of the book, where it makes a bit more sense.

2 Goethe is the god-like being who dwells on Mount Parnassus, the home of the muses in Greek mythology and, thus, a place sacred to poetry. The reference here is to his positive review of *Letters of a Dead Man* (see pages xxv and xxxvii, note 12).

3 Justinus Kerner, *Die Seherin von Prevorst: Eröffnungen über das innere Leben des Menschen und über das Hineinragen einer Geisterwelt in die unsere* (Stuttgart and Tübingen: J. G. Cotta'schen Buchhandlung, 1829). There is an English translation by Catherine Crowe, published under the title *The Seeress of Prevorst: Being Revelations Concerning the Inner-Life of Man and the Inter-Diffusion of a World of Spirits in the One We Inhabit* (London: Moore, 1845). This book describes Kerner's observations of Friederike Hauffe, a young woman from the village of Prevorst. Bedridden with various illnesses for the final ten years of her life, she was believed to be possessed by spirits, to see clairvoyantly, and to know a secret, universal language.

4 *Nonne,* the German word for "nun," has been given the masculine suffix, *-rich,* to comic effect.

5 A fabricated name intended as a witticism.

6 Goethe again, who exhibited the wisdom of Solomon.

7 There were three levels of pasha, a high rank in the Ottoman Empire. The status of a pasha was distinguished by the number of horsetails in his standard, pashas of the highest rank bearing three.

8 Pückler's given name was Hermann Ludwig Heinrich, both the "Hermann" and the "L——" here.

9 Goethe was about eighty-two years old when Pückler wrote the Second Preface by the Editor.

10 "Rhadamanthus": son of Zeus and Europa and wise king in Greek mythology. Virgil represents him as a judge of the damned in the underworld.

11 Another reference to Goethe's review, in which he praises the idea of publishing the second two volumes first. He feels that this gives the entire undertaking an epic turn, since for each event the reader must imagine what went before.

12 An allusion to Goethe's autobiography, *Dichtung und Wahrheit,* usually translated as "poetry and truth." *Dichtung* can also mean "fiction," however.

13 A volt is a small circle used in training horses. Traditionally, a volt was twelve strides long, but it was later reduced to six or eight strides; the accepted diameter of a volt in competition is six meters. A three-by-three volt would have been very tight.

14 A Spanish walk is a trained gait in which the horse raises each foreleg up and out in an exaggerated reach.

15 A wordplay, since *Freimütiger* can mean "outspoken man," but here alludes to the Berlin periodical *Der Freimütige oder Berlinisches Unterhaltungsblatt für gebildete und unbefangene Leser,* which published two reviews by Willibald Alexis of *Letters of a Dead Man,* in October 1830 and May 1832.

16 Probably M. G. Saphir, a feuilletonist who wrote a positive review of *Letters of a Dead Man.*

17 A nickname for Sir Walter Scott, who continued to publish his novels anonymously, even after they became enormously successful and his identity an open secret.

18 The identities of all these men are shrouded in obscurity. The Man in the Iron Mask was a Frenchman imprisoned for over three decades whose face was always masked. King Sebastian of Portugal was last seen riding directly into enemy lines at the Battle of Alcácer Quibir in 1578, but his body was not recovered, sparking long-term rumors that he was still alive. The False Waldemar was an imposter who in 1348 claimed to be the Margrave of Brandenburg-Stendal, the legitimate Waldemar, who had died in 1319. Cagliostro was the alias of a sixteenth-century Italian occultist, forger, and adventurer. The Count of Saint Germain was an adventurer, charlatan, inventor, and much more, whose actual background is not known.

NOTES TO THE POSTSCRIPT

1 The first two published volumes were riddled with misprints. And when the intaglios for the first edition were transferred to stone (lithography being a cheaper process), many of the illustrations were disfigured.

2 Franckh was the Munich publishing house that released the initial two volumes of the *Letters of a Dead Man* in 1830.

3 "The sweet habit of being." This is a near-quotation from act 5 of Goethe's *Egmont*: "Süßes Leben! schöne freundliche Gewohnheit des Daseins und Wirkens!" Also see page xxv.

4 The Postscript accompanied the publication of the third and fourth volumes, which contained letters one through twenty-four.

Annotated Index of Names

Page numbers in *italics* refer to illustrations.

A

Abbas Mirza (ca. 1789–1833), Qajar crown prince of Persia and the second son of emperor Fath-Ali Shah, 320

Abelard, Peter (1079–1142), French philosopher and theologian known also for his tragic affair with Héloïse d'Argenteuil, 307

Aberdeen, Lord = George Hamilton-Gordon, 4th Earl of Aberdeen (1784–1860), Scottish politician and prime minister of the United Kingdom from 1852–1855; he resided at Bentley Priory, 103

Abufar, a character in a 1795 play by French dramatist Jean-François Ducis, 456, 713n15 (Letter 28)

Adair, Maurice, a piper in an Irish folktale, 536–38

Adam, Mr., the director of a trick-riding academy in Dublin, 474

Adelaide, Queen. *See* Clarence, Duchess of

Adelheid, Princess of Carolath-Beuthen, née Pappenheim (1797–1849), Lucie's daughter from her first marriage and Pückler's stepdaughter, whom he also calls Emilie; Pückler was infatuated with her before his marriage, 337, 704n22 (Letter 15)

Agrippa, Marcus Vipsanius (ca. 63–12 BC), Roman general and statesman, friend and son-in-law to Augustus, 664

Aladdin, a character in a story from *One Thousand and One Nights,* 132

Alba, 3rd Duke of (Fernando Alvarez de Toledo, 1507–1582), Spanish general under Charles V and Philip II, 28, 120, 649

Albert, the stage name of the French ballet dancer François-Ferdinand Decombe (1789–1865), 663

Alcibiades (ca. 450–404 BC), Athenian politician, orator, and general, 170

Alexander I (1777–1825), emperor of Russia from 1801 to 1825, 139–40, 216, 255, 259, 697n16 (Letter 1), 698n2 (Letter 3), 706n4 (Letter 17)

Alexander the Great (356–323 BC), Greek king of Macedon who was said to have set fire to Persepolis during a drunken feast, 138, 143, 169, 319, 613, 664–65, 720n30 (Letter 47)

Alexander von Humboldt (1769–1859), Prussian botanist, explorer, and writer, 100, 664, 700n19 (Letter 7)

Alexis, Willibald, pseudonym of Georg Wilhelm Heinrich Häring (1798–1871),

German writer of historical novels and idylls, 406, 722n14 (second preface)

Alfred the Great (849–899), king of the West Saxons, defended the Anglo-Saxon kingdoms of southern England against the Vikings, 141

Almack, William (d. 1781), purportedly founded in 1765 the Almack's Assembly Rooms, a London social club, where Almack's balls were the hub of a social whirl, 170–71, 172, 183–84, 206, 210, 212, 216, 228, 337, 376, 378, 455, 702n9–10 (Letter 12), 704n10 (Letter 14). *See also* Lady Patronesses

Alopaeus, Jeanette Caroline von, Countess (1787–1869), one of Pückler's early passions, the wife of Count David Alopaeus (1769–1831), a Russian diplomat and ambassador to Berlin, 164

Amphitryon, a figure from Greek mythology who appeared in numerous comedies from the sixteenth century on, notably in Molière's play of 1668 (adapted by Kleist in 1808), 86, 562

Anastasius. *See* Hope, Thomas

Angelus Silesius (born Johann Scheffler, 1624–1677), German priest known for his mystical poetry, 323, 708n4 (Letter 21)

Angely, Louis (1787–1835), German dramatist and comic actor, 150, 701n39 (Letter 10)

Anglesey, Lord = General Paget = Henry William Paget (1768–1854), 1st Marquess of Anglesey, Lord Uxbridge, and (when Pückler visited him at Phoenix Park) Lord Lieutenant of Ireland, 415, 423–24, 581, 707n7 (Letter 19), 712n3 (Letter 27), 717n6 (Letter 40)

Anne, Queen of Great Britain (1665–1714), daughter of James II, queen from 1702–1714, 118, 138, 141

Annibale. *See* Carracci, Annibale

Antoinette, Queen. *See* Marie Antoinette

Antony, Mark (83–30 BC), Roman general who committed suicide with his lover Cleopatra, 238

Apis, a sacred bull in Egyptian mythology, 423, 465

Aragon, Joanna of (1454–1517), queen of Naples, not the sitter for the portrait admired by Pückler, 118, 700n4 (Letter 9)

Arbuthnot, Harriet (1793–1834), English diarist (whose diaries were published as *The Journal of Mrs. Arbuthnot* only in 1950) and close friend of the Duke of Wellington in the 1820s, 214

Archenholz, Johann Wilhelm von (1741–1812), German historian who published numerous books and periodicals, 349

Archimedes of Syracuse (ca. 287–212 BC), Greek scientist and mathematician, 449

Argüelles, Agustín (1776–1844), Spanish liberal politician exiled in England from 1823–1834, 347

Aristophanes (ca. 446–386 BC), Athenian playwright, 61

Aristotle (384–322 BC), Greek philosopher, 614

Arthur, Prince of Wales (1486–1502), first son of King Henry VII of England, 387, 707n6 (Letter 19)

Arthur, Sir. *See* Sir Arthur Clarke

Arundel, Edmund FitzAlan, 9th Earl of (1285–1326), opponent of King Edward II and involved in the death of the king's favorite, Piers Gaveston, 124

Asclepius, the god of medicine and healing in ancient Greek mythology, 185

Atholl, Duke of = John Murray, 4th Duke of Atholl (1755–1830), 173

Auber, Daniel François Esprit (1782-1871), French composer, 720n22 (Letter 42)

Augusta Sophia, Princess (1768–1840), daughter of George III, 231

Auguste von Harrach, Countess, second wife of Frederick William III of Prussia, 709n27 (Letter 21)

Augustine of Hippo, or Saint Augustine (354–430), an influential bishop and father of the Catholic Church, 623, 718n7 (Letter 44)

Augustus = Gaius Julius Caesar Augustus (63–14 AD), first emperor of the Roman Empire, 561, 664

Ayton, Fanny (1804–after 1832), a celebrated English soprano who made her debut in London at the King's Theatre in 1827, 160–61

B

Baillie, Matthew (1761–1823), Scottish physician and pathologist, 314–15

Baker, Irish magistrate murdered ca. 1825, 574–75

Baleine, Parisian chef known for his restaurant "Rocher de Cancale," 660, 720n14 (Letter 47)

Ballerino, Pückler's pet crane at Muskau, 112

Balzer, Pückler's name for the Traveled Monkey, 239

Banquo, a character in *Macbeth,* 310–11, 313

Bantry, Lord. *See* White, Richard

Barent-Cohen, Hannah (1783–1850), wife of Nathan Mayer Rothschild, 710n20 (Letter 23)

Barnage. *See* Burbage, Richard

Barnett. *See* Montagu, George Browne

Barrington, Sir Jonah (1760–1834), Irish judge and memoirist; the tale Pückler recounts can be found in Barrington's *Personal Sketches of His Own Times* (1827–1832), 575

Barth, Kaspar von (1587–1658), German humanist and philologist, 143

Bartolozzi, Gaetano Stefano (1757–1821), Italian engraver and merchant, father of Madame Vestris, 69

Bassompierre, François de, Maréchal de (1579–1646), French courtier and marshal of France under King Louis XIII, 88

Batthyány, Count = Gusztáv Batthyány-Strattman (1803–1883), Hungarian nobleman who emigrated to England as a young man, becoming a horse breeder and friend of Pückler's, 55–56, 128, 698n2 (Letter 4)

Bavaria, King of. *See* Maximilian I

Beauchamp, Guy de (10th Earl of Warwick). *See* Warwick, Earls of

Beauchamp, Richard de, 13th Earl of Warwick (1382–1439), English nobleman and warrior, 115, 116, 125, 700n2, 12 (Letter 9)

Beaufort, Cardinal = Henry Beaufort (ca. 1374–1447), English clergyman, uncle of King Henry V, and regent to King Henry VI, 301

Beaufort, Henry Charles Somerset, 6th Duke of (1766–1835), 626, 629, 707n29 (Letter 19), 718n11 (Letter 44)

Beaujeu, J. A., introduced gymnastics to Dublin ca. 1824, 608

Becket, Thomas (1118–1170), archbishop of Canterbury, 652

Beckford, William Thomas (1760–1844), a politician and art collector who built Fonthill Abbey and Lansdown Tower, 637–40, 719n14, 16 (Letter 45)

Bedford, John of Lancaster, 1st Duke of (1389–1435), third son of Henry IV, brother of Henry V, 301, 707n29 (Letter 19)

Bedford, John Russell, 6th Duke of Bedford (1766–1839), resided at Woburn Abbey, 110–11

Belloni, Francesco (1772–1863), Roman artist, trained in mosaics at the Vatican, who went to France in 1797, where he became the director of the Imperial School of Mosaics in Paris, 664

Belvidera, a character in the play *Venice Preserved* by Thomas Otway, 603–4

Benoist, Georges (1641–1717), followed his father as the *écuyer de la bouche du roy* (head cook to the king) at Versailles under Louis XIV, 703n7 (Letter 13)

Beresford, Marquis de = William Carr, Viscount, 1st Marquis of Campo Maior (1768–1854), British general and Portuguese marshal, 352, 710n4 (Letter 23)

Bermingham, Captain, and his son, James, likely members of the Bermingham family that had a long history in the area near Tuam, Ireland, and was also affiliated with the title baron of Athenry, 478, 484, 488

Berndt, a manservant who accompanied Pückler to England but failed to adjust and returned to Muskau in the summer of 1827, 18, 37, 59, 199, 217, 222, 228, 268

Bernhard, Duke. *See* Karl Bernhard of Saxe-Weimar-Eisenach

Bernis, Cardinal = François-Joachim de Pierre de Bernis (1715–1794), French statesman and cardinal, 104

Bernoulli, Johann (1744–1807), Swiss child prodigy, mathematician, and astronomer royal in Berlin who was known for his numerous writings, including travel accounts, 212

Beroldingen, Count, Joseph Ignza Graf von (1780–1868), military man, Württemberg diplomat, and envoy in London from 1814 to 1816, 154, 702n3 (Letter 11)

Bias of Priene (sixth century BC), one of the so-called Seven Sages of Greece, 715n3 (Letter 34)

Bishop, Sir Henry Rowley (1786–1855), English composer and director, 83, 313

Black Prince. *See* Edward, the Black Prince

Blake, Anna. *See* Lynch, James

Blindemann, Professor, likely a pun on "blind man," 402

Bloomfield, Lord = Benjamin Bloomfield, 1st Baron Bloomfield (1768–1846), English member of parliament and private secretary to George IV from 1817 to 1822, 216

Blücher, Gebhard Leberecht von, Prince of Wahlstatt (1742–1819), Prussian field marshal who led the Prussian forces against Napoleon at the battles of Leipzig and Waterloo, 140, 207, 716n5 (Letter 38)

Boccaccio, Giovanni (1313–1375), Renaissance humanist, 143

Böhme, Jakob (1575–1624), German Christian mystic and theologian, 418

Bohrer brothers: Anton (1783–1852), violinist, and Maximilian (1785–1867), cellist, 359, 370

Boleyn, Anne (ca. 1501–1536), queen of England, second wife to Henry VIII, 120

Bolívar, Simón (1783–1830), Venezuelan military leader who led Latin America's revolution against Spain, 659

Bonaparte, Letizia (1804–1871), Napoleon's niece and the daughter of Lucien Bonaparte, who divorced Irish politician Thomas Wyse and attempted suicide in 1828 by throwing herself into the Serpentine, 379–81, 711n24 (Letter 24)

Bonaparte, Letizia Ramolino (1750–1836), Napoleon's mother, called Madame Mère and Empress Mother, 671–72, 686

Bonaparte, Lucien (1775–1840), Napoleon's younger brother and the father of Letizia Bonaparte, 671, 672–73, 721n4 (Letter 48)

Bonneau, chamberlain to King Charles X, 361

Bordogni, Marco (1789–1856), a popular Italian tenor based in Paris, 684

Borghese, Prince = Camillo Borghese, 6th Prince of Sulmona (1775–1832), husband of Pauline Bonaparte (1780–1825) and brother-in-law to Napoleon, 212, 227

Borgia, Cesare (ca. 1475–1507), Italian politician, nobleman, and cardinal, 219

Börne, Ludwig (1786–1837), a liberal journalist known for his satirical writings, 692

Bösenberg, Johann Heinrich (1745–1828), German actor and comedian, primarily in Dresden, 67

Boufflers, Stanislas de (1738–1815), French writer, soldier, and academician, 165, 702n27 (Letter 11)

Bourrienne, Louis Antoine Fauvelet de (1769–1834), French diplomat who attended military school with Napoleon, although their amicable relationship did not last, 96

Boursault, Edmé (1638–1701), French playwright, 721n10 (Letter 48)

Braham, John (ca. 1774–1856), English tenor who became one of Europe's leading stars, his origins are obscure beyond that he was Jewish and married into the British aristocracy, 72, 699n10 (Letter 5)

Bramarbas, a name of uncertain origin indicating a boastful man, popularized in Germany by the comedy *Bramarbas oder der groásprecherische Offizier* ("Bramarbas or the boastful officer"), the translation published 1741 in Gottsched's *Deutsche Schaubühne,* from the Danish play by Ludvig Holberg, *Jacob von Tyboe eller den stortalende Soldat* (1723), 601

Brambilla, Marietta (1807–1875), Italian contralto, 358

Brandon, Lord = William Crosbie, 4th Baron Brandon (1771–1832), Irish peer, 715n11 (Letter 33)

Braybrooke, Lord = Richard Griffin-Neville, 3rd Baron Braybrooke (1783–1858), owner of Audley End, 56

Brentano, Clemens (1778–1842), major writer of German Romanticism, 423

Bridge, John. *See* Rundell, Philip

Bridgewater, 8th Earl of = Francis Henry Egerton (1756–1829), owner of Ashridge Park, 107

Brighella, a figure from the commedia dell'arte, 154

Brongniart, Alexandre-Théodore (1739–1813), French architect, 721n14 (Letter 48)

Brooke, Lord = Robert Greville, 2nd Baron Brooke (ca. 1607–1643), a general in the English Civil War, member of parliament for Warwickshire, and ardent puritan who was killed during the siege of Lichfield, 121

Brougham, Henry, 1st Baron Brougham and Vaux (1778–1868), British liberal Whig politician and reformer famous for his speaking gifts; he designed the carriage that bears his name, 207–8, 342, 379

Brown, John (1735–1788), Scottish doctor whose publication *Elementa medicinae* (1780) described a new art of healing, soon known as the Brunonian system, 699n6 (Letter 7)

Brown, Lancelot "Capability" (1716–1783), landscape designer whom Pückler calls the "Garden Shakespeare," 98, 136, 294, 698n16 (Letter 3), 699n6 (Letter 7), 700n3 (Letter 10), 719n7 (Letter 45)

Brühl, Carl Friedrich Moritz Paul von, Count (1772–1837), a friend of Goethe's and director of the Prussian royal theaters and Berlin museums, 387

Brummell, George Bryan, known as "Beau" (1778–1840), set the tone for men's fashion in England and became the epitome of an English dandy, 654–56, 720n21 (Letter 46)

Brunet, Marguerite (1730–1820), French actress and theater director with the stage name Mademoiselle Montansier, 721n16 (Letter 48)

Brunet, the stage name of Jean-Joseph Mira (1766–1853), a popular comic actor at the Théâtre des Variétés in Paris, 681, 721n16 (Letter 48)

Buckingham, 1st Duke of = George Villiers (1592–1628), a favorite of James I and his successor Charles I, 138, 299, 585

Bulkeley, Captain, a London acquaintance of Pückler's and member of the Horse Guards, 262, 268

Bulkeley, Mr. = Sir Richard Williams-Bulkeley, 10th Baronet (1801–1875), owner of Beaumaris Castle, 420

Bull, John, a personification of England who originally appeared in a series of early eighteenth-century pamphlets (*The History of John Bull*) by the satirist John Arbuthnot (1667–1735), 371, 448, 643, 650

Bülow, Heinrich, Baron von (1792–1846), Prussian statesman and ambassador to England from 1827 to 1841, 356

Bulwer-Lytton, Edward (1803–1873), popular English novelist, poet, playwright, and politician, 705n29 (Letter 16), 706n50 (Letter 16), 710n10 (Letter 24)

Burbage, Richard (1567–1619), actor and presumed painter of the so-called Chandos portrait of Shakespeare, now attributed to John Taylor, 146, 701n31 (Letter 10)

Burdett, Sir Francis (1770–1844), English reformist politician who was imprisoned for three months at King's Bench, 230, 354

Bürger, Gottfried August (1747–1794), German poet whose poem "Leonore" is quoted twice by Pückler, 179, 703n34 (Letter 12), 718n2 (Letter 44)

Burghley (also Burleigh), William Cecil (1520–1598), English statesman, close advisor to Queen Elizabeth I, and builder of Burghley House, 140, 270, 360

Buridan, Jean (ca. 1300–1358), French priest and writer, 717n8 (Letter 40)

Burke, Edmund (1729–1797), British statesman and writer, 449

Burke, Joseph (1818–1902), Irish actor and musician who was famous as a child actor under the name "Master Burke," 322–23

Bury, Lady Charlotte Bury, née Campbell (1775–1861), popular English author of many anonymously published works, including *Flirtation* (1828), 96, 309–10, 699n5 (Letter 7), 708n18 (Letter 20)

Bussy, Comte de, Roger de Rabutin (1618–1693), French memoirist, cousin and frequent correspondent of Madame de Sévigné, 697n1 (Letter 1)

Butler, Lady Eleanor. *See* Llangollen, the Ladies of

Byron, Baroness = Anna Isabella Milbanke Noel (1792–1860), Byron's wife, whose relationship with her husband was exceptionally stormy, 264, 466, 706n11 (Letter 17), 713n9 (Letter 29)

Byron, Lord = George Gordon Noel Byron (1788–1824), British Romantic poet, 23, 45, 55, 169, 214, 264, 300, 381, 466, 580, 697n13 (Letter 1), 704n31 (Letter 15), 706n11 (Letter 17), 707n24 (Letter 19), 712n8 (Letter 27), 713n9–10 (Letter 29)

C

Caesar, Julius (100–44 BC), 82, *84*, 95, 154, 613

Cagliostro, Count Alessandro di, an alias for Joseph Balsamo (1743–1795), alchemist and swindler who practiced his trade in all of Europe, 163, 693, 722n17 (second preface)

Callenberg, Graf = Georg Alexander Heinrich Hermann von Callenberg (1744–1795), Pückler's maternal grandfather, 163, 391, 702n21 (Letter 11), 711n10 (Letter 25)

Callenberg-Muskau, Clementine von (1770–1850), Pückler's mother, 163, 219

Camville, Isabel de. *See* Harcourt, Guillaume de

Canning, George (1770–1827), British statesman and liberal Tory known for his brilliant oratory, he rose steadily through the government in various posts and was named prime minister but, already suffering from ill health, he served only 119 days, from April to August 1827, 24, 111, 200, 204, 207–9, 210, 214, 236, 252, 260, 267, 307–8, 699n8 (Letter 7), 706n45 (Letter 16)

Canova, Antonio (1757–1822), Italian neoclassical sculptor, 111, 162, 219, 668

Caracalla (188–217), Roman emperor notorious for his brutality, 235

Caraccioli, Domenico (1711–1789), ambassador of the king of Naples to England in 1763, 480

Caradori, Maria Caterina Rosalbina (1800–1865), French soprano who performed for most of her life in London, beginning in 1822, 358

Caratacus, first-century British chieftain who led the resistance against the Romans under Claudius, 393

Carl von Carlsberg, the main figure in a six-volume epistolary novel by Christian Gotthilf Salzmann, 447

Carlisle, Lord = George Howard, 6th Earl of Carlisle (1773–1848), British statesman and owner of Castle Howard, 278

Carnarvon, Lord = Henry George Herbert, 2nd Earl of Carnarvon (1722–1833), a politician and vice president of the Royal Horticultural Society, 223

Carolath, Princess. *See* Adelheid, Princess of Carolath-Beuthen

Carr, William Holwell (1758–1830), vicar of Menheniot in Cornwall; he never visited his parish but stayed in London, where he assembled an extraordinarily fine collection of paintings, all thirty-five of which he bequeathed to the National Gallery, London, 343, 709n5 (Letter 22)

Carracci, Annibale (1560–1609), Italian painter of the baroque, 279, 343

Carrington, Lord = Robert Smith, 1st Baron Carrington (1752–1838), who resided at Wycombe Abbey, 148–49

Cartwright, Mr., Pückler's dentist in London, whom some called the most celebrated dentist in Europe, 192

Cassidy, Dick, a character in an Irish folktale, 572

Castlemaine, Countess of = Barbara Palmer, 1st Duchess of Cleveland (1640–1709), wife of Roger Palmer, 1st Earl of Castlemaine, and mistress of King Charles II, with whom she had five children (all but the last acknowledged and ennobled by the king); her other lovers included her second cousin John Churchill, later Duke of Marlborough, who was likely the father of her youngest child, 139, 701n7 (Letter 10)

Castlereagh, Lord = Robert Stewart, 2nd Marquess of Londonderry, Viscount Castlereagh (1769–1822), husband of Lady Londonderry, a leading Irish and British politician, and principal British diplomat at the Congress of Vienna; ultimately deemed repressive and widely disliked, he became irrationally paranoiac and committed suicide, 184, 703n8 (Letter 14)

Catherine, Empress = Catherine the Great, empress of Russia (1729–1796), 575, 717n4 (Letter 39)

Catherine of Medici (1519–1589), wife of Henry II of France; she had enormous influence as regent for her son Charles IX and is often held responsible for the Saint Bartholomew's Day Massacre of 1572, which occurred during her son's reign, 138, 141

Catherine Pavlovna, Grand Duchess of Russia (1788–1819), daughter of Emperor Paul I and sister-in-law of the grand duke, married King Wilhelm I of Württemberg in 1816, 697

Cecil. See Burghley, William Cecil

Cellini, Benvenuto (1500–1571), Italian sculptor and goldsmith, 650

Chambers, Sir William (1723–1796), English architect and garden designer, 144

Chambre, Mrs., and her daughters, acquaintances of Pückler's in Windsor, 264, 265, 268

Chamisso, Adelbert von (1781–1838), German writer. See Schlemihl

Charles I (1600–1649), king of Great Britain, 138, 140, 141, 148, 493, 585, 631, 718n1 (Letter 45)

Charles II (1630–1685), king of England, Scotland, and Ireland, 39, 83, 97, 141, 267, 353, 396, 585, 631, 698n8 (Letter 3), 701n7 (Letter 10), 708n6 (Letter 20), 710n7 (Letter 23), 718n1 (Letter 45)

Charles IV (1748–1819), king of Spain, 672, 721n3 (Letter 48)

Charles VI (1368–1422), king of France, 684

Charles X (1757–1836), king of France from 1824 to 1830, 160, 361, 663

Charles XII (1682–1718), king of Sweden, who was initially successful against the Russian army but ultimately suffered a great defeat at the Battle of Poltava, 141, 319, 665, 701n18 (Letter 10), 708n26 (Letter 20)

Charleville, Lady = Catherine Maria Dawson (1762–1851), wife of Charles Bury, 1st Earl of Charleville, 95, 192–93, 699n1 (Letter 7), 703n8 (Letter 13)

Charlotte, Princess of Wales (1796–1817), only daughter of King George IV, wife of Prince Leopold of Belgium, 265

Cheops, Egyptian king of the 4th dynasty (ca. 2500 BC) who built the Great Pyramid of Giza, 307

Chernyshyov, Alexander Ivanovich (1786–1857), Russian military leader and statesman, 163

Chesterfield, Lord = Philip Dormer Stanhope, 4th Earl of Chesterfield (1694–1773), English statesman and writer whose famous *Letters to His Son* (1774) was reissued eight times in the first year and is still in print today, 228, 252, 710n16 (Letter 24)

Child, English coachman and groom who had worked for Pückler in Muskau and was later part of Lord Darnley's household, 367, 368

Churchill, John. See Marlborough, 1st Duke of

Churchill, Lord. See Spencer-Churchill

Cigoli = Ludovico Cardi (1559–1613), Italian painter known as the "Florentine Correggio," 135–36

Cinti, Madame = Laure Cinti-Damoreau (1801–1863), French soprano especially known for her Rossini roles, 663

Clanronald. See MacDonell

Clanwilliam = Richard Meade, 3rd Earl of Clanwilliam (1795–1879), British diplomat who served as envoy to Berlin from 1823 to 1827, 70, 205

Clarence, Duchess of (1792–1849), Princess Adelaide of Saxe-Meiningen, duchess from 1818–1830, thereafter Queen Adelaide of England, married Prince William, Duke of Clarence, in 1818, 211, 222, 342, 362, 379, 704n18 (Letter 15)

Clarence, Duke of, Prince William Henry (1765–1837), reigned from 1830 until his death as King William IV of the United Kingdom of Great Britain and Ireland and of Hanover; he was succeeded by his niece, Victoria; he left no surviving legitimate children (there had been two), but of the ten illegitimate ones he had with his mistress—the actress Mrs. Jordan, with whom he cohabited for twenty years, from 1791 to 1811—eight survived and were granted the title Fitzclarence, 213, 226, 267, 326, 367, 379, 704n24 (Letter 15)

Clarke, Lady Olivia, née Owenson (ca. 1785–1845), younger sister of Lady Morgan, wife of Sir Arthur Clarke, and mother of daughters Sydney and Josephine, 594, 596, 601, 717n3, 12 (Letter 41)

Clarke, Sir Arthur (1778–1857), Irish physician, fellow of the Royal College of Surgeons, medical writer, close friend of his sister-in-law Lady Morgan, 605, 717n10 (Letter 41), 718n3 (Letter 43)

Claude Gellée, known as Claude Lorrain (1600–1682), French artist renowned for his landscape paintings, 136, 227, 343, 360, 485, 649, 719n11 (Letter 46)

Clauren, Heinrich, pseudonym of Karl Gottlieb Samuel Heun (1771–1854), Prussian civil servant and prolific writer of popular literature, known especially for his sentimental novel *Mimili* and the literary annual *Vergiámeinnicht* (Forget-Me-Not) published from 1808–1834, 348, 406, 709n12 (Letter 22), 712n35 (Letter 25)

Cleopatra (69–30 BC), queen of Egypt and lover of Mark Antony, 29, 238

Clifford, Charles, 6th Baron Clifford of Chudleigh (1759–1831), owner of Ugbrooke House, 634

Clift, William (1775–1849), the first conservator of the Hunterian Museum and likely the guide Pückler identifies as "Clist," 258

Clifton, Mrs., a Brighton acquaintance of Pückler's, 183

Cochrane, Thomas, 10th Earl of Dundonald (1775–1860), British naval officer who was dismissed from the Royal Navy in 1814 after he was convicted for his part in manipulating prices in the "Great Stock Exchange Fraud of 1814," 230, 705n17 (Letter 16)

Cockburn, Sir George (1772–1853), British naval commander and admiral of the fleet who after the war was given the job of conveying Napoleon to Saint Helena, where he remained for some months as governor of the island and the emperor's jailer, 213

Cocotte, French for a prostitute or promiscuous woman, the name given one of the monkeys in the "Travelled Monkey" painting, 239

Codrington, Edward (1770–1851), British admiral, hero of the Battles of Navarino and Trafalgar, 450

Colburn, Henry (ca. 1784–1855), major publisher and bookseller in London who published works by Walter Scott, Lady Bury, and many others, 699n7 (Letter 7)

Columbus, Christopher (1450–1506), 610–11, 718n9 (Letter 43)

C'Omack. See Cormac

Condillac, Etienne Bonnot de (1715–1780), French philosopher of the Enlightenment, follower of John Locke, 455

Conqueror, the. See William the Conqueror

Conyngham, Elizabeth, Marchioness Conyngham (1769–1861), English noblewoman and the last mistress of King George IV, 706n38 (Letter 16)

Cook, James = Captain Cook (1728–1779), English seaman and explorer, 133

Cook, Thomas Potter (1786–1864), English actor, 45

Coriolanus, a Shakespearean hero, 451, 713n10 (Letter 28)

Cork, a maker of counterfeit coins, 274

Cormac (836–908), king of Cashel from 900 on; secular and religious leader of southern Ireland; Pückler spells this M. C'Omack. *See* Mac Carthaigh, Cormac; Mac-Cuilennáin, Cormac

Correggio, Antoio da (1489–1534), Italian painter of the Renaissance, 219

Corsican, the Great. *See* Napoleon

Cotton, Henry (1789–1879), an ecclesiastical writer who went to Ireland in 1823 as chaplain to his father-in-law Richard Laurence, archbishop of Cashel (1822–1839); he served as archdeacon of Cashel from 1824–1832, 551

Coutts, Thomas (1735–1822), English banker of enormous wealth whose second wife, the actress Harriot Mellon (later Duchess of St Albans), inherited his entire fortune upon his death, 304

Cowper, Lady = Emily Mary Lamb (1787–1869), who became Countess Cowper through her marriage to Peter Leopold Louis Francis Nassau Cowper, 5th Earl of Cowper; she lived at Panshanger Park, 210, 319

Crockford, William (1775–1844), son of a fishmonger who became proprietor of Crockford`s Club, a fashionable London gambling establishment through which he amassed an enormous fortune in just a few years, 356–57, 710n10 (Letter 23)

Croesus, King of Lydia (595–ca. 547 BC), renowned for his great wealth, 69, 339

Croker, Thomas Crofton (1798–1854), Irish antiquary who published collections of ancient Irish poetry and folklore, 519, 715n5, 18 (Letter 34), 717n3 (Letter 39)

Cromwell, Oliver (1599–1658), a political leader and Lord Protector of the Commonwealth, 121, 124, 126, 128, 141, 144, 148, 302, 319, 413, 420, 438, 479, 561, 585, 619, 628–29, 646, 701n36 (Letter 10)

Curioni, Alberico (1785–1875), Italian tenor, 358–59

Curtin, Johnny, a character in an Irish folktale related by Pückler, 570–73

Curtius = Quintus Curtius Rufus, a first-century Roman historian whose only surviving work is *The History of Alexander,* 143

Cyrus, the Great, Persian king of the sixth-century BC who was defeated by the troops of Queen Tomyris, who then had his corpse beheaded in revenge for her son's death, 164, 702n25 (Letter 11)

Czartoryski, Adam Jerzy, also knows as Adam George Czartoryski (1770–1861), Polish nobleman and statesman who published several books, 90

D

Dalai Lama, the head of the main order of Tibetan Buddhists, 425

D'Alembert, Jean le Rond (1717–1783), French mathematician, philosopher, and coeditor with Diderot of the *Encyclopédie,* 104

Dalgetty = Captain Dugald Dalgetty, a character in Walter Schott's *The Legend of Montrose* (1819), 415

Daniell, Thomas (1749–1840), English landscape painter and engraver who published a number of illustrated books, including *Hindoo Excavations in the Mountain of Ellora* (1803), 329

Dannecker, Johann Heinrich von (1758–1841), German sculptor, 668

Danneskiold-Samsoe, Christian, Count (1800–1886), Danish nobleman and estate owner who married the Englishwoman Elizabeth Brudenell-Bruce (1807–1847) in 1833, 200

Dante Alighieri (ca. 1265–1321), Italian poet, 636, 719n9 (Letter 45)

Darius III (ca. 380–330 BC), king of Persia, 143

Darnley, Lady = Elizabeth Brownlow (ca. 1767–1831), wife of Lord Darnley, 165, 166, 367–68

Darnley, Lord = John Bligh, 4th Earl of Darnley (1767–1831), resided at Cobham Hall; his son was Edward, 5th Earl of Darnley (1795–1835), who was killed by a falling tree shortly after Pückler's visit, 161–63, 164, 165, 166, 216, 367, 368, 702n16 (Letter 11)

Darnley Lord = Henry Stuart (1545–1567), second husband of Mary Queen of Scots, born at Temple Newsam, 298

David, Jacques-Louis (1748–1825), French painter in the neoclassical style, 667

Dawkins-Pennant, George Hay (ca. 1763–1840), owner of the Penrhyn estate and quarry in Wales, 711n28–29 (Letter 25), 713n21 (Letter 27)

Deffand, Madame du = Marie Anne de Vichy-Chaumrond, Marquise du Deffand (1697–1780), had a leading salon in Paris and carried on personal and epistolary relationships with many important figures of her day, including Voltaire and Walpole; she lost her sight in 1754, 359, 531

del Sarto, Andrea (1486–1530), Italian painter of the Renaissance, 649

Delanglard, Charles, French inventor of the georama installed in Paris in 1825, 721n31–32 (Letter 48)

Denon = Dominique Vivant, Baron de Denon (1747–1824), French artist, writer, minister of arts under Napoleon, and director of the Musée Napoléon (the name given to the Louvre from 1803 to 1814), 104, 663, 664, 720n25 (Letter 47)

Desaix, Louis = Louis Charles Antoine Desaix de Veygoux (1768–1800), French general, 686

D'Esterre, John (d. 1815), Irish Protestant and crack shot who challenged O'Connell to a duel, at which he was killed, 524

Deville, James (1776–1846), phrenologist and sculptor who produced marked-up phrenological busts, including one of William Blake, 232–36, 240, 248, 250, 705n22 (Letter 16), 713n5 (Letter 29)

Devonshire, William George Spencer Cavendish, 6th Duke of (1790–1858), British peer who resided at Chiswick House, his London estate, 38, 189, 212, 270, 356, 379, 700n17 (Letter 7), 713n8 (Letter 29)

Devrient, Ludwig (1784–1832), German character actor in Berlin, 86

Diavolo Antonio, Il, Portuguese tightrope walker and acrobat, 683–84, 721n17 (Letter 48)

Diderot, Denis (1713–1784), French Enlightenment philosopher, writer, and compiler of the the *Encyclopédie* (with D'Alembert), 104, 718–19n6 (Letter 45)

Digby, Jane. *See* Ellenborough, Lady

Diogenes of Sinope (ca. 410–323 BC), Greek philosopher, 713n16 (Letter 27)

Disraeli, Benjamin (1804–1881), British politician and writer, 706n47 (Letter 16), 706n51 (Letter 17)

Dolci, Carlo (1616–1686), Italian painter of the baroque, 138, 250

Dom Miguel. *See* Miguel I

Domenichino, Il = Domenico Zampieri (1581–1641), Italian painter of the baroque who was active in Rome and Naples, 280, 343, 709n5 (Letter 22)

Don Juan (Don Giovanni in Italian), a colorful figure of legend and fiction known as an amoral seducer of women, 223, 306

Don Quixote, the protagonist of the novel by Miguel Cervantes (1547–1616), 109, 141, 319, 439, 518, 595, 601, 665, 715n4 (Letter 34)

Döring, Theodor (1803–1878), German comic actor, 67

Drayton, Michael (1563–1631), English poet, 713n13 (Letter 27)

Drovetti, Bernardino (1776–1852), Italian diplomat, lawyer, explorer, and antiquarian who was appointed French consul to Egypt by Napoleon, 668

Duchesnois, Catherine-Joséphine (1777–1835), French actress, 679

Ducis, Jean-François (1733–1816), French writer, poet, and playwright, 713n15 (Letter 28)

Ducrow, Andrew (1793–1842), British circus performer famous for his elaborate poses atop the rumps of horses and for his flesh-colored body stockings, 585–86, 593

Dundas, Robert, 2nd Viscount Melville (1771–1851), British statesman, member of Parliament, and first lord of the admiralty from 1812 to 1827, when he resigned; he was reappointed in 1828, and resigned again in 1830, 162, 165, 200, 204

Dürer, Albrecht (1471–1528), German Renaissance artist, 148, 648

Duroc, Géraud Christophe Michel, Duke of Frioul (1772–1813), French general and marshal, Napoleon's closest confident and almost constant companion, 255

E

Ebrahim Khan Kalantar (d. 1801), chancellor to the shahs of Persia for fifteen years until he was executed by the Shah, 226, 705n11 (Letter 16)

Edward, the Black Prince (1330–1376), prince of Wales, eldest son of King Edward III, and father of King Richard II; he was victorious over the French at Poitiers in 1356, one of the major battles of the Hundred Years' War, 266–67, 414, 700n9 (Letter 9), 712n7 (Letter 26)

Edward I (1239–1307), king of England who built Caernarfon Castle and Harlech Castle in Wales, 413, 414, 420, 438, 552, 716n4 (Letter 37)

Edward II (1284–1327), prince and king of Wales who was removed by Parliament and murdered, 124, 281, 414

Edward III (1312–1377), king of England from 1327 to 1377, 266–67, 712n7 (Letter 26)

Edward VI (1537–1553), son of Henry VIII and Jane Seymour; the first Protestant king of England, 700n2 (Letter 10)

Egmont, Count = Lamoral, Count of Egmont, Prince of Gavere (1522–1568), Flemish general and statesman, immortalized in Goethe's tragedy *Egmont* (1788) and in the music Beethoven wrote for the play's revival in 1810, 649, 709n20 (Letter 21), 722n3 (postscript)

Egremont, 3rd Earl of = Sir George O'Brien Wyndham (1751–1837), British peer, patron of the arts, and owner of Petworth House

where he lived with about fifteen mistresses and their forty children, 172, 304

Ekhof, Konrad (1720–1778), German actor and theater director who earned the sobriquet "the father of German acting," 348–49

El Empecinado (The Undaunted), the nickname of Juan Martín Díez (1775–1823), a leader of the Spanish revolution of 1820, 345

Eldon, Lord = John Scott, First Earl of Eldon (1751–1838), served as lord chancellor of Great Britain between 1801 and 1827, 200, 209

Eleanor of Castile (ca. 1241–1290), wife of Edward I and mother of Edward II; she was born in Caernarfon Castle, Wales, 414

Elisa, the daughter of the innkeeper at Caernarfon, 415, 419

Elizabeth I (1533–1603), daughter of King Henry VIII and his second wife, Anne Boleyn, queen of England and Ireland from 1558 to 1603, 39, 56, 115, 120, 121, 122, 140, 141, 148, 213, 270, 297, 319, 457, 479, 575, 700n7 (Letter 9), 704n26 (Letter 15), 717n4 (Letter 39)

Ellenborough, Edward Law, 1st Earl of (1790–1871), politician who in 1828 was made Lord Privy Seal in the Duke of Wellington's government, 208, 210

Ellenborough, Lady = Jane Digby (1807–1881), widely known for her beauty and notorious life; her first marriage to the Earl of Ellenborough (his second), which was dissolved by an act of Parliament in 1830, was followed by numerous scandals, affairs, and additional marriages on the Continent, in the Middle East, and in Asia, 208, 210, 212

Elliot, Hugh (1752–1830), British soldier and diplomat who spent considerable time in Bavaria, Prussia, Sweden and, beginning in 1792, Dresden, 85–86

Emilie. See Adelheid, Princess of Carolath-Beuthen

Enghien, Duc d' = Louis Antoine de Bourbon, Duke of Enghien (1772–1804), executed on Napoleon's orders for alleged conspiracy, but the charges were fabricated and his death widely regarded as a murder, 95

Erasmus of Rotterdam or Desiderius Erasmus (1466–1536), Dutch humanist and theologian, 29, 267

Essex, 2nd Earl of = Robert Devereux (1565 [?] –1601), English nobleman and a favorite of Elizabeth I; he was executed after a failed coup d'état, 113

Essex, 5th Earl of = George Capell-Coningsby (1757–1839), whose son-in-law, Richard Ford, toured Pückler around Cassiobury Park, 104

Esterházy, Paul-Anton, Prince (1786-1866), Hungarian prince and ambassador in London during the time of Pückler's visit,

70, 153, 204, 206, 212, 223, 224, 261, 306, 324, 326, 370, 705n10 (Letter 16)

Esterházy, Princess = Princess Maria Theresia of Thurn and Taxis (1794–1874) married Paul-Anton, Prince Esterházy, in 1812

Eulenspiegel, Till, a fictional, impudent character in many tales circulating from the sixteenth century on, 242, 699n10 (Letter 6)706n34 (Letter 16)

Eyck, Jan van (ca. 1390–1441), Flemish painter of the Renaissance, 667

Eynard, Jean-Gabriel (1775–1863), a wealthy Swiss banker who was an enthusiastic supporter of the Greeks during their war of independence, 223

F

Falck, Baron = Anton Reinhard Falck (1777–1843), Dutch statesman and ambassador in London, 708n8 (Letter 21)

Falck, Madame = Rose Amour Barones de Roisin, married Baron Falck in 1818, 328

Falstaff, a corpulent, roguish character in Shakespeare's *Henry IV* and *Merry Wives of Windsor*, 76, 86, 87, 88, 308–9, 436, 622, 623

Fane, John. See Westmorland, John Fane, 10th Earl of

Fane, Miss, a character in Benjamin Disraeli's *Vivian Grey*, 253

Fanferluche, a wicked fairy in *Babiole*, a French literary fairy tale by Madame d'Aulnoy, 508

Fanny. See Hughes, Colonel

Farquhar, Lady (1782–1875), née Maria Frances Geslip, wife of Sir Robert Farquhar, 172, 361–62, 702n13 (Letter 12)

Farquhar, Sir Robert Townsend (1776–1830), British merchant and first governor of Mauritius (Ile de France) who resided at Richmond Terrace, Whitehall, 172, 361, 702n13 (Letter 12), 710n19 (Letter 23)

Farren, Percy (1780–1843), English actor and stage manager, 345, 709n7 (Letter 22)

Fay, Léontine, French actress very popular in London in the 1820s and 1830s, 660, 720n15 (Letter 47)

Ferdinand Friedrich, Duke of Anhalt-Köthen (1769–1830), German prince, 590, 717n9 (Letter 41)

Ferdinand VII (1784–1833), king of Spain who spent 1808–1814 in French imprisonment while Napoleon's brother, Joseph Bonaparte, occupied the Spanish throne; the Spanish revolted, seeking the return of "the Desired" Ferdinand, but the remainder of his reign was filled with unrest, 347

Fergus (Mór), reputedly the first king of Scotland and connected to the Stone of Scone in a fifteenth-century text by Andrew of Wyntoun, 552

Fin, Mr., Irish parliamentarian, 595

Fionn mac Cumhaill, a warrior hunter in Irish myth who in some tales is also a benevolent giant with magical powers, 463

Fischer, Caroline Auguste (1764–1842), German writer, 700n18 (Letter 7)

fitz Stephen. *See* Lynch, James

Fitzclarence, Colonel = George Augustus Frederick Fitzclarence, 1st Earl of Munster (1794–1842), eldest of ten illegitimate children of the Duke of Clarence, later King William IV, and his mistress, Dorothea Jordan; he served as a military officer in the Peninsular War and also in India, 704n25 (Letter 15)

FitzHerbert, Alleyne, 1st Baron St Helens (1753–1839), British diplomat, friend of George Vancouver who named Mount Saint Helens after him, 699n12 (Letter 6)

FitzHerbert, Mrs. = Maria Anne FitzHerbert (1756–1837), whose second husband, Thomas FitzHerbert, died in 1781, and who began a lengthy relationship with the future George IV in 1784, becoming his secret, illegitimate wife in 1785; their rocky relationship went on for years, only ending in 1808, 184, 203, 703n7 (Letter 14)

Fitzpatrick, Kearns, a celebrated Irish piper who performed on August 22, 1821, for George IV during the king's visit to Dublin, 568–69, 576–77

Fitzwilliam, William, 4th Earl Fitzwilliam (1748–1833), British statesman who inherited Wentworth House in 1782, 298

Flahaut, Charles Joseph, Count of (1785–1870), French general and diplomat who was thought to be the illegitimate son of Tallyrand; lover of the queen of Holland, with whom he had an illegitimate son; lived in Germany and then England, where he married the Baroness Keith, 170, 176, 184

Flahaut, Countess of = Margaret Mercer Elphinstone, Baroness Keith (1788–1867), married the Count of Flahaut in 1817, 172, 184, 200, 203

Fleck, Ferdinand (1757–1801), German actor and director who played Shakespearean roles in Berlin and elsewhere, 348–49

Fleury, the stage name of Abraham-Joseph Bénard (1750–1822), French actor of the Comédie-Française and one of the great comedians of his era, 674

Folko = Sir Folko de Montfaucon, a knight in Friedrich de la Motte-Fouqué's *Der Zauberring*, 3 vols. (1812; translated into English as *The Magic Ring*, 1825), in which golden vulture wings appear on Folko's helmet, 541

Ford, Mr., Irish parliamentarian, 595

Ford, Richard (1796–1858), English writer who was married to Harriet Capel, the daughter of the 5th Earl of Essex, 104, 107

Fortunatus, the hero of a popular German chapbook from the fifteenth and sixteenth centuries; he had a wishing hat that, when he put it on, could transport him anywhere, 385

Fouqué, Friedrich de la Motte (1777–1843), German writer of Romantic fiction, 541

Fox, Charles James (1749–1806), long-serving and radical English statesman, uncle of Lord Holland, 111, 176, 260

Francis I (1494–1547), king of France, 280, 596, 698n18 (Letter 3)

Franckh, Friedrich Gottlob (1802–1845), publisher of the first German edition of *Letters of a Dead Man*, 695, 711n25 (Letter 25), 722n2 (postscript)

Françoise d'Orléans de Valois = Françoise Madeleine d'Orléans (1648–1664), married her first cousin Charles Emmanuel II, Duke of Savoy in April 1774 and died that same year at the age of fifteen, 148

Franconi, Antonio (1738–1836), circus performer known for his trick riding; born in Venice, he gained fame in Paris, where he had his own amphitheaters. *See also* Franconi's, *in Annotated Index of Places*

Frederick I (1754–1816), king of Württemberg, 698n11 (Letter 3)

Frederick II (1712–1786), king of Prussia who was sometimes called a Philosopher King because of his great interest in music, philosophy, and the arts, 62, 139, 712n12 (Letter 26)

Frederick the Great. *See* Frederick II

Frederick William III (1770–1840), king of Prussia, under whose rule Prussia lost many territories to Napoleon, including Muskau. He was, like Pückler, infatuated with Lucie's daughters, Adelheid and especially Helmine; his first wife was Louise of Mecklenburg-Strelitz, and his second, morganatic wife was August von Harrach, 582, 700n19–20 (Letter 7), 709n14 (Letter 21)

Fremantel, Miss, a young woman admired by Pückler as the "Beauty of Brighton," 183–84

Frideswide, Saint (ca. 650–727), abbess and patron saint of Oxford and Oxford University, 143–44, 701n27 (Letter 10)

Froissart, Jean (ca. 1337–1405), French chronicler of medieval France, 143

Frömmel, Mr. (and Dr.) von, one of Pückler's invented names, in this case implying an excess of sanctimony, 416, 425, 528, 712n5 (Letter 27), 715n15 (Letter 34)

Fust, Johann (ca. 1400–1466), a wealthy German businessman who lent money to Johann Gutenberg to publish his 42-line Bible; perhaps Fust was acting as a benefactor, but he later brought suit against Gutenberg when the latter could not repay his debts, eventually taking over the Bible-printing firm, 143, 701n22 (Letter 10)

G

Gall, Franz Joseph (1758–1828), German neuroanatomist and physiologist who practiced in Paris and developed "cranioscopy" (later called "phrenology"), a method of determining the personality and development of mental and moral faculties on the basis of the external shape of the skull, 232, 464, 705n20–21, 24 (Letter 16)

Galli, Filippo (1783–1853), a renowned Italian opera singer who performed in London from 1827 to 1833, 204

Ganymede, a beautiful boy in Greek mythology whom Jupiter, in the guise of an eagle, abducts to Mount Olympus, 529

García. *See* Malibran, Madame

Garnerin, Mademoiselle = Elisa Garnerin (1791–1853), niece of Andre-Jacques Garnerin, the inventor of the parachute; as the first female parachutist, she made over three dozen parachute descents from 1815 to 1836, 686

Garofalo, Il = Benvenuto Tisi (1481–1559), Italian painter from Ferrara, 343, 709n5 (Letter 22)

Garrick, David (1717–1779), English actor, poet, and playwright who was a rival and friend of Quin, 73, 135, 141, 186, 349, 637

Garvagh, Lady = Isabella Charlotte Rosabelle Bonham (1804–1891), eldest daughter of Henry Bonham of Titness Park. In 1824, she married George Canning, 1st Baron Garvagh (1778–1840), the first cousin of Prime Minister Canning; Pückler, who sometimes calls her "Lady R(osabelle), was very smitten with her, 221, 267, 269–70, 316

Gaveston, Piers, 1st Earl of Cornwall (ca. 1284–1312), favorite of King Edward II of England; he was captured and held at Warwick Castle by Guy de Beauchamp, and he was executed by Beauchamp and others, 124, 281

Gelert, a hound in a Welsh tale, 432–33, 713n14 (Letter 27)

Gellert, Christian Fürchtegott (1715–1769), German writer known particularly for his fables, stories, and poems, 432, 713n14 (Letter 27)

George III (1738–1820), king of Great Britain from 1760 to 1820; signs of his mental illness were noticed in 1765, and, beginning in 1811, his eldest son ruled as prince regent until his father's death, 441, 564

George IV (1762–1830), prince of Wales and king of Great Britain and Hannover from 1811; he built the Brighton pavilion and enjoyed a secret marriage to Mrs. Fitzherbert, 82–83, *84*, 220, 328, 372, 524, 624, 699n17 (Letter 6), 702n2 (Letter 12), 703n7 (Letter 14), 706n38, 52 (Letter 16), 709n3 (Letter 23), 714n4–5 (Letter 30), 719n19 (Letter 46)

Gérard, François Pascal Simon (1770–1837), French painter, 667

Getti, Jean-André (ca. 1738–1819), the officially sanctioned maker of plaster casts for the new Louvre museum, 667

Gibbings, Mary Woolley (ca. 1799–1889), an heiress whose parents Pückler found "unpalatable," 337, 709n28 (Letter 28)

Gibbon, Edward (1737–1794), English historian of the Enlightenment; his *History of the Decline and Fall of the Roman Empire* (6 vols., 1776–1788; German translation, 1805–1807), chronicled the fall of Rome and the rise of Christianity, 615

Gibson, Thomas (ca. 1680–1751), English portrait painter and copyist, 141

Gilray, James (1757–1815), British caricaturist and printmaker, 91

Girodet de Roussy-Trioson, Anne-Louis (1767–1824), French painter of the early Romantic period who studied with Jacques-Louis David, 667, 685

Glendower, Owen. *See* Glyndwr, Owain

Glengall, Lord = Richard Butler, 2nd Earl of Glengall and 11th Baron Cahir (1794–1858), who ultimately exhausted his fortune trying to improve his estates and restore the family residence, Cahir Castle, 548

Gloucester, Duke of = Humphrey of Lancaster, 1st Duke of Gloucester (1390–1447), served as one of many regents to the young Henry VI and was rumored to have been poisoned, 707n29 (Letter 19)

Gloucester, Duke of = William Frederick (1776–1834), husband of the Duchess of Gloucester, 196

Gloucester, Mary, Duchess of (1776–1857), daughter of George III, married to the Duke of Gloucester, 213, 220

Glyndwr, Owain (ca. 1349–1416), a Welsh hero who led a lengthy revolt against the English, 391

Goderich, Lord = Frederick John Robinson, Viscount Goderich, 1st Earl of Ripon (1782–1859), a British statesman, 209

Godoy, Manuel (1767–1851), twice prime minister of Spain, 673, 721n3 (Letter 48)

Goethe, August von (1789–1830), son of Johann Wolfgang von Goethe, 24

Goethe, Frau von = Ottilie von Pogwisch (1796–1872), wife of August von Goethe; she took care of her father-in-law, Johann Wolfgang von Goethe, until his death in 1832, 24

Goethe, Johann Wolfgang von (1749–1832), a celebrated German writer, civil servant, and garden designer, 20, 21–23, 25, 55, 98, 172, 179, 217, 332, 398, 509, 580, 611, 649, 691, 697n6–7, 9, 13 (Letter 1), 698n12 (Letter 3), 703n33 (Letter 12), 705n37 (Letter 15), 706n35, 42 (Letter 16), 708n3 (Letter 21), 713n22 (Letter 27), 713n6 (Letter 28), 714n10 (Letter 29), 715n19 (Letter 33), 715n13 (Letter 34), 715n5 (Letter 35), 718n10, 14 (Letter 43), 718n4 (Letter 45), 721n40 (Letter 47), 722n2, 6, 8, 10–11 (second preface), 722n3 (postscript)

Gomez. *See* Lynch, James

Gondomar, 1st Count of = Diego Sarmiento de Acuña (1567–1626), Spanish ambassador to England from 1613–1622 and an expert in Spain on English affairs, 148

Gonzalvo. *See* Lynch, James

Gore, Sir. *See* Ouseley, Gore

Gort, Lord = Colonel Charles Vereker, 2nd Viscount Gort (1768–1842), British soldier and politician who developed Lough Cutra Castle and Estate, 500

Gramont, Count of = Philibert, comte de Gramont (1621–1707), French nobleman infamous for his *Mémoirs,* which (though actually written by his brother-in-law) expose the count's witty but mercurial personality and his bad habits, such as cheating and gambling, 650

Granby, a criminal, 24, 274, 697n19 (Letter 1)

Grand Duchess. *See* Karl August, Grand Duke of Saxe-Weimar-Eisenach

Grand Duke. *See* Karl August, Grand Duke of Saxe-Weimar-Eisenach

Grävell, Maximilian Karl Friedrich (1781–1860), a lawyer, politician, writer of political-sociological tracts (including *Der Regent,* 2 vols., 1823), and administrator of Pückler's estates from 1825–1834, 396

Great Agitator. *See* O'Connell, Daniel

Grenville, Lord = William Wyndham, 1st Baron Grenville (1759–1834), British statesman and owner of Dropmore House, 260

Greville, George, 2nd Earl of Warwick (1746–1816), British politician, 278, 700n10 (Letter 9)

Greville, Lady = Charlotte Maria Cox (d. 1841), wife of Algernon Frederick Greville, the private secretary to the Duke of Wellington, 200

Grey, Lord = Charles Grey, 2nd Earl Grey (1764–1845), Whig member of Parliament

who served as prime minister from 1830 to 1834, 209

Grignan, Madame de = Françoise-Marguerite de Sévigné, Comtesse de Grignan (1646–1705), daughter of Madame de Sévigné and recipient of the famous letters her mother wrote to her for three decades, 17

Grillparzer, Franz (1791–1872), Austrian writer and dramatist, 45, 698n14 (Letter 3)

Grimm brothers = Jacob (1785–1863) and Wilhelm (1786–1859), German philologists, writers, and folklorists, 715n18 (Letter 34), 717n3 (Letter 39)

Gros, Baron Antoine-Jean (1771–1835), French neoclassical and early pre-Romantic painter, 721n26 (Letter 48)

Grosvenor, Robert, 2nd Earl and 1st Marquess of Westminster (1767–1845), English member of Parliament and a major art collector; in 1827, he added an art gallery to his London residence, Grosvenor House, and rebuilt Eaton Hall, his country estate, as well as restored the gardens, 60, 128, 360

Grotius, Hugo (1583–1645), an important Netherlandish legal scholar, historian, poet, and statesman, 141

Guido. *See* Reni, Guido

Guise, Duc Henri de = Henry I, Prince of Joinville (1550–1588), who was assassinated at Blois by order of Henry III, 148, 701n35 (Letter 10)

Guises = Claude de Lorraine, duc de Guise (1496–1550), and Francis de Lorraine II, duc de Guise (1519–1563), the subjects of two portraits that Pückler could have seen at Temple Newsam, 298

Gustavus Adolphus (1594–1632), king of Sweden, 19, 128

Guy de Beauchamp (10th Earl of Warwick). *See under* Warwick, Earls of

Gwynn, Nell (Eleanor) (1650–1687), actress and mistress of Charles II, who acknowledged their son, Charles Beauclerk, 1st Earl of Burford, as his illegitimate child and granted him the title Duke of St Albans, 306, 396, 708n6 (Letter 21)

H

Hahnemann, Christian Friedrich Samuel (1755–1843), German physician from Saxony who was the founder of homeopathy, 717n7 (Letter 40)

Halévy, Léon (1802–1883), French playwright and historian, 721n12 (Letter 48)

Hamilton, Duke of = Alexander Hamilton, 10th Duke of Hamilton (1767–1852), Scottish politician, 173

Handel, George Frideric (1685–1759), German-born British composer, 141, 216, 704n34 (Letter 15)

Hannibal (247–ca. 183 BC), Carthagian military commander in Carthage during the Second Punic War, 345, 610, 714n14 (Letter 32)

Harcourt, Amédée d', Marquis d'Olonde (1771–1831), French nobleman and general in the English army, whose family inherited St Leonard's Hill, 264

Harcourt, Countess = Mary Harcourt, née Danby (1749/1750–1833), wife of William Harcourt, 261–62, 263, 706n9 (Letter 17)

Harcourt, Edward. See Venables-Vernon, Edward

Harcourt, Guillaume (William) de, Knight (ca. 1175–1223), from Stanton Harcourt, Oxfordshire; he was the son of Robert d'Harcourt and Isabel de Camville (ca. 1152–1208), 387, 711n4 (Letter 25)

Harcourt, Marie-Augusta d'Harcourt (1813–1892), daughter of the Marquis de Harcourt, 264, 706n10 (Letter 17)

Harcourt, Robert d' (ca. 1152–1202), English nobleman from Stanton Court, Oxfordshire, 387, 711n4 (Letter 25)

Harcourt, William, 3rd Earl Harcourt, Field Marshall (1743–1830), British soldier, owner of St Leonard's Hill, and deputy ranger of Windsor Park; upon his death, most of his holdings went to his cousin Edward Venables-Vernon-Harcourt, Archbishop of York, but St Leonard's Hill went first to his wife Mary and, upon her death, to the family of his French relative Amédée d'Harcourt, 261–64, 267, 706n8 (Letter 17)

Hardenberg, Karl August, Fürst von (1750–1822), liberal statesman, chancellor of Prussia from 1810 until his death, and Pückler's father-in-law, 360, 710n15 (Letter 23), 711n22 (Letter 25)

Hardenberg, the maiden name of Pückler's wife Lucie and reportedly of the black woman he meets in Athenry, Ireland, 480, 714n4 (Letter 31)

Harewood, Lord = Henry Lascelles, 3rd Earl of Harewood (1797–1857), British member of Parliament and owner of Harewood Park, 294–96

Harford, John Scandrett (1785–1866), British banker and philanthropist who owned Blaise Castle House and built Blaise Hamlet for his employees, 635, 719n8 (Letter 45)

Harrowby, Lord = Dudley Ryder, 1st Earl of Harrowby (1762–1847), British politician, 167, 702n1 (Letter 12)

Harvey, Willliam (1578–1657), English physician who first described the mechanics of blood circulation, 299

Hastings, Marquess of = Francis Rawdon-Hastings (1754–1826), British politician and military officer; he served in the American War of Independence, as governor-general of India and later Malta, 97

Hauff Wilhellm (1802–1827), German writer, 398, 711n25 (Letter 25)

Hauffe, Friederike (1801–1829), German somnambulist and clairvoyant, 722n3 (second preface)

Hebe, Greek goddess of youth and cupbearer of the gods, 413

Hegel, Georg Wilhelm Friedrich (1770–1831), German philosopher, 613, 712n8 (Letter 27)

Heine, Heinrich (1797–1856), German poet and writer, 708n3 (Letter 21)

Heinse, (Johann Jakob) Wilhelm (1746–1803), German writer, 275, 706n7 (Letter 18)

Helmine von Lanzendorf (ca. 1801–1846), Lucie von Pückler-Muskau's ward and adoptive daughter; Pückler became deeply enamored of her early on (as did King Frederick William III), which led Lucie to marry her off (to a Lieutenant von Blücher) as quickly as possible, 178–79, 684, 703n30 (Letter 12)

Héloïse d'Argenteuil (ca. 1100–1164), French nun and writer known for her tragic affair with Peter Abelard, 307

Helvétius, Claude Adrien (1715–1771), French philosopher of the Enlightenment, 104, 455, 480

Henri IV (1553–1610), first king of the Bourbon branch in France, 106, 148, 346, 667, 685

Henrietta, the given name of the African woman whom Pückler is so impressed with in Ireland, 491, 493

Henry III (1207–1272), king of England, 124, 132, 700n2 (Letter 10)

Henry IV (ca. 1366–1413), king of England and lord of Ireland, 272, 308, 652, 711n11 (Letter 25), 721n25 (Letter 48)

Henry V (1386–1422), king of England, 622, 623, 707n29 (Letter 19), 718n6 (Letter 44)

Henry VI (1431–1471), king of England, 260, 707n29 (Letter 19), 709n11 (Letter 22)

Henry VII (1457–1509), king of England, 646

Henry VIII (1491–1547), king of England, 39, 45, 46, 120, 140, 142, 280, 287, 291, 303, 304, 305, 479, 628–29, 698n18 (Letter 3)

Herbert, Mr., owner of Muckross estate; at the time of Pückler's visit, Henry Arthur Herbert (1815–1866), successor to his father Charles John Herbert (1785–1823), was still at Eton, although it was he who

began improving the estate and building Muckross House in the late 1830s, 85, 506

Herder, Johann Gottfried (1744–1803), German writer and philosopher, 238, 561

Herodias, identified in the Gospels as the mother of Salome and the force behind the execution of John the Baptist, 164

Herschel, Sir Frederick William (1738–1822), German-born British composer and astronomer who was famous for discovering Uranus in 1781, 705n22 (Letter 16)

Hertford, Francis Seymour-Conway, 3rd Marquess of (1777–1842), British politician and art collector; he was the son of the Marchioness of Hertford, 195, 199

Hertford, Marchioness of = Isabella Anne Ingram (1759–1834), wife of the 2nd Marquess of Herford (d. 1822), mother of the 3rd Marquess of Herford, and mistress of King George IV when he was Prince of Wales; Pückler visited her at Temple Newsam, which she inherited in 1807 upon her mother's death, 191, 297

Hesse, Elector of = likely William I (1743–1821), 326

Hester, Lady. See Stanhope, Lady

Hill, Sir Rowland Hill (1495–1561), Lord Mayor of London, 700n2 (Letter 10)

Hippocrates (ca. 460–370 BC), the ancient Greek physician called the father of western medicine, 47

Hobbema, Meindert (1638–1709), Dutch landscape painter, 219

Hodson. See Hudson, Thomas

Hoffmann, E. T. A. (Ernst Theodor Wilhelm, 1776–1822), a well-known and multitalented German Romantic author, 217, 328, 475, 663, 705n35 (Letter 15), 708n22 (Letter 20), 708n11 (Letter 21), 720n24 (Letter 47)

Hoffmann, Johann Gottfried (1765–1847), German professor and political scientist, 720n24 (Letter 47)

Hohenhausen, Elise von (1789–1857), a writer with a successful salon in Berlin, 397–98, 711n24 (Letter 25)

Hohenhausen, Leopold von (1779–1848), Berlin writer and journalist, and the husband of Elise von Hohenhausen, 397–98, 711n24 (Letter 25)

Holbein, Hans the Younger (ca. 1497–1543), German Renaissance artist, 39, 120, 121, 141, 148, 267, 280, 304, 648, 700n7 (Letter 9), 719n9 (Letter 46)

Holberg, Ludvig (1684–1754), Danish writer of the Enlightenment who was especially known for his thirty-three comedies, 654, 719n18 (Letter 46)

Holland, Lord = Henry Richard Fox Vasall (1773–1840), an important liberal politician and the nephew of Charles James Fox, 209

Holofernes, biblical general who was beheaded by Judith, 173

Homer, ancient Greek author of the *Iliad* and the *Odyssey*, 23, 718n4 (Letter 44)

Hookes, Nicholas (ca. 1550–1637), named on an inscription on a seventeenth-century slab in the Church of Saint Mary and All Saints in Conwy as the forty-first child of his father and himself the father of twenty-seven children, 438–39

Hope, Mrs. = Louisa de la Poer Beresford, married Thomas Hope in 1806, 187, 196, 219, 703n9 (Letter 13)

Hope, Thomas (1769–1831), Dutch and British merchant banker, author, interior designer, and art collector who was known for his very successful novel, *Anastasius: Or Memoirs of a Greek* (which was originally published anonymously) as well as for *Household Furniture and Interior Decoration* (1807) and books on costume, architecture, and philosophy, 90, 187, 196, 219, 703n9 (Letter 13)

Hopper, Thomas (1776–1856), English architect known especially for his designs for country houses, such as Penrhyn Castle, 711n30 (Letter 25)

Horace (65–8 BC), Roman poet, 39, 104, 179, 698n9 (Letter 3), 700n2 (Letter 8), 703n32 (Letter 12)

Horatius Cocles (sixth century BC), officer in the Roman army, 613

Horn, Franz Christoph (1783–1837), German writer and literary historian whose five-volume commentary on Shakespeare's plays (*Shakespeares Schauspiele*) appeared in 1823–1831, 348

Hotspur, Percy. *See* Percy, Sir Henry

Houwald, Christian Ernst, Freiherr von (1778–1845), German writer and dramatist, 304

Howth, Thomas St Lawrence, 3rd Earl of Howth (1803–1874), a descendent of the medieval knight Sir Armoricus Tristram, 585, 606

Hudson, Thomas (1701–1779), English portrait painter, 141, 701n19 (Letter 10)

Hughes, Colonel = William Lewis Hughes (1767–1852), colonel in the Anglesey Milita, member of Parliament, philanthropist, and owner of the Parys Mines and Kinmel Park, where he founded a free school for local girls in 1830; his brother, whom Pückler refers to on page 446, was probably James Hughes (1778–1845); his daughter Fanny (Frances Margaret) Hughes, (1814–1847) would have been not yet fourteen when

she toured Pückler around, although she was not the youngest, as there were other daughters still alive at the time, 439, 442–43, 445, 446, 713n25 (Letter 27)

Humboldt, Alexander von (1769–1859), Prussian naturalist, explorer, and a founder of modern geography, 664, 700n19 (Letter 7)

Hume, Joseph (1777–1855), Scottish doctor and member of Parliament, 204

Hunt, Henry, won a hundred guineas on 17 January 1826 in a wager that he could drive the van of his father's company, Hunt's Matchless Blacking, across Hyde Park's frozen Serpentine, 160, *161*

Hus, Jan (ca. 1372–1415), Catholic priest from Czechoslovakia, burned at the stake for heresy by the Roman Catholic Church, 600

Huysum, Jan van (1682–1749), Dutch painter of landscapes and still lifes, 219

Hymenaios, the Greek god of marriage ceremonies, 406

Hyperion, one of the horses Pückler brought to England, named after the Greek god, 269

I

Ibrahim Pasha of Egypt = Ibrahim Basha (1789–1848), Egyptian general who was defeated at the Battle of Navarino, 449

Iffland, August Wilhelm (1759–1814), German playwright, actor, and theater director, from 1779 in Mannheim and from 1796 in Berlin, 135, 348, 573, 663

Irving, Washington (1783–1859), American diplomat and writer, 200, 610, 718n9 (Letter 43)

Isabel de Requesens (1500–1577), wife of Ramón de Cordona, viceroy of Naples, *119*, 700n4 (Letter 9)

Isolani, Johann Ludwig Hektor von (1586–1650), the imperial general of the Croats in the Thirty Years' War and a character in Schiller's *The Death of Wallenstein*, 395

J

Jackson, Andrew (1767–1845), president of the United States beginning in 1829, 397

Jacquet, François-Henri (1778–after 1848), successor to Jean-André Getti as the maker of plaster casts for the Louvre, 667

Jahn, Friedrich Ludwig (1778–1852), introduced the importance of physical exercises to Germany in 1811, gaining renown as the "father of gymnastics"; he was arrested, kept in confinement, and sentenced to two years in prison when gymnastics was banned as politically suspect from 1820 to 1842, 712n33 (Letter 25), 718n5 (Letter 43)

James, a friend of Pückler's, 491, 494

James I (1566–1625), king of England, Ireland, and Scotland, 148, 360, 539

James II (1633–1701), the last Catholic king of England, Ireland, and Scotland, 637, 714n4 (Letter 33), 719n12 (Letter 45)

Jaquier, Lewis (his will dated 1828) was the "Gentleman" of Clarendon Hotel in New Bond Street; Pückler may be referring to his son, 32

Jaquotot, Marie-Victoire (Madame J) (1772–1855), French porcelain painter who worked at the Sèvres factory until 1842, 148

Javoureck, Constance (also Jawureck) (1803–1858), French mezzo-soprano, 663

Jean Paul, pen name of Johann Paul Friedrich Richter (1763–1825), German writer of the Romantic era, 425, 714n3 (Letter 32)

Jeremias, perhaps a reference to an excessively pious Berlin preacher, 335

Jersey, Lady = likely Sarah Villiers, Countess of Jersey (1785–1867), one of the Lady Patronesses of Almack's, 210, 227

Joanny, the stage name of French actor Jean-Bernard Baptiste Brisebarre (1775–1849), 679, 684

John (1166–1216), king of England, the youngest and favorite son of Henry II, he also held the title "Lord of Ireland" from 1185–1216, 289, 386–87, 483, 548, 707n6 (Letter 19), 716n15 (Letter 36)

Johnson, Dr. = Samuel Johnson (1709–1784), publisher of the first English dictionary, 387

Johnston, Alexander (1775–1849), British colonial official who served as chief justice of Ceylon and participated in the founding of the Royal Asiatic Society, 193

Joseph, Emperor = Joseph II, Holy Roman Emperor (1741–1790), eldest son of Maria Theresa, 293

Josephine. *See* Lady Olivia Clarke

Josephine de Beauharnais, Empress (1763–1814), Napoleon's first wife, who was crowned empress in 1804, 361, 671, 672

Julie, the pseudonym Pückler uses for his wife Countess Lucie von Pappenheim, née Hardenberg (1776–1854), daughter of Karl August von Hardenberg, 18, 23, 24, 71, 104, 107, 110, 115, 132, 144, 149, 151, 153, 161, 166, 170, 174, 181, 182, 183, 189, 193, 194, 199, 211, 212, 216, 222, 224, 239, 240, 242, 248, 253, 259, 265, 268, 269, 272, 275, 280, 285, 316, 332, 335, 337, 358, 365, 383, 411, 412, 415, 422, 423, 430, 434, 436, 485, 489, 510, 513, 516, 533, 535, 538, 540, 544, 555, 562, 567, 573, 577, 587, 588, 590, 593, 597, 605, 617, 619, 621, 631, 648, 671, 708n25 (Letter 20), 717n5 (Letter 41)

Jupiter, the king of the gods in Roman mythology, 232, 526, 667, 688, 721n35 (Letter 48)

K

Kamehameha II (1797–1824), the second king of the kingdom of Hawaii, 404

Kant, Immanuel (1724–1804), German philosopher, 613

Karl August, Grand Duke of Saxe-Weimar-Eisenach (1757–1828), under whom Pückler served in the wars against Napoleon; he was known for the brilliance of his court; his wife was the Grand Duchess Louise Auguste of Hesse-Darmstadt (1757–1830) and his son was the Hereditary Grand Duke Karl Friedrich von Saxe-Weimar-Eisenach, 697n6, 15 (Letter 1), 708n9 (Letter 21)

Karl Bernhard of Saxe-Weimar-Eisenach, Prince and Duke (1792–1862), travel writer, military commander, mathematician, and the seventh son of Grand Duke Karl August, 20, 697n9 (Letter 1)

Karl Friedrich of Saxe-Weimar-Eisenach, Hereditary Grand Duke (1783–1853), the eldest son of Grand Duke Karl August; he was married to the Grand Duchess Maria Pavlovna (1786–1859), the daughter of Emperor Paul I of Russia and sister of Emperor Alexander I of Russia, 23–24, 697n15–16 (Letter 1)

Kaunitz = Wenzel Anton, Prince of Kaunitz-Rietberg (1711–1794), Austrian prince and statesman who served in various influential posts under the Habsburgs, 293

Kean, Edmund (1787–1833), English actor, 73, 348, 349–50, 356

Keith, Lady. *See* Flahaut, Countess of

Kemble, Charles (1775–1854), English actor and the director of the theater at Covent Garden, 73, 83, 86, 87, 88, 308, 348, 349–50, 356, 368

Kemble, John Philip (1757–1823), a famous Shakespearean actor and the elder brother of Charles Kemble, 451, 713n10 (Letter 28)

Kenmare, Lady, likely Augusta Anne Wilmot (1798–1873), wife of Valentine Browne, 2nd Earl of Kenmare, 507

Kenmare, Lords of; the title Earl of Kenmare was created in the Irish peerage in 1801; the brothers at the time of Pückler's visit were Valentine Browne, 2nd Earl of Kenmare (1788–1853) and Thomas Browne, 3rd Earl of Kenmare (1789–1871), 510

Kent, (Victoria) Duchess of = Princess Victoria of Saxe-Coburg Saalfeld (1786–1861), mother of the future Queen Victoria, 213, 229

Keppel, George Thomas, 6th Earl of Albemarle (1799–1891), British soldier, writer, and politician who published several accounts of his travels to India, Assyria, and the Balkans, 220

Kerner, Justinus (1786–1862), German poet and physician who wrote about medical subjects and animal magnetism, 722n3 (second preface)

Kevin, Saint (d. 618), the abbot of Glendalough, Ireland, 463, 713n4 (Letter 29)

Kiesewetter, Raphael Georg (1773–1850), Austrian singer, pianist, and music historian, 370

King, Lord Peter (1776–1833), English politician who served in the House of Lords, 209

King, Mary Elizabeth (ca. 1780–1819), the third daughter of the 2nd Earl of Kingston, 546, 716n12–13 (Letter 36)

Kingston, Lord = George King, 3rd Earl of Kingston, Lord Kingsborough (1771–1839), son of Robert; when not yet twenty, he ran off with a young woman to the West Indies, returning in 1794 to marry Lady Helena Moore; inheriting Mitchelstown upon his father's death, he demolished the family residence and replaced it with the neo-Gothic Mitchelstown Castle that Pückler criticizes in some detail, 546–47, 716n14 (Letter 36)

Kingston, Lord = Robert King, 2nd Earl of Kingston (1754–1799), father of George; he acquired Mitchelstown estate through his 1769 marriage to his cousin, Caroline Fitzgerald (1755–1823), with whom he had ten children; in 1798 he was tried and acquitted of murdering Henry Gerald FitzGerald for having run off with King's daughter, Mary Elizabeth, 545–47, 716n11 (Letter 36)

Kirkpatrick, a criminal, 274

Kitty, a daughter of Captain Bermingham, 489–90, 491

Kotzebue, August von (1761–1819), a popular and prolific German playwright who ridiculed the liberal ideals of the new student associations and was assassinated by the student Karl Sand, 222, 248, 350, 654, 699n23 (Letter 6), 709n11 (Letter 22), 711n20 (Letter 24), 712n32–33 (Letter 25), 719n18 (Letter 46)

Kotzebue, Otto von (1787–1846), German navigator and the son of August von Kotzebue; he undertook three voyages around the world as a Russian marine officer and published several volumes describing his voyages, 404

Krug, Wilhelm Traugott (1770–1842), German philosopher and follower of Kant; he was a prolific and widely read writer and a professor at the University of Leipzig, 582, 708n3 (Letter 21)

Kruse, Laurids (1778–1840), Danish-born writer known for his crime stories; he published what some consider to be the first detective story in the German language, *Der krystallene Dolch* (The Crystal Dagger), 398

Kühleborn, a water spirit in the novella *Undine* by Fouqué, 458

L

La Touche, Peter (1775?–1830), Irish politician, banker, and owner of the estates of Luggala and Bellevue, 713n6 (Letter 29)

Lady Patronesses, the official distributors of tickets to Almack's balls, 171, 172, 206, 376, 378–79

Lainé. *See* Lenné, Peter Joseph

Lalande, Jérôme (1732–1807), French astronomer and writer, 530, 614

Lamothe-Langon, Etienne-Léon de (1786–1864), French writer, 684, 721n19 (Letter 48)

Lancaster, Joseph (1778–1838), the founder of the so-called Lancasterian schools, which were elementary schools in which advanced students taught less advanced ones; these schools were established in several countries and were particularly important in England from 1798 to 1830, when they were superseded by a system that grouped students by age and employed lecturers, 367, 368, 687–88, 710n1 (Letter 24)

Landaff, Earl = Francis James Mathew, 2nd Earl Landaff (1768–1833), Irish politician who transformed the family residence into the neo-Gothic Thomastown Castle, 552, 565

Landseer, Sir Edwin Henry (1802–1873), English painter and sculptor, 239, 705n27 (Letter 16)

Langsalm, Herr von, a character in a farce by Kotzebue, 348, 709n11 (Letter 22)

Langschwert, Richard. *See* Longespée, William

Lannoy, Heinrich Eduard Josef von (1787–1853), a gifted Viennese amateur composer of several melodramas, 720n7 (Letter 47)

Lansdowne, Lady = Mary Arabella Marchioness of Lansdowne (1764–1833), widow of John Petty, 2nd Marquess of Lansdowne (1765–1809); she was Pückler's fiancée but jilted him in 1815 (though remained his friend); she resided at Hampton Court at the time of Pückler's visit, 45, 154

Lansdowne, Lord = Henry Petty-Fitzmaurice, 3rd Marquess of Lansdowne (1780–1863), a half brother of Lady Lansdowne's deceased husband and an important politician in the administration of George Canning, 209, 709n1 (Letter 23)

Laocoön, a tragic figure of Greek and Roman myth, 194

Laporte, Pierre-François (1799–1841), French actor who became manager of the King's Theatre (now called Her Majesty's Theatre) in London in 1828, 96

Lauderdale, James Maitland, 8th Earl of (1759–1839), Scottish politician, member of Parliament, friend, and adviser to Lady Lansdowne, 347

Lavater, Johann Kaspar (1741–1801), Swiss poet and physiognomist, 233, 661

Lawless, John (ca. 1773–1837), Irish nationalist and newspaper publisher, 595

Lawrence, Thomas, Sir (1769–1830), English portrait painter, 139–40, 211, 238, 239, 295

Le Sueur, Eustache (1617–1655), French painter and one of the twelve founders of the Académie Royale, 667

Leeds, Duke of = George Osborne, 6th Duke of Leeds (1775–1838), British politician, 285

Lees, Edward Smith (1783–1846), secretary of the Irish Post Office, 605, 606

Leicester, Earl of = Dudley, Robert, 1st Earl of Leicester (1532–1588), a favorite of Queen Elizabeth I and a figure in Schiller's *Maria Stuart;* she lived at Kenilworth Castle in Warwickshire and was buried in the Collegiate Church of St Mary, Warwick, 126, 141, 213, 704n26 (Letter 15)

Lejeune = Louis François, Baron Lejeune (1775–1848), French painter, lithographer, and general who participated in many Napoleonic campaigns that later became the subjects of his battle paintings, 343, *344, 345,* 709n6 (Letter 22)

Lely, Sir Peter (1618–1660), a painter born in Westphalia to Dutch parents whose career was spent in England, where he was the major painter to the court of Charles I and Charles II, 141

Lenclos, Anne "Ninon" de (1620–1705), French beauty, courtesan, writer, and patron of the arts known for the intellectual quality of her salon and for her many famous lovers, 148, 364

Lenné, Peter Joseph (1789–1866), renowned landscape architect, general director of the Royal Prussian Gardens, and designer of the English Garden in Munich, 129

Lennox, Lord William Pitt (1799–1881), British army officer, unexceptional and impecunious writer, and first husband of soprano Mary Ann Paton, 72

Lenore, the title figure in a ballad by Gottfried August Bürger, 179, 703n34 (Letter 12)

Lenz, Jakob Michael Reinhold (1751–1792), German writer of the Sturm und Drang who was friendly with Goethe; he followed him to Weimar in 1776, but was expelled from court shortly thereafter, 22

Leonardo da Vinci (1452–1519), Italian Renaissance painter, sculptor, and scientist, 343, 667, 709n5 (Letter 22)

Leopold, Prince = Leopold Prince of Saxe-Coburg and Gotha (1790–1865), and Leopold I of Belgium from 1831 until his death, 359

Leopold III, Frederick Franz, Duke of Anhalt-Dessau (1740–1817), created the enormous landscape park at Wörlitz, 712n1 (Letter 27)

Lesage, Alain-René (1668–1747), French translator, novelist, and playwright best known for his novel *Gil Blas,* 718n4 (Letter 43)

Lesage, pseudonym of Emmanuel, comte de Las Cases (1766–1842), French historian who published *Atlas historique généalogique chronologique géographique* in 1802–1804, 337

Lessing, Gotthold Ephraim (1729–1781), German writer and philosopher of the Enlightenment, 323, 708n3 (Letter 21), 712n8 (Letter 27)

L'Estrange, Father = Francis Joseph L'Estrange" (d. 1833), for many years O'Connell's confessor, 524–25, 597, 600

Letizia, Madame. *See* Bonaparte, Letizia

Lewis, Matthew (1775–1818), English writer and dramatist, 720n7 (Letter 47)

Lieven, Prince, Russian ambassador to London from 1812 to 1834, 327, 364, 708n11 (Letter 20)

Lieven, Princess = Dorothea von Lieven, née Benckendorff (1785–1857), Prussian-born wife of Prince Lieven and a major London hostess; she gave Pückler a voucher to his first Almack's and was his supporter until their falling out, 171, 229, 327, 708n11 (Letter 20), 710n12 (Letter 24)

Linwood, Miss = Mary Linwood (1755–1845), English schoolmistress who gained international fame for her embroidered copies of Old Master paintings, 250–51, 706n43 (Letter 16)

Lister, Thomas Henry (1800–1842), English novelist, 697n19 (Letter 1)

Liston, John (ca. 1776–1846), English comic actor whose impersonation of Paul Pry (in the farce *Paul Pry* by John Poole) became so famous that images of him in that role were legion, even found stamped on butter, 67, 68, 205–6, 509

Listowel, Countess of = Anne Latham (1778–1859), London hostess who was married to William Hare, 1st Earl of Listowel (Irish peer and member of Parliament), and who resided at Kingston House, Knightsbridge, 211–12

Liverpool, Lord = Robert Jenkinson, 2nd Earl of Liverpool (1770–1828), British politician and prime minister of the United Kingdom from 1812 until April 1827, when he suffered a massive stroke; he died eight months later, 82, 184

Llangollen, Ladies of = Eleanor Charlotte Butler (1739–1829) and Sarah Ponsonby (1755–1831), celebrated Irish spinsters who fled to Wales, where they lived together in semi-seclusion, 389, *390, 391*

Llywelyn = Llywelyn the Last, prince of Gwynedd (ca. 1223–1282), grandson of Llywelyn the Great and last prince of Wales before it was conquered by Edward I, 412

Llywelyn the Great (ca. 1172–1240), prince of Gwynedd and ruler of Wales, often linked to the legendary story of his faithful hound, Gelert, 432–33

Locke, John (1632–1704), English philosopher, known as the Father of Liberalism, 141

Londonderry, Lady = Amelia Anne Stewart, Marchioness of Londonderry (1772–1829), often referred to as Emily Stewart; she was a sister-in-law of Frances Vane, and the wife of Lord Castlereagh, 2nd Marquess of Londonderry, who served as British Ambassador to Austria (1814–1823) and assisted in the negotiations at the Congress of Vienna; the Russian Emperor, Alexander I was a great admirer, contributing generously to her very extensive collection of jewels, 191

Londonderry, Lady = Frances Anne Vane, Marchioness of Londonderry (1800–1865), heiress, society hostess, and business-woman; she was the second wife of Charles Vane, 3rd Marquess of Londonderry (married 1819), with whom she developed extensive coal mining operations, 214, *215,* 216, 220, 232

Longespée, William, 3rd Earl of Salisbury (ca. 1176–1226), the first person known to be buried in Salisbury Cathedral; the half brother of King John and the illegitmate son of Henry II, he brought the Magna Carta to Salisbury, 646, 719n7 (Letter 46)

Longsword, Richard. *See* Longespée, William

Lorrain. *See* Claude Gellée

Lot, an Old Testament figure seduced by his daughters, 138

Lottum, Count = likely Hermann Friedrich von Wylich und Lottum (1796–1847), career diplomat and later ambassador at The Hague; Lottum was Pückler's best friend in England and secured him entrée into the Travellers Club, 67, 71, 91, 100, 113, 255, 259, 261, 269, 294, 310, 316, 321, 325, 326, 402–7, 415, 425–26, 712n5 (Letter 27)

Louis le Grand. *See* Louis XIV

Louis XIV (1638–1715), king of France from 1643–1715, known as Louis the Great and the Sun King, 92, 153, 185–86, 271, 276, 278, 357, 365, 680, 686, 703n7 (Letter 13), 720n13 (Letter 47)

Louis XV (1710–1774), great-grandson of Louis XIV and king of France from 1715–1774, 205, 372, 660, 720n9, 21 (Letter 47)

Louis XVIII (1755–1824), a Bourbon who lived in exile for twenty-three years, six of which were in England at Hartwell House in Buckinghamshire; he returned to France after Napoleon I's abdication in 1814, when the Bourbons were invited to re-assume the throne, and he reigned as king of France from 1814–1824, except for the Hundred Days in 1815 when he fled Paris after Napoleon's return from Elba, 145, 701n30 (Letter 10)

Louise, Queen of Prussia (1776–1810), wife of Frederick William III, 703n18 (Letter 12)

Louise Auguste. *See* Karl August, Grand Duke of Saxe-Weimar-Eisenach

Loulé, Duchess of = Infanta Ana de Jesus Maria, Marquesa de Loulé (1806–1857), daughter of John VI of Portugal, sister of Dom Miguel, and husband of the Marquis de Loulé (the future Duke of Loulé, married in 1827); scandal followed her nonroyal marriage and the birth of their first child only days after their wedding, 352

Love, Lady, perhaps an oblique reference to Princess Lieven, 307

Lovelace = Robert Loveless, the aristocratic seducer and decadently evil antagonist in the 1748 novel *Clarissa* by Samuel Richardson (1689–1761), 320

Loyola, (Saint) Ignatius of (1491–1556), Spanish knight, priest, and theologian; he founded the Society of Jesus (Jesuits) and was canonized in 1622, 121

Lucien = Lucien Bonaparte (1775–1840), Napoleon's younger brother, 671, 672–73, 711n24 (Letter 24), 721n4 (Letter 48)

Ludwig I (1786–1868), king of Bavaria, 667

Luther, Martin (1483–1546), German monk who ignited the Protestant Reformation, 141, 142, 148, 267, 426, 582, 590, 600, 614, 704n16 (Letter 14)

Luttrell, Henry (1765–1851), popular English writer of fashionable verse prized for his wit, 353

Lynch, Edward. *See* Lynch, James

Lynch, James = James Lynch fitz Stephen, mayor of Galway from 1493 to 1494; according to legend he hanged his own son for murder in 1493; the other characters in Pückler's retelling of the story are the son, Edward Lynch; Edward's sister (unnamed); Gomez, a Spanish merchant; his son Gonzalvo; and Anna Blake, Edward's wife, 495–99, 500, 714n15 (Letter 32)

Lysicrates, a wealthy Athenian who erected a monument celebrating the dramatic arts, known as the Choragic Monument of Lysicrates, in 335 BC, 638

Lytton. *See* Bulwer-Lytton, Edward

M

Macbeth, the tragic hero of Shakespeare's play *The Tragedy of Macbeth*, 308–11, 326, 346, 708n19 (Letter 20)

Macbeth, Lady, the wife of the title character in Shakespeare's tragedy, 309–11, 708n21 (Letter 20)

Mac Carthaigh, Cormac (d. 1138), king of Munster, who built a palace (now in ruins) and Cormac's Chapel (ca. 1130) on the Rock of Cashel, 551, 716n1 (Letter 37)

Maccarnell, in some editions the spelling for Cormac, king and archbishop of Cashel. *See* Mac Carthaigh, Cormac; Mac-Cuilennáin, Cormac

Mac-Cuilennáin, Cormac (d. 908), Irish bishop and king of Munster, who is often associated with the Rock of Cashel, 716n1 (Letter 37)

MacDonell, an eccentric Scotsman whom Pückler meets and calls Mr. MacDonell, Duke of Clanronald and Glengarry; he was likely the flamboyant Alexander Ranaldson MacDonell of Glengarry (1773–1828), the model for Scott's wild chieftain in *Waverley*, 173, 174, 703n17, 22 (Letter 12)

Macduff, a character in Shakespeare's *Macbeth*, 311, 361, 708n19 (Letter 20), 710n17 (Letter 23)

MacFarlane, O'Connor, Irish fortune hunter, a role played by Lady Clarke in a skit performed at Lady Morgan's, 601

Machiavelli, Niccolo (1469–1527), Italian historian and political theorist, 118, 120, 700n6 (Letter 9)

Macpherson, James (1736–1796), Scottish writer now best known for publishing wildly successful translations of poems by a third-century Gaelic bard named Ossian, which were, in fact, essentially his own compositions, 449

Macready, William Charles (1793–1873), English actor whose performance of Macbeth Pückler greatly admires, 310–11, 313

Madocks, William Alexander (1773–1828), born into a wealthy London family, he inherited land in North Wales, purchased more, and undertook an ambitious plan, which almost ruined him, to reclaim a large area from the sea by constructing an embankment and building a model town, Tremadog, on the reclaimed land across Traeth Mawr, 434

Maintenon, Madame = Françoise d'Aubigné, Marquise de Maintenon (1635–1719), the second, morganatic wife of King Louis XIV of France in 1684; she began a long correspondence with the Princess des Ursins that was published as *Lettres inédites de Mme de Maintenon et de Mme la princesse des Ursins* (4 vols., 1826); it was translated into English the following year

as *The Secret Correspondence of Madame de Maintenon, with the Princess des Ursins* (3 vols.), 271, 276

Maistre, Xavier de (1763–1852), French writer and general who served under Tsar Alexander I, 721n33 (Letter 48)

Malcolm = Sir John Malcolm (1769–1833), Scottish statesman and historian who served many years in the Middle East and wrote several books about Persia and India, 249, 706n41 (Letter 16)

Malibran, Madame Maria, née García (1808–1836), Spanish mezzo-soprano who was born into a musical family in Paris and who first performed at the age of eight; she returned to Europe after successes in London and New York, debuting in Paris at the Théâtre-Lyrique Italien in 1828, 684

Malone, Edmond (1741–1812), English scholar who, in 1793, persuaded the vicar of Holy Trinity Church, Stratford-upon-Avon, to whitewash the bust of Shakespeare on the poet's funerary monument; the original colors were restored in 1861, 135

Mansfield, Lord = David William Murray, 3rd Earl of Mansfield (1777–1840), husband of Frederica Markham (1774–1860); he inherited Kenwood House in 1796 and proceeded to alter and improve it, 98

Maria II of Portugal (1819–1853), 692n8 (Letter 7)

Maria Pavlovna, Grand Duchess of Russia (1786–1859), daughter of Paul I of Russia and Sophie Dorothea of Württemberg, wife of Karl Friedrich, Grand Duke of Saxe-Weimar-Eisenach, 697n16 (Letter 1)

Marie Antoinette (1755–1793), archduchess of Austria and the last queen of France, 146, 685

Marie Louise (1791–1847), second wife of Napoleon, empress of France from 1810 to 1814, and later duchess of Parma, 229, 705n16, 25 (Letter 16)

Marlborough, 1st Duke of = John Churchill (1650–1722), English general and politician, ancestor of Sir Winston Churchill; his residence, Blenheim Palace, was originally intended as a gift to the duke in gratitude for his military victory over the French, and subsequently became the residence of the dukes of Marlborough for three centuries; his affair with the Countess of Castlemaine generated many tales, 137, 138–39, 273, 699n3 (Letter 6), 701n7 (Letter 10), 716n7 (Letter 38)

Marlborough, 5th Duke of. *See* Spencer-Churchill

Mars, Mademoiselle = Anne Françoise Hyppolyte Boutet (1779–1847), French actress, 660, 673

Marten, Henry (1602–1680), one of the commissioners who signed the death warrant of Charles I in 1649; he was later exiled and imprisoned in Chepstow Castle from 1668 until his death, 631, 718n1 (Letter 45)

Mary, Queen of Scots (1542–1587), also known as Mary Stuart, queen of Scotland; her first marriage to the dauphin of France ended in his death in 1560; she returned to Scotland and married her cousin Lord Darnley (d. 1567) in 1565 and James Hepburn, 4th Earl of Bothwell in 1567; fleeing an uprising, she fled south to seek protection from her cousin Elizabeth I, but she was suspected of treachery, held captive for eighteen years, and executed on Elizabeth's orders, 121, 141, 298, 460, 585, 700n8 (Letter 9)

Mary I (1516–1558), daughter of Henry VIII and queen of England and Ireland from 1553 until her death in 1558; known as "Bloody Mary" by her critics, she had her successor, Elizabeth I, imprisoned in the Tower of London for two months and then returned to house arrest at Hatfield House, 319, 614

Masséna, André (1758–1817), Duke of Rivoli, Prince of Essling, and commander during the Revolutionary and Napoleonic wars, 672

Mathews, Charles (1776–1835), English actor who became famous for his one-man performance *At Home*, 93–94

Maurice, Prince of Orange (1567–1625), military leader and stadtholder of the republic of the Netherlands, 304

Maury, Abbé = Jean-Sifrein (1746–1817), French cardinal and archbishop of Paris, 104

Maximilian I (king of Bavaria), 20, 229

Mazurier, Charles-François (1798–1828), French mime and comic acrobatic performer, 327

Meath, Earl of = John Brabazon, 10th Earl of Meath (1772–1851), Irish peer and owner of Killruddery, 457

Megaera, the "jealous one," one of the Furies in Greek mythology, 311

Meiningen, Duchess of (1763–1837), Louise Eleanore of Hohenlohe-Langenburg, Saxe-Coburg-Meiningen, mother of the Duchess of Clarence, 362

Melpomene, the Greek muse of tragedy, 640, 664

Melville, Lady, perhaps Anne Saunders (d. 1841), wife of Robert Dundas, Viscount Melville, with whom she had two daughters, 192

Melville, Lord. *See* Dundas, Robert

Mengs, Anton Raphael (1728–1779), German painter who worked in Italy; he was influenced by Johann Joachim Winckelmann and a precursor to neoclassical painting, 141

Merkel, Garlieb (1769–1850), German writer who strove to improve the plight of Baltic peasants, 329–30, 709n18 (Letter 21)

Merlin, a wizard in the legends of King Arthur, 393, 430–32, 433, 712n11 (Letter 27)

Merrilies, Meg, an old gypsy woman in *Guy Mannering*, a novel by Sir Walter Scott that was published anonymously in 1815, 486

Merveldt, Maximilian, Count von (1764–1815), Austrian military envoy to the Court of Saint James from 1814 to 1815, and a popular figure in English society, 154, 702n3 (Letter 11)

Metastasio, Pietro (1698–1782), Italian poet and librettist, 713n12 (Letter 28)

Metternich, Klemens Wenzel, Prince of (1773–1859), an influential conservative politician and statesman who served as foreign minister of the Holy Roman Empire and the Austrian Empire, 37, 214, 346, 698n6 (Letter 3)

Michelangelo (1475–1564), Italian Renaissance artist, 135

Middleton, Lord = Henry Willoughby, 6th Baron Middleton (1761–1835), whose family seat was Wollaton Hall, 301

Miguel I, usually known as Dom Miguel (1802–1866), king of Portugal from 1828 to 1834; he met Pückler while briefly in London (December 30, 1827, to January 13, 1828) before returning to Portugal to assume the role of regent and then king, 326–27, 352, 673, 699n8 (Letter 7), 710n6 (Letter 23), 721n4 (Letter 48)

Mina, Francisco Espoz y (1781–1838), Spanish guerrilla leader and general who fought against the French intervention in Spain in 1823 and was allowed to escape to England, where he stayed for about a decade, 347

Minellius, Johannes (1625 1683), influential Dutch grammarian, 697n3 (first preface)

Minto, Lady = Mary Brydone, Countess of Minto (1786–1853), 172

Mirabeau = Honoré Gabriel de Riqueti, comte de Mirabeau (1749–1791), renowned writer, diplomat, orator, and leading figure in the French Revolution, 293

Moeller, Ludwig (Lewis), K. H. C. privy counselor of the Hanoverian legation in London (1829–1834) and secretary to the Hanoverian Guelphic Order, 249, 326

Monk, George, Duke of Albemarle (1608–1670), English general under Cromwell and Charles II, 298

Montagu, Elizabeth Robinson (1720–1800), a social leader, writer, and friend of many intellectuals, who hosted an annual May Day party for London chimney sweeps; the story that Pückler tells about her kidnapped

son (*see* Montagu, George Browne) is apocryphal, 43, 45

Montagu, George Browne, 8th Viscount (1769–1793), an Englishman who drowned, along with his friend Charles Sedley Burdett (possibly Pückler's Mr. Barnett), when they tried to ride a boat over the Rhine Falls; this seems the basis for the story Pückler hears from his cicerone, Mr. Tournier; there is, however, no connection between this man and Elizabeth Montagu of Montagu House on Portman Square, Mayfair, whose only son died in infancy, 42–45, 698n13 (Letter 3)

Montagu, Lay Mary Wortley (1689–1762), English writer, known especially for her letters about Turkey, where she lived from 1716 to 1718, when her husband was the British ambassador, 359

Montaigne, Michel de (1533–1592), French philosopher, 593, 717n21 (Letter 41)

Montgomery, Roger de, 1st Earl of Shrewsbury (d. 1084), a major counselor to William the Conqueror and founder of Shrewsbury Abbey in 1094, 619

Montmorency, Anne, duc de (1493–1567), French soldier, statesman, and diplomat who became constable of France; it has been shown that the armor that Pückler admired at Wilton House (now in the Metropolitan Museum of Art, New York) belonged to Henry VIII, not to Montmorency, 648

Montrond, Monsieur de = Casimir, comte de Montrond (1766–1843), French diplomat and author who was famous for his successes in the fashionable world; he resided several times in England, 176, 220

Montrose, Duchess of = Lady Caroline Maria, the second wife of James Graham, 3rd Duke of Montrose, 192

Moore, Thomas (1779–1852), Irish poet and songwriter whom Pückler claims the Irish liked to call "Tommy," 347, 407, 463, 464, 466, 491, 709n10 (Letter 22), 712n37 (Letter 25)

Moravians, a Protestant ecclesiastical brotherhood, 404, 479

Morgan, Lady = Sydney Morgan, née Owenson (ca. 1781–1859), a well-known and prolific Irish novelist; although she was initially friendly with Pückler, she became outraged at his depiction of her in *Letters of a Dead Man*, 96, 128, 157, 454–56, 584, 588, 589, 591, 592, 593, 601, 603, 699n6 (Letter 7), 702n8, 24 (Letter 11), 717n3–4, 12–13, 21 (Letter 41), 718n1 (Letter 42)

Morgan, Thomas Charles (1783–1843), physician, philosopher, and husband of Lady Morgan, 588, 601, 717n7 (Letter 41), 718n1 (Letter 42)

Morier, James Justinian (1780–1849), British diplomat and author who went to Persia in 1810 as embassy secretary to the ambassador, Sir Gore Ouseley; he is known for novels about the Qajar dynasty in Iran, especially the *Hajji Baba* series (1824), 90, 226

Moscheles, Ignaz (1794–1870), Bohemian pianist, composer, and conductor in London from 1825 to 1846, 214, 359

Moseley, Mr., a dandy "of second rank" who Pückler meets at Chippenham, 55

Mount Charles, Lord = Henry Conyngham, 1st Marquess Conyngham, Earl of Mount Charles (1766–1832), British politician, 327

Mowbray, Roger de, 1st Baron of (d. 1297/1298), English member of parliament buried at Fountains Abbey, 290

Moynihan, an Irish family involved in a feud with the O'Donoghues, 506–7

Mozart, Wolfgang Amadeus (1756–1791), Austrian composer, 83, 216, 313, 528, 708n22 (Letter 20)

Mulgrave, Lord = Henry Phipps, 1st Earl of Mulgrave (1755–1831), British statesman; Pückler admires his alum mines and his park and castles at Mulgrave, where he is toured by the earl's sons, Constantine Phipps and Charles Beaumont Phipps, 287, 288, 289, 707n7–8 (Letter 19)

Müllner, Amandus Gottfried Adolf (1774–1829), German lawyer, dramatist, and writer from Weiáenfels who was known for being a pugnacious critic, 19

Münchhausen, a fictional character famous for his tales of mind-boggling exploits, was based on Hieronymus Carl Friedrich, Baron von Münchhausen (1720–1797), himself known for telling outrageously tall tales about his military adventures, 217, 411

Münster, Count = Ernst Friedrich Herbert Reichsgraf zu Münster-Ledenburg (1766–1839), German statesman who served as minister for Hanover in London from 1805 to 1831; his family seat in Germany was Castle Derneburg, 195, 213, 227, 326, 328

Murat, Joachim (1767–1815), a dandified, flamboyant figure who was marshal of France, king of the Two Sicilies, and husband of Napoleon's youngest sister, Caroline, 83, 343, 699n9 (Letter 6)

Murillo, Bartolomé-Esteban (1617–1682), Spanish painter of the Baroque, 138, 353

Murray, Mrs. Scott, likely August Eliza (ca. 1784–1862), a London hostess and the wife of Charles Scott Murray (1777–1827), 227

N

Nagler, Karl Ferdinand Friedrich von (1770–1846), Prussian diplomat who served as postmaster general from 1823 to 1836, quickly making the Prussian postal service a model for all Germany, 18, 650

Napier, William (1785–1860), British soldier and military historian, 710n4 (Letter 23)

Napoleon II, "King of Rome" (1811–1832), son of Napoleon and his second wife, Marie Louise of Austria, *666*, 705n16 (Letter 16)

Napoleon = Napoleon I, Napoleon Bonaparte (1769–1821), 20, 22, 33, 39, 73, 95–96, 120, 121, 163, 169–70, 176, 187, 192, 193, 207, 208, 212, 213, 228, 229, 232, 236, 250–51, 251, 255, 268, 293, 307, 323, 326, 374, 379, 380, 381, 385, 426, 466, 502, 510, 524, 544, 545, 548, 593, 594, 609, 617, 658, 659, 665, 666, 667, 671–72, 673, 680, 685, 690, 697n6 (Letter 1), 699n9 (Letter 6), 699n4 (Letter 7), 703n8 (Letter 13), 705n16, 25 (Letter 16), 706n43 (Letter 16), 709n6 (Letter 22), 710n4 (Letter 24), 712n33 (Letter 25), 716n9 (Letter 36), 716n5 (Letter 38), 718n43 (Letter 43), 720n11, 16, 21, 25, 31 (Letter 47), 721n36 (Letter 47), 721n14, 25 (Letter 48)

Napoleon's niece. *See* Bonaparte, Letizia

Nash, John (1752–1835), architect and city planner who laid out much of London, including Regent's Park, Green Park, and Saint James's Park; he also designed the Royal Pavilion in Brighton, 33, 38, 237, 254, 706n52 (Letter 16), 716n16 (Letter 36)

Nash, Richard "Beau" (1674–1762), a British dandy who served as a very influential master of ceremonies at Bath from 1705 until his death, 637, 719n10–11 (Letter 45)

Nayler, George, a man murdered on the road to Doncaster, 274

Nelson, Horatio Lord, 1st Viscount (1758–1805), English admiral who led Britain to its greatest naval victory over the Franco-Spanish fleet at the Battle of Trafalgar (October 21, 1805), where he was mortally wounded, 448, 713n8 (Letter 28)

Nemesis, an ancient Greek goddess of divine retribution, 381, 405, 604

Nero, a lion on display at the Exeter Change, *40, 42, 44,* 213

Nero (37–68), Roman emperor, 235, 292, 671

Nestor, a king and hero known in ancient Greek legend for his bravery, 280

Neville, Richard. *See* Warwick, Richard Neville, 16th Earl of

Newcastle, Duke of = Henry Pelham-Clinton, 4th Duke of Newcastle, a vehement conservative and leader of the "Ultra-Tory" faction, 352

Newton, Sir Isaac (1642–1727), English physicist, mathematician, and astronomer, 304, 599, 614

Noblet, Lise, stage name of Marie-Élisabeth Noblet (1801–1852), French ballerina who performed the role of Fenella in *La Muette de Portici* at the Paris Opera Ballet in 1828, 661, 663

Noel, Anne Isabella Milbanke (1792–1860), wife of Lord Byron, 264, 466, 706n11 (Letter 17), 713n9 (Letter 29)

Norfolk, Duke of = Bernard Edward Howard, 12th Duke of (1765–1842), resided at Arundel Castle, 303–4, 707–8n3 (Letter 20)

Norfolk, Duke of = Charles Howard, 11th Duke of (1746–1815), cousin of the 12th Duke, was responsible for major rebuilding of Arundel Castle, 303–4, 707–8n3 (Letter 20)

Northumberland, Duke of = Hugh Percy, 3rd Duke of (1785–1847), Tory politician and aristocrat; the London residences of the Percy family included Syon House and Northumberland House, 98, 214, 224

Nourrit, the elder = Louis (1780–1831), French tenor, 661

Nourrit, the young = Adolphe (1802–1839), renowned French operatic tenor who was especially associated with works by Rossini; he followed his father as the principal singer of the Paris Opéra in 1826, 663

Nürnberger, Joseph Emil (1779–1848), German writer of articles and books of astrological-astronomical fantasy, 358, 687, 710n11 (Letter 23)

O

Oakeley, William Griffith (1790–1835), owner of the Tan-y-Bwlch estate in Wales, 713n19 (Letter 27)

O'Brien, Donal Mór (Domhnall Mór O Briain) (1168–1194), king of Limerick who founded a cathedral (Holy Cross Abbey) on the Rock of Cashel in ca. 1170; Saint Patrick's Cathedral, now occupying the site, was built in the thirteenth century, 551, 557, 571, 716n2 (Letter 37)

O'Connell, a relative of Daniel O'Connell, 501–2, 528

O'Connell, Daniel (1775–1847), Irish politician who fought for Catholic emancipation; he was elected to the British House of Commons in May 1828, but, as a Catholic, he could not take the Protestant oath and was at first refused a seat in Westminster, 474, 511, 515, 517, 519, 520, 521–22, 523, 524–26, 535, 547, 548, 553, 554, 594–96, 600, 714n6 (Letter 30), 715n9, 11 (Letter 34), 716n12 (Letter 38)

O'Donoghue, legendary Irish chieftain said to rise annually from the lakes of Killarney, 505–6, 509, 510, 714n9 (Letter 33)

O'Donovan, Dermot (or Diarmaid), Irishman hanged in 1581 by Donal Cam O'Sullivan Beare at Lathach-na n-Damh from an oak tree called Dairiheen Diarmada, 529

Odry, Charles-Joseph (1781–1863), French comic actor, 681, 721n16 (Letter 48)

O'Neill, Eliza (1791–1872), Irish actress who became a favorite on the London stage but retired from the theater after her marriage in 1819, 73, 311, 349, *602*, 603–4

Orange, friend from. *See* William I, Prince of Orange

Origen Admantius of Alexandria (185–254), an important Christian theologian, 334, 709n24 (Letter 21)

Orléans, Louis Philippe, Duke of (1773–1850), king of France from 1830 to 1848; he was responsible for major changes at the Palais Royal, his birthplace, 659

Orléans, Philippe I, Duke of (1640–1701), a younger brother of Louis XIV, 92

O'Rourke, Daniel, the titular hero of a fairy tale by Thomas Croker in *Fairy Legends and Traditions of the South of Ireland* (1825–1827), which was translated into German by the Grimm brothers in 1826, 529, 715n18 (Letter 34)

O'Rourke, Thomas. *See* O'Rourke, Daniel

Os, Jan van (1744–1808), Dutch painter known for his still life paintings, 219

Osbaldeston, George (1786–1866), revered English sportsman, 363

Ossian. *See* Macpherson, James

O'Sullivan = Donal Cam O'Sullivan Beare (1561–1613), the "last prince of Ireland," who hanged Derot O'Donovan in 1581, 529

Othello, the tragic hero of Shakespeare's play *The Tragedy of* Othello, 347–48

Otway, Thomas (1652–1685), English dramatist and author of *Venice Preserved,* which was first staged in 1682, 603

Ouseley, Gore (1770–1844), English linguist and diplomat who served as ambassador to Persia from 1810 to 1814; he resided at Woolmers, 226–27, 317–18

Ouseley, Lady = Harriet Georgina Whitelocke, wife of Sir Gore Ouseley, 320

Oxenstierna, Axel (1583–1654), an influential Swedish statesman and confidant of Gustavus Adolphus and later Queen Christina; he played an important role in the Thirty Years War, and his son, Johan, took part in negotiating the Peace of Westphalia, 590, 717n8 (Letter 41)

P

Paddy, a slang term for an Irishman, 250, 506, 569

Paget, General. *See* Anglesey, Lord

Palmela, Marquis of = Pedro de Sousa Holstein, 1st Duke of Palmela (1781–1850), Portuguese diplomat who served twice as ambassador to London, 97, 326

Palmela, Marquise of = Eugénia Francisca Xavier Teles da Gama (1798–1860), wife of the Marquis of Palmela, 211

Pangloss, an optimistic, Leibniz-inspired character in Voltaire's *Candide,* 587

Papageno, a character from Mozart's "Magic Flute," 111, 576

Pappenheim, Countess Lucie von, née Hardenberg (1776–1854), Pückler's wife, to whom these letters were addressed, 703n30 (Letter 12), 703n6 (Letter 13), 704n17 (Letter 14), 707n23 (Letter 19), 707n2 (Letter 20), 708n25 (Letter 20), 710n17 (Letter 24), 711n6 (Letter 25), 712n4 (Letter 26), 714n1 (Letter 30), 714n4 (Letter 31), 717n16 (Letter 41)

Parry, William Edward (1790–1855), English admiral and Artic explorer, 190, 287, 617, 703n3 (Letter 14)

Passeroni, Giancarlo (1713-1803), Italian priest, poet, and author of *Il Cicerone* (6 vols., 1755–1774), 159

Pasta, Giuditta (1797–1865), Italian soprano, considered the supreme opera singer of her time, 204, 213, 217, 223, 358–59, 370, 684

Paton, Mary Ann (1802–1864), Scottish soprano who divorced Lord William Lenox in 1831 when she married the tenor Joseph Wood, 72

Patrick, Saint (ca. 385–461), patron saint of Ireland, 506

Paul = Antoine Paul (1798–1871), noted French ballet dancer who debuted at the Paris Opéra in 1820 and retired from dancing in 1831, 663

Paulus, Heinrich Eberhard Gottlob (1761–1851), German rationalist theologian who was professor at the University of Heidelberg, 582, 603

Pavlovna, Catherine. *See* Catherine Pavlovna

Pavlovna, Grand Duchess Maria. *See* Maria Pavlovna

Peel, Sir Robert (1788–1850), Conservative member of Parliament, who was first elected in 1809 to represent a "rotten borough" in Ireland (with only twenty-four voters on the polls) and who rose quickly through the ranks, becoming prime minister in 1834, 207, 342, 709n4 (Letter 22)

Pellegrini, Felice (1774–1832), Italian baritone, 358–59

Pembroke, Countess of = Ekaterina Semyonovna Vorontsov (1784–1856), daughter of the Russian ambassador in Britain and second wife of George Herbert, 11th Earl of Pembroke, 648

Pembroke, Earl of = George Augustus Herbert, 11th Earl of Pembroke (1759–1827), British peer, army officer, and politician who resided at Wilton House, 648

Penn, John (1700–1746), son of William Penn and the owner of Stoke Park in South Buckinghamshire, now part of Stoke Poges, 259, 706n6 (Letter 17)

Penn, William (1644–1718), English Quaker and founder of the Pennsylvania colony, 259

Percy, Sir Henry, known as "Harry Hotspur" (ca. 1364–1403), English warrior who led a rebellion against Henry IV, 290, 304, 308, 707n10 (Letter 19)

Perlet, French actor who performed in London in the early nineteenth century, 96

Perugino, Pietro (ca. 1446/1450–1523), Italian painter of the Renaissance, 138

Pestalozzi, Johann Heinrich (1746–1827), Swiss humanistic teacher and educational reformer, 23

Petitot = either Jean (1607–1691), a French-Swiss enamel painter, or Jean Louis (1652–1730), his son, whose works are hard to distinguish from those of his father, 148

Petty-Fitzmaurice. *See* Lansdowne, Lord

Philadelphia, Jacob (ca. 1735–1795), English magician, alchemist, and juggler; he was born Jacob Meyer, and was also known as Meyer Philadelphia, 218

Philip II (1527–1598), king of Spain and the Netherlands, attempted to force Spanish absolutism on the Netherlands; he lost the Armada against England, 28, 138

Phipps. *See* Mulgrave, Lord

Pickle, Peregrine, an egotistical dandy who is the eponymous hero of a picaresque novel published in 1752 by Tobias Smollett, 61, 698n1 (Letter 5)

Pillet, General = René Martin Pillet (1768–1816), French satirical writer whose 1815 book, *L'Angleterre vue à Londres et dans ses provinces: Pendant un séjour de six années,* was translated as *Views of England, during a Residence of Ten Years, Six of Them as Prisioner of War* in 1818, 307, 708n10 (Letter 20)

Pinetti = Giuseppe Pinetti de Wildalle (1750–1800), a conjurer who founded the classical school of magic, 218

Pitt, William, the Younger (1759–1806), English statesman, political reformer, and prime minister, 149, 192

Pixis, Johann Peter (1788–1874), German composer and pianist, 359

Plato (ca. 428–348 BC), an ancient Greek philosopher, 489, 713n16 (Letter 27), 718n4 (Letter 45)

Plunket, William Conyngham, 1st Baron Plunket (1765–1854), Irish politician who was lord chancellor of Ireland from 1830 to 1841, 583–84

Polidori, John William (1795–1821), English writer, 698n15 (Letter 3)

Polignac, Armand Jules Marie Héracle, duc de (1771–1847), elder brother of the Prince de Polignac, 171

Polignac, Jules (Auguste Jules Armand Marie), Prince de (1780–1847), a royalist French politician who was involved in an attempt to assassinate Napoleon; given the title prince after the Bourbon restoration, he served as French ambassador to London and briefly (1829–1830) as prime minister of France, where he worked to overthrow the constitution; his unconstitutional ordinances, such as restricting press freedom, led to the July Revolution of 1830, 93, 171, 211

Polignac, Princess de, Charlotte Parkyns, the daughter of Lord Rancliffe, Marquise de Choiseul, and the second wife of Prince de Polignac, 211

Polonius, the figure from *Hamlet* who was famous for giving frequent and often long-winded advice, 336

Poniatowski, Josef (1763–1813), Polish commander who was born and raised in Vienna and was made a marshal of France in 1813 for his service to Napoleon, 170, 662–63

Ponsonby. *See* Llangollen, the Ladies of

Pope, Alexander (1688–1744), English poet, 632

Portland, Duke of = William Bentinck, 4th Duke (1768–1854), inherited Bulstrode Park in 1809 and sold it in 1810, 149, 163

Portsmouth, Duchess of = Louise de Kérouaille (1649–1734), French-born mistress of Charles II of England, who elevated her to the rank of duchess, 585

Potier, Charles-Gabriel (1775–1838), a celebrated comic French actor, 177, 528, 686, 703n25 (Letter 12)

Potter, Paulus (1625–1654), Dutch landscape painter, 219

Powerscourt, Richard Wingfield, 5th Viscount (1790–1823), owner of Powerscourt Park in Ireland, whom Pückler blames for allowing no access to the park on Sundays, although the responsible person at the time would have been the Dowager Lady Powerscourt (Theodosia Howard, 1800–1836), because the 6th Viscount (1815–1833), Wingfield's son by his first wife, would have been just thirteen years old, 465

Procrustes, a figure from Greek mythology, a blacksmith who forced passers-by to spend the night in his iron bed, stretching or cutting off their legs so they would fit, 89

Proteus, the god of rivers and seas in Greek mythology, and hence a symbol of change and mutability, 394

Punch and Judy, main protagonists in a traditional puppet show, 75–81, 699n1 (Letter 6)

Pygmalion, a sculptor in Greek legend (and, most famously, in Ovid's *Metamorphoses*) who falls in love with his own creation and is eventually transformed into a living woman by Aphrodite, 29

Q

Queensberry, Marchioness = Lady Caroline Scott (1774–1854), descended from a Scottish noble family; she was the wife of Charles Douglas, 6th Marquess of Queensberry (1777–1837) with whom she had eight daughters, three of whom Pückler meets, 172, 174

Queensbury (also spelled Queensberry), Duchess of = Catherine Hyde (1701–1777), wife of Charles Douglas, 3rd Duke of Queensbury; she was known for her beauty and frankness, 637, 719n11 (Letter 45)

Quin, James (1693–1766), English actor who late in life reconciled with his sometime rival Garrick, 637

R

Rabelais, François (ca. 1494–1553), French writer and scholar of the Renaissance, 720n34 (Letter 47)

Rabutin, Roger de. *See* Bussy, Comte de

Radcliffe, Ann (1764–1823), English author and one of the founders of the Gothic novel, 521, 715n8 (Letter 34)

Radcliffe, John (1650–1714), English physician after whom many Oxford buildings are named, 142, 701n21 (Letter 10)

Radnor, Earl of = William Pleydell-Bouverie, 3rd Earl of (1779–1869), British politician and owner of Longford Castle and park, 648, 650

Radziwill, Anton Heinrich Prince of (1775–1833), Polish-Lithuanian and Prussian nobleman, music lover, and musician, whose score for *Faust* was first performed in 1835 in Berlin, 23

Raleigh, Sir Walter (ca. 1554–1618), English seafarer, explorer, and writer, 148

Raphael = Raffaello Sanzio da Urbino (1483–1540), Italian Renaissance painter and architect, 45, 118, 121, 136, 138, 141, 144, 237, 238, 276, 319, 359, 667, 700n4 (Letter 9), 701n6, 16–17 (Letter 10)

Rauch, Christian Daniel (1777–1857), German sculptor, 296, 668

Regulus, Marcus Atilius (ca. 307–250 BC), Roman general and statesman whose career became legendary, 164, 613

Rehder, Jacob Heinrich (1790–1852), Pückler's head gardener at Muskau, 98, 100, 103, 124, 127, 128–29, 132, 133–34, 139, 140, 151, 153, 160, 178, 297, 699–700n10 (Letter 7)

Rembrandt Harmensz von Rijn (1606–1669), Dutch artist, 148, 319, 493

Reni, Guido (1575–1642), Italian painter of the Baroque, 138, 164, 649

Repton, Humphry (1752–1818), English landscape designer and writer; he was famous for his "Red Books," each of which described his plans for a specific garden and were presented to its owners so they could visualize what he had in mind, 52, 107, 110, 149, 161–62, 700n6 (Letter 8), 702n17 (Letter 11), 707n5 (Letter 19)

Repton, John Adey (1775–1860), the eldest son of Humphry Repton; he collaborated with his father on numerous projects and was invited by Pückler to contribute to the plans for Muskau Park, 162, 700n6 (Letter 8), 702n17–18 (Letter 11)

Reynard the Fox, a clever and conniving fox who is the hero of various European fables, 332, 535

Reynolds, Sir Joshua (1723–1792), English painter and one of the most famous portraitists of eighteenth-century English society, 138, 295

Richard de Beauchamp. *See* Warwick, Earls of

Richard III (1452–1485), king of England from 1483 to 1845; he was described by Shakespeare as being hunchbacked, 76, 356

Richardson, Jonathan (1665–1745), English art collector, writer, and portrait painter, 148

Richelieu, Cardinal = Armand Jean du Plessis, duc de (1585–1642), French clergyman, statesman, and patron of the arts who founded the Académie Française; he was the author of religious and political works as well as literary works and memoires, 140, 373, 561, 716n6 (Letter 38)

Richelieu, Marshal = Armand de Vignerot du Plessis (1696–1788), French soldier and statesman, 64

Rienzi, Cola di (ca. 1313–1354), Roman tribune and hero of *Rienzi, A Tragedy*, by Mary Russell Mitford (1787–1855), first performed in 1828 at Drury Lane, 640

Ries, Adam (1492–1559), German mathematician who wrote influential books on accounting and calculation, 236

Rivière, Duc de = Charles François de Riffardeau, marquis de Rivière (1763–1828), French ambassador to the Ottoman Empire and instrumental in the Louvre's acquisition of the *Venus de Milo*, 663

Romano, Giulio (ca. 1499–1546), Italian painter, architect, and student of Raphael, 141, 700n4 (Letter 9), 701n16 (Letter 10)

Rome, king of. *See* Napoleon II

Rosa, Salvator (1615–1673), Italian Baroque painter, poet, and printmaker, 157, 164, 588, 702n8, 24 (Letter 11)

Unknown" and "The Wizard of the North"; his identity was an open secret fairly early in his career, but he did not officially "reveal" himself until 1827; his 1826 novel *Kenilworth* brought widespread fame to the castle ruins, 21–22, 55, 88, 96, 117, 126, 136, 173, 174, 213, 244, 276, 310, 314, 328, 354, 389, 398, 415, 463–64, 486, 551, 596, 697n12 (Letter 1), 699n7 (Letter 7), 700n13 (Letter 9), 701n4 (Letter 10), 704n26 (Letter 15), 706n37 (Letter 16), 710n9 (Letter 23), 712n8 (Letter 26), 714n7–8 (Letter 31), 717n22 (Letter 41), 722n16 (second preface)

Scrope, Richard (ca. 1350–1405), bishop of Lichfield and archbishop of York, builder of the great castle of Bolton in the North Riding; he was executed for participating in an uprising against Henry IV, and was buried at York Minster, 272, 706n3 (Letter 18)

Scully, Sergeant, a heavy-drinking Irishman in legends and stories of the nineteenth century, 575–76

Seaford, Lord, perhaps Charles Ellis, 6th Baron Howard de Walden, 2nd Baron Seaford (1799–1868), 278

Sebastian of Portugal, (1554–1578), king of Portugal and the Algarves, 693, 722n17 (second preface)

Ségur, Louis Philippe, comte de (1753–1830), French general, diplomat, and historian whose *Mémoires ou souvenirs et anecdotes, par m. le comte de Ségur* [Memoirs and Recollections of Count Ségur], appeared in 1824, 85, 672, 699n12 (Letter 6)

Semiramis, legendary Assyrian queen, claimed by some to have created the Hanging Gardens of Babylon, sometimes referred to as the "Gardens of Semiramis," 196

Seneca the Younger (ca. 4 BC–AD 65), Roman philosopher, tutor, and adviser to Nero who was forced to commit suicide because of his supposed participation in a plot against the emperor, 138

Sévigné, Madame de = Marie de Rabutin-Chantal, marquise de Sévigné (1626–1696), famous for her letters—first published in the eighteenth century—to her daughter Françoise-Marguerite, contesse de Grignan, written over a period of nearly thirty years, 17, 23, 579, 697n1 (Letter 1)

Sexaginta, an invented name that perhaps indicated the age of sixty but also had negative connotations concerning the devil, 416, 492

Seydlitz, Friedrich Wilhem von (1721–1773), famous Prussian cavalry officer under Frederick the Great, 83, 455, 713n11 (Letter 28)

Shakespeare, William (1564–1616), English poet and playwright, 23, 43, 83, 88, 134–35, 136, 146, 147, 272, 289, 309, 310–13, 327, 348, 349–50, 391, 466, 528, 603–4, 622, 680, 702n4 (Letter 11), 707n6 (Letter 19), 708n21 (Letter 20), 709n11 (Letter 22), 710n17 (Letter 23), 711n11, 26 (Letter 25), 713n10 (Letter 28), 718n4 (Letter 45)

Shelley, Mary (1797–1851), English writer most known for *Frankenstein* (1818), 698n15 (Letter 3)

Shiel, Richard Lalor (1791–1851), Irish writer and politician, 474, 595–96, 601

Siddons, Mrs. Sarah (1755–1831), a famous Shakespearean actress and sister to the Kemble brothers, 73, 311

Sidney, Sir = Philip Sidney, 1st Baron de L'Isle and Dudley (1800–1851), British politician, husband of Sophia Fitzclarence Sidney, illegitimate daughter of the Duke of Clarence, and sister of Colonel Fitzclarence, 213

Sir Arthur Clarke, 605, 717n10 (Letter 41), 718n3 (Letter 43)

Sligo, Lady, probably Hester Catherine de Burgh (ca. 1800–1878), wife of Howe Peter Browne and 2nd Marquess of Sligo, 213

Smith, Horace (1779–1849), English poet and novelist who authored *Zillah*, 703n21 (Letter 12)

Smollett, Tobias George (1721–1771), Scottish writer especially known for his picaresque novels, 254, 698n1 (Letter 5), 720n12 (Letter 47)

Socrates (ca. 470–399 BC), Greek philosopher, 600

Solomon, ancient king of the Hebrews and the reputed author of parts of the Old Testament, 78, 217, 309, 493, 686, 691, 699n5 (Letter 6), 722n6 (second preface)

Somerset, Duke of = Edward Adolphus St Maur, 11th Duke of (1775–1855), mathematician and landowner; he leased the Spencer House in Wimbledon as his country residence from the 1820s to the 1840s; he lived at Somerset House, Park Lane, in London, 351, 364–65

Sontag, Henriette (1806–1854), German soprano who was likely Pückler's lover in Berlin and certainly his lover in London; she secretly married Count Carlo Rossi, the Sardinian ambassador to The Hague in 1828, and shortly thereafter she was made a countess by the king of Prussia, on the understanding that she would abandon her stage career (which she did for nineteen years), 72, 355, 356, 357, 358–59, 370, 375, 508, 509–10, 684–85, 714n9 (Letter 33)

Spencer-Churchill, likely George, 5th Duke of Marlborough and Marquess of Blandford (1766–1840), or his son George Spencer-Churchill, 6th Duke of Marlborough (1793–1857), known as Marquess of Blandford from 1817 until 1840, when he succeeded to the dukedom; he was the owner of Blandford Park, 701n6 (Letter 10)

Spieá, Christain Heinrich (1755–1799), German writer of popular Gothic novels, 411

Spiker, Samuel Heinrich (1786–1858), Berlin journalist, librarian, writer, and translator of Shakespeare, 311

Spring-Rice, Thomas, 1st Baron Monteagle of Brandon (1790–1866), British politician, 361

Spurzheim, Johann Gaspar (1776–1832), German physician and major advocate of phrenology (a term he coined); he worked initially with Gall but then went his own way, traveling extensively, spreading his ideas throughout Europe, 94, 705n24 (Letter 16)

Staël, Madame de = Germaine de Staël, née Uecker (1766–1817), French intellectual, writer, and critic of Napoleon; she described the considerable time that she spent in Germany in *De l'Allemagne* (3 vols., 1810; an English translation appeared in London in 1813), the first edition of which was destroyed by order of Napoleon, 55, 412, 489, 714n3 (Letter 32)

Stanhope, Lady Hester (1776–1839), an eccentric, adventuresome Englishwoman who, in her twenties, served as hostess and secretary to her uncle William Pitt; after his death, she traveled extensively in the Near and Middle East, finally settling in what is now Lebanon, where she lived until her death, 192–93, 704n14 (Letter 14)

Steevens, Miss. *See* Stephens, Catherine

Stephen, an unidentified murderous criminal, 274

Stephens, Catherine (1794–1882), English singer and actress, probably the "Miss Steevens" mentioned by Pückler, 354

Sterne, Laurence (1713–1768), Anglo-Irish novelist and clergyman, 713n13 (Letter 28)

Stigo. *See* Sligo, Lady

Strafford, Lord. *See* Wentworth, Thomas

Strangford, Lord = Percy Clinton Smythe, 6th Viscount Strangford (1780–1855), Anglo-Irish diplomat and ambassador to Portugal, Sweden, Constantinople, and Russia, 317, 318–19

Suffolk, Thomas Howard, 1st Earl of (1561–1626), built Audley End, 56

Sultan, the = Mahmud II (1789–1839), sultan of the Ottoman Empire, 318–19, 708n13 (Letter 20)

Surrey, Lord = Henry Howard, Earl of (ca. 1517–1547), English courtier and poet who was beheaded by Henry VIII for treason, 303

Sussex, Prince Augustus Frederick, Duke of (1773–1843), son of George III and brother of George IV; known for his progressive political views, he supported Catholic emancipation and the abolition of slavery, 220, 356, 442

Suvorov, Alexander Vasilyevich (1729–1800), Russian field marshal renowned for his eccentricities as well as his undefeated record, 365, 432

Swift, Jonathan (1667–1745), Anglo-Irish author, essayist, and satirist, 449, 714n6 (Letter 31), 716n1 (Letter 38)

Sydney. *See* Lady Olivia Clarke

T

Taglioni, Marie (1804–1884), celebrated ballerina who was born in Sweden to an Italian father (a choreographer) and a Swedish mother (a dancer); she debuted at l'Opéra in Paris around 1828, 663

Talbot, an English family with the title Earls of Shrewsbury who owned Malahide Castle in Ireland since the twelfth century, 348, 505, 585, 709n11 (Letter 22)

Tallien, Madame = Thérésa Tallien, née Cabarrus (1773–1835), Spanish-born beauty whose second husband, the French revolutionary Jean-Lambert Tallien, saved her from the guillotine and subsequently married her, 329

Talma, François-Joseph (1763–1826), French actor known for his early advocacy of realism in setting and costume, 94, 255, 596, 674, 679, 684

Tankerville, Lady = Emma Colebrooke (1752–1836), wife of Charles Bennet, 4th Earl of Tankerville; she was known for her large collection of exotic plants, 356

Tartuffe, a proverbial hypocrite who is the eponymous antihero of the 1664 comedy by Molière, 377

Tattersall, Richard (1724–1795), the main auctioneer of race horses in the United Kingdom and an intimate of sporting men as well as of the Prince of Wales, with whom he was a joint proprietor of the *Morning Post* for some time; his grandson Richard (1785–1859) succeeded his father in 1810 and would have been head of the firm at the time of Pückler's visit, 50, 462, 713n2 (Letter 29)

Taylor, Robert, Reverend (1784–1844), a free-thinking English clergyman imprisoned for his radical beliefs, 206, 704n10 (Letter 15)

Telford, Thomas (1757–1834), designed the Menai Suspension Bridge in Wales, 422, 713n24 (Letter 27)

Telluson. *See* Thellusson family

Temple, Sir, conveys a letter from Lucie to Pückler, 178

Teniers, David the Younger (1610–1690), Flemish painter, 148

Tettenborn, Friedrich Karl Freiherr von (1778–1845), cavalry general in the Napoleonic Wars who entered the Russian army in the war of 1812 and occupied Hamburg in 1813, 39

Tharp, John (ca. 1775–1851), a wealthy sugar baron who purchased Chippenham Park in 1791 and greatly enlarged the estate; he and his wife, Anna Maria Phillips, had a son and three daughters, 698n4 (Letter 4)

Thellusson family: the will of Peter Thellusson (1737–1797), a very wealthy Swiss banker living in London, stipulated that none of his living family could inherit his wealth, thus granting it to a third generation of heirs; the will held, although Parliament changed the laws of inheritance for the future, 339, 697n3 (Letter 2), 709n1 (Letter 22)

Themis, the Greek goddess of divine order, custom, and law; the protector of justice, 394

Theresel, the name of the clairvoyant who assists the Editor in conjuring up the spirit of Pückler, 689–93

Thielemann, Johann Adolf Freiherr von (1765–1824), a general in the Saxon and then Prussian service, 298

Thomason, Edward (ca. 1769–1849), an English manufacturer with a buckle-making plant in Birmingham, England; he was appointed vice-consul to Prussia and seven other countries, 127, 134

Thomond, 2nd Marquess of = William O'Brien (1765–1848), an Irish peer, 352, 501

Thomonds, the rulers of the Irish kingdom of Thomond, beginning with the O'Brien clan in the twelfth century, 501

Thorvaldsen, Bertel (d. 1844), Danish sculptor, 196, 668, 704n23 (Letter 14)

Thurn and Taxis, Maximilian Karl, 6th Prince of (1802–1871), a member of the noble German family that developed the Imperial Postal Service in Europe in the sixteenth century and held it as a monopoly until the end of the Holy Roman Empire in 1806 and as a private company until 1867, 650

Tiberius (42 BC–AD 37), Roman emperor, 671

Tieck, Ludwig (1773–1853), major German writer of the Romantic period, 311, 348, 398, 708n21 (Letter 20)

Till. *See* Eulenspiegel, Till

Timur (1336–1405), often called "Tamerlane," the Turkic conqueror of much of Western and Central Asia, 317, 321

Tipu Sahib (1750–1799), Muslim ruler of the kingdom of Mysore, India, as well as a scholar, poet, and soldier; a life-long

enemy of the British in India, he kept a book where he recorded and analyzed his dreams, 193, 329

Titian = Tiziano Vecelli or Tiziano Vecello (ca. 1488/1490–1576), Venetian painter, 118, 120, 135, 138, 148, 164, 193, 673, 704n18 (Letter 14)

Todd, William, an English timber merchant who built a picturesque group of thatched cottages, known as the "Swiss cottages," on his property in Cranham Woods, Gloucestershire, ca. 1815–1820, 385

Tonne, Frau von, likely an invented name containing a pun: "Lady of the Barrel," whose work is "very substantial," 399

Tournier, Mr., Pückler's guide who tells him the story of the Montagu family. *See* Montagu, George Browne

Tradescant, John the Elder (ca. 1575–1638) and the Younger (1608–1662), English naturalists and gardeners to various noble and royal families; their large collection of curiosities became the core of the Ashmolean Museum in Oxford, 140, 701n13 (Letter 10)

Traugott. *See* Krug, Wilhelm Traugott

Trench, Sir Frederick William (1775–1859), a general known for his ambitious plans for improving London; his proposals, which included building a huge pyramid to celebrate Waterloo and an embankment along the north side of the Thames, were constructed after his death, 34

Tristram, Sir Armoricus (d. 1189), a Norwegian who defeated the Irish in battle at Howth in 1177, at which time he was granted the barony of Howth; his sword is still at Howth Castle, 585

Turenne, Vicomte de, Henri de la Tour d'Auvergne (1611–1675), a marshal of France, 319

U

Ude, Louis Eustache (ca. 1769–1846), a celebrated chef under Louis XVI who was lured to Crockford's club in London by the enormous annual salary of £1,200, 357

Ugoni, Camillo (1784–1855), Italian freedom fighter and literary figure, 159, 702n10 (Letter 11)

Unzelmann, Karl Wilhelm Ferdinand (1753–1832), German actor, comedian, and tenor, 67

Unzelmann, Mrs. = Friederike Bethmann-Unzelmann (1760–1815), German actress and singer who divorced Karl Wilhelm Ferdinand Unzelmann in 1803 to marry the actor Heinrich Eduard Bethmann (1774–1857), 348

Urbino, Duke of (1490–1538), duke from 1508 to 1516 and from 1521 until his death, 141, 701n16 (Letter 10)

Ursins, Marie Anne de La Trémoille, princesse des (1642–1722), a powerful figure at the Spanish court whose long correspondence with Madame de Maintenon was first published in French in 1826, 271

V

Valdés y Flores, Cayetano (1767–1834), Spanish naval officer who served in the French Revolutionary and Napoleonic Wars; he was exiled to Gibraltar in 1823 and then to England, where he stayed for ten years, 347

Vallance, John, English brewer and inventor who patented new methods for heating and cooling interior spaces in the 1820s, 336

Van Dyck, Sir Anthony (1599–1641), Flemish artist who became the most prominent court painter in England, 56, 118, 121, 138, 148, 298, 648, 707n21 (Letter 19)

Vanbrugh, Sir John (1664–1726), English architect and dramatist who designed Castle Howard and Blenheim Palace, 278

Varney, Richard, the villain in Walter Scott's *Kenilworth*, 127, 700n13 (Letter 9)

Varnhagen von Ense, Karl August (1785–1858), German writer and biographer, admirer, supporter and close friend of Pückler who encouraged the publication of *Letters of a Dead Man* and helped edit them; he was the uncle of Pückler's biographer Ludmilla Assing, 467, 714n1 (Letter 30), 719n18 (Letter 45)

Vatel, François (1631–1671), a famous French maître d'hôtel, 660, 720n13 (Letter 47)

Velásquez, Diego Rodríguez de Silva y (1599–1660), Spanish painter, 148

Velluti, Giovanni Battista (1780–1861), Italian castrato whose 1825 London debut was greeted with some hostility but drew large crowds; Pückler calls him "old," but he was only five years older than the prince himself, 223

Venables-Vernon, Edward (1757–1847), English clergyman and archbishop of York from 1807 until his death; in 1831, he added "Harcourt" to his name when he inherited most of the family estates upon the death of his cousin, William Harcourt, 3rd Earl of Harcourt, 707n13 (Letter 18)

Vermeer, Jan (1632–1675), Dutch painter, 219

Vernet, Horace (1789–1863), French painter, 667

Vernon. *See* Varney, Richard

Very, likely the owner of a celebrated, sumptuous Parisian restaurant at the Palais Royal known as Véry's, 686

Vestris, Auguste-Armand (1788–1825), French dancer married briefly to Madame Vestris, 69, 683

Vestris, Madame = Lucia Elizabeth, née Bartolozzi (1797–1856), a widely-admired English actress and opera singer who was briefly married to the dancer August-Armande Vestris and later to the actor Charles Mathews; she was the daughter of the artist Gaetano Bartolozzi and the German pianist Theresa Jansen Barrolozzi, 67, 69, 161, 306, 698n5 (Letter 5)

Vieuville, Charles, marquis de la (ca. 1582–1653), superintendent of finance and minister for foreign affairs under Louis XIII until his fortunes turned in 1624 and he fled to Holland and later Brussels; his son, Vincent de la Vieuville, died in battle at Newbury in 1643, 148, 701n34 (Letter 10)

Voisenon, Claude-Henri de Fusée, abbé de (1708–1775), French dramatist and writer known for his libertine novels and fairy tales, 171

Voltaire, the nom de plume of François-Marie Arouet (1694–1778), French writer of the Enlightenment, 30, 104, 118, 562, 587, 597, 697n5 (Letter 2), 705n18 (Letter 16), 706n54 (Letter 16), 709n3 (Letter 22), 710n18 (Letter 23), 711n18 (Letter 25), 716n8 (Letter 38), 717n2, 25 (Letter 41), 718n7 (Letter 43), 719n21 (Letter 45)

Vortigern, a legendary fifth-century British warlord, 430, 712n11 (Letter 27)

W

Wach, Karl Wilhelm (1747–1845), Berlin portrait painter, 719n18 (Letter 45)

Wada, a Saxon chief of the eighth century; the remains of his castle lie near the Mulgrave, 289

Waldemar, the False (d. 1356), an impostor who appeared a quarter century after the death of Waldemar, Margrave of Brandenburg-Stendal, and claimed his identity, convincing many people, 693, 722n16 (second preface)

Wales, Prince of. *See* George IV

Walker, Robert (1599–1658), English portrait painter, 701n36 (Letter 10)

Wallenstein, Albrecht von, Duke of Friedland and Mecklenburg (1583–1634), major military leader in the Thirty Years' War, 329, 517, 702n12 (Letter 11), 704n19 (Letter 14), 709n15 (Letter 21), 711n8 (Letter 25), 715n2 (Letter 34)

Waller, William (ca. 1598–1668), English parliamentarian and general, 637, 719n12 (Letter 45)

Walpole, Horace, 4th Earl of Oxford (1717–1797), English writer, art historian, and politician whose residence at Strawberry Hill in the Gothic revival style kindled an enthusiasm for neo-Gothic architecture in Europe and America, 359

Warwick, Earls of, an English title extending back to the eleventh century and including a number of family names such as Beaumont, Beauchamp, Neville, Dudley, and Greville. Guy de Beauchamp, 10th Earl of Warwick (ca. 1272–1315), is best known for opposing Edward II and eliminating his favorite, Gaveston. Pückler seems to conflate him with Guy of Warwick, a legendary figure of English and French literature from the thirteenth to the seventeenth century who was known for his chivalric valor and his success in slaying monsters and giants; the earl living in the castle at the time of Pückler's visit was Henry Richard Greville (1779–1853), 3rd Earl of Warwick, 115, 117, 123, 124, 126, 278, 281, 700n2, 10–12 (Letter 9)

Warwick, Richard de Beauchamp, 13th Earl of. *See* Beauchamp, Richard de

Warwick, Richard Neville, 16th Earl of (1428–1471), powerful English nobleman, administrator, and military commander known as Warwick the Kingmaker, whom Pückler conflates with Beauchamp, 700n2, 12 (Letter 9)

Warwick, "the old" Earl of. *See* Greville, George

Weber, Carl Maria von (1786–1826), German composer and pianist who died during a performance tour in London; his *Der Freischütz* (*The Marksman* or *The Freeshooter*), considered the first important Romantic opera, premiered in Berlin in 1821 and was a runaway success, 90–91, 241, 313–14, 370, 706n33 (Letter 16), 714n8 (Letter 33), 717n9 (Letter 39), 719n4 (Letter 46), 721n40 (Letter 47)

Weimar, Grand Duchess of. *See* Maria Pavlovna

Weimar, Grand Duke of Saxe-Weimar. *See* Karl August, Grand Duke of Saxe-Weimar-Eisenach

Wellington, Duke of = Arthus Wellesley (1769–1852), British soldier and influential Tory who twice served as prime minister, 82, 200, 204, 208–9, 210, 214, 223, 232, 352, 357, 378, 396, 450, 618, 704n12 (Letter 15), 705n8 (Letter 16), 711n19 (Letter 24)

Wentworth, Thomas, 1st Earl of Strafford (1593–1641), English statesman, lord deputy of Ireland, and adviser to King Charles I, whom he supported in his struggle against Parliament, which ultimately impeached and condemned him to be beheaded, 298, 299, 707n20 (Letter 19)

Wentworth, William, 2nd Earl of Strafford (1626–1695), son of Thomas Wentworth, 298, 707n20 (Letter 19)

Werner, Zacharias (1768–1823), German dramatist who was a Pietist and a Free Mason before converting to Catholicism in 1811 and becoming a priest in 1814, 175, 703n19 (Letter 12)

Werther, the titular hero of Goethe's famous novella *Die Leiden des jungen Werthers* (1774), 527–28, 715n13–14 (Letter 34)

West, Benjamin (1738–1820), American-born painter who worked in England from 1763 until his death; he was the cofounder and later president of the Royal Academy, 129, 266–67

West, Sarah, née Cooke (1790–1876), British actress who played Lady Macbeth opposite Macready's Macbeth in the performance Pückler saw at Drury Lane, 311, 708n20 (Letter 20)

Westmorland, John Fane, 10th Earl of (1759–1841), British politician and Lord Privy Seal, 200, 202, 203, 704n4 (Letter 15)

White, Colonel = Simon White (1768–1838), brother of the 1st Earl of Bantry and husband of Sarah Newenham with whom he had four children, one a daughter named Fanny Rosa Maria (1805–1857); he built Glengarriff Castle (where Pückler enjoyed an extended stay) in the 1790s, 513–15, 529–30, 533–35, 540, 545, 715n13 (Letter 33)

White, Richard, 1st Earl of Bantry (1767–1851); the White family owned most of the Beara Peninsula and the town of Bantry; it was the earl's son, while still Viscount Berehaven, who developed the house and gardens as known today, 513–15. *See also* Bantry House and Glengarriff Lodge, *in Annotated Index of Places*

Wieland, Christoph Martin (1733–1813), German poet and writer, 715n3 (Letter 35)

Wilhelm Meister, the eponymous her of three novels by Goethe, 528

William I, Prince of Orange (1533–1584), also known as William the Silent; he was a statesman, founder of Dutch independence, and fellow conspirator of Count Egmont, 649

William III of Orange (1650–1702), king of England, Ireland, and Scotland (where he was William II), from 1689 until his death, 45, 62, 448, 701n21 (Letter 10)

William IV. *See* Clarence, Duke of

William the Conqueror = William I, king of England and Duke of Normandy from 1027/1028 until 1087, 131, 368, 400, 619, 646

Williams, Hugh, the name, according to various Welsh legends, of the sole survivors of two, three, or four different shipwrecks in the Menai Strait over the course of one to three centuries, 419

Williams, Owen (1764–1832), member of Parliament, owner of the estate Craig-y-Don in Wales, and member of the yacht club at Cowes; he was the father of Thomas Peers Williams, 713n5 (Letter 28)

Williams, Thomas Peers (1795–1875), member of Parliament and son of Owen Williams, 713n5 (Letter 28)

Wilmot-Horton, Mrs. = Anne Beatrix Horton (1788–1871), wife of British politician Robert Wilmot-Horton, 3rd Baronet (1784–1841), 96

Wisotzky, the proprietor of a popular working-man's bar in Berlin, 72, 407, 712n36 (Letter 25)

Wittgenstein, Field Marshall = Ludwig Adolph Peter of Sayn-Wittgenstein (1769–1843), Russian general and field marshal born in Berleburg, Germany, 169, 702n4 (Letter 12)

Wollstonecraft, Mary (1759–1797), English writer and early feminist who served for a time as governess of the daughters of the 2nd Earl of Kingston, 716n12 (Letter 36)

Wolsey, Thomas (1473–1530), cardinal of the Roman Catholic Church and lord chancellor under Henry VIII, 45, 140, 299, 359

Wouwerman, Philips (1619–1668), Dutch landscape and history painter, 219

Wren, Sir Christopher (1632–1723), architect of fifty-three churches in London, 646, 701n9 (Letter 10)

Wurm, Albert Aloys Ferdinand (1783–1834), a popular comic actor in Berlin, 67

Württemberg, King of. *See* Frederick I

Württemberg, Pauline Therese Luise, Queen of (1800–1873), third wife of William I of Württemberg, her first cousin, 264, 267

Württemberg, Queen of = Catherine Pavlovna, Grand Duchess of Russia (1788–1819), daughter of Emperor Paul I and sister-in-law of the grand duke; she married King Wilhelm I of Württemberg in 1816, 23, 697n17 (Letter 1)

Wyatt, James (1746–1813), architect of both the neoclassical and neo-Gothic styles who designed Wycombe Abbey and Fonthill Abbey, 646, 719n9, 12 (Letter 46)

Wyattville, Sir Jeffrey (1766–1840), English architect and landscape designer known for extending and remodeling Windsor Castle (starting in 1824) and Chatworth House, 260

Wyndham, Lady, a niece of the Earl of Egremont, 172

Wyse, Lady. *See* Bonaparte, Letizia

Y

Yermolov, Aleksey Petrovich (1777–1861), a charismatic Russian military hero in the Napoleonic Wars and in the Caucasus, 504

York, Archbishop of. *See* Venables-Vernon, Edward

York, Duke of = Prince Frederick, Duke of York and Albany (1763–1827), second son of King George III and heir presumptive to the throne until his death, 1827, 153–54

Young, Charles Mayne (1777–1856), English actor renowned for his Shakespearean roles, 308–9, 348, 349–50

Young, Edward (1681–1785), English poet and playwright, 713n10 (Letter 28)

Z

Zambeccari, Count Francesco (1752–1812), Italian aviation pioneer who launched an unmanned gas balloon in London in 1783 and later invented a balloon that could be steered, lowered, or raised by the pilot; after several near disasters, he died when his airship caught fire shortly after takeoff, 190, 703n4 (Letter 14)

Zanga, a Moorish priest in Edward Young's play *The Revenge*, 451, 713n10 (Letter 28)

Zieten, Hans Joachim von (1699–1786), Prussian cavalry general who served under Frederick the Great, 83

Zuccaro, Federico (ca. 1540–1609), Italian painter who traveled in 1574 to England, where he painted several royal portraits, perhaps one of Mary Queen of Scots, 141

Zucchelli, Carlo (1793–1879), an opera singer born in London to an Italian father and an English mother; he sang in Italy, Paris, and London, 358, 684

Annotated Index of Places

Berlin, capital of Prussia, 23, 26, 50, 56, 67, 72, 86, 100, 101, 129, 134, 160, 164, 172, 174, 205, 243, 276, 301, 308, 311, 313, 325, 326, 328, 335, 348, 349, 381, 387, 402, 406, 407, 421, 423, 593, 650, 663, 680, 697n8 (Letter 1), 698n4, 5 (Letter 3), 700n19 (Letter 7), 700n14 (Letter 9), 702n13 (Letter 11), 703n33 (Letter 12), 706n36 (Letter 16), 711n13, 22 (Letter 25), 712n36 (Letter 25), 712n12 (Letter 27), 718n3 (Letter 44), 722n14 (second preface)

Berlin City Palace (Berliner Stadtschloss), dating from the eighteenth to the mid-nineteenth century, 421

Bermingham House, an eighteenth-century house in County Galway, western Ireland, 477–79, 484, 488, 489–90

Birmingham, England, 124, 127–28, 129, 133, 134, 140, 155, 384, 650

Bishopthorpe Palace, the residence of the archbishop of York, 276–78, 277, 707n14 (Letter 18)

Blackrock Castle, a late sixteenth-century castle built to guard against pirates entering the Cork Harbor; the castle was destroyed by fire in 1827, but it was rebuilt within two years and would have been nearing completion at the time of Pückler's visit, 541, 542, 715n3 (Letter 36)

Blackwater Bridge, over the Blackwater River in Ireland, 518, 518

Blaise Hamlet, a group of picturesque cottages designed by John Nash for John Harford in 1811, 635, 635, 719n8 (Letter 45)

Blandford Park, Oxfordshire, originally Cornbury Park; it was renamed when owned by the Duke of Marlborough (see Spencer-Churchill, Marquess of Blandford, in Annotated Index of Names) but is once again known as Cornbury Park, 135

Blenheim, an eighteenth-century palace and famous landscape garden by Capability Brown in Woodstock, Oxfordshire, that was the residence of the dukes of Marlborough, 128, 135, 136–38, 137, 144, 278, 651, 701n5 (Letter 10)

Blocksberg, a peak in Germany's Harz Mountains, 668, 721n40 (Letter 47)

Boherlahan, a village near Cashel, Ireland, 560

Bordeaux, France, 33, 54

Bosworth Field, the site of the penultimate battle of the Wars of the Roses in 1485, 646

Botany Bay, the site of the first English penal colony in Australia; the colony was founded in 1788, and although it was soon abandoned in favor of Port Jackson (situated farther north), it was long referred to as "Botany Bay" in England, 231, 340, 474, 574

Boulogne, a city in northern France, 169, 554, 702n3 (Letter 12)

La Bourse, the Paris stock exchange housed in the Palais Brongniart, 680, 681, 721n14 (Letter 48)

Boyne, a river on the east coast of Ireland where a major battle was fought in 1690, 502

Brandon Castle, not the remains of the medieval fortress in Warwickshire, but a site in County Kerry, Ireland, that Pückler misidentifies; what he saw was the tower belonging to a place known as Lord Brandon's Cottage, which served as a hunting lodge for William Crosbie, 4th Baron Brandon, 508–9, 715n11 (Letter 33)

Branksome Hall, an ancient Scottish residence in a poem by Sir Walter Scott, 55

Bray, a town in County Wicklow, Ireland, 457, 464, 466, 468, 470–73, 477

Brighton, England, 166, 167, 168, 170, 172, 176, 181, 182, 183, 185, 186, 192, 199, 200, 203–4, 206, 217, 218, 293, 303, 332–33, 339, 702n2 (Letter 12)

Bristol, England, 626, 631–32, 633–34, 636, 637

British Museum, London, 47

Brody (German Pförten), a village in Lusatia near the western border of Poland; the village was part of Prussia from 1815 until 1945, 143

Brunswick Theater, London, 345, 346, 709n7 (Letter 22)

Buckingham, a town in Buckinghamshire, England, 144

Buckingham House = Buckingham Palace, London, 38

Buenos Aires, Argentina, 714n2 (Letter 30)

Bulstrode Park, a large park in Buckinghamshire, England, that was much admired by Repton but was "a scene of devastation" when Pückler visited, 149

Burghley (also Burleigh) House, a grand sixteenth-century house in Lincolnshire, England, that was built for Sir William Cecil; its park was designed by Capability Brown, 270

C

Cádiz, a city in southwestern Spain that was the home port of the Spanish navy, 347, 496

Caer Caradoc, the site of the final confrontation between the Romans and the Britons, 393

Caernarfon (Caernarvon), a town in Gwynedd, northwest Wales, on the mainland just across from the Isle of Anglesey; it is the site of a late thirteenth-century castle built by Edward I, 409, 411, 413–15, 414, 420, 433, 435

Café Anglais, a famous and elegant Parisian restaurant, 661

Cahir Castle, a thirteenth-century castle in Cahir, Ireland, that belonged to the earls of Glengall in the eighteenth and nineteenth century, 548, 716n15 (Letter 37)

Calais, France, 160, 178, 652–56, 657, 659, 698n18 (Letter 3)

Calcutta, India, 214, 330

Canterbury, England, 204, 651–52

Canton, China, 187

Capel Curig, a village in Wales, 392, 428–30, 712n10 (Letter 27)

Cappawhite, a village near Cashel, Ireland, 560

Capua, a prosperous city in southern Italy, 493, 714n14 (Letter 31)

Cashel, a town in Ireland that was home of the famous Rock of Cashel, or "Devil's Rock," 502, 547, 548, 549, 551–52, 552, 553, 557, 560, 564–65, 570, 571, 579, 606, 716n1 (Letter 37)

Cassiobury Park, a large estate near Watford, Hertfordshire; around 1800 the owner, the 5th Earl of Essex, had the house remodeled by James Wyatt and the park newly designed by Humphry Repton; finances led the Essex family to sell parts of the property in the twentieth century, hence the staircase that Pückler so admired is now in The Metropolitan Museum of Art, New York, 104, 105, 106–7, 106, 108, 109, 110

Castell Dinas Bran, a stone fortress overlooking Llangollen in Wales; usually translated as Crow Castle, 388

Castle Hackett, a thirteenth-century tower house near Tuam, Ireland, with legendary associations, 484–85

Castle Howard, a grand country residence with extensive gardens in North Yorkshire; the house was designed by John Vanbrugh and was the home of the earls of Carlisle for over three hundred years, 278–80, 707n18 (Letter 18)

Castle Howard, a large country house in County Wicklow, Ireland, built in 1811, 460

Catalonia, a region in northeastern Spain, 345

Cernioge Mawr Inn, a farmhouse in County Wonwy, Wales, that was used as an inn from the late eighteenth century, 392

Chatham, a port town in Kent, England, 368, 369

Chelsea, London, 37

Cheltenham, a town in Gloucestershire, England, 383–84, 385–86

Chepstow, a town in Monmouthshire, Wales, known for its Norman castle, 623, 624, 626, 628–29, 628, 631, 718n1 (Letter 45)

Chester, a city in Cheshire, England, and the site of Chester Castle, a medieval structure transformed into a prison in the late eighteenth century, 128, 129–30, 431

Chimborazo, the highest mountain in Ecuador, 530

Chios, a Greek island, 222

Chippenham Park, a country house owned by John Tharp, 698n4 (Letter 4)

Chiswick House, a neo-Palladian villa in London, completed in 1729 by the Earl of Burlington; the villa boasts one of the earliest examples of an English landscape garden, designed by William Kent; at the time of Pückler's visit, it was owned by the Duke of Devonshire, 99, 713n8 (Letter 29)

Cirencester, a market town in Gloucestershire, England, 383

Clare, a county in Ireland, 485, 500, 524, 715n9 (Letter 34)

Clifford's Tower, the thirteenth-century keep (now in ruin) of the castle of York, 274

Clifton, a suburb of Bristol, England, 633–34, 636

Clonoulty, a village near Cashel, Ireland, 560

Cobh (formerly Cove), a town on Cork Harbor, Ireland, 541, 542–43

Cobham Hall, a country house (now a school) in Cobham, Kent, that was the residence of Lord Darnley; the house dates from the sixteenth century, with important improvements by James Wyatt and others, while the grounds (ca. 1790) were designed by Humphry Repton, who spent more time working there than at any other park of his career, 161–62, 162, 164–66, 367–69, 370, 702n16 (Letter 11)

Coleman's Leap, a narrow and deep chasm at the entrance to the upper lake of Killarney, so named because of the tradition that a certain Coleman once leapt over it, 509

College of Surgeons, Royal, at Lincoln's Inn Fields, London, 257–58

Collmberg, a small mountain in Saxony, 18

Cong, a village in western Ireland near the Cong Caves, which are famous for stalactites and stalagmites, 486, 500

Connacht, a province in the west of Ireland, 477

Connemara, a district in the west of Ireland, 484, 485, 487

Constantinople (modern Istanbul), Turkey, 317, 450, 561

Conwy, a walled market town in Wales that was known for its castle and suspension bridge, 437–39, 438, 444, 713n24 (Letter 27)

Cook's Folly, an isolated tower overlooking the Avon River near Bristol, 634

Cork, Ireland, 515, 528, 540, 541, 542, 545, 547, 574, 715n11 (Letter 33), 715n2 (Letter 36)

Corrib, Lough, the second largest lake in Ireland, 485, 486, 487

Courtfield, a house in Welsh Bicknor, Hertfordshire, 718n6 (Letter 44)

Covent Garden = the Royal Opera House in Covent Garden, London, 83, 149

Craig-y-Don, an estate near Beaumaris on the Isle of Anglesey in North Wales; the estate was the residence of Owen Williams and his son Thomas Peers Williams, 420, 444–45

Cross Bones, a house in Galway, Ireland, where, according to legend, James Lynch hanged his son, 495–99

Cumberland, a county in northwest England, 294

Cumnor Place, the scene of the death of Robert Dudley in Sir Walter Scott's novel *Kenilworth* (1821), 700n13 (Letter 9)

Cutra. *See* Lough Cutra

D

Dargle, a river and valley in Ireland, 468, 469

Dee, a river in Wales, 388

Delft, Holland, 29

Demerara, a former Dutch colony in South America, now part of Guyana, 31

Denbigh Castle, a village and castle ruins in Wales, 441–42, 442

Deptford, a district on the Thames in London, 190

Derneburg, the German seat of Count Ernst zu Münster, 704n22 (Letter 14)

Derrynane Abbey, a ruined abbey on an island in County Kerry, Ireland, near Derrynane, the home of Daniel O'Connell, 517, 521, 522, 525

Devil's Bridge, near Beddgelert, Wales, 132, 433, 700n1 (Letter 10)

Devil's Glen, a rocky chasm near Dunran Hill in Wicklow, Ireland, 458, 459

"Devil's Rock." *See* Cashel

Devonshire House, the London residence of the Dukes of Devonshire, 357

Dinas Emrys, a rocky and wooded hill near Beddgelert, Wales, 430, 431–32, 712n11 (Letter 27)

Ditchley Park, a country estate in Oxfordshire, 135

Donaskeigh, a village near Cashel, Ireland, 560, 716n2 (Letter 38)

Doncaster, a town in Yorkshire known for its race course, 270–71, 274, 707n6 (Letter 19)

Donnybrook, a district of Dublin, 467–68, 468

Douai, France, 524

Dover, England, 651, 652

Dresden, Germany, 17, 18, 19–21, 67, 86, 104, 294, 634, 707n16 (Letter 19)

Drogheda, Ireland, the birthplace of Eliza O'Neill, 718n5 (Letter 42)

Dropmore House and Park, a residence built in the 1790s for Lord Grenville, 260

Druid's Head, an isolated rock near Monmouth, Wales, 623

Drury Lane = the Theatre Royal, Drury Lane in Covent Garden, London, 72, 83, 306, 347

Dublin, Ireland, 447, 448–51, 451, 452, 453, 455, 457, 467, 474–75, 524, 539, 549, 577, 579, 587, 592, 597, 599, 603, 604, 605, 615, 617, 713n6 (Letter 29), 715n5 (Letter 36)

Dunran, Valley of, a deep glen in County Wicklow, Ireland, 458

E

Eastcheap, a street in London that was the location of Falstaff's inn in Shakespeare's *Henry IV*, 309

Eaton Hall, Cheshire, the home of the Grosvenor family; rebuilt several times, it was an elaborate "Gothic" folly known as "Porden Hall" when Pückler saw it, 129

Eatrop Park, a park that Pückler locates between Stratford-upon-Avon and Ditchley Park, 135

Edinburgh, Scotland, 160

Egham, a town near Windsor in southeast England; horse races were held there at Runnymeade Meadows from 1734 until 1884, 267

Egypt, fleshpots of, 583

Egyptian Museum, Paris, a department of the Louvre inaugurated in late 1827, 671

Eisenach, Germany, 25

Elbe, a river in Germany, 403

Elberfeld, Germany, 430

Ellora, the site of ancient cave temples in the Indian state of Maharashtra, 329, 709n17 (Letter 21)

Elysium, a park in the Gwynant valley in Snowdonia, Wales, 431

Ems = Bad Ems, a spa town in Germany, 252–53

Epping Place, an inn on the High Road in Epping, England, 56

Epsom, a town in Surrey known for its race course, the Epsom Downs, 359–60

Erfurt, Germany, 255

Erie, a "Great Lake" of North America, 339

Etna, a mountain in Sicily, 29

Eton, a college in Eton, England, 260

Exeter Change = Exeter Exchange, a building on the Strand in London known for the menagerie on its upper floors, 42, 43, 44, 213, 698n10 (Letter 3)

F

Fethard, a village near Cashel, Ireland, 560

Ffestiniog, a parish in Wales, 434

Filey, a seaside town in North Yorkshire, 282

Flamborough Head, an eight-mile-long promontory on the Yorkshire coast, 282–83, 447

Fonthill Abbey, an extravagant Gothic revival country house in Fonthill, Wiltshire, with a large park, also known as "Beckford's Folly" (*see* Beckford, William, *in Annotated Index of Names*); it was designed by James Wyatt and built with excessive haste at the end of the eighteenth century, 637–40, *638*, *639*

Forge Valley, Yorkshire, 280–81

Fountains Abbey, a well-preserved ruin of a twelfth-century Cistercian monastery in North Yorkshire, 289–93, *290*, *291*, *292*, 707n10 (Letter 19)

Franconi's, a circus amphitheater in Paris established by Antonio Franconi; initially the Amphithéâtre Franconi (housed in Astley's Amphiteater) it became the Cirque Olympique de Franconi in 1805, 160, 241, 585–86, 682–83

Frankfurt, Germany, 23

Frères Provençaux, Salon des, a restaurant in the Palais Royal, Paris; founded in 1786, it had the reputation of being one of the best in the city, 686

Frogmore, an estate and gardens adjoining Windsor Castle and a royal residence since the late eighteenth century, 266–67

G

Gaîté, Théatre de la, Paris, 673–74, 721n5, 7–8 (Letter 48)

Galtee Mountains, Ireland, 547–48, 562, 569, 571

Galway, Ireland, 478, 480, 483, 493, 494–99, 500, 563–64, 714n15 (Letter 32)

Geneva, Switzerland, 252

Giant's Causeway, a pavement-like mass of basalt columns on the northeast coast of Ireland, 449, 522

Glen of the Downs, a wooded valley near Bellevue House in Ireland, 458

Glendalough, "Glen of the Two Lakes," a town in County Wicklow, Ireland, famous for its ruins of seven churches, 713n4 (Letter 29)

Glengarriff, a village situated on a bay of the same name, which is an arm of Bantry Bay in County Cork, Ireland, 510, 518

Glengarriff Castle, a castle built in the 1790s by Colonel Simon White, 513–14, 715n13 (Letter 33)

Glengarriff Lodge, the residence of Richard White, 1st Earl of Bantry, 525, 528, 533–34, 715n16 (Letter 33)

Glenmalure, a glacial valley in the Wicklow mountains of Ireland, 462

Gloucester, a city in southwest England, 385, 622

Golconda, a ruined city of India that became a metaphor of great wealth because of its connection with the diamond trade, 218, 474, 714n3 (Letter 30)

Golden, a village near Cashel, Ireland, 560, 571

Goodrich Castle, a ruined Norman castle in Herefordshire, England, 621, 622

Gort, a town in County Galway, Ireland, 500

Gotha, Germany, 25

Gouda, Holland, 28

Granada, Spain, 688

Grandson, the site of a 1476 battle in which the Swiss defeated Charles the Bold, 684, 721n21 (Letter 48)

Gravesend, a town on the south bank of the Thames, 166

Green Park, a royal park in London, 254

Greenwich, a London borough and the site of the Royal Observatory, 358

Grotto, The, a series of caves in Hawkstone Park, Shopshire, 132

Guildhall, a building in the City of London that has served as town hall and as an administrative and ceremonial center, 200, *201*, 704n2 (Letter 15), 705n27 (Letter 16)

Guisborough, a town in North Yorkshire, 287

Guyana, a former Dutch colony that became part of British Guiana on the north coast of South America, 32

Guy's Cliffe, a country house and estate on the River Avon, 124–25, *125*

Gwynant = Nant Gwynant, a valley in Snowdonia, North Wales, with two lakes, Llyn Gwynant and Llyn Dunas, 430–31

H

Hackett, Castle, a ruined castle at the foot of Cnoc Meddha (Knockma Hill) in County Galway, Ireland, the legendary abode of the king of the Connacht fairies, 484–85

Hague, The, Holland, 29, 678–79

Halifax, Nova Scotia, 478

Hampton Court, a royal palace in the London borough of Richmond where Pückler visits Lady Lansdowne, 45–46, 698n16 (Letter 3)

Harewood Park = Harewood House, a country house in West Yorkshire, with a landscape designed by Capability Brown in 1772; its 140 acres of gardens are surrounded by 1,000 acres of ornamental parkland, 294–96, *295*

Harlech Castle, a medieval fortress built by Edward I during his conquest of Wales, 434, *435*

Harrogate, a spa town in North Yorkshire, England, 293

Hartwell, a house in Buckinghamshire that served as the residence of Louis XVIII during his exile from France, 145

Harwich, a port town in England, 153, 160, 178

Harz Mountains, a storied mountain range in northern Germany, 195, 721n40 (Letter 47)

Hatfield House, a Jacobean country house and estate in Hertfordshire; it was the family seat of the earls and marquesses of Salisbury; a large fire destroyed part of the house and took the life of Lady Salisbury in 1835, 317–19, *318*

Haulbowline Island, Cork Harbor, Ireland, 542

Le Havre, France, 169, 702n3 (Letter 12)

Hawk River, a large manmade lake in Hawkstone Park, 131

Hawkstone Park, a landscape park in Shropshire, 131–33, 700n2 (Letter 10)

Haymarket Theatre, London, 67, 69, 242

Helgoland, German island in the North Sea, 325

Hereford, a cathedral city in England, 620–21, 622

Herrnhut, a small town about fifty miles south of Muskau that was the headquarters of the Moravian church, 31

Himalayas, a mountain range in Asia, 301, 688

Holly Lodge, Highgate, the home of the Duchess of St Albans, 352–53

Holycross, a village in North Tipperary, Ireland, that was the site of Holy Cross Abbey, 570

Holyhead, a town in the country of Anglesey, Wales; it was the major port serving Ireland, 388, 445, 447, 617, 619, 643

Hore Abbey, the ruins of a thirteenth-century monastery near the Rock of Cashel in Ireland, 552

Hotel Bourbon, a hotel in Calais, France, 652

Hôtel St-Maurice, the Paris hotel where Pückler stays on his way back to Müskau, 659, 661

Hougoumont, a large farmhouse below an escarpment where Wellington faced Napoleon's army at the Battle of Waterloo on 18 June 1815, 232

Howth, a hilly headland at the north end of Dublin Bay and site of a castle, 448, 450, 453, 585, 617, 713n9 (Letter 28)

Hungry Hill, a mountain on Bantry Bay, Ireland, 514, 529, 535, 715n18 (Letter 34)

Hunterian Museum, part of the Royal College of Surgeons at Lincoln's Inn Fields, London, 706n3 (Letter 17)

Hyde Park, London, 39, 160, 229

Manchester, England, 155

Marengo, the site of a battle fought in June 1800 in northwest Italy, in which Napoleon was victorious over the Austrians, 343, *344*, 345

Marienburg. *See* Malbork Castle

Mark Brandenburg, a margraviate of the Holy Roman Empire, then a province of Prussia, and now the state of Brandenburg, Germany, 27, 38

Mauritius, an island off the southwest coast of Africa; it was called the Ile de France from 1715 to 1810, when it was a French colony, 701n14 (Letter 10), 702n13 (Letter 12), 710n19 (Letter 23)

Medway, a river in southwest England, 368, 369

Meeting of the Waters, in County Wicklow, Ireland, where the rivers Avonbeg and Avonmore join to form the Avoca river, 460, *461*

Meissen, Germany, 18

Melrose Abbey, a ruined monastery in Scotland, 354

Melton, a town in Suffolk, England, 56

Menai Strait, a narrow stretch of water dividing the Isle of Anglesey from the mainland of Wales; it was famous for its 1826 bridge designed by Thomas Telford, which was the first modern suspension bridge in the world, *421*, 712n14 (Letter 26)

Mickarky, a village near Cashel, Ireland, 716n2 (Letter 38)

Micklegate Bar, the most important of York's four main medieval gateways, 706n6 (Letter 18)

Milan, Italy, 272, 702n10 (Letter 11)

Milos, the Greek island where the *Venus de Milo* statue was found, 663

Mitchelstown, a small country town in County Cork, Ireland, and site of Mitchelstown Castle, the largest neo-Gothic house in Ireland, built by the 3rd Earl of Kingston in 1823, 545

Monkstown, Ireland, a village in County Cork, southeast of the city of Cork on the estuary of the River Lee, 542

Monmouth, a town in Wales, 621, 622, 623–24

Mont Blanc, the highest mountain in the Alps, 252

Montpellier, France, 605

Moritzburg, a Baroque castle and park near Dresden; it was a hunting lodge of Augustus the Strong, 294

Moscow, Russia, 206, 213

Moss Cottage, a thatched and moss-clad summerhouse near the Wye River built by the Duke of Beaufort, 626

Mouse Island, a small island in the Lough Leane, the largest of the three Killarney Lakes, 505

Moycarkey, a village near Cashel, Ireland, 560, 716n2 (Letter 38)

Muckross Abbey, a fifteenth-century Franciscan friary on the Herbert estate, now the centerpiece of Killarney National Park, Ireland, 506–7, *507*

Mulgrave, a large estate in Yorkshire belonging to Henry Phipps, 1st Earl of Mulgrave, 287–89, *288*, 707n5–8 (Letter 19)

Muskau, Pückler's estate and the location of his famous park, *xxiv*, 21, 22, 31, 38, 67, 98, 162, 163, 170, 199, 270, 287, 391, 697n3 (Letter 1), 699n1 (Letter 6), 699–700n10 (Letter 7), 700n8 (Letter 8), 702n18 (Letter 11), 703n6 (Letter 13), 705n36 (Letter 15), 705n13 (Letter 16), 714n1, 3 (Letter 30), 716n6 (Letter 37)

N

Naples, Italy, 64, 171, 192, 343, 619, 699n9 (Letter 6), 700n4 (Letter 9)

Navarino, an historical name for Pylos, the site of a major battle on 20 October 1827 in the Greek War of Independence, 449–50, 708n13 (Letter 20), 716n7 (Letter 37)

New Inn, a village near Cashel, Ireland, 560, 716n2 (Letter 38)

Newbury, a town in the county of Berkshire, England; it was the site of two civil war battles in 1643 and 1644, 148, 701n34 (Letter 10)

Newcastle (upon Tyne), a city in northeast England, 283, 352

Newgate Prison, London, a prison from 1188 to 1902, 229, 231

Newmarket, a town in Suffolk, England, famous for its horse races, 47–52, *48–49*, 56

Newport, a town in Shropshire, England, 133

Newstead Abbey, Nottinghamshire, a monastery that was converted to a country house and estate in the sixteenth century; it was the ancestral home of Lord Byron, 300

Normandy, France, 368

Northumberland House, London, a large Jacobean mansion that was the residence of the Duke of Northumberland, 98, 214, 224, 225, 226

Nottingham, England, 300–301, 707n25 (Letter 19)

Notre Dame, an early Gothic cathedral in Paris, 685–86

Nuremberg, Germany, 148, 662

O

Odessa, Ukraine, 211

Oschatz, a town in Saxony, 18

Osnabrück, a city in Lower Saxony, 25

O'Sullivan's Cascade, a waterfall in Tomies Wood, Killarney National Park, Ireland, 507

Ouse, a river in North Yorkshire, 273

Oxford, England, 128, 135, 139–44, 701n9, 11, 13, 18, 27 (Letter 10)

P

Palais du Luxembourg, Paris, 667, 721n36 (Letter 47)

Palais Royal, Paris, a seventeenth-century palace with a large inner courtyard, 659, 662, 686

Palmyra, an ancient Syrian city that was an important stop for caravans crossing the desert; its extensive ruins now cover six square kilometers, 37, 160

Panshanger Park, near Hertford, England, designed by Humphry Repton 1801; it was the residence of Lady Cowper, 319

Panthéon, a neoclassical building in Paris, initially a church but a mausoleum since the late eighteenth century, 685–86, 721n26 (Letter 48)

Paris, France, 20, 25, 39, 55, 56, 63, 93, 97, 118, 128, 150, 176, 178, 185, 190, 200, 205, 208, 214, 229, 231, 237, 241, 264, 273, 308, 357, 364, 368, 372, 374, 378, 381, 401, 443, 464, 465, 482, 484, 536, 554, 584, 593, 601, 615, 655–56, 657, 659–65, 667–69, 671, 673–88, 682, 683, 687, 698n8 (Letter 4), 700n19 (Letter 7), 702n14 (Letter 11), 704n20 (Letter 14), 705n16 (Letter 16), 720n14–15, 22–23 (Letter 47), 721n2, 5, 12, 15, 19, 31 (Letter 48)

Parys Mines, Wales, the largest copper mine in Europe in the late eighteenth century, 445–46, *446*

Passage = Passage West, Ireland, a village on the west bank of Cork Harbor, 542

Passage Vivienne, Paris = the Galerie Vivienne, a covered shopping gallery built in 1823, 688

Pavia, the site of the decisive engagement (on 24 February 1525) of the Italian War of 1521–1526, 140

Penmaenmawr, a mountain in Wales meaning "Head of the Great Stone"; in Pückler's time, this 1,600-foot granite bluff arose almost perpendicularly out of the sea, but it has since been reduced by more than one-third due to quarrying, 437

Penrhyn Castle, a neo-Norman castle near Bangor, Wales, designed by Thomas G. Hopper as a country house for Dawkins-Pennant in the 1820s and 1830s; it was built of a dark limestone called Anglesey marble, 437, 711n12, 27, 29 (Letter 25)

Penrhyn quarry, an enormous slate quarry in North Wales owned by Dawkins-Pennant, 711n28 (Letter 25)

Persepolis, an ancient Persian capital, 169, 330

Petworth House, a late seventeenth-century mansion in West Sussex, England, with a park designed by Capability Brown; the Earl of Egremont, a serious patron of the arts, owned it at the time of Pückler's visit, 304, 306, 708n4 (Letter 20)

Pfaueninsel, an island on the Havel River in Berlin, 301

Phoenix Park, a large walled park in Dublin; it was the site of the Viceregal Lodge (now Aras an Uachtarain), the residence of Henry Paget, Lord Anglesey, when he was lord lieutenant of Ireland; George IV stayed here during his visit to Ireland in 1821, 450, 451, 452, 580, 581, 714n5 (Letter 30)

Piercefield Park, near Chepstow, Wales, an early example of a picturesque landscape in the style of Capability Brown; the house, now a ruin, was designed in a neoclassical style by Sir John Soane, 628, 631

Pigeon Hole, one of the best known of the caves near Cong, Ireland, 486

Pillnitz, the baroque summer palace of Elector Augustus the Strong near Dresden, with an extensive park, 294

Pisa, Italy, 28

Place de l'Étoile, Paris (now Place Charles de Gaulle), 660

Place de Louis XV, Paris (now Place de la Concorde), 660, 720n9 (Letter 47)

Place des Victoires, a large public square in Paris, 686

Plas Newydd, a house and estate located in Anglesey, Wales that was the country seat of the Marquess of Anglesey, 423–24, 424

Plata, Rio de la, an estuary formed by the confluence of the Uruguay River and the Paraná River on the border between Argentina and Uruguay, with Montevideo on its northern shore and Buenos Aires on its southern shore, 467

Plauenscher Grund, a valley near Dresden, 634

Poitiers, France, 652

Poltava, a city in the Ukraine that was the site of a major battle (1709) in which Peter I of Russia defeated Sweden, 319, 610, 708n26 (Letter 20)

Pompei, Italy, 274, 385

Pont de Louis XVI, Paris, now known as the Pont de la Concorde, 660

Pont Neuf, once the newest, now the oldest, bridge over the Seine in Paris, 685

Pont-y-Glyn, also called Pont Glyn Diffwys, a stone bridge over the River Dee near Corwen, Wales, 391–92

Port Jackson, a natural harbor in Australia, with a small bay, Sydney Cove, that was the site of the English penal colony, 574

Porte Saint-Martin, a theater in Paris, 668, 721n39 (Letter 47)

Potsdam, Germany, 33, 129, 173, 402, 697n8 (Letter 1), 712n12 (Letter 27)

Powerscourt Park, a large country estate, with an eighteenth-century house and landscaped grounds, in County Wicklow, Ireland, 465, 468–70, 470, 471

Prague, Czech Republic, 484

Prior Park, near Bath, England, an eighteenth-century house with a landscape garden designed with advice from Alexander Pope and Capability Brown, 641

Priory. *See* Bentley Priory

Pylos. *See* Navarino

R

Radcliffe Library, now Radcliffe Camera, an eighteenth-century building that is now part of the Bodleian Library at Oxford University, 142, 701n21 (Letter 10)

Red Castle, a Norman castle in Hawkstone Park, 131, 133

Redcliffe Church, a Gothic church in Bristol now known as St Mary Redcliffe, dating from the twelfth to the fifteenth century, 634

Regent's Park, London, 33, 101, 330, 352

Reims Cathedral, France, 160

Rhine, a major European river, 44–45, 697n11 (Letter 1), 698n6 (Letter 3)

Richmond, a London borough, 99, 222–23

Richmond, Virginia, 702n24 (Letter 11)

Riesengebirge, a high mountain range along the Czech-Polish border, 392

Rio de Janeiro, Brazil, 252

Ripon, a town in North Yorkshire, 289, 293

Rocher de Cancale, a famous restaurant in Paris, 660, 720n14 (Letter 47)

Rochester, a town in Kent, England, and the site of the twelfth-century Rochester Castle, 368, 369, 400

Rome, Italy, 64, 92, 104, 115, 118, 204, 219, 229, 702–3n19 (Letter 12), 705n16 (Letter 16), 707n17 (Letter 18)

Rosanna, a valley in Ireland, 458

Ross (Ross-on-Wye), a small town in Herefordshire, England, 621

Ross Castle, a fifteenth-century fortress near Killarney, Ireland, and the ancestral home of the O'Donoghue clan, 503, 508

Rossbach, a German village that was the site of a major battle (1757) in the Seven Years' War in which the Prussians under Frederick the Great defeated the armies of France and the Holy Roman Empire, a victory overturned at Jena-Auerstedt, 19

Rotherham, a town in South Yorkshire, 297, 298

Rotterdam, Holland, 26, 28–30, 31, 697n6 (Letter 2)

Roundwood, a village in County Wicklow, Ireland, 460

Royal Exchange, a commercial center in London; the building Pückler saw was destroyed by fire in 1838, 39, 40, 42

Ruhr, a river in western Germany, 26

S

Sadler's Wells, a theater in London that introduced an aquatic stage in 1804, 363, 710n22 (Letter 23)

Saffron Walden, a town in Essex, England, 698n9 (Letter 4)

St Albans Abbey, a large church in the Gothic style, begun in Norman times, that became a cathedral in 1877, 301–2, 302, 707n29 (Letter 19)

St Asaph, a Welsh town with a small fourteenth-century cathedral, 439, 441

St Eustache, a Gothic church in Paris, 686

Saint Gotthard, a mountain range in the Swiss Alps, 688

Saint Helena, an island in the south Atlantic where Napoleon was exiled, 236, 379, 617

St James's Park, London, 203, 254

St Leonard's Hill, a house and park near Windsor owned by Earl Harcourt, now a ruin, 261–62, 261, 706n9 (Letter 17)

St Margaret's Church, York, 707n12 (Letter 18)

St Mary, Church of, a parish church in Whitby, 286, 707n2 (Letter 19)

St Mary, Collegiate Church of, a parish church in Warwick, 700n12 (Letter 9)

St Mary the Virgin, Church of, a gothic church in Saffron Walden, 698n9 (Letter 4)

St Mary's Abbey, a ruined Benedictine abbey in York, England, 273

St Mary's Cathedral, Limerick, 501, 714n1 (Letter 33)

St Mary's, Church of, York, 276

Saint-Omer, a town in northern France, 524

St Patrick's Cathedral, Cashel, Ireland, 552, 716n2 (Letter 27)

Saint Petersburg, Russia, 23, 227, 702n12 (Letter 12)

St Stephen's Cathedral, Vienna, 646

Salisbury, a cathedral city in Wiltshire, England, 643, 644, 645–48, 645, 647, 719n5, 7 (Letter 46)

Salt Hill, a village just west of Slough, England, 259, 264

Salzbrunn, a spa town in lower Silesia, today Szczawno-Zdrój, Poland, 483

Sandomich, a pun on Sandomir. *See* Sandomir

Sandomir, the German spelling of Sandomierz, a town in southeast Poland; Pückler uses the name as an ironic reference to Berlin, its sandy soil, and its accent, 61, 402, 416, 692, 711n13 (Letter 25)

Sandwich Islands, an early name for the Hawaiian Islands, 404, 445

Saragossa, Spain, the site of a major battle (1710) in the Spanish War of Succession, 594

Scarborough, a town in North Yorkshire with the ruins of a medieval fortress overlooking the harbor, 278, 281, *281*, 285

Schaffhausen, a city in northern Switzerland, 43–44

Schönbrunn, a former Hapsburg palace and gardens on the outskirts of Vienna, 23

Schulpforta (also Pforta), a former monastery near Naumberg, Germany, 19

Scone, a village in Scotland, 552, 716n4 (Letter 37)

Segontium, the ruins of a Roman fort near Caernarfon, Wales, 415

Seine, a river in France, 685

Serpentine, a large lake in Hyde Park, London, 160, *161*, 380, 711n24 (Letter 24)

Seven Churches. *See* Glendalough

Severn River, Wales, 628, 632, 633, 634

Sèvres, a town near Paris known for its porcelain, 148

Shannon, the longest river in Ireland, 502, 503

Sheffield, an industrial center in Yorkshire, 298, 299

Sheldonian Theatre, the official ceremonial hall of the University of Oxford, designed by Christopher Wren, 701n9 (Letter 10)

Shelton Abbey, the neo-Gothic ancestral seat of the earls of Wicklow, Ireland, 460

Short Grove Park, an estate near Audley End, 59

Shrewsbury, a town in Shropshire, England; its abbey church was founded in 1084 by the Earl of Shrewsbury, 131, 619–21, 709n11 (Letter 22)

Silesia, a central European region, now mainly in Poland, 31, 434, 483

Snowdon, the highest mountain in Wales, 409–13, *410*, *413*, 415, 419, 424, 428, 430, 462, 712n1 (Letter 26)

Spessart, a low mountain range in Bavaria and Hesse, 240

Stainbrook Castle, an estate in Yorkshire, 298

Stanmore, a village in a northwest borough of London, 103, 336

Star and Garter, an inn on Richmond Hill overlooking the Thames Valley, built in 1738 and regularly expanded, 99

Steele an der Ruhr, a town on the Ruhr River, and since 1929 a suburb of Essen, 26

Stockholm, Sweden, 650

Stoke Park, a mansion and estate (with park by Capability Brown) in South Buckinghamshire, England, now part of Stoke Poges, 259–60

Stonehenge, the ruins of prehistoric monument in Wiltshire, England, 141, 644–45

Stowe, a grand house and landscape park in Buckinghamshire, England, 128, 144–46, *145*, 148, 701n31, 34, 35 (Letter 10)

Strasbourg, France, 169, 646, 719n5 (Letter 46)

Stratford-upon-Avon, Warwickshire, the birthplace of Shakespeare, 134–35

Strawberry Hill, an eighteenth-century Gothic revival house in Twickenham, London, built by Horace Walpole, 359

Studley Park, a large estate in North Yorkshire containing the ruins of Fountains Abbey, 289–93

Suir, a river in Ireland, 549, 557, 572

Surrey Theater, London, 322

Syon House, a garden designed by Capability Brown and house in west London that belonged to the Duke of Northumberland, 98

T

Tahiti, French Polynesia, 404

Tan-y-Bwlch ("under the pass"), a valley in Wales that was the location of an estate owned by the Oakeley family, 433

Tehran, the capital of Iran, 321

Teltow, a town between Berlin and Potsdam, 407

Temple de la Victoire (now Church of the Madeleine), 660, 720n11 (Letter 47)

Temple Newsam, a Tudor-Jacobean house, with grounds by Capability Brown, in Leeds, West Yorkshire, owned by the Marchioness of Hertford, 297–98

Terni, Italy, a city a few miles from the towering cascades known as the Cascata delle marmore (Marmore's Falls) that were built by the ancient Romans, 529

Tewkesbury, a town in Gloucestershire and site of an important battle in the Wars of the Roses, 386

Thames River, London, 31, 39, 98, 162, 166, 228, 237, 241, 242–43, 248, 368, 384, 705n32 (Letter 16)

Théâtre de l'Ambigu-Comique, a theater in Paris; the original structure of 1769, which was destroyed by fire in 1827, was replaced by a new building in 1828 that Pückler visited; the theater was demolished in 1966, 684

Théâtre-Lyrique Italien (Italian Lyric Theater), 684, 721n22 (Letter 48)

Théâtre de Madame, Paris, 660–61

Théâtre Français, Paris, 673–74, 679–80, 684

Thebes, Egypt, 505

Thomastown Castle, the neo-Gothic residence of Earl Landaff, 716n5 (Letter 37)

Thurles, a village near Cashel, Ireland, 560

Tintern Abbey, a ruined Cistercian monastery on the Wye River in Wales, 625, 626, 627

Tipperary, a town and parish in Ireland, 547, 553, 571

Titness Park, an estate near Ascot (Sunninghill), Berkshire, demolished after 1923 (*see also* Garvagh, Lady, *in Annotated Index of Names*), 221

Tivoli, Italy, 700n10 (Letter 9)

Tivoli Gardens, a public garden and amusement park in Paris from 1766 to 1842, 150, 231

Tollamane. *See* Tullamaine

Torgau, a town on the Elbe River in northwest Saxony, 402, 403

Tournai, Belgium, 197, 328

Tralee, a town in southwest Ireland, 502

Travellers Club, an exclusive gentlemen's club in London, 62, 63–64, 65–66, 269

Tremadog, a planned town in Wales founded by William Madocks, who began building the first embankment to drain the fens in 1800, 434

Tryfan (also Tryfaen or Trivaen), a mountain in Snowdonia, Wales, 392–93, *393*, 428–29

Tuam, a town in County Galway, Ireland, 479, 494, 582

Tuileries, a royal palace with gardens in Paris, home to most French monarchs until it was destroyed by fire in 1871, 659

Tullamaine, a small town in Ireland, 560, 716n2 (Letter 38)

U

Udolpho, a castle where the heroine is imprisoned in Ann Radcliffe's most popular Gothic novel, *The Mysteries of Udolpho* (1794), 521, 715n8 (Letter 34)

Ugbrooke House and Park, Devon, the seat of the Clifford family for over four centuries, with gardens laid out by Capability Brown and a house designed by Robert Adam, 719n7 (Letter 45)

Ulster, a province in Ireland, 250, 501

Utrecht, Holland, 27–28

Uxbridge, a town on the western edge of London, 148